HUMAN RESOURCE SELECTION

HUMAN RESOURCE SELECTION

SEVENTH EDITION

ROBERT D. GATEWOOD
Professor Emeritus, University of Georgia

HUBERT S. FEILD
Auburn University

MURRAY BARRICK
Texas A&M University

SOUTH-WESTERN
CENGAGE Learning

Australia • Brazil • Japan • Korea • Mexico • Singapore • Spain • United Kingdom • United States

SOUTH-WESTERN
CENGAGE Learning

Human Resource Selection, Seventh Edition
Robert D. Gatewood, Hubert S. Feild, Murray Barrick

VP/Editorial Director: Jack W. Calhoun

Editor-in-Chief: Melissa S. Acuna

Senior Acquisition Editor: Michele Rhoades

Developmental Editor: Elizabeth Lowry

Senior Editorial Assistant: Ruth Belanger

Marketing Manager: Clinton Kernen

Marketing Coordinator: Julia Tucker

Senior Marketing Communications Manager: Jim Overly

Senior Art Director: Tippy McIntosh

Production Manager: Jennifer Ziegler

Media Editor: Danny Bolan

Production Technology Analyst: Emily Gross

Senior Manufacturing Buyer: Kevin Kluck

Permissions Acquisitions Manager—Text: Mardell Glinski Schultz

Permissions Acquisitions Manager—Image: Deanna Ettinger

Content Project Management: PreMediaGlobal

Production House/Compositor: PreMediaGlobal

Internal Designer: PreMediaGlobal

Cover Designer: Kim Torbeck, Imbue Design

Cover Image: iStock

For product information and technology assistance, contact us at **Cengage Learning Customer & Sales Support, 1-800-354-9706.**

For permission to use material from this text or product, submit all requests online at **www.cengage.com/permissions**. Further permissions questions can be e-mailed to **permissionrequest@cengage.com**.

Library of Congress Control Number: 2010925790

Student Edition:

ISBN-13: 978-0-538-46994-4

ISBN-10: 0-538-46994-3

South-Western
5191 Natorp Boulevard
Mason, OH
USA

Cengage Learning is a leading provider of customized learning solutions with office locations around the globe, including Singapore, the United Kingdom, Australia, Mexico, Brazil, and Japan. Locate your local office at **www.cengage.com/global**.

Cengage Learning products are represented in Canada by Nelson Education, Ltd.

To learn more about **South-Western**, visit **www.cengage.com/South-Western**

Purchase any of our products at your local college store or at our preferred online store **www.cengagebrain.com**

Printed in the United States of America
2 3 4 5 6 7 14 13 12 11

DEDICATION

*To those whom we love and who have made our lives very, very, happy —
Chris, Claire, Courtney, Eithne, Huon, Ivy, Jenn, Jennifer, Mason,
Mikaela, Nat, Owen, Sarah, and Taylor.*

———————

*And to the first time each of us realized that there were individual
differences in people and, thus, were the beginnings of our interest
in psychology and selection and our careers —*

*My 4th grade summer reading program displayed a map of the United States.
Cars moved from New York City to Los Angeles as readers finished a book.
Each book counted for 200 miles. When my car got to Los Angeles, I was
amazed to see that there were cars all over the map—from Pennsylvania
to California. It was a giant surprise and a puzzle. Why weren't all
those cars in Los Angeles with me?*

—Robert D. Gatewood

*I started playing baseball when I was very young, so I knew that boys were
different in how well they played. I learned to measure individual
differences when my coach told me how he figured batting averages,
counted speed from first to second on a steal, and kept track of the number
of balls and strikes for each pitcher. I then understood that when choosing
players for a team, I should get those who had a high batting average,
were fast, and threw a lot of strikes. It was my first and most predictive
selection battery of performance with which I've worked. I learned
then what I learned later: past behavior is a pretty good predictor
of future behavior.*

—Hubert S. Feild

*In first grade, I learned that students with blue stars on their lapels could
go outside during recess; those without a star had to stay in and continue to
work on addition and subtraction. I thought at first that they had bought
shirts with blue stars, but my mother said no. Then I found out that the
"blue star people" had gotten perfect scores on a math test; the ones
still inside working had not. I then developed "conscientiousness"
and studied math.*

—Murray Barrick

BRIEF CONTENTS

CONTENTS

PART 2   FOUNDATIONS OF MEASUREMENT FOR HUMAN RESOURCE SELECTION   65

CHAPTER 3

Human Resource Measurement in Selection   67

PART 4   HUMAN RESOURCE RECRUITMENT   305

CHAPTER 8
Recruitment of Applicants   307

PART 5   PREDICTORS OF JOB PERFORMANCE   333

CHAPTER 9
Application Forms and Biodata Assessments, Training and Experience Evaluations, and Reference Checks   337

CHAPTER 10

The Selection Interview   415

PREFACE

All of us have been involved in the human resource selection program of an organization at one time or another. We have applied to schools and for internships, we have applied for part-time and full-time jobs with organizations, and we have been on the other side as organizational members making decisions about applicants. From either perspective, a common reaction to selection is uneasiness and uncertainty. How many times have we heard an applicant say something like, "I wonder what she was looking for?" How many times have we heard a decision maker mutter, "How can I tell the difference among all these applicants? I hope I made the right choice."

The general procedures of selection are familiar to most of us. We all know that information from applicants is gathered through such devices as resumes, applications, interviews, and various kinds of tests. We also know that this information is then used to make comparisons among applicants in the hopes of identifying strong future performers. Despite this familiarity the question still arises, "If selection procedures are so commonly known, why does such uneasiness and uncertainty still exist?"

We think there are two important reasons: (a) there are some inherent features of selection—in evaluating applicants and predicting future performance—that cannot be totally controlled; and (b) even though selection procedures are well known, the more important parts of selection are not well understood. These are complex operations such as determining what applicant characteristics should be evaluated, which devices should be used to collect information, and how this information should be combined to choose the most desirable applicants. These complex operations are rarely taught in college courses or executive education programs. Understanding each of these aspects of selection is critical to building an effective selection program and being confident in its operation. We think of these aspects as the technical components of selection—technical in the sense that psychometric procedures, statistical analyses, conceptual frameworks of selection, findings of previous research studies, and various legal and organizational constraints all contribute to an understanding of the process.

It is the purpose of this book to present technical information in a manner that we hope will be useful for and interesting to those who are or will be involved in the development and implementation of a selection program for an organization. We have summarized important research in selection and have incorporated these results into recommendations for the development of a selection program. This book is intended to be useful to those working in selection. The text is divided into the following sections, which systematically present the technical aspects of selection.

PART I: AN OVERVIEW OF HUMAN RESOURCE SELECTION. This section presents the nature of selection programs and their legal context. Chapter 1 describes the purpose of selection—the identification of high-performing individuals—and outlines the major steps that must be taken to develop an effective selection program; it concludes with the limitations that must be addressed in these programs. Chapter 2 presents the legal constraints that must be considered in selection—laws, federal guidelines, and court cases that are used to determine employment discrimination in selection.

PART II: FOUNDATIONS OF THE MEASUREMENT FOR HUMAN RESOURCE SELECTION. These chapters treat the measurement concepts that are fundamental to selection. Chapter 3 introduces the topic of measurement and its application to selection. Chapter 4 is devoted to the importance of and methods for estimating reliability. Chapter 5 discusses validation strategies and focuses on the interpretation and meaning of validation information. Chapter 6 presents the methods and strategies for using information in selection decision making.

PART III: JOB ANALYSIS IN HUMAN RESOURCE SELECTION. Chapter 7 describes the first steps in developing a selection program: the most common job analysis methods such as task analysis and standardized questionnaires; the identification of essential worker knowledge, skills, and abilities, necessary for successful performance of a job; and how these job analysis data are translated into selection measures.

PART IV: HUMAN RESOURCE RECRUITMENT. Chapter 8, Recruitment, is new to this edition and it discusses several important topics. one is how selection and recruitment, parts of the process of influencing appropriately skilled individuals to apply for employment, are closely linked. Other topics are the main objectives of recruitment and how these may be reached and the various operations of recruitment and how they should be carried out.

PART V: PREDICTORS OF JOB PERFORMANCE. This section is the longest in the book. The discussion of a major selection predictor in each chapter reviews research about the reliability and validity of the predictor and examines its appropriate construction and use. Chapter 9 discusses ways to more effectively use application forms, training and work experience evaluations, reference information, and biographical information. Chapter 10 reviews ways to improve the ubiquitous employment interview. Chapter 11 presents information about ability tests, especially cognitive ability tests, that have been used extensively. Chapter 12 addresses the assessment and use of personality data during the selection decision. Chapter 13 is about performance tests and assessment centers that mimic job activities. The final chapter of this section, Chapter 14, discusses methods that have been used to screen out applicants with potentially detrimental characteristics or behaviors.

PART IV: CRITERIA MEASURES. This final section covers only one topic: measures of job success or criteria. Chapter 15 is an overview of the essential characteristics and methods of measuring work performance for use as criteria measures. Criteria measures are an essential component in developing and implementing a complete selection program; they help in identifying what selection instruments work for choosing future successful employees within an applicant pool.

New to This Edition

In the seventh edition of *Human Resource Selection*, we introduce several new topics. One of these is the differences between selection and staffing. These two words are frequently used incorrectly as interchangeable terms. Another new topic is why there are differences between what is known about how to conduct selection programs and what organizations often do in carrying out selection. A third is the new chapter on Recruitment and a fourth is the detailed discussion of two Supreme Court cases that could have far reaching implications for selection. In addition to these new topics, we summarize recent research and examine the implications of that research on the design and implementation of selection programs.

Acknowledgments

One of the nicest aspects of writing a book is that it presents a formal opportunity for the authors to thank individuals who have had positive influences on both them and this text.

Bob Gatewood I would like to thank my father, Maurice Gatewood, who has always been an excellent model for me in terms of responsibility and professionalism. For 92 years, Maurice has helped me with every mechanical, electrical, and automotive problem I ever faced. Without this help, I would have wasted my life trying to fix stuff I messed up rather than doing important things like writing this book and hanging with my family. I also would like to thank my very smart and loving wife, Chris, for her advice on how to present some of the material in this book in an understandable way (rather than the way that I originally wrote it). Chris has amazing insights into how to present academic knowledge in useful and interesting ways to those who work in organizations and hopefully make use of the information in this book. Each of my four children has contributed to the various editions of this book in different ways. My oldest two, Jennifer and Nat, actually worked on building the topic and author indices for the first several editions. They have by now trained their children, my grandchildren, to ask what grandfather's book is about. Of course, I tell them in great detail. They seem very interested, even though I know they do not have the slightest idea of what I am saying. I guess in that way they are preparing for college. My younger two children, Mikaela and Mason, often ask "How is your book going, Dad?" They then congratulate me on any progress and tell me to hang in there because I am almost finished. They also ask what the book is about and have the same reaction as the grandchildren. Maybe this is because they all are about the same ages. At any rate, the interest and assistance of all of these people have been valuable and important to me. It is good to have personal and professional parts of one's life mix so well.

Hubert (I prefer "Junior") Feild Since joining Exxon in June 1967 and quitting Exxon in October 1967, I have wondered about the process organizations go through in assessing individuals for employment. Given the misfit that I experienced with Exxon, I knew there must be better means for assessing and predicting who fits particular organizations and I wanted to know about them. During my career many of my interests have centered on examining such methods of assessment, particularly in human resource selection settings. I'm particularly grateful to Art Bedeian, who gave me the opportunity to work with Bob Gatewood, a wonderful friend and colleague, and Murray Barrick, a good man and one of the top names in our field, to explore some of the mysteries of human resource selection. Without Art's encouragement, this book would not have been published, and I would have missed the opportunity to work with two great colleagues. My co-authors and I have been able to laugh together through 7 editions of this book during a period spanning almost 25 years. In learning about assessment, several former professors of mine were most instrumental—William Owens, Lyle Schoenfeldt, Bob Teare, and Jerry Bayley. My colleagues at Auburn have been particularly helpful in "keeping the buzzards off" and "keeping me vertical and on this side of the dirt." These include Art Bedeian (now at LSU), Achilles Armenakis, Bill Giles, Stan Harris, Bill Holley, and Kevin Mossholder. My past doctoral students, namely Brett Becton, Michael Cole, Robert Hirschfeld, and Jack Walker, have made me very proud; I learned and continue to learn so much from them. Thanks, gentlemen. Finally, I thank my family. First, is Claire, my wife. She's listened to my moaning and groaning regarding chapter write and rewrites, put up with my idiosyncrasies and shenanigans (e.g., wearing shorts every day for over 3 years; installing a 50-foot tall ham radio tower beside our house with a 25-foot horizontal beam antenna with 5 elements at the top), and yet has always loved and supported me; what more can you ask of a person? Taylor (my main man) is a wonderful son, professional colleague, and close friend. He has provided guidance, counsel, support, and simply brought joy to me throughout my life in ways he could never imagine. My grandchildren, Huon (my man) and Ivy (my girl) are lights of my life. In the future, I look forward to watching Owen light my life as well. I simply did not know one could feel like I do about these kids. Eithne, my daughter-in-law who is like a daughter to me, has, among many roles, played "cheerleader" for me. Eithne is Ms. Can Do and Jack (rather, Jill) of all trades; she is the best. Finally, I thank Bernice and Hubert Feild (my parents) and Carole and Ridley Parrish (my sister and brother-in-law) for their unwavering support throughout my 65 years.

Murray Barrick I would like to thank all the teachers, mentors, friends, and colleagues who enriched my educational experiences from elementary school to Ph.D. I would single out five outstanding mentors as particularly influential: Mrs. Anfinson, David Whitsett, Ralph Alexander, Frank Schmidt, and Mick Mount. Your advice and counsel enabled me to accomplish more than I ever thought possible. No acknowledgment would be complete without highlighting the love, encouragement, and sacrifice unflaggingly provided by Ray and Marietta Barrick and Jack and Bea Burt. You are my role models. I continue to draw unconditional support, inspiration, and love from Sarah, my wife, and Courtney and Jenn, my daughters. I cannot emphasize enough your impact on everything I do. Finally, the opportunity to work with outstanding Ph.D. students and colleagues has enriched my life and career in incalculable ways. Through all of your contributions, I have been able to see and do more than I ever imagined in my wildest childhood dreams. I am forever indebted to you all.

Several people have been instrumental in reviewing this book. We especially thank the following reviewers for their time and comments, which improved the various editions:

Steven E. Abraham—*Oswego State University of New York*

James Breaugh—*University of Missouri at St. Louis*

Cynthia F. Cohen—*University of South Florida*

Kristl Davison—*The University of Mississippi*

Fritz Drasgow—*University of Illinois, Champaign*

Mary Gowan—*Elon University*

Jerald Greenberg—*The Ohio State University*

Hank Hennesssey—*University of Hawaii, Hilo*

Susan Key—*University of Alabama, Birmingham*

Elliot D. Lasson—*Maryland Department of Budget and Management, Recruitment and Examination Division; and University of Baltimore*

Mark L. Legnick-Hall—*University of Texas, San Antonio*

Mary Lewis—*PPG Industries*

William Ross, Ph.D—*University of Wisconsin–La Crosse*

Joseph Rosse—*University of Colorado*

Craig J. Russell—*University of Oklahoma*

Lyle F. Schoenfeldt—*Appalachian State University*

Ken Schultz—*California State University, San Bernardino*

Brian Steffy—*Franklin and Marshall College*

John Veres—*Auburn University, Montgomery*

Patrick Wright—*Cornell University*

Over the years, other people provided aid, support, and assistance that ranged from discussing the interpretation of relevant research to drinking Cokes and sharing humor during the day: Dwight Norris, Sharon Oswald, Jim Ledvinka, Vida Scarpello, Jim Lahiff,

Mary Evans, John Hollenbeck, Brad Kirkman, Wendy Boswell, Greg Stewart, and Amy Kristof-Brown.

The people at Cengage were, of course, a main force behind this edition. Special thanks goes to those who made the seventh edition a reality: Michele Rhoades (Acquisitions Editor) Elizabeth Lowry (Developmental Editor), Clint Kernan (Marketing Manager), and Karunakaran Gunasekaran (Senior Project Manager, PreMediaGlobal).

Robert D. Gatewood
Denver, Colorado

Hubert S. Feild
Auburn, Alabama

Murray R. Barrick
College Station, Texas

ABOUT THE AUTHORS

ROBERT D. GATEWOOD received his Ph.D. in industrial psychology from Purdue University. After accomplishing this, he first worked as a consultant for American Institutes for Research and then joined academia. His first position was as a member of the Department of Management at the Terry College of Business, University of Georgia. As has been indicative of his well-planned career, Bob thought that he would stay at Terry for maybe five years because it would only take a few years for a smart person with three liberal arts degrees to get used to business schools and then move on to bigger and better things. Thirty-four years later, he decided that maybe it was time to move on, even if he still didn't understand why business school faculty were not as vitally concerned about reliability and validity as he had been taught in his Ph.D. program. During these years, Bob climbed the academic ranks from assistant to full professor and pursued an administrative career at Terry as a department chair and associate dean in the College of Business. An indication of how well he did these jobs is contained on a plaque that he received when he retired; it thanked him "… for his creative solutions to problems and unfailing sense of humor." To his puzzlement, nothing was said about how good these solutions were. Bob was also elected to five executive positions, including President, within the Human Resources Division of the Academy of Management. In 2005, Bob moved to the Neeley School of Business at Texas Christian University as the Director of the Executive MBA Program when his wife, Chris Riordan, was recruited as an Associate Dean at Neeley. In 2008 he moved to Denver, Colorado when Chris became Dean of the Daniels School of Business at the University of Denver. He had the good sense to retire from faculty life at that point, mainly because he didn't want to risk Chris' reputation on anything that he may or may not do at the Daniels School. Since then he has coached his son's various teams, enjoyed a Taylor Swift concert with his daughter, learned to cook (four recipes), and attended many kids' birthday parties. He spends his remaining time on some professional projects.

Bob used to find delight in reading at bedtime to Mikaela and Mason, his two youngest children, from his many articles published in journals such as the *Journal of Applied Psychology, Academy of Management Journal, Academy of Management Review*, and *Personnel Psychology*. As Mikaela and Mason grew older, they yearned for new material, hence the seventh edition of *Human Resource Selection*. The parts they seem to like best are the dedication page and his graphology report.

As a consultant, Bob has worked with a number of companies; for example, PPG Industries, Westinghouse, BellSouth, and Ford. Some of these are still in business—if somewhat iffy, especially the various states' human resource departments with which he has worked. Now he offers his advice about education programs to the various schools that Mikaela and Mason have attended. He is somewhat surprised when people smile, nod, and thank him for his advice. He has not been asked back, but he attributes that to his ability to explain his ideas so clearly that those listening must immediately understand what to do. He thought the same about his students who also had the same reactions to his lectures.

HUBERT S. FEILD earned his Ph.D. in industrial psychology from the University of Georgia. He has been a faculty member in the Department of Management at Auburn University for his whole adult life (at least measured chronologically rather than in psychological maturity, which is doubted by many). Known as "Junior" to both of his friends, Hubert has done many things at Auburn (some of which we can mention). For example, he is now the Torchmark Professor of Management. Junior earned this distinction because he has published many articles in such journals as *Academy of Management Journal, Journal of Applied Psychology*, and *Personnel Psychology*. He has also done many projects for companies such as SONY, PPG Industries, GE, and AmSouth Bank. He has been successful in these because he finds excellent coworkers and gets out of their way.

Some people consider Junior to be individualistic. (Can you say "eccentric"?) He played baseball at Mississippi State; went to work for Exxon; saw the movie, *The Graduate;* and quit Exxon after three months. He's been at Auburn for more than 37 years—whenever, that is, he isn't wherever his son Taylor happens to be when working on plant ecophysiology projects. Their latest adventure was in New Caledonia. Junior spent his time in the South Pacific putting up antennas and speaking on ham radio to N6XMW, a federal judge and childhood friend in California, as well as to others around the world. He and his wife Claire threw out all material possessions that smacked of formality: china, silver, tablecloths, suits, ties, and shoes (other than tennis). The one rational thing that Junior has done has been to stay off of every committee, professional panel, and journal review board that he could. This is why he has been able to do a bunch of fun stuff. This makes Gatewood, the senior author of the book, wonder where his own life went wrong.

MURRAY BARRICK obtained his Ph.D. in industrial and organizational psychology from the University of Akron. He is the Head of the Department of Management, as well as a Distinguished Professor and the Robertson Chair at the Mays Business School at Texas A&M. He has also been a faculty member at the University of Iowa and Michigan State University. Although all this job switching could indicate he cannot hold a job, Barrick believes this simply illustrates the rationality of the labor market. He was asked to become a coauthor of this book when Gatewood and Feild realized that they were old and needed someone who was famous and could still write. Murray has turned out to be a good selection decision. His first publication, in *Personnel Psychology* in 1991, was recognized as the most frequently cited article in that journal during the 1990s. More recently, it was reported to be the most highly cited article in Industrial Psychology between 2001 and 2005. By April 2010, this one article had been cited more than 2,500 times (Google Scholar). Barrick has certainly gotten a lot of mileage out of his one good idea. Mainly due to his good selection of coauthors, he also has been recognized as the 5th most published author in *Journal of Applied Psychology* and *Personnel Psychology* in the 1990s (based on category rank) and the 39th most cited author in *Management* between 1981 and 2004. He has even surprised everyone by winning several awards: "the Outstanding Published Paper" and the "Owens Scholarly Achievement Award." The most notable award he won, along with Mick Mount, was the 2009 Distinguished Scientific Contributions Award from the Society for Industrial and Organizational Psychology. He also has served as the Associate Editor of *Personnel Psychology* and is on the editorial boards of the *Journal of Applied Psychology, Personnel Psychology,* and *Journal of Management.* As for hobbies, he has been known to ride a bike across Iowa on an annual ride called "RAGBRAI" and to travel and serve as keynote speaker in Pretoria, South Africa and Melbourne, Australia. He has conducted tutorial workshops in Saudi Arabia, Switzerland, Australia, and New Zealand and attended the occasional SIOP Conference. If you have an exotic locale and can't pay much, Barrick can visit and talk about the one thing that he knows about: the impact individual differences in personality and behavior have on success at work and how to accumulate frequent flyer miles. If you really need another topic, he can mumble for a bit about the characteristics of an effective handshake or ways candidates should present themselves in an interview. But all this travel is really just a way to find time to think about the next edition of this book.

AN OVERVIEW OF HUMAN RESOURCE SELECTION

In today's competitive business environment, managers in organizations are quite interested in increasing the performance of their employees. Their hope is that this increased performance will provide a competitive advantage over other firms. Many tactics and methods have been developed to enhance performance. Some, such as customer service and employee involvement programs, are organization-wide tactics. Others, such as the redesign of particular jobs and the improvement of communication between a manager and a work group, are specific to parts of the organization. In either case, almost all of these performance-enhancing tactics are based on the assumption that employees of the organization have the necessary capabilities to do the work. These tactics allow employees to use these capabilities more effectively.

Before getting into this book it's important to realize that selection is the basis for employee performance. It identifies those individuals who have the ability to perform a job well. Programs that companies use after selection to increase performance assume that employees have the abilities to do the work. The purpose of performance-increasing programs is to get employees to use their abilities more effectively. If employees do not have the appropriate talents for the jobs to which they are assigned, programs to improve performance will be unsuccessful. For example, many motivation programs bring about changes such as the increase in employee decision making or the involvement of the employee in customer satisfaction issues. If, however, the employee does not have the necessary abilities to do these tasks, these changes may result in a decrease in job performance.

We know that this description of selection brings an important question to your mind: "Because selection is so important to the performance of employees, all organizations must have excellent selection programs—right?" Unfortunately, there is ample evidence that many selection programs in organizations do not function as well as they should. An appropriate match between worker talents and job demands is frequently not achieved. That is the downside. The upside, at least for us, is that often selection programs can be improved fairly easily, and that creates the purpose for this book. Our basic viewpoint is that selection programs can be useful if (a) proper steps are taken to develop selection instruments that collect job-related information from applicants and (b) this information is then used appropriately in making selection decisions. As you probably have guessed, the purpose of this book is to go into much (some say much-too-much) detail over how to accomplish these two objectives. You have also probably guessed that this first section will present a general treatment of selection. (The word *overview* in the section title also might have given a hint.) We know it's not nice to disappoint readers early in a book (that usually happens later), so what is coming is an introductory treatment of selection. The two chapters in this opening section should give you an understanding of these four specific topics:

1. The importance of selection in conjunction with other human resource functions, especially human resource planning and recruitment.

2. The steps to be taken in developing a useful selection program.

3. The inherent difficulties and constraints of selection that must be addressed in developing a program.

4. The specific legal demands of selection. These take the form of laws, executive orders, court decisions, and guidelines for selection practices.

An Introduction to Selection

DEFINITION OF SELECTION

In a time of increasing global competition, every organization is concerned about the level of work performance of its employees. This is because the performance of employees is a major determinant of how successful an organization is in reaching its strategic goals and developing a competitive advantage over rival firms.[1] Therefore, influencing the work performance of employees is a major objective of organizations. Fortunately, there is agreement about how this can be accomplished. Organizational specialists have determined that an individual employee's work performance is made up of two factors: the ability of the individual and the effort that the individual puts forth.[2]

Both of these factors can be influenced by the organization. Ability is a function of two organizational practices, selection and training. An organization either finds individuals with the abilities to do the work or it teaches those abilities to existing employees. Effort is a function of the organization's numerous practices for motivating employees. These practices include every topic found in an introductory management course, such as compensation, goal setting, job design, and communication between managers and subordinates. However, all of these motivation practices assume that the employee has the abilities to perform the job. Motivation practices are intended to get the employee to use these abilities in a concerted and continuous manner.

Selection, in our unbiased view, is critical for an organization. It is one of only two ways of ensuring that employees have the abilities to do work, and it helps provide the base for effective motivational practices.

In this text we will use the following definition of human resource (HR) selection:

Selection *is the process of collecting and evaluating information about an individual in order to extend an offer of employment. Such employment could be either a first position for a new employee or a different position for a current employee. The selection process is performed under legal and environmental constraints and addresses the future interests of the organization and of the individual.*

This is a long definition. To make it more understandable, we will break down this definition and discuss what it means.

Collecting and Evaluating Information

A basic objective of selection is to separate from a pool of applicants those who have the appropriate knowledge, skills, and abilities to perform well on the job. We cannot assume that everyone who applies for a job is qualified to actually perform it. Therefore, to separate the qualified applicants from those who are not, the selection specialist must systematically collect information from the applicants about how much of the necessary knowledge/skills/abilities (KSAs) each possesses. (The term *KSA* is shorthand for the factual information about how to do the job [knowledge] that the individual possesses and the degree to which the individual can perform the activities of the job [skills and abilities]. If we said all that each time we used the term *KSA*, this book would be about 50 pages longer. How bad would that be?)

This systematic collection of information from applicants can range from fairly simple to very complex. For some jobs, a brief interview may provide all the data necessary to evaluate the applicant. For complex managerial jobs, it may be necessary to use interviews, tests, job simulations, or other measures to properly assess candidates. A major purpose of this book is to discuss the various devices that are used to evaluate applicants.

Our use of the term *selection* does not include all offerings of employment that may occur within a firm. We make a distinction between selection and hiring. Selection, as we have just said, occurs when job-related information is collected from applicants and offers of employment are given to those who apparently possess the necessary KSAs to do well on the job. Often, however, offers of employment are given with no evaluation of the applicant's job-related qualifications. We refer to this type of employment as *hiring*. One example of hiring occurs when family members, friends, or relatives of customers are given jobs. In these cases, employment is based primarily on one's relationship to a member of the organization, not on the possession of job-related qualifications. Such hiring is not necessarily inappropriate, nor does it always lead to employing incompetents. It is simply not selection as discussed in this text. Hiring also often occurs when a company desperately needs individuals to fill unskilled or semiskilled positions within a very short period of time. As a result, the organization does little or no evaluation of the applicants' KSAs. Availability is the critical variable.

Selection for Initial Job and Promotion

You may think that selection only refers to choosing people for their first jobs with the organization, and not to the promotion or transfer of existing employees. We don't think that way. The basic objective is common in both selection situations. The company should be trying to collect job-related information from applicants for open positions so that it can identify individuals who have the best chance of performing well in the job activities and have a high level of productivity. There are, however, differences between selection for an initial job and selection for promotion.

Initial Job.   Selection for an initial job involves applicants who are external to the organization. These applicants are usually recruited through formal mechanisms such as media advertisement, internet contact, use of employment agencies, and urging from present or former employees of the organization. These recruitment mechanisms frequently produce a large number of applicants, especially when jobs are in short supply as happened in 2008 and 2009. When there is a large number of applicants, the costs of selection become an important factor for an organization. It cannot possibly afford to test and evaluate all applicants using all the instruments in the selection program, nor can it take the time to do so. So as you can guess or know from your own experience, the number of applicants has to be reduced dramatically at the very beginning of the selection program. This reduction is frequently done by using selection instruments that do not cost very much to administer, such as application forms. The irony of this is that these instruments are somewhat limited in the amount of information that can be collected. Most application forms don't allow for more than job titles, brief descriptions of activities and accomplishments, limited education summary, and minimal job history. So ……. many people are rejected by the company based on little information. As we discuss later in this book, the information collected at the initial stage of a selection program should be job-relevant because so many people are negatively affected. We will tell you how this can be done and you will feel better for having that knowledge.

Because the applicants for intial jobs are all external to the organization, selection programs are usually formalized. That is, there are usually specific steps that applicants must go through in the same order. For example, application forms, graded tests, interviews, and job simulations could be used. The number of applicants is reduced at each stage, which reduces costs and time. The most expensive selection instruments are used at the latter stages of the program. The main reason for this formalization is that the organization usually knows nothing or very little about each applicant before selection begins. Therefore, selection must systematically gather job-related information about each applicant that can be useful for acceptance/rejection decisions. It is also necessary to collect the same information about applicants so that comparisons between applicants can be directly made. Comparisons using different information begin to look like guesses. Finally, because the applicants are unknown to the organization, impressions and evaluations about the applicants are formed by decision makers during the selection process and ideally when candidates are operating under similar or nearly identical circumstances. Everyone is given an equal chance to demonstrate job-related KSAs.

Promotion.   Selection for promotion within an organization has characteristics that are very different from those of selection for an initial job. You have probably already guessed that, because there wouldn't be so many words in this section if they were the same. Candidates for promotion, by definition, are already internal to the company; some may have worked in the company for several years. A limited few recruitment techniques are used to generate applicants: postings of job vacancies either online or on bulletin boards, announcements by human resource specialists or managers higher in the organization than the open position, or requests for nominations from managers or employees (including self-nomination). These techniques commonly produce only a small number of employees who express an interest in the promotion opportunity. Usually, those interested are in the same functional area as the promotion position or in the same physical location; they possess commonly accepted backgrounds for the position. Each of these characteristics reduces the number of applicants.

Because the applicants are members of the organization, much information about them exists. This information includes evaluations made during their selection into an initial job; performance reviews made by managers; human resource records of attendance, compensation, training completed, reprimands, and so on; and observations made by others in the organization when working with the applicant in previous assignments. All of this information has two effects. One is that someone making the promotion decision often has formed impressions of the applicants before the promotion process begins. That decision maker frequently has continuous access to the work and HR records of the individuals and often has worked with them or at least has closely observed their work actions. Given such information, it is common that the decision maker forms a detailed evaluation of the strengths and weaknesses of each applicant even before any formalized evaluation occurs. The second effect of previous information is that the actual evaluation of candidates often is not very extensive or formalized. Sometimes the decision maker simply reviews existing information; sometimes managers connected to the open position meet to discuss applicants; other times the decision maker interviews candidates. Rarely are scored tests or job simulations used. One notable exception is the use of assessment centers, which we will discuss in Chapter 14. Assessment centers are detailed and are systematically planned and scored. Those who score applicants are extensively trained; they meet to discuss candidates and then write a formal evaluation of each candidate. Such emphasis on job relatedness and systematic review and scoring is usual in most evaluations of applicants for promotion.

Are the Two Fundamentally Different?   Our view is that because internal and external applicant pools are so different, it is inevitable that the characteristics of the selection process will differ. However, the fundamental task is the same in both of these types of employment decisions. There are more applicants than positions available. The decision maker must choose among applicants and identify the individuals with the most developed work-related KSAs. It is necessary to collect job-related information systematically for each applicant so direct comparisons of candidates can be made. Unfortunately in both initial job and promotion, selection decisions are often made without job-related data (we will discuss this a bit later), with inconsistent information about the candidates, and using nonformalized decision rules. Often scores for selection instruments and decisions are made using intuition rather than data. In promotion, scoring and decisions take the form of promotion based on such variables as seniority, nonsystematic opinions from others in the organization, and the ill-defined reputations of candidates. Unfortunately, many of these variables are not related to future job performance. For example, a recent study found that neither the applicants' current job performance nor demographic characteristics were closely related to future job performance in a higher level job.[3] Another research study looked at a situation in which both internal candidates and managers perceived that organizational citizenship behavior (generally the willingness to do a wide variety of useful activities not strictly defined by a job description) was related to obtaining a promotion. The surprising finding was that when employees were promoted, their organizational citizenship behaviors declined.[4] Obviously this was not the desired effect of promotion and the study indicated that this variable is not related to future job performance. We believe that the use of variables in promotion that are not systematically collected and scored and that are not clearly related to future job performance is similar to what we described earlier as hiring for initial jobs. It should be no surprise to you that we think selection principles and instruments contained in this book apply to both initial selection and promotion. Matching the KSAs of individuals with the demands of the job is desirable and fair and should lead to a stronger economy. What more could you want out of life—or a textbook?

Constraints and Future Interests

From an organization's viewpoint, the selection decision is ideally made in circumstances in which the organization has a great deal of control over the number of applicants who seek the job, the information that can be gathered from these applicants, and the decision rules used by the organization in evaluating this information. However, the world is not perfect for selection. For example, there are great fluctuations in the number of applicants, frequently due to general economic or educational conditions over which the organization has little control. Also, numerous federal and state laws and administrative rulings restrict both the information that can be gathered from applicants and the way this information can be evaluated. Equal Employment Opportunity laws and guidelines regarding discrimination in selection are good examples.

There is also a growing realization that the usefulness of the selection decision should be viewed in terms of its effects over time. The future interests of both parties must be considered in the selection process or the result will be less than optimal. Rapid and costly turnover, lower performance levels, and friction between an employee and the organization are among the results of a mismatch of interests.[5]

Now that you have a better understanding of what is meant by selection, our next task is to provide a clear overview of the various parts of this subject. To do this, the first chapter of a textbook frequently follows one of two paths: It either traces the history of the subject matter back to the Greeks, Romans, and Egyptians, or it goes into detail about how the subject relates to all that is important in the universe. We could only trace selection back to the Chinese, somewhere around 200 B.C. That reached only the Romans. Falling short of the Greeks and Egyptians, we were forced to adopt the second path for this chapter. The following sections, therefore, describe how selection relates to other human resource management (HRM) activities, what HRM specialists must do to develop an effective selection program, and, finally, what problems are inherent in the selection process. We know you will be amazed. We hope you will gain a better understanding of the complexity of this field and the technical knowledge it requires. Our goal for the first chapter of the next edition of this book is to follow both paths—just to make the book longer, and, undoubtably, more interesting. So please buy that edition too. We think that Plato included his thoughts about selection when he wrote *The Republic*. That gets us back to the Greeks. Now if we can just find something about the Egyptians and selection!

SELECTION AND STRATEGIC HUMAN RESOURCE MANAGEMENT

Firms regularly set goals for future performance and develop plans to reach those goals. For example, a medium-sized software development firm in Texas may set the goal of increasing its sales by 50 percent over the next three years. To reach this goal, the firm, which specializes in health care, plans to develop software for a new market (gerontology institutions) and expand its sales offices into Tampa, Florida, and Charlotte, North Carolina. To implement these plans, the firm will rely on its three types of resources: financial, physical, and human. It must obtain more money to secure additional sales locations and to pay the other costs necessary for increasing sales (financial resources). It also must obtain more computers, office furnishings, transportation, storage facilities, and office supplies (physical resources). Finally, it must both add employees and retrain existing staff (human resources).

The first step in addressing the human resource issues necessary for reaching the goal of this software firm is to make two forecasts about employees. One of these is to forecast the firm's future demand for labor. That is, how many employees will be needed in the various jobs in order to increase sales by 50 percent, develop software for a new market, and open the two new sales offices? Moreover, the firm must forecast when, over the next three years, these people should be employed. The second forecast concerns the labor supply—the number of individuals the organization will have in each of its jobs if the firm continues its present human resource programs. In other words, if employees enter, leave, and are transferred at the present rate over the next three years, how many will there be in each of the necessary jobs?

As you can probably guess, the last step in this analysis is to compare the results of the demand forecast with the labor supply forecast. As you can also probably guess, with the goal of a 50 percent increase in sales and plans to open new locations, the firm will probably have to employ a significant number of additional people and make sure that current employees successfully move into new positions. This example is about expansion, but we know that firms sometimes plan to downsize. In such cases, the two forecasts will most likely indicate that the labor supply forecast is larger than the labor demand forecast. The firm then must develop activities to reduce the number of employees yet retain enough individuals in each job category to meet its goals.

The activities that are used to align the number of employees and their performance with the goals of the firm constitute strategic human resource management (SHRM).[6] Ultimately, employees must perform the work necessary for reaching the goals of the firm.[7] In most cases, the firm's financial and physical resources enable the workers to work better. SHRM requires that the HR systems of the firm are coordinated and interact smoothly with one another.[8] We have already discussed how selection affects employee performance. In addition to selection, other HR systems important for employee performance are recruitment, training, compensation, and job performance review. The relationships among these human resource systems are shown in Figure 1.1. To get the maximum benefits from the HR systems shown in this figure, firms must design the systems so they greatly enhance employees' work performance.[9] Therefore, selection should be coordinated with the activities the firm carries out under recruitment, training, compensation, and job performance review.

For example, training is designed to teach necessary job skills and abilities to those individuals who have accepted a job offer as a result of the selection process. The content, length, and nature of training are affected by the level of the skills and abilities of the individuals selected. If these skills and abilities are well developed for the job, then minimal training should suffice. If the new employees' job skills and abilities are low, then training should be more extensive. Compensation and selection interact; on the one hand, the specific qualifications possessed by the individual selected may affect the amount that he or she is paid. On the other hand, the salary offer that is determined through the organization's recruitment and selection activities affects the applicant's decision to accept the offer or not. As we will frequently point out, selection and work performance measurement are also linked. The purpose of selection is to identify those individuals who will perform well on the job. Work performance data are used to examine the effectiveness of the selection

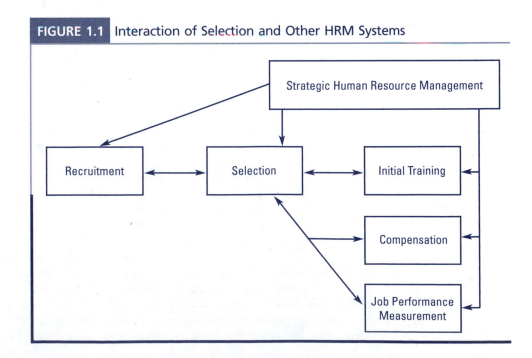

FIGURE 1.1   Interaction of Selection and Other HRM Systems

program. This topic is discussed in both Chapter 5, "Validity of Selection Measures," and Chapter 15, "Measures of Job Performance."

Selection is more closely related to recruitment than it is to the other HRM programs, because both recruitment and selection are concerned with placing individuals into jobs. Both concern individuals who are not working for the firm. Other HRM activities deal with individuals after they are employed. We will define recruitment as those organizational activities (such as choosing recruiting sources, developing recruitment ads, and deciding how much money will be spent) that influence the number and types of individuals who apply for a position—and that also affect applicants' decisions about whether or not to accept a job offer.[10] We use this definition because it is important to think not only about attracting people, but also about increasing the probability that those people will accept a position if it is offered. It is senseless to motivate people to apply and then turn them off when they do—but we all know this happens. Sara Rynes, in an extensive review of recruitment, points out the relationship between selection and recruitment.[11] At the very least, the selection requirements of a firm affect both the recruitment sources used and some of the specific information about the job that is included in the recruitment message. For example, an entry-level HR manager's position in a unionized manufacturing plant may require applicants to know about Equal Opportunity Employment laws, the interpretation of union contracts, and employee benefit plans. These requirements could limit recruitment sources to law schools, industrial relations programs, and human resource programs. In a reverse example, the applicant pool serves as the limiting factor in selection. If this pool is inappropriate for the position, the probability that selection will identify superior workers is low. We will go into much detail about recruitment in Chapter 9. See if you can control your curiosity and hunger to know about this topic until then.

Effects of Strategic Human Resource Management

You may ask yourself two logical questions at this point: "Well, this stuff about strategic HRM makes sense, but is there any evidence that it actually relates to the performance of a firm? Is it really important?" The answers, of course, are *yes* and *yes* (or we would not have asked).

Recently there has been a consistent series of research findings clearly indicating that strategic HRM is related to positive outcomes of organizations. Mark Huselid, in one of the first studies, found that HR practices he called high-performance work systems were related to turnover, accounting profits, and firm market value.[12] Other studies have found additional evidence across various industries. For instance, one study found that HR practices were related to productivity and quality in a sample of worldwide auto assembly plants.[13] Another found significant relationships between HR practices and accounting profits among a sample of banks.[14] Yet another found that certain combinations of HR practices were related to operational performance indicators among a sample of manufacturing firms.[15] Finally, a survey of corporations in New Zealand found that their HR practices were related to turnover and profitability.[16]

Although these studies found that various measures of firm performance are correlated to HR practices, the data for performance and HR practices were collected at the same point in time. Because correlation does not indicate causality, it is not possible to say that HR practices definitely led to increases in firm performance. Pat Wright and his colleagues tried to examine possible causality by collecting data on both HR systems and six measures of organizational performance for 45 food service units over different periods of time.[17] Even with this type of longitudinal design, it was still not clear whether HR practices caused increased organizational performance or whether high-performing firms increased the effectiveness of their HR practices. So ... although the evidence clearly suggests that strategic HR is related to firm performance, we cannot say that it causes higher levels of performance. The best test would be to find several low-performing companies, implement strategic HR in some of these, and measure firm performance some time later. In the absence of such data, we can give our consulting opinion that the correlation between HR and performance is consistent enough to argue for its implementation within organizations. As partial support for this conclusion, Murray Barrick and his colleagues found that it is possible to predict voluntary turnover among an applicant pool using selection measures.[18] That is, selection applied to applicants could predict future staying or leaving the firm.

DEVELOPING A SELECTION PROGRAM

We turn now to the way effective selection programs should be developed. A good deal of work must be completed by human resource specialists before the selection process is applied to those who are being recruited. We contend that the adequacy of these developmental steps, illustrated in Figure 1.2, strongly influences the adequacy of the selection process. If little attention and effort are devoted to developing the selection program, its usefulness will be limited. If these developmental steps are seriously addressed, the usefulness of the selection program is enhanced. Another way of viewing this issue is that a selection process itself can be implemented quite readily. An application form can quite easily be printed or purchased; interviews can be conducted without too much prior work; employment tests (with descriptions indicating that they should produce useful information for selection) can be purchased and administered to applicants. The crucial issue, however, is not whether an organization can collect information from applicants and then decide who are to be given employment offers. Obviously this is possible. Rather, the issue is whether the organization can collect information from applicants that is *closely* related to job performance and *effectively* use this information to identify the best applicants. It is the developmental steps of the selection program that make selection useful. The following paragraphs briefly describe these steps.

Job Analysis Information

If the purpose of the selection program is to identify the best individuals for a job within the organization, then information about the job should be the starting point in the development of this program. *Job analysis* is the gathering of information about a job in an organization. This information includes the tasks, results (products or services), equipment, material used, and environment (working conditions, hazards, work schedule, and so on) that characterize the job. This information serves two main purposes. The first is to convey to potential applicants information about the nature and demands of the job. This helps minimize inappropriate expectations. The second purpose is actually the more critical for the development of selection programs: The job analysis information provides a database for the other steps in the developmental process.

Identifying Relevant Job Performance Measures

A second type of information important for developing the selection program is determining how job performance is measured and what level of performance is regarded as successful. The main purpose of selection is to identify those applicants who will be

FIGURE 1.2 Steps in the Development of a Selection Program

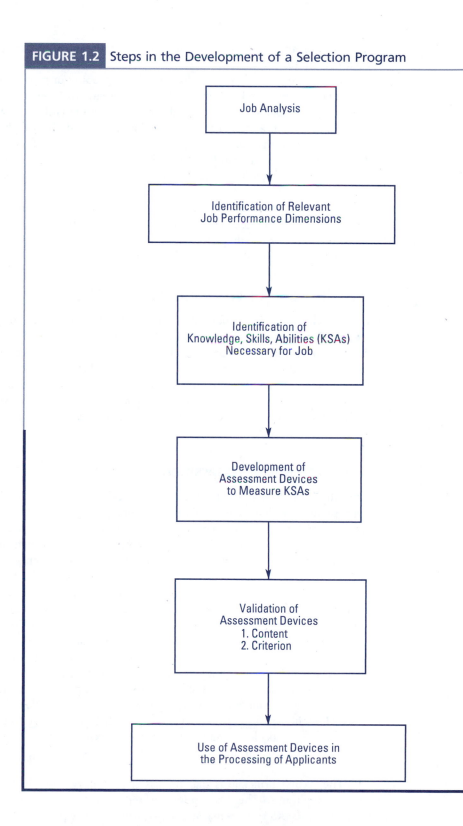

successful on the job. In order to build such a program, selection specialists must know what constitutes success.

In many jobs in which individuals produce an object or meet customers, finding what should be measured and how much of this equals success is relatively straightforward. The objects can be counted and inspected for quality or the customers who receive a service (for example, from a teller) can be counted and surveyed about their satisfaction with the service. However, there are other jobs in which measurement of job performance is not as direct. For example, in team-based jobs, it is difficult to determine how much any one individual has accomplished. And in research and development work, it may take an extended time to translate an idea into a product. In situations such as these, the best source of information about job performance is usually the judgment of the supervisor or the other work team members. Whatever its source or nature, the information as to what constitutes successful job performance is used in the next step of the developmental process.

Identification of Worker Characteristics

Using both job analysis information and job performance data, the HR specialist must identify the KSAs and other employee characteristics that a worker should possess in order to perform the job successfully. These KSAs become the basic pool of characteristics to be evaluated in applicants. This identification is difficult. As we discuss in Chapter 7, a few job analysis methods attempt to identify these KSAs. In most cases, however, HR specialists rely on their own judgments. *Work requirements, worker attributes, worker characteristics,* and *job requirements* are terms frequently used in the same context that we use the term *KSAs.*

Development of Assessment Devices

After the KSAs have been identified, it becomes necessary to either find or construct the appropriate selection devices. These instruments can be classified into the following groups: application blanks, biographical data forms, and reference checks; the selection interview; mental and special abilities tests; personality assessment inventories; and simulation and performance measures. There are two requirements for choosing selection devices to be used. The first is that the device must measure the KSAs the selection specialist has identified as needed for the job. "Duhhh!!!" you say. The problem is that many selection devices that can be purchased or that have been developed by companies measure broad KSAs rather than the specific KSAs for a particular job. For example, application forms usually ask for brief information about previous job titles and job duties but do not collect enough detailed information to clearly determine whether the previous work experience matches the present job. Similarly, interviews frequently attempt to measure general skills such as leadership, attitude, motivation, and personal interaction. These skills are difficult to measure and often not closely related to the specific skills necessary for doing the job, such as the verbal ability to discuss computer hardware and software topics in a way that will be understandable to employees. Selection specialists use test construction principles, which we will discuss in later chapters, to determine the matching of KSAs with the selection device.

The second principle is that the assessment device should be able to differentiate among applicants. The assumption in selection is that applicants possess *different amounts of the KSAs necessary for job performance.* The purpose of the assessment device is to measure these differences (usually by means of numerical scores). It is in this way that promising applicants can be distinguished from unpromising applicants. If nearly all applicants perform about the same on these assessment devices, selection decisions are difficult because the applicants appear to be equal. Choosing a few applicants from a large group of equals is tenuous. The problem of lack of applicant differentiation often occurs when interviews use general questions about career goals and self-assessment of strengths and weaknesses; personality inventories are transparent in purpose (for example, scales measuring the amount of social interaction preferred, or attitudes toward stealing or dishonesty); or simple math or clerical tests are used. Knowing how tests are constructed will help the professional develop—or choose among—tests.

Let us briefly summarize the steps completed by an organization at this point in the selection program development process. Information has been collected describing important aspects of both job activities and outcomes. This information has been used to identify a set of KSAs a worker needs to succeed on the job. A set of selection instruments has been identified that will measure the amount of the KSAs possessed by applicants. If these steps are performed with care, an organization should reasonably expect to obtain the information needed for choosing the right applicants. Frequently, however, the developmental work of the selection program stops at this point. When this happens, there is very little direct evidence available for verifying the accuracy of the above steps. Robert Guion likens these first steps to the development of hypotheses.[19] That is, the HR specialist has formulated testable statements as to the worker characteristics that should be related to successful job performance. The last steps in the development of a selection program can be viewed as a testing of these hypotheses. Technically referred to as *validation,* these steps focus on the collection and evaluation of information to determine whether the worker characteristics thought to be important are, in fact, related to successful job performance. If they are related, then the selection program should be useful to the organization. If, on the other hand, it turns out that the identified worker characteristics are not related to job performance, it is better to learn this as early as possible so that alternatives can be developed.

Validation Procedures

There are several ways to validate the selection process. In *empirical validation,* for example, two types of data are collected: (a) the scores on the selection devices from a representative sample of individuals and (b) measures of how well each of these individuals is performing in important parts of the job. The purpose of validation is to provide evidence that data from the selection instruments are related to job performance. Statistical data analysis, usually correlational analysis (which measures how closely related two different sets of scores are), is the most straightforward manner of producing this evidence. Empirical validation involves calculating correlation coefficients between scores on the selection instruments and on the job performance measure.

In addition to empirical validation, other validation procedures, such as *content* validation, can be used. Content validation systematically takes the data produced by the judgments of workers and managers and uses them to determine the relationship between the selection test and job performance. We will discuss validation in more detail in Chapter 5. No matter which type is employed, it is really only after the validation phase has been completed that one has evidence that the information collected by the selection devices is indicative of job performance and, therefore, useful for choosing among applicants. It is these steps from job analysis to validation that we are referring to when we say that much developmental work must precede the installation of the selection program. If all these steps are not completed, then, in Guion's terms, the organization is using a set of selection instruments that are thought to be useful for the identification of potentially successful workers—but without proper evidence to support this belief.

If the instruments are not related to job performance, their use can be costly because a less than optimum group of workers is being selected for employment. However, organizations often choose not to fully carry out these steps in the development of their selection programs. Less time-consuming and less rigorous procedures are adopted. In such cases, long-term consequences and costs are downplayed or ignored.

CONSTRAINTS IN DEVELOPING A SELECTION PROGRAM

The essence of selection is *prediction* or forecasting. Specifically, we wish to use the information gathered from the selection devices to determine differences among applicants with regard to job-related KSAs and then choose those applicants that we predict will do well in the future in the job under consideration. In HR selection—as in medicine, stock market analysis, meteorology, and economics—prediction is an uncertain activity. Even with a well-developed selection program, not all of the decisions about future job performance will be correct. A number of factors greatly affect the quality of the selection process.

Limited Information on Applicants

The quality of selection decisions depends in part on the accuracy and completeness of data gathered from the applicants. In general, the greater the amount of accurate data obtained, the higher the probability of making an accurate selection decision. However, especially early in the processing of applicants, the amount of the data collected is often severely limited by the cost of obtaining the data. The organization incurs costs for such things as materials and facilities, staff time, travel expenses for staff and applicants, and data storage and analysis. For example, a college campus interviewer frequently spends only 30 minutes with each applicant, and part of this time is devoted to presenting information about the organization. In other cases, application forms and résumés are used extensively as major screening devices. However, campus interviewing and application and résumé forms obtain only limited, basic information about applicants. When there are many applicants for only a few positions, a great many applicants will be dropped. With the limited information gleaned from application blanks or interviews, mistakes can be made both with those selected and those rejected.

Measurement of Jobs, Individuals, and Work Performance

A basic assumption of this book is that the development of a selection program requires the measurement of characteristics of jobs, individuals, and work performance. By *measurement* we mean quantitative description—that is, the use of numbers. Numbers are used to represent information such as the amount of time an applicant has spent in a job activity, or the level of mathematical knowledge an applicant needs to perform a task, or an applicant's score on a verbal skills test, or the quality of a worker's performance in preparing an advertisement. Numbers are necessary because they facilitate the comparison of people. They transmit information more succinctly than words, and they permit statistical manipulation (such as the adding of scores across selection tests to get a total score for each applicant), which provides even more information about the selection program. For example, assume that there are 12 applicants for an entry-level position in the loan department of a bank. All are interviewed and all complete a brief test on financial terms and analysis. Quantifying the performance of each candidate on each of the two selection instruments is the most practical way of comparing them. If scores are not developed, the selection specialist is placed in a complex situation; differences must be determined among the 12 using descriptive information such as "He seemed able to express himself pretty well," or "She knew most of the financial terms but did not seem comfortable judging the risk of the loan." Obviously, when there are such statements about a number of individuals, the difficulty in identifying the most promising of the applicants is enormous.

The problem of measurement for the HR specialist, however, is to ensure that the numbers generated are accurate descriptions of the characteristics of the applicant, the job, or the job performance under study. We address specific measurement issues throughout this text, especially in Chapters 3 through 5. For now we can say that the measurement of many KSAs is difficult and not as precise as we would wish.

A comment is necessary at this point to make sure that we do not give you a false impression. We have mentioned that it is important, when making selection decisions, to use selection instruments that generate scores about the characteristics of applicants. That is not to say, however, that selection decisions are always made by counting the scores and offering employment only to those who score the highest, even though some maintain that the best results occur when this is done. It is common that other factors also enter into the decisions—for example, a desire to balance the demographic composition of the workforce or an intuition about a specific applicant. In this type of situation, our position is that these additional factors should come into play only after the applicants have been measured on the selection devices and a group has been identified as being appropriate for the job. These other factors can then be used in choosing individuals from this group. Very different, and much less desirable, results can occur if these other factors are used early in selection, before the applicant pool has been measured. In such situations, a great number of errors can be made before the selection instruments are even used.

Other Factors Affecting Work Performance

A third issue to keep in mind regarding selection programs is that many factors affect work performance. The primary purpose of selection is to enhance the probability of making correct employment decisions—extending offers to those persons who will perform well in the organization and not extending job offers to those who will not do well. Typically, any evaluation of the adequacy of the selection program is made in terms of job performance.

However, it is apparent that the KSAs of those hired are not the sole determinants of job performance. Practitioners and researchers have identified numerous other factors in an organization that affect individual performance. Among these organizational factors are training programs for employees, appraisal and feedback methods, goal-setting procedures, financial compensation systems, work design strategies, supervisory methods, organizational structure, decision-making techniques, and work schedules.

The implication of these findings for the evaluation of selection programs is clear. A selection program focuses on a few of the many variables that influence performance. Often it is difficult to adequately assess its effectiveness. At times, a thoughtfully developed program might seem to have only a minimal measurable relationship to performance. It is possible in such cases that one or more of the other variables that we have mentioned is adversely affecting performance levels and negating the contribution of the selection program. The conclusion is that it is advisable, in judging selection programs, to examine several other organizational systems when attempting to diagnose deficiencies in employee performance.

Selection Research vs. Selection Practice

Both selection researchers and organizational specialists who implement selection programs have realized during the last several years that the two groups differ in how they treat selection. Edward Lawler III, an academic researcher who works with organizations, has made this statement:

> A great deal that passes as "best practice" in HRM most likely is not. In some cases, there simply is no evidence to support what is thought to be best practice. In other cases, there is evidence to support that what are thought to be best practices are, in fact, inferior practices. In short, most organizations do not practice evidence-based human resource management. As a result, they often underperform with respect to their major stakeholders: employees, investors, and the community.[20]

This difference between what academic research has shown and what often is implemented in organizations is true of many fields in addition to HRM. *Evidence-based management* is a term that means managing by translating principles based on evidence into organizational practice. Through evidence-based management, practicing managers develop into organizational experts who make decisions informed by social science and organizational research. They move professional decisions away from personal preference and unsystematic experience toward those based upon the best available scientific evidence.[21] Said another way, evidence-based management means that managers should become knowledgeable about research results in specific topics of management and how this research is translated into practice. Knowing this will help guide the decision making of managers so that more decisions are based upon evidence and data rather than intuition and hunch.

Unfortunately, evidence-based management is not universal in organizations. Some organizations practice it while many others do not. This divide between research findings and organizational practice occurs in many areas of management, not just in HRM. It is relatively common that practicing managers do not know about academic research and instead base decisions on their own experience, that of close associates, or common practices within their organizations. There are many reasons for this discrepancy. Most basic is that management is not an occupation like medicine, law, or teaching in which entrants to the field must pass some exam, or provide a specific degree, or pass a specific test. As we know, managers come from all educational backgrounds. Some have little education, and some resist academic research findings as too theoretical and impractical. Another reason is that courses that make up a management major can vary greatly between colleges. Some majors require HRM courses; others do not even offer such courses. Related to this, some faculty are quite good at translating HRM research into practice and others are unable to make this translation. Another reason is that practice managers usually do not have the research, statistical, and content knowledge to be able to read published academic research, understand the findings, and recognize the practice implications of these findings. This lack of understanding is to be expected; the knowledge of research and the specialized content of academic areas is what Ph.D. programs teach. Managers do not often attend Ph.D. programs. It is for this reason that some firms, including State Farm Insurance, recommend that some executives employ academic consultants who can discuss relevant research findings with them.

What this means is that this book makes recommendations about selection that you may not find implemented by a specific organization with which you are familiar. However, we know that many organizations do practice the recommendations we make here. Think of the book as your basis for evidence-based selection (EBS). After you finish this course, send us a copy of your final grade and a blank, signed check; we will send you an official EBS button in the day-glow color of your choice. Wearing that button will add a nice touch when you interview for jobs.

Selection and Staffing

Although *selection* and *staffing* are often used interchangeably, we think the two terms describe very different concepts. Staffing is a broad concept that can refer to the various HR programs and techniques used to manage the employees of an organization. Staffing defines the process of systematically filling positions within the organization and then monitoring the performance of individuals in those positions. It includes the process of developing the important KSAs of these people in order to increase both present and future performance. Activities associated with staffing include recruitment, selection, training, work performance measurement, succession planning, job reassignment, termination, and compensation. In many ways, staffing is closer to strategic human resource management as we have previously described it than it is to selection.

We think that knowledge of selection is an essential foundation for staffing. It is not possible to practice effective staffing without a complete understanding of selection. Specific topics we will cover—such as measurement of job components, identification of KSAs, understanding the strengths and weaknesses of various selection instruments, measurement principles, legal employment issues, and essentials of quantifying work performance—must be understood and used correctly in order for staffing to work as it should. The essence of staffing is to determine job demands and the level of KSAs individuals possess and then using this information in various ways to increase workers' performance. Staffing applies the knowledge of selection in a wide variety of ways.

CURRENT ISSUES IN SELECTION

Broadly Defined and Team-Based Jobs

The human resource selection procedures and research that we describe in this text are a product of the steady development of this field over the course of almost 100 years. During most of this time, the makeup of jobs in organizations has remained essentially the same. That is, a job has generally included a small group of related activities designed to be performed by an individual who, for the most part, works alone. An organization's product or service was developed in stages, usually by individual workers who passed the work on to other employees. Although it took a group of workers to make a product or service, this group did not function as an interactive group but rather as a collection of individuals. Most of the existing selection procedures were developed for this traditional model of work. Many jobs included a small number of tasks that remained constant over time. In addition, KSAs were usually thought of in terms of technical knowledge, the application of that knowledge in problem-solving work activities, and various cognitive abilities. These KSAs were the most important factors for success in these individual-oriented jobs.

Recent changes in the way work is done in organizations, however, has prompted an examination of the adequacy of traditional selection procedures for these new work methods. Current management philosophies that emphasize continuous improvement, employee involvement, and autonomous work teams demand that the work processes within an organization be performed by individuals sharing work assignments within work teams. That is, organizations are increasingly designing work that is done interactively by groups of employees. Structuring work in this way has major implications for selection programs. The most obvious of these is that often the success of a work team depends not only on technical knowledge and ability but also on the interaction abilities of members.

Selection specialists have recently addressed these issues in the development of selection programs. The research on the selection of individuals into interactive work teams has mainly focused on measuring applicants on the characteristics that are related to the interaction among team members, characteristics that lead to effective team performance. These characteristics are regarded as different from the KSAs that are necessary for doing the work tasks of the team. Michael Stevens and Michael Campion have developed a selection test that measures 14 characteristics of team-oriented work interaction, regardless of the specific team task.[22] These 14 characteristics can be grouped into five categories: conflict resolution, collaborative problem solving, communication, goal setting and performance management, and planning and task coordination. The two authors refer to these characteristics as KSAs necessary for teamwork and clearly indicate that these are not personality or technical KSAs. One research study has supported the relation of these teamwork KSAs to individuals' performance in team interaction. That is, three observers of interactive teams rated individuals with high scores on Stevens' and Campion's test as high also in how well each interacted with others in accomplishing work tasks.[23]

Other research on the selection of work team members starts with the assumption that contextual performance (activities that support the organization's social and psychological environment) are necessary for successful team performance.[24] To study this, researchers developed an interview that measured a variety of social skills; used a personality test that measured four traits; and used Stevens' and Campion's Teamwork KSA Test described previously. They found that scores on all three selection devices were related to contextual work performance, which, in turn, was strongly related to team work performance. These research findings point out that overall work performance of interactive work teams is dependent on KSAs of both technical business operations and team interaction. Both should be incorporated into selection programs used for employing interactive team members.

Given changes over time in the nature of work and the obvious conclusion that selection procedures will change to correspond to these new work designs, you may be wondering about the value of learning about selection procedures that have been developed and applied to jobs designed under the traditional philosophy. Our job is to convince you that the rest of this book is useful. Let's try these arguments. First, as in all fields based on technical knowledge, future developments in selection will be based on what is previously known about the field. That is, no one has indicated that selection methods for interactive work teams will be so different from traditional selection methods that it will be necessary to start from ground zero. Selection in any form will use information about the characteristics of work activities and people. What we currently know about work activities and people will be the basis for the future evolution of selection.

Second, it seems that many of the specific techniques and measurement instruments that have been used in selection may continue to be used in team-based selection. We have already discussed, for example, how current research into team-based selection practices has described the use of interviews, personality tests, and even paper-pencil tests. The use of these instruments for teams can be directly adapted from their traditional use in selection.

Third, selection in any form will still be based on measurement principles—rules about how to assign numbers to characteristics of work activities and individuals. Measurement has been central to selection throughout its development. The principles of measurement will certainly be continued in future forms of selection.

Fourth, although the philosophy of work may change in organizations, the legal environment in which selection decisions are made will not change as fast or as radically. As we discuss throughout this text, the evidence and proof that are necessary in legal questions about selection practices require the production of data about work activities, employee characteristics, and work performance. These measurement data will be important regardless of the future nature of work and the nature of the employee characteristics measured.

All this has been a long way of saying that even though changes in organizations will be reflected by changes in selection, these changes will be based on what we currently know and do. Understanding the principles of selection currently being used is essential for developing future selection principles and techniques.

Selection in Small Business

The number of open positions in large and small organizations has shifted dramatically in the recent past. That is, large organizations have been reducing the number of employees, and small businesses have been increasing the number of employees. In fact, small businesses provided most of the recent growth in numbers of jobs. These employment patterns mean that a large percentage of selection decisions are made for small businesses. However, many individuals believe that formalized selection programs were developed by large organizations and can only be used by such organizations because of the cost of development and the necessity of using selection specialists. We agree with only half of that statement. For the most part, formalized selection programs were developed by large organizations. However, we strongly disagree with the conclusion that these selection programs can be used only by large firms.

We think much of the knowledge that has been developed about selection can be directly applied to small organizations. Think about the steps in selection that we previously described. In these, a job analysis is completed, successful job performance is defined, and, based on this information, KSAs are identified. Finally, selection instruments are developed and validated. Nothing about these steps presupposes that they can be followed only within large organizations. Small business owners and managers usually know the activities of the jobs in their companies very well. Often the owner has performed all of these activities. Recording this information by writing task statements (doing a job analysis), using these statements to identify KSAs, and developing appropriate selection instruments to measure these KSAs can certainly be accomplished by one or two people in a small business—if they have the proper knowledge. In fact, a survey of the recruitment and selection practices of small businesses found that these companies use multiple practices that are very similar to those used by large firms.[25]

Many of the selection instruments that we discuss in this book are appropriate for small businesses.[26] For example, training and experience evaluation forms and structured, behavior-based interviews and work sample tests can quite easily be developed for small businesses. Basic information necessary for content validity can also be gathered.

We know that selection in small organizations has usually consisted of informal decision making by the owner or manager. However, there is nothing inherent in small business operations or selection to indicate that this has to be the case. Knowledge about the steps and instruments of selection can be very useful to these organizations.

PLAN OF THIS BOOK

The major purpose of this book is to discuss each of the steps necessary for developing selection programs within organizations. We will concentrate on the characteristics of the data that should be gathered and the types of decisions the HR specialist should make at each step. We incorporate research about selection and discuss its implications for the development of HR selection programs. There is no one blueprint for the development of selection programs, and we do not wish to give that impression. The steps we refer to are different stages in the accumulation and processing of information about jobs, individuals, and job performance. At each step, the HR specialist must make a number of decisions, not only about the kind of data needed, but also about the statistical analyses that should be done and about what decisions can be made based upon that data. The particular selection needs of the organization will dictate the appropriate actions; we hope this book will provide information necessary for evaluating options at each stage.

The book is divided into five parts. The first two chapters present an overview of the selection program and its legal environment. Chapters 3 through 6 are devoted to the major measurement issues in selection. These chapters provide the basic information necessary for measuring characteristics of applicants, jobs, and job performance—within the legal direction of the courts. They also discuss how to use measurement data in selection decision making. Chapters 7 explains job analysis and the identification of KSAs. This information is the basis of selection. Chapter 8 discusses recruitment purpose, strategy, and techniques in detail. As we have previously mentioned, recruitment is critical to selection because it provides the applicant pool from which individuals are selected and offered employment. Chapter 9 through 14 discuss in detail the various selection instruments. They present common forms of each instrument, indicate measurement concerns, and suggest the most appropriate use of each instrument. Chapter 15 summarizes the methods of measuring job performance for use in selection programs.

REFERENCES

1. David E. Bowen and Cherrie Ostroff, "Understanding HRM—Firm Performance Linkages: The Role of the 'Strength' of the HRM System," *Academy of Management Review* 29 (2004): 203–221. See also Patrick M. Wright, B. B. Dunford, and S. A. Snell, "Human Resources and the Resource-Based View of the Firm," *Journal of Management* 27 (2001): 701–721.

2. Patrick M. Wright, K. Michele Kacmar, Gary C. McMahan, and Kevin Deleeuw, "P-f(MxA): Cognitive Ability as a Moderator of the Relationship between Personality and Job Performance," *Journal of Management* 21 (1995): 1129–1139.

3. Irene E. DePrater, Vianen Van, E. M. Annelies, Myriam N. Bechtoldt, and Ute-Christine Klehe, "Employees' Challenging Job Experiences and Supervisors' Evaluations of Promotability," *Personnel Psychology* 62 (2009): 297–325.

4. Chun Hui, Simon S. K. Lam, and Kenneth K. S. Law, "Instrumental Values of Organizational Citizenship Behavior for Promotion: A Field Quasi-Experiment," *Personnel Review* 35 (2006): 66–77.

5. Steven L. Premack and John P. Wanous, "A Meta-Analysis of Realistic Job Preview Experiments," *Journal of Applied Psychology* 70 (1986): 706–719.

6. Christopher J. Collins and Kevin D. Clark, "Strategic Human Resource Practices, Top Management Team Social Networks, and Firm Performance: The Role of Human Resource Practices in Creating Organizational Competitive Advantage," *Academy of Management Journal* 46 (2003): 740–752.

7. Bowen and Ostroff, "Understanding HRM—Firm Performance Linkages: The Role of the 'Strength' of the HRM System." *Academy of Management Review* 29 (2004): 203–221. See also Patrick M. Wright, B. B. Dunford, and S. A. Snell, "Human Resources and the Resource-Based View of the Firm," *Journal of Management* 27 (2001): 701–721.

8. Abraham Cameli and John Schaubreck, "How Leveraging Human Resource Capital with Its Competitive Distinctness Enhances the Performance of Commercial and Public Organizations," *Human Resource Management* 44 (2005): 391–412.

9. Collins and Clark, "Strategic Human Resource Practices, Top Management Team Social Networks, and Firm Performance: The Role of Human Resource Practices in Creating Organizational Competitive Advantage."

10. Derek S. Chapman, Krista L. Uggerslev, Sarah A. Carroll, Kelly A. Piasentin, and David A. Jones, "Applicant Attraction to Organizations and Job Choice: A Meta-Analytic Review of the Correlates of Recruiting Outcomes," *Journal of Applied Psychology* 90 (2005): 928–944.

11. Sara L. Rynes, "Recruitment, Job Choice, and Post-Hire Consequences: A Call for New Research Directions," in *Handbook of Industrial and Organizational Psychology*, 2nd ed., vol. 2, ed. M. D. Dunnette and L. M. Hough (Palo Alto, CA: Consulting Psychologists Press, 1991).

12. Mark A. Huselid, "The Impact of Human Resource Management Practices on Turnover, Productivity, and Corporate Financial Performance," *Academy of Management Journal* 38 (1995): 635–672.

13. J. P. MacDuffie, "Human Resource Bundles and Manufacturing Performance: Organizational Logic and Flexible Production Systems in the World Auto Industry," *Industrial and Labor Relations Review* 48 (1995): 197–221.

14. John E. Delery and D. Harold Doty, "Modes of Theorizing in Strategic Human Resource Management: Tests of Universalistic, Contingency and Configurational Performance Predictions," *Academy of Management Journal* 39 (1996): 802–835.

15. Mark A. Youndt, Scott A. Snell, James W. Dean Jr., and David P. Lepak, "Human Resource Management, Manufacturing Strategy, and Firm Performance," *Academy of Management Journal* 39 (1996): 836–866.

16. John P. Guthrie, "High Involvement Work Practices, Turnover, and Productivity: Evidence from New Zealand," *Academy of Management Journal* 44 (2001): 180–192.

17. Patrick M. Wright, Timothy M. Gardner, Lisa M. Moynihan, and Matthew R. Allen, "The Relationship between HR Practices and Firm Performance: Examining Causal Order," *Personnel Psychology* 58, no. 2 (2005): 409–446.

18. Murray R. Barrick and Ryan D. Zimmerman, "Reducing Voluntary, Avoidable Turnover through Selection," *Journal of Applied Psychology* 90 (2005): 159–166.

19. Robert M. Guion, "Personnel Assessment, Selection, and Placement," in *Handbook of Industrial and Organizational Psychology*, 2nd ed., vol. 2, ed. M. D. Dunnette and L. M. Hough (Palo Alto, CA: Consulting Psychologists Press, 1991), 327–398.

20. Edward E. Lawler III, "Why HR Practices Are Not Evidence-Based," *Academy of Management Journal* 50 (2007): 1033–1044.

21. Denise M. Rosseau, "Is There Such a Thing as 'Evidence-Based Management'?' *Academy of Management Review* 31 (2006): 256–269.

22. Michael J. Stevens and Michael A. Campion, "The Knowledge, Skill, and Ability Requirements for Teamwork: Implications for Human Resource Management," *Journal of Management* 20 (1994): 503–530. See also Michael J. Stevens and Michael A. Campion, "Staffing Work Teams: Development and Validation of a Selection Test for Teamwork Settings," *Journal of Management* 25 (1999): 207–228.

23. A. C. McClough and S. G. Rogelberg, "Selection in Teams: An Exploration of the Teamwork Knowledge, Skills, and Ability Test," *International Journal of Selection and Assessment* 11, no. 1 (2003): 56–66.

24. Frederick P. Morgeson, Matthew H. Reider, and Michael A. Campion, "Selecting Individuals in Team Settings: The Importance of Social Skills, Personality Characteristics, and Teamwork Knowledge," *Personnel Psychology* 58, no. 3 (2005): 583–611.

25. Herbert G. Heneman III and Robyn A. Berkley, "Applicant Attraction Practices and Outcomes among Small Businesses," *Journal of Small Business Management* 37 (1999): 53–74.

26. Robert D. Gatewood and Hubert S. Feild, "A Personnel Selection Program," *Journal of Small Business Management* 25 (1987): 16–25.

Legal Issues in Selection

As discussed in Chapter 1, the development of a selection program is a formidable task even when we deal only with the measurement issues. It becomes even more complex when we add the legal policies that must be considered. These legal policies influence the records that must be kept on all employment decisions, the determination of fair treatment of all applicants, and the methods for identifying the job relatedness of selection devices.

If the organization does not attend to these legal policies in the development and use of selection programs, it will be vulnerable to charges of discrimination. A court judgment against the organization in such a case can be extremely costly. Courts can order organizations to make back-pay settlements to individuals they had not hired, to pay punitive damages, to change selection devices and decision rules, and to maintain specified percentages of women and minority group members in future employment patterns. It is imperative that HR specialists have a thorough understanding of the legal guidelines for. selection decisions. Actually, every selection program should have two objectives: (a) maximizing the probability of making accurate selection decisions about applicants and (b) ensuring that these selection decisions are carried out in such a manner as to minimize the chance of a judgment of discrimination being made against the organization. The two are not mutually exclusive objectives and overlap considerably in necessary procedures and data. However, it is also true that there are examples of apparent conflict between these two objectives, which we will discuss in appropriate parts of the book. One example is affirmative action programs that, to many, seem to provide an advantage to minorities by specifying numerical goals for selecting among demographic groups. Another is the use of certain paper-pencil tests that, while valid, almost always produce lower average scores for minority applicants than for nonminority applicants. Seemingly, these score differences provide advantage to nonminority applicants.

Chapter 1 addressed the major background issues that lead to the first objective of selection, making accurate selection decisions. This chapter does the same for the second objective by discussing the following:

1. The basic principles of federal regulation of HR activities

2. An overview of the specific laws and executive orders appropriate to selection

3. The types of evidence used in deciding when discrimination has occurred

4. The types and characteristics of affirmative action programs

5. Major court cases in selection

6. The most important legal issues to consider in developing and implementing a selection program

FEDERAL REGULATION OF BUSINESS

Federal regulation can be traced back to the creation of the Interstate Commerce Commission (ICC) in 1887. For many years, coping with government regulation has been a part of business activities. What is different in recent years is the nature of that regulation. Traditionally, regulation was confined to a given industry. For example, the ICC regulates the railroad and trucking industries, and the Federal Communications Commission (FCC) regulates the radio, telephone, and television industries. For the most part, these traditional agencies act to increase competition and to prevent a monopoly from developing. One of their major purposes is to promote the well-being of the industry by preventing domination by a few members. In this sense, industry companies are actually the constituents of the regulatory agency, because the agency works on their behalf.

Regulatory Model

Newer regulatory agencies have a very different approach. James Ledvinka and Vida Scarpello presented a regulatory model of this approach (see Figure 2.1). Understanding this model is useful to HR specialists, enabling them to explain and even anticipate actions of regulatory agencies.

The thrust of federal regulation for HR activities is equal employment opportunity (EEO). The major characteristic that differentiates regulation in this area from traditional regulation is that it is not specific to one industry; it is applied to many. Rather than being directed to the well-being of a particular industry, as in the past, regulation now attempts to solve social and economic problems, as shown in the left column of Figure 2.1. Equal Employment Opportunity (EEO) regulation is directed toward the solution of employment inequalities. The constituents of EEO regulatory agencies are not business organizations but political and social groups devoted to insuring employment for various groups of workers. Realizing this is key to understanding employment regulation.

The various components of this regulation process are depicted in Figure 2.1. As Ledvinka and Scarpello explain the model:

> *(1) Regulation begins with social political problems, which cause lawmakers to pass laws; (2) those laws empower agencies to take the regulatory actions that trigger management responses; and (3) the courts oversee this process by settling disputes between the parties to it.*[1]

To fully understand EEO regulation it is necessary, therefore, to be familiar with two factors: (a) the laws and executive orders that state general principles and empower regulatory agencies, and (b) the court decisions that interpret these general principles in specific situations. Both of these factors create employment guidelines for organizations. We treat both of these topics, starting with the laws and directives, and discuss the court cases later in the chapter.

EEO Laws and Executive Orders

EEO laws are federal laws whose purpose is the elimination of discrimination in HR management decisions. EEO executive orders are statements made by the executive branch of the government intended for the same purpose but aimed at organizations that do business directly with the government. The scope of EEO laws and executive orders affects other HRM decisions in addition to selection, although selection decisions

FIGURE 2.1   Regulatory Model of EEO

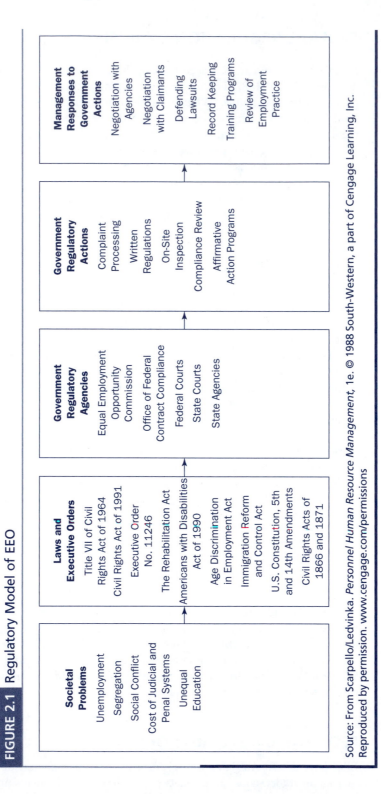

Societal Problems	Laws and Executive Orders	Government Regulatory Agencies	Government Regulatory Actions	Management Responses to Government Actions
Unemployment	Title VII of Civil Rights Act of 1964	Equal Employment Opportunity Commission	Complaint Processing	Negotiation with Agencies
Segregation	Civil Rights Act of 1991	Office of Federal Contract Compliance	Written Regulations	Negotiation with Claimants
Social Conflict	Executive Order No. 11246	Federal Courts	On-Site Inspection	Defending Lawsuits
Cost of Judicial and Penal Systems	The Rehabilitation Act	State Courts	Compliance Review	Record Keeping
Unequal Education	Americans with Disabilities Act of 1990	State Agencies	Affirmative Action Programs	Training Programs
	Age Discrimination in Employment Act			Review of Employment Practice
	Immigration Reform and Control Act			
	U.S. Constitution, 5th and 14th Amendments			
	Civil Rights Acts of 1866 and 1871			

Source: From Scarpello/Ledvinka. *Personnel Human Resource Management*, 1e. © 1988 South-Western, a part of Cengage Learning, Inc. Reproduced by permission. www.cengage.com/permissions

TABLE 2.1	Major EEO Laws and Executive Orders Regarding Selection

Law	Demographic Characteristics	Employers Covered
Title VII Civil Rights Act of 1964	Race, color, religion, sex, or national origin	Private employers with at least 15 employees, governments, unions, employment agencies, employers receiving federal assistance
Civil Rights Act of 1991	Race, color, religion, sex, or national origin	Same as Title VII
Executive Order No. 11246	Race, color, religion, sex, or national origin	Federal contractors and subcontractors
Age Discrimination in Employment Act of 1967	Age (over 40 years)	Private employers, governments, unions, employment agencies
The Rehabilitation Act of 1973	Physical and mental disability	Federal contractors, federal government
Americans with Disabilities Act of 1990	Physical and mental disability	Private employers, labor unions, employment agencies
ADA Amendments Act of 2008	Physical and mental disability	Private employers, labor unions, employment agencies
Immigration Reform and Control Act of 1986	Citizenship, national origin	Private employers with 4 or more employees, governments
U.S. Constitution 5th Amendment	All demographic characteristics	Federal government
U.S. Constitution 14th Amendment	All demographic characteristics	State and local governments
Civil Rights Act of 1866	Race, national, and ethnic origin	Private employers, unions, employment agencies
Civil Rights Act of 1871	All demographic characteristics	State and local governments

have received a great deal of publicity, especially early in the history of the enforcement of EEO laws.

In the following pages we will summarize major employment laws and explain their purposes and implications for employment decisions, especially selection. Table 2.1 lists ten employment laws and one executive order and includes a brief summary of the major provisions of each.

Title VII Civil Rights Act of 1964

Under Title VII, private employers, unions, employment agencies, joint labor-management committees that direct apprenticeship and training programs, and federal, state, and local governments are prohibited from discriminating on the basis of *sex, race, color, religion,* or *national origin.* These are the only personal characteristics covered by Title VII. The law has been amended several times. In 1972 enforcement powers were strengthened and coverage was expanded to include governmental and educational system employers as well as private employers with more than 15 employees. A 1978 amendment prohibited discrimination based on pregnancy, childbirth, or related conditions. The only employers not covered by Title VII are private clubs, religious organizations, places of employment connected with an Indian reservation, certain departments in the District of Columbia, and corporations wholly owned by the government of the United States.

The Equal Employment Opportunity Commission (EEOC) is the enforcement agency for Title VII. Basically, it acts in response to a charge of discrimination filed by one of the EEOC commissioners or initiated by an aggrieved person or someone acting on behalf of an aggrieved person. In most cases, the charge of discrimination must be filed within 180 days of the alleged act. After the EEOC has assumed jurisdiction, the first step is the no-fault settlement attempt, an invitation to the accused to settle the case without an admission of guilt. If this option is not accepted, the case is taken to the second step, that of investigation. During this period the employer is prohibited from destroying any records related to the charge and is invited to submit a position paper regarding the charge, which becomes part of the investigatory data. At the completion of this phase, the district director of EEOC issues a statement of "probable cause" or "no probable cause." In the case of a probable-cause decision, an attempt is made at conciliation between the two parties. This usually involves some major concessions on the part of the employer regarding the employment practice under question. If it fails to obtain a conciliation agreement, the EEOC can either undertake litigation itself or issue a right-to-sue notice to the charging party, informing this party that it may bring its own action in federal court.

In one example of the enforcement of the Civil Rights Act of 1964, in December, 2009 the EEOC and Outback Steakhouse restaurants agreed to a $19 million settlement for alleged gender discrimination in promotion. EEOC filed the suit on behalf of several women who alleged that they could not move above low-level management positions while men with less experience and less education were promoted to higher levels of management. Among the allegations was that a joint venture partner had said that female managers "let him down" and "lost focus" when they had children. He also allegedly said that women managers had trouble "saying no" and that he wanted "cute girls" to work in the front as servers. A managing partner was alleged to have told a female employee that she should be a teacher instead of working in the restaurant business.

In settling the case, Outback Steakhouse did not admit to any wrongdoing. However, the company agreed to not discriminate on the basis of gender or retaliate against any employee who "participated in the EEOC process." In addition to posting the terms of the consent decree in all its restaurants, Outback must display the terms of the agreement on its in-house computer system. Further, the restaurant chain must train management staff, directors, and human resources personnel on the settlement's terms and conditions and tell them they could be fired for breaching the agreement. Outback also agreed to provide letters of reference for four women who brought the suit. When contacted for a job reference for any former employee covered by the consent decree, Outback will provide only dates of employment, salary, and position held.

Outback and the EEOC also picked a consultant to:

- Analyze information on hiring and promotions and provide periodic reports

- Review the company's summary of employee complaints of discrimination, harassment, and retaliation

- Make recommendations for meeting the settlement's goals

- Decide whether Outback has "appropriate and reasonable" procedures in place to protect female employees from discrimination, harassment, and retaliation[2]

Civil Rights Act of 1991

The Civil Rights Act of 1991 amends the Civil Rights Act of 1964. Its most important provisions address the extent of evidence that must be demonstrated in discrimination cases, the ceiling for damages for discrimination, the adjustment of scores on selection tests for different races, and the establishment of the Glass Ceiling Commission, which will recommend ways to remove barriers to women and minorities that limit advancement in organizations. Concerning the provision that treats the extent of evidence of discrimination, Congress passed the Civil Rights Act of 1991 to counter a series of Supreme Court rulings. These rulings—by increasing plaintiffs' burdens of proof and reducing those of defendant organizations—were considered to have a negative effect on those filing charges of discrimination. In essence, this act returned the burdens of proof to be similar to those that were mandated in early Supreme Court discrimination decisions. We will explain these burdens of proof later in this chapter.

Even though this act did return to early requirements for burdens of proof, it nevertheless had a large effect on the information that plaintiffs must include in any charge of discrimination: The complaining party must identify the particular selection practice in question and demonstrate the adverse impact caused by that practice. The only exception to this stipulation is when the plaintiff can demonstrate that the employer's selection decisions cannot be separated according to each selection instrument. In other words, the selection decision is based on scores from all selection instruments. This requirement to present evidence in reference to a specific selection practice is in contrast to previous selection court cases. That is, plaintiffs usually had only to demonstrate that adverse impact occurred after the whole selection program was completed; they did not have to identify the specific part of the program that caused this adverse impact.

This act also allows victims of intentional discrimination, including sexual harassment, to sue for both compensatory and punitive damages. Punitive damages may be recovered against a respondent (but not a government or its agency) if the complainant demonstrates that the respondent engaged in a discriminatory practice with malice or "reckless indifference." The sum of compensatory damages is capped at between $50,000 and $300,000, depending on the number of employees with the company. The act also allows for more extensive use of jury trials. Many legal experts think that the use of jury trials may increase the probability of the plaintiff being successful in discrimination lawsuits. This is because, historically, juries have been more sympathetic to plaintiffs than to defendants.

Another part of the act, section 106 (1), makes it unlawful for an employer "in connection with the selection or referral of applicants or candidates for employment or promotion, to adjust the scores of, use different cutoff scores for, or otherwise alter the results of employment-related tests on the basis of race, color, religion, sex, or national origin."[3] This prohibits race norming: the practice of ranking test scores of minorities separately from nonminorities, and of choosing high scorers within each group in order to create or maintain a more diverse workforce. This practice originated within the U.S. Department of Labor in the early 1980s when the U.S. Employment Service decided to promote the use of its General Aptitude Test Battery (GATB) to individual state employment services.[4] The GATB is a general cognitive ability test composed of 12 subtests. The Employment Service found evidence that the use of the GATB inevitably led to significant between-group differences in average test scores. Blacks as a group typically scored well below the group of white applicants; Hispanics, on average, scored between these two groups.[5] Therefore, in order to promote federal equal employment opportunity and affirmative action goals, race norming of test scores was invented.[6]

Selection specialists have been mixed in their views of norming. Supporters point to the major benefit of helping employers hire a qualified but diverse workforce. Supporters' belief in this benefit is backed by the opinion that selection tests usually measure no more than 25 percent of how well people perform in jobs. Detractors have pointed out that minorities usually score lower than nonminorities on many valid selection tests, and any adjustment in the ranking of applicants can be expected to lower overall job performance.[7]

Part of the act is based on Congress's findings that even though the number of women and minorities in the workforce has grown dramatically, they continue to be underrepresented in management and decision-making positions. The so-called glass ceiling effect, then, refers to artificial barriers that impede their advancement to these higher positions. Under the act, a Glass Ceiling Commission was established to study (a) the manner in which business fills these higher positions, (b) the developmental and skill-enhancing practices used to foster necessary qualifications for advancement into these positions, and (c) the compensation programs and reward structures utilized in the workplace.

Executive Order 11246

This order is directed toward contractors who do more than $10,000 per year in business with the federal government. Enacted in 1965, it prohibits the same discriminatory acts as Title VII. In addition, it requires contractors who have more than $50,000 in business with the government and more than 50 employees to develop *affirmative action plans*. These are formal, specific HR programs that are designed to increase the participation of protected groups. We discuss affirmative action plans later in the chapter. An affirmative action program is not a requirement of Title VII.

Enforcement of executive orders is the responsibility of the Department of Labor, specifically the Office of Federal Contract Compliance Programs (OFCCP). Investigations by the OFCCP are not dependent on charges of discrimination being filed, but, instead, are a product of the OFCCP's administrative review of contractors. The OFCCP can issue a statement of noncompliance that can adversely affect the contractor's participation in government business. When a statement of noncompliance is issued and the deficiencies are not corrected, an administrative hearing procedure before an administrative-law judge can be initiated. The whole procedure can take several years. During this time, the government can impose sanctions on the organization.

Age Discrimination in Employment Act of 1967 (ADEA)

This act, which has been amended several times, has the intention of promoting employment of older persons based on their ability and eliminating barriers to employment based on age. The underlying premise of the act is that there are large individual differences among workers of all ages; some older workers are superior to some young workers. Age, therefore, is not a valid indicator of ability to perform. The act prohibits discrimination against individuals who are 40 years old or older. This act applies to private industry, federal and state governments, employment agencies, and labor organizations.

Enforcement of the ADEA resides in the EEOC, and is usually initiated by the filing of a charge of discrimination. For example, EEOC brought suit against Freudenberg-NOK General Partnership, an auto parts manufacturer based in Michigan, when Freudenberg refused to hire a man for a controller position because of his age. According to the EEOC lawsuit, Timothy Poh applied for and was interviewed for the controller position in the fall of 2006. After Poh followed up several times, Freudenberg called him back on Jan. 3, 2007. At that time the company told him that although he was well qualified, it was looking for someone "not quite so old with as much experience." Freudenberg offered the position to two younger applicants and eventually hired a younger, less qualified person for the position.[8]

The EEOC has the authority to review organizations when there is no charge. The act also provides for trial by jury. This is thought to be potentially beneficial to the person bringing suit because the plaintiff's age and other personal characteristics may elicit a sympathetic reaction from the jury. For example, the EEOC won a jury trial on behalf of four employees of the University of Wisconsin Press. The plaintiffs were awarded $430,427.[9] The four employees, all older than 46 and the oldest employees of the organization, were discharged and replaced by four much younger employees. The company's rationale was that the older employees lacked necessary computer skills; they were terminated as part of a more general reduction in the workforce. The EEOC argued that the four were willing to undergo computer training and should have been given that opportunity.

The Rehabilitation Act of 1973

This act, directed toward the federal government and federal contractors, requires both nondiscrimination in employment practices and also affirmative action toward the disabled. The Americans with Disabilities Act (ADA) of 1990, which we discuss next, essentially replaces the Rehabilitation Act, whose major importance is that its wording is similar to critical sections of the ADA. Therefore, court decisions regarding the Rehabilitation Act have important bearing on the ADA of 1990.

Americans with Disabilities Act of 1990

This act prohibits discrimination against qualified people with disabilities in all areas of employment. It is enforced by the EEOC and applies to employers with 25 or more workers.

Definition of Disability. An individual with a disability is someone who (a) has a physical or mental impairment that substantially limits one or more major life activities, (b) has a record of such an impairment, or (c) is regarded as having such an impairment. According to the ADA, a physical impairment is "any physiological disorder or condition, cosmetic disfigurement, or anatomical loss affecting one or more of the following body systems: neurological, musculoskeletal, special sense organs, respiratory (including speech organs), cardiovascular, reproductive, digestive, genito urinary, hemic and lymphatic, skin, and endocrine."[10] The act also defines a mental impairment as "any mental or psychological disorder such as mental retardation, organic brain syndrome, emotional or mental illness, and specific learning disabilities."[11] It is worth noting that some groups are specifically excluded under ADA: homosexuals and bisexuals; transvestites, transsexuals, pedophiles, exhibitionists, voyeurists, and those with other sexual behavior disorders; and compulsive gamblers, kleptomaniacs, pyromaniacs, and those currently using illegal drugs. Furthermore, active alcoholics who cannot perform their job duties or who present a threat to the safety or property of others are excluded. However, those individuals who have been rehabilitated and are no longer using drugs or alcohol are covered.

Physical or mental impairment is only a part of the ADA's definition of disability. In addition, the impairment must also substantially limit one or more major life activities such as walking, speaking, breathing, performing manual tasks, seeing, hearing, learning, caring for oneself, or working. The phrase "substantially limit" means that the impairment has significantly restricted an individual's ability to perform an entire class of jobs, or a broad range of jobs in various classes, as compared to the average person with similar training, skills, and abilities.

As one example of the enforcement of ADA, the EEOC obtained a settlement agreement with Wal-Mart for $19 million. The EEOC suit was on behalf of Glenda D. Allen, who had been employed with Wal-Mart as a pharmacy technician since July 1993. As a result of a gunshot wound sustained during the course of a robbery at a different employer in 1994, Allen suffered permanent damage to her spinal cord and other medical issues, including an abnormal gait requiring the use of a cane as an assistive device. EEOC charged that despite Allen's successful job performance throughout her employment, Wal-Mart declared her incapable of performing her position with or without a reasonable accommodation, denied her a reasonable accommodation, and then unlawfully fired her because of her disability. The lawsuit was settled shortly after the court denied Wal-Mart's motion for summary judgment and also found that Wal-Mart had no undue hardship defense.[12]

In another example, the EEOC resolved a lawsuit against Sears, Roebuck and Co. for $6.2 million and significant remedial relief. The case arose from a charge of discrimination filed with the EEOC by a former Sears' service technician, John Bava. Bava was injured on the job, took workers' compensation leave, and, although remaining disabled by the injuries, repeatedly attempted to return to work. According to EEOC, Sears refused to provide Bava with a reasonable accommodation that would have put him back to work and, instead, fired him when his leave expired. EEOC also discovered more than one hundred former employees who wanted to return to work with an accommodation, but were terminated by Sears. Some learned of their terminations when their discount cards were rejected while shopping at Sears.[13]

ADA's broad definition of disability and its interpretation by EEOC has been substantially limited in some notable Supreme Court decisions. In *Sutton v. United Air Lines,* Karen Sutton and Kimberly Hinton applied for employment as global airline pilots.[14] Both of them had severe myopic vision (uncorrected visual acuity of 20/200 or worse) that was correctable to 20/20 or better with eyeglasses or contact lenses. United Airlines required a minimum uncorrected visual acuity of 20/100 for global pilots. Because of this requirement, each of the plaintiffs was denied employment. The two filed a complaint against the airline, claiming that its denial of employment violated the ADA. The Supreme Court did not support this claim, ruling that the two individuals did not adequately prove that they were disabled within the meaning of ADA. This was because their visual impairments could be fully corrected, and they were therefore not substantially limited in any major life activity. Further, the court's opinion stated that the determination of whether an individual is disabled, under the ADA, should take into account measures that mitigate the individual's impairment (for example, eyeglasses). In fact, one judge expressed the view that the ADA does not apply to those people with correctable disabilities.

A similar judgment was made in *Murphy v. United Parcel Service* (UPS).[15] Murphy suffered from high blood pressure. When UPS erroneously hired him, his blood pressure was so high that he was not qualified for the Department of Transportation health certification for drivers. Later the company learned of its error and requested that Murphy have his blood pressure retested. Upon retesting, UPS fired Murphy on the basis that his blood pressure exceeded the DOT's requirements for drivers of commercial motor vehicles. Murphy filed suit under the ADA, claiming that he was a disabled person and that he had been fired because UPS regarded him as disabled. The district court, appeals court, and supreme court disagreed. They held that in order to determine whether an individual is disabled under the ADA, the impairment should be evaluated in its medicated state. The courts then noted that when Murphy was medicated, he was inhibited only in lifting heavy objects but otherwise could function normally. In his medicated state, Murphy was not limited in life functions and should not be regarded as disabled. He was fired because he did not meet the legal standard for employment (blood pressure lower than the DOT requirement). Having high blood pressure, however, does not meet the ADA's definition of disabled.

Toyota Motor Mfg., Ky., Inc. v. Williams is a third case in which the Supreme Court restricted the definition of disability as applied to ADA.[16] Ella Williams began working in a Toyota manufacturing plant in a position that required the use of pneumatic tools. Use of these tools eventually led to pain in her hands, wrists, and arms and she was diagnosed with bilateral carpal tunnel syndrome and bilateral tendonitis, which prevented her from doing tasks that required the movement of weighted objects. She worked for two years in a position that did not require such movement. When Toyota changed the tasks of her position to include such movement, Williams worked at the changed position until she again suffered from pain in her hands, wrists, and arms. After a period of discussion between Williams and Toyota, she was dismissed for poor attendance. Williams charged that Toyota had violated ADA. She argued that she was "disabled" under the ADA on the ground that her physical impairments substantially limited her in (1) manual tasks; (2) housework; (3) gardening; (4) playing with her children; (5) lifting; and (6) working, all of which, she argued, constituted major life activities under the Act. She also argued that she was disabled under the ADA because she had a record of a substantially limiting impairment and because she was regarded as having such impairment. The Supreme Court ruled against this claim, indicating that to be substantially limited in performing manual tasks, an individual must have an impairment that prevents or severely restricts the individual from doing activities that are of central importance to most people's daily lives. The impairment's impact must also be permanent or long-term. It is insufficient for individuals attempting to prove disability status to merely submit evidence of a medical diagnosis of impairment. Instead, the claimant must offer evidence that the extent of the limitation [caused by their impairment] in terms of their own experience is substantial. These three decisions that limited the definition of disability caused Congress to pass an amendment to ADA, which we will discuss shortly.

ADA's Impact on Selection.   The ADA prohibits the use of qualification standards, employment tests, or selection criteria that tend to screen out individuals with disabilities unless the standard is job-related and consistent with business necessity. Specifically, section 102 states that tests must be selected and administered to ensure that "test results accurately reflect the skills, aptitude, or whatever other factor … that such test purports to measure, rather than reflecting the [impairment]."[17] This may require that the test administration be modified in accordance with the disability of the applicant.

An important part of the use of any modified selection test is that employers provide enough employment test information to applicants to help them decide whether they will require accommodations in order to take the test. This information should be exchanged early in the application process[18] and should address what is required by the test, how information is presented, response format, and time limits. Test accommodation may be relatively simple and inexpensive, such as larger type required for those with impaired vision. However, accommodation may raise serious questions about the validity of the test and about how to compare the scores obtained on the "accommodated" test to those of the original test. For example, a written test that is usually self-administered might have to be read to a severely sight-impaired applicant. How do we know that the two tests are, in fact, measuring the same KSAs? On the surface, they would seem to differ in terms of short-term memory, oral and written verbal ability, and the ability to make an immediate response. Similar arguments can be made when tests are administered through a language interpreter. In other words, reliability, validity, and norms of the test could be significantly altered due to an accommodation. If the employer determines that accommodation of the existing testing procedure is not reasonable, substitute methods for measuring KSAs should be explored. Some of these methods might include structured interviews, work samples, job trials, rehabilitation expert evaluation, or certificates and references.

The ADA also prohibits preemployment inquiries about a person's disability. If a disability is obvious to the employer, questions about the nature or severity of the disability cannot be asked unless they are limited to the performance of specific job-related tasks. Generally, the disabled person is responsible for informing the employer that accommodation is needed. However, employers may ask that individuals with disabilities request in advance any accommodations necessary for taking employment tests.

Preemployment medical examinations are restricted to those that are job related and consistent with business necessity and should be undergone only after an employment offer has been made to the applicant. Furthermore, the employment offer may be contingent on the results of the examination *only* if the examination is required of all employees, regardless of disability, and if the information obtained is kept confidential and maintained in separate files. It is important to note that the ADA does not consider drug testing a medical examination.

Reasonable Accommodation.   Another important statement of the ADA is that it pertains to "qualified individuals with a disability." This is an individual with a disability who meets the job-related requirements of a position and who, with or without reasonable accommodation, can perform the essential functions of the job. The first important part of this statement is "reasonable accommodation." This means that the organization is required to make changes in the work process for an otherwise qualified individual with a disability unless such accommodation would impose an "undue hardship" on the business. Common examples of reasonable accommodation are making facilities readily accessible (ramps, larger rest rooms), restructuring jobs, altering work schedules or equipment, reassigning jobs, modifying examinations and training materials, and providing interpreters. Although no hard and fast rules exist concerning whether an accommodation would impose an undue hardship, generally the nature and cost of the accommodation as well as the size, type, and finances of the specific facility and those of the parent employer are considered. Accommodation is judged on a case-by-case basis and is related to both the job itself and the nature of a disability.

Reasonable accommodation is not specifically defined in the ADA, and the reasonableness of the accommodation is judged against imposition of an undue hardship. Elliot Shaller has offered his opinion of requirements, which is based on legislative history and the interpretation of the Rehabilitation Act of 1973 as well as on other state statutes.[19] First, an employer is not required to create a job for a disabled employee or maintain quotas. Second, reasonable accommodation does not require that preferences be awarded to persons with disabilities. However, if the choice is between a disabled individual who, without reasonable accommodation, cannot perform a task as fast or as well as a nondisabled person—but who, with accommodation, could perform better—the employer risks ADA liability if the nondisabled applicant is hired. Third, an employer is not required to hire a "shadow" employee, someone who actually performs the majority of essential functions of the disabled employee's position. Fourth, if an employee can be accommodated by a relatively simple and inexpensive redesign or piece of equipment, the employer will likely be required to make such accommodation.

The second important part of reasonable accommodation is the reference to "essential job activity." Job analysis, as used by selection specialists, does not define the term *essential*. Instead, job characteristics have usually been measured in terms of "importance" or "being necessary for job performance." However, neither of these two terms addresses the construct of *essential* as defined by the ADA. The following are several reasons why an activity could be considered essential to a job according to the ADA:

- The position exists to perform the activity.

- Only a limited number of other employees are available to perform the activity or among whom the activity can be distributed.

- The activity is highly specialized, and the person in the position is hired for the special expertise or ability to perform it.

Further, according to the ADA, a company may use various data to determine whether a job activity is essential. Among these are the employer's judgment, supported by job analyses; a written job description; the amount of time spent performing the activity; and the consequences of not hiring a person to perform the activity.

Supreme Court decisions have more clearly defined the extent of reasonable accommodation necessary for organizations. For example, in *U.S. Airways v. Barnett,* the Court held that reasonable accommodation could not violate the provisions of a seniority system.[20] In other words, a seniority system can limit the company's options of reasonable accommodation under the ADA. In *PGA Tour v. Martin,* the issue was whether or not Casey Martin could ride a golf cart during PGA-sponsored tournaments.[21] He suffered from a physical ailment that prevented him from walking the course, a PGA rule, while playing in tournaments. The Court ruled that allowing Martin to use a golf cart was not a modification that would "fundamentally alter the nature" of PGA tournaments.

ADA Amendments Act of 2008

As we mentioned previously, the Supreme Court's judgments that limited the definition of disability caused a strong opposition among enough members of Congress to pass the ADA Amendments Act of 2008.[22] The express intent of this act was to reword the definitions of critical terms in the ADA of 1990 to explicitly counteract the decisions of the Supreme Court. The ADA Amendments Act contains the following statement of this disagreement with the Supreme Court's decisions:

> *Congress expected that the definition of disability under the ADA would be interpreted consistently with how courts had applied the definition of a handicapped individual under the Rehabilitation Act of 1973, but that expectation has not been fulfilled; the holdings of the Supreme Court in* Sutton v. United Air Lines, Inc., *and its companion cases have narrowed the broad scope of protection intended to be afforded by the ADA, thus eliminating protection for many individuals whom Congress intended to protect;*[23]

In this act, the term *disability* was defined to mean: (a) a physical or mental impairment that substantially limits one or more major life activities of an individual; (b) a record of such impairment; or (c) being regarded as having such impairment. In addition, the law states that the definition of disability shall be construed in favor of broad coverage of individuals under this Act, to the maximum extent permitted.

The term *major life activities* was written to include, but not limited to, caring for oneself, performing manual tasks, seeing, hearing, eating, sleeping, walking, standing, lifting, bending, speaking, breathing, learning, reading, concentrating, thinking, communicating, and working. The term *major bodily functions* was written to include, but not limited to, functions of the immune system, normal cell growth, and digestive, bowel, bladder, neurological, brain, respiratory, circulatory, endocrine, and reproductive functions. An impairment that substantially limits one major life activity need not limit other major life activities in order to be considered a disability. An impairment that is episodic or in remission is considered a disability if it substantially limits a major life activity when active.

This Act includes the following statements:

"An impairment occurs when an individual meets the requirement of 'being regarded as having such an impairment' if the individual establishes that he or she has been subjected to an action prohibited under this Act because of an actual or perceived physical or mental impairment whether or not the impairment limits or is perceived to limit a major life activity."

"The determination of whether an impairment substantially limits a major life activity shall be made without regard to the corrective effects of measures such as medication, medical supplies, equipment, or appliances, low-vision devices (which do not include ordinary eyeglasses or contact lenses), prosthetics including limbs and devices, hearing aids and cochlear implants or other implantable hearing devices, mobility devices, or oxygen therapy equipment and supplies."

"The use of assistive technology; reasonable accommodations or auxiliary aids or services; or learned behavioral or adaptive neurological modifications."

These words may mean that a person should be considered disabled if he/she is diagnosed as having an impairment as defined by this act regardless of whether corrective devices can correct the disability.

As of the writing of this book, we could not find any cases that used the definitions referred to in this law. However, the intention of the law is very clear, making it easier for plaintiffs to make a case for disability.

Immigration Reform and Control Act of 1986

Employers can face civil and criminal sanctions for knowingly employing any alien not authorized to work in the United States. Antidiscrimination provisions were added to address concern that the employer sanctions might lead to discrimination against "foreign-looking" job applicants.

Regarding employment, the act states that it is unlawful for a person or other entity to hire or continue to employ an alien knowing that the alien is unauthorized. The company is required to verify authorization by attesting that it has examined any of the following documents produced by the individual being employed: a U.S. passport, a certificate of U.S. citizenship, a certificate of naturalization, an unexpired foreign passport with the proper endorsement of the attorney general, a resident alien card, or specified combinations of social security card, certificate of birth in the United States, documentation evidencing authorization of employment in the United States, driver's license, and documentation of personal identity.[24] A company has complied with these requirements "if the document submitted by the individual reasonably appears on its face to be genuine."[25]

Regarding discrimination, rules issued by the Department of Justice ban only those immigration-related employment practices in which an employer "knowingly and intentionally" discriminates.[26] In terms explained later in this section, unintentional discrimination that creates adverse impact is not covered by this act. Also, it is not an unfair employment practice to prefer to select or recruit an individual who is a citizen or national of the United States instead of another individual who is a noncitizen, if the two individuals are equally qualified. The antidiscrimination provisions apply to any employer with four or more employees.

Complaints of discrimination are processed in the Justice Department by the Office of Special Counsel for Unfair Immigration-Related Employment Practice. Complaints must be filed within 180 days of discriminatory action, and the special counsel must investigate each charge within 120 days. All cases are heard by an administrative-law judge. An employer guilty of discrimination may be assessed back pay for up to two years, along with civil fines of up to $2,000 for subsequent violations.

One example of this type of discrimination was a settlement that the EEOC reached with Woodbine Health Care Center in 1999. Woodbine petitioned the Immigration and Naturalization Service (INS) to allow it to employ foreign registered nurses in its nursing home, claiming a shortage of registered nurses in the Kansas City area. Woodbine promised to employ the Filipinos as registered nurses and pay them the same wages it paid U.S. registered nurses. Contrary to its pledge, Woodbine paid the Filipino nurses about $6.00 an hour less than their U.S. counterparts. Moreover, rather than being employed as registered nurses, the Filipinos were assigned as nurses aides and technicians.

In 1996, two of the Filipino nurses filed discrimination charges with EEOC. Woodbine rejected efforts to conciliate the matter, and one of the Filipino nurses, Aileen Villanueva, filed a private discrimination lawsuit. The EEOC intervened in the suit and Woodbine agreed to a settlement. Under the settlement, Woodbine agreed to pay $2.1 million to 65 Filipino nurses and their attorneys. The nurses shared compensatory damages of approximately $1.2 million and back pay and interest of approximately $470,000. The back pay was based on the average rate of pay that U.S. nurses earned while working for Woodbine.[27]

Constitutional Amendments and Civil Rights Acts of 1866 and 1871

In addition to these EEO statutes, discrimination complaints can be pursued on the basis of the Fifth and Fourteenth Amendments to the Constitution and the Civil Rights Acts of 1866 and 1871, which were part of reconstruction after the Civil War. Both constitutional amendments prohibit the deprivation of employment rights without due process. The Fifth Amendment covers the federal government and the Fourteenth Amendment addresses state and local governments. Unlike the EEO statutes, protection under these amendments applies to all citizens, not only to specific demographic groups. Therefore, discrimination charges can be filed for actions not covered by EEO statutes—for example, discrimination against homosexuals. Pursuit of a charge requires that the plaintiff establish discriminatory intent by the accused, not merely unequal effects of employment actions. This, of course, is often difficult to do.

The Civil Rights Act of 1866 states that "all persons … shall have the same right, to make and enforce contracts … as is enjoyed by white citizens…."[28] Because of this wording, discrimination charges have been limited to racial and, to a lesser extent, ethnic and national background complaints. Sexual, religious, and other forms of discrimination are not considered to be appropriate. Charges can be filed against private employers, unions, and employment agencies. Whereas Title VII requires a minimum of 15 employees in an organization, no such limitation exists with this act. The Civil Rights Act of 1871 is similar to provisions of the Fourteenth Amendment. By its wording, it applies to state and local governments. It does not apply to purely private business or federal agencies unless there is state involvement in the questioned employment practices. Thus this act has been applied to police and fire departments, public schools, colleges, hospitals, and state agencies. A broad range of bases for discrimination is applicable—for example, ethnicity, gender, sex, religion, age, sexual preference, citizenship, and physical attributes.

This brief review of the important EEO laws highlights the major points of the regulatory model. These laws are clearly addressed to societal problems; they focus on safeguarding the fair treatment of demographic groups that traditionally have not had access to the American dream of success. These laws created agencies designed to monitor the compliance of organizations in various industries and to represent the claims of individuals who think that they were unfairly treated. Such actions require the evaluation of organizations' employment practices. In most cases the well-being of the organization itself is not of major concern.

EMPLOYMENT DISCRIMINATION

The previously cited laws and orders clearly prohibit discrimination in selection and other HR actions. The difficulty for managers of organizations is to identify when discrimination is present. As we have said, laws state principles. Putting these principles into operation is another step. As the regulatory model indicates, this step is partially based on court decisions in discrimination cases and partially on actions by regulatory agencies such as the EEOC. The court decisions set legal precedent and yield specific comments about the treatment of evidence of alleged discrimination in specific situations. These legal precedents serve as benchmarks for subsequent legal interpretation. In 1978 the EEOC published the *Uniform Guidelines on Employee Selection Procedures,* which, while being neither law nor court decisions, are important because they represent the joint statement of the agencies empowered by law to enforce the EEO laws. The *Uniform Guidelines* describe what evidence will be considered in judging discrimination and how an employer may defend a selection program. In addition, the guidelines are given "great deference" by the courts when considering discrimination cases. We now discuss the definition and evidence of discrimination.

Discrimination Defined

It is important to understand the difference between two terms that are frequently used in reference to equal employment laws: adverse impact and discrimination. *Adverse impact* means that there are differences between demographically different individuals or groups with regard to the outcome of some selection procedure or process. For example, male applicants may score higher on a physical ability test than do female applicants. Whites may score higher on a written selection test than do blacks or Hispanics. *Discrimination* means that there is not a valid, job-related explanation for the adverse impact. That is, the difference between the two individuals or groups is due to a non-job-related reason. For example, a male is selected for a manual labor position rather than a female because all other workers are males. In such a case, it would be difficult to prove that the gender of fellow workers is an important factor in job performance. Therefore basing the selection decision on gender similarity would not be job related and could result in a judgment of discrimination. Similarly, it would not be job related if an employer declined to select minority group members as wait staff because of a fear that customers would refuse to deal with such individuals.

Disparate Treatment

The first form of discrimination is *disparate treatment.* This form of discrimination describes those situations in which different standards are applied to various groups or individuals even though there may not be an explicit statement of intentional prejudice. Examples are such practices as not hiring women with young children while hiring men with such children, or hiring minority group members to fill cleaning jobs in a restaurant while similarly qualified white people are made cashiers or waiters. The effect of such decisions, even though they may be prompted by the employer's idea of good business practice, is to subject a specific group to negative treatment because of a personal characteristic. The major factor that must be taken into account with regard to this form of discrimination is the intention of the employer.

Disparate Impact

The second form of discrimination is that of *disparate impact.* In this form, organizational selection standards are applied uniformly to all groups of applicants, but the net result of these standards is to produce differences in the selection of various groups. The employer's intention is not the issue in this form of discrimination. Instead, the issue is the relevant data reflecting the percentages of selected applicants from different demographic groups. Two classic examples of such discrimination are the requirement of a high school diploma, which has been used extensively for entry-level positions, and of height minimums, which have been used for police and some manual labor positions.

Both standards are usually applied to applicants consistently and might not seem to be discriminatory.

The problem is that such standards have been demonstrated to have the effect of disqualifying from employment a much larger percentage of some groups than others. High school diplomas are one example. Traditionally, more white people have high school diplomas than do most minority groups. The requirement of a diploma would limit the percentage of minority applicants in comparison to white applicants. Similarly, a minimum height requirement usually limits the number of women, Asian American, and Latin American applicants, even though they could otherwise be found acceptable for employment. A number of other frequently used and seemingly valid selection requirements have been the subject of disparate impact discrimination charges, including arrest records, type of military discharge, various educational degrees, scores on mental evaluation tests, years of previous work experience, and financial history. The use of each of these has been linked to the disqualification of a high percentage of at least one demographic group of applicants.

Evidence Required

One major consequence of these two forms of employment discrimination is their differential effect on both plaintiffs and defendants when charges are brought to court. That is to say that the legal burdens for plaintiffs and defendants are different depending on whether the case is heard as disparate treatment or disparate impact discrimination. In discussing this, we frame our points within Title VII litigation because that is the most prevalent.

In both types of cases, a logical sequence of events should occur. To start, the burden of proof is on the plaintiff to present arguments and facts that, if not rebutted, would convince the judge or jury hearing the case that the employer has engaged in practices in violation of one of the EEO laws. If this is done, the plaintiff is said to have established a *prima facie* case of discrimination. If this is not done, the case should be dismissed for lack of grounds. Once a prima facie case has been established, the burden of proof switches to the defendant. It is necessary to present arguments and facts that rebut the charges and provide a legally permissible explanation for the employment practices under question. If this is done, the burden shifts back to the plaintiff, who has a final opportunity to attack the defendant's evidence and otherwise challenge previous arguments.

Disparate Treatment Evidence

As indicated in Table 2.2, there are major differences in specific data, evidence, and arguments that must be made during this general trial process for the two types of discrimination cases. For disparate treatment cases, a guideline for establishing a prima facie case was specified in the *McDonnell Douglas v. Green* (1973) case, commonly known as the McDonnell Douglas rule. This rule states that the plaintiff must show that the following conditions exist:

1. He or she belongs to a protected class.

2. He or she applied and was qualified for a job for which the company was seeking applicants.

3. Despite these qualifications, he or she was rejected.

4. After this rejection, the position remained open and the employer continued to seek applicants from persons with the complainant's qualifications.[29]

TABLE 2.2   Presentation of Evidence in Title VII Discrimination Cases

Sequence of Steps	Disparate Treatment	Disparate Impact
Plaintiff	Demonstrates that ▪ He or she belongs to a protected class, ▪ He or she applied and was qualified for the job, ▪ He or she was rejected by the company, ▪ The job remained open.	Demonstrates statistically that this HRM practice affects various groups differently in comparison to their distribution in the relevant labor market.
Defendant	Provides a clear and specific job-based explanation for actions.	Demonstrates at least one of the following: business necessity bona fide occupational qualification validation data
Plaintiff	Proves that the defendant's argument is a pretext and the true reason for rejection was prejudice.	Proves that an alternative practice is available that has less adverse impact.

This rule reflects a basic premise of disparate treatment cases: The employer's *intention* to discriminate *must* be shown. The demonstration that a specific, qualified member of a demographic group was passed over and a member of a different demographic group with equal or fewer qualifications was selected suffices to prove intention if not rebutted.

When intent to discriminate is shown, the employer must provide a legitimate, nondiscriminatory reason for rejecting the plaintiff in order to rebut. This is relatively easy to do. For example, in the *McDonnell Douglas* case, the reason was that Green had participated in a protest by illegally stalling his car during a shift change at the McDonnell Douglas plant. In other cases, arguments have been made and accepted that the qualifications of the plaintiff were inferior to those of individuals selected. In general, if the argument is clear and specific, the employer meets its burden of proof. The employer need not persuade the judge that it actually used this as the basis for rejecting the plaintiff. Rather, it is up to the plaintiff to prove that the employer did *not* use it. The employer's argument is usually more acceptable if it shows that the employer used numerical scores in making selection decisions. The argument is less acceptable, however, if the reasons are based on subjective judgments (opinion), especially if these are made without clear definition and procedures.

If the company is successful, the plaintiff must then refute these statements. In essence this means that he or she must show that the company's defense is really a pretense, and that discrimination was being practiced. Examples of evidence that courts have accepted are sexual or racial slurs made by company managers, records that the company's treatment of the plaintiff was inconsistent with that of individuals of other demographic groups, and statistics showing the demographic group of the plaintiff was underrepresented in the company's workforce. If the data presented are not acceptable, the plaintiff is unsuccessful in countering the defense of the company.

Disparate Impact Evidence

In trials of this form of discrimination (see Table 2.2), the focus for establishing a prima facie case shifts from the intention of the employer to an evaluation of the results of an employment decision with regard to various demographic groups. That is, evidence mainly addresses whether various groups have been affected in the same manner by employment decisions. For this reason, statistical data are a major part of these cases. Intention of the employer is normally not addressed, only the outcomes of decisions. Statistics, which we discuss in the following section, are used to analyze the pattern of selection decisions over a period of time. If these analyses do, in fact, indicate that a pattern of adverse impact has occurred, the prima facie case has been established. Once a prima facie case has been accepted, the company has the opportunity of presenting evidence to show that the results of the selection process in question are job related and not, therefore, illegal discrimination. To do this, the company traditionally has three options: proving *business necessity, bona fide occupational qualifications* (BFOQ), or *validity*.

We discussed validation generally in Chapter 1 and go into detail about its procedures in Chapter 5. The requirements for the other two defenses are strict and apply only in limited cases. Business necessity has been viewed by the courts primarily in regard to safety of either workers or customers of the organization. It is necessary to present evidence that if the selection requirement were not used, the risk to members of these groups would be substantially raised. Ordinarily, the courts have not judged business necessity in terms of economic costs or profits. Therefore, demonstrating that not using the selection requirement would result in great cost or loss of business to the firm has not been acceptable.

A BFOQ defense means that a demographic group is disqualified from employment because no one person from that group could adequately or appropriately perform the job. This defense is almost exclusively used for sex or religious discrimination. For example, a company may have a requirement that only women can serve as attendants in women's restrooms. The company could use a BFOQ defense (no man could appropriately serve as such an attendant) if a male brought a discrimination charge against it. Similarly, a Presbyterian church could use a BFOQ defense in order to disqualify all applicants for a minister's position who were not practicing members of the Presbyterian faith. It is not possible to frame a BFOQ defense for race or color. For example, a school district with a predominately white student body could not use a BFOQ defense to disqualify all minority applicants for teaching positions.

If the company is successful in defending the adverse impact, the plaintiff has a chance to present another argument to refute this defense. The nature of this is to establish whether another selection procedure could be used that would have less adverse impact. This topic is not well developed, however, because courts seldom get to this stage in the weighing of evidence.

As a historical note, the Supreme Court decision made in June 1989, concerning the *Wards Cove Packing Company, Inc. et al., Petitioners v. Frank Atonio et al.,* marked a major change in the evidence needed by both parties in disparate impact cases.[30] The Court held that in disparate impact cases the defendant's burden of proof should be similar to evidence characteristic of disparate treatment. For example, under the principles of the *Wards Cove* decision, a plaintiff can meet her level of evidence of adverse impact by showing that a significantly lower percentage of female applicants were hired for entry managerial positions than of male applicants. Under *Wards Cove,* a company may meet its burden of proof by stating a plausible business reason for such results, that is, males scored higher on a profit–loss calculation problem than did females. Before *Wards Cove,* the organization may have had to prove that there were significant statistical differences between the male and female average scores and that the calculation problem was valid (that is, related to job performance). Obviously, the latter burden of proof is much more difficult to demonstrate. The Civil Rights Act of 1991 returned the burden of proof of both the plaintiff and the defendant in disparate impact cases to that specified previously in this section, specifically negating part of the *Wards Cove v. Atonio* decision.

The Use of Statistics

As should be evident from the previous discussion, statistics are used in cases of both forms of discrimination. In disparate treatment cases, statistics are mainly used to assist the plaintiff in rebutting the defendant's explanation of the selection practice under question. In disparate impact cases, statistics are most often used by the plaintiff in demonstrating that a pattern of adverse effect has occurred. Two main types of statistics have been used: *stock* and *flow* statistics.

Stock Statistics

Statistics are used in discrimination cases mainly to compare proportions of various demographic groups with regard to the results of selection decisions. Stock statistics compare groups at one point in time. For example, the most common stock comparison is between the percentage of a specific demographic group in the workforce of the organization and the percentage of that same demographic group in an appropriate comparison group, such as total applicants or the relevant labor force. Here is a specific example:

$$\frac{\text{number of women managers in organization}}{\text{total number of managers in organization}} \quad \text{vs.} \quad \frac{\text{number of appropriately skilled women managers in labor force}}{\text{total number of appropriately skilled managers in labor force}}$$

If the percentage of women managers in the company's workforce is significantly smaller than the percentage in the comparison group, in this case the labor force, then evidence of discrimination in selection practices exists.

The term applied to the comparison group is *relevant labor market* (RLM). To better understand the various statistical comparisons that are used in discrimination cases, it is important to know more about the concept of RLM.

EEO laws require employers to keep and update various records about the composition of the organization's workforce and the results of managerial decisions. One of these records is the Revised EEO-1 Form (see Figure 2.2), which must be filed by employers with 100 or more employees. In this form, data must be reported for ten specific job categories as well as for the total organization. For each job category, the company must report the number of individuals in each demographic group listed on the Revised EEO-1 Form.

In stock analyses, the data from the Revised EEO-1 Form (or similar data) are compared to the RLM, and this result is used as evidence. It is in this context that the RLM becomes important. The RLM has two components: geographical location and skill level. The geographical location is that region from which applicants for the specific job category would likely come, absent any discrimination.[31] In general, determination of this region depends on the scope of the employer's recruiting efforts, the interest among prospective employees in working for the employer in question, and the availability of public transportation.[32] Typically, the geographic region will be smallest for lower-paying jobs and broadest, sometimes nationwide, for high-level executive positions.

Within a region there is still the issue of who shall be counted. At this point, skill level becomes important. Skill level means the special qualifications needed to fill a specific job. Obviously, the number of individuals qualified to serve as electrical engineers is greatly different from that of the general population. The courts recognize that, in calculating stock statistics, it would not be relevant to compare the demographic composition of the company in each of the ten EEO-1 job categories with that of the population as a whole. In general, as the skill level of the job category increases, the percentage of minorities and women in that job category decreases. Table 2.3 describes some of the relevant labor markets that have been used in selection discrimination cases.

FIGURE 2.2 Revised EEO-1 Form

Employment at this establishment—Report all permanent full- and part-time employees including apprentices and on-the-job trainees unless specifically excluded as set forth in the instructions. Enter the appropriate figures on all lines and in all columns. Blank spaces will be considered as zeros.

Number of Employees
(Report employees in only one category)

Race/Ethnicity

Job Categories		Hispanic or Latino		Not Hispanic or Latino												Total Col A–N
				Male							Female						
		Male	Female	White	Black or African American	Native Hawaiian or Other Pacific Islander	Asian	American Indian or Alaskan Native	Two or more races	White	Black or African American	Native Hawaiian or Other Pacific Islander	Asian	American Indian or Alaskan Native	Two or more races	
		A	B	C	D	E	F	G	H	I	J	K	L	M	N	O
Executive/Senior-Level Officials and Managers	1.1															
First/Mid-Level Officials and Managers	1.2															
Professionals	2															
Technicians	3															
Sales Workers	4															
Administrative Support Workers	5															
Craft Workers	6															
Operatives	7															
Laborers and Helpers	8															
Service Workers	9															
Total	10															
Previous Year Total	11															

Source: Federal Register, November 28, 2005 (70 FR 712 94).

41

TABLE 2.3	Some Relevant Labor Markets Used for Statistical Comparisons

General population data

Labor force data (civilian, nonfarm, or total)

Qualified labor market data

Actual applicant flow data

Qualified actual applicant flow data

Employer's own workforce composition (promotion cases)

Employer's own qualified and interested workforce composition (promotion cases)

The labor market chosen for comparison has frequently been the subject of intensive debate between plaintiffs and defendants in court cases. This is because the percentage of various demographic groups can change depending on which combination of geographical region and skill level is used. For example, according to 2003 EEOC employment data, the distribution of officials and managers in the metropolitan Seattle, Washington area is 87.3 percent white, 2.7 percent black, 2.3 percent Hispanic, 7.0 percent Asian American, and 0.7 percent Native American. The same data for Miami, Florida shows the distribution to be 45.2 percent white, 10.5 percent black, 41.7 percent Hispanic, 2.5 percent Asian American, and 0.2 percent Native American. Obviously, the demographic compositions of officials and managers for companies in the two cities can be vastly different but still be legally permissible.

The difficulty in identifying a relevant labor market is the operational one of gathering the appropriate data. In most cases, existing data in the form of census, chamber of commerce, industry, and similar reports are used. In these reports, geographical units are usually reported in three forms: (1) the nation, (2) a state, or (3) the Standard Metropolitan Statistical Area (SMSA), which is the region surrounding a central city or town. Appropriate skill level is expressed in numbers reported as holding or qualified to hold specific jobs. In the U.S. census data, several different types of sales, technical, managerial, and other categories of jobs are reported. The selection of an RLM, in many cases, becomes a judgment as to the most appropriate geographical region and the most similar types of jobs available in existing data sources.

Flow Statistics

The second type of statistic used is referred to as flow statistics. The term is used because this type of statistic compares proportions taken at two points in time. A common flow statistic in selection is the following:

$$\frac{\text{number of minority applicants selected}}{\text{number of minority applicants}} \quad \text{vs.} \quad \frac{\text{number of nonminority applicants selected}}{\text{number of nonminority applicants}}$$

The comparison is made from numbers gathered at two different points in time—before and after selection has taken place. The purpose of the comparison is obviously to determine how minority members fared in the selection process in comparison to nonminority members. If the percentage for the minority group is significantly smaller than the percentage for the nonminority group, evidence of discrimination is present. Because the comparison is made between groups that are both being acted upon by the company, the RLM is usually not an issue.

In making the comparison between the proportions previously discussed, the final step is for the court to decide whether any difference between the proportions is important enough to matter. This is the crux of deciding whether evidence of discrimination exists. If the proportions are close enough, insufficient evidence exists and the case should be dropped. If the proportions are different enough, sufficient evidence exists. To assist them in making this decision, the courts have used statistical tests. By far, the most commonly used test is the *Four-Fifths Rule*.[33] This test uses the basic flow statistic and adds that the ratio of any group must be at least 80 percent of the *ratio of the most favorably treated* group. For example, if 60 percent of white applicants are selected, then the selection proportion of any minority group should be at least 48 percent (0.80 × 0.60). Let us say that there are numerous entry-level retail clerk positions to be filled for a large department store. Through recruiting, 120 white applicants are processed and 72 (60 percent) are selected. Through the same recruiting process, 50 black people apply for the positions. If blacks were hired at the same rate as the whites, we would expect that 30 black applicants would be selected (50 × 0.60). However, according to this guideline, exact parity is not expected. The minimum number of black hires would be expected to be 24 (30 × 0.80), which is 80 percent of the 60 percent hire rate of whites. If the number is smaller, the *initial* conclusion is that adverse impact in selection has occurred. Even though we have discussed this statistic in terms of a flow analysis, it can also be used in a stock analysis. While the Four-Fifths Rule has legal standing with enforcement agencies and courts, there is evidence that it is statistically flawed. This flaw occurs when the Four-Fifths Rule is applied to small samples, which is frequently the case when minority applicants and selectees are compared with nonminority applicants and selectees.[34] For example, think about a situation in which there are 30 nonminority applicants of which 20 are selected and 10 minority applicants of which 5 are selected. The selection rate for nonminority applicants is approximately 67%. The selection rate for minority applicants is 50%. If we apply the Four-Fifths Rule, the threshold for an acceptable selection rate for minorities would be approximately 54% (67% × .80). Using 54% as the standard, the employment of 6 minority applicants would be acceptable but the employment of 5 minorities would not. Therefore a decision about a single minority applicant could make the difference between an acceptable selection pattern and one that seems to indicate adverse impact.

Because it is problematic to use the Four-Fifths Rule with small samples, one research study concluded that the Rule should be combined with another statistical test to accurately indicate when the selection percentages of two different demographic groups are statistically different.[35]

A second statistical analysis that has been mentioned as being appropriate for testing differences in the selection ratios among demographic groups is the Standard Deviation Rule. This rule has been included in various texts as an indicator of adverse impact and has been shown on various Web sites that provide guidelines for testing for significant differences between the selection rates of demographic groups. The general idea of a standard deviation test is to calculate the standard deviation of the variance in scores and compare that to the difference in mean scores between the two demographic groups. If the difference in means is greater than 1.96 standard deviations, the difference in means is considered to be significant between the two groups. However Craig Russell, who has worked in selection for many years, has pointed out that the standard deviation is not the appropriate statistic to use when comparing the selection ratios of two demographic groups and it, therefore, is incorrect to calculate this statistic. Rather the standard error should be calculated or Fisher's Exact Test used (with small samples). Phil Bobko adds that the Binomial test can be also be used with large samples. None of these tests are mentioned in any of the EEOC information that we could find about testing for significant differences in selection ratios between demographic groups, although they have been used in some court cases. No matter which of these tests one uses, it must be kept in mind that the result of its application will yield information that contributes to the conclusion about the comparison of selection rates between two or more demographic groups. The statistical test should not solely dictate the conclusion.

Definition of Internet Applicant

We have previously pointed out that statistics measuring the applicant selection rates for various demographic groups are important for the determination of adverse impact. That is, the selection rates for all demographic groups should be approximately equal. If the selection rates between two groups are very large, this difference can serve as evidence of adverse impact. One key component of examining selection rates is the definition of what is meant by an applicant. Should someone who briefly inquires about open jobs be considered an applicant? Should someone who fills out an application blank but does not follow with any other actions be considered one?

The use of Internet recruitment and selection has made the definition of an applicant very important. By using the Internet, an individual can easily contact an organization and indicate some interest in employment or complete preliminary employment forms. Many of these individuals withdraw from the application process—but that may not matter if they are legally regarded as applicants and must be included in a calculation of selection rates.

In an attempt to clarify who must be counted, the Office of Federal Contract Compliance (OFCCP) has released a definition of who is considered to be an Internet applicant.[36] This definition includes the following points:

1. The person must submit an expression of interest in employment through the Internet or related electronic devices. The term "expression of interest" is not strictly defined, but examples include information about an individual that is gathered from e-mails, résumé databases, job banks, electronic scanning devices, applicant tracking systems, and applicant screeners. Apparently, if any individual from these or related sources is considered an applicant, all individuals from these sources should also be considered applicants.

2. The organization is considering employing the individual for a particular position. This means that the employer evaluates any characteristic of the individual against any qualification needed for a particular position, even those considered to be basic requirements. However, individuals may be excluded from consideration if they do not use the organization's defined application procedure or if they do not apply for a specific position.

3. The individual's expression of interest indicates that the person possesses the basic qualifications for the position. Qualifications are those characteristics used to advertise the position or that the organization has predetermined should be used in the selection of candidates. Qualifications must also be objective (not dependent on subjective judgment), non-comparative (not relative), and job related.

4. The individual must not remove herself from consideration for the position. The most obvious way to do this is to notify the company that she is withdrawing as an applicant. An organization may infer that an individual has removed herself if she does not respond to company inquiries, or if she has made statements in the application reflecting expectations that are incompatible with the employment conditions of the position (for example, salary, work location, or job duties). If the organization decides to remove individuals from the applicant roll for any of these reasons, the organization must be consistent in removing them. That is, all individuals that provide similar statements must be removed. Removal cannot be selective and limited to specific individuals.

OFCCP's definition is very broad and possibly could impose on employers not only the great effort required for compliance, but also the cost of monitoring applicants who apply for employment.

THE UNIFORM GUIDELINES ON EMPLOYEE SELECTION PROCEDURES (1978)

The *Uniform Guidelines on Employee Selection Procedures* (1978) represent a joint statement of the Equal Employment Opportunity Commission, the Civil Service Commission, the Department of Labor, and the Department of Justice as to the characteristics of acceptable selection procedures.[37] As such, these guidelines are not themselves legally binding. However, because they represent the viewpoints of the federal agencies charged with the enforcement of EEO laws, the guidelines serve as a primary reference for court decisions and have been cited in various cases. The most important aspects of the *Uniform Guidelines* are summarized in this section.

Determination of Adverse Impact

The *Uniform Guidelines* clearly state that the decision rule in judging discrimination in selection is whether the use of a selection procedure leads to adverse impact as demonstrated by the statistical tests we have reviewed. However, it must be noted that in certain cases the *Uniform Guidelines* provide exceptions to this. When large numbers of applicants are being selected, discrimination could be indicated even if comparison proportions of applicants are within the Four-Fifths rates. In such cases, enforcement agencies are quite concerned with differences in which large numbers of individuals are affected. Conversely, in cases in which very small numbers of applicants are processed, the Four-Fifths Rule may not always be accepted as indicating discrimination. With small samples, differences in decisions about one or two applicants could greatly change the comparison ratios. This factor is thus taken into account, and in such cases differences greater than the Four-Fifths ratio may not be viewed negatively.

Selection Methods

The *Uniform Guidelines* also state that *any* method of selection that results in an employment decision is covered. Many individuals have incorrectly assumed that only scored selection tests are addressed in the guidelines. This is clearly incorrect, as the following statement in the *Uniform Guidelines* indicates:

> When an informal or unscored selection procedure that has an adverse impact is utilized, the user should eliminate the adverse impact or modify the procedure to one which is a formal, scored, or quantified measure.[38]

Defense of Selection Program

The *Uniform Guidelines* are not concerned, except with respect to record keeping, with selection programs that do not demonstrate adverse impact. For those selection programs that do have adverse impact, the options of the organization are specified. First, the organization may cease to use the selection devices under question and adopt other devices that do not result in adverse impact. If this is not acceptable, the organization may defend its practices in one of the ways we discussed previously. If validation evidence is used, it should specifically address the use of the selection instrument with regard to all groups for whom the test is to be used. At a minimum, this means that statistical validation should include a representative number of women and minorities. In criterion validation, the steps should address the issue of "test fairness" or the comparative performance of various groups on the test. A large portion of the *Uniform Guidelines* is in fact devoted to the steps, data, and procedures of validation strategies. An added provision, however, is that the organization should demonstrate that there are no other alternative selection programs that are both valid and have less adverse impact.

Selection Requirements

Several other aspects of selection programs are specifically addressed by the *Uniform Guidelines*. Skills and abilities easily learned during a brief training program are not acceptable as selection requirements. Requirements drawn from higher-level jobs are permissible only if it can be documented that a majority of individuals move to the higher-level job within a reasonable time. This time period is not precisely defined, but the *Uniform Guidelines* state that "a reasonable period of time will vary for different jobs and employment situations but will seldom be more than five years."[39] The various forms of selection cutoff scores are also discussed. The least stringent cutoff is a score above which all applicants are judged equally acceptable. A second form of cutoff scores is one in which similar scores are grouped together (for example, 81–90, 91–100). The first applicants considered for selection are those with scores in the highest group. Selection proceeds downward along score groups until all open positions are filled. This could result in selection being completed before some score groups are even considered. A third form of cutoff scores is to rank all applicants individually and proceed down this list of individuals. The *Uniform Guidelines* indicate when the second and third forms of cutoff scores are used; if adverse impact results, the organization must not only demonstrate the validity of the selection devices but also justify the contention that scores above a minimum are indicative of higher job performance.

Job Performance Measures

The *Uniform Guidelines* allow a variety of measures of job performance to be used for demonstrating validity. For example, production quantity or quality, supervisors' ratings, turnover, and absenteeism records can be used. Whatever measures are used, however, they must represent important work behaviors or work outcomes that are free from factors that would unfairly alter the scores of any particular groups. We discuss performance measures in Chapter 15 to fully develop this issue. The *Uniform Guidelines* also permit validation evidence to be gathered by means of a multiunit study or evidence borrowed from other companies, as long as data are produced indicating that the job being considered is similar to the job examined by the other companies or studies. The necessary procedures used for such job analyses will be discussed in Chapter 7.

Record Keeping

Another major requirement of the *Uniform Guidelines* is record keeping. All organizations are required to keep information about the demographic characteristics of applicants and hires and to produce such information if requested. This requirement applies only to the groups that constitute at least 2 percent of the relevant labor market. All organizations are technically required to record such data; however, if adverse impact is not characteristic of the selection program, the probability of a request by an enforcement agency for this documentation is almost zero. Organizations with fewer than 100 employees should record by sex, race, and national origin the number of persons selected, promoted, and terminated for each job level. Data indicating the number of applicants for both entry-level positions and promotion are also necessary. These data should also be categorized by sex, race, and national origin. Finally, selection procedures should be described. Organizations with more than 100 employees must develop records indicating whether the total selection process for each job, or any part of that selection process, has had adverse impact on any group that constitutes at least 2 percent of the relevant labor market. For cases in which there is an insufficient number of selections to determine whether an adverse impact exists, the organization should continue to collect, maintain, and have available the information on individual components of the selection process until the information is sufficient to determine whether adverse impact has occurred, or until the job changes substantially. In the latter case, presumably a new round of record keeping would begin.

In summary, the *Uniform Guidelines on Employee Selection Procedures* direct HR specialists as to appropriate selection program features and records. The determination of adverse impact as indicated by the Four-Fifths Rule and other statistical analyses is of primary importance. When such impact is determined, the company must either cease the use of the selection procedure and adopt a nondiscriminatory one or produce evidence of the job relatedness of the selection procedure that produces the adverse impact.

Comments about the *Uniform Guidelines*

As mentioned, the *Uniform Guidelines* were published in 1978. Over that time, they have been referred to in many selection court cases and have been given "great weight." This means that judges and juries have used the information in the *Guidelines* when making decisions. However, selection researchers and managers have advanced our knowledge of several issues that are incorporated into the *Guidelines*. For example, the *Guidelines* argue for performing a validation study in each selection site to insure that all factors that may affect employees' performance are included in the validation effort. Research has clearly contradicted this argument and has demonstrated that validity can be generalized from several previous studies. As a matter of fact, the evidence is that a single validation study is not a very good indicator of validity and could err by either overestimating or underestimating the validity coefficient. We will discuss this issue in detail in Chapter 11. Similarly, researchers have shown that relying heavily on the Four-Fifths Rule and other statistical measures as methods for identifying signs of adverse impact is more fruitful when these methods are combined with additional statistical tests. Using the measures alone could lead to incorrect conclusions above adverse impact. Clearly the *Uniform Guidelines* must be revised to include such research findings.

AFFIRMATIVE ACTION PROGRAMS

Another aspect of EEO laws and regulations that has importance for companies is affirmative action programs (AAP). Generally, AAP applies to a set of specific actions taken by an organization to actively seek out and remove unintended barriers to fair treatment in order to achieve equal opportunity.[40] For example, an organization's AAP for the selection of women and minority college graduates might include identifying and visiting colleges with large proportions of women and minority students, staffing recruiting teams with women and minority members, developing internship programs, and training interviewers and other selection decision makers in appropriate techniques. An affirmative action plan is a written document produced by the company that explicitly states steps to be taken, information to be gathered, and the general baseline for decision making for each area of HRM. It is to serve as a guideline for actions to ensure that EEO principles are implemented within the organization. Such a plan is to be under the direction of a top-level manager and to be communicated to all within the organization.

Basically, there are three situations in which a company would adopt an AAP: (a) the company is a government contractor, (b) the company has lost a court discrimination case or has signed a consent decree, or (c) the company is voluntarily attempting to implement EEO principles. Let's discuss each of these.

Federal Contractor

Most of the EEO laws and executive orders dealing with federal contractors contain the requirement of affirmative action for those with contracts of at least $10,000. The Office of Federal Contract Compliance Programs (OFCCP), a subdivision within the Department of Labor, is usually set up as the regulatory agency. It can review the employment practices of contractors and levy specified penalties if it finds a contractor to be out of compliance with AAP requirements. Three main activities must be carried out by a contractor in an AAP.[41] The first is a utilization analysis. Conceptually, this is similar to previously described stock statistical analyses, because it requires a comparison of the company's workforce to the relevant labor market. If there is a smaller percentage of a specific demographic group in the company's workforce than there is in the labor market, that group is said to be underutilized. The complete determination of underutilization, however, also includes additional information such as the size of the minority unemployed group, the availability of promotable and transferable minorities within the company, the existence of appropriate training institutions, and the degree of training that the contractor may deliver.

The numerical results of a utilization analysis are important because they indicate the discrepancy between the workforce and the company's available labor force. This discrepancy then serves as the basis for the second activity, determining the "goals" that a company should strive to achieve in its employment practices. For example, if Hispanic skilled craft workers constitute 8 percent of the RLM and only 2 percent of the company's workforce, the company would be expected to set a specific numerical goal to achieve a balance between the two numbers, or, at least, to reduce the discrepancy substantially. In addition, a timetable should be developed that would indicate the dates at which the company expects to achieve milestones in reducing the discrepancy. As an example, the percentage in the company's workforce would be expected to increase by 2 percent for each of the next three years. There is a major debate on this topic concerning (a) the extent to which these goals should be considered to be desirable ends that are achievable within the specified timetable, and (b) the extent to which they should be considered to be "quotas" that must be achieved. This has historically been a source of conflict between contractors and OFCCP regulators. Theoretically, the contractor is to "put forth every good faith effort to make his overall affirmative action program work."[42] Obviously, the concept of "good faith effort" is open to interpretation and disagreement. It is a common opinion that, in order to reduce underutilization, pressure has often been exerted on contractors to give preferential treatment to women and minorities.

The third major aspect of these AAPs is the actual steps that are required. Among these are publishing job openings through meetings with various minority organizations, taking ads in media with a high percentage of minorities as a target audience, and publicizing the company's affirmative action policy. Also included are conducting reviews of selection practices and instruments for adverse impact, and training organization members in the objectives of the AAP and procedures necessary for fulfilling its objectives.

Court Order and Consent Decree

When a company is acting under a court order and consent decree, it is legally required to engage in HRM actions that will directly, and in a specified period of time, lead to a balance between its workforce and the relevant labor market. The activities just discussed relative to AAPs for government contractors become, in this situation, part of the AAP for companies. However, even less freedom of action exists for these companies. A primary requirement is that the company must meet specific numerical goals that have been stated and agreed to in the court order or consent degree. These numerical goals are considered to be mandatory, as opposed to desirable, achievements. Often in order to reach these goals, a company must give preferential treatment to minority applicants in selection or in promotion (if the issue concerns internal movement within the company).

For example, part of the agreement signed by Ford Motor Company in its sexual discrimination case required the company to pay female employees $8 million in damages. Ford also agreed to train all of its employees in the prevention of job discrimination and to take appropriate measures to increase female representation in supervisory positions. The goal was to have women in 30 percent of the entry-level supervisory openings at the Chicago Stamping and Assembly Plants within a three-year period. This meant that a number of women were moved into supervisory positions ahead of men.[43]

Voluntary AAP

The most controversial AAPs have been those initiated by an organization without the direct requirement of a court or government agency. The problem with these is the potential conflict between their results and the wording of Title VII of the Civil Rights Act of 1964. Part of this act expressly states that it is "an unlawful ... practice ... to fail or refuse to hire ... any individual with respect to ... race, color, religion, sex, or national origin."[44] Further it is written that "nothing contained in this title shall be interpreted to require any employer ... to grant preferential treatment to any individual."[45]

The potential difficulty with a voluntary AAP is that in order to increase the employment of minority groups, the company may bend over backward by discriminating against other groups and violate the parts of Title VII just cited. We have already mentioned that in the two previous AAP situations, a company is in the direct review (some would say control) of a court or government agency and can legitimately grant preferential treatment to specific groups to meet goals or quotas. In voluntary AAPs, any preferential treatment given one group may be translated into disparate treatment against another group. Because white males are usually the group negatively affected in such instances, the term *reverse discrimination* has been used.

The resolution of such conflicts between voluntary AAPs and disparate treatment of other groups has been the subject of U.S. Supreme Court rulings. These rulings have determined that voluntary AAPs must have the following characteristics: be temporary, have no permanent adverse impact on white workers, and be designed to correct a demonstrable imbalance between minority and nonminority workers. The importance of these characteristics was made clear in *Lilly v. City of Beckley.*[46]

In 1975 the city of Beckley, West Virginia, undertook to remedy the lack of minority and women employees in city departments. In April 1976, a formal AAP was adopted to achieve this. This case arose over selection decisions made in the police department in January 1976, before the formal AAP was adopted. Lilly applied for a patrol officer position at that time and passed the essay test portion of the selection program but failed the interview. He was told that his chance of obtaining employment would be much greater if he were a minority member. He brought suit against the city. (Surprise, huh!) The city's argument in the case was that it was operating under an informal AAP pursuant to the formal adoption of the AAP in April 1976. The Fourth Circuit Court of Appeals compared the circumstances of this informal AAP with the Supreme Court's decisions and found for Lilly. In essence, the informal plan was rejected for lack of a) specific goals and timetables, b) evidence that it was used to remedy past discrimination; and c) evidence that the informal AAP did not result in the hiring of unqualified applicants or unnecessarily trammel the interests of the white majority.

Another Supreme Court decision, however, took a different viewpoint. The *Adarand Constructors, Inc. v. Pena* decision addressed only federal-contract situations but may influence future decisions in private industry. The basic issue of the case was that in 1989 the U.S. Department of Transportation (DOT) awarded the prime contract for construction of a Colorado highway to Mountain Gravel & Construction Company. Mountain Gravel then solicited bids from subcontractors for the guardrail portion of the highway. Among the competing subcontractors were Gonzales Construction Company and Adarand Constructors, Inc. Adarand submitted the lowest bid. However, because of a clause in the contract from DOT that stated that "monetary compensation is offered for awarding subcontracts to small business concerns owned and controlled by socially and economically disadvantaged individuals,"[47] Mountain Gravel awarded the contract to Gonzales Construction.

The Court decided on behalf of Adarand Constructors and stated that affirmative action programs must be very narrowly tailored in order to achieve very specific purposes. In the case of *Adarand v. Pena,* the government's purpose of encouraging contracts to be given to minority subcontractors and presuming that such an action was directed at socially and economically disadvantaged individuals was remanded back to the district court. In the various judges' opinions of the case, the view was expressed that the relationship between being socially and economically disadvantaged and being of a particular race or ethnic group is not clear. Such membership is, therefore, questionable as a basis for a federal affirmative action program.

Employees' Reactions to AAPs

In addition to knowing about the legal aspects of AAPs, employers should also know how employees react to these plans. This is because employees' attitudes and perceptions about AAPs and about the individuals who are selected as a result of them are very important for the plan's success. David Harrison, David Kravitz, and their colleagues did an extensive study of how employees have reacted to AAPs.[48] Not surprisingly, they found that the design of a program and the employees' existing attitudes are strongly related to their reactions to AAPs.

The researchers identified four types of AAPs that have been used by organizations. *Opportunity Enhancement AAPs* typically offer focused recruitment or training directed toward target groups. *Equal Opportunity AAPs* simply forbid assigning negative weights to members of target groups. In *Tiebreak AAPs,* members in target groups are given advantage only in selection situations in which applicants are tied in terms of selection measures. Finally, *Strong Preferential Treatment AAPs* give preference to target members even if they have inferior qualifications. The researchers considered these four categories of AAPs to be in ascending order of prescriptiveness.

The following briefly summarizes the main findings:

- Individual characteristics of employees (gender, race, self-interests, political orientation) are all strongly related to attitudes toward AAPs, especially highly prescriptive programs.

- The type of AAP moderates the relationship between the individual characteristics mentioned in the previous point and employee attitudes toward AAPs. For example, more prescriptive AAP programs widen the differences in attitudes between whites and blacks and men and women.

- Employees' attitudes are influenced by how explicitly an AAP is described. There are smaller differences in the attitudes of whites and blacks and men and women when the AAP is clearly described in detail by the company than when the AAP is only generally described.

- Justifying the use of an AAP can lead to more positive evaluations by employees but can lead to more negative reactions if the justification focuses only on the under-representation of the target group.

SELECTION COURT CASES

In this section we review some of the major court decisions about selection practices. The cases presented in this section are not all of the major cases that deal with selection issues. Rather, they are a cross section chosen to represent demographic issues (age, ethnicity, gender, disability, and so on), measurement issues (job-relatedness, test construction, principles, and so on), and different selection applications (entry-level and promotion). This section will both familiarize you with the manner in which courts review discrimination charges and present important decisions that affect selection practices in organizations.

Griggs v. Duke Power (1971)

The first landmark case decided by the Supreme Court under Title VII was *Griggs v. Duke Power*.[49] The case began in 1967 when 13 black employees filed a class-action suit against Duke Power, charging discriminatory employment practices. The suit centered on recently developed selection requirements for the company's operations units. The plaintiffs charged that the requirements were arbitrary and screened out a much higher proportion of blacks than whites. The requirements, which were implemented in 1965, included a high school diploma, passage of a mechanical aptitude test, and a general intelligence test. When the requirements were initiated, they were not retroactive and so did not apply to current employees in the company's operations units. The company made no attempt to determine the job relatedness of these requirements.

A lower district court found in favor of the company on the grounds that any former discriminatory practices had ended and there was no evidence of discriminatory intent in the new requirements. An appellate court agreed with the finding of no discriminatory intent and in the absence of such intent the requirements were permissible. The Supreme Court, in a unanimous decision, reversed the previous decisions. The court ruled *that lack of discriminatory intent was not a sufficient defense against the use of employment devices that exclude on the basis of race*. In North Carolina at that time, 34 percent of white males had high school degrees whereas only 12 percent of black males did. The court acknowledged that tests and other measuring devices could be used but held *that they must be related to job performance*. Duke Power had contended that its two test requirements were permissible because Title VII allowed the use of "professionally developed tests" as selection devices.

Because there were employees already working in the operational units of the company who did not have a high school diploma or had not taken the tests and were performing their duties in a satisfactory manner, Duke Power had no evidence relating these requirements to job performance. The court stated that if "an employment practice that operates to exclude [blacks] cannot be shown to be related to job performance, it is prohibited."[50]

Two important precedents were set by the *Griggs* case, both of which are related to burdens of proof. The first is that the applicant carries the burden of proving the adverse impact of a particular selection device. Once adverse impact has been determined, the burden shifts to the employer to prove the validity or job relatedness of the device. The second is that the court said that the 1970 *EEOC Guidelines* were entitled to deference for proving validity.

United States v. Georgia Power (1973)

Because the Supreme Court held in the *Griggs* decision that employment tests must be job-related, attention in later cases was directed to the question of just what an employer must do to demonstrate job relatedness and the extent to which the *Guidelines* define that. For example, in February 1973, the Fifth Circuit Court of Appeals upheld the 1970 *EEOC Guidelines* in *United States v. Georgia Power*.[51]

In 1969 the attorney general brought suit against the Georgia Power Company for discrimination against black employees. Evidence was presented that at that time only 543 of the company's 7,515 employees were black (7.2 percent), despite the existence of a large pool of black applicants. Moreover, blacks were classified exclusively as janitors, porters, maids, and laborers; almost all white employees occupied higher positions. Beginning in 1960, in order to qualify for employment, all new employees were required to have a high school diploma or evidence of equivalent educational accomplishment. Then in 1963, all new employees were required also to pass a battery of tests developed by the Psychological Corporation. This requirement was instituted less than one month after the discontinuance of formal job segregation. In 1964 the company imposed the diploma requirement on all incumbent employees who wanted to transfer from the position of janitor, porter, or maid, but did not add that requirement for transferring from elsewhere in the company's structure. No study of these tests to determine job relatedness had been conducted prior to the filing of the suit.

Recognizing its obligation under *Griggs* to provide proof of the job relatedness of its test battery, the company began a validation study after the initiation of the suit. An official of the company conducted a validity study using an all-white sample. The study collected supervisors' ratings on employees who had earlier been hired on the basis of the tests to be validated and then compared those ratings with the test scores. This sample was admittedly small and excluded the 50 percent of the applicants who failed the test. Nevertheless, statistical evidence produced by Georgia Power supported the relationship of its selection test scores to the job performance ratings of supervisors, thereby demonstrating job relatedness.

The court, however, held that the validation study did not meet the minimum standards recommended for validation strategy by the EEOC Guidelines. One failure was the absence of blacks from the validation study. With an applicant population that was one-third black, the court concluded that such a study could at least have been attempted. The court also held that there were black employees in three of the company's job classifications in numbers as large as some of the all-white samples used by Georgia Power; therefore, the company could have attempted separate validation studies and, even though the studies would have been conducted on different job categories, some data could have been generated indicating whether the tests treated both races equally. The

1970 *EEOC Guidelines* also required that the sample of subjects be representative of the normal applicant group for the job or jobs in question. Since there was an absence of black people in the sample, the court ruled that this requirement had not been fulfilled. Also, according to the *Guidelines,* tests must be administered under controlled and standardized conditions. In this case, the court found that testing of new applicants was uniform, but that testing of incumbents was not.

Finally, in accordance with the *Griggs* decision, *the court struck down the company's use of diploma requirements on the grounds that there was no evidence relating the possession of a diploma to job performance.*

Spurlock v. United Airlines (1972)

The case of *Spurlock v. United Airlines* involved a demonstration of the job relatedness of selection instruments other than tests.[52] In this case, Spurlock filed suit against United Airlines after his application for the job of flight officer had been rejected. Spurlock charged the airline with discrimination against blacks and offered as evidence the fact that only 9 flight officers out of 5,900 were black. In the suit, Spurlock challenged two of the requirements for the job: a college degree and a minimum of 500 hours of flight time.

United contended that both these selection requirements were job related. Using statistics, United showed that applicants with a greater number of flight hours were more likely to succeed in the rigorous training program that flight officers must complete after being hired. Statistics also showed that 500 hours was a reasonable minimum requirement. In addition, United contended that, because of the high cost of the training program, it was important that those who begin the training program eventually become flight officers. United officials also testified that the possession of a college degree indicated that the applicant had the ability to function in a classroom atmosphere. This ability is important because of the initial training program, and because flight officers are required to attend intensive refresher courses every six months.

The 10th Circuit Court of Appeals accepted the evidence presented by United as proof of the job relatedness of the requirements. In a significant ruling, the court stated that when a job requires a small amount of skill and training and the consequences of hiring an unqualified applicant are insignificant, the courts should closely examine selection instruments that are discriminatory. On the other hand, *when the job requires a high degree of skill and the economic and human risks involved are great, the employer bears a lighter burden to show that selection instruments are job related.*

Watson v. Ft. Worth Bank & Trust (1988)

The case of *Watson v. Ft. Worth Bank & Trust* addressed the important question of whether discrimination cases focusing on the interview could be heard as disparate impact cases, even though traditionally these cases had been tried as disparate treatment.[53] Clara Watson, a black woman, was hired by Ft. Worth Bank & Trust as a proof operator in August 1973, and she was promoted to teller in January 1976. In February 1980, she sought to become supervisor of the tellers in the main lobby; a white male, however, was selected for the job. Watson then sought a position as supervisor of the drive-in bank, but this position was given to a white female. In February 1981, after Watson had served for about a year as a commercial teller in the bank's main lobby and informally as assistant to the supervisor of tellers, the man holding that position was promoted. Watson applied for the vacancy, but the white female who was the supervisor of the drive-in bank was selected instead. Watson then applied for the vacancy created at the drive-in;

a white male was selected for that job. The bank, which had about 80 employees, had not developed precise and formal criteria for evaluating candidates for the positions for which Watson unsuccessfully applied. It relied instead on the subjective judgment of supervisors who were acquainted with the candidates and with the nature of the jobs to be filled. All the supervisors involved in denying Watson the four promotions were white.

The U.S. District Court that heard the case addressed Watson's claims under the standards applied to disparate treatment cases. It concluded that Watson had established a prima facie case, but that the bank had met its rebuttal burden by presenting legitimate and nondiscriminatory reasons for each of the promotion decisions. Finally, Watson had failed to show that these reasons were pretexts, and her case was dismissed.

Watson appealed the decision on the basis that the district court had erred in failing to apply disparate impact analysis to her claim. From our previous discussion, we understand the significance of this argument. Under disparate treatment, the burden of proof required of the bank to defend its practices is lighter than under disparate impact processes. If the case were heard as disparate impact and Watson established a prima facie case, the bank would most likely have to provide validation evidence as a defense. Given its situation, with no defined criteria and no scored selection instruments, this would be difficult to do. The Fifth Circuit Court of Appeals, however, held that "a Title VII challenge to an allegedly discretionary promotion system is properly analyzed under the disparate treatment model rather than the disparate impact model."[54] In so ruling, citations were given to various courts of appeals decisions that held that disparate treatment analysis was proper when subjective criteria (the interview) were of issue. In essence, this court said that disparate impact analysis should be applied only to objective selection devices (for example, tests), and disparate treatment to opinion or judgment devices. The implication for selection practices is obvious: The use of interviews and related instruments would be easier to defend in discrimination cases; they should, therefore, be extensively used. Anything else would be far riskier.

The Supreme Court, however, took an opposing view and made several important statements. *One was that the ultimate legal issue in the two forms of discrimination cases is similar.* The ruling also stated the following:

> *We are persuaded that our decisions in* Griggs *and succeeding cases could largely be nullified if disparate impact analyses were applied only to standardized selection practices. However one might distinguish " subjective" from "objective" criteria, it is apparent that selection systems that combine both types would generally be considered subjective in nature. Thus, for example, if the employer in* Griggs *had consistently preferred applicants who had a high school diploma and who passed the company's general aptitude test, its selection system could nonetheless have been considered "subjective" if it also included brief interviews.... If we announced a rule that allowed employers so easily to insulate themselves from liability under* Griggs, *impact analysis might effectively be abolished.*[55]

Rudder v. District of Columbia (1995)

In the case of *Rudder v. District of Columbia,*[56] the most important part of this decision made by the U.S. District Court for the District of Columbia was the comments about appropriate procedures for demonstrating the content validity of selection measures. In content validity, the relationship between selection test performance and job performance is demonstrated through a number of judgments of experts. Other cases that we have summarized have discussed empirical validation, in which statistical evidence is used to link test performance to job performance.

The charge in this case was that the examinations for the positions of captain, lieutenant, and sergeant used by the District of Columbia Fire Department adversely affected black firefighters. There were three examinations for these positions. The Job Knowledge Test was a multiple-choice test of knowledge based on manuals, orders, and other material specified on a reading list that was made available to applicants. The Assessment Center was composed of exercises designed to test for behavioral characteristics essential to Fire Department officers. The Fire Scene Simulation presented two fire scenarios. Each scenario presented a drawing of a fire scene and its surroundings, and quotations from the dispatcher. The applicants responded to a series of questions about each scenario, writing down the decisions they would make and the orders they would give on the scene. To develop these examinations, extensive job analyses were conducted of the three different jobs. The job analyses began with interviews with a biracial group of approximately 20 Fire Department officers. These interviews resulted in a nine-page description of the tasks of fire sergeant, lieutenant, and captain. This document was distributed to a biracial sample of 54 officers for review and correction. Based on these steps, it was determined that the jobs of the three officers were essentially the same. They differed in level of authority at a fire scene, but did not differ in task activities. Therefore, the Job Knowledge Test and the Assessment Center exercises were the same for all three jobs. The Fire Scene Simulation did differ for each of the ranks. The Job Knowledge Test was developed in six phases:

1. Twenty officers reviewed the department's manuals and operating procedures and pinpointed those areas that were particularly relevant to their jobs.

2. Another sample of officers generated the same information, including managerial tasks performed at the firehouse.

3. A third sample of officers reviewed the information generated by the first two groups.

4. Multiple-choice items were written based on the information generated by the three groups of officers.

5. These items were carefully reviewed over a period of months by a consultant.

6. Another group of officers did a final review of items.

The Assessment Center exercises were developed using the following steps:

1. Based on the job analysis information, a consultant and groups of officers identified several behavioral dimensions that should be measured, including dealing with people, decisiveness, judgment, leadership, planning and organizing, verbal communication, and written communication.

2. The same individuals developed a number of simulations that were designed to measure these behavioral dimensions.

3. A racially balanced group of assessors (judges) were recruited from fire departments across the United States and Canada.

4. These assessors participated in a two-day training program.

The following steps were used in developing the Fire Scene Simulation:

1. Information was collected during the job analysis, including the frequency of different types of fires, procedures used in responding to emergency calls, the types of equipment used, and communication procedures.

2. These data were used, in various combinations, to create each fire scene and its accompanying information. These combinations were reviewed by various groups of officers.

The three tests were administered under controlled, standardized conditions. The Job Knowledge Tests were graded by employees of the Metropolitan Police Department using a scoring key. The Fire Scene Simulations were graded by 34 battalion fire chiefs, who worked in pairs and were all present in the same classroom during grading. This grading used a double-blind procedure, so that test-takers could not be identified. Answers were based on published Fire Department materials. The Assessment Center was scored by the trained assessors.

In its ruling, the district court explicitly stated that *these procedures "produced more than sufficient evidence that the ... examination was valid and job related...."*[57]

The major points of each of these cases are summarized in Table 2.4. We can see that the result of the various court decisions is to identify selection practices that are either acceptable or unacceptable. Unfortunately for selection specialists, most decisions identify unacceptable actions. We, therefore, know more about what *not* to do than about what we can do. This is somewhat unsettling. It would be more convenient if the courts could assemble a description of acceptable selection practices. From all that has been said in this chapter, however, you should realize that such an action by the courts is not possible. Selection practices are too varied and too interrelated. As regards the regulatory model, the main responsibility of the courts and agencies is to stop organizations from perpetuating the societal problems that prompted the EEO laws. It is the responsibility of those who design selection programs to develop the various parts of their programs so they comply with the laws. Government regulation is a major reason why, as we said at the beginning of Chapter 1, selection has increasingly become such a complex activity

Frank Ricci et al. v. John DeStefano et al. (2009)

The case of *Frank Ricci et al. v. John DeStefano et al.* was about the use of a written selection test and an interview that were used for identifying candidates for promotion into the ranks of lieutenant and captain in the New Haven, Connecticut Fire Department. Under its charter, the city of New Haven requires such examinations of candidates for promotion; then, after the examinations are scored, the department must draw up a list of candidates in the rank order of their scores. The top three are considered for the next open position and all other promotions within a specified time also use a group of three who have the highest scores on the selection exams.

These tests and interviews were developed for the fire department by a consulting firm that had extensive experience in developing promotion examinations for police and fire departments throughout the country. The consulting firm started the test development process by doing a job analysis to determine specific tasks of each position and also the KSAs required for each position. As part of this job analysis, the firm rode with experienced officers currently in the positions, interviewed many officers and firefighters, and developed written job analysis questionnaires that were distributed to officers within the department for completion. Minority officers were oversampled in each of these steps. When writing the test questions, which were all below the 10th grade reading level, the firm gathered written policies, tactics, rules, and factual information to use as sources. After the items were written, all source materials were made available to those who wished to use it to prepare for the written test. The consulting firm also used similar procedures for the construction of the interview, which largely asked about behaviors to be taken in fire situations. The firm also chose and trained

TABLE 2.4	Key Issues in Major Selection Court Cases
Griggs v. Duke Power (1971)	1. Lack of discriminatory intent not sufficient defense 2. Selection test must be job related if adverse impact results 3. Employer bears burden of proof in face of apparent adverse impact
U.S. v. Georgia Power (1973)	1. Validation strategy must comply with EEOC guidelines 2. Validation must include affected groups 3. Validation must reflect selection decision practices 4. Testing must occur under standardized conditions
Spurlock v. United Airlines (1972)	1. College degree and experience requirements are shown to be job related 2. Company's burden of proof diminishes as human risks increase
Watson v. Ft. Worth Bank & Trust (1988)	1. Cases focusing on subjective selection devices, such as interviews and judgments, could be heard as disparate impact 2. Organization may need to validate interview in same manner as objective test
Rudder v. District of Columbia (1995)	1. Content validity is acceptable defense for adverse impact 2. Job analysis, ensuring adequate representation of minority groups in data collection, is essential 3. Clear links must be shown between job analysis information, test questions, and correct answers 4. Attention to test security and administration are important
Ricci v. DeStefano (2009)	1. Adverse impact present as blacks scored less well on tests than whites and Hispanics. 2. Discrimination directed toward whites and Hispanics 3. Threat of lawsuit is not defense for disregarding job-related selection tests 4. Adverse impact can be defended by job relatedness of selection tests
OFCCP v. Ozark Air Lines (1986)	1. In disability cases, organization must prove that individual cannot perform job 2. Reasonable accommodation must be given to disabled individual
Gross v. FBL Financial Services (2009)	1. Central question was how much evidence must plaintiff produce in age discrimination claim to force defendant to provide evidence that it did not use age in decision. 2. Plaintiff must provide clear evidence that age was "but-for" reason for decision 3. Ruling significantly increases the amount of evidence that plaintiff must provide to obtain judgment that age discrimination occurred.

30 individuals who would serve as interviewers. Twenty of the 30 interviewers were minority group members and each of the nine interview panels had two minority group members of the total three.

After the scores were computed, all ten of those immediately eligible for consideration for promotion to lieutenant were white. Of the nine immediately eligible for promotion to captain, seven were white and two were Hispanic. None of the black applicants were immediately eligible for promotion. Not surprisingly, these results caused much consternation among applicants, the legal counsel of the city, its Director of Human Resources, and the Civil Service Board that was ultimately responsible for the usage of the testing. Black applicants threatened a lawsuit based on the adverse impact of the test results. After extensive consideration, the Civil Service Commission voided the exam and its results. Subsequently, a group of white and Hispanic applicants filed a suit against this decision, claiming that race and color were the deciding factors in the decision to void the exams.

The Supreme Court agreed with the white and Hispanic applicants, finding that the decision to void the exam scores violated Title VII of the Civil Rights Act of 1964. Specifically, the court commented that:

1. The threat of a lawsuit is not sufficient reason to void the results of the tests.

2. The adverse impact of test results can be defended by the job relatedness of tests.

3. There appears to be enough evidence in terms of the tests' construction to indicate that the tests in this case were job related.

4. There was no evidence that an alternative testing procedure would have less adverse impact than did the tests that were given.

5. Adjusting the test scores of black applicants would have violated Title VII.

The case was remanded back to a lower court for reconsideration with the implicit understanding that the results of the test could be used to identify candidates for consideration for promotion.[58]

OFCCP v. Ozark Air Lines (1986)

The case of *OFCCP v. Ozark Air Lines* concerns the Rehabilitation Act of 1973 and the refusal of the airline to employ a disabled person as an airline technician.[59] Gary Frey had a nonfunctioning left ear because of a childhood accident. His right ear was unimpaired. Ozark agreed that Frey had the necessary qualifications for the position, but refused to hire him because of his hearing disability and his failure to prove that he could carry out the job duties without endangering himself and others. Because Ozark Airlines was regarded as a federal contractor, the case was decided by the OFCCP. Frey won the decision and was also awarded back pay. In so doing, the OFCCP argued that *it was Ozark's burden to prove that Frey's employment would have endangered him and others,* not the burden of Frey and OFCCP to prove that he could do the work successfully. Second, it stated that *a disabled person is "qualified for employment if he [or she] is capable of performing a particular job with reasonable accommodation to his or her handicap."*[60] The only evidence that Ozark submitted was the testimony of its personnel director who, responding to questioning as to whether he had given any thought to accommodating Frey or putting restrictions on his duties, stated that this was not possible because of limitations in the union contract. A related Ozark argument that the noise levels of the facility would endanger Frey's remaining hearing was also dismissed. Citing specific decibel levels, the OFCCP commented that Ozark failed to show that Frey's hearing could not be protected by wearing ear protectors. This case was about the use of a written selection test and an interview in the promotion into the ranks of lieutenant and captain in the New Haven, Connecticut Fire Department.

Jack Gross v. FBL Financial Services (2009)

In *Jack Gross v. FBL Financial Services*, the central issue was about how much evidence a plaintiff must produce about age discrimination in an employment decision in order for the defendant (company in most cases) to be forced to provide evidence that it did not use age as a factor in making the employment decision in question.

Jack Gross began working for FBL Financial Services in 1971 and by 2001 had become a claims administration director. In 2003, when he was 54 years old, Gross was reassigned as a claims project coordinator. Many of his previous job tasks were reassigned to a a 43-year-old woman in a new claims administration manager position. Gross filed suit against the company, arguing that its action violated ADA 1990 in that the decision to reassign him was at least partially due to his age. A suit in which age is one of several motives being used in an alleged illegal employment decision is referred to by the courts as a *mixed-motive* case. At the conclusion of the trial, the judge instructed the jury that it must return a judgment for Gross if it found that age was a motivating factor in FBL's decision to reassign him. *Motivating factor* meant that age played a role or was part of the reason that FBL made its decision regarding Gross. Following these instructions, the jury found on behalf of Gross.

The Supreme Court disagreed with the instructions given to the jury and reversed and remanded the decision. In explaining its decision, the Court stated that the burden of proof is different in cases filed under ADEA of 1967 than it is for Title VII of the Civil Rights Act of 1964. In ADEA cases, the plaintiff must provide clear evidence that age was the "but for" reason for the employment decision. That is, the employment decision would have been different (presumably more favorable to the plaintiff) but for the fact that age was used in the decision. In a mixed-motive case, this would mean that the plaintiff must offer evidence that age was the dominant or only motive for the negative decision. Further, the burden of proof does not shift to the employer to provide an argument that legitimate reasons (in this case an organizational restructuring) was the reason for the decision if age is shown by the plaintiff to be part of or one factor in the decision. In explaining its ruling, the Supreme Court interpreted actions of Congress, previous case decisions, and the wording of ADEA 1967.

The obvious result of this decision is that it is much more difficult for a plaintiff to win a case of age discrimination under ADEA 1967. In essence, the plaintiff must offer direct evidence, for example written documents or oral statements, that the decision against the plaintiff was made primarily because of age. Absent this kind of evidence, the plaintiff has not met his or her burden of proof—has not produced sufficient evidence to make a claim that age discrimination occurred. Expectedly, many organizations representing older citizens have urged Congress to make changes to ADEA 1967 to lessen the burden of proof necessary to pursue a claim of age discrimination.[61]

EEO SUMMARY

This chapter has presented the major EEO principles and discussed their impact on HR selection programs. This last section summarizes the major legal concepts regarding discrimination that HR specialists must be aware of either in reviewing an existing selection program or developing a new one.

Basis of Discrimination

Charges of discrimination in selection practices must be linked to one of the personal characteristics specified in EEO law. The federal laws and directives identify such characteristics as race, color, religion, sex, national origin, age (over 40), and physical or mental handicaps. Although this is indeed a long list, it clearly means that, unless there is a state or local law, many charges of discrimination threatened against private organizations (for example, discrimination based on homosexuality, hair or clothing style, or school affiliation) are not feasible according to EEO law unless the charge can be linked to one of the specified characteristics. A broader accountability exists for governmental employers, however, because of the wording of constitutional amendments. The specification of these personal characteristics defines the groups HR specialists should consider when reviewing the vulnerability of a selection program to discrimination charges. An analysis of possible discrimination can be conducted on those groups with characteristics that are both specified in EEO law and constitute at least 2 percent of the relevant labor market. Although this may become a lengthy list, it has the advantage of defining the scope of compliance to EEO law.

Evidence of Discrimination

A charge of discrimination can be brought against an organization with little substantiating evidence other than the fact that an individual was not selected for a position. In many cases such a charge is a public embarrassment for the organization. Many organizations do not wish to bear the cost of legal action, especially if such action may be prolonged. The result is that the organization frequently will negotiate a settlement to the charge. Although this may be a pragmatic solution to a particular situation, it does little to resolve a potentially recurrent problem. It is important for HR specialists to realize that judicial rulings about discrimination in selection practices generally have been based on patterns of selection decisions over a period of time rather than on an isolated instance. A particular selection decision means that one (or a few) individuals have been hired from a pool of applicants. The others have been denied employment. Perhaps several of these rejected applicants differ from the one who was selected on a personal characteristic specified in EEO law—for example, color, race, or religion. This difference and the denial of employment could serve as an *indicator* of discrimination in selection. Courts have generally recognized, however, that selection decisions are favorable to some applicants and unfavorable to others. The crucial information is the pattern that is evident when one views the overall result of a series of decisions. If such data indicate that one group—for example, white males—is selected in more cases than one would expect to find, given the relevant labor market's demographic characteristics, then the usual judgment has been that the questioned selection decision could be discriminatory. However, if the review of this series of selection decisions indicates that over time the demographic pattern of those selected is similar to the demographic profile of the relevant labor market, the usual judgment is that the questioned selection decision is not an indicator of discrimination. Furthermore, the consequences of a particular selection decision are a natural and nondiscriminatory by-product of the selection process.

Options of the Organization

If, after reviewing selection patterns for specific jobs and applying the appropriate statistical analysis (for example, the Four-Fifths Rule or the Standard Deviation Rule and accompanying statistical tests) to the demographic groups specified in EEO law, the HR specialist notes large selection differences, the organization has two options for reducing its vulnerability. The first is to discontinue the current procedures and develop alternatives that would result in small differences in selection among the various demographic groups. At first this may seem a formidable task, but for many situations such a change is actually fairly straightforward. We previously discussed the interaction between recruitment and selection. Some organizations have found that, especially for entry-level positions, a broadening of recruitment activities to systematically include women and minorities has provided a sufficiently qualified applicant pool to change selection patterns substantially. Other examples include the reevaluation of selection requirements, such as the number of years of experience and education degrees, to determine their necessity for job performance. Such requirements, especially if they are used stringently at an early stage of the processing of applicants, can have a large effect on the applicant pool. The second alternative, if large selection differences exist, is to conduct a validation study to support the organization's contention that the selection instruments are job related. As the *Uniform Guidelines* indicate, such studies must conform to professional standards for criterion or content validity. Chapter 5 presents the steps in these validation methods.

A final important point to keep in mind is that there is no legal requirement either to demonstrate the job relatedness of all selection devices or to hire unqualified applicants in order to increase the "numbers" of specific groups. As has been pointed out, proof of job relatedness becomes necessary only if adverse impact is evidenced. However, if an organization goes through the process of building job relatedness into the data that are used for selection decisions, it is not obligated to ignore that process and hire only because the applicant belongs to a certain demographic group. This point is often overlooked, and it frequently results in hiring decisions made primarily to increase the employment of certain groups. If these individuals are not qualified for the jobs into which they are hired, their selection is not a service to either themselves or the organization.

LEGAL ISSUES IN SMALL BUSINESS

Many owners and managers of small businesses generally think that EEO regulations are especially burdensome to them, and that many of the defenses for selection practices are available only to large organizations that have the personnel and resources to gather appropriate data. Although we agree that compliance with federal regulations may be time-consuming, such compliance is not beyond the reach of small businesses.

One important fact is that very small businesses are exempt from many of the EEO laws and directives because they have fewer than 15 employees. Second, many businesses with fewer than 100 employees are exempt from most of the reporting requirements associated with these laws and directives. Third, reasonable steps can be taken to estimate whether disparate treatment or impact may occur and to build a reasonable case for validity of selection instruments.

Regarding this third point, we think that the technical demands on small business owners and managers related to selection are similar to those burdens associated with the financial management, marketing, and production of the firm. That is, small business operators must assume many roles and complete many activities for which they are not formally trained and which may not be their primary interest or expertise. However, we regard the selection of employees to be important for the overall productivity of the small business. Because training is usually not a very well developed component of small businesses, selection becomes a crucial activity in obtaining employees with appropriate KSAs.

As we have said, the objectives and activities associated with the selection of appropriate employees to a large degree coincide with requirements associated with EEO laws and directives. Therefore, almost all of the technical work necessary for developing a selection program also applies to meeting legal demands. Specifically, Steven Maurer and Charles Fay have described how content validity can be carried out within small businesses.[62] They have pointed out that job analysis is the basis for such validity, and that legal defenses based on content validity have been accepted by courts. We agree with these authors' position and point out that content validity (which we will describe in detail in Chapters 5 and 7) is essential to the development of a useful selection program.

Being able to judge the possibility of potential claims of discrimination is also useful for small businesses. The possibility for discrimination through disparate treatment can be estimated by using the discussion of evidence and proof presented in this chapter. In this discussion, the initial burden of proof of the plaintiff and the burden of the defendant should be carefully noted. That is, selection procedures should be examined to determine whether they present the conditions necessary for the plaintiff's initial claim. Further, the use of selection instruments based on job analysis, and developed according to the material presented in other chapters of this text, should provide a reasonable business-based explanation of selection decisions that can be used to meet the defendant's burden of proof. It is unclear to what extent discrimination through disparate impact may be applied to small businesses. The small numbers of employees in specific jobs often makes statistical analyses questionable or inappropriate. A more viable question may be the ability of recruitment efforts to reach a diverse applicant pool. Consideration should be given to inexpensive ways of advertising job openings in outlets used by various demographic groups.

REFERENCES

1. James Ledvinka and Vida Scarpello, *Federal Regulation of Personnel and Human Resource Management*, 2nd ed. (Boston: PWS-Kent, 1991), 17.

2. U.S. Equal Employment Opportunity Commission, "Outback Steakhouse Agrees to Pay $19 Million for Sex Bias against Women in 'Glass Ceiling' Suit by EEOC," December 29, 2009, http://www.eeoc.gov/eeoc/newsroom/release/12-29-09a.cfm.

3. Public Law 102–166 102d Congress—Nov. 21, 1991, 105 STAT. 1075.

4. Paul S. Greenlaw and Sanne S. Jensen, "Race-Norming and the Civil Rights Act of 1991," *Public Personnel Management* 25 (1996): 13–24.

5. J. A. Hartigan and A. K. Wigdor eds., *Fairness in Employment Testing: Validity Generalization, Minority Issues and the General Aptitude Test Battery* (Washington, DC: National Academy Press, 1989), 20.

6. Greenlaw and Jensen, "Race-Norming and the Civil Rights Act of 1991."

7. *APA Monitor* 23 (January 1992): 13.

8. U.S. Equal Employment Opportunity Commission, "Auto Parts Manufacturer Settles EEOC Age Discrimination Suit for $80,000," August 19, 2009, http://archive.eeoc.gov/press/8-19-09e.html.

9. U.S. Equal Employment Opportunity Commission, "EEOC Wins Age Discrimination Suit against University of Wisconsin Press," May 10, 2001, http://archive.eeoc.gov/press/5-10-01-a.html.

10. U.S. Equal Employment Opportunity Commission, *A Technical Assistance Manual on the Employment Provisions of the Americans with Disabilities Act* (U.S. Equal Employment Opportunity Commission, 1992).

11. Ibid.

12. U.S. Equal Employment Opportunity Commission, "Wal-Mart to Pay $250,000 for Disability Bias," June 9, 2008, http://www.eeoc.gov/eeoc/newsroom/release/6-9-08.cfm.

13. U.S. Equal Employment Opportunity Commission, "Sears, Roebuck to Pay $6.2 Million for Disability Bias," June 29, 2009, http://www.eeoc.gov/eeoc/newsroom/release/9-29-09.cfm.

14. *Sutton v. United Airlines, Inc.* 119 Sup. Ct. 2139 (1999).

15. *Murphy v. United Parcel Service*, 527 U.S. 516 (1999).

16. *Toyota Motor Mfg., KY., Inc. v. Williams (00-1089)*, 534 U.S. 184 (2002).

17. Act S102; 29CFR S1630.11.

18. Cheryl Mahaffey, *Accommodating Employment Testing to the Needs of Individuals with Disabilities* (Burbank, CA: Psychological Services, Inc., August 1992).

19. Elliot H. Shaller, "'Reasonable Accommodation' under the Americans with Disabilities Act— What Does It Mean?" *Employee Relations Labor Journal* 16 (Spring 1991): 431–451.

20. *U.S. Airways v. Barnett*, 535 U.S. 391 (2002).

21. *PGA Tour v. Martin*, 532 U.S. 661 (2001).

22. ADA Amendments Act of 2008, PL 110-325 (S 3406).

23. Ibid.

24. The *Immigration and Nationality Act*, sec. 274B, 274C.

25. Ibid., 402.

26. Ibid., 366.

27. U.S. Equal Employment Opportunity Commission, "EEOC Announces $2.1 Million Settlement of Wage Discrimination Suit for Class of Filipino Nurses," March 2, 1999, http://www.eeoc.gov/eeoc/newsroom/release/3-2-99.cfm.

28. The *Civil Rights Act of April 9*, 1866, Chap. 31, 1, 14 Stat. 27.

29. *McDonnell Douglas v. Green*, 411 U.S. 792 (1973).

30. *Wards Cove Packing Company v. Atonio*, 490 U.S. 642 (1989).

31. Barbara Lindemann Schlei and Paul Grossman, *Employment Discrimination Law*, 2nd ed. (Washington, DC: Bureau of National Affairs, 1983), 1361.

32. Ibid., 1362.

33. Philip Bobko and Philip L. Roth, "An Analysis of Two Methods for Assessing and Indexing Adverse Impact: A Disconnect between the Academic Literature and Some Practice," in *Adverse Impact: Implications for Organizational Staffing and High Stakes Selection*, ed. James L. Outtz (New York: Routledge, Taylor and Francis Group, 2010).

34. Sheldon Zedeck, "Adverse Impact: History and Evolution," in *Adverse Impact: Implications for Organizational Staffing and High Stakes Selection*, ed. James L. Outtz (New York: Routledge, Taylor and Francis Group, 2010).

35. Philip L. Roth, Philip Bobko, and Fred F. Switzer, "Modeling the Behavior of the 4/5th Rule for Determining Adverse Impact: Reasons for Caution," *Journal of Applied Psychology* 91, (2006): 507–522.

36. Federal Register Vol. 70, No. 194, October 7, 2005, Rules and Regulations.

37. U.S. Equal Employment Opportunity Commission, Civil Service Commission, Department of Labor, and Department of Justice, *Adoption of Four Agencies of Uniform Guidelines on Employee Selection Procedures*, 43 Federal Register 38, 290–38, 315 (August 25, 1978).

38. Ibid.

39. Ibid., 1607.5(1).

40. John P. Campbell, "Group Differences and Personnel Decisions: Validity, Fairness, and Affirmative Action," *Journal of Vocational Behavior* 49 (1996): 122–158.

41. Ledvinka and Scarpello, *Federal Regulation of Personnel and Human Resource Management*, 124.

42. Revised Order of No. 4, 41 Code of Federal Regulations, Part 60, at sec. 2. 10 (1979).

43. U.S. Equal Employment Opportunity Commission, "EEOC and Ford Motor Sign Multi-Million Dollar Settlement of Sexual Harassment Case," September 7, 1999, http://www.eeoc.gov/eeoc/newsroom/release/9-7-99.cfm.

44. The *Civil Rights Act of 1964*, Title VII, sec. 703(a).

45. Ibid., sec. 703(j).

46. *Lilly v. City of Beckley*, 797 F.2d 191, 41 FEP 772 (4th Cir. 1986).

47. *Adarand Constructors, Inc. v. Pena*, 115 Sup. Ct. 2097 (1995).

48. David A. Harrison, David A. Kravitz, David M. Mayer, Lisa M. Leslie, and Dalit Lev-Arey, "Understanding Attitudes toward Affirmative Action Programs in Employment: Summary and Meta-Analysis of 35 Years of Research," *Journal of Applied Psychology* 91 (2006): 1013–1036.

49. *Griggs v. Duke Power Co.*, 401 U.S. 424 (1971).

50. Ibid.

51. *United States v. Georgia Power*, 474 F. 2d 906 (1973).

52. *Spurlock v. United Airlines*, 475 F. 2d 216 (10th Cir. 1972).

53. *Watson v. Ft. Worth Bank & Trust*, 47 FEP Cases 102 (1988).

54. Ibid., 104.

55. Ibid., 107.

56. *Rudder v. District of Columbia*, 890 F. Supp. 23 (1995).

57. Ibid.

58. *Ricci et al. v. DeSafano et al.* 557 U.S. ___ 2009, No. 07-1428 & No. 08-328.

59. *OFCCP v. Ozark Air Lines*, 40 FEP 1859 (U.S. Department of Labor, 1986).

60. Ibid., 1862.

61. *Jack Gross v. FBL Financial Services Inc.* 557 U.S. ___ 2009, No. 88-441.

62. Steven D. Maurer and Charles H. Fay, "Legal Hiring Practices for Small Business," *Journal of Small Business Management* 24 (1986): 47–54.

PART 2

FOUNDATIONS OF MEASUREMENT FOR HUMAN RESOURCE SELECTION

Collecting information about job candidates through selection measures is central to any HR selection system. Information is the basis for all decisions concerning the selection of job applicants. Sometimes, however, HR selection decisions turn out to be wrong. Perhaps individuals predicted to be outstanding performers actually contribute very little to an organization. Others who were forecast to stay with an organization for a lengthy period of time leave after only a few weeks. And, in cases that are not verifiable, persons who were thought to be a poor fit for a firm and not hired would have been valuable contributors had they been employed. In each of these situations, we would conclude that inappropriate selection decisions had been made. Yet when we analyze the situation, we may find that the decisions themselves were not wrong; it may be that the data on which they were based were faulty. Thus it is essential that managers have sound data on which to base selection decisions. What do we mean by "sound data"? The three chapters in Part 2 address this question. Specifically, the objectives of this section are as follows:

1. To explore the role of HR *measurement* in selection decision making.

2. To examine the concepts of *reliability* and *validity* of selection data as well as their role in choosing useful selection measures and making effective selection decisions.

Human Resource Measurement in Selection

FUNDAMENTALS OF MEASUREMENT: AN OVERVIEW

An important assumption in selection decision making is that information is available for making selection decisions. But what types of information can be used? Where does this information come from? What characteristics should this information have in order to be most useful for selection purposes? These are only a few of the questions this chapter addresses. Specifically, we focus on (a) the basics of psychological measurement as they apply to HR selection and (b) the location, development, and interpretation of measures commonly used in HR selection.

THE ROLE OF MEASUREMENT IN HR SELECTION

If you have watched competent carpenters build a house or a piece of furniture, you cannot help being impressed by how well the various pieces fit together. For example, when a door is hung in place, it has a snug fit with its frame. Or perhaps you made a trip to the clinic where you watched the veterinarian save Pepe, your toy poodle, who had swallowed a Christmas tinsel. What makes your vet so skilled and successful? Although many things contribute to the success of a carpenter installing a door and a veterinarian dealing with a pet emergency, one of the factors common to the success of both is their ability to employ *measurement*. How could a door be made to fit if a carpenter could not determine the exact dimensions of the opening? How could your vet operate on Pepe if she did not understand anatomy and physiology? Neither could be done without measurement. As we will see, measurement is also essential to the successful implementation and administration of an HR selection program.

The Nature of Measurement

Let's imagine for a moment that we are in charge of employment for a large company. We have an opening for the position of sales representative. Because of current economic conditions and the nature of the job, many people are interested. Numerous candidates submit an application, complete a test, and interview by phone. After several days of assessing applicants, we can draw at least one obvious conclusion: *People are different.* As we think about the applicants, we notice that some are talkative, some are shy, some are neat and professionally dressed, and others are sloppy and shabbily dressed. After interviewing them, we see that some applicants seem intelligent and others dim-witted; some seem dependable and achievement-oriented, while others appear irresponsible and aimless. Although our usual system of classifying individuals in these extreme categories may be useful for *describing* people in general, it may not be useful for choosing among applicants. In a personnel selection context, we find that few people fall into these extreme categories. For example, only a few of our applicants will be extremely bright and only a few extremely dull. For the many others, we will need some way to make finer distinctions among them with regard to the various characteristics that are of interest to us (intelligence, conscientiousness, and so on). We will need to use measurement to make these discriminations and to study in detail the relationship between applicant characteristics and employee performance on the job.

A Definition

But what is measurement? Numerous writings have examined the topic; some emphasize the meaning of measurement, others address methods involved in applying measurement. From the perspective of human resource selection, we can offer one definition. Simply put, *measurement* involves the systematic application of rules for assigning numerical values to objects to represent the quantities of a person's attributes or traits.[1] Let's explore this definition. *Rules* suggest that the basis for assigning numbers is clearly specified and consistently applied. For any measures we might use in selection, let's say a test, it is important that different users who employ the measure obtain similar results. Thus when job applicants take a test, differences among applicants' scores should be due to individual differences in test performance and not to the way in which different scorers scored the tests or to different test-taking conditions. Rules for assigning numbers to our selection measures help to standardize the application of these measures. The use of rules shows that measurement is not an end but a means in the process of assessing an individual's standing on a characteristic.

A second point in our definition involves the concept of an *attribute*. In reality, when we measure a person, we do not measure the person per se; rather, we assess an attribute or trait of the person. Physical attributes such as gender can be assessed through direct observation. However, *psychological* attributes are not directly observable. Psychological attributes such as conscientiousness, intelligence, job knowledge, and mathematical and verbal abilities must be inferred from an observable score (consisting of numbers or units of measurement) that represents an individual's standing on these unobserved psychological attributes.[2] A score on a mathematics test is a number that reflects a job applicant's mathematical ability. With our test, we are measuring not the applicant but the applicant's mathematical ability. Notice in our description we have not talked about *how well* we measure an attribute. Obviously, if we want to measure mathematical ability, we want a score (a test, for example) that is a good measure of this ability. Obtaining a good measure of these elusive but nevertheless critical psychological attributes (such as various knowledge, skills, abilities, personality, and other traits) is not always easy. Yet it is psychological traits that will typically be identified as important indicators of how well an applicant can perform a job, not just physical attributes.

When we use tests or interviews to obtain measurements of psychological attributes, we must draw inferences from these measures. Because inferences are involved, however, we are on much shakier ground than when we can directly observe an attribute. Someone conducting a selection interview might believe that the extent of an applicant's eye contact with the interviewer reflects the applicant's interest in the company or that the firmness of a handshake reflects the interviewee's self-confidence. But are these inferences warranted? It's important to answer this question if we are to use numbers in a meaningful way to evaluate important psychological attributes when making selection decisions.

A third and final point in our definition of measurement is that *numbers* or units represent attributes. Numbers play a useful role in summarizing and communicating the degree, amount, or magnitude of an assessed attribute. Thus, if applicant A scores 40 out of 50 on an achievement test and applicant B scores a 30, we conclude that applicant A has more "achievement" than applicant B. Although these numbers signify degrees of difference in achievement, one must remember that achievement itself is not measured directly; it is instead inferred from the test score. Nevertheless, this score is used as an indicator of the construct. In this sense, numbers can provide a convenient means for characterizing and differentiating among job applicants. For this reason, numbers play an important role in selection.[3]

Criteria and Predictors in Selection Research

A fundamental challenge in personnel selection is choosing, from a large group of job applicants, the smaller group that is to be employed. The goal of personnel selection is to identify the individuals who should be hired. These individuals are chosen because the selection measures predict that they will best perform the job in question. When the term *predict* is used, it is assumed that a selection expert has the information on which to base these predictions. Where does someone get this information? Basically, the information is derived from an analysis of the job. A *job analysis* is designed to identify the attributes incumbents must possess to perform the job successfully. Once we know the attributes necessary for success on the job, we can measure applicants with respect to these attributes and make our predictions accordingly.

Measurement plays a vital role in helping the selection manager make accurate predictions. Predicting who should be hired generally requires the identification of two types of variables. The first of these is called the *criterion* (or *criteria* when more than one criterion is being considered). A criterion usually serves as a definition of what is meant by employee success on the job. Criteria are defined by thoroughly studying the jobs for which a selection system is being developed. A wide array of variables might serve as criteria. Some criteria deal with issues such as absenteeism, turnover, and other organizational citizenship behaviors. Other criteria represent work-related outcomes including error rates, number of goods produced, dollar sales, amount of scrap produced in manufacturing tasks, and speed of performance. This is just a small sampling of criteria that depict what some workers *do*. The most frequently used performance criteria are supervisory ratings of job performance. Training success and work samples are measured and used when they are meaningfully related to job performance.

Numerous types of criteria can be predicted. Nevertheless, criteria should not be defined or chosen in a cavalier, unsystematic, or haphazard manner. They *must* be important to the job, and they *must* be appropriately measured. Because criteria are the basis for characterizing employee success, the utility of a selection system will depend to a significant degree on their relevance, definition, and measurement.

A second category of variable required in predicting applicants' job success comprises *predictor* variables. Predictors represent the measures of those employee attributes identified through a job analysis as being important for job success. Thus, a predictor should be used if there is a good reason to expect that the employee attributes assessed by the measure will predict the criteria that define job success. This book discusses a wide variety of predictors that have been found to be useful in predicting employee performance. Tests, interviews, biographical data questionnaires, application blanks, and assessment centers are just some of the types of predictors you will read about. As with criteria, there are two important requirements for developing and using predictors: (a) they *must* be relevant to the job and (b) they *must* be appropriate ways to measure the employee attributes identified as critical to job success.

Measurement and Individual Differences

Earlier in this chapter, we noted a basic law of psychology applicable to human resource selection: People fundamentally differ. Furthermore, we said that one goal of selection is to identify those individuals who should be hired for a job. Measuring individual differences with our predictors and criteria helps us to meet our goal. Suppose, for instance, you were charged with the responsibility for hiring workers who could produce high quantities of work output. The workers individually manufacture wire baskets. After looking at some recent production records, you plot graphically the quantity of output per worker for a large number of workers. Figure 3.1 shows the results of your plot. This bell-shaped, or normal, curve is a typical distribution for a variety of biological characteristics, such as height and weight, and for psychological test scores, when sufficiently large numbers of observations are available.

Our plot suggests several things. First, because the productivity scores show a level of variability, individual employees differ in their levels of productivity. Second, relatively few produce a very large or very small number of baskets. Many, however, fall between these two extremes. If we can assume that quantity of production is a suitable criterion, our objective is to obtain a predictor that will detect the individual differences or

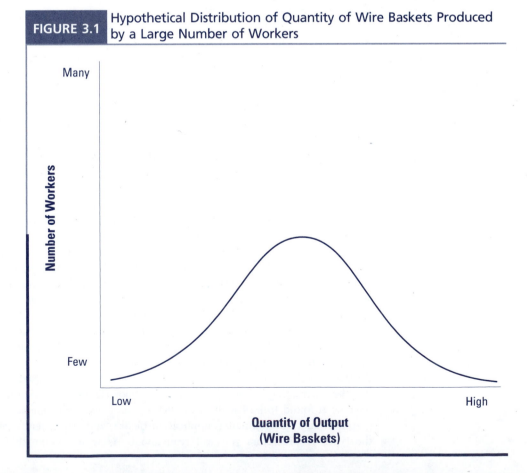

| FIGURE 3.1 | Hypothetical Distribution of Quantity of Wire Baskets Produced by a Large Number of Workers |

variance in productivity. If our predictor is useful, individuals' scores on the predictor will be associated with their productivity scores.

The preceding example highlights the important role of measurement in selection research. Numbers assigned to predictors and criteria enable us to make the necessary fine distinctions among individuals. Subsequent analyses of these numbers help us meet one of our goals: developing a system for predicting job performance successfully. Without measurement, we would probably be left with our intuition and personal best guesses. Perhaps, for a very small number of us, these judgments will work. For most of us, however, deciding "by the seat of our pants" will simply not suffice.

Scales of Measurement

The use of predictors and criteria in selection research requires that these variables be measured, and measured rigorously. Because our ability to distinguish one person from another is determined by the precision with which we measure the variables, rigorous measurement is a prerequisite for performing any statistical analysis in a selection study. (By *precision,* we mean the number of distinct scores or gradations permitted by the predictor and criterion used.) The level of precision will dictate what statistical analyses can be done with the numbers obtained from measurement. Greater precision enables us to use more sophisticated statistical analyses.

In the context of selection research, a *scale of measurement* is simply a means by which individuals can be distinguished from one another on a variable of interest, whether that variable is a predictor or a criterion. Because we use a variety of scales in selection research, the specific predictor or criterion variables chosen can differ rather dramatically in their precision. For example, suppose we were developing a selection program for bank management trainees. One criterion we want to predict is *trainability,* that is, trainee success in a management training program. We could measure trainability in several ways. On one hand, we could simply classify individuals according to who did and who did not graduate from the training program. (Graduation, for example, may be based on trainees' ability to pass a test on banking principles and regulations.) Our criterion would be a dichotomous category, that is, unsuccessful (fail) and successful (pass). Thus our predictor variable would be used simply to differentiate between those applicants who could and those who could not successfully complete their training.

On the other hand, we could evaluate trainability by the *degree* of trainee success as measured by training performance test scores. Our test might be used to assess how much trainees know at the end of their training program. But notice that in this case our criterion is not a categorical measurement (that is, success or failure) but rather a way to more precisely describe the degree of success experienced in training.

Figure 3.2 shows the distributions of trainees' scores for the two methods of measuring trainability. Notice that our simple "*classification* of success" criterion is not measured as precisely as our "*degree* of success" criterion. Greater individual differences in trainability can be mapped for the latter criterion than for the former one. The variable *trainability* is the same in both examples. But the two examples differ with respect to the level of measurement involved. *It is the manner in which the criterion is measured and not the criterion itself that determines level of measurement.* We can draw more precise conclusions with one measure of trainability than we can with the other.

Four types of scales or levels of measurement exist: (a) nominal, (b) ordinal, (c) interval, and (d) ratio. The degree of precision with which we can measure differences among people increases as we move from nominal to ratio scales. Increased precision provides us with more detailed information about people with regard to the variables being studied— whether those variables are employee attributes such as mental ability and personality, or

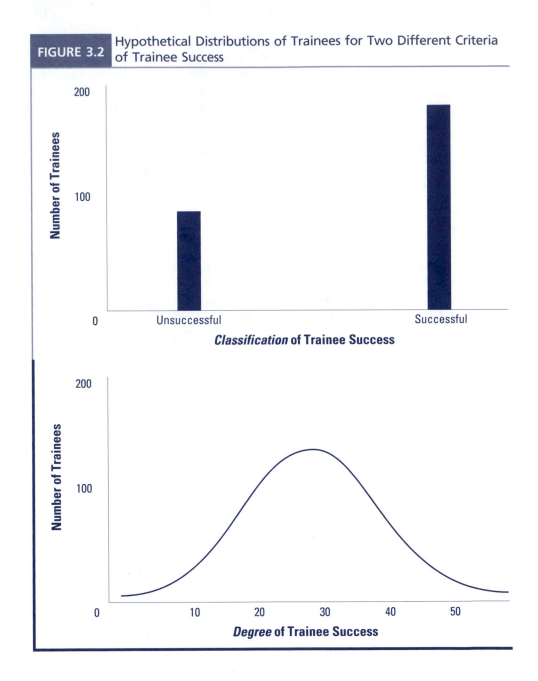

FIGURE 3.2   Hypothetical Distributions of Trainees for Two Different Criteria of Trainee Success

criteria such as trainability and performance. More powerful statistical analyses can then be performed with our data.

A *nominal scale* is one composed of two or more mutually exclusive categories. The numerical values serve merely as "labels" for the category and do not imply any ordering of the attributes. For example, coding male applicants "1" and female applicants "2" does not signify females are twice whatever males are. These numbers, although meaningful and useful, carry no numerical rating. We could use other numbers as well (such as 0 and 1) to identify females and males. Both scoring schemes have the same meaning. The numerical codes themselves do not indicate how males and females differ. The only information we have through our numerical codes is an applicant's sex. Because we cannot state *how* members assigned to nominal scale categories differ, this type of scale is the simplest form of measurement.

Some statistical analyses can be performed with nominal scale data. For example, we can count and obtain percentages of members assigned to our scale categories. Other statistical procedures are possible, but we will not discuss them here because they are beyond the scope of our treatment. Examples of nominal scale measurement for the variables of applicant sex, applicant race, and job title include the following:

A. *Applicant Gender*
   1. Male
   2. Female

B. *Applicant Race*
   1. Black
   2. White
   3. Other

C. *Job Title*
   1. Sales Manager
   2. Sales Clerk
   3. Sales Representative
   4. Salesperson
   5. Other

An *ordinal scale* is one that rank-orders objects, such as individuals, from "high" to "low" on some variable of interest.

Numerical values indicate the relative order of individuals for the variable on which they are ranked. One example is shown in Figure 3.3, where supervisors have rank-ordered their subordinates' performance. Figure 3.3 shows that M. K. Mount, ranked 1, was ranked highest in quality of work completed. Furthermore, we know that each individual on the scale produces better quality work relative to the following individual. However, an ordinal scale does not provide information on the *magnitude* of the differences among the ranks. Thus, we do not know whether the distance between 1 and 2 is of equal interval to the distance between 3 and 4. In our personnel ranking example, M. K. Mount, the employee ranked 1, may be only marginally more productive in quality of work than A. DeNisi, who is ranked 2. However, A. DeNisi may be considerably better than F. L. Schmidt, the employee ranked 3. Thus, the differences between rankings indicate only that higher numbers mean more of whatever attribute the scale is based on, here *more* quality of work.

Another example of an ordinal scale often encountered in selection involves test scores. Percentiles are sometimes used to interpret the results of a test. A percentile represents the proportion of persons taking a test who make below a given score. If we know that a job applicant scored at the 76th percentile, we know that 76 percent of the individuals who took the test scored lower and 24 percent scored higher. As in our previous example, we do not know how much better or worse the next individual performed in terms of a specific test score.

From our two examples, we can draw only "greater than" or "less than" conclusions with ordinal data; we do not know the amount of difference that separates individuals or objects being ranked. Information relative to magnitude differences is provided by our next two scales.

With an *interval scale*, differences between numbers take on meaning. In addition to rank-order information, the scale uses constant units of measurement, affording a meaningful expression of differences with respect to characteristic. For example, when we measure a group of job applicants with the mathematics ability test (scores range from 0 to 100), a difference between scores of 40 and 60 is equal to the difference between 60 and 80. The interval between scores can be interpreted. However, we cannot conclude that an

---

FIGURE 3.3 | Example of an Ordinal Scale of Measurement

Ranking of Employees

Below are listed the names of your ten subordinates. Read the list and then rank the individuals on the quality of work completed in their jobs. By "quality of work completed" we mean the minimum amount of rework necessary to correct employee mistakes. Give the subordinate you believe is highest in quality of work performed a rank of "1," the employee next highest in quality of work a "2," the next a "3," and so on until you reach the employee who is lowest in quality of work completed, a "10."

> Note:
> 1 = Highest Quality
> • •
> • •
> • •
> 10 = Lowest Quality

Employee	Rank on Quality of Work Completed
R. Kanfer	4
A. DeNisi	2
M. K. Mount	1
R. G. Folger	7
F. Drasgow	9
W. C. Borman	5
F. L. Schmidt	3
P. R. Sackett	6
R. D. Pritchard	8
K. Murphy	10

---

applicant with a score of 0 on the test does not have any mathematical ability. Such a conclusion would imply that our test covered *all* possible items of mathematical ability; in fact, our test is only a *sample* of these items. Obviously, we cannot make this statement, because zero is set only by convention. Also, because of the absence of an absolute zero, we cannot state that an individual who scores 80 on our test has twice as much ability as one who scores 40.

Rating scales are frequently used as criterion measures in selection studies. For example, many job performance measures consist of performance appraisal ratings. An example of an interval rating scale is shown in Figure 3.4. When these ratings are treated as an interval scale, the magnitude of the difference between rating points is assumed to be the same. Thus raters are expected to view the difference between points 1 and 2 on the scale in the same way as they view the difference between points 4 and 5.

Because the underlying psychological construct (for example, mental ability) typically is normally distributed, most of the predictors (and criteria) we use in selection can be measured with an interval scale. To preserve the normal distribution, the resulting measurement scale will be an equal interval scale. Thus, if the underlying characteristic is normally distributed and the scores we use give you a normal distribution, then the predictor is using an equal interval scale. Predictors or criteria measured by interval scales tap the differences,

FIGURE 3.4 Example of an Interval Scale Used in Rating Employee Job Performance

Rating Factors				Ratings

1. Accuracy of Work: the extent to which the employee correctly completes job assignments

1	2	3	4	5
Almost always makes errors, has very low accuracy	Quite often makes errors	Makes errors but equals job standards	Makes few errors, has high accuracy	Almost never makes errors, has very high accuracy

Comments: _____

2. Quality of Work: the extent to which the employee produces a volume of work consistent with established standards for the job

1	2	3	4	5
Almost never meets standards	Quite often does not meet standards	Volume of work is satisfactory, equals job standards	Quite often produces more than required	Almost always exceeds standards, exceptionally productive

Comments: _____

3. Attendance/Punctuality: the extent to which the employee adheres to the work schedule

1	2	3	4	5
Excessively absent or tardy	Frequently absent or tardy	Occasionally absent or tardy	Infrequently absent or tardy	Almost never absent or tardy

Comments: _____

4. Coworker Assistance: the frequency with which the employee assists coworkers in the completion of their job assignments

1	2	3	4	5
Never provides assistance to coworkers	Seldom provides assistance to coworkers	Sometimes provides assistance to coworkers	Often provides assistance to coworkers	Always provides assistance to coworkers

Comments: _____

5. Timely Completion of Work Assignments: the extent to which the employee uses time to accomplish job tasks effectively and efficiently

1	2	3	4	5
Almost never completes assignments on time	Seldom completes assignments on time	Sometimes completes assignments on time	Often completes assignments on time	Almost always completes assignments on time

Comments: _____

order, and equality of the magnitude of the differences in the data. Interval scales offer more precision than nominal and ordinal scales; therefore, researchers can employ more powerful statistical methods with them. Interval data can be analyzed by many of the statistical procedures important in personnel research. For example, researchers can employ means, standard deviations, and various correlation procedures.[4] We cannot discuss here the various statistical procedures one could use, but we will soon (see Chapter 5 and Chapter 6). The critical point is that the precision of measurement determines the meaningfulness of the numbers or scores derived from our predictors and criteria. There is no substitute for using high-quality measures in selection, and because most predictors and criteria used in selection are measured close to interval scales, the statistical analyses that can be conducted are useful in making selection decisions.

A *ratio scale* has an *absolute* zero point; as on the interval scale, differences between numerical values on a ratio scale have meaning. The presence of an absolute zero point permits us to make statements about the ratio of one individual's scores to another based on the amount of the characteristic being measured. Thus if one worker produces 100 wire baskets in an hour while another produces 50, we can then state that the second worker produces only half as much as the first.

The numerical operations that can be performed with the data suggest the origin of the name *ratio* scale. Numerical values on a ratio scale can be added, subtracted, multiplied, and divided. Ratios of scale numbers can be used, and the meaning of the scale will be preserved.

Most scales involving physical measurements (such as height, weight, eyesight, hearing, and physical strength) or counting (such as amount of pay, number of times absent from work, months of job tenure, number of promotions received, and number of goods produced) are ratio scales. However, ratio scales are not often encountered in the field of human resource selection. As we discussed earlier, many of our measures are psychological rather than physical in nature; they do not lend themselves to ratio measurement because it is not meaningful to say, for example, that an applicant has "0" mathematical ability. Table 3.1 summarizes the general characteristics of the four types of scales of measurement.

From the preceding discussion, you can probably surmise that interval and ratio scales are the most desirable for conducting sophisticated statistical analyses. Because of the precision of the scales and the statistical analyses they permit, results based on interval and ratio scales are capable of being rigorously and usefully interpreted. Thus, our conclusions using the numbers or scores obtained from the selection predictors or criteria are dependent on the measurement scale. Most measurement in selection is indirect. That is, we cannot directly assess the person's actual level of mental ability or achievement motivation or even attitude toward a proposed career. Instead, the person's standing on the unobservable trait (intelligence or work motivation) is inferred from the score on the test or the predictor itself. Although the unit of measurement for the underlying construct may use an interval or even a ratio scale, the specific score used to measure the construct (a 25-item test assessing mental ability or achievement motivation) may only use an ordinal scale. Thus, the critical issue is whether the scores—not the hypothetical construct—use an ordinal or interval scale.

Measurement is critical, because the use of meaningless numbers will result in meaningless conclusions, no matter how complex the statistical analyses. Ultimately, there is no substitute for high-quality measurement methods. In selection, if the number signifies degrees of differences in units that reflect nearly equal interval units (that is, interval), not just "more than" or "less than" (that is, ordinal), then you have a quality predictor or criterion. Keep in mind that such a conclusion is grounded upon the assumption that these numbers can be meaningfully interpreted as representing the unobservable construct underlying the number. If this is true, you can reasonably subject these numbers to useful interval scale statistical analyses (for example, the use of parametric statistics, including means, standard deviations, Pearson product moment correlations, and F-statistics—all explained later).

The selection practitioner should be aware that there has been controversy about levels of measurement and the use of statistical analysis.[5] The essence of the critic's argument is that unless the number clearly represents an equal interval scale, one should

TABLE 3.1 General Characteristics of the Four Scales of Measurement

Type of Scale	Example of Scale Use in Selection Research	Scale Characteristics			
		Classification	**Order**	**Equality of Difference**	**Absolute Zero**
Nominal	***Classifying*** applicants by their gender	Yes	No	No	No
Ordinal	Supervisory ***ranking*** of subordinates	Yes	Yes	No	No
Interval	Employee ***rating*** of job satisfaction	Yes	Yes	Yes	No
Ratio	***Counting*** employee number of units produced	Yes	Yes	Yes	Yes

Source: Based in part on Uma Sekaran, *Research Methods for Managers* (New York: John Wiley, 1984), p.134.

strictly adhere to the assumption that the numbers are ordinal at best. This means the type of statistics that are "permissible" are severely restricted—even, for example, that the use of means and standard deviations (explained later) are not appropriate. Yet, a pragmatic view is that given the state of measurement in selection research, it is reasonable to treat most selection measures as if they were based on an interval scale. To treat the resulting numbers from these measures as if they were solely on an ordinal level would result in the loss of useful information. We mention this to draw your attention to the importance of carefully examining whether your actual numbers have nearly equal intervals across units. To the extent they do, conclusions based on interval level statistics will likely be quite useful.

STANDARDIZATION OF SELECTION MEASUREMENT

As discussed in the next section, a variety of measures are used in human resource selection, and these differ in the quality of measurement. When we refer to a measurement method in the context of selection, we mean the *systematic application of preestablished rules or standards for assigning scores to the attributes or traits of an individual.* A selection measure may provide information to be used as either a predictor (such as a test) or a criterion (such as a supervisor's performance appraisal rating). It may also involve any one of our four scales of measurement. An important characteristic of any selection measure is its ability to detect any true differences that may exist among individuals with regard to the attribute being measured. For example, if true differences in knowledge of disease prevention exist among job candidates applying for a nurse practitioner's job, then a disease prevention knowledge test must be able to detect these differences. If test score differences in disease prevention are found, these score differences should be due to differences in the candidates' knowledge and not due to extraneous factors such as differences in the manner in which the test was given to the job candidates or the way in which it was scored. To help control such factors, systematic, or *standardized,* measurement is needed in human resource selection. A predictor or criterion measure is standardized if it possesses each of the following characteristics:

1. **Content**—All persons being assessed are measured by the same information or content. This includes the same format (for example, multiple-choice, essay, and so on) and medium (for example, paper-and-pencil, computer, video).

2. **Administration**—Information is collected the same way in all locations and across all administrators, each time the selection measure is applied.

3. **Scoring**—Rules for scoring are specified before administering the measure and are applied the same way with each application. For example, if scoring requires subjective judgment, steps should be taken (such as rater training) to ensure inter-rater agreement or reliability.[6]

No matter how many times a measure is administered or to whom it is given, the same content, administration, and scoring results from the use of a standardized measurement procedure. When viewed from the standpoint of professional practice, however, a measure that is truly standardized is more of an ideal than a reality. Standardization is a goal we strive for but do not always attain. Sometimes it may even be necessary to alter the standardization procedure. For example, it may be necessary to modify the administration of a test in order to accommodate the special needs of a disabled job applicant.

Measures Used in HR Selection

One of the principal roles of a manager involved in HR selection is deciding whether applicants should or should not be hired. Managers use the predictor and criterion variables that we defined earlier in the chapter when making selection decisions. Predictors are measures (such as a test or interview) that managers employ when deciding whether to accept or reject applicants for a specific job. Criteria (such as supervisory ratings of job performance or the number of errors) are employed as part of a research study designed to determine whether the predictors are really measuring those aspects of job success that the predictors were designed to predict. This type of research study is known as a *validation study*. We have more to say about validity and validation studies in Chapter 5. For now, you should understand that criterion measures really help serve as a standard for evaluating how well predictors do the job they were intended to do. Predictors have a *direct* impact on the decisions reached by a manager involved in HR selection decisions. A manager actually reviews an applicant's scores on a predictor and uses this information in deciding whether to accept or reject the applicant. Criteria play an *indirect* role in that they determine which predictors should actually be used in making selection decisions.

We began this chapter by reviewing the impact of scales of measurement on the application and interpretation of data collected by predictors and criteria. The rest of the chapter discusses additional measurement principles that apply to the use of these two types of variables. These principles are important for understanding the application of the selection techniques and issues you will encounter in the remaining chapters. Before we continue our discussion in any meaningful way, it might be helpful to give you a brief overview of the various types of predictors and criteria employed in research involving HR selection. Later chapters will go into greater detail about specific measures. As you read, remember that when we talk about "selection measures," we mean *both* predictors and criteria. Now, let's look at some of the more common predictors and criteria in use.

Predictors

Numerous types of predictors have been used to forecast employee performance. In general, the major types tend to fall roughly into three categories. Keep in mind as you read these descriptions that our intention is not to give a complete account of each type of predictor. We simply want to acquaint you with the variety of predictors currently being used in selection. Subsequent chapters will provide a more detailed review of these measures. The predictor categories are:

1. *Background information*—Application forms, reference checks, and biographical data questionnaires are generally used to collect information on job applicants and their backgrounds. *Application forms* typically ask job applicants to describe themselves and their previous work histories. Applicants are usually asked about current address, previous education, past employment, relevant licenses, and the like. Prospective employers make *reference checks* by contacting individuals who can accurately comment on the applicant's characteristics and background. These checks are often used to verify information stated on the

application form as well as to provide additional data on the applicant. *Biographical data questionnaires* consist of questions about the applicant's past life history. Past life experiences are assumed to be good indicators of future work behaviors.

2. *Interviews*—Employment interviews are used to collect additional information about the applicant. The employment interview principally consists of questions asked by a job interviewer. Responses are used for assessing an applicant's suitability for a job and fit to the organization.

3. *Tests*—Literally hundreds of tests have been used for selection purposes. There are many different ways to classify the types of tests available; the descriptive labels indicated here will give you a feeling for the range of options available. *Aptitude,* or *ability,* tests, for example, are used to measure how well an individual can perform specific parts of a job. Abilities measured by aptitude tests include intellectual, mechanical, spatial, perceptual, and motor. *Achievement* tests are employed to assess an individual's proficiency at the time of testing (for example, job proficiency or knowledge). (For the purposes of this book, you will see in Chapter 11 that we have combined aptitude and achievement tests into the general category "ability" tests.) *Personality* tests in the context of selection are used to identify those candidates who will work harder and cope better at work, which should also relate to success on the job (discussed in Chapter 12).[7]

Most of the tests you encounter will probably fall into one of these categories. Keep in mind, though, that you will find some differences among tests within each of these categories. Some may require an individual to respond with a paper and pencil or a computer; others may require the manipulation of physical objects. Some will have a time limit; others will not. Some can be administered in a group setting, whereas others can be given to only one applicant at a time.

Criteria

Criterion measures usually assess some kind of behavior or performance on the job (for example, organizational citizenship behaviors, sales, turnover, supervisory ratings of performance) that is important to the organization. They are called "criterion measures" because they are used to evaluate the predictors used to forecast performance. Thus, they are the criteria for evaluating selection procedures. Although these measures are based on behavior—what the employee does—the observed behavior is a measure of a theoretical construct (for example, "true" job performance). Consequently, criterion measures are susceptible to the same measurement concerns as are written tests or employment interviews. However, the criterion is also concerned with measuring things that can be used to assess the usefulness of the predictors (later we will extensively discuss construct and criterion validity). And again, the quality of these inferences is based on the scale of measurement. Consequently, it is critical that the selection expert ensures the criterion approximates at least an interval scale. Numerous criteria are available to assess important aspects of work behavior. One way to classify these criteria is by the measurement methods used to collect the data.[8] These categories include the following:

1. *Objective production data*—These data tend to be physical measures of work. Number of goods produced, amount of scrap left, and dollar sales are examples of objective production data.

2. *Personnel data*—Personnel records and files frequently contain information on workers that can serve as important criterion measures. Absenteeism, tardiness,

voluntary turnover, accident rates, salary history, promotions, and special awards are examples of such measures.

3. *Judgmental data*—Performance appraisals or ratings frequently serve as criteria in selection research. They most often involve a supervisor's rating of a subordinate on a series of behaviors or outcomes found to be important to job success, including task performance, citizenship behavior, and counterproductive behavior. Supervisor or rater judgments play a predominant role in defining this type of criterion data.

4. *Job or work sample data*—These data are obtained from a measure developed to resemble the job in miniature or sample of specific aspects of the work process or outcomes (for example, a typing test for a secretary). Measurements (for example, quantity and error rate) are taken on individual performance of these job tasks, and these measures serve as criteria.

5. *Training proficiency data*—This type of criterion focuses on how quickly and how well employees learn during job training activities. Often, such criteria are labeled *trainability* measures. Error rates during a training period and scores on training performance tests administered during training sessions are examples of training proficiency data.

Criteria for Evaluating Selection Measures

Now that we have provided an overview of some measures used in selection, let's assume that you have already conducted a thorough analysis of the job in question to identify those worker attributes thought to lead to job success. (In Chapter 7 we provide some details on the job analysis process.) This step is important because it enables us to identify the constructs or knowledge domains that the selection tests or measures should assess. At this point, you are interested in choosing some measures to be employed as predictors and criteria indicative of job success. One of several questions you are likely to ask is, "What characteristics should I look for in selecting a predictor or a criterion?"

You should consider a number of factors when choosing or developing a selection measure. Although it is not an exhaustive list, some of the factors that you should carefully examine are listed in question form in Table 3.2. Some are more important for predictors, some more essential for criteria, and some important for both types of measures. As you read these factors, you might think of them as a checklist for reviewing for each measure you are considering. Unless you can be sure that a measure meets these standards, you may not have the best measure you need for your selection research. In that case, you have at least two options: (a) determine whether you can adjust your data or the way you calculate the score itself so it will meet each measurement evaluation criterion (for example, ask the supervisor to rate each employee's performance on a 9-point scale instead of rank-ordering the employees); or (b) if this option is not viable, find or develop another, more suitable measure for the underlying construct.

The factors are not of equal importance. Issues concerning reliability, validity, and freedom from bias are obviously more critical than administrative concerns such as acceptability to management. Other factors will vary in importance depending on the specific selection situation. Regardless, the wise selection manager will give serious consideration to each one.

TABLE 3.2	Factors to Consider when Choosing or Developing Measures for Use in HR Selection Research

For Predictors:

1. *What does the predictor measure?* Is it likely to predict the criterion? A predictor is more likely to relate to the criterion if there is empirical research, a good theory, or a logical reason to expect a meaningful relationship between the predictor measure and the outcome of interest. A quality predictor will have a clear and concise definition of what underlying construct (for example, personality, mental ability) is measured.

2. *Is the predictor cost-effective?* The cost of purchasing or developing a predictor, as well as the cost of scoring and conducting validation studies, should be considered.

3. *Has the predictor been "standardized"?* If the predictor is distorted by extraneous, systematic variance (such as giving one group of applicants more time to complete a test than another group), then the meaning of differences in individual scores may be compromised. Consistent "standardized" administration, content, and scoring of a selection predictor across all locations and administrators is critical. There should be procedures for covering how to deal with any nonstandard administration of the predictor, including sessions that were disrupted (for example, computer malfunction, local emergency, illness of candidate) and other human errors (such as failure to track time accurately, non-matching test and answer sheets, and so on). Furthermore, employers should decide how to provide opportunities to reassess applicants or accommodate an applicant's known disability (if it is unrelated to the predictor construct being assessed). Standardization also extends to scoring. For example, if the selection procedure (such as an interview) requires subjective scores, the standardization of training becomes especially important.

4. *Is the predictor easy to use?* A predictor that can be administered and scored by persons who do not have high levels of training is less expensive than one that must be scored by those with higher training levels. Group predictors are more economical than individual predictors. Group predictors can be given to individuals, but many individual predictors cannot be given to groups. These are just a couple of factors that can affect how easy a predictor is to use.

5. *Is the predictor acceptable to the organization? To management? To the candidate?* An organization's past experiences with a selection procedure may mean it is unacceptable to—or is seen as controversial by—others (for example, investors, management, unions, and so on). Candidate reactions should also be considered. Content that is offensive or seen as an invasion of privacy may lead candidates to refuse to participate or to reject an employer's offer of employment.

For Criteria:

6. *Is the criterion relevant to the job for which it is chosen?* Important work-related activities, behaviors, or outcomes of the job should be relevant to the criterion. Trainability, for example, is a relevant criterion for an entry-level job.

7. *Is the criterion acceptable to management?* If management doesn't accept the criterion as worthwhile, managers will not support the system that may predict it. For example, if top executives value increasing revenues, actual sales will be more acceptable to management than will judgments of future trainability.

8. *Are work changes likely to alter the need for the criterion?* Jobs and situations change. Thus, measures of success today may be inappropriate a year later. Criteria should be periodically reviewed for their relevancy. When work changes are rapid or fluid, organization-wide criteria (such as turnover or effectively dealing with time deadlines) may be a better reflection of successful performance.

9. *Is the criterion uncontaminated and free of bias, so that meaningful comparisons among individuals can be made?* Unless jobs and work environments are identical, comparisons among individuals will be biased. Examples of contaminating variables include differences between sales territories, differences in tools and equipment, differences in work shifts, and differences in the physical conditions of the job. It is possible for the researcher to measure and account for possible sources of contamination. Systematic error that differentially affects the criterion performance of different subgroups (bias) must be minimized or eliminated insofar as possible. Group bias occurs when a group characteristic is assumed to relate to individual employee performance. Common examples of this kind of bias include age and job tenure, which are often assumed to be related to performance.

10. *Will the criterion detect differences among individuals if differences actually exist (discriminability)? Are meaningful differences among individuals actually scored with respect to the criterion?* A useful criterion will reflect the relative standing of employees with respect to work outcomes. If variance or individual differences in criterion scores cannot be obtained, then no predictor can be found to predict it. Hence, it is not possible to predict a criterion if all employees get the same performance rating (outstanding), when only 20% of the employees are actually outstanding performers.

(Continued)

TABLE 3.2	*(Continued)*

For Predictors and Criteria:

11. *Does the measure unfairly discriminate against sex, race, age, or other protected groups?* Significant differences among protected groups on a measure do not necessarily mean discrimination. However, if predictor or criterion scores systematically differ across groups, one should carefully examine for predictive bias (that is, is the predictor equally predictive of performance for both men and women?).

12. *Does the measure lend itself to quantification?* For purposes of personnel selection, quantitative data are more desirable than qualitative data (for example, saying that the temperature is 105° F—rather than just saying that it is hot outside). Analysis and confirmation is more meaningful if the characteristic is systematically assessed using "assigned numbers." Numbers on an interval or ratio scale are preferred, because one can use more sophisticated statistical analyses.

13. *Is the measure scored consistently?* Specific rules and procedures should be available for scoring individuals on the measure. Different scores of an individual's performance should obtain the same score. All raters should receive the same training and have the same opportunities to observe and evaluate the applicant or employee.

14. *How reliable are the data provided by the measure?* A measure should provide dependable information. Individuals should consistently retain their relative position in the group across the predictor or criterion measures. Repeated application of a measure (if the context of measurement is the same with each application) should yield the same scores. Thus, if you get a 95 today on a mental ability test, you should get near 95 tomorrow if you retake the same test.

15. *How well does the device measure the construct for which it is intended (construct validity)?* The obtained scores on the predictor or criterion should assess what they are meant to (for example, intelligence or job performance).

Sources: Arne Evers, Neil Anderson, and Olga Voskuijl, *The Blackwell Handbook of Personnel Selection*, pp. 73–97 and 354–375. Copyright © 2005 by Blackwell publishers. Reprinted with permission; and Susana Urbina, *Essentials of Psychological Testing*, pp. 64–116. Copyright © 2004 by John Wiley & Sons, Inc. Reproduced with permission of John Wiley & Sons, Inc.

Finding and Constructing Selection Measures

The process of identifying selection measures to be used in an HR selection study should not be taken lightly. Identification of measures is not accomplished simply by familiarity with or personal whims about what measures are best in a specific situation. As we see in our later chapter on job analysis, systematic work is conducted to identify what types of measures should be used. Thorough analyses of jobs are made to identify the necessary knowledge, skills, abilities, and other characteristics necessary for successful job performance. Once we know the qualifications needed to perform the job, we are ready to begin the process of identifying and implementing our selection measures. Obviously, the identification of selection measures is an important one. It is also one for which a consultant, usually an organizational psychologist or HR specialist, may be needed. Selecting predictors requires an understanding of relevant empirical research and theory; consequently, unless you have read this book closely, a consultant may provide a more informed professional judgment. However, whether selection measures are identified by a consultant or by personnel staff within an organization, you must be familiar with the basic approach. In identifying these measures, we have two choices: (a) we can locate and choose from existing selection measures, or (b) we can construct our own. In all likelihood, we will probably need to take both options.

Locating Existing Selection Measures

There are several advantages to finding and using existing selection measures. These advantages include the following:

1. Use of existing measures is usually less expensive and less time-consuming than developing new ones.

2. If previous research was conducted, we will have some idea about the reliability, validity, and other characteristics of the measures.

3. Existing measures often will be superior to what could be developed in-house.

In searching for suitable selection measures, you will find that many types of measures are available. The vast majority of these, such as tests, are intended to be used as predictors. A variety of predictors are commercially available—for example, intelligence, ability, interest, and personality inventories. Other predictors, such as application blanks, biographical data questionnaires, reference check forms, employment interviews, and work sample measures, will probably have to be developed. Criteria measures are generally not published and will probably have to be constructed by a user.

Information Sources for Existing Measures

Sources in print and on the Internet (see Table 3.3) offer information on existing measures that can be used in personnel selection studies.[9] Although most of these sources will not present the measures themselves, they will provide descriptive information on various options to consider. These sources are described here. Another way to select pre-employment tests is to work with one of the major test publishers. Although a comprehensive list of all available tests is beyond one text, Table 3.4 indicates some of the larger test publishers.

TABLE 3.3	**Internet Sources for Information on Existing Selection Measures**
http://www.unl.edu/buros	Buros Center for Testing
http://www.proedinc.com	Pro-Ed Inc.
http://www.ets.org	Educational Testing Service
http://eric.ed.gov	Education Resources Information Center
http://testpublishers.org	The Association of Test Publishers
http://www.apa.org	American Psychological Association
http://www.siop.org	Society of Industrial & Organizational Psychologists

TABLE 3.4	**Selected List of Pre-Employment Test Publishers**
https://www.cpp.com	Consulting Psychologists Press
http://www.hoganassessments.com	Hogan Assessment Systems, Inc
http://www.ipma-hr.org	International Personeel Management Association
http://www3.parinc.com	Psychological Assessment Resources
http://psychcorp.pearsonassessments.com	Pearson Assessments
http://corporate.psionline.com	Psychological Services, Inc
http://www.shl.com	Saville & Holdsworth, Inc.
http://www.shrm.org	Society of Human Resource Management
http://www.valtera.com	Valtera Corporation
http://wonderlic.com	Wonderlic Personnel Test, Inc.

Text and Reference Sources.   There are several books that provide excellent reviews of predictors and other measures that have been used in hiring for a variety of jobs. Some of the books are organized around the types of jobs in which various measures have been used. Others center on types of selection measures. Still others are organized around the technical aspects of the human resource selection process. Many relevant books on personnel selection are cited in this text.

In addition, users should consult the *Annual Review of Psychology* and *Research in Personnel and Human Resources Management,* both published annually. On occasion, reviews of current selection research are published. These reviews offer an excellent, up-to-date look at research on measures and other issues relevant to personnel selection.

Buros Mental Measurements Yearbooks.   The *Mental Measurements Yearbook* is the most important source for information on tests for personnel selection. It contains critical reviews by test experts and bibliographies of virtually every test printed in English. Oscar Buros was editor of the *Yearbook* for many years; following his death, the Buros Institute of Mental Measurements was moved to the University of Nebraska, where his work is being carried on. Historically, a new edition was published every six years; going forward, it will be published in print and on CD-ROM every 18 to 24 months. The most recent edition is the *Sixteenth Mental Measurements Yearbook* (2005).[10] Unquestionably, the Buros publications present valuable information about existing tests that can be used in personnel selection applications.

In addition, the Buros Institute has published several supplementary books containing additional bibliographies and reviews. One of the most useful is *Tests in Print (TIP) I–VI,* which serves as a comprehensive bibliography to all known commercially available tests currently in print. These reviews provide vital information to users, including test purpose, test publisher, in-print status, price, test acronym, intended test population, administration times, publication dates, and test authors. A score index permits users to identify the specific characteristics measured by each test.

Other Reference Sources

Pro-Ed, a testing corporation in Austin, Texas, offers a series of testing sources referencing a variety of psychological measures. These sources include the following:

1. *Tests: A Comprehensive Reference for Assessments in Psychology, Education, and Business* (Fifth Edition)—Describing more than 2,000 assessment instruments categorized in 90 subcategories, this reference includes information on each instrument's purpose, scoring procedures, cost, and publisher. It does not critically review or evaluate tests. Evaluations are provided in the companion volume, *Test Critiques.*

2. *Test Critiques, Volumes I–XI*—An eleven-volume series that provides evaluations of more than 800 of the most widly used tests in terms of practical applications and uses and technical aspects (validity, reliability, normative data, scoring); it also provides a critique of the instruments.

Educational Testing Service (ETS) of Princeton, New Jersey, has several reference sources available for identifying suitable selection measures. For instance, the *Test Collection* database has a library of more than 25,000 tests and surveys. The database includes information about tests used to assess abilities, aptitudes, interests, and personality as well as other variables related to various vocational and occupational fields. Use of the database is similar to that of the *Mental Measurements Yearbook Database* described earlier.

Another valuable source for test information is the Education Resources Information Center (ERIC), sponsored by the Institute of Education Sciences (IES) of the U.S. Department of Education. This Web site contains a bibliographic database of more than 1.1 million citations going back to 1966. Today, it may be the largest of its kind in the world.

Journals.   Several journals are suitable sources for information about selection measures. In particular, the *Journal of Applied Psychology (JAP)* and *Personnel Psychology* are most relevant. *JAP* has a long history as a major journal in the field of industrial psychology, focusing on empirical research in applied psychology. *JAP* includes articles about various predictors, criteria, and other issues related to personnel selection. Any search for measures should definitely include *JAP* as a source. A second well-respected source is *Personnel Psychology*, which has a long history of publishing articles concerned with personnel selection and related topics. Articles emphasize the practical application of research.

Other journals occasionally publish articles dealing with the application of selection measures. These include the *International Journal of Selection and Assessment, Human Performance, Journal of Occupational and Organizational Psychology, The Industrial-Organizational Psychologist (TIP), Educational and Psychological Measurement, and Applied Psychological Measurement.* At times, reviews of specific tests that may be relevant to industrial personnel selection can also be found in the *Journal of Educational Measurement, Journal of Vocational Behavior*, and the *Journal of Counseling Psychology*. As part of a thorough search, researchers should review these journals for possible ideas. Resources available through many libraries can also help to identify potential selection measures. These include *Psychological Abstracts, Personnel Management Abstracts*, and computerized literature searches (for example, PsycLIT, PsycINFO, or Abstracted Business Information Database). For example, searching the PsycINFO database for a specific test name can provide bibliographic references and articles that discuss the test.

Test Publishers.   A number of organizations publish tests that are used in HR selection. Each publisher provides a catalog describing the various tests offered. A comprehensive list of test publishers and addresses is presented in the *Mental Measurements Yearbook*. The Association of Test Publishers (ATP), a nonprofit organization since 1992, represents a large number of test publishers and providers of assessment services. The Industrial/Organizational Division focuses on the use of tests in selection, placement, development, and promotion and tries to uphold a high level of professionalism and business ethics related to the publishing of assessments. The ATP has links to many test publishers and assessment tools or services on its Web site. The most relevant information is likely to be found in the Industrial/Organizational Division.

These sources present information on the most current tests available. Once a test that appears to meet a specific need is located, qualified users can order a test manual and specimen set. (Typical costs for specimen sets range from $25 to $75.) The test manual provides information on what the test measures and on the administration, scoring, and interpretation of results. In addition, reliability and validity data are also presented. These materials help users decide whether a test is appropriate before adopting it.

However, just because a test is identified for use does not mean that it is available for purchase. Some publishers use a framework for classifying their tests and for determining to whom tests can be sold. This framework was originally developed by the

American Psychological Association, but the Association's testing standards no longer use it. There are three levels of classification:

Level A—This level consists of those tests that require very little formal training to administer, score, and interpret. Most selection practitioners may purchase tests at this level. A typing test is representative of tests in this classification.

Level B—Tests classified in this category require some formal training and knowledge of psychological testing concepts to properly score and interpret. Aptitude tests designed to forecast an individual's performing potential are of this type. Individuals wishing to purchase Level B tests must be able to document their qualifications for correctly using such tests. These qualifications usually include evidence of formal education in tests and measurement as well as in psychological statistics.

Level C—These tests require the most extensive preparation on the part of the test administrator. In general, personality inventories and projective techniques make up this category. A Ph.D. in psychology and documentation of training (such as courses taken on the use of a particular test) are required. Tests in this category tend to be less frequently used in selection contexts than tests in levels A and B.

Another approach to describing test selection practices, an approach more complex than the classification scheme just described, can be found in the *Standards for Educational and Psychological Testing,* published by the American Psychological Association (APA).[11] Although it is not a source of selection measures per se, APA's *Standards* provides an excellent treatment of the considerations in selecting and using tests.

Professional Associations.   Various professional associations may be a source of selection measures. For example, the American Banking Association has supported research to develop selection measures for use in hiring for customer service, operations, and administrative jobs in banking. LIMRA, an association for insurance companies, has sponsored research to review the use of tests in the selection of sales management and so forth. The American Foundation for the Blind Web site (http://www.afb.org) contains a variety of information and even some selection measures for individuals with visual problems. Other trade and professional associations should be contacted as possible sources for selection measures or research on such measures.

Certain management associations may be able to provide guidance in locating selection measures for specific situations. The Society for Human Resource Management (SHRM) and the International Personnel Management Association (IPMA) are two potential sources of information. The Association of Test Publishers (ATP) has developed and published guidelines and standards. In 2002, ATP issued the *Guidelines for Computer-Based Testing,* a set of standards intended to supplement and elaborate on the most recent version of the *Standards for Educational and Psychological Testing* (1999, APA). Finally, the Society of Industrial and Organizational Psychologists, division 14 of the APA, recently revised the *Principles for the Validation and Use of Personnel Selection Procedures* (4th ed., 2003).[12]

In summary, there are minimum recommendations for choosing an existing selection measure:

1. Be sure you clearly and completely understand the attribute or construct you want to measure. Decide on the best means for assessing the attribute, such as a paper-and-pencil test, a work sample test, and so on.

2. Search for and read critical reviews and evaluations of the measure. References mentioned earlier (such as Buros Institute and Pro-Ed publications) are excellent

sources of such reviews. These sources should be able to provide background information on the test, including answers to relevant questions: What theory was the test based on? What research was used to develop the test? This is important because it provides information on the logic, care, and thoroughness with which the test was developed. It should allow you to assess how relevant this information is with regard to your organization's applicants or employees.

3. If a specimen set of the measure (including a technical manual) is available, order and study it. Ask yourself, "Is this measure appropriate for my intended purpose?" In answering this question, study carefully any information relative to the measure's reliability, validity, fairness, intended purpose, method of administration, time limits, scoring, appropriateness for specific groups, and norms. If such information is not available, you may want to consider other measures.

4. Once you have completed steps 1 through 3, ask yourself, "Based on the information I reviewed, are there compelling arguments for using this measure? Or, on the other hand, are there compelling arguments against using it?"

Constructing New Selection Measures

The advantages to using existing selection measures are obvious; when suitable measures can be found, they certainly should be used. But sometimes selection researchers are not able to find the precise measure needed for their purposes. At this point, they have no choice but to develop their own. In this section, we outline the steps involved in developing any selection measure.

Before proceeding, we must consider some important issues. HR professionals raise legitimate concerns about whether it is reasonable to expect practitioners to develop selection measures, particularly in light of the technical and legal ramifications associated with them, and whether an organization has the resources, time, and expertise to develop such measures. In addition, we might ask, "Can't a little knowledge be dangerous? That is, won't some well-meaning practitioners be encouraged to attempt to develop and use measures that 'appear' to be 'good' but really are worthless?" Our intention is not to prepare you nor even encourage you to develop selection measures yourself, but to enable you to work productively with a selection specialist or expert. The development of such measures is a complex, resource-consuming process that usually requires expert advice. The risks associated with the process can be quite high. Most HR managers simply do not have the resources or the skills necessary to engage in the development of selection measures. Consultants will likely be needed.[13] The material presented in this and related chapters is intended to serve as a means by which an organization can monitor and evaluate the work of a consultant as well as study and review the literature describing selection measures. Knowledge of the basic issues involved in selection measure development, validation, and application can help bridge any possible communications gap between the organization and the consultant.

Steps in Developing Selection Measures

Although the details may vary somewhat depending on the specific selection measure being developed, six major steps are typically required:

1. Analyzing the job for which a measure is being developed

2. Selecting the method of measurement to be used

3. Planning and developing the measure

4. Administering, analyzing, and revising the preliminary measure

5. Determining the reliability and validity of the revised measure for the jobs studied

6. Implementing and monitoring the measure in the human resource selection system

Now, let's examine each of these steps.

Analysis of Work. The first step in the instrument development process is perhaps the most crucial. After analyzing the work itself, one should be able to specify the constructs or knowledge, skill and ability domains the predictor will assess. This is a critical step; if it is inappropriately carried out, then all subsequent steps will be flawed. Historically, traditional job analysis methods were used to assess the demands specific jobs or job families make on employees. Today, organizations often find that the nature of the work their employees perform is changing too rapidly to permit a traditional job analysis. Technological advances, the changing nature of the social setting at work (for example, greater interaction with customers, team members, or independent contract workers), and the external environment (for example, the outsourcing or offshoring of work and other changes in the competitive landscape). In such cases, one would focus on a broader analysis of work common across jobs or to the entire organization, rather than on a specific job. In a recent review of job analyses, Paul Sackett and Roxanne Laczo[14] effectively summarize the status of work analysis by stating that today, there are no "one size fits all" job analysis procedures. Consequently, the role of a job or work analysis in the context of selection is to determine the knowledge, skills, abilities, and other characteristics necessary for adequately performing a specific job, or to identify employee competencies and types of work activities from a broader analysis of the work. Irrespective of the specific work analysis procedure adopted, an analysis of work must be performed as an initial step. This is true whether a measure is being developed or whether existing measures are being considered. From this analysis, the developer of a selection measure gains insights and forms hypotheses as to what types of measures may be needed.

In addition to its role in developing and selecting selection measures, analysis of work also provides the foundation for developing criteria measures of job performance. We cannot do systematic research on the selection of personnel until we know which of our selected applicants have become successful employees. Intimate knowledge of the work gained through analysis of work will help us to identify or develop measures of job success. Ultimately, through validation research we will determine the extent to which our selection measures can actually predict these criteria.

As you will see in Chapter 7, many approaches to job analysis exist. Today, there is no single job analytic method that is "correct" for every situation. Nevertheless, the more researchers know about a specific job, the more likely it is that their hypotheses and ideas about selection measures will have predictive utility for that job. Therefore, researchers must choose the method of analysis they believe will yield the most useful information about work.

Selecting the Measurement Method. Once we have identified what to measure, whether it is knowledge, skills, abilities, or other characteristics for performing a job adequately, we are ready to consider the approach we will use in selection. A host of methods are available, including paper-and-pencil tests, job or work sample tests, ratings, interviews, and biographical data questionnaires, to name only a few. The specific nature of the job (such as tasks performed or level of responsibility); the skill of the individuals responsible for administering, scoring, and interpreting selection measures, the number and types of applicants making application (such as level of reading and writing skills or presence of physical handicaps); the costs of testing; and the resources (such as time and dollars) available for test development are just some of the variables that will affect the selection of a measurement medium. If large numbers of applicants are making application for the job, paper-and-pencil measures will be carefully considered. If applicant social skills are critical, then some form of a behavioral exercise might be proposed. If finger dexterity skills appear to be critical to job success, then tests involving the manipulation of a physical apparatus may be necessary to measure applicants' motor responses. The method chosen will ultimately depend on the job and the organizational context in which the job is performed.

Figure 3.5 presents an example of a checklist used to match selection methods with job requirements for industrial electricians. The listing under "Job Requirements" consists of elements of the job, identified through a job analysis, that were found to be critical to the success of a company's industrial electricians. The requirements are the knowledge, skills, and individual attributes that a newly hired electrician must have upon entry into the job. The listing under "Selection Method" represents the possible means by which the essential job requirements can be assessed. After studying the job and the organization, the selection researcher decided that certain methods would be suitable for assessing some requirements, whereas other measures would be appropriate for other job requirements. The suitable methods for specific job requirements are indicated by a check mark. For example, it was decided that a paper-and-pencil test was most suitable for determining an applicant's knowledge of the principles of electrical wiring, whereas a work sample test was chosen to determine an applicant's ability to solder electrical connections. Chapters 9 through 15 discuss predictor and criterion measures in detail and give you more insight into choosing appropriate instruments.

FIGURE 3.5	Checklist Used to Match Selection Methods with Job Requirements for the Job of Industrial Electrician

Job Requirements	Selection Method				
	Work Sample test	Paper-and-pencil test	Selection interview	Biographical data form	Reference check
1. Knowledge of principles of electrical writing		✓			
2. Ability to solder electrical connections	✓				
3. Ability to trouble-shoot electrical wiring problems using a voltmeter	✓				
4. Knowledge of maintenance and repair of electrical equipment		✓			
⋮			⋮		
N. Previous work experience in hazardous work environments			✓	✓	✓

Planning and Developing the Selection Measure.   After a job has been analyzed and some tentative methods considered for assessing the important aspects of the work, the selection researcher probably has some vague mental picture of what each method may be like. In this step, the researcher attempts to clarify the nature and details of each selection measure and prepares an initial version of our measure. The specifications required for each measure considered should include the following:

1. The purposes and uses the measure is intended to serve.

2. The nature of the population for which the measure is to be designed.

3. The way the behaviors or knowledge, skills, abilities, and other attributes (KSAOs) will be gathered and scored. This includes decisions about the method of administration, the format of test items and responses, and the scoring procedures.[15]

   1) Generating behavioral samples or items to assess content domain to be measured. Substantial work is involved in selecting and refining the items or questions to be used to measure the attribute of interest. This often involves having subject-matter experts (SMEs) create the items or rewrite them. In developing these items, the reviewers (for example, SMEs) should consider the appropriateness of item content and format for fulfilling its purpose, including characteristics of the applicant pool; clarity and grammatical correctness; and consideration of bias or offensive portrayals of a subgroup of the population.

   b) Administration methods and scoring procedures should also be developed. It is important to take into consideration the types of formats for eliciting responses from test takers. Broadly, there are two types of formats—the first uses objective or fixed-response items (multiple-choice, true-false); the second elicits open-ended, free-response formats (essay or fill-in-the-blank). The fixed-response format is the most popular; it makes efficient use of testing time, results in few (or no) scoring errors, and can easily and reliably be transformed into a numerical scale for scoring purposes. The primary advantage of the free-response format is that it can provide greater detail or richer samples of the candidates' behavior and may allow unique characteristics, such as creativity, to emerge. Primarily due to both the ease of administration and objectivity of scoring, fixed-response formats are most frequently utilized today, particularly if the measure is likely to be administered in a group setting. Finally, explicit scoring of the measure is particularly critical. Well-developed hiring tools will provide an "optimal" score for each item that is uniformly applied.

   c) Ways to standardize administration of the measure, including the time limits for completion. Consideration must be given to reasonable accomodations to administration based on the Americans with Disabilities Act. For example, allowing oral administration of a written questionnaire to blind applicants is called for, or opportunity to clarify instructions for those applicants with inadequate written comprehension skills. Standardizing procedures during assessment is critical to ensure a more accurate, fairer assessment than if the procedure varies from one person to another. Thus, steps must be taken to control the conditions and procedures of test administration and to keep them constant, even unvarying. Any aspect that may potentially influence scores should be standardized. The challenge is that standardization must be balanced with fairness to reasonably accommodate all candidates.

4. The sampling designs and statistical procedures to be used in selecting and editing items, questions, and other elements on the measure.[16] Selection devices require a number of steps to ensure more accurate measurement. Among the steps often taken are administering items or questions from the device to a panel of subject matter experts. These SMEs typically assure job-relevance and help screen out objectionable items that might produce bias against some respondents. Development may include pilot-testing the selection device with an initial group that is comparable to the applicants the device will be used with. It may even involve a second, holdout sample to double-check findings. Robert Guion, among others, has argued that distorted results can be obtained when the usefulness of a selection device is evaluated for the *same* groups on whom the device was evaluated.[17]

Referring again to the analysis results of the electrician's job, we can see how job content might be translated into selection measure content. Among other requirements, the job analysis identified two important types of knowledge essential to the job: knowledge of the principles of electrical wiring and knowledge of maintenance and repair of electrical equipment. Because these two knowledge characteristics lend themselves to assessment with a paper-and-pencil test, let's assume we have decided to use such a test to measure what an industrial electrician must know to perform the job. In preparing the test, the first step is to develop a content outline. From discussions with incumbents and supervisors as well as additional job analysis information, we know that the two job knowledge components are broken down into more specific details. Figure 3.6 illustrates these details for one of the knowledge characteristics identified from the job analysis—that is, knowledge of the principles of electrical wiring.

In assessing these details, we determine that applicants must know the definitions of terms, safety principles, the correct steps to take in implementing electrical wiring procedures, and how to make specific computations involving electrical measurements (such as voltage, current, or amperage). Figure 3.7 helps us to specify the test item budget—that is, the specific number of items to be prepared for measuring the components of the job. In general, be wary of tests that consist of a limited number of items—for example, a 15-item test that purports to measure five different factors. Measuring an attribute or trait consistently and accurately typically requires more than just a couple of items. In this example, it was decided that 50 multiple-choice items would be used to assess knowledge of the principles of electrical wiring. Theoretically, multiple items could be developed for each cell in the chart shown in Figure 3.7. Our test, however, is only a *sampling* of behavior; we cannot ask all possible questions covering all possible elements of information. By using the chart in collaboration with knowledgeable and competent current employees and managers involved with the job, we can specify a reasonable number of test items

---

FIGURE 3.6 What an Industrial Electrician Needs to Know to Perform the Job

Knowledge of Principles of Electrical Wiring

- Reading schematic drawings
- Choosing appropriate gauges of wire for different electrical applications
- Installing circuit-breaker panels
- Selecting electrical fuses for different electrical applications
- Installing electrical grounds
- Checking voltages in electrical receptacles
- Computing voltage drops for various lengths and gauges of wiring
- Using copper and aluminum wiring

FIGURE 3.7	Form Used to Determine Item Budget for Knowledge Topics in the Industrial Electrician Test

Knowledge Topic	Knowledge Information				
	Definition of Terms	Safety Information	Procedural Applications	Computations	Total Items
Reading schematics	8				8
Choosing wire gauges			4		4
Installing circuit-breaker panels		4	4	3	11
Selecting electrical fuses		3		4	7
Installing electrical grounds		2	4		6
Checking electrical receptacle voltages		2	3	2	7
Computing voltage drops				3	3
Using copper and aluminum wiring			4		4
Total Items	8	11	19	12	50

NOTE: The knowledge topics listed in the chart were developed from the knowledge of principles of electrical wiring listed in Figure 3.6. Cells in the chart show the number of test items devoted to specific knowledge topics for various types of knowledge information.

for each cell (job requirement) chosen to be sampled by the test. Test items would be constructed in proportion to the number identified in the cells of the chart.

Administering, Analyzing, and Revising. Following development, the initial form should be pilot-tested. The measure should be administered to a sample of people from the same population for which it is being developed. Choice of participants should take into account the demographics, motivation, ability, and experience of the applicant pool of interest. To provide data suitable for analyzing its contents, the measure should be given to a sizable sample. For example, if a test is being developed for which item analyses (for example, factor analyses or the calculation of means, standard deviations, and reliabilities) are to be performed, a sample of at least a hundred, preferably several hundred, will be needed.

Based on the data collected, item analyses are performed on the preliminary data. The objective is to revise the proposed measure by correcting any weakness and deficiencies noted. Item analyses are used to choose the content, permitting it to discriminate between those who know and those who do not know the information covered.

Data analyses begin with a description of summary statistics including central tendency and variability (mean and standard deviations) for the total group and for relevant subgroups (if large enough). This informs the meaning of a score on the predictor. A number of psychometric characteristics should also be considered. These include evidence supporting:

1. *The reliability or consistency of scores on the items.* In part, reliability is based on the consistency and precision of the results of the measurement process and indicates whether items are free from measurement error. This is discussed in more detail in the next chapter.

2. *The validity of the intended inferences.* Do responses to an item differentiate among applicants with regard to the characteristics or traits that the measure is designed to assess? For example, if the test measures verbal ability, high-ability individuals will answer an item differently than those with low verbal ability. Often items that

differentiate are those with moderate difficulty, where 50 percent of applicants answer the item correctly. This is true for measures of ability, which have either a correct or incorrect answer. This is discussed in Chapter 5.

3. *Item fairness or differences among subgroups.* A fair test has scores that have the same meaning for members of different subgroups of the population. Such tests would have comparable levels of item difficulty for individuals from diverse demographic groups. Panels of demographically heterogeneous raters, who are qualified by their expertise or sensitivity to linguistic or cultural bias in the areas covered by the test, may be used to revise or discard offending items as warranted. An item sensitivity review is used to eliminate or revise any item that could be demeaning or offensive to members of a specific subgroup.

As this suggests, a number of considerations must guide the item analysis and revision process. To successfully navigate this step, the developer of the test must possess extensive technical knowledge about test development, the discussion of which is beyond the scope of this book.

In conclusion, the quality of the items used in the test has a significant impact on the overall quality of the measure. Consequently, this is a critical step in the development of a new measure.

Determining Reliability and Validity.   At this point, we have a revised measure that we hypothesize will predict aspects of job success. Thus we are ready to conduct reliability and validity studies to test our hypothesis. In the next two chapters we examine how to conduct reliability and validation research. Essentially, we want to answer three questions: Are the scores on our selection measure dependable for selection decision-making purposes? Is the selection measure predictive of job success? Does the test measure what we think it measures?

Implementing the Selection Measure.   After we obtain the necessary reliability and validity evidence, we can then implement our measure. Cut-off or passing scores may be developed. Norms or standards for interpreting how various groups score on the measure (categorized by gender, ethnicity, level of education, and so on) will be developed to help interpret the results. Once the selection measure is implemented, we will continue to monitor its performance to ensure that it is performing the function for which it is intended. Ultimately, this evaluation should be guided by whether the current decision-making process has been improved by the addition of the test.

As you can see, a great deal of technical work is involved in developing a selection measure. Shortcuts are seldom warranted; in fact, they are to be discouraged. This is a complicated process; it can easily take three to five years to develop a commercially successful test. As this implies, significant costs are associated with developing selection measures. Do not approach the development of a new measure in a flippant way. The technical ramifications, associated costs, and potential for legal action are three principal reasons why selection researchers frequently use suitable, existing measures rather than develop their own.

INTERPRETING SCORES ON SELECTION MEASURES

Using Norms

If you took a test, had it scored, and then were told that you achieved a 69, how would you feel? Probably not very good! A moment after receiving your score, you would probably ask how this score compared to others. Your question illustrates one of the basic principles of interpreting the results of selection measurement procedures. That is, in order to interpret the results of measurement intelligently, we need two essential pieces of information: (a) how others scored on the measure and (b) the validity of the measure.[18]

Let's return to your test score of 69 for a moment. Suppose you were told that the top score was 73. You might suddenly feel a lot better than you did a few moments ago. However, you are also told that everyone else who took the test scored 73. Now how do you feel? Without relevant information on how others scored, an individual score is practically meaningless. In order to attach meaning to a score, we must compare it to the scores of others who are similar with regard to characteristics such as level of education, type of job applied for, amount of work experience, and so on. Thus a score may take on different meanings depending on how it stands relative to the scores of others in particular groups. Our interpretation will depend on the score's relative standing in these other groups.

Scores of relevant others in groups are called *norms*. Norms are used to show how well an individual performs with respect to a specified comparison group. For example, standardized norms reported in test manuals are designed to rank-order examinees from high to low on the characteristic that is being assessed. The purpose is to determine how much of the measured characteristic a person has in relation to others for whom the same test information is available. This group of persons, for whom test score information is available and used for comparison purposes, is referred to as a *normative sample* or *standardization group*. The *Wonderlic Personnel Test,* for example, reports norms based on groups defined by the following variables: age of applicant, educational attainment, gender, position applied for, type of industry, and geographical region.

Normative data can be useful in understanding and evaluating scores on selection measures. However, you should keep several points in mind when using norms to interpret scores. First, the norm group selected should be *relevant* for the purpose it is being used. Norms will be meaningless or even misleading if they are not based on a group that is relevant (comparable) to those individuals being considered for employment. For example, suppose individuals applying for the job of an experienced electrician took the *Purdue Test for Electricians*. Let's assume that normative sample data were available for recent trade school graduates who had taken the test as well as for the employer's experienced electricians. If the company is trying to hire experienced electricians, the relevant norm group would be the experienced electricians rather than the norm group representing recent trade school graduates. Clearly, the former is more relevant to company needs for experienced personnel. If the norm group consisting of inexperienced personnel had been used, misleading results, perhaps some with serious consequences, could have occurred. Many different norm groups can be reported in selection manuals. Care must be exercised to ensure the appropriate group is chosen when interpreting scores on measures.

Second, rather than using norms based on national data, an employer should accumulate and use *local* norms. A local norm is one based on selection measures administered to individuals making an application for employment with a particular employer. Initially, when a test is implemented, appropriate norms published in a test manual may be used, but local norms should be developed as soon as 100 or more scores in a particular group have been accumulated. Passing test scores should then be established on the basis of these local data rather than just taken from published manuals.[19]

A third point to consider is that norms are *transitory*. That is, they are specific to the point in time when they were collected. Norms may, and probably do, change over time. If the attribute being assessed is not likely to change, then older norms will continue to be more or less relevant. However, the more likely the attribute is to change over time, the more current the normative data should be. For example, individuals tend to score higher on general mental ability tests than test takers of 10 to 20 years ago.[20] Thus an individual's mental ability test scores would appear higher using older norms than if current norms were used.

There is no prescribed period of time for publishers of selection measures to collect new normative data. Some collect such information every four or five years; others collect normative data every ten years. Norms that appear dated should be interpreted cautiously. Where feasible, normative data should be continuously collected by the user of selection measures; the time frame over which the normative results were established should be stated.

Norms are not always necessary in HR selection. For example, if five of the best performers on a test must be hired, or if persons with scores of 70 or better on the test are known to make suitable employees, then a norm is not necessary in employment decision making. One can simply use the individuals' test scores. On the other hand, if one finds that applicants' median selection test scores are significantly below that of a norm group, then the firm's recruitment practices should be examined. The practices may not be attracting the best job applicants; normative data would help in analyzing this situation.

In using normative information, we rely on statistical methods to aid our interpretation of what a test score means. The two basic methods we use frequently for expressing and interpreting test scores with respect to norms are *percentiles* and *standard scores*.

Employers using norms in selection decision making should be cautious when considering norms based on protected-group characteristics such as race and gender. Prior to the 1991 Civil Rights Act, some federal agencies and private employers engaged in a practice called *race norming* when reviewing job applicants' test scores.[21] Race norming is the practice of adjusting scores on a selection test to account for job applicants' race or ethnicity. Black, White, and Hispanic applicants who take a test are graded only against members of the same group. Percentile scores are then computed separately for each of these groups. Consequently, minority candidates may obtain higher percentile scores than majority candidates who actually outperformed them based on raw test scores. The 1991 Civil Rights Act made this practice illegal. Employers making selection decisions would be wise not only to avoid using percentile test score norms based on race or ethnicity but also to avoid norms based on any group characteristic protected by the Civil Rights Act. Although normative data are helpful in interpreting scores on selection measures, what we really want to know is how well a selection measure predicts future job performance. Norms do not tell us what a score means in terms of important job behaviors or criteria of job performance.

Using Percentiles

The statistic most frequently used in reporting normative data is the percentile. Because the purpose of a norm is to show relative standing in a group, percentile scores are derived to show *the percentage of persons in a norm group who fall below a given score on a measure*. Thus if an individual makes a 75 on a test and this score corresponds to the 50th percentile, that individual will have scored better than 50 percent of the people in a particular group who took the test. A percentile score is not a percentage score. A percentage score is like a *raw* or *obtained* score. For instance, if 1 person out of 200 people taking a 100-item test correctly answered 50 questions, that person's score would be 50, or 50 percent correct. But is this score high or low? By using percentiles, we can compare that score with the other 199 test takers' scores to make that determination. Thus 50 percent correct may correspond to a percentile score ranging from 0 to 100, depending on others' test performance.

In general, the higher the percentile score, the better a person's performance relative to others in the normative sample. Scores above the 50th percentile indicate above-average performance; scores below this percentile represent below-average performance. Figure 3.8 illustrates how normative percentile data are typically reported in test manuals.

FIGURE 3.8	Illustration of How Percentile Norms Are Frequently Reported in Test Manuals

Test Raw Score	z Score	Percentile
50	3.0	99.9
45	2.0	97.7
40	1.0	84.1
35	0.0	50.0
30	−1.0	15.9
25	−2.0	2.3
20	−3.0	0.1

Percentile scores are useful in interpreting test scores; however, they are subject to misuse. Charles Lawshe and Michael Balma point out there is a tendency for some users to interpret these percentile scores as if they were on a ratio scale.[22] For instance, if Susan Dustin, an applicant for a job, scores 5 percentile points higher on a selection test than Jack Fiorito, another job applicant, some may want to conclude that Susan is 5 percent better than Jack for the job. However, percentile scores should not be used in this way—for at least two reasons.

First, a difference of five percentile points may not indicate a real difference in people; the difference may be nothing but chance, resulting from unreliability of the test. (In the next chapter, you will see how the standard error of measurement can be used to make such a determination.) Second, percentile scores are based on an *ordinal* scale of measurement, not a ratio scale. Thus we can make greater-than or less-than statements in comparing scores, but we cannot say how much higher or how much lower one percentile score is from another. For instance, a percentile score of 60 is not twice as good as a percentile score of 30. For a number of reasons, test scores are frequently expressed as *standard* scores. One example of standard scores is entered as a *z* score, which represents the difference between an individual score and the mean, in units of the standard deviation (shown in Figure 3.8).

Using Standard Scores

Many different types of standard scores are reported in manuals accompanying commercially available tests used in selection. Some of the more common are *z, T,* and *stanine* scores. We will not go into all of the statistical details of these standard scores, but we want to comment about their role with regard to interpreting scores on selection measures.

In general, standard scores represent adjustments to raw scores, so it is possible to determine the proportion of individuals who fall at various standard score levels. These scales indicate, in common measurement units, how far above or below the mean score any raw score is. By *common measurement unit,* we mean these scores are on a scale that shows score differences having equal intervals; they can be added, subtracted, multiplied, and divided. Let's look at a few types of standard scores.

One of the most common standard scores is the *z* score. The formula is

$$z = \frac{(X - M)}{SD}$$

where

z = the standard score

X = an individual's raw or obtained score

M = the mean of the normative group's raw scores

SD = the standard deviation of the normative group's raw scores

Using this formula, z scores can be obtained for all individuals for whom test score data are available. The computations result in scores that range from -4.0 to $+4.0$; they can be directly interpreted regarding their distance from the normative group mean in standard deviation units. For example, a person with a z score of 1.0 is 1 standard deviation above the group mean; a person with a z score of -1.5 is 1 1/2 standard deviations below the group mean.

To avoid negative numbers, T scores are often used. These scores are similar to z scores, but they are adjusted so that all T scores are positive. One common form of T scores has a mean of 50 and a standard deviation of 10. To compute such a T score, we simply compute the z score and then use the following formula: $T = 10z \pm 50$. Thus a person's z score of 1.0 is equivalent to a T score of 60.

Stanine scores are another form of standard score. In this case, a single number ranging from 1 to 9 is used to represent individuals' normative score performance. Stanines are computed by rank-ordering scores from lowest to highest. The 4 percent with the lowest scores get a stanine score of 1, the next 7 percent get a stanine of 2, and so on. The higher the stanine score, the better the performance on a selection measure. As you might expect, there is an interrelationship among percentiles and the various standard scores we have mentioned. Figure 3.9 depicts the relationships among these scores. The figure shows a normal distribution of scores made on a test. Under the normal curve are various standard scores expressed as percentiles, z scores, T scores, and stanines. As you can see, the mean score of this distribution corresponds to the 50th percentile, a z score of 0, a T score of 50, and a stanine of 5. An individual who scores 1 standard deviation above the mean would have a percentile score of 84, a z score of 1, and so forth. Many other comparisons are also possible using the concepts described in Figure 3.9.

The biggest problem with the use of standard scores is that they are subject to misinterpretation. For this reason, percentiles are the most common score presented by publishers of selection measures. Although percentile scores show an individual test taker's relative position compared to a reference group, percentiles do not tell us what a score means in terms of success on the job.

We believe it important to reiterate what was said in the beginning of this chapter, that the quality of information used when making selection decisions is fundamental to an effective selection system. Rigorous measurement of our predictors and criteria, particularly regarding the role of precision in the level of measurement (for example, use of interval scales), has a substantial impact upon the quality of our measures. However, in order to identify good measures and weed out the bad ones, we must consider other standard measurement criteria (that is, validity and reliability). Employers sometimes assume that a relationship exists between selection measures and job performance criteria, but without reliability and validity evidence, we do not know whether this assumption is warranted. In the next two chapters, we will review methods for determining the reliability of selection measures and methods for examining the link between predictors and job success.

FIGURE 3.9 Relationships Among the Normal Curve, Percentiles, and Standard Scores

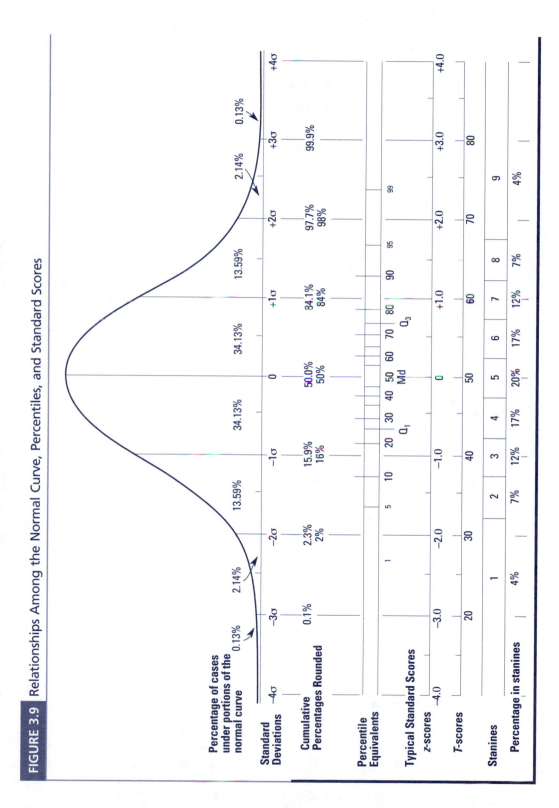

REFERENCES

1. Susana Urbina, *Essentials of Psychological Testing* (Hoboken, NJ: John Wiley, 2004), 64–116.

2. Elazur J. Pedhazur and Liora Pedhazur Schmelkin, *Measurement, Design, and Analysis: An Integrated Approach* (London: Lawrence Erlbaum Associates, 1991), 15–29.

3. Lewis R. Aiken, *Tests and Examinations* (New York: John Wiley, 1998), 30–52.

4. The *mean* is the average score of a group of scores on a variable such as a test. The *standard deviation* is a number that represents the spread of scores for a group of scores around the group's average score on a variable. As the standard deviation increases, the spread or differences among scores becomes larger. *Correlations* show the degree of relationship between variables. Chapter 5 gives a more thorough description of correlation procedures used in selection research.

5. Pedhazur and Schmelkin, *Measurement, Design, and Analysis: An Integrated Approach*; Hart Blanton and James Jaccard, "Arbitrary Metrics in Psychology," *American Psychologist* 61 (2006): 27–41; Susan E. Embretson, "The Continued Search for Nonarbitrary Metrics in Psychology," *American Psychologist* 61 (2006): 50–55; and Anthony G. Greenwald, Brian A. Nosek, and N. Sriram, "Consequential Validity of the Implicit Personality Test: Comment on Blanton and Jaccard (2006)," *American Psychologist* 61 (2006): 56–61.

6. Wayne F. Cascio and Herman Aquinis, *Applied Psychology in Human Resource Management*, 6th ed. (Upper Saddle River, NJ: Pearson Prentice Hall, 2005), 122–134; and Society for Industrial and Organizational Psychology, Inc., *Principles for the Validation and Use of Personnel Selection Procedures*, 4th ed. (Bowling Green, OH: Society of Industrial-Organizational Psychology, 2003), 8–18.

7. Murray R. Barrick and Michael K. Mount, "Select on Conscientiousness and Emotional Stability," in *Handbook of Principles of Organizational Behavior*, ed. E. A. Locke (Oxford: Blackwell Publishers, 2000), 15–28.

8. Robert M. Guion, *Assessment, Measurement, and Prediction for Personnel Decisions* (London: Lawrence Erlbaum Associates, 1998), 211–295; and *Principles for the Validation and Use of Personnel Selection Procedures*, 5–8.

9. Urbina, *Essentials of Psychological Testing*.

10. James C. Impara and Barbara S. Plake, *Thirteenth Mental Measurements Yearbook* (Lincoln, NE: Buros Institute of Mental Measurements, University of Nebraska Press, 1998).

11. American Psychological Association, *Standards for Educational and Psychological Testing* (Washington: American Psychological Association, 1999).

12. *Principles for the Validation and Use of Personnel Selection Procedures*, 42–43.

13. In several places throughout the book, we suggest that it may be necessary to hire a consultant to perform certain tasks or to accomplish specific selection objectives. Ideally, these tasks and objectives could be accomplished *within* the organization. However, access to needed organizational resources is not always possible. External consultants may be required. When should outside advice be sought? Ask yourself the following question: *Does the organization have the expertise, time, and other resources to adequately solve the selection problem?* If the answer is no, then a consultant is necessary.

    Assuming a selection consultant is needed, we might ask, What qualities should we look for? *At a minimum*, a selection consultant should

    1. Hold a Ph.D. in industrial/organizational psychology or human resources management with training in psychological measurement, statistics, and selection-related content areas such as job analysis, test construction, and performance evaluation

2. Have experience conducting selection, test validation, and job analysis research projects in other organizations

3. Provide references from client organizations where selection research projects have been completed

In addition to these criteria, a selection consultant will likely have published books or selection-oriented articles in the industrial–organizational or human resources management literature. Find additional resources for choosing a selection consultant on the SIOP web page under the consultant locator link (http://www.siop.org/conloc/default.aspx).

14. Paul R. Sackett and Roxanne M. Laczo, "Job and Work Analysis," in *Handbook of Psychology: Industrial and Organizational Psychology*, vol. 12, ed. Walter C. Borman, Daniel R. Ilgen, and Richard Klimoski (Hoboken, NJ: John Wiley, 2003), 21–37.

15. Urbina, *Essentials of Psychological Testing;* Thomas M. Haladyna, *Developing and Validating Multiple-Choice Test Items*, 3rd ed. (Mahwah, NJ: Lawrence Erlbaum Associates, 2005), 82–111; and Arlene Fink, *How to Ask Survey Questions*, 2nd ed. (Thousand Oaks, CA: Sage Publications, 2002), 39–63.

16. Robert L. Thorndike, *Personnel Selection* (New York: John Wiley, 1949), 50.

17. Robert M. Guion, *Assessment, Measurement, and Prediction for Personnel Decisions* (London: Lawrence Erlbaum Associates, 1998), 211–295.

18. Cascio and Aquinis, *Applied Psychology in Human Resource Management;* and Guion, *Assessment, Measurement, and Prediction for Personnel Decisions*, 125–137.

19. Harold G. Seashore and James H. Ricks, *Norms Must Be Relevant* (Test Service Bulletin No. 3C) (New York: The Psychological Corporation, May 1950), 19.

20. William T. Dickens and James R. Flynn, "Heritability Estimates versus Large Environmental Effects: The IQ Paradox Resolved," *Psychological Bulletin* 108 (2001): 346–369.

21. "States Forbidden to Use Race-Norming in Job Test," *Atlanta Constitution*, December 14, 1991, A-8; and "Job Tests for Minorities Thrown a Curve," *Atlanta Constitution*, May 6, 1991, A-2.

22. Charles H. Lawshe and Michael J. Balma, *Principles of Personnel Testing* (New York: McGraw-Hill, 1966), 75.

Reliability of Selection Measures

WHAT IS RELIABILITY?

The use of physiological tests by physicians is a common practice in the United States; the most commonly performed test measures blood pressure. Elevated blood pressure is associated with a number of problems, including an increased risk of developing heart disease, kidney disease, hardening of the arteries, eye damage, and stroke.[1] Because hypertension affects one in four adults in the United States, Americans are routinely encouraged to have their blood pressure tested. Measuring blood pressure accurately, however, has proven difficult.[2] Why is it so hard to reliably measure blood pressure? One reason is that patients often experience elevated blood pressure simply due to being subjected to the test in the doctor's office. This problem is so common it has been labeled "white coat" hypertension. It has been estimated that as many as 20 percent of diagnosed hypertensive patients (some estimates range up to 73 percent) have "white coat" hypertension—hypertension caused by anxiety about having their blood pressure checked.[3] Furthermore, blood pressure varies over the course of the day. A single blood pressure measurement is estimated to result in overdiagnosis of hypertension in 20–30 percent of cases, yet it misses a third of those who truly have the disease.[4] Accurate blood pressure measurement also depends on correct handling by medical personnel. Noise or talking can result in errors, as can using the wrong-sized cuff or releasing pressure too quickly during a manual assessment. In addition, inadequate equipment maintenance and calibration can result in inaccuracy. A recent study suggested that only 5 percent of these devices were properly maintained in one major teaching hospital, while another showed unacceptable measurement inaccuracy in up to 60 percent of devices evaluated.[5] The point is, there are a number of reasons why blood pressure tests contain a margin of error and can produce inaccurate and misleading information.

These data show that a test many view as essential produced results that, in many cases, were not dependable or reliable. Because of the unreliability of test results, people who underwent faulty blood pressure tests could have faced serious consequences. That is, persons falsely testing normal could have forgone needed dietary and lifestyle changes or the use of blood pressure-reducing drugs prescribed by their physicians. Those testing falsely high could have suffered unnecessary anxiety and unpleasant side effects from prescribed drugs that were not needed, as well as the expense of unnecessary drug therapy.

The measures we use in HR selection do not have the same physiological implications as do tests used in medicine. However, as in our blood pressure testing example, we have similar concerns regarding the dependability of measures commonly used in selection decision making. That is, we want to be sure we have measures that will produce dependable, consistent, and accurate results when we use them. If we will be using data to make predictions concerning the selection of people, we must be sure that these decisions are based on data that are reliable and accurate. We do not want to use measures where the score obtained on one occasion differs from another due to some chance fluctuation rather than from some true difference in the underlying construct. Obviously, we need accurate data to identify the best people available. We need accurate information for moral and legal reasons as well. Let's look at another example involving the dependability of information, but in this case, in the context of selection.

Robert Newmann, HR manager at Info Sources, Inc., had just finished scoring a computer programming aptitude test that was administered to 10 individuals applying for a job as a computer programmer. Because it was almost 5 p.m. and he had errands to run, he decided to carry the tests home and review them that night. While on his way home, Robert stopped by a store to pick up office supplies. Without thinking, he inadvertently left his briefcase containing the 10 tests on the front seat of his car. When he returned, the briefcase was missing. After filing a report with the police, Robert went home, wondering what he should do. The next day, Robert decided that all he could do was to locate the applicants and have them return for retesting. After a day of calling and explaining about the lost test scores, he arranged for the 10 applicants to come in and retake the programming aptitude test. But wouldn't you know it; the day after readministering the tests, Robert received a visit from the police. His briefcase was returned with contents intact. Robert removed the 10 original tests and set them beside the stack of 10 tests just taken. He muttered to himself, "What a waste of time." Out of curiosity, Robert scored the new exams, wondering how the applicants had done on the retest. He carefully recorded the two sets of scores. His recorded results are shown in Figure 4.1.

After reviewing the data, Robert thought, "What a confusing set of results!" The scores on the original tests were dramatically different from the retests. Robert pondered the results for a moment. He had expected the applicants' test scores to be the same from one testing to the next. They were not. Each of the 10 persons had different scores for the two tests. "Now why did that happen? Which of the two sets of scores represents the applicants' actual programming aptitudes?" he asked himself.

The situation we've just described is similar to that represented by our blood pressure testing illustration. Robert, too, needs dependable, consistent data for selection decision making. Yet from our selection example we can see that his test scores are different for no apparent reason. Thus it appears he does not have the consistent, dependable data

FIGURE 4.1	Summary of Hypothetical Test and Retest Results for 10 Applicants Taking the Programming Aptitude Test		

Applicant	First Test	Second Test
T. R. Mitchell	35	47
G. L. Stewart	57	69
J. W. Johnson	39	49
H. M. Weiss	68	50
D. V. Day	74	69
M. Kilduff	68	65
J. Kevin Ford	54	38
A. M. Ryan	71	78
F. L. Oswald	41	54
L. M. Hough	44	59

he needs. These characteristics of data we have mentioned—that is, consistency, dependability, and stability—all refer to the concept of reliability.

A Definition of Reliability

Reliability of scores from selection measures is a characteristic necessary for effective HR selection. In our earlier example, the computer programming aptitude test was apparently an unreliable measure; it is this unreliability in test scores that makes it difficult for Robert to know each applicant's actual level of programming aptitude.

A host of definitions have been given for the term reliability. In our discussion, we will touch on several of these. But for now we want to consider a fundamental definition of the concept. In the context of HR selection, *reliability* simply means the degree of dependability, consistency, or stability of scores on a measure used in selection research (either predictors or criteria). In general, reliability of a measure is determined by the degree of consistency between two sets of scores on the measure. In our earlier selection example, we would have expected the programming aptitude test to have yielded similar results from one testing period to the next if the test produced reliable data. Because the results were not similar, we would probably conclude that the test contained errors of measurement. Thus a careful study of the reliability of the test should be made.

Errors of Measurement

It is important to keep in mind that reliability deals with errors of measurement. In this sense, a measure that is perfectly reliable is free of errors. None of our selection measures, whether predictor or criterion, will be free of measurement errors (although such errors tend to be less frequent with measures of physical attributes relative to measures of unobservable psychological characteristics). Selection measures designed to assess important job-related characteristics (such as knowledge, skills, and abilities) may be prone to error due to the test taker, the examiner, and the situation in which testing takes place. In general, the greater the amount of measurement error, the lower the reliability of a selection measure; the less error, the higher the reliability. Thus if errors of measurement can be assessed, a measure's reliability can be determined. What, then, are "errors of measurement"?

When we use selection devices such as tests, we obtain numerical scores on the measures. These scores serve as a basis for selection decision making. Because we are using scores as a basis for our decisions, we want to know the "true" scores of applicants for each characteristic being measured. For example, if we administer a mathematics ability test, we want to know the "true" math ability of each test taker. But unless our measure is perfectly reliable, we will encounter difficulties in knowing these true scores. In fact, we may get mathematics ability scores that are quite different from the individuals' true abilities. Let's see why.

The score obtained on a measure—that is, the *obtained* score—consists of two parts: a *true* component and an *error* component. The components of any obtained score (X) can be summarized by the following equation:

$$X_{\text{obtained}} \;=\; X_{\text{true}} + X_{\text{error}}$$

where

X_{obtained} = obtained score for a person on a measure

X_{true} = true score for a person on the measure; that is, the actual amount of the attribute measured that a person really possesses

X_{error} = error score for a person on the measure; that is, the amount that a person's score was influenced by factors present at the time of measurement that are unrelated to the attribute measured. These errors are assumed to represent random fluctuations or chance factors.

This notion of a score being composed of true and error parts is a basic axiom of measurement theory.[6]

True Score

The true score is really an ideal conception. It is the score individuals would obtain if external and internal conditions to a measure were perfect. For example, in our mathematics ability test, an ideal or true score would be one for which both of the following conditions existed:

1. Individuals answered correctly the same percentage of problems on the test that they would have if all possible problems had been given and the test were a construct valid measure of the underlying phenomenon of interest (see next chapter).

2. Individuals answered correctly the problems they actually knew without being affected by external factors such as lighting or temperature of the room in which the testing took place, their emotional state, or their physical health.

Another way of thinking about a true score is to imagine that an individual takes a test measuring a specific ability many different times. With each testing, his or her scores will differ somewhat; after a large number of testings, the scores will take the form of a normal distribution. The differences in scores are treated as if they are due to errors of measurement. The average of all test scores best approximates the test taker's true ability. Therefore, we might think of a true score as the mean or average score made by an individual on many different administrations of a measure.

This idealized situation does not exist. The notion of a true score, however, helps to define the idea that there is a specific score that would be obtained if measurement conditions were perfect. Because a true score can never be measured exactly, the obtained score is used to estimate the true score. Reliability answers this question: How confident can we be that an individual's obtained score represents his or her true score?

Error Score

A second part of the obtained score is the error score. This score represents errors of measurement. Errors of measurement are those factors that affect obtained scores but are not related to the characteristic, trait, or attribute being measured.[7] These factors, present at the time of measurement, distort respondents' scores either over or under what they would have been on another measurement occasion. There are many reasons why individuals' scores differ from one measurement occasion to the next. Fatigue, anxiety, or noise during testing that distracts some text takers but not others are only a few of the factors that explain differences in individuals' scores over different measurement occasions.

Figure 4.2 shows the relationship between reliability and errors of measurement for three levels of reliability of a selection measure. Hypothetical obtained and true scores are given for each of the reliability levels. Errors of measurement are shown by the shaded area of each bar. With decreasing errors of measurement, reliability of the measure increases. Notice that with increasing reliability, more precise estimates of an individual's true score on the measure can be made. Less random error is present. For example, suppose an individual's true score on the measure is 50. For a measure that has low reliability, a wide discrepancy is possible between the obtained scores (40 to 60) and the true score (50). That is, on one occasion a person might score as low as 40

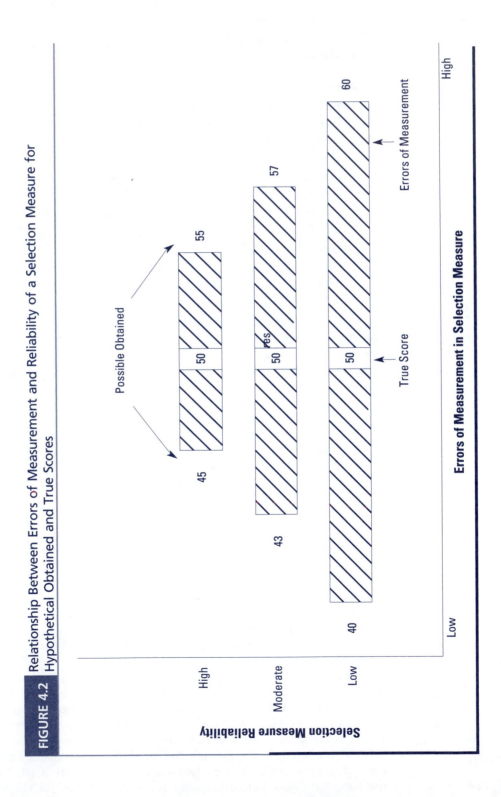

FIGURE 4.2 Relationship Between Errors of Measurement and Reliability of a Selection Measure for Hypothetical Obtained and True Scores

and on another earn a score as high as 60. In contrast, in a measure with high reliability, the possible obtained scores (45 to 55) yield a closer estimate of the true score (50).

How much error exists in a score is an important attribute of the selection measure. If scores on a selection measure are due to chance or reflect an inconsistant or unpredictable error, we cannot have much confidence in the selection device. If we use a test that claims to measure general mental ability, but the reported reliability is so low that the test scores consist mostly of error, then our so-called "intelligence test" cannot possibly measure mental ability. With excessive error, a selection measure will not be useful. If there is little error present, the measure may be applicable in selection. (The next chapter discusses other characteristics of a measure that make it effective.)

Where do these errors come from? Several different sources exist. The importance of any particular source will depend on factors such as the nature of the measure itself (for example, a paper-and-pencil measure, a behavior, the degree of standardization), what is being measured (an ability, a personality trait, an attitude), the test taker and test administrator, the situation in which the measure is being used, and the method of estimating reliability. Table 4.1 summarizes some of the more common sources of error that contribute to the unreliability of selection measures.[8] As you examine the table, keep in mind that these errors can affect predictors (such as tests) as well as criteria (such as performance evaluations).

An important objective in developing and using selection measures is to reduce errors of measurement as much as possible. When these errors are reduced, individual differences in scores on selection measures will more likely be due to true differences rather

TABLE 4.1	Examples of Sources of Errors of Measurement Contributing to Unreliability In Human Resource Selection Measures	
Source of Error	**Conditions under Which an Error May Occur**	**Example of Error**
Individual responding to a selection measure	Where an individual's physical and mental health, motivation, mood, level of stress, understanding of instructions, content of the items, etc., affect how the individual responds to a selection measure	An applicant has an accident on the way to take a test. During the test, he is distracted by worries that his car insurance will not cover all of the expenses.
Individual administering a selection measure	Where the administrator of a selection measure affects the responses of the individual completing the measure	Two employment interviewers interview the same job applicants using the same interview questions. One interviewer frequently smiles and nods approvingly during the interview; the other does not.
Individual scoring a selection measure	Where judgment and subjectivity on the part of the scorer of a selection measure play a role in scoring	A supervisor does not attend a training session prior to using a new performance appraisal instrument. Thus when giving ratings, she completes the performance evaluation forms as soon as possible with no consistent or precise rules for evaluating each employee's actual job performance.
Physical conditions under which a selection measure is administered	Where *heating, cooling, lighting, noise, etc., affect how an individual responds to a selection measure*	While taking a test, respondents are interrupted by a power failure that affects the cooling and lighting in the room.

NOTE: By use of the term *selection measure,* we mean both predictors and criteria.

than chance (or error) differences. The degree to which we are willing to trust differences among individuals' scores as being a real difference depends on the measure's reliability. Reliable measures that are useful in HR selection minimize the presence of these errors of measurement. Because errors are minimized, reliable measures give us more confidence in making decisions such as the suitability of one job applicant over another or the prediction of an applicant's future job performance. Selection decisions based on reliable measures are also fairer to the applicants involved.

Methods of Estimating Reliability

Reliability is generally determined by examining the relationship between two sets of measures measuring the same thing. Where the two sets of measures yield similar scores, reliability will be raised. If scores from the measures tend to be dissimilar, reliability will be lowered. Referring again to our earlier example involving Robert Newmann, HR manager of Info Sources, Inc., we saw that he had two sets of programming aptitude test scores. In Taylor's case, the two sets of test scores were different from each other, even though they were produced by the same programming aptitude test. The fact that the two sets of scores across occasions were different suggested that the stability of measurement of programming aptitude was low. Where scores are generally consistent for people across two sets of measures, reliability of a measure will be enhanced. For example, if a person's math ability score remains the same for two different administrations of a test, this fact will add to the reliability of the test. However, if factors such as fatigue or inconsistent administration procedures cause differential changes in people across sets of measures, the factors will contribute to unreliability. These factors are then considered sources of errors of measurement, because they are chance factors influencing responses to a measure.

Because reliability theory is only an idealized concept of what does or does not contribute to reliability, we cannot measure reliability per se. We can only estimate it. Thus we should not think of the reliability of a measure, but rather an estimate of reliability. We will see that alternative procedures can be used to provide different estimates of reliability. One of the principal ways in which these procedures differ is in how they treat the various factors (see Table 4.1) that may alter measurements of people. Some procedures will consider these factors to be error, while others will not. You might ask, "Which method should be used?" There is no one best method. The choice will depend on each specific situation for which a reliability estimate is desired.

Statistical procedures are commonly used to calculate what are called reliability coefficients. Oftentimes, techniques involving the Pearson product-moment correlation coefficient are utilized to derive reliability coefficients. We do not go into the statistical details of the correlation coefficient here (those are discussed in the next chapter), but we do describe briefly how the coefficient is obtained. Specifics concerning the interpretation of the reliability coefficient are given in the next section.

A reliability coefficient is simply an index of relationship. It summarizes the relation between two sets of measures for which a reliability estimate is being made. The calculated index varies from 0.00 to 1.00. In calculating reliability estimates, the correlation coefficient obtained is regarded as a direct measure of the reliability estimate. The higher the coefficient, the less the measurement error and the higher the reliability estimate. Conversely, as the coefficient approaches 0.00, errors of measurement increase and reliability correspondingly decreases. Of course, we want to employ selection measures having high reliability coefficients. With high reliability, we can be more confident that a particular measure is giving a dependable picture of true scores for whatever attribute is being measured.

Many methods of estimating reliability exist. We discuss four principal methods most often employed in selection research studies: (a) test-retest, (b) parallel or equivalent forms, (c) internal consistency, and (d) interrater reliability estimates. As Milton Blum and James Naylor have pointed out, an important characteristic that differentiates among these procedures is what each method considers to be errors of measurement.[9] One method may treat a factor as error while another treats the same factor as meaningful information. The method chosen will be determined by what factors a researcher wants to treat as error and which of the following questions are to be addressed by reliability procedures.

1. How dependably can an individual be assessed with a measure at a given moment?

2. How dependably will data collected by a measure today be representative of the same individual at a future time?

3. How accurately will scores on a measure represent the true ability of an individual on the trait being sampled by a measure?

4. When individuals are being rated by more than one rater, to what degree do evaluations vary from one rater to another? Or, to what extent is an individual's score due to the rater rather than to the individual's behavior or other characteristics being rated?

As you examine these questions, you can see that each one considers reliability to be the degree of consistency between two or more measurements of the same thing.

Test-Retest Reliability Estimates

One obvious way to assess the reliability of scores obtained on a selection measure is to administer the measure twice and then correlate the two sets of scores using the Pearson product-moment correlation coefficient. This method is referred to as test-retest reliability. It is called test-retest reliability because the same measure is used to collect data from the same respondents at two different points in time. Because a correlation coefficient is calculated between the two sets of scores over time, the obtained reliability coefficient represents a coefficient of stability. The coefficient indicates the extent to which the test can be generalized from one time period to the next.

As an example of test-retest reliability estimation, suppose we wanted to determine the reliability of our mathematics ability test mentioned earlier. First, we administer the test to a representative group of individuals. After a period of time, say eight weeks, we readminister and score the same test for the same individuals. To estimate test-retest reliability, we simply correlate the two sets of scores (test scores at Time 1 correlated with scores at Time 2) using the Pearson product-moment correlation.

Figure 4.3 illustrates the basic design for test-retest reliability determination. The figure also shows the effect on the reliability coefficient when the relative positions of individuals change from one testing to the next. (Of course, we would use many more than the five people listed in the figure for estimating reliability; we are showing their scores simply for illustration purposes.)

Time 1 in the figure shows the five individuals' scores on the mathematics ability test for the initial administration of the test. At a later date, Time 2, the test is readministered to the same individuals. Figure 4.3 shows two possible outcomes (Case A and Case B) that could result from this retesting. (Only one retest is needed to compute reliability.) Case A presents one possible set of scores for the individuals. Notice two points in Case A. First, the scores have changed slightly from Time 1 to Time 2 testing.

FIGURE 4.3   Illustration of the Design for Estimating Test-Retest Reliability

Job Applicant	Test Scores Time 1 (t1)		Retest Scores Time 2 (t2)					
	Time 1	Rank	Case A		Rank	Case B		Rank
	t1	t1	$t2_a$	$t1 - t2_a$	$t2_a$	$t2_b$	$t1 - t2_b$	$t2_b$
J. R. Hollenbeck	96	1	90	−6	1	66	−30	2
M. A. Campion	87	2	89	2	2	52	−35	3
F. L. Morgeson	80	3	75	−5	3	51	−29	4
M. K. Burke	70	4	73	3	4	82	12	1
P. R. Sackett	56	5	66	10	5	50	−6	5

NOTE: Test-retest reliability for Time 1—Time 2 **(Case A)** = 0.94; test-retest reliability for Time 1—Time 2 **(Case B)** = 0.07.

J. R. Hollenbeck's original test score of 96, for instance, fell to 90 upon retesting, a loss of 6 points. Some of the other applicants' scores also fell slightly, while others slightly increased. Second, the rank-ordering of the applicants' scores remained the same from one testing to the next. Hollenbeck's score (96) was the highest on the original test; and even though it fell upon retesting, his score (90) was still the best for the group. The others' rank-ordering of scores also remained the same across the two testings. Because of the relatively small changes in applicants' absolute test scores and no changes in the ranks of these scores over time, a high reliability coefficient would be expected. A test-retest reliability coefficient computed between the Time 1 scores and the Time 2 (Case A) scores is 0.94. This estimate confirms our expectation. It represents a high test-retest reliability coefficient with little error present. Reduced errors of measurement increase the generalizability of individuals' mathematics ability as measured by the initial testing.

Now look at Case B. When you compare this set of retest scores with those originally obtained at Time 1, you can see rather large differential rates of change among the individuals' scores. (Some individuals' scores changed more than others. Compare, for example, Campion's 35-point test score change with Sackett's 6-point change.) These differential rates of change have also altered the individuals' relative rank-orderings in the two sets of scores. Due to these differential test score and rank-order changes between Time 1 and Time 2 (Case B), the test-retest reliability is very low, only 0.07. This coefficient suggests a great deal of error in measurement. The obtained scores on the test represent very little of the mathematics ability of those taking the test.

The higher the test-retest reliability coefficient, the greater the true score and the less error present. If reliability were equal to 1.00, no error would exist in the scores; true scores would be perfectly represented by the obtained scores. A coefficient this high would imply that scores on the measure are not subject to changes in the respondents or the conditions of administration. If reliability were equal to 0.00, a test-retest reliability coefficient this low would suggest that obtained scores on the test are nothing more than error. Any factor that differentially affects individuals' responses during one measurement occasion and not on the other creates errors of measurement and lowers reliability. As we saw in Table 4.1, many sources of error change scores over time and, hence, lower test-retest reliability. Some of these errors will be associated with differences within individuals occurring from day to day (such as illness on one day of testing), whereas others will be associated with administration of a measure from one time to the next (such as distracting noises occurring during an administration). Further, two additional factors affect test-retest reliability: (a) memory and (b) learning.

Recall that earlier we said any factor that causes scores within a group to change differentially over time will decrease test-retest reliability. Similarly, any factor that causes scores to remain the same over time will increase the reliability estimate. If respondents on a selection measure remember their previous answers to an initial administration of a measure and then on retest respond according to memory, the reliability coefficient will increase. How much it increases will depend on how well they remember their previous answers.

The effect of memory, however, will be to make the reliability coefficient artificially high—an overestimate of the true reliability of scores obtained on the measure. Rather than reflecting stability of a measure's scores over time, a test-retest reliability coefficient may tend to reflect the consistency of respondents' memories. In general, when considering reliability we are not interested in measuring the stability of respondents' memories. Instead we are interested in evaluating the stability of scores produced by the measure. One way of lessening the impact of memory on test-retest reliability coefficients is to increase the time interval between the two administrations. As the length of time increases, respondents are less likely to recall their responses. Thus with increasing time intervals, test-retest reliability coefficients will generally decrease. How long a period should be used? There is no one best interval; from several weeks to several months is reasonable depending on the measure and the specific situation.

Although a lengthy interval between two administrations would appear to be a viable alternative for countering the effects of memory, too long a period opens up another source of error—learning. If respondents between the two time intervals of testing learn or change in such a way that their responses to a measure are different on the second administration than they were on the first, then test-retest reliability will be lowered. For instance, if respondents recall items asked on an initial administration of a test and then learn answers so their responses are different on the second administration, learning will have changed their scores. In another example, respondents may have been exposed to information (such as a training program) that causes them to alter their answers the second time a test is administered. Whatever the source, when individual differences in learning take place so that responses are differentially affected (that is, individuals learn at different rates), reliability will be lowered.

Notice that because of learning, our selection measure scores may appear to be unstable over time. Yet their unreliability is not really due to the errors of measurement we have been discussing. In fact, systematic but different rates of change among respondents through learning may account for what would appear to be unreliability. Nevertheless, the calculation of a test-retest reliability coefficient will treat such changes as error, thus contributing to unreliability. Therefore, with a long time interval between administrations of a measure, test-retest reliability may underestimate actual reliability because learning could have caused scores to change.

In addition, the test-retest approach will not provide meaningful estimates of reliability if the trait or characteristic underlying the measure is unstable. For example, selection measures that involve attitudes or self-esteem or measures of self-concept are likely to be in a state of change. Here it may be inappropriate to use test-retest reliability because any changes found will be treated as error. Yet some of those changes reflect the instability of the trait itself (for example, the tendency of self-esteem to change over time). In contrast, reliability of measures involving characteristics that are relatively stable over time (such as mental ability) may be estimated with test-retest reliability.

Given some of the potential problems with test-retest reliability, when should it be used? There are no hard and fast rules, but some general guidelines can be offered. These guidelines include the following:

1. Test-retest reliability is appropriate when the length of time between the two administrations is long enough to offset the effects of memory or practice.[10]

2. When there is little reason to believe that memory will affect responses to a measure, test-retest reliability may be employed. Memory may have minimal effects in situations where (a) a large number of items appear on the measure, (b) the items are too complex to remember (for example, items involving detailed drawings, complex shapes, or detailed questions), and (c) retesting occurs after at least eight weeks.[11]

3. When it can be confidently determined that nothing has occurred between the two testings that will affect responses (learning, for example), test-retest can be used.

4. When information is available on only a single item measure, test-retest reliability may be used.

If stability of measurement over time is of interest, test-retest reliability is a suitable method. If a measure has high test-retest reliability, we can conclude that the test is free of error associated with the passage of time. However, if the reliability coefficient is low, we will not know whether the low coefficient is because of low reliability or the lack of stability in the attribute being measured. If, on the other hand, our interest is in the dependability with which scores are provided by a measure at one point in time, then other reliability procedures (for example, internal consistency) are needed.

Parallel or Equivalent Forms Reliability Estimates

To control the effects of memory on test-retest reliability (which can produce an overestimate of reliability), one strategy is to avoid the reuse of a measure and to use equivalent versions of the measure instead. Each version of the measure has different items, but the questions assess the attribute being measured in precisely the same way. One form of the measure would be administered to respondents; the other form would be administered to the same respondents at a later time. Like our test-retest procedure, a Pearson correlation would be computed between the two sets of scores (Form A correlated with Form B scores) to develop a reliability estimate. Estimates computed in this manner are referred to as *parallel* or *equivalent forms* reliability estimates. The reliability coefficient itself is often called a coefficient of equivalence because it represents the consistency with which an attribute is measured from one version of a measure to another. As the coefficient approaches 1.00, the set of measures is viewed as equivalent or the same for the attribute measured. If equivalent forms are administered on different occasions, then this design also reflects the degree of temporal stability of the measure. In such cases, the reliability estimate is referred to as a *coefficient of equivalence and stability*. The use of equivalent forms administered over time accounts for the influence of random error to the test content (over equivalent forms) and transient error (across situations).

To achieve a parallel forms reliability estimate, at least two equal versions of a measure must exist. Looking again at the math ability test we referred to earlier, we can review the basic requirements of parallel forms of a measure. The basic process in developing parallel forms is outlined in Figure 4.4. As shown in Figure 4.4, the process of developing equivalent forms initially begins with the identification of a universe of possible math ability items, called the universe of possible math items. Items from this domain are administered to a large sample of individuals representative of those to

FIGURE 4.4	Basic Measurement Procedures and Requirements for Developing Parallel Forms (A and B) of a Math Ability Test

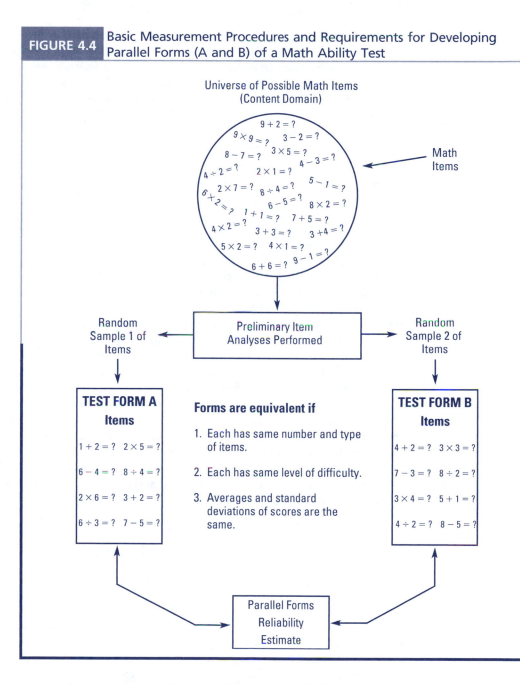

whom the math ability test will be given. Individuals' responses are used to identify the difficulty of the items through item analyses and to ensure the items are measuring the same math ability construct (for example, the ability to add). Next, the items are rank-ordered according to their difficulty and randomly assigned in pairs to form two sets of items (form A and B). If our defining and sampling of math ability item content has been correctly conducted, we should have two equivalent forms of our math ability test.

One form is administered after the other form has been given. The time interval between the two administrations can be brief (within a day or so) or long (for instance, two months). In this manner, we can obtain a reliability estimate rather quickly without being concerned about the effects of memory on responses.

In practice, equivalency of forms is not easy to achieve. Chance or the random effects of sample item selection can produce item differences in the forms. As a consequence, the forms will be different, thus curtailing reliability. For example, item differences on the two forms of our math ability test could result in one form being more difficult than the other. Form-to-form differences will cause changes in scores from one administration to the next, and reliability of test scores will be lowered. Because it is difficult to meet all of the criteria of equivalent forms, some writers use the term *alternate forms* to refer to forms that approximate but do not meet the criteria of parallel forms.[12]

For some selection measures (such as math, spelling, vocabulary, and others), it is possible to obtain reasonably equivalent forms. These and other ability measures are commercially available. They are often used to prevent individuals from improving their scores on a second testing simply due to memorization and to lessen the possibility that test content will be shared with others. The construction of equivalent forms that obtain the same true scores of a biographical data or personality inventory requires considerable effort, time, skills, and other resources.

Because genuine or true equivalent forms are nearly impossible to obtain, and because differences may exist from one administration to another, reliability coefficients computed between parallel forms tend to be conservative estimates. Yet where equivalent forms can be obtained, this estimate of reliability is almost always preferable to test-retest reliability. This is particularly true when completion of the two forms is accomplished across time. If a high parallel forms reliability estimate is obtained over time, the coefficient suggests that individuals' scores on the measure would be as similar as if they had taken an equivalent test on a different occasion.

So far, we have discussed reliability in the context of two administrations of a measure. But what if we want to control the effects of memory on responses and do not have time to wait for memory to be diminished before administering a retest? Or what if an equivalent form of a selection measure does not exist? Or if the underlying trait is too unstable to measure over time (for example, day-to-day mood)? Or if it is not possible to get people to respond twice? Options are available to handle those situations where retests or equivalent forms are not feasible.

Internal Consistency Reliability Estimates

One important characteristic of a reliable measure is that the various parts of a total measure are so interrelated that they can be interpreted as measuring the same thing. An index of a measure's similarity of content is an internal consistency reliability estimate. Basically, an internal consistency reliability estimate shows the extent to which all parts of a measure (such as items or questions) are similar in what they measure.[13] Thus a selection measure is internally consistent or homogeneous when individuals' responses on one part of the measure are related to their responses on other parts. For example, if we have five simple addition items on a test (12 + 23 = ?), individuals who can answer one of the items correctly (excluding guessing) can probably answer the remaining four also. Those who cannot answer one correctly will likely be unable to answer the others correctly. If this assumption is true, then our five-item test is internally consistent or homogeneous; individuals' performances on the test items are related. When a measure is created to assess a specific concept, such as mathematics ability, the items chosen to measure that concept represent only a portion of all possible items that could have been selected. If the sample of selected items truly assesses the same concept, then respondents should answer these items in the same way. What must be determined for the items chosen is whether respondents answer the sample of items similarly. Internal consistency reliability shows the extent to which the data are free from error due to the ways the items were phrased, interpreted by respondents, and so on.

To test the internal consistency hypothesis, we can examine the relationship between similar parts of a measure. The internal consistency hypothesis can be tested by simply correlating individuals' scores on these similar parts. A high estimate suggests that respondents' answers to one part are similar to their responses on other parts of the measure; hence, the measure is internally consistent. Like our other methods for estimating reliability, internal consistency reliability is applicable to many different types of selection measures, including predictors and criteria.

Internal consistency estimates tend to be among the most popular reliability procedures used. In general, the following three procedures are applied most often: (a) split-half reliability, (b) Kuder-Richardson reliability, and (c) Cronbach's coefficient alpha (α) reliability.

Split-Half Reliability Estimates

One of the internal consistency options is referred to as split-half or subdivided test reliability estimates. Split-half reliability involves a single administration of a selection measure. Then, for reliability calculation purposes, the measure is divided or split into two halves so that scores for each part can be obtained for each test taker. Because it is assumed that all items are measuring the same attribute, performance on one half of the test should be associated with performance on the other. To assess split-half reliability, the first problem we face is how to split the measure to obtain the most comparable halves. The most common method for creating these two halves of a measure is to score all even-numbered items as a "test" and all odd-numbered items as a "test." When split in this manner, the distribution of the items into the two test parts approximates a random assignment of items. Then, as in our previous estimates, the Pearson correlation is used to determine the extent of relation between the two test part scores. The resulting correlation coefficient is the reliability estimate.[14] A problem with split-half estimates is that there are many ways to split a measure into two halves; often, different "splits" do not yield the same reliability estimate. This probably explains why this procedure is not as common today. In fact, strictly speaking, a split-half reliability estimate is not a pure measure of internal consistency.[15] Like the parallel forms reliability coefficient, the obtained coefficient primarily represents a coefficient of equivalence. Thus the coefficient tends to show similarity of responses from one form to an equivalent one when administered at one time.

Figure 4.5 illustrates how two parts of a measure may be developed and split-half reliability determined. However, this example is a bit different from some of our earlier illustrations. We employed predictors in previous examples, but in Figure 4.5 we are using a criterion measure. As we specified earlier in the chapter, reliability estimates are important for all variables being studied.

Let's assume that we wanted to know the reliability of an employee productivity measure that was serving as a criterion in a selection research study involving bicycle assemblers. Basically, the measure is the total number of bicycles assembled by each employee during a 28-day period. For purposes of brevity, Figure 4.5 shows the total number of bicycles assembled by employees during an abbreviated 28-day period.

Once we have complete data for our employees on each of the 28 days, we can subdivide our measure into two parts. The odd-numbered days (Days 1, 3, 5, ... , 25, 27) and the associated production for each employee compose Part 1, and the even-numbered days (Days 2, 4, ... , 24, 26, 28) and their associated employee productivity data are assigned to Part 2, as is shown in Figure 4.5. We next obtain total scores or total productivity for each part by summing the respective daily production rates. Next, we

FIGURE 4.5 Representation of Odd-Even (Day) Split-Half Reliability Computed for a Job Performance Criterion Measure

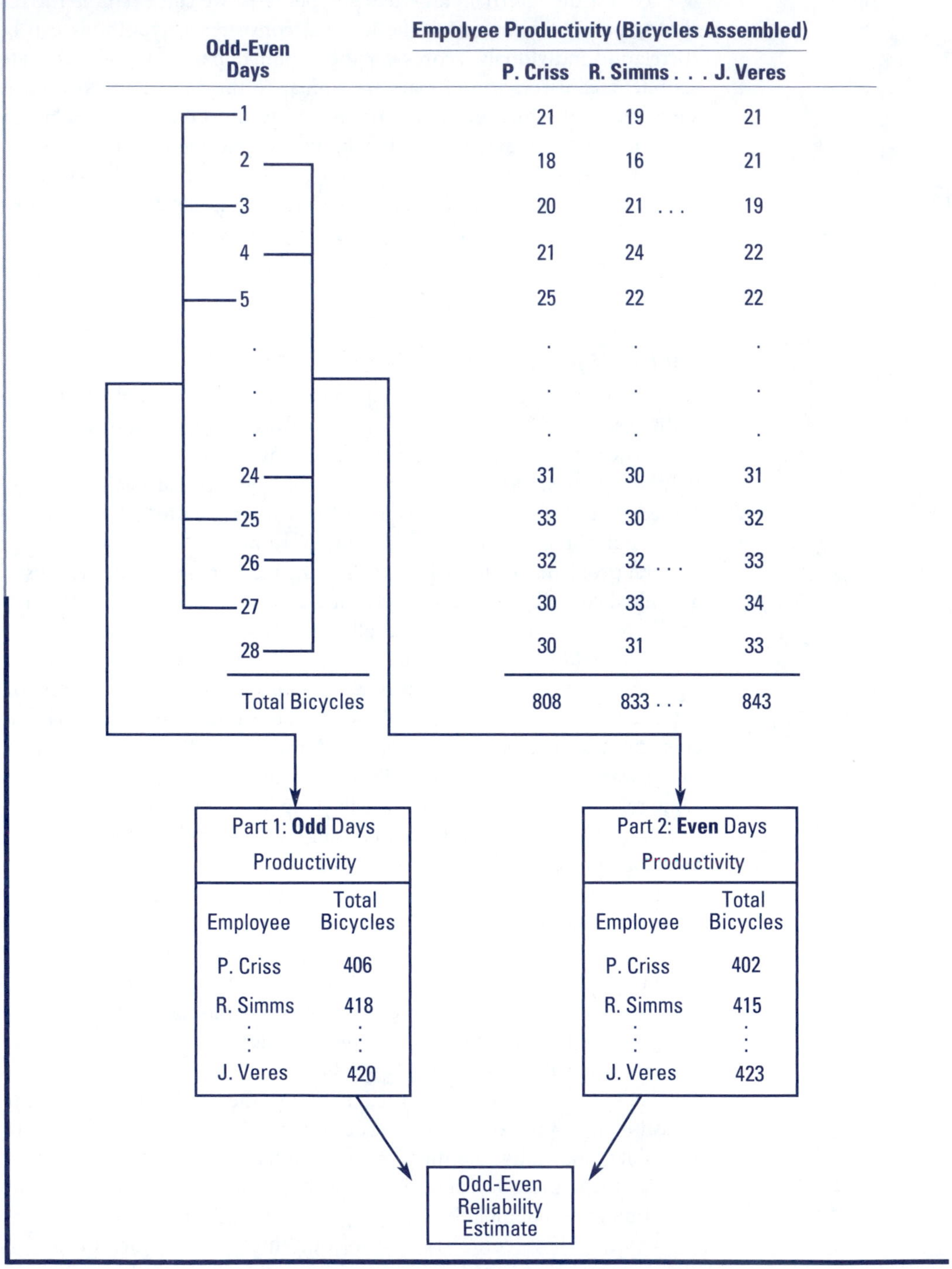

Odd-Even Days	Empolyee Productivity (Bicycles Assembled)		
	P. Criss	R. Simms . . .	J. Veres
1	21	19	21
2	18	16	21
3	20	21 . . .	19
4	21	24	22
5	25	22	22
.	.	.	.
.	.	.	.
.	.	.	.
24	31	30	31
25	33	30	32
26	32	32 . . .	33
27	30	33	34
28	30	31	33
Total Bicycles	808	833 . . .	843

Part 1: **Odd** Days Productivity

Employee	Total Bicycles
P. Criss	406
R. Simms	418
:	:
J. Veres	420

Part 2: **Even** Days Productivity

Employee	Total Bicycles
P. Criss	402
R. Simms	415
:	:
J. Veres	423

Odd-Even Reliability Estimate

compute a correlation between the employees' production rates (Part 1 correlated with Part 2) to obtain a reliability estimate of the employee productivity measure (total bicycles assembled). We could apply this same procedure to a predictor, such as a test, as well. Rather than using odd- and even-numbered days, we would use odd- and even-numbered items on the test. We would then apply identical procedures as outlined in Figure 4.5.

The obtained reliability coefficient developed on two halves of a measure is not a very precise estimate. In practice, we want to use the full measure, not half of it. What we want to know is the reliability of the whole measure.

Other things being equal, reliability increases with increasing length of a measure. Our split-half reliability estimate, however, is based on a correlation between scores on only half of the measure; it underestimates actual reliability. The length of the measure was reduced when we split it into two halves, odd-numbered and even-numbered parts. Therefore, a correction is needed to determine the reliability of the full or complete measure. A special formula, the Spearman-Brown prophecy formula, is used to make the correction.[16] Essentially, the formula shows what the reliability estimate would have been if the correlation had been based on the full rather than the part measures.

The Spearman-Brown formula used to correct a split-half reliability coefficient is as follows:

$$r_{ttc} = \frac{nr_{12}}{1 + (n-1)r_{12}}$$

where

r_{ttc} = the corrected split-half reliability coefficient for the total selection measure

n = number of times the test is increased in length

r_{12} = the correlation between Parts 1 and 2 of the selection measure.

For instance, let's examine the corrected split-half reliability of the criterion measure of bicycle assembler productivity. Part 1 of the productivity measure consisted of total bicycles assembled on all odd days of the month; Part 2 consisted of total bicycles assembled on all even days. Assume that the correlation between Parts 1 and 2 was 0.80. This correlation is the reliability coefficient for half the criterion measure (bicycles assembled). By applying the Spearman-Brown formula, the corrected reliability for the total criterion measure (bicycles assembled) is as follows:

$$r_{ttc} = \frac{2(0.80)}{1 + (2-1)0.80} = 0.89$$

With the corrected reliability estimate of 0.89, we have a more precise estimate of the reliability of the total criterion measure.

Because it is computed from a one-time-only administration of a measure, split-half reliability does not detect any of the errors of measurement that can occur over time (such as changes in individual respondents or changes in administration of a measure). Therefore, this procedure tends to result in a liberal or inflated estimate of reliability.

This method of reliability estimation is not appropriate for any measure that has a time limit associated with its completion. In many cases, for example, timed tests have rather easy questions; scores are a function of how many items are completed. If questions are very simple, then individuals are likely to correctly answer nearly all items that are attempted. As a result, individuals are likely to differ only in the number of questions they complete. Odd and even scores will be similar up until the point that time has expired, because most items will be answered correctly. Beyond that point, responses will also be similar because they were not answered. Consequently, a split-half reliability estimate computed on a test with a time limit will be spuriously high and meaningless.

Kuder-Richardson Reliability Estimates

Many methods other than an odd-even split are used to divide a measure to compute a split-half reliability estimate. Because the Kuder-Richardson reliability procedure takes the average of the reliability coefficients that would result from all possible ways of subdividing a measure, it helps solve the problem of how best to divide a measure for calculating reliability. (Kuder-Richardson formulas come in several different types. The most popular and the one on which this discussion is based is called K-R 20; it is the 20th formula in a series of reliability formulas discussed by George Kuder and Marion Richardson.[17]) It, too, involves the single administration of a measure. The procedure is used to determine the consistency of respondents' answers to any measure that has items scored in only two (dichotomous) categories, for example, questions on a verbal achievement test that are scored as either "right" (= 1) or "wrong" (= 0). Whereas the split-half method examines consistency of response between parts or halves of a measure, the Kuder-Richardson method assesses inter-item consistency of responses. The resulting coefficient estimates the average of the reliability coefficients that would result from all possible ways of subdividing a test.[18] Because it represents an average of all possible splits, Kuder-Richardson reliability estimates are usually lower than those obtained from split-half estimates.

In order to compute K-R 20, several pieces of information are needed on the test results for a group of individuals. As long as we can determine (a) how the group performed on each item of the test as well as (b) each individual's total test score, the coefficient can be computed. Data such as those shown in Figure 4.6 are needed to compute K-R 20. The formula for computing K-R 20 is as follows:

$$r_{tt} = \frac{k}{k-1} \left(\frac{\Sigma p_i(1 - p_i)}{\sigma_{y^2}} \right)$$

where

k = number of items on the test

p_i = proportion of examinees getting each item (i) correct

$1 - p_i$ = proportion of examiners getting each item (i) *in*correct

σ_{y^2} = variance of examiners' total test scores.

FIGURE 4.6 An Example of Data Used in Computing K-R 20 Reliability Coefficient

Applicant	Test Items								Test Score
	1	2	3	4	5	6	7	8	
Neil Anderson	1	1	1	1	1	1	1	1	8
Tammy Allen	0	0	0	1	1	1	0	1	4
Gilad Chen	1	0	1	1	1	0	1	1	6
Richard DeShon	0	0	0	0	0	0	1	1	2
Sharon Parker	1	0	1	1	0	0	0	0	3
Robert Ployhart	1	0	0	1	1	1	1	0	5
Number Correctly Answering Item	4	1	3	5	4	3	4	4	

NOTE: 0 = incorrect response; 1 = correct response.

Cronbach's Coefficient Alpha (A) Reliability Estimates

K-R 20 is a suitable approach for estimating internal consistency reliability when the items on a measure are scored with only two categories (for example, 0 = incorrect response; 1 = correct response). However, items or questions are often scored on a continuum or range of response options representing an interval scale. In Figure 3.4, for instance, we presented an example of an employee performance appraisal rating form for which total scores on the form could be used as a criterion in a selection research study. Returning again to the form, suppose that overall job performance is obtained by summing the five items on the rating form. If we want to determine how well those items, when combined, reflect an overall picture of job performance, we need a method to estimate the internal consistency of these five combined items. Kuder-Richardson reliability would not be appropriate, because each item on the rating form involves more than two response categories on an interval scale. In those cases in which we are interested in knowing the internal consistency of responses to a measure but in which responses are based on an interval scale, we can employ Cronbach's coefficient alpha (α).[19] Alpha is a general version of K-R 20 reliability. K-R 20 reliability can be used only with dichotomously scored items (for example, correct or incorrect), whereas coefficient alpha can be used with any set of items regardless of the number of points on the response scale. Like K-R 20, it represents an average reliability coefficient computed from all possible split-half reliabilities.[20] Put another way, it represents the average correlation of each item with every other item on a measure. Coefficient alpha helps us answer questions such as these: "To what degree do items on the measure seem to be measuring the same attribute?" or "How well do items on a measure hang together?" When the items are measuring the same attribute, then we expect individuals' responses across these items to be highly consistent, that is, a high coefficient alpha. If coefficient alpha reliability is unacceptably low, then the items on the selection measure may be assessing more than one characteristic. [Technical Note: We must make a few cautionary comments regarding the interpretation of coefficient alpha reliability.[21] First, alpha is a function of the number of items. With a sufficiently large number of items comprising a selection measure score (for example, 20 or more), alpha may be high even though the interrelatedness among these items is low (r = 0.30) and the score is multidimensional in nature. Second, although coefficient alpha reflects the interrelatedness among a set of items, it does not mean that the item set is necessarily unidimensional or homogeneous. If alpha for the set is low, the coefficient suggests that more than one dimension probably exists. However, if the coefficient is high (for example, in the 0.80s), then only one general dimension may be present, although it is also quite possible for several dimensions to underlie the set of items. Additional analyses are needed to make the determination.]

Let's consider in more detail another example of the use of coefficient alpha. Figure 4.7 shows the results of two sets (Case 1 and Case 2) of applicant scores on four items assessing conscientiousness. The purpose of the four items was to identify job applicants who had the "right" personality, that is, were likely to be conscientious and achievement oriented.

Case 1 illustrates the scores for one set of eight applicants, A through H. For each individual in Case 1, read down the columns and examine the scores obtained on the four items. For example, applicant A received scores of 4, 5, 5, and 4. Notice that although there were differences among the applicants on the scores received, the scores given to any one applicant were quite similar. That is, individuals in Case 1 who received high scores on one item tended to receive high scores on the other items. A similar pattern is found for those rated low on any one of the items.

FIGURE 4.7   An Example of Applicant Data in Computing Coefficient Alpha (α) Reliability

Items Used to Assess Applicant Conscientiousness—A Personality Trait	Case 1 Applicants									Case 2 Applicants						
	A	B	C	D	E	F	G	H	I	J	K	L	M	N	O	P
Item 1. Dependability	4	1	4	2	4	3	5	2	1	4	4	5	3	2	1	2
Item 2. Organized	5	1	4	2	4	4	5	2	2	3	1	4	3	3	1	5
Item 3. Hardworking	5	1	4	2	5	3	5	3	4	1	3	3	4	4	3	4
Item 4. Persistence	4	1	5	3	5	2	5	3	2	5	5	2	1	5	3	3
Total Score	18	4	17	9	18	12	20	10	9	13	13	14	11	14	8	14

NOTE: Applicants rate their behavior using the following rating scale: 1 = Strongly Disagree, 2 = Disagree, 3 = Neither Agree nor Disagree, 4 = Agree, and 5 = Strongly Agree. Case 1 coefficient alpha reliability = 0.83; Case 2 coefficient alpha reliability = 0.40.

Case 2 is different. As you read down the columns of data for applicants I through P, you can see that the scores show no apparent pattern. That is, an individual may obtain a high score on one item (such as applicant I on Item 3) yet be rated low on another (Item 1). This same, almost random pattern of ratings is true for the remaining applicants as well.

To check the internal consistency reliability of these scores, we must compute coefficient alpha reliability for both Cases 1 and 2. Because the item scores tend to go together in Case 1, there is the indication that whatever is being measured is being measured consistently. The computed coefficient alpha reliability of 0.83 confirms our conclusion that the item scores tend to hang together and measure the same construct—the underlying measure or trait. (We may not be sure just exactly what that construct is. That is a question to be answered by a validation study.) As you probably expected, coefficient alpha reliability of the scores in Case 2 is low, only 0.40. A coefficient this low suggests that the scores are unreliable and do not assess one common trait. Thus our total score does not reflect an overall assessment of an interviewee's conscientiousness. The data used in Case 2 must be improved (for example, by adding items assessing conscientiousness) prior to consideration of their use. The formula for computing coefficient alpha is conceptually similar to that of K-R 20. The only informa-tion needed is (a) individuals' total scores and (b) their responses to each item or question on the measure. The following formula summarizes the computation of coefficient alpha:

$$\alpha = \frac{k}{k-1}\left(1 - \frac{\Sigma \sigma_{i^2}}{\sigma_{y^2}}\right)$$

where

   k = number of items on the selection measure

   σ_{i^2} = variance of respondents' scores on each item (i) on the measure

   σ_{y^2} = variance of respondents' total scores on the measure.

A more convenient computational formula for coefficient alpha is

$$\alpha = \frac{k}{k-1}\left(1 - \frac{n\Sigma i^2 - \Sigma T^2}{n\Sigma X^2 - (\Sigma X)^2}\right)$$

where

   k = number of items

   n = number of persons for whom data are available

   Σi^2 = sum of the squared individual scores

   ΣT^2 = sum of the squares of the k item total scores

   ΣX^2 = sum of the squares of the n person total scores

   ΣX = sum of the n person total scores.

Data such as those shown in Figure 4.7 can be used with this formula to compute coeffi-cient alpha reliability.

K-R 20 and, in particular, coefficient alpha are two of the most commonly reported re-liability procedures in the HR selection literature today. At a minimum, users and develo-pers of selection measures should routinely compute and report these reliability estimates.

Interrater Reliability Estimates

In some measures employed in HR selection, scoring is based on the individual judg-ment of the examiner (the interviewer). In these situations, scoring depends not only on what is being rated, such as the behavior of a person, but also on the characteristics of the rater, such as the rater's biases and opinions. These two sources of scoring information contribute to errors of measurement. The rating of jobs by job analysts, the rating of subordinates' job performance by supervisors, the rating of candidates' performances in a selection interview by interviewers, and the judging of applicants' performances on a behavioral-based measure (such as answering a telephone in a simulated emergency call) are applications of measures that involve degrees of judgment in scoring. Subjective ratings of employee performance by raters pose a double problem for reliability. Unreliability of employee performance is being piled on top of the unreliability of ratings given by the rater.[22]

Conceptually, the way to estimate interrater reliability is to have at least two different ratings for the applicants or jobs being examined. If the trait or attribute is measured reliably, the two ratings should be similar or should at least roughly agree on the relative order of the applicants or jobs. However, as mentioned earlier, there are two sources of measurement error in ratings: randomness (error) in the judgments made by each judge due to the context, the candidate, and rating scales and idiosyncratic differences in rater perception (for example, halo).[23] If there is one thing we know, it is that perceptions of other people are replete with idiosyncratic biases arising from the rater's attitudes, motives, values, and the like. In fact, ratings seem to tell more about the raters than about the people they rate. *Halo error* occurs when the rater's general impressions about the candidate distorts or biases ratings of distinct traits or attributes of the person. This is one of the most serious and pervasive sources of rating errors. The tendency to consistently rate others too high or too low is another. Because the idiosyncratic biases associated with each rater are not part of the trait or attribute being measured, this form of measurement error lowers reliability. When raters agree on the rank order of applicants, their judgment is reliable as far as consistency is concerned. The determination of consistency among raters has been termed *interrater reliability.*[24] Other terms used to describe interrater reliability are *interobserver* and *interjudge* reliability.

The purpose of calculating interrater reliability estimates is to determine whether multiple raters are consistent in their judgments. Determining the proper reliability estimate, however, is quite complex, in part because of the need to account for idiosyncratic errors across raters as well as random measurement error in their judgments. Complexity is further increased because interrater agreement is often used as a form of reliability, even though it is not. The conundrum is that rater agreement is important, too; two raters should agree in their ratings or categorizations. Nevertheless, although interobserver agreement about the degree to which a job requires teamwork may be quite high, interrater reliability may be low. Although this shows that agreement is not an index of reliability, it's important to know the degree of reliability and agreement among raters performing judgmental ratings.

The computation of interrater reliability can involve any of a number of statistical procedures. Most of these procedures tend to fall into one of three categories: (a) interrater agreement, (b) interclass correlation, and (c) intraclass correlation. (A similar system of categorizing interrater reliability methods as applied to job analysis data has been developed by Edwin Cornelius.[25])

Interrater Agreement

In some rating situations, a reliability coefficient for raters is not computed; rather, rater agreement is determined. For instance, two job analysts may be observing an employee performing her job. The analysts are asked to observe the individual's task activities and then indicate whether specific job behaviors are performed. Rater agreement indices are often used in such rating situations. Percentage of rater agreement, Kendall's coefficient of concordance (W), and Cohen's kappa $(\kappa)^{26}$ are three of the most popular indices for estimating interrater agreement. Unfortunately, as has already been pointed out, some of the interrater agreement indices are not good estimators of rating reliability. For example, when the behavior being examined occurs at a very high or very low frequency, indices such as percentage of rater agreement and the coefficient of concordance may produce a spuriously high indication of agreement between raters. This is because they fail to take into consideration the degree of rater agreement due to chance. In addition, interrater agreement indices are generally restricted to nominal or categorical data that reduce their application flexibility. Although interrater agreement indices have their limitations, they are still widely employed in selection research. Percentage of rater agreement is probably the most often reported estimate in this research.

Interclass Correlation

Interclass correlations are employed when two raters make judgments about a series of targets or objects being rated (such as interviewees, jobs, subordinates). Most often, these judgments are based on an interval rating scale. The Pearson product-moment correlation (r) and Cohen's weighted kappa $(\kappa)^{27}$ are the two procedures most commonly reported as an interclass correlation. Essentially, the interclass correlation shows the amount of error between two raters. Relatively low interclass correlations indicate that more specific operational criteria for making the ratings, or additional rater training in how to apply the rating criteria, may be needed to enhance interrater reliability.

Intraclass Correlation

When three or more raters have made ratings on one or more targets, intraclass correlations can be calculated. This procedure is usually viewed as the best way to determine whether multiple raters differ in their subjective scores or ratings on the trait or behavior being assessed. Intraclass correlation shows the average relationship among raters for all targets being rated. Figure 4.8 illustrates the basic research design of a study that computed an intraclass correlation. (If only two raters were involved, the figure would depict the typical design for an interclass correlation.) In this example, each of three employment interviewers interviewed a group of job applicants. After interviewing the applicants, each interviewer rated each applicant's performance in the interview. Intraclass correlation can be used to determine how much of the difference in interviewees' ratings

FIGURE 4.8 Example of a Research Design for Computing Intraclass Correlation to Assess Interrater Reliability of Employment Interviewers

Interviewee	Interviewer		
	1	2	3
A. J. Mitra	9	8	8
N. E. Harris	5	6	5
R. C. Davis	4	3	2
•	•	•	•
•	•	•	•
•	•	•	•
T. M. Zuckerman	7	6	7

NOTE: The numbers represent hypothetical ratings of interviewees given by each interviewer.

is due to true differences in interview performance and how much is due to errors of measurement. Intraclass correlation typically reveals two types of reliability information on the raters: (a) the average reliability for one rater and (b) the average reliability for all raters making ratings. Benjamin Winer outlined the basic model and process for computing intraclass correlations. He also showed how the procedure could be used with ordinal as well as dichotomous rating data.[28]

The challenge with any indicator of interrater reliability is that the "unreliability" or disagreement can occur due to many different reasons, including (a) raters view the same behavior differently or at different times, (b) raters interpret the same behavior differently, (c) the role of idiosyncratic halo for each rater, that general impressions bias ratings of specific behaviors, (d) the sample of behavior itself may be inappropriate or misleading, or (e) error in rating or recording each impression. Yet, the problem is that any measure of interrater reliability yields only a single index, which ignores the fact that there are many potential sources of errors in observational ratings. To compound this problem, there are many different ways to calculate interrater agreement or consistency and the results they produce may markedly differ for the same data or given use. Due to this, the reader must recognize that accurately estimating interrater agreement and reliability is particularly challenging; it may require more expertise than can be conveyed in a single chapter.

Table 4.2 provides a descriptive summary of the methods we have discussed for estimating the reliability of selection measures. In addition to the questions each method addresses, the table presents information on the assumptions as well as the procedural aspects of the methods.

INTERPRETING RELIABILITY COEFFICIENTS

The chief purpose behind the use of measures in HR selection research is to permit us to arrive at sound inferences or selection decisions concerning the people to whom these measures are applied. For these judgments to have any value, they must be based on dependable data. When data are not dependable, any decisions based on this information are of dubious worth. Thus one goal of selection managers is to utilize measures that will provide dependable information.

Reliability analyses help us to determine the dependability of data we will use in selection decision making. Through reliability we can estimate the amount of error included in scores on any measure we choose to study. Knowing reliability, we can estimate how precisely or loosely a score for a measure can be interpreted. But how do we go about interpreting a reliability coefficient? What exactly does a coefficient mean? How high or low must a coefficient be for a particular measure to be used? These are but a few of the questions that can be asked while interpreting a reliability coefficient. Next we examine some of the issues that bear on the interpretation of reliability.

What Does a Reliability Coefficient Mean?

Selection measures are not simply "reliable" or "not reliable." There are degrees of reliability. As we said earlier, calculation of reliability estimates results in an index or a coefficient ranging from 0.00 to 1.00. A variety of symbols are used to indicate reliability; typically, reliability is represented by an "r" followed by two identical subscripts. For example, the following would be the reliability symbols for the four measures of X,

TABLE 4.2 Descriptive Summary of Major Methods for Estimating Reliability of Selection Measures

Reliability Method	Question Addressed	Number of Forms	Number of Administrations	Description	Assumptions	Sources of Error That Lower Reliability
Test-Retest	Are the scores on a measure consistent over time?	1	2	One version of a measure is given to the same respondents during two sessions with a time interval in between.	• Respondents do not let answers on first administration affect those on second administration. • Respondents do not "change" (for example, through learning) from one administration to the other.	• Any changes in respondents and differences in answers for test and retest due to changes occurring over time.
Parallel Forms (immediate administration)	Are the two forms of a measure equivalent?	2	1 or 2	Two versions of a measure are given to same respondents during one session.	• The two forms are parallel. • Respondents do not let completion of first version affect completion of second.	• Any differences in similarity of content between the two forms.
Parallel Forms (long-term administration)	Is the attribute assessed by a measure stable over time? Are the two forms of a measure equivalent?	2	2	Two versions of a measure are given to the same respondents during two sessions with a time interval in between.	• The two forms are parallel. • Respondents do not let completion of first version affect completion of second. • Respondents do not "change" (for example, through learning) from one administration to the other.	• Any differences in similarity of content between the two forms. • Any differences in learning with respect to topics covered by the test.

(Continued)

TABLE 4.2   (Continued)

Reliability Method	Question Addressed	Number of Forms	Number of Administrations	Description	Assumptions	Sources of Error That Lower Reliability
Split-Half (Odd-Even)	Are respondents' answers on one half (odd items) of a measure similar to answers given on the other half (even items)?	1	1	One version of a measure is given to respondents during one session.	• Splitting a measure into two halves produces two equivalent halves. • Measure is not speeded (answers are not based on a time limit).	• Any differences in similarity of item content in one half of the measure versus the other half.
Kuder-Richardson and Coefficient Alpha	To what degree do items on the measure seem to be measuring the same attribute? How well do items on a measure hang together?	1	1	One version of a measure is given to respondents during one session.	• Only one attribute is measured. • Measure is not speeded (answers are not based on a time limit). • K-R 20 is suitable for dichotomous items. • Coefficient alpha is suitable for dichotomous items and items on a continuum.	• Any differences in similarity of item content. • More than one attribute, concept, or characteristic assessed by a measure.
Interrater (Interobserver/ Interjudge)	What is the correlation between any two raters rating a group of people?	1	1	One version of a measure is given to two or more raters during one session.	• Raters are equal or interchangeable. • Raters base their ratings on what is rated; extraneous factors do not influence ratings.	• Any biases of the raters that influence the ratings that are given. • Raters who are not knowledgeable of what to rate and how to make ratings.

Y, 1, and 2: r_{xx}, r_{yy}, r_{11}, and r_{22}. (The symbol r followed by identical subscripts implies that a measure is correlated with itself.)

After the symbol, a numerical coefficient is reported. Again, the values will range from 0.00, indicating no reliability (a measure composed entirely of error), to 1.00 or perfect reliability (no error present in the measure). Without going through too many of the technical details, let's see what the coefficient means. Harold Gulliksen showed that the reliability coefficient is equivalent to the squared correlation between true and obtained scores for a measure and can be directly interpreted as the coefficient of determination.[29] Or,

$$r_{xx} = r^2_{tx}$$

where

r_{xx} = reliability coefficient

r^2_{tx} = squared correlation between true and obtained scores

x = obtained scores

t = true scores.

Therefore, the reliability coefficient can be interpreted as the extent (in percentage terms) to which individual differences in scores on a measure are due to "true" differences in the attribute measured and the extent to which they are due to chance errors. For example, if we have a test called "X," and the reliability of Test X equals 0.90 (that is, r_{xx} = 0.90), then 90 percent of the differences in test scores among individuals who took the test are due to true variance and only 10 percent due to error. The reliability coefficient provides an indication of the proportion (percent) of total differences in scores that is attributable to true differences rather than error.

The reliability coefficient summarizes the dependability of a measure for a group of individuals. It does not indicate which individuals within the group are or are not providing reliable data. When we examine a reliability coefficient, we should understand that the estimate refers to the scores of a group of individuals on a specific measuring device and not to a specific person. Thus it is quite possible to have a high reliability estimate for scores obtained from a reliable selection measure, but one or more people within the group may provide responses that contain considerable error. Unreliable performance by a respondent on a reliable measure is possible, but reliable performance on an unreliable measure is impossible.

In summary, when examining any particular reliability coefficient, consider that it is[30]

- specific to the reliability estimation method and group on which it was calculated,

- a necessary but not a sufficient condition for validity,

- based on responses from a group of individuals,

- expressed by degree, and

- determined ultimately by judgment.

How High Should a Reliability Coefficient Be?

This question has been asked many times. Different opinions exist. Unfortunately, there is no clear-cut, generally agreed upon value above which reliability is acceptable and below which it is unacceptable. Obviously, we want the coefficient to be as high as possible; however, how low a coefficient can be and still be used will depend on the purpose for which the measure is to be used. The following principle generally applies: The more critical the decision to be made, the greater the need for precision of the measure on which the decision will be based, and the higher the required reliability coefficient.[31]

In the practice of HR selection, employment decisions are based on predictors such as test scores. From the perspective of job applicants, highly reliable predictors are a necessity. In many selection situations, there are more applicants than job openings available. Competition can be keen for the available openings. Thus a difference of a few points in some applicants' scores can determine whether they do or do not get hired. Any measurement error in a predictor could seriously affect, in a negative and unfair way, some applicants' employment possibilities. You might be asking, but isn't it possible this same measurement error could produce higher scores for some applicants than might be expected, thus helping them obtain employment? Yes, it is possible for some scores to be inflated through error; yet here again, these scores could be unfair to the applicants "benefited" by errors of measurement. Because of misleading scores, organizations may be hiring these individuals and placing them in job situations they won't be able to handle. Job requirements may be too high relative to their true abilities. Although they may get the job, they may not be able to cope with it, leading to frustration and dissatisfaction for both employee and employer.

From the perspective of the organization attempting to hire executives or other key personnel (whose decisions may affect the success of the entire organization), reliable evidence of applicants' qualifications is also a necessity. The cost of being wrong in the assessment of key managerial personnel can be very high. Imprecise predictors can have long-term consequences for an organization. Dependable predictors are essential for accurately evaluating these key personnel.

But what about criteria? Isn't it just as important that criterion measures be reliable? Of course, criterion measures (such as employees' performance appraisal ratings) should be reliable. However, in the context of personnel selection decision making, their reliability need not be as high as that of predictors for them to be useful.[32] When predictors are used, they are generally employed to make individual decisions, for example, "How does one applicant's score compare with another?" or "Did the applicant make a passing score?" When scores are used for making decisions about individuals, it is critical that the measure used to produce these scores be highly reliable.

In contrast, selection researchers often employ criterion data to examine attributes that may be related to job performance. Employment decisions about individuals are not made with criteria; therefore, reliability coefficients need not be as high. However, as we see in the next chapter, it will not be possible to show empirical validity of a predictor if the criterion with which it is being correlated is not reliable.

Several writers have offered some rough guidelines regarding desirable magnitudes of reliability coefficients for selection measures.[33] Although these guidelines are based on astute logic, we do not believe it is prudent to propose a specific set of guidelines (for example, reliability must be 0.70 or higher) because they soon become self-propagating "crutches" applied without sufficient thought about the problems created by measurement error. A reliability estimate reflects the amount of error in a set of scores from a measure specific to the group on which it is calculated. It can be higher in one situation than another because of situational circumstances that may or may not affect the preciseness (reliability) of measurement. (For further information on this point, see the following sections on factors influencing the reliability of a measure and the standard error of measurement.) We believe test users must consider the specific circumstances surrounding their situations to determine how much measurement error they are willing to put up with. Stated another way, the user must use her best judgment to determine whether it is feasible or important to strive to reduce the influence of random error on her measures. A number of factors can influence the size of an observed reliability coefficient. By accounting for the impact of these factors, such as the range of talent in the respondent group, a specific test user should be able to determine whether a reliability coefficient is adequate for the purpose being considered. To clarify how these factors can influence reliability in a context involving selection measures, let's briefly examine several factors.

Factors Influencing the Reliability of a Measure

As we have discussed, a reliability coefficient is an estimate. Many factors can have an effect on the actual magnitude of a coefficient. Here, we mention nine important factors that can affect estimated reliability: (a) method of estimating reliability, (b) stability, (c) sample, (d) individual differences among respondents, (e) length of a measure, (f) test question difficulty, (g) homogeneity of a measure's content, (h) response format, and (i) administration and scoring of a measure.

Method of Estimating Reliability

We have seen that different procedures for reliability account for different errors of measurement. One result is that different reliability estimates will be obtained on a measure simply from the choice of procedure used to calculate the estimate. This makes sense because each procedure focuses on a different subset of errors that can occur. For example, test-retest examines consistency of results on retesting, while equivalent forms focuses on errors from form to form. Consequently, some methods will tend to give higher (upper-bound) estimates, whereas others will tend to be lower (lower-bound) in their estimates of the true reliability of a measure. Therefore, it is important for any individual evaluating a particular selection procedure to know which procedure was used and to know what methods tend to give higher and lower estimates, and why that is so.

Figure 4.9 presents a rough characterization of relative reliability in terms of whether methods tend to give upper- or lower-bound estimates of a measure's true reliability, other things being equal. We discuss a few of these "other things"—factors that can affect reliability—in this section. It is important to emphasize that the hierarchy in Figure 4.9 is based on general results reported for selected measures. In any one specific situation, it is possible that the rank order of methods may vary; a method characterized as usually providing lower-bound reliability may in fact give a higher estimate than one generally ranked above it.

Parallel forms reliability usually provides a lower estimate than other techniques because it may account for changes occurring over time as well as differences from one form or version of a measure to another. These changes contribute to errors of measurement. If a test is measuring more than one attribute, Kuder-Richardson or coefficient alpha reliability will underestimate true reliability; if a measure has a time limit, reliability will be overestimated by the procedure. Because of memory, test-retest reliability will likely be high, but as the time interval between administrations lengthens, memory will have less impact and estimated reliability will fall. The effect on reliability of lengthening the time interval between administrations will be similar for parallel forms reliability as well.

Individual Differences Among Respondents

Another factor influencing a reliability estimate is the range of individual differences or variability among respondents on the attribute measured. If the range of differences in scores on the attribute measured by a selection device is wide, the device can more reliably distinguish among people. Generally speaking, the greater the variability or standard deviation of scores on the characteristic measured, the higher the reliability of the measure of that characteristic.

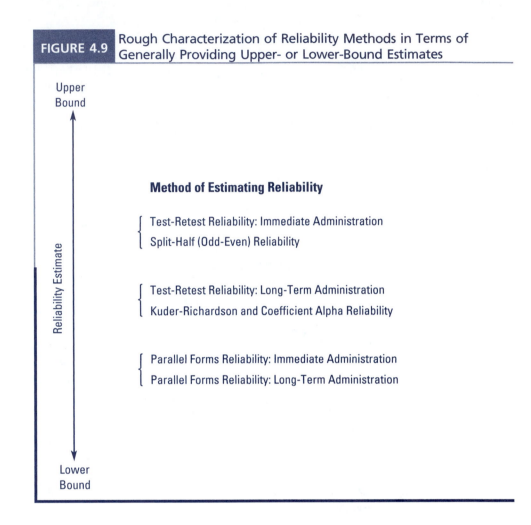

FIGURE 4.9 Rough Characterization of Reliability Methods in Terms of Generally Providing Upper- or Lower-Bound Estimates

Upper Bound

Reliability Estimate

Method of Estimating Reliability

{ Test-Retest Reliability: Immediate Administration
Split-Half (Odd-Even) Reliability

{ Test-Retest Reliability: Long-Term Administration
Kuder-Richardson and Coefficient Alpha Reliability

{ Parallel Forms Reliability: Immediate Administration
Parallel Forms Reliability: Long-Term Administration

Lower Bound

In part, this finding is based on the conception of reliability and its calculation by means of a correlation coefficient. Change or variation within a person, such as changing a response from one administration to another, detracts from reliability; we have already discussed this issue as errors of measurement. On the other hand, differences among respondents are considered to be true differences. Such true variation contributes to reliability. Therefore, if variability or individual differences increase among respondents (true) while variation within individuals (error) remains the same, reliability will increase. Range of ability in the group of individuals being assessed is not something that can usually be controlled or manipulated. However, it should be kept in mind when reviewing reliability coefficients. For example, our criteria are often relatively homogeneous; low performers are fired or quit and high performers are transferred and promoted. In such settings, the total variance is likely to be smaller while the error variance is not reduced. Thus, the ratio of error to total variance increases, resulting in an underestimate of criterion reliability. Consequently, a reliability coefficient of 0.75 for a predictor might be acceptable in a very homogeneous group of people but unacceptable in a very heterogeneous group. Because individual differences can vary a great deal for some groups, such as those differences based on educational level or age, it is imperative that the user of selection measures review reliability data for relevant groups of respondents. Developers and publishers of commercially available predictors should report, at a minimum, separate reliability coefficients and predictor standard deviations for such respondent groups.

Stability

Reliability estimates that examine whether scores of a given test are consistent from time to time (test-retest) may be affected by the stability on the construct assessed by the test itself, as well as stability in measurement over time. That is, some of the characteristics and behaviors assessed through selection tests or job-relevant criteria may be subject to theoretically relevant change over time. For example, measures of anxiety or emotion are usually seen as less stable than constructs related to mechanical verbal abilities. Instability in scores on a test of mood over time would reflect "true" variance as well as measurement error. This underscores a point made earlier, that judgments about the reliability of test scores must be made in relation to what the predictor or criterion attempts to assess. To the extent scores of a given test assess relatively enduring characteristics or stable behaviors, fluctuations in scores from time to time are more likely to be due to measurement error. This is an important consideration, since the *Principles for the Validation and Use of Personnel Selection Procedures*[34] encourages employers to provide opportunities for reassessment of applicants, whenever technically and administratively feasible.

Sample

Results obtained from a sample should be "representative" of the population or situation in which the measure is to be used. Representativeness depends on both the choice of participants and the number of respondents. Individuals should be selected to be similar to the population with respect to sex, race, religion, and so forth, as well as ability, motivation, and prior experience with the measures. Of equal importance is precision of estimates. The precision of a reliability coefficient, like any other statistical parameter estimate (mean, standard deviation, and so on) is significantly affected by sample size. Larger sample sizes are important to ensure the influence of random errors is normally distributed, and therefore enables the sample estimate to better reflect the population parameter. As this suggests, the size and representativeness of the sample, not the size of the population itself, is the critical issue. A good sample estimate requires a sample size of at least 100 and preferably 200 participants.[35]

Length of a Measure

In general, as the length of a measure increases, its reliability also increases. One way of thinking about this relationship is to look out a window for a second or two and then try to describe in detail what you saw. As you increase the number of times you look out the window in one- to two-second intervals, you will probably find that the accuracy and details of your description increase. With increasing measurement, that is, observations, your description begins to approximate the true situation outside the window. A similar effect occurs when a selection measure is lengthened. Only a sample of possible items is used on a given measure. If all possible questions could be used, a person's score on the measure would closely approximate his or her true score. Therefore, as we add more and more relevant items to our measure, we get a more precise and reliable assessment of the individual's true score on the attribute measured. Figure 4.10 illustrates the link between selection measure length, probability of measuring the true score, and test reliability. Initially, we have a universe of all possible test items. As we select test items from the universe and double the test length from 5, 10, 20, … , 80 items, we see that the probability of measuring the true score increases. Using the Spearman-Brown prophecy formula we discussed earlier, we can see that reliability also increases, from 0.20 for a 5-item test to 0.80 for an 80-item test. If we were to continue these calculations, we would see that the

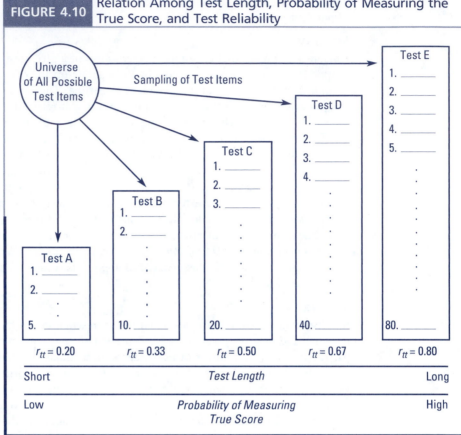

| FIGURE 4.10 | Relation Among Test Length, Probability of Measuring the True Score, and Test Reliability |

reliability of an unreliable short test increases rapidly as similar test items are added. However, after a point, these improvements in reliability begin to diminish with increasing test length.

A variation of the Spearman-Brown formula mentioned earlier and shown here can be used to determine how much a measure must be lengthened to obtain a desired reliability:

$$n = \frac{t_{ttd}(1 - r_{tt})}{r_{tt}(1 - r_{ttd})}$$

where

n = number of times a measure must be lengthened

r_{ttd} = desired level of reliability *after* the measure is lengthened

r_{tt} = reliability of the test *before* the measure is lengthened.

Suppose, for instance, the reliability of a 10-item test is 0.75. The selection researcher desires that the reliability should be 0.90. Substitution in the formula shows that to obtain the desired level of reliability, the test must be three times as long, or 30 items. It should be noted however, that gains in reliability due to test length are also influenced by the interrelations among the items. Thus, if one adds items that measure different things than those intended by the test, this will also affect reliability and it should. Other item characteristics that affect reliability estimates are discussed next.

Test Question Difficulty

When an employment test, such as an ability test, contains questions that are scored as either "right" or "wrong," the difficulty of the questions will affect the differences among job applicants' test scores. If the items are very difficult or very easy, differences among individuals' scores will be reduced because many will have roughly the same test score, either very low or very high.

As an example, refer to Figure 4.11. Suppose we administered a single test question to a group of 10 applicants. Upon answering the question, applicants fell into one of two

FIGURE 4.11	Illustration of the Relation Between Test Question Difficulty and Test Discriminability

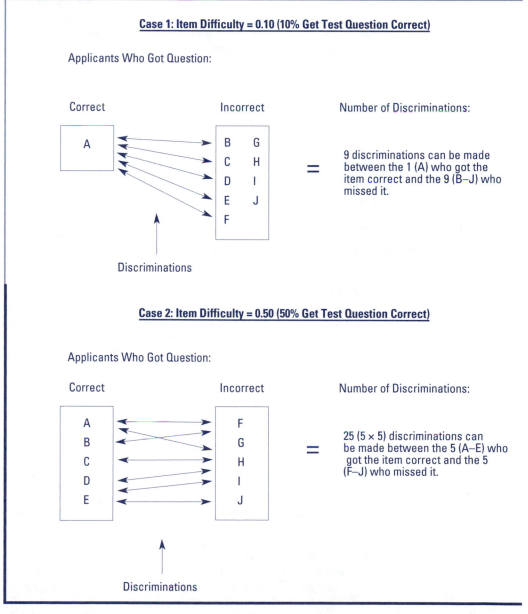

Case 1: Item Difficulty = 0.10 (10% Get Test Question Correct)

Applicants Who Got Question:

Correct   Incorrect   Number of Discriminations:

A   B G   = 9 discriminations can be made between the 1 (A) who got the item correct and the 9 (B–J) who missed it.
C H
D I
E J
F

Discriminations

Case 2: Item Difficulty = 0.50 (50% Get Test Question Correct)

Applicants Who Got Question:

Correct   Incorrect   Number of Discriminations:

A   F   = 25 (5 × 5) discriminations can be made between the 5 (A–E) who got the item correct and the 5 (F–J) who missed it.
B   G
C   H
D   I
E   J

Discriminations

categories: those who answered the question correctly and those who missed it. In Case 1, only 1 person (10 percent of the applicants) answers correctly. We can discriminate between that 1 individual and the 9 who missed it, a total of 9 comparisons or discriminations ($1 \times 9 = 9$ discriminations). We can also make the same number of discriminations if 9 answer correctly and only 1 misses the question ($9 \times 1 = 9$ discriminations).

If, as in Case 2, 5 applicants (50 percent) answer the question correctly and 5 miss it, we can make significantly more discriminations. In this case, we can make 25 discriminations (5×5 discriminations) between pairs of applicants from the two groups. We learned earlier that increasing variability in scores increases reliability. Therefore, because variability or variance in scores increases with greater numbers of discriminations, reliability of a selection test is enhanced.

Test questions of moderate difficulty (where roughly half or 50 percent of the test takers answer a question correctly) will spread out the test scores. Due to the greater range in individual scores, finer distinctions among test takers can be made. Test questions of moderate difficulty permit these finer distinctions, and tests that contain many items of moderate difficulty tend to be more reliable than those tests with many items that are either very difficult or very easy.

Homogeneity of a Measure's Content

In our discussion of Kuder-Richardson and coefficient alpha reliability, we noted that both of these internal consistency methods represent the average correlation among all items on a measure. To the extent that items on a measure do not relate to all other items on the same measure, internal consistency reliability will fall. Internal consistency reliability can be enhanced in several ways. First, new items can be added to a measure that are comparable in quality to and measure the same construct as the original items that compose the measure. Second, items on the measure that do not correlate with each other or with the total score on the measure can be eliminated. Either of these steps will enhance the homogeneity of a measure's content and, therefore, increase internal consistency reliability.

Response Format

Any factor that systematically contributes to differences among individuals' scores on a measure will enhance the reliability of the measure. One factor that will contribute to these differences is the response format for recording answers to a selection measure. As the number of response options or categories on a measure increases, reliability also increases. Suppose interviewers are using a 10-item rating form to judge the suitability of interviewees for a job. Answers to the 10 items are summed to obtain an overall employment suitability score for each interviewee. If each item has only two rating options (for example, 1 = unsuitable; 2 = suitable), then the only possible total scores range from 10 to 20. However, if five rating options are given for each of the 10 items, then possible scores can range from 10 to 50. Finer distinctions among interviewees can potentially be made with the latter scale. This scale can produce a greater spread in interviewees' employment suitability scores, thus enhancing reliability. Up to a point, reliability can be enhanced by increasing the number of possible scores possible for a selection measure. For instance, research has shown that the reliability of rating scales can be improved by offering from five to nine rating categories.[36]

Administration and Scoring of a Measure

As we have noted, various factors we call errors of measurement can have a bearing on the reliability of a measure. For example, emotional and physical states of respondents, lack of rapport with the measure's administrator, unpleasant conditions (too noisy or too cold) during the measure's administration, respondents' inadequate knowledge of how to respond to the measure, and inconsistent scoring of responses can contribute to errors of measurement. Where errors of measurement are present, reliability is lowered. This underscores the importance of standardizing measure administration and scoring, as this helps reduce these errors.

Standard Error of Measurement

We have just seen that reliability coefficients are useful for describing the general stability or homogeneity of a measure. The coefficient gives us some degree of assurance of the dependability of most respondents' scores on a measure. However, the various methods of computing reliabilities that we have discussed do not give us an idea of the error to be expected in a particular individual's score on the measure. Reliability is a group-based statistic.

To obtain an estimate of the error for an individual, we can use another statistic called the *standard error of measurement*. The statistic is simply a number in the same measurement units as the measure for which it is being calculated. The higher the standard error, the more error present in the measure, and the lower its reliability. Thus the standard error of measurement is not another approach to estimating reliability; it is just another way of expressing it (using the test's standard deviation units). The formula for calculating the standard error is as follows:

$$\sigma_{meas} = \sigma_x \sqrt{1 - r_{xx}}$$

where

σ_{meas} = the standard error of measurement for measure X

σ_x = the standard deviation of obtained scores on measure X

r_{xx} = the reliability of measure X.

For example, let's assume that the mathematics ability test that we referred to earlier has a reliability of 0.90 and a standard deviation of 10. The standard error of measurement for a mathematics ability score on this test would be calculated as follows:

$$10\sqrt{1 - 0.90} = 10\sqrt{0.10} = 0.10(0.316) = 3.16$$

To illustrate how the standard error of measurement can be applied, let's look at an example. Suppose an applicant came into our employment office, took our math ability test, and made a score of 50. We could use the standard error to estimate the degree his or her test score would vary if he or she were retested another day. By adding and subtracting the standard error from the math test score (50 ± 3.16), we would obtain a range of math ability scores (46.84 to 53.16). One possible interpretation of this range might be that the chances are two to one that the applicant's true math ability lies somewhere between 46.8 and 53.2. Alternatively, we could say that if he or she were given the test 100 times, we would expect that roughly two-thirds (68 percent) of the time the math ability scores would fall within the range of 46.8 to 53.2.

The standard error of measurement possesses several useful application characteristics. First, the measure is useful in that it forces us to think of scores on a measure not as exact points but as approximations represented by a band or range of scores. Because selection measure scores contain error, an individual's score on a measure is only one of a variety of possible scores the individual could have obtained. We should think of every selection measure score as an approximation.

Second, the standard error of measurement can aid decision making in which only one individual is involved. For instance, suppose a passing or cutoff score on a test was set for a nuclear power facility operator's job. The job itself involves operations that could drastically affect the safety of both workers and citizens. If an individual applicant scores within 2 points of the passing score and the standard error of measurement for the test is 4 points, there is a very good chance that the employment decision will be in error. For this reason, the employer may consider only those applicants that score a minimum of one standard error of measurement above the passing score.

It's important to note that the standard error of measurement can also determine whether scores for individuals differ significantly from one another. For instance, imagine that two job applicants had taken our math ability test. Jacob Farrar scored 50; Alicia Tatum scored 47. Can we conclude that Jacob is the better applicant solely because of math ability as measured by the one test score? The standard error of measurement can help us decide. If our standard error is 3.16 and the difference between our two applicants' scores is 3, then it is entirely possible that the difference in scores is due to chance. On retesting, Alicia may score higher than Jacob.

This same principle also applies to a measure administered to a large group of individuals. If we administer and score a test for 50 job applicants, we can rank the applicants on the basis of their test scores from high to low. If the standard error of measurement is large relative to the differences among these scores (standard deviation), then our rank order is likely to change if the applicants are retested. In general, the higher the standard error, the more susceptible our rank order of test scores is subject to change upon retesting. As you can see, with a large standard error, it may simply be due to chance that one individual scored higher than a group of others. Without an error index, we may assume these differences are meaningful and make employment decisions on the basis of these differences. With this index, however, we are in a better position to determine who really scored significantly higher or lower on a measure.

With respect to interpreting differences in individuals' scores, Lewis Aiken has offered the following guidelines:

1. The difference between two individuals' scores should not be considered significant unless the difference is at least twice the standard error of measurement of the measure.

2. Before the difference between scores of the same individual on two different measures should be treated as significant, the difference should be greater than twice the standard error of measurement of either measure.[37]

The standard error of measurement is also used to establish how confident we may be in scores obtained from different groups of respondents. For example, suppose we had administered a test to 100 male and 100 female job applicants. For the male applicants, reliability for the test was 0.85 (standard deviation = 26); for the female applicants, it was 0.70 (standard deviation = 10). On the face of reliability information alone, we might have more confidence in individual scores obtained for men than in those for women. However, when we use the reliability data and standard deviation information to compute the standard error, we find that the standard error of measurement for men is 10.1, and for women it is 5.5. Therefore, we should have greater confidence in a female applicant's test score than we should in a male applicant's score. This example highlights an important conclusion: Without considering the variability of the group on the attribute measured (the standard deviation), reliability information alone will not permit us to compare relative confidence in scores for individuals in different groups. Because the standard error is not affected by group variability, the statistic can enable us to make this important comparison.

In using the standard error of measurement, we have implicitly made an important assumption: that is, a score on a measure is equally accurate for the complete range of scores. However, it is possible that a test may be more accurate for one range of scores than for another. For example, our math ability test may be a more accurate predictor for individuals scoring about average in math ability than for those scoring high. Yet, even where this assumption may be violated, the standard error of measurement offers many advantages as an overall estimate of error.[38]

The standard error of measurement is a statistic you will likely come across in reading and studying various commercially available predictors (in particular, tests) to be used in selection. It is one of the most popular measures used in reporting test results because it serves as a corrective for the tendency to place undue weight on one measurement. The measure has become so popular that the College Board includes information on the standard error of measurement and its interpretation when it sends results to people who take the college admissions Scholastic Aptitude Test (SAT)[39]

Because of its importance, the statistic should be routinely reported with each reliability coefficient computed for a measure. In practice, if you want to make a cursory comparison of the reliability of different measures, you can use the reliability coefficient. However, to obtain a complete picture of the dependability of information produced by a measure and to help interpret individual scores on the measure, the standard error of measurement is essential.

Evaluating Reliability Coefficients

From our discussion of reliability, you probably recognize that many issues must be considered in evaluating reliability coefficients. We have noted throughout our discussion that the estimation of the reliability of selection measures is one essential requirement in appropriately applying these measures. Some users may believe that commercially available measures will provide all requisite information, and the determination and assessment of reliability data will not be necessary. Past experience with some commercially available measures suggests otherwise. The Buros Institute of Mental Measurements reviewed more than 1,000 commercially available tests published in *The Eighth Mental Measurements Yearbook*. Its results on the availability of reliability information were not encouraging. For the tests listed, the Institute found that

- over 22 percent appeared without any reliability information,

- 7 percent showed neither reliability nor validity data,

- 9 percent showed no reliability data for certain subtests or forms, and

- 28 percent did not report any normative data.[40]

These facts suggest that one should not assume reliability information will be provided just because a user purchases a test from an apparently reputable test publisher. Any user should carefully search for and insist on reliability information about selection measures. Without such information, scores on tests are, essentially, uninterpretable.

Assuming such information can be found, the next step is to systematically evaluate the reported data. To facilitate the evaluation of reliability data, we have summarized, in question form, some of the issues you should consider. These questions are listed in Table 4.3. All of the questions have been addressed in this chapter. When examining reliability coefficients of selection measures, this checklist can serve as a useful means for reviewing the major considerations involved in reliability interpretation.

TABLE 4.3	Questions to Consider in Evaluating Reliability Coefficients

Question	Comment
1. Does the coefficient reflect the precision of a measure by indicating how well items hang together in measuring an attribute?	If interest is in determining the degree to which items on a measure are assessing the same content, an internal consistency estimate is appropriate.
2. Does the coefficient reflect the stability of an attribute as assessed by a specific measure over time?	If stability of performance is of interest, some form of test-retest reliability should be reported.
a. Is the interval between test and retest so short that memory could influence scores?	Depending on the situation, the interval should not be shorter than several weeks.
b. Is the interval between test and retest so long that learning or other changes in respondents could have occurred?	Depending on the situation, the interval should not be longer than six months; a typical interval is six to eight weeks.
c. Is the coefficient based on parallel forms of a measure administered over time?	If so, are data available to indicate that the forms are indeed parallel or roughly equivalent?
d. Is a test-retest coefficient computed for a measure that can be expected to change because of the nature of the attribute being measured?	Some measures can be expected to change over time because of their nature. Examples might include performance ratings and attitudinal measures.
3. Do scores on the measure for which the coefficient is computed depend on how quickly respondents can respond to the measure? Is a time limit involved?	If a time limit for completing a measure is involved, the coefficient should not be based on an internal consistency estimate.
4. Is the coefficient based on respondents like those for whom a measure is being considered?	A coefficient is more meaningful if it is based on a group like the one to which the measure will be administered. For example, if a measure is going to be given to job applicants, a coefficient should be available for similar job applicants.
5. Is the coefficient based on a large enough number of people that confidence can be placed on the magnitude of the coefficient?	The larger the sample size on which the coefficient is based, the more dependable the estimate of reliability. A sample size of at least 100, and preferably 200, is desired.
6. Is information provided on the range of ability for the attribute measured of the group on which the coefficient is based?	Standard deviations and ranges of scores should be given for each group on which a coefficient is reported.
7. Is a standard error of measurement provided for the reliability coefficient?	An index of the standard error of measurement should be given for each coefficient.
Once these questions have been addressed, then a user may ask:	
8. Is the coefficient high enough to warrant *use of the measure*?	The more important the selection decision (that will be based on a specific measure), the higher the required reliability coefficient.

Source: Questions 3, 4, 5, and 7 are based in part on Alexander G. Wesman, *Reliability and Confidence* (Test Service Bulletin No. 44) (New York: The Psychological Corporation, May 1952), p. 7.

Reliability: A Concluding Comment

In this chapter, we have discussed the concept of reliability of measurement and reviewed various approaches to its determination. Although the assessment and interpretation of reliability can be complex, it nevertheless is a fundamental element to the proper use of HR selection measures. As we see in Chapter 5, the validity of a measure depends on its reliability; reliability of predictor scores and criterion scores is necessary, but not sufficient, for a score's validity or interpretation. The validity of a score or the appropriateness of the inferences based on that score cannot be made if the measure is not reliable. Knowledge of reliability information and other associated statistics (such as the standard error of measurement) is critical for making accurate assessments and decisions about individuals seeking employment.

REFERENCES

1. Ulrich Tholl, Klaus Forstner, and Manfred Anlauf, "Measuring Blood Pressure: Pitfalls and Recommendations," *Nephrology Dialysis Transplantation* 19, no. 4 (April 2004): 766–770.

2. Daniel W. Jones, Lawrence J. Appel, Sheldon G. Sheps, Edward J. Roccella, and Claude Lenfant, "Measuring Blood Pressure Accurately: New and Persistent Challenges," *Journal of the American Medical Association* 289, no. 8 (2003): 1027–1030; Anne Marie de Greef and Andrew Shennan, "Blood Pressure Measuring Devices: Ubiquitous, Essential, But Imprecise," *Expert Review of Medical Devices* 5, no. 5 (2008): 573–579.

3. Pater Cornel, "Beyond the Evidence of the New Hypertension Guidelines. Blood Pressure Measurement—Is It Good Enough for Accurate Diagnosis of Hypertension? Time Might Be in, for a Paradigm Shift (I)," *Current Controlled Trials in Cardiovascular Medicine* 6 (2005): 1.

4. Ibid.

5. Tholl, Forstner, and Anlauf, "Measuring Blood Pressure: Pitfalls and Recommendations."

6. Our treatment of reliability is based on a classical reliability theory. Other developments have offered alternative approaches to the study of reliability theory [see, for example, Lee J. Cronbach, Goldine C. Gleser, Harinder Nanda, and Nageswari Rajaratnam, *The Dependability of Behavioral Measurements: Theory of Generalizability for Scores and Profiles* (New York: John Wiley, 1972)]; however, for the beginning student, our approach will suffice. For a full treatment, see Kevin R. Murphy, "Models and Methods for Evaluating Reliability and Validity," in *Oxford Handbook of Personnel Psychology,* ed. Susan Cartwright and Gary L. Cooper (London: Oxford University Press, 2008), 263–290.

7. Our discussion of "errors of measurement" primarily assumes that these errors occur at random. Robert M. Guion, *Assessment, Measurement, and Prediction for Personnel Decisions* (London: Lawrence Erlbaum Associates, 1998), 221–226 distinguishes between random and constant or systematic errors. Constant errors appear consistently with repeated measurement, whereas random errors affect different measurements to different degrees.

8. Guion, *Assessment, Measurement, and Prediction for Personnel Decisions.*

9. Milton Blum and James Naylor, *Industrial Psychology: Its Social and Theoretical Foundations* (New York: Harper & Row, 1968), 41.

10. Susana Urbina, *Essentials of Psychological Testing* (Hoboken, NJ: John Wiley, 2004).

11. Gary Groth-Marnat, *Handbook of Psychological Assessment*, 4th ed. (New Jersey: John Wiley, 2003); Murphy, "Models and Methods for Evaluating Reliability and Validity."

12. John E. Hunter and Frank L. Schmidt, *Methods of Meta-Analysis: Correcting Error and Bias in Research Findings* (Newbury Park, CA: Sage Publications, 2004).

13. Groth-Marnat, *Handbook of Psychological Assessment.*

14. In practice, the coefficient must be "corrected" by use of the Spearman-Brown prophecy formula. The application of this formula is discussed later in this section.

15. Neal Schmitt and David Chan, *Personnel Selection: A Theoretical Approach* (Newbury Park, CA: Sage Publications, 1998).

16. Urbina, *Essentials of Psychological Testing*; Murphy, "Models and Methods for Evaluating Reliability and Validity."

17. George F. Kuder and Marion W. Richardson, "The Theory of the Estimation of Test Reliability," *Psychometrika* 2 (1937): 151–160.

18. Anne Anastasi and Susana Urbina, *Psychological Testing,* 7th ed. (Upper Saddle River, NJ: Prentice Hall, 1997).

19. Lee J. Cronbach, "Coefficient Alpha and the Internal Structure of Tests," *Psychometrika* 16 (1951): 297–334; M. C. Rodriquez and Y. Maeda, "Meta Analysis of Coefficient Alpha," *Psychological Methods* 11 (2006): 306–322.

20. Jose Cortina, "What Is Coefficient Alpha? An Examination of Theory and Applications," *Journal of Applied Psychology* 78 (1993): 98–104. Cortina notes that alpha is equal to the mean of all split-half reliabilities only if selection measure item standard deviations are equal. The greater the differences among item standard deviations, the smaller alpha reliability will be relative to the average of these split-half reliabilities.

21. This discussion is based on Cortina, "What Is Coefficient Alpha? An Examination of Theory and Applications."

22. Hunter and Schmidt, *Methods of Meta-Analysis: Correcting Error and Bias in Research Findings;* James M. LeBreton and Jenell L. Senter, "Answers to 20 Questions about Interrater Reliability and Interrater Agreement," *Organizational Research Methods,* 11 (2008): 815–852.

23. Frank L. Schmidt, Chockalingam Viswesvaran, and Deniz S. Ones, "Reliability Is Not Validity and Validity Is Not Reliability," *Personnel Psychology* 53 (2000): 901–912.

24. For a discussion of interrater reliability issues in the context of collecting personnel selection data (such as job analysis data) through observation methods, see Mark J. Martinko, "Observing the Work," in *The Job Analysis Handbook for Business, Industry, and Government,* ed. Sidney Gael (New York: John Wiley, 1987), 419–431; and Sandra K. Mitchell, "Interobserver Agreement, Reliability, and Generalizability of Data Collected in Observational Studies," *Psychological Bulletin* 86 (1979): 376–390.

25. Edwin T. Cornelius, "Analyzing Job Analysis Data" in *The Job Analysis Handbook for Business, Industry, and Government,* ed. Sidney Gael (New York: John Wiley, 1987), 353–368.

26. Jacob Cohen, "A Coefficient of Agreement for Nominal Scales," *Educational and Psychological Measurement* 32 (1972): 37–46; Maurice G. Kendall and Alan Stuart, *The Advanced Theory of Statistics,* 4th ed. (London: Griffin, 1977).

27. Jacob Cohen, "Weighted Kappa: Nominal Scale Agreement with Provision for Scaled Disagreement or Partial Credit," *Psychological Bulletin* 70 (1968): 213–230.

28. Benjamin J. Winer, Donald R. Brown, and Kenneth M. Michels, *Statistical Principles in Experimental Design,* 3rd ed. (New York: McGraw-Hill, 1991).

29. Harold Gulliksen, *Theory of Mental Tests* (New York: John Wiley, 1950).

30. Guion, *Assessment, Measurement, and Prediction for Personnel Decisions;* Urbina, *Essentials of Psychological Testing;* and Murphy, "Models and Methods for Evaluating Reliabilty and Validity."

31. Elazur J. Pedhazur and Liora Pedhazur Schmelkin, *Measurement, Design, and Analysis: An Integrated Approach* (London: Lawrence Erlbaum Associates, 1991); and Alexander G. Wesman,

Reliability and Confidence, Test Service Bulletin No. 44 (New York: The Psychological Corporation, May 1952), 3.

32. Groth-Marnat, *Handbook of Psychological Assessment;* Guion, *Assessment, Measurement, and Prediction for Personnel Decisions;* and Pedhazur and Schmelkin, *Measurement, Design, and Analysis: An Integrated Approach.*

33. Jum C. Nunnally and Ira Bernstein, *Psychometric Theory* (New York: McGraw-Hill, 1994); and Elliot A. Weiner and Barbara J. Stewart, *Assessing Individuals* (Boston: Little, Brown, and Company, 1984).

34. Society of Industrial-Organizational Psychology, Inc., *Principles for the Validation and Use of Personnel Selection Procedures,* 4th ed. (Bowling Green, OH: Society of Industrial-Organizational Psychology, 2003).

35. Wesman, *Reliability and Confidence.*

36. Paul E. Spector, *Summated Rating Scale Construction: An Introduction* (Newbury Park, CA: Sage Publications, 1992).

37. Lewis R. Aiken, *Psychological Testing and Assessment,* 2nd ed. (Boston: Allyn & Bacon, 1988).

38. Groth-Marnat, *Handbook of Psychological Assessment;* Guion, *Assessment, Measurement, and Prediction for Personnel Decisions;* and Urbina, *Essentials of Psychological Testing.*

39. Anne Anastasi, "Mental Measurement: Some Emerging Trends," in *The Ninth Mental Measurements Yearbook,* ed. James V. Mitchell (Lincoln, NE: Buros Institute of Mental Measurements, University of Nebraska, 1985), xxiii–xxix.

40. James V. Mitchell, "Testing and the Oscar Buros Lament: From Knowledge to Implementation to Use," in *Social and Technical Issues in Testing,* ed. Barbara S. Plake (Hillsdale, NJ: Lawrence Erlbaum Associates, 1984), 114–115.

Validity of Selection Procedures

AN OVERVIEW OF VALIDITY

In the last chapter, we pointed out that *reliability* is one important characteristic we must have from data produced by any test, interview, or other selection procedures we may use. So far, we have examined in some detail various issues regarding the reliability of information from selection measures. Here, we focus on the topic of *validity,* its relation to reliability, and the principal analytic strategies available for determining the validity of selection procedure data. Validity represents the most important characteristic of data from measures used in HR selection. It shows what is assessed by selection measures and determines the kinds of conclusions we can draw from data such measures produce.

Validity: A Definition

When we are concerned with the accuracy of judgments or inferences made from scores on selection measures, such as predictors, we are interested in their *validity.* In this sense, **validity** refers to *the degree to which available evidence supports inferences made from scores on selection procedures.* From the perspective of human resource selection and selection procedure validity, we are most interested in evidence that supports inferences regarding a selection procedure's job relatedness. We want to evaluate our inferences; that is, we want to know how accurate are the predictions we have made (predictions based on data collected from a selection procedure such as an employment interview or personality inventory) about employee work behaviors (such as absenteeism, turnover, dollar sales, service to customers, or other important aspects of job performance).[1]

One way to illustrate the process of inference making from a measure's scores is to think of a common measure that many of us often make—a simple handshake. Think of the last time you met someone for the first time and shook that person's hand. How did the hand feel? Cold? Clammy? Rough? Firm grip? Limp grip? Did you make attributions about that person? For example, if the person's hand was rough, did you conclude, "He must do physical labor"? If it was clammy and cold, did you think, "She must be anxious or nervous"? If you received a "limp" grip, did you deduce, "He must not be assertive"? If you had these or similar feelings, you drew inferences from a measure. (As an aside, you might be wondering: Are job interviewees' handshakes associated with applicant personality characteristics such as extraversion? Are they related to how interviewers judge interviewees? Several studies have confirmed that firmness of handshakes is positively associated with interviewees' level of extraversion and interviewers' ratings of interviewees. Moreover, the relationship between handshake firmness and interviewers' ratings of women was particularly strong. Thus, if you are meeting an interviewer for the first time, it is probably wise to make that first handshake a firm one!)[2] Our next question is, What is the evidence to support the inferences we have drawn? We study validity to collect evidence on inferences we can make from our measures.

In the context of selection, we want to know how well a predictor (such as a test) is related to criteria important to us. If a predictor is correlated with job performance criteria, then we can draw inferences from scores on the measure about individuals' future job performance in terms of these criteria. For example, if we have an ability test that is related to job performance, then scores on the test can be used to infer a job candidate's ability to perform the job in question. Because test scores are related to job performance, we can be assured that, on average, applicants who score high on the test will do well on the job.

Historically, people have tended to think of the validity of a measurement *procedure*. Actually, it is not the procedure itself or the content of the measure (such as test items) that are valid; it is the validity of inferences that can be made from scores on the measure. There is not just one validity; there can be many. The number will depend on the number of valid *inferences* to be made for the criteria available.

You may read or hear someone say, "This test is valid." However, understand that validity is not an inherent property of the test; rather, it depends on the inferences we can legitimately make from scores on the test. A legitimate inference is one in which scores on the selection measure are related to some aspect of job success or performance. In some cases, the validity of inferences is expressed quantitatively; in other cases, judgmentally. Whatever the form, many different validities may exist for data from any one measure. These validities will simply depend on those criteria found or judged to be related to scores on the measure and on the inferences drawn from these relations. Therefore, with respect to a predictor, such as a test we are considering for use in employment decision making, we should always ask ourselves, *Valid for what?*

The research process we go through in discovering what and how well a selection procedure measures is called *validation*. In validation, we conduct research studies to accumulate information (that is, evidence) on the meaning and value of our inferences from a selection procedure.[3]

The results of this process represent evidence that tells us what types of inferences may be made from scores obtained on the measurement device. For instance, let's suppose that a manager believes that a master's degree is essential for satisfactory performance in a job involving technical sales. The manager is inferring that possession of the degree leads to adequate job performance and that lack of the degree results in unacceptable job performance. In validating the use of the educational credential as a selection standard, the manager attempts to verify the inference that the degree is a useful predictor of future job success. The manager is not validating the educational selection standard per se, but rather the inferences made from it. Therefore, many validities may relate to the standard.[4] Thus validation involves the research processes we go through in testing the appropriateness of our inferences.

The Relation between Reliability and Validity

When we discussed the concept of reliability, we used terms such as *dependability, consistency,* and *precision* of measurement. Although these are important characteristics of any measurement device, it is possible to have a measure that is reliable yet does not measure what we want for selection. For example, imagine we have a device that will measure job applicants' eye color in a precise and dependable manner. Now, suppose we try to use the device to predict applicants' job performance, even though research shows that color of applicants' eyes has no relation with how well people perform their jobs. This highly reliable measure is worthless for meeting our objective of predicting job performance. As we saw in our discussion of reliability, the dependability of information produced by a selection procedure is important. However, knowledge regarding what is being measured by this selection procedure and what it means for predicting job performance makes validity information the most important standard for judging the value of a selection procedure.

Rather than existing as two distinct concepts, reliability and validity go hand in hand. Let's see how they are interrelated. With respect to our eye color measure, we may have a highly reliable tool that has no validity in human resource selection applications. However, we *cannot* have high validity if we do not have high reliability. High reliability is a necessary but not a sufficient condition for high validity.

Statisticians have also demonstrated the quantitative interrelationship between validity and reliability.[5] The maximum possible empirical validity of a measure such as a test depends on its reliability as well as the reliability of the criterion with which it is correlated. Stated quantitatively, the relationship between validity and reliability is

$$r_{xy} = \sqrt{r_{xx} r_{yy}}$$

where

$r_{xy} = $ m*aximum possible* correlation between predictor X and criterion Y
    (the validity coefficient)

$r_{xx} = $ reliability coefficient of predictor X

$r_{yy} = $ reliability coefficient of criterion Y

For example, if the reliability of a test (X) is 0.81 and the reliability of the criterion (Y) is 0.60, then *maximum possible* validity of the test is 0.70; that is,

$$r_{xy} = \sqrt{(0.81)(0.60)} = 0.70$$

Notice the formula is not saying what the actual or calculated validity of predictor X is. It is simply saying that actual calculated validity can be no higher than this maximum possible value because both our predictor and criterion scores contain random error. Because random errors are uncorrelated, the more random error present in scores from a predictor *or* a criterion (that is, the more that reliability falls), then the more likely it is that maximum possible validity will also fall.

As you can tell from the formula, if reliability of *either* test X or criterion Y were lower, maximum possible validity would be lower as well. If either our test or criterion were completely unreliable (that is, reliability $= 0.00$), then the two variables would be unrelated, and empirical validity would be zero. (We discuss the meaning of a validity coefficient later in this chapter.) Thus reliability or unreliability limits, or puts a ceiling on, possible empirical validity. Practically speaking, to enhance maximum possible validity, reliability should be as high as possible for our predictors *and* our criteria.

Types of Validation Strategies

A *validation study* provides the evidence for determining the inferences that can be made from scores on a selection measure. Most often, such a study is carried out to determine the accuracy of judgments made from scores on a predictor about important job behaviors as represented by a criterion. A number of different strategies are used for obtaining this evidence to see whether these inferences are accurate and can be supported. For our purposes, we discuss several validation strategies in this chapter. We begin by describing three classical approaches that have been used for validating measures in human resource selection: (a) *content validation,* (b) *criterion-related validation* (including both *concurrent* and *predictive* validation strategies), and (c) *construct validation.* Next, we explore some empirical issues involved in implementing the criterion-related strategies. Following our review of these classical approaches, we briefly examine additional strategies that take a broader perspective; that is, *validity generalization* and *synthetic validity.*

From our overview of the chapter, you probably have the sense that each of the validation strategies just listed represents a separate, distinct way of determining the validity of our selection procedures. We have organized our discussion around these validation strategy groupings because we think that for the student being introduced to validity, organizing our discussion this way may help clarify what the concept entails. However, it is important to recognize that all of the strategies we discuss are interrelated and should not be logically separated. Ultimately, when the results of these strategies for any particular selection measure are taken together as a whole, they form the evidence for determining what is really being measured and what inferences from scores on this measure are warranted. Therefore, where possible, practitioners should rely on multiple validation strategies to support the use of a selection measure in employment decision making.

CONTENT VALIDATION STRATEGY

Content validation is one strategy that has received much interest among practitioners involved in selection. There are several reasons for this interest. First, the strategy is amenable to employment situations where only small numbers of applicants are actually being hired to fill a position. Such a situation is characteristic of many small businesses. When adequate amounts of predictor or criterion data are not available, the applicability of statistical procedures needed in other validation strategies is seriously curtailed.

Second, adequate measures of job success criteria may not be readily available. For some jobs, such as those involving the delivery of services to clients, customers, and so on, a suitable means for measuring employee success may be very difficult and prohibitively expensive to obtain. In such a context, content validation is a viable option because the need for quantitative measures of employee performance is minimized.

Third, selection consultants employing a content validation strategy likely believe use of the strategy will lead to selection procedures that will enhance applicants' favorable perceptions of an organization's selection system. As you will see, content validation attempts to maximize the correspondence between the content of a job and content of selection procedures used for that job. Enhanced correspondence between these two will likely improve applicants' views of an organization's selection methods.

Whatever the reasons, content validation continues to attract growing interest among selection consultants. Because of this interest, we spend some time reviewing this validation method.

Basically, a selection measure has content validity when it can be shown that its content (items, questions, and so on) representatively samples the content of the job for which the measure will be used.[6]

"Content of the job" is a collection of job behaviors and the associated knowledge, skills, abilities, and other personal characteristics (KSAs) that are necessary for effective job performance. The behaviors and KSAs that represent the content of the job to be assessed are referred to as the *job content domain. If a measure is to possess content validity, the content of the measure must be representative of the job content domain.*

This requirement is true for both predictors and criteria. If we want to infer the extent to which a job applicant possesses a skill or knowledge that is necessary to perform a critical job behavior at the present time (that is, present job competence), then a content validation strategy is appropriate.

The more closely the content of a selection procedure can be linked to actual job content, the more likely it is that a content-validation strategy is appropriate. For example, suppose a large trucking company employs drivers of large tractor-trailer rigs. As part of the job, one critical task involves backing a tractor-trailer rig into a warehouse space having only two feet of clearance on each side of the vehicle. A driver must back the truck into the loading dock under heavy traffic conditions, taking no more than three minutes to complete the task. The truck must be backed close enough to a loading dock so that freight can be loaded in a timely manner. Now suppose, as part of the selection program, that applicants for the driver position are asked to actually back up a tractor-trailer rig to a loading dock similar to that actually encountered on the job. While undertaking the selection task, driver applicants experience impatient automobile drivers who blow horns and make verbal comments, events that actually confront truck drivers on the job. For this type of selection situation, a content validation strategy would be particularly appropriate.

Content validation differs from other validation strategies in two important ways. First, the prime emphasis in content validation is on the *construction* of a *new* measure rather than the validation of an existing one. The procedures employed are designed to help ensure that the measure being constructed representatively samples what is to be measured, such as the KSAs required on a job. Second, the method principally emphasizes the role of expert judgment in determining the validity of a measure rather than relying on statistical methods. *Judgments* are used to describe the degree to which the content of a selection measure represents what is being assessed. For this reason, content validation has been called a form of "descriptive" validity. With its emphasis on *description,* content validation contrasts with concurrent and predictive validation strategies, where the emphasis is on statistical *prediction*.

Sometimes, *face* validity is confused with the concept of *content* validity. Whereas content validity deals with the representative sampling of the content domain of a job by a selection measure, face validity concerns the *appearance* of whether a measure is measuring what is intended. A selection test has face validity if it appears to job applicants taking the test that it is related to the job. However, just because a test appears to have face validity does not mean it has content or criterion-related validity—it may or may not. Hence face validity is not a form of validity in a technical sense. But face validity is important. In one study, for instance, participants in France and the United States were asked to rate the favorability of 10 selection procedures. Perceived face validity of the selection procedures was the strongest correlate of participants' beliefs regarding both the procedures' effectiveness in identifying qualified people and the procedures' fairness.[7] If test takers perceive a test to be related to the job, then they are likely to have a more positive attitude toward the organization and its selection procedures. Positive attitudes toward selection measures may yield very positive benefits for an organization. For example, applicants who believe selection procedures are face-valid indicators of their ability to perform a job may be more motivated to perform their best on these procedures. Also, if rejected for a job, applicants may perceive the selection procedures to be less biased than if measures without face validity were used. In this situation, rejected applicants from protected groups may be less likely to file a discrimination charge against an organization that uses face-valid selection measures than an organization that does not. From this perspective, face validity may be thought of as a "comfort factor." Because some job candidates and some managers may be very resistant to the use of selection measures such as tests, they need to "feel" that a measure is fair and appropriate. Face validity of a measure helps to provide this comfort factor.

Major Aspects of Content Validation

There are a number of ways for examining the link between content of a job and content of a predictor. These include the following: (a) showing that the predictor is a representative sample of the job domain, (b) demonstrating that predictor content measures the KSAs required for successful performance on the job, and (c) using subject matter experts to make judgments regarding the overlap between the KSAs required to perform well on a predictor and those KSAs needed for successful job performance.[8] Drawing on some earlier writings, Benjamin Schneider and Neal Schmitt described a number of these key elements for implementing a content validity strategy.[9] We summarize the major aspects of several of these:

1. **Conduct of a Comprehensive Job Analysis**—Job analysis is the heart of any validation study. In particular, job analysis is the essential ingredient in the successful conduct of a content validation study. The results of a job analysis serve to define the *job content domain*. The job content domain consists of the work activities and knowledge, skills, abilities, and any other worker characteristics needed to perform these work activities. The identified job content domain need not include all work activities and KSAs that compose the job. Only those work activities and KSAs deemed most critical to the job need to be considered. By matching the identified job content domain to the content of the selection procedure, content validity is established.

   A number of court cases have affirmed the necessity for analyzing the content and nature of the job for which a selection procedure is used.[10] For example, the U.S. Supreme Court ruled in *Albemarle Paper Co. v. Moody* that job analysis must play an integral role in any validation study.[11] With respect to content validation studies per se, the *Uniform Guidelines on Employee Selection Procedures* specify that a job analysis should result in the following products:

   A. **A description of the tasks performed on the job**

   B. **Measures of the criticality and/or importance of the tasks**

   C. **A specification of KSAs required to perform these critical tasks**

   D. **Measures of the criticality and/or importance of KSAs, which include**

      (1) an operational definition of each KSA

      (2) a description of the relationship between each KSA and each job task

      (3) a description of the complexity/difficulty of obtaining each KSA

      (4) a specification as to whether an employee is expected to possess each KSA before being placed on the job or being trained

      (5) an indication of whether each KSA is necessary for successful performance on the job[12]

   E. **Linkage of important job tasks to important KSAs.** Linking tasks to KSAs serves as a basis for determining the essential tasks to simulate in a behaviorally oriented selection measure, such as a work simulation, or for determining critical KSAs to tap in a paper-and-pencil measure such as a multiple-choice test.

Each important job task identified in the job analysis will likely require at least some degree of a KSA for successful task performance. Here, the KSAs required to perform these tasks are specified. Most often, these KSAs are identified by working with subject matter experts who have considerable knowledge of the job and the necessary KSAs needed to perform it. This step typically involves subjective judgment on the part of participants in identifying the important KSAs. Because inferences are involved, the emphasis in this step is on defining specific KSAs for specific job tasks. By focusing on specific definitions of tasks and KSAs, the judgments involved in determining what KSAs are needed to perform which tasks are less likely to be subject to human error.

2. **Selection of Experts Participating in a Content Validity Study**—As we have noted, the application of content validity requires the use of expert judgment. Usually, these judgments are obtained from job incumbents and supervisors serving as subject matter experts (SMEs). Subject matter experts are individuals who can provide accurate judgments about the tasks performed on the job, the KSAs necessary for performing these tasks, and any other information useful for developing selection measure content. Because of their importance, it is essential that these judges be carefully selected and trained. In using SMEs in a content validation study, it is important to report their qualifications and experience. Ideally, members of protected classes (for example, gender and race/ethnicity) should be represented among the SMEs. Details should also be given regarding their training and the instructions they received while serving as SMEs. Finally, information on how SMEs made their judgments in the validation study—for example, as individuals or in a group consensus—should also be provided.

3. **Specification of Selection Measure Content**—Once the job tasks and KSAs have been appropriately identified, the items, questions, or other content that compose the selection measure are specified. This phase of content validation is often referred to as *domain sampling*. That is, the items, questions, or other content are chosen to constitute the selection measure so they represent the behaviors or KSAs found important for job performance. The content included is in proportion to the relative importance of the job behaviors or KSAs found important for job performance. Subject matter experts who are knowledgeable of the job in question review the content of the measure and judge its suitability for the job. Final determination of selection measure content depends on these experts' judgments.

To aid the review of selection measure content, such as a multiple-choice test or structured interview, Richard Barrett proposed the Content Validation Form II (CVFII).[13] Basically, the form consists of questions that serve as a guide or audit for analyzing the appropriateness of selection measure content in a content validation study. Individuals knowledgeable of the job (for example, incumbents) working with a test development specialist record their evaluations and the rationale behind them for each part of the test being reviewed. The questions on the CVFII are organized into three test review areas. The CVFII review areas and sample questions from each are as follows:

A. Selection Procedure as a Whole

- Is an adequate portion of the job covered by the selection procedure?

- Does the selection procedure, combined with other procedures, measure the most important content of the job?

B. Item-by-Item Analysis

- How important is the ability to respond correctly to successful job performance?

- Are there serious consequences for safety or efficiency if the applicant does not have the information or skills needed to respond correctly?

C. Supplementary Indications of Content Validity

- Are the language and mathematics demands of the test commensurate with those required by the job?

- Would applicants who are not test-wise be likely to do as well as they should?

Predictor Fidelity

In developing a predictor to be used in selection (for example, a selection interview, a work simulation, or a multiple-choice test), one key issue is the fidelity or comparability between the format and content of the predictor and the performance domain of the job in which the predictor will be used. Two types of predictor/job performance fidelity must be addressed: (a) *physical* fidelity and (b) *psychological* fidelity. Physical fidelity concerns the match between how a worker actually behaves on the job and how an applicant for that job is asked to behave on the predictor used in selection. For example, a driving test for truck driver applicants that requires driving activities that an incumbent truck driver must actually perform, such as backing up a truck to a loading dock, has physical fidelity. A typing test requiring applicants to use certain word processing software to type actual business correspondence that is prepared by current employees using the same sofware also has physical fidelity.

Psychological fidelity occurs when the same knowledge, skills, and abilities required to perform the job successfully are also required on the predictor. For example, a patrol police officer may have to deal with hostile and angry citizens. Asking police officer job applicants to write a statement describing how they would handle a hostile individual is not likely to have psychological fidelity. KSAs different from those required on the job, such as the ability to express one's self in writing, may be called for by the written statement. On the other hand, psychological fidelity might be found in a role-playing simulation in which police patrol applicants interact with an actor playing the role of an angry citizen.[14]

Finally, one other point should be made with regard to selection measures—job fidelity. This issue concerns the extent to which a test measures KSAs that are *not* required by the job under study. This problem can be particularly troublesome with multiple-choice tests. Irwin Goldstein and his colleagues pointed out that often the issue with multiple-choice tests is not so much whether they assess job-relevant KSAs; the real issue is whether thay assess KSAs that are not required for successful job performance. For example, candidates being assessed for promotion may be asked to memorize voluminous materials for a knowledge test, but on the job itself incumbents are not required to retrieve the information from memory to perform the job. Necessary information for performing the job can be obtained from available manuals or other reference sources.[15]

Irwin Goldstein and Sheldon Zedeck described another situation in which KSAs covered on the selection procedure were different from those required to perform the job.[16] In this case, a job analysis for the position of lieutenant in a fire department showed that a lieutenant gives short orders orally regarding the placement of personnel and what equipment should be sent to a fire. If a paper-and-pencil selection procedure used with applicants for the position of lieutenant requires them to respond to a hypothetical fire scene by writing down what they would do, then there is a question as to whether writing an essay requires the same KSAs as those required for the actual performance of the lieutenant's job. Then too, if the written exam is scored for grammatical correctness and spelling, additional questions are raised about the job relevance of the selection test. These questions regarding content validity become particularly important when further examination of the job shows that a lieutenant does not write essays or reports. Thus an option to the written test that was developed was to have applicants use a tape recorder and orally give their directions and orders.

In general, when physical and psychological fidelity of the selection predictor mirrors the performance domain of the job, content validity is enhanced. Such a measure is psychologically similar because applicants are asked to demonstrate the behaviors, knowledge, skills, and abilities required for successful incumbent performance.

4. **Assessment of Selection Measure and Job Content Relevance**—Another important element in content validation is determining the relevance of selection measure content for assessing the content of the job.

   After a test or some other measure has been developed, an essential step in determining content validity is to have job incumbents judge the degree to which KSAs identified from the job analysis are needed to answer the test questions. These incumbents actually take the test and then rate the extent of test content-to-KSA overlap. A rating instruction such as the following might be given: "To what extent are each of the following knowledge, skills, and abilities needed to answer these questions (or perform these exercises)?"[17]

   1 = Not at all
   2 = To a slight extent
   3 = To a moderate extent
   4 = To a great extent

   Charles Lawshe proposed a quantitative procedure called the *Content Validity Ratio* (CVR) for making this determination.[18] Basically, the CVR is an index computed on ratings made by a panel of experts (job incumbents and supervisors) regarding the degree of overlap between the content of a selection measure and content of the job. Each panel member is presented with the contents of a selection measure and asked to make ratings of these contents. For example, the panel members are given items on a job knowledge test. Members judge each test item by indicating whether the KSA measured by the item is (a) *essential*, (b) *useful but not essential*, or (c) *not necessary for job performance*. These judgments are used in the following formula to produce a CVR for each item on the test:

$$CVR = \frac{n_e - N/2}{N/2}$$

   where n_e is the number of judges rating the test item as essential, and N is the total number of judges on the rating panel. The computed CVR can range from

1.00 (all judges rate an item essential) to 0.00 (half of the judges rate it essential) to −1.00 (none of the judges rate it essential). Because it is possible for a CVR to occur by chance, it is tested for statistical significance using tables presented by Lawshe. Statistically significant items would suggest correspondence with the job. Nonsignificant items that most of the judges do not rate "essential" can be eliminated from the test. By averaging the CVR item indexes, a Content Validity Index (CVI) for the test as a whole can be also derived. The CVI indicates the extent to which the panelists believe the overall ability to perform on the test overlaps with the ability to perform on the job. Hence the index represents overall selection measure and job content overlap.

Some Examples of Content Validation

Because the content validation approach can have wide applicability in the selection of individuals for jobs requiring generally accepted KSAs (such as reading ability, knowledge of mathematics, ability to read drawings, and so on), we examine some examples of content validation to illustrate the method. Lyle Schoenfeldt and his colleagues were interested in developing an industrial reading test for entry-level personnel of a large chemical corporation. They used job analysis to determine *what* materials entry-level personnel needed to be able to read upon job entry as well as the *importance* of these materials to job performance. These analyses showed that entry-level employees read four basic types of materials: (a) safety (signs, work rules, safety manuals), (b) operating procedures (instruction bulletins, checklists), (c) day-to-day operations (log books, labels, schedules), and (d) other (memos, work agreements, application materials). The safety and operating procedures materials were judged most important because they accounted for roughly 80 percent of the materials read while performing the job. The test was then constructed so that approximately 80 percent of the test items reflected these two types of materials. The test itself was developed from the content of *actual* materials current employees had to read upon job entry.[19]

Silvia Moscoso and Jesus Salgado were faced with the problem of developing a job-related employment interview for hiring private security personnel. They used a content validation strategy in developing the interview questions and scoring procedures.[20] Following the identification of behavioral incidents descriptive of critical aspects of the job, they developed seven interview questions to assess six job performance dimensions (for example, being a good observer, showing firmness, demonstrating initiative). They wrote interview questions to reflect the content of selected incidents identified from the job analysis. Subsequent analyses showed acceptable agreement among subject matter experts rating interviewees' responses to the questions. In addition, they established content validity for five of the seven interview questions.

In a hypothetical example, imagine we want to build content valid measures for use in selecting typist-clerks in an office setting. Again, based on the job analysis procedures discussed previously, we know that incumbents need specific KSAs to perform specific tasks. From the example tasks and KSAs shown in Figure 5.1, we identify two specific job performance domains that we want to be able to predict: (a) typing performance and (b) calculating performance. For our measures to have content validity, we must build them in such a way that their content representatively samples the content of each of these domains. Where should the measures' contents come from? For the contents to be most representative, they should be derived from what incumbents actually do on the job. For example, we might develop a performance measure that would ask an applicant to format an actual business letter in a specific style and then type it

---

FIGURE 5.1   Example Tasks, KSAs, and Selection Measures for Assessing KSAs of Typist-Clerks

	Example Job Tasks of Typist-Clerks		
Example KSAs of typist-Clerks	1. Types and proofreads business correspondence, reports, and proposals upon written instruction	••• 5. Checks and computes travel claims and expenses using a ten-key adding machine	**KSA Selection Measures**
1. Skill in typing reports and correspondence at a minimum of 50 words per minute	√		Speed typing test of business correspondence
2. Ability to read at 12th-grade reading level	√		Reading test involving reports, correspondence, and proposals at 12th-grade reading level
3. Knowledge of business letter styles used in typing business correspondence	√		Formatting and typing test of business correspondence
4. Knowledge of arithmetic at 10th-grade level including addition, subtraction, division, and multiplication		√	Arithmetic test requiring arithmetic calculations on business expense data using a ten-key adding machine
•	•	•	•
•	•	•	•
•	•	•	•
9. Ability to operate a ten-key adding machine		√	Arithmetic test re-quiring arithmetic calculations on business expense data using a ten-key adding machine
Percentage (%) of time performed	75%	••• 15%	

NOTE: A check mark (√) indicates that a KSA is required to perform a specific job task. KSA selection measures are those developed to assess particular KSAs.

---

within a prescribed period of time. Similarly, we might ask applicants to use a ten-key adding machine to compute and check some actual, reported business expenses. Further, in computing scores, we might weigh the measures so that each reflects its relative importance in performing the job. In our example, typing correspondence accounts for approximately 75 percent of the job while 15 percent involves calculating expense claims. (The remaining 10 percent consists of other tasks.) Thus our typing measure should be weighted 75 percent to reflect its relative importance to calculating. As you can tell from our example task statements, KSAs, and measures, we are attempting to develop selection measures whose content representatively maps the actual content of the job itself. To the extent we are successful, content validity of the measures can be supported.

Job incumbents and supervisors serving as subject matter experts play an important role in establishing the content validity of our measures. These experts are used to identify the important tasks performed on the job and the relevant KSAs needed to perform these tasks successfully. Also, as we saw earlier through the computation of the content validity ratio, they may also serve in judging the appropriateness of content for the measures. All of these judgments taken in sum represent the foundation for determining the content validity of the selection measures being developed for our typist-clerk position.

Inappropriateness of Content Validation

As we have seen, content validity provides evidence that a selection measure representatively samples the universe of job content. This evidence is based principally on expert judgment. As long as a selection measure assesses *observable* job behaviors (for example, a driving test used to measure a truck driver applicant's ability to drive a truck), the inferential leap in judging between what a selection device measures and the content of the job is likely to be rather small. However, the more abstract the nature of a job and the KSAs necessary to perform it (for example, the ability of a manager to provide leadership, the possession of emotional stability), the greater the inferential leap required in judging the link between the content of the job and content of a selection measure. Where inferential leaps are large, error is more likely to be present. Therefore, it is much more difficult to accurately establish content validity for those jobs characterized by more abstract functions and KSAs than for jobs whose functions and KSAs are more observable. For these situations, other validation strategies, such as criterion-related ones, are necessary.

Job Analysis and Content Validation

A central concept of content validity is that selection measure content must appropriately sample the job content domain. When there is congruence between the KSAs necessary for effective job performance and those KSAs necessary for successful performance on the selection procedure, then it is possible to infer how performance on the selection procedure relates to job success. Without a clearly established link between these two sets of KSAs, such an inference is unwarranted. Whenever the specific content of the measure and the KSAs required to perform the tasks of a job differ, then an inferential leap or judgment is necessary to determine whether the measure appropriately samples the job. How do we establish this job–KSA link with the selection-procedure–KSA link in a content validity study? A carefully performed, detailed job analysis is the foundation for any content validity study. In a later chapter, we illustrate some of the steps necessary for performing a suitable job analysis for content validity purposes. For now, however, Figure 5.2 descriptively summarizes some major inference points that take place when using job analysis to establish the content validity of a selection procedure.

The first inference point (**1**) in Figure 5.2 is from the job itself to the tasks identified as composing it. Where careful and thorough job analysis techniques focusing on job tasks are used, the judgments necessary for determining whether the tasks accurately represent the job will probably have minimal error. The next inference point (**2**) is from the tasks of the job to identified KSAs required for successful job performance. Here again, complete, thorough job analyses can minimize possible error. The final inference point (**3**) is most critical. It is at this point that final judgments regarding content validity of the selection measure are made. Here we are concerned with the physical and psychological fidelity between the measure and the job performance domain. Specifically, to make the inferential leap supporting content validity, we must address three important issues that contribute to physical and psychological fidelity:

1. Does successful performance on the selection measure require the same KSAs needed for successful job performance?

2. Is the mode used for assessing test performance the same as that required for job or task performance?

3. Are KSAs *not* required for the job present in our predictor?[21]

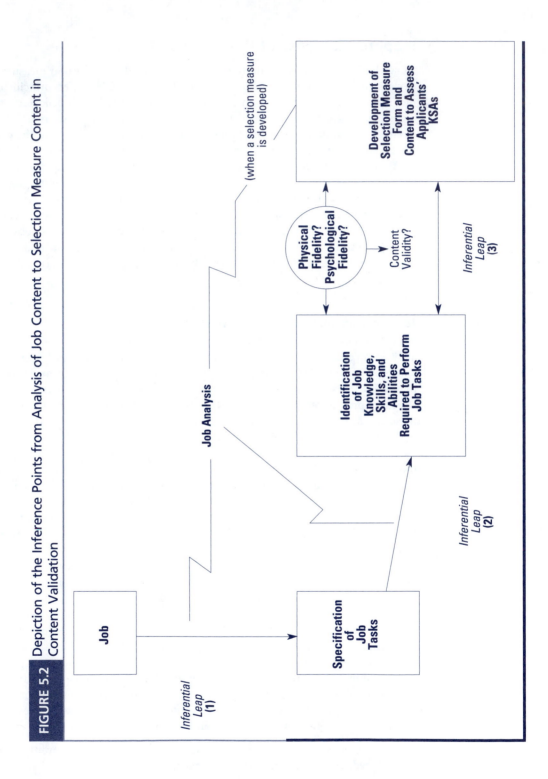

FIGURE 5.2 Depiction of the Inference Points from Analysis of Job Content to Selection Measure Content in Content Validation

If we can deal with these issues successfully, our inferential leaps can be kept small. As long as the inferential leaps are acceptably small—that is, the selection measure is composed of content that clearly resembles important job tasks and KSAs—arguments for content validity inferences are plausible. For jobs involving activities and processes that are *directly observable* (such as for the job of a typist), only *small inferences* may be required in judging the relation between what is done on the job, the KSAs necessary to do the job, and the KSAs assessed by the selection measure. For jobs whose activities and work processes are *less visible* and more abstract (such as those of an executive), greater inferences must be made between job activities, applicant requirements for successful performance, and selection measure content. In general, the greater the inferential leaps being made in a content validity study, the more likely errors will be made, and the more difficult it will be to establish content validity. At this point, other validation strategies are needed, such as criterion-related approaches.

The *Uniform Guidelines* recognize the limits of content validation and specify some situations where content validation alone is *not* appropriate; in these situations, other validation methods must be used. These situations include the following:

1. When mental processes, psychological constructs, or personality traits (such as judgment, integrity, dependability, motivation) are not directly observable but inferred from the selection device.[22]

2. When the selection procedure involves KSAs, an employee is expected to learn on the job.[23]

3. When the content of the selection device does not resemble a work behavior; when the setting and administration of the selection procedure does not resemble the work setting.[24]

As a validation method, content validation differs from criterion-related techniques in the following ways: (a) in content validity, the focus is on the selection measure itself, while in the others, the focus is on an external variable; (b) criterion-related validity is narrowly based on a specific set of data, whereas content validity is based on a broader base of data and inference; and (c) a statement of criterion-related validity is couched in terms of precise quantitative indices (prediction), whereas content validity is generally characterized using broader, more judgmental descriptors (description).[25]

Because content validation emphasizes judgmental rather than statistical techniques for assessing the link between the selection standard and indicators of job success, some writers question its use as a validation strategy. Their main criticism is that content validity is primarily concerned with inferences about the *construction* of content of the selection procedure rather than with predictor scores. Thus because validity of selection standards concerns the accuracy of inferences made from predictors, some have argued that "content validity" is not really validity at all.[26] In contrast to this criticism of content validity, there are situations (as we saw earlier) in which content validation is the only practical option available. For example, small sample sizes, such as when only a few individuals are eligible for promotion into a position, may necessitate a content validation approach. In addition, reliable criterion information may not be available because of existing lawsuits in an organization or union actions that prohibit the collection of job performance data.[27]

Logically, it might seem reasonable to conclude that inferences made from a content-related strategy will overlap those inferences made from criterion-related strategies. Michael Carrier and his associates tested the correspondence between criterion-related and content validation strategies for three structured interview guides used to select insurance agents.[28] They found significant relationships between the two strategies for agents with prior insurance sales experience, but not for those lacking experience. The study suggests that content validity does not automatically mean criterion-related validity. In addition, Kevin Murphy and others concluded that for a set of cognitive predictors (such as psychomotor and performance tests, selection interviews, biographical data scores, knowledge tests, work sample tests) that are positively correlated with one another as well as with a measure of job success, whether there is a match or a mismatch between content of the predictors and content of the job (that is, content validity) is unlikely to have a meaningful influence on *criterion-related* validity. However, for personality inventories, matching predictor and job content (that is, establishing content validity) might be an important determinant of criterion-related validity.[29] In sum, content validity reflects only the extent to which KSAs identified for the job domain are judged to be present in a selection measure. Hence, as our database of inferences regarding validity is built, it is essential we include both content and criterion-related evidence.

CRITERION-RELATED VALIDATION STRATEGIES

Inferences about performance on some criterion from scores on a predictor, such as an ability test, are best examined through the use of a criterion-related validation study. Two approaches are typically undertaken when conducting a criterion-related study, (a) a *concurrent* and (b) a *predictive* validation study. In some respects these approaches are very similar. That is, information is collected on a predictor and a criterion, and statistical procedures are used to test for a relation between these two sources of data. Results from these procedures answer the question, Can valid inferences about job applicants' performance on the job be made based on how well they performed on our predictor? Although concurrent and predictive strategies share a number of similarities, we have chosen to discuss these strategies separately in order to highlight their unique characteristics.

Concurrent Validation

In a concurrent validation strategy, sometimes referred to as the "present employee method," information is obtained on both a predictor and a criterion for a *current* group of employees. Because predictor and criterion data are collected roughly at the same time, this approach has been labeled "concurrent validation." Once the two sets of data (predictor and criterion information) have been collected, they are statistically correlated. The validity of the inference to be drawn from the measure is signified by a statistically significant relationship (usually determined by a correlation coefficient) found between the predictor and measure of job success or criterion.

An Example

As an example of a concurrent validation study, let's imagine we want to determine whether some ability tests might be valid predictors of successful job performance of industrial electricians working in a firm. First, we make a thorough analysis of the industrial electrician's job. Drawing on job analysis methods and techniques such as those we describe in later chapters, we attempt to uncover the critical tasks actually performed on the job. From these identified tasks, we then infer the knowledge, skills, abilities (KSAs), and other characteristics required for successful job performance. Job incumbents then rate the importance of the KSAs in successfully performing the job tasks. Figure 5.3 summarizes three hypothetical tasks and several relevant KSAs that were found to be important in our industrial electrician's job. (Keep in mind, we are providing only

FIGURE 5.3	Selection of Experimental Ability Tests to Predict Important KSAs for the Job of Industrial Electrician

| | Linking of KSAs to Critical Job Tasks (10 = High Relation; 1 = Low Relation) | | | |
| | KSAs | | | |
Critical Job Tasks	**1. Knowledge of Electrical Equipment**	**2. Ability to Design-Modify Mechanical Equipment for New Applications**	**• • •**	**8. Ability to Follow Oral Directions**
1. Maintains and repairs lighting circuits and electrical equipment such as motors and hand tools	9.7	3.4	• • •	1.5
	•	•		•
	•	•		•
	•	•		•
5. Installs equipment according to written specifications and working drawings	9.5	3.3	• • •	2.2
	•	•		•
	•	•		•
	•	•		•
10. Independently constructs basic electrical/mechanical devices	7.2	9.4	• • •	2.2

| | Does Test Appear Suitable for Assessing KSA? | | | |
Selected Tests	**KSA 1**	**KSA 2**	**• • •**	**KSA 8**
A. Bennett Mechanical Comprehension Test (Form AA)	No	Yes	• • •	No
B. Purdue Test for Electricians	Yes	No	• • •	No
C. Purdue "Can You Read a Working Drawing?" Test	Yes	Yes	• • •	No

NOTE: The numbers shown are mean ratings given by subject matter experts used in the analysis of the industrial electrician's job. High ratings indicate that a particular KSA is relevant to the successful performance of a critical job task. "Yes" indicates that a test appears to be useful in assessing a particular KSA.

some example tasks and KSAs; there could be more in an actual job setting.) Two KSAs were found to be critical in performing the three job tasks: (a) Knowledge of Electrical Equipment and (b) Ability to Design/Modify Mechanical Equipment for New Applications. A third KSA, Ability to Follow Oral Directions, was judged to be of less importance in successfully performing the job and was not used as a basis for choosing our selection tests.

After we have identified the requisite KSAs, the next step is to select or develop those tests that appear to measure the relevant attributes found necessary for job success. As shown in Figure 5.3, three commercially available tests were chosen as experimental predictors of electricians' job success. These three tests were (a) *Bennett Mechanical Comprehension Test* (Form AA), (b) *Purdue Test for Electricians,* and (c) *Purdue "Can You Read a Working Drawing?" Test.* How were these three tests selected? We chose the tests based on our knowledge of what KSAs were required on the job and our research on and knowledge of those existing tests that seemed to tap these KSAs. Usually this process of inferring what devices might be used to measure the derived KSAs involves some form of subjective judgment. Expert advice can play an important role in choosing the most appropriate measures. For this reason, experienced selection consultants are often employed in choosing and developing selection measures. Next, our three tests are administered to industrial electricians currently working in the firm. They are told their participation is voluntary, the tests are being given for research purposes only, and their test scores will not affect how they are evaluated or their employment with the company.

As part of our job analysis, we also identify measures of job success that can serve as criteria. In this step, criterion information representing measures of electricians' job performance is collected. Performance appraisal ratings or more objective measures such as the number of errors in equipment repair or in electrical wiring projects might serve as criteria. Whatever the criteria, it is essential that the measures chosen be relevant indicators of performance as identified by the job analysis.

At this point, both predictor and criterion data have been collected. As depicted in Figure 5.4, the final step is to analyze the results using statistical procedures. A common practice is to statistically correlate (using the Pearson product-moment correlation coefficient) the sets of predictor and criterion data. Tests are considered to be valid predictors of performance if statistically significant relationships with criteria exist. If one or more of our tryout tests is found to be significantly correlated with a criterion, we will give serious consideration to incorporating the measures in our selection program. In summary, Table 5.1 outlines the basic steps taken in a concurrent validation study.

FIGURE 5.4 Representation of Relating Predictor Scores with Criterion Data to Test for Validity

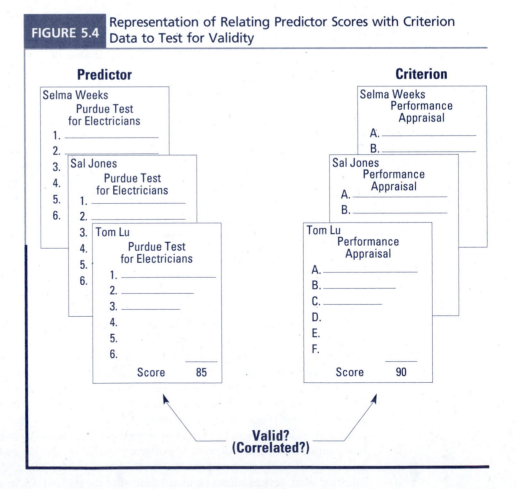

TABLE 5.1	Summary of Major Steps Undertaken in Conducting Concurrent and Predictive Validation Studies	

Concurrent Validation	Predictive Validation
1. Conduct analyses of the job.	1. Conduct analyses of the job.
2. Determine relevant KSAs and other characteristics required to perform the job successfully.	2. Determine relevant KSAs and other characteristics required to perform the job successfully.
3. Choose or develop the experimental predictors of these KSAs.	3. Choose or develop the experimental predictors of these KSAs.
4. Select criteria of job success.	4. Select criteria of job success.
5. Administer predictors to *current employees* and collect criterion data.	5. Administer predictors to *job applicants* and file results.
6. Analyze predictor and criterion data relationships.	6. *After passage of a suitable period of time,* collect criterion data.
	7. Analyze predictor and criterion data relationships.

Strengths and Weaknesses

If it can be assumed that the necessary requirements for conducting an empirical concurrent validation study are met, there is a positive argument for using this method. With a concurrent validation approach, an investigator has almost immediate information on the usefulness of a selection device. However, several factors can affect the usefulness of a concurrent validation study: (a) differences in job tenure or length of employment of the employees who participate in the study, (b) the representativeness (or unrepresentativeness) of present *employees* to job *applicants,* (c) certain individuals missing from the validation study, and (d) the motivation of employees to participate in the study or employee manipulation of answers to some selection predictors.

If job experience is related to performance on the job, then any predictor/criterion relationship may be affected by an irrelevant variable—job tenure. Since most people learn as they perform their jobs, it is entirely feasible that job experience may indeed influence their scores on either a predictor or criterion measure.

Second, if a concurrent validation study is being undertaken for a selection measure, another problem may arise. We want to use the predictor or selection device whose validity is based on current *employees*—in order to predict subsequent job success of *applicants.* If applicants are characteristically different from job incumbents (for example, are younger, have less job experience, have less education), then the generalizability of the results of our study based on incumbents may not apply to applicants. Because of employee turnover or dismissal, our current employee group may be highly select and not at all representative of applicants.

Third, a concurrent validation study excludes certain groups of individuals. For example, applicants who were rejected for employment and employees who left the organization or were promoted out of the job would not be available for the validation study. These factors can restrict the variability or range of scores on the criterion. Because of criterion range restriction, validity will be lowered.

Finally, because we are basing our study on employees who have a job rather than applicants who do not, employee study participants may bring different levels of motivation to the validation study than would applicant participants. For one, employees simply may not want to participate in a study in which they do not see a direct benefit. They may give a poor, unrepresentative effort on the predictor, and this may affect validity.

In addition, on some predictors—for example, a personality inventory—applicants may be more motivated than employees currently on the job to alter responses to create a favorable impression.

Predictive Validation

Rather than collecting predictor and criterion data at one point in time (like our concurrent validation approach), predictive validation involves the collection of data *over* time. In the context of HR selection, job *applicants* rather than job incumbents are used as the source of data. For this reason, it is sometimes known as the "future-employee" or "follow-up" method. The basic steps are also summarized in Table 5.1.

An Example

To illustrate the predictive validation method, let's return to our industrial electrician example. The steps involving job analysis, choice of criteria, and the selection of tests we want to try out are identical to those under the concurrent validation approach. The really significant difference between the two methods occurs at the *test administration step*. Here, our tests are administered to job *applicants* rather than current employees. Once administered, the measures are then filed and applicants employed on the basis of other available selection data (such as other tests, interviews, and so on). Answers to our experimental measures are *not* used in making selection decisions. After our electrician applicants have been selected, trained, placed in their jobs, and allowed enough time to learn their jobs adequately (perhaps as long as six months or more), criterion data representing job success are collected on the applicants. Then, after criterion data have been assembled, the two sets of scores (scores on our experimental predictors and criterion) are statistically correlated and examined for any possible relationships.

Strengths and Weaknesses

There are several important differences between predictive and concurrent validity. Under predictive validation, there is a time interval between the collection of predictor and criterion data. Applicants rather than incumbents serve as the data source and, as such, may have a higher, more realistic level of motivation when they complete the predictor measure. Differences between these individuals and subsequent applicants with respect to job tenure are not a problem with the predictive approach, since the same level of job experience applies to both. Under the predictive validation method, the inference tested or question answered is, Can the predictor predict future behavior as measured by criterion data?

Because of the inference tested by predictive validation, the method is appropriate for measures used in HR selection. The method addresses itself to the basic selection issue as it normally occurs in the employment context—that is, how well job applicants will *be able* to perform on the job. The biggest weakness, of course, with the predictive validation model is the time interval required to determine the validity of the measure being examined. If an organization hires relatively few people a month, it may take many months to obtain a sufficient sample size to conduct a predictive validation study. Moreover, it can be very difficult to explain to managers the importance of filing selection measure information *before* using the data for HR selection purposes.

Our discussion of concurrent and predictive validation strategies may suggest that there is only one way to carry out each of these validity designs. In practice, however, several different ways for conducting concurrent and predictive validation studies are used. Robert Guion and C. J. Cranny, for instance, summarized five variations in which

FIGURE 5.5 Examples of Different Predictive Validation Designs

Type of Predictive Validation Design	Description of Procedure
1. Follow-up—Random Selection	Applicants are tested and selection is random; predictor scores are correlated with subsequently collected criterion data.
2. Follow-up—Present System	Applicants are tested and selection is based on whatever selection procedures are already in use; predictor scores are correlated with subsequently collected criterion data.
3. Select by Predictor	Applicants are tested and selected on the basis of their predictor scores; predictor scores are correlated with subsequently collected criterion data.
4. Hire and Then Test	Applicants are hired and placed on the payroll; they are subsequently tested (e.g., during a training period), and predictor scores are correlated with criteria collected at a later time.
5. Personnel File Research	Applicants are hired and their personnel records contain references to test scores or other information that might serve as predictors. At a later date, criterion data are collected. The records are searched for information that might have been used and validated had it occurred to anyone earlier to do so.

Source: Based on Robert M. Guion and C.J. Cranny, "A Note on Concurrent and Predictive Validity Designs: A Critical Reanalysis," *Journal of Applied Psychology* 67 (1982), 240; and Frank J. Landy, *Psychology of Work Behavior* (Homewood IL: Dorsey Press, 1985), 65.

a predictive study might be conducted.[30] These are illustrated in Figure 5.5. In a similar fashion, different versions of the concurrent validation strategy also exist. These different ways of conducting a criterion-related validation study serve to show that, in practice, a variety of approaches might be used.

At times a particular criterion-related design employed might not fit neatly into our categories of predictive and concurrent validity. For instance, suppose a human resource manager hypothesizes that college grade point average (GPA) is related to job performance of sales personnel. GPA was *not* used in making hiring decisions but is available only for *current employees*. To test her hypothesis, she correlates GPA with first-year sales and finds a relationship between the two variables. Because it was *not* really done with applicants, is this a predictive validity study? Is this a concurrent validity strategy if the data were gathered over time? As you can see, our study design has elements of both predictive and concurrent validation strategies; it does not fall cleanly into either category. Whatever the design employed, the critical issue is not so much the criterion-related validity category to which it belongs. As we have seen, some designs such as that of our college grades and sales performance example may be difficult to classify. Rather, the real question to be answered is, "What inferences will the design of a criterion-related validity study permit?"[31]

Concurrent versus Predictive Validation Strategies

It has generally been assumed that a predictive validation design is superior to a concurrent one. Because of the problems we mentioned earlier in our discussion of the concurrent design, predictive designs have been thought to provide a better estimate of validity. There has been some older as well as newer work on comparing these designs. For example, as might be expected, a review of 99 published criterion-related validity studies showed a greater number of validation studies based on a concurrent validation design than a predictive one.[32] Minimal differences were found, however, in the validation results of the two types of designs. Another review of validity estimates of ability tests also revealed no significant differences in validity estimates derived from the two designs.[33]

For ability tests, results from these studies suggest that a concurrent validation approach may be just as viable as a predictive one. On the other hand, this may not necessarily be true for other predictors. For instance, studies have reported different results for predictive versus concurrent validation designs for both personality and integrity measures.[34]

In a more current review, Chris Van Iddekinger and Robert Ployhart concluded that predictive designs yield validity estimates roughly 0.05 to 0.10 lower than those obtained in concurrent designs for personality inventories, structured interviews, person-organization fit measures, and biographical data inventories.[35] Overall, these conclusions suggest that we consider both the type of predictor used and the validation design when comparing validation study results.

Requirements for a Criterion-Related Validation Study

Just because a criterion-related validation study is desired does not mean that such a study can be conducted. It must first be feasible, and to be feasible certain minimum requirements must be met. In the case of a validation study, "a poor study is not better than none."[36] A poor validation study may cause an organization to reject selection procedures that would have been useful in selecting employees, or accept and use selection procedures that do not predict employee job performance.[37]

At least four requirements are necessary before a criterion-related study should be attempted.

1. The job should be reasonably stable and not in a period of change or transition. The results of a study based on a situation at one point in time may not apply to the new situation.

2. A relevant, reliable criterion that is free from contamination must be available or feasible to develop.

3. It must be possible to base the validation study on a sample of people and jobs that is representative of people and jobs to which the results will be generalized.

4. A large enough, and representative, sample of people on whom both predictor and criterion data have been collected must be available. Large samples (more than several hundred) are frequently required to identify a predictor–criterion relationship if one really exists. With small samples, it may be mistakenly concluded that a predictor is not valid when in fact it is. The probability of finding that a predictor is significantly related to a criterion when it is truly valid is lower with small sample sizes than with larger ones. Therefore large sample sizes are *essential*.[38]

Criterion-Related Validation over Time

After spending time and money on a criterion-related validation study, one might ask, "How long will the validity of my predictor last?" A review by Charles Hulin and his colleagues indicated that the predictive validity of some measures rapidly decayed over time.[39] However, critics of the review noted that only one study reviewed incorporated an ability test to predict actual performance on the job.[40] Another study found that the predictive validity of mental ability tests actually increased over time, job experience validity decreased, and predictive validity remained about the same for dexterity tests.[41] For a weighted application blank scoring key, Steven Brown concluded that the utility of the key for predicting job success held up for a 38-year period.[42] Finally, it has been reported that the validity of mental ability tests for U.S. military occupational specialties remained stable for more than a five-year period.[43] These results suggest that at least for a properly developed and validated mental ability test, it might be expected that a measure's validity should hold up for at least a five-year period.

The Courts and Criterion-Related Validation

We may have given you the impression that, if taken to court, all an employer has to do is to trot out its significant validity coefficient and everything will be okay. Certainly, a statistically significant validity coefficient helps, but there is a lot more involved in the adjudication of employment discrimination cases. Even if proper actions have been taken in a criterion-related validation study, there is no guaranteed outcome of a legal case. Some outcomes hinge on elements of a case that go beyond the technical aspects of criterion-related validity; for example, a judge's personal biases. A review by Lawrence Kleiman and Robert Faley of 12 court cases involving criterion-related validity that were decided after publication of the 1978 *Uniform Guidelines* communicated some of the legal realities faced by employers and selection consultants.[44] Only five of 12 defendants won their case. Among their findings were

1. Rather than considering empirical validity evidence, some courts preferred to judge validity on the basis of format or content of the selection instrument (for example, multiple-choice format, content of an item).

2. Some courts were swayed by a test's legal history (for example, the Wonderlic Personnel Test) even though existing evidence was available on the validity of the test; others were influenced by the type of test used (for example, general aptitude tests such as a vocabulary test).

3. Judges had different preferences with regard to the use of a predictive validation strategy versus a concurrent validation strategy for demonstrating selection procedure validity.

4. A statistically significant validity coefficient alone did not guarantee a judgment for the defendant; some courts also considered the utility of the selection measure. However, they differed as to what evidence is needed to demonstrate utility.

5. Judges differed on their willingness to accept statistical corrections (for example, restriction of range corrections) to predictor scores. Some judges apparently believed that corrections by the defendant were misleading and done to make validity appear higher than it really was.

Certainly, a predictor's validity coefficient that is statistically significant is essential for both practical and legal reasons. A statistically significant validity coefficient is one piece of important evidence that helps to assure users that their inferences from scores on a selection procedure are related to job success. As long as the validity coefficient is statistically significant, using the selection procedure to make employment decisions will be better than using a procedure that is unrelated to job success, a procedure that is no better than flipping a coin and saying: "heads, you're hired; tails, you're not!" But, how high should a validity coefficent be? And, in addition to statistical significance of validity coefficients, how do the courts, namely judges, look at the magnitudes of validity coefficients in judging an employment discrimination claim? As we will see shortly, the higher the validity coefficient, the better for selection practice and the better for legal defense in the event a legal case is brought against an employer.

Daniel Biddle and Patrick Nooren cite a number of legal cases that adopted a value of 0.30 (assuming the coefficient was statistically significant) as a minimally acceptable threshold for a predictor's validity coefficient. (We will see in our discussion of *Utility Analysis,* appearing later in this chapter, that setting an arbitrary value of a validity coefficient for determining if a selection procedure is useful or not is not a wise idea. In addition to the magnitude of the validity coefficient, other factors must be considered as well.) If conditions such as selection procedure scores were used by employers to rank-order job candidates and top/down hiring was based on these ranked scores, and if the degree of disparate impact associated with the procedure were large, this minimum validity threshold would be expected to be higher. Exactly how high a statistically significant validity coefficient would have to be in order to be seen by a judge as acceptable is unknown; it might well vary depending on the judge hearing a case. Thus this conclusion would appear to be "... especially true of judges who have less than adequate statistical training and are sometimes speculative about the statistical sciences (which is arguably most judges)."[45]

Recent research offers some promising guidance to users and even courts facing questions such as "What are the anticipated consequences for adverse impact of various degrees of test validity and test bias?[46] Herman Aguinis and Marlene Smith have offered an online computer program to perform calculations to help with such questions.[47]

Content versus Criterion-Related Validation: Some Requirements

So far, we have discussed several approaches to validation. The choice of a validation strategy implies that certain requirements must first be evaluated and met. Each of the validation strategies discussed up to this point has a particular set of requirements. These requirements must be met for a specific strategy to be viable.

A review of these requirements provides a means for determining the feasibility of a particular validation methodology. We have prepared a summary of requirements in which HR selection issues are in question. Drawing principally from the *Uniform Guidelines,* the *Principles for the Validation and Use of Employee Selection Procedures,*[48] and other sources in the literature, the major feasibility requirements for conducting content and criterion-related (concurrent and predictive) validation methods have been summarized in Table 5.2. The requirements shown are not meant to be exhaustive, only illustrations of major considerations when HR selection is involved. Also, the requirements serve as considerations for deciding the feasibility of a particular validation approach; they are not complete technical requirements.

CONSTRUCT VALIDATION STRATEGY

The next validation strategy we mention is construct validity. When psychologists use the term *construct,* they are generally referring to the postulated psychological concept, attribute, characteristic, or quality thought to be assessed by a measure. When a measure is used in selection research, it is believed that the measure assesses "something." That something is the construct.[49] Thus terms such as *intelligence, sociability,* and *clerical ability* are all theoretical abstractions called constructs. But their measures (such as a clerical ability test) are operational, concrete measures of these constructs.

For example, suppose we have a test called the General Mental Ability Test. The test is *thought* to assess general intelligence. As we review it, we may believe that the test is assessing the construct of intelligence. We look at the test's content and see items involving topics such as verbal analogies, mathematical problem solving, or scrambled sentences. But does this test really assess the construct of intelligence? We hypothesize

TABLE 5.2	Basic Considerations for Determining the Feasibility of Content and Criterion-Related Validation Strategies

Content Validation	**Criterion-Related Validation**[a]
1. Must be able to obtain a complete, documented analysis of each of the jobs for which the validation study is being conducted, which is used to identify the content domain of the job under study. 2. Applicable when a selection device purports to measure existing job skills, knowledge, or behavior. Inference is that content of the selection device measures content of the job. 3. Although not necessarily required, should be able to show that a criterion-related methodology is not feasible. 4. Inferential leap from content of the selection device to job content should be a small one. 5. Most likely to be viewed as suitable when skills and knowledge for doing a job are being measured. 6. Not suitable when abstract mental processes, constructs, or traits are being measured or inferred. 7. May not provide sufficient validation evidence when applicants are being ranked. 8. A substantial amount of the critical job behaviors and KSAs should be represented in the selection measure.	1. Must be able to assume the job is reasonably stable and not undergoing change or evolution. 2. Must be able to obtain a relevant, reliable, and uncontaminated measure of job performance (that is, a criterion). 3. Should be based as much as possible on a sample that is representative of the people and jobs to which the results are to be generalized. 4. Should have adequate statistical power in order to identify a predictor-criterion relationship if one exists. To do so, must have a. adequate sample size; b. variance or individual differences in scores on the selection measure and criterion. 5. Must be able to obtain a complete analysis of each of the jobs for which the validation study is being conducted. Used to justify the predictors and criteria being studied. 6. Must be able to infer that performance on the selection measure can predict future job performance. 7. Must have ample resources in terms of time, staff, and money.

[a]Criterion-related validation includes both concurrent and predictive validity.

Source: Based on Society of Industrial and Organizational Psychology, *Principles for the Validation and Use of Personnel Selection Procedures*, 4th ed. (Bowling Green, OH: Author, 2003); Equal Employment Opportunity Commission, Civil Service Commission, Department of Labor, and Department of Justice, *Adoption of Four Agencies of Uniform Guidelines on Employee Selection Procedures*; 43 Federal Register 38, 295, 300, 301, 303 (August 25, 1989); and Robert M. Guion, *Personnel Testing* (New York: McGraw-Hill, 1965).

that it does, but does it? Construct validation tests our hypothesis. In this sense, construct validation is a research process involving the collection of evidence used to test hypotheses about relationships between measures and their constructs.

Let's use a simple example to illustrate an approach to construct validation of a hypothetical measure called the Teamwork Inventory (TI). Currently, many manufacturing organizations maintain that the ability of employees to work effectively as members of a work team is a critical requirement in manufacturing jobs. Let's assume that we have analyzed such a manufacturing job and found that the performance dimension *Working as a Team Member* (a construct) is important to successful performance. The *Ability to Work with Others* (another construct) is hypothesized to be an important ability employees need for performing this job dimension. As we look at our two constructs, we develop measures that could be used to assess them. For instance, supervisors' ratings are used as a measure of the construct *Working as a Team Member*, whereas a paper-and-pencil test, the TI, is developed to assess the construct *Ability to Work with Others*. Our particular interest is the construct validity of the TI.

Figure 5.6 shows the hypothesized links between the constructs and their measures.[50] Construct validation is an accumulation of evidence that supports the links among the

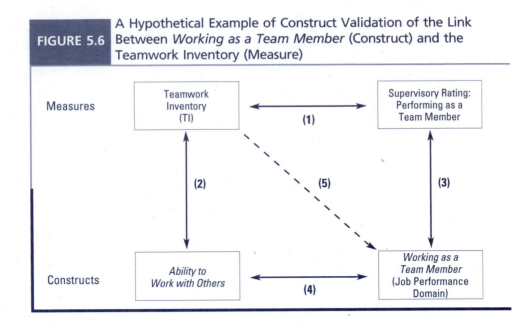

FIGURE 5.6 A Hypothetical Example of Construct Validation of the Link Between *Working as a Team Member* (Construct) and the Teamwork Inventory (Measure)

various measures and constructs. In our current example and from the perspective of personnel selection, we are ultimately interested in the link between the TI measure and the *Working as a Team Member* construct (**link 5**). Evidence of this link can come from several sources. One source might be a criterion-related validation study between the TI and supervisory ratings of performing as a team member (**link 1**). Content validation studies might also provide additional evidence (**links 2** and **3**). However, we can also accumulate other forms of evidence to determine whether our TI test assesses the construct of *Ability to Work with Others*.

Literature reviews might suggest the characteristics of individuals who work effectively on teams. We might hypothesize, for instance, that such individuals would be extraverted, would have a high need for affiliation, would have played/participated extensively in group activities such as team sports while growing up, and would have belonged to a number of social organizations. We would administer measures of these variables, such as personality inventories and biographical data questionnaires, along with the TI to current employees. If our hypothesized associations are found, we have another piece of evidence regarding the construct validity of the TI.

We might design another study in which the TI and other selection measures are given to job applicants. Employees are hired without knowledge of TI scores and placed in work teams. Six months or so later, we ask team members to rate how well individuals fit within their assigned team and collect absenteeism data. Earlier, we hypothesized that individuals possessing the ability to work on a team would show less absenteeism from the work group and be rated by their peers as an effective team member. If we find that employees who scored high on the TI had less absenteeism and were rated more effective than individuals scoring low on the TI, we have more evidence of construct validity.

Additionally, studies investigating the relation between the TI and professionally developed measures of our hypothesized teamwork construct could be conducted. Positive relationships would be expected. Experiments might be designed to determine whether individuals scoring high on the TI behave in ways predictably different from those scoring low. If our anticipated results are found, we have even more evidence of TI construct validity. As you can see, we have suggested a variety of study procedures that could be adopted to test our hypothesis that the Teamwork Inventory effectively predicts the *Working as a Team Member* construct that characterizes the job performance domain.

Our example highlights the major steps for implementing a construct validation study as follows:

1. The construct is carefully defined and hypotheses formed concerning the relationships between the construct and other variables.

2. A measure hypothesized to assess the construct is developed.

3. Studies testing the hypothesized relationships (formed in step 1) between the constructed measure and other, relevant variables are conducted.[51]

Because construct validation may be conducted when no available measure exists, the "thing" or "construct" being validated requires a number of measurement operations. Results of studies such as the following are particularly helpful in construct validation:

1. Intercorrelations among the measure's parts should show whether the parts cluster into one or more groupings. The nature of these groupings should be consistent with how the construct is defined.

2. Parts of the measure belonging to the same grouping should be internally consistent or reliable.

3. Different measures assessing the same construct as our developed measure should be related with the developed measure. Measures assessing different constructs that are not hypothesized to be related to the construct of interest should be unrelated.

4. Content validity studies should show how experts have judged the manner in which parts of the measure were developed and how these parts of the measure sampled the job content domain.[52]

You can probably see from our illustration that construct validation is a process of accumulating empirical evidence of what a selection measure measures. The more evidence we collect, the more assurance we have in our judgments that a measure is really doing what was intended. As such, construct validation represents a much broader definition of validity than we might find in a single criterion-related or content validation study. Through accumulated evidence (that may come from other validation strategies, literature reviews, controlled experiments, and so on), we can answer what and how well a selection measure assesses what it measures. Construct validation is still a developing issue.[53] There is no complete, uniform agreement on the exact methods the strategy entails. Future clarification of the strategy will also clarify its application.

EMPIRICAL CONSIDERATIONS IN CRITERION-RELATED VALIDATION STRATEGIES

Even when we have conducted content validation studies on a selection measure, at some point we probably will want to answer two important questions:

1. Is there a relationship between applicants' responses to our selection measure and their performance on the job?

2. If so, is the relationship strong enough to warrant the measure's use in employment decision making?

Questions such as these imply the need for statistical or empirical methods for determining validity, that is, criterion-related validity. Because of their importance, we review some of the empirical methods and issues most commonly encountered in conducting criterion-related validation research.

Correlation

Computing Validity Coefficients

One of the terms you will often see in reading selection research studies and literature is *validity coefficient*. Basically speaking, a validity coefficient is simply an index that summarizes the degree of relationship between a predictor and criterion. Where does the validity coefficient come from? What does it mean? To answer these questions, let's refer to an example. Consider for a moment that we are conducting a predictive validation study. We want to know whether a sales ability inventory is useful in predicting the job performance of sales personnel. During a one-week employment period, we administered the inventory to 50 job applicants. No employment decisions were based on the inventory scores. Six months later, we can identify 20 individuals who were hired and are still employed.[54] (In practice, we would want to have more than just 20 people in our validation study. Ideally, we need *at least* several hundred people on whom both predictor and criterion data are available. Because of space considerations, we have used a small sample to *illustrate* the data in the accompanying tables and figures. Large sample sizes are *essential* in criterion-related validation research.) As a measure of job performance, we use sales supervisors' ratings of employee performance after the employees have had six months of sales experience. Total scores on the performance appraisal forms are calculated, and they represent employee job performance. Thus for each employee we have a pair of scores: (a) scores on the sales ability inventory (a predictor) and (b) six-month performance appraisal scores (a criterion). These example data are shown in Table 5.3.

We initially make a scattergram or scatterplot of data, like those in Table 5.3, to visually inspect any possible relationships between predictor and criterion variables. An example scattergram of our data is shown in Figure 5.7. Each point in the graph represents a plot of the *pair* of scores for a single salesperson. For instance, employee Q has a sales ability inventory score of 79 and a performance rating of 91. Although a scattergram is useful for estimating the existence and direction of a relationship, it really does not help us specify the *degree* of relationship between our selection measure and job performance. For this purpose, a more precise approach is to calculate an index that will summarize the degree of any linear relationship that might exist. Most often, the Pearson product-moment or simple correlation coefficient (r) is used to provide that index. The correlation coefficient, or in the context of personnel selection the "validity coefficient," summarizes the relationship between our predictor and criterion. Often, the validity coefficient is represented as r_{xy}, where r represents the degree of relationship between X (the predictor) and Y (the criterion).

A validity coefficient has two important elements: (a) its sign and (b) its magnitude. The sign (either $+$ or $-$) indicates the *direction* of a relationship; its magnitude indicates the *strength* of association between a predictor and criterion. The coefficient itself can range from -1.00 to 0.00 to $+1.00$. As the coefficient approaches 1.00, there is *a positive* relationship between performance on a selection measure and a criterion. That is, high scores on a predictor are associated with high scores on a criterion, and low scores on the predictor are related with low criterion scores. As the coefficient moves toward -1.00, however, a negative or inverse relation appears between scores on the predictor and criterion. As the index moves toward 0.00, any relationship between the two

TABLE 5.3	Hypothetical Inventory Score and Job Performance Rating Data Collected on 20 Salespeople	
Salesperson ID	**Sales Ability Inventory Score (Predictor)**	**Salesperson Job Performance Rating (Criterion)**
A	86	74
B	97	91
C	51	67
D	41	31
E	60	52
F	70	70
G	73	74
H	79	59
I	46	44
J	67	61
K	71	52
L	88	75
M	81	92
N	40	22
O	53	74
P	77	74
Q	79	91
R	84	83
S	91	91
T	90	72

NOTE: **Sales Ability Inventory Score (high scores)** = Greater sales ability. **Job Performance Rating (high scores)** = Greater job performance of sales personnel as judged by sales supervisors.

variables decreases. When the validity coefficient is not statistically significant or r is equal to 0.00, then no relationship exists between a predictor and a criterion. Note that *if a validity coefficient is not statistically significant, then the selection measure is not a valid predictor of a criterion.* These predictor/criterion relations are summarized in Figure 5.8.

Using simple correlation, suppose we find that the validity coefficient for our example data in Figure 5.7 is 0.80. Next, after consulting the appropriate statistical table (usually found in psychological measurement or statistics books) or computerized results (that is, the statistical significance of the correlation coefficient as identified by statistical software used in calculating the simple correlation), we test the coefficient to see whether there is a true or statistically significant relationship between the sales ability inventory and job performance or whether the correlation arose simply because of chance. Our significance test will help us determine the probability that the relationship identified for our sample of job applicants can be expected to be found only by chance in the *population* of job applicants from which our sample came. Usually, if the probability is equal to or less than 0.05 (i.e., $p \le 0.05$), we can conclude that a statistically significant relationship exists between a predictor and criterion. That is, a true relationship exists between the predictor and criterion for the population of job applicants. In our example, assume we find that our validity coefficient of 0.80 is statistically significant (usually written as "r = 0.80, $p \le 0.05$"). A statistically significant relationship suggests that we can be 95 percent

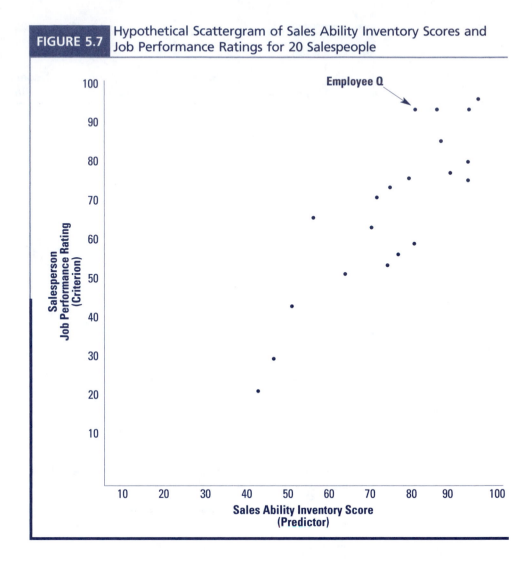

FIGURE 5.7 Hypothetical Scattergram of Sales Ability Inventory Scores and Job Performance Ratings for 20 Salespeople

certain that there is a relationship between how applicants responded to the sales inventory and their subsequent performance on the job. Therefore, we are reasonably confident that the relation did not arise because of chance and that a dependable relationship exists. We can now conclude that our inventory is valid for predicting job performance.

Importance of Large Sample Sizes

The number of people on whom we have both predictor and criterion data for computing a validity coefficient is referred to as the *sample size* (or *N*) of a validation study. There are at least three reasons why it is absolutely essential to have as large a sample size as possible in calculating a validity coefficient:

1. A validity coefficient computed on a small sample (say, for example, $N = 20$) must be higher in value to be considered statistically significant than a validity coefficient based on a large sample (say, for example, $N = 220$).

2. A validity coefficient computed on a small sample is less reliable than one based on a large sample. That is, if we took independent samples of pairs of predictor

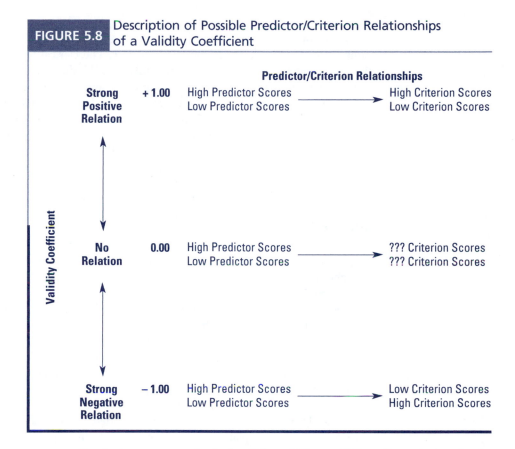

FIGURE 5.8 Description of Possible Predictor/Criterion Relationships of a Validity Coefficient

and criterion scores and calculated the validity coefficient for each sample, there would be more variability in the magnitudes of the validity coefficients for small samples than if the sample sizes were large.

3. The chances of *finding* that a predictor is valid when the predictor is actually or truly valid is lower for small sample sizes than for large ones. A predictor may be truly valid, but the correlation coefficient may not detect it if the sample size on which the coefficient is based is small.[55] The term *statistical power* is often used when describing a validation study. One way of thinking about statistical power is the ability of a validation study to detect a correlation between a selection procedure and a criterion when such a relationship actually exists. Small sample sizes in a validation study have less statistical power than large samples. For example, if a criterion-related validation study had a sample size of 200, then there is about an 80 percent chance of identifying a validity coefficent of .20 or higher as being statistically significant ($p \leq 0.05$). For a sample size of 100, the chances are roughly 50 percent.

You may wonder whether a validity coefficient can be computed for a small sample, and if so, what does it mean? A validity coefficient can be computed on small sample sizes; if it is statistically significant (that is, $p \leq 0.05$), the predictor is considered valid. The coefficient itself is interpreted in exactly the same way as for a large sample size.[56] So, what is wrong with a small sample? The problem is this: As the sample size *decreases,* the probability of *not* finding a statistically significant relationship between predictor and criterion scores *increases.* Therefore, we would be more likely to conclude (and perhaps incorrectly so) that a predictor is not valid and is useless in selection. For this reason, we should use as large a sample size as possible in our criterion-related validation studies.

Research by Frank Schmidt illustrates the effects of using small sample sizes on the variability of validity coefficients.[57] Clerical test validity data were available on a large sample ($N = 1,455$) of post office letter sorters. The clerical test validity coefficient for this large sample was 0.22. They randomly divided the large sample into 63 smaller groups of 68 individuals each. This sample size was chosen because previous research had shown that the average sample size used in test validation studies was 68. Next, they computed test validity coefficients for each of the 63 smaller groups. Their results illustrate that small sample sizes, even with an N of 68, can produce misleading outcomes. Test validity coefficients ranged from -0.03 to 0.48 among the 63 samples. Less than a third of the coefficients were statistically significant ($p < 0.05$) or valid. Because of what is called "sampling error," which is pronounced when we use small sample sizes in validation research, we might not detect the true validity of a predictor.

Interpreting Validity Coefficients

Once we have found a statistically significant validity coefficient, we might well ask, "What precisely does the coefficient mean?" We can take several approaches to answer this question.

When we look at the distribution of our criterion scores shown in Table 5.3, one fact is evident. Some employees perform better than others; some do very well, others not so well. Of course, we expect such differences because people are different. If our predictor is useful, it should help to explain some of these differences in performance. By squaring the validity coefficient (r_{xy}^2), we can obtain an index that indicates our test's ability to account for these individual performance differences. This index, called the *coefficient of determination, represents the percentage of variance in the criterion that can be explained by variance associated with the predictor*. In our case, the coefficient of determination is 0.64 (0.80^2), indicating that 64 percent of the differences (or variance) in individuals' job performance can be explained by their responses to the sales ability inventory. Relatively speaking, our validity coefficient of 0.80 (or coefficient of determination of 0.64) for this sample of employees is high. Only on relatively infrequent occasions do validity coefficients, especially for a single predictor, much exceed 0.50; a more common size of coefficient is in the range of 0.30 to 0.50. Thus coefficients of determination for many validity coefficients will range from roughly 0.10 to 0.25.

In addition to the coefficient of determination, *expectancy tables* and *charts* can be used. Because expectancy tables are frequently employed as an aid in interpreting prediction, we save our discussion of them for the next section.

Finally, *utility analysis* can also be used. Its computation is far more complex than the methods we just mentioned. Yet it offers, perhaps, the ultimate interpretation of a valid predictor and its impact in a selection program for managers in an organization. By translating the usefulness of a validity coefficient into dollars, utility analysis adds an economic interpretation to the meaning of a validity coefficient. Because of its importance in the field of HR selection, we devote a later section of this chapter to a discussion of utility analysis.

Prediction

A statistically significant validity coefficient is helpful in showing that for a *group* of persons a test is related to job success. However, the coefficient itself does not help us in predicting the job success of *individuals*. Yet the prediction of an individual's likelihood of job success is precisely what an employment manager wants. For individual prediction purposes, we can turn to the use of linear regression and expectancy charts to aid us in selection decision making. These should be developed only for those predictors that have proven to have a statistically significant relationship with the criterion. In using these methods, a practitioner is simply taking predictor information, such as test scores, and predicting an individual's job success, such as rated job performance, from this information. For each method, one key assumption is that we are utilizing information collected on a past or present group of employees and making predictions for a *future* group of employees.

Linear Regression

Basically, linear regression involves the determination of how changes in criterion scores are functionally related to changes in predictor scores. A regression equation is developed that mathematically describes the functional relationship between the predictor and criterion. Once the regression equation is known, criterion scores can then be predicted from predictor information. In general, there are two common types of linear regression you are likely to come across: *simple* regression and *multiple* regression.

Simple Regression.   In simple regression, there is only one predictor and one criterion. To illustrate, let's refer to Figure 5.7, which depicted the relationship between sales ability inventory scores and job performance ratings for 20 salespeople. In Figure 5.9, we show the same

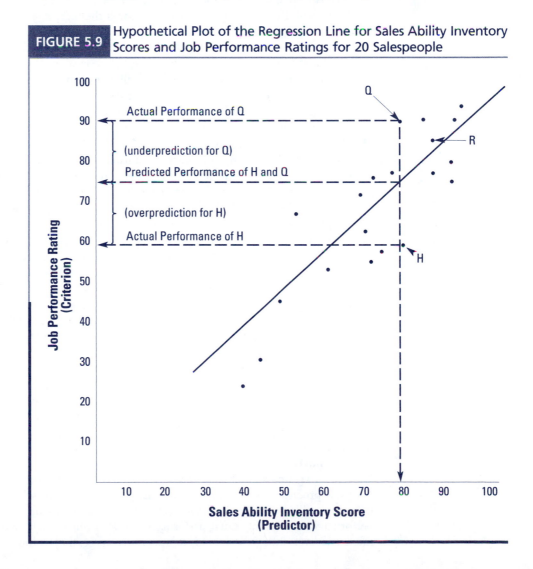

| FIGURE 5.9 | Hypothetical Plot of the Regression Line for Sales Ability Inventory Scores and Job Performance Ratings for 20 Salespeople |

scattergram fitted with a special line to the plotted scores. This line is called the *regression line*. It summarizes the relationship between the inventory scores and the job performance ratings. The line has been fitted statistically so that it is at a minimum distance from each of the data points in the figure. Thus the regression line represents the line of "best fit."

In addition to depicting the fit of the regression line graphically, we can also describe it mathematically in the form of an equation called the *regression* or *prediction equation*. This equation takes the form of the algebraic expression for a straight line, that is,

$$\hat{Y} = a + bX$$

where

$\hat{Y}$ = predicted score of the criterion variable

a = intercept value of the regression line

b = slope of the regression line or regression weight

X = score on the predictor variable.

The data points around the regression line and the validity coefficient are closely related. The validity coefficient represents how well the regression line fits the data. As the validity coefficient approaches + or −1.00, the data points move closer to the line. If a validity coefficient equals + or −1.00, then the data points will fall exactly on the regression line itself, and prediction will be perfect. However, as the coefficient moves away from + or −1.00 (toward 0.00), the points will be distributed farther from the regression line, and more error will exist in our predictions.

To illustrate the role of the regression line and regression equation in prediction, let's look further at our example. The regression line in Figure 5.9 is represented by the equation $\hat{Y} = 3.02 + 0.91(X)$, where $\hat{Y}$ is predicted job performance (our criterion), and X is a score on our sales ability inventory administered to applicants for the sales job. The intercept (3.02) is the value where the regression line crosses the Y-axis. It represents an applicant's predicted job performance if his or her sales ability inventory score were zero. Finally, the slope of the line is represented by 0.91. The slope is often called a *regression weight or regression coefficient* because it is multiplied times the score on the predictor (our sales ability inventory). The slope or regression weight represents the amount of change in the criterion variable per one-unit change in the predictor. Thus for every one-unit increase in an applicant's inventory score, we would expect a 0.91 increase in job performance. A positive validity coefficient indicates a positive slope of the regression line (see Figure 5.9) and, hence, a positive regression weight. A negative validity coefficient means a negative slope and negative regression weight.

Once we have our regression line, we can use it to predict our criterion scores. For example, if an applicant applying for our sales job is given the sales ability inventory, we would locate the score on the X-axis, move upward to the regression line, and then move across to the Y-axis to find his or her predicted job performance score. As you can see in Figure 5.9, individual **R,** who has a test score of 84, is predicted to have a job performance rating of approximately 80. Since individual **R** actually has a performance rating of 83, our prediction is close. As the correlation between the inventory and job performance is not a perfect 1.00, prediction will include some error. For instance, persons **H** and **Q** both scored 79 on the inventory, but notice our predictions have error. For person **H,** we would *overpredict* performance. With an inventory score of 79, performance is predicted to be 73, but it is actually only 59. Conversely, for person **Q,** performance would be *underpredicted*. With the same inventory score (79), predicted performance is 73, but actual performance is 91. Even though errors in prediction are made and even though some may appear rather large, they will be smaller for the *group* of people than if the predictor information and regression line is not used and only random guesses (for example, using an invalid predictor) are made.

Rather than using the regression line, we can use our regression equation to predict job performance. By substituting a person's sales ability inventory score for X in our regression equation, multiplying the score times the regression coefficient (0.91), and then adding it to the constant value (3.02), we can derive a predicted job performance score. Thus for our inventory score of 86, we would predict subsequent rated job performance to be equal to 81. Our calculation would be as follows:

$$\hat{Y} = 3.02 + 0.91(X)$$
$$\hat{Y} = 3.02 + 0.91(86)$$
$$\hat{Y} = 3.02 + 78.26$$
$$\hat{Y} = 81.28 \text{ or } 81$$

As we saw in our preceding example, because our inventory is not perfectly related to job performance, we will have some error in our predictions. Only if all of our data points fall precisely on the regression line ($r_{xy} = \pm 1.00$) will error not be present. In making employment decisions, we must take this degree of error into account. The *standard error of estimate* is a useful index for summarizing the degree of error in prediction.[58] It is determined from the following equation:

$$sd_{y \cdot x} = sd_y \sqrt{1 - r_{xy}^2}$$

where

$sd_{y \cdot x}$ = standard error of estimate

sd_y = standard deviation of criterion scores Y

r_{xy} = validity coefficient for predictor X and criterion Y

The standard error of estimate can be interpreted as the standard deviation of errors made in predicting a criterion from a selection predictor. It is expected that, on the average, 68 percent of *actual* criterion scores will fall within ± 1 standard error of *predicted* criterion scores, and 95 percent of actual criterion scores will fall within ± 1.96 standard errors of *predicted* criterion scores. For example, assume the standard deviation of our job performance ratings is 7.5. Also, assume that the validity of our inventory designed to predict these ratings is 0.80. The standard error of estimate would be computed as follows:

$$sd_{y \cdot x} = 7.5\sqrt{1 - 0.80^2}$$
$$sd_{y \cdot x} = 7.5\sqrt{36}$$
$$sd_{y \cdot x} = 4.50$$

Assume that a person scores 86 on the inventory. Using the regression equation we discussed in the previous section, we calculate that all persons scoring 86 on the inventory would be predicted to have a job performance rating of 81. Notice that we have a *predicted* level of job success, but how confident can we be that individuals' *actual* job success will approximate the predicted level? The standard error of estimate can help us. Basically, it enables us to establish a range of predicted criterion scores within which we would expect a percentage of actual criterion scores to fall. For applicants with a predicted performance rating of 81, we would expect, on the average, 68 percent of them to have *actual* performance ratings between 77 and 86 (81 ±4.50). For this same performance level, we would also expect 95 percent of the applicants' actual job performance ratings to fall between 72 and 90 [81 ±(1.96 × 4.50)].

Multiple Regression.   In addition to simple regression, *multiple* regression can be used to predict criterion scores for job applicants. Whereas the simple regression model assumes only *one* predictor, multiple regression assumes *two or more* predictors are being used to predict a criterion. If the additional predictors explain more of the individual differences among job applicants' job performance than would have been explained by a single predictor alone, our ability to predict a criterion will be enhanced. As our ability to predict improves (that is, validity increases), we will make fewer errors in predicting an applicant's subsequent job performance.

The general model for multiple regression is as follows:

$$\hat{Y} = a + b_1 X_1 + b_2 X_2 + \cdots + b_n X_n$$

where

$$\hat{Y} = \text{predicted criterion scores}$$
$$a = \text{intercept value of the regression line}$$
$$b_1, b_2, b_n = \text{regression weights for predictors } X_1, X_2, \text{ and } X_n$$
$$X_1, X_2, \text{ and } X_n = \text{scores on predictors } X_1, X_2, \text{ and } X_n$$

If, for example, we had administered the sales ability inventory and a biographical data questionnaire, and if these two predictors are related to our job performance measure, we could derive a multiple regression equation just as we did with simple regression. However, in this case, our equation will have two regression weights rather than one. Suppose our multiple regression equation looked as follows:

$$\hat{Y} = 3.18 + 0.77 X_1 + 0.53 X_2$$

where

$$\hat{Y} = \text{predicted criterion scores (job performance measure)}$$
$$3.18 = \text{intercept value of the regression line } (a)$$
$$0.77 = \text{regression weight of the sales ability inventory}$$
$$0.53 = \text{regression weight of the biographical data questionnaire}$$
$$X_1 = \text{score on the sales ability inventory}$$
$$X_2 = \text{score on the biographical data questionnaire}$$

To obtain a predicted job performance score, we would simply substitute an individual's two predictor scores in the equation, multiply the two scores times their regression weights, sum the products, and add the intercept value to obtain predicted performance. For instance, suppose an individual scored 84 on the sales ability inventory and 30 on the biographical data questionnaire. The predicted job performance score would be obtained as follows:

$$\hat{Y} = 3.18 + 0.77(84) + 0.53(30)$$
$$\hat{Y} = 3.18 + 64.68 + 15.90$$
$$\hat{Y} = 83.76 \text{ or } 84$$

The multiple regression approach has also been called a compensatory model. It is called compensatory because different combinations of predictor scores can be combined to yield the same predicted criterion score. Thus if an applicant were to do rather poorly on one measure, he or she could compensate for this low score by performing better on the other measure. Examples of compensatory selection models include those frequently used as a basis for making admission decisions in some professional graduate schools.

Cross-Validation

Whenever simple or multiple regression equations are used, they are developed to optimally predict the criterion for an existing group of people. But when the equations are applied to a new group, the predictive accuracy of the equations will most always fall. This "shrinkage" in predictive accuracy occurs because the new group is not identical to the one on which the equations were developed. Because of the possibility of error, it is important that the equations be tested for shrinkage *prior* to their implementation in selection decision making. This checkout process is called *cross-validation*. Two general methods of cross-validation are used: (a) *empirical* and (b) *formula* estimation. With empirical cross-validation, several approaches can be taken. In general, a regression equation developed on one sample of individuals is applied to another sample of persons. If the regression equation developed on one sample can predict scores in the other sample, then the regression equation is "cross-validated." One common procedure of empirical cross-validation ("split-sample" method) involves the following steps:

1. A group of people on whom predictor and criterion data are available is *randomly* divided into two groups.

2. A regression equation is developed on one of the groups (called the "weighting group").

3. The equation developed on the weighting group is used to predict the criterion for the other group (called the "holdout group").

4. Predicted criterion scores are obtained for each person in the holdout group.

5. For people in the holdout group, *predicted* criterion scores are then correlated with their *actual* criterion scores. A statistically significant correlation coefficient indicates that the regression equation is useful for individuals other than those on whom the equation was developed.

Although the "split-sample" method of cross-validation has been used, Kevin Murphy has argued that the method can produce misleading results.[59] Rather than splitting a sample into two groups, he recommends collecting data on a second, *independent* sample. Of course, finding a second sample for data collection is not easy. As an alternative to empirical cross-validation, *formula* cross-validation can be used. Under this procedure, only one sample of people is used. Special formulas are employed to predict the amount of shrinkage that would occur if a regression equation were applied to a similar sample of people. With the knowledge of (a) the number of predictors, (b) the original multiple correlation coefficient, and (c) the number of people on which the original multiple correlation was based, the *predicted* multiple correlation coefficient can be derived. This predicted multiple correlation coefficient estimates the coefficient that would be obtained if both the predictors were administered to a new but similar sample of people and the multiple correlation were statistically computed. The obvious advantage to these formulas is that a new sample of people does not have to be taken. Philippe Cattin summarized these formulas and the circumstances in which they are appropriate.[60] Kevin Murphy provided additional evidence on the accuracy of such formulas.[61] In general, he concluded that formula cross-validation is more efficient, simpler to use, and no less accurate than empirical cross-validation. More recently, researchers have found that cross validity cannot be accurately estimated when small sample sizes are involved; ideally, the ratio of the number of people in the validation study relative to the number of predictors should be roughly 10:1.[62] With this 10:1 ratio, Burket's cross-validation formula is recommended.[63]

Whatever the approach, cross-validation is *essential*. It should be routinely implemented whenever regression equations are used in prediction. Without it, you should be skeptical of regression equation predictions.

Expectancy Tables and Charts

An expectancy table is simply a *table* of numbers that shows the probability that a person with a particular predictor score will achieve a defined level of success. An expectancy *chart* presents essentially the same data except that it provides a visual summarization of the relationship between a predictor and criterion.[64] As we suggested earlier, expectancy tables and charts are useful for communicating the meaning of a validity coefficient. In addition, they are helpful as an aid in predicting the probability of success of job applicants. As outlined by Charles Lawshe and Michael Balma, the construction of expectancy tables and charts is basically a five-step process:

1. Individuals on whom criterion data are available are divided into two groups: Superior Performers and Others. Roughly half of the individuals are in each group.

2. For each predictor score, frequencies of the number of employees in the Superior Performers and the Others groups are determined.

3. The predictor score distribution is divided into fifths.

4. The number and percentage of individuals in the Superior Performers group and the Others group are determined for each "fifth" of the predictor score distribution.

5. An expectancy chart that depicts these percentages is then prepared.[65]

To illustrate the development of an expectancy table and chart, let's go through a brief example. First, let's assume that we have developed an employment interview to be used in hiring financial advisers who work with a large financial institution. Financial advisers are individuals who provide clients with financial services such as estate planning, personal investments, and retirement planning. In carrying out these activities, they may also sell investment products such as mutual funds to help clients meet their financial needs and objectives.

In hiring financial advisers, we use a number of methods. These range from background and reference checks to administering financial knowledge exams. A most important measure that we also employ is a structured employment interview that takes about 1½ hours to administer. In conducting the interview, we pose a series of specially developed questions that were designed to assess applicants' ability to provide sound financial advice to clients. We use other questions in the interview to assess applicants' ability to choose and sell appropriate financial products to clients. Once an applicant has completed the employment interview, the interviewer rates his or her performance on a series of rating scales. These quantitative ratings are then summed to obtain an overall interview performance score. The higher the applicants' scores on the interview, the better their interview performance.

Now, assume that we have scores from 65 financial adviser job applicants who completed the employment interview, were hired, and have worked as a financial adviser for 12 months. Assume also that we have obtained the annual performance appraisal ratings given by their office managers at the end of their 12-month employment period. For our present purposes, we determine from discussions with these office managers that employees rated 9 or higher are considered to be Superior Performers, while those with scores of 8 or less are classified as Other Performers.

A Pearson product-moment correlation between the sets of interview scores and appraisal data for our 65 financial advisers indicates there is a statistically significant validity coefficient of 0.45 between the interview scores and performance ratings. Figure 5.10 shows the scattergram of the interview scores plotted against the performance ratings. (Note that in comparison to our earlier scattergrams, we have reversed the axes shown in Figure 5.10.) The horizontal lines represent roughly equal fifths of the distribution of predictor scores. Table 5.4 is the expectancy table developed from the plotted data. Basically, it shows the chances out of 100 of an individual's being rated superior on the job, given a range of employment interview scores. For example, persons scoring between 30 and 34 have roughly an 85 percent chance of being rated superior, whereas those scoring between 1 and 6 have only a 33 percent chance. This information can be formatted into a bar chart to form an individual expectancy chart.

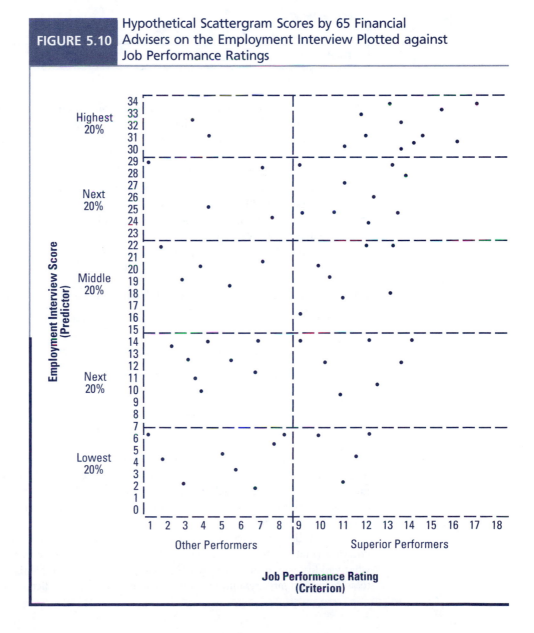

| **FIGURE 5.10** | Hypothetical Scattergram Scores by 65 Financial Advisers on the Employment Interview Plotted against Job Performance Ratings |

TABLE 5.4	Percentage of Financial Advisers Rated as Superior on the Job for Various Employment Interview Score Ratings			
Employment Interview Score Range	**Other Performers**	**Superior Performers**	**Total**	**% Superior Performers**
Top 20%: 30–34	2	11	13	85
Next 20%: 23–29	4	9	13	69
Middle 20%: 15–22	5	7	12	58
Next 20%: 7–14	8	7	15	47
Low 20%: 1–6	8	4	12	33
Total	27	38	65	

Two types of expectancy charts exist: (a) *individual* and (b) *institutional*. The *individual* chart shows the probability that a person will achieve a particular level of performance given his or her score on the test. Thus the individual chart permits *individual* prediction.

The institutional chart indicates what will happen within an organization if all applicants above a particular minimum score are hired. For example, in our study of financial advisers, 77 percent (20/26) of the applicants with a minimum score of 23 on the employment interview will be rated superior; 64 percent of those with a minimum score of 7 will be rated superior. By using the institutional chart, one can estimate what will happen in the organization if various passing or cutoff scores are used for a selection measure.

Factors Affecting the Size of Validity Coefficients

Robert Guion has pointed out that the size of a validity coefficient is dependent on a variety of factors.[66] Any number of factors may have an effect, but four seem to be predominant in determining the magnitude of a validity coefficient.

Reliability of Criterion and Predictor

Earlier we described the intimate interrelationship between reliability and validity. The point is that to the extent a predictor or criterion has error, it will be unreliable. The more error present, the more unreliable and unpredictable these variables will be. *Any unreliability in either the criterion or predictor will lower the correlation or validity coefficient computed between the two.* If *both* predictor and criterion variables have measurement error, error is compounded, and the validity coefficient will be lowered even further. Because of the negative effect of lowered reliability on validity, we should strive for high reliability of *both* the predictor and criterion to get an accurate assessment of what true validity may be.

If the validity coefficient is restricted or attenuated by unreliability of the predictor or criterion (that is, measurement error), it is possible to make statistical adjustments to see what validity would be if the variables had perfect reliability. This adjustment is referred to as *correction for attenuation.* Although unreliability in predictor scores can be corrected, in HR selection situations we have to use predictor data as they normally exist. Selection decisions are made with the actual predictor information collected. Thus correction for attenuation in predictor scores is not made typically. On the other hand, correction for unreliability in criterion data is made in selection using the following formula:

$$\hat{r}_{xy} = \frac{r_{xy}}{\sqrt{r_{yy}}}$$

where

$\hat{r}_{xy} =$ (corrected) validity coefficient of the predictor if the criterion were measured without error

$r_{xy} =$ correlation between the predictor and criterion (that is, the validity coefficient)

$r_{yy} =$ reliability coefficient of the criterion[67]

For example, assume the validity of a test is 0.35 and reliability of the criterion is 0.49. Substituting in the formula shows that with a perfectly reliable criterion, the correlation between the test and criterion would be 0.50, a respectable validity coefficient. The idea behind correction for unreliability in the criterion is that it is unfair to penalize the predictor because of lack of dependability of measurement with the criterion.

Correction for attenuation can be used to evaluate a predictor when we have a criterion that may be highly relevant for our use but having low reliability. In this situation, we will have a clearer picture of the true value of the predictor. Correction can suggest whether the search for another predictor may be worthwhile. For instance, if our original validity coefficient is very low, say 0.20, but correction shows it to be high, say 0.70 or higher, a search for better predictors of our criterion will likely be fruitless. Also, we may have avoided throwing out a valuable predictor.

In using the correction formula, accurate estimates of reliability are essential. From our discussion of reliability, we saw that many factors can affect the magnitude of reliability coefficients. If the correction formula is used with underestimates of true criterion reliability, misleading *over*estimates of corrected predictor validity will result. Performance ratings are often used as criteria in test validation research. Although many selection experts agree that ratings' criteria should be corrected for unreliability, there is currently no uniform agreement as to the best strategy for correcting ratings' criteria. With regard to correcting for unreliability in criterion measures, Chad Van Iddekinger and Robert Ployhart make a number of recommendations.[68] Among these are the following:

1. Report validity coefficients corrected for interrater reliability. However, this step assumes that accurate ratings information on participants can be collected from more than one supervisor.

2. If employees have only one supervisor (which is often the case), collect rating data from peers of those employees in the validation study.

3. If for some reason peer ratings cannot be obtained, other less-than-ideal solutions include (a) correcting validity coefficients based on meta-analytic estimates of interrater reliability (these are 0.52 for supervisor ratings and 0.42 for peer ratings) and (b) computing coefficient alpha for the ratings (which will tend to overestimate ratings' reliability and therefore yield a conservative estimate of corrected predictor validity).

Thus it is important to use and interpret the results of reliability correction formulas with caution when accurate estimates of criterion reliability are unknown.

Restriction of Range

One of the important assumptions in calculating a validity coefficient is that there is variance among individuals' scores on the criterion and predictor. By *variance*, we simply mean that people have different scores on these measures, that is, individual differences. When we calculate a validity coefficient, we are asking, "Do these predictor and criterion score differences co-vary or move together?" That is, are systematic differences among people on the criterion associated with their differences on the predictor? If there is little variance or range in individuals' scores for one or both variables, then the magnitude of the validity coefficient will be lowered. Smaller differences on predictor or criterion scores mean that it will be more difficult for the predictor to identify differences among people as measured by the criterion. Thus lowered validity will occur.

Restriction in range is the term used to describe situations in which variance in scores on selection measures has been reduced. In selection practice, range restriction can occur in a number of circumstances. For instance, in a predictive validation study, *direct* restriction occurs when an employer uses the test being validated as the basis for selection decision making. *Indirect* restriction happens when the test being validated is correlated with the procedures used for selection. Later, when individuals' test scores are correlated with their criterion scores, the validity coefficient will be curtailed. Range restriction occurs because individuals scoring low on the test were not hired. Their test scores could not be used in computing the validity coefficient because criterion data were unavailable.

Criterion scores may also be restricted. Restriction of criterion scores may occur because turnover, transfer, or termination of employees has taken place prior to the collection of criterion data. Performance appraisal ratings might also be restricted because raters did not discriminate among ratees in judging their job performance and gave them very similar ratings.

From our examples, you can see that restriction of scores can happen for either predictor or criterion or for both variables. Any form of restriction will lower computed validity. What we need to know is what validity would be if restriction had not occurred. Fortunately, a number of formulas have been developed to make the necessary statistical corrections in selection practice; however, these formulas correct for restriction on the predictor, not for criteria.[69] To illustrate the application of one formula for estimating the true predictor validity when restriction of range has occurred on the predictor, the following example formula is provided:

$$\hat{r}_{xy} = \frac{r_{xy_r}\left(\dfrac{SD_u}{SD_r}\right)}{\sqrt{1 - (r_{xy_r}) + (r_{xy_r})^2\left[\dfrac{(SD_u)^2}{(SD_r)^2}\right]}}$$

where

$\hat{r}_{xy}$ = estimated validity if restriction had not occurred
r_{xy_r} = validity coefficient computed on restricted scores
SD_u = standard deviation of predictor scores from unrestricted group
SD_r = standard deviation of predictor scores from restricted group

As an example, assume the standard deviation (a measure of individual differences) of applicants' scores on a test was 10. After making selection decisions using the test, the standard deviation of applicants' scores who were hired is 2. The validity coefficient computed for those hired is 0.20. Using the formula, we can estimate the test's validity if all individuals had been hired, and the range of test scores was not restricted. That is,

$$\hat{r}_{xy} = \frac{(0.20)\frac{10}{2}}{\sqrt{1 - (0.20)^2 + (0.20)^2[(10)^2 + (2)^2]}} = \frac{1.00}{1.40} = 0.71$$

The estimated validity of 0.71 is considerably higher than our original validity of 0.20. Thus range restriction had considerable effect. Where range restriction is low (that is, standard deviation of unrestricted predictor scores approximates that of restricted scores), computed validity is very close to estimated validity. But where range restriction is high, estimated validity on unrestricted scores differs substantially from validity computed on restricted scores.

With regard to correction for restriction in range, Chad Van Iddekinger and Robert Ployhart have provided several cautionary actions that should be considered; these include the following:

1. There are 11 types of range restriction that can occur; applying the wrong formula to the specific situation at hand can lead to an overestimate or an underestimate of true predictor validity. Articles by Paul Sackett and his colleagues and Frank Schmidt and John Hunter should be consulted for guidance on using the appropriate formula for a specific situation (see Van Iddekinger and Ployhart's article for these sources).

2. Concerns remain regarding the specific range restriction corrections that should be made. Initial use of sound validation designs and measurement procedures can help mitigate some of these concerns and should be emphasized whenever possible.[70]

Correcting validity coefficients for both range restriction and criterion unreliability are steps that the Society for Industrial and Organizational Psychology has recommended in its *Principles for the Validation and Use of Personnel Selection Procedures*.[71] We have given only one example of range restriction correction, that involving a single variable. Edwin Ghiselli, John Campbell, and Sheldon Zedeck provided formulas for correcting range restriction for one as well as for several variables.[72] In addition, Calvin Hoffman,[73] as well as Deniz Ones and Chockalingam Viswesvaran,[74] have shown how published test norms can be used to obtain unrestricted estimates of the predictor standard deviations to be used in making corrections.

Criterion Contamination

If scores on a criterion are influenced by variables other than the predictor, then criterion scores may be contaminated. The effect of contamination is to alter the magnitude of the validity coefficient. For instance, one criterion frequently used in validation studies is a performance evaluation rating. We may want to know whether performance on a selection measure is associated with performance on the job. However, performance ratings are sometimes subject to contamination or biased by extraneous variables such as gender and ethnicity of ratees or raters or by the job tenure of persons being rated. If criterion ratings are influenced by variables that have nothing to do with actual job performance, then our obtained validity coefficient will be affected. In some cases, the validity coefficient will be spuriously high; in others, spuriously low. Moreover, it is not always possible to know in advance the direction of these effects. Consider another example. One of the authors was engaged in a validation study of a selection measure for bank proof machine operators (sometimes called "item processors"). A proof machine is used by operators to encode magnetic numbers on the bottom of checks so they can be processed by a computer. The bank kept meticulous records of the number of checks processed by operators for specific time periods. Thus it appeared that a sound behavioral measure of performance was available that could be used as a criterion in the validation study. However, further analysis showed that even though the proof machines looked the same externally, some of the machines had different internal components. These different components permitted faster check processing. Our apparently "good" criterion measure was contaminated. Rather than solely measuring differences in operators' performance, the productivity measure was also tapping differences in equipment. Without proper adjustments, the measure would be useless as a criterion because of its contamination.

Another classic example of criterion contamination occurs when "total dollar sales" is being used as a criterion in a validation study of tests designed to measure traveling salespeople's selling ability. Suppose there are differences in the types of geographical territories sales personnel must work. Some territories contain long-term customers, so that all the salesperson has to do is take an order. In other, less mature territories, sales are much more difficult to achieve. A salesperson must really be able to sell in order to make a sale. Without some adjustment in the total dollar sales measure, criterion contamination will be present. Sales performance differences, as measured by total dollar sales, will be due more to territory assignment than to selling ability. The result will be a misleading validation study.

When contaminating effects are known, they should be controlled either by statistical procedures such as partial correlation, by the research design of the validation study itself (for example, including only those employees in a validation study that have the same length of employment), or by adjustments to criterion data such as the computation of ratios. Again, the reason for controlling contaminating variables is to obtain a more accurate reading of the true relationship between a predictor and a criterion.

Violation of Statistical Assumptions

Among others, one important assumption of a Pearson correlation is that a linear or straight-line relationship exists between a predictor and a criterion. If the relationship is nonlinear, the validity coefficient will give an underestimate of the true relationship between the two variables. For example, Figure 5.11 shows two scattergrams summarizing various relations between a selection measure and criterion. Case 1 shows a linear or straight-line relationship. A Pearson correlation coefficient would be appropriate for representing this relationship. However, if a Pearson correlation were calculated on the data in Case 2, the correlation would be equal to 0.00. Yet, we can see that there is a relationship. Low as well as high test performance is associated with high criterion scores. We know that a relation exists, but our Pearson statistic will not detect it; other analyses are called for. If we had simply computed the correlation without studying the scattergram, we could have drawn an incorrect conclusion. Prior to computing a validity coefficient, a scattergram should *always* be plotted and studied for the possibility of nonlinear association.

Utility Analysis

Picture yourself for a moment as an HR manager for a large computer manufacturing plant. Suppose you are looking at the results of a test validation study that shows a statistically significant validity coefficient of 0.50 for a test developed to predict the job performance of computer assembly workers in the plant. Obviously, you are excited about the results, because they suggest that the test can be used as an effective screening tool for computer assembly workers. Tomorrow you will be meeting with the executive staff of the plant; you have been asked to summarize the results and implications of the validation study. As you consider who will be at the meeting and what you will say, it becomes painfully obvious that the individuals in attendance (vice president of operations, vice president of accounting, and

FIGURE 5.11	Appropriateness of Pearson *r* for Various Predictor–Criterion Relationships

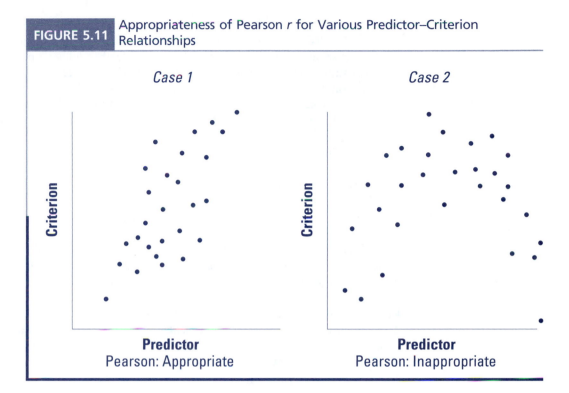

so on) are not likely to understand the meaning of a validity coefficient. You find yourself thinking, "What can I say so they will understand what this validity coefficient means?" "How can I get them to understand the value of the test?"

The situation we just described is not unusual. Frequently, those of us working in the field of HR selection find ourselves in situations where it is difficult to translate our research findings into practical terms that top management will understand. This problem is compounded when validation studies are being conducted and communicated. Few top-level managers outside of HR management understand what a validity coefficient is, much less what it means. Yet, we must find a common terminology to communicate this meaning if we are going to compete with other departments in our organization for scarce resources. It is important that we find a means to translate our research findings into concepts and terms that management can understand and deal with if we hope to see the results of our work implemented.

As you think about a common terminology that most managers will understand, you will probably conclude that a dollars-and-cents terminology is a practical option for communicating results. If we can translate the results of our validation work into economic dollars-and-cents terms or some other metric important to managers, we will probably receive the attention and understanding we want from other managers.

A Definition of Utility Analysis

The concept of *utility analysis* can be used to translate the results of a validation study into terms that are important to and understandable by managers. Utility analysis summarizes the overall usefulness of a selection measure or selection system. *Using dollars-and-cents terms as well as other measures such as percentage increases in output, utility analysis shows the degree to which use of a selection measure improves the quality of individuals selected versus what would have happened had the measure not been used.*[75]

Some Preliminary Work on Utility Analysis

Earlier, we noted that a common characteristic of attributes we measure in human resource selection is that scores on these attributes tend to follow a normal distribution. Normal distributions of job performance, for example, have been found for workers performing a variety of jobs. In general, the more complex the job, the greater the spread or variability in worker job performance. If the variability in worker productivity is large, then the usefulness or utility of valid methods to hire the best-performing workers will also be large.[76]

In examining productivity distributions, a common conclusion is that good workers produce roughly twice as much work as poor workers. This conclusion has naturally led to a series of logical questions such as, "How much is a good worker worth?" and "If we identify and hire applicants who are good workers using a valid selection procedure, what will be the dollar return from using the procedure?" Utility analysis was developed to answer such questions.[77]

Although the validity coefficient, coefficient of determination, and index of forecasting efficiency have been used over the years, these procedures do not readily communicate to practitioners the utility of using valid selection procedures. None of these statistics relate to the economic value of a selection measure or recognize that a measure's usefulness depends on the situation in which it is employed.[78] Early work by Hubert Brogden and H. C. Taylor and J. T. Russell is often recognized as laying the foundation for the development of utility analysis.[79] In sum, they suggested that the percentage of employees who will be identified as successful following the use of a valid test depends on three factors:

1. *Validity coefficient*—The correlation of the test with a criterion.

2. *Selection ratio*—The ratio of the number of persons hired to the number of applicants available. (The smaller the ratio, the more favorable for the organization, because it can be more selective in who is hired.)

3. *Base rate*—The percentage of employees successful on the job without use of the test. (A low base rate suggests that with the current selection system, there is difficulty in identifying satisfactory workers. Use of a valid test should improve the identification of satisfactory employees.)

Taylor and Russell produced a series of tables showing that the utility of a test (that is, the increase in percentage of successful employees selected following use of a valid test) varied substantially depending on the test's validity, selection ratio, and the base rate. Thus by means of the Taylor-Russell model, it was demonstrated that a test could be useful even when the validity coefficient was low.

Subsequent years led to additional, more complex utility models such as those by James Naylor and Lester Shine,[80] Hubert Brogden,[81] and Lee Cronbach and Goldine Gleser.[82] These models refined the concept of utility and led to its translation into definable, measurable payoffs. In particular, the Brogden and Cronbach and Gleser models laid the foundations for most utility models in use today. They proposed that a valid test used in selection be evaluated based on specific (dollar) payoffs. That philosophy underlies much of utility analysis as currently applied in the field of personnel selection.

One of the biggest hurdles to translating the concept of utility analysis from a theoretical idea to a practical method has been in determining how to put a dollar value on differences in workers' productivity. This employee productivity dollar value has been referred to as SD_y or the standard deviation across individuals of the dollar value of employee productivity. SD_y represents how much differences in workers' productivity varies in dollar value to the employer. Or, to put it another way, SD_y shows in dollar terms the difference between good and poor workers' productivity. The tough question is how to estimate SD_y. Although a variety of approaches have been proposed to estimating SD_y, ranging from cost-accounting methods to Wayne Cascio's CREPID[83] procedure, there is still debate as to which one is most appropriate in which situations. One common method that has been used is Schmidt and Hunter's rule: The value in the variability of employee job performance is estimated to be 40 percent of mean salary for the job.[84] Without going through the technical details, the 40 percent rule is based on supervisors' estimates of the dollar value of productivity provided to the employer by good, average, and poor workers on a job. Basically, it says that SD_y for a job is roughly 40 percent of the average salary paid for the job. For example, if an average annual salary of $30,000 is being paid, and if performance on the job is normally distributed, then SD_y = at least $12,000. This means that workers' productivity at the 84th percentile, or +1 standard deviation above the mean, is worth at least $12,000 more per year than that of workers who are average. The difference between good workers at the 84th percentile and poor workers at the 16th percentile, or −1 standard deviation below the mean, is worth $24,000 per year. We should point out that the 40 percent rule has been criticized by some because of its estimates of SD_y. Some research studies have supported the rule; others have not. Research continues in an attempt to further refine the measurement of SD_y.

A number of equations have been proposed for examining selection method utility. One equation that has been used for calculating the utility of a selection program is the following:[85]

$$\text{Expected dollar gain from selection} = N_S\, r_{xy}\, SD_y\, Z_x - N_T(C)$$

where

Expected dollar gain from selection = the return in dollars to the organization for having a valid selection program

N_S = number of job applicants selected

r_{xy} = validity coefficient of the selection procedure

SD_y = standard deviation of job performance in dollars

Z_x = average score on the selection procedure of those hired, expressed in z or standardized score form as compared to the applicant pool (an indication of the quality of the recruitment program)

N_T = number of applicants assessed with the selection procedure

C = cost of assessing each job applicant with the selection procedure

Applying Utility Analysis to Selection: Some Examples

To fully describe a complete application of utility analysis is too involved for our purposes here. However, we have prepared some examples that illustrate the use of utility analysis in determining the value of a valid selection method under various employment situations. The examples are based on the previous utility analysis equation.

Example 1: Costing the Value of a Selection Procedure. We have adapted a utility analysis outlined by Frank Schmidt and his associates.[86] They applied a utility model to examine the gain in dollars obtained by using a valid test for selection as compared to using a predictor that was not valid, or to hiring at random. Figure 5.12 summarizes

FIGURE 5.12	Examples of Utility Analysis Computed under Different Selection Conditions		
Utility Analysis Selection Factor	**Example 1 Mental Ability Test**	**Example 2 Mental Ability Test**	**Example 3 Reference Check**
Number of applicants selected (**N**)	10	10	10
Test validity (**r**)	0.51	0.51	0.26
Standard deviation of job performance ($) (**SD**)	$12,000	$12,000	$12,000
Average test score of those selected (**Z**)	1.00	1.25	1.00
Number of applicants tested (**N**)	100	100	100
Cost of testing each applicant (**C**)	$ 20	$ 20	$ 20
Expected payoff due to increased productivity per year for all employees hired	**$59,200**	**$74,500**	**$29,200**
Expected payoff per year for each employee hired	**$ 5,920**	**$ 7,450**	**$ 2,920**

some hypothetical data for the utility analysis components or factors that we listed earlier. In Example 1, suppose that the validity of a general mental ability test we are using is 0.51. (This is the average validity of general mental ability tests in predicting job performance as reported by Frank Schmidt and John Hunter.[87]) Of every 100 applicants that apply for the job under study, 10 are hired; therefore, the selection ratio is 0.10 or 10 percent. Assuming that individuals are hired on the basis of their test scores, and the top 10 percent is hired, the average test score of the 10 hired—relative to our 100 in the applicant pool in standardized z-score form—is 1.00 (+1 SD), or at the 84th percentile. The standard deviation in dollars for job performance is estimated to be at least $12,000 per year (0.40 × $30,000 average annual salary). An individual who is one standard deviation above the mean on job performance is worth $12,000 more to the company than an individual with average job performance. Finally, suppose that the cost of purchasing, administering, scoring, interpreting, and filing the test is $20 per applicant. When these values are substituted in our utility analysis equation, the result is

$$\begin{aligned} \text{Expected dollar payoff due to increased productivity} \\ \text{per year for all employees hired} = 10(0.51)(\$12,000)(1.00) - 100(\$20) \\ = \$59,200 \end{aligned}$$

Using the valid general mental ability test (versus using random selection or a nonvalid predictor) for one year to select workers would yield the company an expected net gain in productivity worth $59,200 for every 10 employees hired. Dollar gain each year per worker selected using the general mental ability test would be $5,920.

With the utility gain equation, it is possible to examine the effects of the equation's components on test utility. By systematically varying these components, impacts on expected gain can be seen. For example, increased testing costs, lowered validity, or an increased selection ratio will lower utility. Now, let's look at two more of these changes.

Example 2: Enhancing Recruitment.   In this example, let's assume that all of the utility analysis components that we just described are the same, with one exception. Assume that the average test score in standardized z-score form is increased from 1.00 to 1.25. How might this occur? With an enhanced recruitment campaign that attracts better-quality applicants, we will have higher-quality applicants to choose from. Therefore, we can hire those who have test scores indicating higher general mental ability. Because the mental ability test is valid—that is, higher test scores are associated with higher job performance—we will have better performers on the job and enhanced productivity. As you can see from Example 2 in Figure 5.12, this change leads to an annual expected dollar payoff—in increased productivity for the 10 employees hired—of $74,500 or $7,450 per year per employee.

Example 3: Using a Method with Low Validity.   Now, assume that we use a scored reference check rather than the general mental ability test in making selection decisions. In this case, the validity of the reference check is 0.26. (This is the average validity of reference checks in predicting job performance as reported by Frank Schmidt and John Hunter.[88]) The average reference check score in standardized z-score form in this case is 1.00. Notice that even using a selection method with low validity, it is still useful in selection decision making. Use of the valid reference check produces an annual dollar payoff of $29,200 or $2,920 per employee per year. This example illustrates how a method with even low validity can still be useful. By manipulating the other components of our utility analysis, we can determine when the costs associated with the use of a measure would exceed its return on our investment in it.

In a published account of an actual utility analysis, Frank Schmidt and his associates examined the dollar payoff of using a valid test (the Programmer Aptitude Test) in selecting computer programmers employed by the federal government.[89] Results of their analyses showed that under the most conservative selection conditions, an estimated productivity increase for one year's use of the test was $5.6 million. Other researchers have also translated selection procedure utility into dollar payoffs.[90]

It is important to recognize that utility analysis is a developing concept. For instance, some debate has centered on the size of economic returns found when estimating the utility of a valid selection procedure. In part, these estimates have been questioned when utility assumptions may not have been met and factors affecting the estimates have not been taken into account.

Utility analysis is based on several assumptions.[91] The first is that the relationship between a predictor and criterion is linear. Because the vast majority of ability and job performance relationships are linear, this assumption is not likely to be a troublesome one. A second assumption is that selection using the predictor is based on top-down hiring. That is, the top scorer is hired, followed by the rank-order hiring of other applicants until all positions are filled. Use of methods other than a valid predictor in hiring results in a loss of utility. Finally, when using top-down hiring, it is assumed that all applicants who are offered jobs accept their offers. When this result does not occur, lower-scoring applicants on the predictor must be hired. Because of our first assumption (that a linear relation exists between test performance and job performance), hiring lower-scoring applicants with less ability (rather than higher-scoring applicants) will result in lower job performance and lower selection procedure utility.

Wayne Cascio has suggested that a truer picture of actual gains from a selection program will be obtained only by including additional factors in utility analysis equations. Factors affecting the economic payoffs of selection programs include job tenure of hires, recruitment costs, effects of taxes, and time lags in developing new-hire competence in performance, to name only a few.[92] However, others appear to have played down the significance of some of these factors regarding the usefulness of utility estimates.[93]

In addition, some debate has developed and research is continuing on the methods for deriving the suitable standard deviation of job performance measures (SD_y).[94] Some of these methods involve cost accounting approaches,[95] whereas others involve subject matter experts making ratings of performance.[96] These data are then used for computing standard deviations of performance.

Acceptance by Practitioners

As you recall, we began this discussion by noting that a means was needed for translating the value of a valid selection method into terms that could be understood by practicing managers. Utility analysis is one means for dealing with this need. Certainly, translating outcomes into economic gains would seem to be important to practicing managers. However, the method is not always seen positively. One survey of applied psychologists and human resource professionals reported they found utility analysis difficult to understand and explain.[97] In two studies by Gary Latham and Glen Whyte, they concluded that the presentation to experienced managers of utility analysis results *decreased* managerial support for implementing a valid selection procedure.[98] Managers' lack of support was likely due to the managers' difficulties in understanding what the utility analysis results meant. Sole reliance on utility analysis results alone does not appear to be a guarantee that practitioners will be persuaded to adopt a particular selection program. In addition to technical considerations, political, social, and institutional factors should be considered when implementing and communicating utility analysis results.

BROADER PERSPECTIVES OF VALIDITY

Content, concurrent, and predictive validity have been the strategies traditionally employed in validation studies involving predictors used in personnel selection. However, other approaches have been developed that take a broader view of selection measure validity. Two such approaches are *validity generalization* and *job component validity*. Validity generalization relies on evidence accumulated from multiple validation studies that shows the extent to which a predictor that is valid in one setting is valid in other similar settings. Job component validity is a process of inferring the validity of a predictor, based on existing evidence, for a particular dimension or component of job performance. In this section, we will see how important these methods are to the future directions of validation research.

Validity Generalization

An Overview

For many years, selection specialists noted that validity coefficients for the same selection instruments and criteria measures varied greatly for validation studies performed in different organizational settings. This was even true when the jobs for which the selection program had been designed were very similar. It was concluded that the idiosyncrasies of jobs, organizations, and other unknown factors contributed to the differences in results that were obtained. Therefore, it was assumed that the validity of a test is specific to the job or situation where the validation study was completed. This assumption was based on what was called the *situational specificity hypothesis*. In the mid-1960s and early 1970s, Edwin Ghiselli published some classic studies involving hundreds of validation studies and validity coefficients classified by test and job types for two groups of criteria: job proficiency and training criteria.[99] Results from his work showed wide variations in magnitudes of validity coefficients across validation studies, even when the same test had been used to predict the same criteria for practically identical jobs. Ghiselli's results as well as those of others appeared to confirm the situational specificity hypothesis—validity of a test is specific to the job situation on which validity of the test has been determined. Supporters of the hypothesis believed that validity differences were due to dissimilarities in the nature of the specific employment situation or job in which a study was conducted—for example, the nature of the criteria used, the nature of the organization, or the inability of a job analysis to detect "real" job differences. This body of evidence led to the recommendation given by many that a separate validation study should be conducted for a selection measure whenever the measure is used in a different job situation or by a different employer.

In the late 1970s, the situational specificity hypothesis began to be challenged. Frank Schmidt, John Hunter, and their colleagues amassed and presented an impressive amount of evidence that cast considerable doubt on the validity of the situational hypothesis. Results from their analyses of validation studies involving cognitive ability tests led them to conclude that test validity does, in fact, generalize across situations. They argued that much of the differences found in a test's validity for similar jobs and criteria across different validation studies are not due to situational specificity but rather to methodological deficiencies in the validation studies themselves. Schmidt and Hunter hypothesized that these deficiencies that accounted for the differences among the validity coefficients reported in validation studies were due to the following factors:

1. The use of small sample sizes (sampling error)

2. Differences in test or predictor reliability

3. Differences in criterion reliability

4. Differences in the restriction of range of scores

5. The amount and kind of criterion contamination and deficiency

6. Computational and typographical errors

7. Slight differences among tests thought to be measuring the same attributes or constructs[100]

Through a series of studies involving meta-analytic statistical techniques, Schmidt, Hunter, and others conducted a number of investigations called *validity generalization* studies. Their objective was to determine whether these hypothesized deficiencies explained differences found among validity coefficients computed for specific cognitive ability tests used in very similar jobs. If the deficiencies were found to explain a large portion of the differences among the validity coefficients, then the situational specificity hypothesis would be disconfirmed. Such a result would suggest that with appropriate evidence, the validity of a test is generalizable from one situation to another that is very similar (that is, similar in terms of the same type of test and job on which the validity evidence had been accumulated). Conversely, if only a small portion of the differences in validity coefficients were explained by the deficiencies, it would indicate that test validity is situation specific. That is, rather than being generalizable from one situation to another, test validity information must be collected in each new setting in which a test is used.

Validity Generalization Methods

Validity generalization in selection may be defined as follows: *Validity generalization involves the statistical analyses of information accumulated from multiple validation studies involving a predictor whose results are combined to determine the overall effectiveness of the predictor in new employment settings or locations.* By combining data from multiple studies involving larger sample sizes than what would be available in a single validation study, a population validity coefficient can be derived to yield a more accurate picture of the true validity of the predictor.

Several articles have outlined the details of the methodology used by Schmidt, Hunter, and their associates for testing the situational hypothesis and establishing validity generalization. Basically, their methodology corrects for the effects of the first four deficiencies just listed;[101] the remaining three cannot be corrected with the available data. Their major steps are as follows:

1. Obtain a large number of published and unpublished validation studies.

2. Compute the average validity coefficient for these studies.

3. Calculate the variance of differences among these validity coefficients.

4. Subtract, from the amount of these differences, the variance due to the effects of small sample size.

5. Correct the average validity coefficient and the variance for errors that are due to other methodological deficiencies (that is, differences in criterion reliability, test reliability, and restriction in the range of scores).

6. Compare the corrected variance to the average validity coefficient to determine the variation in study results.

7. If the differences among the validity coefficients are very small, then validity coefficient differences are concluded to be due to the methodological deficiencies and not to the nature of the situation. Therefore, validity is generalizable across situations.

Schmidt and Hunter's early validity generalization work focused on the generalizability of cognitive ability paper-and-pencil tests.[102] Additional work has suggested that validity generalization extends beyond mental ability testing. Validity generalizability has also been reported to exist for predictors such as biographical data,[103] personality inventories,[104] and assessment centers.[105] Current work continues with other predictors.[106]

Conclusions from Validity Generalization Studies

From a body of validity generalization investigations, Schmidt and Hunter rejected the "situational specificity hypothesis" regarding test validity in selection. They have used results of these analyses to draw some far-reaching conclusions. First, they concluded that it is not necessary to conduct validity studies within each organization for every job. If the job of interest for the selection program is one of those for which validity generalization data have been reported, then the selection instruments reported in the validity generalization study can be used in the organization for selection.[107] This is because there are no organization effects on validity; therefore, the same predictor can be used across all organizations for the relevant job or jobs. To set up the selection program, it is only necessary to show that the job with the organization is similar to the job in the validity generalization study. If job similarity can be shown, then the selection measure can be used; a separate validation study is not needed. Obviously, this reduces the time, effort, and cost of establishing a valid selection program.

Second, mental ability tests can be expected to predict job performance in most, if not all, employment situations.[108] However, their usefulness as a predictor depends upon the complexity of the job in question. Validity coefficients of these tests will be higher for jobs that are more complex than for less complex jobs. In other words, the more complex the job, the better mental ability tests will be able to predict job performance.

Criticisms of Validity Generalization

The findings of Schmidt, Hunter, and their colleagues have not gone without challenge.[109] As we have mentioned, validity generalization studies apply correction formulas to the results of previous validity studies in order to correct the measurement deficiencies of these studies. Conclusions regarding the validity of the predictor and the generalizability of this validity estimate across organizations are based on the results of these correction formulas.

Ideally, these corrections should be made to each study in the validity generalization analyses using data supplied by that study. However, the validity studies usually do not report enough data to permit the corrections to be made in this manner. Instead, correction formulas use hypothetical values derived from other research work that are assumed to be appropriate for validity generalization analyses.

For the most part, criticisms of validity generalization studies have focused on the appropriateness of the correction formulas. Many of these critical studies have used computer simulation as the method for examining appropriateness. In doing this, samples are generated from various populations of validation studies. For example, the population could be of studies in which the difference in validity coefficients among studies is actually zero; all differences are actually due to measurement errors. In other cases, the validity studies used for analyses are drawn from two populations that, in fact, differ in the magnitude of the validity coefficient. In this way, the researcher knows at the start of the study whether the validity coefficients are the same or different across situations (for example, organizations). The correction formulas are then applied to the data generated by the simulation model. The researcher can then determine whether the results of the correction formulas agree with what is already known about the validity coefficients being tested. If agreement exists, the formulas are thought to be appropriate; if disagreement exists, the formulas are thought to be in error.

As an overall summary, it has been a common finding of these simulation studies that, under many conditions, the validity generalization correction formulas overestimate the amount of variance attributable to study deficiencies. The result of overestimates may be the rejection of the proposition that organizational differences affect validity coefficients more often than would be appropriate. The authors of these simulation studies, therefore, have generally cautioned restraint in the interpretation of the results of validity generalization studies, as well as careful consideration of the conclusions that have been drawn from them. We briefly summarize some of the points made in these critical studies. To obtain a more complete idea of the nature and extent of the criticism, it is necessary to read these studies directly.

Some studies have investigated the power of validity generalization analyses and the related concept of Type II error associated with these procedures. Power refers to the property of the statistical test for identifying differences when they do exist. In the case of validity generalization, power refers to the rejection of generalizability and the determination of effects of organizational variables on the validity coefficients among the data. Type II error refers to the failure to determine situation specificity when it exists and, therefore, to finding no differences among the validity coefficients under study.

Two variables that seemingly affect the power of validity generalization analysis are the number of coefficients used in the analysis and the size of the samples on which these coefficients are calculated. Paul Sackett, Michael Harris, and John Orr concluded that "true population differences of 0.1 will not be consistently detected regardless of [sample size and number of correlations], and differences of 0.2 will not be consistently detected at small values [of these same two variables]."[110]

Other studies have questioned whether the conclusions drawn from the statistical formulas of the Schmidt-Hunter procedures are appropriate. For example, Lawrence James and his associates have criticized several aspects of the Schmidt-Hunter procedures.[111] Among these are that the lines of evidence arguing for validity generalization are not nearly as strong as stated by Schmidt and Hunter; that the procedures call for double corrections for some measurement deficiencies; and that the use of sample validity coefficients in several formulas (as opposed to the Fischer z-transformations for these coefficients) is inappropriate. They concluded that "the prudent scientist/practitioner should be circumspect in interpreting results of [validity generalization] studies, especially those that support an inference of cross-situational consistency."

In partial response to some of these criticisms, Larry Hedges developed an unbiased alternate correction for sampling error.[112] Central to this correction is the use of unbiased estimators of the population validity parameters that had been developed in previous research. Hedges demonstrated that while the correction formula for sampling error used in the Schmidt and Hunter technique is biased, the bias is usually quite small. Consequently, there is little reason to discount the results of existing validity generalization studies solely because of the bias in the correction of sampling error.

More recently, Neal Schmitt has acknowledged that the contributions of meta-analyses and validity generalization have transformed the field of human resource selection. However, he notes that the corrections made for both direct and indirect range restriction in selection measures' scores appear overly optimistic and based on far too few actual studies. He also argues that the assumption that organizations use top/down hiring in making employment decisions is simply not the case in most organizations. Thus, Schmitt suggests that these assumptions regarding the level of range restriction and use of top/down hiring are simply untenable, and as a consequence, population validity estimates are very much inflated as compared to observed validity coefficients.[113]

Other criticisms have also been aimed at validity generalization. A few of the major ones are summarized here:

1. *Lumping together good and bad studies.* Mark Cook reported that some critics have charged that validity generalization mixes together both good and bad studies when accumulating validity evidence. However, as Cook commented, a major problem in selection research is that no single study is perfect, particularly when it comes to sample size. Therefore, useful conclusions about validity may be reached only by pooling results of many investigations, as is done in validity generalization.[114]

2. *File drawer bias.* Another claim has been that journals are less likely to publish negative results; that is, results showing that a selection procedure is not valid. For this reason, some have alleged that many studies have been tucked away in file drawers, and their negative results are not known. Most validity generalization studies attempt to locate such studies for inclusion. Some attempts have been made to derive a statistic for estimating the effect of file drawer bias on validity generalization results.[115]

3. *Criterion unreliability.* The larger the estimate of criterion unreliability, the larger the increase in estimated true validity of the selection measure. Another criticism of validity generalization has been that its advocates have used underestimates of criterion reliability in their studies. A common estimate used for supervisory ratings, the most frequently used criterion in empirical validation studies, has been 0.60.[116] In contrast, others have used 0.80 as the reliability estimate and, as might be expected, have found smaller increases in estimated true validity of ability tests. On the other hand, research appears to support the use of 0.60 as an estimate for supervisor rating criteria.[117]

Schmidt and his associates have concluded that such criticisms are concerned more with fine-tuning the method of validity generalization and do not detract significantly from its overall methodology and conclusions.[118] Some independent evidence seems to support their contention. The National Research Council Committee on the General Aptitude Test Battery of the U.S. Employment Service reviewed the statistical and measurement procedures of validity generalization and generally concluded that they were scientifically sound.[119]

Obviously, more research is necessary before the issues concerning assumptions and procedures of validity generalization studies can be completely agreed upon. Nonetheless, validity generalization studies have produced some of the most important statements regarding selection in recent years.

The work of Schmidt, Hunter, and their associates has important implications for the future of validation research in HR selection. The numerous validity generalization studies available suggest that the validity of a test is more generalizable across *similar situations* and *similar jobs* than has been previously thought. This conclusion should not be interpreted to mean that a test that is valid for one job will be valid for *any other* job. However, sufficient validity information on one job may be generalizable to other, very similar jobs. Ultimately, if validity generalization evidence for a test or some other predictor is available, a validation study may not be needed. Instead, it may be possible to use previous validation research to support the validity and use of the test for certain jobs.

Validity Generalization Requirements

In using validity generalization evidence to support a proposed selection procedure, a user would need to take a number of steps. Assuming that an appropriate validity generalization study does not exist, the first step is to gather all relevant validation studies, both published and unpublished, that investigate the relationship between the proposed selection procedure and the relevant criteria. Once these studies have been collected and proper meta-analytic methods have been applied to the studies, the following conditions must be met:

1. The user must be able to show that the proposed selection procedure assesses the same knowledge, skill, ability, or other characteristic, or that it is a representative example of the measure used in the validity generalization study database.

2. The user must be able to show that the job in the new employment setting is similar (in job behaviors or knowledge, skills, and abilities) to the jobs or group of jobs included in the validity generalization study database.[120]

If these conditions can be met, then the new employment setting shows evidence of selection procedure validity.

To meet these conditions, specific supporting information is needed. This information includes the following:

1. Validity generalization evidence consisting of studies summarizing a selection measure's validity for similar jobs in other settings.

2. Data showing the similarity between the jobs for which the validity evidence is reported and the job in the new employment setting (an analysis of the job in the new employment setting is mandatory).

3. Data showing the similarity between the selection measures in other studies that compose the validity evidence, and those measures that are to be used in the new employment setting.[121]

So what is the future for validity generalization? At this point, it is another procedure or strategy that can be used to justify the use of a selection procedure.[122] However, rather than conducting a local single validation study, this approach implies that one analyzes the accumulated validity evidence to develop generalized validity inferences. Professional judgment is needed to evaluate the results of meta-analytic research, which underlies validity generalization. As previously noted, the researcher must consider the meta-analytic methods used and the tenability of the underlying assumptions, particularly regarding the role of sampling error and other statistical artifacts. Although it is likely to be more useful to generalize validity evidence from a meta-analysis than from a local individual study, there are a number of interpretational difficulties, particularly if the meta-analytic results are based on common methods (for example, employment interviews) instead of being organized around a set of traits (for example, cognitive ability measures or personality traits such as conscientiousness). These interpretational difficulties suggest this strategy will require a relatively high level of expertise, in part because meta-analytic techniques are still evolving. Further research on the validity generalization model; future versions of federal and professional guidelines on employee selection; future decisions in employment discrimination cases involving validity generalization as a validation strategy; and agreement among selection researchers on the technical details underpinning validity generalization will inform us as to when the method has matured as a fully accepted, welcomed validation strategy.

An obvious advantage to using validity generalization—as compared to using traditional criterion-related validation research—is that resources saved in time and money could be considerable. The cumulative predictor-criterion relationship evidence collected in a validity generalization study should be more accurate than any single validation study involving the same predictor.[123]

Although much of the controversy that characterized the application of validity generalization to personnel selection issues appears to have abated, and there is probably at least general acceptance of validity generalization methods among personnel selection scientists, important legal questions may remain. Frank Schmidt and John Hunter concluded that validity generalization has received generally favorable treatment by the courts.[124] In contrast, however, Frank Landy noted that a 1989 Sixth Circuit Court of Appeals conclusion that validity generalization was totally unacceptable under relevant case law and professional standards would have a chilling effect on the sole use of validity generalization as a legal defense for using a selection measure.[125]

Similarly, depending on validity generalization evidence alone to argue support for a predictor to a conservative court can produce some significant burdens for a defending organization. Daniel Biddle and Patrick Nooren theorize that conservative courts would rather see an *actual* validity coefficient that is derived at the defendant's specific locale than an *inferred* value derived from validity generalization procedures. They note that employers face an uphill climb in such courts because they must (a) show that factors specific to the applicant pool, the predictor itself, and the job itself do not limit the predictor from being valid in the employer's specific location and (b) demonstrate that the validity generalization study and the predictor's inferred validity are large enough to be used for its intended purpose and will offset any disparate impact found with the selection procedure by the employer.[126]

After reading our previous discussion on validity generalization, you may ask, "If validity generalization can save time and resources in the undertaking of validation efforts—as well as produce more meaningful results than a single validation study could—why not just use a validity generalization strategy to study all of our selection procedures?" Certainly, this is a reasonable question, and some may very well agree with the sentiment implied. But, in addition to the political concerns we alluded to earlier, and some legal issues remaining to be addressed (for example, the level of detail required by the courts in a validity generalization job analysis), other factors may limit the implementation of validity generalization as a sole validation strategy. Calvin Hoffman and Morton McPhail have noted two of these factors.[127] First, existing validity generalization studies have not examined all jobs in the world of work. There are probably jobs in which few or no validity generalization results exist for use as validity-supporting arguments for implementing selection procedures. Second, the amount of job analysis information collected in a typical validity generalization study may be too sparse to meet the requirements of the courts. Due to these concerns, Hoffman and McPhail concluded that "because the demands of practice sometimes necessitate more detail than required by the best wisdom of the profession ... sole reliance on VG evidence to support test use is probably premature."[128]

Job Component Validity

An Overview

Job component validity is a validation strategy that incorporates a standardized means for obtaining information on the jobs for which a validation study is being conducted. Whereas validity generalization typically involves a more global assessment of a job, job component validity incorporates a more detailed examination of the job.[129] The procedure involves inferring validity for a given job by analyzing the job, identifying the job's major functions or components of work, and then choosing tests or other predictors—based on evidence obtained through previous research—that predict performance on these major work components. Notice that selection procedure validity for a work component is inferred from existing validation research evidence rather than by directly measuring validity through the traditional methods we have discussed (for example, criterion-related or content-related strategies). Two important assumptions underlie this strategy: (a) when jobs have a work component in common, the knowledge, skills, or abilities required for performing that component are the same across these jobs; and (b) a predictor's validity for a knowledge, skill, or ability required for performing a work component is reasonably consistent across jobs.[130]

Conducting a Job Component Validity Study

Briefly, the major steps involved in conducting a job component validation study are as follows:

1. *Conduct an analysis of the job using the Position Analysis Questionnaire (PAQ).* The PAQ is a commercially available, paper-and-pencil questionnaire that contains a comprehensive listing of general behaviors required at work. A respondent (for example, a job analyst) responds to the PAQ by indicating the extent to which these descriptions accurately reflect the work behaviors performed on a particular job.

2. *Identify the major components of work required on the job.* Once the PAQ has been used to analyze a job, the most important work behaviors or components of the job are identified.

3. *Identify the attributes required for performing the major components of the job.* Using ratings from experts, the developers of the PAQ established links between 76 job attributes (including those related to mental ability, perceptual ability, psychomotor ability, interest, and temperament) and the work behaviors listed on the PAQ for approximately 2,200 job titles in the U.S. labor force.[131] This expert ratings' database serves as a basis for identifying which of the 76 attributes are needed to perform the most important work components of a new job being analyzed. For instance, when a new job is analyzed with the PAQ, results of the analysis show the importance of specific attributes, relative to the 2,200 jobs in the PAQ database, in performing the identified components of the job.

4. *Choose tests that measure the most important attributes identified from the PAQ analysis.* Strictly speaking, actual validity coefficients are not computed in job component validity. Predicted validity coefficients and scores for selected general aptitude tests are estimated from an existing database of test scores and PAQ

information. These coefficients estimate what the validity of a test would have been had an actual criterion-related validation study been performed. The results show which ability tests are likely to be most useful and valid for selecting among applicants for the job being analyzed.

Recall the two job component validity assumptions we mentioned earlier. These assumptions form the foundation for which test validity is argued under the job component validity approach. Most important, if a test has been found to predict performance for a job component across a wide array of jobs, it is assumed the test should be valid for jobs in which that same component is most salient. The results of a job component validity analysis identify which tests to use for the job being analyzed.

Accuracy of Job Component Validity Studies

Several studies have investigated the correspondence between predicted validity coefficients of tests using job content validity and actual computed validity coefficients. Studies by Morton McPhail[132] and L. M. Holden[133] reported that job component validity estimates were generally lower and more conservative than validity coefficients obtained in actual validation studies.[134] Calvin Hoffman and Morton McPhail compared predicted job component validity coefficients for 51 clerical jobs with actual validity coefficients computed for similar jobs in a prior validation study.[135] They concluded that the job component validity procedure produced predicted validity coefficients that were very similar to those that had been determined statistically. They reasoned that if the job component validity procedure were used to infer validity of tests for clerical jobs, the conclusions reached would be similar to those that had been drawn from actual validation studies.

We have seen how the PAQ can be used to conduct a job component validation study. Richard Jenneret and Mark Strong have extended the job component validation concept by using the Department of Labor's O*NET database.[136] The O*NET database consists of job analysis information collected on a large array of occupations. Among the many job data available is information on 42 generalized work activities that occupations may involve. A generalized work activity represents a work behavior used in performing major work functions such as analyzing data or information. In their research, Jenneret and Strong found that the O*NET's generalized work activity information was useful for identifying tests to be used in selection for jobs requiring specific types of aptitudes such as verbal aptitudes.

At this point, use of the O*NET for job component validation is in its infancy. More developmental research is needed. However, assuming this research is completed, all an employer might have to do is to analyze a job using the generalized work activities and, perhaps, other O*NET information. This information would then be used to obtain estimates of useful predictors for the job of interest. Again, assuming that the necessary developmental research takes place, O*NET may offer a promising option for those organizations, both large and small, that seek guidance in choosing selection procedures.

Criticisms of Job Component Validity Strategy

Among several specific criticisms, Kevin Mossholder and Richard Arvey have raised several general points concerning the job component validity approach.[137] Although there is limited evidence to the contrary, they noted that the method has been less successful in predicting actual validity coefficients. Second, the strategy has been relatively less useful in predicting psychomotor test data. Finally, the strategy has generally reported results for tests from the General Aptitude Test Battery that are available only to public employers. Results are available for only a relatively limited number of commercially available tests.

In spite of criticisms, the job component validity strategy offers another tool for examining the validity of predictors used in selection. A practitioner may use the method in several ways. A conservative use would be to apply the job component validity approach and then conduct a local validation of the tests identified. Another way the method could be used is to simply apply the job content validity approach and implement the recommended tests without a local validation study. Although this option apparently has not undergone a lot of legal scrutiny, there is at least one court case (*David Taylor v. James River Corporation*, 1989)[138] in which the method received a favorable review.

The method provides a unique approach for small organizations where sample sizes for criterion-related validity are inadequate, or for those jobs yet to be created or undergoing significant change. Richard Jeanneret described two cases illustrating the versatility of the strategy when implemented in a situation unsuited for use with conventional criterion-related approaches.[139] In the first case, a preemployment test battery was developed using the job component validity strategy for workforce selection in a state-of-the-technology manufacturing facility that was under construction. In a second application, the strategy was implemented to design selection test specifications for space station personnel who would spend extended periods in an orbiting space station. These may seem to be unusual employment situations that are different from the typical employment context. Tests are being validated before the actual employment setting exists. Yet, situations such as these depict the future needs in many of today's technologically driven organizations; many do not lend themselves to study using traditional validation strategies. Such situations may very likely be the norm in coming years.

VALIDATION OPTIONS FOR SMALL BUSINESSES

We have reviewed a number of strategies for validating selection measures, all of which are suitable for use in organizations. However, some of these strategies are practical only for large organizations that have large numbers of job incumbents and applicants on whom validation data can be collected. What about small organizations in which there are only small numbers of people available for data collection? Small businesses can pose particular methodological challenges for those contemplating a validation study. But, these challenges do not mean selection measure validation should be ignored. Selection measure validation is probably more critical for a small business than it is for a large one. Small businesses often hire applicants who possess job-specific KSAs and work habits and who must immediately begin a job without completing an extensive training program. Large businesses generally have the resources to compensate for a hiring "mistake"; in small businesses, one or two bad hires could be financially devastating (for example, because of poor job performance, theft, a negligent hiring suit brought against the business, or even a discrimination lawsuit brought by an aggrieved applicant). Recall from our earlier reading that small businesses with 15 or more employees are covered by many equal employment opportunity laws.[140] Given these issues, validation evidence is essential for small businesses. However, what validation options are available?

Of the strategies we have discussed, there are several options. Content validity is one. We noted earlier that criterion problems—and the smaller numbers of people available to participate in a criterion-related validation study in many organizations—are two reasons for the increased use of content validity strategies. As Robert Guion pointed out, when a small organization of 50 or so people is hiring only one or two people a year, ordinary empirical validation cannot be performed.[141] Content validity, however, does not necessarily mean criterion-related validity.

Assuming that validity generalization continues to mature as an acceptable means for validating predictors, it is a second option. To implement a validity generalization study, a small business has two main requirements: (a) to show that the measure used in selection assesses the same constructs as a measure used in a previous validity generalization study, and (b) to show that the jobs for which the measure is used are similar to those jobs in the validity generalization study. If a suitable, existing validity generalization study cannot be found, then one would have to be conducted following the steps we outlined earlier.

Finally, as we just discussed, job component validity or some other form of synthetic validity is a third option. *Synthetic validity* is a logical process of inferring test validity for components of jobs. Charles Scherbaum has discussed the major approaches to synthetic validity as well as the future trends and legal issues involving these methods.[142] Whatever the specific approach, all synthetic approaches tend to involve the following steps: (a) analyzing jobs to identify their major components of work, (b) determining the relationships of selection predictors with these job components using content, construct, or criterion-related validity strategies, and (c) choosing predictors to use in selection based on their relationships with important job components.

To illustrate a form of synthetic validity that incorporates criterion-related validity, let's look at a simple example. Suppose an organization wanted to validate some tests for three different jobs, Typist, Clerk, and Receptionist, using a criterion-related strategy. The problem is that the largest number of people in any one of the three jobs is 60 (Typist); the smallest number of people is 40 (Receptionist). Recall that, in our discussion earlier in the chapter about computing empirical validity, we said it was essential to use as large a sample size as possible in computing a validity coefficient. With small sample sizes, there is a greater likelihood of not finding that a test is valid than there is of finding it valid, even when the test is truly valid.

Using a job analysis questionnaire, it is found that even though job titles are different, some of the jobs share some components of work. Figure 5.13 illustrates three jobs and job performance components that are common to each. The three jobs and the number of their incumbents are as follows: (a) Typist ($N = 60$), (b) Clerk ($N = 50$), and (c) Receptionist ($N = 40$). Three job performance components characterizing these jobs include (a) *Following Directions,* (b) *Typing,* and (c) *Dealing with the Public.* The Xs in the matrix represent the job performance components common to each job. For instance, *Following Directions* and *Typing* characterize the job of Typist, while *Typing* and *Dealing with the Public* are most descriptive of the Receptionist job.

The lower half of Figure 5.13 lists the measures that were developed or chosen from commercially available ones to assess each of the job components. For example, the Oral Directions Test was selected to determine whether it could predict the job component, *Following Directions.* Criterion measures (such as performance ratings) are developed for each job dimension. Jobs sharing a common job performance component are combined for validating the selection measure. For instance, for the job component *Following Directions,* the Typist and Clerk jobs are combined (combined sample size = 110); for the job component *Typing,* the Typist and Receptionist jobs are grouped together (combined sample size = 100); and, finally, for the job component *Dealing with the Public,* the jobs of Clerk and Receptionist are combined (combined sample size = 90). Notice that by combining jobs that require the same work activity, we are able to increase our sample sizes substantially over those samples we would have had using only one job. We can collapse jobs together because we are studying a common work activity. In this sense, validity is "synthetic"; we are not creating validity per se, but rather creating a situation that will permit a better estimate of validity. The major advantage of this is that selection measures are validated across several jobs in an organization, rather than for only one job.

FIGURE 5.13 Illustration of Test Validation Using Synthetic Validity

Job	Number of Employees	Job Performance Component		
		Following Directions I	Typing II	Dealing with the Public III
Typist	60	X	X	
Clerk	50	X		X
Receptionist	40		X	X
Total number of employees in combined jobs		110	100	90

Predictor	Job Performance Component		
	I	II	III
Oral Directions Test	√		
Typing Test		√	
Public Relations Test			√
Total number of employees available for test validation	110	100	90

NOTE: X represents job dimensions characteristic of a job. Jobs sharing an X for the same dimension require the same job function. √ indicates the selection measure chosen for predicting success on a particular job dimension.

Once the jobs have been combined on common job performance components, criterion measures (such as performance ratings) have been collected on each employee performing the job components, and selection measures have been administered, then test and criterion data are correlated. Statistically significant relationships indicate a valid selection measure. As you can see, rather than validating a measure for a whole job, we have broken jobs down into component job performance dimensions and validated our selection measures against these specific components. Because our sample sizes are larger than they would have been for any one job, we can more appropriately perform a criterion-related validation study. Our example illustrates only one approach to synthetic validation. John Hollenbeck and Ellen Whitener have offered another synthetic validation option for small sample size situations.[143]

For the small firm with jobs in which there are a number of incumbents, synthetic validity may offer one solution to the thorny problem of small sample size. The principal assumption in employing a synthetic validity approach is that our analyses of jobs will identify job dimensions common to those jobs studied.

For the small organization, building a database sufficiently large to conduct an empirical validation study is a particularly difficult problem. Additional options include (a) combining similar jobs or components of jobs across different organizations such as in a cooperative validation study, (b) combining similar jobs or components of jobs within and across organizations, and (c) accumulating data over time. Using experts to judge the relationship between selection system and job content is another possibility.[144]

As compared to large organizations, the types of evidence available for showing job relatedness are often quite different in small organizations. Rational judgment is likely to play a far more important role in validity studies within small organizations than large ones. In such cases, the more evidence we can collect on job relatedness, even judgmental evidence, the better.

THE FUTURE OF VALIDATION RESEARCH

In 1983, a survey of 437 organizations by the Bureau of National Affairs revealed that only 16 percent of the firms had validated one or more of their selection techniques.[145] Ten years later, corporate use of validation strategies such as those we have discussed in this chapter had shown little change. A random sample survey of 1,000 companies listed in *Dun's Business Rankings* with 200 or more employees indicated that of the 201 firms responding, only 24 percent stated they had conducted validation studies of their selection measures.[146] Unfortunately, we do not have current survey data showing the extent to which organizations are undertaking validation efforts. Nevertheless, if the older survey results still apply, the results are surprising in light of both the current legal mandates to validate selection predictors and the productivity gains that can be reaped by organizations using valid predictors in selection.

For the most part, we have taken a classic approach in this chapter to discussing validity and the strategies used for validity assessment. Much of our focus has assumed that predictor and criterion data are available on individuals, that data are available on sizable numbers of individuals, and that jobs and the requirements for performing them are remaining relatively constant over time. However, a number of writers have noted that yesterday's workplace is not today's, and it will not be tomorrow's.[147] Changes are occurring, and they will likely affect the assumptions we have made and the future of validation research. Such changes include the following:

1. Increasing numbers of small organizations without the resources (for example, time or money) or technical requirements (for example, large sample sizes) to undertake traditional validation strategies

2. Increasing use of teams of workers rather than individuals[148]

3. Changes in the definitions of job success to include criteria such as organization and job commitment, teamwork, and quality of service delivered to customers

4. The changing nature of work—in that jobs and the requirements for performing them are becoming more fluid, requiring job analytic methods that focus on broader work capacities rather than on molecular requirements of tasks

Because of changes such as these, nontraditional approaches to examining selection measure validity are being called for. For example, in the case of small organizations, Frank Schmidt has argued that complex, expensive validation studies are not necessary.[149] He suggests that through validity generalization research, we already know what works. According to Schmidt, ability tests, assessment centers, interviews, and the like can be implemented in such small organizations and can produce an immediate payoff in their selection systems. But will such strategies as validity generalization be widely adopted? As we suggested earlier, only time will tell. Before widespread adoption of these strategies, however, a balance must be struck between the competing issues, a balance involving (a) the technical requirements of validation research, (b) organizations' needs and the changing nature of work and work contexts, (c) societal demands, and (d) current laws and legal interpretations of the federal and professional guidelines and requirements that determine appropriate validation strategies. Until that balance is reached, we have chosen to provide you with a foundation of knowledge on the subject of those validation methods that have a proven record of usefulness. This foundation should help to prepare you for future needs, challenges, and developments that you may encounter with regard to the study of selection measure validity.

REFERENCES

1. Society for Industrial and Organizational Psychology, *Principles for the Validation and Use of Personnel Selection Procedures*, 4th ed. (Bowling Green, OH: Author, 2003), 4.

2. Greg L. Stewart, Susan L. Dustin, Murray R. Barrick, and Todd C. Darnold, "Exploring the Handsake in Employment Interviews," *Journal of Applied Psychology* 93 (2008): 1139–1145; and William F. Chaplin Jeffrey B. Phillips, Jonathan D. Brown, Nancy R. Clanton, and Jennifer L. Stein, "Handshaking, Gender, Personality, and First Impressions," *Journal of Personality and Social Psychology: Personality Porcesses and Individual Differences* 79 (2000): 110–117.

3. Samuel Messick, "Validity," in *Educational Measurement*, ed. R. L. Linn (New York: American Council on Education and MacMillan Publishing Co., 1989), 13–104.

4. Charles H. Lawshe, "Inferences from Personnel Tests and Their Validity," *Journal of Applied Psychology* 70 (1985): 237–238.

5. Theresa J. B. Kline, *Psychological Testing: A Practical Approach to Design and Evaluation* (Thousand Oaks, CA: Sage, 2005), 212–213.

6. Lawrence S. Kleiman and Robert H. Faley, "The Implications of Professional and Legal Guidelines for Court Decisions Involving Criterion-Related Validity: A Review and Analysis," *Personnel Psychology* 38 (1985): 803–834.

7. Dirk D. Steiner and Stephen W. Gilliland, "Fairness Reactions to Personnel Selection Techniques in France and the United States," *Journal of Applied Psychology* 61 (1996): 134–141.

8. Kevin R. Murphy, Jessica L. Dzieweczynski, and Yang Zhang, "Positive Manifold Limits the Relevance of Content-Matching Strategies for Validating Selection Test Batteries," *Journal of Applied Psychology* 94 (2009): 1018.

9. Benjamin Schneider and Neal Schmitt, *Staffing Organizations* (Glenview, IL: Scott, Foresman, 1986).

10. Lawrence Kleiman and Robert Faley, "Assessing Content Validity: Standards Set by the Court," *Personnel Psychology* 31 (1978): 701–713.

11. *Albemarle Paper Company v. Moody*, 422 U.S. 405 (1975).

12. Equal Employment Opportunity Commission, Civil Service Commission, Department of Labor, and Department of Justice, *Adoption of Four Agencies of Uniform Guidelines on Employee Selection Procedures, 43 Federal Register* 38, 305 (August 25, 1978).

13. Richard S. Barrett, *Challenging the Myths of Fair Employment Practice* (Westport, CT: Quorum Books, 1998), 62–76.

14. Irwin L. Goldstein, Sheldon Zedeck, and Benjamin Schneider, "An Exploration of the Job Analysis–Content Validity Process," in *Personnel Selection in Organizations*, ed. Neal Schmitt and Walter C. Borman (San Francisco: Jossey-Bass, 1993), 7–10.

15. Ibid., 9.

16. Irwin Goldstein and Sheldon Zedeck, "Content Validation," in *Fair Employment Strategies in Human Resource Management*, ed. Richard S. Barrett (Westport, CT: Quorum Books, 1996), 29.

17. Goldstein, Zedeck, and Schneider, "An Exploration of the Job Analysis–Content Validity Process," 21.

18. Charles Lawshe, "A Quantitative Approach to Content Validity," *Personnel Psychology* 28 (1975): 563–575.

19. Lyle F. Schoenfeldt, Barbara B. Schoenfeldt, Stanley R. Acker, and Michael R. Perlson, "Content Validity Revisited: The Development of a Content-Oriented Test of Industrial Reading," *Journal of Applied Psychology* 61 (1976): 581–588.

20. Silvia Moscoso and Jesus Salgado, "Psychometric Properties of a Structured Behavioral Interview to Hire Private Security Personnel," *Journal of Business and Psychology* 16 (2001): 51–59.

21. Goldstein, Zedeck, and Schneider, "An Exploration of the Job Analysis–Content Validity Process."

22. Equal Employment Opportunity Commission et al., *Adoption of Four Agencies of Uniform Guidelines on Employee Selection Procedures*, 303.

23. Ibid., 302.

24. Ibid.

25. Robert M. Guion, "Recruiting, Selection, and Job Placement," in *Handbook of Industrial and Organizational Psychology*, ed. Marvin D. Dunnette (Chicago: Rand McNally, 1974), 786.

26. Mary L. Tenopyr, "Content-Construct Confusion," *Personnel Psychology* 30 (1977): 47–54. See also Robert M. Guion, "Content Validity—the Source of My Discontent," *Personnel Psychology* 30 (1977): 1–10; Robert M. Guion, "Content Validity: Three Years of Talk—What's the Action?" *Public Personnel Management* 6 (1977): 407–414; and Robert M. Guion, "Content Validity in Moderation," *Personnel Psychology* 31 (1978): 205–213.

27. Goldstein and Zedeck, "Content Validation," 36.

28. Michael R. Carrier, Anthony T. Dalessio, and Steven H. Brown, "Correspondence between Estimates of Content and Criterion-Related Validity Values," *Personnel Psychology* 43 (1990): 85–100.

29. Murphy, Dzieweczynski, and Zhang, "Positive Manifold Limits the Relevance of Content-Matching Strategies for Validating Selection Test Batteries," 1018, 1028.

30. Robert M. Guion and C. J. Cranny, "A Note on Concurrent and Predictive Validity Designs: A Critical Reanalysis," *Journal of Applied Psychology* 67 (1982): 239–244.

31. Frank J. Landy, *Psychology of Work Behavior* (Homewood, IL: Dorsey Press, 1985), 65.

32. Neal Schmitt, Richard Z. Gooding, Raymond A. Noe, and Michael Kirsch, "Metaanalyses of Validity Studies Published between 1964 and 1982 and the Investigation of Study Characteristics," *Personnel Psychology* 37 (1984): 407–422.

33. Gerald V. Barrett, James S. Phillips, and Ralph A. Alexander, "Concurrent and Predictive Validity Designs: A Critical Reanalysis," *Journal of Applied Psychology* 66 (1981): 1–6.

34. D. S. Ones, C. Viswesvaran, and F. L. Schmidt, "Comprehensive Meta-analysis of Integrity Test Validities: Findings and Implications for Personnel Selection and Theories of Job Performance," *Journal of Applied Psychology* 78 (1993): 679–703; and R. P. Tett, D. N. Jackson, and H. M. Rothstein, "Personality Measures as Predictors of Job Performance: A Meta-analytic Review," *Personnel Psychology* 44 (1991): 703–742.

35. Chad H. Van Iddekinge and Robert E. Ployhart, "Developments in the Criterion-Related Validation of Selection Procedures: A Critical Review and Recommendations for Practice," *Personnel Psychology* 61 (2008): 897.

36. Society for Industrial and Organizational Psychology, *Principles for the Validation and Use of Personnel Selection Procedures*, 3rd ed. (College Park, MD: Author, 1987), 7.

37. Society for Industrial and Organizational Psychology, *Principles for the Validation and Use of Personnel Selection Procedures* (2003), 10.

38. Society for Industrial and Organizational Psychology, *Principles for the Validation and Use of Personnel Selection Procedures* (1987).

39. Charles Hulin, R. A. Henry, and S. L. Noon, "Adding a Dimension: Time as a Factor in the Generalizability of Predictive Relationships," *Psychological Bulletin* 107 (1990): 328–340.

40. Gerald Barrett, Ralph Alexander, and D. Dorerspike, "The Implications for Personnel Selection of Apparent Declines in Predictive Validities Over Time: A Critique of Hulin, Henry, and Noon," *Personnel Psychology* 45 (1992): 601–617.

41. D. L. Deadrick and R. M. Madigan, "Dynamic Criteria Revisited: A Longitudinal Study of Performance Stability and Predictive Validity," *Personnel Psychology* 43 (1990): 717–744.

42. Steven H. Brown, "Long-Term Validity of a Personal History Item Scoring Procedure," *Journal of Applied Psychology* 63 (1978): 673–676.

43. Frank L. Schmidt, John E. Hunter, and A. N. Outerbridge, "Impact of Job Experience and Ability on Job Knowledge, Work Sample Performance, and Supervisory Ratings of Job Performance," *Journal of Applied Psychology* 71 (1986): 432–439.

44. Lawrence S. Kleiman and Robert H. Faley, "The Implications of Professional and Legal Guidelines for Court Decisions Involving Criterion-Related Validity: A Review and Analysis," *Personnel Psychology* 38 (1985): 803–834.

45. Daniel A. Biddle and Patrick M. Nooren, "Validity Generalization vs Title VII: Can Employers Successfully Defend Tests Without Conducting Local Validation Studies?" *Labor Law Journal* 57 (2006): 29.

46. Herman Aguinis and Marlene A. Smith, "Understanding the Impact of Test Validity and Bias on Selection Errors and Adverse Impact in Human Resource Selection," *Personnel Psychology* 60 (2007): 165.

47. Ibid., 165–199.

48. Society for Industrial and Organizational Psychology, *Principles for the Validation and Use of Selection Procedures* (2003).

49. Robert M. Guion, *Personnel Testing* (New York: McGraw-Hill, 1965), 128.

50. Based on John F. Binning and Gerald V. Barrett, "Validity of Personnel Decisions: A Conceptual Analysis of the Inferential and Evidential Bases," *Journal of Applied Psychology* 74 (1989): 478–494.

51. W. Bruce Walsh and Nancy E. Betz, *Tests and Assessment* (Englewood Cliffs, NJ: Prentice Hall, 1990), 67.

52. Edwin E. Ghiselli, John P. Campbell, and Sheldon Zedeck, *Measurement Theory for the Behavioral Sciences* (San Francisco: Freeman, 981).

53. Paul R. Sackett and Richard D. Arvey, "Selection in Small *N* Settings," in *Personnel Selection in Organizations*, ed. Neal Schmitt and Walter C. Borman (San Francisco: Jossey-Bass, 1993), 431–432.

54. In some employment settings, an organization may not have as many applicants or employ as many people as given in our example. Thus empirical validity may not be technically feasible. Under such circumstances, other approaches to validity—such as content validity, validity generalization, and synthetic validity—may need to be considered.

55. Richard D. Arvey and Robert H. Faley, *Fairness in Selecting Employees* (Reading, MA: Addison-Wesley, 1988), 164–165.

56. Ibid., 167.

57. Frank L. Schmidt, Benjamin P. Ocasio, Joseph M. Hillery, and John E. Hunter, "Futher Within—Setting Empirical Tests of the Situational Specificity Hypothesis in Personnel Selection," *Personnel Psychology* 38 (1985): 509–524.

58. Ghiselli, Campbell, and Zedeck, *Measurement Theory for the Behavioral Sciences*, 145; also see Philip J. Bobko, *Correlation and Regression* (New York: McGraw-Hill, 1995), 142–143.

59. Kevin Murphy, "Fooling Yourself with Cross Validation: Single Sample Designs," *Personnel Psychology* 36 (1983): 111–118.

60. Philippe Cattin, "Estimation of the Predictive Power of a Regression Model," *Journal of Applied Psychology* 65 (1980): 407–414.

61. Kevin R. Murphy, "Cost-Benefit Considerations in Choosing among Cross-Validation Methods," *Personnel Psychology* 37 (1984): 15–22.

62. Van Iddekinge and Ployhart, "Developments in the Criterion-Related Validation of Selection Procedures: A Critical Review and Recommendations for Practice," 887.

63. Ibid., 889.

64. Charles H. Lawshe and Michael J. Balma, *Principles of Personnel Testing* (New York: McGraw-Hill, 1966), 301.

65. Ibid., 306–308.

66. Guion, *Personnel Testing*, 141–144.

67. J. P. Guilford, *Psychometric Methods* (New York: McGraw-Hill, 1954), 400–401.

68. Van Iddekinge and Ployhart, "Developments in the Criterion-Related Validation of Selection Procedures: A Critical Review and Recommendations for Practice," 883.

69. Robert L. Thorndike, *Applied Psychometrics* (Boston: Houghton Mifflin, 1982); and C. A. Olson and B. E. Becker, "A Proposed Technique for the Treatment of Restriction of Range in Selection Validation," *Psychological Bulletin* 93 (1983): 137–148.

70. Van Iddekinge and Ployhart, "Developments in the Criterion-Related Validation of Selection Procedures: A Critical Review and Recommendations for Practice," 884.

71. Society for Industrial and Organizational Psychology, *Principles for the Validation and Use of Personnel Selection Procedures* (2003).

72. Ghiselli, Campbell, and Zedeck, *Measurement Theory for the Behavioral Sciences;* see also Paul Muchinsky, "The Correction for Attenuation," *Educational and Psychological Measurement* 56 (1996): 63–75.

73. Calvin Hoffman, "Applying Range Restriction Corrections Using Published Norms: Three Case Studies," *Personnel Psychology* 48 (1995): 913–923.

74. Deniz S. Ones and Chockalingam Viswesvaran, "Job-Specific Applicant Pools and National Norms for Personality Scales: Implications for Range-Restriction Corrections in Validation Research," *Journal of Applied Psychology* 88 (2003): 570–577.

75. Milton L. Blum and James C. Naylor, *Industrial Psychology: Its Theoretical and Social Foundations* (New York: Harper & Row, 1968); and Wayne F. Cascio, *Costing Human Resources: Financial Impact of Behavior in Organizations* (Boston: Kent, 1982), 130.

76. Frank L. Schmidt and John E. Hunter, "The Validity and Utility of Selection Methods in Personnel Psychology: Practical and Theoretical Implications of 85 Years of Research Findings," *Psychological Bulletin* 124 (1998): 262–263; see also John E. Hunter, Frank L. Schmidt, and M. K. Judiesch, "Individual Differences in Output Variability as a Function of Job Complexity," *Journal of Applied Psychology* 75 (1990): 28–34.

77. Mark Cook, *Personnel Selection* (Chichester, New York: John Wiley, 1998), 277–286.

78. Schneider and Schmitt, *Staffing Organizations*, 264.

79. H. C. Taylor and J. T. Russell, "The Relationship of Validity Coefficients to the Practical Effectiveness of Tests in Selection," *Journal of Applied Psychology* 23 (1939): 565–578.

80. James C. Naylor and Lester C. Shine, "A Table for Determining the Increase in Mean Criterion Score Obtained by Using a Selection Device," *Journal of Industrial Psychology* 3 (1965): 33–42.

81. Hubert E. Brogden, "On the Interpretation of the Correlation Coefficient as a Measure of Predictive Efficiency," *Journal of Educational Psychology* 37 (1946): 64–76.

82. Lee J. Cronbach and Goldine C. Gleser, *Psychological Tests and Personnel Decisions* (Urbana: University of Illinois Press, 1965).

83. Wayne F. Cascio and R. A. Ramos, "Development and Application of a New Method for Assessing Job Performance in Behavioral/Economic Terms," *Journal of Applied Psychology* 71 (1986): 20–28.

84. John E. Hunter and Frank L. Schmidt, "Fitting People to Jobs: The Impact of Personnel Selection on National Productivity," in *Human Performance and Productivity: Human Capability Assessment*, ed. Marvin D. Dunne He and Edwin A. Fleishman (Hillsdale, NJ: Lawrence Erlbaum Associates, 1982), 233–292.

85. Frank L. Schmidt, John E. Hunter, Robert C. McKenzie, and Tressie W. Muldrow, "Impact of Valid Selection Procedures on Work-Force Productivity," *Journal of Applied Psychology* 64 (1979): 609–626.

86. Ibid.

87. Frank Schmidt and John Hunter, "The Validity and Utility of Selection Methods in Personnel Psychology: Practical and Theoretical Implications of 85 Years of Research Findings," *Psychological Bulletin* 124 (1998): 265.

88. Ibid.

89. Schmidt, Hunter, McKenzie, and Muldrow, "Impact of Valid Selection Procedures on Work-Force Productivity."

90. Philip Roth, Philip Bobko, and Hunter Mabon, "Utility Analysis: A Review and Analysis at the Turn of the Century," in *Handbook of Industrial, Work, and Organizational Psychology, Volume 1: Personnel Psychology*, ed. Neil Anderson, Deniz S. Ones, Kepir Handan Sinangil, and Chockalingam Viswesvaran (Thousand Oaks, CA: Sage, 2002), 383–404.

91. Wayne Cascio, "Assessing the Utility of Selection Decisions," in *Personnel Selection in Organizations*, ed. Neal Schmitt and Walter C. Borman (San Francisco: Jossey-Bass, 1993), 318–320.

92. Ibid.

93. Frank L. Schmidt, "Personnel Psychology at the Cutting Edge," in *Personnel Selection in Organizations*, 509–510.

94. Michael J. Burke and James T. Frederick, "Two Modified Procedures for Estimating Standard Deviations in Utility Analysis," *Journal of Applied Psychology* 71 (1986): 334–339; and Jack E. Edwards, James T. Frederick, and Michael J. Burke, "Efficacy of Modified CREPID SDy's on the Basis of Archival Organizational Data," *Journal of Applied Psychology* 73 (1988): 529–535.

95. Olen L. Greer and Wayne Cascio, "Is Cost Accounting the Answer? Comparison of Two Behaviorally Based Methods for Estimating the Standard Deviation of Job Performance in Dollars with a Cost-Accounting Approach," *Journal of Applied Psychology* 72 (1987): 588–595.

96. Schmidt, Hunter, McKenzie, and Muldrow, "Impact of Valid Selection Procedures on Work-Force Productivity."

97. John T. Hazer and Scott Highhouse, "Factors Influencing Managers' Reactions to Utility Analysis: Effects of SD_y Method, Information Frame, and Focal Intervention," *Journal of Applied Psychology* 82 (1997): 104–112.

98. Gary P. Latham and Glen Whyte, "The Futility of Utility Analysis," *Personnel Psychology* 47 (1994): 31–46; Glen Whyte and Gary Latham, "The Futility of Utility Analysis Revisited: When Even an Expert Fails," *Personnel Psychology* 50 (1997): 601–610; see also Steven F. Cronshaw, "Lo! The Stimulus Speaks: The Insider's View on Whyte and Latham's 'The Futility of Utility Analysis,'" *Personnel Psychology* 50 (1997): 611–615.

99. Edwin E. Ghiselli, *The Validity of Occupational Aptitude Tests* (New York: John Wiley, 1966); and Edwin E. Ghiselli, "The Validity of Aptitude Tests in Personnel Selection," *Personnel Psychology* 26 (1973): 461–477.

100. Frank Schmidt and John Hunter, "History, Development, and Impact of Validity Generalization and Meta-analysis Methods," in *Validity Generalization: A Critical Review*, ed. Kevin R. Murphy (Mahwah, NJ: Lawrence Erlbaum Associates, 2003), 31–66.

101. Kevin R. Murphy, "The Logic of Validity Generalization," in *Validity Generalization: A Critical Review*, ed. Kevin R. Murphy (Mahwah, NJ: Lawrence Erlbaum Associates, 2003), 1–30.

102. Frank L. Schmidt and John E. Hunter, "The Future of Criterion-Related Validity," *Personnel Psychology* 33 (1980): 41–60.

103. Frank L. Schmidt and H. R. Rothstein, "Application of Validity Generalization Methods of Meta-Analysis to Biographical Data Scales Used in Employment Selection," in *Biodata Handbook: Theory, Research, and Use of Biographical Information in Selection and Performance Prediction*, ed. G. S. Stokes, M. D. Mumford, and W. A. Owens (Palo Alto, CA: CPP Books, 1994), 237–260.

104. Murray R. Barrick and Michael K. Mount, "Impact of Meta-Analysis Methods on Understanding Personality-Performance Relations," in *Validity Generalization: A Critical Review*, ed. Kevin R. Murphy (Mahwah, NJ: Lawrence Erlbaum Associates, 2003), 197–222.

105. Neal Schmitt, J. R. Schneider, and J. R. Cohen, "Factors Affecting Validity of a Regionally Administered Assessment Center," *Personnel Psychology* 43 (1991): 1–12.

106. Hannah R. Rothstein, "Progress is Our Most Important Product: Contributions of Validity Generalization and Meta-Analysis to the Development and Communication of Knowledge," in *Validity Generalization: A Critical Review*, ed. Kevin R. Murphy (Mahwah, NJ: Lawrence Erlbaum Associates, 2003), 115–154.

107. Schmidt and Hunter, "The Future of Criterion-Related Validity."

108. Schmidt and Hunter, "The Validity and Utility of Selection Methods in Personnel Psychology: Practical and Theoretical Implications of 85 Years of Research Findings."

109. Kevin R. Murphy, *Validity Generalization: A Critical Review*.

110. Paul R. Sackett, Michael M. Harris, and John M. Orr, "On Seeking Moderator Variables in the Meta-Analysis of Correlational Data: A Monte Carlo Investigation of Statistical Power and Resistance to Type 1 Error," *Journal of Applied Psychology* 71 (1986): 302–310.

111. Lawrence R. James, Robert G. Demaree, Stanley A. Mulaik, and Michael D. Mumford, "Validity Generalization: Rejoinder to Schmidt, Hunter, and Raju (1988)," *Journal of Applied Psychology* 73 (1988): 673–678.

112. Larry Hedges, "An Unbiased Correction for Sampling Error in Validity Generalization Studies," *Journal of Applied Psychology* 74 (1989): 469–477.

113. Neal Schmitt, "The Value of Personnel Selection: Reflections on Some Remarkable Claims," *Academy of Management Perspectives* 21 (2007): 19–23.

114. Cook, *Personnel Selection*, 119.

115. Ibid., 119–120.

116. Ibid.

117. Ibid., 121.

118. Frank L. Schmidt, Deniz S. Ones, and John E. Hunter, "Personnel Selection," in *Annual Review of Psychology* (Stanford: Annual Reviews, 1992), 631.

119. J. A. Hartigan and A. K. Wigdor, *Fairness in Employment Testing: Validity Generalization, Minority Issues, and the General Aptitude Test Battery* (Washington, DC: National Academy Press, 1989).

120. Society for Industrial and Organizational Psychology, *Principles for the Validation and Use of Selection Procedures* (2003), 28.

121. For a study illustrating the classification of jobs in the context of validity generalization, see Edwin I. Cornelius, Frank L. Schmidt, and Theodore J. Carron, "Job Classification Approaches and the Implementation of Validity Generalization Results," *Personnel Psychology* 37 (1984): 247–260.

122. Schmidt and Hunter, "History, Development, and Impact of Validity Generalization and Meta-Analysis Methods."

123. Ibid., 37.

124. Ibid.

125. Frank J. Landy, "Validity Generalization: Then and Now," in *Validity Generalization: A Critical Review*, ed. Kevin R. Murphy (Mahwah, NJ: Lawrence Erlbaum Associates, 2003), 155–196.

126. Biddle and Nooren, "Validity Generalization vs Title VII: Can Employers Successfully Defend Tests Without Conducting Local Validation Studies?" 230.

127. Calvin Hoffman and S. Morton McPhail, "Exploring Options for Supporting Test Use in Situations Precluding Local Validation," *Personnel Psychology* 51 (1998): 987–1003.

128. Ibid., 990.

129. Kevin W. Mossholder and Richard D. Arvey, "Synthetic Validity: A Conceptual and Comparative Review," *Journal of Applied Psychology* 69 (1984): 322.

130. P. Richard Jeanneret, "Applications of Job Component/Synthetic Validity to Construct Validity," *Human Performance* 5 (1992): 83.

131. Ibid.

132. S. Morton McPhail, "Job Component Validity Predictions Compared to Empirical Studies," in a symposium, *Current Innovations in PAQ-Based Research and Practice*, Annual Conference of the Society for Industrial and Organizational Psychology, Orlando, FL, May 1995.

133. L. M. Holden, "Job Analysis and Validity Study for the Distribution Planning Office Technical Progression," unpublished report (Los Angeles: Southern California Gas Company, 1992).

134. Hoffman and McPhail, "Exploring Options for Test Use in Situations Precluding Local Validation."

135. Ibid.

136. P. Richard Jeanneret and Mark H. Strong, "Linking O*NET Job Analysis Information to Job Requirement Predictors: An O*NET Application," *Personnel Psychology* 56 (2003): 465–492.

137. Mossholder and Arvey, "Synthetic Validity: A Conceptual and Comparative Review," 328.

138. *Taylor v. James River Corporation*, CA 88-0818-T-C (TC) (S.D. AL, 1989).

139. Jeanneret, "Applications of Job Component/Synthetic Validity to Construct Validity," 91–93.

140. Mark N. Bing, H. Kristl Davison, and Richard Arvey, "Using a Repeated-measures Approach to Validating Personality Tests in Small Samples: A Feasibility Study with Implications for Small Businesses," *Journal of Managerial Issues* 21 (2009): 12.

141. Guion, *Personnel Testing*, 169.

142. Charles Scherbaum, "Synthetic Validity: Past, Present, and Future," *Personnel Psychology* 58 (2005): 481–515.

143. John R. Hollenbeck and Ellen M. Whitener, "Criterion-Related Validation for Small Sample Contexts: An Integrated Approach to Synthetic Validity," *Journal of Applied Psychology* 73 (1988): 536–544.

144. Sackett and Arvey, *Personnel Selection in Organizations*, 432–445.

145. Bureau of National Affairs, *Recruiting and Selection Procedures* (Personnel Policies Forum Survey No. 146) (Washington, DC: Bureau of National Affairs, 1983).

146. David E. Terpstra and Elizabeth J. Rezell, "The Relationship of Staffing Practice to Organizational Level Measures of Performance," *Personnel Psychology* 46 (1993): 27–48.

147. Lynn R. Offerman and Marilyn K. Gowing, "Personnel Selection in the Future: The Impact of Changing Demographics and the Nature of Work," in *Personnel Selection in Organizations*, ed. Neal Schmitt and Walter C. Borman (San Francisco: Jossey-Bass, 1993), 385–417.

148. José M. Prieto, "The Team Perspective in Selection and Assessment," in *Personnel Selection and Assessment: Individual and Organizational Perspectives*, ed. Heinz Schuller, James L. Farr, and Mike Smith (Hillsdale, NJ: Lawrence Erlbaum Associates, 1993), 221–234.

149. Schmidt, "Personnel Psychology at the Cutting Edge," 501–502.

Strategies for Selection Decision Making

Roger selects about 100 employees each year for various positions at the plant. He is proud of his skill in selection and boasts that he knows a good applicant when he sees one. However, an examination of employee records reveals a different story. The turnover rate of good employees is quite high; many of the employees Roger hired turned out to be poor performers and were later terminated; and one applicant who Roger rejected was hired by a competitor and is now their most productive manager. What went wrong with the selection process? Why is Roger so overconfident about his hiring prowess?

The mystery is even more perplexing because Roger's company uses job-related selection devices in its hiring process. In fact, the company hired consultants to help design its current selection system, which is considered state-of-the-art and capable of withstanding legal challenges. Applicant data are carefully collected and documented throughout each phase of the selection process.

In an interview with Roger, flaws of the selection process emerged. Investigators discovered that although Roger systematically collects various information about each applicant using valid selection devices, he makes his final hire/no hire decisions by gut feelings, or intuition. He sizes up applicants using the collected data and then compares them to his own mental image of a good employee.

Two primary reasons can be cited for the low quality of Roger's selection decisions. First, although he uses data collected from valid selection instruments, he combines the information from these various sources unsystematically. In fact, unknown to him, Roger is inconsistent in many selection decisions. Second, Roger is unaware of his true hits and misses as a decision maker because he does not keep records of his own decision making, and the company does not audit his selection decisions periodically. Together, these practices lead to suboptimal selection decision making for both Roger and his firm. It is important to realize that even when an organization employs valid and reliable selection procedures, poor implementation of these procedures in selection decision making can undermine the entire selection system.

How can faulty selection decision making such as Roger's be improved? To begin, we must focus on selection decision making as much as we do on developing and administering valid selection devices. By following sound, systematic decision-making procedures and studying decision outcomes, managers can improve their effectiveness. In this chapter, we first focus on characteristics of selection decisions. Then we outline and assess eight different methods for combining collected predictor information. Next, we list five systematic decision-making strategies for using combined predictor information that can improve selection decision making. We conclude the chapter with practical advice for making selection decisions.

Selection decisions come in two basic varieties: simple and complex. Simple selection decisions involve one position with several applicants. Applicants are assessed on the KSAs important to job success. The applicant who most closely approximates the requirements of the job is selected. Complex selection decisions are those involving several applicants and several positions. Here the decision is not only whom to select, but which candidate is best for each job.

In either case, simple or complex, selection information can be overwhelming at times. The information processing demands placed on a selection decision maker can be represented by the following equation:

Selection information processing demands

= Number of applicants × Amount of selection data collected

These selection information processing demands become great when there are many applicants, and many types of selection data are collected on each one. When time and other costs are factored into the decision, even simple selection decisions become costly. Imagine a situation that occurred in Duluth, Minnesota, a few years ago when 10,000 applicants applied for 300 operator positions at a paper mill. The paperwork alone must have been staggering!

Managers, supervisors, and others who hire employees have several decision options. They can decide to select (or promote or train) an applicant or to reject the applicant from further consideration. Another alternative is to defer the decision and gather more information. This may be done, for example, when all applicants for a position have been interviewed but no clear choice emerges. Additionally, a decision maker may choose to select an applicant on probation. If the employee does not meet expectations during the probationary period, the relationship is terminated. Whatever option is chosen may result in either desirable or undesirable outcomes for the organization.

Ideally, selection decisions result in desired outcomes; that is, employing those who will succeed and rejecting those who will not succeed in the job. However, even under the best circumstances, errors will be made. There are two types of selection decision errors: false positives (or erroneous acceptances) and false negatives (erroneous rejections). *False positive errors* occur when applicants successfully pass through all of the selection phases and are employed, but prove to be unsuccessful on the job. These errors are costly and sometimes disastrous depending on the nature of the job. Additionally, it may be difficult to terminate some false positives once they are hired, adding further to an organization's costs. Many organizations use a probationary period (for example, six weeks for nonexempt employees or six months for exempt employees) in order to reduce the long-term consequences of false positive errors.

False negative errors are equally problematic. These errors occur when applicants who would have been successful on the job are rejected. These applicants might have been rejected at any phase of the selection process. Although these errors are almost impossible to detect as compared to false positive errors, they can be equally damaging to the organization. For example, a design engineer applicant rejected at one organization may prove costly if she develops a new marketable product for a competitor. Likewise, an applicant from a legally protected group who was inappropriately rejected for a position may successfully challenge the incorrect decision in a costly EEO lawsuit.

As decision makers, we obviously want to minimize our false positive and false negative errors. We are most interested in identifying *true positives* (applicants who successfully pass our selection measures *and* perform the job successfully) and *true negatives* (applicants who fail our selection measures *and* would not have performed the job successfully had they been hired). How do we do this? We begin by using standardized selection procedures that have the highest validity for our selection situation. Then we employ proven decision-making strategies when using scores obtained from valid selection procedures as a basis for hiring job applicants. Answering three questions related to these points will enhance managers' employment decision making:

1. For a specific selection situation, what are the best methods for collecting predictor information on job applicants?

2. Because we often collect applicant information using more than one predictor (for example, a test and a structured interview), how should we combine scores on the predictors to give applicants an overall or total score for selection decision-making purposes?

3. Once a total score on two or more predictors is obtained, how should this overall score be used to make selection decisions?

Decision makers cannot avoid selection errors entirely, but they can take precautions to minimize them. Addressing the three questions raised here helps a decision maker take appropriate precautions. Systematic decision-making strategies such as those we discuss in this chapter can improve the chances of making correct decisions; intuition, gut instincts, premonitions, or other such subjective decision-making procedures are not successful.

Methods for Collecting and Combining Predictor Information

Although you may not have selected someone for employment, you probably have participated in other types of selection situations—choosing a roommate, asking someone out, or voting on an individual's suitability for membership in a club. You may not have realized it at the time, but you collected "information" on these individuals. In some cases, your information came from something as formal as an application. In other cases, your information was collected informally while observing a person's physical traits (for example, physical attractiveness), style of dress, or conversation (for example, an accent). Once you obtained your selection information (and this may have been done over a very brief period of time), you somehow combined everything in order to reach your selection decision.

In personnel selection, we can collect information on job applicants using several different methods, and we can combine the collected information using a number of procedures. In this section, we describe eight methods based on whether predictor information was collected either mechanically or judgmentally and whether the collected information was combined for selection decision making either mechanically or judgmentally.[1] As we will see, it is advisable to use some of these methods more than others.

Table 6.1 describes two modes of collecting predictor information from job applicants (*mechanical* and *judgmental* data collecting) that are used by selection decision makers. Predictor information collected *mechanically* refers to applicant data collected without the use of human judgment by selection decision makers. Objective data (such as that from a mental ability test) fall into this category. Predictor data collected *judgmentally* involves the use of human judgment by selection decision makers. For example, an unstructured employment interview is a subjective means for collecting predictor data judgmentally. In this case, questions may vary from one applicant to the next; interviewers think of questions at the time of the interview, and there is no formal means of scoring interviewees' answers.

Once predictor data have been collected, the different pieces of information must be combined in order to reach a selection decision. Table 6.2 summarizes two modes (*mechanical* and *judgmental*) for combining predictor information for selection decision-making

TABLE 6.1	Modes of *Collecting* Predictor Information from Job Applicants	
	Mode of *Collecting* Predictor Information	
	Mechanical	**Judgmental**
Description	*No use* of human judgment by selection decision makers in collecting applicant information	Use of human judgment by selection decision makers in collecting applicant information
Example	Administration of a mental ability test	Administration of an unstructured employment interview

TABLE 6.2	Modes of *Combining* Predictor Information from Job Applicants	
	Mode of *Combining* Predictor Information	
	Mechanical	**Judgmental**
Description	*No use* of human judgment by selection decision makers in combining applicant information	Use of human judgment by selection decision makers in combining applicant information
Example	Entering applicant's test and interview scores in a statistically determined equation developed to predict future job performance	Briefly reviewing applicants' test and interview scores, and from this information, forming a "gut impression" of applicant future job performance

purposes. For example, predictor information can be combined mechanically by entering applicants' test and interview scores into a statistical equation developed to predict job performance When applicants' predictor data are added together using human intuition or "gut instincts," then the data have been combined *judgmentally*. For example, a selection decision maker who looks at applicants' employment interview and ability test score results—and then forms a subjective, overall impression of the applicants—has combined predictor data judgmentally.

The Methods

In this section, we describe eight methods used for collecting and combining predictor information from job applicants. These methods describe whether human resource selection decision makers collect and combine predictor information mechanically, judgmentally, or both. Table 6.3 lists the eight methods. As we will see, some methods are more effective than others.

Pure judgment is a method in which judgmental predictor data are collected and combined subjectively for selection decision making. No objective data (for example, tests) are collected. The decision maker forms an overall impression of the predicted success of the applicant. The overall judgment may be based on some traits or standards in the mind of the decision maker (for example, beliefs about what it takes to make a good employee on the job), but these standards are usually not objective. The decision maker's role is to both collect information and make a decision about the applicant. For example, after several unstructured applicant interviews, a hiring manager selects a corporate recruiter based on the manager's cursory review of the applicants' resumes and his impressions of them. No formal assessments of applicants are made; in making a decision, the

	Method of *Combining* Predictor Information	
Method of *Collecting* Predictor Information	**Mechanical**	**Judgmental**
Judgmental	Trait Ratings	Pure Judgment
Mechanical	*Pure Statistical*[a]	Profile Interpretation
Both	*Mechanical Composite*[a]	Judgmental Composite
Either/Both	*Mechanical Synthesis*[a]	Judgmental Synthesis

TABLE 6.3 Methods of *Collecting* and *Combining* Predictor Information

[a]Indicates (usually) superior methods for collecting and combining predictor information.

NOTE: ***Judgmental***—Involves collecting/combining predictor information using human judgment. ***Mechanical***—Involves collecting/combining predictor information *without* using human judgment.

hiring manager subjectively combines the collected resume and interview information. "Gut feelings" regarding the combined information are the basis for the decision.

Trait ratings are a method in which judgmental data are collected and then combined mechanically. The decision maker rates applicants based on interviews, application blanks, and so on. Ratings are then entered into a formula and added together and an overall score is computed for each applicant. The decision maker's role is to collect information (that is, the ratings), but the decision is based on the results of the formula calculations. For example, applicants for a sales representative job are assessed in several interviews. Judgmental ratings are entered into a formula, and an overall score is computed across the interviews. The highest-scoring applicant receives the job offer.

Profile interpretation is a method in which objective data are collected mechanically but combined judgmentally. The decision maker reviews all the objectively collected data (from tests and other objective measures) and then makes an overall judgment of the applicant's suitability for the job. For example, a manager of a telemarketing firm selects telephone operators based on scores on three tests. The test data are combined judgmentally by the manager, who looks over the three test scores and forms an overall impression of whether the applicants would make successful operators.

A *pure statistical* method involves collecting data mechanically and combining data mechanically. For example, an applicant applies for an administrative assistant position by responding to a clerical skills test and personality inventory via computer. The data collected are then scored and combined by a formula calculated by the computer. The selection supervisor receives a printout that lists applicants in the order of their overall combined scores.

A *judgmental composite* method is one in which both judgmental and mechanical data are collected and then combined judgmentally. This is probably one of the most commonly used methods, and the one used by Roger in the example at the beginning of the chapter. The decision maker judgmentally combines all information about an applicant and makes an overall judgment about the applicant's likely success on the job. For example, test (mechanical) information and unstructured interview (judgmental) information are collected on auto mechanic applicants. The selection manager looks at the information and makes an overall judgment of whether to employ the applicant, but uses no formula or other formal means to calculate an overall score.

Mechanical composite is a method that collects both judgmental and mechanical data and then combines them mechanically. Test scores, biographical data scores, interview ratings, or other predictor information are combined using a formula that predicts job success. For example, assessment centers used for managerial promotion decisions typically use a mechanical composite strategy for making decisions about whom to promote.

A *judgmental synthesis* approach is one in which all information (both mechanical and judgmental data) is first mechanically combined into a prediction about the applicant's likely success. Then this prediction is judged in the context of other information about the applicant. For example, engineering applicants are scored on the basis of tests and biographical data. A formula is used to compute an overall score. A panel of interviewers discusses the applicants' characteristics and makes its decisions about whom to hire based on both their predicted success (from the formula) and judgments of the interviewers on how well the applicants will fit in the organization.

Mechanical synthesis is a method that first combines subjectively all information (both mechanical and judgmental) into a prediction about the applicant's likely success. This prediction is then mechanically combined with other information (for example, test scores) to create an overall score for each applicant. For example, test scores and interview information are reviewed by a work team. Members of the work team make their individual predictions of the likely success of each applicant. These predictions are then entered with other information into a formula to score and predict the applicant's likely success on the job.

Which Method Is Best?

In 1954, Paul Meehl released the most well-known and controversial publication on the role of clinical judgment in predicting human behavior.[2] Meehl concluded from his work that clinical experts' intuitive predictions of human behavior were significantly less accurate than predictions made using more formal, mechanical means (for example, using a statistical equation for combining predictor information). More than 30 years later, Meehl reflected that no more than 5 percent of his findings in 1954 could be retracted. In fact, he noted that any retractions would give more support to what we have termed "mechanical" approaches.[3] Clearly, Meehl's work favored the use of mechanical approaches.

Another review examined 45 studies in which 75 comparisons were made regarding the relative efficiency (superior, equal, or inferior in prediction) of the eight methods of collecting and combining selection information just described.[4] It found that the *pure statistical, mechanical composite,* and *mechanical synthesis* methods were always either equal or superior to the other methods. These results have been replicated in numerous other studies.[5]

Why does mechanical combination of data yield better results than judgmental combination? Bernard Bass and Gerald Barrett[6] suggested several reasons for the superiority of mechanical over judgmental methods for making selection decisions. First, accuracy of prediction depends on the proper weighting of predictor scores to be combined, regardless of which approach is used. Because it is almost impossible to judge what weights are appropriate with any degree of precision, even mechanical approaches that use equal weightings of predictor scores are more likely to make better decisions than methods relying on human judgment.

Second, as data on additional applicants are added to already available data, more accurate models can be created statistically. This makes it possible to improve the decision-making model continuously and adapt it to changing conditions in the environment. Decision makers relying solely on judgment have cognitive limits in their ability to improve their prediction models. In fact, many decision makers rely on a judgmental model developed early in life and never changed, thus leading to increasing rather than decreasing selection errors. In our opening example, Roger may have developed his model of "the ideal employee" in the early 1960s and continues to adhere to it to this day.

Third, decision makers relying on judgment can do as well as a statistical model only if they have been thorough, objective, and systematic in both collecting and combining the information. Because many managers and supervisors make selection decisions only sporadically, it is less likely they will be thorough, objective, and systematic in collecting and combining selection information. Consequently, their decisions will not equal those of a statistical model.

Fourth, decision makers are likely to add considerable error if they are allowed to combine judgmentally subjective data (for example, interview assessments) and objective data (for example, test scores). Their implicit theories (derived from past experience as well as other sources) of good applicants may bias their evaluations and ultimately decisions to select or reject an applicant. Inconsistency across decisions can have numerous causes: time pressure to make a decision, a bad day at home, or even comparisons with the most recently selected applicants.

Finally, there is the problem of the overconfidence of many selection decision makers. Overconfident decision makers tend to overestimate how much they know. Overconfidence contributes to decision makers overweighting, or selectively identifying, only those applicant characteristics that confirm the decision makers' beliefs or hypotheses about those characteristics' association with some behavior. Disconfirming information that might not fit the overconfident decision makers' hypotheses is largely ignored. Such decision makers do not learn from experience and therefore do not modify their methods.[7] Statistical models make an allowance for such errors and reduce the impact of individual biases on decision outcomes.

Implications for Selection Decision Makers

In summary, using standardized, more objective selection procedures in collecting applicant information, and then statistically combining the collected information, is better than using more subjective selection procedures and then subjectively judging how this information should be combined. Numerous studies in a wide variety of disciplines have generally confirmed this conclusion. Although subjective judgments resulting from gut feelings or intuition probably give selection decision makers both a feeling of control over the process and confidence in their judgments, use of subjective judgments is usually not warranted by the quality of decision outcomes.

In human resource selection, many of our most frequently used predictors (for example, the interview) will involve some degree of judgment.[8] Judgment may play a role in how an applicant responds to a question or how the interviewer interprets the response to that question. When additional predictor information is collected from applicants, judgment can also play a role as selection decision makers combine the information to reach a decision. As we have seen, better selection decision making is more likely to occur when judgment plays less of a role in the collecting and combining of selection procedure information. With this thought in mind, we recommend that selection decision makers do the following:

1. Be particularly careful about relying too heavily on resumes and other initial information collected early in the selection process. Research has shown that even experts are prone to placing too much emphasis on preliminary information, even when such information is questionable.[9] For example, one experimental study involved actual human resource managers. Asking these managers to ignore preliminary information on job applicants, and even rewarding them for ignoring such information, failed to keep the managers from emphasizing preliminary information in their selection decision making.

2. Use standardized selection procedures (that is, procedures in which content, administration, and scoring are the same for all applicants) that are reliable, valid,

and suitable for the specific selection purpose (for example, reducing absenteeism from work).

3. When feasible, use selection procedures that minimize the role of selection decision maker judgment in collecting information. For example, where appropriate—and assuming the measures meet point #2 above—use structured employment interviews, weighted application blanks, objective personality inventories, mental ability tests, work sample tests, physical ability tests and computer-administered skill tests that have specific keys for scoring desirable and undesirable responses.

4. Avoid using judgment in *combining* data collected from two or more selection procedures and used for determining applicants' overall scores. When combining selection procedure information that has been systematically derived and applied, applying a mechanical formula or a statistical equation (such as a multiple regression equation) will generally enhance selection decision making. Even very simple formulas used for combining information obtained from different sources, when properly developed and applied, have been found to produce more accurate decisions than even the decisions of experts—when, that is, those expert decisions have been based on a subjective combining of information.[10]

Although ample evidence supports the use of mechanical approaches for making selection decisions, both managers and applicants continue to resist using them. Often managers resist change, and feel threatened when asked to use formulas for making selection decisions rather than their own simple judgment. Because the role of the manager shifts to providing input rather than making judgmental decisions, some selling may be necessary to convince managers that superior decisions will result from following such systematic procedures.[11]

Applicants are also likely to resist use of statistical models for making selection decisions. For instance, one young woman was overheard complaining that she had been rejected from a graduate program without even an interview.[12] She did not believe decision makers could possibly know what she was like when they used a mechanical procedure for making their decision.

STRATEGIES FOR COMBINING PREDICTOR SCORES

For most jobs in many organizations, applicant information is obtained using more than one predictor. For instance, a company may collect application blank and reference check information, administer an ability test, and conduct an employment interview with all applicants for its position openings. In the preceding section, we categorized a number of strategies for combining predictor information obtained from two or more selection procedures. We concluded that mechanical strategies are better than judgmental ones for collecting and combining predictor scores. In this section, we describe several strategies that conform to our prescription for using mechanical methods for *combining* predictor information. These strategies are (a) multiple regression, (b) multiple cutoffs, (c) multiple hurdle, and (d) combination method. No assumptions are made by the strategies about how the data are collected (either mechanically or judgmentally). Each focuses on systematic procedures for combining predictor information. In addition, each makes implicit assumptions about the nature of job performance and the relative importance of multiple predictors.

To make these strategies easier to understand, let's look at an example that shows how decisions are made using each approach. Table 6.4 presents the data for the job of patient account representative. The job involves processing patient records, billing customers, filing

TABLE 6.4	Patient Account Representative Selection Procedure and Application Score Data

Selection Procedure

Selection Procedure Characteristic	Math Test	Filing Test	Spelling Test	Perceptual Accuracy Test	Structured Interview
Maximum Possible Score	15	30	65	15	25
Regression Weights[a]	1	0.8	0.9	0.7	0.5
Cutoff Scores	7	22	50	6	10

Applicant Selection Procedure Scores

Applicant	Math Test	Filing Test	Spelling Test	Perceptual Accuracy Test	Structured Interview
Amanda Maale	6	30	55	15	25
Dave Mason	14	21	63	10	11
Carl Sagan	9	29	60	8	12
Rebecca Malpa	15	22	50	5	24
Cyndy O'Roarke	8	23	55	14	13

[a]The regression equation is $\hat{Y} = x_1 + 0.8x_2 + 0.9x_3 + 0.7x_4 + 0.5x_5$. The intercept value has been omitted.

NOTE: The higher an applicant's score on a predictor, the better the applicant's performance on the predictor.

insurance forms, and filing patient records. Four ability tests and a structured interview are used to obtain predictor information on applicants. The math test requires computing answers to problems involving addition, subtraction, multiplication, and division. Scores can range from 0 to 15. The filing test requires applicants to separate a deck of index cards into two decks (one by name and the other by number) and then sort them (alphabetically for the name stack and numerically for the number stack). Scores can range from 0 to 30. The spelling test requires applicants to circle the correctly spelled word in each pair of words provided. Scores can range from 0 to 65. The perceptual accuracy test requires applicants to compare simulated patient charts with simulated printouts of patient records and identify errors. Scores can range from 0 to 15. On each of the four tests, higher scores indicate better performance. The structured interview has five questions. It is scored numerically; a rating of 5 represents an excellent answer, 3 an average answer, and 1 a poor answer. Ratings of applicants' responses to the five questions are added; total scores can range from 5 to 25, with higher scores meaning better applicant interview performance.

Strategy One: Multiple Regression

We briefly discussed multiple regression in our chapter on validity. As you recall, in this method each applicant is measured on each predictor or selection procedure. Applicants' predictor scores are entered into an equation (called the regression prediction equation) that weights each score to arrive at a total score (for example, predicted job performance). Regression weights are determined by each predictor's influence in determining criterion performance. Using this model, it is possible for applicants with different individual predictor scores to have identical overall predicted scores.

For example, suppose we give two tests, X_1 and X_2, to all job applicants. Suppose further that we previously developed the following regression equation to predict job performance ($\hat{Y}$) using applicants' scores on the two tests (X_1 and X_2):

$$\hat{Y} = 5 + 2X_1 + 1X_2$$

where

$\hat{Y} =$ predicted job performance
$5 =$ a constant or intercept value of the regression line
$2, 1 =$ regression weights for test X_1 and test X_2
$X_1, X_2 =$ applicants' scores on the tests

Now, assume we have three job applicants. Each takes both tests. Here are the applicants' scores on test 1 and test 2: John Meadows (50, 0), Sally Menkowski (0, 100), and Simi Mandu (10, 80). To get their predicted job performance, we simply substitute each applicant's test scores in the preceding regression equation. Our computations show all three applicants have the same predicted job performance, 105. Because it is possible to compensate for low scores on one predictor by high scores on another, multiple regression is sometimes referred to as a *compensatory* method.

Multiple regression makes two basic assumptions: (a) the predictors are linearly related to the criterion, and (b) because the predicted criterion score is a function of the sum of the weighted predictor scores, the predictors are additive and can compensate for one another (that is, performing well on one of the predictors compensates for performing not so well on another predictor).

The multiple regression approach has several advantages. It minimizes errors in prediction and combines the predictors to yield the best estimate of applicants' future performance on a criterion such as job performance. Furthermore, it is a very flexible method. It can be modified to handle nominal data, nonlinear relationships, and both linear and nonlinear interactions.[13] Regression equations can be constructed for each of a number of jobs using either the same predictors weighted differently or different predictors. The decision maker then has three options: (a) if selecting for a single job, then the person with the highest predicted score is selected; if selecting for two or more jobs, the decision maker has the following additional options: (b) place each person on the job for which the predicted score is highest, or (c) place each person on that job where his or her predicted score is farthest above the minimum score necessary to be considered satisfactory.[14]

The multiple regression approach has disadvantages as well. Besides making the assumption that scoring high on one predictor can compensate for scoring low on another, there are statistical issues that are sometimes difficult to resolve. For example, when relatively small samples are used to determine regression weights, the weights may not be stable from one sample to the next.[15] For this reason, cross validation of the regression weights is essential. Moreover, the multiple regression strategy requires assessing all applicants on all predictors, which can be costly with a large applicant pool.

The multiple regression approach is most appropriate when a trade-off among predictor scores does not affect overall job performance. In addition, it is best used when the sample size for constructing the regression equation is large enough to minimize some of the statistical problems just noted. However, as the size of the applicant pool increases, costs of selection become much larger.

Table 6.4 provides the regression equation. Overall scores indicating predicted success for each applicant are first calculated by entering the individual predictor scores into the equation. Once overall scores have been calculated, then applicants can be rank-ordered based on their overall predicted scores. Ordering applicants based on their overall predicted scores would result in the following ranking: **1** = Amanda Maale [predicted score = 102.5], **2** = Dave Mason [predicted score = 100], **3** = Carl Sagan [predicted score = 97.8], **4** = Rebecca Malpa [predicted score = 93.1], and **5** = Cyndy O'Roarke [predicted score = 92.2].

Strategy Two: Multiple Cutoffs

In this method, each applicant is assessed on each predictor. All predictors are scored on a pass-fail basis. Applicants are rejected if any one of their predictor scores falls below a minimum cutoff score. This method makes two important assumptions about job performance: (a) a nonlinear relationship exists among the predictors and the criterion—that is, a minimum amount of each important predictor attribute is necessary for successful performance of a job (the applicant must score above each minimum cutoff to be considered for the job), and (b) predictors are not compensatory. A lack or deficiency in any one predictor attribute cannot be compensated for by having a high score on another (an applicant cannot have "0" on any single predictor).

The advantage of this method is that it narrows the applicant pool to a smaller subset of candidates who are all minimally qualified for the job. In addition, it is conceptually simple and easy to explain to managers.[16] This approach has two major disadvantages. First, like the multiple regression approach, it requires assessing all applicants using all predictors. With a large applicant pool, the selection costs may be large. Second, the multiple cutoff approach identifies only those applicants minimally qualified for the job. There is no clear-cut way to determine how to order those applicants who pass the cutoffs.

A multiple cutoff approach is probably most useful when physical abilities are essential for job performance. For example, eyesight, color vision, and physical strength are required for such jobs as police, fire, and heavy manufacturing work.[17] Another appropriate use of multiple cutoff scores would be for jobs in which it is known that a minimum level of performance on a predictor is required in order to perform the job safely.

Table 6.4 provides the cutoff scores for each predictor. Carl and Cyndy pass the cutoffs; Amanda, Dave, and Rebecca do not.

Strategy Three: Multiple Hurdles

In this strategy, each applicant must meet the minimum cutoff or hurdle for each predictor before going to the next predictor. That is, to remain a viable applicant, applicants must pass the predictors sequentially. Failure to pass a cutoff at any stage in the selection process results in the applicant being dropped from further consideration.

In a variation of the multiple hurdle approach, *called the double-stage strategy*,[18] two cutoff scores are set, C1 and C2 (see Figure 6.1). Those whose scores fall above C2 are accepted unconditionally, and those whose scores fall below C1 are rejected terminally. Applicants whose scores fall between C1 and C2 are accepted provisionally, with a final decision made based on additional testing. This approach has been shown to be equal or superior to all other strategies at all degrees of selectivity.[19]

In the multiple hurdle approach, like the multiple cutoff method, it is assumed that a minimum level of each predictor attribute is necessary for performance on the job. It is not possible for a high level of one predictor attribute to compensate for a low level of another without negatively affecting job performance. Thus the assumptions of the multiple hurdle approach are identical to those of the multiple cutoff approach. The only distinction between the two is in the procedure for gathering predictor information. In the multiple cutoff approach the procedure is nonsequential, whereas in the hurdle approach the

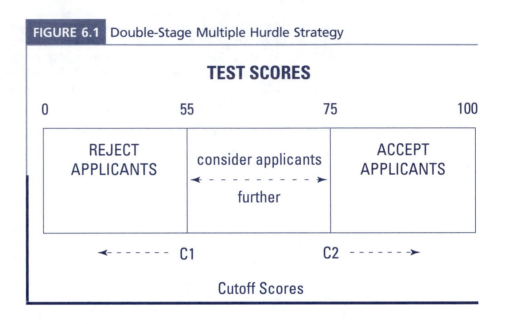

FIGURE 6.1 Double-Stage Multiple Hurdle Strategy

TEST SCORES

procedure is sequential. That is, applicants must achieve a minimum score on one selection procedure before they are assessed on another procedure. If they fail to achieve that minimum score, they are rejected.

The multiple hurdle approach has the same advantages as the multiple cutoff approach. In addition, it is less costly than the multiple cutoff approach because the applicant pool becomes smaller at each stage of the selection process. More expensive selection devices can be used at later stages of the selection process on only those applicants likely to be hired. For example, we might use an inexpensive selection procedure, such as a weighted application blank, to prescreen large numbers of applicants before conducting any employment interviews (an expensive selection procedure). Interviews can then be conducted with the smaller number of applicants who pass the weighted application blank hurdle.

One major disadvantage of this approach relates to establishing validity for each predictor. Because each stage in the selection process reduces the applicant pool to only those on the high end of the ability distribution, restriction of range is a likely problem. As in concurrent validation strategies, this means the obtained validity coefficients may be underestimated. An additional disadvantage is the increased time necessary to implement it. This time disadvantage is particularly important for those employment situations in which selection decisions must be made quickly. For example, in many computer software organizations, there may be a high demand for individuals with appropriate programming skills. Employment decisions have to be reached quickly, before competitors attract a viable applicant. In such a situation, a multiple hurdle approach is likely not appropriate. Under this strategy, it takes time to administer a predictor, score it, and then decide whether to give the next predictor to the applicant. Good applicants may be lost before a final employment decision is reached.[20]

The multiple hurdle approach is most appropriate in situations where subsequent training is long, complex, and expensive.[21] It is also a useful decision-making approach when an essential knowledge, skill, or ability (that cannot be compensated for by the possession of higher levels of other KSAs) is necessary for job performance. For example, typing is an essential skill for a clerical job. Better-than-average filing skills cannot compensate for the inability to type. An organization has no reason to further evaluate applicants who cannot pass the typing test. The multiple hurdle approach is also appropriate when there is a large applicant pool and some of the selection procedures are expensive to administer. For example, when hiring for an information systems manager job, you may use a resume review as the first hurdle in order to narrow the applicant pool before administering more expensive assessment devices later to a smaller pool of applicants. Table 6.4 provides the cutoffs for each predictor. Assume the predictors are administered sequentially in the following order: math test, filing test, spelling test, accuracy test, and structured interview. Amanda would be eliminated from the applicant pool after the math test. Dave would be eliminated after the filing test. Rebecca would be eliminated after the accuracy test. Carl and Cyndy would pass all hurdles and thus be equally acceptable for the job.

Strategy Four: Combination Method

In this strategy, each applicant is measured on each predictor. An applicant with any predictor score below a minimum cutoff is rejected. Thus the combination method is identical to the multiple-cutoff procedure to this point. Next, multiple regression is used to calculate overall scores for all applicants who pass the cutoffs. Then the applicants who remain can be rank-ordered based on their overall scores calculated by the regression equation. This part of the procedure is identical to the multiple regression approach.

Consequently, the combination method is a hybrid of the multiple-cutoff and multiple regression approaches. The combination method has two major assumptions. The more restrictive assumption is derived from the multiple-cutoff approach. That is, a minimal level of each predictor attribute is necessary to perform the job. After that level has been reached, more of one predictor attribute can compensate for less of another in predicting overall success of the applicants. This assumption is derived from the multiple regression approach.

The combination method has the advantages of the multiple cutoff approach. But rather than merely identifying a pool of acceptable candidates, which is what happens when using the multiple cutoff approach, the combination approach additionally provides a way to rank-order acceptable applicants. The major disadvantage of the combination method is that it is more costly than the multiple hurdle approach, because all applicants are screened on all predictors. Consequently the cost savings are not afforded by the multiple hurdle approach's reduction of the applicant pool.

The combination method is most appropriate when the assumption of multiple cutoffs is reasonable and more of one predictor attribute can compensate for another above the minimum cutoffs. It is also more appropriate to use this approach when the size of the applicant pool is not too large and costs of administering selection procedures do not vary greatly among the procedures.

In the example in Table 6.4, the cutoffs for each predictor are provided. Carl and Cyndy pass all of the cutoffs; Amanda, Dave, and Rebecca do not. Overall scores indicating the predicted success for each applicant who passes all cutoffs are then calculated by entering the individual predictor scores into the regression equation. Once the overall scores have been calculated, the applicants can be rank-ordered based on their overall predicted scores. Ordering the applicants based on their overall predicted scores results in the following ranking: **1** = Carl [predicted score = 97.8] and **2** = Cyndy [predicted score = 92.2].

APPROACHES FOR MAKING EMPLOYMENT DECISIONS

After selection predictors have been administered to job applicants, employment decisions must be made as to which of the applicants will be extended offers of employment. If only one predictor is used, then decisions are made based on applicants' scores on this predictor. Usually, however, more than one predictor is employed. When multiple predictors are used for selection, we can use one of the strategies just discussed for combining predictor information.

At this point, let's assume that we have administered our selection measures and derived a final selection measure score for each applicant. We are now ready to make a hiring decision, but how should we evaluate applicants' selection procedure scores? Numerous methods concerned with selecting individuals for jobs have been reported in the human resource selection literature. We will devote our attention to three basic approaches: (a) top-down selection, (b) cutoff scores, and (c) banding.

Top-Down Selection

With the top-down selection approach, applicants' scores are rank-ordered from highest to lowest. Then, beginning with the applicant at the top of the list (the one who has the highest and best score on the selection procedure) and moving to the bottom, applicants are extended job offers until all positions are filled. If an applicant turns down a job offer, the next applicant on the list is offered the job.

Ranking applicants by their selection scores assumes that a person with a higher score will perform better on the job than a person with a lower score. If we assume that a valid predictor is linearly related to job performance (usually a safe assumption, particularly when the selection procedure is of a cognitive nature), then the higher applicants' scores are on a predictor, the better their job performance. The economic return of employing an applicant who scores at one standard deviation above the average score on a valid predictor can be as much as 40 percent more than employing an applicant scoring at the average on the valid predictor.[22] As far as job performance is concerned, maximum utility will be gained from a predictor when top-down hiring is used.[23]

The importance of top-down selection is illustrated in one case involving U.S. Steel Corporation.[24] The plant changed from using top-down selection to using only employee seniority and minimum scores (equivalent to about the 7th grade) on a battery of valid cognitive ability tests. The tests were used for selecting entrants for the company's apprentice-training program. After using the new minimum selection criteria, U.S. Steel found that (a) performance on mastery tests given during training fell dramatically, (b) apprenticeship trainee failure and dropout rates rose significantly, (c) for those trainees completing the program, training time and training costs increased substantially, and (d) later job performance of program graduates fell.

The biggest problem with top-down selection, however, is that it will likely lead to adverse impact against legally protected racial/ethnic groups. This troublesome outcome is most likely when cognitively based predictors are used in selection such as mental ability tests. Because white people tend to score higher, on average, than black and Hispanic people, adverse impact is likely to occur under top-down selection. When adverse impact occurs, using cutoff scores in making employment decisions is one alternative.[25]

Cutoff Scores

In addition to top-down hiring, another strategy for using predictor scores in selection decision making is to use cutoff scores. A cutoff score represents a score on a predictor or combination of predictors below which job applicants are rejected. Before discussing several approaches to developing cutoff scores, we must address a few points. First, there is not just one cutoff score; a cutoff score can vary from one employment context to another. Judgment will necessarily play a role in choosing the method for setting the cutoff score and for determining the actual cutoff score value to be employed in selection. These decisions will be affected by any number of considerations—such as the number of applicants and percentage of those applicants hired for the position in question, the costs associated with recruiting and employing qualified applicants, consequences of job failure (that is, error in predicting applicant job performance due to a cutoff score set too low), workforce diversity concerns, and so on.

Second, there is no single method of setting cutoff scores. A number of approaches can be used; their successful use will depend on how appropriate the procedure chosen is for a particular situation and how effectively the specific procedures are applied. Finally, when a cutoff score is developed and used, the rationale and specific procedures for identifying that particular score should be carefully documented. Written documentation of cutoff score determination is particularly valuable in an employer's defending against a claim of employment discrimination.

In setting cutoff scores, employers must maintain a delicate balance. That is, an employer can expose itself to legal consequences when cutoff scores are set too high and many qualified applicants are rejected. Conversely, cutoff scores can lose utility if they are set so low that a selection procedure fails to screen out unqualified job applicants.[26]

Cutoff scores can be established in at least two general ways: (a) basing the cutoff score on how job applicants or other persons performed on a selection procedure (sometimes labeled *empirical* score setting procedures) and (b) using the judgments of knowledgeable experts regarding the appropriateness of selection procedure content (such as items on a written test) to set the cutoff score. Now, let's take a brief look at some of these ways for determining cutoff scores.

Basing Cutoff Scores on Applicants' or Others' Performance

Empirical methods used to set cutoff scores are generally based on the relationship between scores on predictors and performance on the job as measured by a criterion.[27] Below, we briefly highlight several of these methods.

Local norms developed for an organization's own applicants can be helpful in some cutoff score setting methods. Thorndike's *"predicted yield" method*[28] requires obtaining the following information for establishing a cutoff score: (a) the number of positions available during some future time period, (b) the number of applicants to be expected during that time period, and (c) the expected distribution of applicants' predictor scores. The cutoff score is then determined based on the percentage of applicants needed to fill the positions. For example, if 20 machinists are needed and 250 people are expected to apply for the 20 position openings, then the selection ratio is 0.08 (20/250). Because 92 percent of the applicants will be rejected, the cutoff score should be set at the 92nd percentile on the local norms (norms based on the company's past experience with a selection procedure administered to the company's job applicants applying for similar positions) minus one standard error of measurement.

In the *expectancy chart method*,[29] the same analytical procedure is used as in the Thorndike method to determine the expected selection ratio. Once the expected percentage of applicants that will be rejected is determined, the score associated with that percentile is identified minus one standard error of measurement. As mentioned earlier in our discussion of selection procedure norms, care must be taken to see that local norms are periodically updated because applicant pool members' abilities and other qualifications can change over time.

Cutoff scores can also be determined by administering the selection procedure to individuals (such as job incumbents) other than applicants and using the information as a basis for score development. In one study, undergraduate students were administered tests to be used in selecting emergency telephone operators. The students' distribution of test performance scores (later verified by actual applicants' test scores) served as a basis for setting the cutoff scores. One note of caution: When a group of individuals other than applicants serves as a basis for deriving cutoff scores, care should be taken in determining that the group of individuals is comparable to the applicant pool for the job. When the groups are not comparable, legal questions concerning the fairness and meaningfulness of such scores can arise. For example, in hiring patrol police officers, physical tests of lung capacity have sometimes been used. In setting a minimum lung capacity cutoff score for patrol police officers, it would not be appropriate to determine a cutoff score based on how a group of university track athletes performed on the lung capacity measure. If discrimination is judged to have resulted from cutoff score use, legal concerns regarding the score are likely to involve the following question: Is the discriminatory cutoff score used in screening applicants measuring the *minimum* qualifications necessary for successful performance of the job?[30] In addition to validation information, an affected employer would also need to be able to demonstrate that the chosen cutoff score does, indeed, represent a useful, meaningful selection standard with regard to job performance, risks, costs, and so on.

Contrasting the two distributions of predictor scores made by successful and unsuccessful job incumbents is another empirical approach. Subject matter experts judge the overlay or overlap of the two score distributions and set the cutoff score where the two distributions intersect. This method is most useful when there is a strong relationship between scores on the predictor and job performance.

Finally, simple regression (one predictor) or multiple regression (two or more predictors), which we mentioned earlier, can also be used to set cutoff scores. Assuming that an adequate number of individuals' predictor and criterion scores is available, correlational methods permit cutoff scores to be set by determining that specific predictor score associated with acceptable or successful job performance as represented by the criterion. Of course, regression methods also assume an adequate relationship between the selection procedure and the criterion as well as a representative (of the applicant pool), large sample on which the statistical correlation is based. Thus the assumptions that we described with regard to criterion-related validation strategies in our chapter on validity also apply to regression methods in setting cutoff scores.

Using Experts' Judgments

Cutoff scores are often set using judgmental or rational methods when empirical methods are not feasible. Under judgmental methods of cutoff score determination, the assessments of subject matter experts (for example, job incumbents, supervisors) serve as the basis for establishing the relationship between predictor scores and job success. These assessments, in turn, serve as a basis for cutoff score development. In most cases, these approaches are used with multiple-choice written tests (such as job knowledge tests); some judgmental approaches have been applied to other selection procedures as well. Next, let's review several of these judgmental methods and how they are used.

The *Ebel method*[31] is based on an analysis of the difficulty of test items. First, experts rate all test items on the following basis: (a) difficulty (hard, medium, easy) and (b) relevance to job performance (essential, important, acceptable, and questionable). These ratings produce 12 categories of items. For each of the categories of items, judges are asked what percentage of the items a borderline test taker would be able to answer correctly; for example, "If a borderline test taker had to answer a large number of questions like these, what percentage would he or she answer correctly?" The cutoff score is calculated by multiplying the percentage of items correct times the number of questions in each category and then summing the products across all of the separate categories. Table 6.5 provides an example of this method.

TABLE 6.5 The Ebel Method for Setting Cutoff Scores

	Difficulty of Test Items					
	Easy		**Medium**		**Hard**	
	Items	**% Correct**	**Items**	**% Correct**	**Items**	**% Correct**
Relevance to Job Performance						
Essential	22, 17, 10, 5, 2	90	12, 19	80	11, 15, 25	70
Important	1, 8, 23, 30	85	16, 26, 27, 29	70	4, 24	65
Acceptable	3, 6, 13	80	14, 21	65	18	55
Questionable	7	60	21, 32	50	none	—

Item Category	% Correct	Number of Items	Expected Score for Category
Essential			
easy	90	5	$0.90 \times 5 = 4.5$
medium	80	2	$0.80 \times 2 = 1.6$
hard	70	3	$0.70 \times 3 = 2.1$
Important			
easy	85	4	$0.85 \times 4 = 3.4$
medium	70	4	$0.70 \times 4 = 2.8$
hard	65	2	$0.65 \times 2 = 1.3$
Acceptable			
easy	80	3	$0.80 \times 3 = 2.4$
medium	65	2	$0.65 \times 2 = 1.3$
hard	55	1	$0.55 \times 1 = 0.55$
Questionable			
easy	60	1	$0.60 \times 1 = 0.60$
medium	50	2	$0.50 \times 2 = 1.0$
hard	0	0	0
		Sum (Expected Cutoff Score)	$= 21.55$

In the *Angoff method*,[32] judges or subject matter experts, usually numbering 10 to 15, estimate the probability that a minimally qualified applicant could answer a specific test item correctly. These estimates are used to establish cutoff scores for the test. As William Angoff described it, "the judges would think of a number of minimally acceptable persons, instead of only one such person, and would estimate the proportion of minimally acceptable persons who would answer each item correctly. The sum of these probabilities, or proportions, would then represent the minimally acceptable score." Table 6.6 illustrates this procedure.

A modification of this procedure, described as the *modified Angoff method,* reduces the score calculated by the Angoff method by one, two, or three standard errors of measurement. This adjustment has been accepted in numerous court cases.[33]

For example, a modification of the Angoff procedure was accepted in *U.S. v. South Carolina* for use with written tests. The modification lowered the average Angoff estimate from one to three standard errors of measurement. The court based its acceptance on several considerations: the risk of error (that is, the risk that a truly qualified

TABLE 6.6	The Angoff Method for Setting Cutoff Scores
Item Number	**Proportion Answering Correctly**
1	0.90
2	0.55
3	0.70
4	0.80
5	0.85
6	0.60
7	0.55
8	0.75
9	0.95
10	0.60
11	0.75
12	0.60
13	0.55
14	0.80
15	0.70
16	0.70
17	0.70
18	0.75
19	0.65
20	0.55
	Sum = 14.0
Unmodified Cutoff Score	14.0
Modified Cutoff Score (with 1 SEM = 2.1)[a]	11.9

[a]SEM = Standard Error of Measurement.

applicant might be excluded compared to the risk of including an unqualified applicant), the degree of agreement among subject matter experts in their evaluations of minimum competency, the workforce supply and demand for the job, race and gender composition of the jobs, and the standard error of measurement.[34]

Neal Schmitt and Richard Klimoski proposed a variation of the Angoff method.[35] Their variation was applied to a 25-item in-basket examination used as part of a promotional procedure in a governmental organization. Each of the 25 items was scored on a 4-point scale with 4 indicating a superior answer and 1 judged a clearly inferior response. Subject matter experts (job incumbents) were asked to review the in-basket items and provide responses to the following question for each item: "Consider a *minimally competent applicant* for a middle-level manager's position in state government. This is not an outstanding candidate or even an average applicant, but one who could perform on tests at a *minimally* satisfactory level. Now look at each item and the scoring instructions for that item. What percentage of these *minimally competent* applicants would receive a score of 4 on these items? What percentage would receive a score of 3? Of 2? Of 1?" For example, one judge might rate an item as follows: 4 = 0 percent, 3 = 30 percent, 2 = 60 percent, and 1 = 10 percent. This judge indicates that most (60 percent) of the minimally competent applicants can write a response to this in-basket item that would receive a score of 2. Average scores of judges for each item would be calculated. Then these averages would be totaled across all items to determine the cutoff score. This method would also be useful for other selection instruments, such as for determining cutoff scores for structured interviews.

The Angoff procedure often produces higher cutoff scores than might be expected. To address this issue, the cutoff score is commonly lowered by one, two, or even three standard errors of measurement to limit the number of false negatives. However, these kinds of adjustments can produce unknown consequences for the employing organization.[36]

The *contrasting groups method* uses judgments of test takers rather than the test items as the basis for determining cutoff scores.[37] The first step is to divide test takers (usually job incumbents) into qualified and unqualified groups based on judgments of their knowledge and skills. The next step is to calculate the percentage of test takers who are qualified and unqualified at each test score. The cutoff score is chosen at that point where the proportion of qualified test takers is equal to the proportion of unqualified test takers. This assumes that rejecting unqualified candidates is as important as accepting qualified candidates. If it is desired to minimize either false positive or false negative errors, then the cutoff score is either raised or lowered.

When using judgments from subject matter experts to develop cutoff scores, a key concern of the courts is who served as an expert. For example, when physical ability tests are developed and validated, women and minority group members must be represented among the experts used. Ideally, their percentage representation among the subject matter experts would match their representation in the qualified applicant pool. Although it may be necessary to oversample women and minority group members to have adequate representation, random selection of full-time, non-probationary job incumbents should generally be employed.[38]

Legal and Psychometric Issues

Some guidance on setting cutoff scores is given in the two principal documents referred to for legal and psychometric selection standards. The *Uniform Guidelines on Employee Selection Procedures*[39] states the following about setting cutoff scores:

> *Where cutoff scores are used, they should normally be set so as to be reasonable and consistent with normal expectations of acceptable proficiency within the work force. Where applicants are ranked on the basis of properly validated selection procedures and those applicants scoring below a higher cutoff score than appropriate in light of such expectations have little or no chance of being selected for employment, the higher cutoff score may be more appropriate, but the degree of adverse impact should be considered.*

The *Principles for the Validation and Use of Personnel Selection Procedures* states, "If based on valid predictors demonstrating linearity ... throughout the range of prediction, cutoff scores may be set as high or as low as needed to meet the requirements of the organization."[40]

The *Principles* also note that some organizations choose to use a cutoff score rather than top-down selection. They may do this to enhance workforce diversity. However, use of minimum cutoff scores rather than top-down selection may result in a loss of job performance and consequent higher labor costs.[41] In summarizing earlier research by John Hunter in the 1970s, Frank Schmidt and John Hunter concluded that if the federal government as an employer had used top-down hiring with valid ability tests, one year's labor savings for hires would have been $15.6 billion. If a low cutoff score strategy had been adopted, one year's labor savings would have been $2.5 billion, a loss of 84 percent of labor costs that would have been achievable from using top-down selection.[42]

In reviews of the legal and psychometric literatures on cutoff scores, Wayne Cascio and his colleagues have offered a number of useful guidelines regarding score use. Any

TABLE 6.7	Selected Guidelines for Using Cutoff Scores in Selection Procedures

- Cutoff scores are not required by legal or professional guidelines; thus, first decide whether a cutoff score is necessary.
- There is not one best method of setting cutoff scores for all situations.
- If a cutoff score is to be used for setting a minimum score requirement, begin with a job analysis that identifies levels of proficiency on essential knowledge, skills, abilities, and other characteristics. (The Angoff method is one that can be used.)
- If judgmental methods are used (such as the Angoff method), include a 10 to 20 percent sample of subject matter experts (SMEs) representative of the race, gender, shift, and so on of the employee (or supervisor) group. Representative experience of SMEs on the job under study is a most critical consideration in choosing SMEs.
- If job incumbents are used to develop the cutoff score to be used with job applicants, consider setting the cutoff score one standard error of measurement below incumbents' average score on the selection procedure.
- Set cutoff scores high enough to ensure that at least minimum standards of job performance are achieved.

NOTE: The guidelines are based on Wayne F. Cascio and Herman Aguinis, "Test Development and Use: New Twists on Old Questions," *Human Resource Management* 44 (2005): 227; and Wayne F. Cascio, Ralph A. Alexander, and Gerald V. Barrett, "Setting Cutoff Scores: Legal, Psychometric, and Professional Issues and Guidelines," *Personnel Psychology* 41 (1989): 1–24.

user seriously considering cutoff scores in selection should consider these guidelines. Several of these guidelines are listed in Table 6.7.

Banding

As we mentioned earlier, one problem facing human resource selection decision makers is the fact that adverse impact frequently occurs against racial minorities with selection procedures such as mental ability tests. Race norming was one means developed for dealing with the problem of adverse impact arising from the use of selection procedures. However, the Civil Rights Act of 1991 prohibited race norming of selection procedure scores by employers.[43] In fact, the Act prohibits adjustment of scores, use of different cutoff scores, or alteration of results of employment-related tests on the basis of ethnicity, religion, gender, or national origin.

An alternative in dealing with the problem of selection procedure adverse impact is the use of *banding* of selection procedure scores, which has received legal support.[44] Banding involves establishing ranges of selection procedure scores where applicants' scores within a range or band are treated the same. Within a band, any selection procedure score differences are seen as due to measurement error and thus equivalent. The rationale behind banding is that scores on selection procedures do not have perfect reliability and, therefore, these scores do not perfectly reflect individuals' true scores on the characteristic measured by the selection procedure. Because small differences among applicants' scores on a selection procedure are due to measurement errors (that is, selection procedure score unreliability), these differences are not meaningful.

We saw in our discussion of the standard error of measurement that small differences in predictor scores may not reflect true or real differences in the attributes measured by the predictor. As a result, several banding procedures have been developed to take into account selection procedure measurement error and incorporate that information in selection decisions. For those scores within a band, other means or attributes (for example, random selection or applicant job experience) are used to choose among applicants from within a band.

Establishing Bands

Two forms of statistical methods have generally been used for determining whether selection procedure scores differ: (a) the standard error of measurement method and (b) the standard error of differences method. Both of these methods take into account two pieces of information: (a) the standard error of measurement (composed of the reliability and standard deviation of predictor scores), and (b) the level of confidence necessary for determining that predictor scores do or do not differ. These values affect the width of the band.[45] In the *standard error of measurement method,* the standard error of measurement is calculated for the test or predictor. Then the standard error of measurement is multiplied by 1.96 and the product is subtracted from an applicant's selection procedure score. This results in a range of scores that are basically equivalent 95 percent of the time. For example, assume that the standard error of measurement (SEM) is equal to 2.98. Multiplying 2.98 by 1.96 gives a product of 5.84. If the top applicant score on the predictor is 95, subtracting 5.84 results in a score of 89.16. Thus applicants' predictor scores between 89.16 and 95 are not significantly different and are considered equivalent.

In the *standard error of differences method* (the most frequently discussed method), the standard error of measurement is determined. Then 1 standard error of measurement is multiplied by the *square root* of 2 ($\sqrt{2} = 1.414$). (Technical Note: The $\sqrt{2} \times$ SEM = the standard deviation of the *difference* between two independent predictor scores.)[46] This number is then multiplied by 1.96 to determine the range of scores where it is 95 percent certain that the difference is real. For example, assume that the SEM = 2.98. The standard error of differences (SED) calculation is $1.96 \times 2.98 \times 1.414 = 8.26$. If the top selection procedure score is 95, subtracting 8.26 results in a score of 86.74. Applicants' scores between 86.74 and 95 are not significantly different.

Fixed and Sliding Bands

In *fixed bands* (also called *top-score referenced bands*), the range of the top band is determined from the highest selection procedure score achieved by an applicant. All applicants within the top band must be selected before applicants in lower bands can be chosen.

Fixed bands use the top applicant score attained as the starting point. The top score minus the band width (for example, 1.96×1 standard error of measurement $\times \sqrt{2}$) constitutes the band. Individuals within this band can be selected in any order because all scores within the band are considered equivalent. If more individuals must be selected than are in the first band, a second band is created. The highest remaining score is now the basis for determining the band of score values using the same procedure.

In Figure 6.2, we use the standard error of differences method to compute the relevant bands. For the fixed band example, three bands are shown. The first fixed band is created by taking the top applicant score (95) and subtracting the band width (8.26). This results in a band range from 86.74 to 95. One applicant is within the first band. After that applicant has been selected, the second band is created by subtracting the band width (8.26) from 86.73 (the next highest score after selecting all applicants in the first band). This results in a band range from 78.47 to 86.73. Nine applicants are within the second band, and any one of them can be selected. After all of the applicants in the second band have been selected, the third band is created by subtracting the band width from 78.46. This results in a band range from 70.20 to 78.46.

Sliding bands are also based on the top applicant's selection procedure score. However, once that applicant is selected, the band is recalculated using the next highest applicant score on the selection procedure. With sliding bands, each decision is based on those applicants still available for selection. This method recognizes that selection

---

FIGURE 6.2 | Illustration of Fixed and Sliding Bands for Comparing Test Scores

Example of Fixed Bands

Test Score Band	Applicant Test Scores
95.00 to 86.74	95
86.73 to 78.47	86 86 86 85 83 82 82 82 79
78.46 to 70.20	78 78 77 77 77 76 76 74 73 73 72 71

Example of Sliding Bands

Test Score Band	Applicant Test Scores
95.00 to 86.74	95
86.00 to 77.74	86 86 86 85 83 82 82 82 79 78 78
77.00 to 69.74	77 77 77 76 76 74 73 73 72 71

Note: Test scores *within* the same band are *not* considered to be significantly different; test scores in *different* bands are considered to be significantly different. Band widths were established by the standard error of differences method (SED), where $SED = 1.96 \times 2.98 \times \sqrt{2} = 8.26$.

---

decision making is a sequential process. When one person is chosen, the next selected candidates are chosen relative to those candidates remaining in the applicant pool. To implement the procedure, the highest scorer determines the band range, as in the previous procedure. Once the top scorer is selected, the highest remaining scorer is used to establish the new band. Thus the band slides down each time the top scorer in a band is chosen. The top scorer is the reference point used to identify those who are not reliably different. Use of sliding bands makes it possible to consider more applicants than would have been available under the fixed band method.

In Figure 6.2, the first band is created by taking the top applicant score (95) and subtracting the band width (8.26). This results in a band range from 95 to 86.74. After the top scorer (95) has been selected, the second band is created by subtracting the band width from the next highest remaining score (86). This step results in a range from 86 to 77.74. Notice, as compared to our fixed band example, we pick up two additional applicants—that is, the two individuals who scored 78. After the three applicants with the next highest scores have been selected, the band changes again. This time the band width is subtracted from 77, resulting in a band range of 77 to 69.74. Consequently, the band slides downward, including more applicants each time the high scorer is selected. (In this explanation, we described a situation in which selection decisions are made on the basis of the highest test score. Next, we describe other decision rules that have been used with banding.)

Selecting Within a Band

Once a band has been created, the next step is to choose a procedure for selecting individuals within a band. If selection decisions are based on a rank-ordering of raw test scores and top scorers are offered jobs first, white people generally receive a disproportionate number of job offers compared with minority group members because white people tend to score, on average, higher than some minority group members on some paper-and-pencil tests commonly used in personnel selection.[47] This result leads to an adverse impact of the test on minority groups. Some selection researchers have advocated the banding of selection procedure scores as one remedy to the problem of adverse impact. However, banding does not correct for selection procedure score differences among protected groups; it does, however, provide some flexibility in selection decision making.[48]

Once bands have been created, other selection specifications are used in choosing individuals within the same band. For example, a number of public sector organizations have used criteria such as the following:

- Interpersonal skills (ability to interact with people having diverse backgrounds)

- Job experience

- Job performance

- Training

- Work habits (attendance, punctuality, relationships with coworkers)

- Professional conduct (absence of citizen complaints, absence of disciplinary actions)[49]

To choose among those within the same band, race of applicants generally cannot be used.[50] Wayne Cascio and his colleagues raise an interesting question with regard to the use of various selection specifications for choosing among applicants within the same band. They wonder why, if a specification is reliable and valid, it is not used in the overall selection process along with other selection procedures.[51]

Advantages of Banding

Advocates of banding see a number of strengths that can result from incorporating banding procedures in hiring decisions. Sheldon Zedeck and his colleagues have noted several.[52] Among those mentioned are that an employer has more flexibility in making hiring decisions. For instance, an employer could identify women, minorities, or other underemployed applicant groups within a band. Preferences could be given to applicants falling within the same band, because all applicant scores within the band are considered equal. In addition to obtaining a more diverse workforce, an employer can emphasize secondary hiring factors that may be important, such as past attendance records, possession of special skills, types of training received, and so on. On the other hand, giving emphasis to a protected group characteristic when it is not legally mandated could legally jeopardize an organization.

Second, because performance on many selection measures explains only a relatively small percentage of the differences in criterion performance, use of secondary hiring factors helps an employer take into account those factors not measured by traditional selection methods. Finally, banding advocates have argued that simply basing the utility of a selection program on maximum economic gain resulting from top-down selection procedures views selection from a very narrow perspective. Utility calculations ignore the social and financial impacts that can accrue to an employer for not having a diverse workforce. Moreover, they concluded that use of banding procedures does not result in substantial economic losses to an employer. As noted in the following section, this conclusion has been questioned by others.

Concerns Regarding Banding

Use of banding in giving job offers to protected group members can make it possible to choose a larger number of minorities than would be feasible under top-down hiring based on rank-ordering of applicants' test scores. However, there is debate as to whether using banding to identify equally qualified individuals and then choosing on the basis of minority status within the band will withstand legal challenge.[53]

Banding itself may not be illegal, but what occurs when selecting among applicants after the band has been created may be. Selecting applicants within a band on the basis of random selection, previous job performance, or some standard not associated with protected group status may be legal. However, using protected-group status (for example, race) as the sole basis for choosing among applicants may be illegal because of Section 106 of the 1991 Civil Rights Act. That section prohibits hiring on the basis of protected-group status (for example, race, sex, color, or national origin).[54] Of course, random selection within a band could be used, but that strategy seems to do little to increase minority employment.[55]

Research by Christine Henle has shed some light on the legal issues surrounding banding. She reviewed eight court cases involving the application of banding in public sector organizations. Among other findings, the courts did not support banding when applicant minority status was solely used to select from within the bands, even if it was done to remedy past discrimination in the organization. However, when minority preferences were coupled with other selection criteria (for example, job experience), the courts supported banding. Thus, from Henle's work, it appears the courts support the practice of banding with the caveat that minority status is used with other selection specifications in selecting from within bands.[56]

In addition to legal issues, there have been other concerns regarding banding as a selection practice. For one, any departure from top-down hiring based on applicants' ranked test scores leads to a loss of economic utility as reflected in job performance. Because test scores are, in most cases, linearly related to job performance,[57] any deviation from top-down hiring necessarily leads to a decrease in job performance of the group hired.[58]

Another concern with banding involves the value of banding in reducing adverse impact if preferential treatment cannot be given to minority group members. As we noted, preferential treatment of minorities within bands can lessen adverse impact. Without this treatment, however, banding would seem to have reduced effects on adverse impact and would decrease economic utility.[59] Wayne Cascio and his colleagues concluded that using banding has generally yielded modest reductions in adverse impact with little negative effects on selection procedure validity or utility. However, banding is not the final answer to the problem of adverse impact of selection procedures.[60]

Additionally, banding may involve an incomplete system for weighting factors other than test scores in selecting individuals within a band. Other than random selection, all banding systems involve ranking members within a band on some basis other than test scores (for example, education, training, or personal characteristics). These factors are assumed to be associated with job performance. However, the weights given these factors are rarely specified and may vary across bands and applicants. An explicit and consistent system for weighting these factors (for example, through multiple regression) would be a better approach.[61]

Another concern arises when bands are used that are perceived by some to be too wide. Several research studies have argued that current statistical procedures connected with banding produce bands that are inappropriately wide. The result is that too many applicants are judged as equal with respect to their scores on selection procedures. Moreover, many of such scores within a band are statistically different and should be considered as such in selection decision making.[62]

In addition, bands that appear too wide make it difficult to explain how two scores appearing to be very different from one another are essentially equivalent. When this happens, it is a particular problem to describe to those negatively affected how a lower-scoring applicant is hired over a higher-scoring one.[63] Because it has been shown that reactions to banding are largely a function of the perceived relationship of banding with affirmative action,[64] this problem is probably magnified when affected individuals hold negative attitudes toward affirmative action programs.

Frank Schmidt has argued that a basic principle used in developing bands—that scores not significantly different from each other should not be treated differently—is not applied consistently in banding. Large score differences within a band are ignored, whereas small differences that may occur between scores in one band and scores in another are viewed as meaningful.[65] In response, Wayne Cascio and his associates have argued that Schmidt's viewpoint does not accurately describe banding, because the reference point is the highest remaining score in a band. This is because those individuals are the ones chosen in top-down hiring.[66]

A PRACTICAL APPROACH TO MAKING SELECTION DECISIONS

Several issues should be considered when choosing among selection decision-making procedures: (a) Should the procedure be sequential (for example, multiple hurdle) or nonsequential (for example, multiple regression or multiple cutoff)? (b) Should the decision be compensatory (for example, multiple regression) or noncompensatory (for example, multiple cutoff, multiple hurdle)? (c) Should the decision be based on ranking applicants, or should it be based on banding acceptable applicants?

In making the choice among decision-making options, begin by assessing the job and nature of job performance. What determines success on the job? What factors contribute to success, and how are they related? After answering these questions, consider additional issues: (a) the number of applicants expected, (b) the cost of selection devices used, and (c) the amount of time you can devote to the selection decision.

Having decided on a selection decision-making strategy, implement the strategy systematically in order to reap the potential benefits. Results of numerous studies of decision making are clear: *If you can develop and use a mechanical selection decision-making strategy such as we have described in this chapter, you can improve your personnel selection decision making.* Many selection decisions meet the criteria[67] necessary for building such a model: (a) the same decision is made repeatedly (normal turnover requires hiring for the same position numerous times), (b) data are available on the outcomes of past decisions (applicants are hired and their performance can be tracked over time), and (c) you have good reason to expect the future will resemble the past (many jobs change very little, if at all, over time). When these decision-making strategies are built using sound validation strategies as discussed in this book, powerful decision aids become available to decision makers.

Because of the sporadic nature of selection and the small number of applicants employed, it is often not possible to build objective strategies. This is especially true for small businesses, where selection is but one of many important activities competing for the the time of owners and managers. What can decision makers in this situation do to improve their selection decisions? Suppose a small business owner needs to employ an assistant.[68] First, she specifies what tasks this assistant will be asked to perform and the standards of performance that the assistant will be judged against. Next, she thinks of activities she could ask an applicant to do during the interview and selection process that are similar to, if not exactly, what the assistant would do on the job. After identifying some suitable job-related activities, the owner next thinks about what weights she should attach to each of the activities used for selection. Although these weights are subjective and not based on an empirical analysis of previous hires, they are at least made explicit before the selection process begins. By using some simplified rating process to assess each applicant on each selection activity, the owner has a systematic procedure for collecting data on applicants and ensuring that applicants are evaluated on the same criteria. Once the applicants have been processed in this manner, the final selection decision can be based on a "subjective linear model."[69] By multiplying the weights attached to each selection activity times the rating she gave each applicant, and then summing these products, an overall score can be calculated for each applicant that yields a systematically derived judgment of the applicant's probability for success on the job.

An even better subjective decision-making procedure than the one just described uses a technique called *bootstrapping*.[70] Bootstrapping is based on the assumption that even though people can often make sound judgments, they are not typically able to articulate how they made those judgments. Using this technique requires having the decision maker make judgments on a series of cases (for example, selection decision judgments based on a number of applicant files). Then, through regression analysis, it is possible to infer the weights used by the decision maker to arrive at a particular ranking. The regression analysis shows how much weight, on average, the decision maker puts on each of the underlying factors. As J. Edward Russo and Paul Schoemaker described it, "In bootstrapping, you seek to build a model of an expert using his or her own intuitive predictions, and then use that model to *outperform* the expert on new cases."[71] This method works because when you ask a person to make a prediction, "you get wisdom mixed in with random noise." Judgments based on intuition suffer greatly from random noise caused by an array of factors ranging from fatigue and boredom to stress and anxiety. Bootstrapping produces a standard procedure for decision making that eliminates the random noise while retaining the "core wisdom." Consequently, by using bootstrapping, the decision will be made in the same way today, tomorrow, next week, and next year. Numerous studies support the finding that bootstrapped models consistently do better at prediction than simple intuitive judgments. This leads us to the fascinating conclusion that models of our own subjective decision-making processes can be built that outperform us! Nevertheless, when an objective strategy can be used, it still outperforms both bootstrapped models and simple intuition. It is always best to use an objective strategy whenever possible.

One last issue we must address when discussing a practical approach to selection decisions is procedural fairness. Whether you use a systematic objective strategy of decision making or a simple intuitive approach, it is critical that the procedures be perceived as fair. For selection procedures, we have used the term *face validity* to describe selection practices that applicants believe to be reasonable. In addition to selection instruments having face validity, decision-making procedures, too, must be seen as fair.

One factor that seems to affect whether decision-making procedures are viewed as fair is how well they are justified.[72] This seems especially important for dealing with applicants who are rejected during the selection process. Rejected applicants will accept their rejection better if they believe they were treated justly, they had a fair chance to obtain the job, and someone better qualified received the job. Objective decision-making models built on solid evidence should be easier to justify to applicants than intuitive models that cannot be clearly articulated. Regardless of the approach used, ensuring procedural fairness should be a major consideration when developing selection procedures.

AUDITING SELECTION DECISIONS: LEARNING FROM YOUR SUCCESSES AND FAILURES

The only way you can improve your selection decision making is to learn from what you have done in the past. This dictum applies at both the organizational level and at the individual level. At the organizational level, validation studies can help improve overall organizational selection decision making by identifying scientifically those factors that predict job success and eliminating those factors that do not predict job success. Using validation strategies merely to comply with legal requirements is a gross underutilization of this powerful technology. Organizations that routinely validate their selection practices set the context in which good decisions can occur. Organizations that do not routinely validate their selection practices create a decision-making context that may or may not lead to desirable outcomes.

At the individual level, most managers do not think about their success and failure rate when it comes to making selection decisions. This is not surprising, when you consider the number of selection decisions that must be made over many years. Yet it is surprising that managers are not held as accountable for their selection decisions as they are for other decisions such as capital equipment purchases. Are not a high number of bad selection decisions as damaging to an organization as the purchase of an unreliable piece of machinery? Several bad selection decisions can lead to lower productivity and high separation and replacement costs, as well as to potentially damaging litigation. How can managers be held accountable for their selection decisions and learn from their successes and failures?

The decision-making literature suggests that a simple box-score tally of successes and failures can improve decision making over time.[73] Decision makers learn from feedback that either supports or disconfirms their predictive models. Remember Roger from the beginning of the chapter? This simple procedure may not have prevented him from making selection errors, but it would certainly have reduced his overconfidence about his decision-making ability! If these individual decision audits are made throughout the organization, both good and bad decision makers can be identified for either reinforcement or remedial training.

RECOMMENDATIONS FOR ENHANCING SELECTION DECISION MAKING

Even the best-designed selection systems will not produce sound selection decisions unless good selection decision-making procedures are used as well. To ensure that an organization maximizes the effectiveness of its selection system, we suggest the following prescriptions:

1. Use reliable and valid selection procedures for collecting information on job applicants.

2. Encourage managers and others making selection decisions to participate in the data collection process (for example, rating an applicant's interview performance using valid, standardized methods), but discourage them from combining scores on selection instruments or from making decisions based on intuition or gut feelings.

3. Train managers and others making selection decisions to make systematic decisions, preferably using one of the objective (mechanical) strategies described in the chapter.

4. Although it is difficult for small organizations to adopt some decision-making strategies, small businesses can specify, in advance, (a) the weight of standards to be used in evaluating candidates (for example, performance of activities similar to those on the job), (b) the procedures used for judging whether applicants meet those standards (for example, a rating system for evaluating performance of these simulated activities), and then (c) the procedures for combining the standard weights × the ratings given in order to arrive at an overall applicant score.

5. For organizations using cutoff scores, the modified Angoff procedure is acceptable.

6. Assuming that a selection procedure predicts job performance, and assuming that all applicants who are extended an offer of employment accept the offer, maximum job performance among the group hired will occur when top-down selection is used.

7. Banding of selection procedure scores has been supported in the courts. However, using minority status alone as a basis for selecting within bands is probably not legal in most employment settings. Overall, banding has had a minor but positive effect on reducing adverse impact.

8. For jobs in which selection has taken place, decide on a standard for defining a successful hire (for example, the selected person stayed on the job six months or more) and an unsuccessful hire (for example, the selected person's dollar sales fall below a minimum standard or their supervisory performance appraisal ratings fall below an acceptable level). Then, have managers keep track of their hits (correct selection decisions) and misses (incorrect selection decisions). Of course, it is generally infeasible to track the effects of false negatives that occur in selection decision making (that is, those individuals who were not hired because of their low scores on a selection procedure but who would have been successful on the job had they been employed).

9. Periodically audit selection decisions throughout the organization to identify areas or individuals needing improvement.

These prescriptions do not guarantee that you will always make correct decisions in selecting personnel for your organization, but they are guaranteed to tilt the odds in your favor.

REFERENCES

1. Jack Sawyer, "Measurement *and* Prediction, Clinical *and* Statistical," *Psychological Bulletin* 66 (1966): 178–200.

2. Paul Meehl, *Clinical versus Statistical Prediction* (Minneapolis: University of Minnesota Press, 1954).

3. Paul Meehl, "Causes and Effects of My Disturbing Little Book," *Journal of Personality Assessment* 50 (1986): 370–375.

4. Sawyer, "Measurement *and* Prediction, Clinical *and* Statistical."

5. For a review, see Benjamin Kleinmuntz, "Why We Still Use Our Heads Instead of Formulas: Toward an Integrative Approach," *Psychological Bulletin* 107 (1990): 296–310.

6. Bernard M. Bass and Gerald V. Barrett, *People, Work, and Organizations,* 2nd ed. (Boston: Allyn & Bacon, 1981), 397–398.

7. Kleinmuntz, "Why We Still Use Our Heads Instead of Formulas: Toward an Integrative Approach," 298.

8. Drew Westen and Joel Weinberger, "When Clinical Description Becomes Statistical Prediction," *American Psychologist* 59 (2004): 608.

9. Talya Miron-Shatz and Gershon Ben-Shakhar, "Disregarding Preliminary Information When Rating Job Applicants' Performance: Mission Impossible?" *Journal of Applied Social Psychology* 38 (2008): 1271–1294.

10. Lewis Goldberg, "Diagnosticians vs. Diagnostic Signs: The Diagnosis of Psychosis vs. Neurosis from the MMPI," *Psychological Monographs* 79 (1965).

11. In the book by J. Edward Russo and Paul J. H. Schoemaker, *Decision Traps* (New York: Simon & Schuster, 1989), the authors provide several compelling strategies for convincing people to adopt mechanical approaches for combining predictive information.

12. Max Bazerman, *Judgment in Managerial Decision Making* (New York: John Wiley, 1990), 175.

13. Wayne F. Cascio, *Applied Psychology in Personnel Management,* 4th ed. (Englewood Cliffs, NJ: Prentice Hall, 1991), 286.

14. Milton L. Blum and James C. Naylor, *Industrial Psychology: Its Theoretical and Social Foundations* (New York: Harper & Row, 1969), 68–69.

15. See Wayne F. Cascio, E. R. Valenzi, and Val Silbey, "Validation and Statistical Power: Implications for Applied Research," *Journal of Applied Psychology* 63 (1978): 589–595; and Wayne F. Cascio, E. R. Valenzi, and Val Silbey, "More on Validation and Statistical Power," *Journal of Applied Psychology* 65 (1980): 135–138.

16. Cynthia D. Fisher, Lyle F. Schoenfeldt, and James B. Shaw, *Human Resource Management* (Boston: Houghton Mifflin, 1990), 231.

17. Neal W. Schmitt and Richard J. Klimoski, *Research Methods in Human Resource Management* (Cincinnati: South-Western, 1991), 302.

18. Cascio, *Applied Psychology in Personnel Management,* 289.

19. Lee J. Cronbach and Goldine C. Gleser, *Psychological Tests and Personnel Decisions,* 2nd ed. (Urbana: University of Illinois Press, 1965).

20. Joann S. Lubin, "Speediest Companies Snaring Top Candidates," *Atlanta Journal-Constitution,* August 11, 1999, D1.

21. Richard R. Reilly and W. R. Manese, "The Validation of a Minicourse for Telephone Company Switching Technicians," *Personnel Psychology* 32 (1979): 83–90.

22. Wesley A. Scroggins, Steven L. Thomas, and Jerry A. Morris, "Psychological Testing in Personnel Selection, Part II: The Refinement of Methods and Standards in Employee Selection," *Public Personnel Management* 37 (2008): 190.

23. Frank L. Schmidt, Mack J. Murray, and John E. Hunter, "Selection Utility in the Occupation of U.S. Park Ranger for Three Modes of Test Use," *Journal of Applied Psychology* 69 (1984): 490–497.

24. As described in John Hunter and Frank Schmidt, "Ability Tests: Economic Benefits versus the Issue of Fairness," *Industrial Relations* 21 (1982): 298.

25. Lorin Mueller, Dwayne Norris, and Scott Oppler, "Implementation Based on Alternate Validation Procedures: Ranking, Cut Scores, Banding, and Compensatory Models," in *Alternative Validation Strategies,* ed. S. Morton McPhail (New York, NY: John Wiley, 2007), 357.

26. Ibid., 365.

27. Ibid.

28. Robert L. Thorndike, *Personnel Selection: Test and Measurement Techniques* (New York: John Wiley, 1949).

29. Cascio, *Applied Psychology in Personnel Management,* 288.

30. *U.S. v. Delaware,* U.S. District LEXIS 4560 (2004). *Lanning v. SEPTA,* 308 F. 3d 286 (3rd Cir. 2002).

31. Robert L. Ebel, *Essentials of Educational Measurement* (Englewood Cliffs, NJ: Prentice Hall, 1972).

32. William H. Angoff, "Scales, Norms, and Equivalent Scores," in *Educational Measurement,* ed. Robert L. Thorndike (Washington, DC: American Council on Education, 1971), 508–600.

33. Richard E. Biddle, "How to Set Cutoffs for Knowledge Tests Used in Promotion, Training, Certification, and Licensing," *Public Personnel Management* 22 (1993): 63–80.

34. Dan Biddle and Nikki Sill, "Protective Service Physical Ability Tests: Establishing Pass/Fail, Ranking, and Banding Procedures," *Public Personnel Management* 28 (1999): 218–219.

35. Schmitt and Klimoski, *Research Methods in Human Resource Management,* 303.

36. Wayne F. Cascio, Rick Jacobs, and Jay Silva, "Validity, Utility, and Adverse Impact: Practical Implications from 30 Years of Data," in *Adverse Impact: Implications for Organizational Staffing and High Stakes Selection*, ed. James L. Outtz (New York, NY: Routledge, 2010), 271–322.

37. The contrasting groups method is described in detail in the discussion of setting cutoff scores for weighted application blanks. See George W. England, *Development and Use of Weighted Application Blanks* (Minneapolis: Industrial Relations Center, University of Minnesota, 1971).

38. Biddle and Sill, "Protective Service Physical Ability Tests: Establishing Pass/Fail, Ranking, and Banding Procedures," 218.

39. U.S. Equal Employment Opportunity Commission, Civil Service Commission, Department of Labor, and Department of Justice, *Adoption of Four Agencies of Uniform Guidelines on Employee Selection Procedures,* 43 Federal Register 38, 290–38, 315 (August 25, 1978).

40. Society of Industrial-Organizational Psychology, Inc., *Principles for the Validation and Use of Personnel Selection Procedures,* 4th ed. (Bowling Green, OH: Society of Industrial-Organizational Psychology, 2003), 46.

41. Ibid., 47.

42. Hunter and Schmidt, "Ability Tests: Economic Benefits versus the Issue of Fairness," 298.

43. Lawrence Z. Lorber, "The Civil Rights Act of 1991," in *Legal Report* (Washington, DC: Society for Human Resource Management, Spring 1992), 1–4.

44. Herman Aguinis, ed., *Test-score Banding in Human Resource Selection: Legal, Technical, and Societal Issues* (Westport, CT: Quorum, 2004).

45. Scientific Affairs Committee, "An Evaluation of Banding Methods in Personnel Selection," *The Industrial-Organizational Psychologist* 32 (1994): 80.

46. Philip Bobko and Philip Roth, "Personnel Selection with Top-Score-Referenced Banding: On the Inappropriateness of Current Procedures," *International Journal of Selection and Assessment* 12 (2004): 293.

47. Frank L. Schmidt, "The Problem of Group Differences in Ability Test Scores in Employment Selection," *Journal of Vocational Behavior* 33 (1998): 272–292.

48. Cascio, Jacobs, and Silva, "Validity, Utility, and Adverse Impact: Practical Implications from 30 Years of Data."

49. Christine A. Henle, "Case Review of the Legal Status of Banding," *Human Performance* 17 (2004): 428.

50. *Chicago Firefighters Local 2 v. City of Chicago*, 249 F. 3d 649 (7th Cir. 2001).

51. Cascio, Jacobs, and Silva, "Validity, Utility, and Adverse Impact: Practical Implications from 30 Years of Data," 281.

52. Sheldon Zedeck, Wayne F. Cascio, Irwin L. Goldstein, and James Outtz, "Sliding Bands: An Alternative to Top-Down Selection," in *Fair Employment Strategies in Human Resource Management,* ed. Richard S. Barrett (Westport, CT: Quorum Books, 1996), 228–230.

53. Gerald V. Barrett, Dennis Doyerspike, and Winfred Arthur, "The Current Status of the Judicial Review of Banding: A Clarification," *The Industrial-Organizational Psychologist* 33 (1995): 39–41.

54. Ibid.

55. Paul Sackett and L. Roth, "A Monte Carlo Examination of Banding and Rank Order Methods of Test Score Use in Personnel Selection," *Human Performance* 4 (1991): 279–295.

56. Henle, "Case Review of the Legal Status of Banding," 415–432.

57. W. M. Coward and Paul R. Sackett, "Linearity of Ability Performance Relationship: A Reconfirmation," *Journal of Applied Psychology* 75 (1990): 297–300.

58. Frank L. Schmidt, "Why All Banding Procedures in Personnel Selection Are Logically Flawed," *Human Performance* 8 (1995): 165–177.

59. Sackett and Roth, "A Monte Carlo Examination of Banding and Rank Order Methods of Test Score Use in Personnel Selection."

60. Cascio, Jacobs, and Silva, "Validity, Utility, and Adverse Impact: Practical Implications from 30 Years of Data."

61. Scientific Affairs Committee, "An Evaluation of Banding Methods in Personnel Selection."

62. Bobko and Roth, "Personnel Selection with Top-Score-Referenced Banding: On the Inappropriateness of Current Procedures" Philip Bobko, Philip Roth, and Alan Nicewander, "Banding Selection Scores in Human Resource Management Decisions: Current Inaccuracies and the Effect of Conditional Standard Scores," *Organizational Research Methods* 8 (2005): 259–273.

63. Zedeck, Cascio, Goldstein, and Outtz, "Sliding Bands: An Alternative to Top-Down Selection," 230.

64. Donald M. Truxillo and Talya N. Bauer, "Applicant Reactions to Test Store Banding in Entry-Level and Promotional Contexts," *Journal of Applied Psychology* 84 (1999): 322–339.

65. Schmidt, "Why All Banding Procedures in Personnel Selection Are Logically Flawed."

66. Wayne F. Cascio, James Outtz, Sheldon Zedeck, and Irwin L. Goldstein, "Statistical Implications of Six Methods of Test Score Use in Personnel Selection," *Human Performance* 8 (1995): 133–164.

67. Russo and Schoemaker, *Decision Traps,* 138.

68. This procedure is similar to one described in Benjamin Schneider and Neal Schmitt, *Staffing Organizations* (Glenview, IL: Scott, Foresman, 1986), 416.

69. Russo and Schoemaker, *Decision Traps,* 131–134.

70. Ibid., 134–137.

71. Ibid., 135.

72. See, for example, R. J. Bies and D. L. Shapiro, "Voice and Justification: Their Influence on Procedural Fairness Judgments," *Academy of Management Journal* 31 (1988): 676–685.

73. Kleinmuntz, *"Why We Still Use Our Heads Instead of Formulas: Toward an Integrative Approach,"* 296–310.

JOB ANALYSIS IN HUMAN RESOURCE SELECTION

In selecting personnel to fill job vacancies, managers are ultimately faced with important questions that must be addressed: What tasks are new employees required to perform? What knowledge, skills, and abilities must new employees possess in order to perform these tasks effectively? If certain specifications are used, is it then possible to find or develop selection procedures such as tests or employment interviews that could be used in making selection decisions? For any job under study, what factors or measures exist that represent job success? These are but a few of the questions that confront managers involved in human resource selection. Answers are not always obvious and are seldom easy. Yet, whatever the issue in human resource selection, one managerial tool can and should be used first in addressing selection considerations—*job analysis*. This chapter provides an overview of the job analysis process in the context of human resource (HR) selection. Our objectives are fourfold:

1. To explore the role of job analysis as applied in an employee selection context

2. To describe several techniques used in collecting job information for employee selection purposes

3. To examine how job information can be used to identify employee specifications (such as knowledge, skills, and abilities, or KSAs) necessary for successful job performance

4. To examine how these employee specifications can be translated into the content of selection procedures including predictors (such as tests, employment interviews, and application forms) and criterion measures (such as performance appraisal rating forms and objective measures of productivity)

Job Analysis in Human Resource Selection

When we come to this section of the book, several of the authors are accustomed to hearing a common refrain from many of our students (and even from some of our academic colleagues, for that matter!). That refrain goes something like this: "*Job analysis*! That is the most boring topic in selection. Can not we do something that's more interesting, like watching paint dry or grass grow?" We have to admit that our discussion of job analysis may not be a life changing event for you. If you think it might put you to sleep, do not read this chapter while lying down, before driving a car, or before operating heavy equipment. But trust us, job analysis is important in selection. We hope to persuade you of its importance in this chapter. Hang in there; the fun is just beginning! Now, tighten your safety belt so you do not fall out of your chair when you read the following sections.

JOB ANALYSIS: A DEFINITION AND ROLE IN HR SELECTION

There are probably as many definitions of job analysis as there are writings on the topic. For our purposes though, when we refer to job analysis, we simply mean *a purposeful, systematic process for collecting information on the important work-related aspects of a job.* Some possible aspects of work-related information to be collected might include the following:

1. Work activities—what a worker does; how, why, and when these activities are conducted

2. Tools and equipment used in performing work activities

3. Context of the work environment, such as work schedule or physical working conditions

4. Requirements of personnel performing the job, such as knowledge, skills, abilities (KSAs), or other personal characteristics (physical characteristics or personality)[1]

Job analysis information has been found to serve a wide variety of purposes. For example, almost 70 years ago Joseph Zerga identified more than 20 uses of job analysis data.[2] More recently, job analysis data have been used in HR areas such as compensation, training, and performance appraisal among others. Of particular interest here is the application of job analysis data in HR selection.

Broadly speaking in the context of HR selection, job analysis data are frequently used to

1. Identify employee specifications (KSAs) necessary for success on a job.

2. Select or develop selection procedures that assess important KSAs and can be administered to job applicants and used to forecast those employees who are likely to be successful on the job.

3. Develop criteria or standards of performance that employees must meet in order to be considered successful on a job.

By examining factors such as the tasks performed on a job and the KSAs needed to perform these tasks, one can obtain an idea of what ought to be measured by predictors used in employment screening. As an example, consider the job of a bank teller. An analysis of a teller's job might identify a number of tasks that are critical to successful job performance. Examination of these tasks as well as the KSAs needed to perform them might reveal some important findings. For instance, a job analysis may reveal that balancing receipts and disbursements of cash, performing arithmetic operations on numbers involving dollars and cents, and entering transaction information into a computer are critical teller tasks. Conversely, notarizing legal documents, opening savings accounts, and handling transactions involving customer loans are tasks that may not be performed by a teller. Further analysis of such job information may indicate that one important criterion of successful teller performance is the dollar balance of a teller's receipts and disbursements for a workday. That is, a teller should not take in more dollars (an "overage") or fewer dollars (a "shortage") than he or she has disbursed. An examination of the KSAs associated with a teller's balancing of receipts and disbursements might show that the ability to use an electronic calculator to add, subtract, multiply, and divide monetary numbers involving decimals is *one* important requirement. In searching for a predictor of teller success, one would consider locating or developing a selection procedure that provides information about a teller's ability to use a calculator to perform arithmetic operations on monetary values.

When predictors and criteria are developed based on the results of a job analysis, a selection system that is job-related can be developed. As we suggested in earlier chapters, by using a job-related selection system we are in a much better position to predict who can and who cannot adequately perform a job. With a job-related selection system, we are far more likely to have an employment system that will be viewed by job applicants as well as the courts as being "fair."

Figure 7.1 outlines a general framework for the application of a job analysis in the context of HR selection. Initially, an analysis is conducted using any of a number of available techniques. Most often, information on the critical job tasks, duties, or work behaviors performed on the job will be identified initially. Identification of these critical job tasks is needed to produce two important products: (a) criterion measures such as performance appraisals or productivity assessments and (b) selection procedures or predictors such as tests, application forms, or employment interviews. Oftentimes, criterion measures are developed or identified directly from job task information. However, the development of predictors typically requires some intermediate steps. For example, employee specifications (that is, the KSAs and other personal characteristics) needed to perform the critical job tasks are specified from job task information. Usually this step involves the judgment of job experts (such as supervisors or key job incumbents) to infer the necessary employee specifications. Once employee specifications have been identified, it is possible to develop measures of these employee requirements; these measures will serve as job applicant screening tools.

FIGURE 7.1 Role of Job Analysis in Human Resource Selection

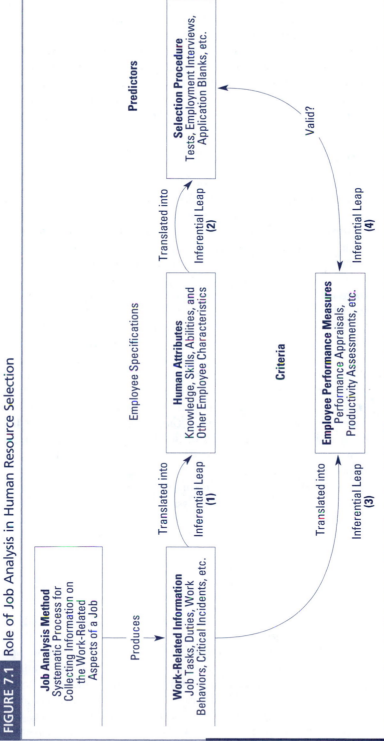

Assuming that predictor and job performance measures are derived from a job analysis, it is expected that job applicants' performance on the predictors will be related to their performance on the job (as represented by the criterion measures). As we learned earlier, a validation study tests this hypothesized relationship. Important here is the recognition that it is the job analysis process that is the foundation of the effectiveness of any HR selection system. Where job analysis is incomplete, inaccurate, or simply not conducted, a selection system may be nothing more than a game of chance—a game that employer, employee, and job applicants alike may lose.

Growth in Job Analysis

Within the last three decades or so, job analysis has received considerable attention from employers. This attention has focused on the use of job analysis not only in the basic personnel areas we mentioned earlier, but in selection as well. At least three interrelated reasons account for this renewed interest. First, many have realized that jobs are not static entities; that is, the nature of jobs may change for any number of reasons, such as technological advancements, seasonal variations, or the initiatives of incumbents.[3] Thus, as managers have recognized the importance of job information in HR decision making, there has been an accompanying recognition of the need for up-to-date information on the jobs themselves.

In addition to the need for current, accurate job data, two other factors have influenced the role of job analysis in selection. Federal guidelines (namely, the *Uniform Guidelines on Employee Selection Procedures*[4]) have had a significant effect.[5] In addition, professional standards (for example, the *Principles for the Validation and Use of Personnel Selection Procedures*)[6] produced by the Society for Industrial and Organizational Psychology have also emphasized the important role of job analysis in human resource selection programs. The *Uniform Guidelines* and the *Principles* have advocated that job analyses be performed as part of the development, application, and validation of selection procedures. Each of these documents has elevated the legal as well as the practical importance of job analysis.

Similarly, court cases involving employment discrimination in selection have underlined the significance of job analysis.[7] We discuss selected cases in the section that follows. Generally speaking, rulings in various cases have held that job analysis *must* play an integral role in any research that attempts to show a correlation between job performance and a selection measure.

Legal Issues in Job Analysis

Job analysis has become a focal point in the legal context of HR selection. The principal source for this development can be traced to the passage of Title VII of the 1964 Civil Rights Act. Title VII makes it illegal for an organization to refuse to select an individual or to discriminate against a person with respect to compensation, terms, conditions, or privileges of employment because of the person's race, sex, color, religion, or national origin. Because many Title VII cases have concerned the role of discrimination in selection for employment, job analysis has emerged as critical to the prosecution or defense of a discrimination case. Thus job analysis and its associated methodologies have become intertwined with the law. Within this legal vein, two developments have amplified the importance of job analysis in selection research: (a) the adoption of the *Uniform Guidelines on Employee Selection Procedures* by the federal government and (b) litigation involving discrimination in selection, arising under Title VII as well as the Fifth and Fourteenth Amendments to the U.S. Constitution.

Court Cases Involving Job Analysis

Although a number of cases involving job analysis have been heard in the courts, two early Supreme Court cases are particularly important. Perhaps the seminal one with respect to job analysis is *Griggs v. Duke Power Co.*[8] Even though the term *job analysis* is not mentioned per se, *Griggs* gave the legal impetus to job analysis. The case implies that an important legal requirement in a selection device validation program is an analysis of the job for which the device is used.

In *Griggs,* Duke Power was employing a written test and a high school diploma as requirements for entry into a supervisory position. The Court noted that these selection standards were used "without meaningful study of their relationship to job-performance ability. Rather, a vice president of the company testified, the requirements were instituted on the company's judgment that they generally would improve the overall quality of the work force."[9] The Court ruled that "What Congress has commanded is that any test used must measure the person *for the job* and not the person in the abstract."[10] The ruling in *Griggs* implied that for employers to attempt to meet this job-relatedness standard, they must first examine the job. Measurement of the job is accomplished through job analysis. *Albemarle Paper Co. v. Moody* is equally important.[11] In *Albemarle,* the Court, for the first time, expressly criticized the lack of a job analysis in a validation study. It was noted by the Court that "no attempt was made to analyze the jobs in terms of the particular skills they might require."[12] As with *Griggs,* the Court gave weight to the use of job analysis.

Albemarle is noteworthy for its support of job analysis. Like *Griggs,* its predecessor, *Albemarle* was a U.S. Supreme Court case. Plaintiffs and lower courts look for guidance from rulings of the Supreme Court. Thus it can be expected that the Court's insistence on job analysis in selection cases will encourage other courts to look for the presence (or lack) of a job analysis.

This case is also significant for a second reason. The Court supported the *EEOC Guidelines on Employee Selection Procedures,*[13] which required that a job analysis be performed in a validation study. As we see in the next section, the Court's endorsement of these guidelines, as well as the subsequently issued *Uniform Guidelines,* has emphasized the role of job analysis in HR selection.

Numerous court cases could be cited in addition to *Griggs* and *Albemarle.* On the whole, decisions and remedies in these cases emphasize the importance of job analysis. An examination of these cases would be helpful in isolating the standards used by the courts in evaluating job analysis in validation research. In this light, Duane Thompson and Toni Thompson reviewed 26 selected federal court cases to determine the criteria the courts used in assessing job analyses conducted in the development and validation of tests. Their review produced a set of job analysis characteristics, which they suggest are capable of withstanding legal scrutiny. Although these characteristics may vary depending on issues such as type of job analysis, type of validation strategy, and purpose of the analysis, the standards serve as a useful guide for understanding the judicial view. The legal standards identified by Thompson and Thompson are as follows:

1. Job analysis must be performed and must be for the job for which the selection instrument is to be utilized.

2. Analysis of the job should be in writing.

3. The job analysts should describe in detail the job analysis procedures used.

4. Job data should be collected from a variety of current sources by knowledgeable job analysts.

5. Sample size of individuals serving as subject matter experts should be large and representative of the jobs for which the device will be used.

6. Tasks, duties, and activities should be included in the analysis.

7. The most important tasks should be represented in the selection device.

8. Competency levels of job performance for entry-level jobs should be specified.

9. KSAs should be specified, particularly if a content validation model is followed.[14]

Federal Guidelines on Employee Selection

From 1966 to 1978, various sets of federal regulations on employee selection were issued.[15] The Equal Employment Opportunity Commission (EEOC), the Office of Federal Contract Compliance (OFCC), the Civil Service Commission (currently the U.S. Office of Personnel Management), and the Department of Justice offered guidelines for employers to follow in their selection procedures. Although some employers treated these guidelines as nothing more than a guide, the *Albemarle* case enhanced their role. As noted earlier, the Court gave deference to the EEOC guidelines, at least to the portion that discussed job analysis. The impact of the Court's opinion has been to make it mandatory for HR selection practitioners to be intimately familiar with their content.

Current federal regulations noted in the *Uniform Guidelines* supersede previous regulations and represent a joint agreement among the EEOC, Department of Justice, Department of Labor, and Civil Service Commission (now the U.S. Office of Personnel Management). Given the substantial weight accorded to the *Uniform Guidelines* in cases, the courts can be expected to continue to emphasize the importance of job analysis in the foreseeable future.

Many of the legal issues surrounding job analysis have concerned the necessity for employing these methods when developing and implementing a selection program. Since the early 1980s, however, another set of legal questions has arisen concerning the actual application of job analysis procedures. Because most of these methods involve some degree of human judgment, cases have been appearing in the courts in which technical aspects of job analysis implementation are involved. In many instances, the issue has been to determine whether the inferences made from job analysis data based largely on human judgments have discriminatory impact on protected classes of job applicants. Returning to Figure 7.1, you will see there are four points where judgment may be involved in the use of job analysis information in personnel selection. These judgments are referred to in the literature as "inferential leaps." For instance, at inference point **1** in Figure 7.1, the KSAs and other personal characteristics are inferred from the job tasks performed on a job. Because humans are involved in the process of inferring human attributes from work-related information, there is the possibility of error. The greater the role of human judgment, the larger the inferential leap, and, therefore, the greater the opportunity for discriminatory impact. In particular, inference points **1** and **2** represent areas where much equal opportunity litigation has centered when job analysis issues are in question.

Of course, the extent of inferential leaps to be made in any one job analysis application will depend on the particular situation. Factors such as the validation strategy being used (for example, content versus criterion), the type of job (for example, hourly versus managerial), the job analysis method, and the personal attribute assessed (for example, a physical skill versus a personality trait) affect the degree of inferential leaps made.

Although it would be convenient, it is simply impossible to specify one clear, suitable, standard means for meeting *all* the technical and legal considerations of a job analysis. Situations, problems, and technical issues are so varied that proper conduct of a job analysis is a complex, resource-consuming process. No one way is standard.

Collecting Job Information

Earlier we said that one principal role of job analysis in HR selection is to assess job content so that knowledge, skills, abilities (KSAs), and other requisite employee specifications can be identified. It is these employee specifications that we want to translate into selection measures such as tests, interviews, and the like. Assuming our selection measures are valid, they, in turn, may be used for selection decision-making purposes. The process of developing valid selection measures or procedures that assess employee specifications requires that judgment or inferences be made at several points. Figure 7.2 summarizes these inferential points.

At the first inference point, data collected from a job analysis are used to infer KSAs and other relevant employee specifications. A second inference point is then reached concerning the content of selection measures that reflect these identified specifications. An important goal is to minimize the chance of error at each inference point. Our resulting specifications will be useful only to the extent that our inferences are accurate and complete. If our inferences are wrong, our selection measures will be useless for predicting successful job performance.

Obviously, the process depends on the data derived initially from the job analysis. If these data are incomplete, inaccurate, or otherwise faulty, subsequent judgments based on these data will be incorrect. In the end, we will likely have an inappropriate, invalid, perhaps illegal selection procedure. Thus we must be very careful in our choice and implementation of methods for collecting job information.

At this point, we should note that many of the methods we review and discuss tend to focus on the tasks performed by job incumbents. Other researchers in the field of HR selection do not necessarily agree with using these detailed job-task approaches for all HR selection applications. In particular, writers in the area of validity generalization have tended to support more holistic methods of job analysis.[16] Their argument is that task-oriented job analysis is not of much value for selection when measures of employee ability and aptitudes are concerned. On the other hand, when noncognitive attributes of applicants are being assessed or content validation strategies are being used with job knowledge or work sample tests, task-oriented job analysis is needed.[17] We will have more to say about a more holistic job analysis approach later in the chapter when we discuss the future of job analysis.

A SURVEY OF JOB ANALYSIS METHODS

We divide our review of specific job analysis methods into two parts. The first part of the chapter covers the following job analysis methods: (a) job analysis interviews, (b) job analysis questionnaires (including task analysis inventories), (c) Critical Incidents Technique, and (d) subject matter expert (SME) or job expert workshops. We describe each technique, its application, and its advantages and disadvantages. We do not advocate one particular method to the exclusion of others. Many methods are available to the user; our omission of a specific method should not be interpreted as a condemnation of it. In this book we concentrate on those methods that seem to be most popular in current HR selection practice. However, because all of the methods depend on interviews, questionnaires, or a combination of the two for collecting job information, we begin with and focus our discussion on these methods. Finally, in the last portion of the chapter, we illustrate one method of how job analysis information can be used for HR selection purposes.

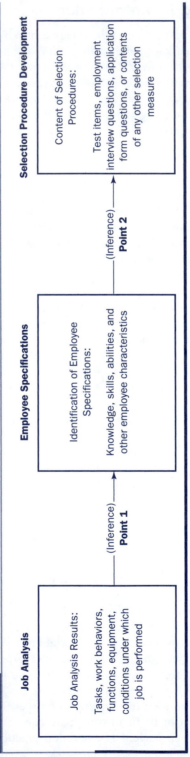

FIGURE 7.2 Points of Inference in the Job Analysis → Employee Specifications → Selection Measure Development Process

Job Analysis

Job Analysis Results:

Tasks, work behaviors, functions, equipment, conditions under which job is performed

——— (Inference) ———
Point 1

Employee Specifications

Identification of Employee Specifications:

Knowledge, skills, abilities, and other employee characteristics

——— (Inference) ———
Point 2

Selection Procedure Development

Content of Selection Procedures:

Test items, employment interview questions, application form questions, or contents of any other selection measure

JOB ANALYSIS INTERVIEWS

Description

The interview is one of the most frequently used methods of job analysis, capable of meeting a wide array of purposes. Essentially, a job analysis interview consists of a trained analyst asking questions about the duties and responsibilities, KSAs required, and equipment and/or conditions of employment for a job or class of jobs.

Job analysis data collected through interviews are typically obtained through group or individual interviews with incumbents or supervisors. A key assumption of the method is that participants are thoroughly familiar with the job being studied. Large groups (10 to 20) of incumbents may be used when it is certain that all incumbents are performing the same major activities. Supervisors are sometimes employed to verify incumbent information and to provide information unavailable to employees in the job. In other cases, supervisors are used because they may feel less threatened than incumbents in discussing an incumbent's job activities with a stranger, or they may be better able to comment on the necessary employee characteristics required to perform these activities successfully.

A job analysis interview may be structured or unstructured. For selection purposes, a structured interview in which specific questions are asked and means are available for recording answers to these questions (such as rating scales or interview answer forms) is essential. An unstructured interview consists of a job analyst collecting information about a job without a specific list of questions developed prior to the interview. Because of the technical and legal issues involved in job analysis, a structured interview is much more likely than an unstructured one to provide the kind of job analysis data that can be used effectively in selection applications. When we speak of a job analysis interview, we are referring to one that is structured.

In the context of HR selection, a job analysis interview is typically performed for one or more of the following reasons:

1. To collect job information—for example, information on job tasks—that will serve as a basis for developing other job analysis measures, such as a job analysis questionnaire

2. To serve as a means for clarifying or verifying information collected previously through other job analysis methods

3. To serve as a method, perhaps as one of several used, for collecting relevant job data for developing a selection system

Considerations on Applicability

The interview can be applied to a variety of jobs, from those with activities that are basically physical in nature, such as a laborer's, to those with activities that are primarily mental, such as a manager's. When used with knowledgeable respondents, the interview makes it possible to identify activities that may go unobserved or occur over long time periods.

An important step toward effective application of an interview is to plan the interview itself. Plans should be formulated so that objectives of the interview are clear (for example, the identification and rating of job tasks), individuals to be interviewed are known (for example, incumbents with six or more months of job experience), questions and means for recording answers are clearly specified (for example, an interview schedule listing the questions and forms for recording responses), and those who will conduct the interviews are identified (for example, consultants or staff members).

With regard to the interview questions themselves, numerous approaches can be taken in phrasing and posing questions. Figure 7.3 presents a sample job interview schedule for use with a single job incumbent. The schedule shown illustrates only some of the types of questions that might be asked. Supplementary forms would also be used with the schedule to systematically record incumbents' responses to the questions.

FIGURE 7.3 An Example of a Job Analysis Interview Schedule for Use with an Incumbent

Name of Employee _____   Payroll Title _____

Job Analyst _____   Department _____

Date _____   Work Location _____

Important Job Tasks

1. Describe your job in terms of what you do.
2. How do you do your job? Do you use special tools, equipment, or other sources of aid? If so, list the names of the principal tools, equipment, or sources of aid you use.
3. Of the major tasks in your job, how much time does it take to do each one? How often do you perform each task in a day, week, or month?

Knowledge, Skills, and Abilities Required

What does it take to perform each task in terms of the following:

1. Knowledge required

    a. What subject matter areas are covered by each task?
    b. What facts or principles must you have an acquaintance with or understand in these subject matter areas?
    c. Describe the level, degree, and breadth of knowledge required in these areas or subjects.

2. Skills required

    a. What activities must you perform with ease and precision?
    b. What are the manual skills that are required to operate machines, vehicles, and equipment, or to use tools?

3. Abilities required

    a. What is the nature and level of language ability, written or oral, required of you on the job? Are complex oral or written ideas involved in performing the task, or do you use simple instructional materials?
    b. What mathematical ability must you have?
    c. What reasoning or problem-solving ability must you have?
    d. What instructions must you follow? Are they simple, detailed, involved, abstract?
    e. What interpersonal abilities are required? What supervisory or managing abilities are required?
    f. What physical abilities such as strength, coordination, or visual acuity must you have?

Physical Activities

Describe the frequency and degree to which you are engaged in such activities as pulling, pushing, throwing, carrying, kneeling, sitting, running, crawling, reaching, climbing.

Environmental Conditions

Describe the frequency and degree to which you will encounter working conditions such as these: cramped quarters, moving objects, vibration, inadequate ventilation.

Typical Working Incidents

Describe the frequency and degree to which you do the following:

1. Work in situations involving interpretation of feelings, ideas, or facts in terms of personal viewpoint.
2. Influence people in their opinions, attitudes, or judgments about ideas or things.

(Continued)

FIGURE 7.3 *(Continued)*

3. Work with people beyond giving and receiving instructions.
4. Perform repetitive work, or continuously perform the same work.
5. Perform under stress when confronted with emergency, critical, unusual, or dangerous situations or situations in which work speed and sustained attention are make-or-break aspects of the job.
6. Perform a variety of duties, often changing from one task to another of a different nature, without loss of efficiency or composure.
7. Work under hazardous conditions that may result in violence, loss of body parts, burns, bruises, cuts, impairment of the senses, collapse, fractures, or electric shock.

Records and Reports

What records or reports do you prepare as part of your job?

Source of Job Information

What is the principal source for instructions you receive on how to do your job (for example, oral directions or written specifications)?

Supervisory Responsibilities

1. How many employees are directly under your supervision?
2. Do you have full authority to assign work; correct and discipline; and recommend pay increases, transfers, promotions, and discharge for these employees?

Other

Are there any additional elements about your job that would help me better understand what you do? If so, please describe them.

An Example

An approach adopted by the U.S. Office of Personnel Management is one possibility when a job analysis interview will be used.[18]

The key initial step in characterizing a job with this interview procedure is the identification of critical job tasks. Once identified, each task is described in terms of factors such as KSAs required for task performance and environmental conditions surrounding task performance. Because of the task's importance to the interview method, it may be helpful to review how job tasks are analyzed and structured with this method. After all, it is the task statement from which worker specifications are ultimately developed.

Task statements are written so that each shows the following:

1. What the worker does, by using a specific action verb that introduces the task statement

2. To whom or what he or she does it, by stating the object of the verb

3. What is produced, by expressing the expected output of the action

4. What materials, tools, procedures, or equipment are used[19]

Using these task characteristics, let's see how they are applied in an actual interview context for the purpose of developing appropriate task statements.

Suppose, for example, an analyst is reviewing the job of welfare eligibility examiner in a state human services agency. Assume further that background and supplementary data have been obtained from the incumbent. The interviewer asks the respondent to describe his or her job in terms of what is done—and how, for what purpose, and using what equipment or tools. The interviewee then describes the job as follows:

I interview applicants for food stamps—ask the applicants all the pertinent questions that will help to determine their eligibility. For example, are they working part time, receiving other assistance, and so on. To carry out the job I have to interpret regulations, policies, and actually make decisions about eligibility. Some applicants are referred to other assistance units. Some applicants need detailed explanations of policies at a level they can understand, to avoid an unpleasant reaction over a decision. They also get advice about their appeal rights from me. I visit homes to evaluate a client's circumstances and make determinations. I verify what the client has said on the application: household composition, shelter arrangements, income, and so on. This helps me determine whether the food stamp costs have been correctly or incorrectly determined.

At times, I work in outreach centers and homes of applicants to make determinations. I make personal appearances at high schools, colleges, and civic organizations to outline and explain the food stamp program.[20]

Following these comments, the analyst uses the task statement criteria listed earlier to produce task statements representing important task activities. Table 7.1 summarizes the classification of content for one important task. Once classified, the content is rewritten to produce an easy-to-read, understandable statement. The goal of the rewriting process is to produce task statements that people unfamiliar with the job will understand. For example, the task content classified in Table 7.1 could be rewritten as follows:

1. Asks client questions, listens, and records answers on standard eligibility form, using knowledge of interviewing techniques and eligibility criteria in order to gather information from which client's eligibility for food stamps can be determined.[21]

If the analyst follows through with the process just described, 10 to 20 important task statements are typically identified. From the interview response given earlier, additional tasks might include the following:

2. Determines eligibility of applicant (using regulatory policies as a guide) in order to complete client's application for food stamps.

3. Decides on and describes other agencies available in order to assist and refer client to appropriate community resources using worker's knowledge of resources available and knowledge of client's needs.

TABLE 7.1	Classification of Interview Content for the Purpose of Developing a Task Statement		
Performs What Action? (Verb)	**To Whom or What? (Object of Verb)**	**To Produce What? (Expected Output)**	**Using What Tools, Equipment, Work Aids, Processes?**
Asks questions, listens, records answers	To/of applicant on eligibility form	In order to determine eligibility	Eligibility form; eligibility criteria in manual; interviewing techniques

Source: U.S. Civil Service Commission, *Job Analysis: Developing and Documenting Data* (Washington, DC: U.S. Government Printing Office, 1973), p. 6.

4. Explains policies and regulations appropriate to applicant's case in order to inform applicants of their status.

5. Evaluates information gained from home visit, interview, and observation in order to decide whether home conditions are consistent with original application, using original application and agency's housing standards as a guide.

6. Meets with, talks to, answers the questions of, and has discussions with members of high schools, colleges, and civic organizations in order to outline and explain food stamp program using knowledge and experience of food stamp program.[22]

After the important job tasks have been stated, the analyst then characterizes each statement with regard to frequency of performance, KSAs required, physical activities required, environmental conditions, and other factors thought to be important to task performance. Questions such as those in the sample interview schedule shown in Figure 7.3 can be used to make these determinations for each task. An illustration may help to clarify the task characterization process. For the moment, let's reexamine the second task identified in the study of welfare eligibility examiner. The task was stated as follows: "Determines eligibility of applicant (using regulatory policies as a guide) in order to complete client's application for food stamps." Describing the task using the interview schedule might be accomplished as shown in Figure 7.4. In addition to those characteristics illustrated in Figure 7.4, additional task data, such as ratings of task importance or task frequency, may also be obtained. These ratings may be made by the job incumbent, using rating scales, to further describe the job task. (We discuss such scales later in the chapter.) This same process is then carried out for each task statement. In the end, we should have a clearer picture of the demands, activities, and conditions of employment for the job being studied.

The success of the interview as a job analysis technique depends, to a large extent, on the skill of the interviewer. A successful interviewer must possess several important skills—the ability to listen, put individuals at ease, probe and prompt for answers from reluctant interviewees, and control the direction of an interview—all vital to a successful job analysis.[23] With such skills, an interviewer may be able to tease out job information that goes undetected by other forms of analysis. To enhance the likelihood of success in using the technique, certain guidelines should be followed. Suggestions for improving the chance of success in using job analysis interviews are given in Figure 7.5.

Limitations of the Job Analysis Interview

The job analysis interview is one option for collecting job data; however, it has its limitations. The interview often suffers from a lack of standardization and has limited possibilities for covering large numbers of respondents, particularly if they are spread over a wide geographical area. If thorough documentation is not collected as the interview is conducted, important legal requirements of job analysis information will likely go unmet. The skills and procedures used by the individual analyst principally determine the utility of the interview.

In addition, the job analysis interview has other limitations. Unless group interviews can be conducted, the technique requires a great deal of time and may not be cost efficient if many jobs need to be studied. Depending on the interviewee and the type of job being reviewed, an interviewer may literally be required to track through an entire job in specific detail. Such a process is not only expensive, but may require a highly skilled interviewer to identify the needed content.

Another major problem is that the technique may be plagued with a distortion of information. If interviewees believe conveying certain information may be beneficial

---

FIGURE 7.4   Example Characterization of a Selected Job Task: The Job of Welfare Eligibility Examiner

> **Task 2:**
>
> **Determines eligibility of applicant (using regulatory policies as a guide) in order to complete client's application for food stamps.**

Task Characterization

Knowledge Required:

1. Knowledge of content and meaning of items on standard application form
2. Knowledge of Social-Health Services food stamp regulatory policies
3. Knowledge of statutes relating to Social-Health Services food stamp program

Skills Required:

None

Abilities Required:

1. Ability to read and understand complex instructions such as regulatory policies
2. Ability to read and understand a variety of procedural instructions, written and oral, and convert these to proper actions
3. Ability to use simple arithmetic—addition and subtraction
4. Ability to translate requirements into language appropriate to laypersons

Physical Activities:

Sedentary

Environmental Conditions:

None

Typical Working Incidents:

Working with people beyond giving and receiving instructions

Interest Areas:

1. Communication of data
2. Business contact with people
3. Working for the (presumed) good of people

Source: U.S. Civil Service Commission, *Job Analysis: Developing and Documenting Data* (Washington, DC: U.S. Government Printing Office, 1973), p. 13–14.

---

for them (for example, a wage increase), they may exaggerate their activities and responsibilities to reflect a more complex job. It can be difficult to identify distorted job information. Verification from the supervisor or other incumbents can be used as a check. However, comparisons among subjective data are difficult and expensive to make.

In general, a job analysis interview should *not* be relied on as the *sole* method when the analysis is being conducted for selection purposes. When employed as a supplementary source, however, interview data can be helpful. For example, interviews can be used to identify content for other job analysis methods, such as the development of task analysis inventories or the clarification of responses to other methods.

FIGURE 7.5	Guidelines for Conducting a Job Analysis Interview

Opening the Interview

1. Put the worker at ease by learning his or her name in advance, introducing yourself, and discussing general and pleasant topics long enough to establish rapport. Be at ease.

2. Make the purpose of the interview clear by explaining why the interview was scheduled, what is expected to be accomplished, and how the worker's cooperation will help in the production of tools for use in personnel selection.

3. Encourage the worker to talk by always being courteous and showing a sincere interest in what he or she says.

Steering the Interview

1. Help the worker to think and talk according to the logical sequence of the duties performed. If duties are not performed in a regular order, ask the worker to describe the functional aspects of the duties by taking the most important activity first, the second-most important next, and so forth. Request the worker to describe the infrequent duties of his or her job—duties that are not part of the worker's regular activities, such as the occasional setup of a machine, occasional repairs, or infrequent reports.

2. Allow the worker sufficient time to answer each question and to formulate an answer.

3. Phrase questions carefully, so that the answers will be more than "yes" or "no."

4. Avoid the use of leading questions.

5. Conduct the interview in plain, easily understood language.

6. Control the interview with respect to the economic use of time and adherence to subject matter. For example, when the interviewee strays from the subject, a good technique for bringing him or her back to the point is to summarize the data collected up to that point.

Closing the Interview

1. Summarize the information obtained from the worker, indicating the major duties performed and the details concerning each of the duties.

2. Close the interview on a friendly note.

Miscellaneous Dos and Don'ts for Interviews

1. Do not take issue with the worker's statements.

2. Do not show any partiality to grievances or conflicts concerning the employer-employee relations.

3. Do not show any interest in the wage classification of the job.

4. Do not talk down to the worker.

5. Do not permit yourself to be influenced by your personal likes and dislikes.

6. Be impersonal. Do not be critical or attempt to suggest any changes or improvements in the organization or methods of work.

7. Talk to the worker only with permission of her or his supervisor.

8. Verify completed job analysis interview with an appropriate individual—such as a supervisor.

Source: U.S. Civil Service Commission, *Job Analysis: Developing and Documenting Data* (Washington, DC: U.S. Government Printing Office, 1973), p. 12–13.

JOB ANALYSIS QUESTIONNAIRES

Description

The job analysis questionnaire or survey is one way to handle some of the problems of the job analysis interview. This method consists of a questionnaire distributed to respondents through various means—in person by a job analyst or via email sent to participants including a link to the questionnaire. The questionnaire lists job information such as activities or tasks, tools and equipment used to perform the job, working conditions in which the job is performed, and KSAs or other characteristics incumbents need to perform the job successfully. Participants are asked to make some form of judgment about job information presented on the questionnaire. Respondents often use some form of a rating scale to indicate the degree to which various aspects of job information listed on the questionnaire apply to their jobs.

Numerous forms of job analysis questionnaires can be used, but most fall into one of two classes: (a) *tailored* questionnaires developed for a specific purpose or a specific job, or (b) *prefabricated* or existing questionnaires. Tailored job analysis questionnaires are typically prepared by an organization (or its consultants) for application to a *specific* job. Like prefabricated instruments, these questionnaires also include tasks or other aspects of jobs (for example, skills and abilities) to be rated by a respondent. Because the focus of tailored questionnaires is usually on one job, the aspects of the job listed on the questionnaire are more specific than those given on an existing measure.

Prefabricated questionnaires are usually generic measures developed for use with a variety of jobs. These inventories usually consist of a preestablished set of items describing aspects of a job that respondents (incumbents, supervisors, or observers) judge using a rating scale. Frequently, the aspects of jobs that respondents are asked to rate deal with job activities or functions performed. Because these questionnaires are already developed, many are designed to be taken "off-the-shelf" and applied by a knowledgeable user. Here are some examples of prefabricated job analysis questionnaires that are suitable for use in HR selection applications:

1. *Common Metric Questionnaire*[24] (http://cmqonline.com/)

2. *Professional and Managerial Position Questionnaire*[25] (http://www.paq2.com/pmpqmain.html)

3. *Management Position Description Questionnaire*[26]

4. *Managerial and Professional Job Functions Inventory*[27] (http://www.creativeorgdesign.com/tests_page.htm?id=152)

5. *Position Analysis Questionnaire*[28] (http://www.paq.com/)

6. *Threshold Traits Analysis System*[29]

7. *Occupation Analysis Inventory*[30]

8. *Personality-Related Position Requirements Form*[31]

We turn our attention now to one popular type of tailored job analysis questionnaire employed in HR selection, the task analysis inventory.

The Task Analysis Inventory

A task analysis inventory is a questionnaire or survey that includes a listing of tasks (100 or more tasks is not unusual) for which respondents make some form of judgment. Usually these judgments are ratings given by respondents using a task rating scale, such as frequency of task performance.

Because many different tasks exist in any job, this type of job analysis questionnaire is typically directed toward only one job or a class of very similar jobs. Most often, the inventory is intended for use by incumbents. Nevertheless, supervisors and observers can complete it—assuming they are knowledgeable about the job being studied.

Historically, the method has been widely used in military settings, in particular by the U.S. Air Force.[32] Although the origin of task inventories may be traced to the military, their use for selection purposes by both public and private employers has grown substantially. One important reason for the increasing use of these inventories is that many employers have adopted a content validation strategy for selection measures, for which the inventories are particularly helpful.

The Nature of Task Inventories

A task inventory often contains three major categories of information: (a) background information on respondents, (b) a listing of the job tasks with associated rating scales, and (c) other or miscellaneous information. Information on respondents such as name, gender, ethnicity, tenure on the job being rated, tenure with the employing organization, job location, and title of the job being rated should be included on the task inventory. Identifying information is useful should the need arise to contact respondents (for example, for clarifying responses), and demographic information is valuable for performing analyses—such as a comparison of how different types of respondents view the job being rated. In addition, respondent demographic information can be important in dealing with any legal questions that may arise about a job analysis. For example, it may be necessary to show that respondents to the task inventory are representative of minority or other protected groups or that the respondents have the necessary qualifications to serve as job analysis agents. The second part of a task analysis inventory includes the job tasks and their rating scales. Figure 7.6 presents a condensed example of this portion of a task analysis inventory.

The inventory shown is one used to analyze the various tasks associated with the job of personnel analyst. Since most inventories are similar to the one exhibited, we use it to point out two important characteristics: (a) the *phrasing of tasks* to be rated and (b) the use of *rating scales* for judging the tasks.

First, we see that the item being judged is a *task*. If we compare the phrasing of the tasks shown in Figure 7.6 with those developed by the Office of Personnel Management interview procedure discussed earlier, we find that the two sets of tasks differ. From our comparison, we see that the task statements developed previously appear to be more complex. Tasks that were identified under the interview procedure described what the tasks consisted of as well as the results of those tasks. Work aids, materials, methods, and other requirements of a job incumbent were noted. In contrast, in our task inventory example the tasks are not as fully developed. Most statements on a task analysis inventory are concerned with *what* gets done. Tasks listed on some inventories provide no information about the situation surrounding the activity. Tasks developed by other job analysis methods (for example, the Office of Personnel Management interview) usually provide information on what, how, and why. Some task analysis inventories also include these kinds of detailed task statements. Because of the detail provided in these statements, inventories with detailed statements can be particularly helpful in selection applications. For instance, they are useful in planning specific selection procedures to employ and developing the actual content of these procedures.

Another important characteristic of any task inventory is the *rating scale* used by the respondent for judging the given tasks. A rating scale provides a continuum or range of options (most often consisting of five to seven steps) that respondents can use to express their perceptions of a task. Numbers are employed to define degrees of respondents' views. For example, *Relative Time Spent on Task Performance* is an often-used task rating measure.[33] One form of such a scale is as follows:

Relative to the time you spend in your job doing other tasks, how much time do you spend on this job task?

0 = This task is not performed

1 = Much below average

FIGURE 7.6   A Condensed Example of a Task Analysis Inventory for the Job of Personnel Analyst

Directions: We are interested in knowing more about your job. Below we have listed a number of tasks you might perform on your job. Using the rating scales given below, rate each task as to (a) how *frequently* you perform it and (b) how *important* it is for newly hired workers in a job like yours to be able to perform this task when they first begin work. Read each task and then place your rating in the two spaces to the right of each task.

Frequency of Performance	**Importance for Newly Hired Employees**
1 = Not performed at all	1 = Not performed at all
2 = Seldom	2 = Somewhat important
3 = Occasionally	3 = Important
4 = Frequently	4 = Very important
5 = Almost all of the time	5 = Extremely important

Job Tasks	Frequency of Performance	Importance for Newly Hired Employees
1. Prepare job descriptions for secretarial jobs.	[ ]	[ ]
2. Check file folders for disposition of medical and dental records.	[ ]	[ ]
3. Initiate requests for identification cards from terminated personnel.	[ ]	[ ]
4. Describe company policies to newly hired employees.	[ ]	[ ]
5. Write computer programs using SPSS in order to analyze personnel absenteeism and turnover data.	[ ]	[ ]
•	•	•
•	•	•
•	•	•
105. Plan and develop training programs for newly hired clerical personnel.	[ ]	[ ]

---

  2 = Below average

  3 = Slightly below average

  4 = About average

  5 = Slightly above average

  6 = Above average

  7 = Much above average

This illustration is just one way of phrasing the rating scale for time spent on task performance. Many other forms can be used. Regardless of the scale, the objective of a rating scale is to identify the *degree* to which a task is perceived to possess a rated characteristic.

Quite often, respondents use more than one rating scale to assess job tasks. The scales chosen depend on any number of issues, such as the number of tasks to be rated, the time available, the capabilities of incumbents (for example, educational level, reading ability), the complexity of the job (the more complex, the more scales needed to assess the job adequately), and the purpose of the task analysis. Regarding purpose, if the analysis is being performed as part of a validation study, specific rating scales will be needed. For example, in a content validation study, the following task-rating categories should be considered:

   1. Frequency of task performance

   2. Task importance or criticality

3. Task difficulty

4. Whether the task can be learned on the job relatively quickly[34]

The third portion of the task inventory may focus on parts of the job, other than tasks, that also account for job performance. For instance, this last section is sometimes used to assess the physical working conditions of the job (degree of heating and cooling; amount of lifting, standing, sitting, walking, and so on; degree of job stress; or equipment and tools used for performing the job).

Development of Task Inventories

Because most task inventories are aimed toward a specific job, they may have to be developed by the user. This process is time-consuming and often expensive. Access to previous inventories or analyses of the job in question—as well as use of technical experts in job analysis and questionnaire development—are important determinants of the cost and success of the method. For those organizations committed to the development and administration of a task inventory, there are a number of steps to be taken.[35] Some of the major steps and guidelines for developing task inventories are listed in Table 7.2. Basically, development of a task inventory should be carried out in a sequential fashion such as the one outlined in the table. There is no one best way. However, suggestions like those noted increase the chances that the resulting questionnaire will meet the objectives for which it is intended.

Once developed, the inventory is ready for application. In using task analysis inventories, several issues should be considered. First, respondents' names and other identifying information should be collected. Using identifying information (a) helps ensure high-quality information, (b) is necessary if follow-up studies will be conducted, and (c) is useful when combined with personnel file data (such as scores on selection measures and demographic characteristics). Second, the inventory should be distributed to large numbers of incumbents, which improves data reliability. Finally, optical scanning sheets are recommended for minimizing time, cost, and errors in coding and data entry. In some cases, it may be possible to administer the inventories using the World Wide Web.

Application of Task Analysis in Selection

A task analysis inventory is used to define the most important tasks or activities that compose incumbents' jobs. It is this core group of job tasks that serves as the basis for inferring the KSAs and other characteristics needed to perform the job successfully. Since jobs we are interested in studying may be reasonably complex, lists of task statements and accompanying rating scales are one of the principal means used for assessing job tasks. Once the task rating data have been collected, subsequent statistical analyses of the ratings are used to identify the most important or most critical aspects of the job.

To identify important job tasks, any of several statistical techniques can be applied to the rating data.[36] In many cases, these techniques involve the calculation of simple descriptive statistics (such as means, standard deviations, and percentages) and the application of decision rules for defining critical job tasks. Let's look at a simple example. Assume for a moment that we have given a comprehensive task analysis inventory to a large sample of bank clerks. Among other judgments, the clerks were asked to use a seven-point rating scale (1 = Of No Importance to 7 = Of Major Importance) to judge each task. Analyses of the data were conducted and descriptive information obtained. We will use two of the rated tasks to illustrate our point. Figure 7.7 shows the two example tasks and some associated descriptive statistics computed on the task ratings.

TABLE 7.2	**Summary of Steps and Guidelines for Developing Task Analysis Inventories**

Sequential Steps for Developing Content of Task Inventories

1. Technical manuals, previous job analyses, and other job-related reports are reviewed for possible task-item content.
2. Technical job experts (consultants, selected incumbents/supervisors) prepare lists of job tasks known to be performed.
3. Interviews are held with job incumbents and supervisors in order to identify additional tasks.
4. Tasks identified are reviewed for duplication, edited, and incorporated into an initial version of the inventory. Tasks are described according to task-writing guidelines.
5. First draft is prepared and submitted to a panel of experts (or incumbents and/or supervisors) for review.
6. Panel of reviewers adds, deletes, or modifies tasks for the development of another draft of the inventory.
7. Steps 5 and 6 are repeated, using the same or a similar panel, until an acceptable draft has been developed.
8. Task inventory is then pilot-tested on a sample of respondents to whom the final version will be given.
9. Appropriate modifications are made as needed.
10. Steps 8 and 9 are repeated until a final, acceptable version is developed.

Guidelines for Writing Task Statements

When task statements are identified, they should

1. Characterize activities, not skills or knowledge.
2. Have an identifiable beginning and ending.
3. Represent activities performed by an individual worker, not activities performed by different individuals.
4. Have an identifiable output or consequence.
5. Avoid extremes in the phrasing of activities; statements should not be too broad or too specific.
6. Be developed by full-time inventory writers (preferably); supervisors/incumbents should serve as technical advisers.

When task statements are written, they should

1. Mean the same thing to all respondents.
2. Be stated so that the rating scale to be used makes sense.
3. Be stated so that the incumbent is understood to be the subject of the statement. The pronoun "I" should be implied. For example "(I) number all card boxes."
4. Be stated so that an action verb is in the present tense.
5. Be stated so that the action verb has an object.
6. Use terms that are specific, familiar, and unambiguous.

Source: Based on Ernest J. McCormick, "Job Information: Its Development and Applications," *ASPA Handbook of Personnel and Industrial Relations*, ed. Dale Yoder and Herbert G. Heneman (Washington, DC: BNA, 1979), 4–66; and Joseph E. Morsh and Wayne B. Archer, *Procedural Guide for Conducting Occupational Surveys in the United States Air Force* (PRL-TR-67-11, AD-664 036) (Lackland Air Force Base, TX: Personnel Research Laboratory, Aerospace Medical Division, 1967), 8–11.

In deciding which tasks should be classified as important to the job, some *minimum* statistical criteria are chosen that a task must meet to be considered critical. As a possibility, we could set the following (in this example, arbitrary) cutoff points:

1. A task must receive a mean rating of 4.00 or higher (the higher the mean, the more important the task).

2. A task rating must have a standard deviation of 1.00 or lower (the lower the standard deviation, the greater the degree of agreement among employees in their task ratings).

3. Most employees (75 percent or more) must perform the task.

Using these standards, Task 9 would be chosen and Task 67 omitted (see Figure 7.7). The task "Use basic arithmetic to add, subtract, divide, and multiply monetary figures with

| FIGURE 7.7 | Example Task Statements and Associated Descriptive Statistics Used in Identifying Important Job Tasks |

Task Statement	Mean Importance[a]	Standard Deviation	% Employees Performing Task
9. Use basic arithmetic to add, subtract, divide, and multiply monetary amounts with decimals.	6.74	0.68	99.2
•	•	•	•
•	•	•	•
•	•	•	•
67. Recommend to customers investment account options for investing savings.	1.21	1.56	8.9

[a]The ratings of task importance were made using a rating scale ranging from 1 = Of No Importance to 7 = Of Major Importance.

decimals" would be added to other tasks that meet our evaluation criteria. These would be deemed the most important tasks that compose the job. Inferences concerning the content of selection measures would be based on the pool of tasks derived from application of these criteria to the task ratings.

Oftentimes, several rating scales are employed by raters when judging job tasks. That is, employees are asked to judge job tasks on several different criteria, such as frequency of task performance, importance of the task, and difficulty of the task. When multiple rating scales were used, some researchers simply arithmetically combined all of the rating scores for each task.[37] As in our previous example, the results of these arithmetic procedures are used to determine task importance.

Whatever the analyses used, the most important tasks are the basis on which inferences regarding the content of our selection measures rests. The major idea behind the application of task analysis inventories is to define *important* job content. That determination can serve as the source of statements about requisite worker specifications and the development or selection of devices for choosing among job applicants. In addition, the defined job content can also serve as one basis for applying specific validation models such as content validity.

Advantages and Disadvantages of Task Analysis

Any job analysis technique will have unique assets and limitations; task analysis is no different. On the positive side, task inventories offer an efficient means for collecting data from large numbers of incumbents in geographically dispersed locations. Additionally, task inventories lend themselves to quantifying job analysis data. Quantitative data are invaluable in analyzing jobs and determining core job components.

Development of task inventories can be time-consuming and expensive. Motivation problems often become significant when inventories are long or complex. Ambiguities and questions that arise during administration of the inventory may not be addressed; however, in a method such as the interview, problems can be resolved as they come up. As these difficulties become magnified, one can expect respondents to become less cooperative, with a concomitant decline in the quality of data collected.[38] With regard to data quality, a problem that can plague the use of task inventories, as well as other job analysis methods involving respondents who voluntarily participate, is the respondent representativeness of the desired employee population. When actual respondents to a job analysis survey are not representative of the desired employee population (for example, in terms of gender, race, age), the results obtained from those participants may be biased. Potential for bias in job analysis studies can lead to legal concerns. Steps may be needed to encourage participation in job analysis surveys—requiring names on surveys, conducting follow-up contacts with nonrespondents, and requiring survey participation.[39]

CRITICAL INCIDENT TECHNIQUE

Description

The Critical Incident Technique approach involves the development of a series of behavioral statements developed by supervisors and other subject matter experts (SMEs). The SMEs develop these behavioral statements based on direct observation or memory, describing incidents of good and poor job performance. These statements are important because they describe those behaviors that differentiate successful job performance from unsuccessful performance. Critical incidents can provide valuable information about important components of the job. These components can serve as a basis for developing descriptive information about a job.

The Critical Incident Technique was originally developed to gather information to determine training needs and develop performance appraisal forms.[40] The process is designed to generate a list of especially good and especially poor examples of performance (incidents) that job incumbents exhibit. The object of the Critical Incident Technique is to gather information regarding specific behaviors that actually have been observed, not judgmental or trait-oriented descriptions of performance. These behaviors are then grouped into job dimensions. The final list of job dimensions and respective critical incidents provides a great deal of qualitative information about a job and the behaviors associated with job success or failure. The basic elements of information collected are job behaviors rather than personal traits. Each critical incident consists of (a) a description of a situation, (b) the effective or ineffective behavior performed by a job incumbent, and (c) the consequences of that behavior. The result of the Critical Incident Technique is a list of events where employees performed tasks poorly or exceptionally well. A representative sample of all job tasks may not be in the list, but the range of incidents provides information from which performance dimensions and worker specifications can be inferred.

Application of Critical Incidents

The Critical Incident Technique can be used for a variety of selection purposes. Here, we examine the use of the technique to generate a list of job-related behaviors from which inferences are based regarding worker specifications. Job information collected from critical incidents is helpful in developing the content of task analysis surveys. In addition, critical incidents are particularly helpful in developing selection procedure content such as the Situational Interview, the Behavioral Description Interview, Assessment Center tasks, and Situational Judgment Tests.[41] Information derived from critical incidents can facilitate the development of content comprising employee performance evaluations that often serve as criterion measures of job success. Implementing the method involves the following steps:

1. *Selecting the Method for Critical Incidents Collection*. Critical incidents can be gathered from job experts (a) in a group setting, (b) in individual interviews, or

(c) by administering a questionnaire. The most efficient method of gathering critical incidents is by working with a group of job experts. Each job expert in the group is asked to write as many critical incidents as he or she can. This approach entails less time for the analysts, and job experts may help jog each other's memories and subsequently generate a greater number of critical incidents. At times it is not possible to gather the information in a group setting. For example, job experts may not be skilled at writing. In this case, individual or group interviews are conducted and incidents recorded as the job experts remember them. Individual interviews may be used when the information is confidential or embarrassing and should not be discussed in a group. Also, if the job experts are managers or executives, it may be difficult for them to find a common time to meet as a group. The final method, the questionnaire, should be used only with individuals who are skilled at expressing themselves in writing and excited about participating in the process. Otherwise, the resulting critical incidents obtained may be insufficient in content and number.

2. *Selecting a Panel of Job Experts.* The Critical Incident Technique is frequently applied by a job analyst working with subject matter experts. With this particular procedure, it is important to think carefully about the job experts chosen to participate in the process. Job incumbents, subordinates, and supervisors are likely to provide different types of information. Individuals should be chosen who have had the opportunity to observe others' performance on the job. Normally, this would include supervisors and job incumbents who have been in the position for a long period of time (four to five years).[42]

3. *Gathering Critical Incidents.* Use of a structured format for generating critical incident statements is best. A structured format should be used whether a questionnaire or interview is being conducted. Job experts are asked to recall actions workers have taken while performing the job that illustrate unusually effective or ineffective performance. Then job experts write statements describing effective and ineffective performance that meet the following four characteristics of a well-written critical incident:

   a. It is specific (a single behavior).

   b. It focuses on observable behaviors that have been, or could be, exhibited on the job.

   c. It briefly describes the context in which the behavior occurred.

   d. It indicates the consequences of the behavior.[43]

A resulting critical incident should be detailed enough to convey the same image of performance to at least two individuals who are knowledgeable about the job. The following is an example of a critical incident for a supervisory job:

> *Nontoxic waste was being picked up by a disposal company. The order ticket was in error and read that the waste was toxic and to be disposed in a manner only suitable for nontoxic waste. The supervisor signed the disposal order without taking time to read it. As a consequence, EPA fined the company $5,000 for improper disposal of waste.*

In this incident, there is only one critical behavior exhibited by the supervisor: signing the disposal ticket without reading it. It is an observable behavior that could be exhibited on the job. It is also phrased in behavioral terms, not in reference to any personal traits of the supervisor (for example, careless, lacks attention to detail, hasty, trusting). There is enough detail for the reader to understand the situation, and the consequences of this behavior are clear.

4. ***Rating and Classifying Critical Incidents into Job Dimensions***. Ratings of the developed incidents are typically made by subject matter experts. The goal of the ratings is to identify those behaviors that are most relevant in differentiating among behaviors leading to job success or failure. Those incidents passing various rating screens are then classified into job dimensions. Job dimensions are determined by judges analyzing the content of the critical incidents and identifying common themes among the incidents. One way to do this is to write each critical incident on a separate card. These cards are sorted by a judge into piles representing common themes. The sorting continues until all incidents are in piles, and all piles are of a reasonable size. (Piles that are too big may be representative of more than one theme, and those with only one or two incidents may not really be a theme.) Once the incidents have been sorted by theme, each theme is given a label that names the dimension. To help establish confidence in clustering incidents into dimensions, other job analysts or experts are asked to re-sort the incidents into the dimensions. If there is not agreement about the dimension to which a critical incident belongs, it is prudent to drop that critical incident.

Advantages and Disadvantages of Critical Incidents

The Critical Incident Technique clearly results in a great deal of interesting, specific, job-related information. This information is behavioral in nature, not trait based. The described behaviors are "critical" incidents, so the information most likely represents important aspects of the job. On the other hand, it is not clear that the incidents reported represent the full scope of the job.[44] Consequently, dimensions based on these critical incidents may not be representative of the entire job. Further, the dimensions may not be stable, given that they are the product of the analysts' judgments. The process is labor intensive, and results are very situation specific. Considerable effort is required for each new endeavor, since it is doubtful that the information is transferrable from one setting to another.

Subject Matter Expert (SME) Workshops

The Subject Matter Expert (SME) workshop, our final job analysis method, is not really a distinct job analysis method per se. Many different job analysis formats and methods, such as task analysis inventories and group interviews, can be used in the context of SME workshops. Because of their use, particularly in content validation studies, we briefly outline how SME workshops are used to produce job analysis data.

Description

SME workshops consist of groups or panels of 10 to 20 job incumbents who work with a group leader to produce a job analysis. Because participants are selected for their knowledge of the job, they are referred to as subject matter experts or SMEs.

Although there is no one particular format for conducting the workshops, the following general steps seem to characterize most workshops: (a) selecting and preparing SMEs to participate, (b) identifying and rating job tasks, and (c) identifying and rating KSAs associated with these job tasks. When a content validation study is being conducted, a fourth step is added. The fourth step requires that the SMEs judge the relevance of a selection measure's content (for example, items on an employment test, or selection interview questions) to the job domain. In carrying out these steps, questionnaires and group interviews are often used to collect relevant job data. The steps are as follows:

1. Selecting and Preparing SMEs. SME workshop panelists should possess several important characteristics—a willingness to participate in the workshop, a minimum period of tenure in the job, a position representative of the employees on the job under study, reading, writing, and speaking skills, and so forth. Once SMEs are selected, the panelists are oriented in the workshops' purpose and procedures and trained in how to develop and rate task and KSA statements.

2. Identifying and Rating Job Tasks. Following training, the workshop leader serves as a group facilitator. The facilitator's role is to solicit from the group descriptions of the major tasks performed on the job. The group describes these major activities, and the facilitator records their comments on a projection screen or large sheets of paper so that the entire group can read what is being written. The goal is to prepare the task statements to accurately capture the group's descriptions. Once prepared, the task statements are assembled into a rating booklet whose format is like that of a task analysis inventory. Then, panelists use rating scales to make judgments about the task statements listed in the booklet.

3. Identifying and Rating KSAs. After rating job tasks, SMEs identify KSAs required for successful performance of these tasks. These ratings may be made by the same panelists participating in the task ratings or by different panelists. Following a group process similar to that used for generating task statements, SMEs specify KSAs required on the job. Then, as with the task statements, the panelists rate these KSAs using rating scales. The purpose of these ratings is to identify the most essential KSAs that must be possessed by those applying for the job.

4. Judging Selection Measure—Job Content Relevance. Whether or not to undertake this last step is determined by the purpose of the job analysis and the validation strategy being used. It is essential that it be undertaken in content validation. As we described in our chapter on validity, SMEs use rating scales to indicate the relevance of selection measure content to the job domain. These ratings help to establish content validity.

Use of Multiple Job Analysis Methods

For some users, a review of methods may show that one job analysis approach will not be sufficient in the context of HR selection. Instead, multiple methods of job analysis may be needed. Edward Levine and associates, who surveyed 93 experienced job analysts' attitudes toward using multiple job analysis methods, observed support for a multiple-method approach. Their survey results showed that of 93 respondents, 80 preferred a combination of methods, 9 preferred a single approach, and 4 were not sure.[45]

In addition, Gary Brumback and his colleagues noted that job analysis is still a relatively imprecise endeavor, and that the results of any one method should be corroborated by the results of another. They recommend that whatever the job, whatever the measure, whatever the validation strategy to be used, a multi-method approach is preferable to reliance on a single method. From their view, the costs involved in using multiple methods are more than offset by the advantages of their use. They concluded, "In this period of legislated employment, this risk of having what may be an otherwise valid qualification requirement overturned is certainly not worth the modest cost of an independent verification of the job analysis results."[46] In general, we agree with these comments. Yet it is important to remember that HR job analysts may be faced with the problem of developing a means to reconcile any differences they find in the results produced by two or more job analysis methods. If these differences cannot be reconciled, then job analysis results may be open to both technical and legal challenges.

INCORPORATING JOB ANALYSIS RESULTS IN SELECTION MEASURES

To this point, we have explored in some detail the actual application of job analysis in terms of collecting job information through various job analysis methods. But by this time you may be wondering, How do we actually use our collected data for developing or choosing selection measures? Recall for a moment Figure 7.1. In that figure, we showed that job analysis results are used to determine the relevant knowledge, skills, abilities (KSAs), or other employee specifications needed for effective performance on the job. Once identified, these specifications, in turn, serve as the basis for *constructing* (such as in developing questions for an employment interview) or *choosing* (such as in selecting a commercially available ability test) the needed selection measures. In this section, we study the last two elements of Figure 7.1, that is, (a) the identification of KSAs and other characteristics from job analysis data (determination of employee specifications) and (b) the incorporation of employee specifications in our selection procedures (determination of selection measure content). These two elements are key steps in implementing job analysis results for HR selection purposes.

IDENTIFICATION OF EMPLOYEE SPECIFICATIONS

Filip Lievens and Juan Sanchez note that in estimating employee specifications such as KSAs, *direct* or *indirect* methods are used.[47] Indirect methods involve the use of specific steps in order to break down the large inferential leaps involved in deriving critical KSAs from job tasks. We described those inferential leaps in our earlier discussion of Figure 7.1. Direct methods of KSA identification require larger inferential leaps than indirect methods because SMEs simply rate the importance of KSAs for a specific job. SMEs do not engage in the more manageable, step-by-step processes of indirect methods.

In Figure 7.1, we noted that judgments or inferences play an important role in identifying employee specifications. However, the resulting specifications will be useful only to the extent that the inferences are accurate and complete. If the inferences are wrong, the selection measures will not be useful for predicting job performance. Given current federal laws and executive orders, inappropriate selection measures may produce a situation that is ripe for charges of adverse impact against certain applicant groups, or one in which new employees are unqualified for the job for which they were employed. Both situations are unfair to employers and employees alike. The probability of situations such as these arising can be minimized by taking appropriate steps to ensure, as much as possible, that the inferences are accurate. In this section, we address the inference problem by describing one approach to inferring KSAs to incorporate in selection procedures.

The method we describe below is an indirect procedure for KSA determination. It is derived from task analysis and makes use of SMEs' judgments concerning the important tasks and KSAs required for a job. Under this method, a series of steps are taken to collect SMEs' opinions through the use of surveys. The surveys, some composed of work behaviors or job tasks and others consisting of KSAs, are given to subject matter experts who judge aspects of a job using various rating scales. Structured interviews with groups of job incumbents in SME workshops are often used in conjunction with these surveys to obtain task and KSA data. Generally speaking, this method of KSA determination is specific to one job. Because it is job specific, the method is particularly appropriate in a content validation study involving the development of selection procedures such as a written test or a structured employment interview. Implementation of the method's sequential steps facilitates the identification of appropriate selection procedure content that representatively samples the job content domain. As we saw in our validity chapter, representative job content domain sampling by a selection procedure is essential in content validation work.

Before describing how employee specifications are identified, we must make several general comments. First, just as there are numerous job analysis methods other than those we have reviewed, there are also job analysis/employee specifications approaches other than the one we describe. For example, Frank Landy[48] has illustrated how the tasks of a patrol police officer's job can be analyzed using Edwin Fleishman's taxonomy of human abilities.[49] The identified abilities required to perform the tasks on a job serve as the basis for choosing the type of selection predictor to use (for example, a paper-and-pencil test or an interview) as well as the specific content of the measure (for example, test items requiring deductive reasoning). Use of the Position Analysis Questionnaire (PAQ) offers another means for deriving job attributes and identifying paper-and-pencil tests to measure these identified attributes for use in personnel selection in a wide variety of jobs.

Second, like all methods for developing selection procedures, the development of employee specifications we describe involves the use of judgment on the part of users. Although judgment is involved, our approach involves a series of steps designed to lead *systematically* from analyzing the job to identifying employee specifications to determining selection measure content. It is this methodical, step-by-step sequence that enhances the validity of SMEs' final KSA judgments.[50]

Third, our method is suitable for small as well as large organizations. It lends itself to the development of selection measure content (such as test items) and as such plays an important role in establishing the content and, possibly, face validity of these measures. In addition, the sequence of steps taken in the method are designed to help comply with certain requirements as described in the *Uniform Guidelines*.

Determination of Employee Specifications

The various approaches to the development of KSAs and other employee specifications using the results of a task analysis typically follow similar procedures. Generally speaking, task or work behavior data are collected and these data, in conjunction with SME panels' judgments, are used to identify the KSAs that will compose the content of selection measures for the job.

The following sequential steps are taken in developing KSAs and selection procedure contents:

1. Identifying job tasks/work behaviors

2. Rating job tasks/work behaviors

3. Specifying KSAs necessary for successful job performance

4. Rating the importance of identified KSAs

5. Identifying other employee specifications necessary for successful job performance

6. Linking KSAs and other employee specifications to job tasks/work behaviors

7. Developing the content areas of selection procedures

Ultimately, the goals of these seven steps are to (a) identify job-related information that should compose the content of selection procedures and (b) identify the selection procedures that should be used to assess the identified information. Before we see how we implement these steps, we need to clarify one point. As you read about the steps taken, you will see the terms "tasks" and "work behaviors" used. Understand that a *work behavior* is a broad description of the major activities of a job while a *task* is a more specific action associated with these work behaviors. Some strategies used in implementing the task analysis approach deal exclusively with job tasks while others focus initially on work behaviors and then focus on tasks composing those behaviors. Nevertheless, many of the general procedures we discuss in this section of the chapter are the same, whether they are applied to tasks or work behaviors. Although we use the word *tasks* in our discussion, understand that our discussion applies to *work behaviors* as well. We now describe how these steps are applied to accomplish our goals.

1. Identifying and Rating Job Tasks/Work Behaviors. The first step is the specification job tasks. This initial step is crucial because it serves as the foundation from which KSAs are developed and selection measures are produced. A number of the different approaches we have mentioned can be used to identify task content. For example, observing and interviewing job incumbents and supervisors, and conducting brainstorming sessions with SMEs in SME workshops, are two methods that can be used for deriving task content. Whatever the methods used, the goal of this step is to produce a survey questionnaire that SMEs can use to rate their job tasks.

Because of the importance of task data, proper development of task statements is critical. Rules such as those we discussed earlier for developing task statements are important for generating the type of task information we need. In sum, task statements (a) begin with an action verb and (b) describe *what* the worker does, for *whom* or *what* the worker does it, *why* the worker does it, and *how* the worker does it. The following example portrays an incorrect and a corrected task statement:

Incorrect: *"Assists with inspection of construction projects."*

Comment: *First, the What is ambiguous and gives no real information as to the action. Second, neither the Why nor the How questions have been answered.*

What

Corrected: *"Inspects/construction operations (erosion control, Portland cement concrete paving, asphaltic concrete paving, painting, fencing, sign placement)*

Why

in order to ensure compliance with construction specifications

How?

by comparing visual observations with construction specifications and plans, and by following verbal instructions; while under daily review by the supervisor."[51]

Another example of task development is a procedure used by Katherine Jackson and her colleagues.[52] Job analysts work with SMEs to write work behavior statements (that is, broad descriptions of the major aspects of a job) and task statements (that is, narrow descriptions of the actions associated with these work behaviors) for a specific job. These actions lead to a precise description of the work activities involved on the job. For example, Figure 7.8 shows one work behavior and the associated task statements that were identified for the job of police sergeant. As you can see, the level of detail is quite precise. For the sergeant's job, a total of 24 work behaviors and an accompanying 497 task statements were developed. Although this information seems massive, it is this level of precision in the identified work behaviors and task statements that facilitates the development of selection procedure content that accurately maps job content. Therefore, content validity of resulting selection procedures is enhanced.

FIGURE 7.8	Example of a Work Behavior and of Associated Task Statements for the Job of Police Sergeant

Work Behavior 3

Responds to life-threatening emergencies or critical incidents such as a plane crash, explosion, train wreck, tornado, flood, hazardous chemical spill, shooting, accident with injuries, hostage situation, bomb threat, and fire—using mobile data terminal (MDT), Fire and Rescue, robots, police vehicle, K-9, barricades, helicopter, radio, traffic vest, outside agencies, fire trucks, personal protective equipment, body armor, first aid kit, fire extinguisher, and firearms—following the Airport Aircraft Emergency Plan, County Police Department Critical Incident Response Plan, County Employee Manual, special orders, general orders, and HAZMAT guide in order to ensure the safety of property, self, and others during dangerous or hazardous situations. Stabilizes injured individuals until medical assistance arrives, and prevents the escape of an offender.

Associated Task Statements

1. Provides assistance to other agencies (e.g., State Police, local police department)
2. Extinguishes small fires (such as grass or vehicle fires) to prevent or minimize damage and prevent injury
3. Rescues people from dangerous situations such as burning buildings, damaged vehicles, and drowning
4. Administers first-aid to the injured at emergency scenes until medical help arrives
5. Evaluates an emergency or disaster scene to determine what assistance is required, whether evacuation is necessary, whether the ordinance disposal unit is necessary, whether the dispatching of emergency personnel is necessary, or if additional medical assistance is needed
6. Evacuates occupants of buildings and surrounding areas during emergencies or disasters
7. Maintains security in an emergency area and controls gathering crowds
8. Searches buildings and/or areas for bombs or other indications of criminal activity
9. Provides on-scene counseling to assist persons in dangerous situations or during emergencies, and reassures injured individuals that medical assistance is on the way
10. Determines if backup is necessary, and if so, requests backup assistance
11. Establishes a perimeter and if necessary diverts traffic and bystanders
12. Notifies the chain-of-command of the status of situations
13. Notifies Public Information Officer of the status of situations
14. Establishes a command post
15. Requests additional assistance from other personnel or agencies (HAZMAT, Fire Department, DOT, EPA, SWAT team)
16. Notifies hospitals

Source: Based on the Auburn University-Montgomery Center for Business and Economic Development, *Job Analysis and Content Validation Report: County Bureau of Police Services for the Rank of Sergeant* (Montgomery, AL: Auburn University-Montgomery Center for Business and Economic Development, 2004). Used by permission of Dr. Katherine Jackson.

2. Rating Job Tasks/Work Behaviors.   Once we have task data for a specific job, the next step is to isolate the essential job tasks that compose the job content domain. Typically, we use job incumbents or SMEs' ratings of the tasks to make this determination. In our earlier discussion of task analysis inventories, we described how tasks are often rated on a variety of rating scales such as frequency of task performance or task importance. We can employ these ratings to identify a job's most important activities. For instance, one possible tack is to use statistical indices (for example, averages, percentages, or even more complex calculations) created from the rating scales and decision rules applied to these indices to define important tasks. We might require that important tasks receive a minimum average rating on one or more of our rating scales. Tasks whose ratings exceed our minimum rating requirements are then selected for further study. For example, we might specify that a task composing the content domain of a job is one where (a) the task is performed by 67 percent or more of the SMEs and (b) the task receives an average rating of at least 2.0 (= Important) on a 5-point rating scale, where 0 = Not Important and 4 = Critical. Any one or more of several criteria can be used. The important point is that a common standard is employed so that it is possible to objectively justify the selection of important job tasks.

Based on our earlier example of the police sergeant position (see Figure 7.8), Figure 7.9 illustrates the rating scales used to judge one work behavior and some associated task statements. Whatever the analyses used, the "most important" tasks are the basis on which inferences regarding selection instrument content rest (see Inference Point **(2),** Figure 7.1). The major idea behind the application of task analysis inventories is to define important job content. As illustrated in Figure 7.1, that determination serves as a guideline for defining requisite employee specifications and developing selection procedures for choosing among job applicants.

3. Specifying KSAs Necessary for Successful Job Performance.   Once critical job tasks have been identified, we are ready to specify the KSAs required for successful performance of these tasks. We cannot overemphasize the importance of producing accurate, complete KSA statements. As we will see, correct phrasing of the statements is *essential* to developing useful selection instruments. Several stages are necessary for appropriately specifying these KSAs.

Selection of a KSA Rating Panel.   The first stage is to select a panel of job experts (SMEs) who can identify important KSAs. Such a panel may be composed of those who participated in a job's prior task analysis (Steps 1 and 2), or it may be formed from a new group of individuals. Listed here are several considerations that should be used in forming the KSA rating panel.[53]

1. *A panel of job experts (at least 10 to 20) is preferable over only one or two individuals.* Emphasis, however, should not be given exclusively to *numbers* of experts; we are more interested in the *quality* of their job knowledge and participation. If their assessments and inferences regarding KSAs are incorrect, resulting selection instruments will necessarily suffer.

2. *Characteristics we should seek in job agents are also relevant in choosing the KSA rating panel.* These characteristics include the following: (a) participation should be voluntary, (b) incumbents should have performed adequately on the job in question, and (c) participants should have served on the job a minimum period of time. In addition, women and minority group members should be represented on the panel.

FIGURE 7.9 Example of Rating Scales Used to Rate a Work Behavior (Detailed in Figure 7.8) and Associated Job Tasks for the Job of Police Sergeant

Work Behavior:

Responds to life-threatening emergencies or critical incidents

DO YOU PERFORM THIS WORK BEHAVIOR?

Yes (Y)   No (N)

If **No**, go to the next work behavior, if **Yes**, rate the following associated tasks:

Associated Task:	Perform		Frequency						Importance					Necessary at Entry	
	Yes	No	Rarely	Seldom	Occasionally	Frequently	Continuously	Not	Somewhat	Important	Essential	Critical		Yes	No
1. Provides assistance to other agencies (e.g., State Police, local police department)	Y	N	1	2	3	4	5	0	1	2	3	4		Y	N
2. Extinguishes small fires (such as grass or vehicles to prevent or minimize damage and prevent injury)	Y	N	1	2	3	4	5	0	1	2	3	4		Y	N
• • • •															
15. Requests additional assistance from other personnel or agencies (HAZMAT, Fire Department, DOT, EPA, SWAT team)	Y	N	1	2	3	4	5	0	1	2	3	4		Y	N
16. Notifies hospitals	Y	N	1	2	3	4	5	0	1	2	3	4		Y	N

NOTE: **Perform** = Do you perform this job task? **Frequency** = How often do you perform this job task? **Importance** = How important is it for you to perform this task in your current position? **Necessary at Entry** = Should a new employee, upon starting the job of sergeant, be able to perform this task successfully?

Source: Based on the Auburn University-Montgomery Center for Business and Economic Development, *Job Analysis and Content Validation Report: County Bureau of Police Services for the Rank of Sergeant* (Montgomery, AL: Auburn University-Montgomery Center for Business and Economic Development, 2004). Used by permission of Dr. Katherine Jackson.

Preparation of KSA Panelists. Whatever the data collection methodology, some form of orientation and training of KSA panelists is needed.[54] Panel members will likely require explanations as to what is meant by KSAs, why KSAs are important, and what their roles are to be in identifying and rating KSAs.

Collection of KSA data can take a variety of forms. Survey questionnaires completed independently by panelists can be used. Alternatively, group meetings of panel members can be convened, discussions held, and listings made of KSAs by panelists working independently within groups.

In specifying KSAs, panelists basically review the tasks identified from the job analysis and ask, "What knowledge, skills, or abilities are needed to perform each of these job tasks successfully?" Although the KSAs may not be written at the same level of specificity as task statements, several guides should be followed in their preparation. Again, the appropriate phrasing of the KSA statements facilitates making inferences concerning employee specifications for a job. Criteria that should be considered include the following:

1. *Panelists should have a clear understanding of what is meant* by *knowledge, skills,* and *abilities.* Definitions of these terms can vary, but for our use the following are helpful:
   Knowledge: A body of information, usually of a factual or procedural nature, about a particular domain (for example, information systems) that makes for successful performance of a task.[55]
   Skill: An individual's level of proficiency or competency in performing a specific task (for example, typing speed).[56] Level of competency is often expressed in numerical terms.
   Ability: A more general, enduring trait or capability an individual possesses when he or she first begins to perform a task (for example, inductive reasoning).[57]

Some analysts have difficulty distinguishing between skills and abilities.[58] For purposes of preparing KSA statements, it is not absolutely essential that a statement be correctly classified as a skill or an ability. What is important for us is the content of the statement itself; the statement, not its classification, serves as the basis for inferring selection instrument content.

2. *Statements should be written to show the kind of knowledge, skill, or ability and the degree or level of each that is needed for successful task performance.* For example, in describing "typing skill," it should be specified whether the typing skill requires typing tables of data and complex numbers within a specified time period, typing letters at a self-paced rate, or typing from handwritten manuscripts at the rate of 40 words per minute.[59]

3. *Statements should be written to specify the highest level that is required for the job.* For example, if statistical skills involving the calculation of correlation coefficients are needed to perform a task, there is no need to list an ability to count or a knowledge of basic mathematics as other KSAs. These would be covered in the statistical skill statement.[60]

4. *Specific statements are preferable to broad, general ones that lack clarity as to what actual KSAs are required.* In preparing a statement it may be necessary that job experts probe the exact nature, degree, breadth, and precision of a stated KSA. If, for instance, a statement such as "Knowledge of Mathematics" is offered, it may be necessary to ask, "What kind?" "To what extent?" and "To solve what types of problems?" Use of probing questions should permit the development of more complete and useful statements of what specifications are needed to perform a job.

5. *Although it may be possible to prepare a long list of KSAs for many jobs, emphasis should be given to identifying those that determine "successful" performance on the job.* That is, KSAs rated as most important to job success by KSA-rating panelists should be emphasized.

6. *In preparing knowledge statements, adjective modifiers relative to the degree or extent of knowledge required should not be used (for example, "thorough," "some").* Here are examples of appropriate knowledge statements: "Knowledge of the application of word processing procedures using Microsoft® Word including setting margins, centering text, creating style sheets, and naming and storing files." "Knowledge of the use and interpretation of simple and multiple correlation statistical procedures, including knowing when to use a procedure, knowing the importance of statistical assumptions, and understanding the interpretation of results in the context of human resource selection."

7. *In preparing ability statements, adjective modifiers of level or extent of the ability required should not be used.* Vague adverbs implying some level of performance (for example, "*rapidly*" or "*effectively*") should not be used to modify the action of the statement.[61] Ability statements should avoid confusing the action of the ability with the result of that action. For instance, look at this statement: "Ability to maintain accurate clerical accounting records." The results of the action "Maintain accurate accounting records" is treated as the action itself. The statement would be better written like this: "Ability to log accounting transactions in order to maintain accurate and up-to-date accounting records."

After all KSAs have been suggested, it is quite possible some statements will require editing. When editing is needed, the objective should be to specify important content in as much detail as possible and give examples where appropriate. Several illustrations of KSAs developed in previous job analyses are shown in Figure 7.10.

Potential Problems in KSA Determination. The development and specification of KSA statements is not always as straightforward a task as we have presented it here. Several different problems may occur. For example, if the KSA panelists serving as SMEs are not properly trained, they may produce very broad, undefined KSA statements that are relatively useless in developing a measure. KSA statements such as "Ability to Work under Stress" are not helpful in understanding exactly what is required to be successful on the job. Such KSAs are very likely to be developed when SMEs simply want to take a job task and add words to it such as "Knowledge of," "Ability to," or "Skill at" in defining KSAs. For instance, the task of handling customer complaints becomes "Ability to Handle Customer Complaints." Not only is the KSA undefined and of little use in developing a predictor, but this process assumes a unique KSA for each job task. Realistically, a particular KSA may underlie several job tasks.[62]

4. Rating the Importance of Identified KSAs. For selection instruments to be useful, they should reflect the importance of different KSAs required for a specific job. That is, those KSAs that are most important for a job should account for more selection instrument content than less important ones. Determination of KSA importance is usually based on SMEs' ratings of KSAs.

Methods of Judging KSA Importance. The methods used in rating KSA importance are similar to those used in assessing the importance of job tasks. That is, some form of survey questionnaire consisting of a listing of KSA statements and relevant rating scales

FIGURE 7.10	Examples of Knowledge, Skills, and Abilities (KSAs) Statements Developed in Previous Job Analyses

Knowledge:

"Knowledge of building materials including the uses, storage, and preparation of materials such as aluminum siding, Masonite®, concrete block, and gypsum board" (building materials company supervisor)

"Knowledge of the development, scoring, and application of employee performance appraisal techniques such as behaviorally anchored rating scales, 360-feedback, and graphic rating scales" (human resources consultant)

"Knowledge of basic and advanced first-aid procedures to include CPR techniques" (state police corporal)

"Knowledge of aircraft nomenclature (type, number of engines, manufacturer, jet/non-jet engine) and performance characteristics such as speed, climb/descent rates, turning radius, and weather and radio capabilities" (air traffic controller)

Skills:

"Skill in using a bank proof machine to process 50 checks per minute without error" (bank proof machine operator)

"Skill in typing business correspondence at 50 words per minute without error" (secretary)

"Skill in the use of handguns as needed to pass annual departmental qualifying standards" (state police corporal)

Abilities:

"Ability to give oral testimony in court as an expert witness in an employment discrimination suit regarding test validation issues" (human resources consultant)

"Ability to use basic arithmetic to calculate flow of current through an electrical circuit" (lighting company technician)

"Ability to obtain facts and information by using interviewing skills and techniques" (state police corporal)

is used by respondents (KSA panel members) in judging KSA importance. Actual questionnaire formats, including rating scales, can vary from one application to the next. However, most KSA rating scales employed resemble those shown in Figure 7.11.

5. Identifying Other Employee Specifications Necessary for Successful Job Performance. Other than KSAs, jobs may require that applicants possess certain personal specifications that are necessary for adequate performance. Such specifications typically include the following types: (a) physical requirements, (b) licensure/certification requirements, and (c) other/miscellaneous requirements.[63]

Physical Requirements.   Physical requirements are those qualifications workers must possess in order to physically perform their jobs. These requirements can involve a number of physical abilities requiring specific levels of hearing, seeing, speaking, or lifting, to name a few. For example, the ability to lift, pull, or carry a specific amount of weight must be set for firefighters. Minimum levels of corrected visual acuity could be used in choosing nuclear plant operators, who must visually monitor dials and meters at a distance. Operative or physically demanding jobs will likely require more physical abilities for adequate performance than will managerial positions. Thus when setting employee specifications for operative positions, physical ability qualifications should routinely be considered. Be sure that any specified physical abilities are *essential* to the job. Careful review will help to ensure compliance with the Americans with Disabilities Act (ADA).

The relevance of physical qualifications can be assessed in either of two ways: (a) by listing and rating physical abilities required for a job or (b) by rating a pre-established set of physical abilities. Where a listing and rating of physical abilities is concerned, the

FIGURE 7.11	Examples of Typical Ratings Scales Used in Rating Knowledge, Skills, and Abilities (KSAs)

A. How important is this KSA in performing your job effectively?

0 = **Not important**—You can *definitely* perform your job effectively even if you do not possess this KSA. There is *no* problem if you do not possess this KSA.

1 = **Somewhat important**—You can *probably* perform your job effectively even if you do not possess this KSA. There is a *minor* problem if you do not possess this KSA.

2 = **Important**—It is *unlikely* that you can perform your job effectively unless you possess this KSA. There is a *problem* if you do not possess this KSA.

3 = **Essential**—You *cannot* perform your job effectively unless you possess this KSA. There is a *major problem* if you do not possess this KSA.

4 = **Critical**—You *cannot* perform your job effectively unless you possess this KSA. There is a *serious problem* if you do not possess this KSA.

B. Should a newly hired employee possess this KSA on their first day of work in this job?

Y = **Yes**; individuals on this job *should* possess this KSA on their first day of work.

N = **No**; individuals on this job do *not* need this KSA on their first day of work.

C. To what extent do individuals in this job who have *more* of this KSA do a better job than individuals in this job who have *less* of this KSA?

0 = **Not at all**—Having more of this KSA does *not* lead to better overall job performance.

1 = **Slightly**—Having more of this KSA leads to *slightly* better overall job performance.

2 = **Moderately**—Having more of this KSA leads to *moderately* better overall job performance.

3 = **Considerably**—Having more of this KSA leads to *considerably* better overall job performance.

D. At what level of recall must you remember this knowledge in order to perform your job effectively?

0 = **No recall**—I do *not* need to remember this knowledge to perform my job effectively.

1 = **General familiarity**—I must be aware of the general principles. For specific details, I can look in source documents or seek guidance from others.

2 = **Working knowledge**—I must be able to remember both general principles and specific details to perform routine tasks. In unusual situations, I can look in source documents or seek guidance from others for specific details.

3 = **Full recall**—I must be able to remember both general principles and specific details to perform all tasks. I cannot look in source documents or seek guidance from others.

same methods described for generating and rating KSAs can be used. Emphasis is placed on developing specific, observable, and measurable statements descriptive of physical job requirements. Examples of such statements include the following:

"Be able to read a voltmeter dial from a distance of five feet."

"Be able to carry a 180-pound deadweight down a 50-foot ladder."

"Be able to carry on a telephone conversation without electronic amplification."

Once listed, these characteristics can be rated using appropriate scales like those utilized in judging KSAs. For example, ratings of physical abilities might be based on variables such as importance or criticality to performance. Analyses can then be made of the ratings to determine those physical abilities most important for a job. Selection procedures comprising important physical abilities can next be developed or chosen.

Rather than developing a rating scale of physical requirements, existing measures, such as Edwin Fleishman's *Physical Abilities* scales, can be employed.[64] The *Physical Abilities* scales are designed to examine the extent to which job performance requires various physical abilities. The *Physical Abilities* scales consists of an analyst making ratings of a job on nine rating scales, one for each of nine physical abilities (for example, static strength, dynamic flexibility, stamina). Each rating scale has a set of definitions that includes examples of tasks representing differing amounts of an ability. The scales are first applied by an analyst observing a job or specific job task. Each scale is then studied, and the job or task is rated by assigning the most descriptive scale point value (1 to 7).

The *Physical Abilities* scales have been used in several different selection situations. For example, they have been used for identifying the physical requirements of jobs such as firefighter, sanitation worker, and police officer.[65] The scales have served as a valuable foundation for determining which physical abilities are critical to a job. From such a foundation, a rationale is created for developing selection instruments for measuring these critical abilities.

Licensure/Certification Requirements.   The next set of specifications that may be legally necessary for job performance are special licensure or certification requirements. If these requirements are critical in performing a job, then they are important specifications that should be used in selection. Examples of licensure/certification requirements are a driver's license, a teaching certificate, and a first-class Federal Communications Commission (FCC) radiotelephone license. Because there may be a variety of such requirements, a particular questionnaire or form for determining these specifications is not provided. Instead, provision can be made on a survey questionnaire for a job analyst to list any important licensure or certification requirements. Like tasks and KSAs, these specifications can be rated on a scale to determine their importance in performing the job under study or simply listed as a mandatory requirement.

Other Miscellaneous Requirements.   It is possible for requirements other than KSAs, licenses, or certificates to be critical to a job. More than likely, these requirements will be unique to a job; if they are critical to job success, they should be evaluated. Examples of these "other" requirements might be ownership of specific tools, equipment, or vehicle. Some jobs may require a willingness on the part of an applicant/incumbent to work under unusual conditions of employment, such as frequent relocation, frequent overtime, specific shifts, or frequent travel. These requirements can be listed and rated for their significance to job performance.

6. Linking KSAs and Other Employee Specifications to Job Tasks/Work Behaviors.
It is critical to a job analysis that a clear relationship between KSAs and other employee specifications be established with the most important tasks performed on a job.[66] Provision must be made for showing that *each* identified KSA is tied to *at least* one important task for which it is required. Tying KSAs and other specifications to job tasks is important for several reasons. First, KSA → job task/work behavior link information may be needed in the legal defense of a selection procedure. The *Uniform Guidelines* state that a relation be shown between each identified KSA and an important work behavior. By tying these specifications to important job tasks, evidence can be provided on how these specifications are required on a job. Second, specifications can improve the efficiency and effectiveness of selection instruments. If unnecessary specifications are included in selection instruments, they are wasteful of resources, and they may fail to identify the most

qualified job applicants. By linking KSAs with important tasks, it is possible to check the appropriateness of selection specifications and associated selection instruments.

Methods of Establishing KSA → Job Task/Work Behavior Links. Documentation of KSA → job task/work behavior links can be accomplished in several ways. All involve using SMEs to review job tasks or work behaviors and then rate the extent to which a KSA is required for successful performance of that activity. For example, one format used involves presenting a listing of each important KSA for each important task or work behavior. (Important KSAs and tasks/work behaviors are determined from previous steps in the task analysis process that we have described.) Then, raters judge how important each KSA is in performing a specific task. Another format presents a Job Task X KSA rating matrix and then has SMEs rate the degree to which a KSA is necessary for performing each task successfully. Again, these linkage ratings are made only for those KSAs and tasks/work behaviors that have been judged to be important.

Whatever the format, SMEs use rating scales such as the following to make their judgments:

0 = **Not important**—You can *definitely* perform this task (or work behavior) effectively even if you do not have this KSA.

1 = **Somewhat important**—You can *probably* perform this work task (or work behavior) effectively even if you do not have this KSA.

2 = **Important**—It is *unlikely* that you can perform this task (or work behavior) effectively unless you have this KSA.

3 = **Essential**—You *cannot* perform this task (or work behavior) effectively unless you have this KSA.

KSAs would be successfully linked to an important job task or work behavior when the average SME rating equals or exceeds a specific rating scale value.

Licensure/certification and other characteristics that may be treated as employee specifications should also be tied to job tasks. When these specifications are used, they can be judged along with KSAs. However, in certain situations, it may not be meaningful to tie a specification to a job task. In those cases, reasons justifying their criticality should be listed. For example, if it is specified that a suitable applicant for a radio technician job should hold a first-class FCC radiotelephone license, it should be noted that this specification is required by federal law. The idea behind this documentation is to provide evidence that the specification is indeed required to perform a job.

The linking of KSAs, licensure/certification, and other specifications to job tasks is a critical step in job analysis. This linking step should not be taken lightly. The data obtained will ultimately help to justify the job analysis efforts and content of selection measures. From the perspective of content validity, these links help to identify the tasks to be simulated by a selection measure. They provide job-specific and task-specific cues as to the design and content of selection measures that will have greatest fidelity with the job.

7. Developing the Content Areas of Selection Procedures. So far, in our exploration of the process of developing appropriate employee specifications, we have studied the tasks performed on a job, the KSAs and other specifications needed for job performance, and the relationships between these specifications and job tasks. Our final step is to both combine and screen the task and KSA information in order to identify the employee specifications to be covered in our selection procedures. Once established, selection procedures can be constructed or, where possible, chosen to match these specifications. More is said about actually incorporating these specifications in selection measures later in the chapter. For now, however, we give attention to finalizing our identification of selection procedure content as reflected in chosen KSAs.

We are pretty sure you are sitting there wondering, "If someone collects all this information, how do they possibly wade through it to determine what a selection procedure ought to measure?" This is where our SME rating information comes into play. We use SME ratings of tasks, KSAs, and the links between them to screen out those tasks and KSAs not centrally important to our selection procedures. To identify these, we require relevant tasks and KSAs to pass multiple screens such as the following:

1. Tasks or work behaviors must be performed by at least 67 percent of SMEs.

2. At least 67 percent of SMEs must judge that a new employee must be able to perform the task or work behavior at the start of the job.

3. Tasks or work behaviors must have an average importance rating of at least 2.0 (= Important).

4. KSAs must be given a mean importance rating of at least 2.0 (= Important) by SMEs.

5. KSAs must be rated as necessary at job entry by at least 67 percent of SMEs.

6. KSAs must be linked by SMEs to an important job task or work behavior that meets rating criteria (1) through (3) above with a mean linkage rating of at least 1.5.[67]

These are just a few of the screens that might be used. Whatever the criteria employed, our use of standardized, objective screening procedures in the task analysis process will enhance our chances of producing selection procedures that reflect the content of the job.

An Example

To summarize and, perhaps, clarify the task analysis approach, let's look at an example of the entire process. Suppose we are attempting to develop selection procedures for the job of HR selection analyst. Individuals in this job work for a state government, and they are generally responsible for helping to produce and implement selection procedures to be used by state agencies.

Assume that a job analysis of the HR selection analyst position has been performed, and 15 major job tasks have been identified. Figure 7.12 summarizes the results of the ratings given by a large group of SMEs to a number of these tasks. (Note that in order to conserve space, we have shortened the task statements.) For a task to be judged as important to the job, the SME ratings must meet the following criteria: (a) at least 67 percent of the SMEs must indicate that they perform the task and that successful performance of the task is necessary at job entry, and (b) SMEs must give a task a mean importance rating of 2.0 or higher. An examination of the summarized ratings indicates that five tasks (Tasks 1, 2, 3, 4, and 15) meet the above criteria and are deemed as essential job tasks. The remaining tasks do not meet the criteria and are eliminated from our study.

In the next step, important job-related KSAs are identified. Figure 7.13 shows the ratings given to 6 of the 12 KSAs that the SMEs had previously identified for the job. (Note that the KSA statements have been shortened to conserve space.) Like the job tasks, KSAs must meet several criteria in order to be judged as representing the job content domain. These are (a) SMEs must give a KSA a mean importance rating of 2.0 or

FIGURE 7.12   SMEs' Average Ratings of Abbreviated Job Tasks for the Job of HR Selection Analyst

Abbreviated Job Tasks ↓	Task Performed? (Yes)	Task Frequency?[a] ↓	Task Importance?[b] ↓	Necessary at Job Entry? (Yes)
1. **Computes adverse impact statistics for selection procedures**	70%	3.9	2.0	67%
2. **Constructs written tests for use in selection**	67%	4.1	3.0	88%
3. **Conducts job analyses on entry-level jobs**	75%	4.0	2.8	84%
4. **Develops affirmative action plans and programs and monitors impact**	69%	3.5	2.2	70%
5. Gives oral testimony in court regarding state selection procedures	10%	1.2	2.0	20%
6. Trains department managers in use of acceptable selection practices	27%	2.2	1.9	25%
•				
•				
15. **Maintains job applicant applications and selection test records**	71%	3.7	2.0	67%

NOTE: The task statements have been abbreviated to conserve space. Task statements shown in **bold** print are those passing the SME task rating screens.

[a]Task **Frequency** ratings were made using the following scale: 1 = Rarely, 2 = Seldom, 3 = Occasionally, 4 = Frequently, 5 = Continuously.

[b]Task **Importance** ratings were made using the following scale: 0 = Not Important, 1 = Somewhat Important, 2 = Important, 3 = Essential, 4 = Critical.

FIGURE 7.13   SMEs' Average Ratings of Abbreviated KSAs for the Job of HR Selection Analyst

Abbreviated KSAs	KSA Importance?[a]	Necessary at Job Entry? (Yes)	Relatedness to Job Performance[b]
1. Knowledge of record-keeping procedures	2.0	50%	1.0
2. **Knowledge of applied statistics**	3.0	90%	3.0
3. **Knowledge of test validation requirements**	3.0	100%	3.0
4. **Knowledge of development of task inventories**	2.4	77%	2.0
5. **Ability to read and understand technical written material**	2.1	67%	2.1
•			
•			
12. **Skill in using computerized data analysis packages (SPSS)**	2.0	67%	1.8

NOTE: The KSA statements have been abbreviated to conserve space. KSA statements shown in **bold** print are those passing the SME KSA rating screens.

[a]KSA **Importance** ratings were made using the following scale: 0 = Not Important, 1 = Somewhat Important, 2 = Important, 3 = Essential, 4 = Critical.

[b]KSA **Relatedness to Job Performance** ratings were made using the following scale: 0 = Not At All, 1 = Slightly, 2 = Moderately, 3 = Considerably.

FIGURE 7.14 Mean Ratings of KSA Importance Linked to Task Performance for the Job of HR Selection Analyst

Abbreviated Job Tasks	KNOWLEDGE, SKILLS, ABILITIES (KSAs)					
	Knowledge of Applied Statistics	Knowledge of Test Validation Requirements	Knowledge of Development of Task Inventories	Ability to Read and Understand Technical Material	•	Skill in Using Computerized Data Analysis Packages (SPSS)
1. Computes adverse impact statistics for selection procedures	3.7	2.0	0.9	0.0	•	3.8
2. Constructs written tests for use in HR selection	3.5	3.0	2.7	2.0	•	1.7
3. Conducts job analyses on entry-level jobs	2.9	3.7	3.9	0.0	•	2.1
4. Develops affirmative action plans and programs and monitors impact	0.7	1.2	0.8	1.0	•	1.3
•	•	•			•	•
•	•	•			•	•
•	•	•			•	•
15. Maintains job applicant applications and selection test records	0.5	0.3	0.0	0.0	•	0.0

NOTE: The task and KSA statements have been abbreviated to conserve space. KSA linkage to task ratings were made using the following rating scale:
How important is this KSA in performing this task?
0 = Not Important
1 = Somewhat Important
2 = Important
3 = Essential

FIGURE 7.15	Summary of KSA Tabulations for Determining Content Areas of Selection Procedures for the Job of HR Selection Analyst

	KSA IMPORTANCE CRITERIA		
KSAs and Other Employee Specifications	Mean Importance of KSA to Job Success[a]	Percentage Indicating a New Employee Should Possess This KSA[b]	Task Statements (Numbers) and Mean Ratings of Task Importance for Which a KSA is Necessary[c]
1. Knowledge of record-keeping procedures	2.0	50%	**2**(3.1), **3**(3.3), **4**(2.4), **15**(3.8)
2. Knowledge of applied statistics	2.0	90	**1**(3.7), **2**(3.5), **3**(2.9)
3. Knowledge of test validation requirements	3.0	100	**1**(2.0), **2**(3.0), **3**(3.7)
4. Knowledge of development of task inventories	2.4	77	**2**(2.7), **3**(3.9)
5. Ability to read and understand technical written material	2.1	67	**2**(2.0)
•	•	•	•
•	•	•	•
•	•	•	•
12. Skill in using computerized data analysis packages (e.g., SPSS)	2.0	67	**1**(3.8), **3**(2.1)

NOTE: The KSA statements have been abbreviated in order to conserve space. KSA statements shown in **bold** print are those selected for defining the content of selection measures.

[a]Important KSAs are those receiving a rating of **1.5** or higher on the following scale:
0 = Not Important
1 = Somewhat Important
2 = Important
3 = Essential

[b]KSAs that should be possessed by newly hired employees are those chosen by **67%** or more of the SMEs.

[c]Numbers *outside* of the parentheses are task statement numbers. Numbers *inside* the parentheses are average importance ratings of a KSA for that task's performance. The mean ratings are taken from Figure 7.14.

higher, and (b) at least 67 percent of the SMEs must indicate the KSA is necessary at job entry. As can be seen, five of the six KSAs were judged as being essential in performing the job; Knowledge of Record-Keeping Procedures was eliminated because it did not pass the required screen of 67 percent of SMEs judging that the KSA is necessary at job entry.

Next, the SMEs link the KSAs to the important job tasks by rating how important the screened KSAs were for each of the tasks. Figure 7.14 illustrates the SMEs' mean ratings of KSA importance for performing the five job tasks. Based on the requirement that each KSA must receive a mean rating of at least 1.5 for at least one job task, Figure 7.14 shows that each of the five KSAs were tied to at least one important job task.

At this point, those KSAs that should be included in our selection measures can be identified. These are the KSAs that will serve as the basis for deriving the content of our selection measures. Determination of these areas can be made by comparing the KSA ratings summarized on our rating form with the preestablished rating criteria that we mentioned earlier. Content areas of our selection procedures are defined by those KSAs that meet all of the prescribed rating criteria. That is, (a) if a KSA is rated by SMEs as

FIGURE 7.16	KSA Content Areas Identified for Measurement by Selection Procedures for the Job of HR Selection Analyst

	SELECTION PROCEDURE CONTENT AREA CRITERIA			
KSAs and Other Employee Specifications	Is This KSA an Important One?	Is This KSA Necessary for Newly Hired Employees to Possess?	Is This KSA Necessary for an Important Job Task?	Should This KSA Serve as a Selection Procedure Content Area?[a]
1. Knowledge of applied statistics	Yes	Yes	Yes	**Yes**
2. Knowledge of test validation requirements	Yes	Yes	Yes	**Yes**
3. Knowledge of development of task and inventories	Yes	Yes	Yes	**Yes**
4. Ability to read and understand technical written material	Yes	Yes	Yes	**Yes**
•	•	•	•	•
•	•	•	•	•
•	•	•	•	•
12. Skill in using computerized data analysis packages (e.g., SPSS)	Yes	Yes	Yes	**Yes**

NOTE: The KSA statements have been abbreviated in order to conserve space. KSA statements shown in **bold** print are those selected for defining selection measure content.

[a]For a KSA to be chosen as a selection content area, each of the selection instrument content area criteria must show "Yes" as an answer. These KSAs are identified in this column by a **bold "Yes."**

important, (b) if two-thirds of SMEs believe that new employees should possess the KSA upon job entry, and (c) if the KSA is linked by SMEs to performance of an important job task, then the KSA should be represented in the selection measure content. Figure 7.15 summarizes the final tabulations of the KSAs being evaluated.

In our HR selection analyst example and as shown in Figure 7.16, five KSAs meet all of the screening criteria (that is, Knowledge of Applied Statistics, Knowledge of Test Validation Requirements, Knowledge of Development of Task Inventories, Ability to Read and Understand Technical Material, and Skill in Using Computerized Data Analysis Packages [SPSS]). Therefore, these five KSAs should be employed to define the selection measure content for the job of HR selection analyst. Next, we see how we might take these results and translate them into the content of the selection measures.

Determination of Selection Procedure Content

Now that we know what is required to perform a job (the employee specifications), how do we translate these specifications into selection procedures? The answer to this question can be technical and detailed. The development of assessment methods requires the use of specially trained individuals such as industrial psychologists or test development specialists. Yet job analysts and others working in HR management can play an integral role in developing selection measures. The experience and information obtained during a job analysis is valuable for suggesting selection methods that reflect important KSAs and other employee specifications.

Before building or choosing our selection instruments, we must decide on the relative importance of our KSAs and other worker requirements as well as the type of measure that would be most appropriate for collecting this information (for example, a test or a selection interview). This process of specifying the relative KSA weights and choosing the appropriate procedures for measuring them is referred to as *developing a selection plan.* The preparation of a selection plan is accomplished in two phases:

1. Determining the relative importance of employee specifications

2. Choosing the selection methods that will assess these employee specifications

Determining Relative Importance of Employee Specifications. Previously in this chapter, employee specifications such as KSAs important to a job were identified. For most jobs, however, it is unlikely that all specifications will be equally critical to job success. Some specifications will be more important than others, and it is these specifications that should play a more dominant role in determining the content and use of selection instruments. Before choosing tests or other selection devices, it is important to determine the relative importance of employee specifications that these measures are intended to assess.

Relative importance of employee specifications can be defined in a number of ways. For example, job experts might be administered a survey questionnaire and asked to make relative determinations of KSA importance.[68] The questionnaire might consist of a listing of previously identified KSAs. Respondents could be asked to assign a relative importance weight to each KSA, from 0 to 100 percent, so that the sum of the weights totals 100 percent. The product of this process would be a relative weighting of the critical KSAs. Based on the example job of HR selection analyst, relative KSA importance weights might look as follows:

	KSA	Mean Weight Assigned
1.	Knowledge of applied statistics	15%
2.	Knowledge of test validation requirements	15%
3.	Knowledge of development of task inventories	10%
4.	Ability to read and understand technical written material	10%
•	•	•
•	•	•
•	•	•
12.	Skill in using computerized data analysis packages (e.g., SPSS)	10%
	Total Weight	**100%**

Rather than administering a separate questionnaire that will define relative importance of KSAs, we can use another option. For instance, because we used a task analysis survey, we have already collected KSA and task importance information. We might assume that KSAs rated by SMEs as more important for several job tasks should represent more selection measure content than KSAs judged less important for fewer tasks. Then we can simply multiply our *KSA importance* ratings by the *task importance* ratings for those tasks requiring the KSA. This calculation will yield points for each KSA. Relative weights can be determined by obtaining the proportion of each KSA's points for all total KSA points computed. The relative weight will indicate the extent of KSA coverage that should be present in the selection measure. By using methods such as these, KSAs needed for a variety of important tasks will be represented in more selection measure content than KSAs used for only a few or less important tasks. Shortly, we will see the role these importance weights play in developing and choosing among predictors of job success.

Choosing Selection Methods to Assess Employee Specifications. A wide variety of means are available for assessing applicants. The remaining chapters discuss the nature and application of many of these methods. Choosing ways to assess relevant KSAs requires that a number of factors be considered. Inferences and judgments play an important role in deciding which means are best for measuring which specification. In considering the possible alternatives, a consultant, HR manager, or any personnel decision maker choosing a selection measure should ask questions such as the following:[69]

1. **Have job applicants demonstrated past behaviors or had experiences prior to taking the job that are associated with successful performance of the tasks of the job?** If so, evaluation of such past behaviors, such as through a structured interview or biographical data questionnaire, may be appropriate.

2. **Can job applicants be observed performing the job or part of it? Is there a means for simulating the job in a test situation that is likely to require important behaviors as defined by the job? If so, is there a practical way of measuring simulated job performance?** When demonstration of successful performance is possible and measurable for a job applicant, a work sample or performance test might seriously be considered.

3. **Would a written test be best for examining worker requirements in terms of eliciting desired reactions and providing practical scoring?** If so, a written test should be proposed. A paper-and-pencil or computer-administered test is often appropriate for assessing job knowledge.

4. **Would giving job applicants an opportunity to express themselves orally through an interview cover job requirements that might go unassessed using other means?** In this case, a structured selection interview that can be objectively scored could be administered.

5. **Can the assessment method produce reliable and valid data for evaluating job applicants' possession of a KSA?** If not, the method should be dropped from consideration and replaced by one that is reliable and valid for the desired inference.

6. **Is it practical and within our resources to use a particular method for measuring a KSA?** If not, an alternative method should be considered.

John Campbell has illustrated how such a questioning approach might suggest alternative means for assessing the same KSA. For instance, suppose an ability such as "Ability to Relate Verbally to Persons of Varied Socioeconomic Levels" was found to be important for the job of social worker. Campbell has noted that in studying this ability, several selection methods might be considered.

1. The applicant may have performed the same, or very similar, kinds of tasks in previous jobs. We could then try to find out how effective he or she was on that task in the past....

2. If previous experience does not exist, one might try to "simulate" the task in some fashion. For example, one might contrive a role-playing situation and include as many of the real-life dynamics as possible....

3. Several steps further removed from a direct sample of job behavior is the response of the applicant to open-ended questions when interviewed by members of the target group. [The interview] could pose hypothetical situations and focus on the content of the answers; minority group interviewers could play the role of a hostile minority group member to see how the applicant handled the hostility....

4. Some paper-and-pencil predictor could be used that poses a number of hypothetical situations for the applicant....

5. One could use a test such as Rokeach's Dogmatism Scale in the belief that it has something to do with how people relate to ... minority group members.[70]

Practical considerations will play a role in choosing the type of selection measure to use. For example, if an organization has hundreds of applicants applying for a position such as that of a bank teller in a large urban bank, the possibility of using a multiple-choice, paper-and-pencil or computer-administered test will be given careful consideration because of its low cost and relative ease of administration to large groups of applicants.

An Example Selection Plan for the Job of HR Selection Analyst

Figure 7.17 shows a selection plan for the example job of HR selection analyst. For illustration purposes, it is assumed that only five KSAs are critical to this job. At the top of our plan, a variety of selection procedures that could be used for this or any other job has been listed. You may be unfamiliar with some of these techniques; however, for our present purposes, complete understanding is not necessary. We deal with these procedures in later chapters. What is important is understanding that we have chosen different methods for assessing different KSAs. In practice, fewer methods would likely be used for any one job.

Let's study the example in more detail. With respect to the first two KSAs, "Knowledge of Applied Statistics," and "Knowledge of Test Validation Requirements," we are dealing with specific bodies of information and knowledge in two related technical fields. Because we are interested in the extent to which applicants possess knowledge of these technical areas, a written multiple-choice test is recommended. Because the two content areas are judged to be equally important, roughly half of the exam should concentrate on test validation issues and the remainder on applied statistics.

With respect to "Knowledge of Test Validation Requirements," we may be interested in applicants' knowledge and actual experiences with test validation matters. Three additional assessment methods are suggested. The application form could ask applicants for a list of previous experiences in test validation research. We may contact previous employers through reference checks to verify certain stated test validation capabilities. A structured oral interview could be used to let applicants describe in detail their experiences or, possibly, respond to technical questions or situations concerning their knowledge of test validation research. Our selection method weights show that more emphasis should be placed on the interview than on the application form or reference check in appraising this KSA.

"Knowledge of Development of Task Inventories" could be assessed through a selection interview and a training and experience evaluation. In addition to questions about test validation, our selection interview should also incorporate questions involving applicants' knowledge about the development of task inventories. Training and experience evaluations should play a role in the objective judgment of applicants' experiences with task inventories.

Applicants' "Skill in Using Computerized Data Analysis Packages" should be evaluated. Relative to some KSAs, this skill plays a less critical role in accounting for job

FIGURE 7.17 An Example Selection Plan for the Job of HR Selection Analyst

KSAs to be Used in Selection	KSA Weight	Selection Procedures					
		Application Form	Reference Check	Selection Interview	Work Sample (Performance) Test	Written Objective Test	Training and Experience Evaluation
1. Knowledge of applied statistics	15%					15	
2. Knowledge of test validation requirements	15	5%	5%	15%		15	
3. Knowledge of development of task inventories	10			5			5%
4. Ability to read and understand technical written material	10			• • •		10	
• • •							
12. Skill in using computerized data analysis packages (e.g., SPSS)	10	5			5%		
Total KSA Weight	100%	10%	5%	25%	5%	50%	5%

NOTE: The KSA percentage weights do not sum to 100% because other relevant KSAs and their weights are not shown.

success as a selection analyst. An application form could ask for information on formal training, experience, or self-rated expertise with data analysis packages. Applicants could be scored objectively on their skill by actually using a statistical or data analysis software package to solve a realistic problem. This skill would be assessed through a work sample or performance test.

Besides suggesting alternative methods for appraising job-relevant KSAs, a selection plan has an additional value. That is, the weights assigned to a selection method for each KSA are useful in determining the relative emphasis that should be placed on the content areas of the measures. For instance, think back to the job of HR selection analyst. Let's say we plan to allocate two hours for assessing each HR selection analyst applicant. Some of our assessments will occur in groups (for example, a written test), while other assessments will be made with regard to individuals (for example, an interview). From examining our selection plan shown in Figure 7.17, we see that half of our time allocated for selection (50 percent of the KSA weights) should be assessed through a written, multiple-choice test. From previous experience, we know that roughly 50 multiple-choice items can be completed in an hour. Thus we decide to use 50 items on our written test. How do we determine the proportion of these items that should be allocated to each KSA? Again, referring to our selection plan, we see that two KSAs are to be measured with our test; each has the same importance weight (15 percent). Therefore, 8 of the 50 multiple-choice items should be written to measure "Knowledge of Test Validation Requirements" and 8 written to measure "Knowledge of Applied Statistics." We would follow this same procedure in deciding how we want to allocate our remaining time to our other selection methods.

As you look at our proposed selection plan, you may notice an interesting result. Our job analysis appears to have produced a selection program whose contents seem to reflect the major contents of the job. Selection procedure/job content overlap is precisely what we want. The more we can ensure a match between content of our selection methods and demands of the job, the more confident we can be of the value of our selection program. Of course, we would not stop with a job analysis as final evidence of selection method usefulness; job analysis is really the first step. Where feasible, we would want to plan validation research studies to examine empirically how well our proposed measures actually predict successful job performance.

Some experts in the field of job analysis have questioned whether incumbents are capable of making the kind of inferences needed to identify the relevant worker attributes needed to perform a job, particularly when such attributes such as traits are abstract in nature.[71] There is evidence that job incumbents have greater difficulty in making reliable job analysis ratings than professional job analysts.[72] However, recent research has shed some light on the ability of incumbent SMEs to make accurate ratings of stimuli such as KSAs. For example, Erich Dierdorff and Frederick Morgeson used a sample of more than 47,000 incumbents in more than 300 occupations to examine incumbents' ratings of tasks, responsibilities, knowledge, skills, and traits.[73] One of several conclusions they reached was that incumbents were capable of providing reliable and discriminating ratings of knowledge and skills. However, on less specific, less observable descriptors, namely abstract traits, the raters could not make reliable ratings. Other research points to the important finding that certain forms of training, that is, frame-of-reference training, can enhance the quality of ratings given by job incumbents, even on abstract traits such as personality traits.[74] Taken in total, when developing employee specifications, recent research seems to suggest that

1. A structured, systematic approach, such as the one we have described, should be used to reduce the size of inferential leaps made by job incumbents when rating their jobs.

2. Incumbents can reliably and validly rate the specifications for their position when the specifications deal with specific, more observable job descriptors such as knowledges and skills.

3. Ratings of more abstract traits are improved when raters are properly trained using methods such as frame-of-reference training.

EMPLOYEE SPECIFICATIONS FOR JOBS THAT ARE CHANGING OR YET TO BE CREATED

We have mentioned throughout our discussion that selection procedures must be based on a job analysis. We have discussed at length the use of methods to analyze jobs as they are *currently* being performed. But suppose a job does not yet exist or is about to undergo a drastic change; for example, through organizational restructuring. How do you develop employee specifications for a job about to change? How do you identify these specifications when a job that does not yet exist is being created? In these cases, selection procedures must be able to distinguish between individuals who can and who cannot perform the job as it *will* be performed in the future.

Conducting a job analysis of "future jobs" in our hypothetical situation is a problem. One option for handling current jobs that will change in the future is what Benjamin Schneider and Andrea Konz refer to as "strategic job analysis."[75] The purpose of their approach is to define the tasks and KSAs thought to be needed for a job as it is predicted to exist in the future. In essence, the method consists of the following steps:

1. An analysis of the job is made to identify current tasks and KSAs.

2. Subject matter experts (for example, job incumbents, supervisors, managers) knowledgeable about the job are assembled in a workshop to discuss how future issues (for example, technological change) are likely to affect the job.

3. Information on expected future tasks and KSAs is collected from individuals knowledgeable about these expected job changes.

4. Differences between present and future judgments about the job are identified to isolate those tasks and KSAs where greatest change is anticipated. It is this task and KSA information that serves as the basis for selecting incumbents in a job that does not currently exist.

Obviously, a key component of the entire process is the subject matter expert who is asked to predict future job change. If a current job is being changed, incumbents, supervisors, managers, and other experts are asked to forecast changes in job activities and KSAs.

If a new job is being created it will be necessary to use a more creative approach to selecting experts to make future job task and KSA predictions. Select individuals within the organization who can envision what the job will be like. Consider others outside the organization who have specific technical knowledge about the needed changes. For example, persons in the organization familiar with corporate strategy and technological change might be helpful. Supervisors and incumbents of jobs that have tasks similar to those predicted for the new one can also participate. If the new job entails running a new piece of equipment, a technical representative of the manufacturer may provide useful information regarding the tasks and worker requirements necessary.

The process of strategic job analysis has many yet-to-be-resolved issues. For example, what is the reliability and validity of experts' future job predictions? What experts are most helpful and accurate in forecasting change? What is the best way to conduct workshops and job analyses to collect the data needed? Will this approach be accepted if challenged in the courts? These are but a few of the unanswered questions that remain. Richard Arvey, Eduardo Salas, and Kathleen Gialluca have taken a different, empirical tack with regard to analyzing future jobs.[76] Rather than tasks, their concern is with statistically forecasting future skills and abilities needed to perform job tasks. The need-to-know skills and abilities could occur, for instance, when the skills and abilities for operating new equipment in the future are unknown, when new plants with new jobs are being started, or when job redesign efforts involving reconfigurations of tasks into new jobs are occurring.

Using comprehensive task and ability inventories obtained from 619 skilled-trade incumbents, Arvey and his colleagues sought to determine if it were possible to predict required abilities from job tasks. Results from their analyses suggested that it was possible to forecast some needed KSAs from task data. Other KSAs, however, were not particularly predictable. Nevertheless, results from their research were encouraging enough to suggest that when it is possible to build a comprehensive database of links between job tasks and KSAs, forecasting future KSAs from existing task information should be considered. All that would be needed for future jobs is to estimate the key tasks that might be performed; required KSAs could then be predicted. A major problem with such an approach is that collecting task and ability data on a large-scale basis is likely to be feasible only in large organizations.

Another approach to estimating the requirements of future jobs involves use of the Occupational Information Network or O*NET (http://online.onetcenter.org/) developed by the Department of Labor. O*NET is a comprehensive database of information that describes characteristics of workers and the work they do in jobs representative of the national labor force. Richard Jeanneret and Mark Strong conducted a study to determine if it were possible to identify selection instruments by using information on occupations' generalized work activities that is stored in the O*NET database.[77] Generalized work activities are essentially groups of job behaviors used in performing major work functions (for example, identifying objects, actions, and events; teaching others; and thinking creatively). Results of their research showed that the generalized work activities were particularly helpful in choosing selection measures for occupations requiring intelligence and verbal and numerical aptitudes; they were less useful for occupations requiring manual dexterity. If it is possible to estimate generalized work activities required in an occupation, then knowledge of these activities might be used in selecting appropriate selection instruments.

With regard to O*NET, we suspect that future research will draw upon this database to examine the efficacy of using current O*NET data to infer required KSAs to use in selection. Current research using O*NET data has suggested the efficacy of these data in future research on employee specifications.[78] Use of O*NET for specifying future work requirements is still being developed, and additional research is needed, but O*NET may hold particular promise for specifying selection procedures. Given the rapid technological change that many organizations are experiencing, the need to conduct some form of future-oriented job analysis is likely to become a necessity. At this point, the details of application have yet to be refined. Clearly, more research is needed on methods for identifying employee specifications of future jobs and job tasks.

THE FUTURE OF JOB ANALYSIS

Revolutionary changes are occurring in many organizations in the United States. Global competition, smaller companies employing fewer people, reengineering of businesses, increased use of teams to do the work in organizations, and the shift from manufacturing products to providing services are just a few of the trends that seem to be redefining the nature of work.[79] This redefinition of work has produced a growing disappearance of the traditional job comprising a fixed bundle of tasks.[80] To compete, some organizations have found it necessary to move away from the concept of organizing work around individual job tasks and to view work more in terms of processes. A *process* consists of groupings of activities that take inputs and create outputs of value to customers, for example, product development or order fulfillment.[81] Our concern here is with the potential implications that such changes in the nature of work have for the future of job analysis and personnel selection as we have presented it. Wayne Cascio posed the following questions for consideration:

> *What will be the future of traditional task-based descriptions of jobs and job activities? Should other types of descriptors replace task statements that describe what a worker does, to what or whom, why, and how? Will "task" cluster ... become the basic building blocks for describing work? ... Will job specifications (which identify the personal characteristics—knowledge, skills, abilities, and other characteristics—necessary to do the work) supersede job descriptions? ... Will emphasis shift from describing jobs to describing roles?*[82]

Critical questions have been raised concerning the current practice and relevancy of job analysis. One criticism points out that many job analysis methods fail to identify the importance of factors such as requirements for teamwork[83] or personality variables that are potentially important in selection systems for many jobs. Moreover, some selection researchers have argued that detailed, comprehensive analyses are not necessary for test validation. Specifically, validity generalization advocates point out that the only thing needed from a job analysis is to show that the job under study is from the same job family on which validity generalization data have been collected.[84] Therefore, task analyses and other detailed approaches are unnecessary.

As a consequence of these questions regarding job analysis, some have suggested that our traditional job analysis methods are no longer suitable for tomorrow's world of work; other methods will be needed.[85] For example, it has been proposed that these new methods be labeled "work analysis" methods to move away from the concept of "the job."[86]

At this point, you are probably wondering, "Why, then, have I spent all this time reading a chapter and learning about something that may already be out of date?" The questions raised about the need for and adequacy of current job analysis methods are relevant issues; we should be concerned about them. However, for several reasons, do not despair. First, newer methods for analyzing work will be developed and will be useful; at this point, concrete procedures for work analysis in the context of personnel selection are still being developed and, therefore, not widely agreed upon. Many organizations still need and use methods like those we have presented in this chapter. Many organizations will need these methods in the foreseeable future, particularly for jobs at lower organizational levels (skilled trades, clerical, retail, and production/operations). Second, even though new analysis methods may be created, many will likely follow one or more of the formats we have discussed; that is, they will use questionnaires, rating scales, SME workshops, and the like. The fundamentals you have learned in this chapter should serve you well in understanding, evaluating, using, and, perhaps, helping design new methods for assessing work. Finally, with regard to the issue of the necessity for job analysis in selection procedure validation studies, we still have legal constraints that require our use of job analysis methods. Much of the *Uniform Guidelines,* for example, is oriented around the concept of a job and the *essential* requirement of conducting a job analysis. Although one advantage of validity generalization may be that less job analysis information is required, this advantage may also be its greatest potential limitation.

Robert Guion, in commenting on the amount and comprehensiveness of job analysis information needed in selection research, noted

> *The level of detail desired may also be determined by the likelihood of litigation. Prudent personnel researchers attend not only to the best wisdom of their profession but to the realities of the court room. In a specific situation, a detailed job analysis may not be necessary technically, but failure to have evidence of an 'adequate' job analysis, in the view of the trial judge, may result in an adverse decision in court.*[87]

Before widespread use of newer means for analyzing work can be adopted, changes may be necessary in existing employment law and federal selection guidelines. This is not to say that these changes should not occur; rather, to comply with existing guidelines, knowledge of traditional job analysis methods is still needed. At this point in the development of job analysis methods, we believe prudent developers and users of selection systems would be wise to consider job analysis methods such as those we have mentioned in this chapter.

THE FUTURE OF KSAs AND EMPLOYEE CORE COMPETENCIES

Because KSAs grow out of a job analysis, the changing nature of work will necessarily influence our notion of KSAs. Some jobs, technologies, and organizations are changing quite rapidly. Employee specifications developed for such jobs are less likely to be stable over time. Some writers are now suggesting that rather than tying KSAs to jobs likely to change, we should think more broadly about longer-term organizational needs.[88] That is, employee specifications should be based on stable organization requirements as opposed to soon-to-change job requirements. Organizationally defined employee specifications should ideally facilitate the flexible movement of employees into and out of jobs as opportunities open up that require their skills and abilities.

Because of the perceived need for more broadly defined worker KSAs, some writers are calling for the identification of a common core of organizationally defined *employee competencies* that many, if not all, employees should possess—in addition to job-specific KSAs.[89] These competencies would consist of attributes that cut across job tasks, linked to organizational strategies and required of employees in the broader organizational culture. How might this be accomplished? What will these competencies be like? These questions, of course, are critical. Although final answers are simply not yet available, proposals have been made. One approach emphasizes that an outcome of job analysis is to identify broader work *functions* that are composed of clusters of the tasks performed on many jobs.[90] Competencies characterizing these functions would then be sought. Of special importance would be topics such as tasks and competencies associated with cross-functional teams, total quality management, and other forms of customer and supplier involvement.[91] As regards the specific competencies required for the changing world of work, constructs such as the ability to learn or be trained, self-management, self-motivation, teamwork skills, managing change, adaptability, handling conflict, and an ability to work under stress, to name a few, might be required.[92]

Juan Sanchez and Edward Levine have discussed the differences between competency modeling and traditional job analysis.[93] They note that for a number of human resource functions, the use of competency modeling in developing employee competencies has replaced traditional job analysis. However, in the context of personnel selection, Sanchez and Levine suggest caution to those organizations planning a staffing system based solely on competency modeling. In their view, attempting to use competency validation strategies, such as criterion-related and content validation, in order to comply with the *Uniform Guidelines*, which calls for explicit links between KSAs and important job tasks, is the wrong way to proceed. They state, "…. making such inferences concerning the job relatedness of strategic competencies on 'the slippery floor of behaviorally-fuzzy competencies' is akin to performing acrobatic gymnastics on an icy floor." By integrating competency modeling with traditional job analysis (including the use of SMEs, workshops, interviews, and so on), a clearer picture may emerge of the appropriate roles of employee competencies and KSAs in the context of personnel selection.

The dynamics we have described should not be interpreted to mean that our current methods of KSA determination have no place in tomorrow's world of work. Jobs will still exist.[94] There will still be a need to define KSAs and other employee characteristics for these jobs. Methods for determining meaningful employee competencies remain to be developed and tested in a wide array of organizations. Until viable approaches can be developed, the procedures we have discussed will likely continue to play an important role in defining organizations' employee specifications.

IDENTIFYING EMPLOYEE COMPETENCIES: AN EXAMPLE

As we mentioned, some companies have initiated programs for identifying core employee competencies. This company has developed a set of core competencies applicable to all employees throughout its organization. In developing these competencies, a task

---

FIGURE 7.18 Examples of Employee Competencies

Competitive Advantage through People

I. Achieving Competitiveness

1. **Customer Focus:** Aggressively monitors and anticipates customer requirements and responds to them in an appropriate manner.
2. **Business Focus:** Strategically monitors business performance and external environment to enhance the organization's competitive position.
3. **Innovation and Change:** Actively seeks out new ideas and displays creativity in adapting to changing conditions.
4. **Results Orientation:** Demonstrates drive and persistence to meet and exceed job goals for self or others.
5. **Analysis and Planning:** Uses critical thinking and diagnostic skills to solve problems and develop effective work plans.
6. **Systems Thinking:** Designs, improves, and integrates business and operational processes in order to achieve the organization's strategic goals.
7. **Technical/Functional Expertise:** Demonstrates, enhances, and shares job knowledge and skills.

II. Succeeding through People

1. **Valuing People:** Demonstrates respect for others regardless of personal background.
2. **Commitment to Development:** Acts in a purposeful manner to develop own and/or others' capabilities to better meet organizational needs.
3. **Professionalism:** Demonstrates candor, composure, objectivity, and commitment to obligations in all working relationships.
4. **Empowerment:** Delegates or accepts responsibility to expand own and/or others' capabilities to take appropriate risks and make decisions.
5. **Influence:** Uses appropriate methods and strategies to motivate others to meet individual, department, or company goals.
6. **Team Orientation:** Accepts the team approach and takes necessary action to support its processes and goals.

Note: We thank Dr. Dave Smith, Anheuser-Busch Companies.

FIGURE 7.19   An Example of Employee Behaviors Descriptive of a Team Orientation Competency

13. Team Orientation: Accepts the team approach and takes necessary action to support its processes and goals.

Individual Contributor	Manager	Senior Manager/Executive
13A. Team Orientation	**13B. Team Orientation**	**13C. Team Orientation**
a. Recognizes that own success is linked to team success	a. Creates and monitors teams as appropriate to meet business objectives	a. Develops and fosters an organizational culture that supports a team environment
b. Supports team roles, norms, and decisions	b. Sets clear expectations for teams	b. Ensures that performance feedback, recognition, and reward systems support a team environment
c. Speaks up when he/she feels the team is heading in the wrong direction	c. Works to build commitment toward common goals	c. Encourages cross-functional cooperation among teams
d. Seeks and maintains positive relationships with teams and others outside of own group	d. Provides resources for team projects to the business objectives	d. Understands how each team contributes
e. Keeps others informed of decisions and information that may impact them	e. Recognizes team for contributions to goal accomplishment	
	f. Measures own success by team's success	

Note: We thank Dr. Dave Smith, Anheuser-Busch Companies.

force was assembled to review the company's vision, mission, business objective, and values. The task force was led by the corporate human resources staff and advised by an external consultant well known for his work on developing competency models for business. Among others, one important goal of the task force was to identify the key business imperatives or challenges the corporation would face over the next 5 to 10 years (for example, competition in global markets or commitment to employee development). For each of these identified challenges, the task force derived a list of personal competencies needed by employees at all levels of the organization. Focus groups consisting of managers representing various divisions of the company were assembled to (a) review and narrow the list of competencies created by the task force and (b) confirm or edit four to five specific employee behaviors reflecting each competency. Questionnaires, including the finalized behavior list, were then distributed to selected company supervisors from various levels of the organization. The supervisors rated the frequency with which they saw these behaviors demonstrated by three employee groups: (a) top-performing or "role model" employees, (b) employees identified as competent and satisfactory in their performance, and (c) employees needing to improve their performance. The goal of this step in the Anheuser-Busch competency development process was to identify employee behaviors descriptive of employee competencies—behaviors that would differentiate among top performers, satisfactory performers, and those needing to improve job performance. Competencies discriminating among these groups represented the employee competencies judged to be most critical to the future success of the company.

Figure 7.18 lists these competencies. In this figure, the heading with roman numerals represents two competency groupings or structures identified through factor analyses, for example (a) achieving competitiveness and (b) succeeding through people. The Arabic-numbered entries such as "customer focus" are the employee competencies that were linked to each business imperative mentioned earlier.

Figure 7.19 illustrates how one of these competencies, "team orientation," was translated into specific behaviors important for the success of three groups of employees: (a) individual contributors, (b) managers or supervisors, and (c) senior managers/executives. Anheuser-Busch has used the framework of competencies to begin building and integrating its human resources programs, starting with recruiting employees and selecting the most qualified through performance management, training and development, and succession planning.

REFERENCES

1. Ernest J. McCormick, "Job and Task Analysis," in *Handbook of Industrial and Organizational Psychology*, ed. Marvin Dunnette (Chicago: Rand McNally, 1976), 652–653.

2. Joseph E. Zerga, "Job Analysis, A Resume and Bibliography," *Journal of Applied Psychology* 27 (1943): 249–267.

3. Marvin D. Dunnette, *Personnel Selection and Placement* (Belmont, CA: Wadsworth, 1996).

4. Equal Employment Opportunity Commission, Civil Service Commission, Department of Labor, and Department of Justice, *Adoption of Four Agencies of Uniform Guidelines on Employee Selection Procedures*, 43 *Federal Register* 38,290–38,315 (August 25, 1978).

5. Paul Sparks, "Legal Basis for Job Analysis," in *The Job Analysis Handbook for Business, Industry, and Government*, ed. Sidney Gael (New York: John Wiley, 1988), 37–47.

6. Society for Industrial and Organizational Psychology, Inc., *Principles for the Validation and Use of Personnel Selection Procedures* (Bowling Green, OH: Society for Industrial and Organizational Psychology, Inc., 2003).

7. Duane E. Thompson and Toni A. Thompson, "Court Standards for Job Analysis in Test Validation," *Personnel Psychology* 35 (1982): 872–873.

8. *Griggs v. Duke Power Co.*, 401 U.S. 424, 436 (1971).

9. Ibid.

10. Ibid.

11. *Albemarle Paper Co. v. Moody*, 422 U.S. 405 (1975).

12. Ibid.

13. Equal Employment Opportunity Commission, *Guidelines on Employee Selection Procedures*, 35 *Federal Register* 12,333–12,336 (1970).

14. Thompson and Thompson, "Court Standards for Job Analysis in Test Validation," 872–873.

15. Equal Employment Opportunity Commission, Civil Service Commission, Department of Labor, and Department of Justice, *Adoption of Four Agencies of Uniform Guidelines on Employee Selection Procedures*, 43 *Federal Register* 38,290–38,315 (August 25, 1978), referred to in the text as the *Uniform Guidelines*; Equal Employment Opportunity Commission, Office of Personnel Management, and Department of Treasury, *Adoption of Questions and Answers to Clarify and Provide a Common Interpretation of the Uniform Guidelines on Employee Selection Procedures*, 44 *Federal Register* 11,996–12,009 (1979); and Equal Employment Opportunity Commission, *Guidelines on Employee Selection Procedures*, 41 *Federal Register* 51,984–51,986 (1976).

16. See, for example, Frank L. Schmidt, John Hunter, and Kenneth Pearlman, "Test Differences as Moderators of Aptitude Test Validity in Selection: A Red Herring," *Journal of Applied Psychology* 66 (1981): 166–185.

17. Frank L. Schmidt, Deniz S. Ones, and John E. Hunter, "Personnel Selection," *Annual Review of Psychology* 43 (1992): 627–670.

18. U.S. Civil Service Commission, *Job Analysis: Developing and Documenting Data* (Washington, DC: U.S. Civil Service Commission, Bureau of Intergovernmental Personnel Programs, 1973).

19. Ibid., 5.

20. Ibid., 11–12.

21. Ibid., 6.

22. Ibid., 12.

23. Sidney Gael, "Interviews, Questionnaires, and Checklists," in *The Job Analysis Handbook for Business, Industry, and Government*, ed. Sidney Gael (New York: John Wiley, 1988), 394–402.

24. Robert J. Harvey, *CMQ, A Job Analysis System: Directions for Administering the CMQ* (San Antonio, TX: The Psychological Corporation, 1992).

25. Ernest J. McCormick and P. Richard Jeanneret, "Position Analysis Questionnaire (PAQ)," in *The Job Analysis Handbook for Business, Industry, and Government*, ed. Sidney Gael (New York: John Wiley, 1988), 840.

26. Ronald C. Page, "Management Position Description Questionnaire," in *The Job Analysis Handbook for Business, Industry, and Government*, ed. Sidney Gael (New York: John Wiley, 1988), 860–879.

27. Melany E. Baehr, "The Managerial and Professional Job Functions Inventory (Formerly the Work Elements Inventory)," in *The Job Analysis Handbook for Business, Industry, and Government*, ed. Sidney Gael (New York: John Wiley, 1988), 1072–1085.

28. McCormick and Jeanneret, "Position Analysis Questionnaire (PAQ)," 825–842.

29. Felix M. Lopez, "Threshold Traits Analysis System," in *The Job Analysis Handbook for Business, Industry, and Government*, ed. Sidney Gael (New York: John Wiley, 1988), 880–901.

30. Joseph W. Cunningham, "Occupation Analysis Inventory," in *The Job Analysis Handbook for Business, Industry, and Government*, ed. Sidney Gael (New York: John Wiley, 1988), 975–990.

31. Patrick H. Raymark, Mark J. Schmit, and Robert M. Guion, "Identifying Potentially Useful Personality Constructs for Employee Selection," *Personnel Psychology* 50 (1997): 723–736.

32. Jimmy L. Mitchell, "History of Job Analysis in Military Organizations," in *The Job Analysis Handbook for Business, Industry, and Government*, ed. Sidney Gael (New York: John Wiley, 1988), 30–36.

33. This scale is typical of the relative scales that have been used in job analysis in the military.

34. Duane E. Thompson and Toni A. Thompson, "Court Standards for Job Analysis in Test Validation," *Personnel Psychology* 35 (1982): 872–873; and Edward L. Levine, James N. Thomas, and Frank Sistrunk, "Selecting a Job Analysis Approach," in *The Job Analysis Handbook for Business, Industry, and Government*, ed. Sidney Gael (New York: John Wiley, 1988), 345. Redundancy in task ratings can be an issue when considering rating scales to be used. See Lee Friedman, "Degree of Redundancy between Time, Importance, and Frequency Task Ratings," *Journal of Applied Psychology* 75 (1990): 748–752.

35. Ernest J. McCormick, "Job Information: Its Development and Applications", in *ASPA Handbook of Personnel and Industrial Relations*, ed. Dale Yoder and Herbert G. Heneman (Washington, DC: BNA, 1979) 4-66–4-67.

36. For a review of statistical techniques that can be used in analyzing job analysis data, see Edwin T. Cornelius III, "Analyzing Job Analysis Data," in *The Job Analysis Handbook for Business, Industry, and Government*, ed. Sidney Gael (New York: John Wiley, 1988), 353–368.

37. Wayne Cascio and Robert Ramos, "Development and Application of a New Method for Assessing Job Performance in Behavioral/Economic Terms," *Journal of Applied Psychology* 71 (1986): 20–28. See also Patrick Manley and Paul Sackett, "Effects of Using High versus Low-Performing Job Incumbents as Sources of Job Analysis Information," *Journal of Applied Psychology* 72 (1987): 434–437, for an example of the application of empirical criteria for defining important job tasks.

38. Thomas A. Stetz, Mathew Beaubien, Michael J. Keeney, and Brian D. Lyons, "Nonrandom Response and Rater Variance in Job Analysis Surveys: A Cause for Concern?" *Public Personnel Management* 37 (2008): 223–239.

39. Ibid.

40. John C. Flanagan, "The Critical Incident Technique," *Psychological Bulletin* 51 (1954): 327–358.

41. Anna Koch, Anja Strobel, Guler Kici, and Karl Westoff, "Quality of the Critical Incident Technique in Practice: Interrater Reliability and Users' Acceptance Under Real Conditions," *Psychology Science Quarterly* 51 (2009): 3–15.

42. David A. Bownas and H. John Bernardin, "Critical Incident Technique," in *The Job Analysis Handbook for Business, Industry, and Government*, ed. Sidney Gael (New York: John Wiley, 1988), 1120–1137.

43. Ibid., 1121.

44. Ibid.

45. Edward L. Levine, Ronald A. Ash, Hardy L. Hall, and Frank Sistrunk, "Evaluation of Job Analysis Methods by Experienced Job Analysts," *Academy of Management Journal* 26 (1983): 339–347.

46. Gary B. Brumback, Tania Romashko, Clifford P. Hahn, and Edwin A. Fleishman, *Model Procedures for Job Analysis, Test Development, and Validation* (Washington, DC: American Institutes for Research, 1974), 102–108.

47. Filip Lievens and Juan Sanchez, "Can Training Improve the Quality of Inferences Made by Raters in Competency Modeling? A Quasi-Experiment," *Journal of Applied Psychology* 92 (2007): 812–813.

48. Frank J. Landy, "Selection Procedure Development and Usage," in *The Job Analysis Handbook for Business, Industry, and Government*, ed. Sidney Gael (New York: John Wiley, 1988), 271–287.

49. Edwin A. Fleishman and Marilyn K. Quaintance, *Taxonomies of Human Performance: The Description of Human Tasks* (Orlando: Academic Press, 1984).

50. Lievens and Sanchez, "Can Training Improve the Quality of Inferences Made by Raters in Competency Modeling? A Quasi-Experiment."

51. Iowa Merit Employment Department, *Job Analysis Guidelines* (Des Moines: Iowa Merit Employment Department, 1974), 10.

52. Center for Business and Economic Development, Auburn University—Montgomery, Montgomery, Alabama.

53. U.S. Civil Service Commission, *Job Analysis for Improved Job-Related Selection* (Washington, D.C.: U.S. Civil Service Commission, Bureau of Intergovernmental Personnel Programs, 1976) 1–2.

54. Lievens and Sanchez, "Can Training Improve the Quality of Inferences Made by Raters in Competency Modeling? A Quasi-Experiment."

55. Equal Employment Opportunity Commission, Civil Service Commission, Department of Labor, and Department of Justice, *Adoption of Four Agencies of Uniform Guidelines on Employee Selection Procedures*, 43 *Federal Register* 38,307–38,308 (August 25,1978).

56. Ibid.

57. Ibid.

58. For an excellent discussion of the similarities and differences among knowledge, skills, abilities, and other employee characteristics, see Robert J. Harvey, "Job Analysis," in *Handbook of Industrial and Organizational Psychology*, ed. Marvin D. Dunnette (Palo Alto, CA: Consulting Psychologists Press, 1990), 75–79.

59. Richard E. Biddle, *Brief GOJA: A Step-by-Step Job Analysis Instruction Booklet* (Sacramento, CA: Biddle and Associates, 1978), 27.

60. Ibid., 28.

61. Ibid.

62. Landy, "Selection Procedure Development and Usage," 272.

63. U.S. Civil Service Commission, *Job Analysis for Improved Job-Related Selection*, 27.

64. Edwin A. Fleishman, *Rating Scale Booklet F-JAS Fleishman Job Analysis Survey* (Palo Alto, CA: Consulting Psychologists Press, 1992).

65. Ibid., 89.

66. Equal Employment Opportunity Commission et al., "Uniform Guidelines," 43 *Federal Register* 38,302.

67. These are rating criteria used by the Center for Business and Economic Development, Auburn University—Montgomery, Montgomery, Alabama.

68. Stephan J. Mussio and Mary K. Smith, *Content Validity: A Procedural Manual* (Chicago: International Personnel Management Association, 1973), 24–27.

69. U.S. Civil Service Commission, *Job Analysis for Improved Job-Related Selection*, 10–11.

70. John P. Campbell, "Comments on Content Validity: A Procedural Manual" (unpublished report prepared for the Minneapolis Civil Service Commission), as cited in Stephan J. Mussio and Mary K. Smith, *Content Validity: A Special Report* (Chicago: International Personnel Management Association, 1973), 30–31.

71. Robert J. Harvey and Mark A. Wilson, "Yes Virginia, There is an Objective Reality in Job Analysis," *Journal of Organizational Behavior* 21 (2000): 829–854.

72. Erich C. Dierdorff and Mark A. Wilson, "A Meta-Analysis of Job Analysis Reliability," *Journal of Applied Psychology* 88 (2003): 635–646.

73. Erich C. Dierdorff and Frederick P. Morgeson, "Effects of Descriptor Specificity and Observability on Incumbent Work Analysis Ratings," *Personnel Psychology* 62: 601–628.

74. Herman Aguinis, Mark D. Mazurkiewica, and Eric D. Heggestad, "Using Web-Based Frame-of-Reference Training to Decrease Biases in Personality-Based Job Analysis: An Experimental Study," *Personnel Psychology* 62 (2009): 405–438; and Lievens and Sanchez, "Can Training Improve the Quality of Inferences Made by Raters in Competency Modeling? A Quasi-Experiment."

75. Benjamin Schneider and Andrea Konz, "Strategic Job Analysis," *Human Resource Management* 28 (1989): 51–63.

76. Richard Arvey, Eduardo Salas, and Kathleen Gialluca, "Using Task Inventories to Forecast Skills and Abilities," *Human Performance* 5 (1992): 171–190.

77. P. Richard Jeanneret and Mark H. Strong, "Linking O*NET Job Analysis Information to Job Requirement Predictors: An O*NET Application," *Personnel Psychology* 56 (2003): 465–492.

78. Erich C. Dierdorff, Robert S. Rubin, and Frederick P. Morgeson, "The Milieu of Managerial Work: An Integrative Framework Linking Work Context to Role Requirements," *Journal of Applied Psychology* 94 (2009): 972–988; Dierdorff and Morgeson, "Effects of Descriptor Specificity and Observability on Incumbent Work Analysis Ratings"; Christelle C. Lapolice, Gary W. Carter, and Jeff W. Johnson, "Linking O*NET Descriptors to Occupational Literacy Requirements Using Job Component Validation," *Personnel Psychology* 61 (2008): 405–441; Paul J. Taylor, Wen-Dong Li Kan Shi, and Walter C. Borman, "The Transportability of Job Information across Countries," *Personnel Psychology* 61 (2008): 69–111.

79. Wayne Cascio, "Whither Industrial and Organizational Psychology in a Changing World of Work?" *American Psychologist* 50 (1995): 928–939.

80. William Bridges, "The End of the Job," *Fortune*, September 19, 1994, 62–64, 68, 72.

81. Cascio, "Whither Industrial and Organizational Psychology in a Changing World of Work?" 932.

82. Ibid.

83. Michael A. Campion, "Job Analysis for the Future," in *Personnel Selection and Classification*, ed. Michael G. Rumsey and Clinton B. Walker (Hillsdale, NJ: Lawrence Erlbaum Associates, 1994), 1–12.

84. Kenneth Pearlman, Frank L. Schmidt, and John E. Hunter, "Validity Generalization Results for Tests Used to Predict Job Proficiency and Training Success in Clerical Occupations," *Journal of Applied Psychology* 65 (1980): 373–406.

85. Karen E. May, "Work in the 21st Century: Implications for Job Analysis," *The Industrial-Organizational Psychologist* 33 (1996): 98–100.

86. Ibid.

87. Robert M. Guion, "Personnel Assessment, Selection, and Placement," in *Handbook of Industrial and Organizational Psychology*, ed. Marvin D. Dunnette and Leatta M. Hough (Palo Alto, CA: Consulting Psychologists Press, 1992), 332.

88. May, "Work in the 21st Century: Implications for Selection," 80–83.

89. Allan H. Church, "From Both Sides Now: The Changing of the Job," *The Industrial-Organizational Psychologist* 33 (1996): 52–61.

90. L. Shankster, B. Cawley, M. Olivero-Wolf, and F. Landy, *Organizational Re-Design Final Report* (US West Learning Systems, 1995), as reported in May, "Work in the 21st Century: Implications for Job Analysis," 100.

91. Church, "From Both Sides Now: The Changing of the Job."

92. K. P. Carson and G. L. Stewart, "Job Analysis and the Sociotechnical Approach to Quality: A Critical Examination," *Journal of Quality Management* 1 (1996): 49–64.

93. Juan I. Sanchez and Edward L. Levine, "What Is (or Should Be) the Difference between Competency Modeling and Traditional Job Analysis?" *Human Resource Management Review* 19 (2009): 60.

94. Church, "From Both Sides Now: The Changing of the Job."

HUMAN RESOURCE RECRUITMENT

Perhaps the most essential ingredient to any effective human resource selection program is an organization's ability to attract quality job applicants. By "quality applicants," we mean those individuals who possess the requisite characteristics desired by the recruiting organization. Without qualified or at least qualifiable applicants, the best selection procedures a firm could possibly have will be useless. Thus, attracting and recruiting viable job applicants is vital to a firm's success. Assuming such applicants can be attracted, we can then make use of our selection procedures to identify those job candidates most appropriate for our open positions.

In this part of the book, we examine the recruitment process. We focus on a variety of strategies used to attract those applicants most desirable to a recruiting organization. We will see how recruitment messages and the media used to communicate such messages can affect applicants' perceptions of recruiting organizations. We offer recommendations to enhance the likelihood that organizations' recruitment activities will meet their desired objectives.

Recruitment of Applicants

RECRUITMENT AND SELECTION

Let's fast-forward to your career after you have finished this course. You are now an HR Selection Specialist with a six-figure salary (not counting the decimal places, we hope). Your manager comes into your office (which has a great view of the ocean) and tells you that she is about to put you in charge of solving a big problem. The company has decided to diversify its product lines by going into programming for video games. You are to recruit the first set of applicants for this new unit. That means you must write the job descriptions, decide on how to attract a qualified pool of applicants, and then design the selection program. (Lucky you did so well in this course! ☺) You already know how to write job descriptions. This is the chapter that will help you plan how to attract qualified applicants for those jobs. The chapters that follow this one address selection procedures you will need to set up and implement the selection program. Aren't you glad you took this course so seriously?

Selection is more closely related to recruitment than it is to other HR functions, because both recruitment and selection are concerned with placing individuals into jobs. We define recruitment as those organizational activities that influence the number and types of individuals who apply for a position (such as choosing recruiting sources, developing what will be stated in recruitment ads, and deciding how much money will be spent). These same organizational activities also affect applicants' decisions about whether or not to accept a job offer.[1] We use this definition because it is important to think not only about attracting appropriate people for open positions, but also about increasing the probability that those people will accept a position if one is offered. It is senseless to motivate people to apply and then turn them off when they do—but we all know this happens. Although firms can engage in both internal and external recruitment, our focus is on external recruitment. That is, our interest is those potential job applicants who are not currently employed by the recruiting organization.

Sara Rynes, in an extensive review of recruitment, describes the relationship between recruitment and selection.[2] At the very least, the selection requirements of a firm affect both the recruitment sources used and some of the specific information about the organization and position openings that are included in the recruitment message. For example, an HR manager's position in a unionized manufacturing plant may require applicants to know about Equal Employment Opportunity laws, the interpretation of union contracts, and employee benefit plans. These requirements could limit recruitment sources to law schools, industrial relations programs, and human resource programs. In a reverse example, the applicant pool serves as a limiting factor in selection. If this pool consists of applicants inappropriate for the position, the probability that selection will identify superior workers is low. In the following, we summarize some of the major characteristics of a recruitment program to indicate its critical importance to selection.

Purposes of Recruitment

Recruitment has three major purposes:

1. To develop an appropriate number of minimally acceptable applicants for each open position while keeping costs reasonable.

2. To meet the organization's legal and social obligations regarding the demographic composition of its workforce.

3. To help increase the success rate of the selection process by reducing the percentage of applicants who are either poorly qualified or who have the wrong KSAs (knowledge, skills, and abilities) for the recruiting organization.

Referring to the first purpose, it has been demonstrated that the value of selection to an organization increases as the pool of qualified applicants grows. Essentially, a larger pool of qualified applicants means that there are more appropriate applicants for the same number of positions. We can be more selective in filling position openings, and if we are using job-related selection procedures, our new employees should, on average, demonstrate value to the firm. (Of course, we assume that if we offer applicants a position, they will accept, that we can provide proper training and equipment, and that we can retain these employees.) A viable selection program, therefore, has an excellent probability of identifying well-qualified individuals. On the other hand, if the recruitment program produces only a small number of applicants relative to the number of available positions, then rather than *selection,* the situation approaches what we have referred to as *hiring*. (In other words, if applicants can "fog a mirror placed under their nose," hire 'em!)

Earlier, we discussed the various laws and directives that are part of the second purpose of recruitment. An organization's compliance with such laws and directives has often been judged by the demographic characteristics of those recruited and selected. The demographic characteristics of those selected are directly related to the characteristics of the applicant pool. If the recruitment program does not provide a demographically balanced set of applicants, it is unlikely that the selection program will produce a demographically balanced set of hires.

The third purpose of recruitment refers to the costs of selection. Attracting and processing applicants can be expensive. Expenses such as staff time, recruitment materials, travel and related per diem costs for both applicants and recruiters, and physical facilities are incurred by most organizations. If the recruitment program produces applicants who do not match the requirements of open positions, the results can be disastrous (for example, poor job performance, absenteeism, early voluntary turnover). Money spent on evaluating unsuitable candidates is wasted. Moreover, the extra time needed for continued personnel recruitment and selection is an added cost to the organization.

Our point regarding wasted recruitment dollars is illustrated by an actual incident involving one of your authors who was working in the Department of Management at a southern university located in a small, rural town. Years ago, prior to the World Wide Web and other high-tech recruitment methods, we advertised an assistant professor position in labor relations. The ad, which basically described the position (course load) but not the community where the university is located, appeared in a printed academic placement document, sponsored by a professional organization, along with other open positions in university management departments. That document was mailed to members of the Academy of Management (the professional organization to which many management doctoral students and faculty members belong). Academy members interested in available academic positions read the placement document and use the information presented in deciding whether to apply.

After our ad appeared, our department head received an application letter and an accompanying resume from a doctoral student (we will call him "Stanley") just finishing his Ph.D. at a prestigious Ivy League university. The department head liked what he saw on the applicant's resume and invited him to the university for an interview. Four of us (all newly minted assistant professors) got into a car and drove roughly 30 miles to pick up Stanley at the airport in a nearby city. As we left the airport and drove toward the university community, Stanley remarked, "The smallest city I've ever lived in is Washington, D.C.; the smallest city my wife has ever lived in is Cincinnati." For a moment, we four "recruiters" got quiet and looked at each other. A few miles later, Stanley asked about our town's public transportation system. He didn't have a driver's license. The only public transportation we knew about was a vehicle, seating about 10 people, that shuttled between our rural community and a similar one adjoining ours. Some would ride our "public transportation system" to get to work in the other community. One of us muttered, "We really don't have much of a public transportation system." By this time, as you can imagine, several of us were uncomfortable and beginning to squirm. About five miles from our university's city limits, Stanley queried us further. "Can you tell me something about the local synagogue?" Not only did we not have a public transportation system, but we did not have a synagogue. Finally, as we entered and drove through the middle of town to a guest house where Stanley was staying, he said, "I thought you were going to drive me through the center of town?" Our driver replied, "We just did!" Later that evening, the four of us discussed the evening's "events." The next morning when we picked him up for his job interviews, one member of our group asked Stanley, "How did things go last night at the guest house?" Stanley replied, "I read the telephone directory." At that point, the most senior person in our recruitment group said, "Stanley, I don't think we're going to have what you are looking for. Why don't you sit back, relax, and experience a two-day tour of a southern town and university." And, that's basically how the two-day "interview" went. In essence, we provided a $1,000 "visit" for Stanley (back then, $1,000 was BIG money), but we did not produce a viable applicant. In addition to being professionally embarrassing (in our eyes, anyway), our recruitment dollars were wasted.

We can imagine that after reading the incident above, you are probably smiling, and asking "Couldn't you have avoided all of this by simply planning and properly designing your recruitment program and by communicating relevant community information to job candidates?" Obviously, you are correct, but we didn't; we learned a lesson the expensive way.[3]

Given the close interrelationship between recruitment and selection, you are probably ready to ask us, "What is the best way to carry out recruiting so that it meets our objectives and helps selection?" In response, we say to you, "That's a difficult question; why don't you ask your instructor?" The reality is that many of the processes of recruitment are only partially understood. HR professionals have described anecdotal recruiting practices, but limited objective research is available on "what works." Although the amount of such research is certainly increasing, some recruitment-related issues are unresolved; there are few definitive research findings about many of the actions that organizations should take. Let's learn a bit more about recruitment and see what we can do to avoid recruitment mistakes such as the incident involving Stanley detailed earlier.

Conflicts Between Recruitment and Selection Objectives

Motivated job seekers attempting to attract the interest of organizations often engage in a number of "impression management" activities—that is, those actions applicants take to make themselves appear attractive to recruiting organizations. Some of these activities are mundane, such as getting a haircut or buying a new suit prior to a job interview. Other impression management activities, however, more directly conflict with what recruiting organizations need to know about applicants in order to make good selection decisions. For example, some applicants exaggerate previous job titles, responsibilities, and achievements on their resumes. Others, knowing there is "no way" they could live in certain regions of the United States respond "Open" when asked on a pre-employment screening application whether they have a geographical preference.

Like many applicants, some organizations use impression management tactics in conducting their recruitment activities. They may imply that applicants will be on a career "fast-track" or show pictures in employment brochures only of the most desirable company locations. In one case involving a nationally prominent accounting firm, the firm's recruitment Web site presents a series of employee interviews describing what a typical work day is like. One young woman living in California describes her typical work day as beginning with time devoted to surfing prior to office hours. She gives the impression that one has plenty of freedom and control over how one's time will be spent. Although many of us are not surfers, her description of a typical work day certainly has appeal. But realistically, how likely is it that work-time options such as she describes will present themselves to most new college graduates considering an accounting job with the firm?

Again, the motivation of most organizations is to create a favorable impression among job seekers. Just as applicants would like to receive numerous offers of quality job opportunities, organizations would like to choose from numerous highly qualified applicants for their position openings. Thus, both applicants and organizations have incentives to present their best qualities to attract one another. Negative information is viewed by many as lowering the attractiveness of organizations to applicants and as lowering the attractiveness of applicants to organizations. Yet, in order for the selection system to work both groups must know what the other is *really* like. These attraction-selection objectives sought by both job seekers and recruiting organizations often lead to conflicts. These conflicts, in turn, can have dysfunctional consequences for both individuals and organizations because they affect the quality of information upon which selection decisions are based (selection decisions on the part of both organizations *and* applicants). Such dysfunctional consequences can include job dissatisfaction, absenteeism, lowered job performance, early voluntary turnover, and employee termination.

Based on the work of Lyman Porter and his colleagues, Figure 8.1 summarizes four conflicts that can arise when job seekers are attempting to attract recruiting organizations, and recruiting organizations are attempting to attract job seekers.[4] For our needs in this chapter, two of these conflicts (**A** and **D**) are probably less important than the other two. Conflict **A** suggests that applicants might avoid gathering certain information they would like to obtain for selecting organizations. For example, individuals might decide not to ask about pay or benefits during an initial interview for fear the organization will find such questions "unattractive." Yet individuals need that information to decide whether a particular company is suitable. Conflict **D** indicates the conflicting objectives between organization activities involving attracting and selecting individuals. For example, employers might mix recruiting activities with structured selection interviews even though research suggests recruitment activities be kept separate from selection interviews. Because organizations might fear structured selection interviews will be seen by applicants as a "test," employers conduct recruiting activities during selection interviews,

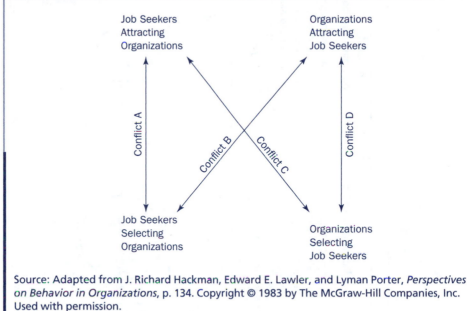

FIGURE 8.1 Conflicts Between Organizations and Job Seekers

Source: Adapted from J. Richard Hackman, Edward E. Lawler, and Lyman Porter, *Perspectives on Behavior in Organizations*, p. 134. Copyright © 1983 by The McGraw-Hill Companies, Inc. Used with permission.

making the organization more attractive to applicants. However, the interview information they collect might not be as valid as information they could have obtained had they used the interview time for selection purposes.

Conflict **B** describes a situation alluded to earlier; that is, individuals need accurate information from organizations in order to select employers with whom they fit. However, some organizations accentuate only the positive aspects of jobs and the organization in order to remain attractive. When expectations communicated by organizations' recruiting activities do not comport with reality, dysfunctional consequences are likely. Much of this chapter deals with issues relevant to Conflict **B**.

Finally, Conflict **C** taps into the issue regarding the accuracy of information organizations need about individuals in order to select them. However, some job seekers engage in activities to make themselves look more attractive, such as falsifying educational information on a resume. Thus a conflict ensues between job seekers trying to attract organizations and organizations needing accurate information in order to choose among applicants. Many of our chapters on selection procedures confront the issue about how employers can use selection procedures to produce valid information for more productive selection decision-making.

Planning and Executing Recruitment by the Organization

James Breaugh and Mary Starke have described a model of the recruitment process. We have adapted their model for our purposes and summarized some of the major components of it in Figure 8.2.[5] In this chapter, we use Figure 8.2 as a framework to (a) identify issues that recruitment managers should consider when developing a recruitment program, (b) summarize some of what is known from recruitment research that managers might consider for recruitment program implementation, and (c) emphasize that the recruitment process has a strong impact on the selection process. We rely principally

FIGURE 8.2   The Recruitment Process and Interplay with Selection

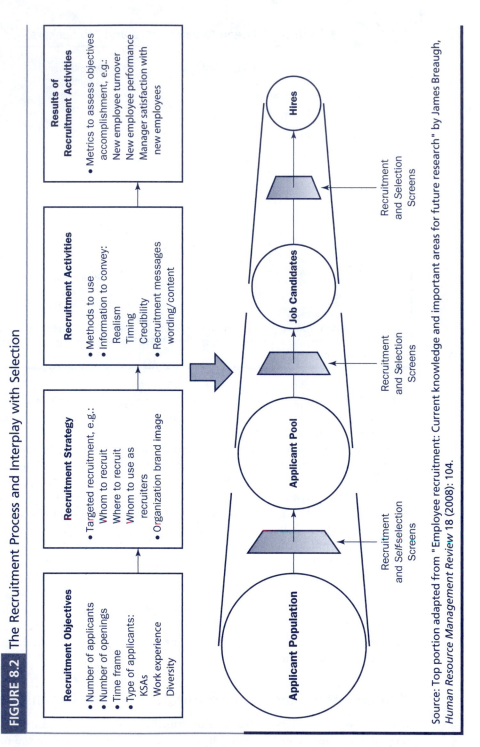

Recruitment Objectives

- Number of applicants
- Number of openings
- Time frame
- Type of applicants:
  KSAs
  Work experience
  Diversity

Recruitment Strategy

- Targeted recruitment, e.g.:
  Whom to recruit
  Where to recruit
  Whom to use as
  recruiters
- Organization brand image

Recruitment Activities

- Methods to use
- Information to convey:
  Realism
  Timing
  Credibility
- Recruitment messages
  wording/content

**Results of
Recruitment Activities**

- Metrics to assess objectives
  accomplishment, e.g.:
  New employee turnover
  New employee performance
  Manager satisfaction with
  new employees

Applicant Population

Recruitment
and *Self*-Selection
Screens

Applicant Pool

Recruitment
and Selection
Screens

Job Candidates

Recruitment
and Selection
Screens

Hires

Source: Top portion adapted from "Employee recruitment: Current knowledge and important areas for future research" by James Breaugh, *Human Resource Management Review* 18 (2008): 104.

on several reviews of the research literature on recruitment.[6] If you want more details regarding what is known about the effects of various recruitment actions, please read these reviews. Note that we discuss the issues in Figure 8.2 as if they were discrete events. In reality, many of the topics listed in the figure necessarily overlap and interact dynamically with one another. For example, a firm's recruitment objectives affect the types of strategies it should adopt.

1. Recruitment Objectives

First, an organization should start its recruitment efforts by specifying its objectives: How many individuals does it want to attract for how many positions? With what KSAs, competencies, experience, or other characteristics? With what demographic diversity? When should these positions be filled? Answers to these questions should control the actions taken by the firm. Often recruitment starts with the general objective of attracting as many people as possible with as little cost as possible. However, such a general objective does not provide much guidance for implementing recruitment; it can lead to increased costs during recruitment and selection and even discourage highly talented people. Thus, the recruitment objectives that are set serve as an important basis for determining the nature of the "screens" (including both self-selection and selection procedures) we want to use in narrowing the potential applicant population to an appropriate applicant pool.

Look again at Figure 8.2. By *potential applicant population* we mean all individuals who could possibly have an interest in an open position and who might consider applying for a position opening. These individuals have not yet decided to apply for a position and might choose not to do so. The *applicant pool* is a subset of the potential applicant population, those who have chosen to apply for a position; they might not accept a position offer if one were made. Recruitment screens (for example, a video on a company recruitment Web site showing what activities a job incumbent performs; comments made by an employee about an employer) serve as applicant "self-selection screens." They help potential applicants decide whether to move into or out of the applicant pool. In that sense, self-selection screens, in contrast to selection procedures, play a dominant role early in the recruitment process. As you will read in the following sections, recruitment screens can take a variety of forms; they play an important role in both the recruitment *and* selection processes and they occur at different points in these processes. When meaningful recruitment screens are tied to requisite KSAs, worker competencies, or other job-related characteristics, the ratio of minimally qualified applicants to all applicants should be enhanced. These initial recruitment screens, along with others that occur during the recruitment process, help determine who is eventually hired (and, perhaps, even who stays or succeeds in the organization). Carefully considering issues such as the content, use, timing, type, and media for communicating these screens can reduce recruiting costs considerably; time and other resources will not be allocated to undesirable applicants who are unlikely to succeed with the firm. By ensuring, wherever possible, that all recruitment screens are indeed job related or have a justified business need, employers will be in a better position to (a) select from among high-quality candidates and (b) successfully defend themselves if an employment discrimination suit were filed.

2. Recruitment Strategy

The second part of the recruiting process is deciding on a strategy for reaching these objectives. A strategy is the plan for choosing which recruitment activities the organization will use (for example, using a business social network such as WWW.Linkedin.com, visiting college campuses, writing recruitment ads, building a recruitment Web site), when/how these activities will be done, whom to use as recruiters, and what theme or message to convey. Careful consideration must be given to the strategy to achieve the previously defined recruitment objectives. For example, a firm with a favorable reputation (for example, SAS, Inc., #1 in *Fortune's* 2010 "Best Companies to Work For" with 100 applications for each position opening[7]) might emphasize reputation in its chosen recruitment media because firm reputation is associated with increased numbers of applicants.[8] A firm such as Wal-Mart or McDonald's might selectively target certain groups, for example older applicants, in order to reduce turnover among service personnel. Organizational recruitment practices aimed at affecting specific types of individuals who are willing to apply or accept a position if offered is referred to as *targeted recruiting*.[9] Targeted recruiting is aimed at groups such as those defined by certain demographic (race, gender) or psychological characteristics (personality, mental ability). Such a strategy can be used to enhance the diversity of a firm's applicant pool. Often, this strategy is used to address potential problems regarding adverse impact in selection, which can arise due to the use of certain selection procedures (for example, a mental ability test). Targeted recruiting designed to minimize adverse impact arising from the use of such selection procedures is generally legally defensible. For example, the *Uniform Guidelines on Employee Selection Procedures* focus mainly on *selection* procedures, not as much on recruitment procedures. The *Uniform Guidelines* recognize that targeted selection is often necessary.[10]

As another aspect of a firm's recruitment strategy, consider the role of *organizational branding*. Employers and researchers alike have recognized that job applicants' reactions to early recruitment activities frequently affect their initial organizational perceptions; these, in turn, influence their job acceptance offers. *Organizational branding* is one part of a recruitment strategy that organizations can use to positively influence job applicants' early organizational perceptions.[11] Derived from the field of product branding in marketing, organizational branding suggests that companies can influence applicants' decisions by creating a favorable and unique organizational brand or image.[12] A positive organizational brand image affects the kinds of inferences that potential job applicants make and influences their initial attraction to potential employers.[13] Applicants use these images to distinguish among organizations and in making application and job choice decisions. Research has shown that organizational image attributions explain applicants' attraction to recruiting organizations beyond specific job and organizational characteristics (for example, employee benefits).[14]

One means organizations can use to manage image is by tailoring their recruitment strategies and methods to communicate the kind of brand or image they wish to portray to applicants. Recruiting organizations should carefully consider the exact nature of their recruitment strategy as well as the design of recruitment media such as Web sites; media can influence applicants' perceptions of an employer's organizational culture.[15] For example, organizations wishing to convey a culture of teamwork would use different images and messages than would organizations wishing to convey a culture of diversity, high achievement, high energy, and high rewards. As another example, job seekers viewing technically advanced recruitment Web sites (those including the use of video, audio, color, and graphics) tend to perceive such organizations as more technologically advanced than organizations without such sites.[16]

Where to recruit is another issue in recruitment strategy development. Depending on other aspects of a firm's recruitment strategy, targeting a specific recruiting message can be very important. For example, to enhance racial diversity among technically trained job applicants, a company might target engineering programs at historically black colleges and universities or the National Society of Black Engineers. To attract conscientious and intelligent job applicants, a company can target specific groups of university students such as those in Phi Beta Kappa or on Dean's or President's lists.

3. Recruitment Activities

The third portion of the recruitment process involves key components of recruiting that a firm must consider and implement. These include (a) recruitment sources (how potential applicants are reached), (b) recruitment personnel (who does the recruiting), (c) content of the recruitment message (what information is presented), and (d) administration of recruitment (when activities are done).

Recruitment sources.   Some of the major sources of recruitment are presented in Table 8.1. These vary by a number of important characteristics that affect how organizations use these sources. One characteristic is *cost* of use. Generally speaking, employee referral sources and advertising, especially when only local media are used, are relatively inexpensive, meaning that cost per person contacted is usually low. Sources that require a good deal of travel and personnel time, such as college recruiting, are much more expensive.

Another important characteristic is the *amount of information that can be presented* to potential applicants. The cost of television and newspapers is a direct function of the timing, geographical coverage, and length of the recruitment message. Most companies restrict the amount of information provided in these sources, even though it is possible to provide much more. College recruitment is usually quite expensive—because of the recruiters' travel expenses and because each recruiter usually contacts only 8 to 12 applicants each day. Use of company recruitment Web sites, corporate links on social networking sites (such as Facebook, MySpace, Twitter), and current employees making referrals are often more cost-effective recruiting approaches.

A third factor is the *predictability of the number of applicants.* It is commonly thought that advertising and employment agencies are less consistent in both the numbers and qualifications of applicants generated than are sources more directly under the control of the organization, such as school recruiting and employee referral. Variability in the numbers recruited can be caused by factors such as time of year, general economic and employment conditions, amount and intensity of competitors' recruiting efforts, applicants' perceptions about the specific media or agencies used, and the recruiting organization itself. A major part of the design of recruitment programs and the implementation of the recruitment strategy is deciding which combination of recruiting sources to use for specific jobs.

One obvious question about recruitment sources that we know you are thinking about is, "What are the differences in results among recruitment sources?" Much research has been done to investigate differences, and differences have been found.[17] However, the results have not been consistent across studies. In part, this lack of consistent findings occurred because firms often use more than one recruitment source and it is not possible to isolate the effects of any single source. However, James Breaugh identified three studies that used job applicants, collected data on specific recruiting methods, and involved only one employer.[18] In general, companies that obtained applicants from employee referrals and received unsolicited applications tended to yield more applicants and hires. Explanations for these differences include the realistic information hypothesis (some methods such as employee referrals provide more accurate information about a job) and the individual difference hypothesis (different recruitment sources bring information on a job opening to different types of people who differ on key characteristics).[19]

In terms of voluntary turnover among new hires, a recent study helped clarify why conflicting results have been found among some types of recruiting sources.[20] Ingo Weller and associates theorized that when applicants gather information about jobs they tend to weigh information obtained from more personal recruitment sources (referrals from current employees, family, or friends; rehires) more heavily than that obtained from more formal sources (newspaper ads, employment agencies). Informal, more personal recruitment source information is valued by potential applicants because personal sources are thought

TABLE 8.1	Characteristics of Recruitment Sources

Recruitment Source	Cost	Amount of Information Given	Predictability Number of Applicants	Internal/ External Recruitment Source	Principally Used for Professional Positions	Principally Used for Non-professional Positions
Advertisements:						
Local newspapers	Moderate	Little	Low	External		√
National newspapers	High	Little	Low	External	√	
Trade publications/ magazines	Moderate	Little	Low	External	√	
Television or radio	High	Little	Low	External		√
Agencies and Organizations:						
Targeted minority recruiting	Moderate	Little	Low	External	√	
Private employment agencies	Moderate	Little	Low	External		√
State employment agencies	Low	Little	Low	External		√
Temporary help agencies	Moderate	Little	Low	External		√
Universities	Moderate	Moderate	Low	External	√	
Community organization partnerships	Low	Little	Low	External		√
Technical/community college	Low	Moderate	Low	External		√
Search firms	High	Little	Low	External	√	
Job fairs	Moderate	Little	Low	External	√	√
Professional Associations:						
Professional conferences	Moderate	Little	Low	External	√	
Professional organizations	Low	Little	Low	External	√	
Inside Organization Resources:						
Previous employees	Moderate	High	Low	Internal	√	
Employee referrals	Low	Moderate	Moderate	Internal		√
Job posting to current employees	Low	High	Moderate	Internal		√
Company Web sites	Low	High	Moderate	External	√	
Internships	Low	High	Moderate	Internal	√	
Other Sources:						
Online job boards	Low	Moderate	Low	External	√	
Walk-ins/unsolicited resumes	Low	Moderate	Low	External	√	√
Word-of-mouth	Low	Little	Low	External		√
Retiree job bank	Low	Little	Low	External		√

to provide more accurate and complete information about jobs and employers. Better information received by applicants leads them to perceive better personal outcomes if hired (better fit with the organization; higher quality of job held). Weller and colleagues reasoned that voluntary turnover should be lower for those individuals relying on personal recruitment sources than those relying on formal sources. However, these personal *vs.* formal recruitment source differences in voluntary turnover rates were predicted to diminish over time. They reasoned that individuals new to an organization seek information in a very deliberate manner when uncertainty is highest (that is, early in new employees' tenure). Better quality information obtained from personal sources gives individuals a better picture of what to expect from a new job. Over time, however, as individuals become more knowledgeable about their jobs, differences in turnover rates between personal recruitment sources and formal recruitment sources were expected to diminish.

To examine their expectations, they collected data on more than 2,700 individuals over a nine-year period to test for the effects of recruitment source differences on employee turnover. After studying turnover rates for two types of recruitment source (personal *vs.* formal sources), they found roughly 25 percent less turnover among employees relying on personal recruitment sources for employment information versus those relying on formal sources. This pattern was particularly evident during the first 24 months of employment, when voluntary turnover was particularly high. They concluded that use of personal recruitment sources is beneficial for those firms experiencing high turnover rates during the first 24 months of new hires' careers. For example, when Weller and colleagues computed the impact of personal recruitment sources (versus formal sources) on voluntary turnover in large national franchise operations such as in the fast-food industry (for example, Taco Bell; Burger King), they estimated a $20,000,000 savings in turnover-related costs.[21]

The take-away point regarding recruitment sources seems to be this: use informal, personal recruitment sources where voluntary turnover is a problem during employees' first two years of employment. There is a cautionary note, however. Although we are unaware of any recent research, past evidence has indicated that minorities, perhaps because of historic employment patterns in many industries, use formal recruitment sources more frequently than informal ones.[22] If this is the case, employers overemphasizing personal recruitment sources over formal ones might reduce the number of minority applicants in their applicant pools.

A related point about personal recruitment sources is that word-of-mouth information about jobs and employers has also been identified as an important source of recruits. Word-of-mouth recruitment involves personal communication about an employer, independent of the employer, that is received by a potential job applicant. Research has demonstrated that potential applicants receiving positive word-of-mouth information about an employer early in the recruitment process tend to view that employer as more attractive and are more likely to submit an employment application.[23] Word-of-mouth recruitment information is particularly important when the recruit has close ties with the individual (a personal friend) providing positive employer information. For this reason, organizations might broaden their recruitment activities to include potential applicants' family and friends—sponsoring "refer-a-friend" programs for vacant positions on a recruitment Web site; ensuring that a company's employees have complete information about vacant positions, and rewarding employee referrals.[24] Organizations must be careful that word-of-mouth recruiting does not lead to minority underrepresentation in applicant pools. Table 8.2 summarizes some general guidelines on how employers can avoid discrimination against protected groups in their recruitment activities.

Understanding how individuals process information from recruitment sources is as important as tracing the effectiveness of separate sources of recruitment. Christopher Collins and Cynthia Stevens found that recruitment sources interacted with one another.[25] These sources affected two perceptions of potential applicants: general company image and specific job attributes. These perceptions, in turn, were related to applicants' intention to apply for a job. One conclusion that can be drawn is that recruitment sources should complement one another. For example, if a company wishes to emphasize in its recruitment process its goal of furthering the career development of employees, then its recruitment sources should emphasize this theme (using different examples and wording, as appropriate). This strategy helps to incorporate some of the principles behind organizational branding that we mentioned earlier.

TABLE 8.2	How Can Employers Avoid Discrimination When Recruiting?

> **EEOC General Guideline:** It is illegal for an employer to recruit new employees in a way that discriminates against them because of their race, color, religion, sex (including pregnancy), national origin, age (40 or older), disability, or genetic information.

- **When Writing Job Advertisements:** Generally, employers should not express a preference for a protected group characteristic, e.g., race, in job advertisements (including newspapers, Web sites, or other media). Employers can indicate that they are "equal opportunity employers."

- **When Using Employment Agencies:** Employment agencies may not honor employer requests to avoid referring applicants in a protected group. If they do so, both the employer and the employment agency that honored the request will be liable for discrimination.

- **When Using Word-of-Mouth Employee Referrals:** Word-of-mouth recruitment is the practice of using current employees to spread information concerning job vacancies to their family, friends, and acquaintances. Unless the workforce is racially and ethnically diverse, exclusive reliance on word-of-mouth should be avoided because it is likely to create a barrier to equal employment opportunity for certain protected groups that are not already represented in the employer's workforce. For example, an employer's reliance on word-of-mouth recruitment by its mostly Hispanic workforce may violate the law if the result is that almost all new hires are Hispanic.

- **When Using Homogeneous Recruitment Sources:** Employers should attempt to recruit from diverse sources in order to obtain a diverse applicant pool. For example, if the employer's primary recruitment source is a college that has few African-American students, the employer should adopt other recruitment strategies, such as also recruiting at predominantly African-American colleges, to ensure that its applicant pool reflects the diversity of the qualified labor force.

Sources: http://eeoc.gov/laws/practices/index.cfm and http://www.eeoc.gov/policy/docs/qanda_race_color.html

The World Wide Web is the source of recruiting that has become the most dominant medium in recent years. It is relatively inexpensive, allows for the presentation of large amounts of information, and can be accessed by individuals at any time and in almost any place. Some research has reported savings of up to 90 percent of the costs associated with traditional recruiting methods and 25 percent reductions in time in the hiring cycle.[26]

Companies can use the Web in a number of ways for recruiting. Some of the more popular ways include

- posting jobs on a company's home page

- posting jobs on Web sites devoted to job announcements (WWW.Monster.com; WWW.CareerBuilder.com)

- posting links on social networking Web sites (WWW.Twitter.com; WWW.Facebook.com; WWW.YouTube.com) to a recruiting company's corporate Web sites (see, for example, Developmental Dimensions International (DDI®) corporate Web site at WWW.DDI.com)

- screening for applicants using available search options on business social networks such as WWW.Linkedin.com (approximately 2,000,000 professionals join Linkedin each month; Boolean search terms and phrases can be used with keywords, job titles, current and past company employers, and geographic location fields to find both passive and active applicants); training/consultation on the use of Linkedin for recruitment purposes is available on the Web site[27]

- searching for candidates in materials posted on Web sites (other companies' employee listings, member lists of associations, online news articles)

Popular press writings about using the Web for recruiting discuss several actions leading to best results.[28] These actions include the following:

- Use individuals who know your firm to refer applicants—All firms have both current employees and past employees who have left the firm but are still positive toward it. These individuals can be sources for referrals of new employees. Keeping current with ex-employees' e-mail addresses is the biggest challenge for this activity.

- Develop a recruiting Web site—Most companies have home Web sites. Some have effective recruiting or career center links to their site. A recruiting Web site that is properly constructed (for example, making use of color, video, and audio) and easy to access and navigate can provide many well-qualified applicants. Such a Web site should display much more than minimal information about open positions. For example, a description of company culture, statements by existing workers at all levels, success stories of individual workers or teams, a discussion of advancement/career development opportunities, a philosophy of employee rights and treatment, and a demographic summary of employees can all be used to present an inviting message to those that inquire.

- Organizations using a recruiting Web site might specifically consider using employee testimonials on the Web site itself. Jack Walker and his associates reported that video-with-audio employee testimonials (*vs.* those presented with an employee picture and text *vs.* no testimonials presented) included on an organization's Web site were particularly beneficial. Testimonials delivered via video and audio had higher organizational attractiveness and information credibility ratings among Web site viewers than those given via picture with text.[29] Finally, with regard to taking job applications via a corporate recruiting Web site, applicants' perceptions of the efficiency and user-friendliness of the Web site is an important characteristic associated with applicant satisfaction.[30]

- Find active candidates—There are more than 50,000 active job boards populated by job candidates actively seeking employment. These range from very large boards with several hundred thousand applicants at any one time to niche boards that specialize in particular industries, occupations, or jobs. Although time consuming, it is beneficial to learn about the various boards and the profiles and general skill levels of the typical applicants appearing on these boards. This knowledge can be used for targeting the search to those job boards that are the best matches for finding the desired employees. WWW.Monster.com; WWW.CareerBuilder.com; and WWW.Datafrenzy.com are examples of such boards.

- Find passive candidates—Passive job candidates are those individuals, usually employed by another firm, who are not actively seeking a job. However, they often possess certain KSAs that are desirable to a potential employer. It's possible to find much electronic information about individuals who are employed by other firms. These people are not actively seeking another position, but often respond positively to being approached for new employment. This is the tactic that executive search firms or "headhunters" have traditionally used. Many search firms build listings of individuals in particular positions throughout the world and use these listings when the search firm is employed to find executives for open positions. Lists of potential applicants (passive candidates) can be built using information found on companies' Web sites, in news stories, on professional association membership rolls, and on meeting or convention registration and speaker lists.

- A more efficient way to identify candidates is to use a Web site such as WWW. Linkedin.com. This particular site is best described as a business social networking site. It is not like a social networking site such as MySpace, a more personal option. By using options available on the Linkedin Web site, recruiters can access a vast database to identify passive job candidates. One small anecdotal survey of 40 employers in the United Kingdom showed that more than 8 out of 10 employers used Linkedin for recruitment purposes; roughly 6 of 10 used Facebook. Less than half of the employers used any of the other social networking options (MySpace, Twitter, or Blogs).[31]

- According to anecdotal evidence, Nike has successfully used Internet-recruiting strategies in recruiting its European sales force, both in terms of attracting qualified applicants and in reducing its recruiting costs by approximately 50 percent.[32] Similarly, Xerox developed a Web-recruiting vehicle for its European sales force. Reportedly, the Web site annually receives more than 100,000 contacts for 2,000 open positions. Applicants are supplied job and organization information; applications are sourced to appropriate administrative units; and some initial evaluation of applicants' KSAs is done.[33]

- Another way to identify passive candidates with the desired qualifications is to use Internet data mining methods. Jean Phillips and Stanley Gully[34] describe three methods. The first of these is to use *Boolean search terms and statements* to search for individuals possessing certain characteristics (for example, those living in Chicago with a degree in human resource management). These Boolean search terms can be used with Web sites such as WWW.Infoseek.com, WWW.HotBot.com, and WWW.AltaVista.com. A second method is *flip searching,* which identifies people who visit a specific Web site. However, flip searching can raise ethical issues for the user. Finally, Web sites such as WWW.ZoomInfo.com use *Web crawlers* to collect and store information about people having specific talent qualifications and characteristics. These sites sell access to their talent databases.

Very little research has been done on the effectiveness of Web recruiting, but empirical research is beginning to appear. One study developed a Web site for a fictitious company including information about the company, the company's open positions, and company values. The Web site also provided feedback to applicants about their fit with the organization. (One of the proposed advantages of Web recruiting is the low cost of providing such information.) Results of this study indicated that the feedback information about applicants' potential fit with the organization generally influenced their attraction to the firm.[35] Another study using a Web site for a fictitious company manipulated the demographic diversity shown in various scenes on the site. White viewers were not affected by the diversity shown in the ad. Black viewers were attracted by ad diversity, but only when it included supervisory-level positions. Viewer reactions were also related to viewers' openness to racial diversity.[36] We conclude that Web-recruiting can be a more effective and less costly recruiting source than almost all others.

It's important to consider several factors when determining what recruitment sources to use: (a) costs associated with various recruitment sources, (b) nature of the job being recruited, (c) image of the company in the external labor market, (d) attitudes of current employees, and (e) demographic mix of applicants being sought.

Recruitment costs are a key consideration. In general, Web-based recruitment methods tend to yield the greatest return on investment. Recruiting for complex jobs requires providing detailed information about the job, the company, and selection qualifications.

This kind of detailed information can be given best by recruiters or a Web site. A strong, positive image of the organization is related to individuals' willingness to apply for employment. Image can be strengthened by written and graphic brochures and by television, newspaper, and Internet advertisements.

The fourth factor to consider is worker attitudes, which affect the extent to which an organization can rely on worker referrals. Referrals can be an important recruitment source, but only if the employees are positive about their jobs and the company. All employee referrals are not equal. There is evidence to suggest that the performance level of individuals making a referral is associated with the quality of the persons referred.[37]

Various recruitment sources are better suited than others for reaching particular demographic groups that are sought by the organization. Some, such as the Hispanic Chamber of Commerce newsletters or electronic resources such as WWW.Hirediversity.com and WWW.Minorityjobs.net, focus on specific minority groups. Usually these contact vehicles will provide information about job openings as well as information on minority job candidates.

Recruitment personnel. Logically, recruiters should have an important influence on the attitudes and behavior of applicants; recruiters are usually the first real people applicants encounter after they get through the Web site, brochures, media ads, and broadcasts. Much research has been conducted on the effects recruiters have and the strength of these effects. The general conclusion is that recruiters do influence applicants, both positively and negatively, but that (surprise!) it is not crystal clear how this influence works.[38]

Research has examined the demographic characteristics, behaviors, personality, and training of recruiters to determine whether these characteristics affect the attitudes and behaviors of recruits (for example, their interest in the firm, whether they apply to the firm, or whether they accept job offers). The following is a brief summary of what has been concluded.[39]

- Recruiters usually influence the early opinions and behaviors of recruits. That is, recruiters affect applicants' decisions about whether to seek out more information or continue with recruitment. Recruiters have little effect upon recruits' actual decisions about whether to accept the job or not.

- Recruiters who have race and gender in common with applicants may have some influence on those applicants, but such influence is neither consistent nor strong.

- Job and organization characteristics have a stronger influence on recruits than do recruiters.

- The training of recruiters in interviewing and in the management of the social interaction of recruitment interviews is important.

- Often recruiters are seen as less trustworthy and credible than members of the intended work group, perhaps because they have less knowledge about work operations.

- Recruiters perceived as warm, enthusiastic, personable, and concerned are generally regarded favorably.

- Recruiters can have a strong, negative influence on applicants. This can cause applicants to discontinue pursuit of the firm.

- Recruiters vary in the way they mix the recruitment ("selling" of the firm) and selection (evaluation of the applicant) components of their applicant interviews. The best mix seems to be a combination. Heavy emphasis on recruitment is negatively regarded.

Derek Chapman and his fellow researchers have concluded that firms should select recruiters on the basis of personableness and other positive interpersonal behaviors and train them in interviewing and interpersonal conduct.[40] In the actual recruitment interview, recruiters should combine the process of describing the job and organization with a preliminary screening of the applicants' characteristics. In addition, they should explain the recruitment and selection process and address any questions or concerns the applicants have.

One limitation of much of the research on recruiter effects on applicants is that it is based on the initial impressions of college students interviewing for jobs at university placement centers. The generalizability of research based on well-educated, inexperienced college students to less-educated or more-experienced recruits in other recruitment contexts is unknown.[41] James Breaugh and his colleagues suggest that the conclusion that certain recruiter characteristics (for example, recruiter experience) makes little difference to recruits might be premature.[42] There are several reasons why different types of recruiters might matter, particularly for more experienced job applicants, than what has been reported in past studies. For one, recruiters often differ in the job-related information they have and can share with job applicants. Secondly, recruiters are likely to differ more in the eyes of different types of job applicants. Third, because of these differences, they are likely to convey different things to different job candidates. Thus, future research should consider the ways in which both recruiters and applicants differ when studying recruiter effects.

Content of the Recruitment Message.   An obvious consideration when designing recruitment programs is the effect on recruits of various kinds of information. Traditionally, recruitment programs have been regarded as an opportunity to sell the organization as a favorable place to work; the message has, therefore, been universally positive. Pay excellence, coworkers, physical facilities, advancement, benefits, and job challenge have been stressed. As we suggested in Figure 8.1, because no work situation is without negative aspects, such traditional messages can instill false expectations in recruits that cannot be fulfilled in actual employment.

Inflated expectations happen to some degree in most recruitment situations. Many now think that it is unproductive to create expectations in the applicant that cannot be fulfilled. Once employed, some individuals find the differences between their expectations and the actual job to be unpleasantly large. Such discrepancies can cause both dissatisfaction with the organization and rapid job turnover. Obviously, in such cases the whole cost of recruitment and selection must be repeated as other applicants are processed. In place of such unrealistic recruitment messages, some recruitment researchers have recommended a "Realistic Job Preview" (RJP).[43] In RJPs applicants are given the negative aspects of the job as well as the positive. For example, in a film for potential operators, Southern New England Telephone made clear that the work was closely supervised, repetitive, and sometimes required dealing with rude or unpleasant customers. In theory, such information should lead to a self-selection process whereby those candidates who regard these job aspects negatively remove themselves from further consideration. Those that remain make up a recruitment pool of individuals having fairly accurate expectations of job demands and characteristics.[44]

Although several studies have shown that a reduction in subsequent employee turnover is associated with the use of RJPs, the size of the reduction has usually been fairly small. Recently, the argument has been made that RJPs should be included throughout various parts of the recruitment process (that is, a multi-step RJP)—talks with recruiters, company visits, discussions with employees—rather than only through a designated film or brochure.[45] However, there is the possibility that applicants may think that such distinct, separate presentations mean that the company or job has too many major deficiencies. It has been found that some applicants with job choices are influenced by negative RJP information and choose instead the company with traditional recruitment messages.[46]

James Breaugh[47] attributes one research study of RJPs as having a detrimental effect on RJP research. In that study, the author generally showed minimal relationships between the use of RJPs and variables such as voluntary turnover and job satisfaction.[48] From Breaugh's identification of possible flaws in this research (for example, laboratory studies involving students, using studies where RJPs are provided to employees who have already started work, possibly incorporating participants who could not self-select out of the job in question) as well as research of his own, Breaugh concluded that RJPs can have powerful effects.[49] RJP positive effects are most likely to occur when an employment situation involves

- Applicants who have not formed an opinion about the job (if individuals have opinions, it is difficult for them to change their opinions)

- People who are able to accurately predict how they will react to the job based on characteristics presented in the RJP (that is, they have relevant experience with such job attributes)

- Individuals who have self-insight (that is, aware of their own abilities/interests) and know how they will react to job characteristics presented to them in the RJP[50]

All in all, RJPs seem to have a slightly positive relationship to job satisfaction and a slightly negative one to turnover. Historically, several studies have concluded that RJP relationships are not strong. Possibly, a firm should not view RJPs as more important than job characteristics or supervisory behavior in reducing turnover. Future research on RJPs, taking into account the variables that Breaugh has suggested and that we have mentioned, may reveal more powerful RJP effects than what some studies have found. But even if very strong effects are not found, perhaps it is more appropriate to view RJPs as "a right thing to do."[51] In other words, providing somewhat balanced information about the job and organization is the correct way of treating applicants.

Another important factor in the content of recruitment messages is the amount of specificity and detail in the message. Two factors are important, especially very early in the recruitment process: potential applicants' decision about whether to maintain interest in a firm based upon (a) their perceptions of a firm's image and (b) their familiarity with a firm.[52] This should not be surprising; during the early stage of recruitment, applicants often have little specific information about the job, salary, benefits, working conditions, or organizational characteristics. Therefore, applicants choosing the firms that they will pursue from among many possible firms must make this choice based upon general information and perceptions. A specific organizational image can favorably influence applicants' perceptions of the positions they are applying for and help them imagine the pride they would feel in becoming a member of the organization. In this sense, organizational image is like a brand image in marketing. By enhancing activities such as publicity and advertising, an employer can enhance organizational attractiveness among recruits, particularly among those making early contact with an organization. Such practices can influence both applicant quality and quantity.[53]

Even at later stages of recruitment, research has shown that specific, detailed information about an organization is viewed positively by applicants.[54] There is some evidence that applicants regard the amount and specificity of information to be a signal of the company's regard for employees. It has also been found that applicants, when presented with inadequate information, make inferences about the company from the company's statements about its size and industry—and transfer those inferences to other characteristics of the company and job.[55] However, the consequences stemming from such inferences (with regard to subsequent applicant behavior) are not consistent across individuals.

These general principles for the presentation of information at various stages in the recruitment process have traditionally been used for recruitment messages displayed in costly printed media. Use of the World Wide Web permits the inexpensive display of large quantities of information about the company and the job. No one really knows what applicants' reactions will be to the presentation of such detailed information early in the recruitment process. However, research has shown that job advertisements with more detailed information were seen as more attractive[56] and more credible.[57] Logical arguments can be made that such a presentation will enhance the image of the company, which, in turn, will influence many recruitment Web site viewers to become applicants.

With regard to recruiting message content, research by David Newman and Julie Lyon is quite interesting. Their experimental work indicated that using certain adjectives to describe a job and the company attracted applicants having a specific job-related personality and ability as well as demographic characteristic. From their results, they suggested that firms undertaking targeted recruiting to attract candidates from a racial minority or recruits who are conscientious and high in cognitive ability incorporate the following in their recruitment messages:

- To target applicants with high cognitive ability, describe the job or work environment using terms such as *challenging* and *stimulating; say* that the job requires *quick thinking, intelligence*, and *knowledge*.

- To attract those high in conscientiousness, message content should incorporate terms such as these to describe a desirable recruit: *reliable, works hard, well-organized, self-disciplined*, and *conscientious*.

- To attract racial minorities who are conscientious, message content should characterize companies as *innovative* and *progressive*.[58]

One caution, however, is that the recruitment message must accurately represent the true characteristics of the company and job. Otherwise, low job performance and employee attrition is likely to ensue.

From an overall recruitment perspective, they recommended that firms generally recruit applicants high in cognitive ability combined with recruiting racial minorities high in conscientiousness. They concluded that this particular strategy enhances average job performance among hires as well as the percentage of hires from racial minority groups. Of course, recruitment message content alone would not be the only strategy that a firm should use to recruit those possessing these desired attributes. Other actions should be used to supplement recruitment message content.

Administration of Recruitment. The small amount of research on recruitment administration indicates that the promptness of follow-up contacts with applicants between the various stages of recruitment is positively related to whether applicants stay in the recruitment pool.[59] Employers giving timely responses are associated with applicants' perceptions of an employer's organizational attractiveness.[60] Prompt responses by the company may indicate to the applicant that the company is efficient and, therefore, a desirable place to work—or that the applicant has very favorably impressed the company and has a good chance of getting a job offer. It is important to note that highly qualified applicants who have multiple job alternatives are most strongly affected by delays in communications with them.

No relationship between expenditures on recruiting (in the form of dinners, receptions, gifts, hotels, and so forth) and applicant response has been found.[61] However, ignoring such a strategy when competing firms in the same industry are doing it (as large accounting and consulting firms do) would probably not be a wise decision. Applicants' visits to the physical site of the organization is also an important component of recruiting effectiveness. Applicants note the importance of the people they meet, how they are treated by the people they meet, and the organization's professionalism.[62] Reactions to the job site visit have been found to be related to applicants' ultimate decision to accept the job.[63] Finally, some preliminary data suggest that increasing the information that an applicant must supply—for example, university transcripts, additional letters of reference, diplomas, or writing samples—reduces the number of applicants.[64] Such demands, however, have not produced any noticeable changes in the quality of applicants.

4. Results of Recruitment Activities

The last part of recruiting is to determine the results of recruiting: the number of people who applied, their skill levels, their diversity, the time it took to hire recruits, and how many actually became employed by the firm. Several metrics have been suggested for use in evaluating recruitment effectiveness. Among these are the following:[65]

- *New employee job performance*—Performance appraisal ratings for new employees 6–12 months after being hired

- *New employee turnover*—Percentage of employees who voluntarily leave the organization after 6–12 months of employment

- *Manager satisfaction with new employees*—Percentage of managers satisfied with new employees

- *New employee training success*—New employees' performance on training measures such as performance tests

- *Cost per hire*—Costs associated with hiring new employees; typically involves costs such as (a) internal costs such as employment/recruiting office salaries and benefits, staff members' travel, lodging and entertainment; (b) external costs such as lodging, entertainment, and other recruiters' salaries; (c) company visit expenses such as candidate travel, lodging, meals, interview expenses; and (d) direct fees such as advertising, Web site hosting, job fairs, agency search fees, cash awards for employee referrals

Usually, a series of recruitment metrics is necessary to get a more complete picture of recruitment effectiveness. These metrics can serve as a means for diagnosing and remedying problems in recruitment. For example, suppose a firm finds that it takes 94 days, on average, to hire for a position and that the average new employee stays 40 days. By enhancing recruitment materials and methods, improving application and other pre-screening procedures, refining the interview and other applicant selection methods, streamlining new employee orientation/training procedures, and altering compensation packages, the firm reduces the time-to-hire period to an average of 35 days. New hires now stay an average of 9 months. Such a needed change brought by an analysis of recruitment metrics can have a large financial impact on a firm. One recruitment metric by itself may have little value, but when viewed along with other metrics, they can serve an important diagonostic role, not only for recruitment but other HR functions as well. In sum, recruitment metrics can aid in determining whether a firm's recruitment strategy and execution are appropriate. If they are not, adjustments can be made in future recruiting efforts.

In addition to these metrics, employers should consider analyzing the recruitment Web site visitation patterns made by applicants—the time users spend on a Web site or an associated Web site link, the number of mouse clicks made during a visitation session, and visitors' associated navigation patterns. Results from these analytics can be used to improve Web site design. For example, if it were found that job applicants had to make too many mouse clicks to navigate through the recruitment Web site to submit an application, that information can be used to improve applicants' ease of navigating and using the Web site.

OTHER FACTORS AFFECTING THE ATTRACTION OF APPLICANTS

We have discussed that selection and recruitment are interrelated, and that organizations can structure the four parts of recruitment to help them meet their needs for new employees. However, recruitment is not the only activity that affects an organization's ability to attract potential employees. Sara Rynes and Alison Barber have pointed out some other important factors.[66] Among these are the inducements offered by the firm (for example, salary, benefits, child care, flexible work schedules, and career paths), the firm's targeted applicant pools (for example, education level, experience level, and applicant demographics such as age, gender, race, and ethnicity), external labor market conditions, and job and organizational characteristics. These authors clearly indicate that a firm's ability to attract candidates for employment depends on all of these factors rather than on recruitment practices alone. For example, a small business that pays minimum wage, has no benefits or child care arrangements, and does not offer training or a career path may have great difficulty attracting the candidates it desires. In the face of these other characteristics, changing only its recruitment practices may not alter the company's success in attracting and retaining desirable applicants.

SUMMARY RECOMMENDATIONS FOR ENHANCING RECRUITMENT

Listed below is a summary of the major issues and suggestions we have discussed for attracting applicants to organizations. Although our list is not exhaustive and, in some cases, we depend on anecdotal evidence, we believe that carefully implementing these recommendations will facilitate recruitment program effectiveness. Our recommendations are

1. Carefully consider the sometimes competing objectives of attracting *vs.* selecting job seekers; the ratio of qualified applicants applying per position opening is one measure. Selection procedure norms (preferably, local norms—see Chapter 2) and performance evaluations are examples of measures used for monitoring changes in applicant quality.

2. Identify specific objectives of a recruitment program—the number of positions to be filled, KSAs required for those positions, when positions should be filled.

3. Formulate a specific strategy for accomplishing recruitment program objectives.

4. Insure that recruitment screens (including *self*-selection screens) reflect the desired job-related characteristics of job candidates.

5. Identify who represents the potential applicant population; the relevant labor market likely mirrors that population.

6. Use targeted recruitment to identify underrepresented protected groups in an organization. Search recruitment Web sites targeting such underrepresented

groups and contact specific organizations representing such groups to find possible sources of applicants.

7. Develop a recruitment Web site that is attractive, easy to navigate, and easy to use for submitting application materials.

8. Incorporate color, pictures, audio, and video (for example, podcasts, employee testimonials) on a recruitment Web site; all narrative content on the site should be well written in an engaging style. Be sure all materials (including pictures and themes presented) accurately reflect the true nature of the organization.

9. For organizations using recruitment Web sites and receiving large numbers of resumes, consider using resume screening and applicant tracking software to manage the number of resumes that must be individually reviewed and applicant contacts that must be made. As a form of prescreening, consider incorporating applicant assessments (team orientation; personal fit with the recruiting organization) as part of the recruitment program.

10. Evaluate an organization's image being communicated by recruitment and related media. Insure that image is the desired organizational "brand."

11. Consider using recruitment Web sites for organizations searching for employees. If a recruitment Web site is used, establish links to it on popular social networking sites, particularly, WWW.Linkedin.com and WWW.MySpace.com

12. Encourage referrals of potential applicants from employees; particularly valuable are those individuals recommended by high-performing employees.

13. Recruiters can play an important role in attracting initial interest in organizations. Select them on characteristics associated with dealing with people; they should be enthusiastic, personable, and extraverted. At a minimum, train them in interviewing and managing social interactions in recruitment and on knowledge of work operations for those jobs being recruited.

14. Using technology to aid in recruiting is an asset; however, use more personal means of communications (for example, making telephone calls) to applicants who are particularly desirable. Stay in touch with desired applicants throughout the recruitment process.

15. Use realistic job previews (RJPs). Positive results are most likely to occur when (a) applicants have not formed an opinion of what a job is like; (b) applicants can predict how they will react to certain job characteristics presented in the RJP (for example, standing for an 8-hour day); and (c) applicants are aware of the KSAs they possess and their interests.

16. Finally, use metrics and other measures to evaluate recruitment programs and associated activities to identify "what works."

REFERENCES

1. Derek S. Chapman, Krista L. Uggerslev, Sarah A. Carroll, Kelly A. Piasentin, and David A. Jones, "Applicant Attraction to Organizations and Job Choice: A Meta-Analytic Review of the Correlates of Recruiting Outcomes," *Journal of Applied Psychology* 90 (2005): 928–944.

2. Sara L. Rynes, "Recruitment, Job Choice, and Post-Hire Consequences: A Call for New Research Directions," in *Handbook of Industrial and Organizational Psychology*, Vol. 3, 2nd ed.,

Marvin D. Dunnette and L. M. Hough (Palo Alto, CA: Consulting Psychologists Press, 1991).

3. We thank Achilles Armenakis, Bill Giles, and Art Bedeian for helping us recall the details of this incident.

4. J. Richard Hackman, Edward E. Lawler, and Lyman Porter, *Perspectives on Behavior in Organizations*. (New York: McGraw-Hill, 1983) 134.

5. James A. Breaugh and Mary Starke, "Research on Employee Recruitment: So Many Studies, So Many Remaining Questions," *Journal of Management* 26 (2000): 405–434.

6. James A. Breaugh, "Employee Recruitment: Current Knowledge and Important Areas for Future Research," *Human Resource Management Review* 18 (2008): 109; Robert E. Ployhart, "Staffing in the 21st Century: New Challenges and Strategic Opportunities," *Journal of Management* 32 (2006): 868–897; Chapman et al., "Applicant Attraction to Organizations and Job Choice: A Meta-Analytic Review of the Correlates of Recruiting Outcomes"; Sara L. Rynes and Daniel M. Cable, "Recruitment Research in the Twenty-First Century," in *Handbook of Psychology*, vol. 12, *Industrial and Organizational Psychology*, ed. Walter C. Borman, Daniel R. Ilgen, and Richard J. Klimoski, (Hoboken, NJ: Wiley, 2003), 55–76; and Breaugh and Starke, "Research on Employee Recruitment: So Many Studies, So Many Remaining Questions."

7. Retrieved from http://money.cnn.com/2010/01/21/technology/sas_best_companies.fortune/

8. Daniel B. Turban and Daniel M. Cable, "Firm Reputation and Applicant Pool Characteristics," *Journal of Organizational Behavior* 47 (2003): 733–751.

9. Daniel A. Newman and Julie Lyon, "Recruitment Efforts to Reduce Adverse Impact: Targeted Recruiting for Personality, Cognitive Ability, and Diversity," *Journal of Applied Psychology* 94 (2009): 299.

10. Ibid.

11. Filip Lievens, "Employer Branding in the Belgian Army: The Importance of Instrumental and Symbolic Beliefs for Potential Applicants, Actual Applicants, and Military Employees," *Human Resource Management* 46 (2007): 51–69.

12. Scott Highhouse, Erin E. Thornbury, and Ian S. Little, "Social-Identity Functions of Attraction to Organizations," *Organizational Behavior and Human Decision Processes* 103 (2007): 134–146.

13. Jerel E. Slaughter and Gary J. Greguras, "Initial Attraction to Organizations: The Influence of Trait Inferences," *International Journal of Selection and Assessment* 17 (2009): 1–18.

14. Jerel E. Slaughter, Michael J. Zickar, Scott Highhouse, and David. C. Mohr, "Personality Trait Inferences about Organizations: Development of a Measure and Assessment of Construct Validity," *Journal of Applied Psychology* 89 (2004): 85–103.

15. Phillip W. Braddy, Adam W. Meade, J. Joan Michael, and John W. Fleenor, "Internet Recruiting: Effects of Website Content Features on Viewers' Perceptions of Organizational Culture," *International Journal of Selection and Assessment* 17 (2009): 19–34.

16. Karen H. Ehrhart and Jonathan C. Ziegert, "Why Are Individuals Attracted to Organizations?" *Journal of Management* 31 (2005): 901–919.

17. Rynes and Cable, "Recruitment Research in the Twenty-First Century."

18. Breaugh, "Employee Recruitment: Current Knowledge and Important Areas for Future Research," 107.

19. Ibid.

20. Ingo Weller, Brooks C. Holtom, Wenzel Matiaske, and Thomas Mellewigt, "Level and Time Effects of Recruitment Sources on Early Voluntary Turnover," *Journal of Applied Psychology* 94 1146–1162.

21. Ibid., 1157.

22. J. P. Kirnan, J. A. Farley, and Kurt F. Geisinger, "The Relationship Between Recruiting Source, Applicant Quality, and Hire Performance: An Analysis by Sex, Ethnicity, and Age," *Personnel Psychology* 42 293–308.

23. Greet Van Hoye and Filip Lievens, "Tapping the Grapevine: A Closer Look at Word-of-Mouth as a Recruitment Source," *Journal of Applied Psychology* 94 341–352.

24. Ibid., 349.

25. Christopher J. Collins and Cynthia K. Stevens, "The Relationship between Early Recruitment-Related Activities and the Application Decisions of New Labor-Market Entrants: A Brand Equity Approach to Recruitment," *Journal of Applied Psychology* 87 (2002): 1121–1133.

26. Hella Sylva and Stefan T. Mol, "E-Recruitment: A Study into Applicant Perceptions of an Online Application System," *International Journal of Selection and Assessment* 17 (2009): 311.

27. See http://talent.linkedin.com/blog/index.php2009//12/save-a-search/

28. Michael Foster, *Recruiting on the Web: Smart Strategies for Finding the Perfect Candidate* (New York: McGraw-Hill, 2003).

29. Harvel J. Walker, Hubert S. Feild, William F. Giles, and Achilles A. Armenakis, "Displaying Employee Testimonials on Recruitment Web Sites: Effects of Communication Media, Employee Race, and Job Seeker Race on Organizational Attraction and Information Credibility," *Journal of Applied Psychology* 94 (2009): 1354–1364.

30. Sylva and Mol, "E-Recruitment: A Study into Applicant Perceptions of an Online Application System."

31. Anonymous, "Recruiting and Marketing are Top Benefits of Social Media," *HRfocus* 87 (2010): S1–S4.

32. "E-Recruitment Gets the Nike Tick of Approval," *Human Resource Management International Digest* 13, no. 2 (2005): 33–35.

33. "E-Recruitment Helps Xerox to Pick Cream of the Crop," *Human Resource Management International Digest* 13, no. 5 (2005): 33–35.

34. Jean M. Phillips and Stanley M. Gully, *Strategic Staffing* (Upper Saddle River, NJ: Pearson, 2009), 161–162.

35. Bruce R. Dineen, Steven R. Ash, and Raymond A. Noe, "A Web of Applicant Attraction: Person-Organization Fit in the Context of Web-Based Recruitment," *Journal of Applied Psychology* 87 (2002): 723–734. See also Derek S. Chapman and Janie Webster, "The Use of Technology in the Recruiting, Screening, and Selection Processes of Job Candidates," *International Journal of Selection and Assessment* 11 (2003): 113–120.

36. Derek R. Avery, "Reactions to Diversity in Recruitment Advertising—Are Differences Black and White?" *Journal of Applied Psychology* 88 (2003): 672–679.

37. Valery Yakubovich and Daniela Lup, "Stages of the Recruitment Process and the Referrer's Performance Effect," *Organization Science* 17 (2006): 710–723.

38. Breaugh and Starke, "Research on Employee Recruitment: So Many Studies, So Many Remaining Questions."

39. Rynes and Cable, "Recruitment Research in the Twenty-First Century."

40. Chapman et al., "Applicant Attraction to Organizations and Job Choice: A Meta-Analytic Review of the Correlates of Recruiting Outcomes."

41. Breaugh, "Employee Recruitment: Current Knowledge and Important Areas for Future Research," 111.

42. James A. Breaugh, Therese. H. Macan, and Dana. M. Grambow, "Employee Recruitment: Current Knowledge and Directions for Future Research," *International Review of Industrial and Organizational Psychology* 23 (2008): 45–82.

43. John P. Wanous, *Organizational Entry: Recruitment, Selection, and Socialization of Newcomers* (Reading, MA: Addison-Wesley, 1980), 34.

44. Ibid., 329.

45. Breaugh, "Employee Recruitment: Current Knowledge and Important Areas for Future Research," 108.

46. Robert D. Bretz and Timothy A. Judge, "Realistic Job Previews: A Test of the Adverse Self-Selection Hypothesis," *Journal of Applied Psychology* 83 (1998): 330–337.

47. Breaugh, "Employee Recruitment: Current Knowledge and Important Areas for Future Research," 106.

48. Jean M. Phillips, "Effects of Realistic Job Previews on Multiple Organizational Outcomes: A Meta-Analysis," *Academy of Management Journal* 41 (1998): 673–690.

49. Breaugh, "Employee Recruitment: Current Knowledge and Important Areas for Future Research," 106.

50. Ibid., 106–107.

51. Michael R. Buckley, Don B. Fedor, Sean M. Carraher, Dwight D. Frink, and Marvin D. Dunnette, "The Ethical Imperative to Provide Recruits Realistic Job Previews," *Journal of Managerial Issues* 9 (1997): 468–484.

52. Robert D. Gatewood, Mary A. Gowan, and Gary L. Lautenschlager, "Corporate Image, Recruitment Image, and Initial Job Choice Decision," *Academy of Management Journal* 36 (1993): 414–427.

53. Christopher J. Collins and Jian Han, "Exploring Applicant Pool Quantity and Quality: The Effects of Early Recruitment Practice Strategies, Corporate Advertising, and Firm Reputation," *Personnel Psychology* 57 (2004): 685–717.

54. Rynes and Cable, "Recruitment Research in the Twenty-First Century."

55. Allison E. Barber and Mark V. Roehling, "Job Postings and the Decision to Interview: A Verbal Protocol Analysis," *Journal of Applied Psychology* 78 (1993): 845–856.

56. David G. Allen, Raj V. Mahto, and Robert F. Otondo, "Web-Based Recruitment: Effects of Information, Organizational Brand, and Attitudes Toward a Web Site on Applicant Attraction," *Journal of Applied Psychology* 92 (2007): 1696–1708.

57. David G. Allen, James R. Van Scotter, and Robert F. Otondo, "Recruitment Communication Media: Impact on Prehire Outcomes," *Personnel Psychology* 57 (2004): 143–171.

58. Newman and Lyon, "Recruitment Efforts to Reduce Adverse Impact: Targeted Recruiting for Personality, Cognitive Ability, and Diversity."

59. Richard D. Arvey, Michael E. Gordon, Douglas P. Massengill, and Stephan J. Mussio, "Differential Dropout Rates of Minority and Majority Job Candidates Due to 'Time Lags' between Selection Procedures," *Personnel Psychology* 28 (1975): 175–180; Sara L. Rynes, Robert D. Bretz Jr., and Barry Gerhart, "The Importance of Recruitment in Job Choice: A Different Way of Looking," *Personnel Psychology* 44 (1991): 487–521.

60. Chapman et al., "Applicant Attraction to Organizations and Job Choice: A Meta-Analytic Review of the Correlates of Recruiting Outcomes."

61. M. Susan Taylor and Thomas J. Bergmann, "Organizational Recruitment Activities and Applicants' Reactions at Different Stages of the Recruitment Process," *Personnel Psychology* 40 (1987): 261–285.

62. Rynes, Bretz Jr., and Gerhart, "The Importance of Recruitment in Job Choice: A Different Way of Looking."

63. Ibid.

64. Wayne F. Gersen, "The Effects of a Demanding Application Process on the Applicant Pool for Teaching Positions," *Dissertation Abstracts International* 36 (1976): 7773A.

65. Phillips and Gully, *Strategic Staffing*, 191.

66. Sara L. Rynes and Alison E. Barber, "Applicant Attraction Strategies: An Organizational Perspective," *Academy of Management Review* 15 (1990): 286–310.

PREDICTORS OF JOB PERFORMANCE

Predicting future events is a common part of our lives. We have all tried to guess the winner of a sporting event, who might ask us out, or what the questions on our next test may be. Some people, such as fortune-tellers, meteorologists, stock brokers, and selection specialists, also make prediction a large part of their jobs. They use some limited amount of currently available information to make judgments about future events. Although all four of these types of practitioners could use our help in improving the accuracy of their predictions, we predict that this section will be of more value to selection specialists than to the other three. Information the selection specialist uses to predict future job performance can be obtained from several different types of devices: application forms, interviews, tests, work simulations, and so on. Each of the chapters of this section treats a major type of device in detail. Our viewpoint is that if selection devices are properly developed, administered, scored, and interpreted, the information about applicants that is obtained and used in predicting job performance improves. As this happens, the success rate of prediction should also get better.

Of course, successful prediction in selection is complex; hiring high performers depends on three factors described in Chapter 5 as part of our discussion about the utility of a predictor.[1] They are:

1. Validity coefficient—the correlation between the predictor scores and job performance or other criterion.

2. Selection ratio—the number of hires divided by number of applicants. The smaller the ratio of people hired from all applicants available, the greater the chance of choosing really top performers, because a company can "skim the cream" of the applicant pool.

3. Base rate of success—also a ratio, reflecting the proportion of employees who would be successful on the job if selection decisions were made by random choice among the applicants. In this case, the predictor is not referred to or used when making the hiring decision.

The effectiveness of predictions during selection varies with the size of the correlation, the selection ratio, and the base rate of success. Not surprisingly, the higher the correlation or validity coefficient of the predictor, the better the predictor will be at identifying applicants who will be high performers on the job. This relationship is straightforward; it simply means that prediction improves as validity rises. The other two factors' effect on prediction is not quite so obvious.

A smaller selection ratio means fewer applicants are hired. When the "best" available candidates are hired (top down selection), these few hires will be the highest scoring applicants on the test, interview, application blank, or other selection device. As long as these selection devices are valid predictors of job success, top scoring candidates have the best chance of being high performers if selected. Thus, the lower the selection ratio (.05 versus .60), the more useful the test becomes. Although a smaller proportion of those in the applicant pool are hired when jobs are given to only the top 5% with the highest scores (versus the top 60%), more of those hired are higher performers, other things being equal. Because many of the rejected applicants could have succeeded if they had been hired, there is a cost to rejecting a larger proportion of the applicants. If only the top 5% are hired, you will not be surprised to hear that there are more who would have been successful among the 95% who are rejected. Typically, the firm ignores the cost of rejecting these candidates because the gain is higher performance from those selected, which has obvious value to the firm. The cost is less visible to the firm and typically borne primarily by the applicant (who suffers through the rejection and loss of a job opportunity). Yet there is a cost to the firm. They lose the potential contributions of talented people who are not hired. If Motorola failed to hire the person who developed the next innovative feature for the Apple cell phone, such a decision could be very costly. Nevertheless, it is typically assumed that there is no cost to the firm for rejecting qualified applicants. Instead, to maximize prediction, we focus on selecting a greater proportion of qualified, successful applicants and downplay the cost of our "misses." Although it may seem heartless, we agree with this assumption in nearly all cases—except those rare instances when we have been turned down for a job. Then the science is less compelling.

Finally, the third factor, accounting for the effect of the base rate of success on selection decisions, is even less obvious than the effect for selection ratio just described. Base rate accounts for the "quality" of the applicant pool. That is, it recognizes the proportion of applicants in the pool who could do the job well if the predictor were not used to help make the selection decision. Predictors are most useful when 50 percent of the applicants are likely to be high performers and 50 percent likely to fail if hired. To understand this, think about the extremes. If 100 percent of the applicants would be successful if hired, there is no added information provided by the predictor; one would randomly pick from the pool of superstar candidates. Conversely, if every applicant in the selection pool would fail if hired, the predictor cannot help identify even one applicant who would be successful; none are available. Thus, when the base rate is either very high (most would be successful) or very low (few would be successful), using the predictor does not significantly improve the quality of the decision; the additional information gained by the selection device does not improve our guess about future performance very much. There is only limited gain from using the predictor, less than we might expect. However, when the ratio of high performers to low performers is about 50/50, the predictor is able to improve the 50/50 ratio considerably if the test has high predictive validity and a small selection ratio. When making hiring decisions, we can be more accurate than a coin flip (a 50/50 chance) by making available additional information provided by the predictor (test, interview, and so on).

As this illustrates, it's not easy to predict which candidate has the most potential as an employee. Taylor and Russell tables are available that enable one to calculate the percentage of new hires who will be successful, given knowledge of these three factors.[2] Part of their tables are reported below in Table 9.1. The number embedded in the table represents the percentage of those hired who will be high performers or correctly hired candidates, given the base rate of success, the selection ratio, and validity coefficient. Take a moment to consider what proportion of candidates hired will be successful if the following is true: a) current base rate of success is .20, b) the firm is quite selective (selection ratio = .05) and c) the predictor has high validity (r_{xy} = .65). Then look what happens if the base rate goes up to .90 while everything else remains the same. What happens if the firm cannot be selective and must hire 95% of the applicants, all else being equal? Finally, what happens when the predictor is not very valid (r_{xy} = .10)? Are there situations when a predictor with relatively low validity is still useful?

This last question, at first blush, seems ridiculous. Why would you ever want to use a predictor with relatively low validity? (Such a good question!) To develop and use selection devices with high predictive validity typically requires considerable resources (time, money, or expert personnel) all of which can be in short supply. For instance, early in the selection process, when we have a very large number of applicants, it can be quite daunting to figure out how to reduce the number of applicants to a manageable number of candidates. Consider the case where we want to hire 10 mid-level managers.

TABLE 9.1	Excerpts from the Taylor-Russell Tables[a]

A. Base Rate of Success = .20

Validity (r_{xy})	Selection Ratio			
	0.05	0.30	0.60	0.95
0.10	26%	23%	22%	20%
0.25	37%	29%	24%	21%
0.45	54%	36%	28%	21%
0.65	73%	45%	31%	21%

B. Base Rate of Success = .40

Validity (r_{xy})	Selection Ratio			
	0.05	0.30	0.60	0.95
0.10	48%	45%	42%	40%
0.25	61%	51%	46%	41%
0.45	77%	61%	51%	42%
0.65	92%	72%	57%	42%

C. Base Rate of Success = .70

Validity (r_{xy})	Selection Ratio			
	0.05	0.30	0.60	0.95
0.10	77%	74%	72%	70%
0.25	86%	80%	76%	71%
0.45	94%	87%	81%	72%
0.65	99%	94%	86%	73%

D. Base Rate of Success = .90

Validity (r_{xy})	Selection Ratio			
	0.05	0.30	0.60	0.95
0.10	93%	92%	91%	90%
0.25	97%	95%	93%	91%
0.45	99%	98%	95%	91%
0.65	100%	99%	98%	92%

Note: The percentage embedded in the table reflects the percent of applicants hired who are successful performers.

[a]From H.C. Taylor and J.T. Russell, "The Relationship of Validity Coefficients to the Practical Effectiveness of Tests in Selection," *Journal of Applied Psychology*, © 1939, 23, pp. 565–578.

We certainly won't be able to administer our assessment center ($5,000 per applicant) to all 100 people who applied for our 10 new openings. More important, its not necessary to have each applicant participate in the assessment center in order to make a good employment decision; we often can screen out a large proportion of the applicants simply by using a few basic characteristics or qualifications. Applicants who could be screened out relatively quickly include those who lack minimal experience or qualifications as-sessed in a resume or application blank, who get poor references from prior bossess, and who lack the "right" personality. These predictors (applications, letters of reference, personality tests) can be efficiently administered to large groups of applicants and, even though they do not predict job performance as well as the assessment center, they can still be extremely useful and valuable if the selection ratio is small and/or the base rate of success is near the ideal 50/50 ratio.

This explains why, early in selection, predictors with only modest valitity can be quite effective (such as application blanks, reference checks, and personality tests). In contrast, by the time we get around to choosing the best finalist to hire from the remain-ing candidates, even a predictor with moderate validity (such as college grades) may not add useful information to the hiring decision. Our intent here is not to overwhelm you, but to simply underscore why selection is such a complex process—and why some pre-dictors might be useful (the application blank or resume), even though they may not have a very high predictive validity coefficient. Given this, our purpose is to familiarize you with a variety of selection devices in the following chapters. For each of the chapters, the major objectives are as follows:

1. Describe the appropriate information about applicants that may be gathered by each type of selection device or instrument.

2. Point out the important measurement principles of each type of instrument and review legal implications in using the instrument.

3. Present specific points about the proper development and use of each type of instrument. Where appropriate, this discussion will include considering how these three factors (validity, selection ratio, and base rate) may affect their application.

Application Forms and Biodata Assessments, Training and Experience Evaluations, and Reference Checks

APPLICATION FORMS AND BIODATA ASSESSMENTS

Nature and Role of Application Forms in Selection

When candidates apply for a job in an organization, they are usually asked to complete an *application form*. Most organizations utilize employment applications as a means for collecting preemployment information to assess an applicant's likelihood of success. These forms are a way to begin to learn about the candidate's qualifications and job-relevant personal experiences.

An application form typically consists of a series of questions designed to provide information about the general suitability of applicants for jobs to which they are applying. Questions usually concern the applicant's educational background and previous job experiences and other areas that may be useful in judging a candidate's ability to perform a job. The form itself may be brief and general or long and detailed. Whatever its exact nature, its principal purpose is to serve as a preemployment screen regarding the future job success of job applicants. As such, it serves as a means for (a) deciding whether applicants meet the minimum requirements of a position and (b) assessing and comparing the relative strengths and weaknesses of individuals making application.

Taken at face value, an application form may appear to be innocuous; it may seem to offer no real threat to any particular group. However, when used as a basis for selecting among job applicants, these forms can provide information that unfairly discriminates against some individuals. For example, when application information unrelated to a person's ability to perform a job (such as gender, ethnicity, age) is used to screen applicants, that application data can be used for discriminatory selection practices.

Because application forms have been used to discriminate unfairly against protected groups, federal and state laws (such as Title VII of the 1964 Civil Rights Act and Fair Employment Practice statutes) were passed to prevent discrimination by means of preemployment inquiries. These legal restrictions will be discussed later.

Appropriately designed application forms can provide much useful information about job applicants. Even though this information might help managers make selection decisions, a key issue facing any application reviewer is in deciding *what* application data are most beneficial in choosing successful job applicants. Where clear guidelines are not provided, selection decisions focusing on application information may be based on the personal biases, prejudices, and whims of each application reviewer. For example, in considering applicants for first-line supervisory jobs, some managers believe only applicants possessing a high school diploma should be hired; others may not hold this view. Is a minimum level of education mandatory for successful performance as a supervisor? Unless relationships between application data and job success are known, this information may be of limited help to managers involved in selection decisions.

This creates a conundrum: most firms collect applicant personal history information on some type of application form. Yet surprisingly few firms systematically structure and standardize that information in order to exploit its full value to predict later employee performance and turnover.[3] In part, this is because practitioners are concerned about its practicality, its potential to create legal "issues," even its ability to validly predict job performance.[4] Although gathering information from some types of application forms does require large sample sizes and considerable expertise, that's not true in all cases. Furthermore, with forethought and care in selecting items focused on the demands of the work or outcomes of interest, it's possible to minimize or eliminate concerns about legal complications. Of course, another reason practitioners have not commonly used well validated application blanks is because even researchers have not been able to reach a consensus as to what consititutes useful applicant information.

An application form is a tool for gathering self-report data. In nearly all cases, application forms are a paper-and-pencil measure, although other methods (phone, web-based) are used.[5] There is little agreement as to what constitutes relevant application information.[6] Some researchers argue the information should be restricted to prior work experience: time in prior positions, the number of jobs held and so forth.[7] Other researchers have taken a much broader perspective to personal history information and include personality, preferences, and interests; future expectations; values; and self-assessed skills.[8] Without a clear understanding of what application data is or means, it will be difficult to conclude that this information does or does not predict later job performance or turnover.

To clarify matters, in the remainder of this book we refer to application information that is developed and scored in a way to maximize prediction as *biodata*, to distinguish it from run-of-the-mill application form data. The core feature of biodata is that it is self-report data provided by the applicant. It is historical data that reflects the applicant's past behaviors and experiences—in a work context (for example, held 10 jobs in the past 5 years), in an educational setting (high grades in math, graduated from college), as part of a family (mother worked outside the home), and regarding community activities (coached 5-year- old children in soccer)—yet predicts outcomes at work. This definition excludes directly assessing personality traits, values, interests, skills, and abilities, though such attributes are likely to be related to applicants' personal history experiences.[9] For example, the applicant's interests and personality would influence what kinds of settings the person seeks out (a highly extraverted, social person prefers sales to a job working alone). Certain experiences provide opportunities to develop specific knowledge and skills (leading the local United Way campaign develops leadership skills). By separating biodata from measures of personality, interests, and abilities, it is possible to better understand why and when biodata will be an effective predictor.

More than fifty years ago, organizations began to develop scoring keys that isolate specific individual items on the application form that distinguished between successful and unsuccessful employees.[10] Once identified, items related to employee job success are then weighted to reflect their degree of importance in differentiating good and poor performers. The *weighted application blank* (WAB) has a total score determined by summing the collective weights for responses to the items; it can be used like any HR selection test to predict probable job success. The use of WABs has waned since the mid-1970s, primarily because many of these items resemble personality questions and their development requires considerable technical expertise and large sample sizes.[11] Nevertheless, they can be quite effective, particularly for a variety of lower-skilled jobs.

Biographical Information Blanks (BIB) are another specific type of biodata based on the notion that a deeper study of applicants and their employment backgrounds and life experiences can be employed as an effective predictor.[12] Use of BIBs is based on the cliché that the best predictor of future behavior is past behavior.[13] For example, if an applicant has held 15 different jobs over the past five years, it seems reasonable to anticipate that person wouldn't remain long at your firm either.[14] Similarly, if the applicant has prior experience with skills needed to successfully perform your job, it seems logical that using items to assess these skills will predict future job performance.[15]

Various labels have been given to biodata (BIBs, WABs, personal or life history information, and background data). These differ as to whether the items are empirically validated and optimally weighted statistically. Ideally, the items appearing on the application were developed from an analysis of the job, have validity evidence, and have been screened for possible discriminatory impact against protected groups.

There are at least two other ways to categorize biodata: (a) based on the type of response options offered to a respondent (*response*-type), and (b) based on the specific behavioral content of the item itself (*behavior*-type). Response-type classification refers to the kind of scale a respondent is asked to use in answering biodata items.[16] Table 9.2 classifies exampler items into seven categories of response type. The type of rating scale employed on a biodata questionnaire can significantly affect the subsequent scoring and analysis of items. Preferable (and the most common item format) is a biodata item having an underlying continuum and requiring a single choice (see Category 2 in Table 9.2). This item is the most amenable to various kinds of statistical analyses; the other item types require special steps for scoring and analysis. At times when constructing biodata, it is not possible to put all items in the continuum, single-choice format; it may make more sense to use something different. In these instances, other item formats should be considered (such as those shown in Table 9.2). Scoring (through dummy variable coding and treating each item option as a separate variable) and statistical provisions can be made to handle these variations.

Table 9.3 presents another taxonomy of biodata items. This particular classification categorizes items according to behaviors to be judged by respondents.[17] With this system, biodata items can be classified along one or more of the following dimensions: (a) verifiable/unverifiable, (b) historical/futuristic, (c) actual behavior/hypothetical behavior, (d) memory/conjecture, (e) factual/interpretive, (f) specific/general, (g) response/response tendency, and (h) external event/internal event. Each of these dimensions represents a continuum. The categories are not mutually exclusive because it is possible for any single item to be characterized by more than one dimension. At any rate, the items listed provide some typical examples of those in a biodata questionnaire.

What makes a clear definition of biodata even more confusing is that it can be assessed by means other than an application blank, which makes it somewhat challenging to specify what exactly should be called biodata. Craig Russell, for example, used a system of structured interviews to gather biographical information on 66 candidates for general manager positions in a *Fortune 500* firm. Interview questions focused on three background areas of each applicant: (a) accomplishments and disappointments and what was learned from those experiences both in college and in positions held since entering the workforce; (b) accomplishments, disappointments, and situational experiences in the applicants' current position relative to nine performance dimensions that had been identified for the general manager's job; and (c) career aspirations, prior formal developmental activities, self-perceptions, and how others were believed to perceive the applicant.[18] In another biodata application, Russell

TABLE 9.2	Classification of Exampler Application or Biographical Data Items by Response Type

1. **Yes-No Response:**
   Are you satisfied with your life?
   a. Yes
   b. No

2. **Continuum, Single-Choice Response:**
   About how many fiction books have you read in the past year?
   a. None
   b. 1 or 2
   c. 3 or 4
   d. 5 or 6
   e. More than 6

3. **Noncontinuum, Single-Choice Response:**
   Which one of the following would you most prefer to do in your leisure time?
   a. Read a book
   b. Work crossword puzzles
   c. Attend a party
   d. Play golf, tennis, or softball
   e. Repair a broken appliance or make minor home repairs

4. **Noncontinuum, Multiple-Choice Response:**
   Check each of the following activities you had participated in by the time you were 18.
   a. Shot a rifle
   b. Driven a car
   c. Worked a full-time job
   d. Traveled alone more than 500 miles from home
   e. Repaired an electrical appliance

5. **Continuum, Plus Escape Option:**
   When you were a teenager, how often did your father help you with your schoolwork?
   a. Very often
   b. Often
   c. Sometimes
   d. Seldom
   e. Never
   f. Father was not at home

6. **Noncontinuum, Plus Escape Option:**
   In what branch of the military did you serve?
   a. Army
   b. Air Force
   c. Navy
   d. Marines
   e. Never served in the military

7. **Common Stem, Multiple Continuum:**
   In the last five years, how much have you enjoyed each of the following? (Use the rating scale of 1 to 4 shown below.)
   a. Reading books
   b. Watching TV
   c. Working at your job
   d. Traveling
   e. Outdoor recreation
      (1) Very Much
      (2) Some
      (3) Very little
      (4) Not at all

Source: Based on William A. Owens, "Background Data," In *Handbook of Industrial and Organizational Psychology*, ed. Marvin Dunnette (Chicago: Rand Mcnally, 1976), 613.

coded biographical information from life history essays written by cadets at the U.S. Naval Academy. The biodata information was found to predict leadership and academic performance among cadets at the academy.[19] More commonly, biodata questions are presented in a self-report questionnaire. The questionnaire is usually in a standardized multiple-choice format that asks applicants to characterize themselves using past life experiences. What these methods have in common is that information is collected from the applicant. As we will soon see, there are legitimate concerns about the accuracy of this information when collected in a high-stakes employment context. Concerns about accuracy have important implications for reliablity and validity.

Based on our earlier definition and description of biodata information, you are probably thinking at this point, "It seems to me that this information could measure a number of different attributes or constructs. Is that so?" The short answer to that question is yes. Although in this chapter we talk about personal history information as if it assesses a particular construct, in reality it can measure a host of attributes suitable for assessment by a predictor used in selection. What these forms measure simply depends on what constructs the biodata questionnaire was constructed to measure. It is preferable to think of application information more as a method than as a means for assessing one substantive construct, such as cognitive ability, which is assessed through a general mental ability test.[20] As we discuss various findings and compare various studies that use this

TABLE 9.3	Classification of Exampler BioData Items Based On Behavioral Content

1. Verifiable: Did you graduate from college?	**Unverifiable:** How much did you enjoy high school?
2. Historical: How many jobs have you held in the past five years?	**Futuristic:** What job would you like to hold five years from now?
3. Actual Behavior: Have you ever repaired a broken radio?	**Hypothetical Behavior:** If you had your choice, what job would you like to hold now?
4. Memory: How would you describe your life at home while growing up?	**Conjecture:** If you were to go through college again, what would you choose as a major?
5. Factual: How many hours do you spend at work in a typical week?	**Interpretive:** If you could choose your supervisor, what characteristic would you want him or her to have?
6. Specific: While growing up, did you collect coins?	**General:** While growing up, what activities did you enjoy most?
7. Response: Which of the following hobbies do you enjoy?	**Response Tendency:** When you have a problem at work, to whom do you turn for assistance?
8. External Event: When you were a teenager, how much time did your father spend with you?	**Internal Event:** Which best describes the feelings you had when you last worked with a computer?

Source: Based on James J. Asher, "The Biographical Item: Can It Be Improved?" *Personnel Psychology*, 25 (1972): 252; and Wayne F. Cascio, *Applied Psychology in Personnel Management* (Englewood Cliffs, NJ: Prentice-Hall, 1991), 266.

information, it's important to keep in mind that different biodata forms may measure different constructs.

EVALUATING APPLICATION BLANKS AS PREDICTORS

There is value in evaluating past behavior to identify which applicant is likely to perform well if hired. One fundamental problem is identifying which information provides a useful assessment. This is illustrated by research that shows scored evaluations of personal life experiences using unweighted data are only moderate predictors of later job performance (average r_{xy} ranges from .10 to .20[21]). In contrast, when the application blank is systematically scored and weighted when summing job-related items or devloped and scored like biodata responses, the evidence for validity or prediction is compelling. For example, considerable meta-analytic evidence demonstrates average predictive validities for biodata questionnaires range between .30 and .40.[22] This shows that information obtained from application blanks can be useful, but to realize its potential, the form must either rely on an empirical analysis to identify items that predict the outcome of interest or begin with a job analysis to ensure that only job-related questions are posed. Besides focusing on attributes demanded by the work, it also requires consideration of the specific criterion to be predicted. Biodata can predict supervisory ratings of performance, productivity, promotion, tenure, turnover, and training success (see Table 9.4), but only when the criterion is taken into account when identifying items to rely on.

| | TABLE 9.4 | Summary of BioData Validation Studies for a Variety of Criteria |

Criterion	Investigator	Number of Validity Coefficients	Total Sample Size	Average Validity Coefficient
Performance Rating	Dunnette[a]	115	N.A.	0.34
	Hunter and Hunter[b]	12	4,429	0.37
	Reilly and Chao[c]	15	4,000	0.36
	Schmitt et al.[d]	29	3,998	0.32
Productivity	Schmitt et al.[d]	19	13,655	0.20
Promotion	Hunter and Hunter[b]	17	9,024	0.26
Tenure	Hunter and Hunter[b]	23	10,800	0.26
Turnover	Schmitt et al.[d]	28	28,862	0.21
Training Success	Hunter and Hunter[b]	11	6,139	0.30

Note: N.A. Data were not available.

[a]Marvin D. Dunnette, *Validity Study Results for Jobs Relevant to the Petroleum Refining Industry* (Washington, DC: American Petroleum Institute, 1972). The data reported in the table were taken from John E. Hunter and Rhoda F. Hunter, "Validity and Utility of Alternative Predictors of Job Performance," *Psychological Bulletin*, 96 (1984): 83.

[b]John E. Hunter and Rhonda F. Hunter, "Validity and Utility of Alternative Predictors of Job Performance," *Psychological Bulletin*, 96 (1984): 72–98.

[c]Richard R. Reilly and Georgia T. Chao, "Validity and Fairness of Some Alternative Employee Selection Procedures," *Personnel Psychology*, 35 (1982): 1–62.

[d]Neal Schmitt, Richard Z. Gooding, Raymond A. Noe, and Michael Kirsch, "Metaanalyses of Validity Studies Published between 1964 and 1982 and the Investigations of Study Characteristics," *Personnel Psychology*, 37 (1984): 407–422.

A validity generalization study by Hannah Rothstein and her colleagues showed that biodata instruments can be developed and validated so they lead to validity generalizability.[23] They selected and scored biographical items from the *Supervisory Profile Record* found to be related to the job performance of roughly 11,000 first-line supervisors in 79 different organizations. Mean estimated validities for the criteria of supervisory ability ratings and supervisory performance ratings were 0.33 and 0.32. These validities were judged to be stable over time and generalizable across groups based on age, gender, education, previous experience, tenure, and ethnicity. These results should not be interpreted to apply to every biodata instrument, since conventional methods of biodata construction and validation differ from Rothstein's approach.

Hannah Rothstein's work employed a biodata questionnaire developed for first-line supervisors employed in multiple organizations. Kevin Carlson and his coworkers sought to develop a biodata measure in one organization whose validity would be generalizable to managers above the first-line supervisor level in different organizations.[24] Following development, the biodata component of the *Manager Profile Record* was given to a sample of more than 7,300 managers working in 24 organizations. The biodata inventory was designed to predict managers' level of progression within their employing companies. Results showed that estimated true validity (following correction for range restriction on the predictor and criterion unreliability) was 0.53 and was generalizable across organizations. Like Rothstein's research, Carlson and coworkers concluded that when properly developed, biodata inventory validities are not restricted to a specific organization and are, in fact, generalizable to other organizations. They posed the following guidelines for developing biodata inventories with generalizable validities:

- Are there sound reasons to expect that the validity of a biodata instrument should generalize to other populations and situations? No methods can make an instrument generalize more than is theoretically possible. Some predictive relationships would not be expected to generalize outside limited populations or situations.

- Has a valid criterion been selected and has a reliable measure of that criterion been constructed for use in [scoring] key development? The greater the validity of the criterion measure, the more accuracy is possible in identifying relationships between items and the criterion.

- Has the validity of each item been determined? Assuring that both empirical and conceptual justifications exist for each item's validity reduces the sample dependence of an instrument. Sample dependence is increased when strictly empirical analyses are performed.

- Does an adequate sample exist? The larger the sample, the more representative that sample is likely to be of the larger population and the more likely that validities in the development sample will generalize to [the] population.[25]

Results from both Rothstein's and Carlson's work show that with large samples available, it is possible to produce a biodata instrument that is predictive of performance across organizations and employee groups. Organizations without the resources for developing their own biodata questionnaires now have access to a generalizably valid one for use in selection.

It's important to note that Rothstein's and Carlson's studies were based on *incumbent* supervisors and managers already on the job. Do their results generalize to job *applicant* groups? Common practice has been to develop biodata scoring keys on incumbents and assume they are generalizable to applicants. Some results suggest that this assumption may not be valid. Garnett Stokes and her coworkers compared the scoring keys of a biodata questionnaire for both applicant and incumbent groups.[26] They concluded there was little overlap in the scoring keys for the two groups. The implication is that biodata scoring procedures developed on job incumbents do not necessarily generalize to applicant groups.

The magnitude of this problem was effectively illustrated by Thomas Bliesener, who found that 135 of 165 biodata studies (82%) he reviewed collected biodata responses from current employees (concurrent validity design).[27] Thus, conclusions about the validity of biodata are primarily based on collecting responses from current employees, not applicants. The problem Bliesner found was that the average validitiy coefficient was .35 when involving current employees but only .29 or .21 when collecting information from applicants and either relying on, or better yet, not relying on, the information obtained from the application blank to make selection decisions (a predictive validity design). In a recent large scale study, 20 biodata items were administered to 425 current call center employees and 410 applicants.[28] The predictive validity of those responses was significantly higher for current employees than it was for applicants ($r_{xy} = .27$ versus .17, respectively). If those validity coefficients are meaningfully higher with current employees, the experiences they gain while working on the job appear to contribute to gains in predicting job performance. Until further research has shown otherwise, it seems that scoring procedures of biodata forms should be based on job applicants rather than incumbents. Although a biodata predictor is likely to be effective, particularly when used to screen out unqualified applicants, the actual validity coefficients basaed on current employees may overestimate the validity of applying the procedure to select applicants.

Based on the data we have presented so far, we can conclude that biodata measures are valid predictors of job performance. But do these measures add to our ability to predict job performance over predictions made from measures such as mental ability tests? Frank Schmidt and John Hunter reported from their analyses that biodata measures did not significantly enhance the prediction of job performance over that attributed to general mental ability measures.[29] They reasoned that this was due, in part, to the substantial correlation (0.50) found between biodata and general mental ability measures. They imply that as far as the prediction of overall job performance is concerned, an employer would do about as well by simply using a readily available general mental ability test and avoiding a biodata inventory.

The prediction of job performance is important to most organizations. However, practitioners now recognize that the job performance domain includes broader aspects than specific performance of job tasks. These broader aspects include both contextual performance factors and organizational citizenship behaviors. Measures such as biographical data inventories often predict these broader aspects of job performance better than mental ability measures.[30]

Overall, research results suggest that biodata is an effective predictor for a wide diversity of measures of job success. In fact, for entry-level selection, biodata has been found to be one of the best predictors of job performance when compared to other types of predictors such as employment interviews, training and experience ratings, reference checks, personality inventories, and some ability tests.[31]

Given the positive results that recent research on biodata has produced, application blanks should at least be considered for adoption in selection programs, particularly as an early screen to help identify the viable candidates from which the finalists will be drawn. But as this section illustrates, there is considerable work to be done to obtain application form items that are as useful as the biodata results reported in Table 9.4.

One other problem associated with the use of personal life and work experiences is how to get information that is not embellished or otherwise distorted. When people are competing for a job, self-report application data are susceptible to distortion; applicants believe it is advantageous to "look good." Falsification of application data can range from inflation of college grades to outright lies involving types of jobs held, past salaries received, companies worked for, or educational degrees earned. Applicants may attempt to conceal gaps in their employment histories.

A common distortion seen by many HR managers involves reported college background. At some executive levels, applicants frequently misrepresent a specific degree such as the master of business administration (MBA). Research results suggest that applicants are most likely to distort those items believed to be related to whether a job offer will be made or whether a specific salary given; not surprisingly, an applicant's education can influence such outcomes.

How prevalent is the practice of giving fraudulent data on job applications? Few studies have explored the problem in detail. However, some limited investigations have addressed the issue. One conclusion from this research is that when people are directed to "fake good," they consistently skew their application responses toward what they believe an employer wants to hear.[32] Such distortion, however, is not a good indication of the *likelihood* of distortion or faking by real job applicants. On this question, researchers are split; some find little evidence of faking in actual selection contexts, whereas others report substantial evidence of faking.[33] Although it is not possible to draw a definitive conclusion based on the research evidence, the popular press believes false information is more common than you might think. For example, ResumeDoctor.comSM reports that 42.7 percent of 1,000 resumes it vetted over six months contain major misstatements, while popular press articles suggest that about one-third to one-half of applicants list inaccurate dates of employment or exaggerate their accomplishments.[34] When the stakes are high (a job opportunity exists), it appears that some applicants give distorted answers to questions—particularly when the correct, job-related answer is fairly obvious and burnishing one's credentials is seen as providing that last "nudge" to get the job offer. What is not known with certainty is how common such behavior is. However, a surprising amount of research on non-cognitive predictors reveals that faking does not reduce predictive validity.[35] In fact, the study by Neal Schmitt and Fred Oswald concluded that even by removing 30 percent of those applicants who fake their responses, the mean gain in job performance would only be about 0.1 SD.[36] Consequently, it is unclear how distortion on application forms affects hiring decisions.

Several empirical studies have identified the specific application items where distortion is most prevalent as well as their frequency of occurrence. This research shows that when items are verifiable ("What was your cumulative grade point average in college?"), historical ("How many cars did you sell in the past year?"), and factual ("How many times were you late for work over the past six months?"), there is less faking by applicants (refer to Table 9.3).[37] The type of question asked and the likelihood of "getting caught" influence applicant responses.

A recent U.S. Supreme Court ruling (*McKenna v. Nashville Banner Publishing Co.*, 513 U.S. 352 [1995]) illustrates the risks an applicant assumes by distorting or exaggerating qualifications for a job. In this case, the Court concluded that evidence of application/resume fraud or misconduct—in cases where the individual would have been either terminated or not hired in the first place if the firm had known the truth—could limit the employer's liability on discrimination claims (that is, could limit the damages recovered by an employee). Such evidence, however, referred to as "after-acquired evidence," is not an absolute defense against discrimination, as the employee's wrongdoing may not bar the employee from winning a lawsuit. Nevertheless, an employer can fire the offending individual immediately for misrepresentation on the application or resume. Furthermore, if this wrong information was material to the selection decision, or the employer directly relied upon such information when making the selection decision, the employer may (as we have noted above) employ these circumstances as a defense in a wrongful termination case.

Taking all of these factors into consideration, it is reasonable to conclude that some distortion of application form answers does take place. Most likely, distortion of these data is due to pressure on an applicant to obtain a desired job. However, it should not be concluded that employment applications are not useful. Even though distortion is a problem, application forms, with certain characteristics, can provide valid information for comparing and predicting the success of job applicants. This is particularly true for items that require verifiable, historical, and factual information. In the next section we show how the accuracy of application form data can be enhanced, even without such information.

Enhancing Application Form Accuracy.   As we have seen, accuracy of application form data can be a problem. Employers can take several steps to lessen the problems of applicant errors, distortion, and omission of data on the form. First, applicants should be told, preferably both verbally and in writing, that the information they give will affect their employability. Recent research demonstrates that the extent of faking can be reduced through instructions that include statements about the consequences of faking (invalidating a score or resulting in termination). For example, a statement such as this could be included: "Deliberate attempts to falsify information can be detected and may be grounds for either not hiring you or for terminating you after you begin work." Such instructions have been found to reduce attempts to fake responses by nearly half.[38]

Second, applicants should be explicitly informed that the data they provide will be thoroughly checked.[39] For example, a statement such as the following should be included on the form:

All information you provide on this application will be checked. Driving, educational, employment, and any military records will be checked with appropriate individuals and groups such as local and state police, previous employers, or previous schools attended. Be sure to review your application to ensure that it is complete and that you did not omit any information.

The statement should be printed on the form so that it is easily seen and readable.

Applicants should be required to sign and date their application. They should be required to sign a statement certifying the accuracy of the information they provided on the form. Such a statement should warn applicants that misstatements or omission of relevant information are grounds for termination if uncovered after their employment. An example of such a statement is as follows:

By signing this application, I declare that the information provided by me is complete and true to the best of my knowledge. I understand that any misrepresentation or omission on this application may preclude an offer of employment, may result in a withdrawal of an employment offer, or may result in my discharge from employment if I am already employed at the time the misrepresentation or omission is discovered.[40]

Note, however, that if applicants are required to sign the application, some state labor codes require that a copy of a company's application be filed with a specific state department governing labor issues. A state labor code may also require that applicants be given a copy of their signed application if they request it. As we mentioned earlier, review all state labor codes, statutes, and fair employment practice regulations for state-specific information that may apply to the use of employment applications.

Finally, in states covered by an employment-at-will doctrine, an employer should be sure that no contract of permanent employment is implied in the employment application or any resulting job offer letter. Including a statement on the application informing applicants that the application does not create a binding obligation of employment for any specific period of time will help protect an employer. For example, the following statement that was included on an application helped an employer successfully defend against a subsequent wrongful discharge claim:

I, the undersigned, understand that I am being considered as a potential employee of Eastern Capital Corp. dba Fitness USA Health Spas (the "Company"), and hereby certify that:

1. *I understand that if I am hired, such hiring will not be for any definite period of time. Even though, if hired, I will be paid my wages on a monthly, semi-monthly, or weekly basis, I understand that this does not mean I am being hired for a definite period of time.*

2. *I understand that if hired, I will be an employee-at-will and I can be terminated at any time, with or without cause, with or without notice....*

3. *I understand that this agreement cannot be changed except in a written document signed by me and the Company President.*

4. *I have been given an opportunity to ask questions regarding Company rules and my potential status as an employee-at-will. No representative of Fitness USA Health Spas has made any promises or other statements to me which imply that I will be employed under any other terms than stated above.*

5. *I understand that if hired, this Statement is part of the employment arrangement between the Company and me, and will be binding on me.*[41]

Recent research suggests that one other approach to reducing score inflation is to require applicants to provide written support to the answers to biodata items. Two studies show that requiring elaboration to answers significantly reduces biodata scores.[42] Although this technique is a promising way to reduce embellishment, continued research is needed to establish whether predictive validity is also enhanced. These strategies underscore the importance of systematically approaching the planning, development, and use of application blank information in order to realize the substantial value that is possible when using biodata or personal history information as a predictor.

Legal Implications of Application Forms

Some employers think it desirable to obtain as much information as possible on the application form. With a lot of information available, it would seem easier to set up an initial screen for choosing among applicants. However, this "the more information, the better" mentality can create major problems for an employer. As we have said, federal and state laws affect the kinds of information that can be requested on the application blank. Under these laws, it is generally assumed that *all* questions asked on an application form are used in making hiring decisions. Under a charge of discrimination, the burden of proof may be on the employer to demonstrate that *all* application questions are indeed fair and not discriminatory. The law, according to EEOC preemployment guidelines, cautions against questions on the application form that (a) disproportionately screen out minority group members or members of one sex, (b) do not predict successful performance on the job, or (c) cannot be justified as a business necessity.[43] In judging the suitability of a potential item, an employer should thoroughly review each question. The rating criteria listed in Table 9.5 are useful for examining the appropriateness of application form questions.

An employer has the right to establish and use job-related information for identifying the individuals qualified for a job. With respect to an employment application, an

TABLE 9.5	Questions to Be Asked in Examining Appropriateness of Application Form Questions

Yes	No	Question
[ ]	[ ]	1. Will answers to this question, if used in making a selection decision, have an adverse impact in screening out members of a protected group (that is, disqualify a significantly larger percentage of members of one particular group than of others)?
[ ]	[ ]	2. Is this information really needed to judge an applicant's competence or qualifications for the job in question?
[ ]	[ ]	3. Does the question conflict with EEOC guidelines, federal or state laws, or statutes?
[ ]	[ ]	4. Does the question constitute an invasion of privacy?
[ ]	[ ]	5. Is information available that could be used to show that responses to a question are associated with success or failure on a specific job?

Sources: Questions 1 and 2 are based on Equal Employment Opportunity Commission, *EEOC Guide to Pre-Employment Inquiries* (Washington, DC: Equal Employment Opportunity Commission, August 1981); questions 3 through 5 are based on Ernest C. Miller, "An EEO Examination of Employment Applications," *Personnel Administrator*, 25 (March 1981): 68–69.

organization is free to ask almost any question it regards as important in selecting among job applicants. However, as we discussed in Chapter 2, if a complainant can show adverse impact resulting from selection practices, then the burden of proof is on the employer to demonstrate that the information provided by the application questions is not used in a discriminatory manner prohibited by law. Most often a complainant will argue that application items result in (a) *adverse impact* or (b) *disparate treatment*. Under *adverse impact,* members of a protected minority group may respond differently to a question than members of a majority group (for example, "Do you own your home?") White people may respond "yes" in greater proportion than black people. If persons responding "no" are screened out of employment consideration, then the question will have an adverse impact on minority applicants. When *disparate treatment* is involved, different questions may be posed for different groups. For instance, it is disparate treatment if only women are asked, "Do you have children under school age and, if so, what arrangements have you made concerning child care?" In response, an employer has two basic options to show that application form items do not unfairly discriminate among applicants. An employer can either demonstrate (usually with statistics) that (a) the questions being challenged are predictive of job success, or (b) the questions represent a bona fide occupational requirement. An item on an application form is justified as being a bona fide occupational requirement by showing "that it is necessary to the safe and efficient operation of the business, that it effectively carries out the purpose it is supposed to serve, and that there are no alternative policies or practices which would better or equally well serve the same purpose with less discriminatory impact."[44]

Because many of the laws that affect the content of application forms have existed for 35 to 45 years, it might be assumed that most forms companies currently use comply with the law. However, research consistently has shown that numerous public and private sector employers continue to request information that could be viewed as "inadvisable." (The term inadvisable does not mean that questions are illegal and cannot be asked. However, due to their phrasing, the courts would view the questions in such a light as to make a user vulnerable to charges of discrimination if an investigation of unfair discrimination were conducted. Then, it would be up to each employer to justify use of these questions.)

During the early 1980s, three research studies illustrated that many application forms reviewed had at least one inadvisable question; the average was 7.7 to 9.74 inadvisable questions per form.[45] In the first study of its kind, Ernest Miller reviewed the applications of 151 randomly sampled *Fortune 500* firms.[46] Only two used applications judged in an initial review to be completely fair. The applications used by almost 4 out of 10 firms (38 percent) had more than 10 inadvisable inquiries, and Miller reported an average of 9.74 inadvisable items per form. Following are two of the most frequently used inadvisable questions, and the percentage of firms in Miller's study that included these questions in application forms:

1. Have you ever been arrested for a misdemeanor or felony? Describe. (Used by 64.7 percent of firms surveyed; the EEOC has advised the answer might adversely impact minorities.)

2. During what dates did you attend grammar school? High school? (Used by 61.4 percent of firms surveyed; applicant age can be inferred from the answer and used in a discriminatory manner.)

Two other studies were published at about the same time that substantiate Miller's findings regarding the frequency of inadvisable questions on the application. Whether examining application forms from the state personnel office in each of the 50 states,[47] or from 50 large, well-known businesses,[48] nearly all (98 of 100 forms) contained at least one inadvisable item. On average, the states had 7.7 such inquiries per application. At that time, employers were just becoming aware that there could be problems with the content of application forms. Given that these laws have existed for so long, today one would expect application forms to comply with the law. However, research suggests there are a number of inadvisable items still being requested by organizations today.

In 2004, Craig Wallace and Stephen Vodanovich[49] reported that nearly all application forms they examined still contained at least one inadvisable question, with an average of 5.35 from 109 firms using customer service application forms and 2.99 inadvisable items, on average, from 191 *Fortune 500* Web application forms. Such results correspond to earlier findings, which reported similar results after examining 42 online state general employment applications in 2000,[50] 85 retail applications in 1992,[51] and 283 random application forms from American Society of Public Administration members in 1989.[52] Taken together, these studies reveal that today, although there are fewer inadvisable items than found in the early 1980s, a number of employers continue to ask questions the EEOC strongly advises against.

A recent study of more than 300 federal court cases involving the use of application forms powerfully demonstrates the relative frequency of employment discrimination litigation associated with various types of preemployment inquiries. This study found that questions associated with applicant sex and age were most likely to lead to litigation (53 percent of cases), and the plaintiff won over 40 percent of these cases. Furthermore, nearly 20 percent of the cases involved questions addressing educational requirements, convictions, height or weight requirements, and work history or experience requirements.[53] This evidence, when coupled with the finding that firms continue to ask inadvisable questions, underscores the severity of these concerns.

These research studies illustrate rather impressively that many organizations continue to use existing application forms that do not fully comply with current equal employment opportunity law. Resources must be directed toward reviewing and, where needed, revising these forms to ensure full compliance with the law while at the same time meeting an organization's selection needs. Although it is important to get as complete a picture of the candidate as possible, the information requested on the application form cannot be used in a discriminatory manner. As previously stated, the rating criteria listed in Table 9.5 are useful for examining the appropriateness of application form questions. Considering these criteria when screening biodata items should minimize concerns about adverse impact.[54]

The value of using empirical scoring, statistical analyses, and job analyses to isolate those specific application factors predictive of job success—that is using biodata items instead of formally scored application questions—becomes even more obvious when one considers legal issues involved in relying on information derived from the application blank. Once a case has been established against an employer (that is, a prima facie case of discrimination), users of information from application forms must provide evidence of validity and fairness of the item, total, or dimension score. Reliance on biodata-like procedures increase the likelihood the scores have validity, and thus, there use is more defensible since they predict future job success.

Because some biodata items involving topics such as education and socioeconomic background may very well be associated with applicant gender or ethnicity, caution is needed. If Title VII burden of proof requirements are carried out with regard to specific biodata items, such caution must include reviewing items to determine whether they show both logical *and* empirical evidence of appropriate biodata use. Thus reasonable care in selecting items would include undertaking an empirical review of item fairness. Validity and fairness should not be taken for granted. Job analysis and item review panels, as well as other steps, could be used to produce content-valid measures that may have less adverse impact on protected applicant groups.[55]

Another legal issue that could arise with the use of biodata is that of invasion of privacy. Although many writers suggest that an application blank is an innocuous selection device, some questions appearing on some biodata forms could be considered offensive. For example, items that involve relationships with siblings and parents, socioeconomic status, or community activities (for example, politics or religious activities) could be viewed by some respondents as highly personal. Using rational item screening by subject matter experts to minimize biodata item bias and objectionability is one way to handle this problem.[56] Another proposed strategy is simply to have applicants omit items that they consider personal or offensive. However, questions left blank by job applicants may produce negative perceptions on the part of prospective employers.[57]

Invasion of privacy and job applicant rights are issues likely to grow in importance in the future. Research must be directed toward invasion-of-privacy implications, particularly where biodata questionnaires composed of very personal items are being used as selection measures.

It is impossible to answer in the abstract and with complete certainty the question of whether biodata are discriminatory. Previous research on the matter is far from conclusive. William Owens found from his review that "all in all, the available evidence would seem to suggest that the major dimensions of biodata response are quite stable across cultures, age, race, and sex groups."[58] On the other hand, Richard Reilly and Georgia Chao summarized some studies reporting race and sex differences in biodata scoring keys.[59]

At a minimum, given that cognitive ability often results in adverse impact and given evidence that biodata correlates with cognitive ability, there is cause for concern.[60] Futhermore, given evidence of the continued use of inappropriate or inadvisable questions, firms must examine each biodata item for fairness and discrimination.[61]

Little published literature exists regarding the relationship of protected group characteristics with biodata measures. There have been, however, at least two large validity generalization studies that reported the validity of a biodata measure for race and gender groups.[62] One of these investigations noted that the biodata measure's estimated true validities were higher for men than women and higher for white people than black people.[63] Both investigations concluded that the biodata measures' validity generalized across racial and gender groups. In other words, the measures were valid for both white and black people as well as for men and women. A recent study by Murray Barrick and Ryan Zimmerman supports this, as they reported minimal adverse impact with biodata.[64] This led Leatta Hough and colleagues to conclude that, compared to other selection devices, biodata can have low adverse impact against members of protected groups.[65]

Composition of Application Forms

Application forms can be valid and fair predictors, although job-relevant forms are typically called biodata rather than application blanks. Yet whether an application form is valid and fair or not, the composition of the form is relatively similar, although development of a biodata form requires the expenditure of a great deal of time, effort, and resources. As your mother used to say, "Do the work up front, you'll be thankful later." Our description of the composition of the application form below is based on the premise you are trying to develop a job-relevant and fair application form or biodata questionnaire; hence we will use the terms interchangeably. We realize this simplifies things too much, as there are many types of biodata forms. Nevertheless, we assume you will strive to enhance the predictive validity and fairness of your application form and there are some general steps involved in doing so. These are discussed next.

Most job applications consist of two major parts. The first part includes instructional information for completing and submitting the application. The second consists of questions whose answers are used in deciding applicant suitability for a position in the organization.

Instructions for Applicants

Instructions are important because they tell applicants how to complete the necessary forms. They should be clear and understandable. These instructions, however, serve another important purpose: They may help shield an employer from an unlawful employment charge. For instance, employers should consider stating in the instructions that an applicant giving unsolicited information on the application will be rejected. Extraneous information can be used by rejected applicants to argue that they were turned down for an unlawful reason. For instance, Timothy Bland and Sue Stalcup noted that some union organizers, when applying for a job, have written on the employment application that they are union organizers, even though such information was not requested.[66] Then—when they were not employed—they sued, arguing that they were unlawfully denied employment because of their union activity.

The Americans with Disabilities Act (ADA) requires reasonable accommodation during the selection process. Employers should state in the instructions that disabled applicants can request reasonable accommodation in completing the application.

Recent research also illustrates that instructions may influence whether applicants react favorably or unfavorably to a firm's selection methods, which in turn determines whether they are willing to accept an offer and to work for that organization.[67] The most important factors that influence applicant reactions to selection procedures used by organizations include evidence that the selection procedure is useful, valid, and fair.[68] These results have implications for the instructions included on an application form, as applicant reactions should be accounted for whenever feasible. Consequently, there is merit in clearly stating that the application form has been reviewed to ensure it is job-related and fair, if such a review has indeed been conducted. Because many applicants are concerned about privacy issues, there is value in clearly stating who will see the information or how applicant responses will be used to arrive at a decision.[69]

As a selection *and* recruitment measure, the form should be reviewed for its attractiveness, fairness, and ease of use. In general, when applicants do not like application forms it is largely because they are seen to be less fair and less job related than other selection methods (such as interviews and assessment centers).[70] Particularly during periods of low unemployment, employers must consider candidate reactions to the application form.

Employers covered by various federal and state requirements must collect and report demographic information (for example, gender, ethnicity, physical disability) on job applicants. Although it may appear efficient to simply collect the data on the application form, this strategy could lead to a discrimination charge. Collecting descriptive data separately from the application form or on a tear-off portion of the application form—together with a disclaimer that the information is voluntary and will be separated and stored anonymously—would be a more effective strategy.[71] Whether employers follow procedures established by state laws or develop procedures on their own, they would be wise to adopt policies for handling demographic data on job applicants.

Questions for Applicants

Requesting information, other than that necessary for initially judging applicants' qualifications to perform a job, opens an organization to the possibility of a discrimination charge. Organizations should ask job-related questions only and avoid those relating to personal information. It is in the interest of an organization to carefully review the necessity of information requested on the application form.[72]

Research has shown that including discriminatory questions on an application form influences applicants' perceptions of the employing organization. One study found that applicants who completed an application form having discriminatory questions viewed the company as less attractive, were less motivated to pursue employment with the organization, were less likely to accept an offer of employment, and were less likely to recommend the organization to friends than were individuals who completed a form without such questions.[73]

Selecting Application Form Content

What information is necessary? How does an organization decide whether the information is in fact essential? These are important questions. Answers depend on the job for which an application form will be used. Some essential data should be assessed in all forms, including (a) name, (b) current address, (c) telephone number, (d) work experience, (e) level of education and training received, (f) skills possessed, and (g) social security number.[74] What other data should be collected? In general, the lower the organizational level of a job or job class, the shorter, less detailed the content of the application. Using job analysis methods such as those discussed in Chapter 7, we can identify items that could be useful in screening applicants for a job. However, job analysis alone will not completely resolve the problem of which items should be included on an application form. Once we have identified the possible questions to appear on the form, it's important to review each one for its fairness and usefulness.

In reviewing application form items, employers should first research the fair employment practice laws that exist for their state. An employer conducting business in more than one state should review carefully each state's laws, regulations, and guidelines concerning the use of preemployment inquiries. State fair employment practice laws determine the legal status of preemployment inquiries, such as application form items, used by employers doing business within the state. One excellent source for review is *The Commerce Clearing House Employment Practice Guide,* Volume 3, State FEP Laws. A state-by-state review is important, because what is legal in one state may be illegal in another.[75] Furthermore, where state laws and regulations exist, the EEOC gives them more weight than federal standards, which are generally more permissive.

Employers might rightfully ask, "What do we do if it is permissible to ask a job application question in one state but not permissible in another state where we do business?" There are several options employers in this situation might consider. Of course, the option chosen will depend on the specific situation (for example, the specific application question, the specific state in question). Some of these options are

1. Use a generic job application composed of items permissible in all relevant states.

2. Develop state-specific supplements that can be used with a generic job application.

3. Use an application instructing applicants from relevant states to ignore specific questions.

Using the rating criteria noted earlier in Table 9.5 and mandated by any state fair employment practice laws, employers should carefully review all items for their necessity and for their possible discriminatory impacts. For some questions under review (such as ethnicity), the answer is obvious. For others, discriminatory impact is not so evident yet discriminatory effects may be present. The way the questions themselves are used determines the legality of the application form. Of critical importance is the phrasing of the questions on the form. A miscast question can undermine the usefulness and legality of the form and leave an organization vulnerable to a lawsuit.

Using the research of a number of writers, we have summarized in Table 9.6 examples of some appropriate and inappropriate application form questions. In reviewing the table, keep several points in mind. First, phrase items to elicit information related to the specific job for which the application form is being used. Wallace and Vodanovich suggest that simple rephrasing using job-related language can eliminate some "inappropriate" items.[76] For example, a form could ask, "Are you at least 18 years old?" rather than, "What is your date of birth?" Second, an item that is unacceptable in some situations might not be acceptable in others. For example, an item may be usable if it can be shown that it provides information useful for predicting the success of a new employee with regard to the job for which application is being made. Or, an item may provide information that represents a bona fide occupational requirement for a specific job. The example items listed are not an exhaustive treatment of what should and should not be asked on the application form. The items shown are meant to be illustrative of what can be used. Thus the examples serve as a guide to planning, developing, and using application forms.

Of course, whether an item is appropriate will also depend on laws enacted by the various states. For example, although federal law permits questions regarding criminal convictions, a few states limit the use of conviction records in the employment context. For example, in Ohio applicants cannot be required to disclose convictions for minor misdemeanor violations (Ohio Rev. Code Ann. Tit. 29 § 2925.11). Employers must be aware of relevant state nondiscrimination laws as well as federal laws. Although the review in Table 9.6 is not an exhaustive treatment of items that could be included on an application form, it does provide some guidelines and comments to consider in preparing or revising a biodata questionnaire to be used in selection.

Developing and Revising Application Forms

Biodata, like application forms, consists of questions about the applicant's work and life experiences. As we have seen, the questions asked on a job application form determine its effectiveness in selecting the best, most appropriate job applicants. Some questions may result in a discrimination charge against the user or employer. It is imperative that employers study carefully the development or revision of their biodata forms. Similar to the development of any selection device, several steps are involved in the development of a biodata questionnaire. The steps include the following:

1. **Because There Are Many Types of Job, More Than One Application Form Will Probably Be Needed.** At the extreme, there could be one application form for each job. More realistically, however, one form will likely be used to cover a class or family of jobs, that is, jobs that require similar types of knowledge, skills, abilities, or tasks. For example, different versions of application forms may be used for job classes such as clerical/office personnel, sales personnel, operation workers, professional and technical personnel, executives, and managers[77] Bryan Kethley and David Terpstra report that more than half of the lawsuits filed in federal court associated with application forms involved service (29 percent) or professional jobs (22 percent). Three other categories of jobs were associated with legal challenges: executive/administrative/managerial (13 percent), operations/fabrication/laborers (13 percent), and administrative/support/clerical (10 percent).[78] These findings underscore the need to tailor application forms to various jobs or classes of jobs.

TABLE 9.6	Examples of Appropriate and Inappropriate Questions Asked on Application Forms

Subject of Question	Appropriate Questions	Inappropriate Questions	Comments
Name	"What is your name?" "Have you worked for this company under another name?" "Have you used a name (such as an assumed name or nickname) the company would need to know to check your previous work and educational records? If so, please explain."	"What was your maiden name?" "Have you ever used another name?"	Questions about an applicant's name that may indicate marital status or national origin should be avoided.
Age	"Are you at least 18 years old?" "Upon employment, all employees must submit legal proof of age. Can you furnish proof of age?"	"What is your date of birth?" "What is your age?"	The Age Discrimination in Employment Act of 1967, amended in 1986, prohibits discrimination against individuals 40 years of age and older. A request for age-related data may discourage older workers from applying. Age data should be collected only when it can be shown to be a bona fide occupational requirement.
Race, Ethnicity, and Physical Characteristics	"After employment, a photograph must be taken of all employees. If employed, can you furnish a photograph?" "Do you read, speak, or write Spanish [or other language required for the job]?"	"What is your race?" "Would you please submit a photograph with your application for identification purposes?" "What is the color of your hair? Your eyes?" "What language do you commonly use?" "How did you acquire your ability to read, write, or speak a foreign language?"	Information relative to physical characteristics may be associated with sexual or racial group membership. Thus, unless such information can be shown to be related to job performance, the information may be treated as discriminatory.
Height and Weight	"After employment, all employees are required to submit a physical description (eye color, hair color, height, and weight)."	"What is your height and weight?"	Questions regarding height and weight should be asked only if an employer can demonstrate that minimum height/weight requirements are necessary for successful job performance.
Religion	The employer may state the days, hours, and shifts to be worked.	"What is your religious faith?" "Does your religion prevent you from working on weekends?"	Questions that determine an applicant's availability have an exclusionary effect because of some people's religious practices (e.g., whether an applicant can work on holidays or weekends). Questions should be used only if they can be shown not to have an exclusionary effect, if they are justified by business necessity, or where religion is a bona fide occupational qualification (BFOQ).

(Continued)

| TABLE 9.6 | (Continued) | | |

Subject of Question	Appropriate Questions	Inappropriate Questions	Comments
Gender, Marital Status, Children, Child Care	"If you are a minor, please list the name and address of a parent or guardian."	"What is your sex?" "Describe your current marital status." "List the number and ages of your children." "If you have children, please describe the provisions you have made for child care." "With whom do you reside?" "Do you prefer being referred to as Miss, Mrs., or Ms.?"	Direct or indirect questions about marital status, number and ages of children, pregnancy, and childbearing plans frequently discriminate against women and may be a violation of Title VII. Information on child care arrangements should not be asked solely of women. Questions about an applicant's gender should be avoided, unless gender is a BFOQ.
Physical or Mental Health	"Are you able to perform these job tasks (attach a list of specific tasks to the application) with or without an accommodation? If so, how would you perform the tasks, and with what accommodations"? "Can you meet the attendance requirements of this job?"	"Do you have any physical or mental disabilities, defects, or handicaps?" "How would you describe your general physical health?" "When was your last physical exam?" "Have you received workers' compensation or disability income payments?" "Have you any physical defects that could preclude you from performing certain jobs?"	The Americans with Disabilities Act prohibits any preemployment inquiries about physical or mental disability.
Citizenship[a] or National Origin	"If you are offered and accept a job, can you submit proof of your legal right to work in the United States?" "Do you have the legal right to live and work in the United States?"	"What is your country of citizenship?" "Please list your birthplace."	Consideration of an applicant's citizenship may constitute discrimination on the basis of national origin. The law protects citizens and noncitizens with legal authorization to work in the United States from discrimination on the basis of sex, race, color, religion, or national origin.
Military Service	"Please list any specific educational or job experiences you have acquired during military service that you believe would be useful on the job for which you are applying."	"Please list the dates and type of discharge you received from military service."	Minority service members have a higher percentage of undesirable military discharges. A policy of rejecting those with less than an honorable discharge may be discriminatory. This information may discourage minorities from applying for employment.

[a] The Immigration Reform and Control Act of 1986 contains specific language regarding the employment of citizens, impending citizens, and legal aliens. The act has a bearing on the questions that can be asked on the application form concerning citizenship and the use of citizenship information in selection. In addition, questions on the application that involve citizenship status must be worded carefully to avoid discrimination due to national origin covered by the Civil Rights Act of 1964.

(Continued)

| TABLE 9.6 | (Continued) |

Subject of Question	Appropriate Questions	Inappropriate Questions	Comments
Arrest and Conviction Records	"Have you ever been convicted of a felony or, during the last two years, of a misdemeanor that resulted in imprisonment? If so, what was the felony or misdemeanor?" (A conviction will not necessarily disqualify you from the job for which you are applying. A conviction will be judged on its own merits with respect to time, circumstances, and seriousness.)	"Have you ever been arrested?" "Have you ever been convicted of a criminal offense?"	Arrest information is illegal. Federal courts have held that a conviction for a felony or misdemeanor should not automatically exclude an applicant from employment. An employer can consider the relationship between a conviction and suitability for a job. When questions are used, there should be a statement that factors such as age at time of offense, seriousness of violation, and rehabilitation will be considered, along with the factor of how the nature of the job relates to the conviction(s).
Hobbies, Clubs, and Organizations	"Do you have any hobbies that are related to the job for which you are making application?" "Please list any clubs or organizations in which you are a member that relate to the job for which you are applying." "While in school, did you participate in any activities or clubs that are related to the job for which you are applying?"	"Please list any hobbies you may have." "Please list all clubs or other organizations in which you are a member." "In what extracurricular activities or clubs did you participate while in school?"	Applicant information on membership in clubs and organizations can be discriminatory. If membership is associated with the age, sex, race, or religion of the applicant, the data may be viewed as discriminatory. If questions on club/organizational memberships are asked, a statement should be added that applicants may omit those organizations associated with age, race, sex, religion, or any other protected characteristic.
Education	"Did you graduate from high school? From college?"	"When did you attend high school? Elementary school?"	On average, minority members tend to have lower levels of education than nonminority group members. Where educational requirements disqualify minority group members at a higher rate than nonminority group members and it cannot be shown that the educational requirement is related to successful job performance, the courts have viewed educational requirements as discriminatory.
Credit Rating and Bonding	"Do you have the use of a reliable car?" (if car travel is required by the job)	"Do you own your own car?" "Do you own or rent your residence?" "Have you ever filed for bankruptcy?"	Use of credit rating questions tends to have an adverse impact on minority group applicants and women and has been found unlawful in some cases. Unless shown to be job-related, questions on car ownership, home ownership, length of residence, garnishment of wages, etc., may violate Title VII.
		"Have you ever been refused an application for bonding or had your bonding canceled?"	The federal Bankruptcy Code prohibits discrimination against job applicants who may have been bankrupt.

(Continued)

TABLE 9.6	(*Continued*)		
Subject of Question	**Appropriate Questions**	**Inappropriate Questions**	**Comments**
Off-the-Job Conduct	None.	"Do you smoke?" "Do you drink alcoholic beverages?"	In general, employers cannot inquire into applicants' off-the-job conduct unless the conduct is associated with a BFOQ or conflicts with the employer's primary mission. However, a statement regarding an employer's policy for on- the-job behavior can be included; for example, "Our organization provides a smoke-free work environment for its employees."
Driver's License	"Do you have a current driver's license?"	"Do you have a driver's license?"	Employers should only ask this question if a driver's license is required for performance of the job.
Emergency Contact	"Please give a name and address of a person to be notified in case of an emergency."	"Please give a name and address of a relative to be notified in case of an emergency."	If this information is collected in order to have a contact in case of an emergency, request this after employment.

Sources: Based on Craig Wallace and Stephen J. Vodanovich, "Personnel Application Blanks: Persistence and Knowledge of Legally Inadvisable Application Blank Items," *Public Personnel Management*, 33 (Fall 2004): 331–349; J. Craig Wallace, Mary G. Tye, and Stephen J. Vodanovich, "Applying for Jobs Online: Examining the Legality of Internet-Based Application Forms," *Public Personnel Management*, 4 (Winter 2000): 497–504; Stephen J. Vodanovich and Rosemary H. Lowe, "They Ought to Know Better: The Incidence and Correlates of Inappropriate Application Blank Inquiries," *Public Personnel Management*, 21 (1992): 363–370; Herbert G. Heneman and Timothy A. Judge, *Staffing Organizations*, 5th ed. (Mendota House, Middleton, WI, 2006); Bureau of National Affairs, *Equal Employment Opportunity Commission Guide to Pre-Employment Inquiries* (Washington, DC: Equal Employment Opportunity Commission—periodically updated), pp. 65–80; and Bureau of National Affairs, *BNA Handbook: Personnel Management* (Washington, DC: Bureau of National Affairs, 2003).

2. **Job Analysis Data Should Serve as One Basis for Choosing Employment Application Questions.** Although job analysis data are commonly used in developing other selection devices such as tests, few users consider these data in constructing their application forms. Not only should these analyses suggest useful items for the forms, but they should also serve as a basis for their legal justification. This suggests that while empirical data have traditionally been used to justify the validity of applicant information (for example, WAB), recent research has begun emphasizing whether items can be theoretically linked to job-relevant attributes and performance.[79] Thus, this approach relies on job analytic data to establish the content-validity of the inquiries used on application forms.

This step is crucial to developing highly valid biodata items. To know what antecedent behavior or life experiences to measure, it is important to identify the criterion or measure of job success or job performance we are interested in predicting. Many different types of criteria can be employed: (a) job tenure (or turnover), (b) absenteeism, (c) training program success, (d) rate of salary increase, (e) supervisory ratings, or (f) job performance. Criteria involving *behavioral* measures of performance such as job tenure, dollar sales, absenteeism, tardiness, compensation history, and job output are likely to provide more reliable data than subjective measures such as ratings. However, care should be taken to ensure that these behavioral measures provide reliable, uncontaminated, and meaningful assessments. In many cases, the most readily available criterion may not be the most useful. Biodata items may then be written or selected to reflect those attributes that can be used to predict our criterion or measure of success on the job.

3. ***Developing a Pool of Biodata Items.*** After hypothesizing life history experiences that may predict our identified criteria, we select or construct biodata items to reflect these experiences. Our hypotheses guide the development of specific life history items that will appear on the application form. As we have noted, the items can be selected from previous biodata research studies or be originally developed. Available publications can serve as sources of items. For example, James Glennon, Lewis Albright, and William Owens have prepared a compendium of life history items.[80] Their catalog consists of more than 500 biodata items classified into the following categories: (a) habits and attitudes, (b) health, (c) human relations, (d) money, (e) parental home, childhood, teenage years, (f) personal attributes, (g) present home, spouse, and children, (h) recreation, hobbies, and interests, (i) school and education, (j) self impressions, (k) values, opinions, and preferences, and (l) work. Items from the catalog can be selected if it appears that they may be useful in measuring the hypothesized life experiences thought to be predictive of success. Bibliographies of biographical data research can also be a valuable source of references with potentially useful items.[81]

Another approach to selecting items relies on empirical analyses (for example, WAB). In this approach, items statistically correlated with various criteria such as tenure, absenteeism, and job performance are retained. Example items include (a) size of hometown, (b) number of times moved in recent years, (c) length of residence at previous address, (d) years of education, (e) courses taken and preferred during high school, (f) types of previous jobs, (g) number of previous jobs, (h) tenure on previous jobs, (i) distance of residence from company, (j) source of reference to company, (k) reason for leaving last job, (l) length of time before being available for employment, and (m) whether current employer can be contacted. Many other item examples could be cited. Keep this in mind when items are being proposed. The simplest and most apparent form of an item on the application may not be the most useful. It may be possible to develop several potential items from one question appearing on an application. For instance, if a question asks about previous jobs within a specified period, we may be able to develop items on the *number* as well as the *type* of jobs held.

Michael Mumford, William Owens, Leatta Hough and colleagues have provided excellent reviews of research studies investigating various aspects of writing and formatting biodata items.[82] These investigations have important implications for the validity and reliability of biodata questionnaires. We do not review those studies per se, but we summarize some item-writing guides distilled from the research. These guidelines should be followed as biodata items are formatted into an application form:

1. Biodata items should principally deal with past behavior and experiences.

2. Items dealing with family relationships or other issues of a personal nature (for example, religion) are usually viewed as offensive.

3. Specificity and brevity of items and response options are desirable.

4. Numbers should be used to define a biodata item's options or alternatives.

5. All possible response options and an "escape" option (for example, "other") should be given; where possible, response options that form a continuum should be used.

6. Item options should carry a neutral or pleasant connotation.

7. Items dealing with past and present behaviors and with opinions, attitudes, and values are generally acceptable.

Fred Mael suggested two additional guides in preparing biodata items:[83]

8. Items should reflect historical events that are important in shaping a person's behavior and identity. (In contrast to Mael's recommendation, Lawrence Kleiman and Robert Faley reported that a set of biodata items measuring present behavior were as valid in predicting reenlistment in the Air National Guard as biodata items measuring past behavior.[84])

9. To lessen the effect of individuals responding in ways considered to be socially desirable (that is, faking), biodata items should reflect external events (that is, prior behaviors occurring in real-life situations), be limited to firsthand recollections, be potentially verifiable, and measure unique, discrete events (such as age when first licensed to drive).

4. Prescreening and Pilot-Testing Biodata Items. Like items appearing on other selection measures, biodata items can be objectionable and produce bias against some respondents. In this step, the biodata items developed are reviewed by a panel of judges for objectionability and potential bias against certain groups of respondents (for example, with regard to gender and ethnicity). Item content and response option review by a panel of subject matter experts has been found to reduce objectionability and bias and enhance the clarity and job relevance of biodata items.[85]

Once a relevant group of items has been developed and its content prescreened, it should be tried out on an appropriate group of respondents. Ideally, this group should be large and representative of the applicant or employee population for which the biodata form will be used. Although biodata forms have been developed using sample sizes of 300 or so, more dependable, generalizable results are found with larger sample sizes (>500). In general, the larger the sample size, the better.

After administering the items to an appropriate sample, analyses are performed in order to choose those items that are most useful. For example, items are eliminated from the biodata inventory using one or more item specifications such as the following:

- Items exhibiting little response variance

- Items having skewed response distributions

- Items correlated with protected-group characteristics such as ethnicity

- Items having no correlation with other items thought to be measuring the same life history construct

- Items having no correlation with the criterion (that is, no item validity)

Those biodata items passing the prescreening and pilot-testing reviews are retained for inclusion in the final version of the application form.[86]

5. Scoring the Biodata Form. After collecting responses to the biodata questionnaire from a large, representative sample, procedures for determining scores on the inventory are developed. The various options for scoring biodata measures tend to fall into two categories: (a) the calculation of a *single*, empirically-keyed overall score that is predictive of employee success[87] or (b) the development of multiple scores for dimensions or groups of related items appearing on a biodata inventory.[88] As we have noted before, there are many types of biodata. A fundamental distinction is whether the scores require the computation of a single score based on empirical keying. Several methods of empirical keying are available, including (a) vertical percentage,[89] (b) horizontal percentage,[90] (c) correlation,[91] (d) differential regression,[92] (e) deviant response,[93] and (f) rare response.[94] Of these, the vertical percentage method has been the most popular and useful. This method of scoring corresponds to what is also called weighted application blank (WAB). That is, each item on the biodata form is analyzed to determine its relation with some criterion of job success, such as job tenure or turnover. Items related to the criterion are identified, and weights are assigned to the item alternatives to reflect the strength of their relationship. Scores are obtained for individuals by summing the weights corresponding to their responses.

The other approach is to score clusters or groups of related or homogeneous items into dimensions or constructs reflecting a common life experience or behavior. Scores are derived for each of the biodata factors (usually 10 to 15 factors). A study by Robert Morrison and his associates illustrates how dimensions of biodata can be used to predict and understand aspects of employee job performance.[95] One of the purposes of their research was to examine how dimensions of life history were related to industrial research scientists' job performance. They factor analyzed 75 biodata items and three criteria (creativity ratings, overall job performance ratings, and number of patent disclosures) collected on 418 petroleum research scientists. The five biodata dimensions identified and brief descriptions of individuals with high scores on each dimension follow:

1. *Favorable Self-Perception*

   In the top 5 percent of performance in their occupation

   Could be a highly successful supervisor if given the chance

   Work at faster pace than most people

   Desire to work independently

2. *Inquisitive Professional Orientation*

   Completed Ph.D. degree

   Belong to one or more professional organizations

   Devote much time to reading with broad interests

   Have high salary aspirations

3. *Utilitarian Drive*

   Desire extrinsic rewards from business and society

   Prefer urban dwelling

   Feel free to express self and perceive self as influencing others

   Do not desire to work independently

4. *Tolerance for Ambiguity*

   Desire to have many work activities

   Are not single

   Have solicited funds for charity

   Have friends with various political views

5. *General Adjustment*

   Feel that school material was adequately presented

   Came from happy homes

   Express their opinions readily; feel effective in doing so

An examination of the association of the five dimensions or factors with the three criteria revealed some interesting findings. *Different* biodata factors were associated with *different* types of performance on the job. For example, scientists who received high ratings on overall job performance tended to be those with high scores on the biodata factors of *Favorable Self-Perception, Utilitarian Drive,* and *General Adjustment.* Scientists with many patent awards had an opposite life history profile. They scored high on *Inquisitive Professional Orientation* and *Tolerance for Ambiguity.* Among others, these results suggest that different types of life experiences (that is, biodata factors) might be used to predict different types and levels of job performance (criteria). By weighting some biodata factors more than others in selection decisions, we could affect subsequent performance in our organization. For instance, in the current example, if greater weight were given to hiring applicants high in *Inquisitive Professional Orientation* and *Tolerance for Ambiguity,* we would expect higher performance in number of patents awarded than if other factors such as *General Adjustment* were emphasized.

A recent study showed four empirically-keyed, cross-validated biodata dimensions that not only predicted different unique criteria, further supporting the results described above, but also showed incremental validity above and beyond that accounted for by personality (using the five-factor model) and intelligence or general mental ability.[96] As this suggests, the approach popularized by William Owens and Lyle Schoenfeldt, to score biodata by identifying life history dimensions, appears to be the contemporary trend.[97] Their research program supports the idea that prediction, as well as greater understanding of the relation between life history and employee job success, can be enhanced by scoring biodata in terms of dimensions. Whatever scoring option is taken, cross-validation of any scoring procedure is essential. In addition, validity and reliability information should be collected on any biodata measure.

The developmental approach just outlined can enhance the effectiveness of biodata as a predictor as well as our understanding of how and why biodata works. This method, or one similar to it, is also likely to enable you to develop a legally defensible approach for employing biodata in HR selection.

Applications and Resumes

The first impression many employers have of applicants for professional positions is from their resumes. Applicants often initially submit a resume to a prospective employer rather than an application form. Resumes are subject to the same kinds of distortions that plague many application forms. In one study, for example, 95 percent of college students surveyed said they were willing to tell at least one false statement to get a job; 41 percent had previously done so.[98] For this reason, resume reviewers are encouraged to carefully consider the following as indicators of possible "resume fraud":

- Inflated educational credentials (grades achieved, degrees attained)

- Omitted or inconsistent periods of employment or stretched employment dates

- Gaps in time periods listed (Where was the applicant? Prison?)

- Exaggerated claims of expertise and experience

- Claims of self-employment

- Claims of work as a consultant

- Claims of work with firms that are now out of business

- Evidence of a regressive work history (for example, moving down in levels of responsibility or compensation)

- Use of qualifiers such as "had exposure to," "assisted with," "attended a university"

- Use of vague answers (such as indicating a state or city rather than the company's complete address)

In many of these cases, verification of the self-report information (through background checks of application and resume information) is likely warranted.

Little research has been done on the validity of inferences employers make in judging applicants' skills and abilities from their resumes. In one study, recruiters' perceptions of resume content were found to be predictive of the applicant's mental ability, as well as personality attributes such as conscientiousness and extraversion. These results are important; prior research has shown that these applicant traits, particularly mental ability and conscientiousness, are important predictors of job success. These findings show that recruiters can use resume information to screen applicants on characteristics that are likely to be predictive of job performance.[99] A second study focused on the attributes inferred from resume information. Barbara Brown and Michael Campion obtained ratings from 113 recruiters of the degree to which 20 resume items represented six job applicant abilities and skills—language ability, math ability, physical abilities, interpersonal skills, leadership ability, and motivation.[100] The resume items that were used by recruiters to infer job applicant attributes, regardless of the job under consideration, are shown in Table 9.7. Moderate interrater reliability (0.60s to 0.70s) was found among recruiters for the inferences made. In general, recruiters inferred language and mathematics abilities from items related to educational achievement; physical abilities were judged from athletics or sports participation items; and leadership and interpersonal attributes were seen from items dealing with authority positions held and social activities participated in. Recruiters' inferences, such as those identified in these two studies, appear to have face validity; however, there is little evidence regarding the empirical validity of recruiters' inferences from resume information.

Online and Internet-Based Resume Screening

The typical employer receives hundreds, if not thousands of resumes. The rate of unsolicited resumes has exploded along with growth in internet useage, which is increasingly relied on by applicants and employers as a way to search for job opportunities and qualified candidates. To indicate the scale of internet usage, Monster.com, one of the largest internet employment sites, reports more than one million unique job postings each month and 28 million unique visitors. As usage online has surged, so has the number of firms catering to these needs. For example, it is possible to screen only from a pool of "Aggies" from Texas A&M University by searching on http:www.AggieCareers.com or http:www.HireAggies.com. Given the volume of resumes companies receive, the challenge is to quickly screen out applicants who are clearly unsuited for the job in a way that is fair and efficient and relies on job-requirements. We will use the resume to discuss issues that arise from using online tools to facilitate searching (or screening) for jobs or applicants, and legal considerations that may emerge in this context.[101]

Companies are increasingly using technology to optically scan resumes and using keyword searches to identify specific attributes that meet minimum qualifications or credentials—work experience, training or education, even whether the candidate currently resides near the job opportunity or is willing to relocate. As we noted previously, a problem with resumes is controllability; the applicant controls what information is reported. Although automating the process aids in extracting relevant

TABLE 9.7 Resume Items Used by Recruiters to Infer Job Applicant Abilities and Skills for Sales and Accounting Positions

Resume Item	Inferred Job Applicant Attribute					
	Language Ability	Math Ability	Physical Abilities	Interpersonal Skills	Leadership Ability	Motivation
Education Items:						
1. Pursuing job-related degree						
2. Grades obtained in major		✔				(✔)
3. Overall grades obtained						✔
4. Earned college expenses						✔
5. Has computer experience						✔
6. Has foreign language skills	✔					
Work Experience Items:						
7. Has full-time work experience						
8. Has supervised others				(✔)	✔	(✔)
9. Individual job achievements						✔
10. Held summer internship						(✔)
11. Worked while in college						(✔)
12. Served as dorm advisor				(✔)	✔	✔
Activities/Honors/Interests:						
13. Professional society member						✔
14. Held elected office				(✔)	✔	✔
15. Varsity athletics captain				(✔)	✔	✔
16. Participant in recreational sports			✔			
17. Participant in community activities				(✔)		✔
18. College clubs member				(✔)		✔
19. Social fraternity member				(✔)		
20. Has been on Dean's list						✔

Note: Definitions of job applicant abilities and skills: **Language ability**—capacity to read, write, and speak; **Math ability**—capacity to perform mathematical manipulations (addition, subtraction, statistics); **Physical abilities**—physical strength and fitness; **Interpersonal skills**—capacity to interact with and relate to others; **Leadership ability**—capacity to direct, control, and coordinate others; **Motivation**—drive and level of energy. A ✔ indicates that a resume item was used by recruiters to infer a particular job applicant attribute for *both* sales and accounting applicants. The results are based on ratings of 113 recruiters.

Source: Copyright © 1994 by the American Psychological Association. Based on Barbara K. Brown and Michael A. Campion, "Biodata Phenomenology: Recruiters' Perceptions and Use of Biographical Information in Resume Screening," *Journal of Applied Psychology*, 79 (1994): 901–902. Reproduced with permission. No further reproduction or distribution is permitted without written permission from the American Psychological Association.

information, verification of experience, education, and other qualifications is typically not feasible at this early stage; it is dealt with at a later step during the hiring process.[102] To ensure the information being collected is standardized (obtained from all applicants), more and more firms are requiring preformatted resume builders with preset fields and check boxes. The trade-off is convenience; applicants must spend more time cutting and pasting qualifications as prompted rather than simply submitting an existing resume. Such a requirement will reduce the number of applicants who submit a resume or application, but those who do respond are likely to be more motivated and committed to the opportunity. The firm will at least have the same information on each applicant.[103]

Two legal issues are particularly salient with online screening. First, to the extent qualified applicants from minority groups do not have equal access to the internet, and consequently are overlooked during the screening process, there may be disparate impact. Employers using online screening techniques must make every effort to actively recruit minority members and use fair procedures during their assessment. The second concern relates to privacy. Sensitive data may be tracked by third-party vendors or the web sites themselves without the knowledge of the applicant or employers.[104] J. M. Stanton reports that some legal cases (*Bohach v City of Reno et al.,* 1996; *State v Bonnell,* 1993) indicate selection related websites should provide "disclaimers that explicitly tell applicants what happens to their data, who has (and will have) access to their data, and the degree to which their data and their involvement in the hiring process are kept private and confidential" (p. 15).[105] Considerably more research is needed to establish the validity and usefulness of data obtained online. As it is, this is a new arena in a relatively uncontrolled environment. Consequently, many issues must be examined. At a minimum, an employer should utilize the same rigorous approach detailed above for successfully developing and administering an application form.

Using Application Forms in HR Selection

An employment application represents only one means for evaluating a job applicant's ability to perform a job. Certainly, other types of measures such as tests and interviews can be used in conjunction with the application form. For the moment, however, we are concerned with *how* the application might be used in selection. This is a critical issue, one that deserves more attention than it typically receives. Recent research shows that the application information managers say they rely on to make the initial screening decision often differs from what they actually use, as is reflected through a policy capturing analysis.[106] Some managers relied on gender, for example, rather than actual applicant qualifications for the job, when they evaluated candidates. How this information is assessed warrants careful consideration, because information from applications can be useful for predicting job performance.[107] As we have seen, the alternatives for utilizing application data can range from those that are objective in their treatment of information to those that are more or less subjective. These approaches can be general or detailed. Furthermore, even though various scoring options are available for handling application data, the methods that have been demonstrated to provide valid information tend to be either based on an empirical scoring key, resulting in an overall score, or they rely on multiple job-relevant constructs, as identified through job analysis, and each of these dimensions has a separate score.

Application forms can be used like a checklist. Because most checklists emphasize applicants' training, education, and experience, they are usually referred to as training and experience evaluations (or simply "T&E" evaluations). Because training and experience evaluations are important and used frequently, we treat T&E evaluations as another selection predictor.

TRAINING AND EXPERIENCE (T&E) EVALUATIONS

Nature and Role of T&E Evaluations in Selection

T&E evaluations are a way to rationally assess previous experience, training, and education information given by job applicants. The information is reported by the applicant on the resume, on the application form itself, or on a separate questionnaire completed along with the application. Whatever the form, applicants provide job-related information in areas such as previous performance of specific tasks; work history; prior education and training received; credentials such as licenses; self-report ratings of the knowledge, skills, and abilities they possess; and past accomplishments at work. This information is then evaluated by a rater or HR selection specialist using a scoring plan. Scores from the evaluations can be used in a number of ways: (a) as the sole basis for deciding whether an individual is qualified, (b) as a means for rank-ordering individuals from high to low based on a T&E score, (c) as a basis for prescreening applicants prior to administering more expensive, time-consuming predictors (for example, an interview), and (d) in combination with other predictors used for making an employment decision. The objective of using the scores is to predict future job performance, and this information can be helpful in determining the minimum qualifications needed to perform a job.[108]

Examples of T&E Evaluations.   To better understand T&E ratings, some examples may help. Our first example might be suitable when only a brief check is needed of relevant portions of a job application for minimal qualifications. The second example shows that a T&E evaluation may be appropriate when a more thorough review of minimum qualifications is being made.

Figure 9.1 illustrates an example of a brief check. It is a checklist to be completed by a company HR specialist for applications submitted for the job of clerk. The form is brief and simple, but it encourages the application reviewer to attend to those aspects of the

---

FIGURE 9.1 Brief Training and Experience Evaluation Used for Appraising Applications Submitted for the Job of Clerk

Name of Applicant: _____

Directions: Before completing this form, review the minimum qualifications for the job of Clerk that are listed below. Then, study each application form submitted for the job. After reviewing each application, indicate if the applicant possesses each minimum qualification. If an applicant meets the necessary requirements, check "Yes"; if not, then check "No." When there are job openings, applicants meeting all minimum qualifications will be invited in for additional consideration. After completing the checklist, please attach it to the application form and return the application to the personnel file.

Minimum Applicant Qualifications		
Yes	No	
☐	☐	1. Maintained a filing system of letters, reports, documents, etc.
☐	☐	2. Used a personal computer and Microsoft Word® for Windows® 2007 word processor to type letters and reports.
☐	☐	3. Used a Dictaphone® or other digital recording device in transcribing correspondence.

Note: This form is completed by a selection specialist.

application that are important for identifying a successful clerk. These aspects important to the job were identified in a previous job analysis. If an applicant meets each of the minimum qualifications listed, an employment decision may be made or additional testing offered. For example, if a candidate possesses all basic qualifications for the job, the applicant might then be administered a filing or typing test or given an interview.

A T&E evaluation such as that in Figure 9.1 can be helpful in making a quick, cursory screening of job applicants. In particular, it is useful in initial screening for those jobs for which large numbers of people make application. When used in this context, the checklist can help to minimize unnecessary HR selection costs by ensuring that only suitable applicants receive further employment consideration. For example, if experience with Microsoft Word® for Windows® 2007 word processing software is a necessary requirement for successfully performing the job of clerk, our checklist might include "Used a personal computer and Microsoft Word® for Windows® 2007 word processor to type letters and reports." An applicant must have at least this much relevant job experience, in addition to meeting other minimum qualifications, before being hired or asked to complete another selection measure such as a filing test. It is important to emphasize that the minimum qualifications listed on any preemployment checklist should meet the criteria for establishing employee specifications that we discussed earlier in Chapter 7.

Figure 9.2 presents an example of a separate T&E evaluation form for the job of personnel research analyst. This form is representative of those training and experience assessment methods that are based on job tasks. Using a previous job analysis, tasks critical to the job were identified. We have listed only a few. For each of the important job tasks, applicants are asked to indicate their specific work experiences and/or any training received. With regard to work experience, for example, applicants might be asked to list dates of employment, previous employers, previous job titles, and supervisory responsibilities. Applicants might also be asked to describe their educational background, specialized training, or specific skills acquired that might have prepared them to perform each of these tasks. In addition, applicants must provide names of persons who can be contacted to verify their self-reported information. Verification information helps to discourage applicants from inflating their training and job experiences.

One product of the job analysis is the determination of what experience, education, and training are relevant for successful task performance.[109] For instance, for the task "Computed and monitored applicant flow statistics for nonexempt job applicants using computerized statistical packages (for example, SPSS, SAS)," we may require knowledge of college-level introductory psychological statistics and training in the use of SPSS, SAS, or equivalent computerized statistical packages. The reviewer of the T&E would simply study the applicant's reported experience, education, and training descriptions to determine whether the applicant met minimum standards. Each task would be reviewed in a similar manner; that is, applicant descriptors would be compared with job task qualifications. These comparisons would be recorded using a summary form like that in Figure 9.3. Individuals who meet or exceed these minimum qualifications would be recommended for further consideration.

Evelution of Work-Related Experience, Education, and Training.   T&E ealuations are based on ratings. This rules out empirically keying life history responses like those used in WABs. Thus, a critical question is *which* aspects of experience, education, and training are judged relevant by raters. Consider experience. It can be measured by the frequency or length of time on the task or job, (that is, quantity) or by the challenge, complexity, or

FIGURE 9.2	An Example Training and Experience Evaluation Form for the Job of Personnel Research Analyst

Directions: Listed below are some important job tasks performed by a Personnel Research Analyst. Read each of the tasks. If you have had experience or training in performing a task, check the box marked "Yes." If you have not, then check the box marked "No." For the task(s) marked "Yes," please describe any experience and training you have had that you believe to be associated with each task. All of your responses are subject to review and verification.

Have you had experience or training with this task?

Yes	No	Task
❑	❑	1. Computed and monitored applicant flow statistics for nonexempt job applicants using computerized statistical packages (for example, SPSS, SAS).

Describe Your Relevant Experience:

Employer: _____ Title: _____
Dates of employment: From _____ To _____
Describe your experience with this task: _____
_____
_____

Describe Your Relevant Training:

Formal coursework and location: _____
_____

Training programs attended and location: _____

On the job training: _____

Name and address of person(s) who can verify this information: _____
_____
_____

Yes	No	Task
❑	❑	2. Designed and conducted test validation studies for entry-level jobs.

· · ·

Yes	No	Task
❑	❑	3. Supervised research assistants in collecting data for human resource studies.

· · ·

Yes	No	Task
❑	❑	4. Trained personnel assistants in the use of personnel tests (for example, typing, basic math, and verbal tests) for entry-level jobs.

· · ·

(Continued)

FIGURE 9.2 *(Continued)*

	Yes	No

☐ Yes   ☐ No

5. Made oral presentations to line and/or upper-level managers on the results of personnel research studies.

- •
- •
- •

- •
- •
- •

Describe Your Relevant Experience:

Employer: _____ Title: _____
Dates of employment: From _____ To _____
Describe your experience with this task: _____
_____
_____
_____

Describe Your Relevant Training:

Formal coursework and location: _____
_____

Training programs attended and location: _____
_____

On the job training: _____
_____

Name and address of person(s) who can verify this information: _____
_____
_____

Note: This form is completed by the job applicant.

---

quality of instruction/feedback given while doing the task or job (that is, quality). Prior research shows that quantity of experience is a useful predictor for up to five years for highly skilled work experience but only up to three years on routine jobs. In contrast, quality of experience that is based on challenging experiences may continue to increase competency and self-efficacy for years. Thus, measures of quality may predict beyond the five-year limit of quantity measures. In addition to quantity and quality, relevancy is important; it may be the preferred approach to assessing aspects of work experience. In large part, relevancy is gauged in two ways: in terms of fit, based on similarity between prior job and the job the candidate is applying for, including size and kind of organization (large, private or public, small, family owned) and the level of supervisory responsibility, technical knowledge required, and complexity and criticality of those experiences.

Similar issues are associated with education and training. Both of these deal with learning, the former with general, non-job specific learning and the latter with specific job or task training. Brown and Campion (1994) found college recruiters differentiate facets by: job-related experiences including degree and grades in major; computer experience; foreign language; and more general experiences including overall grades, Deans Lists, scholarships, whether an applicant earned college expenses, varsity athletics, elected offices, college clubs or social fraternities.[110]

Another way to categorize assessment experiences is to consider the inferences guiding these assessments. These evaluate the relationship between experience, education, and training have and job knowledge and task proficiency.[111] These past ratings are, to a surprising degree, seen as assessing the candidates motivation and work atitudes; along with skill and ability, these predict job performance and career development. As this shows, determining which measures to focus on requires some thought. Below, we show how useful this selection device can be, based on accumuluted reliability and validity evidence.

Reliability and Validity of T&E Evaluations

Reliability.   As far as reliability is concerned, T&E evaluations tend to reflect rather high interrater reliability estimates. Ronald Ash and Edward Levine reported average

FIGURE 9.3	An Example Rating Form for Use in Evaluating Training and Experience of Applicants for the Job of Personnel Research Analyst

Directions: Read the minimum qualifications required to perform the job of Personnel Research Analyst. Then, compare these qualifications to the applicant's training and experience evaluations. If an applicant's qualifications meet or exceed the requirements for the job, check "Meets Requirements." If not, check "Does Not Meet Requirements."

Name of Applicant _____

Task	Minimum Qualifications	Applicant Rating
1. Computes and monitors applicant flow statistics for nonexempt job applicants using computerized statistical packages (for example, SPSS, SAS).	1. Has knowledge of college-level introductory psycho-logical statistics course; formal coursework training or on-the-job training in use of SPSS, SAS, or equivalent statistical packages.	❑ Meets Requirements ❑ Does Not Meet Requirements
2. Designs and conducts test validation studies for entry-level jobs.	2. Was responsible for conducting empirical vali-dation studies or selection tests. Is knowledgeable of the content of the Uniform Guidelines.	❑ Meets Requirements ❑ Does Not Meet Requirements
3. Supervises research assistants in collecting data for personnel selection studies.	3. Directed or was primarily responsible for the work of others involving the collection of empirical data.	❑ Meets Requirements ❑ Does Not Meet Requirements
4. Trains personnel assistants in the use of personnel tests (for example, typing, basic math, and verbal tests) for entry-level jobs.	4. Had college-level course or training in testing and test administration.	❑ Meets Requirements ❑ Does Not Meet Requirements
5. Makes oral presentations to line and/or upper-level managers on the results of personnel research studies.	5. Made formal oral presentations of 15 to 30 minutes duration involving the presentation of quantitative data and results to a non-technical audience.	❑ Meets Requirements ❑ Does Not Meet Requirements

Based on the information shown, the applicant

❑ Meets Requirements

❑ Does Not Meet Requirements for the job of Personnel Research Analyst

Notes: _____   Rater: _____
_____   Date: _____
_____
_____
_____

Note: This form is completed by a selection specialist.

interrater estimates in the 0.80s. The task-based method produced the highest reliability coefficient; the grouping method produced the lowest.[112] Frank Schmidt and his associates also reported interrater reliability estimates of T&E ratings in the 0.80s.[113]

Validity.   Although most organizations use prior training and work experience as a first cut in selecting applicants, there are surprisingly few studies examining the validity of these predictors. Given evidence this can lead to litigation,[114] there is a need for more research on the validity of these procedures. When such evidence is collected, it often shows that using evaluations of training and experience as a predictor of productivity can pay off.

In one of the most comprehensive reviews to date, Michael McDaniel, Frank Schmidt, and John Hunter conducted a meta-analysis of the validity of four methods for rating training and experience.[115] With overall job performance as the criterion, they examined a total of 132 validity coefficients based on more than 12,000 observations. They found that the validity of T&E ratings varied with the type of procedure used. The behavioral consistency method demonstrated the highest validity with a mean corrected validity coefficient of 0.45. Lower validities were found for the Illinois job element, point, and task methods with mean validities of 0.20, 0.15, and 0.11, respectively. Validity generalization was concluded to exist for the behavioral consistency and Illinois job element methods but not for the point-based and task-based approaches. However, Ronald Ash and associates have concluded that the point-based and task-based methods show useful validities for applicant groups having low levels of job experience (for example, three years or less).[116]

Other meta-analyses have been conducted of specific types of experience or training measures. One such predictor is work experience, which was found to have an overall correlation of 0.27 with job performance[117] and to correlate with salary ($\rho = 0.27$)[118] in two separate, large scale meta-analyses. The study by Miguel Quinoñes and his associates is particularly informative.[119] They proposed that measurement of work experience is multidimensional. Different relationships between experience and job performance should be found depending on (a) how work experience is measured, that is, by amount, time, or type of experience; and (b) how specific the experience is to the task, job, or organization. An analysis of 22 studies examining work experience-job performance relationships showed the following:

1. Overall, the correlation between the two variables was 0.27, as previously stated.

2. Relationships varied among the studies depending on how work experience was measured and the level of experience received.

3. The amount of work experience had higher relationships with performance than those factors involving time or type of experience.

4. Task experience was more highly related with performance than job or organizational-level experience.

Practitioners and researchers developing systems to assess applicants' previous work experience should carefully consider exactly how they want to define and measure it. Based on reasearch by Quinoñes and his associates, this decision may impact the prediction of subsequent performance on the job.

Work experience has been operationalized using years of tenure. Two recent meta-analyses find the correlation between job tenure and job performance is 0.18[120] and 0.20 or 0.24 with salary and job performance,[121] depending on whether tenure is measured as organizational tenure or hours worked. As Paul Tesluk and Rick Jacobs have pointed out, there are a number of ways to operationalize tenure, including tenure in the job, organization, or occupation.[122] Here we find that two very different ways of measuring time on the job (organizational tenure and hours worked) result in similar predictive validities with salary.

Two meta-analyses that examine educational achievement illustrate that variation in how education is defined and measured differentially predicts work outcomes. Frank Schmidt and John Hunter[123] found that years of education was not a good predictor of future job performance ($\rho = 0.10$). Put another way, the validity coefficient of 0.10

suggests that the average job performance of those on a typical semi-skilled job with, say, 12 years of education will only be slightly higher than the performance of those on the same job having 9 or 10 years of education. However, if one were to measure educational achievement using Grade Point Average (GPA), a recent meta-analysis demonstrates that this measure *is* correlated with job performance ($\rho = 0.32$).[124] Compounding this confusion, another meta-analysis finds educational level relates to later salary ($\rho = 0.29$); yet another finds education is unrelated to turnover ($\rho = 0.05$).[125] Thus, even if educational attainment doesn't predict job performance or turnover, it can predict how much a person makes during his or her career. These results suggest that the strength of the relationship to job performance depends on how educational achievement is measured. Furthermore, the usefulness of a measure is also influenced by the outcome being evaluated (for example, job performance, salary, or turnover).

Why do measures of experience and training provide useful information? Those applicants who are judged to be more experienced or to have more training relevant to the job have had more opportunities to learn in the past, which increases job performance even on the first day. Furthermore, greater experience and training enable applicants to acquire job knowledge faster, which in turn increases job performance. Consequently, applicants with more experience and training perform better on the job.[126] However, there is also evidence that these gains increase in a linear fashion up to a certain point; beyond this point the gains plateau. The meta-analysis by Michael McDaniel and his associates powerfully illustrates this; they show that the experience of newly hired employees (three or fewer years of job experience) correlates highly with supervisory ratings of job performance ($\rho = 0.49$). This true-score correlation drops to 0.15 for incumbents with 12 or more years of experience.[127] That is, for the first few years of job experience there is a strong linear relationship with performance. However, at some point (generally thought to be at approximately three to five years of job experience, depending on the job's degree of complexity) the relationship begins to level off, showing that additional years of experience result in little increase in job performance. This nonlinear relationship between experience and performance has been supported by others;[128] it suggests that beyond a certain point, more time and experience does not enhance learning or job performance. Thus experience and training is thought to predict future job experience only for the first few years of work.

These findings also illustrate why there is often concern about those candidates who are overqualified; the additional experience or training will not result in commensurate "one-to-one" gains in performance. A recent study published in the *Annals of Internal Medicine* examined the relationship between years of experience in practice and the quality of care provided by medical doctors. The authors concluded that "Our results suggest physicians with more experience paradoxically may be at risk for providing lower-quality care."[129] This conclusion is based on a review of 59 studies that examined the link between a physicians' years of experience and patient care. They found that more than half of these studies (52 percent) found a decreasing quality of care associated with a doctor's increasing years in practice for all outcomes assessed; only 4 percent of the studies reported an increasing quality of care associated with a doctor's increasing experience for some or all outcomes. The authors argue these findings suggest that more experienced doctors possess less factual knowledge, are less likely to adhere to appropriate standards of care, and are less likely to adopt more proven therapies. These findings, which differ from those we just reviewed in the previous paragraphs about the experience-performance relationship, suggest that there is a decreasing performance—in other words, a concave relationship (where performance initially increases with experience, peaks, and than decreases)—associated with increasing experience, not just a "leveling off" of this relationship. Such results imply that hiring an overqualified person may be as harmful as hiring an underqualified applicant. Interestingly, these results contradict the findings from another meta-analysis, which concluded that "experience becomes more predictive of job performance in high complexity jobs" (medical doctor is a highly complex job).[130] Thus, we clearly need more research to fully understand the nature of the relationship between experience, age, and performance. Suffice it to say that this issue requires considerably more research before we fully understand implications of being "overqualified."

Taken together, these results reveal that measures of experience and training (a) consistently predict important work outcomes; (b) vary significantly in the strength of predictive validity found (some methods exhibit substantial correlations with success, for example, the "behavioral consistency" method and GPA, while others reflect low validities, for example, the point method); and (c) are particularly valuable for the first three to five years on the job. To ensure that a company is effectively screening out the least-qualified applicants, and to be able to successfully refute a disparate impact claim of discrimination, practitioners must give careful consideration to the specific measures they utilize and assess the validity of those measures. As we have seen, empirical validity generally shows that these measures predict job performance, especially early in one's career.

One can illustrate validity without relying on empirical validity. This approach emphasizes content validity that relies on an understanding of the tasks and knowledge, skills, and abilities required by the job. The challenge is to identify the minimum, not preferred, qualifications an employee must possess at job entry in order to perform on the job at an adequate or barely adequate level. The problem, of course, is how to set and validate minimum qualifications. For example, in the grouping method, where years of experience may substitute for years of education and vice versa, how is it determined what combinations of education and experience are most relevant for a job? Two recent articles address this issue and detail the application of the content validity approach as a way to create procedures that ultimately were agreed to by the courts as part of a settlement from a lawsuit.[131] These studies highlight the importance of job analysis for identifying minimum qualifications in content-valid education and experience. Subject matter experts (SMEs) are relied on to rate whether the personal attribute reflects that needed to perform at a barely acceptable level (that is, to exceed or match the level required of a barely acceptable employee). Obviously, it matters who the SMEs are; the group should include non-probationary job incumbents and supervisors who vary by race and gender and who represent the various functional aspects of the job. Their performance on the job should also meet or exceed the level of "satisfactory" job performance. Although published research about content validity approaches are not common, these articles show that application of these approaches can result in the development of minimum qualifications for training and experience that withstand judicial scrutiny.

Legal Implications

Training and experience are often used as an initial screen focusing on the minimum qualifications needed for performing at a barely acceptable level on the first day of the job. Although it makes sense that the knowledge, skills, and prior work experience a candidate possesses should impact their level of productivity in the new job, evaluating training and experience is not as easy as one might expect. From a legal perspective, this information may be used to unfairly discriminate against certain individuals. For example, college GPA, which can be used as an indicator of educational achievement, was found in one recent large-scale study to result in fairly large differences in group means.[132] These results suggest that using GPA cut scores may produce disparate impact due to differences in mean GPA across minority groups, when compared to the majority (white) group. For example, if the average GPA for graduating accounting majors is 2.92 for whites and 2.52 for blacks and the accounting firm decides to only interview students with GPAs greater than 3.0, significantly fewer blacks would be interviewed (only 11 percent of the blacks, but 34 percent of the whites). Bryan Kethley and David Terpstra examined the degree of federal litigation associated with the application form by studying more than 300 court cases between 1978 and 2004. A number of these cases dealt with information that would typically be considered representative of training and experience criteria. For example, education requirements (6 percent of total cases), experience requirements (7 percent of cases), and work history (3 percent of cases) were found to be common types of information involved in litigation. Further analyses revealed the plaintiff prevailed in nearly 30 percent of those cases.[133] Although it is not known whether these criteria were part of a training and experience evaluation, they could have been.

One conclusion that should be drawn from these studies is that as with application forms, organizations should ensure that the training and experience qualifications they rely on for initial selection decisions are fair and not discriminatory. The inference is that organizations should avoid collecting information that disproportionately screens out members of one sex or minority group, particularly when that information (a) does not predict successful performance on the job, (b) is not related to the requirements of the job, or (c) cannot be justified as a business necessity. To minimize legal exposure, these predictors should be based on a competent job analysis, have some validity evidence available, and be uniformly applied to all applicants. The maximum amount of minimum qualification should usually be limited to no more than five years and should exclude qualifications that are developed after a brief training period. Finally, to assure compliance with the Americans with Disabilities Act, consider oral administration for blind applicants and provide instructions that can be read and understood by applicants with suspect composition and reading skills.[134]

Methods of Collecting T&E Evaluation Information

There are many approaches to T&E evaluations. In general, most have in common the following characteristics: (a) a listing or description of tasks, KSAs, or other job-relevant content areas, (b) a means by which applicants can describe, indicate, or rate the extent of their training or experience with these job content areas, and (c) a basis for evaluating or scoring applicants' self-reported training, experience, or education. Paul Tesluk, Rick Jacobs, Edward Levine, Ronald Ash, and their associates have published excellent reviews of these methods.[135] We draw on their work to describe in the following sections some of the major methods in use.

Holistic Judgment.   This particular method is not really a T&E evaluation as we have defined the term. Rather, it is an informal, unstructured approach that an individual takes when reviewing an application or T&E form. It merits a brief description because of how frequently it is used. Essentially, an individual receives an application, resume, or some other form on which training, experience, and education information are reported. The individual makes a cursory review of the information and arrives at a broad, general judgment of the applicant's suitability. These judgments might be no more specific than "qualified" or "not qualified for this position." Judgments made are individualistic; that is, the standards used for evaluating T&E information exist in the mind of the individual evaluator. Thus they will vary from one evaluator to the next.[136]

As you can probably tell, an evaluator's judgments in the holistic approach are not formally recorded on a standardized form and scored; they are simply made by an individual after a brief review of training and experience information. Because of its unstandardized nature and unknown reliability and validity, it should be avoided as an approach to T&E evaluations.

Point Method. Wayne Porter, Edward Levine, and Abraham Flory described the point method as a T&E evaluation alternative often used in the public sector.[137] Essentially, this method consists of a preestablished rating system for crediting applicants' prior training, education, and experience considered relevant to the job. Points are assigned based on the recentness of training experience, amount of job experience, and amount of education received. Ideally, the specific points credited for job experience and education are determined through a job analysis.

Applicants meeting the minimum qualifications for the job are assigned a passing score of 70. For individuals who exceed the minimum qualifications, additional points are added to the score of 70 based on the length and recentness of experience (in months or years completed) or the amount (for example, in semester credit hours) of education received.

Although widely used, the point method has been criticized for its lack of validity and its specious precision in the manner in which points are assigned for experience and education. Another complaint against the method centers around its disparate impact on women, minorities, and younger applicants.[138] These groups have historically not had the opportunities and time older white males have had to attain the same level of experience and education.

Grouping Method. The objective of the grouping approach is to divide applicants into groups that represent levels of qualification. The number of groups used will depend on the particular situation. More often than not, three or four groups are used:

High Group = applicants who are clearly suited and well qualified for the job

Middle Group = applicants who do not fit either the high or low group

Low Group = applicants who meet minimum qualifications but appear poorly suited for the job because of limited experience or training

Unqualified Group = applicants who do not meet minimum qualifications

In classifying applicants to groups, the rater considers training and experience information simultaneously. The combinations of training and experience chosen to define the groups should distinguish among the groups in terms of job success. Subject matter experts participating in a job analysis are used to determine the combinations that best describe each group.

Because individuals in a group receive the same score, ordinal ranking of applicants (as in the point method) does not occur. As Wayne Porter and others have noted, the grouping of applicants conforms better to the actual level of precision of T&E evaluations and measurement. That is, T&E evaluations are more like a blunt ax than a surgeon's scalpel in measurement precision.[139]

Behavioral Consistency Method. The behavioral consistency method assumes past performance is the best predictor of future success on the job. With this method, applicants describe things they have done that relate to key requirements or competencies for the job. These achievements are formally scored using scales derived from subject matter experts. This approach is also called the accomplishment record approach; it requires job applicants to describe past accomplishments in several job-related areas (usually five to seven) that have been judged to distinguish superior from marginal job performance.

The description is a written narrative that includes examples of past achievements applicants believe demonstrate their skills and abilities in each of these job-related areas. In writing their descriptions, applicants are asked to answer questions such as the following: What are examples of your past achievements that demonstrate the necessary abilities and skills for performing these job behaviors? What was the problem on which you worked? What did you do (in terms of an achievement) to solve the problem, and when did you do it? What percentage of credit do you claim for this achievement? What are the names and addresses of persons who can verify the achievement and credit you claim? Rating scales that describe levels of performance on job-related behaviors that distinguish superior from marginal job performance are used by raters to evaluate applicants' written descriptions.

As an example of the behavioral consistency method, consider the problem of graduate school admissions committees. Most graduate programs want students who can perform well. Obviously, academic grades, test scores such as those from the Graduate Record Examination, and faculty recommendations can be used to predict performance. Assume we have a graduate program and wish to have scores on a T&E measure to use with these measures in evaluating student applications.

After analyzing the "job" of graduate student, we uncover five behaviors considered particularly important that graduate student applicants have displayed in the past. Examples include thinking independently, conducting empirical research, and others. Let's take one of these behaviors, *conducting empirical research,* as an example.

Figure 9.4 gives an example of the behavioral consistency T&E method for describing an applicant's past accomplishments and activities in *conducting empirical research.* The applicant wrote a description of his senior thesis research activities as being representative of the behavior conducting empirical research.

Figure 9.5 shows a rating scale used for evaluating the applicant's research description shown in Figure 9.4. Using the rating scale as a standard, the applicant is given a score of 6. Similar descriptions and ratings are made for the remaining four job-relevant graduate student behaviors. Scores on these behaviors are summed, and the total score represents the applicant's behavioral consistency score.

A similar technique, one that also attempts to capture the qualitative nature of the candidate's accomplishments (for example, level of challenge or responsibility in the assignment), is the "accomplishment record" method, developed by Leaetta Hough.[140] This technique, which is particularly suited for selecting professionals and upper-level managers, gets at what the accomplishment entailed, not just the amount or length of time of the accomplishment. The first study to apply the "Accomplishment Record" method involved selecting and promoting attorneys working in the federal government. More than 300 attorneys working in a large federal agency described the major accomplishments they deemed illustrative of their competence in performing eight critical job behaviors (for example, planning/organizing, researching/investigating, and hard work/dedication). Raters were used to score their written descriptions by applying rating scales that described levels of competence in performing these eight job behaviors. Analysis of the Accomplishment Record showed it to be correlated with job performance (0.25) and uncorrelated with other selection measures such as aptitude tests, academic performance, and so on. These results imply that the Accomplishment Record may be measuring a construct that is not assessed by traditional predictors of attorney job performance. Preliminary analyses also suggested that the method was fair for women, minorities, and white men.[141] C. W. Von Bergen and Barlow Super have also reported developing an Accomplishment Record Inventory used in selecting for positions in personnel management. Similarly, Cynthia D. McCauley and associates have proposed the Developmental Challenge Profile as a way to systematically measure and evaluate the life history

---

FIGURE 9.4   An Example of the Behavioral Consistency Method of T&E Evaluation

---

Job Behavior: Conducting Empirical Research

Concerns the conduct of research activities including designing a research study, collecting and analyzing data to test specific research hypotheses or answer research questions, and writing up research results in the form of a formal report.

For the behavior **Conducting Empirical Research** that is defined above, think about your past activities and accomplishments. Then write a narrative description of your activities and accomplishments in the space below. In your description, be sure to answer the following questions:

1. What specifically did you do? When did you do it?

2. Give examples of what you did that illustrate how you accomplished the above behavior.

3. What percentage of credit do you claim for your work in this area?

Description:

During my senior year (2005–2006), I wrote a senior research thesis as a partial requirement for graduation with honors in psychology. I designed a research study to investigate the effects of interviewer race on interviewee performance in a structured interview. I personally designed the research study and conducted it in a metropolitan police department. White and African-American applicants for the job of patrol police officer were randomly assigned to white and African-American interviewers. After conducting an analysis of the patrol police job, a structured interview schedule was developed. The various interviewee-interviewer racial combinations were then compared in terms of their performance in the structured interview.

I consider the vast majority of the work (80 percent) to be my own. My major professor accounted for about 20 percent of the work. His work consisted of helping to obtain site approval for the research, helping to design the study, and reviewing my work products.

Name and Address of an Individual Who Can Verify the Work You Described Above:

Name: Dr. David Whitsett

Address: Department of Psychology

            Univ. of Northern Iowa; Cedar Falls, IA

Phone: 515-555-0821

Note: This form is completed by the job applicant.

---

experiences associated with learning and managerial development.[142] As a result, even though the Accomplishment Record method has not been widely adopted, it has been found to be a useful way to screen professionals and managers early in the selection process.

With its emphasis on job-related behaviors, the behavioral consistency approach to evaluating training and experience has some obvious advantages; however, it has limitations as well. One is that applicants must be able to communicate in writing. This likely explains why the "Accomplishment Record" method may be more appropriate for selecting managers and professionals. Another limitation is that the level of detail required in the descriptions and the mandatory verification discourage some prospective applicants from applying. Ronald Ash and Edward Levine, for instance, found that only slightly over half (56 percent) of their study participants chose to describe their achievements under the behavioral consistency method.[143] They also reported that in an earlier study by Frank Schmidt and his colleagues, only 20 percent of the study participants completed their descriptions.[144] Of course, there is the possibility that behavioral consistency methods may actually discourage individuals from applying whom we would *not* want in the job in the first place (for example, individuals not sincerely interested in the job). Finally,

FIGURE 9.5	An Example Rating Scale for Scoring the Behavioral Consistency Method of T&E Evaluation

Instructions for Scoring the Job Behavior: Conducting Empirical Research

Read the handwritten narrative the job applicant wrote describing activities and accomplishments in conducting empirical research. Then study the scale below. Choose the score you believe best represents or characterizes the applicant's narrative description of past empirical research work.

Score   **Empirical Research Behaviors**

1 = Worked as a member of a student team. Helped design a study, helped collect and analyze data, and/or wrote a report describing the study and its results.

2 = Independently designed a study, collected and analyzed data, and/or wrote a report describing the study and its results. The study was conducted as a class requirement.

3 = Independently designed a study, collected data, and analyzed the data. The study was not an academic requirement.

4 = Worked as a research assistant for a professor. Helped with the collection and/or analysis of the data. The study was or will be submitted for presentation at an academic or professional meeting or will be submitted for journal publication.

5 = Wrote or coauthored a paper that was submitted for presentation at an academic or professional meeting. The paper involved the collection and analysis of data.

6 = Wrote a research thesis as a graduation requirement that involved the collection of data, analysis of data, and tests of research hypotheses or research questions.

7 = Wrote or coauthored a paper that was accepted for publication in a professional or academic journal. The paper involved the collection and analysis of data.

Note: This form is Used by a Selection Specialist.

the behavioral consistency method can be time-consuming and expensive to develop, administer, and score. Nevertheless, for upper-level positions, the expense may be worth it. Of all the T&E methods discussed here, this method likely offers the best prediction of later job performance. It also has the intuitively appealing advantage of letting the candidate's record "speak for itself." This is because the method is based on a relatively objective biodata measure that reflects self-reported prior accomplishments.

Task-Based Method.   Following a comprehensive analysis of the job for which a T&E method is desired, critical job tasks are identified. These critical job tasks serve as the basis for the task-based method. The tasks are listed on a form, and applicants are asked to rate each task listed. The rating may be nothing more than an indication of whether the applicant has or has not performed the task before. An example of a modified form of the task-based method was shown in Figure 9.2. Applicants may also be asked to rate task performance in terms of frequency, such as with a frequency rating scale (for example, 0 = Have Not Done to 5 = Have Done Every or Almost Every Workday), closeness of supervision received in task performance, or some other rating criterion. Furthermore, the applicant may be asked to give the name of an individual who can verify the applicant's reported task performance. Verification is used in an attempt to reduce the obvious inflation factor in such self-ratings. As another means for controlling inflation, some staffing experts incorporate bogus tasks into the listings in an attempt to identify applicants who are inflating their task ratings.[145]

KSA-Based Method.   The KSA-based method is quite similar to that of the task-based method. Rather than tasks, questionnaires list KSAs such as specific computer programming skills or knowledge of the application and interpretation of specific statistical techniques. Ratings that evaluate whether a KSA is possessed, or determine the level of a skill possessed, can also be used. Verification through listings of previous jobs held, dates, and names of individuals are used to limit as much as possible the inflation factor in the ratings.

In the next section, we review reliability and predictive validity evidence for T&E evaluations.

Recommendations for Using T&E Evaluations

Most formal applications of T&E evaluations have occurred in the public sector rather than the private sector. Previous studies suggest that T&E evaluations tap job performance dimensions not assessed by other predictors.[146] By tying minimum job requirements to essential job tasks and KSAs through a well-developed T&E evaluation, minimum qualifications predictive of job performance can be set.

To apply T&E evaluations effectively, the following guidelines are recommended:

1. Minimum amounts of training, experience, and education are among the most frequently used selection standards. **Use T&E evaluations to set specific minimum qualifications job candidates should hold, rather than using a selection standard such as a high school diploma (unless the diploma can be justified).** These minimum qualifications may be expressed through job-relevant KSAs applicants possess, or by applicants' prior performance of job-relevant tasks. Consequently, the utility of any good T&E evaluation system will depend on a thorough job analysis.

2. **Employers using the holistic method of T&E evaluation should replace it with competency-based approaches such as the behavioral consistency and grouping methods.**[147]

3. **T&E evaluations are subject to the *Uniform Guidelines*.** Like all selection devices, validation studies should be conducted on their job relatedness. Studies by Edward Levine, Maury Buster, and their associates illustrate applications of content validity procedures that withstand court scrutiny.[148]

4. Although typical validity coefficients may be relatively low, the available evidence is reasonably clear that some T&E ratings are valid predictors of job performance. **Nevertheless, it has been recommended that these procedures be used only as rough screening procedures for positions where previous experience and training are necessary for job performance.** For those entry-level jobs where only minimal levels of previous experience or training are required, other predictors should be considered.[149]

5. **Forms and procedures for collecting and scoring T&E evaluations should be standardized as much as possible.**

6. **Because T&E evaluations involve self-report data, some form of data verification, particularly of data given by applicants who are going to be offered a job, should be made.**

7. **Where distortion of self-evaluation information is likely to be a problem, final hiring decisions based on other selection measures, such as ability, job knowledge, and performance tests, can minimize the inherent risks associated with T&E evaluations.**

REFERENCE CHECKS

Nature and Role of Reference Checks in Selection

Another technique that is nearly always used to select among job applicants is the checking of applicants' references or recommendations. This method requires the employer to collect information about prospective job applicants from people who have had contact with the applicants. Information collected is used for the following purposes: (a) to *verify* information given by job applicants on other selection measures (such as application forms, employment interviews, or T&E evaluations), (b) to serve as a basis for either predicting the job success of applicants or screening out unqualified applicants, and (c) to *uncover* background information (for example, a criminal record or unsafe driving record) about applicants that may not have been provided by applicants or identified by other selection procedures. The principle that underlies the use of reference checking is simple; the best way to find out about an applicant is to ask those who know him or her well.[150]

We saw in our earlier review of the accuracy of application form data that distortion can be a very real problem. Some job applicants give inaccurate information on prior employment, education, and acquired job skills in order to enhance their employability. Therefore, one principal purpose of a reference check is to verify what applicants have stated on the application form. The method is useful only when it fails to confirm previous selection measure information given by applicants. Thus *reference checking serves more as a basis for negative selection—that is, detection of the unqualified—rather than identification of the qualified.*

The second purpose of the reference check is to serve as a predictor of job success. Like application form data, a reference check used in this way assumes that past performance is a good predictor of future performance. While an application form may summarize what applicants say they did, a reference check is meant to assess how well *others* say the applicants did. It is presumed that information provided by others can be used to forecast how applicants will perform on the job in question.

Some applicants distort application information, others omit background information such as a criminal record. Applicants often fail to report background information when they believe it will affect their chances for employment. However, because unreported background information affects job performance or perhaps endangers the mental or physical well-being of coworkers, clients, or customers, a prospective employer may use reference checks for a third purpose—to identify applicants' job-relevant, but unreported, background histories. Uncovering potential problems is one way a firm can defend itself against negligent-hiring lawsuits.[151]

Reference checking is a common practice of many employers. It is one of the most popular preemployment procedures for screening job candidates. Several surveys have documented that over 95 percent of the firms they sampled said they engaged in checking references.[152] When reference information is collected, a significant number of organizations state they use the data for prediction rather than just for verification purposes. For example, a survey of 345 public and private organizations showed that more than half found the reference-checking method always (19 percent) or sometimes (51 percent) useful for obtaining additional information about the applicant's previous job performance or overall employability. This compares to those organizations reporting that reference checks always (68 percent) or sometimes (30 percent) provided adequate verification information, such as dates of employment. This method helps the employer get a more complete picture of the candidate, as indicated by the fact that more than half of the 345 firms using reference checks found the method very (18 percent) or somewhat (55 percent) effective in identifying poor performers.[153]

Types of Reference Data Collected

Generally speaking, four types of information are solicited through reference checks: (a) employment and educational background data, (b) appraisal of an applicant's character and personality, (c) estimates of an applicant's job performance capabilities, and (d) willingness of the reference to rehire an applicant.[154] With the passage of the Illegal Immigration Reform and Immigrant Responsibilities Act of 1996, ensuring that applicants are legally eligible to be employed in the United States became the most common kind of information verified by employers.

Table 9.8 illustrates the usefulness of employment and personal background information collected through reference checks. The data are based on a nationwide survey of HR professionals from 345 organizations conducted by the Society for Human Resource Management (SHRM).[155] Nearly all (96 percent) conducted reference checks; the most frequent information sought and received were dates of employment (98 percent at least sometimes) and whether an ex-employee was eligible for rehire (83 percent at least sometimes). Most of the employers said that information they received on personality traits (47 percent) and violent or "bizarre" behavior was inadequate (69 percent). Nevertheless, almost three out of four respondents said that reference checking was very or somewhat effective and only 2 percent said it was not at all effective. Even though employers want this information, more than half of the organizations contacted (53 percent) refused to provide the information for fear of legal action; 25 percent had a policy in prohibiting them from supplying any information beyond employment verification.[156] These findings probably account for some of the results presented in Table 9.8. As you can see from the table, the types of information HR professionals receive drops off rather dramatically after "dates of employment." This is likely due to reference givers' unwillingness to comment on applicants' personal backgrounds for fear of being held legally accountable.

TABLE 9.8 Getting Adequate Employment Information on Job Applicants

Employment Information	Always	Sometimes	Rarely or Never
Dates of employment	68%	30%	2%
Eligibility for rehire	23%	60%	17%
Prospective hire's qualifications for a specific job	16%	54%	30%
Overall impression of employability	19%	51%	30%
Salary history	13%	48%	39%
Reason candidate left previous employer	12%	55%	33%
Candidate's work ethic (absences, tardiness, etc.)	14%	54%	33%
Interpersonal skills	17%	47%	36%
Personality traits	9%	45%	47%
Malpractice, professional disciplinary action, etc.	9%	26%	65%
Violent or bizarre behavior	6%	25%	69%

Source: Data are based on a survey—*report for Reference and Background checks*—conducted by the Society for Human Resource Management, January 2005.

With regard to types of reference data requested, we should make one comment concerning legal guidelines established by the Americans with Disabilities Act (ADA) and reference checking on disabled applicants. Employers are prohibited from asking any questions of references that they may not request of applicants. (For example, see our earlier discussion on employment applications.) Employers may not inquire about applicants' disabilities, illnesses, or compensation histories. Employers may make inquiries concerning previous job tasks performed, job performance, attendance records, and other job-related issues not associated with applicants' disabilities.[157]

Usefulness of Reference Data

We have studied several aspects of the reference check, including the reference check's role in selection, approaches to collecting reference data, and sources of reference data. The next question is, how valuable are these data in predicting the success of job applicants? Although not many empirical studies have examined the effectiveness of the method, we present some of the limited results that are available on the reliability and validity of reference data.

Reliability and Validity of Reference Data.   Despite the widespread use of reference checks, there is surprisingly little research evidence available regarding their reliability and effectiveness in predicting applicants' subsequent job performance. Studies of reference data reliability have been rare. When reliability data have been reported, they have typically involved interrater (for example, among supervisors, acquaintances, and coworkers) reliability estimates of 0.40 or less.[158] Although these estimates are low, they are not all that surprising. We might anticipate that different groups of raters focus on different aspects of candidates and judge them from different perspectives. These differences will contribute to different ratings and, thus, lower reliability. Furthermore, the lack of agreement between two reference givers for the same person restricts the predictive validity of the reference check.

Michael Aamodt and Felice Williams conducted a meta-analysis of 30 studies reporting validity data between references or letters of recommendation and performance and reported a mean sample-weighted correlation of 0.18, with a corrected true score correlation of 0.29.[159] This result is comparable to the meta-analytic results reported in two influential studies conducted in the early 1980s. John and Rhonda Hunter's meta-analysis showed a true-score correlation of 0.26 for supervisor ratings of performance,[160] which is remarkably similar to the 0.29 estimate reported by Aamodt and Williams more than 20 years later. Furthermore, the mean sample-weighted correlation of 0.18 found by Aamodt and Williams matches that reported by Richard Reilly and Georgia Chao's meta-analysis (conducted in 1982) of the validity of reference checks.[161] Taken together, these findings show that the relationships between reference ratings and measures of employee success (performance ratings and turnover) are low to moderate at best. Other predictors such as biographical data and cognitive ability tests generally fare better than reference checks in predicting job success. Nevertheless, reference checks provide information that is related to work performance and can provide evidence of fraud or of other information not disclosed by the applicant (for example, the reason the candidate left a firm), which can be used to screen out undesirable applicants.

You may wonder why reference checks do not perform better than they do in predicting an applicant's subsequent performance. There are several possible explanations. First, the criteria or success measures with which reference checks have been statistically correlated have generally suffered from low reliability. As we saw in Chapters 4 and 5, when a criterion is characterized by unreliable information, we should not expect reference data to predict it statistically. Many of the criteria utilized in reference data validity studies have had poor reliability. Supervisory ratings have frequently served as criteria, and these are notorious for their subjectivity and, sometimes, low reliability.

Another explanation for the apparent low validity of reference data is that applicants preselect who will evaluate them.[162] Because applicants recognize that references may have a bearing on their employability to judge, they are most likely to choose those who will have something positive to say about them. As we have noted, leniency is the rule rather than the exception. The result is a narrow or restricted range of scores characteristic of many reference reports. Scores tend to be high with little negative information being given on an applicant. If all applicants generally receive the same high reference scores, then it is unreasonable to expect a reference check to predict how applicants will perform on a subsequent job. If we used only positive information, we would predict that all applicants would succeed. Yet we know that differences in job success will exist.

Other factors we have already listed also contribute to the low value of reference measures. Reference givers may not have had sufficient opportunity to observe the applicant on a job; they may not be competent; they may distort their ratings to help the applicant; and they may not be able to adequately communicate their evaluations. One factor emphasized by recent research that appears to have a significant bearing on the utility of references for predicting job success involves the level of structure, with greater structure being found to increase validity. As noted previously, Julie McCarthy and Richard Goffin reported a multiple correlation of 0.42 when using a standardized questionnaire, one that required reference givers to rate the candidate's standing on a number of job-relevant attributes using a standardized scale. This scale ranged from 0 to 100, with a score of 50 representing the performance of an average peer.[163] Similarly, Paul Taylor and his associates found that a structured telephone reference check predicted supervisory ratings of job performance (uncorrected $r = 0.25$; a true-score correlation $= 0.36$).[164] These validities are larger than the mean uncorrected correlations reported in prior meta-analyses. Moreover, the fact that higher predictive validities are obtained using structured rather than unstructured interviews suggests the potential value of structuring reference checks.

Researchers have recently begun to consider the construct validity of the measures that can be assessed in a letter of reference.[165] As mentioned above, Paul Taylor and associates not only relied on more highly structured reference checks, but also assessed three job-related personality/interpersonal dimensions (conscientiousness, agreeableness, and customer focus).[166] This resulted in considerably higher validities than typically are found. Similarly, Ryan Zimmerman, Maria Triana, and Murray Barrick reported five separate constructs that predicted academic and occupational success.[167] These results suggest the inherent value in measuring structured, standardized constructs in references.[168] Providing frame-of-reference training for assessors has been found to be one way to encourage construct validity.[169] Just as with the interview, there is evidence that physical attractiveness and gender can bias the assessment of reference check constructs.[170] Considering what construct is being measured and the rigor involved in assessing it is likely to matter to reference ratings, though there is still a need for continued research to establish predictive validity.[171]

Yet another factor that has the potential to increase the predictive validity of reference information is systematic assessment ratings from others familiar with the candidates' performance in previous work situations (supervisors, customers, coworkers, and subordinates). More and more organizations are using multi-source performance ratings or 360-degree feedback that relies on ratings from diverse organizational perspectives. Results from meta-analyses examining the usefulness of information from raters from different organizational levels illustrates that these raters observe different facets of a ratee's job performance.[172] Systematically incorporating information from these different organizational perspectives should increase the predictive validity of references by adding unique variance. Michael Mount, Murray Barrick, and Judy Perkins Strauss found that observer ratings (supervisor, coworker, and customer) that were based on a questionnaire assessing job-relevant personality traits predicted performance as well as (and perhaps better than) self ratings.[173] Even though these ratings were not collected during reference checking, these results suggest that the use of multiple raters from different organizational perspectives could provide more valid reference information than raters from just one organizational perspective. Nevertheless, it should be noted that researchers are concerned about the reliability or interrater agreement derived from such ratings.[174] Fortunately there is evidence that the underlying applicant characteristics being measured tend to be the same across different sources (that is, tend to have measurement equivalence).[175] Taken together, these findings underscore the need to obtain ratings from multiple observers across organizational levels. Aggregating across multiple raters will provide a more reliable and valid reference measure.

Finally, Frank Schmidt and John Hunter have noted that past validity estimates of reference checks may no longer be accurate.[176] Because of lawsuits by former employees (see our discussion in the next section), many past employers have restricted information given to prospective employers simply to dates of employment and job titles held. However, recent as well as future changes in the legal climate may significantly impact the quantity and quality of information given by past employers. Currently, 40 of 50 states have provided immunity from legal liability for employers giving reference information in good faith, and other states are considering such laws.[177] In the future, these changes may enhance the validity of reference checks in predicting job performance.

Applicant Acceptability. Applicant reactions to references are likely to vary, depending upon how intrusive the information being requested is (for example, credit check versus verifying employment dates). However, a recent meta-analysis examines the perceived favorability of 10 different selection tools, including references. Results show that references are viewed more favorably by applicants than cognitive ability evaluations, personality tests, biodata, honesty tests, and graphology but not as favorably as employment interviews, work samples, and resumes. These reactions suggest applicants view references as a reasonable tool to rely on for making hiring decisions because the information assessed bears a close relationship to how successfully the candidate would perform actual job duties.[178]

Legal Issues Affecting the Use of Reference Checks

As with any HR selection measure, there are important legal concerns an employer should consider when using reference checks for selection or providing reference data to another employer. Two broad categories of legal issues are particularly critical. The first of these comprises two matters: (a) the discriminatory impact reference checks may have on a job applicant and (b) the defamation of a job applicant's character through libel or slander.

The second category is one that is somewhat unique to reference checks. That issue involves complaints filed against employers for "negligent hiring" of employees. As we see in the following sections, the possibility of libel or slander suits *discourages* employers from providing reference information; the possibility of negligent hiring charges *encourages* prospective employers to use reference checks.

Discriminatory Impact and Defamation of Character. A few cases have appeared in the courts dealing with claims of discriminatory impact through reference checks. For example, in *Equal Employment Opportunity Commission v. National Academy of Sciences* (1976), a job applicant was refused employment on the basis of a poor reference by her previous supervisor. It was argued by the plaintiff that the reference check excluded a disproportionate number of black people and was not related to performance on the job. Evidence presented by the defense led the court to conclude that there was no adverse impact, and that the reference check (verified with a validation study) was job related.[179]

Defamation is another problem that can occur in reference checking, but it concerns the former employer giving reference information, not the one using the information for selection decision making. Although defamation is beyond the present scope of this book, it is an important problem for employers giving reference data and it deserves a few comments.

Defamation in this context involves a written (libel) or oral (slander) false statement made by an employer about a previous employee that damages the individual's reputation.[180] For instance, in *Rutherford v. American Bank of Commerce* (1976), an individual brought a charge against her former employer, who mentioned in a letter of recommendation that she had brought a sexual discrimination charge against the firm. She was able to demonstrate that she could not obtain later employment because of the letter of recommendation. The court ruled on her behalf, saying that the employer illegally retaliated against her because she exercised her rights under Title VII.[181]

For defamation to occur, several elements must be present:

1. A written or oral defamatory statement must have been given.

2. There must be a false statement of fact. To be considered not false, the employer must prove that the statement was made in good faith and was believed to be true.

3. Injury must have occurred to the referee, such as the inability of the referee to get another job because of the previous employer's statement.

4. The employer does *not* have absolute or qualified privilege. (Under *absolute* privilege, an employer has immunity from defamation, such as in a legal proceeding. Under *qualified* privilege, an employer will not be held liable unless the information is knowingly false or malicious.) Information that is judged to be truthful, based on facts, limited to the appropriate business purpose (that is, reference information), made on the proper occasion, and given to appropriate parties is likely to be judged as qualified privilege and, therefore, appropriate.[182]

Two additional cases help to illustrate further the impact of libel or slander in reference checking. *True v. Ladner* (1986) is a case in which True, a public high school teacher, brought suit for libel and slander against Ladner, the school superintendent, based on Ladner's statements given during an inquiry by a prospective employer. Ladner characterized True as being a poor mathematics teacher, more concerned with living up to his contract than going the extra mile as a teacher, and unable to "turn students on" as a teacher. Although Ladner argued that these were his personal opinions and protected by his first amendment rights, the jury found from the evidence presented that

Ladner's reference statements were given with "reckless disregard of their truth or falsity" and, therefore, libel and slander were committed against True. Under appeal, the jury's verdict was upheld by the Maine Supreme Judicial Court.[183] In *Hall v. Buck* (1984), Buck, an insurance salesman, was fired by Hall & Co., Inc. Although he had a history of high success in insurance sales, Buck was unable to find employment with several other insurance firms. Buck hired an investigator to find out the real reasons he was fired from Hall, Inc. Several employees of the firm made derogatory statements to the investigator about Buck. Testimony by one of Buck's prospective employers indicated that he did not make a job offer because a reference giver at Hall, Inc. said, among other comments, that he would not rehire Buck. Evidence presented at the trial showed that the reference givers at Hall, Inc. made their statements based on secondhand information, and that the statements made were not substantially true. Thus it was concluded that Hall, Inc. had committed slander and libel against Buck.[184]

The cases cited illustrate some legal ramifications for reference givers. However, a California case illustrates a situation where former employers provided positive references for a problem employee. In this case, a school district obtained letters of reference from four school districts who collectively extolled the candidate's ability and concern for students and recommended him for employment. In each case, the school districts were allegedly aware that the former teacher had engaged in sexual misconduct with female students. The court found all four school districts liable for negligent misrepresentation, noting that although the school was under no duty to provide this information, once the reference givers offered opinions about the teacher's personal qualities ("genuine concern for students" and "high standards") they should also have discussed the alleged inappropriate incidents.[185]

The point in this case is that some reference givers tend to go beyond necessity in describing people. Potential employers would be wise to recognize the signals of defamation and discount such reference data. Because of the *Uniform Guidelines,* Fair Credit Reporting Act (1971), Family Educational Rights and Privacy Act (1974), and some statutes included under state labor codes, there is a growing concern among employers about the legal implications of using reference checks in selection. Libel, slander, or defamation of an applicant's character are becoming significant issues for some employers. As a consequence, some may believe that it is not permissible under the law to check references. *However, it is legal and even the duty of employers to check references.* They have the right to seek job-related reference information, to use such information in an appropriate manner in selection decision making, and to share appropriate information with individuals who have a legitimate need to know.[186]

To limit the civil liability of employers, a number of states have passed laws to offer protection to employers that provide good-faith job references for former employees. As we mentioned earlier, 40 states have passed such legislation. However, from a legal perspective, laws limiting a former employer's liability could increase a hiring employer's responsibility for checking references.[187] Although the details in each law differ state to state, they often require the employer to show the reference to the employee and allow him or her to correct it or provide another version of events.

Negligent Hiring. A charge of negligent hiring occurs when a third party such as a coworker, client, or customer of an organization files suit against an employer for injuries caused by an employee.[188] For example, suppose an exterminator for a pest control company who has come to inspect an apartment physically assaults a resident. The victim in this incident might bring a negligent hiring suit against the pest control company. The focus of the plaintiff's charges in such a suit is that the employer knew or should have known that the employee causing the injuries was unfit for the job and that the employer's negligence in hiring the individual produced the plaintiff's injuries.

For an employer to be held liable in negligent hiring, five points must be covered:

1. Injury to a third party must be shown to be caused by an individual employed by a firm.

2. The employee must be shown to be unfit for the job he or she holds. To address whether the candidate was fit to perform the job duties and responsibilities extends beyond assessing only the employee's technical skills; it includes ascertaining whether the individual is trustworthy, honest, and free from any violent, criminal, or improper tendencies that should have disqualified the candidate for the position.

3. It must be shown that the employer knew or should have known that the employee was unfit for the job, and that had the employer conducted a background check or criminal check, the firm would have discovered the candidate's lack of fitness for the job (for example, a propensity for assaulting coworkers or a third party.

4. The injury received by the third party must have been a foreseeable outcome resulting from the hiring of the unfit employee. This will depend on the type of job in question. Those jobs involving safety or protection of property or those jobs that expose coworkers or customers to unsupervised contact with the employee are particularly likely to lead to a negligent hiring lawsuit.

5. It must be shown that the injury is a reasonable and probable outcome of what the employer did or did not do in hiring the individual.[189]

Suits involving negligent hiring typically encompass the following types of issues: (a) those in which there was intentional employee misconduct, such as a theft committed by an employee with a history of dishonesty; (b) those in which physical harm occurred, such as a physical attack or sexual assault by an employee with a violent past or previously exhibited sexually deviant behavior; or (c) those in which an employee does not possess the skill or ability to perform a job task (for example, an inexperienced truck driver) and an individual is injured as a result.[190] In judging employer negligence, the courts consider the steps an employer has taken to identify whether an employee is unfit, given the nature of the tasks performed by the employee. Reference checks and background investigations are two types of preemployment screens that many courts view as suitable for identifying potential problems. Both of these screens are particularly appropriate for jobs that involve (a) access to others' residences, (b) little supervision, (c) public safety (for example, transportation industry) or substantial personal contact with the general public, and (d) work with individuals receiving personal care (for example, health care industry). For many jobs, documented reference checks alone can serve as important evidence in defending a negligent hiring suit.

As you read and think about reference checks, you may be wondering, "Can't a company find itself in a catch-22 situation? That is, on the one hand, to avoid a negligent hiring lawsuit, it may be important to obtain reference information prior to hiring; on the other hand, many employers do not provide such information for fear of libel or slander suits by past employees. What then?" Certainly, employers are concerned about the type of information released on past employees. For example, the following recommendations are frequently proposed for releasing reference information: (a) do not give out reference information over the telephone, (b) document all information that is released, (c) provide only specific, objective information, (d) obtain written consent from the employee prior to releasing reference information, and (e) do not answer a question involving an opinion as to whether a previous employee would be rehired.[191]

Obviously, if many organizations follow these guidelines, it will be difficult for prospective employers to obtain much more than dates of employment and the last position held in the organization. The results from a survey of 335 public and private organizations supports this concern, as they found that a majority of firms (54 percent) have a policy not to provide references or information about current or former employees. Furthermore, 53 percent of the organizations surveyed had at least one manager or HR professional who refused to provide reference information for fear of legal action, while 25 percent had a policy not to provide any information beyond employment verification.[192] A recent examination of federal court cases revealed there were more lawsuits involving reference checks and background investigations than lawsuits involving medical exams, drug tests, or polygraph tests. Furthermore, the results indicated organizations were more likely to lose reference-check lawsuits.[193]

These results indicate that employer fears of legal liability are certainly not unfounded, particularly since a lawsuit can be expensive in terms of monetary damages and legal fees. Yet, the same survey of 335 employers found that the percentage of organizations that reported a legal issue in the past three years regarding references and background checks was quite small; less than 5 percent reported claims due to defamation (2 percent), negligent hiring (3 percent), or failing to provide adequate warning about the threat posed by a former employer (1 percent). Based on this, it appears that employer concerns may be exaggerated. One way to address these concerns is to have the candidate sign a waiver relieving former employers of liability. The survey found that 66 percent of HR professionals believe that signed waivers by their former employees would increase the odds that they would provide references.[194]

In encouraging former employers to supply information on a past employee, the following strategies have been recommended:

- Submit a written request for information on specific questions that are relevant to making an employment decision, and use the same questions with every applicant (such as "Was the person ever disciplined or discharged for fighting?").

- Include a release form signed by the applicant stating that (a) the applicant has read and approves the information requested, and (b) the applicant requests that the information be given.

If the previous employer refuses to provide such information, then do the following:

- Call the person in charge of human resources and ask why the request was not honored.

- Ask how a request should be made so it will be honored.

If the previous employer still refuses to give the information, then do the following:

- Inform the individual that failure to cooperate is being documented with date, time, and name of the person refusing the request.

- At a minimum, verify the candidate's statements about the position held, the number of years spent in that position, and the final salary.

- If the missing information is so relevant that the applicant will not be hired without it, tell the individual that the applicant will be told that the previous employer's refusal was the reason for the lack of an offer.[195]

Refusing to give information on a past employee does not necessarily shield an employer from a lawsuit. Employers have responsibility to provide relevant information on a past employee who is under consideration for employment by another employer. In fact, refusal to do so may legally jeopardize an employer. Legal jeopardy for such firms may be a particular problem in states that have laws protecting employers giving references. Hiring employers should also be vigilant about noticing abbreviated periods of employment, frequent changes in residences, or gaps in employment. Whenever such "suspicious" employment gaps are revealed, the hiring employer should inquire further into the candidate's background and consider conducting a criminal record search.

Bill Leonard has described a legal case involving reference giving in Florida, a state with a law protecting employers from civil liability when they give reference information.[196] The case, against Allstate Insurance Co., involved a workplace shooting in which two employees of Fireman's Fund Insurance Co. were killed by a coworker who had been fired.

The accused assailant had worked for Allstate but was fired for carrying a pistol in his briefcase. As part of his severance package, Allstate gave him a letter of reference stating that he had not been terminated due to his job performance. Fireman's Fund hired him but fired him two years later. He returned to the company and killed two employees and himself. Families of the slain workers sued Allstate, alleging that Allstate violated its responsibility to fully and truthfully disclose information on the assailant concerning his character and propensity toward violence. The case was settled out of court.

From the perspective of negligent hiring suits, a key element is that written documentation must show that the employer *attempted* to collect background data on prospective employees. Even though necessary reference information was not given by a past employer, a firm using reference checks should carefully document what questions were asked and what information was obtained. From a legal point of view, the important question is this: *Did the employer take reasonable steps and precautions to identify a problem employee, given the risks inherent in the job tasks the employee would be required to perform?* Depending on the nature of these tasks, steps other than reference checks (such as providing comprehensive training, giving close supervision, and conducting an extensive background investigation) may be required. However, for many jobs, verifying and checking references is considered an appropriate degree of care for identifying potential problem employees.

Methods of Collecting Reference Data

Reference information is collected in a number of ways, including (a) by telephone, (b) from the Internet, (c) by e-mail, (d) by fax, (e) by mail, or (f) in person. A recent survey of HR professionals from 345 organizations revealed that the telephone is the most frequently used method of conducting a reference check (98 percent either always or sometimes use it); just over 50 percent always or sometimes use either fax or mail. The Internet is being used more and more (36 percent either always or sometimes use it; 43 percent never use it); e-mail and in-person methods are the least frequently used (less than 5 percent always use either method; 62 percent and 92 percent rarely or never use it, respectively).[197] Organizations can use a number of criteria to decide which reference-checking method to use; three critical factors include the speed with which information can be collected, the type of information being gathered, and the cost associated with collecting the information. Although the weight of each factor will vary depending on the employment position being filled, the telephone appears to be the best way to satisfy these criteria.

Telephone Checks. Telephone checks are relatively fast, result in a relatively high reference return rate, allow the reference checker to ask follow-up questions or clarify what type of information is needed, and are inexpensive to conduct. In addition, the personal nature of the telephone check contributes to greater responsiveness from the reference giver; the way that oral comments are given (voice inflections, pauses) may be useful for revealing what a person really thinks. This should lead to greater disclosure—since information is sometimes given orally that would not be given in writing. Finally, on the telephone it is easier to ensure that reference comments are being given by the person named rather than by a clerk or secretary. The sheer number of advantages attributed to the telephone method probably accounts for its disproportionate use.[198]

It's wise to use prepared questions while conducting the telephone reference check interview. In fact, telephone reference checks should be treated as an "informal" interview. Consequently, you will want to utilize the same principles and techniques that make an interview effective. More will be said about this in Chapter 10, but let us say now that enhanced structure is an important element of successful interviews.[199] If an unstructured approach is used over the telephone, the utility of the data collected will be highly dependent on the skill and training of the telephone interviewer. Table 9.9 lists some questions frequently asked during a telephone reference check; these are not necessarily recommended questions.

Fax, Internet, and E-mail Reference Checks. These methods are also fast and relatively inexpensive, though not as interactive. It is not as easy to ask follow-up questions or clarify ambiguous requests for information. Furthermore, e-mail and fax reference-checking methods are likely to be seen as less desirable because of their lack of privacy and informality. However, these methods may be necessary when searching public records. As organizations continue to integrate their HR management technologies with these new techniques, fax, Internet, and e-mail methods could significantly affect how organizations go about conducting reference checks. One relatively simple way to demonstrate this is to use Internet search engines to "google" the applicant. This approach can yield relevant information about companies the applicant was affiliated with; it may provide news reports, press releases, or even personal "blogs" that disclose connections and personal characteristics that make the applicant an undesirable candidate. Finally, recent federal legislation makes references submitted electronically as legally binding as if the employer used the U.S. mail, a factor likely to increase the use of electronic reference checking.[200]

Mail Checks. Reference checks requested through the mail use a written questionnaire or letter. To increase the likely response rate, the company should have the candidate sign a release form that gives the candidate's former employers permission to release information without liability for doing so. This form is sent with the written questionnaire or letter. With a questionnaire, references are usually asked to rate an applicant on a variety of traits or characteristics. When used in this manner, reference checks resemble traditional employee job performance ratings. Raters provide judgments of individual characteristics using some form of graduated rating scale. Space may also be provided for comments as well. Figure 9.6 presents one example of a typical reference questionnaire.

Reference checks collected through the mail can be a systematic, efficient means for collecting reference data. However, one of the biggest problems associated with mail questionnaires is their low return rate. This can present a significant problem for employers if some applicants have relevant reference information from letters while others do not. This problem is exacerbated if unfavorable and favorable reference responses have different rates of return. In such a case, the resulting information would necessarily

TABLE 9.9	Some Example Questions Frequently Asked in a Telephone Reference Check

1. The candidate states that he or she was employed with your firm in the position of (position) _____ from _____ to _____, and that his or her final salary was $ _____ per annum. Is this correct?

2. Would you rehire the job candidate? Is the candidate eligible for reemployment?

3. Why did the candidate leave your firm?

4. How would you rate the candidate's overall job performance—on a scale of 1 to 10 (10 being high)—compared to the performance of others with similar responsibilities?

5. On average, how many times did the candidate miss work? Come in late? Did he or she fail to meet commitments?

6. Does the candidate work well with others (coworkers, superiors, subordinates, customers)? Is he or she a team player?

7. What were the candidate's responsibilities in order of importance? Describe the candidate's general duties:
   [Or you could ask] Let me read you what the candidate says his or her duties were at your organization. [After reading them ask] Is this accurate?

8. What were the candidate's principal strengths, outstanding successes, and significant failures in his or her job activities?

9. Describe the candidate's last job performance evaluation: _____ What were his or her strengths? What recommended improvement areas were noted?

10. How would you describe the applicant's success in training, developing, and motivating subordinates?

11. What does the candidate need to do for continued professional growth and development? What is the biggest change you have observed in him or her?

12. Were there any vehicle or personal injury accidents while the candidate was employed by you?

13. Do you know of anything else that would indicate whether the applicant is unfit or dangerous for a position such as _____?

14. Is there anything else you would like to tell me about the candidate?

Note: The questions here are those that have frequently been used to collect information on job applicants. These questions are *not* being recommended. In general, any question may be asked, but the user should be sure that the information collected is related to the job for which the applicant is being considered—before using the information in selection decision making.

Source: Questions are based on H. C. Pryon, "The Use and Misuse of Previous Employer References in Hiring," *Management of Personnel Quarterly*, 9 (1970): 15–22; Peter A. Rabinowitz, "Reference Auditing: An Essential Management Tool," *Personnel Administrator*, 24 (1979): 37; Edward C. Andler and Dara Herbst, *The Complete Reference Checking Handbook*, 2d. ed. (New York, NY: AMACOM, 2004); and *Human Resources Guide*, ed. Robert J. Nobile, Sandra King, Steven C. Kahn, and David Rosen (Boston: West Group, A Thomson Company, 2000).

be biased. There may be fewer unfavorable references returned because many employers are concerned that they are more likely to be sued over written information, especially if that information is negative.[201] The other concern with mail is that it tends to be a relatively slow way to get information; it can take weeks to get a reply.

Letters of Recommendation. Another form of mail check is the letter of recommendation. In this case, references write a letter evaluating a job applicant. Reference givers may be asked to address specific questions about an applicant or simply told to express any comments of their choice. Although there do not appear to be comparative data on their frequency of use, letters of recommendation are probably restricted to high-skill or professional jobs. When properly completed by a knowledgeable reference, letters may provide greater depth of information on an applicant than that obtained on a rating scale.

FIGURE 9.6	Example of a Mail Questionnaire Reference Check

Sales Applicant Reference Check

We are in the process of considering *James Ridley Parrish* (SS Number: 123-45-6789) for a sales position in our firm. In considering him/her, it would be helpful if we could review your appraisal of his/her previous work with you. For your information, we have enclosed a statement signed by him/her authorizing us to contact you for information on his/her previous work experience with you. We would certainly appreciate it if you would provide us with your candid opinions of his/her employment. If you have any questions or comments you would care to make, please feel free to contact us at the number listed in the attached cover letter. At any rate, thank you for your consideration of our requests for the information requested below. As you answer the questions, please keep in mind that they should be answered in terms of your knowledge of his/her previous work with you.

1. When was he/she employed with your firm? From _____ to _____. Final Salary: _____.
2. Was he/she under your direct supervision? ☐ Yes ☐ No
3. If not, what was your working relationship with him/her? _____
   _____
4. How long have you had an opportunity to observe his/her job performance? _____
   _____
5. What was his/her last job title with your firm? _____
6. Did he/she supervise any employees? ☐ Yes ☐ No If so, how many? _____
7. Why did he/she leave your company? _____

Below is a series of questions that deal with how he/she might perform at the job for which we are considering him/her. Read the question and then use the rating scale to indicate how you think he/she would perform based on your previous knowledge of his/her work.

8. For him/her to perform best, how closely should he/she be supervised?
   ☐ Needs no supervision
   ☐ Needs infrequent supervision
   ☐ Needs close, frequent supervision

9. How well does he/she react to working with details?
   ☐ Gets easily frustrated
   ☐ Can handle work that involves some details but works better without them
   ☐ Details in a job pose no problem at all

10. How well do you think he/she can handle complaints from customers?
    ☐ Would generally refuse to help resolve a customer complaint
    ☐ Would help resolve a complaint only if a customer insisted
    ☐ Would feel the customer is right and do everything possible to resolve a complaint

11. In what type of sales job do you think he/she would be best?
    ☐ Handling sales of walk-in customers
    ☐ Traveling to customer locations out-of-town to make sales

12. With respect to his/her work habits, check *all* of the characteristics below that describe his/her *best* work situation:
    ☐ Works best on a regular schedule
    ☐ Works best under pressure
    ☐ Works best only when in the mood
    ☐ Works best when there is a regular series of steps to follow for solving a problem

13. Do you know of anything that would indicate that he/she would be an unfit or dangerous choice (for example, for working with customers or coworkers or driving an automobile) for a position with our organization?
    ☐ Yes ☐ No

    If "yes," please explain.

    _____

(Continued)

FIGURE 9.6	*(Continued)*

14. Would you rehire her/him?   ❑ Yes   ❑ No

15. If you have any additional comments, please make them on the back of this form.

Your Name: _____   Your Signature: _____

Your Title: _____

Address: _____

_____

| City | State | ZIP |

Company: _____

Telephone: _____   E-mail: _____

Thank you for your cooperation and prompt response to this inquiry. The information you provided will be very useful as we review all application materials.

Note: This form is completed by the reference giver.

However, since letters of recommendation usually come from writers suggested by a job applicant, negative comments are seldom given.

Letters of recommendation are becoming increasingly positive. For example, a two-part national survey found that though writers of letters of recommendation claimed they would provide relevant negative information about candidates applying as interns to psychology programs, negative characteristics were found to be rarely disclosed.[202] A recent study found that less than 1 percent of references rate applicants as "below average" or "poor."[203] Rodney Miller and George Van Rybroek humorously asked, "Where are the other 90 percent?"[204] This leniency bias occurs for a number of reasons, including fear of diminished rapport with former colleagues and subordinates, retaliation or even violence, and legal repurcussions. Evidence for the latter is shown by the finding that when letters of recommendation are kept confidential (that is, applicants waive their right to see the letter), the letter was rated less positive than those not kept confidential.[205]

There are few empirical studies about the predictive validity of the letter of recommendation method, even though they are commonly used. Julie McCarthy and Richard Goffin uncovered nine studies assessing the predictive validity of this method. They concluded that although the findings from early research (pre-1980) suggested that letters of recommendation have low predictive validity, more recent research reveals that when a more structured, rigorous evaluation approach is used, the validity results are higher.[206] For example, two studies involving graduate students and instructors in an academic setting found that specific traits (for example, mental ability, vigor, dependability, and so on) obtained from letters of recommendation could be reliably classified into general trait categories (for example, intelligence) and that adjectives dealing with these categories were predictive of student and instructor performance.[207] This approach reveals that a seemingly positive letter of recommendation may actually be "damning with faint praise." For example, if your former supervisor says you were "well intentioned" or "an average performer," it probably will not advance your candidacy. Other research suggests that the length of the letter of recommendation was a better indicator of a reference giver's attitude toward the person written about than the content itself. This body of research shows that a long letter is more indicative of a positive attitude than a short letter. For example, one recent study found that the acceptance of candidates by letter of recommendation reviewers was related not only to the lack of negative information in the letter, but to its length as well.[208] These studies suggest that even if only positive comments are given, it may still be possible to obtain some indication of the writer's true feelings, and this information can be used to predict performance in the new job.

In part, an applicant's evaluation from a letter of recommendation depends on the individual reading the letter. George Tommasi and his colleagues found that although information indicative of the quality of an applicant influenced human resource managers' evaluations of applicants, some managers were influenced by job-irrelevant information such as the gender of the applicant and the gender and status of the letter writer.[209] They concluded that letters of recommendation could be improved by imposing a more structured format on the letter writer. In essence, they seem to be suggesting that employers should use a more structured format, such as one incorporating rating scales that the reference giver would then use to evaluate applicants on job-relevant dimensions. McCarthy and Goffin followed just such an approach and found that when referents compared candidates on a scale from 0 to 100 to the candidates' peers doing similar work, they found that ratings derived from 31 job-relevant attributes were significantly predictive of subsequent supervisory ratings of performance (multiple $r = 0.42$).[210]

One recent finding that is particularly troubling is that letters of recommendation may tell us more about the letter writers than about the candidates themselves. In one study, Tim Judge and Chad Higgins demonstrated that letter writers who possess a "positive" personality were more likely to write favorable letters than would reference writers who tended to be more critical or negative.[211] Two other studies found that letters written by the same letter writer about two separate candidates were actually found to be more consistent in content than two different authors describing the same candidate.[212] These results make it difficult to trust letters of recommendation as an accurate evaluation tool.

Consequently, even though there may be some positive aspects to letters of recommendation, there are some important disadvantages associated with them. Some of these disadvantages include the following:

1. Writers have the difficult task of organizing the letter and deciding what to include. Thus, the job relevance of the information will vary across letter writers.

2. Letter quality will depend on the effort expended by the writers and their ability to express their thoughts.

3. Writers tend to be quite positive in their evaluations and often lack specificity and accuracy in letter writing.

4. The same job-relevant information will not be obtained on each applicant, which makes it hard to compare candidates.

5. Information relevant to areas or issues important to the hiring organization may be omitted in the letter.

6. The scoring of the letter is subjective and based on the reader's interpretation.[213]

Despite these disadvantages, the small possibility that letters of recommendation will produce important negative information about an applicant—and the fact that such information can have serious implications for a hiring organization—justify for most users the continued use of letters of recommendation as a reference-checking method.

In-Person Checks. In-person checks involve face-to-face personal contact with a reference giver. This allows high levels of interaction, which may lead to more useful information being exchanged. Most often, these contacts are part of background investigations and concern jobs in which an incumbent is a potential security or financial risk. Although in-person contact may uncover information not captured by written methods, it is expensive, time-consuming, and often impractical. In-person checks are not frequently used in most selection programs.

Sources of Reference Data

Many different types of individuals, including friends, relatives, college professors, teachers, immediate supervisors, coworkers, subordinates, and HR managers, can serve as reference sources. For these data to be useful, reference givers must meet four conditions: (a) they must have had a chance to observe the candidate in relevant situations, (b) they must have knowledge of the candidate, (c) they must be competent to make the evaluations requested and be able to express themselves so their comments are understood as intended, and (d) they must want to give frank and honest assessments. Simply reviewing those whom the candidate has listed as references may provide the employer with useful information. For example, a candidate who lists all former bosses is often most forthright. In the following section, we report typical characteristics of the different sources of reference information that should be considered when conducting a reference check.

Former Employers.   As we have noted, former employers are an important source for verifying previous employment records and for evaluating an applicant's previous work habits and performance. If available, data from former employers will more than likely be released through a personnel office. Information from previous supervisors is particularly valuable, because the supervisor is able to evaluate the candidate's performance in light of the organization's overall objectives and in comparison to others who are similarly situated. A supervisor who has had direct experience with, or firsthand knowledge of, the applicant at work is often the best person to provide the reference. References from employers will be more useful and accurate as the reference givers' experience with and knowledge of the applicant increases.

Personal References.   Personal references supplied by the applicant are another source of information. As might be expected, most applicants choose those individuals they believe they will give a positive evaluation. If personal references are requested, they should be contacted. Through careful questioning, it may be possible to obtain useful information about the applicant. Personal references can provide information about the applicant's prior employment and detailed descriptions of the candidate's qualities and behavior characteristics. It is important to ask how long and in what capacity the reference has known the applicant.

Investigative Agencies.   At a cost of several hundred dollars per applicant, investigative agencies will conduct background checks on applicants. Background checks focus on resume and application information, educational accomplishments, credit ratings, police and driving records, personal reputation, lifestyle, and other information. These investigative agencies often obtain more detailed information about a candidate than other sources can; this may be helpful for making the hiring decision and for building a defense against a claim of negligent hiring (discussed later in this chapter). However, investigative agencies are expensive and require more time for obtaining results. Many of these checks take the form of consumer reports, of which two basic types exist:[214]

1. *Consumer reports*—Any written or oral communication collected by an agency concerning an individual's credit standing, character, general reputation, or personal characteristics used to establish an individual's eligibility for employment. The Fair Credit Reporting Act (15 U.S.C. 1681), as amended by the Consumer Credit Reporting Reform Act of 1996 (CCRRA) and further amended by the Consumer Reporting Employment Clarification Act of 1998 (CRECA), reveals that inquiries about the candidate's financial status and credit rating should be obtained only where there is a legitimate business necessity for the information. Although this is a sensitive area, employment generally qualifies as a legitimate business necessity.[215]

2. *Investigative consumer reports*—A consumer report or part of a consumer report concerning an applicant that is based on personal interviews with an applicant's friends, neighbors, or acquaintances. Federal and state laws impose certain requirements that employers must meet *before* and *when* taking adverse action against a candidate based on information contained in the consumer report. For example, use of a credit check requires that the employer must obtain the candidate's written authorization and provide the candidate with a clear and conspicuous disclosure of how and whether the credit information will be used for employment purposes. Furthermore, if a job offer is not made to an applicant because of information included in a consumer report, the individual must be so informed. The employer must indicate the name, address, and telephone number of the consumer reporting agency making the report and provide information about how to check and correct (if necessary) the agency's report.[216]

Public Records. In addition to the sources just listed, public records also include useful information. As with any application information, an employer should use caution when accessing public records. *The employer should be sure that the information solicited does not discriminate against a protected group and that it can be justified by the nature of the job for which applicant screening is being undertaken.* With this caution in mind, public records can be searched rather easily. These records include the following:[217]

1. *Criminal records*—Before using these records, an employer should check to see whether such use is likely to discriminate against a protected group and whether there is actual business necessity for using criminal record information. Furthermore, employers must be aware of state and local laws regarding criminal conviction inquiries.[218] A search of criminal records is often required for jobs that involve high degrees of public contact, have limited supervision, involve working at private residences or other businesses, involve personal care of others (such as children), or have direct access to others' personal belongings, valuables, or merchandise. Assuming that such information is needed and can be used, there are two ways to collect criminal record data. First, if allowed by law, the employer can access the state's central criminal record repository. Each state has such a repository. Second, criminal record data are available from counties where the candidate has lived or worked. State police records are also sources of information. Whatever the source used, there are several points to keep in mind. Criminal record data may be inaccurate or incomplete. If employment is not offered to an applicant because of his or her criminal record, employers covered by the Fair Credit Reporting Act must disclose to the applicant the name, address, and

telephone number of the agency reporting the criminal record. The applicant must be given an opportunity to check the records. Criminal convictions cannot serve as an absolute bar to employment. Users of criminal record data should consider factors such as the nature and seriousness of the offense, the relation of the offense to the nature of the job sought, the individual's attempts at rehabilitation, and the length of time between the conviction and the employment decision.

2. *Motor vehicle department records*—Driving record information can be obtained from the state department of motor vehicles. Driving records should be obtained only when driving is an essential function of the job. Information is available about traffic violations, license suspension or revocation, and other offenses such as driving under the influence of alcohol or drugs,. In addition, these records can be used to check the name, birthdate, address, and physical description of an applicant. This is useful for identifying falsified information given on the application form and for confirming that applicants are who they claim to be.

3. *Workers' compensation records*—These records are usually available from a state agency, although the organization and completeness of the records can vary from one state to the next. They show the types and number of claims that have been filed by an individual. The Americans with Disabilities Act (ADA) prohibits an employer from asking about a worker's compensation claims during selection. However, a job offer can be contingent upon the candidate passing a medical examination, which could include information about the candidate's workers' compensation history.

4. *Federal court records*—Civil and criminal federal court case information is available through federal court records. If the employer knows where an applicant has lived or worked, it's possible to search federal court records to identify civil, criminal, or bankruptcy cases that an individual has been involved in. Information about violations of federal law can be obtained through the National Criminal Information Center (NCIC) and the National Instant Check System (NICS). A person's name and social security number can be run through both systems to search multiple databases that hold the names of millions of people. At present it is illegal for any employers but the government to use these systems for employment purposes.

5. *Educational records*—We have pointed out the importance of checking educational records. Many universities and colleges will verify an individual's dates of attendance and degrees held. Surveys have shown that a large percentage of colleges will provide the information over the telephone; many will send an applicant's actual transcript when the proper requesting procedures are followed. For example, schools may require a signed authorization from the candidate before releasing educational records to a prospective employer. Employers should obtain written consent on the application or on a separate release form.

Employers sometimes contract with outside firms to run background checks on applicants. A typical check will cost from $50 to $200 and require one to five days to complete. If a background investigation firm is used, employers should understand that the firm is serving as the employer's agent; the employer may be held liable for the agent's actions. It is important to evaluate carefully any firm hired to undertake background investigations. *The Sourcebook to Public Record Information*, available from BRB Publications at http://BRBPub.com, is a comprehensive reference book that many employers find useful for accessing information contained on public records.

Recommended Steps for Using Reference Checks

From legal and practical perspectives, employers wanting to use reference checks should undertake several steps.

1. **Reference data are most properly used when the data involve job-related concerns.** Requested data should address KSAs or other characteristics of the applicant that are necessary for successful job performance. Emphasis should be given to those characteristics that distinguish effective from ineffective performance. How do we identify which KSAs or other characteristics are critical? As we discussed in earlier chapters, we make the determination based on an analysis of the job for which we are selecting employees. If questions or ratings are restricted to those that can be demonstrated as related to the job, then there should be no difficulties.

2. **Because we are tailoring the content of our reference check to the content of a specific job, we will likely need more than one general form for all positions in an organization.** At the very least, we will need a reference form for each cluster or family of jobs that require similar KSAs. Multiple forms obviously add multiple costs and additional work. But if we are going to obtain useful, legal selection data, and if we choose to use reference checks, multiple forms will probably be necessary.

3. **Reference checks are subject to the *Uniform Guidelines*.** As for any selection measure, it's important to monitor the fairness and validity of the reference check. If our reference checking system unfairly discriminates against protected groups or is not related to job success, we should change or eliminate our system. To do otherwise is not only legally foolish but jeopardizes our ability to choose competent employees.

4. **A more structured reference checking system (for example, a system that focuses on factual or behavioral data related to the applicant), rather than an unstructured system (such as one focusing on general overall evaluative judgments), is less likely to be open to charges of discrimination.** Methods that rely on greater structure are more amenable to the development of scoring procedures, reliability, and validity analyses. Such methods consist of those that focus on behaviors and have a specific scoring system. Structured approaches also help to ensure that the same information is obtained systematically on all applicants, and that the information is used in a consistent manner. Information that qualifies or disqualifies one applicant must qualify or disqualify all. Written recommendations (such as a letter of reference) followed by a brief review often lead to subjective impressions and hunches that may not be valid. If we use these measures in our selection program, we should be aware that unstructured ratings are woefully inadequate.

5. **Applicants should be asked to give written permission to contact their references,** including educational institutions, former employers, past and present landlords, credit bureaus, and other sources the employer relies on. When prospective employers actually contact references, the employer should also collect information on how long that reference giver has known an applicant and the position the reference giver holds. This information can be useful for verifying responses or, if necessary, legally proving that the person contacted is in a position to provide the assessments being requested.

6. **Reference takers collecting information by telephone or in person should be trained in how to interview reference givers.** Reference takers must be prepared to formulate questions and record responses systematically. Here again, a structured approach to information collection will improve the quality of the data ultimately collected.

7. **All reference check information should be recorded in writing.** If a legal suit is brought against an employer, reference data may serve as important evidence in defending against the suit. Documentation in writing is essential for the defense.

8. **If a job applicant provides references but reference information cannot be obtained, ask the applicant for additional references.** Consider *not* hiring an applicant if complete reference information is not available. Hiring an applicant without such information can be risky.

9. **Check all application form and resume information.** In particular, focus on educational background (for example, schools attended, degrees earned, academic performance) and previous employment records (for example, dates of employment, job titles, duties performed). Gaps in information reported are red flags that signal a need for special attention. For instance, an individual may have recently spent time in jail for a crime directly related to the position to which he or she is applying.

10. A caveat on the use of negative information: Negative information received during a reference check frequently serves as a basis for rejecting an applicant. Caution is advised in using *any* negative data as a basis for excluding applicants. **Before negative information is employed, prospective employers should (a) verify its accuracy with other sources, (b) be sure that disqualification on the basis of the information will distinguish between those who will fail and those who will succeed on the job, and (c) use the same information consistently for all applicants.**

As you read the literature on reference data, note an apparent pattern. Practitioner-oriented journals tend to view reference checks as playing an important role in HR selection. Apparently, the belief is that reference checks provide information not given by other measures. In contrast, articles in research-oriented journals generally regard reference checks as a relatively minor selection tool. Research studies investigating the utility of selection devices have typically concluded that references are not especially useful. Although reference reports may not be as useful as other measures in predicting employee job success, they may be the *only* basis for detecting some information that would indicate unsatisfactory job performance. In this role, reference data will serve as a basis for identifying a relatively small number of applicants who should not be considered further for a job. However, it may not be efficient to incorporate reference checks in the selection of applicants for every job in an organization. The decision about whether to employ reference checks will vary across organizations and jobs. But we suggest that the higher the responsibility level associated with a particular position—or the greater the risk posed by the position to customers, clients, and coworkers—the greater the need for a reference check.

SUMMARY

Earlier in the chapter, we examined application blanks, training and experience (T&E) ratings, and reference checks as measures that can be used in employee selection. In this final section, we discuss how useful these procedures can be for selection, given the timing of their use. Application forms, resumes, reference checks, and ratings of training, education, and experience are relatively inexpensive and easy to collect. The data can provide useful information for predicting which applicants are likely to be high performers, although these selection devices do not have high predictive validities. Applicants expect to provide this information and see it as having high face validity. Collecting basic background information enables one to ensure the applicant has the minimal skills and qualifications to do the job. Practically, at this point, there are a large number of applicants to consider; one must screen out scores of applicants to reduce the pool to a manageable set of candidates who are suited for the job. At this stage we have a small selection ratio; it is not unusual to eliminate 70 percent to 90 percent of all applicants during the first cut. After these initial cuts, we proceed to more expensive, time-consuming selection devices such as the interview, tests, even an assessment center. Even if the predictive validity for the selection tool (for example, a semi-structured application blank) is only modest, it can still have very high value due to the small selection ratio. In conclusion, we strongly encourage those making hiring decisions to carefully consider each piece of information that is requested in the early stages of selection; there is considerable utility to be gained by rigorously measuring minimum qualifications and applicant ability and motivation at this stage.

REFERENCES

1. H. C. Taylor and J. T. Russell, "The Relationship of Validity Coefficients to the Practical Effectiveness of Tests in Selection," *Journal of Applied Psychology* 23 (1939): 565–578.

2. Ibid.

3. James A. Breaugh, "The Use of Biodata for Employee Selection: Past Research and Future Directions," *Human Resource Management Review* 19 (2009): 219–231.

4. Adrian Furnham, "HR Professionals' Beliefs about and Knowledge of Assessment Techniques and Psychometric Tests," *International Journal of Selection and Assessment* 16 (2008): 300–305.

5. Robert E. Ployhart, Jeff A. Weekley, Brian C. Holtz, and C. Kemp, "Web-based and Paper-and-pencil Testing of Applicants in a Proctored Setting: Are Personality, Biodata, and Situational Judgment Tests Comparable?" *Personnel Psychology* 56 (2003): 733–752; and Chad H. Van Iddekinge, Carl E. Eidson, Jeffrey D. Kudisch, and Andrew M. Goldblatt, "A Biodata Inventory Administered via Interactive Voice Technology (IVR) Technology: Predictive Validity, Utility, and Subgroup Differences," *Journal of Business and Psychology* 18 (2003): 145–156.

6. James A. Breaugh, "The Use of Biodata for Employee Selection: Past Research and Future Directions," *Human Resource Management Review* 19 (2009): 219–231; and Fred A. Mael, "A Conceptual Rationale for the Domain and Attributes of Biodata Items," *Personnel Psychology* 44 (1991): 763–792.

7. B. J. Nickels, "The Nature of Biodata," In Biodata Handbook, eds. Garret A. Stokes, Michael D. Mumford, and William A. Owens (Palo Alto, CA: Consulting Psychologists Press, 1994): 1–16; and Matthew S. O'Connell, Keith Hattrup, Dennis Doverspike, and Alana Cober, "The Validity of 'Mini' Simulations for Mexican Salespeople," *Journal of Business and Psychology* 16 (October, 2004): 593–599.

8. Joel Lefkowitz, Melissa I. Gebbia, Tamar Balsam, and Linda Dunn, "Dimensions of Biodata Items and Their Relationship to Item Validity," *Journal of Occupational and Organizational Psychology* 72 (1999): 331–350; Michael K. Mount, L. A. Witt, and Murray R. Barrick, "Incremental Validity of Empirically Keyed Biodata Scales Over GMA and the Five Factor

Personality Constructs," *Personnel Psychology* 53 (2000): 299–323; M. A. Oviedo-Garcia, "Internal Validation of a Biodata Extraversion Scale," *Social Behavior and Personality* 35 (2007): 675–692; Howard Sisco and Richard R. Reilly, "Development and Validation of a Biodata Inventory as an Alternative Method to Measurement of the Five Factor Model of Personality," *The Social Science Journal* 44 (2007): 383–389; and Chad H. Van Iddekinge, Carl E. Eidson, Jeffrey D. Kudisch, and Andrew M. Goldblatt, "A Biodata Inventory Administered via Interactive Voice Technology (IVR) Technology: Predictive Validity, Utility, and Subgroup Differences," *Journal of Business and Psychology* 18 (2003): 145–156.

9. James A. Breaugh, "The Use of Biodata for Employee Selection: Past Research and Future Directions," *Human Resource Management Review* 19 (2009): 219–231; Fred A. Mael, "A Conceptual Rationale for the Domain and Attributes of Biodata Items," *Personnel Psychology* 44 (1991): 763–792; and Neal Schmitt, Danielle Jennings, and Rebbeca Toney, "Can We Develop Measures of Hypothetical Constructs?" *Human Resource Management Review* 9 (1999): 169–183.

10. George W. England, *Development and Use of Weighted Application Blanks* (Minneapolis: Industrial Relations Center, University of Minnesota, 1971), 60–65.

11. George W. England, *Development and Use of Weighted Application Blanks* (Minneapolis: Industrial Relations Center, University of Minnesota, 1971), 60–65; and Raymond Lee and Jerome M. Booth, "A Utility Analysis of a Weighted Application Blank Designed to Predict Turnover for Clerical Employees," *Journal of Applied Psychology* 59 (1974): 516–518.

12. Fred A. Mael, "A Conceptual Rationale for the Domain and Attributes of Biodata Items," *Personnel Psychology* 44 (1991): 763–792.

13. Paul F. Wernimont and John P. Campbell, "Signs, Samples, and Criteria," *Journal of Applied Psychology* 52 (October 1968): 372–376; and William A. Owens, "Background Data," in *Handbook of Industrial and Organizational Psychology*, ed. Marvin Dunnette (Chicago: Rand-McNally, 1976), 252–293.

14. Murray R. Barrick and Ryan D. Zimmerman, "Reducing Voluntary, Avoidable Turnover through Selection," *Journal of Applied Psychology* 90 (2005): 159–166.

15. Leatta Hough and Cheryl Paullin, "Construct-oriented Scale Construction," in Biodata Handbooks, eds. Garnett Stokes, Micahel D. Mumford, and William A. Owens (Palo Alto, CA: Consulting Psychologists Press, 1994), 109–145; and Neal Schmitt, Danielle Jennings, and Rebbeca Toney, "Can We Develop Measures of Hypothetical Constructs?" *Human Resource Management Review* 9 (1999): 169–183.

16. William A. Owens, "Background Data," in *Handbook of Industrial and Organizational Psychology*, ed. Marvin Dunnette (Chicago: Rand-McNally, 1976), 252–293.

17. James J. Asher, "The Biographical Item: Can It Be Improved?" *Personnel Psychology* 25 (1979): 759.

18. Craig J. Russell, "Selecting Top Corporate Leaders: An Example of Biographical Information," *Journal of Management* 6 (1990): 73–86.

19. J. Russell Craig, Joyce Mattson, Steven E. Devlin, and David Atwater, "Predictive Validity of Biodata Items Generated from Retrospective Life Experience Essays," *Journal of Applied Psychology* 75 (1990): 569–580.

20. Philip Bobko, Philip L. Roth, and Denise Potosky, "Derivation and Implications of a Meta-Analytic Matrix Incorporating Cognitive Ability, Alternative Predictors, and Job Performance," *Personnel Psychology* 52 (1999): 573.

21. John E. Hunter and Rhonda F. Hunter, "Validity and Utility of Alternative Predictors of Job Performance," *Psychological Bulletin* 96 (1984): 72–98; and Neal Schmitt, Richard Z. Gooding, Raymond A. Noe, and Michael Kirsch, "Metaanalysis of Validity Studies

Published between 1964 and 1982 and the Investigation of Study Characteristics," *Personnel Psychology* 37 (1984): 407–422.

22. Thomas Bliesener, "Methodological Moderators in Validating Biographical Data in Personnel Selection," *Journal of Occupational and Organizational Psychology* 69 (1996): 107–120; Kevin D. Carlson, Steven E. Scullen, Frank L. Schmidt, Hannah Rothstein, and Frank Erwin, "Generalizable Biographical Data Validity Can Be Achieved Without Multi-Organizational Development and Keying," *Personnel Psychology* 5 (1999): 731–755; John Hunter and Rhonda Hunter, "The Validity and Utility of Alternative Predictors of Job Performance," *Psychological Bulletin* 96 (1984): 72–98; Frank L. Schmidt, and John E. Hunter, "The Validity and Utility of Selection Methods in Personnel Psychology: Practical and Theoretical Implications of 85 Years of Research Findings," *Psychological Bulletin* 124 (1998): 262–274; Neal Schmitt, Richard Z. Gooding, Raymond A. Noe, and Michael Kirsch, "Metaanalysis of Validity Studies Published between 1964 and 1982 and the Investigation of Study Characteristics," *Personnel Psychology* 37 (1984): 407–422; and Andrew J. Vinchur, Jeffrey S. Shippmann, Fred S. Switzer, and Phillip L. Roth, "A Meta-Analytic Review of Predictors of Job Performance for Salespeople," *Journal of Applied Psychology* 83 (1998): 586–597.

23. Hannah R. Rothstein, Frank L. Schmidt, Frank W. Erwin, William A. Owens, and C. Paul Sparks, "Biographical Data in Employment Selection: Can Validities Be Made Generalizable?" *Journal of Applied Psychology* 75 (1990): 175–184.

24. Kevin D. Carlson, Steven E. Scullen, Frank L. Schmidt, Hannah Rothstein, and Frank Erwin, "Generalizable Biographical Data Validity Can Be Achieved Without Multi-Organizational Development and Keying," *Personnel Psychology* 52 (1999): 731–755.

25. Ibid., 745.

26. Garnett S. Stokes, James B. Hogan, and Andrea F. Snell, "Comparability of Incumbent and Applicant Samples for the Development of Biodata Keys: The Influence of Social Desirability," *Personnel Psychology* 46 (1993): 739–762.

27. Thomas Bliesener, "Methodological Moderators in Validating Biographical Data in Personnel Selection," *Journal of Occupational and Organizational Psychology* 69 (1996): 107–120.

28. Crystal M. Harold, Lynn A. McFarland, and Jeff A. Weekley, "The Validity of Verifiable and Non-Verifiable Biodata Items: An Examination Across Applicants and Incumbents," *International Journal of Selection and Assessment* 14 (2006): 336–346.

29. Schmidt and Hunter, "The Validity and Utility of Selection Methods in Personnel Psychology: Practical and Theoretical Implications of 85 Years of Research Findings," 269.

30. Bobko, Roth, and Potosky, "Derivation and Implications of a Meta-Analytic Matrix Incorporating Cognitive Ability, Alternative Predictors, and Job Performance," 562.

31. Hunter and Hunter, "Validity and Utility of Alternative Predictors of Job Performance."

32. Gary J. Lautenschlager, "Accuracy and Faking of Background Data," in *Biodata Handbook*, ed. Garnett S. Stokes, Michael D. Mumford, and William A. Owens (Palo Alto, CA: Consulting Psychologists Press, 1994), 391–419; Lynn A. McFarland and Ann Marie Ryan, "Variance in Faking Across Noncognitive Measures," *Journal of Applied Psychology* 85 (2000): 812–821; Thomas E. Becker and Alan L. Colquitt, "Potential versus Actual Faking of a Biodata Form: An Analysis Along Several Dimensions of Item Type," *Personnel Psychology* 45 (1992): 389–406; Stephen A. Dwight and John J. Donovan, "Do Warnings Not to Fake Reduce Faking?" *Human Performance* 16 (2003): 1–23; and John J. Donovan, Stephen A. Dwight, and Gregory M. Hurtz, "An Assessment of the Prevalence, Severity, and Verifiability of Entry-Level Applicant Faking Using the Randomized Response Technique," *Human Performance* 16 (2003): 81–106.

33. Lautenschlager, "Accuracy and Faking of Background Data."; and Fred Morgeson, Michael A. Campion, Robert L. Dipboye, John R. Hollenbeck, Kevin Murphy, and Neal Schmitt, "Reconsidering the Use of Personality Tests in Personnel Selection Contexts," *Personnel Psychology* 60 (2007): 683–729.

34. Barbara Kate Repa, "Resume Inflation: Two Wrongs May Mean No Rights," *Nolo.com* (August 8, 2001); Edward C. Andler and Dara Herbst, The Complete Reference Checking Handbook, 2nd ed. (New York, NY: AMACOM, 2004); Lisa Teuchi Cullen, "Getting Wise to Lies," *Time* (May 1, 2006): 59; and Steven D. Levitt and Stephen J. Dubner, *Freakonomics: A Rogue Economist Explores the Hidden Side of Everything,* New York, NY: Harper Collins, 2006.

35. Neal Schmitt and Frederick L. Oswald, "The Impact of Corrections for Faking on the Validity of Noncognitive Measures in Selection Settings," *Journal of Applied Psychology* 91 (2006): 613–621; Margaret A. McManus and Jaci Jarrett Masztal, "The Impact of Biodata Item Attributes on Validity and Socially Desirable Responding," *Journal of Business and Psychology* 12, no. 3 (1999): 437–446; Murray R. Barrick and Michael K. Mount, "Effects of Impression Management and Self-Deception on the Predictive Validity of Personality Constructs," *Journal of Applied Psychology* 81 (1996): 261–272; and Becker and Colquitt, "Potential versus Actual Faking of a Biodata Form: An Analysis Along Several Dimensions of Item Type."

36. Schmitt and Oswald, "The Impact of Corrections for Faking on the Validity of Noncognitive Measures in Selection Settings."

37. Becker and Colquitt, "Potential versus Actual Faking of a Biodata Form: An Analysis Along Several Dimensions of Item Type"; Garnett S. Stokes, James B. Hogan, and Andrea F. Snell, "Comparability of Incumbent and Applicant Samples for the Development of Biodata Keys:? The Influence of Social Desirability," *Personnel Psychology* 46 (1993): 739–762; Lautenschlager, "Accuracy and Faking of Background Data"; and Kenneth E. Graham, Michael A. McDaniel, Elizabeth F. Douglas, and Andrea F. Snell, "Biodata Validity Decay and Score Inflation with Faking: Do Item Attributes Explain Variance across Items?" *Journal of Business and Psychology* 16 (2002): 573–592.

38. Neal Schmitt and C. Kunce, "The Effects of Required Elaboration of Answers to Biodata Measures," *Personnel Psychology* 55 (2002): 569–588; Neal Schmitt, Fred L. Oswald, Brian H. Kim, Tae-Yong Yoo, Michael A. Gillespie, and Lauren J. Ramsay, "Impact of Elaboration on Socially Desirable Responding and the Validity of Biodata Measures," *Journal of Applied Psychology* 88 (2003): 979–988; Dwight and Donovan, "Do Warnings Not to Fake Reduce Faking?"; and Donovan, Dwight, and Hurtz, "An Assessment of the Prevalence, Severity, and Verifiability of Entry-Level Applicant Faking Using the Randomized Response Technique."

39. Dwight and Donovan, "Do Warnings Not to Fake Reduce Faking?"; and Donovan, Dwight, and Hurtz, "An Assessment of the Prevalence, Severity, and Verifiability of Entry-Level Applicant Faking Using the Randomized Response Technique."

40. Timothy S. Bland and Sue S. Stalcup, "Build a Legal Employment Application," *HR Magazine* 44 (1999): 129–133.

41. *Jenkins v. Eastern Capital Corp.*, 846 F. Supp. 864 (N.D. Cal 1994).

42. Neal Schmitt, and Charles Kunce, "The Effects of Required Elaboration of Answers to Biodata Questions," *Personnel Psychology* 55 (2002): 569–587; Neal Schmitt, Fred L. Oswald, Brian K. Kim, Michael A. Gillespie, Lauren J Ramsay, and Lauren J. Tae-Yong Yoo, "Impact of Elaboration on Socially Desirable Responding and the Validity of Biodata Measures," *Journal of Applied Psychology* 88 (2005): 979–988.

43. "Equal Employment Opportunity Commission," *Guide to Pre-Employment Inquiries* (Washington, DC: Equal Employment Opportunity Commission, August 1981), 1.

44. Ibid.

45. Ernest C. Miller, "An EEO Examination of Employment Applications," *Personnel Administrator* 25 (March 1981): 63–70; Debra D. Burrington, "A Review of State Government Employment Application Forms for Suspect Inquiries," *Public Personnel Management* 11 (1982): 55–60; and Richard S. Lowell and Jay A. Deloach, "Equal Employment Opportunity: Are You Overlooking the Application Form?" *Personnel* 59 (1982): 49–55.

46. Miller, "An EEO Examination of Employment Applications."

47. Burrington, "A Review of State Government Employment Application Forms for Suspect Inquiries."

48. Lowell and Deloach, "Equal Employment Opportunity: Are You Overlooking the Application Form?"

49. J. Craig Wallace and Stephen J. Vodanovich, "Personnel Application Blanks: Persistence and Knowledge of Legally Inadvisable Application Blank Items," *Public Personnel Management* 33 (Fall 2004): 331–349.

50. J. Craig Wallace, Mary G. Tye, and Stephen J. Vodanovich, "Applying for Jobs Online: Examining the Legality of Internet-Based Application Forms," *Public Personnel Management* 4 (Winter 2000): 497–504.

51. Stephen J. Vodanovich and Rosemary H. Lowe, "They Ought to Know Better: The Incidence and Correlates of Inappropriate Application Blank Inquiries," *Public Personnel Management* 21 (1992): 363–370.

52. James P. Jolly and James G. Frierson, "Playing It Safe," *Personnel Administrator* 25 (1989): 63–81.

53. R. Bryan Kethley and David E. Terpstra, "An Analysis of Litigation Associated with the Use of the Application Form in the Selection Process," *Public Personnel Management* 34 (2005): 357–373.

54. Garnett S. Stokes, "Introduction to Special Issue: The Next One Hundred Years of Biodata," *Human Resource Management Review* 9 (1999): 111–116.

55. James C. Sharf, "The Impact of Legal and Equal Employment Opportunity Issues on Personal History Inquiries," in *Biodata Handbook*, ed. Garnett S. Stokes, Michael D. Mumford, and William A. Owens (Palo Alto, CA: CPP Books, 1994): 370.

56. Mumford, Cooper, and Schemmer, *Development of a Content Valid Set of Background Data Measures.*

57. Dianna L. Stone and Eugene F. Stone, "Effects of Missing Application Blank Information on Personnel Selection Decisions: Do Privacy Protection Strategies Bias the Outcome?" *Journal of Applied Psychology* 72 (1987): 452–456.

58. Owens, "Background Data," 620.

59. Reilly and Chao, "Validity and Fairness of Some Alternative Employee Selection Procedures," 1–62.

60. Bobko, Roth, and Potosky, "Derivation and Implications of a Meta-Analytic Matrix Incorporating Cognitive Ability, Alternative Predictors, and Job Performance"; and Schmidt and Hunter, "The Validity and Utility of Selection Methods in Personnel Psychology: Practical and Theoretical Implications of 85 Years of Research Findings," 269.

61. J. Craig Wallace and Stephen J. Vodanovich, "Personnel Application Blanks: Persistence and Knowledge of Legally Inadvisable Application Blank Items," *Public Personnel Management* 33 (Fall 2004): 331–349; J. Craig Wallace, Mary G. Tye, and Stephen J. Vodanovich, "Applying for Jobs Online: Examining the Legality of Internet-Based Application Forms," *Public Personnel Management* 4 (Winter 2000): 497–504; Stephen J. Vodanovich and Rosemary H. Lowe, "They

Ought to Know Better: The Incidence and Correlates of Inappropriate Application Blank Inquiries," *Public Personnel Management* 21 (1992): 363–370; James P. Jolly and James G. Frierson, "Playing It Safe," *Personnel Administrator* 25 (1989): 63–81; and R. Bryan Kethley and David E. Terpstra, "An Analysis of Litigation Associated with the Use of the Application Form in the Selection Process," *Public Personnel Management* 34 (2005): 357–373.

62. Rothstein et al., "Biographical Data in Selection: Can Validities Be Made Generalizable?"; and Carlson et al., "Generalizable Biographical Data Can Be Achieved without Multi-Organizational Development and Keying."

63. Carlson et al., "Generalizable Biographical Data Can Be Achieved without Multi-Organizational Development and Keying."

64. Murray R. Barrick and Ryan D. Zimmerman, "Reducing Voluntary, Avoidable Turnover through Selection," *Journal of Applied Psychology* 90 (1999): 159–166.

65. Leatta M. Hough, Fred L. Oswald, and Rob E. Ployhart, "Determinants, Detection and Amelioration of Adverse Impact in Personnel Selection Procedures: Issues, Evidence, and Lessons Learned," *International Journal of Selection and Assessment* 9 (2001): 152–194.

66. Timothy S. Bland and Sue S. Stalcup, "Build a Legal Employment Application," *HR Magazine* 44 (1999): 129–133.

67. John P. Hausknecht, David V. Day, and Scott C. Thomas, "Applicant Reactions to Selection Procedures: An Updated Model and Meta-Analysis," *Personnel Psychology* 57 (2004): 639–683.

68. Brad S. Bell, Ann Marie Ryan, and Darrin Weichmann, "Justice Expectations and Applicant Perceptions," *International Journal of Selection and Assessment* 12 (2004): 24–38; Ann Marie Ryan and Robert E. Ployhart, "Applicants' Perceptions of Selection Procedures and Decisions: A Critical Review and Agenda for the Future," *Journal of Management* 26 (2000): 565–606; Sara L. Rynes and Mary L. Connerley, "Applicant Reactions to Alternative Selection Procedures," *Journal of Business and Psychology* 7 (1993): 261–277; Donald M. Truxillo, Talya N. Bauer, Michael A. Campion, and M. E. Paronto, "Selection Fairness Information and Applicant Reactions: A Longitudinal Field Study," *Journal of Applied Psychology* 87 (2002): 1020–1031; and Donald M. Truxillo, Dirk D. Steiner, and Stephen W. Gilliland, "The Importance of Organizational Justice in Personnel Selection: Defining When Selection Fairness Really Matters," *International Journal of Selection and Assessment* 12, no. 1 (2004): 39–53.

69. Truxillo, Steiner, and Gilliland, "The Importance of Organizational Justice in Personnel Selection: Defining When Selection Fairness Really Matters."

70. Ryan and Ployhart, "Applicants' Perceptions of Selection Procedures and Decisions: A Critical Review and Agenda for the Future"; Hausknecht, Day, and Thomas, "Applicant Reactions to Selection Procedures: An Updated Model and Meta-Analysis"; and Alan M. Saks, Joanne D. Leck, and David M. Saunders, "Effects of Application Blanks and Employment Equity on Applicant Reactions and Job Pursuit Interactions," *Journal of Organizational Behavior* 16 (1995): 415–430.

71. Wallace, Tye, and Vodanovich, "Applying for Jobs Online: Examining the Legality of Internet-Based Application Forms"; and Department of Fair Employment and Housing, "State of California", *Pre-Employment Inquiry Guidelines* (Sacramento, CA: Department of Fair Employment and Housing, May 1982).

72. Wallace and Vodanovich, "Personnel Application Blanks: Persistence and Knowledge of Legally Inadvisable Application Blank Items"; Wallace, Tye, and Vodanovich, "Applying for Jobs Online: Examining the Legality of Internet-based Application Forms"; and Ernest C. Miller, "An EEO Examination of Employment Applications."

73. Alan M. Saks, Joanne D. Leck, and David M. Saunders, "Effects of Application Blanks and Employment Equity on Applicant Reactions and Job Pursuit Interactions," *Journal of Organizational Behavior* 16 (1995): 415–430.

74. *Human Resources Guide;* and Ernest C. Miller, "An EEO Examination of Employment Applications."

75. Andler and Herbst, *The Complete Reference Checking Handbook*, 2nd ed. Sandra King, Steven C. Kahn, and David Rosen, *Human Resources Guide*, ed. Robert J. Nobile (Boston: West Group, A Thomson Company, 2000); and Philip Ash, "Law and Regulation of Preemployment Inquiries," *Journal of Business and Psychology* 5 (1991): 291–308.

76. Wallace and Vodanovich, "Personnel Application Blanks: Persistence and Knowledge of Legally Inadvisable Application Blank Items."

77. Richard R. Reilly and Georgia T. Chao, "Validity and Fairness of Some Alternative Employee Selection Procedures," *Personnel Psychology* 35 (1982): 1–63.

78. Kethley and Terpstra, "An Analysis of Litigation Associated with the Use of the Application Form in the Selection Process."

79. Garnett Stokes and L. A. Cooper, "Content/Construct Approaches in Life History Form Development for Selection," *International Journal of Selection and Assessment* 9 (2001): 138–151; Erich P. Prien and Garry L. Hughes, "A Content-Oriented Approach to Setting Minimum Qualifications, *Public Personnel Management* 33, no. 1 (2004): 89–104; and Elizabeth Allworth and Beryl Hesketh, "Job Requirements Biodata as a Predictor of Performance in Customer Service Roles," *International Journal of Selection and Assessment* 8 (2000): 137–147.

80. James R. Glennon, Lewis E. Albright, and William A. Owens, *A Catalog of Life History Items* (Greensboro, NC: The Richardson Foundation, 1966); Owens and Henry, *Biographical Data in Industrial Psychology*.

81. W. M. Brodie, Lillian A. Owens, and M. F. Britt, *Annotated Biography on Biographical Data* (Greensboro, NC: The Richardson Foundation, 1968); Owens and Henry, *Biographical Data in Industrial Psychology*.

82. Michael D. Mumford and William A. Owens, "Methodology Review: Principles, Procedures, and Findings in the Application of Background Data Measures," 6–8; Leaetta M. Hough, "Development and Evaluation of the 'Accomplishment Record' Method of Selecting and Promoting Professionals," *Journal of Applied Psychology* 69 (1984): 135–146; and Leaetta M. Hough, Margaret A. Keyes, and Marvin D. Dunnette, "An Evaluation of Three 'Alternative' Selection Procedures," *Personnel Psychology* 36 (1983): 261–276.

83. Mael, "A Conceptual Rationale for the Domain and Attributes of Biodata Items."

84. Lawrence S. Kleiman and Robert Faley, "A Comparative Analysis of the Empirical Validity of Past and Present-Oriented Biographical Items," *Journal of Business and Psychology* 4 (1990): 431–437.

85. Williams, "Life History Antecedents of Volunteers versus Nonvolunteers for an AFROTC Program," 8.

86. William A. Owens and Lyle F. Schoenfeldt, "Toward a Classification of Persons," *Journal of Applied Psychology Monograph* 64 (1979): 569–607.

87. See, for example, Sam C. Webb, "The Comparative Validity of Two Biographical Inventory Keys," *Journal of Applied Psychology* 44 (1960): 177–183; Raymond E. Christal and Robert A. Bottenberg, *Procedure for Keying Self-Report Test Items* (Lackland Air Force Base, TX: Personnel Research Laboratory, 1964); and William H. Clark and Bruce L. Margolis,

"A Revised Procedure for the Analysis of Biographical Information," *Educational and Psychological Measurement* 31 (1971): 461–464.

88. Owens and Schoenfeldt, "Toward a Classification of Persons," 569–607; Michael T. Matteson, "An Alternative Approach to Using Biographical Data for Predicting Job Success," *Journal of Occupational Psychology* 51 (1978): 155–162; Michael T. Matteson, "A FORTRAN Program Series for Generating Relatively Independent and Homogeneous Keys for Scoring Biographical Inventories," *Educational and Psychological Measurement* 30 (1970): 137–139; and Terry W. Mitchell and Richard J. Klimoski, "Is It Rational to Be Empirical? A Test of Methods for Scoring Biographical Data," *Journal of Applied Psychology* 67, no. 4 (1982): 411–418.

89. England, *Development and Use of Weighted Application Blanks.*

90. William H. Stead and Carol L. Shartle, *Occupational Counseling Techniques* (New York: American Book, 1940).

91. William B. Lecznar and John T. Dailey, "Keying Biographical Inventories in Classification Test Batteries," *American Psychologist* 5 (1950): 279.

92. Michael P. Malone, *Predictive Efficiency and Discriminatory Impact of Verifiable Biographical Data as a Function of Data Analysis Procedure* (Minneapolis: Doctoral Dissertation, University of Minnesota, 1978).

93. Webb, "The Comparative Validity of Two Biographical Inventory Keys."

94. Paul A. Telenson, Ralph A. Alexander, and Gerald V. Barrett, "Scoring the Biographical Information Blank: A Comparison of Three Weighting Techniques," *Applied Psychological Measurement* 7 (1983): 73–80.

95. Robert F. Morrison, William A. Owens, J. R. Glennon, and Lewis E. Albright, "Factored Life History Antecedents of Industrial Research Performance," *Journal of Applied Psychology* 46 (1962): 281–284.

96. Michael K. Mount, L. Alan Witt, and Murray R. Barrick, "Incremental Validity of Empirically Keyed Biodata Scales Over GMA and the Five Factor Personality Constructs," *Personnel Psychology* 53 (2000): 299–323.

97. William A. Owens and Lyle F. Schoenfeldt, "Toward a Classification of Persons," *Journal of Applied Psychology Monograph* 64 (1979): 569–607.

98. Jane H. Philbrick, Barbara D. Bart, and Marcia E. Hass, "Pre-employment Screening: A Decade of Change," *American Business Review* 17 (1999): 77.

99. Michael S. Cole, Hubert S. Feild, and William F. Giles, "Using Recruiter Assessments of Applicants' Résumé Content to Predict Applicant Mental Ability and Big Five Personality Dimensions," *International Journal of Selection and Assessment* 11, no. 1 (2003): 78–88.

100. Barbara K. Brown and Michael A. Campion, "Biodata Phenomenology: Recruiters' Perceptions and Use of Biographical Information in Resume Screening," *Journal of Applied Psychology* 79 (1994): 897–908.

101. Edward L. Levine, Ronald A. Ash, and Jonathan D. Levine, "Judgemental Assessment of Job-Related Experience, Training and Education for Use in Human Resource Staffing," *Comprehensive Handbook of Psychological Assessment* 16 (2004): 269–293.

102. Ibid. Levine, Ash and Levine.

103. Ibid. Levine, Ash, and Levine.

104. J. M. Stanton, "Validity and Related Issues in Web-Based Hiring," *The Industrial-Organizational Psychologist* 36 (January 1999): 69–77.

105. L. I. Machwirth, H. Schuler, and K. Moser, "Entscheidungsprozesse bei der Analyse von Bewerbungsunterlagen," *Diagnostica* 42, no. 3 (1996): 220–241; and George W. Tommasi, Karen B. Williams, and Cynthia R. Nordstrom, "Letters of Recommendation: What Information Captures HR Professionals' Attention?" *Journal of Business and Psychology* 13, no. 1 (1998): 5–18.

106. Kevin D. Carlson, Steven E. Scullen, Frank L. Schmidt, Hannah Rothstein, and Frank Erwin, "Generalizable Biographical Data Validity Can Be Achieved Without Multi-Organizational Development and Keying," *Personnel Psychology* 5 (1999): 731–755.

107. Paul E. Tesluk and Rick R. Jacobs, "Toward an Integrated Model of Work Experience," *Personnel Psychology* 51 (1998): 321–355.

108. Erick P. Prien and Garry L. Hughes, "A Content-Oriented Approach to Setting Minimum Qualifications," *Public Personnel Management* 33 (2004): 89–98; and Beryl Hesketh and Elizabeth Allworth, "Job Requirements Biodata as a Predictor of Performance in Customer Service Roles," *International Journal of Selection and Assessment* 8 (September 2000): 137.

109. W. R. Porter, Edward L. Levine, and A. Flory III, *Training and Experience Evaluation: A Practical Handbook for Evaluating Job Applicants, Resumes, and Other Applicant Data*, (Tempe, AZ: Personnel Services Orientation, 1976); and Miguel A. Quinones, J. Kevin Ford, and Mark S. Teachout, "The Relationship between Work Experience and Job Performance: A Conceptual and Meta-Analytic Review," *Personnel Psychology* 48 (1995): 887–910.

110. Barbara K. Brown and Michael A. Campion, "Biodata Phenomenology: Recruiters' Perceptions and Use of Biographical Information in Resume Screening," *Journal of Applied Psychology* 79 (1994): 897–908.

111. Walter C. Borman, Mary Ann Hanson, Scott H. Oppler, Elaine D. Pulakos, and Leonard A. White, "Role of Early Supervisory Experience in Supervisor Performance," *Journal of Applied Psychology* 78 (1993): 443–449; and Frank L. Schmidt, John E. Hunter, and Alice N. Outerbridge, "Impact of Job Experience and Ability on Job Knowledge, Work Sample Performance, and Supervisory Ratings of Job Performance," *Journal of Applied Psychology* 71 (1986): 432–439.

112. Ronald A. Ash and Edward L. Levine, "Job Applicant Training and Work Experience Evaluation: An Empirical Comparison of Four Methods," *Journal of Applied Psychology* 70, no. 3, (1985): 572–376.

113. Schmidt et al., *The Behavioral Consistency Method of Unassembled Examining*.

114. Kethley and Terpstra, "An Analysis of Litigation Associated with the Use of the Application Form in the Selection Process."

115. Michael A. McDaniel, Frank L. Schmidt, and John E. Hunter, "A Meta-Analysis of the Validity of Methods for Rating Training and Experience in Personnel Selection," *Personnel Psychology* 41 (1988): 283–314.

116. Ronald Ash, James Johnson, Edward Levine, and Michael McDaniel, "Job Applicant Training and Work Experience Evaluation in Personnel Selection," in *Research in Personnel and Human Resource Management*, ed. Kenneth Rowland and Gerald Ferris (Greenwich, CT: JAI Press, 1989), 187–190.

117. Miguel A. Quinoñes, J. Kevin Ford, and Mark S. Teachout, "The Relationship between Work Experience and Job Performance: A Conceptual and Meta-Analytic Review," *Personnel Psychology* 48 (1995): 887–910.

118. Thomas W. H. Ng, Lillian T. Eby, Kerry L. Sorensen, and Daniel C. Feldman, "Predictors of Objective and Subjective Career Success: A Meta-Analysis," *Personnel Psychology* 58 (2005): 367–408.

119. Miguel A. Quinoñes, J. Kevin Ford, and Mark S. Teachout, "The Relationship between Work Experience and Job Performance: A Conceptual and Meta-Analytic Review," *Personnel Psychology* 48 (1995): 887–910.

120. John Hunter and Rhonda Hunter, "The Validity and Utility of Alternative Predictors of Job Performance," *Psychological Bulletin* 96 (1984): 72–98.

121. Thomas W. H. Ng, Lillian T. Eby, Kelly L. Sorensen, and Daniel C. Feldman, "Predictors of Objective and Subjective Career Success: A Meta-Analysis," *Personnel Psychology* 58 (2005): 367–408.

122. Tesluk and Jacobs, "Toward an Integrated Model of Work Experience."

123. Frank L. Schmidt and John E. Hunter, "The Validity and Utility of Selection Methods in Personnel Psychology: Practical and Theoretical Implications of 85 Years of Research Findings," *Psychological Bulletin* 124 (1998): 262–274.

124. Philip L. Roth, C. A. Bevier, F. S. Switzer, and J. S. Schippmann, "Meta-Analyzing the Relationship between Grades and Job Performance," *Journal of Applied Psychology* 81 (1996): 548–556.

125. Thomas W. H. Ng, Lillian T. Eby, Kerry L. Sorensen, and Daniel C. Feldman, "Predictors of Objective and Subjective Career Success: A Meta-Analysis," *Personnel Psychology* 58 (2005): 367–408.; and Rodger W. Griffeth, Peter W. Hom, and Stefan Gaertner, "A Meta-Analysis of Antecedents and Correlates of Employee Turnover: Update, Moderator Tests, and Research Implications for the Next Millennium," *Journal of Management* 26 (2000): 463–488.

126. Frank L. Schmidt and John E. Hunter, "General Mental Ability in the World of Work: Occupational Attainment and Job Performance," *Journal of Personality and Social Psychology* 86 (2004): 162–173; Malcolm J. Ree, Thomas R. Carretta, and Mark S. Teachout, "Role of Ability and Prior Job Knowledge in Complex Training Performance," *Journal of Applied Psychology* 80 (1995): 721–730; Charles E. Lance and Winston R. Bennett, "Replication and Extension of Models of Supervisory Job Performance Ratings," *Human Performance* 13 (2000): 139–158; and Charles A. Scherbaum, Karen L. Scherbaum, and Paula M. Popovich, "Predicting Job-Related Expectancies and Affective Reactions to Employees with Disabilities from Previous Work Experience," *Journal of Applied Social Psychology* 35 (2005): 889–904.

127. Michael A. McDaniel, Frank L. Schmidt, and John E. Hunter, "A Meta-Analysis of the Validity of Methods for Rating Training and Experience in Personnel Selection," *Personnel Psychology* 41 (2006): 283–309.

128. Bruce J. Avolio, David A. Waldschmidt, and Michael A. McDaniel, "Age and Work Performance in Nonmanagerial Jobs: The Effects of Experience and Occupational Type," *Academy of Management Journal* 33 (1990): 407–422; Rick Jacobs, David A. Hofmann, and S. D. Kriska, "Performance and Seniority," *Human Performance* 3 (1990): 107–121; Frank L. Schmidt, John E. Hunter, and Alice E. Outerbridge, "Impact of Job Experience and Ability on Job Knowledge, Work Sample Performance, and Supervisory Ratings of Job Performance," *Journal of Applied Psychology* 71 (1986): 431–439; and Michael C. Sturman, "Searching for the Inverted U-Shaped Relationship between Time and Performance: Meta-Analyses of the Experience/Performance, Tenure/Performance, and Age/Performance Relationships," *Journal of Management* 29, no. 5 (2003): 609–640.

129. Niteesh K. Choudry, Robert H. Fletcher, and Stephen B. Soumerai, "Systematic Review: The Relationship between Clinical Experience and Quality of Health Care," *Annals of Internal Medicine* 142 (2005): 260–273.

130. Michael C. Sturman, "Searching for the Inverted U-Shaped Relationship between Time and Performance: Meta-Analyses of the Experience/Performance, Tenure/Performance, and Age/Performance Relationships," *Journal of Management* 29, no. 5 (2003): 609–640.

131. Edward L. Levine, Doris M. Maye, Ronald A. Ulm, and Thomas R. Gordon, "A Methodology for Developing and Validating Minimum Qualifications (MQs)," *Personnel Psychology* 50 (2004): 1009–1023; and Maury A. Buster, Philip L. Roth, and Philip Bobko, "A Process for Content Validation of Education and Experienced-Based Minimum Qualifications: An

Approach Resulting in Federal Court Approval," *Personnel Psychology* 58 (August 2005): 771–799.

132. Philip Bobko and Philip L. Roth, "College Grade Point Average as a Personnel Selection Device: Ethnic Group Differences and Potential Adverse Impact," *Journal of Applied Psychology* 85 (2000): 399–406.

133. R. Bryan Kethley and David E. Terpstra, "An Analysis of Litigation Associated with the Use of the Application Form in the Selection Process," *Public Personnel Management* 34 (2005): 357–376.

134. Richard D. Arvey and R. H. Faley, *Fairness in Selecting Employees*, 2nd ed (Reading, MA: Addison-Wesley, 1988); Edward L. Levine, Doris M. Maye, Ronald A. Ulm, and Thomas R. Gordon, "A Methodology for Developing and Validating Minimum Qualifications (MQs)," *Personnel Psychology* 50 (1997), 1009–1023.

135. Tesluk and Jacobs, "Toward an Integrated Model of Work Experience"; Ronald Ash, James Johnson, Edward Levine, and Michael McDaniel, "Job Applicant Training and Work Experience Evaluation in Personnel Selection," in *Research in Personnel and Human Resource Management*, ed. Kenneth Rowland and Gerald Ferris (Greenwich, CT: JAI Press, 1989), 187–190; and Edward L. Levine, Doris M. Maye, Ronald A. Ulm, and Thomas R. Gordon, "A?Methodology for Developing and Validating Minimum Qualifications (MQs)," *Personnel Psychology* 50 (1997): 1009–1023.

136. Scott Highhouse, "Assessing the Candidate as a Whole: A Historical and Critical Analysis of Individual Psychological Assessment for Personnel Decision Making," *Personnel Psychology* 55 (2002): 363–396; and Ronald Ash, James Johnson, Edward Levine, and Michael McDaniel, "Job Applicant Training and Work Experience Evaluation in Personnel Selection," in *Research in Personnel and Human Resource Management*, ed. Kenneth Rowland and Gerald Ferris (Greenwich, CT: JAI Press, 1989), 187–190.

137. Wayne R. Porter, Edward L. Levine, and Abraham Flory, *Training and Experience Evaluation* (Tempe, AZ: Personnel Services Organization, 1976).

138. Ibid.

139. Ibid.

140. Leaetta M. Hough, "Development and Evaluation of the 'Accomplishment Record' Method of Selecting and Promoting Professionals," *Journal of Applied Psychology* 69 (1984): 135–146.

141. Leaetta M. Hough, Margaret A. Keyes, and Marvin D. Dunnette, "An Evaluation of Three 'Alternative' Selection Procedures," *Personnel Psychology* 36 (1983): 261–276.

142. C. W. Von Bergen and Barlow Super, "The Accomplishment Record for Selecting Human Resources Professionals," *SAM Advanced Management Journal* 60 (1995): 41–46; and Cynthia D. McCauley, Marian N. Ruderman, Patricia J. Ohlott, and Jane E. Morrow, "Assessing the Developmental Components of Managerial Jobs," *Journal of Applied Psychology* 79 (1994): 544–560.

143. Ronald A. Ash and Edward L. Levine, "Job Applicant Training and Work Experience Evaluation: An Empirical Comparison of Four Methods," *Journal of Applied Psychology* 70 (1985): 572–576.

144. Ibid.

145. Cathy D. Anderson, Jack L. Warner, and Cassey C. Spencer, "Inflation Bias in Self-Assessment Examinations: Implications for Valid Employee Selection," *Journal of Applied Psychology* 69 (1984): 574–580.

146. Miguel A. Quinoñes, J. Kevin Ford, and Mark S. Teachout, "The Relationship between Work Experience and Job Performance: A Conceptual and Meta-Analytic Review," *Personnel*

Psychology 48 (1995): 887–910; and Tesluk and Jacobs, "Toward an Integrated Model of Work Experience."

147. Edward L. Levine, Doris M. Maye, Ronald A. Ulm, and Thomas R. Gordon, "A Methodology for Developing and Validating Minimum Qualifications (MQs)," *Personnel Psychology* 50 (1997): 1009–1023, and Maury A. Buster, Philip L. Roth, and Philip Bobko, "A Process for Content Validation of Education and Experienced-Based Minimum Qualifications: An Approach Resulting in Federal Court Approval," *Personnel Psychology* 58 (August 2005): 771–799.

148. Ibid.

149. Schmidt and Hunter, "General Mental Ability in the World of Work: Occupational Attainment and Job Performance"; Quinoñes, Ford, and Teachout, "The Relationship between Work Experience and Job Performance: A Conceptual and Meta-Analytic Review"; and Tesluk and Jacobs, "Toward an Integrated Model of Work Experience."

150. David E. Terpstra, R. Bryan Kethley, Richard T. Foley, and Wanthanee Lee Limpaphayom, "The Nature of Litigation Surrounding Five Screening Devices," *Public Personnel Management* 29, no. 1 (2000): 43–53; and Andler and Herbst, *The Complete Reference Checking Handbook*.

151. Andler and Herbst, *The Complete Reference Checking Handbook*.

152. Stephanie L. Wilk and Peter Cappelli, "Understanding the Determinants of Employer Use of Selection Methods," *Personnel Psychology* 56 (2003): 103–124; Ann Marie Ryan, Lynn McFarland, Helen Baron, and Ron Page, "International Look at Selection Practices: Nation and Culture as Explanations for Variability in Practice," *Personnel Psychology* 52 (1999): 359–392; *Reference and Background Checking Survey Report*, Society of Human Resources Research (January 2005): 1–27; and Sara L. Rynes, Marc O. Orlitzky, and Robert D. Bretz, "Experienced Hiring Versus College Recruiting: Practices and Emerging Trends," *Personnel Psychology* 50 (1997): 309–339.

153. *Reference and Background Checking Survey Report*.

154. Wayne F. Cascio and Herman Aguinis, *Applied Psychology in Human Resource Management*, 6th ed. (Upper Saddle River, NJ: Prentice Hall, 2005).

155. *Reference and Background Checking Survey Report*.

156. Ibid.

157. Equal Employment Opportunity Commission, *Disability Discrimination* (Washington, DC: Equal Employment Opportunity Commission, Technical Assistance Program, April 1996), V15–V16.

158. George W. Tommasi, Karen B. Williams, and Cynthia R. Nordstrom, "Letters of Recommendation: What Information Captures HR Professionals' Attention?" *Journal of Business Psychology* 13 (2004): 5–18; Aamodt and Williams, "Reliability, Validity, and Adverse Impact of References and Letters of Recommendation"; and K. Moser and D. Rhyssen, "Reference Checks as a Personnel Selection Method," *Zeitschrift Fur Arbeits-Und Organisationspsychologie* 45 (2001): 40–46.

159. Michael G. Aamodt and Felice Williams, "Reliability, Validity, and Adverse Impact of References and Letters of Recommendation," *Society for Industrial and Organizational Psychology* (Los Angeles, California, April 2005).

160. John E. Hunter and Rhonda F. Hunter, "The Validity and Utility of Alternative Predictors of Job Performance," *Psychological Bulletin* 96 (1984): 72–98.

161. Richard R. Reilly and Georgia T. Chao, "Validity and Fairness of Some Alternative Employee Selection Procedures," *Personnel Psychology* 35 (1982): 1–62.

162. Michael G. Aamodt, *Industrial/Organizational Psychology—An Applied Approach* , 5th ed. (Belmont, CA: Thomson/Wadsworth, 2007).

163. Julie M. McCarthy and Richard D. Goffin, "Improving the Validity of Letters of Recommendation: An Investigation of Three Standardized Reference Forms," *Military Psychology* 13 (2001): 199–222.

164. Paul J. Taylor, Karl Pajo, Gordon W. Cheung, and Paul Stringfield, "Dimensionality and Validity of a Structured Telephone Reference Check Procedure," *Personnel Psychology* 57 (September 2004): 754–772.

165. Jeffrey D. Facteau and Craig B. Bartholomew, "Are Performance Appraisal Ratings from Different Rating Sources Comparable?" *Journal of Applied Psychology* 86 (2001): 215–227; Todd J. Maurer, Nambury S. Raju, and William C. Collins, "Peer and Subordinate Performance Appraisal Measurement Equivalence," *Journal of Applied Psychology* 83 (1998): 693–702; and David J. Woehr, M. Kathleen Sheehan, and Winston Bennett Jr., "Assessing Measurement Equivalence Across Rating Sources: a Multitrait-Multirater Approach," *Journal of Applied Psychology* 90 (2005): 592–600.

166. Taylor, Karl Pajo, Gordon W. Cheung, and Paul Stringfield, "Dimensionality and Validity of a Structured Telephone Reference Check Procedure," *Personnel Psychology* 57 (September 2004): 754–772.

167. Ryan D. Zimmerman, Mary Triana, and Murray R. Barrick, "Predictive Criterion-Related Validity of Observer-Ratings of Personality and Job-Related Competencies Using Multiple Raters and Multiple Performance Criteria," *Human Performance* 22 (in press).

168. Paul R. Sackett and Filip Lievens, "Personnel Selection," *Annual Review of Psychology* 59 (2008): 1–32.

169. Filip Lievens, "Assessor Training Strategies and Their Effects on Accuracy, Interrater Reliability, and Discriminant Validity," *Journal of Applied Psychology* 86 (2001): 255–264; and Deidra J. Schleicher, David V. Day, Bronston T. Mayes, and Ronald R. Riggio, "A New Frame for Frame-of-Reference Training: Enhancing the Construct Validity of Assessment Centers," *Journal of Applied Psychology* 87 (2001): 735–746.

170. Jessica A. Nicklin and Sylvia G. Roch, "Biases Influencing Recommendation Letter Contents: Physical Attractiveness and Gender," *Journal of Applied Social Psychology* 38 (2008): 3053–3074.

171. Paul R. Sackett and Filip Lievens, "Personnel Selection," *Annual Review of Psychology* 59 (2008): 1–32.

172. Dennis P. Bozeman, "Interrater Agreement in Multi-Source Performance Appraisal: A Commentary," *Journal of Organizational Behavior* 18 (1997): 313–316; and James M. Conway, Kristie Lombardo, and Kelley C. Sanders, "A Meta-Analysis of Incremental Validity and Nomological Networks for Subordinate and Peer Rating," *Human Performance* 14 (October 2001): 267–303.

173. Michael K. Mount, Murray R. Barrick, and Judy Perkins Strauss, "Validity of Observer Ratings of the Big Five Personality Factors," *Journal of Applied Psychology* 79 (1994): 272–280.

174. Dennis P. Bozeman, "Interrater Agreement in Multi-Source Performance Appraisal: A Commentary," *Journal of Organizational Behavior* 18 (1997): 313–316; and James M. Conway, Kristie Lombardo, and Kelley C. Sanders, "A Meta-Analysis of Incremental Validity and Nomological Networks for Subordinate and Peer Rating," *Human Performance* 14 (October 2001): 267–303.

175. Jeffrey D. Facteau and Craig B. Bartholomew, "Are Performance Appraisal Ratings from Different Rating Sources Comparable?" *Journal of Applied Psychology* 86 (2001): 215–227;

Todd J. Maurer, Nambury S. Raju, and William C. Collins, "Peer and Subordinate Performance Appraisal Measurement Equivalence," *Journal of Applied Psychology* 83 (1998): 693–702; and David J. Woehr, M. Kathleen Sheehan, and Winston Bennett Jr., "Assessing Measurement Equivalence Across Rating Sources: A Multitrait-Multirater Approach," *Journal of Applied Psychology* 90 (2005): 592–600.

176. Schmidt and Hunter, "The Validity and Utility of Selection Methods in Personnel Psychology: Practical and Theoretical Implications of 85 Years of Research Findings."

177. Donald L. Zink and Arthur Gutman, "Legal Issues in Providing and Asking for References and Letters of Recommendation," *The Society for Industrial and Organizational Psychology Paper* (Los Angeles California, April, 2005).

178. John P. Hausknecht, David V. Day, and Scott C. Thomas, "Applicant Reactions to Selection Procedures: An Updated Model and Meta-Analysis," *Personnel Psychology* 57 (2004): 639–683.

179. *Equal Employment Opportunity Commission v. National Academy of Sciences*, 12 FEP 1690 (1976).

180. Ralph L. Quinoñes and Arthur Gross Schaefer, "The Legal, Ethical, and Managerial Implications of the Neutral Employment Reference Policy," *Employee Responsibilities and Rights Journal* 10, no. 2 (1997): 173–189; and Beverly L. Little and Daphne Sipes, "Betwixt and Between: The Dilemma of Employee References," *Employee Responsibilities and Rights Journal* 12, no. 1 (2000): 1–8.

181. *Rutherford v. American Bank of Commerce*, 12 FEP 1184 (1976).

182. D. L. Zink and A. Gutman, "Legal Issues in Providing and Asking for References and Letters of Recommendation," *The Society for Industrial and Organizational Psychology Paper* (Los Angeles California, April 2005); and Ann Marie Ryan and Maria Lasek, "Negligent Hiring and Defamation: Areas of Liability Related to Pre-Employment Inquiries," *Personnel Psychology* 44 (1991): 307–313.

183. *True v. Ladner*, 513 A. 2d 257 (1986).

184. *Frank B. Hall & Co., Inc. v. Buck*, 678 S.W. 2d 612 (1984).

185. *Randi W. v. Livingston Union School District*, 49 Cal. Rptr. 2d 471 (Cal. Ct. App. 1996).

186. Aamodt, *Industrial/Organizational Psychology—An Applied Approach;* and Cascio and Aguinis, *Applied Psychology in Human Resource Management.*

187. D. L. Zink and A. Gutman, "Legal Issues in Providing and Asking for References and Letters of Recommendation"; and *Human Resources Guide.*

188. Ibid.

189. Ralph L. Quinoñes and Arthur Gross Schaefer, "The Legal, Ethical, and Managerial Implications of the Neutral Employment Reference Policy," *Employees Responsibilities and Rights Journal* (November 2004): 173–189; Beverly L. Little and Daphne Sipes, "Betwixt and Between: The Dilemma of Employee References," *Employees Responsibilities and Rights Journal* (October 2004): 1–8; Charles R. McConnell, "Employment References: Walking Scared between the Minefield of Defamation and the Specter of Negligent Hiring," *Health Care Management* 19, no. 2 (2000): 78–90; and Charlotte Hughes Scholes, "Potential Pitfalls in Providing a Job Reference," *Legal Information Management* 6 (2006): 58–60.

190. *Human Resources Guide.*

191. *Human Resources Guide;* and Andler and Herbst, *The Complete Reference Checking Handbook.*

192. *Reference and Background Checking Survey Report.*

193. David E. Terpstra, R. Bryan Kethley, Richard T. Foley, and Wanthanee (Lee) Limpaphayom, "The Nature of Litigation Surrounding Five Screening Devices," *Public Personnel Management* 29, no. 1 (2000): 43–53.

194. *Reference and Background Checking Survey Report.*

195. *Human Resources Guide;* and Andler and Herbst, *The Complete Reference Checking Handbook.*

196. Bill Leonard, "Reference Checking Laws: Now What?" *HR Magazine* 40 (1995): 58.

197. *Reference and Background Checking Survey Report.*

198. Andler and Herbst, *The Complete Reference Checking Handbook.*

199. Paul J. Taylor, Karl Pajo, Gordon W. Cheung, and Paul Stringfield, "Dimensionality and Validity of a Structured Telephone Reference Check Procedure," *Personnel Psychology* 57 (2004): 745–772; and Tommasi, Williams, and Nordstrom, "Letters of Recommendation: What Information Captures HR Professionals' Attention?"

200. Nancy J. King, "Is Paperless Hiring in Your Future? E-Recruiting Gets Less Risky," *Employee Relations Law Journal* 26, no. 3 (2000): 87.

201. Michael G. Aamodt, *Industrial/Organizational Psychology—An Applied Approach*, 5th ed. (Belmont, CA: Thomson/Wadsworth, 2007); and Andler and Herbst, *The Complete Reference Checking Handbook.*

202. Christopher L. Grote, William N. Robiner, and Allyson Haut, "Disclosure of Negative Information in Letters of Recommendation: Writers' Intentions and Readers' Experiences," *Professional Psychology: Research and Practice* 32 (2001): 655–661.

203. Michael G. Aamodt and Felice Williams, "Reliability, Validity, and Adverse Impact of References and Letters of Recommendation," *Society for Industrial and Organizational Psychology 20th meeting Paper* (Los Angeles, California, April, 2005).

204. Rodney K. Miller and George J. Van Rybroek, "Internship Letters of Reference: Where Are the Other 90 Percent?" *Professional Psychology: Research and Practice* 19 (1988): 115–117.

205. Stephen J. Ceci and Douglas Peters, "Letters of Reference: A Naturalistic Study of the Effects of Confidentiality," *American Psychologist* 39 (1984): 29–31.

206. Julie M. McCarthy and Richard D. Goffin, "Improving the Validity of Letters of Recommendation: An Investigation of Three Standardized Reference Forms," *Military Psychology* 13, no. 4 (2001): 199–222; and Michael G. Aamodt, Devon A. Bryan, and Alan J. Whitcomb, "Predicting Performance with Letters of Recommendation," *Public Personnel Management* 22 (1993): 81–90.

207. Ryan D. Zimmerman, Mary Triana, and Murray R. Barrick, "Predictive Criterion-Related Validity of Observer-Ratings of Personality and Job-Related Competencies Using Multiple Raters and Multiple Performance Criteria," *Human Performance* 22 (in press).

208. Brian T. Loher, John T. Hazer, Amy Tsai, Kendel Tilton, and J. James, "Letters of Reference: A Process Approach," *Journal of Business and Psychology* 13 (1998): 5–18.

209. George W. Tommasi, Karen B. Williams, and Cynthia R. Nordstrom, "Letters of Recommendation: What Information Captures HR Professionals' Attention?" *Journal of Business and Psychology* 13, no. 1 (1998): 5–18.

210. Julie M. McCarthy and Richard D. Goffin, "Improving the Validity of Letters of Recommendation: An Investigation of Three Standardized Reference Forms," *Military Psychology* 13 (2001): 199–222.

211. Timothy A. Judge and Chad A. Higgins, "Affective Disposition and the Letter of Reference," *Organizational Behavior and Human Decision Processes* 75 (1998): 207–221.

212. Michael G. Aamodt, Mark S. Nagy, and Naceema Thompson, "Employment References: Who Are We Talking About?" *Paper presented at the annual meeting of the International Personnel Management Association Assessment Council* (Chicago, Illinois, June 22, 1998).

213. Christopher L. Grote, William N. Robiner, and Allyson Haut, "Disclosure of Negative Information in Letters of Recommendation: Writers' Intentions and Readers' Experiences," *Professional Psychology: Research and Practice* 32 (2001): 655–661; Aamodt, *Industrial/ Organizational Psychology—An Applied Approach*; and Stephen B. Knouse, "Letter of Recommendation: Specificity and Favorability of Information," *Personnel Psychology* 36 (1983): 331–342.

214. Andler and Herbst, *The Complete Reference Checking Handbook*.

215. Ibid.

216. Ibid.

217. Ibid.

218. Ibid.

The Selection Interview

The interview has long been acknowledged as the most frequently used selection device. A reasonable case can be made that it is the most important device in many selection decisions because it is given the most weight. Interviewers certainly believe they can personally do a better job of predicting a candidate's success than they could by using a test score or by relying on a candidate's educational achievements.[1] Practically, few employers are willing to hire an employee sight unseen. However, the interview is also a fairly time-consuming and expensive selection tool, as a survey of members of the Society of Human Resource Managers indicates.[2] For example, based on data from this survey, we estimate that the equivalent of two days of staff time are spent on interviews for each open position.

Partially because of its widespread use and cost, selection researchers have studied the interview for almost 80 years. Until recently, their studies generally produced negative conclusions regarding the interview's reliability, validity, and usefulness in selection. Further, these studies determined that the low reliability and validity were due to a combination of both the use of inappropriate questions and extraneous factors that affected an interviewer's evaluation of an applicant.[3] This research prompted other work, which developed corrections for these deficiencies. These corrections, in turn, were frequently incorporated into the design of the selection interview. As a result, the most recent examinations of this selection instrument have been quite positive. As we will discuss later in this chapter, specific types of interview questions have led to significant validity coefficients. Validity generalization studies (quick, go back and read the validity generalization section in Chapter 5!) have produced strong evidence of the validity of selection interviews. It is accurate to conclude that *designed appropriately and used correctly, the interview is good!* Frank Schmidt and John Hunter conducted a comprehensive review of cumulative empirical findings from research over the past 85 years. They concluded that the corrected validity coefficient for the structured interview ($\rho = 0.51$) is comparable to similar coefficients produced for cognitive ability tests ($\rho = 0.51$)—and higher than one determined for assessment centers ($\rho = 0.37$).[4] In fact, when it is combined in a standardized regression equation with cognitive ability, they found a 24 percent increase in job performance produced by a selection procedure relying solely on cognitive ability. This clearly shows the utility of the (correctly conducted) interview and reveals that using the interview can result in substantially better hiring decisions.

In this chapter we summarize what is currently known about the selection interview by stressing the results of empirical research studies. We also discuss procedures that have been demonstrated through this research to improve the interview. We hope to provide sufficient information so you will be able to design and implement this important selection device.

THE NATURE AND ROLE OF THE INTERVIEW IN SELECTION

The employment interview is an agenda-driven social exchange between strangers. It's necessary to keep this in mind in order to really understand the interview and to realize its full potential. The opportunity to meet and directly interact with the candidate makes the interview distinctive as a selection tool. Often it provides the only opportunity to see how socially "competent" an interviewer is.[5]

The demands of the social exchange does, however, create a number of "challenges." This includes the fact there are competing interests infused throughout the interview. For example, the candidate wants to get a job offer, yet the interviewer wants to get accurate information about the candidate's suitability to do the job. Furthermore, the candidate almost always is a "stranger" to the interviewer, yet the candidate is dependent on the interviewer to recommend he or she be extended a job offer. Such demands generally lead people to try to maximize their own interests. This means candidates actively manage the image they portray in the interview.[6] At times, this leads candidates to intentionally misrepresent past accomplishments, even to the point of making them up.[7] The interview is a complex selection tool and it is challenging to use it effectively. We now look at steps one can take to maximize the utility of the employment interview.

The employment interview is a flexible tool; when properly conducted, interviews provide a wealth of information that can be used by both the interviewer and interviewee for making quality decisions. A first step in understanding the appropriate use of the interview is a discussion of its proposed advantages in selection. Generally, these advantages fall into three main categories: (a) the fact that the interview provides an opportunity for the organization to recruit good candidates and educate them about the job; (b) the fact that the interview is an efficient and practical method for measuring a number of applicant KSAs; and (c) the fact that the interview can help an employer make either an early decision about an applicant's acceptability (that is, screening out an applicant) or a later one (that is, selecting in an applicant). We discuss each of these advantages in the next sections. Our general conclusion is that to utilize these advantages fully and advantageously, organizations must correctly incorporate changes into the interview. If improperly managed, these changes can detract from the usefulness of the selection interview.

Recruiting the Applicant to the Organization

Providing Job Information: Consider the Alternatives.   Often, some of the time spent in selection interviews is used by the interviewer to describe the job and the organization or to sell the job to the applicant. Although the interview can be used for these purposes, some limiting factors should be noted. Both personal anecdotes and communication research studies provide examples of oral discussion between two individuals being subsequently recalled differently by each person. There is thus good reason to give a written job description to applicants that conveys much of the information usually transmitted in the interview. One example would be a permanent statement that could easily be referred to by the applicant after the interview has been concluded. This could save some of the time allocated for recruiting during the interview—time that could be used to obtain more job-relevant information.

Alison Barber and her colleagues reported important research regarding the mixing of recruitment and selection purposes in the interview.[8] Using a sample of undergraduates and a campus job, they manipulated the focus of the interview. One applicant group experienced a recruitment-only interview; the other group received an interview that combined recruitment and selection. The researchers found that applicants clearly retained more information about the position from the recruitment-only interview than from the mixed-focus interview. This effect was especially pronounced for those applicants who were high in anxiety and low in self-monitoring abilities. Apparently, being anxious and not monitoring how others see them reduces candidates' ability to collect and remember information about the job. Moreover, there was a strong relationship between the amount of information acquired in the interview and the amount of information retained two weeks later, which indicated a continuing effect of the recruitment interview. The authors concluded that "strict recruitment focus may be particularly useful to organizations that have a great need to convey information to applicants (for example, organizations that want to counteract negative public images or organizations that are not well known)."[9]

There is another factor to consider. It has been hypothesized that the interviewer's behavior changes depending on the degree to which recruitment is emphasized over selection in the interview. As the recruitment function increases, there is evidence that the interviewer places relatively more emphasis on job rather than applicant characteristics, describes vacant positions in more favorable terms, and asks questions that are less likely to lead to applicant disqualification.[10] Logically, this change in emphasis has costs in terms of the amount and quality of pertinent information that is gathered for selection decisions.

Effect on Applicants: Recruiting Outcomes.   It is commonly assumed that the interview has value as a public relations device. That is, the personal contact between organizational member and applicant positively affects the attitudes of the applicant. This is not always the case. Growing evidence indicates that the interview is only part of the information that applicants use to form impressions about the organization and to make job search and job acceptance decisions. That is, applicants use information from multiple sources (friends, class materials, advertisements, product/service usage, recruitment brochures, site visits, and employer location information, as well as recruiters) to make these decisions.[11] The problem for applicants is that they often have to make a decision with inadequate information about the firm. For example, early in the process, individuals must decide in which companies they will invest the time, effort, and money to continue as an applicant. It is simply not possible to continue with all possible companies. In making the decision to continue or not, the applicant uses whatever information is available in order to infer the organization's characteristics.

Recruiter characteristics and behaviors are only part of this information. However, a recent meta-analysis by Derek Chapman and his associates[12] reveals that recruiters with the "right" qualities (who are personable and skilled in listening and conveying information) who were trained to consistently and fairly provide correct information about the company and job had a significant impact on the candidate's attitudes toward a job. These "right" qualities, to a lesser extent, also influenced whether the applicant actually accepted the job offer. In contrast, the findings reveal that the individual interviewer (organizational function, sex, race) did not affect the candidate's perception of the job or organization or alter intentions to pursue or accept a job. Nevertheless, after controlling for actual job and organizational characteristics, the effect of recruiter behavior on candidate attitudes or intentions to accept an offer becomes a relatively modest effect, albeit one that still remains statistically significant.[13]

One reason the effect of the recruiter may be relatively modest is because it seems to be a function of the personal characteristics of the candidate as well. For example, one study found that recruiters had only a minimal effect on individuals with previous work experience.[14] Other studies found that recruiters had a stronger effect on female candidates[15] and black candidates,[16] who often have less work experience. Although demographic similarity of interviewers and candidates has been found to have small and inconsistent effects on candidate evaluations, attitudinal similarity does appear to increase the candidate's attraction to the job;[17] at the same time, it does not appear to reduce the predictive validity of interviewer ratings of the candidate's likely job performance. These results illustrate the complexity of studying recruiter effects.

Measuring Applicant KSAs

More Is Not Better.   This issue addresses the number and type of applicant characteristics that interviewers often attempt to measure. During the early 1970s, there was a decrease in the use of scored ability and performance selection tests and an increase in the use of unscored interviews. In part this was due to the courts' reviews of selection programs. Early selection discrimination cases revolved around the use of written mental and special ability tests. Courts stated that these tests must be validated before they could be used for selection. Only recently has it become expressly clear that the selection interview is viewed as a selection test and must also be validated before use. In the interim, however, the interview was used to assess a wide variety of applicant characteristics without rigorous scoring associated with specific dimensions. The use of the interview in this way often results in superficial data of limited value. Also, by substituting the interview for other assessment devices, which may be better suited to measure particular applicant characteristics (for example, a test to assess intelligence), an HR specialist may be collecting less accurate, more expensive data than is necessary.

Most major studies that have reviewed the use of the interview have agreed in their conclusions. For example, Lynn Ulrich and Don Trumbo state that "the interviewer is all too frequently asked to do the impossible because of limitations on the time, information, or both, available to him. When the interviewer's task was limited to rating a single trait, acceptable validity was achieved."[18] They further point out that even when the interviewer concentrates on only a few characteristics, some of these are not profitably addressed. For example, they contend that all too often a conclusion about the applicant's mental ability, arrived at during a 30-minute interview, may be less efficient and accurate than one based on the administration of a 10-minute test, the use of which would leave the interviewer time to assess those areas in which his or her judgment was more effective.

Appropriate KSAs.   Which specific characteristics, then, are best assessed in the interview? Allen Huffcutt and colleagues recently conducted a meta-analysis on 47 interview studies and found the interview is designed to evaluate seven major dimensions. Table 10.1 provides a list and brief definition of these dimensions and reports the frequency of use for each of these dimensions. This meta-analysis reveals that the interview is frequently used to assess personality (for example, conscientiousness, extroversion), applied social skills (for example, oral communication and interpersonal skills, leadership, persuasiveness), mental ability (for example, general intelligence and applied mental skills such as judgment and decision making), and knowledge and skills (for example, job knowledge and skills, experience, and general work history).[19] Less than 5 percent of interviews assessed either interests and preferences, physical attributes, or organizational fit. Ironically, interviewer ratings of organizational fit or the match between the candidate and demands of the job had one of the highest mean validities for predicting later job performance ($\rho = 0.49$). They also found that interviewer ratings of personality—particularly agreeableness and emotional stability ($\rho = 0.51$ and 0.47, respectively) and to a lesser extent, conscientiousness and extroversion (both $\rho = 0.33$)—also predicted later job performance. These predictive validities are substantially higher than those

TABLE 10.1 Behavioral Dimensions Frequently Measured in the Structured Interview

Dimension	Frequency of Use	Definition
General Intelligence	16%	Ability to learn and evaluate information quickly; ability to effectively plan and organize work; application of mental ability for solving problems.
Job Knowledge and Skills	10%	Declarative information (i.e., terms, values, names, and dates) and procedural knowledge (i.e., actions, skills, and operations) specific to the job; technical knowledge.
Personality	35%	Long-term disposition to act in certain ways; reflection of habitual behavior with regard to five dimensions: conscientiousness, extroversion, agreeableness, openness to experience, emotional stability.
Applied Social Skills	28%	Ability to function effectively in social situations; includes interpersonal skills, oral communication skills, leadership, and persuasiveness.
Interests and Preferences	4%	Tendency toward certain activities; preference for certain work environments or a particular type of work or profession; interest in certain topics or subjects.
Organizational Fit	3%	Match between candidate and the organization's values, goals, norms, and attitudes; fit with unique organizational culture or climate.
Physical Attributes	4%	Evaluation of stamina and agility; and general characteristics, like an evaluation of physical appearance.

NOTE: Frequency of Use = the relative frequency with which these constructs are evaluated in the Interview.
Source: From Allen I. Huffcutt, James M. Conway, Philip L. Roth, and Nancy J. Stone, "Identification and Meta-Analytic Assessment of Psychological Constructs Measured Employment Interviews," *Journal of Applied Psychology*, 86 (2001): 897–913.

typically found using personality tests (ρ's in the low 0.20s to high teens).[20] Other constructs evaluated in the employment interview were found to significantly predict later performance evaluation, including the assessment of specific job knowledge and skills (ρ = 0.42 for job knowledge and skills and 0.49 for experience and general work history) and applied social skills (ρ = 0.49 for leadership, 0.39 for interpersonal skills, and 0.26 for oral communication skills).

To further illustrate the value of the interview, they concluded that these predictors were not highly correlated with the single-best predictor of performance, measures of general mental ability.[21] A recent meta-analytic study found only a 0.40 correlation between the interview and cognitive ability tests, indicating that the two overlap by only 16 percent of their variance.[22] Moreover, the correlation between the two instruments decreases as the level of structure of the interview increases. Thus, asking the same job-related questions of all candidates and systematically scoring the answers will decrease the correlation with measures of general mental ability. Consequently, interviews are likely to add significantly to the quality of selection decisions, particularly with structured interviews. Robert Dipboye, however, cautions that researchers should not forget that predictive validity will only be achieved if the specific traits assessed in the interview are job-related.[23] Consequently, although creativity had the highest mean validity (ρ = 0.58) in the meta-analysis conducted by Huffcutt and associates, it will not be useful to assess this construct if creativity is irrelevant to the job.[24]

Employment interviews are flexible and can be used to assess a number of different constructs. However, careful inspection of Table 10.1—and consideration of the predictive validity of these dimensions—reveals that the interview, due to its interactive nature, may be uniquely suited for measuring applied social skills (such as interpersonal and communication skills) as well as personality or habitual behaviors (such as conscientiousness, emotional stability, and extroversion), and fit with the job and organization. Applied social skills reflect those characteristics important for successful personal interaction, oral communication, and specific characteristics such as leadership and negotiation. The interview, by its very nature, is an example of such a situation; it should be an accurate indicator of skills in these areas. Personality characteristics are often evaluated after a discussion of work habits, tasks completed in a previous job, and the candidate's typical approach or habitual ways of doing things at work. Interviewer ratings on these attributes strive to assess the candidate's long-term dispositional behavior in specific work environments. Recent research has shown interviewer ratings of personality can predict later job performance.[25] Although it may be somewhat surprising that a stranger can assess personality, we have found that these ratings collected in the interview do predict job performance for candidates who are hired. Finally, the interview is likely to be a particularly effective way to assess whether the candidate's values, norms, goals, and attitudes "fit" or correspond to those of the organization. Such discussions usually require the clarification or elaboration of statements made by the respondent on the application form, cover letter, or resume—or require clarification of statements made by others in letters of reference. The interview, because of its interactive nature, provides a suitable means for such probing by the interviewer.

The characteristic *job knowledge* has been successfully evaluated in interviews. There are some guidelines as to when an interview would be useful for assessing this characteristic. If there are many job knowledge questions, and especially if the answers are fairly short and routine, a written test is preferable to an interview. Such a test is usually less expensive to administer and score, provides a permanent record, and is often a more familiar format for the applicant. If interview questions ask about complex job behaviors such as diagnosing product defects, operating equipment, and manipulating data or information, job simulation instruments are usually more appropriate. One situation that would certainly argue for the use of job knowledge questions in the interview is when the applicant has serious reading or writing deficiencies that would impede selection evaluation but not job performance. The interviewer would be able to determine whether the applicant understands the question and could clarify unclear or poorly worded responses. Another situation that would be appropriate for job knowledge questions is when selecting for jobs that require the verbalization of technical information and work procedures, such as advisory or consulting jobs in which most of the requests for service are oral. In such situations, the interview approximates a job simulation selection device.

One important issue to consider with regard to the behavioral dimensions mentioned in Table 10.1 is how to measure them. Unfortunately, the research does not provide many examples of specific questions that have been used to assess these behaviors or characteristics. However, we will be happy to share our thoughts with you. We think that these characteristics should be measured with questions that are expressly intended for these KSAs. We will discuss specific techniques that can be used to develop such questions later in the chapter. For now we will provide a general example.

Sociability and verbal fluency, in some form, are demonstrated in every interview. For the purposes of selection, these KSAs should be defined to reflect specific behaviors of the job of interest. For example, sociability for a retail clerk may be demonstrated in brief interactions with customers. Thus these characteristics may be assessed using only the general comments and remarks that start most interviews. However, if the behaviors are of interactions that include technical content, then specific questions should be formed. For example, medical sales personnel must meet and interact with the physicians and nurses who order their products. Usually, even initial conversations and interactions include discussion of the technical qualities of the products. Physicians and nurses simply do not have a lot of free time in their schedules. For such a job, questions that require the interviewee to explain some technical topic would be appropriate. In predicting future job performance, it is more appropriate that applicants demonstrate that they can quickly and easily discuss technical information than that they can initiate and continue a general discussion about the weather, the local baseball team, or a hit movie.

When interviews are viewed as a selection tool, the importance of which constructs to focus on becomes particularly salient. This is a chance to ask questions and assess the interpersonal competence of the candidate. However, as emphasized earlier, a single interview will be most effective if it limits the number of attributes to be assessed. Based on this, we strongly encourage that only two or three characteristics be evaluated during an interview. Those characteristics selected should be constructs that are critical to doing the work, cannot be assessed in other ways, and are particularly suited to assessment during the interview.

Making A Selection Decision

Theoretically, one advantage of the interview over other selection instruments is that the data gatherer, interpreter, and decision-maker is a human being who understands the job and organization. However, ratings by an interviewer can reflect the method of measurement (subjective ratings) as much as or more than the construct the rating is thought to be measuring. One common stereotype held by many raters is the "what-is-beautiful-is-good stereotype."[26] If an interviewer's rating of job knowledge is artificially inflated by a particularly attractive candidate *and* the supervisor's later rating of employee performance on the job is also artificially inflated by the employee's attractiveness, then the relatively high validity coefficient reported between the interviewer's rating of candidate job knowledge and supervisor's performance evaluation is not actually based on more job knowledge. Instead, it is based on attractiveness of the individual. This just underscores the complexity of establishing validity – here we see a correlation is not definitive evidence of validity. To establish the validity of a job knowledge question on the interview, we would want to see higher scorers not only lead to more successful performance on the job but be seen by co-workers as actually having more job knowledge and being able to solve more work-related problems.

Concern about method of measurement bias in the interview is a legitimate one.[27] A recent meta-analysis shows interviewer ratings of candidate suitability is significantly affected by physical attractiveness and professional demeanor ($\rho = .42$), use of impression management behavior ($\rho = .44$), and verbal and non-verbal behavior of the candidate ($\rho = .40$).[28] Given that physical attractiveness and impression management have also been found to affect supervisory ratings of performance,[29] it is important that we try to ensure interviewer ratings are focused on job-relevant KSAs, not to non-job relevant attributes such as "good looks." I would emphasize this even if I had not just glanced in a mirror.

Fortunately, the accuracy of the decision-making processes of interviewers has been extensively studied. Evidence clearly illustrates that when the interview is appropriately designed, the interviewer can, in fact, make more valid predictions about job performance. The results of the meta-analytic studies that concerned the increased reliability and validity of interview data (we referred to these studies at the beginning of this chapter) show that decision-making quality is highly dependent on a structured format. The following section describes two important factors that influence the utility of selection decisions when using the employment interview.

Structured versus Unstructured Interviews. Using an unstructured get-acquainted interview results in subjective, global evaluations that are not very useful, even though interviewers have great confidence in their ability to select the best candidate. Thus, the interviewer can become his or her own worst enemy when using an unstructured interview. This occurs because the interviewer's decisions are being influenced by extraneous factors such as physical attractiveness or the strength of a handshake, factors that may have little to do with later job success.[30] We are, after all, pre-wired to quickly form overall impressions of strangers; these ratings are, at best, only moderately valid.

To combat the potential weaknesses of casual conversation that leads to subjective global evaluations or reactions, current evidence stresses the use of structured interactions. Structured interviews rely on a disciplined method for collecting job-relevant information, including the use of a job analysis that identifies questions aimed at attitudes, behaviors, knowledge, and skills that differentiate high performers for a particular job. Interviewers are trained to take notes and record ratings in order to reduce the interviewers' memory distortions and to evaluate candidate responses to each question systematically. In essence, structured interviews rely on more objective evaluation procedures (asking only job-related questions, providing training on interviewing skills, and rating on established scoring formats). This standardization in the gathering, recording, and evaluating of information improves the quality of selection decisions. As you can probably guess, structured interviews make use of standardization and unstructured interviews do not. In reality, structured interviews vary in the use of these evaluation procedures, especially the use of predetermined questions. It is not accurate to refer to interviews as being either highly structured or not. For our purposes, however, we follow the common practice of distinguishing between structured and unstructured types of interviews and encourage the reader to remember that these vary on a continuum from highly structured to highly unstructured.

Recent research has centered on explaining what is meant by the concept of a structured interview. Derek Chapman and David Zweig identified a four-factor model of interview structure consisting of the following: (a) evaluation standardization, which includes scoring each item, relying on anchored rating scales, and summing scores across multiple dimensions; (b) question sophistication focusing on job-related behaviors, including the use of followup probes; (c) question consistency, which is based on asking all applicants the same questions derived from a job analysis, using the same interviewers; and (d) rapport building, which involves getting to know each other through casual conversation at the beginning of the interview.[31] By including rapport building, this factor structure implicitly recognizes the importance of another purpose of the interview—recruitment. Effective rapport building at the start of the interview may help to attract the best candidates or increases the likelihood they will accept a later offer. At the same time, higher levels of rapport building may be seen as a characteristic of less structured interviews. Consequently, future research must examine whether greater rapport enhances predictive validity. To the extent that more rapport elicits greater disclosure (due to the candidate being more comfortable with the interview), such rapport may increase validity. However, if greater rapport results in the inclusion of more contaminated, non-job-relevant information, rapport is likely to bias hiring decisions.

How big an impact does the rapport-building "stage" have on later hiring recommendations? Although there is very little research on the effect of candidate first impressions during the initial stage of the interview, conventional wisdom holds that interviewers make their minds up about the hirability of a candidate within four minutes of starting the interview. This belief is based on a study conducted in 1958, which showed that, on average, the interviewer took four minutes to check the answer sheet on which she indicated whether she would recommend hiring an applicant or not.[32] This conclusion is not surprising, given findings in social psychology that individuals form reactions almost instantaneously and effortlessly—and do this based on minimal information received upon meeting a person for the first time.[33] Murray Barrick, Greg Stewart, and colleagues recently conducted a series of studies that shows the impact of first impressions formed at the start of the interview.[34] In one study, they found the "quality" of the candidate's handshake (firmness, completeness of grip, vigor in shaking, and eye contact) influenced the end of interview suitability rating from the interviewer.[35] In other studies, they found that interviewer evaluations collected after the brief introduction and rapport-building stage of the interview—but prior to the asking of any substantive, job-related questions—were highly correlated with hiring recommendations made after the interview and even affected the proportion of invitations to a second interview or actual job offers received. The results from four separate samples reveal that first impressions formed early in the interview have a substantial effect on whether the interviewer recommended extending a job offer.[36] In these studies, these evaluations were made in the absence of prior information about the candidate. These findings show interviewers do form early impressions of the candidate, and those early impressions appear to establish an anchor for the interviewer that filters all subsequent evaluations of the candidate. These results illustrate that the information collected during the rapport-building stage can have a significant impact on hiring recommendations at the end of the interview.

The other three interview structure factors emphasize the importance of standardized interview content, centered on the kinds of questions asked during the interview (that is, question sophistication and question consistency), and standardized evaluation scoring. Michael Campion and his colleagues have identified and discussed 15 separate characteristics of interviews that have been used to structure an interview.[37] Their findings influenced the work of Chapman and Zweig (mentioned earlier) and show that the most important characteristics of a structured interview include using job analysis as a basis for questions, asking the same questions of all applicants, posing only behavior-based questions, scoring each answer, having multiple KSA scoring scales, using scoring scales that use behavioral examples to illustrate scale points, and training interviewers. Ultimately, the main advantage of a structured interview is that information regarding the major job topics is collected from all applicants, which makes the comparison across applicants easier and minimizes the influence of non-job-related impressions and guesses.

Screening versus Selection Interview. Frequently the interview is used at two different stages of the selection program. At the first stage, the interview is used to assess applicants on general characteristics. Such a first-stage interview is done by a campus recruiter, for example, and is frequently referred to as a *screening* interview. At the second stage, the interview is used to assess specific job-related KSAs. This is the *selection* interview, for which specific job-related questions—such as those developed in a structured interview—would be appropriate. One recent meta-analysis examined the constructs assessed in two different interviews: conventional interviews and behavioral interviews, which correspond to what we are calling (respectively) screening interviews and selection interviews. The conventional or screening interview focuses on the checking of credentials and licensure requirements and the evaluation of an applicant's minimum work requirements and experiences needed for the job. Selection or behavior interviews are composed of questions concerning job-related knowledge, interpersonal skills, problem-solving skills, and other work-related experiences and behaviors.[38]

The meta-analytic results showed that interviewer recommendations from the screening interviews were highly correlated with the applicant's social skills ($\rho = 0.46$), general mental ability ($\rho = 0.41$), and personality traits (on emotional stability, extroversion, openness to experience, agreeableness, and conscientiousness, ρ ranges from 0.26 to 0.38). These results show that these characteristics have a significant impact on interviewer evaluations of the candidate during the screening interview. In the selection interview, successful candidates had higher scores on specific work-related experiences ($\rho = 0.71$), social skills ($\rho = 0.65$), job knowledge ($\rho = 0.53$), and skills assessed by situational judgment tests ($\rho = 0.46$).[39] Based on these findings, the researchers concluded that screening and selection interviews focus on different constructs. The biggest difference is that screening interviews were designed to measure general traits (such as personality and intelligence), whereas selection interviews assess more specific job-related skills and habitual behaviors (such as work-related experiences, job knowledge, problem-solving skills, and so on).

Surprisingly little research has been conducted as to how to develop questions for the screening interview that predict job performance. This is unfortunate; such interviews are often the first step in the selection program and their results determine which members of the applicant pool will complete the other selection instruments. Based on the small amount of relevant research, and even more upon careful thought, we recommend the following options for developing questions for a screening interview:

1. Use job analysis information to identify general or fundamental KSAs that an applicant must possess and for which the organization does not provide training. Examples are the verbal ability to explain instructions, the ability to respond to points made in conversation by others, the ability to work on multiple projects simultaneously, and the ability to analyze problem situations similar to what would occur on the job. In addition, several interpersonal behaviors may be important, especially if work teams are a primary vehicle for work processes. These may include giving a friendly first impression, playing multiple roles in group projects, assisting others in the work group, and changing tasks easily and often.

2. Use "job experts" to identify the most important of these characteristics. That is, job incumbents and supervisors can be asked to rate these characteristics on such

scales as *importance for team interaction, importance for job performance,* or *importance for initial training.* Based on these responses, identify a set of two to three KSAs for use in the screening interview.

3. Use a modified Critical-Incidents Technique to identify questions. That is, job incumbents and supervisors can be asked to supply examples only in reference to the KSAs identified in the previous step. Examples could be obtained about good and poor behaviors related to giving instructions, coordinating one's efforts on multiple projects, and taking action during slack work demands. Questions and scoring systems that reflect typical highly structured interviews could be developed. The following are examples of possible questions:

"Please give me instructions about how to assemble some piece of equipment or how to do some activity that is part of one of your hobbies."

"When you worked with other students on a group class assignment, what would you do when you finished your part of the project?"

"You started a work assignment yesterday, but today you are not sure you are doing it correctly. What would you do at this point?"

Our view is that the screening and selection interviews serve the same purpose—they both measure KSAs relative to the employee requirements of a job. However, the two differ in the type and specificity of behaviors and knowledge assessed. The screening interview evaluates *general* work and interaction behaviors and knowledge. The selection interview is focused on more narrowly defined KSAs, such as specific job knowledge.

Conclusions about the Nature of the Interview

It seems to us that some often-found deficiencies in the interview can be directly attributed to misperceptions about its use in selection. Our examination indicates that it is not appropriate to use a significant portion of the selection interview for attracting applicants, providing detailed employment information, and developing the company's image. We do not intend this to mean that these activities are unimportant. We are simply saying that spending a significant portion of a 30-minute to 40-minute interview on these activities limits the effectiveness of this device in its primary purpose—evaluating the suitability of the applicant's attributes. Alternate vehicles that are primarily designed for providing information about the company and promoting a positive company image, we contend, would be more effective.

It is also clear that the validity of the interview is improved when a limited number of specific applicant characteristics are measured. In reality, this means designing the interview in the same manner as other selection devices. It is generally held that application blanks, tests, and work samples can measure some applicant characteristics. Selection programs are designed to take this into account. However, for some reason the selection interview is often viewed as a general measuring device. Possibly this is because interviewers are overly confident that they can make accurate judgments about a variety of applicant characteristics. The social-perception literature tells us that such judgments are a common part of initial personal interaction. However, it also tells us that such judgments are usually made with very little data and are often inaccurate. Findings clearly show that there is better construct validity when fewer dimensions or attributes are used.[40]

In summary, employment interviews can be used to achieve multiple goals or purposes including recruiting, initial screening and final selection and otherwise exchanging information so that decision makers are more comfortable with the hiring decision. However, these diverse goals can be in conflict, which makes the interview a difficult technique to utilize effectively. For example, using the interview to make a selection decision, whether for initial screening or final selection, will require (due to the money and time needed to interview each applicant) reducing the number of candidates—thereby counteracting the objective of recruiting, which is to increase the number of candidates in the applicant pool.[41] As we have discussed, the structured interview is the best format to use for identifying the best candidate; however, there is some evidence that these interviews are not useful for recruiting, probably because they are seen as impersonal and do not allow candidates to control how they express themselves.[42] Consequently, organizations should recognize that the usefulness of an interview is likely to depend on the importance of pursuing selection or recruitment goals; the format of the interview may need to reflect the most important goal in order to ensure that both organizations and candidates get the most out of the interview.

EVALUATING INTERVIEWS AS PREDICTORS

As we mentioned in the beginning of this chapter, today we have considerable evidence about techniques that enable the employment interview to yield more reliable and valid information for selection decisions. This is due to the concerted effort of a number of researchers over the past 20 years or so, researchers who have enhanced our understanding about what makes the interview an effective selection tool. Knowing that you are probably hungering for more details, we will share with you what we know. The first stream of research revealed that structured interviews were found to be more valid than unstructured interviews. Three meta-analytic studies supported this conclusion, with corrected validity coefficients of 0.44, 0.57, and 0.62 for structured interviews and 0.20, 0.31, and 0.33 for unstructured interviews.[43]

One other meta-analysis directly examined the influence the level of interview structure has on predictive validity for entry-level jobs. Allen Huffcutt and Winfred Arthur assigned prior interview studies to one of four levels of structure. At one extreme, Level I reflected unstructured interviews with no standardized scoring and no constraints on what questions to ask. The other extreme, Level IV, relied on a highly standardized or structured interview complete with a preestablished scoring "key" and a requirement to ask the same question to every candidate with no follow-up questions allowed. The mean observed predictive validity (uncorrected for measurement error) was 0.20 for unstructured interviews (Level I) and increased to 0.35 for Level II, 0.56 for Level III, and 0.57 for highly structured (Level IV) interviews.[44] These results reveal that the substantial gains in predictive validity for structured interviews is due to standardizing the process of gathering, recording, and interpreting applicant suitability. The use of a standardized "instrument," similar to a test, appears to be an effective way to overcome the weaknesses inherent in the unstructured interview. The value of following a script and applying standardized scoring was shown in a meta-analysis of telephone-based interviews. Results showed greater standardization enhanced predictive validity of the interview.[45]

Nevertheless, it is surprising that the corrected validity coefficient for unstructured interviews is as large as it is (ranging from 0.20 to 0.33). Prior to 1990, it had generally been thought that such instruments were useless, that they had zero validity. It may be, however, that the studies identified as unstructured really were structured to some extent. At least each had a formal scoring system from which the validity coefficient was calculated. For example, the study by Mike McDaniel and his associates indicated that the studies classified as unstructured "gathered information in a less systematic manner than do structured interviews."[46] Thus, one might interpret these findings to indicate that even little amounts of structure can yield a valid selection interview.

One explanation of why structured interviews work better than unstructured interviews relates to differences in reliability. The notion is that by improving the structure or standardization of the interview, one increases reliability and—all else being equal—higher reliability leads to higher validity (refer to Chapters 4 and 5 to examine the role of reliability on validity, if this does not sound familiar). A recent meta-analysis provides evidence that structured interviews are more reliable than are unstructured interviews, which may explain why structured interviews have higher predictor validity. In this study, individual interviews using unstandardized questions were found to have a mean reliability of 0.37, which was significantly lower than the mean reliability of 0.66 and 0.59 for the top two highest levels of structure (level 5 and 6).[47] They concluded that reliability creates an upper limit on predictive validity of 0.67 for highly structured interviews and 0.34 for unstructured interviews. Frank Schmidt and Ryan Zimmerman showed that much of the difference in criterion-related validity between structured and unstructured interviews could be reduced by increasing the reliability of the unstructured interview.[48] Because the level of standardization cannot, by definition, be increased for unstructured interviews, the only way to increase reliability is to increase the number of interviews given to each job candidate. The use of multiple independent raters increases the reliability of the interview simply by aggregating overall available ratings. This increases the amount of available information on which a hiring recommendation can be based and should correct for the idiosyncratic biases of individual interviewers. They found that averaging the ratings of three to four independent interviewers who conducted unstructured interviews resulted in the same level of predictive validity obtained from a structured interview conducted by a single interviewer. These results underscore the importance of reliability, which can be enhanced by standardizing the interview or by relying on multiple interviewers arriving at independent evaluations for each candidate.

As noted previously, however, it is misleading to talk about structured interviews as if they were one "type" of interview. For example, one way these interviews fundamentally differ is with regard to the questions asked. Behavior description interviews are past-oriented questions involving prior work experiences. The questions ask the applicant "Can you tell me a time when you did...?" In contrast, situational interviews are future-oriented questions that ask applicants to imagine a work situation. Such questions ask, "What would you do if...?" Two recent meta-analyses have examined the validity coefficients of both the situational and the behavior description interview. Both types of interviews have produced good results, with a corrected correlation of 0.43 (32 studies; $N = 2,815$) or 0.45 (30 studies; $N = 2,299$) for situational interviews and 0.51 (22 studies; $N = 2,721$) or 0.56 (19 studies; $N = 1,855$) for behavior description interviews.[49]

Two additional primary studies have directly compared the two types of interviews. In one of these, Michael Campion, James Campion, and Peter Hudson developed a set of 30 questions, of which 15 were situational-type and 15 were behavior-type.[50] All applicants received all 30 questions. Results indicated strong similarities between the two: (a) a 0.73 correlation between ratings on the two types of interview questions, (b) similar interrater reliabilities of the two (0.94 for situational and 0.97 for behavioral), and (c) significant validity coefficients of 0.51 for the behavioral and 0.39 for the situational. This difference was not statistically significant, and (d) both interview types added incremental validity beyond the validity of a battery of nine tests, which were also part of the selection program. However, the two types of interviews did differ in one interesting way: The behavior-type interview added to the prediction of job performance beyond that provided by the situational interview, but the reverse was not true. In a second study, 120 candidates received either the situational interview or a behavior description interview; Arla Day and Sarah Caroll found the two types predicted performance equally well ($r = 0.37$ and 0.36, respectively) and explained variance in performance beyond that accounted for by prior experience and cognitive ability. Furthermore, they found that both interview types were perceived as equally fair to the candidates.[51] Elaine Pulakos and Neal Schmitt conducted an additional comparison of these two types of interviews.[52] In this test, the authors carefully constructed interviews that were nearly identical in question content, differing only in format. Therefore, exactly the same job-analysis-based KSAs were measured. Panels of three interviewers conducted each interview and rated applicants on eight dimensions. Surprisingly, results identified no significant validity for the situational interview but a significant correlation of 0.32 for the behavior description interview. Although their study was not designed to explain differences between the validities of the two interviews, the authors did note that the failure of the situational interview could be attributed to the nature of the professional job used. We agree with this possible conclusion. Much of the validity evidence of the situational interview has been produced from studies involving entry-level, clerical, and hourly jobs. When it comes to more complex jobs, perhaps using hypothetical questions (in situational interviews) is not as appropriate as using questions about what the candidate has done in actual situations (in behavioral description interviews).

A recent meta-analysis supports this supposition. The corrected correlation for situational interviews was only 0.30 for highly complex jobs, which was significantly lower than the predictive validities found in less complex jobs ($\rho = 0.44$ and 0.51 for less complex and moderately complex jobs).[53] However, another meta-analysis contradicted this finding, as the corrected correlations were similar for less complex ($\rho = 0.46$), moderately complex ($\rho = 0.44$), and highly complex ($\rho = 0.43$) jobs.[54] Although it seems plausible that hypothetical questions are not as useful in highly complex jobs, more research is needed. Nevertheless, with entry-level jobs or moderately complex jobs, it appears that structured interviews using either type of question result in comparably (high) predictive validities.

One potentially important finding about situational interviews is that coaching of interviewees can significantly improve their performance in the interview (as measured by interviewers' ratings).[55] This coaching, given to applicants for four different police and fire jobs, consisted of descriptions of the interview process, logistics of the interview, advantages of structured interviews, the KSA list measured in the interview, participation in and observation of interview role plays, and tips on how to prepare for the interview. Further research illustrated interviewee coaching appears to work by teaching candidates to be more organized, to pause and think before answering, and even to jot notes before answering.[56] This form of coaching is given by many colleges and universities to its students and by many private organizations to its customers. Coaching effects may be greatest for situational interviews, because these request answers to hypothetical questions rather than asking questions about prior experiences as behavioral description interviews do.

This review of the validity of the interview has focused on criterion-related or predictive validity. However, a content validity strategy is also a relevant approach, particularly for structured interviews that rely on questions that are specificly related to the job. The courts have accepted the job-relatedness of structured interviews, and this has proven to be an effective defense against discrimination lawsuits.[57] A recent study illustrates the content validation approach, where expert ratings were converted to a content validity ratio using Lawshe's method.[58] Results showed considerable content validity at both the question and overall evaluation level, with a content validity index (CVI) of 0.89 (a value of 0.59 is necessary for reaching a significant level when there are 11 experts involved). This implies a high degree of overlap between performance during the interview and the capability to effectively do the job on the defined dimension of job performance.[59]

DISCRIMINATION AND THE INTERVIEW

Our viewpoint of the legal issues relative to the interview is similar to our viewpoint about its validity—the interviewer (and organization) could be in big trouble if specific features that closely tie the interview to job activities are not incorporated into the interview. As described in Chapter 2, an organization would be in a vulnerable position with regard to discrimination if two conditions occurred: (a) decisions of the selection interview led, or assisted in leading, to disparate treatment or a pattern of disparate impact; and (b) the interview could not be defended regarding job relatedness.

As noted in the chapter dealing with application forms (Chapter 9), employers should avoid asking questions relating to race, color, religion, sex, national origin, marital status (including family responsibilities), sexual orientation, age, handicap or disability, and status as a Vietnam-era or disabled veteran.[60] In Chapter 9, Table 9.2 lists questions that have been deemed appropriate or inappropriate on an application form or during an employment interview. We encourage the reader to peruse those questions again. Using non-job-related questions to elicit these answers during the interview, even innocently, may provide the basis for an employment discrimination lawsuit. As this suggests, the employment interview today should be viewed as a source of potential liability for employers. The best way to protect the employer from discrimination claims is to ask questions that provide information about the candidate's ability to meet the requirements of the job.

Court Cases

As we discussed in Chapter 2, the *Watson v. Ft. Worth Bank & Trust* case has had a major impact on how the selection interview is treated by courts and companies in discrimination cases.[61] Because unscored interviews were considered to be subjective selection devices, previous to this decision interview cases were most often heard as disparate treatment issues. Disparate impact cases were usually associated with formally scored objective devices such as tests. As we have noted, defending a disparate treatment charge does not require as precise a score as defending a disparate impact charge. It was therefore in the best interest of companies, for legal defense reasons, to keep the interview as a less precisely scored selection instrument. Because of this, a conflict existed between the most effective use of the interview (scoring applicants) and the ease of defending a discrimination charge (not precisely scoring applicants).

The *Watson v. Ft. Worth Bank & Trust* decision changed this by stating that a case in which the selection interview is central to the charge of discrimination could be heard as a disparate impact case if the appropriate data were presented. Because validation is the most common defense of disparate impact, and because such a defense commonly requires statistical data, many companies now use a scored interview.

While the *Watson v. Ft. Worth Bank & Trust* case addresses an important legal procedural issue, other cases have focused on the specific practices used by companies in conducting the selection interview. We discuss some of the more important of these cases in the next paragraphs. Table 10.2 is a summary of these cases.

Discrimination Found. In *Stamps v. Detroit Edison Co.*, the court noted that disparate impact had occurred and that the interview was a subjective process that unnecessarily contributed to this impact.[62] The interviewers had not been given specific job-related questions to follow, nor had they been instructed in either the proper weights to apply to specific pieces of information or the decision rules for evaluating the applicant as

TABLE 10.2	Selected Court Cases Treating the Selection Interview

Cases in Which Discrimination Was Found	Court Comments
Stamps v. Detroit Edison (1973)	All interviewers were white Interviewers made subjective judgments about applicant's personality No structured or written interview format No objective criteria for employment decisions
Weiner v. Country of Oakland (1976)	All interviewers were male Interview questions suggested bias against females Selection decision rule not clearly specified
King v. TWA (1984)	Female applicant did not receive same questions as males History of interviewer's gender bias
Robbins v. White-Wilson Medical Clinic (1981)	No guidelines for conducting or scoring interview Interviewer's evaluation seemed racially biased based on own comments
Gilbert v. City of Little Rock, Ark. (1986)	Content validity inappropriate defense for measurement of mental processes Failure to operationally define KSAs Dissimilarity between exam questions and actual work situations
Bailey et al. v. Southeastern Area Joint Apprenticeship (1983)	Content of questions discriminatory toward women Defense did not conform with EEOC *Uniform Guidelines* Unclear instructions for rating applicant performance
Jones v. Mississippi Dept. of Corrections (1985)	Little evidence of specific questions used No scoring standards No cutoff score for selection

Cases in Which Discrimination Was Not Found	Court Comments
Harless v. Duck (1977)	Structured questionnaire Questions based on job analysis Relationship between interview performance and training
Maine Human Rights Commission v. Dept. of Corrections (1984)	Measurement of personality-related variables permitted KSAs listed Formal scoring system used
Minneapolis Comm. on Civil Rights v. Minnesota Chemical Dependency Assoc. (1981)	Permissible to use subjective measures of certain applicant characteristics that cannot be fully measured with objective tests Additional questions asked only of this applicant were appropriate Qualifications for job were posted A set of formal questions was asked of all applicants
Allesberry v. Commonwealth of Penn. (1981)	Nonscored questions used Written qualifications available to interviewer Posted notice of required qualifications Permissible to use subjective measures of administrative ability that cannot be fully measured with objective tests

acceptable or unacceptable. In addition, all interviewers were white; a high percentage of the people in the applicant pool were black. In *Weiner v. County of Oakland,* the organization partially addressed the issues of the preceding case in that the interview was scored in a systematic fashion.[63] However, the court specifically reviewed the questions asked in the interview. The court ruled that questions such as whether Mrs. Weiner could work with aggressive young men, whether her husband approved of her working, and whether her family would be burdened if she altered her normal household chores were not sufficiently job-related to warrant their use in the interview.

King v. TWA dealt with disparate treatment regarding the questions asked males and females for a job of kitchen helper.[64] A black woman was asked about her recent pregnancy, her marital status, and her relationship with another TWA employee, who had previously filed an EEOC complaint against the company. The interviewer also inquired about her future childbearing plans and arrangements for child care. The company claimed other reasons for her rejection, but the court did not agree for two reasons: (a) the questions at issue were not asked of anyone else; and (b) a previous TWA HR specialist testified that the interviewer in this case had a history of discriminating against women because he felt child care problems created a high rate of absenteeism.

Robbins v. White-Wilson Medical Clinic was a case of racial discrimination in an unscored interview that was intended to measure a pleasant personality and the ability to work with others.[65] The court tentatively accepted the requirement of personality as legitimate, but found the rejection of the plaintiff to be on racial grounds. There were two crucial pieces of evidence: (a) a written comment in the margin of the application blank ("has a bad attitude—has called and asked many questions. She is a black girl. Could cause trouble)" and (b) a response given by the interviewer in cross-examination about a black woman who was employed by the clinic that "she's more white than she is black."

There have also been cases in which discrimination was found despite the use of structured or scored interviews. In *Gilbert v. City of Little Rock,* a formal oral interview was scored, weighted, and combined with scores on other promotion devices.[66] The court ruled that the interview resulted in adverse impact against black officers in promotion evaluations. The police department attempted to justify the interview by content validity, showing that it measured attributes important to the position of sergeant. The court rejected this by pointing out that content validity is normally appropriate to justify specific tasks called for on the job. This interview required inferences to be made about mental processes and failed to define operationally the KSAs it purportedly measured.

A formally scored interview was also the focus of *Bailey v. Southeastern Area Joint Apprenticeship.*[67] In this case formally scored questions were asked of each applicant. These dealt with education, military service, work history, interests, and personal activities and attitudes. Interviewers summarized responses and assigned points to applicants based on these responses. The court held that sex discrimination had occurred, despite these formal procedures. Questions involving military service, prior vocational training, shop classes, and prior work experience in boilermaking caused adverse impact. The defendant did not show the business necessity of these questions. Also, interviewers were inexperienced and used ambivalent instructions in rating applicant performance.

Another related case was *Jones v. Mississippi Department of Corrections.*[68] A scored oral interview was given by members of a promotion interview panel. Applicants were asked about job duties and prison rules and regulations. Each interviewee was rated on a five-point scale for each of the following characteristics: attendance and punctuality, self-improvement efforts, prior performance of duties, current job knowledge, knowledge of new grade responsibilities, command presence/leadership qualities, personal appearance, overall manner, and educational level. This interview was ruled to be racially discriminating because the department could not prove it to be job related. Further, insufficient data were available concerning the actual questions used to measure these characteristics or standards used in scoring responses.

Discrimination Not Found. The interview has also been upheld in a number of court cases. In *Harless v. Duck,* the police department used an interview board to gather responses to approximately 30 questions asked of applicants. These questions tapped such KSAs as the applicant's communication skills, decision-making and problem-solving skills, and reactions to stress situations.[69] The court accepted the defendant's arguments that the interview was valid because the questions were based on dimensions identified through job analysis, and that interview performance was related to performance in training at the police academy.

Maine Human Rights Commission v. Department of Corrections involved an interview designed to measure general appearance, self-expression, alertness, personality, interest in work, public relations ability, and leadership ability.[70] This interview was used in selection for the position of Juvenile Court Intake Worker. Multiple interviewers used a Department of Personnel Form that included a numerical grade for each of seven characteristics. The court regarded personality and the other variables to be acceptable in selection for this position. A major portion of the department's defense of its procedures was a job description for the position that listed necessary entry-level KSAs, such as the ability to maintain composure in stressful situations, the ability to exercise judgment in interpersonal situations, the ability to relate to a variety of people, and the ability to listen and act appropriately in counseling relationships. As this shows, though we would question the wisdom of assessing 7 attributes in one interview, the court accepted the interview as a legally defensible selection procedure.

In *Minneapolis Commission on Civil Rights v. Minnesota Chemical Dependency Association,* the plaintiff, who had a history of gay rights activism, was asked additional questions that were not asked other applicants.[71] Included among these was the comment, "The one thing that bothers me [the interviewer] about it is this, that in this position,… it seems to be that although you have special interests or anyone that took this position would have some special interests, that this job requires someone else to carry the ball of those special interests." While acknowledging that the plaintiff was asked additional questions, the court found that the previous history of extensive involvement in outside activities was a legitimate concern and this justified the additional questions. The fact that the plaintiff indicated that, in his opinion, neutrality might unfairly suppress his interests and that he would resign if the agency's decisions were insensitive to these interests was held to support the use of the additional questions and to properly serve as a basis of rejection.

In *Allesberry v. Commonwealth of Pennsylvania,* an unscored interview was one of several complaints referred to by the black plaintiff, who was not hired when two white applicants were.[72] The court did not find discrimination, judging that the two white applicants were better qualified and citing educational degrees and previous work history in support of this position. In addressing the interview specifically, the court said that "decisions about hiring in supervisory jobs and managerial jobs cannot realistically be made using objective standards alone." Subjective measures were, therefore, acceptable. In this case the interviewer had access to a posted notice of the KSAs required for the position. Included in this notice were statements such as "ability to plan, organize, and direct specialized programs" and "ability to establish and maintain effective working relationships."

Laura Gollub Williamson and her colleagues have analyzed 130 federal court discrimination cases.[73] They found links between interview structure and the way that judges explained their verdicts. Several specific interview characteristics were shown to be important: behavior-based vs. trait-based criteria, specific vs. general criteria, the use of multiple interviewers, interviewer training, the interviewer's familiarity with KSA requirements, validation evidence, guides for conducting interviews, minimal interviewer discretion in decision making, standardized questions, and the review of the interviewer's decisions. These results are supported in a recent analysis of 75 cases involving charges of discrimination in Canada. These findings show that tribunals give great weight to whether the employer used structured interviews or not.[74]

RESEARCH FINDINGS ON DISCRIMINATION

Legal restrictions against using race, ethnicity, sex, age, and disability in employment decisions should minimize or eliminate the influence of these characteristics when making hiring decisions. Several studies have examined the influence these demographic variables have on interview outcomes, and recent reviews of the literature concluded that direct (main) effects due to candidate race, sex, age and other demographic characteristics on interviewer ratings generally are small and inconsistent, particularly structured interviews.[75] A second stream of research focuses on the effects of similarity between the candidate and the interviewer. The basic premise is that interviewers who are of the same race as the candidate will tend to rate the candidate more favorably. Again, research reveals small and inconsistent effects on interviewer evaluations, based on whether the candidate and interviewer share demographic characteristics. This finding is similar to findings in the performance appraisal literature, which show that demographic similarity between employee and interviewer results in mixed or small effects on supervisor performance ratings.[76]

It is possible that the small effects these demographic variables have on interviewer ratings is due to the positive influence of EEO legal restrictions. To support this contention, a few studies show that demographic variables tend to have larger effects on interviewer thoughts and beliefs than on actual hiring decisions.[77] It may well be that if there are causal effects resulting from these demographic variables, they are due to reasons other than discrimination. Such effects may simply reflect more complex underlying factors such as the tendency of an interviewer to make inferences about candidate attitudes and values—and that therefore these demographic variables are one way interviewers draw such inferences.

One area in which research does demonstrate some influence of demographic variables on interview outcomes is the area of physical and mental disabilities. Since the passage of the Americans with Disabilities Act of 1990, there have been a number of studies conducted on this topic. Although the results are not uniform, findings suggest that applicant disclosure of non-obvious disabilities—as well as early discussion during the interview about obvious applicant disabilities—tends to increase the likelihood of a hiring recommendation[78] Although employers are barred from asking candidates questions about their disabilities prior to making a job offer, these results suggest that candidates will receive a favorable response to such disclosures, particularly if the applicants are not seen as threatening (likely to pursue litigation).

Research on demographic characteristics has also suggested two ways to further reduce any effects due to age, race, sex, and other demographic variables: using highly structured interviewers and relying on more experienced interviewers who have more training. The use of structured interviews appears to reduce the influence of biases due to discrimination.[79] For example, Jennifer DeNicolis Bragger, Eugene Kutcher, and their associates found that the use of structured interviews reduced interviewer biases against overweight candidates when hiring decisions were made. This study found that by focusing on job-related factors, the bias against overweight job candidates was reduced.[80] Although the effects are less clear, there is also evidence that the more skilled interviewers are (in experience and training), the less likely they are to be biased by the candidate's demographic characteristics.[81]

Does this mean there is not likely to be disparate impact on race, sex, and so forth in employment interviews? A recent meta-analysis of 31 studies conducted by Allen Huffcutt and Philip Roth showed that black and Hispanic candidates received candidate evaluations that on average were about one-quarter of a standard deviation lower than those for white candidates.[82] Thus, employment interviews show some evidence of disparate impact on the basis of candidate race. Nevertheless, those differences are substantially smaller than the group differences often found when cognitive ability tests are used. Recent research, however, illustrates that the magnitude of the mean standardized difference between the candidate evaluations of white and black or Hispanic candidates is likely to be larger if one accounts for the impact of only interviewing the top 30 percent of applicants (range restriction).[83]

One other finding is particularly important to this discussion; that is, that structured interviews result in smaller subgroup differences ($d = 0.23$ and 0.17, respectively, for black and Hispanic candidates) than structured interviews ($d = 0.32$ and 0.71, respectively).[84] This supports the point made in prior paragraphs. One way to reduce discrimination is to use a structured interview. A recent study examining 158 U.S. federal court cases revealed that unstructured interviews were involved in charges of hiring discrimination in 57 percent of these cases, whereas structured interviews were involved in only 6 percent of cases.[85] Furthermore, although the unstructured interview was ruled to be the cause of discrimination in 41 percent of these cases, the structured interview was never found to be discriminatory (0.00 percent). Not surprisingly, reliance on job-related questions increases the odds of an organization winning a lawsuit. The utility of structured interviews will be discussed more extensively later in this chapter. For now, it is important to recognize that using structured interviews will reduce the likelihood of a disparate impact lawsuit and will provide a job-related basis for defending the selection decision.

A MODEL OF INTERVIEWER DECISION MAKING

Recent research on the interview illustrates that a number of important factors influence interviewer decision making, including social and cognitive factors, individual differences between the applicant and the interviewer, and the interview context itself.[86] As we mentioned previously, early research on the interview pointed out deficiencies in its reliability and validity. Consequently, research over the past 15 to 20 years has attempted to identify which characteristics of the interviewer, the candidate, or the interview process were related to low reliability and validity. While such research produced some interesting and useful results, in general it was disorganized. Many interview factors were unsystematically studied, often because they were easy to measure rather than because they were theoretically important. Consequently, results of studies were often inconsistent. We know in general that structured interviews are superior to unstructured interviews, but we still need a comprehensive model to explain why this is so.

Models that focus on factors that affect decision making during the interview provide a way to organize the conduct of research and the interpretation of results. Basically such models assume that the interviewer and candidate are gathering and processing information about each other as well as the organization and job. Research in cognitive and social psychology becomes the basis for many of the propositions of such decision-making models. Robert Dipboye's model (shown in Figure 10.1) briefly summarizes the existing large body of research that identifies critical factors affecting the decision-making process over the different phases of the interview (before, during, and after the

FIGURE 10.1 A Model of the Selection Interview

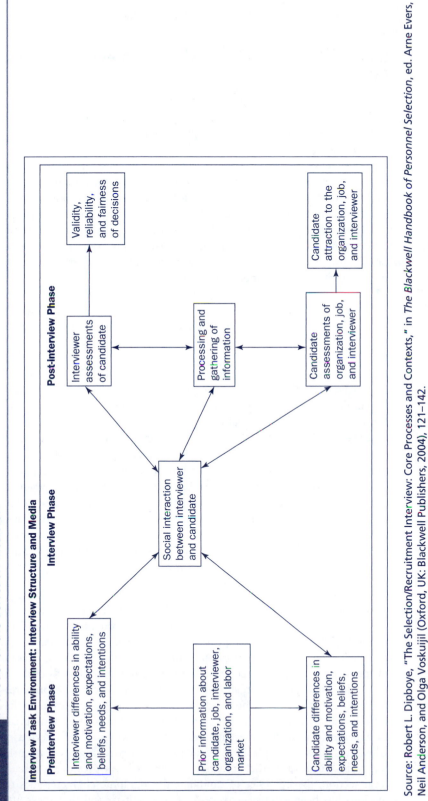

Interview Task Environment: Interview Structure and Media

Preinterview Phase   **Interview Phase**   **Post-Interview Phase**

Interviewer differences in ability and motivation, expectations, beliefs, needs, and intentions

Prior information about candidate, job, interviewer, organization, and labor market

Candidate differences in ability and motivation, expectations, beliefs, needs, and intentions

Social interaction between interviewer and candidate

Interviewer assessments of candidate

Processing and gathering of information

Candidate assessments of organization, job, and interviewer

Validity, reliability, and fairness of decisions

Candidate attraction to the organization, job, and interviewer

Source: Robert L. Dipboye, "The Selection/Recruitment Interview: Core Processes and Contexts," in *The Blackwell Handbook of Personnel Selection*, ed. Arne Evers, Neil Anderson, and Olga Voskuijil (Oxford, UK: Blackwell Publishers, 2004), 121–142.

interview).[87] We hope that familiarizing yourself with this model will help elucidate the recommendations we make at the end of the chapter.

Expectations, Beliefs, Needs, and Intentions Prior to the Interview

Interviewers and candidates bring to the interview their own expectations, beliefs, needs, and intentions with regard to the job, the interview itself, the organization, and each other. These are a product of the previous knowledge, training, education, and experience of the interviewer and the candidate. These expectations, beliefs, needs, and intentions influence all three stages of the interview (see Figure 10.1). In the preinterview phase, these factors have been shown to have a significant impact on impressions held by the interviewer and candidate, which in turn has been found to influence interviewer evaluations of those candidates.[88] Research also shows that interviewers seek out and recall (even distort) information that supports or confirms their preinterview impressions of the candidate,[89] thereby creating a self-fulfilling prophecy. Interview outcomes have been shown to be influenced by interviewer preconceptions about what the ideal candidate or group of applicants should be.[90]

In contrast, there has been little research done on the influence of the candidate's preinterview expectations, beliefs, needs, and intentions. For example, the interview process is likely to be significantly different for those candidates who approach the interview with an expectation that they will receive and accept a job offer than for those who are less likely to pursue an offered position.[91] In one recent study, candidates who thought the interviewer was likely to extend them a job offer after the first few minutes of the interview were less vigilant and motivated to effectively manage their image during the remainder of the interview and thus received lower ratings from the interviewer than those candidates who thought the interviewer had a less favorable reaction.[92] In this case the candidate's beliefs about the interviewer's initial reaction was found to influence how effectively the candidate managed the image projected during the rest of the interview. The lack of research with regard to candidate beliefs and expectations is surprising, given that the cost incurred by an organization can be high when, due to negative or unrealistic expectations or beliefs, a prospective candidate fails to apply for a position or drops out of the hiring process early. As shown in Figure 10.1, what the interviewer and the candidate are thinking prior to the interview has a significant and dynamic effect on both the social interaction that occurs during the interview and on postinterview outcomes.

Individual Differences

A number of individual difference variables of both the candidate and the interviewer have been shown to play a role in the interview process. A candidate's physical attractiveness, for example, has repeatedly been shown to influence interviewer evaluations and hiring decisions.[93] As previously mentioned, the candidate's handshake at the start of the interview has also been shown to affect the interviewer's evaluations.[94] The candidate's personality has been shown to affect whether he or she prepares rigorously for an interview. Furthermore, the candidate's personality is expected to have a direct effect during and after the interview.[95] For example, gregarious, outgoing candidates are likely to experience a much different interview than will shy, introverted candidates. Finally, whether or not a candidate has participated in a coaching program prior to the interview has been found to predict interview outcomes.[96] As previously discussed in this book's legal section, the influence of candidate demographic characteristics on interviewer evaluations has been extensively investigated. Results reveal that these attributes have small and inconsistent effects on actual hiring decisions.[97] These findings show that more research should be done on the individual differences between candidates—and the effects of these differences and their effects before, during, and after the employment interview.

Interviewer individual differences also have a significant effect on the interview. A number of studies have assessed the utility of providing interviewer training; in general, these studies show only modest effects on interviewer evaluations. This is surprising, given the cost borne by organizations to provide such training.[98] Relatively little research has been done about the value of interviewer experience, although increasing experience should positively affect interviewer evaluations. One explanation for the relative dearth of studies about interviewer experience is that the conditions needed for learning (training and feedback) are not present in the typical interviewer's job. Robert Dipboye and Susan Jackson found a positive relationship between interviewer experience and interviewer decisions when the experience was associated with higher levels of cognitive complexity (that is, the ability to deal with complex social situations).[99] This finding, however, may be due to the influence of differences among interviewers' general mental abilities rather than interviewer experience. Further research should examine the effect interviewer intelligence has on decision making. In fact, there is a need for better understanding about how the interviewer's personality, cognitive complexity, emotional intelligence, self esteem, or generalized and specific self-efficacy affect the validity and accuracy of interviewer judgments. The finding that some interviewers are able to render more valid judgments than other interviewers underscores the need to study individual differences between interviewers.[100]

Social Interaction During the Interview

The interview is fundamentally a social interaction between the candidate and interviewer. Because these interactants are almost always strangers and because the candidate is dependent on the interviewer to get a job offer, there is considerable incentive to manage one's image. Consequently, there has been considerable research about factors that influence the quality of this relationship. Two related factors that have been extensively studied involve the similarities between the interviewer and the candidate and candidate fit with the job or organization. Similarity with regard to demographic characteristics (race, sex) and attitudes is expected to increase attraction. This should lead to liking and positive impressions, which lead the interviewer to rate the candidate more favorably.[101] As noted previously, however, research on demographic similarity has led to small and inconsistent effects on the ratings of candidates.[102] In contrast, the findings for attitudinal similarity (similarity in work attitudes and personal values) seems to affect interviewer evaluations of candidates positively, particularly evaluations relating to perception of the candidate's competence. Furthermore, the effect due to similarity does not seem to reduce the predictive validity of interviewer ratings.[103] However, applicant and interviewer perceptions of attitudinal similarity take time to manifest themselves; consequently attitudinal similarity is harder to assess during an interview than similarities that are based on demographic factors. This likely explains why attitudinal similarity effects are not even larger in the interview. In general, research on similarity (both attitudinal and demographic) has shown that effects are much less pronounced when the interview is structured and job requirements are clear.[104]

In addition to similarity, another area that has garnered considerable study is the fit between the candidate and the job or organization. Here, the research focuses on the impact of congruence between the candidate and characteristics of the position or organization rather than characteristics of the interviewer. A recent meta-analysis of person–environment fit conducted by Amy Kristof-Brown, Ryan Zimmerman, and Erin Johnson shows the value of attaining a good fit of the candidate to the position or firm, as the candidate's attraction to the organization is significantly influenced—whether due to person–job fit ($\rho = 0.48$) or person–organization fit ($\rho = 0.46$). Results also show that the employer's intention to hire the candidate ($\rho = 0.67$ and 0.61, respectively, for person–job fit and person–organization fit) increased when the employer thought the candidate was the "right type."[105] Although the meta-analysis by Allen Huffcutt and associates found organizational fit was only rarely measured during the interview (in 3 percent of interviews), it had a relatively high mean validity for predicting performance ($\rho = 0.49$).[106] Furthermore, "fit" is one of those constructs that is relevant to all jobs, whether for an entry-level position or a senior manager job.

Another recent meta-analysis illustrates that what the recruiter does during the interview has a significant effect on candidate attitudes. For example, interviewers who are more personable, competent, and informative increased the candidate's attraction to the job or organization (ρ ranged from 0.29 to 0.42).[107] Recruiter behaviors also influenced whether the candidate chose to actually join the organization, although this effect was smaller. This study also found that demographic characteristics of the interviewer did not influence candidate attitudes or job choices (ρ is less than 0.10). These results show that it does not matter whether the recruiter is from a specific functional area (already does the job being interviewed for) or is of a particular gender or race. Thus, who the interviewer is doesn't matter as much as how the interview is conducted. Research also shows that interviewer ratings of the candidate tend to be higher when the interview itself is longer and the interviewer talks more during the interview.[108] Taken together, these findings suggest that candidates use the behavior of the recruiter to make inferences about the organization, the job, and even the likelihood of receiving a job offer, which in turn affects candidate attitudes about the attractiveness of the position.

Studies examining the influence of the candidate's behavior during the interview have centered on the self-presentation tactics the candidate relies on to influence the interviewer's evaluation. Tactics include the candidate's professional demeanor and physical attractiveness, use of impression management behaviors, and verbal and nonverbal behavior.[109] For example, two recent meta-analyses found that attractive candidates were more likely to be hired than less-attractive individuals, even when decision makers have job-relevant information available about the candidate.[110] Stephen Motowidlo and his associates have studied both verbal and nonverbal behaviors in videotapes of actual interviews. They found that interviewer ratings had greater accuracy when the interviewers had both a high level of verbal cues (voice pitch, pitch variability, speech rate) and moderate to high levels of nonverbal cues (attractiveness, eye contact, head movements, smiling, hand gestures, and so on) from candidates.[111] It appears that interviewer evaluations of candidates are significantly affected by what and how the candidate communicates, verbally and nonverbally.[112] There is some evidence that these behaviors may also predict performance on the job.[113] That is, the same visual and vocal cues that positively influenced interviewers were also positively related to a candidate's future job performance ratings. The authors explain that these cues affect interviewers; they cause liking and trust, which affects job performance by facilitating interpersonal relationships that are important for success in many jobs.

Does this mean that the candidate can manipulate the outcome of the interview through behaviors such as smiling, posture, and hand movements? Such manipulation is part of what is termed "impression management," and a number of studies have shown that these behaviors do, indeed, influence hiring decisions.[114] Studies show that candidates frequently engage in assertive influence tactics (self-promotion or ingratiation tactics) during employment interviews.[115] However, the effects of impression management tactics are not always consistent. One study found that such tactics affect different interviewers in different ways and can, under certain conditions, create negative images of the applicant.[116] Interestingly, the use of such tactics by candidates seems to be more related to how the candidate perceives the interviewer's characteristics (communication skills, age, experience, apprehension) rather than to the candidate's characteristics.[117]

Two recent meta-analyses of the impression management literature shows that both ingratiation (tactics that focus on the interviewer by flattering or agreeing with the target, and which includes nonverbal behavior such as smiling, head nodding, and so on) and self-promotion (describing one's past experience and accomplishments in a positive manner in order to generate a perception of competence) positively affect interviewers' evaluations of job candidates.[118] In fact, these studies found that when ingratiation and self-promotion were studied in the context of employment interviews, the effect sizes were roughly equal. Interestingly, the use of ingratiation was found to positively relate to supervisory ratings of job performance ($\rho = 0.26$), suggesting that these tactics may also be related to success on the job. In contrast, although self-promotion tactics were useful in the interview, these tactics were negatively related to supervisor assessments of performance ($\rho = -0.25$).[119] This may be because a candidate is expected to "brag" about him or herself during the interview, but continuing to do so as an employee leads others to evaluate the person in a less positive way or even negatively. These findings bring into question whether impression management tactics create bias or instead enable the candidate to convey job-related qualifications. This is an important question future research must examine. It should be noted that research shows that the influence of impression management tactics is reduced when structured interviews are used.[120]

One final area that we know is critical to the reliability and validity of the employment interview relates to the nature of the questions asked. If the questions are not related to the job, we should not expect validity to be high. If interviewers ask different questions, we should not expect the interviewers to be reliable in their evaluations of candidates, because each interviewer has in fact collected different information about the applicants. Guess what has often been found when research has examined interviewers' questions? You're right! Susan Taylor and Janet Sniezek found that interviewers often disagreed among themselves about which topics should be covered in an interview.[121] These differences seemed to relate more to individual preferences than to the perceived importance of job requirements. Interviewers also consistently failed to cover topics that they themselves believed to be important; applicants report that the most frequently covered topics are the relatively unimportant ones of university life and extracurricular activities, not topics related to the demands of the job. Even today, many interviewers continue to resist using the structured interview format even though research shows that it is more useful for predicting later job success.[122] It is reasonable to assume that questions tend not to be consistently asked of all candidates if the interview is unstructured.

Information Processing and Decision-Making Factors

The interview ultimately requires that interviewers and candidates make decisions. Considerable research has been conducted on the decision-making process of managers; across multiple theories, we find that decision makers use a two-stage decision process.[123] Robert Dipboye applied this finding to explain how decisions are made during the interview.[124] In the first stage, the decision maker is trying to reduce choices by screening out unsuitable candidates, often using relatively simple decision rules. Dipboye argues that interviewers *categorize* applicants in a relatively unthinking way during this initial screening process. At the second stage, interviewers evaluate choices more rigorously in an attempt to choose the "best" candidate. This stage results in a process called *characterization*. During the *characterization* process, traits are inferred based on a candidate's behavior and answers to interview questions.[125] The model posits that if the interviewer gains information that contradicts his initial categorization, he may engage in a process of *correction* and change his initial impression in order to incorporate this new information. Researchers have found that a number of factors influence decision making within this two-stage evaluation process. The most important of these factors is reviewed next.

Interviewers appear to use *heuristics*, or simple rules of thumb, when making decisions. The tendency to use prior estimations as an anchor around which future judgments revolve is one well-known psychological heuristic commonly used by decision makers. Two other commonly used heuristics, representativeness and availability, are also expected to influence interviewers.[126] Both of these heuristics would lead the interviewer to overestimate the likelihood a candidate possesses a "rare" characteristic because it is similar to another more common attribute (representativeness) or has high emotional impact (availability). Gary Latham and associates found that interviewers were affected by anchoring and adjustment heuristics, just like other decision makers. In this study, interviewers were given either a high or low anchor score (prior estimation) about the candidate's hireability. Those candidates with a high anchor score led to more favorable interviewer evaluations than did candidates with a low anchor score. It should be noted, however, that the effect from the anchoring heuristic was significantly reduced when the interview was structured, again underscoring the importance of using a structured interview.[127]

Order or contrast effects have also been found to influence interviewer judgments. A number of studies have found that interviewers compare or contrast candidates. The contrast effect occurs when an "average" candidate is rated "above average" when contrasted with other candidates who were "below average." However, if the same "average" candidate had been contrasted against other "above average" candidates instead, the interviewer would have rated the candidate below average. Consequently, the rating obtained for a candidate is partly determined by others against whom the candidate is being compared.[128]

There is evidence of a strong primacy effect—that initial information carries considerable weight in the interview.[129] One stream of research, which was discussed earlier, illustrates the effect of first impressions formed about candidates during the initial stage of the interview.[130] Findings in social psychology show that individuals form reactions to strangers rather quickly—and this research suggests we are "pre-wired" to evaluate strangers based on minimal information.[131] The first impression appears to establish an anchor for the interviewer that filters all subsequent evaluations of the candidate.[132] As previously noted, the primacy effect also emerges from preinterview perceptions of candidate competency, based on information from application forms, resumes, and other tests administered prior to the interview. Therese Macan and Robert Dipboye found that preinterview beliefs and impressions interviewers bring to the session, beliefs based on knowledge of an applicant's coursework and job experience, were strongly related to postinterview ratings of the candidate. Nevertheless, they also found that performance during the interview significantly affected interviewer evaluations, even after accounting for this preinterview impression.[133]

The other type of applicant information that is apparently given a disproportionate weight by interviewers is negative information. Somewhat surprisingly, it has been found that even experienced interviewers give more weight to negative information than to positive information in decision making.[134] For example, in one study, unfavorable ratings on only one of several characteristics resulted in the rejection of the applicant in over 90 percent of the cases.[135] In some cases, the source of these negative judgments is not clear. There is evidence that impressions formed during the interview—rather than the facts gathered—are related to these judgments. Such decision making would clearly be at odds with the stated purpose of the interview—but consistent with the evidence that physical attractiveness, liking, and nonverbal cues affect the decision.[136] We can explain this emphasis on negative information by thinking about the costs of the various outcomes of an interview. The greatest cost to the interviewer comes from making the mistake of selecting a candidate who fails on the job. Professional reputation and company expenditures suffer. On the other hand, rejecting an applicant who would in fact be a successful performer if selected has no real costs. Who would know? Therefore, cost is lowered when an interviewer rejects all candidates who appear to be marginal or doubtful, even if they would have been successful in the job.

Another reason ratings are not accurate is due to the amount of information an interviewer can recall after an interview. In one study, managers watched a 20-minute video of an interview. Immediately after the video, they were asked 20 factual questions. The average manager missed 10 of the 20 facts mentioned during the interview. Managers who had taken notes during the interview were much more accurate (some missed none), while those managers without notes missed as many as 15 out of 20 questions. Those managers with notes rated the candidate more critically and demonstrated more variance in their ratings across dimensions. In contrast, managers without notes assumed that the overall applicant evaluation was more favorable and provided comparable ratings across all dimensions. Thus, those interviewers who knew the facts were more accurate and recognized that the candidate could differ from dimension to dimension.[137] However, other research shows that, in order to get the most benefit from note taking, interviewers must be trained on how to take notes.[138]

One conclusion that can be drawn from research on information processing and decision making is that many factors that only marginally relate to job activities often influence an interviewer's evaluation, even when the interviewer is experienced. Does this all mean that the interview is worthless? Of course not; as we have shown, studies have clearly revealed the validity of this device. However, these studies have been conducted on interviews that were designed to counteract many of the problems just discussed. The last section of this chapter develops recommendations for the design of an interview.

Developing Appropriate Interview Questions

The interviewer's evaluation of candidates should be more accurate if more information is obtained about candidates' job knowledge or performance of job activities. The relevant question becomes, "How does an interviewer develop specific job-related questions?" We answer this question using the two types of structured interview (situational and behavior description).

The Situational Interview.   The situational interview method was developed by Gary Latham, Lise Saari, Elliot Pursell, and Michael Campion.[139] Its basic intent is first to identify specific activities representative of the job and then to use this information to form questions that ask applicants how they would behave in the situation. The first step is to do a job analysis of the position using the *Critical-Incidents Technique*. (Go back to Chapter 7 to refresh your memory about this technique. Aren't you impressed with how tightly interwoven this book is?) Critical incidents are descriptions of work behaviors that have actually occurred, examples of particularly good or particularly poor job performance. A well-written incident is a description of the action, not an evaluation. It describes the circumstances leading up to the incident, what actually happened, and the result. These incidents are gathered from job incumbents as well as from supervisors. They can be gathered either through personal interviews or questionnaires. Both methods require that the term *critical incident* be defined, and that examples be provided to focus the respondents' thinking.

Typically, several hundred incidents are obtained for a single job. These incidents are then sorted into groups of similar behaviors, referred to as *behavioral dimensions,* by a small group of judges. Only those behaviors that are reliably sorted are retained. These behavioral dimensions are then named according to the content of the similar behaviors; for example, technical skills, the diagnosing of defects, customer service, and so on.

The next step is to review the incidents for each behavioral dimension, select a small number of the most appropriate incidents, and use these to write interview questions. There appears to be no one best way of selecting the small number of appropriate incidents. The judgments used are frequently provided by supervisors who are experienced in interviewing for the job. The exact number of incidents that are chosen depends on the planned time of the interview and the number of dimensions to be addressed. At least two incidents per dimension is common.

These incidents are then rephrased as interview questions appropriate for job applicants. Table 10.3 contains examples of such questions. This rephrasing is fairly straightforward; it usually includes a brief description of the circumstances of the incident and the question, "What would you do?" Here's an example: "You are to start your shift as convenience store manager at 5 A.M. When you attempt to start your car at 4:45, you realize that your husband left the gas tank nearly empty. What would you do?"

Scoring of applicants' responses to these questions is simplified by the development of scales for each question. Usually, these are five-point scales on which examples of low, average, and high responses are written. Table 10.3 contains examples of such a scale for each question. Developing the examples for each scale also makes use of the judgment of supervisors of the job of interest. Either the supervisors are asked to note actual behaviors they have observed or they are asked to write down applicant responses they have heard in an interview. Again, only those examples showing agreement between low, average, and high behaviors are used on the scale. This scale is not revealed to the applicant but is used only by the interviewer. In scoring the interview, the interviewer places a check on the scale using the example responses as a frame of reference. If the example responses have been carefully prepared, it is common for the applicants' responses to be similar to the examples. A total score for the interview can be obtained by summing the ratings for each scale. Alternatively, a series of separate scores can be generated by treating each scale score independently.

The Behavior Description Interview. This method, first described by Tom Janz, is similar to the situational interview and uses many of the same steps.[140] It starts with generating critical incidents and identifying behavioral dimensions in the same manner as was described for the situational interview. However, unlike the situational interview, the behavior description interview calls for a review of these behavioral dimensions as well as the identification of each dimension as essentially describing either maximum or typical performance of the individual. The difference between these two types is described as follows:

> *If how much the applicant* knows *or* can do *is critical to job performance, the dimension tends toward maximum performance. If what the applicant* typically will do *relates more closely to job performance, the dimension tends toward typical performance.*[141]

Maximum performance dimensions usually deal with technical skills and knowledge. Typical performance dimensions deal with getting along with others, working hard versus wasting time, and being organized, courteous, or punctual. The importance of this

TABLE 10.3	Examples of Situational Interview Questions and Scoring Scales

1. Your spouse and two teenage children are sick in bed with colds. There are no relatives or friends available to look in on them. Your shift starts in three hours. What would you do in this situation?

1 (low)	I'd stay home—my family comes first.
3 (average)	I'd phone my supervisor and explain my situation.
5 (high)	Since they only have colds, I'd come to work.[a]

2. A customer comes into the store to pick up a watch he had left for repair. The repair was supposed to have been completed a week ago, but the watch is not back yet from the repair shop. The customer is very angry. How would you handle the situation?

1 (low)	Tell the customer the watch is not back yet and ask him or her to check back with you later.
3 (average)	Apologize, tell the customer that you will check into the problem, and call him or her back later.
5 (high)	Put the customer at ease and call the repair shop while the customer waits.[b]

3. For the past week you have been consistently getting the jobs that are the most time consuming (e.g., poor handwriting, complex statistical work). You know it's nobody's fault because you have been taking the jobs in priority order. You have just picked your fourth job of the day and it's another "loser." What would you do?

1 (low)	Thumb through the pile and take another job.
3 (average)	Complain to the coordinator, but do the job.
5 (high)	Take the job without complaining and do it.[c]

[a]Gary P. Latham, Lise M. Saari, Elliot D. Pursell, and Michael A. Campion, "The Situational Interview," *Journal of Applied Psychology,* 4 (1980): 422–427.

[b]Jeff A. Weekley and Joseph A. Gier, "Reliability and Validity of the Situational Interview for a Sales Position," *Journal of Applied Psychology,* 3 (1987): 484–487.

[c]Gary P. Latham and Lise M. Saari, "Do People Do What They Say? Further Studies on the Situational Interview," *Journal of Applied Psychology,* 4 (1984): 569–573.

distinction is that, for the *behavior description interview,* it is recommended that maximum performance dimensions be omitted from the interview and almost complete emphasis placed on typical performance dimensions.

The development of questions is essentially the same as discussed previously for a situational interview. However, two aspects are different from the situational interview. First, each question is formed with appropriate probes (follow-up questions). The main question serves to locate a particular instance from the applicant's past and focus the applicant on that type of event. Probes seek out exactly how the applicant behaved and what the consequences were of that behavior. Second, a distinction is made between questions appropriate for applicants who have work experience related to the job of interest and applicants who don't have such experience. The latter type of question should focus on the same behavior as the former, except the type of event or situation is more general and need not be part of a job at all. For example, a question asked of an experienced salesperson might be, "Tell me about the most difficult new client contact you made in the last six months." An equivalent question for an applicant with no sales experience might be, "We have all tried to convince someone we did not know well of the merits of a product or idea we were promoting. I would like you to tell me of a time when this was especially tough for you." Table 10.4 contains examples of the basic and accompanying probe questions using behavior description interviewing.

Scoring is done *separately* for each of the behavioral dimensions. It is recommended that when the interview is completed, the interviewer reviews his or her notes (or the tape recording if one has been used). Based on the judged quality of their responses, applicants are placed in one of five rank-order groups for each dimension (see Table 10.4). Each group on the scale represents 20 percent of all applicants; that is, a score of

---

TABLE 10.4	Examples of Behavioral Description Interviewing Questions and Scoring

1. It is often necessary to work together in a group to accomplish a task. Can you tell me about the most recent experience you had working as part of a group?

   (The following are probe questions.)

   a. What was the task?
   b. How many people were in the group?
   c. What difficulties arose as a result of working as a group?
   d. What role did you play in resolving these difficulties?
   e. How successful was the group in completing its task?
   f. How often do you work as part of a group?

2. Tell me about a time when you aided an employee in understanding a difficult policy.

   (The following are probe questions.)

   a. What was the policy?
   b. How did you know that the employee was having trouble understanding?
   c. What did you do or say that helped?
   d. How did you know that you had been successful?
   e. What steps did you take to change the policy?

Applicant Assessment Form for Scoring Behavioral Description Interview

	1	2	3	4	5
Dimension	**Bottom 20%**	**Next 20%**	**Middle 20%**	**Next 20%**	**Top 20%**
1. Working with group					X
2. Understanding policy					
•					
•					
•					
10.		X			

Dimension	Dimension Score		Weight (optional)		Cumulative Total
1.	5	×	25	=	125
•	•		•		
•	•		•		
•	•		•		
10.	3	×	10	=	325

Source: Janz, *Behavior and Descriptive Interviewing*, 1st Edition, © 1986, Pg. 113, 117, 138, 181. Reprinted by permission of Pearson Education, Inc., Upper Saddle River, NJ.

"1" indicates that the applicant ranks in the bottom 20 percent; a score of "5" means that he or she ranks in the top 20 percent of all applicants. Each dimension is assigned a weight derived from judgments made by the interviewers, judgements that reflect its importance to overall job performance. It is advised that dimensions not be differentially weighted unless some dimensions are at least two to three times more important than other dimensions. If this is not the case, equal weights are recommended. The dimension score described previously is multiplied by this dimension weight to obtain the total score for the dimension. Total score for the interview is obtained by summing all the dimension total scores.

Use of either approach (situational or behavior description interviews) should result in content-valid interview questions, which should be predictive of performance in the job. Taken together, considerable research conducted over the past 15 years documents the predictive validity of structured interviews. If the primary purpose of the employment interview is to select the best candidates in the applicant pool, one would be well advised to utilize a structured interview.

RECOMMENDATIONS FOR USING THE INTERVIEW

We have discussed a lot of information about the selection interview. Let's put this information to use by discussing specific recommendations for how to build a better interview. These recommendations are summarized in Table 10.5.

Restrict the Scope of the Interview

We believe that one of the major weaknesses of the interview is that it is often used to accomplish too many purposes. As we have discussed, the interview is frequently and simultaneously used as a public relations vehicle for projecting an image of the organization, a recruitment vehicle for conveying job description and organization information to potential applicants, and a selection vehicle for evaluating the job-related KSAs of the applicants. Although recruitment, selection, and projecting a good public image all must be dealt wih when hiring, we ought not confuse time similarity with function similarity. Just because these three functions are compressed into a short period at the beginning of the HR management cycle does not mean they should be addressed at the same time. The purposes of and the data for public relations, recruitment, and selection are simply not the same.

We think that recruitment and selection should be systematically separated. If it is decided that the interview, as a process, should be used in either one of these functions, then each separate interview process ought to be planned according to the models for effective use that have been developed for that function. In this way, the selection interview becomes focused and is not a multiple-purpose hybrid activity. This should substantially increase its usefulness.

There is a second way in which the interview suffers from a multiple-purpose use. Earlier in this chapter, we noted that several writers have concluded that often too many KSAs are evaluated in the interview. It has been recommended that the scope of the interview be limited to a much narrower band of applicant characteristics: *job knowledge, applied social and interpersonal skills,* and *personality and habitual behaviors* (work habits, conscientiousness, emotional stability, agreeableness, and so on).

Let us use the information presented in Table 10.5 to demonstrate the appropriate use of the interview in a selection program. Using the procedures previously described in Chapter 7, we have completed a job analysis of the job of maintenance supervisor. The

---

TABLE 10.5 Recommendations for Interview Use

1. Restrict the use of the interview to the most job-relevant KSAs, preferably just 2-3 KSAs.
2. Limit the use of preinterview data about applicants.
3. Adopt a structured format by predetermining major questions to be asked.
4. Use job-related questions.
5. Use multiple questions for each KSA.
6. Rely on multiple independent interviewers.
7. Apply formal scoring that allows for the evaluation of each KSA separately.
8. Train interviewers in the process of the selection interview.

KSAs listed in Table 10.6 have been derived from this job analysis. The remainder of the table illustrates the appropriate way to use various selection instruments for measuring the KSAs; the table shows the percentage of the selection program that should be devoted to each of the selection instruments.

Our judgment is that only three of the eight KSAs are appropriate for assessment in the interview and that, due to the importance of these KSAs, the interview should comprise 45 percent of the selection program. "Ability to give verbal work instructions to laborers regarding construction and repair" is best demonstrated through a verbal exchange process such as the interview. Measurement of "ability to schedule work crews for specific tasks" would frequently entail the exchange of information about specific characteristics of tasks and also an explanation of the reasoning used in making specific assignments. Such an exchange is more appropriate for an interview than for a written test. The "ability to direct multiple work crews and work projects simultaneously" is, perhaps, the most difficult of the KSAs to measure accurately. Ideally, we would use a simulation that creates several situations and evaluates the applicant's responses. However, to be accurate, the simulation should be carried out for an extended period of time. This would not usually be feasible. Our approach, therefore, would be to view this ability as a work habit and to use the interview to determine information about the applicant's behavior in similar, previous situations.

We thus conclude that of the eight KSAs being measured in this selection program, only these three should be assessed by the interview. As Table 10.6 indicates, three other

TABLE 10.6   Selection Plan for the Job of Maintenance Supervisor

	Selection Instruments				
Job: Maintenance Supervisor	**KSA Importance**	**Application Form**	**Interview**	**Performance Test**	**Ability Test**
KSA					
Knowledge of construction principles of small buildings	15%	3%			12%
Knowledge of building systems: heating, electrical, plumbing	15	3			12
Knowledge of inventory control methods	10	3			7
Skill in performing basic carpentry, plumbing, electrical wiring operations	5			5%	
Ability to diagnose defects in building and building systems	10			10	
Ability to give verbal work instructions to laborers regarding construction and repair	20		20%		
Ability to schedule work crews for specific tasks	10		10		
Ability to direct multiple work crews and work projects simultaneously	15		15		
	100%	9%	45%	15%	31%

KSAs are tapped by a combination of the application form and ability tests. The remaining two KSAs are best measured by performance tests.

Limit the Use of Preinterview Data

Perhaps the most common sequence of steps in selection programs is that the applicant first completes an application form or provides a resume and then participates in a screening interview. In most cases, the interviewer has access to this information and uses it, at least initially, to formulate questions and direct conversation during the interview.

There is some question as to whether this preinterview information is of real benefit to the interviewer. Many argue that preinterview information is essential to good interviewing. It provides basic information about previous work and educational experience that can be developed in the interview. Some interview guides even recommend that interviewers develop hypotheses about the type of KSAs possessed by a specific applicant based on application information, and then use the interview to test these hypotheses. Recent research, however, that has closely studied this issue has not supported these proposed advantages of using preinterview data—and in fact has found detrimental effects. We have already presented the model developed by Robert Dipboye, which emphasizes that preinterview information is used to develop assessments of applicants before the interview is conducted. These assessments affect the interview process itself and can serve as sources of error in the evaluation of applicants. The meta-analysis by Mike McDaniel and his associates found higher predictive validities when interviewers do not have access to test scores or other background information.[142] These results indicate the direct effect that preinterview impressions can have on the interviewer. So, do interviewers typically have ancillary information available prior to the interview (test scores, letters of reference)? A recent study of the practices of 79 HR managers showed that 53 percent avoid looking at any preinterview information before making a hiring recommendation, while 27 percent include it when making a recommendation. The remaining 20 percent explicitly review it prior to the interview.[143] Thus, nearly half of the interviewers use preinterview information.

Our recommendation about the use of preinterview data is based on a combination of research and common sense.

Assuming that the interview focuses on a small number of KSAs, our recommendation is to limit to two types the preinterview information that is provided to interviewers. The first type is *complete data about any of the KSAs to be covered in the interview*. This could save time or allow for more detailed questioning. The second type is the *incomplete or contradictory statements presented on the application blank or other similar instruments*: employment gaps, overlapping full-time positions, a nonregular career movement pattern, and so on. This kind of irregularity could be clarified in the interview.

There is enough evidence to indicate that access to data not directly relevant to the purposes of the interview only contributes to deficiencies in interviewers' decisions. Therefore, data such as ability test scores, letters of reference, and brief reactions of others should be withheld until after the interview is completed.

Adopt a Structured Format

As stated previously, one of the most consistent recommendations made by those who have written about ways to improve the use of the interview in selection has been to impose structure on the verbal exchange between the parties. This is done by providing the interviewer with a set of questions that must be asked of all interviewees.

In this format *a set of questions should be formulated for each KSA* identified as appropriate for the interview. Referring to the previous example of the maintenance supervisor job, this would mean a set of questions concerning each of the three KSAs: "ability to give verbal instructions," "ability to schedule work crews," and "ability to direct multiple work crews simultaneously." These questions must be asked of each applicant. However, the interviewers are also permitted to go beyond these questions as they feel necessary, either to clarify a given response, to seek other important details, or to pursue a closely related area. The logic behind imposing this structure is to build consistency in the interview regarding the appropriate KSAs from each applicant. The major benefit of this consistency in questioning is that it makes comparisons among applicants much easier. If done properly, *this method would provide* the HR specialist with information from each applicant on the same KSAs. This would facilitate the identification of those applicants most suitable for the job.

Use Job-Related Questions

Having a structured format for the interview is of limited value if the predetermined set of questions provides information that is only marginally related to job performance. Therefore, another concern in the interview is to ensure that the questions used are job related; that is, information gathered must be useful in measuring the appropriate knowledge, skills, abilities, and other characteristics required in the job.

We have already discussed the two primary techniques that have been used to develop job-related questions: the *situational interview* and the *behavior description interview*. In the following paragraphs, we discuss questions that are useful for each of the three types of KSAs we think are appropriately measured in an interview. The two techniques (situational and behavior description interviews) described previously can be used in developing specific questions for each type of KSA.

Questions of Job Knowledge.   This is the most straightforward KSA, both for measuring and for developing interview questions. Basically, the interviewer is trying to find out whether the applicant knows some specific information. Appropriate questions could be the following:

> *What steps would you take to perform an empirical validation study?*
> *How do you string a 220-volt electric cable in a laboratory building that is under construction?*
> *What are the current tax laws regarding borrowing from an IRA?*

There are a number of important points to remember when asking this type of question. The first is that the knowledge being asked about should be important to the overall performance of the job. It should not be information that is difficult but only peripheral to the job. Asking an applicant for a production supervisor's job about the principles of just-in-time management is appropriate. Asking about the programming features of Microsoft Outlook® software, which might be used in scheduling, usually would not be appropriate. The second is that the question should not ask about material easily learned on the job or material taught as part of a training program for the job. Third, as was mentioned previously, it is not useful to ask questions about a series of specific facts or operations. A written test would be more appropriate.

Commonly, interviewers phrase would-be job knowledge questions something like this:

Have you ever directed a construction crew?
Do you know how to do a performance appraisal?
Have you taken any courses in accounting?

Questions of this type are not very useful for measuring job knowledge, because they require the interviewer to make inferences in order to evaluate the answer. For example, if the applicant responds that he or she had two accounting courses, the interviewer normally would ask what the courses were, what grades were received, and so on. Even at this point, however, there is no direct evidence that the applicant knows specific information necessary for the job. All accounting courses with the same name do not cover the same material. All grades of "B" do not indicate the same mastery of material. The interviewer must infer the applicant's knowledge from this circumstantial data. A better method is to ask questions about material that is important for the job and then judge whether the answer given is correct. Little inference is necessary; the applicant indicates directly whether he or she has the knowledge. In practice, the use of job knowledge questions requires the selection specialist to work with technical specialists in various parts of the organization. This is because the selection specialist usually does not have enough technical knowledge of accounting, engineering, maintenance, and so on to properly formulate and evaluate answers to this type of question. Therefore, it is necessary to involve those persons working in the functional area to develop and score interview questions.

Questions of Social Interaction.   Measuring KSAs related to applied social skills seems to be especially dependent on how the questions are stated. For example, an office receptionist position usually requires short-term, nonrecurring interaction with individuals. The KSAs necessary for such behavior would be evaluated appropriately in an interview. However, if these KSAs are specified by general characteristics such as "poise," "friendliness," "pleasantness," or "professional bearing," assessment becomes more difficult due to the ambiguity of these terms.

A better tactic would be to try to phrase the KSAs as abilities and skills. For example, the receptionist's position may require "the ability to provide preliminary information to angry customers about the resolution of product defects" or "the ability to query customers regarding the exact nature of complaints in order to route them to appropriate personnel." Phrased in this manner, it is easier to develop questions that require the demonstration of these skills and abilities. *Situational interview questions* would be appropriate.

Questions of Personality or Habitual Behaviors.   The group of KSAs encompassing these traits is, perhaps, the most difficult to assess accurately in applicants. This group includes work habits such as persistence in completing assignments, ability to work on multiple tasks simultaneously, and ability to plan future actions. The very general term *motivation* is frequently used to refer to these KSAs. Other attributes included in this category are "helping coworkers with job-related problems, accepting orders without a fuss, tolerating temporary impositions without complaint, and making timely and constructive statements about the work unit."[144]

One method frequently used to measure these attributes is asking the applicant in various ways whether he or she has worked or is willing to work in circumstances requiring these habits or personality traits. The limitation of this type of question is that the information is virtually unverifiable and subject to distortion by the respondent, who wishes to portray favorable characteristics. Most job applicants, especially experienced ones, know that almost all organizations desire employees who cooperate with other workers, can plan ahead, accept orders, and tolerate impositions. It is in the self-interest of applicants to portray themselves as having demonstrated, or being willing to demonstrate, these characteristics. A strategy that is increasingly being used to at least partially avoid such self-enhancement is to question the applicant in detail about participation in activities that are similar to those that are part of the job under consideration. David Grove has described such an interview that was used by the Procter & Gamble Company for entry-level selection.[145] This interview is aimed at forming judgments of the applicant based on five factors that are important for effectiveness at P&G: stamina and agility, willingness to work hard, working well with others, learning the work, and initiative. The applicant is asked to write answers to "experience items" on a special form. These experience items ask the applicant to describe several relevant experiences that may have occurred in either a work or nonwork setting for each of the five factors. For example, one experience item for assessing the factor "working well with others" may be "Describe a situation in which you had to work closely with a small group to complete a project." Responses to these experience items are then probed in each of two separate interviews. The interviews are conducted separately by a member of the plant employment group and a line manager, and each independently rates the applicant on a seven-point scale for each of the five factors.

We have developed a list of questions that could be used in a selection interview for the job of maintenance supervisor that we mentioned previously. These questions, presented in Table 10.7, are intended to gather information about the three KSAs that were identified in Table 10.6 as appropriate for being measured with an interview. The number of questions used for each KSA was determined from the importance assigned to each KSA in Table 10.6.

Finally, as stated previously, recent research shows that the usefulness of the "type" of question asked—whether those questions are focused on past behavior (behavior description interview) or on hypothetical, future-oriented situations (situational interview)—differs as the complexity of the job increases. Although this conclusion has not been universally supported,[146] research does suggest that the predictive validity of situational interview questions may be lower than that of behavioral description questions in complex jobs such as management. One possible explanation is that prior experience may be needed to successfully answer questions related to such jobs. For example, the best candidates for a management position may be those with prior supervisory experience. Nevertheless, in less complex or moderately complex jobs, predictive validity is comparable for both situational interviews and behavior description interviews. In fact, the situational interview should actually be "easier" for those applicants with little or no prior work experience. Although more research is needed, practitioners would do well to keep these findings in mind as they design their employment interview questions.

USE MULTIPLE QUESTIONS FOR EACH KSA

A basic psychological measurement principle that we discussed in Chapter 4 was that, in order for the assessment device to be a useful instrument, *the device should contain several items or parts that gather answers about the same variable.* To a certain extent, both reliability and validity of measurement are generally related to the number of items on the measuring device. In selection this means that, all else being equal, the more items an

TABLE 10.7	Selection Interview Questions for the Job of Maintenance Supervisor

KSA 1: Ability to give verbal work instructions to laborers regarding construction and repair
  1. What instructions would you give a work crew that was about to string a 220-volt electric cable in a laboratory building under construction?
  2. Two laborers, with limited experience, ask about the procedures for tuckpointing and restoring a damaged brick wall. What instructions would you give them regarding what equipment they should use and how they should operate it?
  3. You assign a group of four to inspect the flat tar-and-gravel roofs on four buildings. They are also to make minor repairs and describe to you the major repairs that will need to be made in the future. What instructions do you give them? (Assume that each worker knows how to operate any necessary equipment.)
  4. You will use eight summer employees to do the repainting of the third floor hall, ten private offices, and two public restrooms. What instructions do you give them about both general work and specific painting procedures?

KSA 2: Ability to schedule work crews for specific tasks
  1. You need to send a work crew to the far part of the industrial park to inspect and (if necessary) repair a 40' × 10' brick wall and to prepare a 40' × 60' flower bed. It is Monday morning. Rain is expected Tuesday afternoon. How many people do you assign to which tasks? How long should each task take?
  2. You are in charge of a work crew of twelve. Included in this are four experienced carpenters and two electricians. These six are also permitted to do other jobs. You are to finish a 100' × 200' area that will have five separate offices and a general meeting room. Tell me the first five tasks that you would assign your crew and how many people you would put on each task. How long should each task take?

KSA 3: Ability to direct multiple work crews and work projects simultaneously
  1. Go back to the situation in the previous question. Tell me which tasks you would try to complete in the first two days. Which sequence of tasks would you schedule? How would your work crews know when to start a new task?
  2. Describe a specific experience in the past few years in which you had at least five people reporting to you who were performing different parts of a bigger project. This could either be in work, school, community activities, or the military.
  3. Describe a specific experience in the past few years in which you and a group of others were working under a tight deadline on a project that had several parts. This could either be in work, school, community activities, or the military.

assessment device possesses that measure the same KSA, the greater is its reliability and validity.

Returning once more to our example of the maintenance supervisor in Table 10.7, the use of this principle of multiple questions means that applicants would be asked to respond to four questions to provide examples of instructions given to work crews, to two questions to measure ability to schedule work crews for specific tasks, and to three questions to measure the ability to direct multiple work crews and work projects simultaneously. There is no rule for the exact number of questions to be asked. This is primarily a function of two factors: (a) the information developed from the job analysis and (b) the time available for each applicant. Concerning the information developed from the job analysis, it is necessary to consider first the relative importance of the KSAs being measured in the interview. In our previous example in Table 10.6, "Ability to give verbal work instructions" had the highest weight (20), followed by "ability to coordinate and direct multiple work crews" (15), and "ability to schedule work crews" (10). The number of questions listed in Table 10.7 for each of these KSAs generally reflects these weights. The second consideration is the diversity of the tasks that relate to each KSA being assessed in the interview. If the maintenance supervisor must give instructions about many different types of tasks, it may take more questions to have a representative sample than if these are very similar tasks. Nevertheless, the broader point is the more "items" or questions asked to assess a construct during the interview, the more useful the score for that construct when predicting later job performance.

The total amount of time available for the interview is, in some cases, beyond the control of the interviewer—for example, on-campus interviews or many job fair situations. In these cases an estimate should be made before the interview of the number of questions possible based on the total time allocated for the interview and the estimated length of time required for answering each question.

Rely on Multiple Independent Interviewers

Another basic psychological measurement principle discussed in Chapter 4 is that the use of multiple interviewers will enhance reliability, as long as their ratings are independent of the influence of other interviewers (or managers). This conclusion was supported by the findings of Frank Schmidt and Ryan Zimmerman,[147] who found that the predictive validity of an unstructured interview could be raised to that of a single structured interview by aggregating the hiring recommendations of three to four interviewers who utilized an unstructured interview.

As noted previously, however, meta-analyses have found predictive validities for panel interviews that are comparable to or somewhat lower than the correlations reported for single interviewers. At least two studies that have previously been reviewed found that individual interviewers, using structured interviews ($\rho = 0.63$ or 0.46), had the same or higher validity coefficients than did panel interviews ($\rho = 0.60$ and 0.38).[148] These findings suggest a lack of support for the commonly held opinion that a panel interview (two or more interviewers asking at once) is superior to an individual interview. This counterintuitive finding has likely emerged because these meta-analyses have not distinguished those studies where groups of interviewers make independent decisions based on different interviews from those where the group arrives at an overall consensus decision based on one interview. Pooling or averaging interviewer judgments can only increase reliability in those cases where multiple interviewers have made judgments independently. Pooling or averaging judgments reduces the influence of measurement error, particularly if these judgments are from different interviews of the same candidate. As we know, increasing interrater reliability will enhance the predictive validity of the hiring recommendation, since reliability limits validity. But again, the critical element necessary for successfully using multiple interviewers is that interviewers provide independent ratings based on more than one interview (rather than a group of interviewers who give one interview).

Recent research also illustrates that the same interviewers should be used across all candidates. Allen Huffcutt and David Woehr compared the results from 23 studies in which the same interviewers interviewed all of the candidates with the results from 100 studies in which different interviewers interviewed different candidates. They found that using the same interviewers to rate across all candidates substantially increased the validity of the interview.[149] How frequently does this occur? The survey of the actual practices of HR managers revealed that 80 percent of interviews use two or three interviewers (and 18 percent use only one), and that 73 percent used the same interviewers across all candidates.[150] These results show that many companies are following "best practices," at least with regard to using multiple interviewers, and that the same interviewers are conducting all interviews.

Apply a Formal Scoring Format

The study of the interview has consistently concluded that an interview format that provides a formal, defined scoring system is superior in many ways to a format that does not. This is in terms of legal defensibility as well as the reliability and validity of interviewer judgments. We have made the point that measurement is the essence of a selection program. Without measurement of the KSAs of applicants, any comparison of these applicants becomes too complex to be done accurately. It is simply not possible for a selection specialist to retain all relevant information, weigh it appropriately, and use it to compare a number of individuals—at least in a consistent and effective manner. The issue, therefore, becomes not whether to score the interview but rather how best to score it.

The most commonly used systems require the interviewer to rate the interviewee on a series of interval measurement scales. The number of rating points on such scales varies but usually consists of between four and seven scale points. These scale points have a number at each point that is used to reflect various degrees of the applicant characteristics being judged. These scale points usually have either a set of adjectives describing differences among them (for example, not acceptable, marginal, minimal, good, superior) or a brief behavioral definition for each scale point (for example, instructions given were not understandable, instructions given were understandable but mainly incorrect, instructions were understandable and generally correct). Behavior-based rating scales are preferable—in part because they are based on critical behavioral incidents representative of the performance dimensions in question. A meta-analysis by Paul Taylor and Bruce Small illustrates the value of using behaviorally anchored rating scales; they find that— if they have such rating scales—the predictive validity of behavior description interviews increases ($\rho = 0.63$) in comparison with those interviews without behaviorally anchored rating scales ($\rho = 0.47$).[151] These findings show that there is value in anchoring the scoring format to job-relevant behaviors.

A second aspect of scoring concerns the dimensions to be scored. Table 10.8 contains an example of a scoring form that can be used in interviews for the position of maintenance supervisor discussed previously. It seems best to rate the applicant directly on the KSAs for which the interview was intended and for which the questions were designed. It is not necessary to score each question, just the KSAs that are measured by multiple questions.

The rating form should also provide space for comments about the applicant's performance on the KSA being rated. These comments are usually summary examples of the responses provided by the applicant to the questions that were designed to assess the KSA. The purpose of the comments is to provide not only documentation to support the rating, if it is questioned in the future, but also more information that can be used to compare a series of applicants. Not surprisingly, a recent study shows that note taking significantly improved the predictive validity of the employment interview.[152] Another analysis demonstrates that note taking results in better interviewer recall of what happened in the interview, but did not significantly improve the decisions made by the interviewer.[153] Consequently, interviewers should be trained on how to most effectively take notes in order to enhance their accuracy when scoring the interview.

Finally, if an overall score is sought, this rating should simply be a summation of the interviewer's ratings on each of the candidate's responses to the job-related questions rather than an overall judgment.[154] That is, the interviewer should add the separate ratings together, not simply score the candidate on the basis of his judgment as a whole across all factors of the interview. Evidence consistently shows that statistical aggregation of ratings invariably yields more valid and reliable ratings than does the use of global judgments.[155]

Train the Interviewer

Another point important to reiterate is the value of training the interviewer. Allen Huffcutt and David Woehr compared the results of 52 studies that included interviewer training with results of 71 studies that did not. They found that training should be provided to

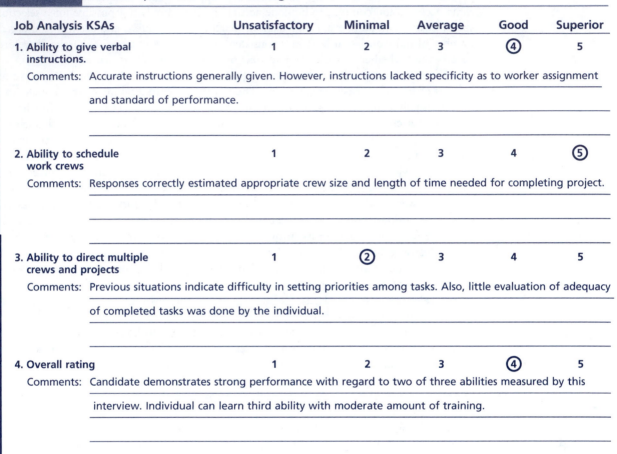

TABLE 10.8 An Example of Interview Rating Scales of KSAs

Job Analysis KSAs	Unsatisfactory	Minimal	Average	Good	Superior
1. Ability to give verbal instructions.	1	2	3	④	5

Comments: Accurate instructions generally given. However, instructions lacked specificity as to worker assignment

and standard of performance.

2. Ability to schedule work crews	1	2	3	4	⑤

Comments: Responses correctly estimated appropriate crew size and length of time needed for completing project.

3. Ability to direct multiple crews and projects	1	②	3	4	5

Comments: Previous situations indicate difficulty in setting priorities among tasks. Also, little evaluation of adequacy

of completed tasks was done by the individual.

4. Overall rating	1	2	3	④	5

Comments: Candidate demonstrates strong performance with regard to two of three abilities measured by this

interview. Individual can learn third ability with moderate amount of training.

interviewers; this was true regardless of whether the interview was structured or unstructured.[156] It is commonly agreed that the focal skills of an interviewer are the abilities to (a) accurately receive information, (b) critically evaluate the information received, and (c) regulate his or her own behavior in the delivering of questions.[157] Most training programs focus on at least one of these areas; many address all three. Although it is not within the scope of this book to present the specific features of such training programs, the following characteristics have frequently been included in successful programs.

Receiving Information.　In training interviewers to receive information accurately, instruction has concentrated on factors that influence (a) hearing what the respondent has said, (b) observing the applicant's behavior, and (c) remembering the information received. In accomplishing this, programs frequently address such topics as learning listening skills, taking notes, reducing the anxiety of the interviewee, establishing rapport with the interviewee, taking measures to reduce the fatigue and loss of interest of the interviewee, and minimizing the effect that interviewer expectations have on perceptions about what the applicant says.

One purpose of this training is to create an interview situation in which the candidate feels relaxed and comfortable. Logically, this should make it easier for the candidate to think of difficult-to-remember information and to provide complete answers about the topics asked. Another purpose of this training is to minimize what may be called *administrative errors* that can occur in the interview. These are errors such as misunderstanding what was said, not correctly remembering information provided by the applicant, tipping off the applicant as to the "best" answers to questions, and being able to deliver questions consistently so as to cover all topics. The general purpose of such training is to increase the amount of information obtained in the interview and to ensure its accuracy.

Evaluating Information.   Training interviewers in the critical evaluation of information obtained from the interviewee usually focuses on improving the decision-making process of the interviewer by pointing out common decision errors and providing methods for overcoming these errors. Common errors include the halo effect (ratings across all performance dimensions influenced by the rating on one "important" dimension), distributional rating errors (including central tendency and leniency error—rating everyone in the middle or high end of the distribution), the similar-to-me effect, the contrast effect, and the first-impressions error. Training programs often rely on videotapes or simulated interviews. The trainees evaluate candidates through these means, then follow this with a group discussion about the reasons for each trainee's ratings. Such programs frequently focus on the effect of candidate appearance and mannerisms and interviewer stereotypes and biases that cause inappropriate weighting. The major point of such training is that learning the nature of typical errors will minimize the distortion caused by these errors in actual interviews. Another type of training program emphasizes how an interviewer weighs various pieces of information about the applicant. In one study, interviewers were trained on the optimal weights for different KSA dimensions based on a multiple regression model. The training significantly improved their predictive validities, often with correlations of 0.40 or higher.[158]

A final theme advocates systematic scoring of the interview. It is almost universally recognized that the intuitive evaluation of a candidate by an interviewer, still very common in interviewing, is to be avoided. Formal evaluation forms usually contain a number of defined candidate characteristics that are related to job performance, a separate rating scale for each characteristic, and a rating of the overall acceptability of the candidate. Research shows that mechanically combining the scores for each characteristic into an overall rating will maximize predictive validity.

Interviewing Behavior.   The third area often addressed by interviewer training is how interviewer behavior influences the conduct of the interviewer–applicant interaction itself. Training sessions often address topics such as techniques for questioning the candidate and the role of interview structure on this interaction. For example, if the interviewer talks excessively, it limits the amount of job-related information obtained from interviewees. More importantly, if the interviewer perceives himself or herself to be similar to the candidate, he or she is likely to interact differently with the candidate. The point is that the interview is fundamentally a social and interpersonal process. Consequently, the behavior of the interviewer can affect the candidate's responses. These training programs focus on improving the interviewer's skill at maintaining control throughout the interview and on enhancing awareness of how the interviewer's behavior is influencing the interaction.

Results of Training.   How much improvement have these changes brought about in the way that interviews are carried out? The results of training have generally been encouraging, but not all problems have been corrected. For the most part, the various training programs have reduced some of the more common rater errors: contrast, halo, leniency, and central tendency. Furthermore, training has been found to enhance the re-liability of interviewer judgments.[159] However, other studies have demonstrated modest effects of training on interviewer behavior, especially when shorter training programs, which are less comprehensive, are examined.[160] This finding corresponds to that re-ported in the training literature, which shows modest incremental gains in actual behav-ioral change.[161] Another explanation is that the length of interviewer training is simply too short to be effective. This is a viable alternative explanation for these mixed effects, as there is evidence that the median interview training program is only six hours long.[162] Nevertheless, many popular interview training programs focus on using structured inter-view questions and systematic scoring; this has been shown to improve the reliability and validity of evaluations among sets of interviewers. Evidence clearly shows that during evaluation, trained interviewers are found to be more standardized and formalized; they consistently use more sophisticated questioning strategies.[163] Thus, training enables the interviewer to more fully realize the benefits of a highly structured interview, which sup-ports the use of training.

It seems obvious that organizations would provide training to interviewers—given the importance of this selection technique on hiring decisions. Yet, two recent studies suggest that this may not be the case, as only about a third of interviewers report receiv-ing formal interviewer training.[164] This underscores a need to emphasize the value of training.

To summarize, it seems that the critical components of training consist of identify-ing the specific behavioral objectives to be addressed in the training program, providing the trainees with opportunities to demonstrate and review their skills, and having a method for evaluating a trainee's demonstrated behavior and offering suggestions for change. Raymond Gordon observes that although practice and analysis can quickly im-prove interviewer skills, these skills deteriorate over time through disuse or lack of criti-cal self-analysis.[165] This implies that interviewers should attend training sessions on a regular basis in order to maintain necessary skills.

SMALL BUSINESS SELECTION

The interview has traditionally been one of the primary instruments used for selecting employees for small businesses. We think that it certainly can be a valid instrument when designed and used as we have discussed in this chapter. We do not want to repeat our previous points, but will simply say that basing the interview on job analysis infor-mation as well as on the development of standardized questions and scoring formats is essential. Many small business owners and operators may be reluctant to spend the time to develop an interview in this manner. However, we believe that all such owners and managers actually possess the knowledge about jobs and workers' characteristics that is necessary for developing a valid selection interview.

Given the steps discussed in this chapter, applying this knowledge to the interview should be straightforward. We realize, of course, that such a statement is easy to make, especially since we are not among the harried individuals who are running small busi-nesses. However, we think that it is appropriate to take a long-term perspective when evaluating the time required. That is, some time will be spent developing and conducting some form of the interview. One can spend less time in the short run and use only a partially job-related, unstructured interview. The evidence is clear that such an interview will yield poor results. On the other hand, the time spent (*after* individuals have been selected) correcting an individual's deficient performance, or, in the worst case, dismissing an individual, can be long and distressing. To the extent that a valid selection interview reduces such future costs, it would seem to be worth the slightly increased initial time spent in development. Taking this argument even further, one could say that a few poor selection decisions will have much larger consequences on a small business than on a larger organization, simply because these few people constitute a larger percentage of all employees. Small businesses have less room for error in selection and, consequently, should spend the preparation time necessary for developing appropriate selection instruments.

REFERENCES

1. Angelo J. Kinicki, Chris A. Lockwood, Peter W. Hom, and Rodger W. Griffeth, "Interviewer Predictions of Applicant Qualifications and Interviewer Validity: Aggregate and Individual Analyses," *Journal of Applied Psychology* 75 (1990): 477–486; Richard A. Posthuma, Frederick P. Morgeson, and Michael A. Campion, "Beyond Employment Interview Validity: A Comprehensive Narrative Review of Recent Research and Trends over Time," *Personnel Psychology* 55 (2002): 1–82; and Steffanie L. Wilk and Peter Cappelli, "Understanding the Determinants of Employer Use of Selection Methods," *Personnel Psychology* 56 (2003): 103–124.

2. Joe A. Cox, David W. Schlueter, Kris K. Moore, and Debbie Sullivan, "A Look behind Corporate Doors," *Personnel Administrator* (March 1989): 56–59; Society for Human Resource Management, "SHRM Poll: Interviewing Do's and Don'ts for Job Seekers," September 15 , 2009, http://www.shrm.org/TemplatesTools/Samples/PowerPoints/Documents/SHRMPollInterviewinglFINAL.pptx.

3. Robert L. Dipboye, "The Selection/Recruitment Interview: Core Processes and Contexts," in *The Blackwell Handbook of Personnel Selection*, ed. Arne Evers, Neil Anderson, and Olga Voskuijil (Oxford, UK: Blackwell Publishers, 2004), 121–142; and Posthuma, Morgeson, and Campion, "Beyond Employment Interview Validity: A Comprehensive Narrative Review of Recent Research and Trends over Time."

4. Frank L. Schmidt and John E. Hunter, "The Validity and Utility of Selection Methods in Personnel Psychology: Practical and Theoretical Implications of 85 Years of Research Findings," *Psychological Bulletin* 124 (1998): 262–274.

5. Posthuma, Morgeson, and Campion, "Beyond Employment Interview Validity: A Comprehensive Narrative Review of Recent Research and Trends over Time."

6. Murray R. Barrick, Jonathan A. Shaffer, and Sandra W. DeGrassi, "What You See May Not Be What You Get: A Meta-Analysis of the Relationship between Self-Presentation Tactics and Ratings of Interview and Job Performance," *Journal of Applied Psychology* 94 (2009): 1394–1411.

7. Julia Levishina and Michael A. Campion, "Measuring Faking in the Employment Interview: Development and Validation of an Interview Faking Behavior Scale," *Journal of Applied Psychology* 92 (2007): 1638–1656.

8. Alison E. Barber, John R. Hollenbeck, Spencer L. Tower, and Jean M. Phillips, "The Effects of Interview Focus on Recruitment Effectiveness: A Field Experiment," *Journal of Applied Psychology* 79 (1994): 886–896.

9. Ibid., 893.

10. Sara L. Rynes, "The Employment Interview as a Recruitment Device," in *The Employment Interview*, ed. Robert N. Eder and Gerald R. Ferris (Newbury Park, CA: Sage Publications, 1989), 127–142.

11. Daniel Turban, James E. Campion, and Alison R. Eyring, "Factors Related to Job Acceptance Decisions of College Recruits," *Journal of Vocational Behavior* 47 (1995): 193–213.

12. Derek S. Chapman, Krista L. Uggerslev, Sarah A. Carroll, Kelly A. Piasentin, and David A. Jones, "Applicant Attraction to Organizations and Job Choice: A Meta-Analytic Review of the Correlates of Recruiting Outcomes," *Journal of Applied Psychology* 90 (2005): 928–944.

13. Posthuma, Morgeson, and Campion, "Beyond Employment Interview Validity: A Comprehensive Narrative Review of Recent Research and Trends over Time."

14. Michael M. Harris and Laurence S. Fink, "A Field Study of Applicant Reactions to Employment Opportunities: Does the Recruiter Make a Difference?" *Personnel Psychology* 40 (1987): 765–784.

15. Sara L. Rynes, Robert D. Bretz Jr., and Barry Gerhart, "The Importance of Recruitment in Job Choice: A Different Way of Looking," *Personnel Psychology* 44 (1991): 24.

16. Robert C. Liden and Charles K. Parsons, "A Field Study of Job Applicant Interview Perceptions, Alternative Opportunities, and Demographic Characteristics," *Personnel Psychology* 39 (1986): 109–122.

17. Posthuma, Morgeson, and Campion, "Beyond Employment Interview Validity: A Comprehensive Narrative Review of Recent Research and Trends over Time"; and Jack L. Howard and Gerald R. Ferris, "The Employment Interview Context: Social and Situational Influences on Interviewer Decisions," *Journal of Applied Social Psychology* 26 (1996): 112–136.

18. Lynn Ulrich and Don Trumbo, "The Selection Interview since 1949," *Psychological Bulletin* 63 (1965): 100–116.

19. Allen I. Huffcutt, James M. Conway, Philip L. Roth, and Nancy J. Stone, "Identification and Meta-Analytic Assessment of Psychological Constructs Measured in Employment Interviews," *Journal of Applied Psychology* 86 (2001): 897–913.

20. Murray R. Barrick, Michael K. Mount, and Timothy A. Judge, "The FFM Personality Dimensions and Job Performance: Meta-Analysis of Meta-Analyses," *International Journal of Selection and Assessment* 9 (2001): 9–30.

21. Huffcutt, Conway, Roth, and Stone, "Identification and Meta-Analytic Assessment of Psychological Constructs Measured in Employment Interviews."

22. Allen I. Huffcutt, Philip L. Roth, and Michael A. McDaniel, "A Meta-Analytic Investigation of Cognitive Ability in Employment Interview Evaluations: Moderating Characteristics and Implications for Incremental Validity," *Journal of Applied Psychology* 81 (1996): 459–473.

23. Dipboye, "The Selection/Recruitment Interview: Core Processes and Contexts."

24. Gary P. Latham and Daniel P. Skarlicki, "Criterion-Related Validity of the Situational and Patterned Behavior Description Interviews with Organizational Citizenship Behavior," *Human Performance* 8 (1995): 67–80; and Posthuma, Morgeson, and Campion, "Beyond Employment Interview Validity: A Comprehensive Narrative Review of Recent Research and Trends over Time."

25. Brian S. Connely and Deniz S. Ones, "An Other Perspective on Personality: Meta-Analytic Integration of Observers' Accuracy and Predictive Validity," *Psychological Bulletin* (in press).

26. Megumi Hosoda, Eugene F. Stone-Romera, and Gwen Coats, "The Effects of Physical Attractiveness on Job-Related Outcomes: A Meta-Analysis of Experimental Studies," *Personnel Psychology* 56 (2003): 431–462.

27. Winfred Arthur Jr. and Anton J. Villado, "The Importance of Distinguishing between Constructs and Methods When Comparing Predictors in Personnel Selection Research and

Practice," *Journal of Applied Psychology* 93 (2008): 435–442; Paul R. Sackett and Filip Lievens, "Personnel Selection," *Annual Review of Psychology* 59 (2008): 419–450.

28. Barrick, Shaffer, and DeGrassi, "What You See May Not Be What You Get: A Meta-Analysis of the Relationship between Self-Presentation Tactics and Ratings of Interview and Job Performance."

29. Hosoda, Stone-Romera, and Coats, "The Effects of Physical Attractiveness on Job-Related Outcomes: A Meta-Analysis of Experimental Studies"; and Chad A. Higgins, Timothy A. Judge, and Gerald R. Ferris, "Influence Tactics and Work Outcomes: A Meta-Analysis," *Journal of Organizational Behavior* 24 (2003): 89–106.

30. Barrick, Shaffer, and DeGrassi, "What You See May Not Be What You Get: A Meta-Analysis of the Relationship between Self-Presentation Tactics and Ratings of Interview and Job Performance"; and Greg L. Stewart, Todd Darnold, Murray R. Barrick, and Susan D. Dustin, "Exploring the Handshake in Employment Interviews," *Journal of Applied Psychology* 93 (2008) 1139–1146.

31. Derek S. Chapman and David I. Zweig, "Developing a Nomological Network for Interview Structure: Antecedents and Consequences of the Structured Selection Interview," *Personnel Psychology* 58 (2005): 673–702.

32. B. M. Springbett, "Factors Affecting the Final Decision in the Employment Interview," *Canadian Journal of Psychology* 12 (1958): 13–22.

33. Soloman E. Asch, "Forming Impressions of Personality," *Journal of Abnormal and Social Psychology* 41 (1946): 258–290; Robert B. Zajonc, "Feeling and Thinking: References Need No Inferences," *American Psychologist* 35 (1980): 151–175; Robert B. Zajonc, "On the Primacy of Affect," *American Psychologist* 39 (1984): 117–123; and Peter Borkenau and Anette Liebler, "Convergence of Stranger Ratings of Personality and Intelligence with Self-ratings, Partner Ratings, and Measured Intelligence," *Journal of Personality and Social Psychology* 65, no. 3 (1993): 546–553.

34. Murray R. Barrick, Brian Swider, and Greg L. Stewart, "The Impact of First Impressions on Interviewer Judgments," (in press) *Journal of Applied Psychology;* and Susan Dustin, Murray R. Barrick, Laura Parks, Greg L. Stewart, Ryan Zimmerman, and Todd Darnold, "The Impact of First Impressions on Interviewer Judgments," the Annual Conference of the Society of Industrial Organizational Psychology, Dallas, 2006.

35. Greg L. Stewart, Todd Darnold, Murray R. Barrick, and Susan D. Dustin, "Exploring the Handshake in Employment Interviews," Journal of Applied Psychology 93 (2008): 1139–1146.

36. Barrick, Sweider, and Stewart, "The Impact of First Impressions on Interviewer Judgments"; and Dustin, Barrick, Parks, Stewart, Zimmerman, and Darnold, "The Impact of First Impressions on Interviewer Judgments."

37. Michael A. Campion, David K. Palmer, and James E. Campion, "A Review of Structure in the Selection Interview," *Personal Psychology* 50 (1997): 655–702.

38. Jesus F. Salgado and Silvia Moscoso, "Comprehensive Meta-Analysis of the Construct Validity of the Employment Interview," *European Journal of Work and Organizational Psychology* 11 (2002): 299–324.

39. Ibid.

40. Paul R. Sackett and Filip Lievens, "Personnel Selection," *Annual Review of Psychology* 59 (2008): 419–450.

41. Posthuma, Morgeson, and Campion, "Beyond Employment Interview Validity: A Comprehensive Narrative Review of Recent Research and Trends over Time."

42. Laura Kohn and Robert L. Dipboye, "The Effects of Interview Structure on Recruiting Outcomes," *Journal of Applied Social Psychology* 28 (1998): 821–843; and Silvia Moscoso, "A Review of Validity Evidence, Adverse Impact and Applicant Reactions," *International Journal of Selection and Assessment* 8 (2000): 237–247.

43. Willi H. Wiesner and Steven F. Cronshaw, "A Meta-Analytic Investigation of the Impact of Interview Format and Degree of Structure on the Validity of the Employment Interview," *Journal of Occupational Psychology* 61 (1988): 275–290; Michael A. McDaniel, Deborah L. Whetzel, Frank L. Schmidt, and Steven D. Maurer, "The Validity of Employment Interviews: A Comprehensive Review and Meta-Analysis," *Journal of Applied Psychology* 79 (1994): 599–616; and Allen I. Huffcutt and Winfred W. Arthur Jr., "Hunter and Hunter (1984) Revisited: Interview Validity for Entry-Level Jobs," *Journal of Applied Psychology* 79 (1994): 184–190.

44. Huffcutt and Arthur Jr., "Hunter and Hunter (1984) Revisited: Interview Validity for Entry-Level Jobs."

45. Frank L. Schmidt and Mark Rader, "Exploring the Boundary Conditions for Interview Validity: Meta-Analytic Validity Findings for a New Interview Type," *Personnel Psychology* 52 (2006): 445–464.

46. McDaniel, Whetzel, Schmidt, and Maurer, "The Validity of Employment Interviews: A Comprehensive Review and Meta-Analysis."

47. James M. Conway, Robert A. Jako, and Deborah Goodman, "A Meta-Analysis of Interrater and Internal Consistency Reliability of Selection Interviews," *Journal of Applied Psychology* 80 (1995): 565–579.

48. Frank L. Schmidt and Ryan D. Zimmerman, "A Counterintuitive Hypothesis about Employment Interview Validity and Some Supporting Evidence," *Journal of Applied Psychology* 89 (2005): 553–561.

49. Paul J. Taylor and Bruce Small, "Asking Applicants What They Would Do versus What They Did Do: A Meta-Analytic Comparison of Situational and Past Behaviour Employment Interview Questions," *Journal of Occupational and Organizational Psychology* 75 (2002): 272–294; and Allen I. Huffcutt, James M. Conway, Philip L. Roth, and Ute-Christian Klehe, "The Impact of Job Complexity and Study Design on Situational and Behavior Description Interview Validity," *International Journal of Selection and Assessment* 12 (2004): 262–273.

50. Michael A. Campion, James E. Campion, and Peter J. Hudson, "Structured Interviewing: A Note on Incremental Validity and Alternative Question Types," *Journal of Applied Psychology* 79 (1994): 998–1102.

51. Arla L. Day and Sarah A. Carroll, "Situational and Patterned Behavior Description Interviews: A Comparison of Their Validity, Correlates, and Perceived Fairness," *Human Performance* 16 (2003): 25–47.

52. Elaine D. Pulakos and Neal Schmitt, "Experience-Based and Situational Interview Questions: Studies of Validity," *Personnel Psychology* 48 (1995): 289–308.

53. Huffcutt, Conway, Roth, and Klehe, "The Impact of Job Complexity and Study Design on Situational and Behavior Description Interview Validity."

54. Taylor and Small, "Asking Applicants What They Would Do versus What They Did Do: A Meta-Analytic Comparison of Situational and Past Behaviour Employment Interview Questions."

55. Todd J. Maurer, Jerry M. Solamon, and Deborah D. Troxtel, "Relationship of Coaching with Performance in Situational Employment Interviews," *Journal of Applied Psychology* 83 (1998): 128–136.

56. Todd J. Maurer, Jerry M. Solamon, Kimberly D. Andrews, and Deborah D. Troxtel, "Interviewee Coaching, Preparation Strategies, and Response Strategies in Relation to Performance in Situational Employment Interviews: An Extension of Maurer, Solamon, and Troxel (1998)," *Journal of Applied Psychology* 86 (2001): 709–717; and Todd J. Maurer and Jerry M. Solamon, "The Science and Practice of a Structured Employment Interview Coaching Program," *Personnel Psychology* 59 (2006): 433–456.

57. David E. Terpstra, A. Amin Mohamed, and R. Bryan Kethley, "An Analysis of Federal Court Cases Involving Nine Selection Devices," *International Journal of Selection and Assessment* 7 (1999): 26–34.

58. Charles H. Lawshe has shown that a form of quantitative analysis may be applied in content validity; see Charles H. Lawshe, "A Quantitative Approach to Content Validity," *Personnel Psychology* 28 (1975): 563–575.

59. Silvia Moscoso and Jesus F. Salgado, "Psychometric Properties of a Structured Behavioral Interview to Hire Private Security Personnel," *Journal of Business and Psychology* 16 (2001): 51–59.

60. *Human Resources Guide*, ed. Robert J. Nobile, Sandra King, Steven C. Kahn, and David Rosen (Cincinnati, OH: West Group, A Thomson Company, 2000), 2-70-2-84; Fred P. Morgeson, Matthew H. Reider, Michael A. Campion, and Rebecca A. Bull, "Review of Research on Age Discrimination in the Employment Interview, " *Journal of Business Psychology* 22 (2008): 223–232.

61. *Watson v. Ft. Worth Bank & Trust*, 47 FEP Cases 102 (1988).

62. *Stamps v. Detroit Edison Co.*, 6 FEP 612 (1973).

63. *Weiner v. County of Oakland*, 14 FEP 380 (1976).

64. *King v. TWA*, 35 EPD 34, 588 (1984).

65. *Robbins v. White-Wilson Medical Clinic*, 660 F.2d 1210 (1981).

66. *Gilbert v. City of Little Rock, Ark.*, 799 F.2d 1210 (1986).

67. *Bailey v. Southeastern Joint Apprenticeship*, 561 F. Supp. 895 (1983).

68. *Jones v. Mississippi Department of Corrections*, 615 F. Supp. 456 (1985).

69. *Harless v. Duck*, 14 FEP 1,616 (1977).

70. *Maine Human Rights Commission v. Department of Corrections*, 474, A.2d 860 (1984).

71. *Minneapolis Commission on Civil Rights v. Minnesota Chemical Dependency Association*, 310 N.W.2d 497 (1981).

72. *Allesberry v. Commonwealth of Pennsylvania*, 30 FEP 1634 (1981).

73. Laura Gollub Williamson, James E. Campion, Stanley B. Malos, Mark V. Roehling, and Michael A. Campion, "Employment Interview on Trial: Linking Interview Structure with Litigation Outcomes," *Journal of Applied Psychology* 82 (1997): 900–912.

74. Rick D. Hackett, Laurent M. Lampierre, and Helen P. Gardiner, "A Review of Canadian Human Rights Cases Involving the Employment Interview," *Canadian Journal of Administrative Sciences* 21 (2004): 215–228.

75. Ellyn Brecher, Jennifer Bragger, and Eugene Kutcher, "The Structured Interview: Reducing Biases toward Job Applicants with Physical Disabilities, " *Employee Responsibilities Rights Journal* 18 (2006): 155–170; Michael M. Harris, "Reconsidering the Employment Interview: A Review of Recent Literature and Suggestions for Future Research," *Personnel Psychology* 42 (1989): 691–726; and Posthuma, Morgeson, and Campion, "Beyond Employment Interview Validity: A Comprehensive Narrative Review of Recent Research and Trends over Time."

76. Paul R. Sackett and Cathy L. DuBois, "Rater-Ratee Race Effects on Performance Evaluation: Challenging Meta-Analytic Conclusions," *Journal of Applied Psychology* 76 (1991): 873–877.

77. Dipboye, "The Selection/Recruitment Interview: Core Processes and Contexts"; Ricardo A. Frazer and Uco J. Wiersma, "Prejudice versus Discrimination in the Employment Interview: We May Hire Equally, but Our Memories Harbour Prejudice," *Human Relations* 54 (2001): 173–191; Benoit Monin and Dale T. Miller, "Moral Credentials and the Expression of Prejudice," *Journal of Personality and Social Psychology* 81 (2001): 33–43; and Posthuma, Morgeson, and Campion, "Beyond Employment Interview Validity: A Comprehensive Narrative Review of Recent Research and Trends over Time."

78. Posthuma, Morgeson, and Campion, "Beyond Employment Interview Validity: A Comprehensive Narrative Review of Recent Research and Trends over Time."

79. Jennifer DeNicolis Bragger, Eugene Kutcher, John Morgan, and Patricia Firth, "The Effects of the Structured Interview on Reducing Biases against Pregnant Job Applicants," *Sex Roles* 46, nos. 7/8 (2002): 215–226; Allen I. Huffcutt and Philip L. Roth, "Racial Group Differences in Employment Interview Evaluations," *Journal of Applied Psychology* 83 (1998): 179–189; and Joshua M. Sacco, Christine R. Scheu, Ann Marie Ryan, and Neal Schmitt, "An Investigation of Race and Sex Similarity Effects in Interviews: A Multilevel Approach to Relational Demography," *Journal of Applied Psychology* 88 (2003): 852–865.

80. Bragger, Kutcher, Morgan, and Firth, "The Effects of the Structured Interview on Reducing Biases against Pregnant Job Applicants"; Ellyn Brecher, Jennifer Bragger, and Eugene Kutcher, "The Structured Interview: Reducing Biases toward Job Applicants with Physical Disabilities," *Employee Responsibilities Rights Journal* 18 (2006): 155–170.

81. Dipboye, "The Selection/Recruitment Interview: Core Processes and Contexts."

82. Huffcutt and Roth, "Racial Group Differences in Employment Interview Evaluations."

83. Philip L. Roth, Chad H. Van Iddekinge, Allen I. Huffcutt, Carl E. Eidson Jr., and Philip Bobko, "Corrections for Range Restriction in Structured Interview Ethnic Group Differences: The Values May Be Larger Than Researchers Thought," *Journal of Applied Psychology* 87 (2002): 369–376.

84. Huffcutt and Roth, "Racial Group Differences in Employment Interview Evaluations."

85. Terpstra, Mohamed, and Kethley, "An Analysis of Federal Court Cases Involving Nine Selection Devices."

86. Cynthia K. Stevens, "Structure Interviews to Hire the Best People," in *Handbook of Principles of Organizational Behavior*, ed. Edwin A. Loeke (Oxford, UK: Blackwell Publishers, 2009), 45–68; Posthuma, Morgeson, and Campion, "Beyond Employment Interview Validity: A Comprehensive Narrative Review of Recent Research and Trends over Time"; and Robert L. Dipboye, "The Selection/Recruitment Interview: Core Processes and Contexts."

87. Dipboye, "The Selection/Recruitment Interview: Core Processes and Contexts."

88. Therese H. Macan, and Robert L. Dipboye, "The Relationship of Interviewers' Preinterview Impressions to Selection and Recruitment Outcomes," *Personnel Psychology* 43 (1990): 745; Therese H. Macan and Robert L. Dipboye, "The Effects of the Application on Processing of Information from the Employment Interview," *Journal of Applied Social Psychology* 24 (1994): 1291–1314; and Daniel M. Cable and T. Gilovich, "Looked Over or Overlooked? Prescreening Decisions and Postinterview Evaluations," *Journal of Applied Psychology* 83 (1998): 501–508.

89. Thomas W. Dougherty, Daniel B. Turban, and John C. Callender, "Confirming First Impressions in the Employment Interview: A Field Study of Interviewer Behavior," *Journal of Applied Psychology* 79 (1994): 659–665; and Anthony T. Dalessio and Todd A. Silverhart,

"Combining Biodata Test and Interview Information: Predicting Decisions and Performance Criteria," *Personnel Psychology* 47 (1994): 303–315.

90. Micki K. Kacmar, Sandy J. Wayne, and Shannon H. Ratcliffe, "An Examination of Automatic versus Controlled Information Processing in the Employment Interview: The Case of Minority Applicants," *Sex Roles* 30 (1994): 809–828; Neil C. Anderson and Vivian J. Shackleton, "Decision Making in the Graduate Selection Interview: A Field Study," *Journal of Occupational Psychology* 63 (1990): 63–76; Cheryl L. Adkins, Craig J. Russell, and James D. Werbel, "Judgments of Fit in the Selection Process: The Role of Work Value Congruence," *Personnel Psychology* 47 (1994): 605–623.

91. Dipboye, "The Selection/Recruitment Interview: Core Processes and Contexts."

92. Brian A. Swider, Murray R. Barrick, T. Brad Harris, and Adam C. Stoverink, "Impression Mismanagement: Self-Presentation Tactics and the Moderating Role of Rapport Building in the Interview," working paper (2010) Texas A&M University.

93. Hosoda, Stone-Romera and Coats, "The Effects of Physical Attractiveness on Job-Related Outcomes: A Meta-Analysis of Experimental Studies," *Personnel Psychology* 56 (2003): 431–462; and Barrick, Shaffer and DeGrassi, "What You See May Not Be What You Get: A Meta-Analysis of the Relationship between Self-Presentation Tactics and Ratings of Interview and Job Performance."

94. Greg L. Stewart, Todd Darnold, Murray R. Barrick, and Susan D. Dustin, "Exploring the Handshake in Employment Interviews," *Journal of Applied Psychology* 93 (2008): 1139–1146.

95. David F. Caldwell and Jerry M. Burger, "Personality Characteristics of Job Applicants and Success in Screening Interviews," *Personnel Psychology* 51 (1998): 119–136.

96. Maurer, Solomon, Andrews, and Troxtel, "Interviewee Coaching, Preparation Strategies, and Response Strategies in Relation to Performance in Situational Employment Interviews: An Extension of Maurer, Solomon, and Troxel (1998)," *Journal of Applied Psychology* 86 (2001): 709–717; and Maurer, Solomon, and Troxtel, "Relationship of Coaching with Performance in Situational Employment Interviews," *Journal of Applied Psychology* 83 (1998): 128–136.

97. Posthuma, Morgeson, and Campion, "Beyond Employment Interview Validity: A Comprehensive Narrative Review of Recent Research and Trends over Time."

98. Ibid.

99. Robert L. Dipboye and Susan J. Jackson, "Interviewer Experience and Expertise Effects," in *The Employment Interviewer Handbook*, ed. Robert W. Eder and Michael M. Harris (Thousand Oaks, CA: Sage Publications, 1999), 259–278.

100. Laura M. Graves and Ronald J. Karren, "Are Some Interviewers Better Than Others?" in *The Employment Interviewer Handbook*, ed. Robert W. Eder and Michael M. Harris (Thousand Oaks, CA: Sage Publications, 1999); and Harris, "Reconsidering the Employment Interview: A Review of Recent Literature and Suggestions for Future Research."

101. Neal Schmitt, Elaine D. Pulakos, Earl Nason, and David J. Whitney, "Likability and Similarity as Potential Sources of Predictor-Related Criterion Bias in Validation Research," *Organizational Behavior and Human Decision Processes* 68 (1996): 272–286.

102. Posthuma, Morgeson, and Campion, "Beyond Employment Interview Validity: A Comprehensive Narrative Review of Recent Research and Trends over Time."

103. Ibid.

104. Wayne F. Cascio and Herman Aguinis, *Applied Psychology in Human Resource Management*, 7th ed. (Upper Saddle Brook, NJ: Pearson Prentice Hall, 2010).

105. Amy L. Kristof-Brown, Ryan D. Zimmerman, and Erin C. Johnson, "Consequences of Individuals' Fit at Work: A Meta-Analysis of Person–Job, Person–Organization, Person–Group, and Person–Supervisor Fit," *Personnel Psychology* 58 (2005): 281–342.

106. Huffcutt, Conway, Roth, and Stone, "Identification and Meta-Analytic Assessment of Psychological Constructs Measured in Employment Interviews."

107. Uggerslev, Carroll, Piasentin, and Jones, "Applicant Attraction to Organizations and Job Choice: A Meta-Analytic Review of the Correlates of Recruiting Outcomes."

108. Cascio and Aguinis, *Applied Psychology in Human Resource Management.*

109. Barrick, Shaffer and DeGrassi, "What You See May Not Be What You Get: A Meta-Analysis of the Relationship between Self-Presentation Tactics and Ratings of Interview and Job Performance."

110. Barrick, Shaffer and DeGrassi, "What You See May Not Be What You Get: A Meta-Analysis of the Relationship between Self-Presentation Tactics and Ratings of Interview and Job Performance"; and Hosoda, Stone-Romera, and Coats, "The Effects of Physical Attractiveness on Job-Related Outcomes: A Meta-Analysis of Experimental Studies."

111. Jennifer R. Burnett and Stephen J. Motowidlo, "Relations between Different Sources of Information in the Structured Selection Interview," *Personnel Psychology* 51 (1998): 963–983; and Timothy DeGroot and Stephen J. Motowidlo, "Why Visual and Vocal Interview Cues Can Affect Interviewers' Judgments and Predict Job Performance," *Journal of Applied Psychology* 84 (1999): 986–993.

112. Barrick, Shaffer and DeGrassi, "What You See May Not Be What You Get: A Meta-Analysis of the Relationship between Self-Presentation Tactics and Ratings of Interview and Job Performance."

113. DeGroot and Motowidlo, "Why Visual and Vocal Interview Cues Can Affect Interviewers' Judgments and Predict Job Performance."

114. Alex P. J. Ellis, West, Ryan, and DeShon, "The Use of Impression Management Tactics in Structured Interviews: A Function of Question Type?" *Journal of Applied Psychology* 87, no. 6 (2002): 1200–1208; Higgins, Judge and Ferris, "Influence Tactics and Work Outcomes: A Meta-Analysis"; and Cynthia K. Stevens and Amy L. Kristof, "Making the Right Impression: A Field Study of Applicant Impression Management During Job Interviews," *Journal of Applied Psychology* 80, no. 5 (1995): 587–606; Barrick, Shaffer and DeGrassi, "What You See May Not Be What You Get: A Meta-Analysis of the Relationship between Self-Presentation Tactics and Ratings of Interview and Job Performance."

115. West, Ryan, and DeShon, "The Use of Impression Management Tactics in Structured Interviews: A Function of Question Type?"; and Stevens and Kristof, "Making the Right Impression: A Field Study of Applicant Impression Management during Job Interviews."

116. Michael J. Crant, "Doing More Harm than Good: When Is Impression Management Likely to Evoke a Negative Impression?" *Journal of Applied Social Psychology* 26 (1996): 1454–1471.

117. John E. Delery and Michele K. Kacmar, "The Influence of Applicant and Interviewer Characteristics on the Use of Impression Management," *Journal of Applied Social Psychology* 28 (1998): 1649–1669.

118. Higgins, Judge, and Ferris, "Influence Tactics and Work Outcomes: A Meta-Analysis"; Barrick, Shaffer, and DeGrassi, "What You See May Not Be What You Get: A Meta-Analysis of the Relationship between Self-Presentation Tactics and Ratings of Interview and Job Performance."

119. Higgins, Judge, and Ferris, "Influence Tactics and Work Outcomes: A Meta-Analysis."

120. Barrick, Shaffer, and DeGrassi, "What You See May Not Be What You Get: A Meta-Analysis of the Relationship between Self-Presentation Tactics and Ratings of Interview and Job Performance"; and Wei-Chi Tsai, Chien-Cheng Chen, and Su-Fen Chiu, "Exploring Boundaries of the Effects of Applicant Impression Management Tactics in Job Interviews," *Journal of Management* 31 (2005): 108–125.

121. M. Susan Taylor and Janet A. Sniezek, "The College Recruitment Interview: Topical Content and Applicant Reactions," *Journal of Occupational Psychology* 57 (1984): 157–168.

122. Filip Lievens and Ananeleen De Paepe, "An Empirical Investigation of Interviewer-Related Factors That Discourage the Use of High-Structure Interviews," *Journal of Organizational Behavior* 25 (2004): 29–46; and Karen I. Van der Zee, Arnold B. Bakker, and Paulien Bakker, "Why Are Structured Interviews Used So Rarely in Personnel Selection?" *Journal of Applied Psychology* 87 (2002): 176–184.

123. Stevens, "Structure Interviews to Hire the Best People."

124. Dipboye, "The Selection/Recruitment Interview: Core Processes and Contexts."

125. Ibid.

126. Posthuma, Morgeson, and Campion, "Beyond Employment Interview Validity: A Comprehensive Narrative Review of Recent Research and Trends over Time"; and Amos Tversky and Daniel Kahneman, "Judgment under Uncertainty: Heuristics and Biases," *Science* 185 (1974): 1124–1130.

127. Heloneida C. Kataoka, Gary P. Latham, and Glen Whyte, "The Relative Resistance of the Situational, Patterned Behavior, and Conventional Structured Interviews to Anchoring Effects," *Human Performance* 10 (1997): 47–63.

128. Herbert G. Heneman III, Donald P. Schwab, D. L. Huett, and John J. Ford, "Interviewer Validity as a Function of Interview Structure, Biographical Data, and Interviewee Order," *Journal of Applied Psychology* 60 (1975): 748–753; and Gary P. Latham, Kenneth N. Wexley, and Elliott D. Pursell, "Training Managers to Minimize Rating Errors in the Observation of Behavior," *Journal of Applied Psychology* 60 (1975): 550–555.

129. Posthuma, Morgeson, and Campion, "Beyond Employment Interview Validity: A Comprehensive Narrative Review of Recent Research and Trends over Time."

130. Springbett, "Factors Affecting the Final Decision in the Employment Interview."

131. Asch, "Forming Impressions of Personality"; Zajonc, "Feeling and Thinking: References Need No Inferences"; Zajonc, "On the Primacy of Affect"; and Borkenau and Liebler, "Convergence of Stranger Ratings of Personality and Intelligence with Self-Ratings, Partner Ratings, and Measured Intelligence."

132. Dustin, Barrick, Parks, Stewart, Zimmerman, and Darnold, "The Impact of First Impressions on Interviewer Judgments."

133. Macan and Dipboye, "The Relationship of Interviewers' Preinterview Impressions to Selection and Recruitment Outcomes"; "The Effects of the Application on Processing of Information from the Employment Interview."

134. Patricia Rowe, "Individual Differences in Selection Decisions," *Journal of Applied Psychology* 47 (1963): 305–307.

135. B. Bolster and B. Springbett, "The Reaction of Interviewers' to Favorable and Unfavorable Information," *Journal of Applied Psychology* 45 (1961): 97–103.

136. Barrick, Shaffer, and DeGrassi, "What You See May Not Be What You Get: A Meta-Analysis of the Relationship between Self-Presentation Tactics and Ratings of Interview and Job Performance."

137. Robert E. Carlson, Paul W. Thayer, Eugene C. Mayfield, and Donald A. Peterson, "Improvements in the Selection Interview, *Personnel Journal* 50 (1971): 268–275.

138. Jeremy C. Biesanz, Steven L. Neuberg, T. Nichole Judice, and Dylan M. Smith, "When Interviewers' Desire Accurate Impressions: The Effect of Note Taking on the Influence of Expectations," *Journal of Applied Social Psychology* 29 (1999): 2529–2549; Jennifer R. Burnett, Chenche Fan, Stephen J. Motowidlo, and Timothy DeGroot, "Interview Notes and Validity," *Personnel Psychology* 51 (1998): 375–396; and Catherine H. Middendorf and Therese H. Macan, "Note Taking in the Employment Interview: Effects on Recall and Judgment," *Journal of Applied Psychology* 87 (2002): 293–303.

139. Gary P. Latham, Lise M. Saari, Elliott D. Pursell, and Michael A. Campion, "The Situational Interview," *Journal of Applied Psychology* 65 (1980): 422–427.

140. Tom Janz, "Initial Comparisons of Patterned Behavior Description Interviews versus Unstructured Interviews," *Journal of Applied Psychology* 67 (1982): 577–580.

141. Tom Janz, Lowell Hellervik, and David C. Gilmore, *Behavior Description Interviewing* (Boston: Allyn & Bacon, 1986), 62.

142. Whetzel, Schmidt, and Maurer, "The Validity of Employment Interviews: A Comprehensive Review and Meta-Analysis."

143. Van der Zee, Bakker, and Bakker, "Why Are Structured Interviews Used So Rarely in Personnel Selection?"

144. Thomas S. Bateman and Dennis W. Organ, "Job Satisfaction and the Good Soldier: The Relationship between Affect and Employee 'Citizenship,'" *Academy of Management Journal* 26 (1983): 587–595.

145. David Grove, "A Behavioral Consistency Approach to Decision Making in Employment Selection," *Personnel Psychology* 34 (1981): 55–64.

146. Taylor and Small, "Asking Applicants What They Would Do versus What They Did Do: A Meta-Analytic Comparison of Situational and Past Behaviour Employment Interview Questions"; and Conway, Roth, and Klehe, "The Impact of Job Complexity and Study Design on Situational and Behavior Description Interview Validity."

147. Schmidt and Zimmerman, "A Counterintuitive Hypothesis about Employment Interview Validity and Some Supporting Evidence."

148. Two other meta-analyses show the same results; see Marc C. Marchese and Paul M. Muchinsky, "The Validity of the Employment Interview: A Meta-Analysis," *International Journal of Selection and Assessment* 1 (1993): 18–26; Willi Wiesner and Steven Cronshaw, "A Meta-Analytic Investigation of the Impact of Interview Format and Degree of Structure on the Validity of the Employment Interview"; and Whetgel, Schemidt, and Manrer "The Validity of Employment Interviews: A Comprehensive Review and Meta-Analysis."

149. Allen I. Huffcutt and David J. Woehr, "Further Analysis of Employment Interview Validity: A Quantitative Evaluation of Interviewer-Related Structuring Methods," *Journal of Organizational Behavior* 20 (1999): 549–560.

150. Van der Zee, Bakker, and Bakker, "Why Are Structured Interviews Used So Rarely in Personnel Selection?"

151. Taylor and Small, "Asking Applicants What They Would Do versus What They Did Do: A Meta-Analytic Comparison of Situational and Past Behaviour Employment Interview Questions."

152. Huffcutt and Woehr, "Further Analysis of Employment Interview Validity: A Quantitative Evaluation of Interviewer-Related Structuring Methods."

153. Middendorf and Macan, "Note Taking in the Employment Interview: Effects on Recall and Judgment."

154. Robert L. Dipboye, "The Selection/Recruitment Interview: Core Processes and Contexts"; and Posthuma, Morgeson, and Campion, "Beyond Employment Interview Validity: A Comprehensive Narrative Review of Recent Research and Trends over Time."

155. Ibid.

156. Huffcutt and Woehr, "Further Analysis of Employment Interview Validity: A Quantitative Evaluation of Interviewer-Related Structuring Methods."

157. Raymond L. Gordon, *Interviewing: Strategy, Techniques, and Tactics*, 3rd ed. (Homewood, IL: Dorsey Press, 1980), 480.

158. Thomas W. Dougherty, Ronald J. Ebert, and John C. Callender, "Policy Capturing in the Employment Interview," *Journal of Applied Psychology* 71 (1986): 9–15.

159. Conway, Jako, and Goodman, "A Meta-Analysis of Interrater and Internal Consistency Reliability of Selection Interviews."

160. Steven D. Maurer and Charles Fay, "Effect of Situational Interviews, Conventional Structured Interviews, and Training on Interview Rating Agreement: An Experimental Analysis," *Personnel Psychology* 41 (1988): 329–344. See also Michael A. Campion and James E. Campion, "Evaluation of an Interviewee Skills Training Program in a Natural Field Experiment," *Personnel Psychology* 40 (1987): 675–691.

161. George M. Alliger, Scott I. Tannenbaum, Winston Bennett Jr., Holly Traver, and Allison Shotland, "A Meta-Analysis of the Relations among Training Criteria," *Personnel Psychology* 50 (1997): 341–358.

162. The Bureau of National Affairs, Inc., *PPF Survey No. 146—Recruiting and Selection Procedures* (Washington, DC: Bureau of National Affairs, Inc., May 1988).

163. Chapman and Zweig, "Developing a Nomological Network for Interview Structure: Antecedents and Consequences of the Structured Selection Interview."

164. Chapman and Zweig, "Developing a Nomological Network for Interview Structure: Antecedents and Consequences of the Structured Selection Interview"; and Van der Zee, Bakker, and Bakker, "Why Are Structured Interviews Used So Rarely in Personnel Selection?"

165. Gordon, *Interviewing: Strategy, Techniques, and Tactics*, 486.

Ability Tests for Selection

HISTORY OF ABILITY TESTS IN SELECTION

The history of the use of ability tests in selection is almost as old as the fields of industrial psychology and HR management. In 1908, Par Lahy described his work in developing tests for use in the selection of street car operators for the Paris Transportation Society.[1] Among the abilities he measured in applicants were reaction time, ability to estimate speed and distance, and ability to choose correct driving behavior in reaction to street incidents. These tests were administered to individual applicants using specially designed equipment in a laboratory. The following nine years saw other ability and performance tests (which we will discuss in Chapter 13) used in selection for jobs such as telegraph and telephone operators, chauffeurs, typists, and stenographers.

World War I, with its need for rapid mobilization of military human resources, became a major impetus in the development of other tests used in selection. In 1917, a five-man Psychology Committee of the National Research Council was formed and chaired by Robert Yerkes. The group decided that the development and use of tests was the greatest contribution that psychology could offer to military efficiency. The immediate objectives of this committee were to quickly develop paper-and-pencil tests that could be administered to large groups of military recruits and that would provide scores to be used as a basis for rejecting recruits thought to be unfit for military service.

The first test developed by this group was a mental ability or intelligence test. The committee required that this test correlate with existing individually administered tests of intelligence. It would have objective scoring methods, a format that could be rapidly scored, alternate forms to discourage coaching, responses that required a minimum of writing, and a structure that permitted an economical use of time.[2] These same requirements have characterized industrial ability tests ever since. The result of the committee's work was the famous Army Alpha (famous, at least, among test specialists). Five forms were developed, each containing 212 items and taking about 28 minutes to administer. Approximately 1.25 million men were tested in 35 examining units located across the United States.

The conspicuous use of this test generated interest in the development of other ability tests for use in vocational counseling and industrial selection. The next two decades saw the development of mechanical, motor, clerical, and spatial relations ability tests, among others. World War II provided another boost to test development: All three U.S. military organizations had extensive psychological testing programs. One emphasis was the development of specialized tests to assist in placing recruits in the most appropriate jobs. By this time the military had tremendously increased both the technical complexity and the diversity of its jobs. Similar tests were used extensively by industrial organizations after the war, partially because many jobs in these organizations closely resembled military jobs and also because a large number of war veterans suddenly became available as applicants; efficient selection devices were needed. The growing use of some ability tests halted abruptly in the late 1960s and 1970s, mainly because of EEO laws and early Supreme Court decisions that specifically addressed a few of the most popular of these tests (especially mental ability tests, see Chapter 2). Recently, the use of ability tests in selection has increased substantially.

In this chapter, we discuss the major types of ability tests that have been used in selection and describe a few representative tests in some detail to show what these tests actually measure. We also discuss their usefulness in present-day selection. Overwhelmingly, evidence indicates that these tests, when used appropriately, are valid selection measures, can be nondiscriminatory in their effects, and can cut costs significantly when used in employment decision making.

Definition of Ability Tests

As a first step, we will discuss briefly what we mean when we use the term *ability test*. Except for physical ability tests, generally these tests measure some form of knowledge. In this chapter, we discuss devices that measure mental, mechanical, clerical, and physical abilities. Although these are the tests most often used, other ability tests—for example, musical and artistic tests—have been included in selection programs. Space does not permit us to discuss them all. Except for physical ability tests in industrial settings, ability tests are almost always paper-and-pencil tests administered to applicants in a standardized manner. They have been developed to be given to several applicants at the same time. Tests of physical abilities, as the name implies, measure muscular strength, cardiovascular endurance, and movement coordination. Usually special equipment is required for these measurements.

The devices we call ability tests have often been referred to as *aptitude* or *achievement* tests. These two terms have been employed to connote slight differences in uses of the two types of tests. Several years ago, ability tests were thought to measure the effects of formal learning experiences such as courses in English grammar or computer programming. Scores were interpreted to be a measure of how much an individual knew as a result of the learning experience. Aptitude tests, on the other hand, were thought to indicate how much knowledge or skill the individual had acquired "naturally" or without formal training. Therefore, aptitude scores were to be indicative of inherent (maybe genetic) levels of KSAs.

In reality, distinctions between achievement and aptitude tests are arbitrary. *All tests measure what a person has learned up to the time he or she takes the test.* A distinction between formal and informal learning is meaningless. A test respondent necessarily must have learned what to write, say, or do before being able to respond to a test question. There must be previous information or acquired actions to draw on. Psychologists agree that test behaviors reflect a large degree of previous learning. Tests cannot be measures of "innate" or unlearned potential.[3]

For these reasons, terms such as *aptitude* and *achievement* have been replaced by the term *ability*. We now take a look at some types of ability tests that have been used in selection.

MENTAL ABILITY TESTS

Mental ability tests were at the center of many of the early Supreme Court decisions regarding the discriminatory effects of the use of tests in selection. As we mentioned previously, after these decisions, the use of mental ability tests in selection dropped significantly. HR managers were reluctant to use tests that had been implicated in disparate impact situations. However, much work in selection indicates that for almost all jobs, mental ability tests are related to job performance. Because of their previous wide use in selection and the fact that many of the principles governing the appropriate use of ability tests in general have been developed for mental ability tests, we spend more time discussing mental ability tests than we do other types of ability tests.

Development of Mental Ability Tests

To fully understand the use of mental ability tests in selection, it is important to know something of the history of their development. What is generally thought to be the first work on mental ability or intelligence tests was done by the French psychologists Alfred Binet and Theodore Simon from 1905 to 1911. They attempted to develop tests that would identify mentally retarded children in the French school system who should be assigned to special education classes. Most of the items that made up the tests were written through consultation with teachers in the school system. Binet and Simon sought to develop an age scale for each year between three and adulthood. An age scale contained a sample of curriculum questions that were appropriate for instruction at each academic grade level. For example, if the average age for children in grade 1 was six years, then the six-year age scale would be composed of items learned in grade 1.

A child's mental age was based on correct answers to the various grade-level scales. For example, if a child correctly answered the items for the first grade and incorrectly answered the items on the second-grade scale, the child's mental age was estimated at six years (average age of first-grade students). Mentally retarded students were identified as those whose calculated mental age was substantially below their chronological age. Mentally superior students (gifted or genius) were those who could correctly answer questions at grade levels above their chronological ages.[4]

Binet and Simon's test items measured a variety of abilities: including omissions in a drawing, copying written sentences, drawing figures from memory, repeating a series of numbers, composing a sentence containing three given words, naming differences between pairs of abstract terms, and interpreting given facts.[5] This mental ability test was designed to be administered by a trained professional to one individual at a time. In 1916, this test was modified for use in the United States and published as the *Stanford-Binet Intelligence Scale*. It is modified periodically and still used extensively today. The first group-administered mental ability test to have widespread use in the industry was the *Otis Self-Administering Test of Mental Ability*. This test took approximately 30 minutes to complete and consisted of written multiple-choice questions that measured such abilities as numerical fluency, verbal comprehension, general reasoning, and spatial orientation. The *Otis* served as the model for several other mental ability tests that have been used in HR selection.[6]

What Is Measured

Three points about the early mental ability tests are important for understanding this type of test. The first is the close association between the content of these tests and academic achievement.[7] As we just mentioned, the first mental ability test was developed using formal educational materials. Many later tests have closely followed the same strategy. Moreover, mental ability tests have commonly been validated using educational achievement as a criterion measure. Early studies correlated scores on a mental ability test with such measures as amount of education completed, degrees obtained, or, occasionally, grade point average. The rationale was that mental ability should be related to success in school. Robert Guion has commented that it seems acceptable to equate this

TABLE 11.1	Abilities Measured by Various Mental Ability Tests
Memory Span	Figural Classification
Numerical Fluency	Spatial Orientation
Verbal Comprehension	Visualization
Conceptual Classification	Intuitive Reasoning
Semantic Relations	Ordering
General Reasoning	Figural Identification
Conceptual Foresight	Logical Evaluation

type of test with scholastic aptitude, meaning that an adequate definition of what is measured by these tests is the ability to learn in formal education and training situations.[8]

The second point is that mental ability tests actually measure several distinct abilities (see Table 11.1 for a list). As we can see, the main abilities included are some form of verbal, mathematical, memory, and reasoning abilities. This clearly indicates that mental ability tests can actually differ among themselves in what is measured. All of the topics in Table 11.1 are mental abilities. However, they obviously are not the same ability. What this means is that *mental ability tests are not interchangeable*. They could differ in the abilities that are measured because the items of the tests differ in content.

Third, a variety of scores can be obtained from tests called mental ability tests. General mental ability tests measure several different mental abilities and report scores on all items as one total score. This total score, theoretically, indicates overall mental ability. Other tests provide separate scores on each of the tested abilities and then add these scores together to report a general ability total score. A third type of test measures each of several separate abilities and does not combine scores into a general ability measure. We now discuss one of the more famous and widely used mental ability tests in order to illustrate the concepts we have mentioned.

The Wonderlic Personnel Test

The *Wonderlic Personnel Test* was developed in 1938 and is still widely used. It is the mental ability test that was used by the Duke Power Company and questioned by Griggs in the landmark EEO selection case. (Yes, you're right—Chapter 2!) The *Wonderlic* is a 12-minute multiple-choice test that consists of 50 items. The items cover vocabulary, "commonsense" reasoning, formal syllogisms, arithmetic reasoning and computation, analogies, perceptual skill, spatial relations, number series, scrambled sentences, and knowledge of proverbs. Table 11.2 contains items similar to those used in the *Wonderlic*. They are not part of the test itself. Statistical analysis has found that the primary factor measured by the test is verbal comprehension; deduction and numerical fluency are the next two factors in order of importance.[9]

Multiple parallel forms of the *Wonderlic* are printed in seven languages, said by the publisher to be "equal and similar to a very high degree."[10] It is recommended that organizations alternate the use of two or more forms of the tests to maintain the security of the items. All forms of the test are easily scored by counting the number of correct answers out of the total of 50 items. No attempt is made to convert this score to an I.Q. score, even though the *Wonderlic* is purportedly a test of general mental ability. On all forms the 50 items are arranged in order of ascending difficulty. These items range from quite easy to fairly difficult; the average difficulty is a level at which approximately 60 percent of the test takers would answer the item correctly.

TABLE 11.2 Example Items Similar to Items on the Wonderlic Personnel Test

1. Which of the following months has 30 days?
   (a) February   *(b) June   (c) August   (d) December

2. Alone is the opposite of:
   (a) happy   *(b) together   (c) single   (d) joyful

3. Which is the next number in this series: 1, 4, 16, 4, 16, 64, 16, 64, 256,
   (a) 4   (b) 16   *(c) 64   (d) 1024

4. Twilight is to dawn as autumn is to:
   (a) winter   *(b) spring   (c) hot   (d) cold

5. If Bob can outrun Murray by 2 feet in every 5 yards of a race, how much ahead will Bob
   be at 45 yards? [Bob, you wish—Murray]
   (a) 5 yards   *(b) 6 yards   (c) 10 feet   (d) 90 feet

6. Bob is to Jr. as
   (a) knowledge is   (b) light is to dark   *(c) both of these
       to blank mind

Note: An asterisk (*) indicates the correct response.

One very appealing feature of the test is the extensive set of norm scores that has been developed through its long history. The test publisher provides tables indicating the distribution of scores by education level of applicants, position applied for, region of the country, gender, age, and ethnicity. Parallel form reliability among the forms is given, ranging from 0.73 to 0.95; test-retest reliability is 0.82 to 0.94.[11] During the many years of its use, many selection programs that use the *Wonderlic* as a predictor device have been described in various academic journals. Data within these journal articles have become part of validity generalization studies, which we discuss later in the chapter. These studies have been used to examine some critical selection issues.

An interesting point for you sports enthusiasts: The *Wonderlic* is given to all players at the NFL Scouting Combine; scores are reported to NFL teams before the annual draft.

The Nature of Mental Ability Tests

As is obvious from the preceding sections, mental ability tests and those that have been called intelligence, or I.Q., tests are the same type of tests. We think that because of widespread misconceptions about the terms *intelligence* and *I.Q.*, selection specialists can more appropriately conceptualize these tests as mental ability. The term *mental ability* makes explicit that these tests measure various cognitive abilities. These cognitive abilities are most directly identified by the general factors that compose the test or, in some cases, from the content of the items themselves. These cognitive abilities should really be thought of in the same manner as the abilities discussed in other parts of this book. That is, these are measures of an individual's ability to mentally manipulate words, figures, numbers, symbols, and logical order.

Following from this, it is fairly easy to understand the strong relationship between mental ability test scores and academic performance. Formal education heavily stresses cognitive exercises and memorization of facts, and these are the components that make up a large part of most mental ability tests. Many mental ability tests have been validated against educational achievement, because it is sensible to think that, in general, those with the greatest mental ability will progress farther and do better in school situations than those with lesser ability. For these reasons it has been said that these tests measure academic ability. This, however, does not mean that mental ability is useful only for academic selection. Almost all jobs in organizations, including managerial, technical, and some clerical jobs, demand the use of mental abilities. We develop this topic next.

THE VALIDITY OF MENTAL ABILITY TESTS

The extensive use of cognitive ability tests has prompted studies of their validity. These studies have uniformly concluded that mental ability tests are among the most valid of all selection instruments. In this section, we summarize that research.

Project A

Project A was a multiple-year effort to develop a selection system appropriate for all entry-level positions in the U.S. Army. John P. Campbell and his associates describe some of the findings of Project A that are important for our discussion of the validity of mental ability tests.[12]

One of the major tasks of this project was the development of 65 predictor tests that could be used as selection instruments. Statistical analyses were applied to the scores on these tests of 4,039 incumbents of entry-level army jobs. These analyses resulted in six categories of predictor instruments: general cognitive ability, spatial ability, perceptual-psychomotor ability, temperament/personality, vocational interest, and job reward preference. Another major task was the development of categories of work performance across entry-level jobs. Five categories were determined: core technical task proficiency; general soldiering proficiency; peer support and leadership, effort, and self-development; maintaining personal discipline; and physical fitness and military bearing.[13]

You can probably guess what a group of selection specialists would do if they found themselves with six predictors and five measures of job performance for 4,000 people. Yep, they conducted a giant validity study. Table 11.3 presents only a small part of the results. The validity coefficients are corrected for range restriction and adjusted for shrinkage. The general cognitive ability predictor category of tests correlated 0.63 and 0.65 with the two factors that most directly measured job task performance. Spatial ability, an ability that sometimes has been included in measures of general cognitive ability,

TABLE 11.3   Project a Validity Coefficients

Job Performance Factor	Predictor					
	General Cognitive Ability	Spatial Ability	Perceptual Psychomotor Ability	Temperament/ Personality	Vocational Interest	Job Reward Preference
Core technical proficiency	0.63	0.56	0.53	0.26	0.35	0.29
General soldiering proficiency	0.65	0.63	0.57	0.25	0.34	0.30

Source: Jeffrey J. McHenry, Laetta M. Hough, Jody L. Toquam, Mary A. Hanson, and Steven Ashworth, "Project A Validity Results: The Relationship between Predictor and Criterion Domains," *Personnel Psychology* 43 (1990): 335–354.

also had high validity coefficients. It is important to remember that these data were calculated across all entry-level jobs in the army. Our conclusion is that these data indicate that general mental ability tests are valid selection instruments across a large variety of military jobs.

Validity Generalization Studies

We discussed validity generalization in Chapter 5. (On the off chance that you don't remember that discussion, you should go back and look it over. It will make the following easier to understand!) For many years, selection specialists had noted that validity coefficients for the same combination of mental ability tests and job performance measures differed greatly for studies in different organizations. This was true even when the jobs for which the selection program was designed were very similar. Selection specialists explained these differences in validity coefficients as caused by undetermined organizational factors that affected the correlation between selection instruments and criteria. They concluded that a validation study is necessary for each selection program being developed.

Importance in Selection.   The conclusions that have been drawn from meta-analytic studies of mental ability tests and job performance are very different from those we just mentioned. Frank Schmidt, John Hunter, and their colleagues conducted many of these studies and state that the differences in validity coefficients among studies that have used mental ability tests for similar jobs are not a function of unknown organizational factors. Rather, these differences are due to methodological deficiencies in the validation studies themselves. When these deficiencies are corrected, the differences among these validity coefficients are close to zero. Validity generalization studies have applied these corrections to validation works conducted previously. These studies corrected for differences in sample size, reliability of criterion measures, reliability of predictor measures, and restriction in range.

Validity Generalization for the Same Job.   One approach of validity generalization studies has been to analyze data from validity studies conducted for the same job—for example, computer programmers—that all used the same type of test as a predictor. Table 11.4 summarizes the corrected mean validity coefficients of some of these studies. The most prominent finding of these studies is that, as Schmidt and Hunter hypothesized, there is evidence that the differences among studies in terms of validity coefficients are greatly reduced. In some instances, all differences have been eliminated. This interpretation means that the validity coefficients for mental ability and other types of tests are stable across organizations.

A second finding of these studies has been that the corrections to the validity coefficients raised the magnitude of these coefficients. This is the same concept we discussed in Chapter 5 regarding the factors that may artificially reduce a validity coefficient. Many validity coefficients from single studies are understatements of the true relationships between predictors and criteria, because they are affected by factors that are corrected in validity generalization studies. As Table 11.4 indicates, some of these corrected coefficients for mental ability tests are relatively high, in the 0.50s and 0.60s. Such coefficients demonstrate a much stronger relationship between mental ability and performance than was previously thought.

A third finding refers to previous statements we have made that selection instruments can predict training results very well. The coefficients for training criteria in Table 11.4 are, as a whole, higher than those for job performance, sometimes reaching 0.70 to 0.90.

TABLE 11.4	Selected Validity Generalization Results for Various Jobs		

| Job | Test Type | Estimated Average Validity Coefficient | |
		Performance Criteria	Training Criteria
Computer programmer[a]	Figure analogies	0.46	—
	Arithmetic reasoning	0.57	—
	Total score all tests	0.73	0.91
Mechanical repairman[b]	Mechanical principles	—	0.78
First-line supervisor[b]	General mental ability	0.64	—
	Mechanical comprehension	0.48	—
	Spatial ability	0.43	—
Computing and account-recording clerks[c]	General mental ability	0.49	0.66
	Verbal ability	0.41	0.62
	Quantitative ability	0.52	0.66
	Reasoning ability	0.63	—
	Perceptual speed	0.50	0.38
	Memory	0.42	—
	Spatial/mechanical	0.42	0.36
	Motor	0.30	—
	Clerical ability	0.53	0.62
Operator (petroleum industry[d])	Mechanical comprehension	0.33	—
	Chemical comprehension	0.30	—
	General intelligence	0.26	—
	Arithmetic reasoning	0.26	—
Police and detectives[e]	Memory	—	0.41
	Quantitative ability	0.26	0.63
	Reasoning	0.17	0.61
	Spatial/mechanical ability	0.17	0.50
	Verbal ability	—	0.64

[a] Frank Schmidt, Ilene Gast-Rosenbery, and John Hunter, "Validity Generalization for Computer Programmers," *Journal of Applied Psychology* 65 (1980): 643–661.
[b] Frank Schmidt, John Hunter, Kenneth Pearlman, and Guy Shane, "Further Tests of the Schmidt-Hunter Bayesian Validity Generalization Procedure," *Personnel Psychology* 32 (1979): 257–281.
[c] Kenneth Pearlman, Frank Schmidt, and JohnHunter, "Validity Generalization Results for Tests Used to Predict Job Proficiency and Training Success in Clerical Occupations," *Journal of Applied Psychology* 65 (1980): 373–406.
[d] Frank Schmidt, John Hunter, and James Caplan, "Validity Generalization Results for Two Job Tests Used to Predict Job Proficiency and Training Success in Clerical Occupations," *Journal of Applied Psychology* 66 (1981): 261–273.
[e] Hannah Rothstein Hirsh, Lois Northrup, and Frank Schmidt, "Validity Generalization Results for Law Enforcement Occupations," *Personnel Psychology* 39 (1986): 399–420.

Note: Data for missing cells are not reported.

Validity across Jobs. A second focus of validity generalization studies has been to examine differences in validity coefficients for the same set of predictor-criterion measures across different jobs. This can be regarded as a logical extension of the previously described studies. If situation specificity within organizations is false, perhaps specificity within jobs is also false. As you might guess from our previous comments, the conclusion of these validity generalization studies has been that mental ability tests are valid across a large variety of jobs and can serve as useful selection instruments.[14] Table 11.5 presents some results obtained by John Hunter that are representative of these studies.

The upper part of Table 11.5 presents the results of the validity correction formulas applied to studies within each of nine occupations. The argument for the validity of mental ability tests is strongly made, because the average coefficient presented in the table is significant for each occupation. One conclusion is that mental ability tests are valid for each of these occupations, although there are differences in the magnitude of the coefficients among the occupations.

The lower part of Table 11.5 extends these conclusions. This part is based on 515 validation studies conducted by the U.S. Employment Service on the validity of the General Aptitude Test Battery (GATB), a mental ability test battery. Data on jobs were reported using six different job analysis systems. All systems had one dimension that measured complexity. Jobs in these 515 validation studies were grouped into low, medium, and high complexity based on their scores on this dimension. A second method of grouping jobs on complexity level was used for jobs in industrial families. Using the

TABLE 11.5	Selected Validity Generalization Results for Mental Ability Tests Across Jobs	
Occupations	**Performance Criteria**	**Training Criteria**
Manager	0.53	0.51
Clerical	0.54	0.71
Salesperson	0.61	—
Sales clerk	0.27	—
Protective professions	0.42	0.87
Service workers	0.48	0.66
Vehicle operators	0.28	0.37
Trades and crafts	0.46	0.65
Industrial	0.37	0.61
Job Families	**Performance Criteria**	**Training Criteria**
General job families		
high complexity	0.58	0.50
medium complexity	0.51	0.57
low complexity	0.40	0.54
Industrial families		
setup work	0.56	0.65
feeding/offbearing	0.23	—

Source: John Hunter, "Cognitive Ability, Cognitive Aptitudes, Job Knowledge, and Job Performance," *Journal of Vocational Behavior* 29 (1986): 340–362.

Note: Data for empty cells are not reported.

"things" scale of the *Dictionary of Occupational Titles*, published by the Department of Labor, these jobs were grouped into setup work (more complex) and feeding/offbearing work (less complex).

Validity generalization analyses were applied to the studies within each complexity level. This meant that many different jobs were grouped together within each of these five complexity categories. As Table 11.5 shows, the GATB was valid for each category with both performance and training criterion measures.

However, there are differences among the performance validity coefficients, with those for more complex jobs being higher than those for less complex jobs. Coefficients for training criteria are uniformly high. These results are interpreted to show that mental ability tests are valid for a great many jobs and increase in the predictability of job performance as the job becomes more complex. For training success, mental ability tests are consistently very high in validity.

Comparison of Mental Ability and Other Selection Tests. In yet another meta-analysis study, Schmidt and Hunter compared the validity of mental ability tests to that of 18 other selection procedures.[15] This study had two purposes. The first was to estimate the validity of each type of selection test. The second was to examine how much increase in validity could be gained by adding these other instruments to a mental ability test in a selection battery. Schmidt and Hunter's findings for some of the types of selection instruments that we discuss in this book are presented in Table 11.6.

The "Validity" column of Table 11.6 states the corrected validity that Schmidt and Hunter determined for each of the selection devices listed. Only one of these devices, the work sample test, has a higher validity than does the mental ability test. However, each of these other selection devices can improve the validity of the selection program when it is added to a mental ability test. The second column of numbers in the table presents the combined validity of a mental ability test and the other selection measure. For example, the combined validity for a mental ability test and a work sample test is 0.63. The third column of numbers presents the increase in validity over the mental ability test obtained by using the second test. In the case of work sample, this gain is 0.12. According to the two authors, these findings clearly indicate that mental ability tests should be regarded as a primary selection device; when combined with other selection tests, they help form a useful selection battery.

TABLE 11.6 Validity of Mental Ability and Other Selection Tests

Selection Test	Validity	Validity of Both Tests	Gain in Validity
Mental ability	0.51		
Work sample	0.54	0.63	0.12
Integrity	0.41	0.65	0.14
Personality (conscientiousness)	0.31	0.60	0.09
T&E application (behavioral consistency)	0.45	0.58	0.07
Biographical data	0.35	0.52	0.01
Assessment center	0.37	0.53	0.02

Source: Frank L. Schmidt and John E. Hunter, "The Validity and Utility of Selection Methods in Personnel Psychology: Practical and Theoretical Implications of 85 Years of Research Findings," *Psychological Bulletin* 124 (1998): 262–274.

Another way of studying the usefulness of mental ability tests in selection was undertaken by Richard Reilly and Michael Warech.[16] They grouped selection instruments into 18 types and examined the data for each type with regard to validity, adverse impact, feasibility (cost of development and use), and fairness to applicant. They also compared each of the 18 types of instruments with the use of cognitive ability tests in selection. Although it is not possible to report their findings for all 18 types of instruments, Table 11.7 presents their major findings for eight commonly used types.

Because we consider validity to be a fundamental property of selection tests, we present the comparisons of validity first. Only four of the eight types are approximately equal to cognitive ability tests: assessment centers, biographical data, trainability tests, and work samples. The other four types, academic performance, personality inventories, projective personality techniques, and interviews, are generally less valid. (However, it should be noted that other studies have concluded that the validity of structured interviews is approximately that of cognitive ability tests.) Regarding differences between demographic groups in test scores, all types except academic performance have demonstrated less adverse impact than have cognitive ability tests.

Regarding feasibility of use, large differences are demonstrated between cognitive ability tests and other types. Usually these differences are clearly in favor of cognitive ability tests. Of the four types that have approximately equal validity and less adverse impact, only biographical data (biodata) is as inexpensive and easy to administer and score as cognitive ability tests. Even so, the development of biodata requires a large-scale empirical study and may need periodic rekeying to avoid deterioration in validity. Assessment centers are among the most expensive of selection devices; they require extensive training for assessors, special physical facilities, and excessive time from assessors and participants. Work samples are appropriate only for experienced applicants. Trainability tests are expensive to administer because they allow time for the applicant to learn necessary skills for test performance. Valid interviews usually require extensive training of interviewers, which is also expensive. Personality inventories and projective techniques may be expensive to administer and may require a trained psychologist to interpret the applicant's responses.

The findings regarding the fairness to the applicant of each type of test are difficult to summarize briefly. Reilly and Warech defined three dimensions of fairness. The first was false rejection rates, for which trainability tests, work samples, biodata, and assessment centers were all judged to have rates equal to or less than cognitive ability tests. The second dimension was perceived relevance by the applicant of test material to the job. Work samples, trainability tests, and assessment centers were all thought to be superior. On the third dimension, potential for improvement of employability for the rejected applicant,

TABLE 11.7 Comparison of Eight Selection Methods with Cognitive Ability Tests

	Selection Methods							
	Academic Performance	Assessment Center	Biographical Data	Interview	Personality Inventories	Projective Techniques	Trainability	Work Sample
Validity	Less	Equal	Equal	Slightly less	Less	Less	Equal	Equal
Adverse impact	Equal	Less	Less	Less	Less	Less	Less	Less
Feasibility	Less	Less	Equal	Equal/Less	Less	Less	Less	Less

Source: Richard Reilly and Michael Warech, "The Validity and Fairness of Alternatives to Cognitive Tests," in *Policy Issues in Employment Testing*, ed. Linda C. Wing and Bernard R. Gifford (Norwell, MA: Kluwer, 1993).

trainability tests and work samples allow for improvement through job-related training. Cognitive ability and biodata permit no such improvement.

Based on Reilly and Warech's report, we conclude that cognitive ability tests are viable selection instruments because of their high validity and low cost. However, biodata, interviews, trainability, work samples, and assessment centers all demonstrate almost equal validity, less adverse impact, and more fairness to the applicant, although each has some deficiency in cost and ease of development and implementation.

A related study used meta-analysis to compare cognitive ability tests, structured interviews, biodata inventories, and the personality measure of conscientiousness on both validity and adverse impact.[17] This study determined that the *uncorrected* validity coefficients for cognitive ability (0.30), structured interviews (0.30), and biodata inventories (0.28) were about the same and higher than that of the conscientiousness test (0.18). The adverse impact of the cognitive ability test was much greater than that of each of the other three. However, each of these three, especially when combined into one selection battery, did cause some adverse impact that favored white people over black people. The conclusion we draw from this study is that there are alternatives to cognitive ability tests, but that these alternative tests do not eliminate adverse impact and can themselves be the cause of claims of discrimination (although that probability is significantly lower than when cognitive ability tests are used).

Another way of comparing the adverse impact associated with various selection tests is to identify federal court cases involving these tests and determine the number of decisions that indicated that discrimination had occurred with their use. One study found that unstructured interviews were the most frequent subject of cases (81) and had the most decisions of discrimination (33). Cognitive ability tests were next, with 24 such cases (of which 8 were found to be discriminatory). Physical ability tests generated 19 cases (8 were discriminatory).[18] Structured interviews (9 cases), work sample tests (7 cases), and assessment centers (1 case) were also examined. Discrimination was found in only one of these three types of tests (a work sample test). Concerning cognitive ability tests in particular, these findings indicate that such tests do cause adverse impact, but they can be successfully defended; courts often rule that although adverse impact is found, discrimination has not occurred. In fact, these overall findings indicate that a relatively large percentage of all cases involving selection instrument and adverse impact can be successfully defended. This is good news, because we have said the same thing at various times in this book and now we have evidence to support us.

Implications for Selection.   The studies we have summarized resulted in some far-reaching conclusions. The first is that it is no longer necessary to conduct validity studies within each organization. If the job of interest for the selection program is one of those for which validity generalization data have been reported, then the selection instruments reported in the validity generalization study can be used for selection. There are no organizational effects on validity; therefore, the same predictor can be used across all organizations. To set up the selection program, it should be necessary only to demonstrate through job analysis that the job within the organization is similar to the job in the validity generalization study. Obviously, this reduces the time, effort, and cost of establishing a valid selection program.

A second conclusion is that task differences among jobs have very little effect on the magnitude of the validity coefficients of mental ability tests. In other words, mental ability tests are valid predictors for a wide variety of jobs. The variable that moderates the relationship between mental ability and job performance is most likely the differing information-processing and problem-solving demands of the job, not task differences themselves. That is, jobs that differ in these demands may differ in the validity of the mental ability test.

Even in such cases, however, the mental ability test should be valid for all jobs; it just has "more predictability" for jobs with greater information-processing and problem-solving demands than for those jobs with less of these characteristics.

One explanation for this is that cognitive ability is highly correlated with job knowledge, and job knowledge is highly correlated with job performance. Moreover, cognitive ability is related to job performance itself, not just to job knowledge. Hunter writes:

> *This may be because high ability workers are faster at cognitive operations on the job, are better able to prioritize between conflicting rules, are better able to adapt old procedures to altered situations, are better able to innovate to meet unexpected problems, and are better able to learn new procedures quickly as the job changes over time.*[19]

A third conclusion is that a score obtained from a general mental ability test is as good a predictor of job performance as is a composite score obtained from a test of specific abilities using multiple scales. In support of this, Hunter analyzed data obtained from military validity studies. He grouped jobs into four categories: mechanical, electronic, skilled services, and clerical. Five tests were examined: general mental ability and four separate composite tests tailored to each job group (mechanical composite, electrical composite, skilled service composite, and clerical composite). Results indicated very little difference between the magnitude of the validity coefficient of the general mental ability test and the appropriate composite test for each of the four job groups. In fact, the coefficient for the general mental ability test was higher than the validity for the composite in three of the four job categories.

A fourth conclusion that can be drawn from this series of meta-analyses is that parts of the *Uniform Guidelines on Employee Selection Procedures* (discussed in Chapter 2) are not appropriate at this point in time. The *Uniform Guidelines* are based upon the premise of situational specificity of validity. That is, they assume that the validity of a selection test is partially dependent upon the characteristics of the organization. The *Uniform Guidelines* require that in order to demonstrate empirical validity, a company must conduct a validity study, using its own applicants or employees and performance measures. As we stated previously, these meta-analyses clearly point out that situational specificity is not correct. Following from that, the requirement of conducting a validity study within a specific organization is not appropriate. In fact, meta-analysis demonstrates that single organization validity studies are usually flawed because of small sample size and other methodological limitations. Because of these limitations, the resulting validity coefficient cannot be regarded as an accurate indicator of the validity of the selection test in question. We are therefore in a quizzical legal arena in which the precedent of court cases and the *Uniform Guidelines*, which should be given "great weight" in legal decisions of discrimination, both argue for a validation strategy that has been discredited by empirical research conducted subsequent to the early court cases and the publication of the *Uniform Guidelines*. Clearly the *Uniform Guidelines* must be updated to include validity generalization as an appropriate validation strategy for the explanation of adverse impact in selection decisions.

MENTAL ABILITY TESTS AND DISCRIMINATION

As we mentioned previously, the widespread use of ability tests that has characterized selection programs since the 1920s has diminished since the early 1970s. In part, this is the direct result of court rulings in early EEO selection cases. Cognitive ability tests were specifically singled out and found to be discriminatory. In the preceding section we pointed out that since those early court decisions, the extensive validity data that have accumulated about cognitive ability tests were analyzed to study their effectiveness in selection programs. Similarly, these data were also used to study the issue of discriminatory effects of cognitive ability tests in selection. In this section, we summarize this work.

Differential Validity

Differential validity is a term that was used to describe the hypothesis that employment tests are less valid for minority group members than nonminorities. The situation is one in which the validities for the same selection test in the two groups are statistically significant but unequal. For example, the test may be significantly more valid for white people than for black people. In many ways, this term is related to the issue of test bias that has often been addressed regarding ability tests.

Most explanations of test bias include hypotheses of differential validity. The argument is that the actual content of ability tests (especially mental ability tests) is based on the content of white middle-class culture and, therefore, does not mean the same thing to other groups as it does to whites. Nonwhite middle-class respondents use different terms and symbols; in essence, this difference reduces their scores on the test. These test scores will not have the same meaning for whites and nonwhites, nor will the pattern of validity coefficients with other measures—such as job performance or school grades—be the same for the two groups. This different pattern of validity coefficients is what is meant by differential validity. Taken a step further, the presence of differential validity would imply that selection managers should develop separate selection programs for each applicant group for each job. This would be necessary to control the differences in terms and symbols of selection tests among the various cultures.

To examine the problem more closely, studies have analyzed data collected from several selection programs simultaneously. It has been a consistent conclusion of these studies that *differential validity does not exist.* Those few selection programs in which differential validity has been observed have been characterized by methodological limitations that seem to account for the observed differences. For example, one investigation examined 31 studies in which 583 validity coefficients were reported.[20] These studies were also scored on methodological characteristics such as sample size, use of criteria measures that were identified as being for research purposes only, and use of a predictor chosen for its theoretical relationship to the criterion measures. For the most part, differential validity was observed only in those studies with several methodological limitations. For the methodologically sound studies, no differences in validity coefficients between black and white groups were observed.

Another study used 781 pairs of validity coefficients. The pairs were made up of the correlation between the same predictor variable (commonly a cognitive ability test) and criterion variable for both a white and a black group of workers.[21] These correlations ranged from approximately −0.37 to +0.55. Figure 11.1 is part of this study; it shows the result of graphing these pairs of validity coefficients. As you can see, the two curves, one composed of validity coefficients for black workers and one of corresponding validity coefficients for white workers, look almost identical. This means that these tests acted in the same manner for both black and white people. The major conclusion of the study was that differential validity was not demonstrated, and that tests that ordered white people successfully with respect to some given job criterion *also* ordered black people with equal success.

Mental Ability Tests and Adverse Impact

Meta-analysis has also been used to examine the tested differences among demographic groups in scores on cognitive ability tests. These analyses have been consistent in

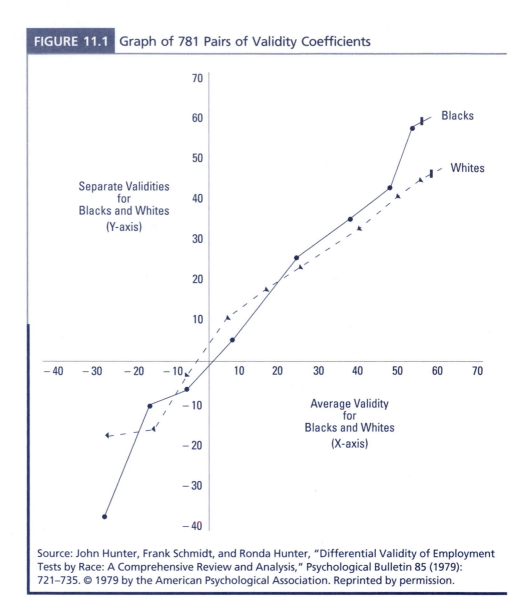

FIGURE 11.1 Graph of 781 Pairs of Validity Coefficients

Source: John Hunter, Frank Schmidt, and Ronda Hunter, "Differential Validity of Employment Tests by Race: A Comprehensive Review and Analysis," Psychological Bulletin 85 (1979): 721–735. © 1979 by the American Psychological Association. Reprinted by permission.

determining that there are significant differences in mean test scores among racial/ethnic groups. Asian people usually score the highest, followed by whites, Hispanics, and blacks.[22] The disagreement among these studies has been in terms of how large the differences are.

Phil Roth and his colleagues completed a thorough meta-analysis of these differences and the following is a brief summary of what was found. The important statistic in measuring differences between demographic groups is the *d-statistic*. This is defined as the difference in means (for example, white mean vs. black mean) divided by the sample-weighted average of the standard deviations. "Of course it is!" you say. This is complex, but it is a way of determining differences among groups as a function of differences within the groups. Large between-group differences are more significant if there are very small differences within each of the groups. Between-group differences are less significant if there are very large differences within each of the groups. At any rate, Roth and his associates found d = 1.10 for the black–white differences and 0.72 for the Hispanic–white differences for studies across both business and educational settings.

Said another way, the mean score for blacks is at approximately the 14th percentile of white scores; the mean score for Hispanics is at approximately the 24th percentile of white scores. The differences between blacks and whites were somewhat lower for business job applicants and even lower for job incumbents. Differences between white and black groups also varied by the level of complexity associated with jobs on which applicants were selected. Perhaps the most appropriate figures from this research are a measured difference of 0.86 between black and white applicants for low complexity jobs and a difference of 0.72 for applicants for medium complexity jobs. Other studies have reported similar findings.[23]

Another study by Denise Potosky and the two prolific Phils (Bobko and Roth) studied how adding applicants' scores on other types of selection tests to their scores on a cognitive ability test would affect measured adverse impact.[24] This follows from a common assumption that developing selection programs including selection instruments thought to produce less adverse impact than cognitive ability tests would inevitably produce a final selection score that would "soften" the demographic differences in scores using the cognitive ability test alone. The hoped-for result would be significantly less, or perhaps no, adverse impact among demographic groups. In three separate analyses, the authors added measures of conscientiousness, biodata, and a structured interview to the cognitive ability score. Their main conclusion was that the validity of the composite battery does not always go up in comparison to the cognitive ability score by itself and the addition of non-cognitive predictors had little if any effect on the occurrence of adverse impact. Although adverse impact was lessened, it still usually resulted in significant adverse impact as measured by the Four-Fifths Rule we discussed in Chapter 2. The authors, in fact, raised the question of whether or not it is possible for organizations to avoid adverse impact if a cognitive ability test is used as part of the selection program.

Another research study took a different approach to examining whether or not the adverse impact of measuring cognitive ability could be reduced. Specially, it looked at adverse impact if a proxy measure of a cognitive ability test score was used (that is, amount of education attained). As we mentioned previously in this chapter, cognitive ability test scores have been related to educational attainment both through the content of items on tests and through various statistical analyses. This study had two main purposes. The first was to determine whether educational attainment could actually be used as a proxy measure for cognitive ability. The second was to compare the adverse impact of using educational attainment vs. cognitive ability test scores for selection. The data used for the study was previously gathered from more than 12,000 individuals between the ages of 35 and 43. Analyses indicated that the correlation between tested cognitive ability and educational attainment was 0.63 and that, therefore, educational attainment could be used as a proxy of cognitive ability as long as the criterion is set at least at one year of college. Setting a lower educational attainment standard (for example, completion of high school) turned out to be not much more effective than random selection among applicants in terms of the resulting mean cognitive ability level of those selected. Setting a standard of one year of college or above yields appreciable differences in mean cognitive ability of those selected vs. random selection among applicants. Not surprisingly, this difference increases as the educational attainment standard increases. However, it was also determined that using educational attainment as proxy results in the group of applicants being selected having a lower mean cognitive ability score than a comparable number of applicants being selected directly on the cognitive ability score. Since cognitive ability test scores are highly correlated with job performance, this result could mean that lower ability and lower performing applicants were selected using educational attainment than by using the cognitive ability test scores. When the researchers compared the adverse impact yielded by educational attainment and the cognitive ability test score, they found that educational attainment lessened the amount of adverse impact. However, in many cases educational attainment still resulted in adverse impact against minorities using the Four-Fifths Rule as the criterion. Among their conclusions, the authors write:

> *The results of this study ... point out that using educational attainment can decrease adverse impact when compared with selecting directly on cognitive ability. For many organizations this may be a very important goal. For other organizations the reduction in cognitive ability of their applicants, and the subsequent loss of criterion-related validity, would be valued more highly than the potential improvements in adverse impact. This is a judgment call to be made by the organization.*[25]

So What?

The importance of these findings for selection is very clear. As we previously discussed, cognitive ability tests have a high correlation with job performance. Some think that they are among the most valid selection tests available. However, using a cognitive ability test will frequently result in lower percentages of black and Hispanic people than white people scoring higher than a cutoff score necessary for selection. If that percentage difference is less than the Four-Fifths Rule used as a guideline by the EEOC, there is evidence of adverse impact. If a discrimination charge is filed in court, the company may have to provide evidence that the mental ability test is job related. The evidence we have summarized about the validity and lack of differential validity of cognitive ability tests should make such a defense feasible. If such a defense is acceptable, the organization would be allowed to use the cognitive ability test in selection. That use of the cognitive ability test may result in a large percentage of jobs being filled by white people, and much smaller percentages being filled by black and Hispanic people. However, these differences among demographic groups can be justified because of the overall validity of cognitive ability tests and the lack of differential validity of these tests. There is also evidence that this adverse impact in the use of cognitive ability test scores cannot be overcome by the use of measures of other selection predictors or another measure of cognitive ability.

It must be clearly noted that the studies summarized above only analyze the cognitive score differences among demographic groups. They do not attempt to explain the causes or possible reasons of such differences. It is not appropriate for anyone to argue for genetic, educational, or cultural factors as the sole cause of differences that are based on the data from the studies we have summarized.

Opinions about the Use of Mental Ability Tests in Selection

It can be said that the majority of selection specialists agree that mental ability tests can be useful in selection. There is not a clear majority opinion, however, regarding how or the extent to which these tests should be used. Kevin Murphy and colleagues surveyed a large number of specialists to try to determine what the consensus was with regard to the use of these tests.[26] The survey consisted of 49 statements about the use of cognitive ability tests in selection. Respondents indicated how much they agreed with each statement. Based upon the responses, the researchers formed three categories of items: those with which the majority agreed, those with which significant percentages both agreed and disagreed, and those that showed neither agreement nor disagreement. In the last group were patterns for which a large percentage of respondents had no opinion about these items.

The items about which the majority agreed generally relate to characteristics and measurement properties of mental ability tests. That is, the majority agreed that such tests are valid and fair, do measure intelligence, are incomplete measures of intelligence, and are not comprehensive indicators of job performance. Many of the items about which there was both significant agreement and disagreement addressed the importance of mental ability in selection and job performance. Examples were items stating that cognitive ability accounts totally for the predictive validity of ability tests, that cognitive ability should always be a part of a selection program, that cognitive ability is the most important individual difference variable, and that the use of cognitive ability tests results in a high proportion of incorrect negative employment decisions for minorities. Items about which there was neither agreement nor controversy covered many topics. Examples of these items stated that large societal changes were needed to significantly affect the adverse effects of cognitive ability tests, that there are combinations of noncognitive measures that can equal the validity of cognitive tests, that the use of cognitive tests leads to more social justice than does their abandonment, and that persons with lower levels of cognitive ability will have to settle for lower-level jobs. The authors concluded that although there seems to be wide agreement that cognitive ability tests are valid and provide useful information for selection, there is disagreement about how they should be used. This disagreement is probably based on the probability of fewer minority applicants being hired when cognitive ability tests are used extensively in selection. This is because minorities would score lower than whites and many would fail to meet cutoff score requirements. Many people apparently believe that such disparities in employment have large societal consequences that outweigh the benefits of selection based on the demonstrated validity of mental ability tests.

Our Comments about Mental Ability Tests.   The research evidence is clear that mental ability tests are among the most valid, if not the most valid, of all selection tests. They predict job performance, no matter how it is measured, across a wide variety of jobs; they are especially useful for complex jobs. This validity is most likely because job performance requires many of the same cognitive activities that are measured in mental ability tests: language fluency, numerical calculation, spatial relations, analysis, and memory. The evidence is that these tests are not culturally biased in terms of the relevance of their content to what is required by organizations for job success. Many selection specialists think that it's important to use mental ability tests if a priority of the selection program is to identify applicants who will have high job performance.

However, one social downside of the use of mental ability tests is that adverse impact usually occurs when these tests are used in selection. As a group, minority applicants score lower on mental ability tests than do nonminority applicants as a group. These group differences usually mean that a larger percentage of majority applicants than minority applicants are selected into the open positions. Compounding this social issue is the fact that there does not seem to be a clear short-term answer to such score differences. One tactic used in the past had been to separate the applicants into two groups, majority and minority, and decide how many of each group should be selected. Frequently this decision reflects an equal percentage of each group. The applicants are ordered within each group according to scores on the mental ability test. Selection begins with the highest-scoring applicant in each group and moves down the rank-order list until the appropriate number within each group is selected. Such a practice is no longer legal based upon the Civil Rights Act of 1991 that forbade race norming. We discussed this topic in Chapter 2.

A second tactic has been to develop score bands starting with the top score among applicants on a mental ability test. Simply stated, the idea underlying score banding is that all tests have some degree of unreliability, or error of measurement. Score banding is a supposed statistical method for specifying a range of scores around (or below) a score that takes error of measurement into account. The band of scores identified are said to be equal in terms of true score. They differ in their actual score because of error of measurement.

Therefore, all individuals with scores within this band should be considered to have scored equally on the selection test. Banding is thought to be advantageous for the selection of minorities because it creates a range of scores that should encompass the scores of minority applicants. Because all scores within the range are regarded as equal, a selection specialist can select minority applicants from the pool of equal scores. However, most test specialists are certain that the measurement and statistical explanations and procedures used to develop score bands are inappropriate or incorrect. Many selection specialists believe that score banding should not be incorporated into a selection program because of the measurement limitations inherent in banding.

If the selection of a diverse workforce is a goal of an organization that wishes to use mental ability tests because of their validity, the main option is to more vigorously recruit minority applicants. Attracting a large number of such applicants should increase the absolute number of minority applicants that pass a cutoff score on a mental ability test. Increased recruiting across many firms would have positive societal effects such as more employment for minorities; it would also signal the need for adequate education and employment training.

Conclusions

How should we interpret the findings of these various studies in light of the specific statements of discriminatory effect in the EEO court decisions we discussed in Chapter 2? One thing to remember is that the court decisions and the studies summarized here reflect different levels of validation work. The studies summarized in this chapter are based on complex validity data collected in many organizations. In contrast, the organizations that were found guilty of discrimination in their use of ability tests for selection had taken only superficial steps in the development of their selection programs. More complete development procedures might have yielded different results.

Second, the analyses reviewed in this section were completed after many of the court decisions regarding the discriminatory use of ability tests were handed down. It is fair to assume that both plaintiffs and defendants in the court cases were using the traditional viewpoint of the necessity of demonstrating a selection device's validity for the job under question. As we have said previously, the results of recent validity generalization studies have radically changed this perspective. Not only has the concept of validity generalization emphasized the necessity of accumulating results across multiple studies, but it argues that studies within a single organization may not be interpretable. This would especially be true if the study was limited by small sample size, restriction of range, or some of the other statistical artifacts that we mentioned previously in this chapter and also in Chapter 5.

The use of validity generalization for establishing the validity of a cognitive ability test has been part of very few court cases and decisions have not been consistent. In one relevant case, *Friend et al. v. City of Richmond*, the court of appeals ruled that the firefighters' jobs in Richmond, Virginia were similar to those of firefighters in California—and allowed data from the California validity study to be used.[27] The court also commented that it was not logical to expect every city to conduct a validation study for firefighters. However in another case involving firefighters, the court did not accept validity generalization as validity evidence and indicated that it was important to demonstrate specific knowledge of the Detroit Fire Department in establishing validity.[28] In a third case, validity generalization was accepted. The court agreed with the argument that even large differences between the duties of the jobs described in a validity research study—and the jobs of an organization at issue in Bolivar County, Mississippi—did not destroy the validity of the General Aptitude Test Battery (a general cognitive ability test).[29] However, shortly after that decision, an appeals court rejected validity generalization in another case and noted that on-site investigation of jobs was necessary for establishing validity.[30]

What can we conclude from all of this information about the use of cognitive ability tests in selection? Two factors must be taken into account when answering this question. The first is that the evidence shows that these tests are among the most valid of all selection tests for a large number of jobs (some selection specialists would say for all jobs). The second factor is the evidence that these tests exhibit adverse impact; that is, mean differences in test scores among demographic groups. But because these tests are also valid, there is a good chance that their use in selection could be defended against claims of discrimination. Therefore, some have thought that cognitive ability tests should be used extensively in selection. Others have expressed deep reservation about their use because the disqualification of larger proportions of minorities than nonminorities has major social implications. These dramatically different viewpoints are the reasons why decisions about the use of cognitive ability tests are among the most difficult for selection specialists to make. To some extent, the decision to use or not use cognitive ability tests should reflect the goals and values of the organization. If maximizing individual performance with minimum cost is the predominant goal of the organization, then the frequent use of cognitive ability tests may be a key to achieving this goal. However, if the organization has multiple goals, which include sustaining high job performance and maintaining a broad demographic base of employees, then it may be feasible to limit the use of mental ability tests and use other, generally more expensive and almost equally valid instruments—biodata inventories, structured interviews, work sample and trainability tests, and assessment centers.

MENTAL ABILITY TESTS AND THE INTERNET

In the interest of reducing the costs of selection, many organizations use electronic delivery systems for gathering data about job candidates. For example, application blanks and resumes are often submitted online. Telephone interviews are frequently conducted at initial stages of applicant screening. Mental ability tests are often used in selection; they consist of multiple-choice questions and do not require interaction between the test administrator and the applicant taking the test. This combination makes them ideal for some form of electronic delivery. There are many questions about gathering online applicant information, especially using electronic tests, that we will discuss next.

Equivalence of Paper-and-Pencil and Electronic Tests.   Testing experts do not know whether transforming a paper-and-pencil test into an electronic form leaves it unchanged. That is, do technology factors change applicants' test performance (waiting for screen changes, not being able to see the complete test, computer familiarity and comfort)? In selection, the relative test performance of applicants is important. Those with higher scores are usually selected before those with lower scores. We are absolutely sure that you remember material from the "reliability" chapter (Chapter 4), so we will put it this way: If the factors mentioned previously affect test scores, then technology may be introducing error variance into the scores of applicants on mental ability tests. No one in selection wants to increase the error component in scores except maybe low-ability people like the authors who could only benefit from errors that raise our scores.

Only a few research studies have examined the equivalence of paper-and-pencil and electronic testing. Denise Potosky and Philip Bobko did such a study of two cognitively based tests, one timed and the other untimed.[31] They collected data from subjects about their reactions to the two versions of each test. In the following we summarize their extensive findings.

Adult subjects from a variety of jobs took both paper-and-pencil and computer versions of two tests. Almost one-half of the subjects indicated that they had applied for a job over the Internet previously. They were paid for participating and were told that the four highest-scoring subjects would receive a bonus of $50. The computer tests were identical to the paper-and-pencil versions in terms of the wording of instructions and items, and the same person was the administrator for all testing situations. One test was the *Test of Learning Ability* (TLA), a 12-minute timed general mental ability test. The second test presented 10 situations and required the subject to choose one of four multiple-choice answers as the best action to take in the situation described. This test did not have a time limit.

Potosky and Bobko's main conclusions are presented in Table 11.8. One very important finding was that the correlation between scores on the two versions of the TLA was 0.60. This clearly indicated that test performance among the subjects, especially for items of spatial reasoning and other abilities that require visual perception, was different on the two versions. The rank order of individuals was different for each test; in a situation in which individuals would be selected according to their test scores, the individuals chosen using one of the versions would be different than those chosen using the other version. The correlation of scores on the two versions of the situational judgment test was 0.84. Because this was approximately the same as the reliability estimate of the paper-and-pencil test, the authors concluded that the electronic version did not introduce error into the test results. The clear implication is that timed tests are much more problematic to translate into an electronic version than are untimed tests. Most mental ability tests are timed. So … their use in electronic screening is not clear at this point. High-quality research about this could make you famous!

The two authors reported other research findings concerning the administration of timed tests, respondents' test-taking behaviors, and Web-based test design principles. We will summarize some of the main findings. It was determined that Internet time and actual time are not equivalent. The time allowed for Internet test taking must be adjusted for the "load time" of screens—and there must be a way of meaningfully presenting that time to

TABLE 11.8   Considerations Regarding the Use of Internet Tests

Timed Tests	Test-Taking Behaviors	Design Considerations
• Virtual time is not equal to actual time.	• Respondents often answer items in order.	• Internet tests usually have fewer items/page and more pages than paper-and-pencil versions.
• Time needed to load Web pages varies within tests and between users.	• Distinction between items and instructions can be blurred.	• Color and graphics may be necessary.
• Timer should be used in Internet tests as a signal to test-takers.	• Respondents attend to instructions differently than do respondents using paper-and-pencil tests.	• User expectations are important for design.
• Time must be appropriate for items and format.	• Role of test proctor differs for paper-and-pencil and Internet tests.	
• Load time may affect test performance.	• Respondents may differ with regard to preference for using mouse clicks vs. key strokes.	

Source: Adapted from Denise Potosky and Philip Bobko, "Selection Testing via the Internet: Practical Considerations and Exploratory Empirical Findings," *Personnel Psychology* 57 (2004): 1003–1034.

test takers. Test takers frequently do not respond the same way to the test instructions and ancillary information presented online as they would in a paper-and-pencil testing situation. Emphasis on the presentation of test titles and instructions should be increased to orient individuals to the test. This may be addressed by having the proctor read instructions or by including audio files with the electronic test. The design of screens for electronic testing is important; graphics and color are useful. There also seemed to be differences between the two versions with regard to test-taking behavior. In electronic testing, subjects more often answered test items in order because it was difficult to move to items on different screens. Note taking or marking among alternative answers is not feasible on electronic tests. A final point is that respondents' beliefs about their computer and Internet abilities had little effect on test scores. However, age did have an effect; older subjects performed less well than young subjects.

Unproctored Internet Testing.   Many selection specialists in organizations favor Internet testing because it allows applicants to answer a selection instrument at any time in any place. This allows the processing of applicants to be completed and applicants to be selected more quickly. However, providing applicants with such flexibility usually means that the applicants are taking unproctored tests. That is, the applicant is taking the test without the presence of an organizational representative who monitors the testing behaviors of the applicant. Such a testing situation means that decisions about applicants are made using test scores of unproctored tests. These scores can be affected by several sources of error: someone other than the applicant completing the test, the use of books or Internet material, and aid from accomplices. In addition, differences among the various computers used by applicants in terms of speed and software functioning may artificially affect scores.

Several writers have addressed issues in unproctored Internet testing.[32] The main issues are the type of test (mental ability vs. other kinds of tests), whether the test is used for selection or development, the importance of the test score to the test taker, the effects of cheating on the test's validity, and the cost and feasibility of measures to reduce cheating. Although writers do not completely agree on most of these issues, there seems to be consensus that brief biodata tests, situational judgment tests, and personality tests are the most appropriate for Internet testing. These are tests for which identifying the correct response is more difficult; they are, therefore, less susceptible to cheating.[33] Knowledge and mental ability tests are not recommended. Some argue that the optimum system for selection is to use unproctored tests as an initial screening followed by a proctored test for those who pass; at this point, applicants' identities can be confirmed. Mental ability tests can be used at that stage. One research study that compared the test results of individuals taking the same test in proctored and unproctored situations found that differences in scores between the two types of test administrations were unsystematic.[34] The authors concluded that the test takers concentrated on test content and that the personality and cognitive ability tests that were studied could be given under either test administration condition. One of the interesting findings was that scores on the cognitive ability test improved between the first and second test taking no matter which of the two testing conditions came first. The authors indicated that the subjects learned about the test by completing the first administration and this learning led to higher scores the second time. We should note that the general finding of no differences in test performance between proctored and unproctored administrations did not examine the existence of cheating—a main concern for unproctored testing.

Some argue that unproctored selection testing should be used very cautiously or be integrated with proctored testing. For example, an organization may review the unproctored scores of applicants and drop those with low scores. All of the remaining applicants may then be required to take a second form of the unproctored selection test at a proctored location. Both assessments would be used in the screening decision. Such procedures could reduce cost significantly because a smaller number of applicants take the more expensive proctored test. It is thought that such a procedure does not reduce the number of highly qualified applicants because those with low scores on the unproctored test are almost always those with low ability. Higher scores, however, could be produced by high-ability applicants or low-ability applicants who cheated. The second form of the test given in a proctored situation should yield data that help to identify those who cheated. Those would be the individuals who scored significantly lower on the proctored test than they did on the unproctored test. (Read the following section on Effects of Practice and Coaching before you decide whether to believe this assumption.) Using this testing scenario may allow the organization to gain the advantages of using Internet tests while still protecting it from cheating and the reduction in the validity of using the test.

Only a few studies have examined the extent to which cheating actually occurs in unproctored Internet testing. The results are inconsistent, but some studies have found that there are no significant changes in mean scores for the same test when it is administered in both proctored and unproctored situations.[35] Research work on the extent of cheating on Internet tests may be another way for you to be famous. It seems obvious that organizations will continue to increase the use of electronic testing because such tests cost less, reduce the time it takes to process applicants, and take into account the increased use of computers by the working population.

EFFECTS OF PRACTICE AND COACHING

Several organizations, especially public organizations, allow applicants to repeat the application and testing process multiple times. For example, many fire and police departments permit those who failed a test to retake it after some period of time. As a result, many applicants take a mental ability test two or more times. It is useful to know how practice affects test scores. Similarly, coaching of applicants who take mental ability tests is a growing industry. You are most familiar with those organizations that teach applicants how to take a standardized test for college admission (the Scholastic Aptitude Test—SAT or the Graduate Management Aptitude Test—GMAT). The success of such organizations has given rise to others that prepare applicants for taking mental ability tests for employment. Advocates of minority groups argue that individuals should be coached on how to respond to mental ability tests in order to overcome what some regard as the cultural bias of mental ability tests.

Studies of the effects of coaching have found that such training has a minimal effect on test scores.[36] For example, coaching has been found to change scores 0.15 to 0.20 standard deviation units on the SAT. If, for example, the standard deviation of a standardized test is 80 points, coaching would only change scores on the average of 12 to 16 points. If the standard deviation is 40 points, the average change would be 6 to 8 points. Another study of the effects of coaching on job applicants found that those who attended a coaching clinic did not score significantly better than did those who did not attend.[37]

The effects of practice (that is, reapplying and taking a specific test two or more times), have been studied using data collected from 4,726 individuals who applied multiple times for law enforcement positions.[38] Scores on mental ability tests were found to increase between the first and second test completions and also between the second and third completions. It was estimated that these increases could result in someone scoring in the 50th percentile in Test 1 but then scoring in the 80th percentile after Test 3. Such a change would definitely improve the applicant's chances of being selected. There are three possible explanations for this improvement in scores. Applicants could develop a better understanding of the test format and methods of responding (this understanding is what many coaching programs emphasize). Second, applicants could reduce test anxiety before taking subsequent tests. Third, applicants could learn the specific skills tested (vocabulary, mathematical operations). Although the study could not determine which one of these explanations was appropriate for the test score increase, it did find related information. The validity coefficient between the mental ability test and job training performance was higher for those individuals who were hired after one test completion than it was for those with two or more test completions. The researchers speculated that those who took the test multiple times improved on specific skills such as vocabulary—but not on general ability that was related to training performance. The logical conclusion from this study is that practice can improve an applicant's score on a mental ability test—but that improvement does not necessarily translate into improved job performance, which is the ultimate goal of the organization and the selection process. Of course, this is only one study; more replication is needed before we can accept these findings as proven fact.

MECHANICAL ABILITY TESTS

There is no strict definition for the construct of mechanical ability, even though the term has long been used by testing specialists. For the most part, mechanical ability refers to characteristics that tend to make for success in work with machines and equipment.[39] One of the earliest tests of this type was the *Stenquist Mechanical Assembly Test*, developed in 1923 by John Stenquist. It consisted of a long, narrow box with ten compartments. Each compartment had a simple mechanical apparatus (mousetrap, push button) that the test taker had to assemble. Stenquist also developed two picture tests designed to measure the same abilities. The *Stenquist* thus demonstrated the two testing methods that have been generally used in mechanical ability tests: manual performance and written problems. Early tests like the *Stenquist* and the *Minnesota Mechanical Assembly Test* (1930) emphasized actual mechanical assembly or manipulation. However, the cost and time involved in administering and scoring such tests for large numbers of individuals can quickly become prohibitive. Therefore, group-administered paper-and-pencil tests that attempted to present problems of mechanical work through pictures and statements were developed. The use of paper-and-pencil tests has greatly exceeded the use of performance tests.

Attempts have been made to more precisely determine the abilities measured by mechanical ability tests. As with mental ability tests, these abilities vary from test to test; in general, the main factors are spatial visualization, perceptual speed and accuracy, and mechanical information.[40] Mechanical ability tests can be thought of as measuring general or specific abilities. We discuss now one of the most frequently used general mechanical ability tests, the *Bennett Mechanical Comprehension Test*. This test has been utilized for a large number of different jobs. Different specific ability tests have been developed and used for jobs such as carpenter, engine lathe operator, welder, electrician, and other skilled crafts.

The Bennett Mechanical Comprehension Test

The *Bennett Mechanical Comprehension Test* is, perhaps, the most widely used mechanical ability test for more than 50 years. Two 68-item parallel forms of this test, *S* and *T*, were developed in 1969. Purportedly, it is most appropriately used for jobs in industries such as manufacturing, production, energy, and utilities and in occupations such as automotive mechanic, engineer, installation, maintenance, repair, skilled trade, technical sales, transportation trade, and equipment operator.

The items of the *Bennett* contain objects that are generally familiar in American culture: airplanes, carts, steps, pulleys, seesaws, and gears. The questions measure the respondent's ability to perceive and understand the relationship of physical forces and mechanical elements in practical situations. Although they require some familiarity with common tools and objects, the questions purportedly assume no more technical knowledge than can be acquired through everyday experience in an industrial society such as ours. Partially supporting this assumption is evidence that formal training in physics only slightly increases test scores. Items are pictures with a brief accompanying question. For example, one item is a picture of two men carrying a weighted object hanging down from a plank; it asks, "Which man carries more weight?" Each figure has a letter below its base. Because the object is closer to one man than to the other, the correct answer is the letter that identifies the closer man. Another item has two pictures of the same room of a house. In one picture the room contains several pieces of furniture, carpeting, and objects on the wall. In the other picture the room contains only few objects and no carpeting. The question is, "Which room has an echo?" Given some basic knowledge or experience, the question can be answered by logical analysis of the problem rather than the mastery of detailed and specific facts.

Each form of the *Bennett* has a 30-minute time limit. A score is the number of items answered correctly. The manuals for the different forms provide percentile norms for various groups including industrial applicants, employees, and students. Reported reliabilities range from 0.81 to 0.93. The test purportedly focuses on spatial perception and tool knowledge rather than manual dexterity. It is best used for assessing job candidates for positions that require a grasp of the principles underlying the operation and repair of complex devices. It is also intended to measure an individual's learning ability regarding mechanical skills. Studies have correlated scores on the *Bennett* with scores on other ability tests in order to further understand the abilities being measured. Results indicate a moderate correlation with both verbal and mathematical mental ability tests and tests of spatial visualization. The relationship to verbal ability and spatial visualization can partially be explained by the fact that it is a written test with pictures as items. As one indication of the validity of this test, Paul Muchinsky found that in a study of 193 employees who produced electromechanical components, the *Bennett*, form S, had the highest correlation with supervisors' performance ratings among three mechanical tests (the *Flanagan Aptitude Classification Test–Mechanics*, the *Thurstone Test of Mental Alertness–Form A*, and the *Bennett*).[41] Finally, we found no studies that reported differences between racial or ethnic groups on the *Bennett*.

CLERICAL ABILITY TESTS

Traditionally, clerical jobs have been thought of as any job that required extensive checking or copying of words and numbers and the movement and placement of objects such as office equipment, files, and reports. Clerical ability tests have predominantly measured perceptual speed and accuracy in processing verbal and numerical data. These tests have traditionally been used in selection for office clerical and staff positions.

The Minnesota Clerical Test

Developed in 1933, the *Minnesota Clerical Test* is generally regarded as the prototype of clerical ability tests and has been the most widely used of these tests for much of its existence. The test is brief, easily administered, and easily scored. It has one form consisting of two separately timed and scored subtests: number checking and name checking.

| TABLE 11.9 | Example Items Similar to Items on the Minnesota Clerical Test |

Name Comparison

Neal Schmitt	_____	Frank Schmidt
Hubert Feild	_____	Herbert Field
Chris Riordan	_____	Kris Reardan
Tim Judge	_____	Jim Fudge
Murray Barrick	_____	Mick Mount

Number Comparison

84644	_____	84464
179854	_____	176845
123457	_____	12457
987342	_____	987342
8877665994	_____	8876659954

Each subtest contains 200 items. Each item consists of a pair of numbers or names. The respondent is asked to compare the two names or numbers and place a check on a line between them if they are identical. If the two entries are different, no mark is placed on the line. The entries in the numbers subtest range from 3 through 12 digits; the entries in the names subtest range from 7 through 16 letters. The tests are timed separately at eight minutes for numbers and seven minutes for names. The score is the number right minus the number wrong; scores are determined for each subtest separately as well as for the total score. Table 11.9 contains items similar to those used in these subtests.

Although the two subtests are related, they do measure separate abilities. The names subtest has been found to be correlated with speed of reading, spelling, and group measures of intelligence. The numbers subtest has been related to the verification of arithmetic computations.[42] Scores on the subtests are only slightly related to either education level or experience in clerical positions. Reliability has been estimated as 0.90 for parallel forms and 0.85 for test-retest. Norm-group scores are provided for various job groups for each gender. Adverse impact has not been reported for scores of this test.

PHYSICAL ABILITY TESTS

Another area of importance for selection specialists is the testing of physical abilities of applicants for placement into manual labor and physically demanding jobs. As Michael Campion has pointed out, there are three reasons for this type of testing.[43] First, EEO legislation has prompted an increase in women applicants for traditionally male-dominated physical labor jobs. Although women, as a group, score lower than men on many physical ability tests, applicants (as we have previously discussed) must be evaluated as individuals, not as members of a group. Individual evaluation is best done by testing all applicants on the specific physical demands that are related to the job. Second, the use of appropriate selection devices for physically demanding jobs can reduce the incidence of work-related injuries. The insurance, compensation, and therapy costs associated with back, knee, and shoulder injuries continue to rise dramatically. Physical ability tests should improve the selection of individuals who are better suited to job demands. Third, because the Americans with Disabilities Act prohibits preemployment medical examinations, the most feasible way to collect data about the physical status of applicants is through the use of specific physical ability tests that measure the worker characteristics required by the job.

A recent example of the use of physical ability tests occurred in the selection of firefighters. Recruits from nine consecutive fire academy classes were assessed on a battery of strength and endurance measures at Weeks 1, 7, and 14 of training. Statistical analyses using Week 1 measures indicated that strength variables were the primary predictors of performance on physically demanding firefighting tasks assessed at the completion of training. Increased validity was obtained with the addition of aerobic capacity, which produced more accurate performance distinctions among recruits with high strength levels. Results also showed a drop-off in performance for recruits with strength levels below the male 25th percentile. The authors concluded that general strength and endurance were useful selection predictors of firefighter performance on physically demanding fire suppression and rescue tasks.[44]

Most physical ability tests require demonstrations of strength, oxygen intake, and coordination. In the next sections we summarize the work of two experts, Edwin Fleishman and Joyce Hogan, who have developed test batteries that measure these characteristics.

PHYSICAL ABILITIES ANALYSIS

Edwin Fleishman and his colleagues have developed a taxonomy of 52 different abilities, both physical and nonphysical, that are necessary for performing work activities.[45] We will discuss only the measurement of the nine physical abilities in the following section.

Fleishman has identified these physical abilities, all of which have been extensively used to select employees for physically demanding jobs:[46]

1. *Static strength*—maximum force that can be exerted against external objects. Tested by lifting weights.

2. *Dynamic strength*—muscular endurance in exerting force continuously. Tested by pull-ups.

3. *Explosive strength*—ability to mobilize energy effectively for bursts of muscular effort. Tested by sprints or jumps.

4. *Trunk strength*—limited dynamic strength specific to trunk muscles. Tested by leg lifts or sit-ups.

5. *Extent flexibility*—ability to flex or stretch trunk and back muscles. Tested by twist-and-touch test.

6. *Dynamic flexibility*—ability to make repeated rapid, flexing trunk movements. Tested by rapid, repeated bending over and touching floor.

7. *Gross body coordination*—ability to coordinate action of several parts of body while body is in motion. Tested by cable-jump test.

8. *Gross body equilibrium*—ability to maintain balance with nonvisual cues. Tested by rail-walk test.

9. *Stamina*—capacity to sustain maximum effort requiring cardiovascular exertion. Tested by 600-yard run-walk.

The following validity coefficients for specific jobs are among the results reported by Fleishman for the use of these abilities in selection: pipeline workers (0.63), correctional officers (0.64), warehouse workers (0.39), electrical workers (0.53), and enlisted army men (0.87).[47] All coefficients represent the correlation of a battery of two to four physical abilities with job performance.

Three Components of Physical Performance

The extensive work of Joyce Hogan has produced the three components of physical performance described in Table 11.10. She combined two lines of research in the development of this taxonomy. The first was data about physical requirements derived from job analysis. The second was data based on physical ability tests already developed for selection. Her idea was that by examining these two sources of information about physical work performance, a comprehensive model of physical abilities could be developed.

Factor analyses were performed on several sets of data. Results consistently identified three factors, or components, of physical abilities.[48] The first, *muscular strength*, is the ability to apply or resist force through muscular contraction. Within this component are three more specific subelements: muscular tension, muscular power, and muscular endurance. The second component is *cardiovascular endurance*, which refers to the capacity to sustain gross (as contrasted with localized) muscular activity over prolonged periods. It is aerobic capacity and general systemic fitness involving the large muscles. The third component, *movement quality*, concerns characteristics that contribute to skilled performance. This component also has three subelements: flexibility, balance, and muscular integration. Hogan concluded that this three-component model describes the true structure of physical abilities necessary for work activities. As such, the model

TABLE 11.10	Three Components of Physical Performance		
Component	**Subelement**	**Sample Work Activities**	**Sample Tests**
Muscular Strength	Muscular tension	Activities of pushing, pulling, lifting, lowering, or carrying a heavy object	Handgrip strength, dynamometer (scored in pounds/kilos)
	Muscular power	Use of hand tools, raising a section of a ladder with a halyard	Ergometer, medicine ball put (scored in pounds)
	Muscular endurance	Repetitions of tool use, loading materials onto pallets	Push-ups, arm ergometer, (scored in number of repetitions)
Cardiovascular Endurance	None	Search and rescue, climbing stairs, wearing protective equipment	Step-up time, distance run (scored in amount of time taken)
Movement Quality	Flexibility	Mining operations, installing light fixtures	Sit and reach, twist and touch (scored in distance of limb displacement, repetitions)
	Balance	Pole climbing, ladder usage, elevated construction	Static rail balance (scored in time or distance)
	Neuromuscular integration	Accessing an offshore platform, intercepting an object	Minnesota rate manipulation (scored in lapsed time or target error)

Source: Based on Joyce C. Hogan, "Physical Abilities," in *Handbook of Industrial & Organizational Psychology*, 2d ed., Vol. 2, edited by Marvin Dunnette and Leatta Hough (Palo Alto, CA: Consulting Psychologists Press, 1991).

could be used as the basis for selection. The major issue in developing a selection program would be to determine which subset of abilities correlates with job performance for the job under study.

The importance of Hogan's work was demonstrated in the development of a selection program for seven jobs in various industries, with a total sample of 1,364 individuals. These jobs were law enforcement officer, firefighter, customer gas service, pipeline construction and maintenance, pipefitter, utility worker, and utility line repair and installation. Job analyses indicated that for each of these jobs muscular strength, one of the three components of Hogan's model, was a major factor necessary for performing several important tasks. A series of tests were developed. Results indicated that these tests were significantly correlated with both supervisors' ratings of physical performance and work simulations of critical job tasks.[49]

Legal Issues in Testing Physical Abilities

Selection specialists working with physically demanding jobs must be especially concerned with three groups of applicants: females, disabled workers, and older workers. Adverse impact for scores on physical ability tests is a common occurrence for each group. Because physical ability tests emphasize strength, aerobic power, and coordination, frequently males will score higher than females, the nondisabled higher than the disabled, and younger workers higher than older. The essential issue is that the tests must clearly be linked to critical job tasks that *require* physical abilities in their completion. However, even this statement is complicated by the question of whether the tasks can be modified to reduce or eliminate these physical demands. Such modification can occur either through the use of additional equipment or personnel. If such modifications can be made, the use of the physical ability test appropriate for the original tasks may be unwarranted. We now briefly discuss some of the main legal issues that have been raised relative to selection for demographic groups that are based on gender, age, and physical condition.

Two selection requirements regarding females that have been treated in court cases are height/weight standards and state laws prohibiting women from lifting items that exceed certain weight. In *Weeks v. Southern Bell*, the court ruled that even though the state of Georgia had protective legislation prohibiting women from lifting 30 pounds, "Title VII of the 1964 Civil Rights Act rejects just this type of romantic paternalism as unduly Victorian and instead vests individual women with the power to decide whether or not to take on unromantic tasks."[50] Similarly, height and weight standards have been equally hard to defend. Usually the argument has been that height and weight are surrogate measures of strength necessary for many jobs. Courts have consistently held that if measuring strength is the objective, then selection requirements should assess that directly rather than using secondary indicators such as height or weight.

Physical ability tests differ in the amount of adverse impact they produce in the testing of women. For example, cardiovascular endurance measures demonstrate mean scores for females that are about two-thirds those of men. For that reason, cutoff scores must be well documented. However, tests of muscular power and endurance, vertical jumps, and sit-ups have shown smaller differences between males and females. Finally, tests of flexibility, balance, and coordination usually show little or no adverse impact.

Joyce Hogan has demonstrated another way of lessening the adverse impact of physical ability tests by allowing applicants to prepare for these types of tests in various ways (such as calisthenic training, total body workouts including the use of weights, and applicant tryouts of the actual physical ability tests used in a selection program for several jobs). She found that women significantly increased their physical performance as a result of these methods of preparation. Also, the differences between men and women on the physical ability tests used in the selection program significantly decreased. For example, for the position of firefighter, more than one-half of 53 female applicants passed the physical ability portion of the selection program. Prior to this study, no woman had successfully completed this part of the selection battery. It should be noted, however, that it is unrealistic, and perhaps undesirable, to develop a selection program for physical abilities that eliminates all test score differences between men and women. The general evidence is that although women score lower than men on strength and endurance tests, they also demonstrate lower performance on jobs that require these abilities. In such cases, the adverse impact may be inherent in the job activities, not in the content of the test. To reduce male-female differences, the appropriate strategy would be to alter the job tasks rather than the tests used for selection.

As discussed in Chapter 2, the Americans with Disabilities Act of 1990 prohibits discrimination on the basis of disability and requires employers to take action to hire and advance the disabled. Such action includes "reasonable accommodation" of the disabled worker in the work processes and physical setting of the job. This has generally been interpreted to mean that adjustments should be made for the known physical and mental limitations of an otherwise qualified disabled applicant or employee unless the organization can demonstrate that the accommodation would cause undue hardship to the firm. Both financial and safety costs are weighed in this consideration of undue hardship.

An employer is not justified in presuming that a disabled worker is unable to perform a job. It is necessary that a thorough job analysis be conducted and physical ability tests be identified for important corresponding job tasks. Even if this is done, the job tasks may still be subject to the reasonable accommodation directive. In general, courts have placed a more stringent demand for reasonable accommodation on employers when the disabled individuals are employees returning to work after illness or injury than when they are new workers. Of direct importance for physical ability testing is the ruling in *E. E. Black, Ltd. v. Marshall*.[51] In this case the plaintiff was rejected for the job of apprentice carpenter, which required a good deal of lifting and carrying, because of a back condition detected in the medical screening for the job. The court ruled, based on other evidence including the examination of an orthopedist, that even though the plaintiff should be considered disabled (the back condition), he still could perform the job. The court expressly disagreed with the company's position that the plaintiff should be denied employment because he constituted a future risk for injury. In this case, an employment decision made on the basis of a valid physical ability test rather than a medical screening test may have avoided the confrontation.

No general presumptions can be made about the physical abilities of older applicants, either. That is, an organization cannot assume that an applicant over the age of 40 (threshold age in the Age Discrimination in Employment Act of 1967) is incapable of any physical demands of a job. However, the use of physical ability tests that correspond to job requirements should be an acceptable basis for selection decisions.

RECOMMENDATIONS FOR THE USE OF ABILITY TESTS IN SELECTION

In this chapter we presented brief descriptions of a few tests that are representative of ability tests. These tests were included because of their extensive use in selection over several years. However, be aware that in this chapter we have not described a large number of other ability tests that are available to HR specialists. For example, the Buros Institute of Mental Measurements provides online reviews of nearly 4,000 tests; its 2007 volume of *The Seventeenth Mental Measurements Yearbook* contains information on more than 200 tests. The sheer number of these tests creates a difficult situation for HR specialists. What is needed is a way to evaluate an ability test in order to assess its potential usefulness. Obviously, the best method of doing this would be to become familiar with the principles of psychological test construction and measurement. We have already presented some—but not nearly all—of these principles in Chapters 3 through 5, which were devoted to the role of measurement in selection. We now apply these concepts to the problem of assessing the potential usefulness of available ability tests.

Review Reliability Data

Our primary assumption is that a useful ability test should have development information available to users. One part of such information should consist of work done to estimate the reliability of the test. As we discussed previously, reliability is a necessary characteristic of a selection test. High reliability is an indication that the test can be expected to yield consistent scores for applicants and that uncontrolled factors that might affect the score of applicants are minimized. Therefore, information about the method of estimating reliability, the size and nature of the sample used to collect these data, and the magnitude of the reliability estimate should all be fully presented to users.

As we know, each of the four major ways of estimating reliability is appropriate for specific circumstances and inappropriate for others. For example, test-retest reliability calculated with a very short intervening period of time (such as a few hours or even a few days) may be an inflated estimate due to the effect of memory factors. It is necessary for the test user to determine whether the appropriate method of estimating reliability was employed, and whether this method was carried out correctly. It is clear that using larger samples (200+) yields better estimates of reliability than using smaller samples. Occasionally, samples of 30 to 50 respondents have been used in reliability studies. We considered the limitations of small-sample correlation estimates when we discussed validity generalization. Essentially the same limitations exist when reliability is calculated.

It is desirable that the sample of respondents used in reliability studies be similar to the individuals for whom the HR specialist intends to use the test. Perhaps the most common way to judge similarity is on the basis of demographic characteristics such as ethnicity, gender, average age, average education level, and occupational background. One can argue that these are not the most accurate indicants of similarity, because similarity between two groups actually means that the test is interpreted and answered in the same fashion by the two groups. However, collecting such data would require work far beyond that normally done in test development. Information about demographic characteristics allows the user to at least note major differences and form hypotheses about the meaning of such differences. For example, if the reliability of a test of English grammar and writing has been estimated using a sample of college students, and the applicant pool in the selection situation is mainly high school students, the reliability may not be the same for the two groups. If the test is of moderate difficulty for the college students, it may be very difficult for high school students. Difficult tests often have low reliability because respondents frequently guess in making their responses, and such guesses are sources of error of measurement. Therefore, the stated reliability of the test may not be accurate for the applicant pool. The same argument can be applied to many craft or mechanical ability tests that have used experienced workers rather than inexperienced ones in reliability estimates.

A minimum reliability estimate of 0.85 to 0.90 is commonly thought to be necessary for selection use. This is because selection involves making a decision for each applicant about whether to extend a job offer. This decision is based on the scores of the selection tests used. If the test is not highly reliable, the large standard error of measurement accompanying a test score would make choosing among applicants very uncertain. For example, using the standard error of measurement information contained in Chapter 4, we would estimate that the range of true scores for a test with an estimated reliability of 0.60 and a standard deviation of 15 is ±9.5 points with a 68 percent confidence level. If an applicant scores an 80 on this test, the true score realistically could be anywhere between 70 and 90. With such a large range, identifying meaningful differences among applicants is very difficult. However, if the same test has a reliability of 0.90, then the standard error becomes ±4.7 points with the same confidence level. The range of probable true scores becomes much smaller, and the test results are more precise and easier for the selection specialist to use.

Review Validity Data

The second major kind of information that should be made available to test users is validity data accumulated during test development and use. Two kinds of validity data are desirable. One kind indicates that the ability test measures what it is said to measure. Frequently this information is reported in terms of statistical analyses of the scores. Two of the most common types of analyses are (a) correlational analyses of the scores of the test with other psychological measures and (b) factor analyses of the items of the test or of the test with other tests. We mentioned examples of such correlational analyses when we discussed mental ability tests. To know that scores on mental ability tests are correlated with various measures of educational achievement greatly improves our understanding of what these tests measure. In some cases, correlations with other tests are conducted. For example, we noted that the *Bennett Mechanical Comprehension Test* was correlated with verbal ability and spatial visualization tests. This indicates that the test measures more than mechanical concepts.

Factor analysis is a technique for analyzing the interrelationships among several tests or a set of test items. For example, if 20 test items have been given to 400 individuals, the first step is to correlate each item with every other item. Further statistical manipulations attempt to identify small groups of items that are highly correlated with one another and minimally correlated with other groups of items. Each group of items is called a *factor* and named by the common psychological characteristic measured. For example, on this 20-item test, one group of 10 basic arithmetic problems might be identified as one factor and 10 vocabulary questions might be identified as a second factor. This test can then be said to measure arithmetic ability and vocabulary. The ability that is measured is identified from the common content of the items that make up the factor. The importance of this type of information is that the HR specialist can examine the correspondence between the factors that are identified and the abilities that are to be tested in the selection program. It is necessary that the test, in fact, match the abilities identified from the job analysis.

The second type of validity information that can be provided is the correlation of the test scores with some measure of training or job performance. This is the criterion-related validity to which we have frequently referred. Demonstration of validity for a measure of training or job performance similar to the one of interest to the test specialist is, obviously, the most desirable data.

Our opinion is that this information about reliability and validity of the ability test, at minimum, must be available to the user. Other test construction data (such as norm group scores, difficulty levels of items, and whether the test measures one or multiple topics) can also be useful. However, such data are usually of secondary importance compared to basic reliability and validity information. If reliability and validity data are not provided or are inappropriately calculated, the HR specialist should be wary of using the ability test. It is not a difficult task physically to construct a purported ability test.

Most intelligent individuals, with a few friends and a long weekend, could write 50 multiple-choice test items that were intended to measure any of several abilities (for example, mathematics, English, logical reasoning or, given enough reference books, technical areas such as computer programming, football analysis, and carpentry). The trick is to make sure that the test is what it is intended to be. The only way an HR specialist who is considering using an ability test can tell this is by examining the reliability and validity information. *No amount of verbal assurance provided by the test seller can substitute for such information.* After all, the test seller has a vested interest in describing the test in favorable terms in order to sell more tests.

Use in Small Business

It is feasible to purchase and use ability tests and job knowledge tests for selection in small businesses. There are, however, two important considerations for such use. The first is to identify tests that are appropriate. To do this, it is necessary to first identify the knowledge and abilities that are necessary for the job through a job analysis. This identification should be made by listing the knowledge/ability and an abbreviated statement of the most important tasks that require this knowledge/ability. For example,

Knowledge of principles of residential electrical wiring.

Task 1: Connecting outside power transformer to household energy supply

Task 2: Stringing 110-volt and 220-volt wires through rooms of the house

Task 3: Wiring household lights and appliances

Task 4: Building the circuit breaker panel

By doing this, the small business manager will obtain adequate, detailed information that will allow him or her to choose the appropriate test. This is done in the following way. After accumulating this information, the manager would contact various test publishers (go back to Chapter 3 to review these organizations) and obtain catalogs (or look at publishers' websites) that describe published tests. The manager would then compare the information about job knowledge, abilities, and tasks with descriptions of tests in order to tentatively identify the appropriate tests for measuring the same knowledge and abilities. (We also discussed doing this in Chapter 3.)

The second consideration is the purchase of relevant tests. As we discussed in Chapter 3, many test publishers categorize their tests into three levels: A, B, and C. Level A tests are the only ones that may be purchased by an individual without demonstrating some specialized training or education. Many job knowledge and ability tests are at this level. Other tests classified as level B or C would not be available to most managers of small businesses. To appropriately use published ability tests, tests must be selected to match the specific knowledge and abilities needed for the job; they must be of such a nature as to be usable by individuals with little formal training in testing.

Chapter Summary

We could tell you much more about ability tests, but you should move on to the remaining chapters so you can become a well-rounded selection expert. We will leave you with the following thoughts to dwell on at your leisure. You can also use this list as a basis for asking your instructor a series of endless questions about ability tests. That would surely affect your grade!

Ability tests are

1. Useful—they are valid predictors for all forms of job performance.

2. Cheap—most can be purchased for a reasonable price from a test publisher.

3. Fast—most take an applicant 30 minutes or less to complete.

4. Easy—they can be administered individually or in group settings.

5. Versatile—many come in several languages.

6. Scorable—publishers usually provide a scoring key that can be used by an organization member.

7. Understandable—many ability tests reflect knowledge that is job based, especially mechanical, skilled crafts, and clerical ability tests. Both applicants and organization members who review scores can usually understand what the test is measuring.

8. Sometimes falsely marketed—because ability tests have worked so well and are familiar to many applicants, sometimes unscrupulous and nefarious individuals make up their own tests. They write items that seem to measure important knowledge or abilities, describe the test in glowing terms, develop elaborate brochures or websites, and aggressively sell these tests to the unwary. Do not be among the unwary (or unwashed, but that is a different story). Look at the test development data! Ask about the reliability and validity studies! Be suspicious! Be wary!

REFERENCES

1. Par Lahy, "La selection psycho-physiologique des machinistes de la société des transports en commun de la région Parisienne," *L'Année Pschologique* 25 (1924): 106–172.

2. Philip DuBois, *A History of Psychological Testing* (Boston: Allyn & Bacon, 1970).

3. Anne Anastasi, *Psychological Testing*, 5th ed. (London: Macmillan, 1982), 393.

4. Lewis Aiken, *Psychological Testing and Assessment*, 2nd ed. (Boston: Allyn & Bacon, 1988), 107.

5. Ibid., 108–109.

6. Anastasi, *Psychological Testing*, 387.

7. Christopher M. Berry, Melissa L. Guys, and Paul R. Sackett, "Educational Attainment as a Proxy for Cognitive Ability in Selection: Effects on Levels of Cognitive Ability and Adverse Impact," *Journal of Applied Psychology* 91 (2006): 696–705.

8. Robert Guion, *Personnel Testing* (New York: McGraw-Hill, 1965), 234.

9. Ibid., 221.

10. Buros Institute of Mental Measurements, *The Fourteenth Mental Measurements Yearbook*, ed. Barbara S. Plake and James C. Impara (Lincoln, NE: Buros Institute of Mental Measurements, 2001).

11. Donald E. Super and John O. Crites, *Appraising Vocational Fitness*, rev. ed. (New York: Harper & Row, 1962), 87–88.

12. John Campbell, "An Overview of the Army Selection and Classification Project (Project A)," *Personnel Psychology* 43 (1990): 243–257.

13. Jeffrey J. McHenry, Leaetta M. Hough, Jody L. Toquam, Mary Ann Hanson, and Steven Ashworth, "Project A Validity Results: The Relationship between Predictor and Criterion Domains," *Personnel Psychology* 43 (1990): 335–354.

14. John E. Hunter, "Cognitive Ability, Cognitive Attitudes, Job Knowledge, and Job Performance," *Journal of Vocational Behavior* 29 (1986): 340–362; see also Gwen E. Jones and Malcom James Ree, "Aptitude Test Score Validity: No Moderating Effect Due to Job Ability Requirement Differences," *Educational and Psychological Measurement* 58 (1998): 284–294.

15. Frank L. Schmidt and John E. Hunter, "The Validity and Utility of Selection Methods in Personnel Psychology: Practical and Theoretical Implications of 85 Years of Research Findings," *Psychological Bulletin* 124 (1998): 262–274.

16. Richard R. Reilly and Michael A Warech, "The Validity and Fairness of Alternatives to Cognitive Tests," in *Policy Issues in Employment Testing*, ed. Linda Wing and Bernard R. Gifford (Norwell, MA: Kluwer, 1993).

17. Philip Bobko, Philip L. Roth, and Denise Potosky, "Derivation and Implications of a Meta-Analytic Matrix Incorporating Cognitive Ability, Alternative Predictors, and Job Performance," *Personnel Psychology* 52 (1999): 561–589.

18. David E. Terpstra, A. Amin Mohamed, and R. Bryan Kethley, "An Analysis of Federal Court Cases Involving Nine Selection Devices," *International Journal of Selection and Assessment* 7 (1999): 26–34.

19. Hunter, "Cognitive Ability, Cognitive Attitudes, Job Knowledge, and Job Performance," 354.

20. Virginia Boehm, "Different Validity: A Methodological Artifact," *Journal of Applied Psychology* 62 (1977): 146–154.

21. John Hunter, Frank Schmidt, and Ronda Hunter, "Differential Validity of Employment Tests by Race: A Comprehensive Review and Analysis," *Psychological Bulletin* 85 (1979): 721–735.

22. Philip L. Roth, Craig A. Bevier, Philip Bobko, Fred S. Switzer III, and Peggy Tyler, "Ethnic Group Differences in Cognitive Ability in Employment and Educational Settings: A Meta-Analysis," *Personnel Psychology* 54 (2001): 297–330.

23. Leatta M. Hough, Frederick L. Oswald, and Robert E. Polyhart, "Determinants, Detection, and Amelioration of Adverse Impact in Personnel Selection Procedures: Issues, Evidence and Lessons Learned," *International Journal of Selection and Assessment* 9 (2001): 152–194.

24. Denise Potosky, Philip Bobko, and Philip Roth, "Forming Composites of Cognitive Ability and Alternative Measures to Predict Job Performance and Reduce Adverse Impact: Corrected Estimates and Realistic Expectations," *International Journal of Selection & Assessment* (2005): 304–315.

25. Christopher M. Berry, Melissa L. Gruys, and Paul R. Sackett, "Educational Attainment as a Proxy for Cognitive Ability in Selection: Effects on Levels of Cognitive Ability and Adverse Impact," *Journal of Applied Psychology* 91 (2006): 696–705.

26. Kevin R. Murphy, Brian E. Cronin, and Anita P. Tam, "Controversy and Consensus Regarding the Use of Cognitive Ability Tesing in Organizations," *Journal of Applied Psychology* 88 (2003): 660–671.

27. *Friend et al. v. City of Richmond et al.*, 588 F. 2d 61 (4th Cir. 1978).

28. *Van Aken et al. v. Young and City of Detroit et al.*, 541 Supp. 448 (U.S. Dist. 1982).

29. *Pegues v. Mississippi State Employment Service*, 488 F. Supp. 239 (N.D. Miss 1980), gaff's 699 F. 2d 760 (5th Cir. 1983), cert. denied, 464 U.S. 991, 78 L. Ed. 2d 679, 104 S. CT. 482 (1983).

30. *EEOC v. Atlas Paper Box Co.*, 868 F.2d 1487; (6th Cir.), cert. denied, 58 U.S. L.W., 3213 (1989).

31. Denise Potosky and Philip Bobko, "Selection Testing via the Internet: Practical Considerations and Exploratory Empirical Findings," *Personnel Psychology* 57 (2004): 1003–1034.

32. Nancy T. Tippins, James Beaty, Fritz Drasgow, Wade M. Gibson, Kenneth Pearlman, Daniel O. Segall, and William Shepherd, "Unproctored Internet Testing in Employment Settings," *Personnel Psychology* 59 (2006): 189–225.

33. William Shepherd, B. R. Do, and Fritz L. Drasgow, "Assessing Equivalence of Online Non-Cognitive Measures: Where Research Meets Practice," *paper presented at the Annual Conference of the Society for Industrial and Organizational Psychologists*, 2003, Orlando, Florida.

34. Klaus J. Templer and Stefan R. Lange, "Internet Testing: Equivalence between Proctored Lab and Unproctored Field Conditions," *Computers in Human Behavior* (2008): 1216–1228.

35. Tippins et. al, "Unproctored Internet Testing in Employment Settings."

36. J. A. Kulik, R. L. Bangert-Downs, and C. C. Kulik, "Effectiveness of Coaching for Aptitude Tests," *Psychological Bulletin* 95 (1984): 435–447.

37. Ann M. Ryan, Robert E. Polyhart, Gary Greguras, and M. J. Schmit, "Test Preparation Programs in Selection Contexts: Self-Selection and Program Effectiveness," *Personnel Psychology* 51 (1998): 599–621.

38. John P. Hausknecht, Charlie O. Trevor, and James L. Farr, "Retaking Ability Tests in a Selection Setting: Implications for Practice Effects, Training Performance, and Turnover," *Journal of Applied Psychology* 87 (2002): 243–254.

39. Super and Crites, *Appraising Vocational Fitness*, 219.

40. Ibid., 220–221.

41. Paul M. Muchinsky, "Validation of Intelligence and Mechanical Aptitude Tests in Selecting Employees for Manufacturing Jobs," Special Issue: Test Validity Yearbook: IL, *Journal of Business and Psychology* 7 (1993): 373–382.

42. R. B. Selover, "Review of the Minnesota Clerical Test," *The Third Mental Measurements Yearbook*, ed. Oscar K. Buros (New Brunswick, NJ: Rutgers University Press, 1949), 635–636.

43. Michael A. Campion, "Personnel Selection for Physically Demanding Jobs: Review and Recommendations," *Personnel Psychology* 36 (1983): 527–550.

44. Norman D. Henderson, Michael W. Berry, and Tomislov Matic, "Field Measures of Strength and Fitness Predict Firefighter Performance on Physically Demanding Tasks," *Personnel Psychology* 60 (2007): 431–473.

45. Edwin A. Fleishman and Michael D. Mumford, "Ability Requirement Scales," in *Job Analysis Handbook for Business, Industry, and Government*, vol. 2, ed. Sidney Gael (New York: John Wiley, 1988).

46. Edwin A. Fleishman, *Physical Abilities Analysis Manual*, rev. ed. (Palo Alto, CA: Consulting Psychologists Press, 1992).

47. Fleishman and Mumford, "Ability Requirement Scales."

48. Joyce Hogan, "Structure of Physical Performance in Occupational Tasks," *Journal of Applied Psychology* 76 (1991): 495–507; see also Joyce Hogan, "Physical Abilities," in *Handbook of Industrial Psychology*, 2nd ed., vol. 2, ed. Marvin D. Dunnette and Leaetta M. Hough (Palo Alto, CA: Consulting Psychologists Press).

49. Barry R. Blakley, Miguel A. Quinones, Marnie Swerdlin Crawford, and Ann I. Jago, "The Validity of Isometric Strength Tests," *Personnel Psychology* 47 (1994): 247–274.

50. *Weeks v. Southern Bell Telephone & Telegraph Co.*, 408 F.2d 228, 1 Empl. Prac. Dec. (CCH) 9970 (5th Cir. 1969).

51. *E. E. Black, Ltd. v. Marshall*, 24 Empl. Prac. Dec. (CCH) 31260 (D. Haw. 1980).

chapter 12

Personality Assessment for Selection

Now that you are well on your way to becoming an expert in selection (which must be true because there are only four chapters left, including this one, and we know what kind of student you are), you will be fascinated to learn about the use of personality measures in selection, one of the most complex and rapidly changing topics in the field. Selection researchers have found that personality data, when gathered appropriately, can provide valid information for making selection decisions.[1] As a result, the use of personality tests in selection is rapidly increasing. For example, a survey published in 2005 by the Society of Human Resource Management indicated that 30 percent of American companies used personality tests to screen job applicants. Larger organizations apparently are more likely than smaller ones to use these instruments; more than 40 percent of *Fortune 100* companies use them to hire at least some job applicants, ranging from entry level to CEO.[2] Nevertheless, a recent study of staffing practices in 20 countries found personality tests are used more frequently in other countries than they are in the United States. In fact, between 50 percent and 80 percent of firms use these tests in New Zealand, South Africa, Spain, and Sweden.[3] In this chapter we summarize the major issues with regard to the use of personality data, along with the relevant research. We conclude that personality data can make an independent contribution to selection decisions. Moreover, there is no evidence that only people with so-called great personalities succeed. That gives me great hope.

DEFINITION AND USE OF PERSONALITY IN SELECTION

In popular usage, personality is often equated with social skill. It is thought of as the ability to elicit positive reactions from others in one's typical dealings with them. Psychologists who study personality professionally have a different concept. Although there is not a single standard definition of the term *personality,* most formal definitions agree that personality refers to the unique set of characteristics that define an individual and determine that person's pattern of interaction with the environment. The term *characteristics* is usually interpreted to include what people habitually think, feel, and act; these attributes are combined distinctly in each person. The environment includes both human and nonhuman elements (organizational demands, work conditions, physical environment, and so on). We can see, then, that personality involves much more than social skill; in fact, many believe that no other area of psychology represents as broad a topic as personality.[4]

Personality would seem, therefore, to be critically important in selection. After all, everyone has a personality and personality influences performance at work. When we review job analysis information, especially for jobs above entry-level positions, we find the employee's personality characteristics are essential for job performance. Two broad personality traits, conscientiousness and emotional stability, are likely to be valid for all or nearly all jobs. These traits relate to how hardworking, persistent, and achievement oriented one is, and they predict the candidate's ability to cope with the stress of hazardous conditions or emotionally demanding work. What manager, after all, sets out to hire a lazy, irresponsible worker who is always stressed out and unable to cope at work? Other personality traits are valid for some but not all jobs or activities. Agreeableness might be such a trait. This trait, which relates to how someone gets along with others, is likely to be important in jobs that emphasize interaction with other people, such as customer service representative, secretary, or even team member.[5]

Given these findings, we should expect to find evidence that personality data are valid for selection. However, until recently this has not proved to be the case. In the mid-1960s, several individuals reviewed the use of personality data in selection. The following comments by Robert Guion and Richard Gottier are typical of the conclusions of this work:

> *It cannot be said that any of the conventional personality measures have demonstrated really general usefulness as selection tools in employment practice.... The number of tests resulting in acceptable statements of validity is greater than might be expected by pure chance—but not much. The best that can be said is that in* some *situations, for some purposes,* some *personality measures can offer helpful predictions.*[6]

Some researchers still generally agree with these earlier conclusions. In fact, Kevin Murphy and Jessica Dzieweczynski would still assert that the problems cited in the mid-1960s have not yet been resolved.[7] Predictive validities of personality traits are still quite low, rarely exceeding 0.20. Furthermore, our theoretical understanding of why specific personality traits are useful in specific jobs is still inadequate.[8] But other work has offered evidence supporting the use of personality data in selection decisions. Murray Barrick and Michael Mount summarized this evidence.[9]

First, there is growing agreement among researchers that personality characteristics can be grouped into five broad dimensions, referred to as the *Five-Factor Model*. These five traits are conscientiousness, emotional stability, agreeableness, extraversion, and openness to experience. We will discuss these traits extensively in the next few pages, but suffice it to say that the emergence of a consensus—and believe me, psychologists rarely agree on anything—enables researchers to develop better theories, addressing the criticism raised by Murphy and Dzieweczynski.

Second, managers intuitively believe personality traits matter at work. Not surprisingly, research shows managers' view relevant personality traits (which depend on the context or demands of the job) as being nearly as important to the candidate as general mental ability.[10] In fact, managers give greater weight to these traits than is warranted by the empirical evidence. Third, recent meta-analytic data show these traits can be relevant predictors of work performance, although the magnitudes of these relationships are modest.[11] This will be discussed later, but again, although these traits do not predict performance as well as some other selection tools (for example, general mental ability, work samples), they are useful predictors of a number of outcomes managers care about, including avoiding counterproductive behavior, reducing turnover and absenteeism, exhibiting more teamwork and leadership, providing more effective customer service, contributing more citizenship behavior, influencing job satisfaction and commitment to the firm, and enhancing safety. Furthermore, because more than one trait is used to predict later performance, we must recognize the multiple correlation, which jointly considers all relevant personality traits and will yield higher predictive validities.[12]

Fourth, because personality is not highly correlated to other useful selection tools (general mental ability, biodata, and so on), personality traits contribute incremental validity to the prediction of success at work—above and beyond what is added by these other predictors.[13] Fifth, there is little or no adverse impact, as mean scores are comparable across racial and ethnic groups and between men and women.[14] And of course, the threat of a discrimination lawsuit is an important consideration for any hiring manager. Finally, even if the effect for personality is small to modest, the employer obtains this benefit every single day the employee shows up for work. Research reveals that personality assessed in high school could predict career success 50 or more years later! This study showed that the multiple correlation or composite validity of the Five Factor traits was over 0.60 when predicting occupational success (status and income) 30 to 50 years after personality was assessed.[15] The fact that these modest effects compound throughout one's career illustrates why we believe personality traits matter.

We will discuss each of these points in more detail. As a start, we present background information derived from writings in personality theory.

Personality Traits

The use of personality data in selection requires classifying and measuring individuals according to some set of personality characteristics referred to as traits. A *trait* is a continuous dimension on which individual differences may be measured by the amount of the characteristic the individual exhibits.[16] *Sociability, independence,* and *need for achievement* are examples of traits. Individuals show large differences in the degree to which they demonstrate such traits.

The concept of traits begins with the common observation that individuals may differ sharply in their reactions to the same situation. For example, one individual enjoys a routine job working with data, whereas another is quite unhappy about the same task features. Similarly, one person is verbal and actively engaged in negotiating with others in a committee meeting while another is reticent. The concept of trait is used to explain these different reactions to the same situation. In these cases, individuals are thought to have different amounts of traits that could be referred to as openness to new experiences and dominance, a facet of extraversion. Traits are used to explain the consistency of an individual's behavior over a variety of situations. It has been observed that an individual who strives for dominance in a committee meeting frequently acts similarly in other group interactions. From this brief description, we can understand that some psychologists and many nonpsychologists frequently regard traits as the cause of a person's reactions to situations. The essence of traits has been conceptualized in many ways. The one element common to these different perspectives is that traits are viewed as the dispositional or relatively stable and enduring ways people tend to think, feel, and act.[17]

The use of personality data in selection requires, first, the specification of job tasks and, second, the identification of traits that are linked to these tasks. Table 12.1, which is derived from several studies, provides examples of personality traits that have been used in selection based on these steps. In previous chapters, we discussed the difficulties associated with the specification of employee knowledge, skills, and abilities (KSAs) in general. The first problem with specifying employee personality traits in particular is determining which personality traits to use.

It is in this regard that the recent work in the Five-Factor Model, which we referred to previously, is important. Generally, personality psychologists now agree there are five general factors of personality that can serve as a meaningful taxonomy for describing traits. In other words, these five factors can be thought of as the five core traits that influence behavior.[18]

Typically, the research that led to the development of the Five-Factor Model involved collecting vast amounts of data. A large sample of subjects completed several personality questionnaires, each of which was designed to measure multiple personality traits.

TABLE 12.1	Personality Traits for a Sample of Jobs Studied in Selection
Job	**Personality Trait**
Executive	Conscientiousness, emotional stability, extraversion, ambition (especially)
Supervisor	Persistence, endurance, emotional stability, nurturance
Salesperson	Conscientiousness, achievement (especially), ambition, extraversion
Secretary	Conscientiousness, dependability (especially), emotional stability, agreeableness
Computer Programmer	Conscientiousness, original thinking, openness to new experiences
Insurance Agent	Conscientiousness, extraversion, original thinking
Newspaper Writer	Conscientiousness, emotional stability, openness to new experiences
Carpenter	Conscientiousness, dependability (especially), emotional stability

Statistical analyses, such as factor analyses, was then used to determine whether all of these measured personality traits can be reduced to a smaller number. Such analyses have consistently identified five traits, each of which is composed of several related traits measured by the various personality questionnaires. The same five traits have been identified using different instruments, in different cultures, and using data obtained from different sources.[19]

Extraversion is the first dimension. Traits frequently associated in forming this dimension include (from the positive pole) sociability, gregariousness, assertiveness, optimism, ambition, and activity. Some personality specialists have interpreted this dimension to represent two basic components: ambition and sociability.[20] The second dimension is called *emotional stability*. Traits usually associated with it are calmness, security, confidence, resistance to upset, and lack of emotion. The third dimension, usually interpreted as *agreeableness*, is made up of courtesy, flexibility, trust, good natured, supportiveness, generosity, cooperativeness, forgiveness, and tolerance. The fourth dimension is labeled *conscientiousness*, characterized by responsibility, organization, dependability, decisiveness, hard work, achievement orientation, and perseverance. The fifth dimension is labeled *openness to experience*; it also has been referred to as *intellect* or *culture*.[21] This dimension includes imagination, culture, curiosity, intelligence, artistic sensitivity, originality, and broad mindedness. A sixth factor, recently found, extends the traditional Five-Factor Model. It has been called an honesty/humility factor, consisting of sincerity, fairness, avoidance of greed, and modesty. This trait seems to be particularly suited to predicting workplace deviance.[22] Many other personality traits relevant to work behavior have been studied but these are not well represented in the Five-Factor Model.

Other Personality Measures

Core Self Evaluation.   Tim Judge and his colleagues have presented considerable empirical evidence that core self-evaluations (CSEs) are important to performance at work. CSEs consist of four frequently studied traits: self-esteem, generalized self-efficacy, locus of control, and emotional stability. Research shows that candidates who have a strong predisposition to confidence, who feel good about themselves, and who can control their anxiety tend to be happier, see their work as more interesting, and are more productive at work. For example, a recent meta-analysis revealed a true-score correlation of 0.30 when predicting job performance.[23]

Emotional Intelligence. The second personality trait that has elicited considerable interest in selection contexts is emotional intelligence (EI). EI is a broad construct, one that appears to be composed of attributes beyond just personality. It includes nearly all noncognitive predictors and some that appear to be cognitive measures. In many respects, this may be the biggest question EI research is focused on: What is EI? EI is purported to measure the candidate's self-awareness and self-regulation, as well as social awareness and relationship management. Thus, this measure includes the ability to recognize one's emotions and to exert control over them, to manage one's disruptive impulses, and to pursue and persist toward one's goals. The trait also assesses interpersonal competence, including one's ability to perceive others' emotions and to anticipate their needs and desires.[24]

Obviously, being able to control one's emotions, to focus one's motivation on critical goals, and to effectively interact with others should contribute to success at work. However, there has not been enough research in work settings to enable us to fully realize the promise of this construct. This led one set of researchers to conclude that "the ratio of hyperbole to hard evidence is rather high, with overreliance on anecdotes and unpublished surveys."[25] This underscores the fact that it is incumbent upon the practitioner to carefully examine evidence of predictive validity and other psychometric evidence to ensure the EI measure relates to important outcomes at work. We believe the field is not currently at an adequate level of understanding to be recommended as a selection tool. It certainly seems promising, but the available research has not yet clearly revealed the value of this predictor in selection settings.

Proactive Personality. The third individual measure is proactive personality. This trait reflects a dispositional approach toward taking initiative at work and effecting environmental changes. This "action-oriented" trait has been shown to predict salary, the rate of promotions, use of transformational leadership, entrepreneurial intentions, and job performance.[26] Proactive personality has been shown to relate to conscientiousness (especially achievement-striving) and extraversion and, to a lesser extent, to openness to experience and emotional stability.[27] However, these Five-Factor Model measures were also found to account for only about 25 percent of the variance in proactive personality. Consequently, proactive personality reflects something more than just the Five-Factor Model. Because employers are increasingly demanding their employees take responsibility for their own career development and be more self-directed at work, we anticipate this construct will continue to garner interest from both researchers and practitioners.

Without doubt, the most frequently used technique to assess personality is to ask for self-reports. However, reliance on self-report questionnaires may limit the validities of these personality traits, and this is not due to the biasing effects of intentional distortion. Rather, self-ratings of personality are influenced by a very broad "frame of reference" that includes non-job-relevant behaviors as well as behaviors at work. In contrast, when we obtain personality ratings from others who observe us at work, their ratings reflect our reputation at work. Self-reports may introduce irrelevant effects that reduce the correlation between trait scores and measures of job performance. In contrast, ratings of supervisors, coworkers, and customers are limited to job behaviors, which are particularly relevant. The authors of one study gathered self-report ratings of the Five-Factor Model from 105 sales representatives, as well as ratings from at least one supervisor, coworker, and customer. Results showed that self-ratings produced either insignificant or lower validity coefficients than those produced from ratings of the other three sources for all traits except conscientiousness.[28] The tentative explanation for this finding is that the frame of reference for self-ratings differed from that of the other ratings, which accounted for the differences in validity coefficients. A related study using personality ratings from high school (ratings were provided by a psychologist) found that the Five Factor dimensions, especially conscientiousness and emotional stability (the universal predictors), were related to career success 50 or more years later.[29] Again, these predictive validities were larger than those typically resulting from self-reports. Taken together, these results underscore the value of considering alternative ways of assessing personality. On the following pages, we review some of these approaches.

PERSONALITY MEASUREMENT METHODS

We stated in Chapters 1 and 3 that the accurate measurement of many human characteristics is difficult because we are trying to quantify intangible constructs through the use of inferred data. This is especially true in the measurement of personality. To fully understand the use of personality in selection, it is necessary to understand the nature and characteristics of these measurement methods. The three most commonly used methods in selection are inventories, the judgment of interviewers, and the judgment of other observers, especially former co-workers or supervisors. We discuss each of these separately.

Inventories in Personality Measurement

Inventories use the written responses of an individual as the information for determining personality. There are literally hundreds of such measures, all differing substantially in their characteristics. Many can be found in the test sources mentioned in Chapter 3— for example, the Buros Institute's *Mental Measurements Yearbook*. Some of these inventories are designed to measure abnormal personality traits; others measure normal traits. Some devices measure several personality dimensions, and others measure only one. It would be impossible to discuss each one of these devices here. Instead, we discuss only two major types of inventories—self-report questionnaires and projective techniques—to illustrate their principal characteristics.

Self-Report Questionnaires. These instruments usually consist of a series of brief items asking respondents to use a multiple-choice answer format to indicate personal information about thoughts, emotions, and past experiences. Typical items begin with statements such as "I am happy" or "I enjoy going to small parties" or "I think good things happen to those who work hard." Respondents are frequently given only three response categories: agree, undecided, or disagree. These questionnaires assume that a correspondence exists between what people say about themselves and what is actually true. They also assume that individuals are aware of their thoughts and emotions and are willing to share them openly. For illustrative purposes, we will discuss one often used self-report inventory. In addition, we will discuss three other measures that have been found to predict work behavior. Each of these measures focuses on a single personality trait. But first, we review the Five Factor personality model.

The Five-Factor Model. We mentioned the Five-Factor Model earlier. Actually there are several different measuring devices of the five core personality dimensions. The two most often used in selection are the *NEO-Personality Inventory,* developed by Paul Costa

TABLE 12.2	Scales and Representative Items of Five Factor Personality Dimensions

Personality Scale[*]	Typical Item
Extraversion	I tend not to say what I think about things.
Agreeableness	I tend to trust other people.
Conscientiousness	I approach most of my work steadily and persistently.
Stability	Whenever I'm by myself, I feel vulnerable.
Openness to Experience	I enjoy eating in new restaurants I know nothing about.

*Based on the revised *Personality Characteristics Inventory* by Murray P. Barrick and Michael K. Mount, published by Wonderlic, Inc., Libertyville, Illinois.

and Robert McCrae, and the *Personality Characteristics Inventory (PCI),* developed by Murray Barrick and Michael Mount. We will discuss the PCI in detail, as at least one of the authors of this book is somewhat familiar with this test (Murray Barrick is a co-author).

The PCI has 150 multiple-choice items derived from empirical research using several Five-Factor Model inventories. Each item has three possible responses: "agree," "undecided," and "disagree." Typically it takes 30 to 45 minutes to complete the PCI. The five personality dimensions measured, together with examples of typical (not actual) items, are presented in Table 12.2. Each of the Five Factors can best be understood in terms of more specific related traits that characterize the broad trait.[30] Think of each of these traits as bipolar: Opposite extreme scores on each dimension represent opposite behaviors of the trait measured.

Other Self-Report Personality Inventories.   A number of different personality inventories using self-report methodologies are available to the practitioner; we have described the PCI as one example. Not all of these measure the Five-Factor Model. For example, the 16 PF contains more than 5 factors—16 "primary" factors, to be precise. Although research has shown that these 16 personality factors can be subsumed into the Five Factor measures, effective prediction also can be obtained using non–Five Factor measures. Later in the chapter, for example, we introduce three such measures. Some frequently used self-report personality inventories and the names of the original authors are reported in Table 12.3.

Forced-Choice Inventories.   As the name implies, forced-choice measures of personality require test-takers to choose the most liked item of two to four equally desirable items. The primary advantage of this is that faking or response distortion tends to be reduced; "faking good" is difficult when the items are equally "desirable." For example, when applying for an engineering job, you are asked to endorse either "I like football" or "I like wii sports." In this case, applicants don't know the right answer; because they happen to live in Texas, they are comfortable answering "I like football." In reality, based on criterion keying, the correct answer is actually the one high-performing engineers select.

The U.S. Navy and Army have recently developed forced-choice computer adaptive personality tests creatively called the Navy Computer Adaptive Personality System (NCAPS) and the Army's Assessment of Individual Motivation (AIM).[31] Answering these types of tests invokes deeper processing and is cognitively more demanding, but

TABLE 12.3	Examples of Personality Inventories and Authors
16 Personality Factor Test (16 PF)	Raymond Cattell
California Psychological Inventory (CPI)	Harrison Gough
Myers-Briggs Type Indicator (MBTI)	Katherine Cook Briggs and Isabel Briggs Meyers
Conditional Reasoning Test (of Aggression)	Lawrence James and Michael McIntyre
NEO-Personality Inventory (NEO-PI)	Paul T. Costa, Jr. and Robert R. McCrae
Hogan Personality Inventory (HPI)	Robert and Joyce Hogan
Global Personality Inventory (GPI)	PDI, Inc.
Gordon Personal Profile (GPP)	Leonard Gordon
Jackson Personality Inventory (JPI)	Doug Jackson
Guilford-Zimmerman Temperament Survey (GZTS)	J. P. Guilford and Wayne Zimmerman

the tests do reduce acquiescent responding and other response biases (as well as faking). One trade-off is that because the tests rely on computer adapted assessment, the number of items answered is shorter. Testing is more efficient because it more accurately measures personality traits; each question asked is dependent on the desired level of the trait measured in the previously answered question (estimated using item response theory).[32]

Forced-choice inventories are psychometrically challenging in a number of ways—including negative intercorrelations as a product of the dependencies between item responses and the fact each applicant responds to a unique set of items.[33] Nevertheless, a few studies yield predictive validities that are as good as or better than more traditional likert-scale self-report personality scales.[34] Although there are issues to be resolved with forced-choice inventories, they do warrant consideration as another way to assess personality.

Projective Techniques.   These devices are similar to self-report questionnaires in that they require verbal responses that are scored to obtain measures of personality characteristics. However, they differ noticeably on several other important aspects. In contrast to the structure of both the questions and the answers of self-report questionnaires, projective techniques are intentionally ambiguous. For example, the respondent is presented with a series of inkblots or pictures and asked to make up a story about each one. Instructions are usually kept brief and vague. Another frequently used technique is to present the respondent with a series of sentence stems such as "My father …" or "My favorite …." Respondents are asked to complete each sentence. In both types, respondents are encouraged to say whatever they wish. The inkblots, pictures, or sentence stems are purposefully chosen to be open to a wide variety of reasonable answers. The assumption underlying projective techniques is that they allow respondents to expose central ways of "organizing experience and structuring life" because meanings are imposed on a stimulus having "relatively little structure and cultural patterning."[35] In this sense, these devices might be classified as "weak testing situations" in which individual differences in personality mainly account for the differences in responses among people. These techniques are called "projective" because, given the ambiguity of the items, the respondent must project interpretation on them. This interpretation is held to be an extension of the personality of the individual. The proposed advantage of these devices for obtaining data on personality is that the respondent is not supposed to realize the possible interpretation of the information provided. This encourages the respondent to make public certain information that might otherwise not be provided. For example, a subject might interpret a picture of two interacting people as a violent argument that will lead to one individual physically assaulting the other. According to the theory of projective techniques, the aggression expressed in this story is more a function of the aggressive impulses of the individual than the context of the picture, which was deliberately chosen to be ambiguous. It would then be hypothesized, given additional data, that the respondent is an angry person with a predisposition to experience the world as peopled by hostile individuals.[36]

Miner Sentence Completion Scale (MSCS). The MSCS was developed by John Miner specifically to assess the motives that are characteristically manifested at work and in the managerial role.[37] The respondent is presented with 40 items or sentences and asked to complete each. Only 35 of the items are scored to form measures on seven different motivation scales. Table 12.4 contains these scales and some representative items. Many of the specific items of this instrument refer to situations that are either outside the work environment entirely or are not specifically related to the managerial job. This is done to minimize the ability of respondents to distort their responses to present a particular image of themselves. Each of the seven scales was developed to measure a particular managerial motive. The *authority figures* scale measures the subject's capacity to meet role requirements in the area of relationships with his or her superior. *Competitive games* and *competitive situations* both focus on occupational or work-related competition. The *assertive role* generally reflects a person's confidence in his ability to perform well and a wish to participate in activities. *Imposing wishes* refers to controlling or directing the behavior of others. The scale for *standing out from the group* uses items describing situations where an individual is highly visible and measures the desire to assume a somewhat deviant position as compared with subordinates. The last scale, *routine administrative functions,* is used as an indicant of the desire to meet job requirements related to day-to-day administrative work.

A complete scoring guide has been developed. Using this guide, each response is scored as positive, neutral, or negative according to whether the response is a positive

TABLE 12.4 Scales and Representative Items from the Miner Sentence Completion Scale

Scale	Items
Authority Figures	My family doctor … Police officers …
Competitive Games	Playing golf … When playing cards, I …
Competitive Situations	Running for political office … Final examinations …
Assertive Role	Shooting a rifle … Wearing a necktie …
Imposing Wishes	Punishing children … When one of my staff asks me for advice …
Standing Out from the Group	Presenting a report at a staff meeting … Making introductions …
Routine Administrative Functions	Dictating letters … Decisions …

Source: John B. Miner, *Studies in Management Education* (New York: Springer, 1965).

or negative emotion in association with the content of the item. In addition, various overall scores can be obtained, one of which compares the respondent's answers to those of a normative sample of individuals. Work with the MSCS has generally focused on describing managerial motivation and success within large, bureaucratic organizations. Test-retest correlations indicate acceptable levels of reliability (about 0.80) for the MSCS. Furthermore, evidence of both construct and criterion-related validation has been reported. For example, one meta-analytic study found that the MSCS demonstrated a predicted pattern of correlations with other personality measures, was positively related to various measures of managerial effectiveness, and was predictive of those individuals who opt for a career in management.[38]

The Interview in Personality Measurement

We discussed the selection interview in Chapter 10 as a device used to predict productivity through the assessment of applicant characteristics. We will not repeat that information here, so this section is brief. However, it is known that the interview serves as a primary device for estimating personality characteristics of applicants.

An interview is frequently used as a convenient way to determine how an applicant would typically act on the job. A recent meta-analysis found that traits are the most frequently assessed constructs in the employment interview.[39] Conscientiousness is the most frequently measured personality trait in the interview; is assessed as often as all other personality traits combined. Since this trait is a universal predictor, we are not surprised that hiring managers want to measure it. Although there are not a large number of studies showing the predictive validity of these measures, the available evidence suggests that interviewer ratings of applicant personality are moderately related to job performance, with true score predictive validities of 0.33 for extraversion and conscientiousness. The predictive validity for the trait of agreeableness was 0.51, although this measure was assessed in less than 10 percent of the studies examining personality in this meta-analysis.[40] We believe these findings highlight the importance of specifying whether a personality trait is likely to be relevant in a specific situation. At least for agreeableness, the predictive validity is quite high when the measure is deemed to be relevant in a specific work setting.

Psychologists and HR managers have studied this personality assessment process and have come up with several important findings that are likely to affect the accuracy and validity of interviewer ratings of personality. First, interviewers need to be aware that there is a natural tendency to attribute others' behavior to personality rather than to situational causes. Such attributions contrast with the way we analyze our own behavior, believing that the conditions of a situation are more often the determinants of our action than are personality traits.[41] To compound this, raters often interpret even small amounts of behavior as signs of underlying traits and motives.[42] This may explain why interviewer ratings of personality often do not correlate very highly with self-reported measures of personality.[43]

Accurate assessment of a job candidate's personality may actually increase when using an unstructured interview rather than a structured interview. The notion is that an unstructured interview relies on questions that are often open-ended and can be answered with a wide variety of responses. Because there are no obvious right or wrong answers to these questions, the responses given are expected to be influenced by the candidate's own personality. Because the interview is less structured, it is likely to be a weaker situation, which also allows the applicant's personality to emerge more. These reasons should allow unstructured interviews to result in more accurate assessment of the candidate's personality. Some recent research supports this notion.[44]

Does this mean that we are encouraging you to use unstructured interviews? As discussed in Chapter 10, structured interviews have higher predictive validity. Furthermore, a recent meta-analysis examining the constructs that are assessed in the employment interview also supported the utility of the structured interview when assessing personality. The researchers found that the predictive validities for personality constructs reported for highly structured interviews were higher than those reported for interviews with less structure (extraversion, $\rho = 0.40$ versus 0.22; conscientiousness, $\rho = 0.37$ versus 0.24). Although interviewer assessments of personality may be more accurate in an unstructured interview, these data show that whatever is influencing interviewer ratings in structured interviews also contains valid job-related information.[45] Future research is needed to examine what information is being used to form impressions of candidate personality during the interview; this research should consider whether that information is useful for predicting later job performance. A recent study by Michael Cole, Hubert Feild, and William Giles shows that recruiters are able to assess candidate personality just from the applicants' resumes.[46] These results suggest it may not be as difficult to form valid judgments about candidate qualifications or "personality" as one might expect.

The Appropriate Use of the Interview. Having said all this, what statements can we make about the use of the interview in personality assessment? Recall from Chapter 10 that we concluded the interview is an appropriate way to assess interpersonal skills and work habits, both of which reflect personality traits. Our first recommendation with regard to such assessments is that the scope of the interview be limited. Instead of attempting to assess the complete personality of applicants, it would be more feasible to measure social interaction patterns and work patterns (such as attention to detail, meeting difficult objectives, and so on) identified through job analysis information. This would limit the number of personality traits that must be judged and identify more carefully the ones that are to be assessed. For example, attention to detail may be an important personal characteristic for clerical or computer system jobs within organizations. The interviewer should, therefore, attempt to find information about this trait rather than attempting a more complete personality description that would include traits such as *ambition, aggressiveness,* and *sociability.* These may seem desirable, but are not directly related to job activities.

The problem, however, is how to successfully accomplish this. One way to assess personality is to concentrate on previous behaviors that seem to depend on the same personality trait. In this case, interview questions and discussion could be addressed to previous instances in which the interviewee demonstrated behaviors requiring attention to detail. The *Behavior Description Interview* discussed in Chapter 10 is appropriate here. It is not necessary that responses be phrased in terms of employment activities. Other activities might include hobbies and academic behaviors. It is hoped that information could be obtained about the nature of the behavior or activity, length of time involved, relevance to the demands of the job or work context, and whether one or multiple instances of the behavior can be cited. In interviews, the interviewer is the measuring device. It is hoped that by limiting the scope of decisions that the interviewer must make, and by maximizing the correspondence between the information gathered and the type of assessment that must be made, personality assessment accuracy will be increased.

Observer Ratings of Personality

As we saw in the interview, observers can rate an applicant's personality, even after brief conversations. This finding corresponds to those reported in social psychology, where even strangers can rate a target person's personality with modestly high agreement with others who know the target person well.[47] Because we routinely make decisions in everyday life based on our observations of people, it makes sense to consider alternative sources when assessing personality. To a large degree these decisions, based on our observations, have a substantial impact in determining how successfully we interact with others. This leads to the notion that we might enhance our understanding and better predict behavior on the job if we also account for observer ratings of the applicant's personality. The results from the employment interview, reviewed above, underscores this notion.

In some respects, observer ratings of personality "get at" a person's public self or social reputation; they reflect the way we are perceived by others. In contrast, self-reports of personality likely reflect perceptions of ourselves over many situations. They incorporate less observable information about the dynamics and processes inside us and include our motives, intentions, feelings, and past behaviors. In many respects, self-reports depict our "identity." We believe ratings of personality, based on reputation, will be a second way to predict the employee's success at work.[48]

Two recent meta-analyses suggest that observer ratings of personality enhance predictions of job performance, with magnitudes often twice as large as the predictive validities for self-report responses.[49] This suggests that personality traits based on observer ratings are psychologically meaningful ways to organize information about people, information that has real implications for understanding and predicting job performance. Does this mean that an individual does not know himself better than his co-workers? While we would not say this, we do believe the research evidence shows co-workers who know us well do know something about how we tend to think, feel, and act; that information, captured in other-reports of personality ratings, can add incremental validity to self-report ratings of personality.

Ryan Zimmerman, Mary Triana, and Murray Barrick found a structured letter of reference, relying on ratings on a number of personality items, predicted later job performance better than typical self-report responses.[50] This, coupled with the meta-analysis data just reviewed, illustrates the potential of obtaining co-worker ratings of the applicant's personality.

Evaluating the Validity of Personality Tests as a Predictor

The Validity of Self-Report Inventories.   Many recent studies have examined the validity of several different self-report inventories. A large number of these studies have focused on inventories that measure the Five-Factor Model. A recent study conducted by Murray Barrick, Michael Mount, and Tim Judge, which relied on a second-order meta-analysis of prior meta-analyses, will be reviewed here because it provides a thorough review of the predictive validity of these Five Factor personality traits.[51] This study quantitatively summarized the findings from 15 prior meta-analyses of the Five-Factor Model's predictive validity across five occupational groups and four specific work criteria, along with an overall measure of work performance. Using sample sizes that at times exceeded 80,000, the authors concluded the following:

1. Conscientiousness and emotional stability were valid predictors of overall work performance over all studies examined (the estimated true correlation at the construct level, $\rho = 0.24$ and 0.17, respectively). This led them to conclude that these two predictors were universal predictors across all jobs. Nevertheless, even though conscientiousness was a valid predictor across all occupations and over all specific criteria, emotional stability was consistently related only to some of the specific criteria.

2. Extraversion was a valid predictor for some occupational groups such as managers ($\rho = 0.21$) and specific criteria such as training performance ($\rho = 0.28$).

3. Agreeableness and openness to experience demonstrated modest validity overall. However, each trait was related to a specific criterion. Agreeableness was related to teamwork ($\rho = 0.27$), whereas openness was associated with training performance ($\rho = 0.33$).

In conclusion, whereas two of these traits are universal or generalizable predictors (conscientiousness, emotional stability), the other three traits (extraversion, agreeableness, and openness) were found to be contingent predictors, predicting success in only a few jobs or specific criteria. Thus, the authors label these "niche" predictors.

Joyce Hogan and Brent Holland extended these findings by illustrating the value of matching specific personality traits to relevant work criteria using a theoretically driven rationale for expecting significant relationships between personality and performance.[52] Given this, the above estimates likely underestimate the true predictive validity of the traits, since they include empirically derived estimates (the researcher reports all relationships, even when there isn't a theoretical rationale) in addition to theoretically based estimates. In the Hogan and Holland meta-analysis, the criterion measured getting along with others or getting ahead of others. Getting along was defined as those behaviors that relate to gaining the approval of others, cooperating more, or building and maintaining relationships. On the other hand, getting ahead related to behavior that involves negotiating, striving to be recognized, and leading others, which enables the person to advance in the job, team, or organization.

Based on theory, the authors expected emotional stability, conscientiousness, and agreeableness to be important predictors of the getting along with others criterion, and the results supported this (true score correlation, $\rho = 0.34, 0.31,$ and 0.23). Theoretically, they expected ambition (a facet of extraversion), emotional stability, and openness (labelled intellectance) to predict getting ahead of others. In general, the results corresponded to the hypotheses ($\rho = 0.26, 0.22, 0.12$, respectively), although conscientiousness had a stronger relationship ($\rho = 0.20$) with getting ahead than did openness to experience ($\rho = 0.12$).[53] The latter finding is not surprising to us, as we would expect conscientiousness (and emotional stability) to predict both criteria, since it is a "universal" predictor. In this case, though, it should be noted that the specific measure of conscientiousness used in this study actually reflected a narrow measure, as it only assessed prudence or dependability, but not striving for achievement. The latter component is likely to be particularly important for the getting ahead criterion; hence the estimate reported here should be viewed as an underestimate of the validity for a broader measure representing all aspects of conscientiousness. The finding that agreeableness matters for one criterion, while extraversion matters for the other, shows "niche" predictors work best when they are carefully matched to relevant criteria or situations. These results also reveal that predictive validities do "improve" when theory is used to identify which personality traits to include in the selection battery. Consequently, selection experts should ensure that the personality test they are using assesses those personality traits that are relevant for the specific demands of the job, and that only these traits are used to make the hiring decision.

A number of other meta-analyses have recently been conducted that examine unique criteria (such as leadership, expatriate success, and so on). To enhance your understanding of when specific traits may be particularly useful, we next summarize the results from these studies:

1. When selecting effective leaders from ineffective ones, results reveal that those candidates high in extraversion, openness to experience, and emotional stability experience the greatest success on the job ($\rho = 0.24, 0.24, 0.22$, respectively).

Conscientiousness and agreeableness are also related to effective leadership (both $\rho = 0.16$). However, if one is interested in identifying those candidates who will most likely *emerge* as leaders, conscientiousness and extraversion were the most important personality traits (both $\rho = 0.33$).[54] Taken together, these results show that great leaders inspire and influence others around them (are extraverted), can manage their own anxiety (are emotionally stable), are able to adapt as needed (open to new experiences), and have an "inner fire" as they strive for achievement (are conscientious).

2. Teamwork is another important criterion. A recent meta-analysis showed that conscientiousness, emotional stability, and agreeableness were useful predictors of teamwork and performance in jobs involving interpersonal interactions ($\rho = 0.26$, 0.27, and 0.33).[55] Not surprisingly, these results correspond to those reported by Hogan and Holland with regard to "getting along" criteria. Nevertheless, they do powerfully illustrate that agreeableness is likely to be a meaningful predictor in jobs requiring teamwork or extensive interpersonal interaction, such as customer service.[56]

3. Two other meta-analyses show how these personality traits relate to expatriate job performance as well as entrepreneurial status. While expatriates are managers working in a country and culture other than that of their upbringing or legal residence, entrepreneurs are owners or managers who undertake and operate a new business venture. In both cases, all Five Factor traits except openness to experience meaningfully predicted success—either as an expatriate or an entrepreneur. Extraversion is a particularly important predictor. This is not surprising, given the "risky" nature of both undertakings. And again, being hardworking and persistent (that is, conscientious) as well as emotionally stable and confident contributes to an individual's degree of success.[57]

4. Two other recent studies examine deviant behavior and turnover. Candidates with higher conscientiousness and agreeableness scores were less likely to exhibit deviant behavior ($\rho = -0.26$ and -0.20).[58] These same two traits, plus emotional stability and extraversion, were found to also predict those who were more likely to stay with the firm ($\rho = 0.31$, 0.22, 0.35, and 0.20, respectively).[59] These results show that organizations can avoid bad "outcomes" (counterproductive behavior or turnover) as well as obtain desirable "outcomes" (for example, higher performance) when selecting for these core personality traits.

5. The final set of meta-analyses we will discuss investigate the process through which personality affects job performance. Although these results are not directly relevant to selection, understanding the way personality influences performance will help you develop more useful theories regarding which traits should be particularly relevant in a specific job. Taken together, these studies show that the primary means through which personality operates is motivation, as these traits influence what makes you happy and what keeps you working at the activity. Tim Judge, Daniel Heller, and Mick Mount found the estimated true score correlation with regard to job satisfaction is meaningful for at least three traits: 0.29 for emotional stability, 0.25 for extraversion, and 0.26 for conscientiousness.[60] Thus, although most researchers focus on ways to change the job to enhance job satisfaction, these results show that one can also select people who are more likely to be satisfied and committed to their work. The second study found conscientiousness and emotional stability were related to three different measures of performance motivation. These two universal predictors influence whether the

person has the confidence to accomplish the task ($\rho = 0.22$ and 0.35), is more likely to set and pursue goals ($\rho = 0.28$ and 0.29), and possesses high expectations about being able to complete the work ($\rho = 0.23$ and 0.29).[61] It is not surprising that these two traits are universal predictors of success at work, since they determine how motivated the person is while doing the job and influence how happy about and committed they are to doing the work.

It should be noted that in some ways, studying individual personality traits may not be the best way to determine the usefulness of the candidate's "entire" personality, at least for selection. Because these personality traits are relatively independent, simultaneously accounting for their effects should add extra predictive power. For example, Tim Judge and his colleagues have reported that the Five-Factor Model had a multiple correlation of 0.48 with leadership, 0.41 with job satisfaction, and an average multiple correlation of 0.49 with performance motivation criteria. Hao Zhao and Scott Seibert found a multiple correlation of 0.37 with entrepreneurial status.[62] These results, which are substantially larger than the validities reported previously trait by trait, powerfully illustrate the utility of personality as a useful selection tool.

And, as just discussed, when people who know you well at work rate your personality, the evidence is clear—these observer-based ratings add incremental validity to predictions solely based on self-reports of personality.[63] In fact, the predictive validities when peers or supervisor's rate your personality are nearly twice as large. However, the ratings these results are based on were collected on employee's, not applicants; the reason for obtaining the ratings was to help employees grow and develop. The point is, these raters had every incentive to tell the whole, unvarnished truth about the personality of the employees they were rating. What is unknown is how accurate such ratings would be if they were collected as part of a letter of reference or other selection tool.[64] Hence, there still are a few unknowns about relying on co-worker ratings in selection contacts. Nevertheless, the results suggest these ratings may be useful as part of a selection battery.

Finally, one other important issue regarding the validity of personality inventories is whether they provide any prediction of job performance over that provided by other selection instruments. Recent studies have yielded evidence that personality data do so when used with cognitive ability measures, biodata, situational judgment tests, and employment interviews.[65] Rather than review each of these studies, the upshot is that adding a personality test is likely to add incremental validity or enhance the accuracy of the selection decision.

Critics have asked, "why does personality matter?" We contend the question should be "who wouldn't care about the candidate's personality?" Hiring managers care about it. Empirical studies show we should care about it if we want to enhance performance and motivation at work. This is particularly evident if we consider the multiple correlation from all relevant personality traits (simultaneously), as they are likely to add incremental validity to other predictors one is likely to use to make a quality hiring decision. Finally, personality predicts many outcomes organizations care about—not just overall job performance, but whether an employee is less likely to steal, quit, or alienate the customer and whether an employee is more likely to be a leader, a team player, and a good citizen while also being happier and more motivated to work every day. Because these are habitual or dispositional predictors that change only slowly over time, the organization obtains these benefits throughout the individual's career. Thus, personality matters at work. By accounting for personality, we will likely enhance the quality of a selection decision.

Validity of Projective Techniques.   On the surface, it would seem that projective techniques could provide more beneficial information than self-report questionnaires in assessing personality. After all, it is not clear what the correct answer is when an applicant is asked to describe what he or she sees in an ambiguous inkblot or photograph. One would expect that socially appropriate answers would not be as evident as they would be in the responses to personality self-report questionnaires, and that responses would be reflective of personality characteristics of the respondent. This is, in fact, the basic assumption of projective techniques. However, various issues have arisen concerning the scoring and use of the information obtained from projective instruments that have questioned their general usefulness in selection. The following points address these issues.

The first issue is the reliability of an individual's responses at two different times. In all other selection devices, it is assumed that the characteristic demonstrated by the respondent is consistently measured. The scores derived from projective tests, however, often have low reliabilities.[66] There is a question about the proper measurement of reliability and if, in fact, this is a useful concept for these techniques. It has been thought that observed changes in test responses over time reflect real changes in the individual, since many of the characteristics measured, like emotion and mood, change over time. The problem this causes for HR selection decisions is significant. Usually, the applicant completes a projective test only once. The information obtained is then generalized to descriptions of the applicant. Even if changes in response patterns are indicative of real changes in the individual, the selection specialist can have little confidence in the usefulness of such personality data in predicting long-term job performance.

The second issue in the use of projective techniques is the impact on an individual's score due to the total number of responses given. This is not a major issue for some devices, such as the MSCS, that limit responses to a relatively constant number for all subjects. However, for those instruments that encourage free response, there is evidence that the scores of personality characteristics are related to the volume of information given.[67] The problem here is that the number of responses given may not be a function of personality but rather of specific verbal or test-taking skills. If this is the case, the accuracy of the personality data would be reduced, as would be its usefulness in selection.

A third major concern is the scoring of the information provided, for which the proposed benefit of projective instruments becomes a liability. The quantity and complexity of the responses make scoring, even using a designated scoring manual, very difficult. This is a greater problem for those instruments that encourage free response and less of a problem for those that limit response. The result is that at times the same answers have not been scored and interpreted identically by different scorers.[68] Such findings cloud the usefulness of the resulting personality scores for selection, because it would appear that the scoring of the information is indicative of the examiner's particular scoring system and judgment as well as of the individual's responses. This adds error to the scores as far as HR specialists are concerned; it is necessary that the scores reflect the applicant only, since the selection decision is to be made about this individual. A fourth and related concern is that few HR specialists are trained in administering, scoring and interpreting data from projective tests. This means that consultants must be hired to administer and score them. At times such consultants are not familiar with the job under consideration, and they evaluate the candidate in comparison to a general profile of a good worker. In many cases, this profile is based only on the opinion of the consultant. However, given the complexity of projective test data and the unfamiliarity of the HR specialist with scoring, it is difficult to find an alternative route. As a result, the personality description is often accepted by the specialist but actually is of little value. These criticisms show that this technique is often based on poorly developed instruments or scoring "keys" and on poorly conducted validity studies. However, there are psychometrically sound instruments, detailed scoring guides, and well-done studies. For example, the Miner Sentence Completion Test is one of these; it warrants consideration for use in selecting managers.

Legal Issues in the Use of Personality Tests

Two large-scale meta-analyses demonstrate mean differences between most subgroup comparisons on personality measured during personnel selection that are relatively small or virtually the same when compared to the "majority" group (for example, whites or males).[69] Blacks, Hispanics, and Asians were found to have nearly the same mean score as whites on extraversion, emotional stability, agreeableness, and conscientiousness. The only issue that might make a practical difference was that black applicants had lower average scores on openness to experience measures than white applicants in one meta-analysis ($d = -.20$), but in the other meta-analysis the difference was small ($d = -.10$). Also, there were small gender differences, favoring women for Agreeableness and favoring men for Emotional Stability. In general, personality tests have no or negligible adverse impact when using the Five-Factor Model. I mention this because some preliminary evidence suggests somewhat more adverse impact or subgroup mean differences at the facet level of Five-Factor Measures.[70]

Although personality tests have not been found to produce an adverse impact on any given demographic group (race, ethnicity, or gender), there are two major legal issues accompany the use of personality tests in selection. The first has to do with the Americans with Disabilities Act. As you might recall from Chapter 2, this act prohibits preemployment medical examinations. It is not clear whether a personality test should or should not be included in such an examination. All tests are reviewed on a case-by-case basis, which includes such questions as (a) Is the test administered by a health care professional? (b) Are the results interpreted by a health care professional? and (c) Is the test designed to reveal an impairment of physical or mental health? Because psychiatrists and clinical psychologists can use personality tests to diagnose mental health deficiencies, such tests could be viewed as medical examinations and therefore deemed inappropriate for use before a job offer has been made.

However, the Equal Employment Opportunity Commission (EEOC) has taken the position that personality tests are more likely to be classified as medical examinations to the extent that they include personality scales with clinical designations of psychiatric disorders such as depression, schizophrenia, and paranoia. If the test focuses on general traits such as positive commitment toward work, responsiveness to supervision, honesty, and loyalty, it is not a medical examination.[71] If the test does focus on these general traits, it should not make disability-related inquiries such as (a) whether an individual has sought mental health services, (b) the extent of prior legal or illegal drug use, and (c) the extent of prior or current alcohol use.

In a recent lawsuit (*Karraker v. Rent-A-Center*, 2005), the Seventh Circuit Federal Court ruled that the company used a personality test, the Minnesota Multi-Phasic Personality Inventory (MMPI), which asked questions that could reveal a mental disability. Based on this finding, the test was held to be a "medical examination" under the ADA; its use was deemed illegal as a preemployment test. The court went on to note that psychological tests that measure personal traits such as honesty, integrity, preferences, and habits do not qualify as medical examinations.[72] The types of tests discussed in this chapter, such as the Five Factor questionnaires, should not constitute a medical examination and therefore would not violate the ADA.

A second issue is the privacy rights of individuals. Although a right to privacy is not explicitly set forth in the U.S. Constitution, individuals are protected from unreasonable government intrusions and surveillance. Therefore, the selection of employees for public institutions may be affected by the use of personality tests, which by their nature, reveal an individual's inner thoughts and feelings. In addition, several states have constitutional privacy protection acts or recognize a statutory right to privacy; these acts affect both private and public employment.[73] To date, litigation about privacy has occurred in reference to questions that dealt with an applicant's sexual inclinations or religious views. In *Soroka v. Dayton Hudson,* the California Court of Appeals stopped Dayton Hudson's Target stores from requiring applicants for store security positions to take a personality test that contained questions about such topics.[74] The court also stated that employers must restrict psychological testing to job-related questions. The ruling was later dismissed as the parties reached a court-approved settlement. Under terms of the settlement, Dayton Hudson agreed to stop using the personality test and established a $1.3 million fund to be divided among the estimated 2,500 members of the plaintiff class who had taken the test.

Faking in Personality Inventories.   One important issue that may affect the validity of personality inventories is the faking of responses by applicants. These personality inventories are self-reports of how the candidate tends to think, feel, and act. Answers can be intentionally distorted or faked and are not objectively verifiable. Do candidates intentionally alter their responses to increase the likelihood of receiving a job offer? Although it seems plausible that candidates would change their responses to increase their chances of being hired, empirical evidence is contradictory. In some studies, but not in others, mean scores for applicants are higher than those for current employees. For example, Jeff Weekley, Rob Ployhart, and Crystal Harold found applicants ($N = 7,259$) scored on average 0.64 SD higher than current employees ($N = 2,989$) on three personality measures from the Five-Factor Model.[75] This is quite similar to the 0.69 SD higher average for applicants over current employees ($N = 270$) reported by Joe Rossé and colleagues, also using Five-Factor Model scales.[76] In contrast, Leatta Hough found no significant mean score differences for applicants and current employees across three large samples of applicants ($N = 40,500$) and current employees ($N = 1,700$).[77] This is supported in a second large study, based on a within-subject design where people completed the personality test as an applicant and another for developmental purposes.[78] Researchers have also examined indirect evidence that applicants are distorting scores by investigating whether the factor structure of the measures changes when using applicant responses. In one study, the dominant factor in applicant personality responses reflects an "ideal applicant" factor. The explanation for this factor was that the job applicant responds as he thinks he should to appear to be a competent or ideal employee, not as he actually sees himself on various personality traits. These responses vary from the self-image that the respondent reports in a nonemployment setting. However, other studies show no evidence that the factor structure of a Five Factor inventory is different for applicants than it is for respondents in a nonemployment situation.[79]

One explanation for these contradictory findings is that the studies differ in one crucial way: Those showing differences for applicants rely on research designs that tell or direct subjects to fake their answers or instruct them to answer in a way to get hired. In contrast, where subjects are allowed to naturally express themselves, even in settings where they have an incentive to distort (that is, in a selection setting where one tries to obtain a job), the evidence that applicants fake is less compelling and suggests that applicants are not faking.[80] Even though research does not clearly show applicants intentionally distort responses, it may be best to approach personality testing as if applicants do fake. A recent study of applicant practices suggest at least some applicants attempt to intentionally distort perceptions of their characteristics and traits. This study found approximately 30 percent of entry-level applicants report faking on selection tests, which presumably would include personality inventories.[81] Thus, it appears that at least some applicants do fake, with estimates ranging from 0 percent to 50 percent.[82]

What are the implications if candidates do fake? A number of studies in organizational settings have found little evidence that such faking affects the predictive validity of personality inventories.[83] Instead, these researchers have concluded that distortion does not significantly alter validity coefficients and may, in fact, relate to real personality differences among individuals. A recent study illustrates that even when all those who are faking are removed, mean performance will only increase by about 0.1 SD.[84] Thus, instead of worrying about faking, these results imply that a selection expert should focus on selecting the test with the highest predictive validity.

Faking may make decisions about *individual* applicants incorrect, however, as applicants who do distort may be hired at the expense of those who do not fake. There is evidence that some (honest) applicants are harmed by those who fake and that this effect is greatest when only a small proportion of applicants are selected (for example, when less than one applicant out of five is hired).[85]

These findings have encouraged researchers to consider ways to reduce the effects of faking. Research suggests that instructions should include a warning that faking may be detected. A recent review of the literature found that warnings not to fake can reduce faking by 0.23 SD.[86] While not having a large impact, warning instructions can reduce applicant scores, particularly if the warning includes a description of the potential consequences of intentionally distorting one's answers. Since this is an inexpensive solution, it is recommended that selection experts include instructions warning about the consequences of faking.

Statistical techniques have been developed to correct for distortion in responses. In one approach, regression is used to account for the effect of response distortion in personality responses. The "corrected" score is assumed to be free of contamination from faking. The second approach is to eliminate applicants who have extremely high scores on scales that are constructed to detect lying. People with scores in the top 2.5 percent or 5 percent on these lie scales are eliminated from the pool, based on the assumption that if they are lying on these items, they will on the other questions too. Research shows these corrections do not affect the predictive validity of the instrument. However, it has been found that even though a correction for distortion may not affect validity coefficients, it may result in different individuals being selected than those who would have been selected on the basis of uncorrected scores.[87] This is because validity coefficients refer to the whole sample of applicants. Correction formulas or the elimination of candidates with high scores on the lie scale change individual scores, but do not change all scores by the same amount. In fact, applying correction formulas fails to produce a corrected score that accurately reflects the score achieved by the individual who is not instructed to fake responses.[88] It seems quite clear that statistical correction techniques do not affect the estimated validity of an instrument. However, they do adjust individual scores. Since an applicant's score after correction is not more strongly related to performance, it is not advisable to base selection decisions on these corrected scores.

RECOMMENDATIONS FOR THE USE OF PERSONALITY DATA

We started this chapter with a discussion about the apparent contradiction of using personality data in selection programs. There is ample evidence that personality should be a worker characteristic related to performance in many jobs. This type of data conceivably should be as useful in selection decisions as data about the applicant KSAs that have been stressed in other chapters. The magnitude of the predictive validities of personality data, however, is not as high as we would like. A possible explanation of this is that the methods of personality assessment in selection often are inadequate. The major focus of the chapter, therefore, has been on the definition and measurement methods of personality assessment. Because personality psychologists have studied these topics in much more depth than HR specialists have, much of the information in this chapter has been drawn from psychology. Given this, it is possible to draw some conclusions that should be useful to selection specialists.

Define Personality Traits in Terms of Job Behaviors

Of fundamental importance is the definition of what personality characteristic should be used in a selection program. We are reminded of the saying, "If you don't know where you are going, any way will take you there." The definition of important worker attributes is something we mentioned before as necessary for all selection measures. However, the lack of definition seems to be more common with personality measurement than with other types of worker attributes.

This lack of definition usually takes one of two forms. In the first, a personality instrument is used without much attention paid to the specific traits being measured. The instrument is used because someone vouches for its effectiveness, or even because it has been used in previous selection work. Such reasons are not proper justification for use. As we have said before, it is necessary to have a job-related basis for whatever KSAs are measured in selection. Personality characteristics should be thought of as another type of KSA.

The second form this lack of definition takes is the use of very generalized statements to describe personality traits; for example, "a manager that fits in well with our staff" or a "salesperson who has a good personality." Given this impreciseness, it is unlikely that different selection specialists would agree about what particular personality traits should be evaluated. Even if only one specialist is involved, there is little assurance that the personality traits evaluated are, in fact, the appropriate ones.

There seem to be two ways that job analysis information could supply information to generate adequate definitions. The first is through the task approach described in Chapter 7. If this approach is carried out completely, it should yield information about job tasks, interaction patterns among the incumbent and others, working conditions, equipment used, and work patterns. From these data, an HR specialist should be able to infer personality traits in much the same way that other KSAs are inferred. That is, for example, traits such as "control of stress caused by steady demands of users for quick answers to programming difficulties" and "diligence in review of details of complex programs" could be identified for a computer programmer's job. The second is by means of those job analysis methods that directly produce worker attributes, some of which are personality dimensions. One such method is the Position Analysis Questionnaire (PAQ) "attributes of an interest or temperament nature" that we presented in Chapter 7. Included in these attributes were *working alone, pressure of time, empathy, influencing people,* and so on. Another method is the Personality-Related Position Requirements Form (PPRF) that has been developed to directly identify the personality dimensions necessary for job performance.[89] This instrument consists of 136 items that measure 12 personality dimensions. These dimensions, in turn, measure the Five-Factor Model traits. Job incumbents complete the questionnaire; analyses of their responses produce scores on these 12 dimensions. These scores indicate how much of each of the 12 personality dimensions—or of the broader Five-Factor Model traits—is associated with job performance.

The Appropriateness of the Selection Instrument

The instruments we have discussed or listed in Table 12.3 are only part of a very large number of self-report inventories used in selection. Many of them, such as the *Edward's Personal Preference Schedule,* the *California F Scale,* and the *Thurstone Temperament Schedule,* are products of extensive pre-testing and developmental work.

From our previous discussion, it should be clear that we think that there are two important characteristics of the personality selection measure to consider. The first is the breadth of the personality trait being measured. Our conclusion is that it seems to be more effective in selection to use traits that affect a wide set of behaviors rather than a narrow set.

Our recommendation is to only use those tests with enough developmental information available to show that the instrument measures broadly defined personality traits. This, of course, means that data should be provided regarding the reliability, item statistics, and statistical analysis of each of the scales measuring a personality dimension. Given the extreme difficulty in constructing personality instruments, it would be foolhardy to use any personality device in selection that does not have supporting information. Without supporting data, an instrument can really be considered only a theory of the writer. The value of such an instrument would therefore be unknown and undocumented. We stress this point because numerous instruments of this type are being sold to organizations for managerial and executive selection. Often these instruments are quite costly, but useless.

The second important characteristic of a personality instrument in selection is whether respondents can learn "correct" responses to the instrument. This topic was part of our discussion about ambiguous measuring devices. It is our opinion that instruments for which appropriate responses are not apparent are preferable to those for which answers are apparent. We mentioned such limitations with regard to the interview (as it is commonly used), and with regard to many self-report, multiple-choice inventories.

Interaction of Personality Traits and Situations

As we have mentioned, an underlying assumption regarding traits is that they are stable characteristics related to an individual's actions in various situations. However, when psychologists began to study this assumption more closely, they soon realized that individuals tended to show some variability in their behavior even across seemingly similar conditions. To be sure, behavior is not random; but the consistency was less than many trait psychologists believed. Some studies of the consistency of trait behavior across different situations are represented by the early work of Hugh Hartshorne and Mark May. In their investigations of the honesty and deception of children in varied situations, these researchers concluded that children's behavior was a function of both traits and the particular situation.[90]

Powerful and Weak Situations. Psychologists have turned their attention to the interaction of traits and situations. The reasoning is that neither can be offered as the major determiner of behavior in all cases; rather, they interact with each other, exerting a different influence on behavior depending on the circumstances.[91] Following this reasoning, one line of work has labeled situations as either powerful or weak. Situations are *powerful* to the degree that they lead individuals to interpret particular events in the same way, create uniform expectancies regarding the most appropriate behavior, provide adequate incentives for the performance of that behavior, and require skills that everyone possesses roughly to the same extent. Peter Herriot has discussed the selection interview from this viewpoint, noting that roles of both the interviewer and interviewee are frequently well known, and that individuals often behave similarly in these situations.[92] A *weak situation* is one with opposite characteristics: It is not uniformly interpreted, does not generate uniform expectations concerning desired behavior, does not offer sufficient incentives for one type of behavior, and is one in which a variety of skills may produce acceptable behavior. Many sales situations could be classified as weak because of the differences in customers' expectations and knowledge, differences in characteristics of products or services, and the manager's inability to closely supervise the sales employee's behavior. Taken together, this gives the sales representative considerable discretion—and in such settings, personality matters.

The general conclusion is that in powerful situations, individual behavior is more attributable to the situation than to individual traits. In our example, knowing that the interview is for an entry-level managerial position in a large financial institution may better explain an interviewee's behavior than inferences about his traits. Herriot has pointed out that many of the differences in interviewee behavior can be explained as inconsistency in perceptions of the proper role of the interviewee in the interview, rather than as trait differences. In weak situations, on the other hand, traits would seem to be important explanations of behavior. In these situations individuals are uncertain about appropriate behavior. It is assumed that they interpret the situation and act in accordance with personality traits. In our sales example, there are noticeable behavioral differences among sales personnel in friendliness, aggressiveness, and persistence. These differences could be thought of as related to the different levels of these traits that are possessed by each salesperson.

These concepts have two implications for the use of personality in selection. One implication concerns the jobs for which the use of personality may be appropriate. For a job in a powerful work situation, personality may not be an important dimension for selection purposes. For example, one study found that the validities of two of the Five Factor personality dimensions were significantly higher for those managers in jobs high in autonomy compared with those jobs low in autonomy.[93] Perhaps concentrating on identifying the abilities necessary for performing the job may be more advantageous in powerful work situations. A second implication addresses which instrument to use. Personality data drawn from powerful testing situations would not seem to yield accurate personality information about the applicant. We have mentioned the interview as an example. Very often these interviews are short, highly structured interactions about which the interviewees have been well coached from classes, articles, and friends. Accordingly, applicant behavior could be more a function of the applicant learning what behavior and responses are appropriate in these sessions than a function of the applicant's personality traits. Alternatively, use of highly structured interviews may create a powerful situation, one that makes it difficult to assess the applicant's personality. Some recent research finds interviewer ratings of candidate personality are "more accurate" in unstructured rather than structured interviews.[94] We hypothesize, therefore, that personality characteristics are more important for selection devices and job assignments in weak situations than in powerful ones.

One way to identify situations as powerful or weak would be to ask several individuals to rate the appropriateness of a variety of behaviors for a specific situation. If one or a very small number of behaviors are rated as appropriate, this would constitute a powerful situation. The rating of many behaviors as appropriate would indicate a weak situation. Such a strategy could be used in selection to identify powerful and weak job performance situations.

Relevance of the Work Context.   As previously noted, behavior is the result of a person's personality and the situation.[95] Thus, extraverted people talk more than shy people. However, even highly extraverted people can be quiet when the situation demands, such as at a funeral. This example shows that personality traits interact with the situation to predict behavior. This is a critical concept; it clarifies that whether specific personality traits matter in selection depends on the relevance of the work context. In other words, when the behaviors linked to specific traits are relevant to the situation or required for high performance, those personality traits matter. Extending the example above to a work setting, extraverts enjoy interacting with people and—not surprisingly—tend to be more effective in sales. In this case, the trait of extraversion enables the sales representative to exhibit behaviors, such as engaging and talking to strangers, that result in higher sales performance. This same trait would not be as important, though, in jobs where these behaviors are not linked to success. Consequently, personality traits are only relevant in specific situations.

Robert Tett and Dawn Burnett have developed a model that seeks to explain, by explicitly accounting for the person-situation interaction, when personality effects on work behaviors are most likely to occur.[96] This model proposes that specific personality traits are "activated" in response to specific trait-relevant situational cues. These cues are a function of task, social, and organizational demands in the work setting. To illustrate how the work context cues specific traits, consider the influence of the organizational reward system. Greg Stewart found that whether highly extraverted sales representatives emphasized customer service behavior that was related to adding new members or retaining current customers depended on the pay system. Specifically, he found that when the firm rewarded sales representatives for identifying and adding new members, extraverted sales representatives achieved higher performance related to new sales but not for customer retention. In contrast, when the firm rewarded representatives for contacting and renewing existing members, extraverted sales representatives had higher performance related to customer retention with no change in new sales.[97] In both cases, the "non-rewarded" behavior, whether it was adding new clients or retaining current customers, did not increase; this suggests that extraverted people are quite sensitive to situational cues. These results reveal that personality traits have the greatest influence on performance when traits lead to are aligned with the specific behaviors associated with high performance and when those behaviors are also elicited by the situational cues or demands of the work environment.

The Nature of Job Performance

We have discussed previously that personality may be less important for technical jobs and more important for nontechnical jobs. Similarly, jobs that are very structured in terms of work behaviors would seem to be less related to personality than those jobs that are unstructured. This is just another way of saying that for some jobs, it appears that the application of knowledge and predetermined ways of doing things is critical for successful job performance. For these jobs, cognitively based KSAs would seem more important for selection than personality traits. Yet—even for these jobs—who wouldn't want to hire a hardworking, dependable candidate who will show up for work every day (be conscientious), approach work with confidence and a general sense of well-being, and manage anxiety and stress effectively (be able to demonstrate emotional stability or core self-evaluation)? Because personality is a dispositional predictor of motivation, personality matters at work, even in technical or highly structured jobs.

Other jobs rely less on specific knowledge or predetermined procedures and have a number of acceptable ways for producing desired performance. It is for these jobs that personality is even more clearly related to job performance. More traits than just the two universal predictors (conscientiousness and emotional stability) will be relevant for success, depending on the specific work context. For example, if the job requires considerable teamwork or customer service, agreeableness or possibly even emotional intelligence will be more important. Conversely, if the job requires negotiating or influencing others, extraversion will be more relevant. If, on the other hand, the job requires creativity and involves considerable uncertainty, we expect that openness to new experiences or proactive personality would matter. Such results underscore the importance of considering the nature of the job under consideration when making a decision about whether to use personality measures in the selection program.

Over the past fifteen years or so, work has been dramatically changing, whether due to changes in information technology or to offshoring or outsourcing work. This has important implications for the use of personality in selection. One implication is that jobs will change more rapidly and become less structured—implying that personality will increasingly predict work behaviors. Another implication is that work will continue to become even more knowledge based or information intensive. This enhances the importance of cognitive ability, but also relates to personality; specific traits (for example, extraversion and openness to experience) can predict employee success in (continuous) training and identify those applicants who will be more committed (that is, conscientious and emotionally stable) to the organization. Third, as organizations continue to eliminate layers of management, they rely more and more on the use of teams to coordinate work efforts. In general, personality predicts success even better in team settings, and a few traits emerge as particularly important: agreeableness, extraversion (in some settings), and emotional intelligence. Thus, the changing nature of work is likely to increase the utility of personality as a predictor in most selection decisions.

Conclusions.   We have introduced much information from the field of personality psychology and have drawn implications from this work for the use of personality in organizations. We have done this because simply administering personality instruments to applicants and attempting to relate the scores on these to job performance is not a worthwhile strategy. Instead, the appropriate use of personality data calls for understanding two important findings in personality research. First is the observation that traits vary greatly in the extent to which they influence behavior. A seemingly small number of core traits have a strong influence on behavior. A larger number of traits have limited or superficial influence. The second major observation is that the situation also has an important influence on individual behavior. All personality traits are more easily expressed in some situations (weak settings) than others (powerful settings). Further, specific personality traits predict valued behaviors at work only in relevant situations. These observations offer a partial explanation for the lack of uniform positive findings in the use of personality data for selection.

Use in Small Businesses

One recent study found that managers of small businesses were concerned more with personality characteristics such as honesty, integrity, and interest in the job than with an applicant's ability.[98] This is perhaps understandable but it presents an awkward situation for selection. The problem is that there are fewer valid ways in which managers of small businesses can identify which traits are relevant or that even measure personality. As we have mentioned, using the interview to assess personality is a process fraught with challenges and difficult to do well. The use of poorly measured traits, of course, does not assist with selection and, in fact, may prove to be detrimental. Furthermore, as we have seen, cognitive ability is one of the most, if not the most important attribute businesses should be evaluating when selecting candidates. Hence, ability tests should be included in any testing battery.

We therefore recommend that the process of selection for small businesses must focus on relevant KSAs and, secondarily, work to incorporate data about personality—whether this is achieved via a short personality inventory or gathered from an interview. Small businesses should strive to use training-and-experience evaluation forms, situational interviews, job knowledge tests, and work sample and trainability tests to measure the employee characteristics necessary for actually performing the tasks of the job. Small businesses should also consider using a personality test focused on the universal predictors (conscientiousness and emotional stability), as these personality traits will be relevant in all of their jobs.[99] One such test, the Wonderlic Productivity Index (WPI), focuses on these universal predictors and takes only about 10–15 minutes to complete. The applicant pool could first be screened using all of these devices, including the WPI. In that way, a smaller pool of individuals who possess the abilities to do the job can be identified. If this pool includes more applicants than the number of positions available, interviews may also be used as a tool for additional personality assessment. In doing this, the recommendations previously discussed should be incorporated into the interview. In other words, the personality traits of interest should be defined in terms of job behaviors, and the interview questions should be phrased in terms of job situations. For example, if cooperation with fellow workers is important, include a question such as this: "Describe a situation in which you worked in a team with others. Specifically, how was work shared between you and others and how did you go about resolving any differences of opinion about work methods?" Follow-up questions would be used to gather full information about what decisions the individual made, how conflict was dealt with, and whether the outcome was appropriate. These recommended approaches enable small businesses to make use of the universal personality traits as a component of an initial screen and, where feasible, allow for a more comprehensive assessment (that might include niche personality predictors) late in the selection program. By such means, the organization's upside potential would be maximized and its downside risk minimized.

REFERENCES

1. Murray R. Barrick, Michael K. Mount, and Timothy A. Judge, "The FFM Personality Dimensions and Job Performance: Meta-Analysis of Meta-Analyses," *International Journal of Selection and Assessment* 9 (2001): 9–30.

2. Matthew Heller, "Court Ruling That Employer's Integrity Test Violated ADA Could Open Door to Litigation," *Workforce Management* 84, no. 9 (2005): 74–77; and Paul B. Erickson, "Employer Hiring Tests Grow Sophisticated in Quest for Insight about Applicants," *Knight Ridder Tribune Business News* (May 16, 2004): 1.

3. Ann Marie Ryan, Lynn McFarland, Helen Baron, and Ron Page, "An International Look at Selection Practices: Nation and Culture as Explanations for Variability in Practice," *Personnel Psychology* 52 (1999): 359–401.

4. Walter Mischel, *Introduction to Personality*, 3rd ed. (New York: CBS College Publishing, 1981), 2.

5. Murray R. Barrick and Michael K. Mount, "Yes, Personality Matters: Moving on to More Important Matters," *Human Performance* 18 (2005): 359–372; Barrick, Mount, and Judge, "The FFM Personality Dimensions and Job Performance: Meta-Analysis of Meta-Analyses"; and Mount, M. K., Barrick, M. R., & Stewart, G. L., "Personality Predictors of Performance in Jobs Involving Interaction with Others," *Human Performance* 11 (1998): 145–166.

6. Robert M. Guion and Richard F. Gottier, "Validity of Personality Measures in Personnel Selection," *Personnel Psychology* 18 (1966): 135–164.

7. Kevin R. Murphy and Jessica L. Dzieweczynski, "Why Don't Measures of Broad Dimensions of Personality Perform Better as Predictors of Job Performance?" *Human Performance* 18 (2005): 343–357.

8. Murphy and Dziewecynski, "Why Don't Measures of Broad Dimensions of Personality Perform Better as Predictors of Job Performance?"; and Fred P. Morgeson, Micahel A. Campion, Robert L. Dipboye, John R. Hollenbeck, Kevin Murphy, and Neal Schmitt, "Are We Getting Fooled Again? Coming to Terms with Limitations in the Use of Personality Tests for Personnel Selection," *Personnel Psychology* 60 (2007): 1029–1050.

9. Barrick and Mount, "Yes, Personality Matters: Moving on to More Important Matters."

10. Wendy Dunn, Michael K. Mount, Murray R. Barrick, and Deniz S. Ones, "The Five Factor Personality Dimensions, General Mental Ability, and Perceptions of Employment Suitability," *Journal of Applied Psychology* 80 (1995): 500–509.

11. Barrick, Mount, and Judge, "The FFM Personality Dimensions and Job Performance: Meta-Analysis of Meta-Analyses."

12. Fred L. Oswald and Leatta Hough, "Personality and Its Assessment: Measurement, Validity, and Modeling," (in press) *APA Handbook of Industrial and Psychology 2*, Part II, Chapter 5; and Deniz S. Ones, S. Dilchert, C. Vishwesvaran, and T. A. Judge, "In Support of Personality Assessment in Organizational Settings," *Personnel Psychology* 60 (2007): 995–1027.

13. Oswald and Hough, "Personality and Its Assessment: Measurement, Validity, and Modeling"; and Paul R. Sackett and Filip Lievens, "Personnel Selection," *Annual Review of Psychology* 59 (2008): 1–16.

14. Oswald and Hough, "Personality and Its Assessment: Measurement, Validity, and Modeling."

15. Timothy A. Judge, Chad A. Higgins, Carl J. Thoresen, and Murray R. Barrick, "The Five Factor Personality Traits, General Mental Ability, and Career Success across the Life Span," *Personnel Psychology* 52 (1999): 621–652.

16. Mischel, *Introduction to Personality*, 18.

17. Robert Hogan, "In Defense of Personality Measurement: New Wine for Old Whiners," *Human Performance* 18 (2005): 331–342; and Mischel, *Introduction to Personality*, 18.

18. John M. Digman and Jillian Inouye, "Further Specification of the Five Robust Factors of Personality," *Journal of Personality and Social Psychology* 50 (1986): 116–123; and Barrick, Mount, and Judge, "The FFM Personality Dimensions and Job Performance: Meta-Analysis of Meta-Analyses."

19. Gerard Saucier and Lewis Goldberg, "The Structure of Personality Attributes," in *Personality and Work: Reconsidering the Role of Personality in Organizations*, ed. Murray R. Barrick and Ann Marie Ryan (San Francisco: Jossey-Bass, 2003), 1–29; and Murray R. Barrick, Terrence R. Mitchell, and Greg L. Stewart, "Situational and Motivational Influences on Trait-Behavior Relationships," in *Personality and Work: Reconsidering the Role of Personality in Organizations*, ed. Murray R. Barrick and Ann Marie Ryan (San Francisco: Jossey-Bass, 2003), 60–82.

20. Saucier and Goldberg, "The Structure of Personality Attributes."

21. R. R. McCrae and P. T. Costa Jr., "Updating Norman's 'Adequate Taxonomy': Intelligence and Personality Dimensions in Natural Language and in Questionnaires," *Journal of Personality and Social Psychology* 49 (1985): 710–721. See also W. T. Norman, "Toward an Adequate Taxonomy of Personality Attributes: Replicated Factor Structure in Peer Nomination Personality Ratings," *Journal of Abnormal and Social Psychology* 66 (1963): 574–583; and Saucier and Goldberg, "The Structure of Personality Attributes."

22. Kibeom Lee and Michael C. Ashton, "Psychometric Properties of the HEXACO Personality Inventory.," *The Journal of the Society of Multivariate Experimental Psychology* 39 (2004): 329–358; Bernd Marcus, Kibeom Lee, and Michael C. Ashton, "Personality Dimensions Explaining Relationships between Integrity and Counterproductive Behavior: Big Five or One in Addition?" *Personnel Psychology* 60 (2007): 1–34.

23. Timothy A. Judge, Annelies E. M. van Vianen, and Irebe E. de Pater, "Emotional Stability, Core Self-Evaluations, and Job Outcomes: A Review of the Evidence and an Agenda for the Future Research," *Human Performance* 17 (2004): 325–346; Timothy A. Judge and Joyce E. Bono, "Relationship of Core Self-Evaluation Traits—Self-Esteem, Generalized Self-Efficacy, Locus of Control, and Emotional Stability—with Job Satisfaction and Job Performance: A Meta-Analysis," *Journal of Applied Psychology* 86 (2001): 80–92; and Timothy A. Judge, Edwin A. Locke, Cathy C. Durham, and Avraham N. Kluger, "Dispositional Effects on Job and Life Satisfaction: The Role of Core Evaluations," *Journal of Applied Psychology* 83 (1998): 17–34.

24. Kenneth S. Law, Chi-Sum Wong, and Lynda J. Song, "Construct and Criterion Validity of Emotional Intelligence and Its Potential Utility for Management Studies," *Journal of Applied Psychology* 89 (2004): 483–496; and David L. van Roy and Chockalingham Viswesvaran, "Emotional Intelligence: A Meta-Analytic Investigation of Predictive Validity and Nomological Net," *Journal of Vocational Behavior* 65 (2004): 71–95.

25. Gerald Matthew, Moshe Zeidner, and Richard D. Roberts, *Emotional Intelligence: Science and Myth* (Cambridge, MA: MIT Press, 2002), 542.

26. Scott E. Seibert, Michael J. Crant, and Maria L. Kramer, "Proactive Personality and Career Success," *Journal of Applied Psychology* 84 (1999): 416–427; Scott E. Seibert, Maria L. Kramer, and Michael J. Crant, "What Do Proactive People Do? A Longitudinal Model Linking Proactive Personality and Career Success," *Personnel Psychology* 54 (2001): 845–874; Michael J. Crant and Thomas S. Bateman, "Charismatic Leadership Viewed from Above: The Impact of Proactive Personality," *Journal of Organizational Behavior* 21 (2000): 63–75; Michael J. Crant, "The Proactive Personality Scale as a Predictor of Entrepreneurial Intentions," *Journal of Small Business Management* 34 (1996): 42–49; Jeffrey A. Thompson, "Proactive Personality and Job Performance: A Social Capital Perspective," *Journal of Applied Psychology* 90 (2005): 1011–1017; and Michael J. Crant, "The Proactive Personality Scale and Objective Job Performance among Real Estate Agents," *Journal of Applied Psychology* 80 (1995): 532–537.

27. Thomas S. Bateman and Michael J. Crant, "The Proactive Component of Organizational Behavior: A Measure and Correlates," *Journal of Organizational Behavior* 14 (1993): 103–118; Crant, "The Proactive Personality Scale and Objective Job Performance among Real Estate Agents"; and Crant and Bateman, "Charismatic Leadership Viewed from Above: The Impact of Proactive Personality."

28. Michael K. Mount, Murray R. Barrick, and J. Perkins Strauss, "Validity of Observer Ratings of the Five Factor Personality Factors," *Journal of Applied Psychology* 79 (1994): 272–280.

29. Judge, Higgins, Thoreson, and Barrick, "The Five Factor Personality Traits, General Mental Ability, and Career Success across the Life Span."

30. Barrick, Mount, and Judge, "The FFM Personality Dimensions and Job Performance: Meta-Analysis of Meta-Analyses."

31. Janis S. Houston, Walter C. Borman, William F. Farmer, and Ronald M. Bearden, "Development of the Navy Computer Adaptive Personality Scales" (NCAPS) (NPRST-TR-06-2) (2006): Millington, TN: Navy Personnel, Research, Studies, and Technology; Deirde J. Knapp, Eric D. Heggestad, and Mark C. Young, "Understanding and Improving the Assessment of Individual Motivation (AIM) in the Army's GED Plus Program (ARI Study note 2004-03) (2004): Alexandria, VA: U.S. Army Research Institute for the behavioral and social sciences.

32. Houston, Borman, Farmer, and Bearden, "Development of the Navy Computer Adaptive Personality Scales"; Oleksandr S. Chernyshenko, Stephen Stark, Matthew S. Prewett, Ashley A. Gray, Frederick R. Stilson, and Matthew D. Tuttle, "Normative Scoring of Multidimensional Pairwise Preference Personality Scales Using IRT: Empirical Comparison with Other Formats," *Human Performance* 22 (2009): 105–127.

33. Oswald and Hough, "Personality and Its Assessment: Measurement, Validity, and Modeling."

34. H. Baron, "Strengths and Limitations of Ipsative Measurement," *Journal of Occupational and Organizational Psychology*, 69 (1996): 49–56.

35. Mark Sherman, *Personality: Inquiry and Application* (New York: Pergamon Press, 1979), 205; and Scott O. Lilienfeld, Jim Wood, and Howard N. Garb, *The Scientific Status of Projective Techniques* (Oxford, UK: Blackwell Publishers, 2000).

36. Sherman, *Personality: Inquiry and Application*, 206.

37. John B. Miner, *Motivation to Manage: A Ten-Year Update on the Studies in "Management Education" Research* (Atlanta, GA: Organizational Measurement Systems Press, 1977), 6.

38. Kenneth P. Carson and Debora J. Gilliard, "Construct Validity of the Miner Sentence Completion Scale," *Journal of Occupational and Organizational Psychology* 66 (1993): 171–175.

39. Allen I. Huffcutt, James M. Conway, Philip L. Roth, and Nancy J. Stone, "Identification and Meta-Analytic Assessment of Psychological Constructs Measured in Employment Interviews," *Journal of Applied Psychology* 86 (2001): 897–913.

40. Ibid.

41. Mischel, *Introduction to Personality*, 490.

42. Ibid.

43. Philip L. Roth, Chad H. van Iddekinge, Allen I. Huffcutt, Carl E. Eidson Jr., and Mark J. Schmit, "Personality Saturation in Structured Interviews," *International Journal of Selection and Assessment* 13 (2005): 261–285; and Murray R. Barrick, Gregory K. Patton, and Shanna N. Haugland, "Accuracy of Interviewer Judgments of Job Applicant Personality Traits," *Personnel Psychology* 53 (2000): 925–954.

44. Melinda C. Blackman, "Personality Judgement and Utility of the Unstructured Employment Interview," *Basic and Applied Social Psychology* 24 (2002): 241–250; "Melinda C. Blackman David C. Funder, "Effective Interview Practices for Accurately Assessing Counterproductive Traits," *International Journal of Selection and Assessment* 10 (2002): 109–116; and Chad H. van Iddekinge, Patrick H. Raymark, and Phillip L. Roth, "Assessing Personality with a Structured Employment Interview: Construct-Related Validity and Susceptibility to Response Inflation," *Journal of Applied Psychology* 90 (2005): 536–552.

45. Huffcutt, Conway, Roth, and Stone, "Identification and Meta-Analytic Assessment of Psychological Constructs Measured in Employment Interviews."

46. Michael S. Cole, Hubert S. Feild, and William F. Giles, "Using Recruiter Assessments of Applicants' Resume Content to Predict Applicant Mental Ability and Five Factor Personality Dimensions," *International Journal of Selection and Assessment* 11 (2003): 78–92.

47. David Watson and Lee A. Clark, "Self- versus Peer Ratings of Specific Emotional Traits: Evidence of Convergent and Discriminant Validity," *Journal of Personality and Social Psychology* 60 (1991): 927–940; and David C. Funder, "On the Accuracy of Personality Judgement: A Realistic Approach," *Psychological Review* 102 (1995): 652–670.

48. David C. Funder and Stephen G. West, "Consensus, Self-Other Agreement, and Accuracy in Personality Judgment: An Introduction," *Journal of Personality* 61 (1993): 457–476; and

Robert J. Hogan and David Shelton, "A Socioanalytic Perspective on Job Performance," *Human Performance* 11 (1998): 129–144.

49. Brian S. Connelly and Deniz S. Ones, "An Other Perspective on Personality: Meta-Analytic Integration of Observers' Accuracy and Predictive Validity," *Psychological Bulletin* (in press); In Sue Oh, Gang Wang, and Michael Mount, "Validity of Observer Ratings of the Five-Factor Model of Personality: A Meta-analysis," working paper (2010) University of Iowa.

50. Ryan D. Zimmerman, Mary Triana, and Murray R. Barrick, "Predictive Criterion-Related Validity of Observer-Ratings of Personality and Job-Related Competencies Using Multiple Raters and Multiple Performance Criteria," Human Performance 22 (in press).

51. Barrick, Mount, and Judge, "The FFM Personality Dimensions and Job Performance: Meta-Analysis of Meta-Analyses."

52. Joyce Hogan and Brent Holland, "Using Theory to Evaluate Personality and Job-Performance Relations: A Socioanalytic Perspective" *Journal of Applied Psychology* 88 (2003): 100–112.

53. Ibid.

54. Timothy A. Judge, Joyce E. Bono, Remus Ilies, and Megan W. Gerhardt, "Personality and Leadership: A Qualitative and Quantitative Review," *Journal of Applied Psychology* 87 (2002): 765–780.

55. Michael K. Mount, Murray R. Barrick, and Greg L. Stewart, "Personality Predictors of Performance in Jobs Involving Interaction with Others," *Human Performance* 11 (1998): 145–166.

56. Murray R. Barrick, Greg L. Stewart, Mitch Neubert, and Michael K. Mount, "Relating Member Ability and Personality to Work Team Processes and Team Effectiveness," *Journal of Applied Psychology* 83 (1998): 377–391.

57. Stefen T. Mol, Marise P. Born, Madde E. Willemsen, and Henk T. van der Molen, "Predicting Expatriate Job Performance for Selection Purposes," *Journal of Cross-Cultural Psychology* 36 (2005): 590–620; Margaret A. Shaffer, David A. Harrison, Hal Gregersen, J. Stewart Black, and Lori A. Ferzandi, "You Can Take It with You: Individual Differences and Expatriate Effectiveness," *Journal of Applied Psychology* 91 (2006): 109–125; and Hao Zhao and Scott E. Seibert, "The Five Factor Personality Dimensions and Entrepreneurial Status: A Meta-Analytical Review," *Journal of Applied Psychology* 91 (2006): 259–271.

58. Jesus F. Salgado, "The Five Factor Personality Dimensions and Counterproductive Behaviors," *Journal of Selection and Assessment* 10 (2002): 117–125.

59. Ibid.; Ryan D. Zimmerman, "Understanding the Impact of Personality Traits on Individual Turnover Decisions: A Meta-Analytic Path Model," *Personnel Psychology*, 61 (2008): 309–348.

60. Timothy A. Judge, Daniel Heller, and Michael K. Mount, "Five-Factor Model of Personality and Job Satisfaction: A Meta-Analysis," *Journal of Applied Psychology* 87 (2002): 530–541.

61. Timothy A. Judge and Remus Ilies, "Relationship of Personality to Performance Motivation: A Meta-Analytic Review," *Journal of Applied Psychology* 87 (2002): 797–807.

62. Judge, Bono, Ilies, and Gerhardt, "Personality and Leadership: A Qualitative and Quantitative Review"; Judge, Heller, and Mount, "Five-Factor Model of Personality and Job Satisfaction: A Meta-Analysis"; Judge and Ilies, "Relationship of Personality to Performance Motivation: A Meta-Analytic Review"; Oswald and Hough, "Personality and Its Assessment: Measurement, Validity, and Modeling"; Zhao and Seibert, "The Five Factor Personality Dimensions and Entrepreneurial Status: A Meta-Analytical Review."

63. Connelly, and Ones, "An Other Perspective on Personality: Meta-Analytic Integration of Observers' Accuracy and Predictive Validity" and In Sue Oh, Wang, and Mount, "Validity of Observer Ratings of the Five-Factor Model of Personality: A Meta-analysis."

64. Zimmerman, Triana, and Barrick, "Predictive Criterion-Related Validity of Observer-Ratings of Personality and Job-Related Competencies Using Multiple Raters and Multiple Performance Criteria." Human Performance 22 (in press).

65. Jeff J. McHenry, Leatta M. Hough, Jody L. Toquam, Mary Ann Hanson, and Steven Ashworth, "Project A Validity Results—The Relationship between Predictor and Criterion Domains," *Personnel Psychology* 43 (1990): 335–354; Margaret A. McManus and Mary L. Kelly, "Personality Measures and Biodata: Evidence Regarding Their Incremental Value in the Life Insurance Industry," *Personnel Psychology* 52 (1999): 137–148; Michael K. Mount, Alan Witt, and Murray R. Barrick, "Incremental Validity of Empirically-Keyed Biographical Scales over GMA and the Five Factor Personality Constructs," *Personnel Psychology* 53 (2000): 299–323; Frederick L. Oswald, Neal Schmitt, Brian H. King, Lauren J. Ramsay, and Michael A. Gillespie, "Developing a Biodata Measure and Situational Judgment Inventory as Predictors of College Student Performance," *Journal of Applied Psychology* 89 (2004): 187–207; Jesus F. Salgado and Filip de Fruyt, "Personality in Personnel Selection," in *The Blackwell Handbook of Personnel Selection*, ed. Arne Evers, Neil Anderson, and Olga Voskuijil (Oxford, UK: Blackwell Publishers, 2004), 174–198; Frank L. Schmidt and John E. Hunter, "The Validity and Utility of Selection Methods in Personnel Psychology: Practical and Theoretical Implications of 85 Years of Research Findings," *Psychological Bulletin* 124 (1998): 262–274; and Jeff Weekley and Robert E. Ployhart, "Situational Judgment: Antecedents and Relationships with Performance," *Human Performance* 18 (2005): 81–104.

66. Richard L. Lanyon and Leonard D. Goodstein. *Personality Assessment*, 2nd ed. (New York: John Wiley, 1982), 144.

67. Ibid., 145.

68. Sherman, *Personality: Inquiry and Application*, 213.

69. Hannah J. Foldes, Emily E. Duehr, and Deniz S. Ones, "Group Differences in Personality: Meta-Analyses Comparing Five U.S. Racial Groups," *Personnel Psychology* 61 (2008): and 579–616; Leatta Hough, Robert E. Ployhart, and Frederick L. Oswald, "Determinants, Detection and Amelioration of Adverse Impact in Personnel Selection Procedures: Issues, Evidence and Lessons Learned," *International Journal of Selection & Assessment* 9 (2001): 152–170.

70. Ibid.; Oswald and Hough, "Personality and Its Assessment: Measurement, Validity, and Modeling."

71. Jonathan R. Mook, "Personality Testing in Today's Workplace: Avoiding the Legal Pitfalls," *Employee Relations* 22 (1996): 65–88.

72. *Karraker v. Rent-A-Center, Inc.*, 411 F.3d 831 (7th Cir. 2005), Case No. 04-2881.

73. Ibid.; Oswald and Hough, "Personality and Its Assessment: Measurement, Validity, and Modeling."

74. *Soroka v. Dayton Hudson*, 18 Cal. App. 4th 1200, 1 Cal. Rptr. 2nd 77 (Cal. App. 1991).

75. Jeff A. Weekley, Robert E. Ployhart, and Crystal M. Harold, "Personality and Situational Judgment Tests across Applicant and Incumbent Settings: An Examination of Validity, Measurement, and Subgroup Differences," *Human Performance* 17 (2004): 433–461; and Joseph G. Rosse, Mary D. Stecher, Janice L. Miller, and Robert A. Levin, "The Impact of Response Distortion of Preemployment Personality Testing and Hiring Decisions," *Journal of Applied Psychology* 83 (1998): 634–644.

76. Rosse, Stecher, Levin, and Miller, "The Impact of Response Distortion of Preemployment Personality Testing and Hiring Decisions."

77. Leatta M. Hough, "Effects of Intentional Distortion in Personality Measurement and Evaluation of Suggested Palliatives," *Human Performance* 11 (1998): 209–244.

78. Jill E. Ellingson, Paul R. Sackett, Brian S. Connelly, "Personality Assessment Across Selection and Development Contexts: Insights into Response Distortion, *Journal of Applied Psychology* 92 (2007): 386–395; Sackett and Lievens, "Personnel Selection."

79. Judith M. Collins and David H. Gleaves, "Race, Job Applicants, and the Five-Factor Model of Personality: Implications for Black Psychology, Industrial/Organizational Psychology, and the Five-Factor Theory," *Journal of Applied Psychology* 83 (1998): 531–544; Jill E. Ellingson, Paul R. Sackett, and Leatta M. Hough, "Social Desirability Corrections in Personality Measurement: Issues of Applicant Comparison and Construct Validity," *Journal of Applied Psychology* 84 (1999): 155–166; and Deniz S. Ones and Chockalingham Vishwesvaran, "Job-Specific Applicant Pools and National Norms for Personality Scales: Implications for Range Restriction Corrections in Validation Research," *Human Performance* 11 (1998): 245–269.

80. Leaetta M. Hough and Frederick L. Oswald, "Personnel Selection: Looking toward the Future—Remembering the Past," *Annual Review of Psychology* 51 (2000): 631–664; and Leaetta M. Hough, "Emerging Trends and Needs in Personality Research and Practice: Beyond Main Effects," in *Personality and Work: Reconsidering the Role of Personality in Organizations*, ed. Murray R. Barrick and Ann Marie Ryan (San Francisco: Jossey-Bass, 2003), 289–325.

81. John J. Donovan and Stephen A. Dwight, "Do Warnings Not to Fake Reduce Faking?" *Human Performance* 16 (2003): 1–23; and John J. Donovan, Stephen A. Dwight, and Gregory M. Hurtz, "An Assessment of the Prevalence, Severity, and Verifiability of Entry-Level Applicant Faking Using the Randomized Response Technique," *Human Performance* 16 (2003): 81–106.

82. Ellingson, Sackett, and Hough, "Social Desirability Corrections in Personality Measurement: Issues of Applicant Comparison and Construct Validity"; and Neal Schmitt and Frederick L. Oswald, "The Impact of Corrections for Faking on the Validity of Noncognitive Measures in Selection Settings," *Journal of Applied Psychology* 91 (2006): 613–621.

83. Murray R. Barrick and Michael K. Mount, "Effects of Impression Management and Self-Deception on the Predictive Validity of Personality Constructs," *Journal of Applied Psychology* 83 (1996): 261–272; Neal D. Christiansen, Richard D. Goffin, Norman G. Johnston, and Mitchell G. Rothstein, "Correcting the 16PF for Faking: Effects on Criterion-Related Validity and Individual Hiring Decisions," *Personnel Psychology* 47 (1994): 847–860; Leatta M. Hough, Newell K. Eaton, Marvin D. Dunnette, John D. Kamp, and Rodney A. McCloy, "Criterion-Related Validities of Personality Constructs and the Effect of Response Distortion on Those Validities [Monograph]," *Journal of Applied Psychology* 75 (1990): 581–595; and Deniz S. Ones, Chockalingham Viswesvaran, and Angela D. Reiss, "Role of Social Desirability in Personality Testing for Personnel Selection: The Red Herring," *Journal of Applied Psychology* 81 (1996): 660–679.

84. Schmitt and Oswald, "The Impact of Corrections for Faking on the Validity of Noncognitive Measures in Selection Settings."

85. Patrick D. Converse, Fred L. Oswald, Anna Imus, Cynthia Hendricks, Radha Roy, and Hilary Butera, "Comparing Personality Test Formats and Warnings: Effects on Criterion-Related Validity and Test-taker Reactions," *International Journal of Selection & Assessment* 16 (2008): 155–169; Christiansen, Goffin, Johnston, and Rothstein, "Correcting the 16PF for Faking: Effects on Criterion-Related Validity and Individual Hiring Decisions"; Ellingson, Sackett, and Hough, "Social Desirability Corrections in Personality Measurement: Issues of Applicant Comparison and Construct Validity"; Rose Mueller-Hanson, Eric D. Heggestad, and George C. Thornton III, "Faking and Selection: Considering the Use of Personality from Select-In and Select-Out Perspectives," *Journal of Applied Psychology* 88 (2003): 348–355; and Rossé, Stecher, Miller, and Levin, "The Impact of Response Distortion of Preemployment Personality Testing and Hiring Decisions."

86. Dwight and Donovan, "Do Warnings Not to Fake Reduce Faking?"

87. Christiansen, Goffin, Johnston, and Rothstein, "Correcting the 16PF for Faking: Effects on Criterion-Related Validity and Individual Hiring Decisions"; Mueller-Hanson, Heggestad, and Thornton III, "Faking and Selection: Considering the Use of Personality from Select-In and Select-Out Perspectives"; Rossé, Stecher, Miller, and Levin, "The Impact of Response Distortion of Preemployment Personality Testing and Hiring Decisions"; and Schmitt and Oswald, "The Impact of Corrections for Faking on the Validity of Noncognitive Measures in Selection Settings."

88. Ellingson, Sackett, and Hough, "Social Desirability Corrections in Personality Measurement: Issues of Applicant Comparison and Construct Validity"; Sackett and Lievens, "Personnel Selection."

89. Patrick H. Raymark, Mark J. Schmit, and Robert M. Guion, "Identifying Potentially Useful Personality Constructs for Employee Selection," *Personnel Psychology* 50 (1997): 723–736.

90. Hugh Hartshorne and Mark May, *Studies in the Nature of Character* (New York: Macmillan, 1928), 384.

91. Murray R. Barrick and Michael K. Mount, "Autonomy as a Moderator of the Relationships between the Five Factor Personality Dimensions and Job Performance," *Journal of Applied Psychology* 78 (1993): 111–118; and Barrick, Mitchell, and Stewart, "Situational and Motivational Influences on Trait-Behavior Relationships."

92. Peter Herriot, "Towards an Attributional Theory of the Selection Interview," *Journal of Occupational Psychology* 54 (1981): 165–173.

93. Barrick and Mount, "Autonomy as a Moderator of the Relationships between the Five Factor Personality Dimensions and Job Performance."

94. Blackman, "Personality Judgement and Utility of the Unstructured Employment Interview"; Blackman and Funder, "Effective Interview Practices for Accurately Assessing Counterproductive Traits," and Van Iddekinge, Raymark, and Roth, "Assessing Personality with a Structured Employment Interview: Construct-Related Validity and Susceptibility to Response Inflation."

95. Greg L. Stewart and Murray R. Barrick, "Four Lessons Learned from the Person-Situation Debate: A Review and Research Agenda," in *Personality and Organizations*, ed. Brent Smith and Benjamin Schneider (Hillsdale, NJ: Lawrence Erlbaum Associates, 2004), 61–87.

96. Robert P. Tett and Dawn D. Burnett, "A Personality Trait-Based Interactionist Model of Job Performance," *Journal of Applied Psychology* 88 (2003): 500–517.

97. Greg L. Stewart, "Reward Structure as a Moderator of the Relationship between Extraversion and Sales Performance," *Journal of Applied Psychology* 81 (1996): 619–627.

98. Dave Bartram, Patricia A. Lindley, Linda Marshall, and Julie Foster, "The Recruitment and Selection of Young People by Small Businesses," *Journal of Occupational and Organizational Psychology* 68 (1995): 339–358; and Murray R. Barrick and Michael K. Mount, "Select on Conscientiousness and Emotional Stability," in *Handbook of Principles of Organizational Behavior*, ed. Edwin E. Locke (Oxford, UK: Blackwell Publishers, 2000), 15–28.

99. Barrick and Mount, "Select on Conscientiousness and Emotional Stability."

Performance Tests and Assessment Centers for Selection

PERFORMANCE TESTS

This chapter describes selection devices that assess applicants by means of testing situations that closely resemble actual parts of the job being considered. In their most common form, these devices are referred to as *performance* or *work sample tests* because they ask the applicant to complete some job activity, either behavioral or verbal, under structured testing conditions. One example of a performance test requires applicants to write a simple computer program to solve a specific problem.

Differences from Other Selection Devices

Performance tests provide *direct* evidence of the applicant's ability and skill to work on the job, whereas other selection devices provide indirect evidence. In well-constructed performance tests, the activities presented to the applicant are representative of job tasks, equipment, and policies that are actually part of the job. In completing these activities, the applicant performs a representative part of the job for which he or she is being evaluated.

When we consider the other types of selection devices we have discussed, we realize that these devices collect primarily either verbal descriptions of activities or verbal indicants of job knowledge. For example, application and biographical data forms concentrate on written descriptions of previous educational or vocational experiences. Interviews are oral exchanges that are primarily descriptions of work and educational experiences or oral demonstrations of job knowledge. Ability tests are primarily written indicants of knowledge, and personality inventories are most often written descriptions of behavior.

In most selection situations, the selection specialist must use the verbal information that is provided by the applicant to make an inference about the applicant's future job performance. There are limitations to these verbal data that hinder this inference. One is that these data are subject to willful distortion or faking by the applicant. The possibility of successful distortion varies—the description of past experience is the most difficult to verify; the demonstration of job knowledge is the least difficult to verify. The second limitation is that the relationship between verbal description and actual behavior is not perfect. Most of us can cite personal examples that demonstrate that we know the correct way to do something, such as hitting a backhand shot in tennis, tuning the motor of a car, or organizing work and study habits more efficiently; yet talking about something does not mean that we can translate that knowledge into actual behavior (at least for the author). The same could be true of applicants who describe work behaviors. To the extent that distortion and lack of translation into behavior occur in the collection of data from applicants, the accuracy of the selection decision becomes more tenuous.

With performance tests the probability of both of these limitations is greatly reduced. In most cases, applicant descriptions are minimized—what to do, what equipment to use, and so on. Instead, the applicant acts in the work situation. These actions and their results are the important outcome. The only time written or oral information is produced is when the actual job activity consists of written or oral components, such as preparing a press release or answering questions posed by an assembled group of consumers.

Limitations

After looking at it in this way, you are probably asking yourself, "If performance tests are so sensible and efficient, shouldn't they be used in all selection situations?" Good question! In fact such instruments are used widely, especially for clerical and skilled manual labor positions. Recently, performance tests have also been used extensively in the form of *assessment centers* for managerial and professional selection. However, a number of factors can limit their use in selection programs. For one, much care must be taken in the construction of work sample tests to ensure that they are representative of job activities. For many complex and multiple-demand jobs, this is difficult. We are all familiar with selection devices that may be intended as work samples but really are not. One example is the attempt by an interviewer to create a stressful situation during the interview by asking questions rapidly, not allowing time for the applicant's response, or acting in a cold, aloof manner. Even if the job of interest is one of high work demands that produces stress, the situation staged in the interview is not representative of those demands. Actually, in very few jobs is stress created by semi-hostile individuals rapidly questioning the job holder. The behavior of the applicant in such an artificial interview situation is not readily generalizable to the job; the interview should not be viewed as a performance test.

A second limitation is that performance tests are usually developed on the assumption that the applicants already have the knowledge, ability, and skill to complete the job behavior required in the test. This assumption is most appropriate for jobs with tasks that are similar to jobs in other organizations, or tasks that can be taught in formal education programs. In other words, the most appropriate tasks for performance tests are those that do not depend on specialized knowledge, abilities, or skills regarding company products, personnel, materials, or customers. When the performance test does require specialized knowledge, the selection specialist must include training in that specialized knowledge before the test begins. That inclusion, obviously, makes the test longer and more difficult to administer.

A third factor limiting the use of performance tests is the cost. Usually, performance tests are much more expensive than other selection devices. Such costs include equipment and materials used only for selection; the time and facilities needed for individual or small group administration of the selection instruments; the staff time spent in identifying representative tasks during job analysis; and the development of test instructions, testing situations, and scoring procedures.

In the following sections, we will discuss in more detail the rationale underlying the use of performance tests, describe examples of successful tests, and present the important steps in their development. Finally, we will describe the use of assessment centers for the selection of managerial and professional jobs. After all this you will be one chapter closer to being a selection expert and able to solve many of the great problems of the world.

Consistency of Behavior

Paul Wernimont and John Campbell made the most direct statement of the principles of performance tests as selection devices.[1] Their major thesis is that selection decisions are most accurate when "behavioral consistency" is the major characteristic of the selection program. To clarify their point, Wernimont and Campbell have categorized all the selection devices as either signs or samples.

Signs are selection tests used as indicators of an individual's predisposition to behave in certain ways. To the extent that these signs differ from the job behaviors being predicted, their ability to relate directly to these job behaviors is limited. *Samples*, on the other hand, are selection tests that gather information about behaviors consistent with the job behaviors being predicted. To the extent these samples are similar to the job behaviors, their ability to predict job behavior is increased.

Two major types of instruments are regarded as samples. One type consists of instruments that gather information about an applicant's work experience and educational history to determine whether the applicant has ever demonstrated the necessary job behaviors. If so, rating methods are then developed to judge the frequency of these behaviors, the applicant's success in performing them, and the similarity of their content to the job situation addressed in the selection program. These data are, in turn, used for rating the probability that the applicant will demonstrate good work performance. These ideas were part of our previous discussions of the appropriate design of training and experience evaluations, biodata forms, and interviews and the gathering of behavioral descriptions in personality assessment. In each of these cases, we emphasized gathering several descriptions of behavior closely related to job activities.

The second type of sample selection instrument discussed by Wernimont and Campbell consists of work-sample tests and simulation exercises. Such devices are in essence what we have called performance tests and require the applicant to complete a set of actions that demonstrate whether the job behavior of interest can be successfully completed. It is this second type of sample that we discuss in this chapter.

Examples of Performance Tests

Work-sample tests, which can be classified as either motor or verbal, are tailor-made to match the important activities of the job being considered.[2] The term *motor* (behavioral) is used when the test requires the physical manipulation of things—for example, operating a machine, installing a piece of equipment, or making a product. The term *verbal* is used when the problem situation is primarily language or people oriented—for example, simulating an interrogation, editing a manuscript for grammatical errors, or demonstrating how to train subordinates.

Examples of various performance tests and the jobs for which they have been used are presented in Table 13.1. As is evident from the table, a wide variety of tests have been used, even for the same job. Traditionally, motor performance tests have been used for selection of skilled craftworkers, technicians, and clerical staff. These jobs usually require an extensive use of equipment and tools. Such jobs often utilize a diversity of equipment, which means that one performance test would not be appropriate for all jobs. Several tests, each directed to a specific set of job tasks, are often necessary for any given job. This has been especially true for the skilled craft positions such as mechanic, electrician, and machine operator.

TABLE 13.1   Examples of Work-Sample Tests Used in Selection

Test	Job
Motor:	
Lathe	Machine operator
Drill press	
Tool dexterity	
Screw board test	
Packaging	
Shorthand	Clerical worker
Stenographic	
Typing	
Blueprint reading	Mechanic
Tool identification	
Installing belts	
Repair of gearbox	
Installing a motor	
Vehicle repair	
Tracing trouble in a complex circuit	Electronics technician
Inspection of electronic defects	
Electronics test	
Verbal:	
Report of recommendations for problem solution	Manager or supervisor
Small business manufacturing game	
Judgment and decision-making test	
Supervisory judgment about training, safety, performance, evaluation	
Processing of mathematical data and evaluating hypotheses	Engineer or scientist
Describing laboratory tests	
Mathematical formulation and scientific judgment	
Oral fact finding	Customer service representative
Role playing of customer contacts	
Writing business letters	
Giving oral directions	

Motor Tests.   James Campion has described one example of a motor performance test used in the selection of maintenance mechanics.[3]

> Motor Performance Test for Maintenance Mechanics—*The development of this test began with extensive job analysis that resulted in a list of task statements. Those statements were job related and could be performed by a large number of applicants. Thus tasks were part of the job and within the repertoire of job applicants. Experts identified two major work activities that differentiated good and poor job performance: use of tools and accuracy of work. Included in the test were tasks such as installing pulleys and belts, disassembling and repairing a gearbox, installing and aligning a motor, pressing a bushing into a sprocket, and reaming the bushing to fit a shaft. A distinct feature of the scoring system was that experts tried to identify all possible task*

behaviors an applicant might demonstrate in the test. Each possible behavior was evaluated and weighted and placed on the list. The rater, therefore, had only to observe the applicant's behaviors and check them off the list. Adding weights assigned to the checked behavior determined the applicant's overall score.

David Robinson has described a second example, a test for the position of construction superintendent.[4]

Blueprint Reading Test—*An architect was instructed to identify common architectural errors in blueprints for drawings that had actually been executed by the company. Applicants were asked to review the blueprints and mark the location of the errors with a felt-tipped pen on copies of the drawings. The test was scored by counting the number of correct markings.*

Verbal Tests. Verbal performance tests are commonly used in selection programs for managers, staff specialists, engineers, scientists, and similar professionals. These jobs require the use of spoken or written messages or interpersonal interaction. It is these components that are simulated in verbal performance tests. The diversity that characterized motor tests also holds true for the sample of verbal tests listed in Table 13.1. The following two examples illustrate verbal performance tests. The first was also reported by David Robinson and was used to select a construction superintendent.

Scrambled Subcontractor Test—*In the construction business, interruption of the critical construction path can be costly. The most important factor in staying on the critical path is that subcontractors appear in the right order to do their work. Knowledge of the proper order of subcontractor appearance is a prerequisite to staying on this path. In order to test this knowledge, applicants were given a list of 30 subcontractors (for example, roofing, framing, plumbing, fencing) and were asked to list them according to order of appearance on the job site. The order of appearance given by the applicant was compared with the order of appearance agreed upon by the company managers. The applicants were given the opportunity to discuss their rationale for particular orders. Minor deviations from the managers' solution were accepted.*

The second example, a reading test developed for packers of explosive materials, was reported by Robert Gatewood (blush) and Lyle Schoenfeldt.[5]

Reading Test for Chemical Packages—*Reading and understanding written material was critical to the job of chemical packager because often explosive chemicals were involved. Job analysis determined that 50 percent of the material read dealt with safety procedures, 30 percent with work procedures, 15 percent with daily operations, and the remaining 5 percent with miscellaneous company material. These four areas were referred to as the content categories of reading material. A reading test was developed that used the actual materials read on the job. In this test the applicant read a short passage drawn from work documents. The content of these passages appeared in the same proportions as did the content categories of the job materials. True-false and multiple-choice items that asked about the behaviors called for on the job were presented after each passage. Answers were scored based on their conformity to the information contained in the passage that had been presented.*

Trainability Tests. Trainability tests are another variation of performance tests. This type of test is most often used in selection for two kinds of jobs: jobs that do not presently exist but are anticipated in the near future and for which extensive training is necessary, and jobs that do exist but are so specialized or technical that applicants could not be expected to possess the knowledge or skill to complete either appropriate ability tests or performance tests.

Richard Reilly and Edmond Israelski described AT&T's development and use of trainability tests, which were known in the company as minicourses.[6] The major purpose of the minicourse is to place the applicant in a test situation that closely resembles the training setting. In this way, an assessment can be made of the applicant's ability to learn critical material and complete the necessary, extensive training program. The strategy is clearly one of selection for performance in training. The applicant is required first to read and study a standardized sample of programmed training material, the minicourse. A typical minicourse has a six-hour time limit; the range is between two hours and three days. After completing the minicourse, the applicant answers test questions designed to measure how well he or she learned the material. A passing score qualifies the applicant to be admitted into the training program. He or she must then successfully complete this training to be offered employment.

Two types of minicourses have been developed. The first type consists of highly specific material that matches training content closely. An example would be a course containing material relevant to learning to use a particular piece of equipment. The second type of minicourse consists of more general material; it is used for jobs that are expected to change frequently because of technological advancement. In this case, the purpose of the minicourse is to present basic information that is appropriate despite the specific technology currently being used on the job. For example, a minicourse was developed about understanding binary, octal, hexadecimal, and decimal numbering systems. This was considered basic information appropriate for a variety of software programs and statistical analyses.

The Development of Performance Tests

Even though performance tests vary considerably in the jobs for which they are used and the problem situations they present to applicants, they are similar in the steps taken to develop them. These steps, listed in Table 13.2, are essential to the construction of performance tests that are both legally defensible and valid for selecting applicants.[7] This section presents the details of these steps.

Perform Job Analysis. The information presented in Chapter 7 on the methods and procedures of job analysis is relevant in developing a performance test. Job tasks must be described in detail in order to identify job-related equipment and material (important for motor performance tests) and pinpoint the kinds of personal interaction required for the job (important for verbal performance tests). To maximize the likelihood that the statement of the job tasks is accurate, one should obtain information from several job incumbents and supervisors. One issue to consider is the proficiency level of the workers and supervisors involved. It is necessary to rely heavily on information supplied by

---

TABLE 13.2	Steps in the Development of Performance Tests

- Perform job analysis
- Identify important tasks to be tested
- Develop testing procedures
- Develop scoring procedures
- Train judges

individuals who perform the job well. If the information in the job analysis is to be used to design and score the performance test, accurate information about the correct method of working is necessary.

Identify Important Job Tasks. Judging job tasks according to frequency, importance, time required, level of difficulty, and/or consequence of error is important. The results of such evaluation should contribute significantly to the identification of the content of a performance test. The test should address those tasks that have a strong bearing on job performance. Usually task ratings provide such information. Special attention must be paid to tasks that are seasonal or not often repeated. Such tasks may be critical and may have major consequences if not performed correctly. For this reason, it is usually recommended that ratings of task importance be obtained from several individuals.

Develop Testing Procedures. Once the tasks that will serve as the basis for the performance test have been identified, another important judgment must be made as to whether an applicant can realistically be expected to perform the task. As we mentioned previously, in most performance tests it is assumed that the applicant can do the task. In other cases in which the job task has some idiosyncratic features and cannot be done except by experienced workers, modifications must be made in the test situation. One modification is to provide the applicant with instructions about the operation of equipment, features of special materials used, or background information about company policy before the test is given. Obviously, this modification will work only in those cases in which the amount of information necessary to perform the job task is relatively simple and easy to learn. In those cases in which this preliminary information is complex or difficult, the performance test is modified to measure the applicant's ability to develop the skill to perform the task. Our previous description of trainability tests is an example of this type of a modification.

Select Tasks. After the most appropriate job tasks have been identified, they must be further studied to make the most efficient use of testing time. The most important considerations in this study are the following:

1. The total time required to perform the task must be reasonable. It is expensive to administer performance tests, and the cost increases as the length of the task to be completed increases.

2. Tasks that can be done by either many applicants or few applicants provide little help in discriminating among good and poor applicants.

3. If there is a choice between two approximately equal tasks in the performance test and one of the two uses less expensive materials, equipment, or facilities, usually this task is chosen.

4. Tasks should be judged on the content of the material that would be scored in a test. All else being equal, tasks that have standardized operations or products or easily defined verbal or interaction components are more appropriate in performance tests than tasks not so characterized. It is usually far easier and less expensive to both develop and score the test for these types of tasks.

Specify Testing Procedures. As with other selection tests, it is important that the performance test be consistently administered to all applicants and graded consistently by all scorers. Standardization of testing conditions requires that a set of instructions be developed to inform the applicant of the nature of the task, what is expected, and the materials and equipment to be used. The same or identical conditions for testing should be provided to each applicant. Information about what actions, products, or outcomes will be scored should be provided. For grading, rules must be developed to specify what constitutes a "correct" response and how many points should be deducted for various deficiencies. All scorers should be thoroughly trained in the interpretation of these rules.

Establish Independent Test Sections.   In developing the task problem used in the performance test, another important consideration is the independence of various parts of the test. All else being equal, it is preferable that the applicant's performance on one part of the test not be closely tied to a previous part of the test. If all errors are independent of one another, it is possible to obtain a large sample of the applicant's behavior. If, on the other hand, the test is developed so that the identification of one or two errors would disclose other errors, there is a strong probability of obtaining a distorted measurement of the applicant's performance. Applicants who do not recognize the one or two central errors have no opportunity to identify the remaining errors correctly; if they do identify the central errors, then the rest become apparent. This actually makes the test only a one- or two-item test for applicants.

Lack of independence is most likely when the performance test is a sequence of steps in a job process such as sewing a garment or constructing a small piece of apparatus. In either case, an error in measuring the materials to be used would adversely affect the remaining steps. To avoid this problem, some tests have been designed to provide a new set of acceptable materials for each phase of the job process. For example, if the first phase of a performance test is measuring and cutting the necessary pieces, the applicant stops after this phase. The pieces are taken to be scored by the judges, and the applicant is provided with a set of acceptable pieces to use in the next phase of the construction task.

Eliminate Contaminating Factors.   In developing a performance test, it is important to ensure that apparatus, jargon, or other testing elements that have only a minor influence on job performance do not interfere with or limit the test performance of applicants who are not familiar with these elements. For example, in a performance test for an HR specialist, some numerical data may be provided from a company's attitude survey. The applicant is asked to make preliminary data analyses and use these results to answer a few specific management questions about the employees' attitudes about company procedures. The data analyses are to be performed on a personal computer. A serious problem could occur if an applicant did not know how to operate the computer provided for the performance test. In cases such as this, it is appropriate to provide a variety of computers, to train the applicant in the use of the computer before the performance test begins, or to provide an operator for the computer. Modifications such as these are not necessary when the operation of a particular apparatus is essential to the job task and not easily learned after one starts on the job. In such a case, the apparatus becomes an essential part of the performance test.

Select the Number of Test Problems.   The final point we address in test construction is the number of times an applicant will be asked to perform a job activity during a performance test. A trade-off usually exists between the time required and the cost of testing and the increased reliability that results from having the applicant demonstrate the task more than once. The general guideline is to have the applicant repeat the task several times within cost limitations. For example, many skilled craft positions, such as typing, sewing, maintenance, or machine operation, have short-cycle tasks. An applicant can provide several products within a relatively brief time period by repeating the cycle of tasks. Obviously, if the task of the performance test is long or costly to stage, a limited number of trials should be scheduled.

Develop Scoring Procedures.   The criteria for scoring performance tests must be clearly defined, because the decisions facing the scorer are often difficult. In many cases a judgment must be made about the acceptability of task performance when multiple factors are present. Scoring generally is a function of comparing the applicant's test task performance to a standard defined by the organization to be satisfactory. Table 13.3 provides examples of several factors that have been used primarily in scoring *motor* performance tests. In this type of test, the *task process* or the *task product* is scored. The task process is the actions or observable behaviors the applicant demonstrates when performing the task. The task product is the result of the task process. In motor performance tests, products are usually physical objects such as a typed document, a piece of sewn clothing, or a set of joined pieces of wood or other building materials. In general, a process is scored when there are clearly a small number of ways to do the job, and these ways invariably lead to an acceptable product. The operation of machinery in a continuous job process is one example. A product is scored in those situations in which a large number of different behaviors can lead to an acceptable product.

Standards.   As Table 13.3 indicates, a number of separate standards can be scored for both process and product categories. Quality is vital, of course, to almost all jobs. Quantity is important for those performance tests in which the amount produced within a given time period is under the control of the worker. One example is the number of sales orders prepared for shipping. Cost becomes important as a scorable standard when there are a variety of options possible to the worker and the options vary in cost. An example

---

TABLE 13.3   Criteria Used in Scoring Motor Performance Tests

Standard	Process Criteria	Product Criteria
Quality	Accuracy	Conformance to specifications
	Error rate	Dimensions or other measures
	Choice of tools and/or materials	Spacing
		Position
	Efficiency of steps taken	Strength
		Suitability for use
		General appearance
Quantity	Time to complete	Quantity of output
Learning time	Number of steps for which guidance is needed	Improvement in meeting quantity standards
		Improvement in meeting quality standards
Cost	Amount of material used	Number of rejects
Safety	Handling of tools	Safety of completed product
	Accident rate	

Source: Lynnette B. Plumlee, I (Washington, DC: Personnel Research and Development Center, U.S. Civil Service Commission, Professional Series 75–1, January 1975).

would be tasks such as the repair of a research apparatus in which several options are available that vary greatly in expense.

The remaining two standards—learning time and safety—are used much less frequently than the other standards. Learning time is a logical standard for tasks that are characterized by the variety of novel demands they place on the incumbent; the technical repair of a variety of sophisticated electronic equipment is one example. In many cases, the task of repair requires the worker to constantly learn and use new methods of diagnosis. The length of time that an employee takes to learn these new methods translates directly into costs for the organization. Scoring the dimension of safety is obviously important if physical injury can be caused by an incorrect process or product.

More than one of these standards can be used in scoring; for example, quantity and quality are often used together. Also, process and product can both be scored in the same performance test. Process dimensions used in scoring can be identified by observing performance of the job. The selection specialist can use both demonstration and descriptions of task steps given by these workers. Most organizations have defined the physical dimensions or properties of satisfactory products. This information is often used in scoring the product dimensions of motor performance tests. For example, the diameter of rolled wire, the strength of welds, and the location of buttons sewn on a blouse are all such standards.

Rules for Scoring. In scoring the motor performance test, the assignment of numbers to the applicant's test performance must be performed according to defined rules. Most often, especially if the performance test has several repetitions or separately scored parts, a simple "0, 1 rule" is used. Performance that meets the standard is scored "1" and performance that does not is scored "0." The total score for the test is obtained by summing across all parts of the test. Another scoring option is to use scales, for example 1 to 5. The highest number on the scale is assigned when the performance meets the desired level; other numbers are assigned to less acceptable performance in descending order of acceptability. It is necessary to determine how much of a deviation from the desired level each number on the scale represents. Finally, if many different standards are scored in the performance test—for example, quality of the products, quantity produced, and cost of the work process—a rule must be stated to allow these separate scores to be combined into one total score.

Scoring verbal performance tests is different from scoring motor performance tests. The general principle is essentially the same—the verbal performance of the applicant is compared against a standard that the organization has deemed satisfactory. The use of words and concepts, however, and the interaction among individuals cannot be as precisely defined as standards of motor performance tests. In many cases the scoring of verbal performance tests depends on the extensive training of judges. We examine such scoring methods later in our discussion of assessment centers, which have a large component of verbal performance tests.

Train Judges. For motor performance tests, training raters in how to judge applicants' performance is relatively straightforward if scoring standards and rules have been well defined. Videotapes of applicant task behaviors have been used to train raters to make judgments about process dimensions.[8] Whether videotapes or live demonstrations are used in training, the rater is given an explanation and a description of appropriate job process behaviors, including the sequence of the behaviors. Emphasis is then placed on demonstrations of appropriate and inappropriate behavior. Videotapes seemingly have an advantage in this phase because they can be used frequently, stopped at critical moments, and replayed to demonstrate specific points. Logically, it is important to present numerous inappropriate behaviors during this training to familiarize the rater with errors before actual testing begins.

Reliability of measurement must be maximized in developing a scoring system and training raters to use it. By using some measure of interrater reliability (discussed in Chapter 4), high agreement among raters in measurement and scoring should be demonstrated. If raters do not demonstrate reliability in their judgments after training, either more training is necessary, the scoring system must be changed, or the raters are replaced.

An Example of the Development of a Performance Test

Neal Schmitt and Cheri Ostroff described the development of a performance test that was used for selecting emergency telephone operators for a police department.[9] Job analysis was conducted through two meetings with experienced workers. The first meeting, with four workers, generated a list of task statements. The second meeting, with three other workers, reviewed and revised this list. This revised list was then submitted to supervisory personnel for final revision. The 78 task statements that were produced were subsequently grouped into categories based on task similarity. All workers were then reconvened in order to generate statements of the KSAs needed to perform the 78 tasks successfully. This meeting resulted in a list of 54 KSAs, which were arranged into similar content groups. The following is an example.

Communication Skills

1. Ability to speak on the telephone in a clearly understandable manner.

2. Ability to control conversations in order to acquire information needed to respond to emergencies.

The next step was to evaluate the importance of these tasks and KSAs to the ability to perform the job. To do this, one questionnaire was written that asked workers to rate each task on three seven-point scales: (a) the relative time spent on the task compared to all others, (b) the relative difficulty of the task compared to all others, and (c) the criticality of the task as judged by the degree to which incorrect performance results in negative consequences. A second questionnaire asked each worker to rate each KSA on three scales: (a) the necessity for newly hired employees to possess the KSA, (b) the extent to which trouble is likely to occur if the KSA is ignored in selection, and (c) the extent to which the KSA distinguishes between superior and average workers. The first scale required a simple yes or no response; the other two used seven-point response formats.

Interrater reliabilities were calculated for all scales; all but one were 0.87 or higher. The data from these scales were then used to identify the KSAs to be measured in selection. To do this, three factors were considered: (a) being linked to important job tasks, (b) being necessary for new workers, and (c) having a high score on the scale measuring likely trouble when this was ignored in selection. The resulting KSAs were grouped into six dimensions (see Table 13.4).

Three tests were developed to use in selection: an oral directions/typing test, a situational interview, and a telephone call simulation. The link between these devices and the KSAs is shown in Table 13.4. To develop these tests, both important job tasks and KSAs were used. Each test measured at least two KSAs and incorporated parts of the important job tasks linked to those KSAs.

Oral Directions/Typing Test.   This test was designed to measure the applicant's memory and technical/clerical skills. The test consisted of four parts: (a) spelling of common street and place names, (b) recording important information from telephone calls, (c) answering questions about the location and movement of police units after monitoring conversations, and (d) typing forms required in report writing. Material for each of

TABLE 13.4	KSAs and Tests Used for Police Operator Selection		

	Selection Test		
KSA	**Oral Directions**	**Interview**	**Simulation**
Communication skills		X	X
Emotional control		X	X
Judgment		X	X
Cooperativeness		X	X
Memory	X		
Clerical/technical skill	X		

Source: Adapted from Neal Schmitt and Cheri Ostroff, "Operationalizing the 'Behavioral Consistency' Approach: Selection Test Development Based on a Content-Oriented Strategy," *Personnel Psychology* 39 (1986): 91–108.

the four parts was obtained directly from job incidents and activities to ensure representativeness of job tasks.

Situational Interview.   The development of questions for this type of interview was described in Chapter 10. Those procedures were used to obtain critical incidents from incumbent workers. These incidents were used to form questions about how the applicant would act in specific situations. Because applicants were unlikely to have direct job experience, the questions were phrased in such a way that applicants could provide answers drawing on their own corresponding experience and knowledge. For example, the following critical incident was identified by the incumbent workers:

A caller becomes abusive when talking to the operator. The operator gets mad and verbally abuses the caller by using derogatory language.

This statement was transformed into the following question:

How would you react if you were a sales clerk, waitress, or service station attendant and one of your customers talked back to you, indicated you should have known something you did not, or told you that you were not waiting on them fast enough?

Seventeen such questions were developed.

Telephone Call Simulation.   This test created a role-playing exercise that required the job applicant to act like an operator taking calls from complainants. An experienced operator played the role of a caller. Six different scripts were prepared for the operator-caller to ensure that the situations were equal for all applicants. The callers were trained in the presentation of their complaints. Each applicant was given one practice trial to become familiar with the test. Applicants recorded information that they gathered from the call on a standardized form used by the department to record information from such calls.

It can easily be understood that these steps resulted in a three-instrument selection program that closely resembled actual on-the-job behaviors. Moreover, the development of these tests relied on the content validation procedure recommended in the *Uniform Guidelines:* The procedure identified important tasks using a job analysis technique that also estimated their importance and criticality. The selection instruments represented these major tasks.

The Effectiveness of Performance Tests

Studies that examine the results of using performance tests in selection have been universally positive and have identified several benefits. For example, Philip Roth, Philip Bobko, and Lynn McFarland's meta-analytic study found a 0.33 validity coefficient for performance tests, after appropriate methodological corrections.[10] The authors also determined only a small difference in validity when objective (usually a measured outcome of the task) or subjective (usually a supervisor's judgment) job performance criteria measures were used. Objective criteria were associated with a 0.30 validity coefficient and subjective criteria with a 0.34 coefficient. They found that performance tests added to the prediction of job performance when cognitive ability was also used as a predictor.

Other studies have compared the use of performance tests and mental ability tests. One of these examined both a verbal performance test and an intelligence test in relationship to success in a police training program.[11] Data were collected from three different samples of cadets. The verbal performance test was found to be valid in all three cases (0.52, 0.72, and 0.64); the intelligence test was valid for only one sample (0.56). Moreover, when prediction of success in training was analyzed, it was determined that the performance test gave adequate prediction and that the additional use of the intelligence test did not improve this predictability. Another study compared a motor performance test for maintenance mechanics with a battery of paper-and-pencil tests. Included in this battery were both mechanical comprehension and intelligence tests. All tests were evaluated against supervisors' ratings of work performance. There were large differences between the two types of tests in terms of validity. All of the motor performance tests were found to be valid; none of the paper-and-pencil tests were.

Adverse Impact. Researchers have examined the adverse impact associated with the use of performance tests in selection. Some studies compared scores of black and white test takers and found that there were no differences between the two groups in either average scores on performance tests or on the percentage of applicants who were selected.[12] In one of these studies, paper-and-pencil tests were also used and adverse impact was found on those tests.

Findings from these and many related studies became the basis for the popular opinion that performance tests are valid and do not yield score differences among ethnic groups. Many selection specialists have said that these tests should be considered when an organization wishes to minimize adverse impact in selection. However, many of the studies of performance tests and adverse impact used job incumbents as subjects. Incumbents have the advantage of having learned the job before the research study started; logically, differences in scores among such individuals should be rather small. However, incumbents are quite different from applicants who have not worked on the job. The incumbents' pattern of scores on performance tests may not be the same as those of applicants.

A meta-analytic study conducted by Phil Roth, Phil Bobko, Lynn McFarland, and Maury Buster examined this very issue as it compared differences in performance of work sample tests between black and white incumbents and black and white applicants.[13] Results were $d = .53$ for incumbent samples and $d = .73$ (or .67 omitting one study). This difference was judged to be large enough to be evidence that differences in score between blacks and whites on work sample tests were moderated by type of sample; the differences were larger for applicants than for incumbents. This finding is important because selection deals with applicants, not incumbents. Equally important is the difference of .73 (or even .67) found between black and white applicants. This difference is close to differences commonly found between black and white applicants on cognitive ability tests when both types of tests are used for moderately complex jobs. The magnitude of this difference contradicts previous findings that determined much smaller differences that were usually in the range of $d = .38$ to $.52$. As the authors point out, a difference of $.73$ will usually lead to a determination of adverse impact when a fairly low percentage of applicants is hired. For example, if the use of a work sample test with a $d = .70$ resulted in the selection of 25% of the majority applicant pool, it would result in the selection of 16.6% of the applicants in the minority pool. This difference in selection rates (25 v. 16.6) means that the selection rate for minorities would be 66% of that for whites. This rate is below the Four-Fifths Rule commonly used by EEOC; therefore this difference could lead to a decision that adverse impact occurred in the use of the work sample test. The results of this study contradict a commonly held belief that work sample tests used with applicants will produce less differences among demographic groups than do cognitive ability tests. Said another way, there is now evidence that two of the most valid selection devices, cognitive ability tests and work sample or performance tests, result in almost equal adverse impact when used with applicants. Because the cost of the development and implementation of work sample tests is very high, these findings give pause to attempts to use work sample tests mainly for the reason of having a valid selection test with low adverse impact.

Other Results of Using Performance Tests.   In addition to being valid, performance tests provide other benefits when used in selection. One study reported that during the first 17 months that performance tests were used, no complaints were lodged about their appropriateness. This was in contrast to the previous applicant complaint rate of 10 to 20 percent that occurred when other types of tests were used.[14] Another study described the development of eight computer-based secretarial work-sample tests. Among these were tests of word processing, mail log entry, letter typing, travel expense form completion, and telephone-message noting. The authors concluded that this battery offered many advantages: (a) test administrators' time was minimized; (b) instructions, materials, and scoring were standardized; (c) test results could immediately be provided to both the applicant and the selection specialist; and (d) candidates were forced to learn simple job activities while completing the test, which provided data about the applicant's ability to learn on the job.[15]

Performance tests can serve as realistic job previews and can lead to the benefits we discussed in Chapter 8. An example of such a benefit concerns the selection of sewer-pumping station operators. During an initial one-hour instruction period, a sewer mechanic explained and demonstrated (as if he were the applicant's supervisor) procedures for the general maintenance of sewer pipes and equipment, for example, how to clean filters, grease fittings, and read a pressure chart. The test was given during the second hour, when each applicant was required to repeat the demonstration as if on the job. Follow-up interviews revealed that those who qualified for and accepted the job had an accurate idea of the job demands. Before the performance test was used, the job turnover rate was approximately 40 percent. During the 9 to 26 months after performance testing was started, this rate dropped to less than 3 percent.[16]

ASSESSMENT CENTERS

When performance tests are used for the selection of managers, professionals, and executives, they are usually referred to as *assessment centers*. The definition of an assessment center (AC) that was developed by the Task Force on Assessment Center Standards is as follows:

> *An* assessment center *consists of a standardized evaluation of behavior on multiple inputs. Multiple trained observers and techniques are used. Judgments about behavior*

are made, in part, from specially developed assessment simulations. These judgments are pooled by the assessors at an evaluation meeting during which assessment data are reported and discussed and the assessors agree on the evaluation of the dimension and any overall evaluation that is made.[17]

In simpler terms, an AC is a procedure for measuring KSAs in groups of individuals (usually 12 to 24) using a series of devices, many of which are verbal performance tests. The performance tests measure KSAs as patterns of behavior that are demonstrated when the applicant completes the performance tests. The devices in an AC, usually called *exercises,* are designed so that the participants have several opportunities to demonstrate each of the KSAs being measured. The evaluators, referred to as *assessors,* are specially trained in observing and recording the behavior of participants in the exercises. This information about behavior is used when the assessors meet as a group to share their observations of each participant and develop consensus evaluations of each applicant.

ACs have been used for both selection and career development. In selection, the emphasis is on identifying those participants who demonstrate behaviors thought necessary for performing the position being considered. When used for career development, the emphasis is on determining those behaviors each participant does well and those in which each needs improvement. Participants who need improvement are then sent to appropriate training programs. For our purposes, we will concentrate on the ACs used for selection. The next sections discuss in some detail the topics we have briefly introduced.

Assessment Centers in Industry

The Management Progress Study of AT&T marked the beginning of the use of the assessment center for industrial organizations.[18] This program was begun in 1956 to study the career development of men (remember, it was the 1950s) hired for managerial positions. According to Douglas Bray, who designed the study, the general questions that prompted the study were:

- What significant changes take place in men as their lives develop in a business career?

- Conversely, are there changes we might expect or desire that do not occur?

- What are the causes of these changes or stabilities? More particularly, what are the effects of company climate, policies, and procedures?

- How accurately can progress in management be predicted? What are the important indicators, and how are they best measured?

The study was to provide information to be used in directing the career development of managers at AT&T.

One major focus of the study was to identify the personal attributes thought to be related to the successful career progress of managers. As a start, Bray and his colleagues measured 25 characteristics (communication skill, goal flexibility, self-objectivity, and so on) and determined whether they were related to career success. These 25 were drawn from research literature, opinions of industrial psychologists specializing in management career patterns, and opinions of senior executives at AT&T. The study measured these characteristics in 274 new managers periodically over several years and related the data to these employees' progress through the levels of management. During this time, none of the data were made available to anyone but the researchers.

The immediate problem for those conducting the study was to develop devices to measure the 25 characteristics of interest. It was decided that it would be necessary to examine each manager thoroughly at each testing period to obtain useful data. To do this, a three-and-a half-day assessment center was devised. Managers were brought together in groups of 12, and several methods were administered to measure personal characteristics. These included tests of general mental ability, personality and attitude questionnaires, interviews, group problems, an individual administrative exercise, and projective tests of personality. It is not within the scope of this book to discuss the results of the study in detail. However, the reports published over the years have provided much useful information about managerial careers. More important for us, the assessment information obtained from the various exercises was shown to be related to subsequent movement through managerial levels. This, of course, prompted much attention to the use of these types of exercises and the whole concept of assessment centers for managerial selection. The use of multiple-day, multiple-exercise testing programs quickly grew. Although there were variations among these programs, they used similar types of assessment devices. These usually paralleled those used in the AT&T study. In the next section we discuss some of these types of exercises, mainly emphasizing the individual and group performance tests that were used.

Assessment Center Exercises

Dimensions.   The development of an AC starts with a job analysis to identify clusters of job activities that are the important parts of the job of interest. Each cluster should be specific and observable, comprising job tasks that are related in some way. These job clusters, referred to as *dimensions*, are measured by the assessment center devices. Table 13.5 provides a list and brief definitions of nine dimensions commonly used in ACs. It is important to note that these dimensions are defined based on actual job activities. As you can see, the definitions in Table 13.5 illustrate such activities. In assessment centers, the definitions are more detailed. For example, the dimension of *tolerance for stress* is often defined by describing the actions taken to meet specific multiple demands (from subordinates, superiors, outside pressure groups, and so on) and the specific multiple roles (negotiator, public relations specialist, performance evaluator, and so on) that characterize the job under study. The behaviors for each dimension serve as the basis for the development of performance tests to measure the dimension. It is easy to understand why ACs have relied heavily on performance tests as a primary measurement device; it is usually a straightforward process to translate these job activities into test activities.

Traditional Assessment Devices.   Following the example of the AT&T assessment center, other ACs often use various types of traditional tests and interviews. These are variations of the selection instruments that we have already discussed. We will briefly describe the use of several of these types of tests, but discuss in detail only the performance tests.

ACs frequently include mental ability, projective personality, and paper-and-pencil personality tests. We have described the uses and validity of these tests in previous chapters. The interview is also employed quite often in ACs; in many ways it is similar to the selection interview we recommended using in Chapter 10. Commonly referred to as the *background interview*, the emphasis of the AC interview is to gather information from the candidate about job activities that represent the behavioral dimensions being evaluated in the AC. The interviewer's objective is to gather as much information as possible about these dimensions. Many of the recommendations made in Chapter 10 for the use of the interview are incorporated in the AC background interview: Each interview is structured and focuses on previous job behaviors; relatively few behavioral dimensions are utilized; multiple questions are prepared to tap each dimension; interviewers are trained to record relevant job actions for each behavioral dimension; and a formal

| TABLE 13.5 | Behavioral Dimensions Frequently Measured in Assessment Centers |

Dimension	Definition
Oral Communication	Effectively expressing oneself in individual or group situations (includes gestures and nonverbal communications)
Planning and Organizing	Establishing a course of action for self or others in order to accomplish a specific goal; planning proper assignments of personnel and appropriate allocation of resources
Delegation	Utilizing subordinates effectively; allocating decision making and other responsibilities to the appropriate subordinates
Control	Establishing procedures for monitoring or regulating the processes, tasks, or activities of subordinates; monitoring and regulating job activities and responsibilities; taking action to monitor the results of delegated assignments or projects
Decisiveness	Expressing a readiness to make decisions, render judgments, take action, or commit oneself
Initiative	Actively attempting to influence events to achieve goals; showing self-starting actions rather than passive acceptance. Taking action to achieve goals beyond those called for; originating action
Tolerance for Stress	Maintaining a stable performance under pressure or opposition
Adaptability	Maintaining effectiveness in varying environments, with various tasks, responsibilities, or people
Tenacity	Staying with a position or plan of action until the desired objective is achieved or is no longer reasonably attainable

Source: George C. Thornton III, *Assessment Centers in Human Resource Management* (Reading, MA: Addison-Wesley Publishing Co., 1992).

scoring system is used to evaluate each candidate on each behavioral dimension. When combined with the information generated from other AC devices, the background interview has been shown to be effective at arriving at a final evaluation of a candidate.

Performance Tests.   It is the use of performance tests, sometimes referred to as *simulation tests*, that distinguishes ACs from other selection programs. The following describes the devices most frequently used.

In-Basket.   The *In-Basket* is a paper-and-pencil test designed to replicate administrative tasks of the job under consideration. The name of the test is taken from the in- and out-baskets on some managers' desks used to hold organizational memos coming to and going from the managers.

The content of the administrative issues included in the set of memos that make up the In-Basket test should be obtained from job analysis information and should be representative of the actual administrative tasks of the position. Examples of typical In-Basket items are presented in Table 13.6. The In-Basket test is completed individually; it usually takes two to three hours. The candidate sits in a private area at a desk on which is found the written material of the test. Usually no oral directions are given by the AC staff, nor is there any interaction between the AC staff and the candidate while the test is being taken.

The In-Basket test includes an introductory document that describes the hypothetical situation. This situation is a variation of this theme: The candidate has recently been placed in a position because of the resignation, injury, vacation, or death of the previous

---

TABLE 13.6 Examples of In-Basket Memos

TO: Philip Bobko
FROM: Philip Roth
RE: Assignments

Do you think that we should find something new to examine other than old studies about validity? Maybe we should get out of this field entirely. Look, you live in Gettysburg and I live in South Carolina. Both of us live in homes of great Civil War events. I think that we should do something about the Civil War!!! We can give talks and you could wear a blue cap and I will wear a gray one. If you really want to continue using those quaint statistics that we have used in our previous work, we can do something with them to identify tactics of generals in Civil War battles. Think of the intellectual value! I bet nobody else has thought much about analyzing the Civil War.

TO: Mick Mount
FROM: Murray Barrick
RE: Can I Get a Job Again?

Mick, as you know, I have been away from Iowa for over two years. Therefore, as is my habit, it is time to come back. I miss the snow, the exodus of the population, biking across the state during the three nice days of the year, and the corn. Who can live without the fresh corn!!! What do you think? Can I talk the Dean into hiring me again at a big raise with a lot of vacation? I am getting tired of working. I really miss all of you guys. Remember how we would sit around all afternoon and watch old movies. That was great – but not too conscientious (Get it!!!!! Ha, Ha, Ha!!!)

TO: Bob Dipboye, Dick Jeanneret, Rich Klimoski, Frank Schmidt, and Neal Schmitt
FROM: Bob Gatewood
RE: Class Reunion

Hey guys, I just got an e-mail from the Department Head at Purdue asking me to organize our class reunion. Apparently she tried to contact each of you to do this but her e-mail got bounced; something about your e-mails being clogged with articles and thoughtful book chapters. She was happy that mine was empty. She wants us to do a skit about being in measurement classes together at Purdue. Rich, you can play the instructor because you know bunches of citations and big words. Dick, you can go off on tangents about measuring job activities. That will add a laugh. Neal, can you write five articles during the 30-minute skit—like old times? Bob, you should interview the audience and see if you can influence their behavior—like make them laugh. Frank, do you remember the lectures that led to the development of validity generalization? You seem to have gotten more out of them than I did.

---

incumbent. A number of memos, describing a variety of problems, have accumulated and must be addressed. The candidate is given organization charts, mission statements, and company policy statements that provide background information about the unit he or she is now managing. The candidate is informed that, unfortunately, previous plans require that he or she be away from the office for the next several days. Before departing, the candidate must indicate what action should be taken concerning the problem issues by leaving written memos in the Out-basket. No other office members can be contacted.

The memos themselves are presented on different types and sizes of paper and are both typed and handwritten to add realism. The candidate is to read the memos and write a recommendation as to what action should be taken and which personnel should be involved. Each candidate is given a standard time period in which to complete the test. After the candidate has finished, he or she may be interviewed by one of the AC staff and asked to explain the overall philosophy used in addressing the memos, as well as the reasoning behind the specific recommendations made for each administrative problem. The AC staff member uses the written and oral information to evaluate behavioral dimensions such as decision making, planning and organizing, ability to delegate, decisiveness, independence, and initiative.

Leaderless Group Discussion (LGD).   The In-Basket and the LGD together are probably the two most often-used performance tests in ACs. The LGD is designed to represent those managerial attributes that require the interaction of small groups of individuals in order to solve a problem successfully. In the LGD, participants are tested in groups of six. These six are seated around a conference table usually placed in the middle of a room. AC assessors are seated along the walls of the room to observe and record the behavior of the LGD participants.

The LGD is so named because no one member is designated as the official leader or supervisor of the group. The meeting is one of equals addressing a common problem. This problem could emphasize either cooperation or competition among the six participants. One example of a "cooperation scenario" is a situation in which the company must issue a public statement in response to a racial discrimination charge made by some of its employees. Competitive problems are usually characterized by a small amount of some organizational resource (money for raises or new equipment, a one-time fund for capital investment, and so on) that is not large enough to satisfy the wishes of all LGD members. In both cases, the group is provided with a written description of the issue and relevant supporting material—for example, individual work performance records, maintenance costs, equipment capacity charts, and so on. The group is then usually charged with producing a written report that specifies the action to be taken by the company. In most cases, 1½ to 2 hours is the maximum time allotted.

In addition to being classified as cooperative or competitive, the LGD problem can have either defined or undefined roles. With defined roles, each group member is given specific information, unknown to the others, that both describes his or her position in the company and provides additional information about the department or the individuals that the LGD participant is supposed to be representing. The participant may use this information as he or she sees fit to influence the actions of the group. Unassigned roles are obviously those for which such information is not provided to each participant. Assigned roles are most commonly used in competitive LGD problems. Each member's role information is used to argue that the scarce resource should be allocated for that participant's purposes. Table 13.7 contains examples of a general problem and two assigned roles that could be used in such LGD situations. The LGD is used to measure behavioral dimensions such as oral communication, tolerance for stress, adaptability, resilience, energy, leadership, and persuasiveness.

Case Analysis. In case analysis exercises, each participant is provided with a long description of an organizational problem that changes according to the job being considered in the AC. For a higher-level position, the case frequently describes the history of certain events in a company, with relevant financial data, marketing strategy, and organizational structure. Frequently, industry data concerning new products, consumer trends, and technology are introduced. The case focuses on a dilemma that the participant is asked to resolve. In resolving it, the candidate must give specific recommendations, present supporting data presented, and detail any changes in company strategy.

The content of the case is varied to make it appropriate for the position being considered. For middle-management jobs, the major issue frequently concerns the design and implementation of operational plans or systems—for example, management information systems or job process systems. For first-level management, the focus often is on either the resolution of subordinate conflicts, subordinate nonconformity with policies, or the reevaluation of specific work methods. After the candidate has been given time to read and analyze the case, he or she may be asked to prepare a written report, make an oral presentation to AC staff members, or discuss the case with other participants. The primary dimensions usually evaluated are oral and written communication, planning and organizing, control, decisiveness, resilience, and analysis.

TABLE 13.7	Example of Leaderless Group Discussion Problem

Problem: All of you are executive vice presidents for the organization World Peace Through Activity. The organization has raised enough money through Hollywood and Bollywood stars to fund another project to further its mission. This project is to compliment its other projects such as Cure Hunger Through Liver (no one is hungry when liver is served!), Education Through Example (uneducated people follow educated people throughout two work days), and Friendliness Through Fitness (groups are formed consisting of one person from each country in the world to go to some remote island and perform fitness exercises for months. A person can leave the island when he/she learns the language of each other person on the island).

This three-person group must decide what the next project is to be.

Assigned: Role #1   Murray Barrick, EVP of Wheel Projects

Your group has decided that the next project should be "Bicycle Through the Bayous." The project would start by choosing a random sample of 1000 people from the world and providing 500 bicycles-built-for-two. Every morning each person would be paired with a different person until all pairs have been completed. When that happens, another group of 1000 random individuals would be flown in to repeat the cycle (pun intended). The ride would start in the bayous around New Orleans and go along bayous all over the world. Of course, there are not bayous throughout a continuous path around the world so your executive group would have to rent plush boats, airplanes, or limos and accompany the bicycles and people to the next starting point.

Assigned: Role #2   Hubert Field, EVP of Floating Words

Your group is in favor of "Chatting Through Chaos." The idea is to give each person in the world a ham radio set, train each of them how to use and repair it, and then get them started in contacting at least 51 other people in the world each day. Your group would also have control of all the food supplies in the world so that any one person would only get food after he/she chatted with the 51 people. Each chat must last for 20 minutes. Of course, your group would also monitor each conversation to make sure that all conversations are discussing independence and world peace. This program has two great advantages. First, if each person in the world has to chat 17 hours a day and then eats for two hours, how much time is there left to get into trouble? Second, your organization would have to employ millions and millions of people to monitor the conversations. That would solve the problem of world unemployment. The world economy would boom!!!!

Assigned Role #3   Robert Gatewood, EVP of Committees

Your group is in favor of a very simple idea. Everyone in the world should be assigned to five committees that meet at least once a week. The purpose of each committee is relatively unimportant—committees never get anything done anyway so what difference does the name make. However, each committee would have to come up with a socially acceptable name just for publicity sake, such as Freedom for Fingered Friends. Not many people could object to that! Your group hasn't decided whether or not each committee name must be an alliteration. You think that you can get your idea approved because you have stolen the best parts of the other two ideas (which you have learned through moles that you planted in the other divisions of the organization). So your committees will be composed by random draws of the world population with no more than one person from each country on a committee (to prevent voting blocks) and each committee member would be paid to be on the committee (thereby providing world employment) but not through your organization. Each committee gets a separate annual budget to pay members. Therefore, you will pitch it as small business development which is a international hot button. You are no dummy!!!!

The Training of Assessors

As we discussed previously, scoring the verbal performance tests that characterize ACs is usually more difficult than scoring motor performance tests. If an AC is to be useful as a selection device, it is crucial that *assessors* (staff members who have the responsibility of observing and evaluating the behaviors of the participants) have the necessary training. As we pointed out, ACs focus on the behavioral dimensions. The exercises require the participants to provide behaviors relative to these dimensions. Each dimension must be measured by more than one exercise. Each exercise usually measures more than one dimension. The major duty of an assessor is to record the behavior of a participant in an exercise and use the data to rate the participant on each behavioral dimension appropriate for the exercise. For example, if the LGD is designed to measure the dimensions of oral communication, adaptability, and persuasiveness, the assessor must use his or her observations of the actions of a participant in the LGD problem to rate the participant on these dimensions. Usually, the rating is done on a 5-point scale.

In most cases, there are half as many assessors in an AC as there are participants. These assessors are usually managers within the organization in positions one level above the position of interest for the AC. In this way the assessors are assumed to be familiar with the job and the behaviors required in the job. After recording and judging the participants' behavior in the AC, and after all exercises have been completed, the assessors come together to discuss their observations. The ratings and data gathered by each assessor are used to develop group or final scores of each participant on each behavioral dimension. These ratings are then used to develop a single, overall rating of the acceptability of each candidate for the position of interest. The major difficulty in having managers within the organization perform these activities is that, even though they are knowledgeable about the job behaviors, they are usually unskilled in systematically observing behaviors representative of each dimension and then using the behaviors to develop ratings. The purpose of assessor training programs is to develop those skills. If assessors are not adequately trained in these observation and rating methods, the value of the AC evaluation is lessened.

William Byham has written an excellent detailed description of the training of assessors.[19] Much of the material in the following paragraphs is drawn from his ideas. Essentially, this training is meant to develop the six key abilities listed in Table 13.8. We describe some methods for doing this.

Understanding the Behavioral Dimensions.   As we mentioned, one fundamental part of an AC is the determination of which behavioral dimensions of the job are to be evaluated. These should be dimensions that are representative of and important to the job. The first step in training assessors, therefore, is to thoroughly familiarize them with the dimensions. Often this is done by providing assessors with a clear and detailed definition of each dimension, and then spending time discussing them. The major goal is to ensure that all assessors have a common understanding of the dimensions. Dimensions such as adaptability, decisiveness, and tolerance for stress may have different meanings for different individuals. The following is an example of a definition that could be used for an AC dimension focused on first-line supervisors:

> Tolerance for Stress—*stability of performance under pressure and/or opposition. A first-line supervisor finds himself in a stressful situation because of three main factors: (a) multiple demands on the work unit that must be completed at approximately the same deadline, (b) the joint roles he must play as both a representative of management to nonmanagement employees and a representative of nonmanagement employees to management, and (c) confrontation by employees who are angry or hostile because of a work situation.*

TABLE 13.8	Types of Abilities to Be Developed in Training Assessors

- Understanding the behavioral dimensions
- Observing the behavior of participants
- Categorizing participant behavior as to appropriate behavioral dimensions
- Judging the quality of participant behavior
- Determining the rating of participants on each behavioral dimension across the exercises
- Determining the overall evaluation of participants across all behavioral dimensions

Observing the Behavior of Participants.   After the assessors have become familiar with the dimensions to be used in the AC, the next step is to train them to observe and record behavior. The initial tendency of most managers when they first become assessors is immediately to make evaluative judgments about the performance of participants in the AC exercises. For example, when observing an LGD problem, a common reaction is to make the judgment that a participant can or cannot handle stress. However, such immediate judgments are dysfunctional with regard to the purpose of the AC. An AC, you will remember, is to provide *multiple* exercises or opportunities for participants to demonstrate behaviors that *exemplify* the dimensions under study.

This step in training, therefore, is designed to overcome the tendency of assessors to form immediate judgments and instead to focus on recording the behavior of the participant. Commonly, this step has two parts. One part explains to the assessors in detail the differences between recording behavior and making judgments; to clarify this difference, examples of each are provided. Often a list of statements is prepared about each of the dimensions, and the assessor is asked to indicate whether the statement reflects behavior or judgment. The following is an example:

Dimension: Tolerance for Stress

Indicate whether each of the following is a statement of a participant's behavior or a statement of an assessor's judgment.

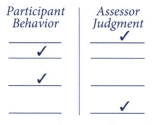

Participant Behavior	Assessor Judgment	
	✓	*Resolved the conflict quietly*
✓		*Listened to the explanations of both parties as to how the conflict started*
✓		*Offered some tentative suggestions as to changes that could be made*
	✓	*Broke down when the argument heated up*

After assessors understand the meaning of the term *behavior*, the second step of training presents examples of participant behavior in the exercises; this allows assessors to practice recording behaviors. These examples can be taken from either live or videotaped exercises. The advantage of a videotaped exercise is that it can be stopped at specific points, or parts can be replayed for discussion.

Categorizing Participant Behavior.   The next phase of training merges the first two steps. In this phase, the assessor learns to record the behavior of the participant under the proper dimension. This ensures that assessors are consistent in recording participant behaviors that are examples of the dimensions. This consistency is also essential to the reliability and validity of the ratings.

For the most part, training in this phase centers on both descriptions and discussions of the behavior representative of each dimension and also demonstrations of these behaviors. For descriptions, assessors are provided with material that briefly defines each dimension and presents a list of behaviors that are representative of both high and low levels of the dimension. Such a list may take the following form:

Tolerance for Stress: *Stability of performance under pressure or opposition.*

Examples:

When engaging the two arguing parties, participant soon began screaming at them.

Suggested that the two arguing parties walk with her to an unoccupied conference room.

Asked the individuals observing the arguing parties to return to work stations.

Physically grabbed the nearest arguing party and pulled him from the area.

A list of the representative behaviors is prepared for each dimension and is reviewed in group discussion among the assessors. Other example behaviors are frequently generated during this time. In some cases, the assessors are then provided with a list of recorded behaviors that have been drawn from previous ACs; they are asked to indicate which dimension is identified by the described behavior. The correct answers are reviewed by the group and differences of opinion discussed. During the last part of training for this step, the assessors observe either a live set of exercises or a videotaped set and record the behaviors that demonstrate each dimension. A group discussion of the records that the members of group generate is then carried out.

Judging the Quality of Participant Behavior. This portion of training attempts to develop consistency among assessors in the use of rating scales to evaluate the behavior of participants on the dimensions. In most ACs, each dimension is rated using the following 6-point scale:

5   A great deal of the dimension was shown (excellent).

4   Quite a lot of the dimension was shown.

3   A moderate amount of the dimension was shown (average).

2   Only a small amount of the dimension was shown.

1   Very little of the dimension was shown, or this dimension was not shown at all (poor).

0   No opportunity existed for this dimension to be shown.

The major objective in using a scale such as this is to develop a common frame of reference among assessors, so that each will assign the same scale point to the same observed behaviors. Developing a common frame of reference across different raters is a problem in other HR activities (performance appraisal, scoring interviews, assessing training needs, and so on). AC training revolves around providing examples of behaviors that are representative of scale points for each dimension. Frequently, these example behaviors are drawn from other ACs.

In training, the group of assessors is presented with either written descriptions or videotapes of examples of behaviors and asked to rate the behaviors on all appropriate dimensions. After each assessor has completed the ratings, a discussion follows that brings out any differences in ratings. This discussion is intended to identify common definitions of each scale point. When practicing managers are used as assessors, this phase of the training is usually completed quite easily. Often such managers have a common viewpoint about what constitutes extremely good or extremely poor behaviors on the dimension. For example, most assessors agree that physically grabbing a person is an unsatisfactory demonstration of tolerance for stress. More difficulty arises in arriving at a consensus for the middle scale points. Even in this case, however, a common understanding is reached fairly quickly, owing greatly to the common work experiences of the assessors.

Determining Dimension and Overall Evaluation Ratings. We will combine the points of discussion of the final two stages of assessor training. The training in these stages is similar in that it involves the use of rating scales and draws heavily on the training previously discussed.

After a participant's behaviors for any one AC exercise are described appropriately on the dimensions, the next task is to combine the data on the same dimension across two or more exercises. For example, say that data about tolerance for stress are gathered on three different exercises. Assessors must learn to combine these data into one *overall dimension rating* for each individual participant. Again, training is primarily based both on group discussions that form a common frame of reference and several examples that serve as trials. Differences in ratings are fully discussed. Important in forming overall dimension ratings are such factors as consistency of demonstrated behavior across exercises, how good each exercise is at bringing out a variety of behaviors, and the strength and duration of behaviors.

The last training step concerns how to use the final dimension ratings to form the *overall rating* of the participant's ability to perform the job. Job analysis information is critical for this. From the job analysis, it can be determined which dimensions are the most critical or the most frequently used in the job. These dimensions are then weighted more heavily than other dimensions in producing the overall rating of acceptability. As a means of training for these last two steps, assessor groups are often required to complete a mock assessment of a small group of candidates under the observation of experienced assessors.

The Effectiveness of Assessment Centers

Validity.   As we have discussed, the major purpose of ACs is to evaluate the potential of individuals for management positions. In many organizations, the overall assessment of each AC participant is placed in corporate files or summarized for the participant's current immediate supervisor and communicated directly to the participant. When these participants are then considered for higher-level positions, this information is made available together with other data. Such practice, however, presents a problem for evaluating the validity of ACs with regard to predicting managerial success. If the AC evaluations are made known, it is impossible to determine what effect these evaluations had on the selection decision. This issue is sometimes referred to as the "Crown Prince Syndrome." If the AC evaluation does affect the selection decision, then the rating creates a self-fulfilling prophecy.

A few studies, many of them at AT&T, have avoided this problem by not releasing the results of the AC to anyone, even the participants themselves. In general, these studies have been supportive of the AC's accuracy in predicting the career advancement of individuals. The most famous of such studies is the AT&T Management Progress Study we discussed previously. In this case, the AC was used to predict the advancement of each participant into middle-level management within 10 years. Eight years after the study had begun, a significantly higher percentage of those individuals predicted to move into middle management had done so as compared with the percentage of those who had been predicted not to move that far. When the sample was categorized into college graduates and noncollege graduates, and each sample analyzed separately, the same patterns of significant differences were identified.

The most often cited indicators of the validity of ACs come from a meta-analysis of 50 different studies containing 107 validity coefficients. This study found a 0.36 correlation between AC ratings and job performance and a 0.36 correlation between ratings and career advancement.[20] A more recent meta-analysis was conducted on 27 validity studies with over 5850 participants. The corrected validity coefficient between OARs and ratings of job performance made by supervisors was .28 which the authors thought to be a conservative estimate due to indirect range restriction.[21]

A study that examined the validity of assessment center ratings on 679 individuals over a seven-year time period produced interesting findings about determining the criterion-related validity of ACs.[22] This study used salary growth as the criterion measure and found that, with regard to the criterion, the correlations of the OAR and the ratings of various AC dimensions were not stable during the seven years of the study. For example, the correlation of the overall AC rating with salary growth was significant for the first and seventh years but not for the other years. A similar pattern was found for other predictor dimensions of the AC. This inconsistent pattern of validity coefficients does not argue for the validity of AC ratings for predicting salary advancement.

ACs and Managerial Behavior.   There is some evidence that the experience of participating in an AC has a positive effect on both the assessors and the individuals who are being evaluated. For example, it has been shown that managers who had served as assessors in their company's AC for at least three months benefited in three ways as compared with inexperienced assessors.[23]

First, they demonstrated greater proficiency in interviewing by being able both to obtain a greater number of relevant facts and to demonstrate a more systematic approach to questioning. Second, they were also more proficient in several aspects of communicating information: orally presenting information about people to another individual, responding effectively when questioned about this information, and communicating information about people in concise written reports. Third, their assessments of the behavior of subordinates showed a decrease in the halo rating error. That is, assessors did not rate individuals at the same (approximate) score across all dimensions.

Regarding assessees, it has been found that participation in an AC was related to changes in self-perceived ability ratings.[24] Data were collected from 1,693 participants who provided self-ratings on eight ability dimensions both before and immediately after the AC. Results indicated significant changes in the ratings of organizing and planning, analyzing, decision making, influencing others, and flexibility.

ACs and Adverse Impact.   A positive feature of ACs is their generally favorable support by the courts and the Equal Employment Opportunity Commission (EEOC) in alleged discrimination cases. For example, in the much-publicized sex discrimination case against AT&T, ACs were identified as a method to use in changing AT&T's promotion policies.[25] The essence of the discrimination charge was the adverse impact against women in promotion through management ranks. Under the agreement between AT&T and the EEOC, ACs were to be used extensively to identify those women who were most likely to be successful in higher management positions.

A few discrimination cases have directly evaluated the use of ACs in selection. In *Berry v. City of Omaha*, ACs were used in selection for the position of deputy police chief. The main issue was whether the three different assessor groups that evaluated candidates used different standards.[26] After reviewing descriptions of the development of the AC and data analysis with regard to reliability among assessors, the court upheld the use of the AC. In another case, *The Richmond Black Police Officers Association v. the City of Richmond,* the use of an AC for selection of supervisory positions in both the police and the fire departments was upheld. Of interest in this case was that a combination of written tests and the AC was used in selection. Evidence indicating that the paper-and-pencil tests resulted in adverse impact was presented. However, final selection decisions were based on both sets of devices, and these final decisions did not result in adverse impact.[27]

However, one study that compared paper-and-pencil tests to AC-type simulations found that simulations did, in fact, produce score differences between black and white respondents, even though these differences were smaller than differences between the groups on written tests.[28] The score difference was 0.61 SD units for the written tests and 0.30 SD units for the simulation tests. The simulations still produced differences, but those were about one-half of the differences that occurred with the paper-and-pencil test. It is probable that this reduction in differences was due to two factors: the subjects' positive reactions to the simulations, and the reduced reading requirements of the simulation in comparison with the written tests. All of the above findings looked at racial differences. Regarding gender differences, differences between males and females on Overall Assessment Ratings have not been consistently identified. However, it has been found that females are rated notably higher on dimensions reflecting inter-personal leadership behaviors (for example, oral communication and interaction, and drive and determination).[29]

Criticism of ACs.   These findings of the general validity of ACs and their lack of adverse impact does not mean their use is without some criticism. Generally, criticism has taken two forms.

Cost.   The first criticism is that an AC is usually expensive to develop and maintain; if selection among applicants is its only use, there might be alternative methods that are much less expensive. One study found that the correlation of AC evaluations with the management level attained by individuals was very close to the correlation of ratings of evaluations of personnel files with a job success measure.[30] Both correlations were statistically significant but not different from one another. If the same accuracy of prediction is possible, it would be more sensible to use the least expensive method. Following similar reasoning, Donald Brush and Lyle Schoenfeldt described an integrated appraisal system for generating information that was comparable to that yielded by assessment centers.[31] The approach consisted of the following parts: job analysis for establishing the critical tasks and abilities of each managerial position, the training of line managers to assess behavior of subordinates on critical dimensions identified in the job analysis, and systematic procedures for obtaining and evaluating the assessment data supplied by these line managers. Brush and Schoenfeldt explained that dimensions closely related to the behavioral dimensions measured in assessment centers can be constructed, and that actual job performance tasks such as management presentations, completion of reports, unit productivity, and quality of employee performance reviews can be substituted for assessment center exercises. The authors' conclusion was that it is possible to use data currently available in organizations. Such selection data is content-valid and available at a lower cost than data obtainable from assessment centers.

Another related study examined the relationship between structured selection interviews, cognitive ability tests, and overall AC ratings of performance.[32] Data were gathered for candidates who were applying for admission into the Israeli police force. Correlations between the interview and AC ratings were significant as were the correlations between cognitive ability tests and AC ratings. The combination of the interview and the cognitive ability tests significantly predicted the decisions as to whom would be accepted into the police force. The authors concluded that the cost of the use of the AC could be greatly reduced by automatically admitting those who scored high on the combination of the interview and the cognitive ability and rejecting those who scored low. The AC, therefore, would only be used for those who had middle range scores.

Construct Validity.   The second area of criticism focuses on the failure of ACs to demonstrate the pattern of correlations among dimension ratings that they were designed to produce. As we mentioned previously, ACs supposedly measure the behavioral dimensions across several exercises. Logically, the ratings given for the same dimension in various exercises should be highly correlated. After all, the same characteristic is being measured. For example, if the dimension of planning and organizing is to be measured with the In-Basket test, the interview, and a case analysis, then the correlations of the ratings for participants for this dimension among these three devices should be quite high. This is commonly referred to as *convergent* validity.

The evidence is quite clear, however, that the correlations among such dimension ratings are very low, often ranging from 0.05 to 0.15.[33] This is puzzling because a lack of convergent validity indicates that behavior on each dimension is either very specific to a testing situation, is not reliably judged by assessors, or both. In any case, the validity of the overall rating of the dimension is questionable. Even more disturbing is the finding that the correlations among dimensions that are measured within the same exercise are very high.[34] This is referred to as a lack of *discriminant validity*; it should not occur. Discriminant validity exists when relatively low correlations are found among dimensions—such as problem solving, leadership, and verbal communication—within a single exercise. The dimensions are regarded as separate characteristics of the participants. For example, an In-Basket may be intended to measure 12 separate dimensions of the participants. The design of an AC assumes that these dimensions are independent. If this is so, the correlations among dimensions should be low to moderate.

In addition, there is other evidence that assessors' ratings do not act as they should. For example, the ratings by the same assessor of the same participants in two similar LGD problems do not correlate very highly.[35] A related study explored how contrast effects influence assessor ratings of candidates.[36] Specifically, a low-performing candidate was rated significantly lower than she actually performed when evaluated in a group consisting of two similar low performers.

There are several possible explanations for both this lack of convergent validity within dimensions and discriminant validity across dimensions. One is that cognitive ability and personality traits underlie participants' performance in ACs. Assessors' ratings merely reflect the amount of these traits that the individuals going through the AC possess. In support of this explanation, one study found that measures of cognitive ability, extraversion, emotional stability, openness, and agreeableness had a multiple correlation of 0.84 with the Overall Assessment Ratings that assessors assigned to participants.[37] The authors speculated that this multiple correlation might have been even higher if measures of conscientiousness had been available. Their conclusion was that organizations should consider using mental ability and personality measures for selection rather than bear the costs of the much more expensive ACs.

A second explanation is that AC exercises intended to measure the same dimensions are too dissimilar to actually do so. That is, exercises such as In-Baskets, LGDs, and role-plays present situations to participants that differ in terms of psychological demands. The exercises cannot be considered to be parallel measures of the same dimensions.[38] Some research has supported this explanation by demonstrating that assessors' ratings of dimensions across similar exercises are higher than those across dissimilar exercises.[39] However, even in these studies the correlations for the same dimension across similar exercises have not been as high as one would anticipate from the intended design of ACs. Related to this last finding is attempts to develop parallel forms of some AC exercises. For example, attempts have been publicized for two parallel form In-Baskets in which parallel items on the two forms presented the same problem and were based on the same critical incidents. They only differed in the situation in which the critical incident was presented.[40] Similarly, parallel forms for a Leaderless Group Discussion, an Interview Simulation, and a Case Presentation were developed. The idea behind this type of work is that the reliability of parallel forms of the same simulation should be quite high and contribute to increased validity of the exercises.

A third explanation is that ACs contain too many dimensions for assessors to successfully distinguish. That is, the information-processing demands of ACs are too high for assessors to be able to separate behaviors and map them onto each of the multiple dimensions that are contained in ACs. Partial support of this explanation was found in a meta-analysis that determined that assessor ratings on four dimensions had a higher correlation with job performance than did correlations based upon more dimensions.[41] Following from this explanation, AC designers have reduced the number of dimensions that assessors are asked to evaluate, or provided assessors with checklists of behaviors to use in scoring.[42] They have also provided more training[43] and used only psychologists and experienced managers as assessors.[44] However, these changes have only marginally improved the convergent and divergent validity issues.

A fourth explanation is that exercises—not dimensions—are important components of ACs. Exercises are specific work-related situations related to work behaviors and performance. The high correlations among dimensions within an exercise are not error but rather represent consistent behavior in a specific testing/work situation. One study found that assessors' ratings could be separated into both exercise and dimension factors.[45] The exercise factors correlated with the Overall Assessor Ratings as well as with measures of cognitive ability, job knowledge, and job performance. The authors concluded that (a) assessors apparently rate overall exercise behavior rather than dimension behavior; (b) assessors may view exercise ratings as evaluations of work samples—in which case they provide global ratings of how well participants perform important job activities; or (c) assessors view exercises as demonstrations of trait behaviors. That is, the assessors may primarily see the LGD as an exercise that measures persuasiveness or leadership and therefore evaluate that trait in participants. This explanation fits with the study (described previously) that found that personality characteristics and cognitive ability correlated very highly with Overall Assessment Ratings. Based upon these findings, ACs could be designed such that exercises become the focus. These exercises should be developed on the basis of content validity of work samples demonstrated through job analysis.[46]

A related study tested the importance of participant behaviors in predicting OAR by developing behavioral checklists to score simulation exercises.[47] Data were collected from a sample of 204 executives. The behavioral checklists were drawn from job analysis of workers in the job under consideration. One example of the type of behaviors included in the checklist is *speaks clearly and enunciates appropriately*. Three behavioral checklists were used, one for each exercise. Factor analysis determined a separate factor for each of the three checklists. Cumulative scores for each factor were determined and multiple regressions among these three predictors and the OARs were run. The authors found that the behavioral checklists could account for over 90% of variance in the OARs. The authors concluded that the OARs are valid because they reflect work behaviors rather than traits. Therefore, dimension ratings should be abandoned in favor of specific work behavior ratings.

Based upon these and other studies, Chuck Lance and his colleagues have concluded that participants' performance in ACs is composed of a General Performance factor that cuts across exercises and exercise factors.[48] The GP factor is a function of stable individual differences and the separate exercise factors that are a function of situational specificity (that is, the characteristics of a particular exercise). Exercise factors are, in fact, job performance-related behaviors and not measurement error. Indirect evidence for this statement is that exercise factors have been shown to relate to other variables that are themselves related to job performance, such as cognitive ability, job knowledge, and personality.

Interestingly enough, one set of authors have questioned the appropriateness of the research on dimension ratings vs. exercise behaviors by arguing that MTMM analysis is not appropriate for use with ACs.[49] The authors' reasoning is that some AC dimensions are clearly composed of heterogeneous behaviors and two or more such dimensions could be correlated to the extent that both dimensions contain some overlapping behaviors. Additionally, MTMM assumes one method. However, the AC is not one method but rather multiple methods (exercises) that share the fact that assessors observe behavior and make ratings. Another indication of inappropriateness is that MTMM nests assessors within exercises and is an inadequate way for teasing out variance components for behavioral dimensions of ACs. The argument that MTMM is inappropriate for analyzing ACs is interesting; if it is true, then the issue of whether exercise factors or dimensions are evidenced in ACs is moot because most of the analyses of correlations within ACs use MTMM.

SITUATIONAL JUDGMENT TESTS

Partially because of the cost and lack of convergent and discriminant validity of ACs, selection specialists have turned their attention to other types of simulation devices. One of these is situational judgment tests (SJTs) or "low-fidelity" simulations. These present a series of written descriptions of work situations and multiple responses to each situation. The participant indicates one of the responses for each situation as being the one that she endorses. (Yes, an SJT is like a multiple-choice exam in college! It just doesn't have a corresponding chapter in a textbook that contains the answers.) This type of test is much less expensive to develop and administer than AC exercises. A meta-analysis study calculated a validity coefficient of 0.34 for SJTs, which is comparable to that of ACs, interviews, and biographical data measures.[50] The evidence about SJTs is that they are valid and cheap, so we are not surprised that they are of great interest to selection experts. Their most apparent deficiencies are that they are job specific and difficult to use for development or training purposes.

Michael McDaniel and Nhung Nguyen have described the steps traditionally taken to develop SJTs.[51] We summarize their work in the following list and add some of our thoughts:

1. Collect stories from incumbents or supervisors about situations encountered on the job that are important for successful performance. For example, for a customer service job, respondents might be asked to write critical incidents concerning understanding customers' needs, promoting the product to customers, and seeking a balance between the needs of the customers and the company's interests.

2. Review the situations that are described. The goal is to identify a series of situations that will serve as item stems for the SJT. This involves grouping the situations according to similarity of content, selecting representative situations, eliminating redundant situations, and ensuring that the situations vary in terms of difficulty or complexity.

3. Edit the situations into item stems. That is, rephrase situations in a simple form that can be used in the item posed as a question on the SJT. It is desirable that all stems be approximately the same length and represent all important aspects of the job. Table 13.9 contains examples of item stems and possible responses that may be contained in an SJT.

TABLE 13.9	Examples of Items of a Situational Judgment Test for Entry-Level Management in Financial Institutions

Item Stem #1. It is Friday afternoon and your immediate manager has just told you to stay until the office is finished compiling its weekly reports—until about 8:30 P.M. However, you have tickets for you and your date for an 8:00 P.M. concert. What would you do?

    a. Tell your manager that you cannot stay because of the concert (−1 point).

    b. Explain the situation to your manager's manager (−2 points).

    c. Tell your manager that you will stay and explain the situation to your date (+2 points).

    d. Try to find someone else at your level to do this, but stay if you cannot find someone else (+1 point).

Item Stem #2. A customer with a relatively small asset base complains to you that the institution does not provide enough appropriate information about financial markets for him to be able to develop his own investment strategy. What would you do?

    a. Listen and tell him that you will speak with your manager about this (−2 point).

    b. Take notes and tell him that you will look into this (−1 points).

    c. Take notes and briefly discuss the situation with the Market-Knowledge manager to determine what can be done (+1 point).

    d. Take notes, speak with the Market-Knowledge manager, and spend time thinking of possible actions (+2 points).

4. Drop inappropriate situations or those that may raise legal concerns. For example, situations including activities that cannot be performed by disabled applicants. Other situations may be excluded because they are too job specific and would be unknown to applicants or because they represent undesirable behaviors (for example, robbery or violence).

5. Perform a job analysis including gathering ratings of the importance of and time spent on specific tasks. Compare these ratings with the written situations in order to determine that the situations address the most important and time-consuming tasks.

6. Assemble the chosen items into a survey. The survey should be formatted, laid out in survey form, and reviewed for grammar and spelling.

7. Administer the survey to a sample of subject matter experts. The purpose of this step is to collect information that can be used to write alternative responses to each item. Respondents for this step could either be job incumbents or supervisors of the job of interest. The SJT developer asks respondents to identify one or more responses to each situation listed as an item stem. The specific instruction is usually either "Describe what you would do in this situation" or "Describe what you should do (or is the best action to take) in this situation." Sometimes respondents are given both instructions and complete two versions of responses. Research has indicated that asking what one "would do" leads to better test development that asking what one "should do." That is, the criterion-related validities of items were substantially higher when the "would do" instructions were used.[52]

8. The test developer reviews all the offered responses to each situation and prepares an edited list of potential responses to each situation. He or she edits the responses to remove duplicates and improve the understandability of the response and may also omit responses that are too obviously socially desirable,

long, complex, or clearly inappropriate for the situation described. Typically, the developer wants to have multiple responses to each situation and responses that span a range of effective reactions to the situation.

9. The list of situations and alternative responses is circulated to the same people who provided alternative responses to the item or an equivalent group. The question for this round of review is essentially "How appropriate is each of these responses to the situation described in the item stem?" Respondents frequently rate each alternative on a 1–3 scale. The test developer selects for inclusion in the survey those responses that: (a) have a high level of agreement among the raters in terms of scaled scores to the item-question and (b) have different average scale scores, which indicates that the alternatives are different in terms of their appropriateness. While this is the method most often used for scoring an SJT, there are other possible ways to do it. The scoring method a developer chooses is important because it may affect the SJT's correlation with criteria measures.[53]

10. If possible, the test developer should perform an empirical validity study for the SJT. This evidence could be important if there were legal questions concerning adverse impact of the test.

As this list indirectly points out, the SJT is a process rather than a content type of test. That is, the content base for SJT questions is not a narrowly defined subject area as is true with cognitive ability or personality tests. We should think about a SJT as analogous to an interview. An interview is a verbal interaction between the person who has prepared and who delivers questions and another person who responds to the questions. The SJT is a written interaction between the person who prepares the questions and the person who provides responses to the questions. Like the interview, the SJT can be about almost any subject (job knowledge) or behaviors (such as how to solve an employee conflict, how to give a presentation, or how to plan and evaluate a training program). In some ways, you can think about a SJT in the same way that you do a structured interview (we know you remember Chapter 10 vividly and will not go into details!). The interviewer asks predetermined questions and the SJT asks predetermined questions. The content of the questions can include a variety of topics.

SJTs are generally considered to be either knowledge based (respondents are asked questions that require the use of technical information to respond) or behaviorally based (respondents are asked what they should or would do).

Compared with many of the selection instruments discussed in this book, the SJT only recently has attracted the attention of selection specialists and researchers. It has not received as much examination as many other instruments. One area of interest has been the validity of SJTs. As we mentioned earlier, one study was a meta-analysis of validity. Because many of the studies that were used for this meta-analysis used concurrent validity samples, a later study compared validity coefficients for applicant and job incumbent samples of SJT usage.[54] Results indicated that although incumbents scored significantly higher than applicants of SJTs, concurrent and predictive validity coefficients for SJTs were not significantly different and were within one standard deviation of the correlation that the meta-analytic study reported. One conclusion was that both predictive and concurrent validation designs were appropriate to measure the validity of SJTs. Another study of SJT validity examined correlates and the validity of a SJT in predicting managerial performance.[55] Measures of cognitive ability, personality, job experience, and a SJT were combined to predict job performance. Analysis indicated that the SJT fully mediated the relationship of ability and general work experience to performance and partially mediated the relationship of personality with performance. Further the SJT seemed to measure general rather than job-specific forms of knowledge. This was because although the SJT fully mediated general cognitive ability and work experience, it did not mediate either job tenure or training. The latter two were regarded as providing specific job knowledge and the first two as providing general job knowledge. It was also found that SJTs accounted for incremental variance above the other three predictors of job performance. Because cognitive ability and experience were fully mediated by the SJT, an argument was made that the SJT, if properly constructed, could be used instead of measures of those variables. Because the SJT did not covary with training and job tenure, it did not rely at all on specific job knowledge and therefore could be used on applicants without question. Further, such an SJT would most likely show less adverse impact than cognitive measures but provide the same information for prediction.

Another topic that has been examined is subjects faking responses on SJTs. One study looked at faking for knowledge- and behavior-based SJTs separately.[56] The researchers found that faking occurred with the use of behavior-based SJTs but not with knowledge-based SJTs. This makes sense because knowledge-based SJTs require technical knowledge to select the correct alternative. It is difficult to fake technical knowledge if you don't have it. Behaviors are often more obvious; when presented in a multiple-choice format, the respondent can often select the most socially acceptable or most logical alternative, which often turns out to be the correct alternative. Secondary findings were that although faking occurred with behavioral SJT, this faking was less than that which can occur with personality tests. Both knowledge-based SJT scores and behavior-based scores correlated with cognitive ability. Knowledge-based scores were more highly correlated than behavior-based scores. This makes sense; knowledge-based tests seemingly require the learning of technical information that may be more cognitive than are behavioral questions. A related study started from the previous finding that some SJTs can be faked. It examined the effect of requiring respondents to elaborate their responses (give reasons to support their answers) on faking.[57] The content of the SJT being examined was mainly behaviors. Results indicated that elaboration reduced faking for items with behavioral responses that were familiar to the respondents and reduced the number of fakers in the high scoring group. Those subjects who were in the elaboration part of the study rated the SJT as providing a better opportunity to demonstrate KSAs than did the nonelaboration group. Finally, there was no difference between the groups in terms of satisfaction with the test.

Two studies by Michael McDaniel and his colleagues examined differences in scores on SJTs by various demographic groups.[58] These two studies indicated that overall whites perform better on SJTs than do blacks, especially on knowledge-based questions rather than behavior-based questions. Females generally score better than do males mainly on the knowledge-based items. However, this difference is not usually smaller than the Four-Fifths Rule. Therefore, SJTs are more likely to have adverse impact based on race but not gender. However, it was found that these difference between blacks and whites were also reflected in differences in job performance (d = .47). The conclusion was that although SJTs may cause adverse impact, they probably were not discriminatory.

We will report one additional study whose findings have implications for writing and interpreting SJTs. This study analyzed the variance of SJT items into trait and situational components.[59] Situation factors accounted for over three times as much variance as individual difference variables. Strong situations (described when we discussed personality measurement) were identified in which the responses of subjects were less varied and more attributable to the situation than weak item situations in which the traits of the respondent influence the responses of subjects, resulting in a wider range of differences among subjects. We can conclude, therefore, that writing items based upon weak situations would lead to scores that describe a characteristic of the respondents rather than characteristics of the situations used in the items.

USE OF PERFORMANCE TESTS AND ACS IN SMALL BUSINESS

We think that performance tests and situational judgment tests can be very useful for the selection programs of small businesses. Assessment centers are, of course, impractical for small businesses because of the cost and difficulty inherent in developing them. However, the performance tests and situational judgment tests described in this chapter are highly recommended and easy to implement. To develop either of these two tests, a small business owner should follow the steps described in this chapter for choosing appropriate job tasks, developing testing procedures, and establishing scoring rules.

One selection strategy that an owner of a small business should consider is linking the four instruments: a training and experience evaluation, a behavior-based interview, a performance test, and an SJT. As we have discussed, each of these instruments emphasizes behaviors that are directly related to those of the job being considered. That is, a training and experience evaluation would ask the applicant for information about his or her previous work and training that is related to the most important tasks of the job. A small business owner could read the applicants' responses, score them, and invite the highest-scoring individuals to return for a situational or behavioral description interview. Either of these types of interview poses questions that require the applicant to provide additional information about behaviors that reflect actual job activities. The owner could score this interview immediately after completion and invite an applicant who has performed well to take a performance test or an SJT. These tests would tap activities that make up part of the actual job (completing the forms for an actual order, interacting with customers, or managing a team of workers doing a particular task). The owner should easily be able to evaluate how well an applicant performed on the performance test or SJT and use this information for selection. The advantage of a selection program consisting of these instruments is that it is inexpensive, fairly easy to develop, job related, and interpretable by the small business owner.

REFERENCES

1.   Paul Wernimont and John Campbell, "Sign, Samples, and Criteria," *Journal of Applied Psychology* 52 (1968): 372–376.

2.   James Asher and James Sciarrino, "Realistic Work Sample Tests: A Review," *Personal Psychology* 27 (1974): 519–533.

3.   James E. Campion, "Work Sampling for Personnel Selection," *Journal of Applied Psychology* 56 (1972): 40–44.

4.   David Robinson, "Content-Oriented Personnel Selection in a Small Business Setting," *Personnel Psychology* 34 (1981): 77–87.

5.   Robert Gatewood and Lyle F. Schoenfeldt, "Content Validity and EEOC: A Useful Alternative for Selection," *Personnel Psychology* 56 (1977): 520–528.

6.   Richard R. Reilly and Edmond W. Israelski, "Development and Validation of Minicourses in the Telecommunication Industry," *Journal of Applied Psychology* 73 (1988): 721–726.

7. Lynnette B. Plumlee, *A Short Guide to the Development of Performance Tests* (Washington, DC: Personnel Research and Development Center, U.S. Civil Service Commission, Professional Series 75–1, January 1975).

8. Joseph L. Boyd and Benjamin Shimberg, *Handbook of Performance Testing* (Princeton, NJ: Educational Testing Service, 1971), 24.

9. Neal Schmitt and Cheri Ostroff, "Operationalizing the 'Behavioral Consistency' Approach: Selection Test Development Based on a Content-Oriented Strategy," *Personnel Psychology* 39 (1986): 91–108.

10. Philip L. Roth, Philip Bobko, and Lynn A. McFarland, "A Meta-Analysis of Work Sample Test Validity: Updating and Integrating Some Classic Literature," *Personnel Psychology* 58 (2005): 1009–1037.

11. Michael E. Gordon and Lawrence S. Kleiman, "The Prediction of Trainability Using a Work Sample Test and an Aptitude Test: A Direct Comparison," *Personnel Psychology* 29 (1976): 243–253.

12. Frank Schmidt, Alan Greenthol, John Hunter, John Berner, and Felicia Seaton, "Job Sample vs. Paper-and-Pencil Trade and Technical Tests: Adverse Impact and Examiner Attitudes," *Personnel Psychology* 30 (1977): 187–197. See also Wayne Cascio and Niel Phillips, "Performance Testing: A Rose among Thorns?" *Personnel Psychology* 32 (1979): 751–766.

13. Philip Bobko, Philip L. Roth, and Maury A. Buster, "Work Sample Selection Tests and Expected Reduction in Adverse Impact: A Cautionary Note," *International Journal of Selection and Assessment* 13 (2005): 1–10.

14. Cascio and Phillips, "Performance Testing: A Rose among Thorns?"

15. Neal Schmitt, Stephen W. Gilliland, Ronald S. Landis, and Dennis Devine, "Computer-Based Testing Applied to Selection of Secretarial Applicants," *Personnel Psychology* 46 (1993): 149–165.

16. Cascio and Phillips, "Performance Testing: A Rose Among Thorns?"

17. Task Force on Assessment Center Guidelines, "Guidelines and Ethical Considerations for Assessment Center Operations," *Public Personnel Management* 18 (1989): 457–470.

18. Douglas W. Bray, Richard J. Campbell, and Donald L. Grant, *Formative Years in Business: A Long-Term AT&T Study of Managerial Lives* (Huntington, NY: R. E. Krieger Publishing Co., 1979).

19. William C. Byham, "Assessor Selection and Training," in *Applying the Assessment Center Method*, ed. J. L. Moses and W. C. Byham (New York: Pergamon Press, 1977), 89–126.

20. Barbara B. Gaugler, Douglas B. Rosenthal, George C. Thornton III, and Cynthia Bentson, "Meta-Analysis of Assessment Center Validity," *Journal of Applied Psychology* 72 (1987): 493–511.

21. Eran Hemelin, Filip Lievens, and Ivan T. Robertson, "The Validity of Assessment Centres for the Prediction of Supervisory Performance Ratings: A Meta-analysis," *International Journal of Selection & Assessment* 15 (2007): 405–411.

22. Paul G. Jansen and Ben A. M. Stoop, "The Dynamics of Assessment Center Validity: Results of a Seven-Year Study," *Journal of Applied Psychology* 86 (2001): 741–753.

23. Robert V. Lorenzo, "Effects of Assessorship on Managers' Proficiency in Acquiring, Evaluating, and Communicating Information about People," *Personnel Psychology* 37 (1984): 617–634.

24. Neal Schmitt, Kevin J. Ford, and Daniel M. Stults, "Changes in Self-Perceived Ability as a Function of Performance in an Assessment Centre," *Journal of Occupational Psychology* 74 (1986): 327–335.

25. "Landmark AT&T-EEOC Consent Agreement Increases Assessment Center Usage," *Assessment & Development* 1 (1973): 1–2.

26. *Berry v. City of Omaha*, 14 FEP 391 (1977).

27. George C. Thornton III and William C. Byham, *Assessment Centers and Managerial Performance* (NY: Academic Press, 1982).

28. Neal Schmitt and Amy E. Mills, "Traditional Tests and Job Simulations: Minority and Majority Performance and Test Validities," *Journal of Applied Psychology* 86 (2001): 451–458.

29. Neil Anderson, Filip Lievens, Karen van Dam, and Marise Born, "A Construct-Driven Investigation of Gender Differences in a Leadership-Role Assessment Center," *Journal of Applied Psychology* 91 (2006): 555–566.

30. John R. Hinrichs, "An Eight-Year Follow-Up of a Management Assessment Center," *Journal of Applied Psychology* 63 (1978): 596–601.

31. Donald R. Brush and Lyle F. Schoenfeldt, "Identifying Managerial Potential: An Alternative to Assessment Centers," *Personnel* 26 (1980): 68–76.

32. Kobi Dayan, Shaul Fox, and Ronen Kasten, "The Preliminary Employment Interview as a Predictor of Assessment Center Outcomes," *International Journal of Selection & Assessment* 16 (2008): 102–111.

33. Paul R. Sackett and George F. Dreher, "Constructs and Assessment Center Dimensions: Some Troubling Empirical Findings," *Journal of Applied Psychology* 67 (1982): 401–410.

34. Peter Bycio, Kenneth M. Alvares, and June Hahn, "Situational Specificity in Assessment Center Ratings: A Confirmatory Factor Analysis," *Journal of Applied Psychology* 72 (1987): 463–474. See also Ivan Robertson, Lynda Gratton, and David Sharpley, "The Psychometric Properties and Design of Managerial Assessment Centres: Dimensions into Exercises Won't Go," *Journal of Occupational Psychology* 60 (1987): 187–195; and David Chan, "Criterion and Construct Validation of an Assessment Centre," *Journal of Occupational and Organizational Psychology* 69 (1996): 167–181.

35. Robert D. Gatewood, George Thornton III, and Harry W. Hennessey Jr., "Reliability of Exercise Ratings in the Leaderless Group Discussion," *Journal of Occupational Psychology* 63 (1990): 331–342.

36. Barbara B. Gaugler and Amy S. Rudolph, "The Influence of Assessee Performance Variation on Assessors' Judgments," *Personnel Psychology* 45 (1992): 77–98.

37. J. M. Collins, F. L. Schmidt, M. Sanchez-Ku, L. Thomas, M. A. McDaniel, and H. Le, "Can Basic Individual Differences Shed Light on the Construct Meaning of Assessment Center Evaluations?" *International Journal of Selection and Assessment* 11 (2003): 17–29.

38. Filip Lievens, Christopher S. Chasteen, Eric A. Day, and Neil D. Christiansen, "Large-Scale Investigation of the Role of Trait Activation Theory for Understanding Assessment Center Convergent and Discriminant Validity," *Journal of Applied Psychology* 91 (2006): 247–258. See also Filip Lievens and James M. Conway, "Dimension and Exercise Variance in Assessment Center Scores: A Large Scale Evaluation of Multitrait-Multimethod Studies," *Journal of Applied Psychology* 86 (2001): 1202–1222.

39. Stephanie Haaland and Neil D. Christiansen, "Implications of Trait-Activation Theory for Evaluating the Construct Validity of Assessment Center Ratings," *Personnel Psychology* 55 (2002): 137–163.

40. Filip Lievens and Fredenik Anseel, "Creating Alternate In-Basket Forms through Cloning: Some Preliminary Results," *International Journal of Selection & Assessment* 5 (2007): 428–433.

41. Winfred Arthur Jr., Eric Anthony Day, Theresa L. McNelly, and Pamela S. Edens, "A Meta-Analysis of the Criterion-Related Validity of Assessment Center Dimensions," *Personnel Psychology* 56 (2003): 125–154.

42. Barbara B. Gaugler and George C. Thornton III, "Number of Assessment Center Dimensions as a Determinant of Assessor Accuracy," *Journal of Applied Psychology* 74 (1989): 611–618. See also Richard R. Reilly, Sarah Henry, and James W. Smither, "An Examination of the Effects of Using Behavior Checklists on the Construct Validity of Assessment Center Dimensions," *Personnel Psychology* 43 (1990): 71–84; A. Jones, Peter Herriot, B. Long, and R. Drakely, "Attempting to Improve the Validity of a Well-Established Assessment Centre," *Journal of Occupational Psychology* 64 (1991): 1–21; and Ted H. Shore, George C. Thornton III, and Lynn McFarlane Shore, "Construct Validity of Two Categories of Assessment Center Dimension Ratings," *Personnel Psychology* 43 (1990): 101–115.

43. Beverly Dugan, "Effects of Assessor Training on Information Use," *Journal of Applied Psychology* 73 (1988): 743–748. See also Deidra J. Schleicher, David V. Day, Bronston T. Mayes, and Ronald E. Riggio, "A New Frame for Frame-of-Reference Training: Enhancing the Construct Validity of Assessment Centers," *Journal of Applied Psychology* 87 (2002): 735–746; and Filip Lievens, "Assessor Training Strategies and Their Effects on Accuracy, Interrater Reliability, and Discriminant Validity," *Journal of Applied Psychology* 86 (2001): 255–264.

44. Filip Lievens, "Trying to Understand the Different Pieces of the Construct Validity Puzzle of Assessment Centers: An Examination of Assessor and Assessee Effects," *Journal of Applied Psychology* 87 (2002): 675–686.

45. Charles E. Lance, Robert D. Gatewood, William H. Newbolt, Mark S. Foster, Nita R. French, and David E. Smith, "Assessment Center Exercises Factors Represent Cross-Situational Specificity, Not Method Bias," *Human Performance* 13 (2000): 323–353.

46. Charles E. Lance, Mark R. Foster, William A. Gentry, and Joseph D. Thoreson, "Assessor Cognitive Processes in an Operational Assessment Center," *Journal of Applied Psychology* 89 (2004): 22–35. See also J. D. Thoresen, "Do We Need Dimensions? Dimensions Limited or Unlimited," paper presented at the meeting of the International Congress of Assessment Center Methods, Pittsburg, Pennsylvania, 2002.

47. Duncan J. Jackson, Andrew R. Barney, Jennifer A. Stillman, and William Kirkley, "When Traits Are Behaviors: The Relationship between Behavioral Responses and Trait-Based Overall Assessment Center Ratings," *Human Performance* 20 (2007): 415–432.

48. Charles E. Lance, Mark R. Foster, Yvette M. Nemeth, William A. Gentry and Sabrina Drollinger, "Extending the Nomological Network of Assessment Center Construct Validity: Prediction of Cross-Situationally Consistent and Specific Aspects of Assessment Center Performance," *Human Performance* 20 (2007): 345–362.

49. Robert G. Jones and Manse Born, "Assessor Constructs in Use as the Missing Component in Validation of Assessment Center Dimensions: A Critique and Directions for Research," *International Journal of Selection & Assessment* 16 (2008): 229–238.

50. Michael A. McDaniel, Frederick P. Morgeson, Elizabeth B. Finnegan, Michael A. Campion, and Eric P. Braverman, "Use of Situational Judgment Tests to Predict Job Performance: A Clarification of the Literature," *Journal of Applied Psychology* 86 (2001): 730–740.

51. Michael A. McDaniel and Nhung T. Nguyen, "Situational Judgment Tests: A Review of Practice and Constructs Assessed," *Journal of International Selection and Assessment* 9 (2001): 103–113.

52. Robert E. Ployhart and Mark G. Ehrhart, "Be Careful What You Ask For: Effects of Response Instructions on the Construct Validity and Reliability of Situational Judgment Tests," *International Journal of Selection and Assessment* 11 (2003): 1–16.

53. Mindy E. Bergman, Fritz Drasgow, Michelle A. Donovan, Jaime B. Henning, and Suzanne E. Juraska, "Scoring Situational Judgment Tests: Once You Get the Data, Your Troubles Begin," *International Journal of Selection an Assessment* 14 (2006): 223–235.

54. Jeff A. Weekley, Robert E. Ployhart, and Crystal M. Harold, "Personality and Situational Judgment Tests across Applicant and Incumbent Settings: An Examination of Validity, Measurement, and Subgroup Differences," *Human Performance* 17 (2004): 433–461.

55. Jeff A. Weekley and Robert E. Polyhart, "Situational Judgment Antecedents and Relationships with Performance," *Human Performance* 18 (2005): 81–104.

56. Nhung T. Nguyen, Michael D. Biderman, and Michael A. McDaniel, "Effects of Response Instructions on Faking a Situational Judgment Test," *International Journal of Selection & Assessment* 13 (2005): 250–260.

57. Filip Lievens and Helga Peeters, "Impact of Elaboration on Responding to Situational Judgment Test Items," *International Journal of Selection & Assessment* 16 (2008): 345–355.

58. Deborah L. Whetzel, Michael A. McDaniel and Nhung T. Nguyen, "Subgroup Differences in Situational Judgment Test Performance: A Meta-Analysis," *Human Performance* 21 (2008): 291–309. See also Matthew S. O'Connell, Nathan S. Hartman, Michael A. McDonald, and Walter Lee Grubb, "Incremental Validity of Situational Judgment Tests for Task and Contextual Job Performance," *International Journal of Selection & Assessment* 15 (2007): 19–29.

59. Alyssa J. Friede Westring, Fredrick L. Oswald, Neal Schmitt, Stephanie Drzakowski, Anna Imus, Brian Kim, and Smriti Shivpuri, "Estimating Trait and Situational Variance in a Situational Judgment Test," *Human Performance* 22 (2009): 44–63.

CHAPTER 14

Integrity Testing, Drug Testing, and Graphology

The previous five chapters focused on those instruments that measure the KSAs that are important for job performance. In this chapter, we take a different tack—we primarily concentrate on characteristics that applicants should *not* have. Yep, we are into the dark side of selection. The first part of the chapter presents information about integrity testing—how to tell which applicants have a higher probability of doing bad stuff (like stealing, sabotage, and punching out supervisors) and even worse stuff (like being late and not ratting on bad guys to management). This is followed by a discussion about drug testing. Yes, the legacy of the 1960s lives on and presents a problem to employers. We regard both types of instruments—*integrity testing* and *drug testing*—to be useful in selection, and we present evidence from various studies indicating that they are valid selection devices. However, we don't have the same thoughts about the third type of instrument discussed in this chapter—graphology, or handwriting analysis. We use graphology as an example of a selection instrument that is used but that does not have ample support for its use. No evidence actually exists to prove that graphology works for selection. In fact, the evidence is quite the opposite—graphology flat out doesn't work. However, the use of this technique keeps popping up so we think of this part of the chapter as our attempt to push back the frontiers of darkness and make the world better—by presenting evidence about the validity (or lack thereof) of graphology. As part of this section, one of the authors, Bob Gatewood, sent a handwriting sample to a graphologist for analysis. As a result, an extra benefit of this chapter is that you get to learn intimate details about him. It is not a pretty thing, so be prepared.

INTEGRITY TESTING

A growing cost to American business has been employee theft. Obviously, estimates of the amount of theft are unverifiable, but a common opinion is that 2 to 5 percent of each sales dollar is a premium charged to customers to offset losses resulting from internal crime. Given the pressure from international competition, often with lower labor costs, and the critical need to reduce the cost of production in order to maintain competitive positions, the interest of American firms in controlling employee theft is acute.

Surveys of applicants or employees who responded to anonymous questionnaires have estimated that 5 percent of the workforce engage in theft.[1] However, a study determined a much higher rate of 58 percent.[2] This difference is so large and the implications of this difference are so important for the use of honesty testing that we must discuss how these estimates were derived. The 58 percent estimate was obtained using more sophisticated measurement techniques than anonymous surveys. As one example, employees in high-theft businesses (fast food, service stations, and convenience stores) were asked to respond to a series of questions. They were also instructed to flip a coin after they read each question and before they marked their responses. The instruction for answering was the following:

> *If your coin flip is a head OR you are/were engaged in the theft from your employer of from $5.00–$9.99 in cash, supplies, or merchandise within a given month, please put an "X" in the box to the right.*

Other questions specified higher ranges of dollar figures. It was thought that this form of questioning would minimize the amount of denial of theft by respondents who had, in fact, stolen from their employers. The rate of theft was determined by subtracting the rate of head flips (50 percent) from the frequency of Xs that were marked.

The authors caution that their estimates of approximately 58 percent must be further investigated because the samples were only from industries known to have high theft rates. Moreover, about 50 percent of those who indicated theft marked the $5.00–$9.99 box that could include paper tablets, pens, and a few long-distance telephone calls.

If accurate, this higher percentage of theft clearly points out the need for honesty tests to address this issue of the high frequency of dishonesty.

We begin this chapter by discussing two forms of tests that have been used extensively to combat this problem: polygraphs and paper-and-pencil honesty, or integrity tests. In this discussion, we describe the nature of both of these forms and present opinions about their use.

Polygraph Testing

A polygraph, or lie detector, is a machine that measures the physiological responses of an individual that accompany the verbal responses he or she makes to the direct questions of a polygraph operator. These data, in conjunction with the opinion of the polygraph operator, are used to evaluate the truthfulness of the individual's responses to the questions. For all practical purposes, the use of polygraphs for selection is now illegal because of a federal law, the Employee Polygraph Protection Act of 1988.[3] However, polygraphs still may be used in specific employment circumstances.

The most common field polygraph examination uses readings of three types of physiological data. One set of readings, the electrodermal channel, displays changes in palmar skin resistance or galvanic skin response. The second set, the "cardio" channel, records changes in upper arm volume associated with the cardiac cycle. From this channel, it is possible to determine heart rate and some changes in pulse volume. The third channel, connected pneumatically or electrically to an expandable belt around the respondent's chest, records respiration. The purpose of these sets of data is to provide the polygraph examiner with information about the examinee's physiological reactions during questioning. The assumption is that the specialist can detect lying by observing changes in the subject's physiological response pattern.

Procedures.   In most polygraph examinations, the examiner conducts a pretest discussion with the examinee that covers all the questions to be used in the test. The purpose is to make sure the examinee understands the wording and the meaning of the questions and can answer them with a simple yes or no. After this discussion, the polygraph is attached to the examinee and the actual interview is conducted. The list of questions is then gone over again and usually repeated once or twice in order to obtain more reliable data. Three types of questions are usually used in the examination. One type is the irrelevant, nonemotional question, such as, "Are you six feet tall?" A second type is the emotional control question. Such questions are designed to elicit an emotional reaction, preferably of guilt. Questions such as, "Did you ever lie to escape punishment?" are frequently asked. The third type is specifically about the behavior of interest. In employment selection, this almost always concerns stealing of company resources. To detect lying, the polygraph operator looks for evidence of autonomic disturbance associated with the answers to the last type of question.[4] When the examinee is lying, there should be a disturbance that is more intense and persistent than that associated with the other two types of questions. Most polygraph examiners make an overall judgment of lying based on the polygraph information and other data, such as the demeanor of the examinee, the examiner's knowledge of the evidence, the respondent's prior history, and so on.[5]

Limitations.   One of the difficulties with such testing, however, is that other reactions besides guilt can trigger an emotional response in the examinee. Specifically, responses can be affected by the examinee's *lability*—the autonomic arousal threshold that differs from individual to individual. Examinees with high lability are more likely to have physiological reactions that may be interpreted as lying behavior than are respondents with low lability.

Another difficulty is the variety of countermeasures that examinees can use to avoid detection. Any physical activity that affects physiological responses is a potential problem for interpretation of polygraph readings. Such movements as tensing muscles, biting the tongue, flexing the toes, and shifting one's position can affect physiological response. Similarly, mental countermeasures such as mental relaxation or attempts to concentrate on exciting memories during the presentation of the emotional control questions can be effective.[6] In general, polygraph examiners try to monitor these attempts. The use of drugs to obscure physiological reaction differences is more difficult to detect unless a urinalysis is conducted. Examinees' experience with polygraphs and biofeedback training have also had demonstrated effects on polygraph results.

The major drawback to using the polygraph in employment testing is the frequency of the false positive. The *false positive* is a test result indicating an individual is lying when, in fact, he or she is not lying. The frequency of the false positive depends on both the validity of the test and the base rate of the lying behavior in the population. To illustrate the possible magnitude of false-positive identification, we make the following assumptions: (a) that the polygraph is 90 percent accurate (commonly regarded as a high estimate), and (b) that the rate of stealing is 5 percent of the working population. (This estimate has been regarded as accurate for many years. However, as we discussed previously, there is some evidence that the dishonesty rate among employees is much higher.) If 1,000 polygraph tests are conducted, we would expect that 50 of the examinees would be lying, and that 45 (90 percent) of them would be detected. The serious problem concerns the remaining 950 examinees. Assuming the 90 percent accuracy rate, 95 of these (950 × 0.10) would be inaccurately identified as lying about their actions. Therefore, a total of 140 individuals would be identified as lying, 68 percent of which would be false positives. The consequence of such examinations is that those singled out for lying are denied employment or, if they are current employees, are commonly terminated from employment. This example clearly shows that unless a polygraph test has perfect validity, a large number of false-positive identifications can occur when the device is used to test for a behavior that has a low incidence in the general population. Given the limitations in the validity of the polygraph, it is reasonable to suppose that the actual frequency of false positives is much greater than this example would indicate.

Another group, false negatives, has also received attention. *False negatives* occur when test results are judged to be truthful when, in fact, they are not. Individuals in this group are, understandably, of much interest to organizations; it is thought that these employees are most likely to be the cause of future theft. In fact, in many ways false negatives are of more immediate concern to organizations than are false positives.

We have mentioned several times in this text that incorrect judgments about applicants occur with the use of all selection devices. That is, some applicants who do not achieve scores high enough to be selected would perform well on the job. In addition, there are applicants who do score high enough to be selected but, subsequently, do not perform well on the job.

The problem with misjudgments in polygraph and other forms of integrity testing is the public statement that is made about individuals who incorrectly fail these tests, the false positives. These individuals could be labeled by an incorrect judgment about a behavior, honesty, that is highly valued in our society. It is obviously much more serious to reject an applicant because he or she has failed an honesty test than it is to reject him or her because the applicant's knowledge and ability do not meet the demands of this job. For this reason, public outcry about false positives grew as the use of polygraphs, and the number of individuals falsely labeled, increased. This outcry resulted in the passage of the Employee Polygraph Protection Act of 1988, which essentially ended polygraph use in selection and greatly restricted its use in other employment situations. The following is a summary of the major parts of this act, under which it is unlawful for employers to take any of the following actions:

1. Directly or indirectly require, request, suggest, or cause any employee to take or submit to any lie detector test, for example, a polygraph, deceptograph, voice-stress analyzer, psychological-stress evaluator, and any similar mechanical or electrical device used to render a diagnostic opinion about the honesty of an individual

2. Use, accept, refer to, or inquire about the results of any lie detector test of any job applicant or current employee

3. Discharge, discipline, discriminate against, or deny employment or promotion to (or threaten to take such adverse action against) any prospective or current employee who refuses, declines, or fails to take or submit to a lie detector test

However, the following employers are exempted from these prohibitions on pre-employment polygraph testing:

1. Private employers whose primary business purpose is to provide security services. Prospective employees may be tested if the positions for which they are applying involve the protection of nuclear power facilities, public water supply facilities, shipments or storage of radioactive or other toxic waste materials, public transportation, currency, negotiable securities, precious commodities, or proprietary information.

2. Employers involved in the manufacture, distribution, or dispensing of controlled substances. Employers may administer polygraph tests to applicants for positions that would provide direct access to the manufacture, storage, distribution, or sale of a controlled substance.

3. Federal, state, and local government employers. The federal government also may test private consultants or experts under contract to the Defense Department, the Energy Department, the National Security Agency, the Defense Intelligence Agency, the Central Intelligence Agency, and the Federal Bureau of Investigation.

Testing of current employees is also permitted if four conditions are met.

1. The polygraph test must be administered in connection with an investigation into a workplace theft or other incident that has resulted in an economic loss to the company.

2. The employee must have had access to the property that is the subject of the investigation.

3. The employer must have a "reasonable suspicion" that the employee was involved in the incident.

4. Prior to testing, the employee must have been given specific written information about the incident being investigated and the reasons for the testing.

One may conclude that the act was intended to restrict preemployment polygraph testing to those situations that have a large public interest, and the testing of current employees to those situations in which there is enough evidence to reasonably implicate an individual of a specific illegal act.

Paper-and-Pencil Integrity Tests

Before the Employee Polygraph Protection Act of 1988 was passed, more than 30 states had enacted legislation to prohibit, or severely limit, the use of polygraphs in employment decisions. Most of these state laws were worded, as is the federal act, to address mechanical or electronic devices only. In recent years several paper-and-pencil tests have been developed to provide a legal means to accomplish the same objective as polygraphs. The market for such tests has grown rapidly and a few states have passed laws that either prohibit or restrict the use of paper-and-pencil integrity tests. These laws have been passed for the same reasons as those prohibiting the use of polygraph testing.

Two forms of these tests have been developed.[7] One form is commonly referred to as an *overt integrity test*. It directly asks for information about attitudes toward theft and the occurrence of previous theft behaviors. The second is commonly labeled *personality-based measures*. This type of test does not ask about theft behaviors directly. Instead it is a personality inventory, measuring traits linked to several related employee behaviors that are detrimental to the organization. Theft is only one of these behaviors.

Overt Integrity Tests. Examples of the first type of test are the *Personnel Selection Inventory,* the *Reid Report*, and the *Stanton Survey*. The rationale underlying this type of test is to measure a job applicant's attitudes and cognitions toward theft that might predispose him or her to steal at work, especially when both the need and the opportunity to steal are present. William Terris and John Jones have explained this testing approach in the following way:

Past research has shown that the "typical" employee-thief (1) is more tempted to steal, (2) engages in many of the common rationalizations for theft, (3) would punish thieves less, (4) often thinks about theft-related activities, (5) attributes more theft to others, (6) shows more inter-thief loyalty, and (7) is more vulnerable to peer pressure to steal than is an honest employee.[8]

Items on this type of test follow directly from these points. Some example items are the following:[9]

- Most people who have had jobs where they handled money or had expense accounts have probably taken some money without their employer's permission.

This includes directly taking cash, borrowing money that is not returned, or padding expense accounts. Estimate how much you have taken from all employers in the past five years.

- Did you ever think about doing something that, if you had done it, would have been a crime?

- In any of your other jobs did you find out a way a dishonest person could take money if a dishonest person had your job?

- Do you believe that making personal phone calls from your employer's place of business without an OK is stealing?

- Have you ever overcharged someone for your personal gain?

- Is it true that to be human is to be dishonest?

Another type of question poses a situation that focuses on dishonest behavior. Here is an example: "A store manager with 15 years of good work performance has an eight-year-old son who is dying of cancer. The manager takes $25 per week from the store for three months in order to buy toys and games for the child. Another employee sees this behavior and tells the district manager." A number of questions follow that ask the respondent's opinions about the theft, the action of the employee who informed the district manager, and his or her choices of alternative actions that can be taken by the district manager.

Personality-Based Measures.   A second type of integrity test takes the form of a general personality test. The central idea for this approach is that employee theft is just one element in a larger syndrome of antisocial behavior or organizational delinquency. Such delinquency includes dishonesty, theft, drug and alcohol abuse, vandalism, sabotage, assault actions, insubordination, absenteeism, excessive grievances, bogus worker compensation claims, and violence. The assumption is that there is a common personality pattern that underlies organizational delinquency and that it is feasible to identify individuals who have this personality pattern through the use of personality inventories used by the general public. Frequently, these personality measures will contain a subset of items that are identified as an integrity scale. These items are part of the personality inventory, but are the only ones scored in order to measure the integrity, honesty, and/or organizational delinquency of the test taker. It is thought that imbedding these items and the integrity scale within a personality inventory has two advantages. First, in comparison with an overt integrity test, the items on a personality integrity test are not as transparent in their intention to measure theft and related transgressions. This reduces the probability of respondents faking responses. Second, applicants who are not selected because of the personality test need not be rejected because of failing an integrity test. Rather, they are rejected for a mismatch between their personality profile and that of successful employees.

The Hogan Personality Inventory (HPI) is one such personality-based integrity measure.[10] It is a 206-item Big-Five type of personality survey that has been developed for use in employment situations. It contains seven primary scales and six occupational scales that are presented in Table 14.1. The publisher provides normative data from more than 30,000 working adults across a wide variety of industries. The primary scales can be regarded as personality dimensions that are measured by the 206 items. The occupational scales are composed of various combinations of the 206 items of the primary scales and were developed to provide information about specific employment topics.

One of these occupational scales is the Reliability scale, composed of 18 items that measure honesty, integrity, and organizational citizenship (for example, assisting others,

TABLE 14.1	Scales of the Hogan Personality Inventory

Primary Scales

Adjustment—Self-confidence, self-esteem, and composure under pressure

Ambition—Initiative, competitiveness, and the desire for leadership roles

Sociability—Extraversion, gregariousness, and a need for social interaction

Interpersonal Sensitivity—Warmth, charm, and the ability to maintain relationships

Prudence—Self-discipline, responsibility, and conscientiousness

Inquisitiveness—Imagination, curiosity, vision, and creative potential

Learning Approach—Enjoying learning, staying current on business and technical matters

Occupational Scales

Service Orientation—Being attentive, pleasant, and courteous to customers

Stress Tolerance—Being able to handle stress, being even-tempered and calm under fire

Reliability—Honesty, integrity, and positive organizational citizenship

Clerical Potential—Following directions, attending to detail, and communicating clearly

Sales Potential—Energy, social skills, and the ability to solve customers' problems

Managerial Potential—Leadership ability, planning, and decision-making skills

Source: © 2010 Hogan Assessment Systems.

engaging in nonmeasured performance). High scores are good; low scores are bad. The authors have reported test-retest reliability as high as 0.90 for the Reliability scale. Concurrent validity studies have been conducted with various groups of workers in a variety of jobs. Table 14.2 contains a list of the various criteria measures that have been used in these studies. The diversity of the measures indicates two points: (a) that the index can predict employee performance as well as organizational delinquency, and (b) that there is a wide scope of employee behaviors that can be included in organizational delinquency. Other research has also supported the validity of the Reliability scale and the HPI.[11]

What We Know About Integrity Tests

Perhaps because integrity tests have so much value to American industry, there has been much research about these intstruments. For example, Paul Sackett and his colleagues have published five extensive reviews of integrity tests since 1979, each of which has addressed several important topics. The following discussion draws from these reviews, especially the latest review that Sackett did with Christopher Berry and Shelly Wiemann.[12] It also relies heavily on a series of studies done by Deniz Ones, Chockalingam Viswesvaran, and Frank Schmidt.[13] We also refer to other research studies that are not included in these reviews.

Constructs Measured.   As mentioned previously, integrity tests were first used to detect employee theft because that is such a large and expensive issue for businesses. Recent research has indicated that it is more appropriate to think of integrity tests as measuring counterproductive work behaviors (CWB) that include a number of actions such as theft, sabotage, restriction of performance, confrontation, and others. It seems appropriate to think of CWB as a hierarchical model with a general CWB factor at the top, mid-range factors (such as interpersonal and organizational deviance) below the general factor, and specific factors such as theft below the mid-range factors.[14] Integrity tests can measure CWBs at all three levels of this model. Therefore, integrity tests should be thought of as

TABLE 14.2	Criteria Measures Correlated with Employee Reliability Index	

Job	Negative Behaviors That Are Correlated	Positive Behaviors That Are Correlated
Truck driver	Discharges from work Grievances filed Claims for equipment failure	Commendations
Psychiatric counselor		Supervisor's ratings of performance
Hospital service worker	Times counseled for aberrant behavior	
Rehabilitation therapist	Injuries sustained Incidents reported to insurance fund State dollars spent for treatment	
Nuclear power plant worker		Supervisor's ratings of attitude, accuracy, punctuality
Service operations dispatchers	Absences	
Navy electronics students		Course time completion
Customer service representatives		Supervisor's ratings of quality, teamwork, performance
Telemarketers		Sales performance Sales lead generation

Source: Based on Joyce Hogan and Robert Hogan, "How to Measure Employee Reliability," in *Employee Testing: The Complete Resource Guide* (Washington, DC: Bureau of National Affairs, Inc., 1988).

multifaceted and the construct they are measuring may be hierarchical in nature (that is, an overall Conscientiousness factor[15]).

Variables Related to Integrity Tests.   Several meta-analytic studies have examined the relationships among integrity tests and the Big Five personality measures. Both overt and personality-based honesty tests significantly correlate with a variety of these personality dimensions.[16] In all cases, personality-based tests correlate more highly with the Big Five dimensions than do overt tests. With both types of tests, however, the correlations are substantial with the three dimensions of conscientiousness, agreeableness, and emotional stability. Recent work in personality measurement has postulated the addition of a sixth personality dimension to the Big Five. The HEXACO model of personality adds the Honesty-Humilty dimension that measures fairness, sincerity, lack of conceit, and lack of greed.[17] One study tested the relationship of the six factor HEXACO model vs. the Five-Factor Model of personality with workplace delinquency in three countries: Netherlands, Canada, and Australia. Results indicated that the HEXACO model significantly outperformed the Five Factor Model in predicting both workplace delinquency and scores on overt honesty tests.

Integrity test scores have also been correlated with cognitive test scores; initial findings were that overall or general integrity test scores are not correlated with cognitive ability test scores and, therefore, they can provide additional predictive validity over cognitive ability tests.[18] However, other work investigated the relationships between cognitive ability and 23 integrity sub factors rather than overall scores.[19] Several sub factors were positively correlated with cognitive ability while others negatively related to cognitive ability. Thus, the near-zero correlation reported using overall integrity scores may be the result of combining positively and negatively related integrity sub factors with cognitive ability. The relationship between integrity measures and cognitive ability may depend on which factors of integrity are measured by a test.

Relationship of Overt and Personality Based Tests.   Research has also examined how similar overt integrity tests are to personality-based integrity tests. That is, do the two forms of integrity tests measure the same constructs? The study used 798 test items (remember that no matter what the developer says the test measures, it measures what the items ask about!) from three overt and four personality-based integrity tests.[20] These items were sorted into 23 distinct, interpretable themes, such as theft thoughts/temptations, self/impulse control, risk taking/thrill seeking, and perception of dishonesty norms. These themes were then statistically analyzed to form four factors or dimensions: antisocial behavior, socialization, positive outlook, and orderliness/diligence. The authors then used data from 1,428 individuals to derive correlations among the 23 behavioral themes, the four dimensions, the seven integrity tests, and the two Big Five personality inventories. The purpose was to determine both how closely correlated integrity tests were to each other and how closely they were correlated with personality measures. The following were some of the authors' conclusions:

1. There are positive correlations among all integrity tests across five themes—theft thoughts/temptations, perception of dishonesty norms, social conformity, association with delinquents, and theft admissions. Therefore, all integrity tests show a great deal of similarity in what is being measured.

2. There are some differences among overt and personality-based tests. Overt tests correlate more highly with honesty attitudes and supervision attitudes. Personality tests correlate more highly with self/impulse control, home life/upbringing, risk taking, diligence, and emotional stability.

Validity.   Determining the validity of integrity tests is difficult because of the problems of measuring a criterion variable. Theft and many other counterproductive work behaviors are not easily detected and recorded in individual workers' employment records. In addition, it is not known whether self-reported dishonesty is an accurate measure of actual dishonesty. As a result, recent work with integrity tests has used theft, absenteeism, disciplinary action, termination, sabotage, and others. Some studies have even used overall work performance. In reviewing validity studies with these various criteria, Sackett and Wanek have estimated the following population validity coefficients: 0.13 for overt tests with theft criterion, 0.39 for overt tests with various nontheft criteria, and 0.29 for personality tests with nontheft criteria.[21] In general, they concluded that there is not enough data from meta-analytic studies to indicate that either overt or personality-based tests are superior to the other. Both types demonstrate validity across different criteria. In related work, another meta-analysis looked at the relationships between both types of integrity tests and voluntary absenteeism. Results were corrected values of .33 and .09 for personality-based and overt tests, respectively. This indicated a considerable difference in the predictive validity of the two types of tests, with personality-based tests more useful in the prediction of voluntary absenteeism than overt tests.[22]

Ones, Viswesvaran, and Schmidt estimated the population validity coefficient between integrity tests and supervisors' ratings of overall job performance to be 0.41.[23] The two possible explanations for this correlation are a) that integrity tests reflect underlying personality dimensions, which are linked to productive work behaviors, and b) that supervisors use the occurrence of unproductive behaviors (to which integrity tests are related) in their judgments of job performance. A related study examined the validity of personality-based integrity scores with maximal work performance (individuals try to perform at their highest levels as opposed to typical or day-to-day performance) and found a correlation of .27.[24] Furthermore, integrity scores correlated .14 with job knowledge and job knowledge had a .36 correlation with maximal work performance. Integrity seems to be related to maximal performance because it taps motivation of individuals; that is, a person exerting maximum effort and also because integrity is related to job knowledge. Both motivation and job knowledge are major components of individual difference in maximal performance. Based on all of these findings, it is possible to conclude that integrity tests are valid for the prediction of theft, general counterproductive behaviors, and various types of work performance.

In order to understand these validity relationships better, Ones and her colleagues investigated the question of whether the relationship between integrity test scores and overall job performance is merely a function of the relationship between both of these variables and conscientiousness.[25] They did this by determining the correlation between integrity test scores and job performance while statistically controlling conscientiousness. The conclusion is that although integrity tests overlap with various personality dimensions, they independently contribute to the prediction of job performance. Sackett and Wanek believe that this contribution occurs because integrity tests emphasize self-control and contain many items that measure this variable. Although self-control is generally considered to be part of the personality dimension of conscientiousness, it is usually measured by relatively few items in most Big Five measures. Therefore, integrity measures add to the prediction of job performance over conscientious measures because self-control is strongly related to job performance.[26]

False Positives.   The issue of false positives is identical to that discussed previously concerning polygraphs. A large percentage of applicants (estimated as 40 percent to 70 percent) commonly fail integrity tests, and a large number of those who fail may be incorrectly classified. Cutoff scores that cause these failure rates are usually set in one of two ways. The test publisher can set the score based on statistics gathered in test development. For the most part, it is in the best interest of the test publisher to set the cutoff score high enough to reduce the number of individuals who pass the test but are subsequently dishonest. In other words, it may be in the best interest of the test publisher to avoid false negatives, even at the cost of increased false positives. Cutoff scores may also be set by the organization using the integrity test. It is commonly in the best interest of the organization to minimize false negatives even at the cost of increased false positives. In such a case, the organization would set high cutoff scores. This would be especially true for those cases in which the applicant pool is large enough to absorb the rejection of high numbers of applicants and yet provide enough individuals to fill the open positions.

It is Sackett and Wanek's opinion that integrity test decision errors should be evaluated based on choosing among *multiple applicants,* rather than on a decision concerning a *single* individual.[27] That is, integrity tests are often used near the end of the selection program and given to applicants who have passed other KSA-related selection measures. If there are more applicants than open positions, and if the integrity test is valid, its use improves selection over the alternative, which is random selection among the remaining applicants.

Related to Sackett and Wanek's opinion is the fact that all selection tests have false positives. Selection specialists have not been very concerned with these decisions and have usually regarded having a valid test as beneficial for the results of selection. No special consideration of false positives is usually given. However, most selection tests do not have the social implications of an integrity test, in which a low score may be seen as an indicant of dishonesty. For this reason, the use of personality-based integrity tests may be more socially acceptable than the use of overt measures. Although the rate of false positives *probably* does not differ between the two types, the implication of a low score is not as socially noticeable to the test taker because he or she may think that the test is a personality measure rather than an integrity test.

Faking.   One concern of test users is that applicants may be able to fake their responses on integrity tests. This may be especially true for overt tests that directly ask about attitudes and previous instances of theft from employers. (That is, it simply doesn't make sense that many people would openly indicate instances of theft. However, we must remember that integrity test scores are not clearly related to cognitive ability test scores.) This concern is similar to the concern about faking on personality inventories, which we discussed in Chapter 12. Research on faking on integrity tests generally comes to the same conclusion we drew about personality tests—faking doesn't seem to make a difference in the validity of the test.[28] One study instructed subjects about how to distort their answers on an integrity test in several ways. The scores of these individuals were compared to those of other subjects who were not instructed to distort and also to those of job applicants who took the test as part of selection programs for various organizations. Subjects who were instructed to distort did score higher on the integrity test than those who were not told to do so. However, they did not score as high as job applicants. The logical conclusions were that (a) individuals can distort their responses and score higher; (b) some applicants use such distortion in their responses, perhaps even to a greater degree; (c) because validity coefficients were determined on samples of job applicants, such distortion does not make the test invalid; (d) distortion by future job applicants will not be greater than it is for those for whom the test has been developed, and it will not affect the test's validity.[29] However, just as in the case of faking of personality inventories, this position may not indicate the full effect of distortion on selection decisions. We should remember that the validity of the test is a group-level statistic. Selection decisions are made on the basis of individual-level data, and distortion may differentially affect applicants' scores. Therefore, those individuals who are selected when taking distortion into account may differ from those who would have been selected if no distortion had occurred.

Legal Issues in Integrity Testing.   The Equal Employment Opportunity Commission (EEOC) has specifically commented that integrity tests, even personality-based ones, should not be considered a medical examination because such tests assess only the propensity for dishonest behavior. Therefore, these tests can be used in selection programs prior to an employment offer. However, any personality test that was designed to detect mental illness and that also is used to determine dishonesty would be treated differently. Such a test would be considered a medical examination. This possibility has not been evidenced at this point in time. Another important issue is whether a specific test includes any items that ask about previous drug or alcohol use. Such items cannot be used, because the Americans with Disabilities Act (ADA) prohibits inquiries about the extent of prior use of these substances. Finally, a metaanalysis of scores on three overt integrity tests found insignificant differences among ethnic and racial groups.[30]

Other Stuff. There have been recent attempts to develop integrity tests in formats other than the traditional true-false questionnaire. These formats include biodata questionnaires, forced choice response formats, interviews, and situational judgment tests.[31] However, these new formats have not been used extensively; given the demonstrated validity of integrity tests, it is unclear as to what the potential advantage of some of these would be. For example, interviews would take much longer to administer than an integrity test and cost significantly more. Biodata forms have traditionally required large samples for validation and some items may very closely resemble those of integrity tests.

There has been some research done on application reactions to integrity testing; many of these studies find that individuals react more negatively to integrity tests than to many other forms of selection testing. However, most studies have used college students participating in research studies. Very few studies have used applicants or incumbent employees, samples that would be reflective of groups to whom the tests would normally be administered.

DRUG TESTING

Employees' use of drugs and alcohol has been of major concern to organizations since the 1960s. During that time period, drug testing has become increasingly common in work organizations, especially those that have safety sensitive jobs or receive government contracts. In addition, research has found that drug use is negatively associated with job performance, accidents, injuries, absences, involuntary turnover, and job-withdrawal behaviors such as too many breaks and sleeping on the job.[32]

It is difficult to precisely know how many individuals or what percentage of the workforce regularly uses drugs. The problem with measuring usage is that it relies on self-report data. That is, individuals must indicate in some way that they have used drugs. Such an indication can be risky to the individual, so there is a general thought that any data gathered through self-report may be an underestimate of actual use. Measuring the deterioration in work performance attributable to drug use is, perhaps, even more difficult to do. The issue with this measurement is that there is not a linear relationship between the amount of a drug consumed and the decline of work performance level. Individuals differ in their reactions to a specific amount of drugs; the same amount of a drug will have differential effects among the individuals in the group of employees. Additionally, some people adapt to consistent use of drugs and over time develop the ability to absorb larger quantities of drugs due to a resistance to the effects of the drug.[33] It is not possible to estimate the effect of a given quantity of a drug on the work performance of an individual. The only sure way to measure deterioration in performance is to establish a standard of performance while an individual is free from drugs and then measure performance after drugs have been consumed. Obviously, such data are pretty much impossible to obtain.

Arguably, the best estimate of drug use among United States workers and also of drug impairment has been collected by Michael Frone.[34] He collected information from a carefully selected representative sample of 2,806 adults working in the 48 contiguous states and the District of Columbia. The data were gathered through a telephone survey that contained many questions about employee health and safety. Each respondent answered two questions about the use of six drugs: marijuana or hashish, cocaine or crack, sedatives, tranquilizers, stimulants, and analgesics. Any use of marijuana or cocaine is illicit. The other four (psychotherapeutic) drugs are legal. Questions were phrased to indicate use other than for prescribed medical purposes.

The first of the two questions asked how often each drug was used during the preceding 12 months. This question was designed to measure the percentage of the workforce who used drugs. The second question asked how often the respondent took each drug and got high or stoned. The answer to this was interpreted as a measure of impairment. Keep in mind that there is a distinction to be made between use and impairment. Use means that some amount of the drug has been consumed. Impairment means that the amount consumed was enough to cause deterioration in performance. Results from Frone's research led to the following estimates:

1. Marijuana had been used by 11.33 percent of the workforce (14.2 million workers).

2. Cocaine had been used by 1.01 percent of the workforce (1.3 million workers).

3. At least one of the four psychotherapeutic drugs had been used by 4.90 percent of the workforce (6.2 million workers).

4. At least one drug had been used by 14.06 percent of the workforce (17.7 million workers).

5. Marijuana use had caused 10.57 percent of the workforce (13.3 million workers) to become impaired.

6. Cocaine use had caused 0.93 percent of the workforce (1.2 million workers) to become impaired.

7. The four psychotherapeutic drugs had caused 2.21 percent of the workforce (2.8 million workers) to become impaired.

8. At least one of the drugs had caused 11.23 percent of the workforce (14.1 million workers) to become impaired.

Illicit drug use was highest in the arts, entertainment, sports, media, and food preparation and serving occupations. Impairment was highest in legal, food preparation and serving, and building and grounds maintenance occupations. Men used and were impaired by drugs more frequently than women, and race was unrelated to use or impairment. Both age and education were negatively related to use and impairment—that is, older individuals and those who had completed more education used drugs less frequently and were impaired less frequently than younger or less-educated individuals. Among those who used a drug, 56 percent used it at least once a week and 41 percent were impaired at least one day a week. Finally, 2.71 percent of the workforce (3.4 million workers) used drugs within two hours of reporting to work, 1.82 percent (2.3 million workers) used during lunch breaks, 1.19 percent (1.5 million workers) used during other kinds of work breaks, and 1.72 percent (2.2 million workers) used while working. Frone concluded that although the absolute numbers for use and impairment are high, "they represent only 1.8 percent of the total workforce." From these data it is feasible to conclude that drug usage, while worrisome, is not rampant in the U.S. workforce.

Drug Tests

Paper-and-Pencil Tests. The simplest, and least controversial, drug test is the paper-and-pencil type. This test is identical in intent to the paper-and-pencil integrity tests discussed previously. Overt-type tests ask directly about drug usage with questions such as the following:

- Do you think that it is okay for workers to use "soft" drugs at work if this does not cause poor job performance?

- In the past six months, how often have you used marijuana at work?

- In the past six months, have you brought cocaine to work even though you did not use it at work?

General-purpose tests are adaptations of personality inventories, analogous to personality-based integrity measures developed to identify drug users. Unlike integrity tests, however, there is almost no public literature that evaluates the reliability or the validity of this type of test. However, one court case ruled that preemployment tests in which applicants were asked to indicate their use of legal and illegal drugs were unconstitutional, based on the Fifth Amendment's prohibition of involuntary self incrimination.[35] Therefore, it seems that a company would be limited in its ability to force an applicant to complete at least the overt-type test. For this reason, perhaps, it seems that organizations use paper-and-pencil tests infrequently.

Urine Tests.   A second type of test, the one used the most often, is the urine test. First used in the 1960s, it was a way for hospital emergency room personnel to diagnose patients in a drug-induced coma for appropriate treatment. In the 1970s, demand for this type of testing increased with the need to monitor clients' compliance with treatment programs for methadone maintenance and other drug therapy programs. The desire of business organizations to control the problems associated with employee drug usage further increased the demand for these tests in the 1980s and 1990s.

Commonly in employment testing, a drug can be reported as present only if it has been detected in two separate tests using different analytic methods. In practice, this means two levels of testing: a *screening test* and a *confirmation test* (used only when the screening test indicates that a drug is present). If the screening test finds no drug presence or if the confirmatory test does not agree with the results of the screening test, the decision is that no drug is present. To conduct these tests, the urine sample is divided into two parts immediately after it is collected. Samples are usually identified by number or code rather than by name of person.

All urine tests are based on the fact that what enters the body through ingestion, injection, or inhalation must be excreted in some form. Most drugs are excreted, wholly or in part, into the urine via the liver, kidneys, and bladder. Although some drugs are excreted unchanged (for example, morphine), most drugs are broken down by the body; the products, or *metabolites*, can be found in the urine. The physical evidence of drug use differs from drug to drug. The testing procedures, then, must also differ for the different drug families, and new tests must be developed as new drugs come into use. To avoid error, standard thresholds (amount of drug present) of detection are set to determine the presence of a drug. If less than the threshold amount is detected, the decision is made that no drug is present. This theoretically reduces the possibility of drug presence being indicated by amounts of a legally permissible drug product.

Hair Analysis.   A third drug testing method is hair analysis, in which samples of hair are taken from the individual to be tested. The basis of hair analysis is similar to that of urine analysis. That is, the use of drugs leaves chemical traces in human hair that remain after drug use. Hair analysis uses screening and confirmatory tests that are similar to those used for urine testing. Theoretically, because of the growth rate of scalp hair, hair analysis can detect drug use over a longer time period than can urine testing. For example, an inch of hair is estimated to contain information relative to 90 days of potential drug use. To perform a hair analysis, the hair is divided into different samples and is washed multiple times to remove external contamination. The use of bleach or dye on the hair may lower drug levels slightly but not completely.

Fitness-for-Duty Tests.   A fourth type of drug test is referred to as a *fitness-for-duty, impairment,* or *competency* test. This test is relatively new and not often used in industry. One form, a two-minute test of eye-hand coordination, resembles a computer game. The individual operates a device according to instructions; time of response and accuracy rate are compared to a previously determined standard based on the individual taking the test 100 times. If the results of any single test indicate that someone is operating significantly below the standard, the individual is either sent home for the day or reassigned to another position. This type of test is considered less intrusive than either urine or hair analysis and is capable of providing immediate results. However, more information is needed about the effect of factors such as fatigue, stress, and prescribed drugs on test performance. Even more important is the variability of normal performance and the ability of an individual to restrict behavior during the testings to establish the standard.

Oral Fluid Test.   The person being tested rubs an oral swab on the inside of the mouth and then seals it in a vial. The liquid on the swab is analyzed for the presence of drugs. Barring lab error, the test is always accurate. This test almost eliminates the risk of adulteration of a sample and makes it virtually impossible for donors to mask drugs in their systems or to use samples from others.

Accuracy of Chemical Tests

Because the physical properties of each drug are invariate, the chemical tests should be completely accurate. False positives (individuals indicated as drug users who, in fact, are not users) may occur in an initial test. However, these individuals should be eliminated by confirmation tests. Errors in confirmation tests occur only when the laboratory conducting the testing does not use standard procedures.

   It is important to realize the limitations of the information obtained from these tests. A positive result means a presence of the drug above the threshold level set for detection. The result does not allow a determination of how much of the drug was used, how frequently it was used, how long ago it was used, the circumstances of its use, or the level of impairment in performance caused by the drug. Individuals differ in their absorption, metabolism, and tolerance of drugs. Also, many drugs leave a metabolite trail long after any performance effects have faded; therefore, it is not accurate to assume automatically that a positive test is an infallible indicant of inability to perform. Finally, the threshold level obviously affects the results. Although commonly accepted threshold levels for detection do exist, some levels are so low that passive inhalation of marijuana can give a positive result.

Legal Issues in Employment Drug Testing

As we mentioned previously, the legal status of using drug tests in employment is unclear. It seems safe to say that organizations have less risk in using such tests for preemployment selection; considerably more legal risk is associated with testing existing workers before making promotion decisions or with testing employees in order to detect drug users for disciplinary or counseling purposes. This is mainly because applicants cannot take advantage of collective bargaining or challenge employment-at-will principles, as can employees who feel they have been wrongly treated.

   The major questions about drug testing have centered on the following six legal arguments:[36]

1. Testing represents an invasion of privacy.

2. Testing constitutes an unreasonable search and seizure.

3. Testing is a violation of due process.

4. Drug users are protected under the Americans with Disabilities Act.

5. Testing may violate the Civil Rights Act.

6. Testing may violate the National Labor Relations Act.

We briefly discuss each of these issues.

By its very nature, the collection of urine, hair, or oral samples for testing is intrusive. Intrusion, physical or otherwise, on the private affairs of an individual has commonly been the basis for civil suits under the doctrine of *right of privacy*. However, this term offers protection only if the employer is a governmental institution or agency. Therefore, this defense is actually open only to a small number of employees. It is not clear to what extent this concept can be applied to private industry, but currently it seems limited. The right of privacy in nongovernmental firms *may* apply only to confidentiality in the collection and reporting of the drug test results. Collection practices should include guarantees of the privacy of the individual regarding the facilities provided as well as the procedures used in monitoring the specimen collection to ensure that it has not been altered. For certain jobs, it may be acceptable to require testing in the interests of public safety even at the cost of employee privacy. These would be jobs in which employees could place themselves or others in substantial danger while under the effects of drug use. Examples of such jobs include airline pilot and other public transportation positions, chemical and nuclear power plant operators, and security officers.

The Fourth Amendment prohibits unreasonable search; the Fifth and Fourteenth Amendments guarantee the right of due process. Although they are frequently applied in public practices, these concepts have limited application to private industry. A central issue is the reason for the testing. It seems important that testing be linked to workplace problems such as accidents, theft, absenteeism, and sabotage. Data that indicate the existence of such problems before testing can serve as evidence the company was pursuing a legitimate self-interest. In the absence of such data, the company is at risk by seeming arbitrary in its actions and seeming to have little actual justification for its claims.

The question of due process, under which a person is innocent unless proven guilty, seems to deal with the validity of drug tests. Presumably, evidence provided by professionally conducted testing would constitute evidence of guilt.

The Americans with Disabilities Act of 1990 prohibits discrimination against the disabled. The act clearly protects former drug users who are in rehabilitation and excludes individuals currently using drugs. Title VII of the Civil Rights Act of 1964 could be a legal basis for discrimination if, as described previously, unequal treatment occurs. It is possible drug testing could also result in adverse impact if a greater percentage of minority than nonminority members are identified. The test would then have to be shown to be job related. Safety of others or demonstration of previous records of high rates of damage, accidents, or absenteeism could serve as evidence. The previously noted difficulty in linking positive results of a drug test with decrements in job performance could limit an organization's defense.

Collective bargaining agreements represent one of the most significant obstacles to drug testing programs in unionized firms. Because drug testing is considered a working condition, and as such is subject to collective bargaining, employers generally cannot implement drug testing without consulting with the union. Even when such testing is accepted by both parties, disciplinary measures prompted by the results of testing can be subject to arbitration. One study reported that arbitrators have overturned more discharges than they have sustained.[37] Also pertinent are court rulings regarding employment-at-will and wrongful discharge. Traditionally, management has had nearly complete discretion in terminating employees under these principles. However, some recent rulings have altered this position.

It is no surprise that drug testing has caused negative reactions among applicants as well as employees. Consequently, it is important for selection and HR specialists to understand how applicants and existing employees may react to a drug testing program.

In general, research has indicated that employees and applicants react more favorably to drug testing when (a) an advance warning of the testing is given, (b) the company uses rehabilitation rather than termination when the presence of drugs is detected,[38] and (c) the drug testing adheres to fair detection procedures and explanation of results.[39] Additionally, researchers have found that employees and applicants are more positive about drug testing when there is a perceived need for the test.[40] In this research, some of the acceptable reasons for testing included perceptions of danger, contact with the public, use of spatial ability in hazardous job tasks, and the performance of repetitive tasks. In addition, a company's restrictive confidentiality policy regarding access to results was associated with intention to apply for employment.[41] Finally, when drug testing was required, individuals were more satisfied with either urinalysis or overt paper-and-pencil tests than with a personality inventory.[42] Not surprisingly, drug users had much more negative reactions to all forms of testing than did nonusers.[43] Most people do not regard the negative reactions of drug users to be a bad thing, however.

Guidelines for Drug Testing Programs

We conclude this section with a brief description of the important features of a drug testing program.

1. The organization is in the most legally defensible position when it limits testing to those positions that have major safety implications or a history of poor performance in specific areas that may be linked to drug usage.

2. Organizations have more flexibility in such testing with applicants than with existing employees.

3. A combination of screening and confirmatory tests are necessary for the testing results to be valid. Such tests increase the cost of the program but are necessary given the seriousness of the matter.

4. The organization should obtain the written consent of the individual before testing and provide the individual with the test results afterward. Particular attention should be paid to those situations in which an individual is informed of positive results from the drug test. At a minimum, the person should be allowed to explain positive results in terms of legal drugs that he or she may have taken. A physician's verification may be required in such explanations. Some have also recommended that the individual who tested positive be offered the opportunity to submit part of the urine sample used in the testing to another laboratory for additional testing. This would be done at the individual's expense.

5. The procedures used in the testing program should be applied to all individuals in the same job status. It would be inadvisable to exempt some persons from testing because it seems obvious that they are not taking drugs.

6. The program should be designed and reviewed periodically to ensure that privacy is afforded to the individuals being tested. This means that urine collection

procedures be standardized and attuned to the privacy of the individual. Also, all results must be kept confidential, especially from supervisors of existing employees, unless there is a defined need to know.

7. Drug testing, especially when used for current employees, should be one part of a larger program. Other features should include some form of education, counseling, and assistance.

GRAPHOLOGY

Because the popular press has periodically given this technique attention in terms of its use in selection, in this section we focus on graphology. The validity of graphology in selection has actually been addressed in research studies. Other intended selection techniques have been used (notice we said intended, not useful or valid), such as eye-reading, face or expression reading, phrenology (the study of bumps on the head), body shape interpretation, and astrological sign interpretation. We find no validity associated with any of these. At the time of this writing, the use of graphology in selection is declining.[44] We like to think that is because we have been relentless in spreading truth to all corners of the selection world (we have written about it in the last four editions of this book). We are overjoyed to see the result of our determined and heroic effort. Maybe in the next edition we will talk about astrological signs in selection (a selection technique that actually had some benefits for at least one of us much earlier in life).

> Graphology *is the analysis of an individual's handwriting in order to infer personality traits and behavioral tendencies. A* graphologist *is the individual who performs the analysis.*

Graphologists link their field to the projective personality assessment devices that were discussed in Chapter 11. That is, it is thought that the idiosyncratic features of a person's handwriting serve as an expression of his or her personality in the same manner as does a story written about ambiguous inkblots or scenes involving human beings. All are projections of the person imposed on a neutral field. No standard form of expression is demanded; therefore, the result is expressive of the individual. In HR selection, graphologists examine handwriting samples of job applicants and evaluate (a) their suitability for employment in general or (b) the match of their personality traits to the demands of a specific position. This type of analysis has been in widespread use in western Europe for many years. Recently, it has attracted some attention in the United States. In this section, we provide example interpretations of some features of handwriting and summarize the few studies that have examined the validity of this technique in selection.

Analysis of Handwriting Features

Although different graphological approaches exist, most of them analyze the following features of handwriting: size of letters, slant, width, zones (top, middle, and bottom), regularity of letter formation, margin, pressure, stroke, line of letters (upward, straight, downward), connections of letters, form of connection, and word and line spacing. The various approaches to graphology differ in the interpretation each assigns to these specific features and how combinations of writing features should be viewed.

The following are illustrations and comments about selected analyses provided by the International Graphoanalysis Society.[45] The writing sample should be a full page or more of spontaneous writing made with a ballpoint pen or pencil on unruled paper. The general procedure for graphoanalysis is based on the following steps. First, a *perspectograph* is developed. This is an analysis of the first 100 *upstrokes* that occur in the writing sample according to set rules of measurement. The result is a percentage value for each of seven different degrees of slant ranging from far forward to markedly backward. Each type of slant is thought to indicate a state of emotional responsiveness. In general, far-forward writing is indicative of extremely emotional individuals, and backward-slanted writing is indicative of emotionally constrained ones. The percentage of each of the seven slants is plotted on a graph for reference as other traits are found. Figure 14.1 presents examples of specific handwriting features and their interpretation.

FIGURE 14.1   Some Examples of Handwriting Features and Their Interpretation

1. Mental Prowess

(a)
Comprehensive
thinking

(b)
Cumulative
thinking

(c)
Exploratory or
investigative
thinking

2. Approach to Achievement

(a)
Lack of
self-confidence

(b)
Strong
willpower

3. Levels of Honesty

(a)
Frankness

(b)
Self-deception or
rationalization

(c)
Intentional
deception

4. Levels of Determinism

(a)
Strong
determination

(b)
Weak
determination

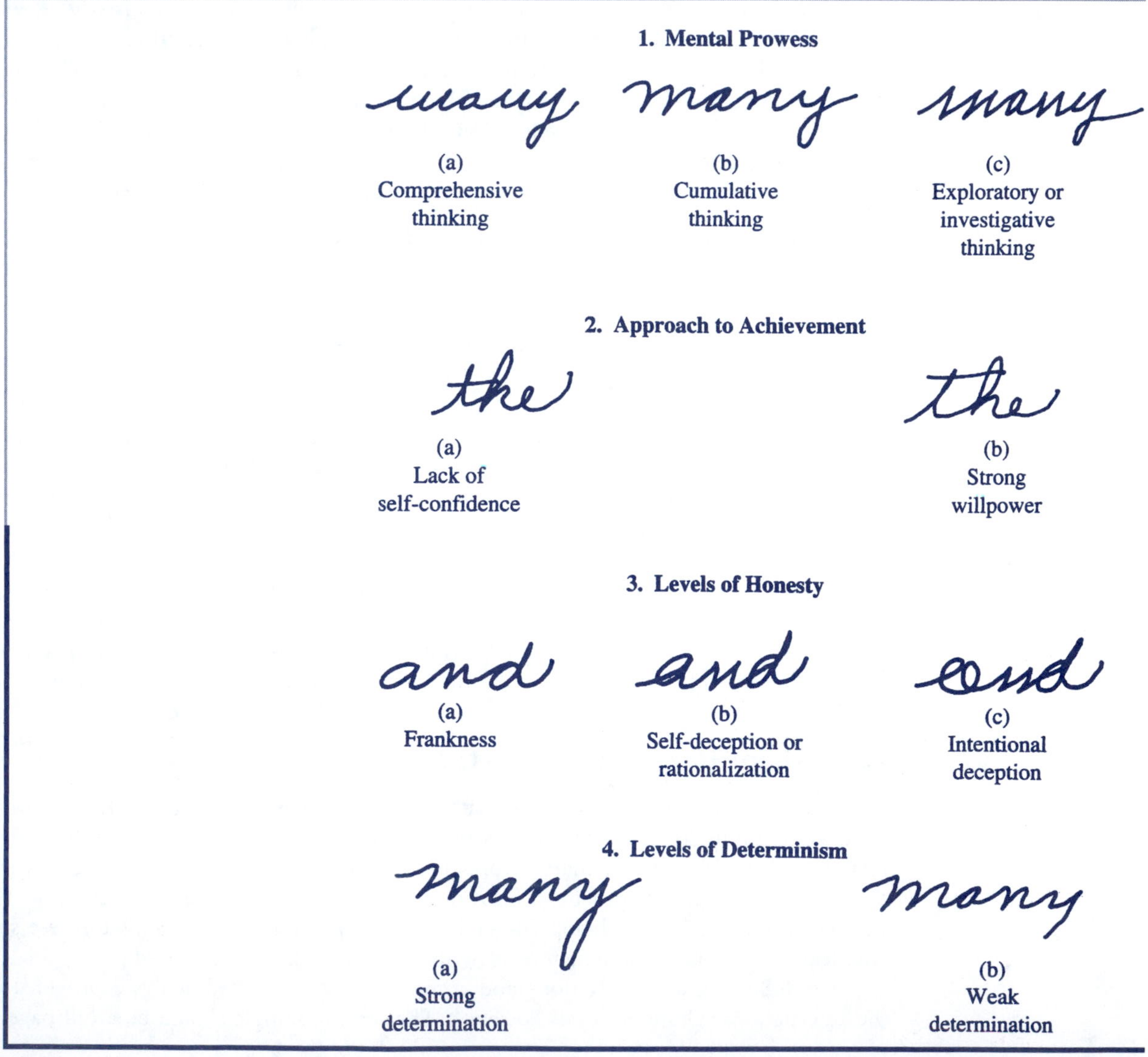

Validity of Graphology in Selection

The few studies of the validity of the technique in selection have concluded that graphoanalysis has no validity as a selection instrument. Anat Rafaeli and Richard Klimoski conducted a well-formulated study.[46] In summary, seventy real estate brokers with at least 18 months of experience in the same firm were asked to supply two samples of their handwriting: The first sample described a neutral topic (a house description), and the second was content laden (an autobiography). Job performance data were collected for each broker in the form of supervisor's ratings and dollar level of sales. Of the 20 graphologists who participated in the study, 12 had previous experience in HR selection. A group of 24 undergraduate students, untrained in graphology, served as a comparison for the graphologists and analyzed the handwriting samples.

The graphologists were allocated ten scripts each, both the neutral and content scripts from two writers and one script each from six additional writers. Each graphologist rated each script on ten personality dimensions: *social confidence, social activity, sales drive, interpersonal communication, work management skills, decision making, health/vitality, economic maturity, empathy,* and *summary.* A separate overall rating of effectiveness was also obtained. The 24 students performed the same evaluation on four or five writing samples. Finally, each real estate broker rated himself or herself on the ten personality dimensions.

The first analysis examined the reliability of the ratings of two different graphologists of the same script. The median correlation for ratings of neutral scripts was low but statistically significant, 0.54. For content-laden scripts, the median was 0.34; overall, it was 0.41. The authors of the study found moderate support for the idea that different graphologists can reliably rate writing samples. They also concluded that content did not have an effect on the graphologists' assessments. It was sometimes thought these assessments would be influenced by what was said in the sample and, therefore, were not assessments only of handwriting features.

No support was found for the validity of the graphologists' ratings. None of the correlations with supervisors' ratings, sales data, or self-ratings of the brokers were significant. The same pattern held true for the student raters. Rafaeli and Klimoski concluded that experienced graphologists were no better than untrained students at selection, and that neither group operated at better than a chance level.

Abraham Jansen reported a series of four experiments on the validity of graphology. The experiments were carried out over a period of almost ten years.[47] The first two experiments used equal numbers of raters from each of three experimental groups consisting of people who analyzed handwriting samples: graphologists, psychologists, and psychologists who had had a short course in graphology. Each rater was to evaluate the writing samples as being either *energetic* or *weak.* The criteria for comparison were scores on a complete psychological test. There were no differences among the three rating groups; each group was correct in about 60 percent of the cases. This level of accuracy was statistically significant above the chance level but was judged to have little practical import.

In the third experiment, the writers were separated into energetic and weak groups on the basis of ratings of job performance. In essence, this experiment became one of concurrent validity of graphological assessments. The accuracy rate of all three groups improved to approximately 70 percent. However, again there were no differences in accuracy among the three groups of writing-sample raters. In the fourth experiment, the three groups of judges were asked to rate writing samples on 18 different dimensions. All 18 dimensions were used for performance ratings of employees in a commercial-administrative contact job. This experiment may also be considered a concurrent validity study. The 18 dimensions fell into groups of energy variables (6), work ability variables (9), contact variables (2), and self-control. A fourth group of judges was used—a group of psychologists who made ratings based on typed versions of the handwriting samples. None of the three groups of handwriting analysts demonstrated significant correlations with the 18 performance ratings. The ratings of the fourth group, who used typed copy, were significantly more accurate on a number of the variables. In none of the four experiments was a high level of reliability attained by any of the groups of analysts. The author concluded that "graphology is a diagnostic method of highly questionable and in all probability minimal practical value."[48] Finally, a meta-analysis was done of 17 graphology studies. Results demonstrated that graphologists were not better than non-graphologists in predicting future performance based on handwritten scripts. In fact, psychologists with no knowledge of graphology outperformed graphologists on all dimensions. Moreover, the nature of the scripts was found to be a moderating variable. Content-laden scripts had a higher validity ($r = 0.16$) than neutral scripts ($r = 0.03$).[49]

Evidence to date does not seem to warrant the use of graphology as a selection instrument. In all fairness to its advocates, the studies supporting this conclusion are few and generally did not use large samples. We have commented several times in this text about the difficulty of making any judgments about validity based on studies with small samples. However, it is also true that the common use of graphology in selection does not involve the use of job analysis data. There also seems to be no linkage of traits to job performance. Instead, the graphologist apparently performs a general assessment of the character of the writer and uses that assessment as the basis for the selection evaluation. Such a procedure is obviously contrary to common professional selection strategy. It is unlikely, then, that the resulting ratings will be related to subsequent job performance.

A Case Example

In our eternal quest for truth and knowledge about selection, one author (Bob Gatewood) sent a handwriting sample to a graphologist who graduated from the program conducted by the International Graphoanalysis Society. Actually, Gatewood does this for each edition. He was able to find the same graphologist who did his analysis in 1993, 1997, 2000, and 2006, so he thinks of this present example as a test-retest–retest-retest-retest reliability exercise. Just the fact that he thought about such a thing and went to the trouble to find this person tells you more about him than the handwriting analysis does. As a result, you will shortly be able to learn about Gatewood's last twenty years of living. (Remember, we told you that this section would not be pretty!) In this most recent review by the graphologist, Gatewood received ratings on 90 personality traits and a qualitative description of his personality and some related KSAs. Gatewood didn't know he had this much personality! (Apparently the graphologist didn't think that he had much either. Each of the 90 traits was scored on a 0–10 scale with 10 being high. Gatewood received a rating of 4 or less on 50 of the scales. This explains his social life!) The following section summarizes the results of this recent analysis and Gatewood's reactions to them. Part of Gatewood's way of developing new friends is to show them this graphological (is that a word?) analysis and ask them to point out the ratings that are wrong. Perhaps this technique also explains his social life. He is puzzled as to why most people he subsequently calls do not want to go to lunch with him. Those who do always bring a friend and the two of them sit at the table and frequently elbow each other in the ribs, wink, and nod their heads a lot. They look as though they are enjoying Gatewood's company because they are laughing, but he wonders why they never call.

Reliability.   We provide both semi-quantitative and judgmental summaries. The semi-quantitative summary is based upon the four analyses done in 1997, 2000, 2006, and 2010. Each used the same Big Twelve and 90 questions. Gatewood's average scores on these 12 scales are presented in Table 14.3. Given that each of the items uses a 10-point scale and

TABLE 14.3	Gatewood's Scores on the Big Twelve			
Trait	**1997**	**2000**	**2006**	**2010**
Reliability	8.17	7.50	7.30	6.80
Integrity	7.37	7.25	7.05	6.50
Conscientiousness	7.30	6.63	7.58	6.50
Organizational Skills	7.00	6.40	7.00	5.40
Confidence	6.20	6.70	6.50	5.80
Energy	4.50	5.30	4.40	3.40
Adaptability	3.32	3.67	3.56	4.00
Mental Processes	3.20	3.00	3.40	2.60
Mental Attributes	2.40	2.80	2.40	2.00
Fears	0.67	0.89	0.67	1.40
Resistance	1.00	1.30	1.00	1.20
Escape (retreating to protect the ego)	0.45	1.27	1.73	1.60

assuming a standard deviation of 1.0 (for no reason), it seems that the graphologist has been pretty consistent in rating Gatewood. That becomes more apparent when a comparison is made of the 90-item differences in ratings between the 2006 and 2010 analyses. Of these 90 items, the graphologist rated 30 of them exactly the same, due partially to the fact that Gatewood scored 0 on a lot of them both times. In addition, the graphologist rated 33 other items with a score difference of 1 between the two time periods, and 14 other items with a score difference of 2. Sticking with our assumed standard deviation of 1.0, about 86 percent of the traits were rated within two units of our made-up standard deviation. That is impressive. Reliability in actual behavior rings true with Gatewood also. It has been said (by an unnamed but reliable source) that he always forgets to make lists, never knows where anything is, and doesn't pay attention to what he has been told. He is self-aware that he doesn't remember names and forgets simple geographic directions within 30 seconds. The overwhelming evidence is that he is reliable in his behavior and so is the graphologist in her ratings of him.

Validity.   This is a tougher call because of the lack of definite criteria against which to judge Gatewood's scores and the graphologist's comments. The difficulty in assessing validity is compounded when one notices the general decline in eight of the twelve scale scores over time. Gatewood is puzzled as to whether or not this is a function of slowly eroding reliability of measurement or the slow erosion of himself. He got almost all of his friends (three) to take a look at these ratings and give him their collective opinions. First these friends grouped the four scales that have either stayed consistent or risen: adaptability, fears, resistance, and escapes. They thought for awhile and concluded that the trend is valid. Over the last 13 years, Gatewood has clearly become more adaptable (or less principled, depending on how one views the behavior), escapes from reality for longer periods of time, resists deadlines about the same as before, and is becoming a bit more resistant to suggestions. They then looked at the scale scores that have shown decline: reliability, integrity, conscientiousness, organizational skills, confidence, energy, mental processes, and mental attributes. After discussing these, they all started to cry (which puzzled Gatewood). After they regained their composure, they told him that essentially they agreed with these ratings also and thought they were valid. His reliability and integrity are clearly near the bottom of any social norms; these friends, as responsible individuals, have learned to do the opposite of what Gatewood decides to do in any moral choice. The same is true of his conscientiousness, organizational skills, and energy. He never got very much done early in life and now it is next to nothing. Because nothing is moving as far as they can tell, they sometimes sneak a small mirror in front of his face to see if he is still there. It was the two mental scales that really made them feel concerned. Although he never did score high on any of the previous years' mental ability scores, they remembered that he could come up with the correct answer at least at a random chance level. Now he has gone below that. They think that the only times he is correct now are a function of Type 1 or Type 2 errors with a large alpha level. They worry about his future. They disagreed only with the confidence scale rating. Unfortunately, Gatewood seems to have become more confident in his judgments and opinions even as his mental processes have deteriorated and he has demonstrated less integrity. As a result, they think that perhaps he could run for a political office and fit in very well with others—maybe even be a star. That made them feel a lot better about his future and left them with an idea for starting a PAC with the slogan … "It's the dollars, stupid!" They didn't explain the slogan to Gatewood; he is puzzled, not knowing whether this is a reference to historical events or a serious political slogan. The only objection Gatewood has with his friends' judgments regarding the scores on the mental ability scales is that he does have a Ph.D. and that his parents always told him that he was smart. However, because his highest scores over the 13 years have only been in the low 3s, he doesn't push the objection too far.

Another look at validity is shown in Table 14.4 in which Gatewood comments on the comments of the graphologist. As you can see, he doesn't always agree with her

---

TABLE 14.4 The Graphologist's and Gatewood's Comments

Graphologist	Gatewood
1. A weakness in your determination is evident. You may not carry through on your projects in the face of obstacles. Projects aren't always finished.	Must have talked with my wife, editor, dean, coauthors, tax accountant ….. most any one I *k*now.
2. You possess the ability to create pictures in your mind about unseen things.	Now I know why girls in high school slapped me all the time.
3. There is a tendency to think that you have been insulted or offended.	You think you're smart, don't you!! This is only when people, disagree with me. I am fine when they agree. How come you don't mention that????
4. Your mind is active and you investigate and analyze all matters.	Hmm! Think this has to do with not getting anything done? I will consider this later.
5. There are times when you can be yielding and gullible to what others wish and not use common sense.	She's talking about those college girls and the things they made me do – and they didn't respect me in the morning either.
6. You are really afraid that you will be taken advantage of.	What do you expect after what the college girls made me do???
7. You are inclined to express disapproving judgments in a sarcastic manner.	Me!! All she has to do is read this table and she will know that she is wrong.
8. When a decision needs to be made, you rely on yourself for your conclusions.	Well, usually everyone else is finished and they won't work with me anyway. They say I procrastinate too much. Can you believe that?
9. Vanity is evident. You feel basically insecure and unappreciated.	Well in defense of my many friends, it is hard to keep track of all of my accomplishments. But you would think that they could keep up with the four or five big ones that I do every day!! Could you say something to them?

assessments. He thinks that he should know better than she does because he has lived with himself for most of his life.

REFERENCES

1. Philip Ash, "Honesty Test Scores, Biographical Data, and Delinquency Indicators," paper presented at the 96th Annual Convention of the American Psychological Association, Atlanta, Georgia.

2. James C. Wimbush and Dan R. Dalton, "Base Rate for Employee Theft: Covergence of Multiple Methods," *Journal of Applied Psychology* 82 (1997): 756–763.

3. Employee Polygraph Protection Act of 1988, Public Law 100–347, 29 USC 2001.

4. David Z. Lykken, "Psychology and the Lie Detector Industry," *American Psychologist* 29 (1974): 725–739.

5. Ibid.

6. Gershon Ben-Shakhar and Karmela Dolev, "Psychophysical Detection through Guilty Knowledge Technique: Effect of Mental Countermeasures," *Journal of Applied Psychology* 81 (1996): 273–281.

7. Paul Sackett, Laura Burris, and Christine Callahan, "Integrity Testing for Personnel Selection: An Update," *Personnel Psychology* 42 (1989): 491–529.

8. William Terris and John Jones, "Psychological Factors Related to Employees' Theft in the Convenience Store Industry," *Psychological Reports* 51 (1982): 1219–1238.

9. Bureau of National Affairs, *Employee Testing: The Complete Resource Guide* (Washington, DC: Bureau of National Affairs, 1988).

10. Joyce Hogan and Robert Hogan, "How to Measure Employee Reliability," *Journal of Applied Psychology* 74 (1989): 273–279.

11. Nathan Luther, "Integrity Testing and Job Performance within High-Performance Work Teams: A Short Note," *Journal of Business and Psychology* 15 (2000): 19–25.

12. Christopher M. Berry, Paul R. Sackett, and Shelly Wieman, "A Review of Recent Developments in Integrity Test Research," *Personnel Psychology* 60 (2007): 271–301.

13. Deniz S. Ones, Chockalingam Viswesvaran, and Frank L. Schmidt, "Comprehensive Meta-Analysis of Integrity Test Validities: Findings and Implications for Personnel Selection and Theories of Job Performance," *Journal of Applied Psychology Monograph* 78 (1993): 679–703. See also Deniz S. Ones, Chockalingam Viswesvaran, and Frank L. Schmidt, "Group Differences on Overt Integrity Tests and Related Personality Variables: Implications for Adverse Impact and Test Construction," *Conference of Society for Industrial and Organizational Psychology* (1996); and Deniz Ones, Frank L. Schmidt, and Chockalingam Viswesvaran, "Integrity and Ability: Implications for Incremental Validity and Adverse Impact," *Conference of Society for Industrial and Organizational Psychology* (1993).

14. Paul R. Sackett and C. J. Devore, "Counterproductive Behaviors at Work," in N. Anderson, Deniz S. Ones, HK Sinangil, and Chocklingam Viswesvaran, *Handbook of Industrial Work and Organizational Psychology*, London Sage 1 (2002): 145–164. See also Christopher M. Berry, and Paul R. Sackett, "Interpersonal Deviance, Organizational Deviance, and Their Common Correlates," *Journal of Applied Psychology* 92 (2007): 410–424.

15. Berry, Sackett, and Wiemann, "A Review of Recent Developments in Integrity Test Research."

16. Paul R. Sackett and James E. Wanek, "New Developments in the Use of Measures of Honesty, Integrity, Conscientiousness, Dependability, Trustworthiness, and Reliability for Personnel Selection," *Personnel Psychology* 49 (1996): 787–829.

17. Bernd Marcus, Kibeom Lee, and Michael C. Ashton, "Personality Dimensions Explaining Relationships between Integrity Tests and Counterproductive Behavior, Big Five, or One in Addition," *Personnel Psychology* 60 (2007): 1–34.

18. Sackett and Wanek, "New Developments in the Use of Measures of Honesty, Integrity, Conscientiousness, Dependability, Trustworthiness, and Reliability for Personnel Selection."

19. Ibid.

20. James E. Wanek, Paul R. Sackett, and Deniz S. Ones, "Toward an Understanding of Integrity Test Similarities and Differences: An Item-Level Analysis of Seven Tests," *Personnel Psychology* 56 (2003): 873–894. See also Bernd Marcus, Stefan Hoft, and Michaela Riediger, "Integrity Tests and the Five-Factor Model of Personality: A Review and Empirical Tests of Two Alternative Positions," *International Journal of Selection and Assessment* 14 (2006): 113–130.

21. Sackett and Wanek, "New Developments in the Use of Measures of Honesty, Integrity, Conscientiousness, Dependability, Trustworthiness, and Reliability for Personnel Selection."

22. Deniz S. Ones, Chockalingam Viswesvaran, and Frank L. Schmidt, "Persoality and Absenteeism: A Meta-Analysis of Integrity Tests," *European Journal of Personality* 17 (2003): 519–538.

23. Ones, Viswesvaran, and Schmidt, "Comprehensive Meta-Analysis of Integrity Test Validities: Findings and Implications for Personnel Selection and Theories of Job Performance."

24. Deniz S. Ones and Chockalingam Viswesvaran. "A Research Note on the Incremental Validity of Job Knowledge and Tests for Predicting Maximal Performance," *Human Performance* 20 (2007): 293–303.

25. Deniz S. Ones, Chockalingam Viswesvaran, and Frank L. Schmidt, "Integrity Tests Predict Substance Abuse and Aggressive Behaviors at Work," *American Psychological Association Meeting*, 1993.

26. Sackett and Wanek, "New Developments in the Use of Measures of Honesty, Integrity, Conscientiousness, Dependability, Trustworthiness, and Reliability for Personnel Selection."

27. Ibid.

28. Ones, Viswesvaran, and Schmidt, "Comprehensive Meta-Analysis of Integrity Test Validities: Findings and Implications for Personnel Selection and Theories of Job Performance."

29. Michael R. Cunningham, Dennis T. Wong, and Anita P. Barbee, "Self-Presentation Dynamics on Overt Integrity Tests: Experimental Studies of the Reid Report," *Journal of Applied Psychology* 79 (1994): 643–658.

30. Deniz S. Ones and Chockalingam Viswesvaran, "Gender, age, and race differences on overt integrity tests: Results across four large-scale job applicant data sets," *Journal of Applied Psychology* 83 (1998a): 35–42.

31. Berry, Sackett, and Wiemann, "A Review of Recent Developments in Integrity Test Research." See also Thomas E. Becker, "Information Exchange Article Development and Validation of a Situational Judgment Test of Employee Integrity," *International Journal of Selection and Assessment* 13 (2005): 225–232.

32. Matthew D. Paronto, Donald M. Truxillo, Talya N. Bauer, and Michael C. Leo, "Drug Testing, Drug Treatment, and Marijuana Use: A Fairness Perspective," *Journal of Applied Psychology* 87 (2002): 1159–1166.

33. Michael R. Frone, "Prevalence and Distribution of Illicit Drug Use in the Workforce and in the Workplace: Findings and Implications from a U.S. National Survey," *Journal of Applied Psychology* 91 (2006): 856–869.

34. Ibid.

35. *National Treasury Employees Union v. Von Raab*, 649 F. Supp 380 (1986).

36. Deborah F. Crown and Joseph G. Rosse, "A Critical Review of Assumptions Underlying Drug Testing," in *Applying Psychology in Business: The Manager's Handbook*, ed. Douglas W. Bray, John W. Jones, and Brian D. Steffy (Lexington, MA: Lexington Books, 1991).

37. Thomas Geidt, "Drug and Alcohol Abuse in the Work Place: Balancing Employer and Employee Rights," *Employer Relations Law Journal* 11 (1985): 181–205.

38. Dianna Stone and Debra Kotch, "Individuals' Attitudes toward Organizational Drug Testing Policies and Practices," *Journal of Applied Psychology* 74 (1989): 518–521.

39. Bennett J. Tepper, "Investigation of General and Program-Specific Attitudes toward Corporate Drug-Testing Policies," *Journal of Applied Psychology* 79 (1994): 392–401.

40. Kevin Murphy, George Thornton, and Kristin Prue, "Influence of Job Characteristics on the Acceptability of Employee Drug Testing," *Journal of Applied Psychology* 76 (1991): 447–453.

41. David A. Sujak, "The Effects of Drug-Testing Program Characteristics on Applicants' Attitudes toward Potential Employment," *Journal of Psychology* 129 (1995): 401–416.

42. Joseph G. Rosse, Richard C. Ringer, and Janice L. Miller, "Personality and Drug Testing: An Exploration of the Perceived Fairness of Alternatives to Urinalysis," *Journal of Business and Psychology* 10 (1996): 459–475.

43. Joseph G. Rosse, Janice L. Miller, and Richard C. Ringer, "The Deterrent Value of Drug and Integrity Testing," *Journal of Business and Psychology* 10 (1996): 477–485.

44. Kristine M. Kuhn and Marsha L. Kristine, "Understanding Applicant Reactions to Credit Checks: Uncertainty, Information Effects and Individual Differences," *International Journal of Selection & Assessment* 16 (2008): 307–320.

45. James C. Crumbaugh, "Graphoanalytic Cues," *Encyclopedia of Clinical Assessment*, vol. 2 (San Francisco, CA: Bass, 1980), 919–929.

46. Anat Rafaeli and Richard Klimoski, "Predicting Sales Success through Handwriting Analysis: An Evaluation of the Effects of Training and Handwriting Sample Content," *Journal of Applied Psychology* 68 (1983): 212–217.

47. Abraham Jansen, *Validation of Graphological Judgments: An Experimental Study* (The Hague, Netherlands: Mouton, 1973).

48. Ibid., 126.

49. Efrat Neter and Gershon Ben-Shakhar, "The Predictive Validity of Graphological Inferences: A Meta-Analytic," *Personality and Individual Differences* 10 (1989): 737–745.

CRITERIA MEASURES

As we have stated more times in this book than any of us would wish to count, the ultimate test of a selection program is how well those selected perform on the job. Just as selection instruments should be properly constructed to obtain the most useful information about applicants, job performance measures should be carefully developed to obtain accurate data. Otherwise, the adequacy of the selection program may be incorrectly evaluated and/or unfairly criticized. That is, the selection program itself could be suitable, but the data used to evaluate the job performance of those selected could be flawed; inevitably, any conclusions about the program would be inappropriate. This chapter has the following objectives:

- To describe the various types of job performance measures

- To discuss the appropriate use of each type of measure

- To detail the important characteristics of each measure

Measures of Job Performance

Well, this is it. We can see the proverbial light at the end of the tunnel, the cows have left the barn, and the rolling stone has gathered moss (or whatever). Our last remaining topic is job performance measures.

In selection, the major purpose of job performance measures is to serve as criteria measures in validation studies. We will discuss which job performance measures can be used in validation and their appropriate characteristics. We will not discuss these measures as management tools for communicating to employees and improving work performance.

In previous chapters, we discussed the other major parts of validation work: (a) the statistical procedures necessary for conducting validity studies (Chapter 5), (b) methods for identifying important job tasks and KSAs (Chapters 7), and (c) methods for developing predictor measures (Chapters 9 through 14). In this chapter we turn our attention to another part of validation, the criteria measures of job performance. There are numerous types of such measures; for example, a supervisor's rating or the number of goods produced by individual workers. Some people (incorrectly) use the term *criterion* to mean the cutoff score on selection tests. That term should be *selection standard* or *cutoff*. We aren't talking about selection measures in this chapter at all—only job performance measures.

The adequacy of the criterion measure is as important to a validation study and to the selection program as is the adequacy of the predictor measure. The criterion measure defines what is meant by job performance. High scores on this measure define what is meant by "successful" job performance. The main purpose of the selection program is to predict which applicants will be successful on the job and thus score high on the criterion measure once the workers are employed by the organization. As we discuss in this chapter, many different types of criteria measures have been used in validity studies. It is up to the selection specialist to decide which of these to use. The importance of this decision should be obvious. In one case, if the criterion measure chosen for the validation study is inappropriate, then the selection program may be inappropriate also. That is, the selection program will be constructed in such a way that it will select applicants who will perform well on an inappropriate measure of job success. In another case, the selection program may be correctly built but the measure of job performance is changed by the organization and the selection program is inadequate because the new measure of success was not included in its design.

As is the case with the development of predictors, the information obtained from the job analysis should serve as the basis for the development of the appropriate criterion measure. For example, using the task approach for job analysis, worker performance on those tasks that are rated as highly important or as requiring the most time to complete should be measured by the criterion. The same principle applies when one of the standardized questionnaire approaches is used; those job characteristics that are rated as important should be covered by the criterion measure. In this chapter we present several topics essential to the development of an appropriate criterion: the strengths and limitations of the major types of job performance measures, the essential characteristics of any measure that is used, and the equal employment opportunity (EEO) implications for these measures.

TYPES OF JOB PERFORMANCE MEASURES

Several different types of job performance measures can be used singly or in combination as a criterion measure. We will present an overview of each of these major types and discuss its use in selection. For a more detailed treatment of each type, books such as these are excellent sources: *The Measurement of Work Performance Methods, Theory, and Application* by Frank Landy and James Farr; *Understanding Performance Appraisal: Social, Organizational, and Goal-Based Perspectives* by Kevin Murphy and Jeanette Cleveland; and *Performance Management, Concepts, Skills, and Exercises* by Robert L. Cardy.[1]

One way of presenting the various types of job performance measures is to group them into the following four categories according to the nature of the data gathered:

1. Production data—quality and/or quantity of output

2. HR personnel—absenteeism, turnover, and related variables

3. Training proficiency—a specially developed test or simulation of training information or activities developed in training

4. Judgmental data—opinions (usually supervisors') of subordinates' performance

Each of these four categories may be further subdivided, as we see in the following discussion.

Production Data

Production data consists of the results of work. The data comprise things that can be counted, seen, and compared directly from one worker to another. Other terms that have been used to describe these data are *output, objective,* and *nonjudgmental performance measures.* Such measures are usually based on the specific nature of the job tasks; quite different measures have been used for the same job title. The variety of measures that can be used is actually so great that it is not possible to summarize them in any representative manner. Instead, Table 15.1 contains a list of job titles and some of the various production criteria measures that have been used for each title. It is apparent from the table that data about both quantity and quality of production have been used. Quantity is usually expressed as the number of units produced within a specified time period. Quality is the goodness of the product; it may be indirectly measured by the number of defects, errors, or mistakes identified either per number of units or per unit of time (for example, one working day).

Many consider the use of production data the most desirable type of measure for a number of reasons. First, such data are often easy to gather because they are collected routinely for business operations such as production planning and budgeting. The importance of such measures is thought to be obvious and easily understood. Production

TABLE 15.1	Examples of Production Criteria Measures for Various Jobs	
	PRODUCTION MEASURE	
Job Title	**Quantity**	**Quality**
University faculty member	Number of student credit hours taught	Rating by students as to amount learned in course
Skilled machine operator	Number of units produced per week Weight of output per week	Number of defects Weight of scrap
Salesperson	Dollar volume of sales Number of orders	Number of customer complaints Number of returns
Manager	Profit of unit	Number of unit returns to his or her department because of defects

data are the direct result of job actions. They are the objectives of the work process. Finally, these data are thought to be unchallengeable and easily accepted by workers. Production output can be seen and counted; therefore, no argument can be made about its measurement. Our opinion is that such enthusiasm about production data serving as criteria measures is overstated. None of these four major categories of work measurement data is without limitation. Each is appropriate in some circumstances and inappropriate in others. To illustrate this point, we will discuss some of the limitations inherent in the use of production data.

Consider first the argument about the ease of gathering data through commonly used business operations. Frequently, such operations are concerned with the records of total work units rather than of individuals. For example, the budgeting operation usually compares a departmental unit's actual production and cost to a prior projection of these variables. Production planning is frequently concerned with the optimum movement of goods through various stages of the manufacturing process. In neither of these cases is attention paid to the individual worker, especially if he or she frequently moves to different work stations. However, data on individuals are essential for validation. As we know, a validity coefficient correlates individual workers' selection test scores with the same individuals' performance scores. Therefore, if accurate *individual* worker data cannot be gathered, then validation is difficult to carry out and interpret.

The assumption that production data are countable, and, therefore, indisputable, is also tenuous. As Table 15.1 indicates, numerous measures are used for sales performance. All seem to be straightforward measures that would be acceptable to those concerned. However, the literature and the practice of sales management contradict such a notion. The consensus in sales work is that the most often used measure of sales performance, dollar sales volume, is closely related to the characteristics of the territory that is worked. Such items as population, store density, socioeconomic status of customers, number of competitors, and amount of advertising are all relevant characteristics.

Various modifications of dollar sales volume have been suggested to control for these differences in territory. One of the most popular is to calculate monthly sales as a percentage of a quota for the territory.[2] Quotas are usually set by the sales manager. However, this assumes that the judgment of the sales manager is accurate and acceptable to all. Another adjustment is to divide sales volume by years that the salesperson has been in the territory.[3] The rationale is that as a salesperson learns the territory, sales should increase rather than merely stay level. This simplified judgment can obviously be inaccurate.

Similar issues have been raised regarding the use of production data that relate to managers. Several studies, especially those of assessment centers, have used rate or level of promotion or salary increase as job performance measures. The assumption is that high performance by a manager will result in promotion and salary increases. Such an assumption is probably not completely accurate, because labor market availability, job tenure, and area of specialization are all known to affect compensation and promotion.

In summary, production measures have frequently been used in validation studies and are desirable mainly because of their direct relationship to job activities. However, these measures are often limited and often must be corrected. Most correction factors require that a manager make a judgment about how to correct the raw data, and these judgments can vary considerably in their effects on performance measurement. There-fore, production data must be reviewed carefully to determine its accuracy as a measure of employee work performance.

HR Personnel Data

Turnover, grievances, accidents, and promotions are variables that have been used in the second type of performance data, HR personnel data. These variables are usually col-lected as part of other HR data files, almost always on an individual basis, and they re-flect important aspects of work behavior. The data for these variables are countable and seemingly objective.

However, some limitations must be considered when using these measures. The first is limited variance in the scores of employees on these measures. That is, it is common for a majority of any given group of workers to have no accidents or grievances and to remain with the company (no turnover). This is especially true if the time period inves-tigated is relatively brief. Even promotions, for many groups of workers, can be very lim-ited. As we discussed in Chapter 5, limited variance will lower the magnitude of the validity coefficient. The second limitation, which we discuss in the following paragraphs, is the different measures that can be used for each of these variables. The problem is that the different measures of absenteeism, for example, do not yield identical data for a group of workers. Therefore, the selection specialist must clearly evaluate the concept that is to be measured as well as the most appropriate method for doing it.

Absenteeism. The most frequently used measures of absenteeism have been the following:

- Number of separate instances

- Total number of days absent

- Number of short absences (one or two days)

- Long weekends (occurrence of a one-day absence on a Monday or Friday)[4]

A major concern regarding these measures has been the distinction between volun-tary and involuntary absences. Involuntary absences are usually thought of as those due to severe illness, jury duty, union activities, death in the immediate family, and accidents. Voluntary absences make up almost all of the other absences. Presumably the distinction is made to differentiate between absences workers have control over and others that they do not have control over. A high level of absenteeism that a worker should be able to control indicates a conscious restriction of output. Other kinds of absences, while not desirable, may only reflect unfortunate circumstances that affect a worker.

We can see how this distinction is reflected in the four measures just identified. For example, counting the number of short absences or the number of Mondays or Fridays missed is clearly an attempt to measure voluntary absences. The number of separate instances of absenteeism, logically, reflects the same idea. Presumably, lower-performing workers are absent more times than their higher-performing counterparts. Therefore, only the frequency of instances is recorded, which is now the most commonly used measure of absenteeism. The number of days missed on each occasion is irrelevant in this measure, as is the reason for the absence. The measure of the total number of days absent makes a different assumption. Time off is undesirable for whatever reason. Moreover, if one assumes that illness is evenly distributed in the population of workers, much of the difference among individuals is a function of voluntary absences.

Even without spending a great deal of effort in examining these various assumptions, it is obvious that each categorizes and counts absences differently. Based on the same set of employee data records, it is possible to construct different sets of absenteeism criteria measures by using each of the four absence measures mentioned previously. Another problem in using any of the four absence measures is the length of time over which the data are collected. In most organizations, absenteeism is controlled within specified limits. Most employees realize that flagrant or repeated absenteeism, especially within a short time period, would prompt a reaction from the organization. Therefore, it has tentatively been concluded that, to be useful, absenteeism data should be accumulated over at least one year.[5]

Another difficulty in using absenteeism data as a criterion is that the distribution of scores on this variable limits its use in correlational analysis. Because of the low base rate of absences in organizations, measures of absenteeism are almost never normally distributed.[6] This lack of a normal distribution severely affects correlations between absenteeism and other variables. Even statistically transformed measures of absenteeism are questionable in linear regression models because of the violation of normally distributed data. In general, correlations between absences and other variables are lowered due to this violation.[7]

Although these problems have been known for several years, the vast majority of research on absenteeism has used linear regression or product-moment correlations. Recently, however, procedures known as *event history analyses* have been proposed as a viable solution to the non-normality problem.[8] These procedures allow many types of predictors to be examined, including individual-level, group-level, and temporal characteristics. As a result of using such procedures, a supervisor may be able to predict whether or not every one of her employees will attend work on the following Monday; whether there will be enough people to fill work stations or assembly lines. (We think that event history analysis is an excellent topic to bring up when you want to make new friends. You will certainly astound them!)

Turnover. This is a measure of permanent separation from the organization. We have mentioned that turnover is a frequently used criterion in validation studies of weighted application blanks. In general, its use in selection is similar to the use of absenteeism data. A primary question is how to separate turnover data into voluntary/involuntary categories. *Voluntary* usually means resignation despite the opportunity for continued employment; *involuntary* means termination by the organization for any of several reasons.

Measures of turnover can confound the two types of turnover. For example, if the company has dismissed employees because of a violation of company rules, these terminations are clearly involuntary. However, it is not always clear how to classify such cases of separation. Some workers are allowed to resign rather than be terminated.

These resignations may look like incidents of voluntary turnover, even though they are not. Similarly, at the perceived threat of dismissal, some employees seek other jobs and resign from the company. These, too, appear to be voluntary, yet this behavior was prompted by the organization's actions and may be reactions to workers' perceptions of the threat of dismissal.

With absenteeism as a criterion, measurement and statistical issues surrounding turnover must be addressed. Voluntary turnover measures represent two different theoretical constructs. One is employee tenure (the continuous variable of length of time a worker stays with an organization), and the other is turnover (a dichotomous variable of stay/quit behavior).[9] A selection specialist must decide which construct he wishes to measure.

Grievances. A grievance is an employee's complaint against some aspect of management's behavior. Grievances have been used occasionally as criteria measures for supervisory and management selection. Theoretically, a large number of grievances would indicate poor treatment of subordinates or inferior management decision making. Grievance systems almost always exist as part of a union-management contract. In these agreements, the steps and procedures for filing a grievance are outlined.

When grievances are used as job performance measures, the assumption must be made that the tendency to file a grievance is equal among all workers, and that the working conditions related to grievances are also equal for all workers. In reality, neither assumption is likely to be true. For example, working conditions can vary dramatically within the same organization. Safety hazards, amount of overtime, job pressure, and ambiguity of task objectives are just a few conditions that could be correlated with grievances. Individuals can differ in their willingness to file grievances and engage in open confrontation. In fact, one study found that the number of grievances is at least as much a function of the union steward's personality as it is an indication of management performance.[10] If this measure is used, it is best to limit the use of grievances to a constant time period during a supervisor's career, job, or assignment to a new work group. For example, the first year may be used. Using a calendar year, in which the manager participants in the validity study are at different points in their work experience, could introduce error into the measure.

Accidents. Accidents are usually measured either in terms of injury to the worker or damage to the equipment being used (car, truck, and so on). In either case, some threshold of damage must be exceeded before the incident is classified as an accident. For personal injury, usually a medical determination of damage that prevents working on the job for some period of time (for example, one day) is required. In the case of equipment damage, frequently some dollar amount of repair must be exceeded before the incident is recorded. The assumption is made that the worker's carelessness precipitated the accident.

Even more than in the use of other HR data, such assumptions are probably not valid. Jobs differ in inherent hazards, equipment differs in its operating condition, and employees differ in the amount of safety training they have received. No easy way can be found to remove these factors from accident rates. The only way to overcome them is to equalize their occurrence within the sample. For example, a group of long-distance truck drivers may be measured on accidents if they receive a standardized training program, drive approximately the same schedules and locations, and operate equally maintained trucks. If such conditions cannot be met, accident rates are questionable as criteria measures. This is underscored by the studies that have failed to find accident proneness a stable worker characteristic and have concluded that a large proportion of accidents are situationally determined.

Promotions. This is a measure of career progress, based on the number of vertical job changes that an individual has experienced as a worker. The term *vertical* means the job change represents a move upward in the organization that results in increased responsibility and authority. The underlying assumption in the use of such a measure as a criterion is that high performance is a prerequisite for promotion. Those individuals who receive more promotions, therefore, have performed better than those individuals with fewer promotions. This measure is most commonly used in validation studies involving managers and professionals, frequently with an assessment center as the predictor. Conceptually, it is feasible to use this measure for lower-level jobs also. However, in actual practice many lower-level jobs have limited career ladders and, therefore, few promotions. Even in these situations, job tenure, not performance, is often the most important factor used to make the promotion decision.

Three possible limitations in the use of promotions should be considered before those data are used. The first is the number of factors besides performance that may affect promotion opportunities. This becomes especially important if the factors differentially affect the employees in the validation study. For example, divisions within an organization grow at different rates. Presumably, managers in high-growth divisions have a much greater chance for promotion than do those with comparable performance in low-growth divisions. The same situation can occur between functional areas within a division; that is, marketing is being enlarged while production remains the same. In such instances, promotion is not just a measure of performance; it includes factors not directly influenced by the individual and therefore it is less useful as a criterion measure.

The second consideration is the difficulty in identifying vertical job changes from HR records. Obviously, not all job changes are promotions. The term *lateral* is commonly applied to those job changes that result in no change in responsibility and authority but rather in a different set of tasks. In many instances, it is difficult to determine accurately whether a given job change is lateral or vertical. In organizations with well-known career paths, the determination is usually straightforward. Even so, organizations occasionally obscure the true details of lateral changes to avoid embarrassing the individual involved. In new or rapidly expanding organizations, the difference between the two types of change is often not apparent or not conceptually appropriate. The third issue is that some promotions are declined because of dual-career implications, children's needs, or other personal issues. If this occurs very often, the data about promotions may be contaminated by factors unrelated to performance.

Training Proficiency

Why Measure Training Proficiency? A seldom used but very desirable criterion measure is training proficiency, that is, a measure of employee performance immediately following the completion of a training program. As we pointed out in our discussion of ability tests in Chapter 11, validity generalization studies found that training proficiency demonstrated higher validities than the measures of job performance.[11] The Equal Employment Opportunity Commission (EEOC) *Uniform Guidelines* explicitly state that training proficiency is legally permissible as a criterion measure. Despite these points, the reported use of this variable in validation studies has been infrequent.

There are strong arguments for the use of training measures as criteria. Essentially, these arguments point out the increased control that the selection specialist has in the measurement process. This control should increase reliability and, in turn, increase the magnitude of the validity coefficient.

The first source of control is the amount of standardization possible. A common sequence is using training measures as criteria is to select the employees, place them in a training program, and—at the end of training but before job assignment— administer some measures of mastery of training. In such a sequence, it is possible to design a formal training program that is consistent for all employees, even if they are at different physical locations. Companies commonly develop instruction booklets, films, and exercises that are sent to several cities or placed on a website. In addition, the training instructors can be given the same specific instructional techniques. Perhaps most important, standardized measures of proficiency can be developed and used. All of these factors would reduce measurement errors that lower validity coefficients.

A second source of control is that validity coefficients between predictors and training measures are oftentimes more direct indicators of the relationship between knowledge, skills, and abilities (KSAs) and work level than are validity coefficients using other criteria measures. To explain this, let us start with a point we made in Chapter 1. In discussing the inherent limitations in developing and evaluating selection programs, we stated that the adequacy of selection is frequently judged by the level of actual job performance achieved. However, the management literature is filled with organizational factors that affect work performance—for example, leadership, specificity of objectives, amount of training, and so on. This means that performance levels could possibly be influenced by these other factors, even though the selection program itself is basically sound. In measurement terms, these factors could artificially lower the validity coefficient between selection devices and job performance measures. This is, in fact, the finding of the studies that we presented in Chapter 11. Validity coefficients using job performance as criteria measures were lower, often greatly lower, than coefficients using training proficiency. One explanation of this difference is that other organizational factors have less opportunity to operate when training proficiency is used, because of the brief time that has elapsed. The training proficiency measure, therefore, is influenced more by the workers' KSAs and less by the organizational factors. This is clearly a desirable state of affairs for attempts to validate selection programs.

Measures.   Three basic measures can be used to quantify training proficiency. All assume that the training program is representative of the job itself. This may seem to be a superfluous statement. However, it is common to find training programs that are really orientation sessions covering general company issues, not job activities; others are intended to teach the main tasks of the job but are improperly designed to do so. The first of these three measures is judgments made by the training instructor about the trainees. Judgments could be made about how well individuals have mastered either the whole training program or parts of it. This method is prone to the common drawbacks of decision making. These drawbacks and appropriate corrections are discussed later.

The second measure uses scores on a paper-and-pencil test. To do this correctly, it's important to follow basic test construction principles in the development of the test. We do not elaborate on these principles, but the following issues are important. There should be a match between the extent of topic coverage in training and the number of questions asked about this topic on the test. It would make little sense, for example, to ask only 5 of 50 questions about how to operate a wine processing machine if one-half of the training program was devoted to this topic. Standardized administration and scoring procedures must be developed and utilized in order to reduce errors in the measurement process.

The third measurement method uses scores on a work sample test, exactly the same kind of device we described in Chapter 13. This may be confusing, because in that chapter we presented work sample tests as predictors. Now we introduce them as criteria measures. Remember the central characteristic of a work sample test is to replicate the major tasks of the job. However, work sample tests cannot be used as a predictor in all selection situations, especially if the assumption cannot be made that the applicants already possess the KSAs necessary to complete the task. Work sample tests do not have similar restrictions when they are used as training proficiency measures. The training program is designed to be representative of the job activities. Work sample tests are similarly designed; each individual in the training program will be exposed to everything in the work sample test. It should be appropriate as a measure of adequacy of training. Those who learned well will do well on the work sample. Those who did not learn well will do poorly.

We will describe two selection programs validated at AT&T that used work sample tests in this fashion.[12] One selection program for telephone operators used 10 specially developed ability tests as predictors. The criterion, administered upon the completion of a formal training program, was a one-hour job simulation. In this simulation, trainers acting as customers initiated calls at a steady pace in the same way for each operator-trainee. Each operator activity that was to be performed for each call was listed on the evaluation form. Supervisors directly observed and assessed the effectiveness of trainees in processing each call during the simulation. The second selection program used 10 different paper-and-pencil tests of mental ability and perceptual speed and accuracy as predictors for clerical jobs. In this case, the criterion was an extensive two-day simulation that was given by a specially trained administrator. This simulation consisted of eight separate exercises. Five were timed clerical activities: filing, classifying, posting, checking, and coding. The remaining three were untimed tests covering plant repair service, punched card fundamentals, and toll fundamentals.

Judgmental Data

In the fourth type of criterion measure, judgmental data, an individual familiar with the work of another is required to judge this work. This measurement is usually obtained by using a rating scale with numerical values. In most cases, the individual doing the evaluation is the immediate supervisor of the worker being evaluated. However, it should be noted that these evaluations can be done by others. The term *360-degree feedback* is used in those cases in which judgments are gathered from supervisors, subordinates, and peers. In any case, the evaluation is based on the opinion or judgment of others, hence the term *judgmental* data.

Because such data rely on opinion, HR specialists and managers are generally skeptical about their use. Many of the deficiencies in decision making that we described in the use of the unstructured interview have also been observed with judgmental performance data. However, as with the selection interview, much effort has been devoted to correcting these deficiencies. In reality, the use of judgmental data is unavoidable in modern organizations. Many jobs such as managerial, service, professional, and staff positions no longer produce tangible, easily counted products on a regular basis—for which the use of production data would be appropriate. In most cases, neither HR nor training performance data are relevant or available. Almost by default, judgmental data are increasingly being used for work measurement. In addition to availability, there are other arguments for using this type of criterion data. The information is supplied by individuals who should know firsthand the work and the work circumstances; after initial development, the use of the judgment scales should be relatively easy.

Types of Judgmental Instruments. Many different types of instruments have been used to collect judgmental data. We discuss four of the most commonly used ones. All four are various forms of rating scales.

Trait Rating Scales. (This is a bad method! Read this section and then never use it.) This method requires the supervisor to evaluate subordinates on the extent to which each individual possesses personal characteristics thought to be necessary for good work performance. The evaluation uses rating scales that contain as few as 3 points or as many as 11. The scale points are usually designated with integers that may also have attached adjectives, for example, *unsatisfactory, average, superior,* or *excellent.* The personal characteristics are most often stated as personality traits such as dependability, ambition, positive attitude, initiative, determination, assertiveness, and loyalty.

Even though this type of judgmental data is commonly collected in organizations, it is regarded as inappropriate criterion data by selection specialists. For a validation study, the criterion must be a direct measure of job performance. Trait ratings are measures of personal characteristics that have no proven relationship to performance. Moreover, the accurate assessment of such traits by a supervisor is nearly impossible. John Bernardin and Richard Beatty have summarized the common viewpoint of these scales: "If the purpose of appraisal is to evaluate *past performance,* then an evaluation of simple personality traits … hardly fits the bill…. Trait ratings are notoriously error-prone and are usually not even measured reliably."[13] Instead of traits, therefore, acceptable judgmental measures require the evaluation of work behaviors. The following three types are examples.

Simple Behavioral Scale. (This is a better method! This scale could be used.) This type of measure is based on information about tasks determined from job analysis. The supervisor is asked to rate each subordinate on major or critical tasks of the job. For example, a manager of information systems within an organization may be evaluated by her supervisor on the task of "Developing software packages to process compensation system data." The number of tasks used in the evaluation differs according to the complexity of the job, but commonly the range is between 4 and 10 tasks. A supervisor scores the subordinate using a rating scale similar to that described for use with trait rating scales, that is, usually 3-point to 7-point scales using integers and adjectives. The following is an example of such a scale.

	Unsatisfactory		Average		Superior
Developing software packages to process compensation system data.	1	2	3	4	5

Scores can be added across all task scales to produce an overall measure of job performance, or an individual task scale can be used to obtain a measure of a specific aspect of job performance. The major limitation in using this type of measure is that supervisors of the same job often disagree on what level of performance on a task is required for a specific score (for example, a score of 3 or "average"). Training the supervisors in developing common interpretations of the performance associated with each scale point can be used to address this limitation.

BARS or BES. (This is an even better method!) *Behaviorally Anchored Rating Scales (BARS)* and *Behavioral Expectation Scales (BES)* are judgmental measures developed to define the scale's rating points in relation to job behaviors.[14] Such definitions are intended to reduce the difficulty for supervisors of consistently interpreting the performance associated with various points on the scale. Figure 15.1 presents an example of one scale representative of this approach. The following steps are necessary in the development of BARS or BES ratings.

1. The Critical-Incidents Technique is used to gather data from groups of 6 to 12 job incumbents/supervisors. A *critical incident* is defined as a description of a worker's job behavior that has four characteristics: (a) it is specific; (b) it focuses on observable behaviors that have been, or could be, exhibited on the job; (c) it briefly describes the context in which the behavior occurred; and (d) it indicates the consequences of the behavior. Each member of the group

FIGURE 15.1 An Example of a BES Rating Dimension for the Job of Bartender

Dimension: Interacting with Customers

7   Employee can be expected to smile, greet a regular customer by name as she approaches, and ask how specific family members are doing.

6

5   Employee can be expected to smile and ask to be of service to the customer.

4

3   Employee can be expected to greet customer by grunting or hissing.

2

1   Employee can be expected to remain silent until customer waves money or yells loudly.

is asked individually to generate as many critical incidents as possible that describe competent, average, and incompetent job behaviors.

2. These critical incidents are then given to other groups of incumbents/supervisors in order to form dimensions. A *dimension* is a group of critical incidents that share a common theme, such as "interacting with customers" for the job of bartender. These dimensions are usually developed through discussion within the group.

3. Other groups of individuals are given the critical incidents and the dimensions, and each person in the group is asked to independently sort the critical incidents into the dimensions. The purpose of this is to determine which critical incidents are reliably viewed as being necessary for inclusion in the dimensions. Usually only those incidents that are assigned to the same category by at least 80 percent of the judges are retained for further work.

4. Other groups of incumbents/supervisors are then given the list of dimensions and the critical incidents assigned to each dimension. Individuals in these groups are asked to rate each of the critical incidents on a 7-point scale ranging from poor performance (scale point of 1) to outstanding performance (scale point of 7). Only those critical incidents for which there is a high agreement among judges (measured using a standard deviation—the smaller the standard deviation, the greater the agreement) are retained.

5. For each dimension, a set of critical incidents is selected that represents various levels of performance on the dimension. Average scores determined in the previous step are used as measures. These selected incidents are then arranged at appropriate places on the scale (see Figure 15.1).

The main difference between BARS and BES is in the wording of the incidents. BARS incidents are worded to reflect *actual* work behaviors, for example, "greets customer as he or she approaches." BES incidents are phrased as *expected* behavior, for example, "can be expected to greet a regular customer as he or she approaches." The wording difference points out to supervisors that the employee does not need to demonstrate the actual behavior of the incident to be scored at that level. The incident is to be interpreted as representative of the performance of the employee. Scores can be obtained for each dimension or summed for a total score of job performance.

In a study that examined behavioral anchors as a source of bias in ratings, Kevin Murphy and Joseph Constans came to the conclusion that the *appropriate behaviors to use as scale points are those that are representative of actual job behaviors.*[15] This should be especially true of behaviors used to anchor the high and low ends of scales. The authors' viewpoint was, for example, that poor performers probably make a series of small errors on the job. Therefore, the behaviors located on the lower end of the scale should be representative of these behaviors rather than an example of one spectacular mistake. Regarding the scale in Figure 15.1, what is your opinion about scale point 1? Is it representative of poor work behavior? If you think not, what would you come up with?

CARS. (This is a very promising approach!) The *Computerized Adaptive Rating Scale* (CARS) technique also uses job behaviors to rate performance but it is specifically designed to be used with computer technology.[16] This technique requires that the rater select between two statements of job performance behaviors that both describe behavior on a specific performance dimension. The two statements, however, differ in terms of their level of performance. That is, one statement is a description of higher work performance on the dimension being measured than is the other statement. The rater chooses the statement that is the most descriptive of the behavior of the person being evaluated. The rater is then shown two more behavioral statements for the same job performance dimension. One of these two is slightly higher in terms of job performance than the statement identified on the previous paired statements and the other is slightly lower than the one chosen. Figure 15.2 provides an example of two rounds of paired statements that may be used in CARS. The presentation of paired statements continues until all appropriate pairs are used. The performance rating is then calculated as a function of all items chosen by the rater. The development of a CARS instrument is complex; it uses the following general steps:

1. *Identify and define work performance dimensions to be measured.* The HR specialist who is developing the CARS evaluation system selects and defines the performance dimensions to be evaluated (for example, customer service—determining the customer's problem and finding solutions or explaining to the customer why the issue cannot be changed).

2. *Generate job behaviors for each performance dimension.* A sample of job incumbents or supervisors writes as many specific behavioral statements as possible for each job performance dimension to be evaluated (for example, a teller inquires whether he may be of help, listens to the bank member's comments about problems related to obtaining loan information, and contacts the loan officer).

3. *Match written job behavior statements to performance dimensions and rate effectiveness of behavioral statements.* Another sample of experts sorts each of the written behavioral statements into the performance categories to be

FIGURE 15.2	Examples of Paired Statements of the Teaching Performance Dimension *Responding to Students' Questions about Class Material*

PAIR #1

1. Rephrases question asked by student to ensure clarity of question.
2. Tells students to read appropriate material from class notes and then ask question.

PAIR #2 (Assuming rater chose statement #2 in previous pair)

1. Rewords student's question as research question and responds in technical detail.
2. Ignores student's question and proceeds with lecture.

evaluated and rates the effectiveness of each behavior statement. (For example, if three performance dimensions were selected—such as customer service, the reporting of financial activities, or maintaining computer security—and 80 behavioral statements were written, this sample of experts would sort the 80 statements into the three performance categories.) Then an individual expert places to the side those behavioral statements that cannot be placed into one of the performance categories. In addition, this group of experts also rates each behavioral statement on a scale (usually 1–5 or 1–7) that indicates how effective the behavioral statement is in demonstrating the performance dimension in which it is placed. For example, a behavioral statement such as "Teller takes notes about member's complaint" may be rated with a score of 4 on a 7-point scale within the performance category of Customer Service.

4. *Eliminate those behavior statements which have limited agreement.* The HR specialist omits those behavioral statements that the experts from the previous step: (a) have not consistently placed into the same performance dimension or (b) have consistently set aside because the statement does not belong to any of the performance dimensions. Generally, 85 percent is used as the desired level of agreement among experts for retaining the behavioral statement as part of a performance dimension. It is important to retain only those behavioral statements for which experts agree on the effectiveness rating. A decision rule may be that the standard deviation among experts' on the effective rating should be less than 0.51 for the behavioral statement.

5. *Repeat the sorting and rating of remaining behavioral statements.* Another sample of experts repeats the sorting of behavioral statements into job performance categories using those statements that have been retained from the previous step. This group of experts also rates each behavioral statement on the effectiveness scale used previously.

6. *Retain those statements that indicate a high level of agreement for both the job performance dimension and the effectiveness ratings.* The HR specialist uses the same agreement criterion that was used after the first sorting of behavioral statements. For example, 85 percent of the second group of experts must place the behavioral statement in the same performance category as did the previous group of experts. The second group of experts must also agree on the scale rating of effectiveness for the behavioral statement to be retained. That is, the standard deviation among these experts' ratings should be less than 0.51 for the behavioral statement to be retained.

7. *Write CARS form.* The HR specialists places the items that are retained into the appropriate performance dimensions and pairs items such that each pair has one behavioral statement that has an effectiveness rating higher than the other behavioral statement. These pairs of statements should vary in terms of the difference in rated effectiveness between the two statements. In some pairs, the difference in effectiveness ratings should be large, the difference in other pairs should be small.

The CARS instrument was found to demonstrate both higher reliability and validity than did the BARS scales or the traditional 1–7 rating scales of job dimensions. The major drawback with using CARS is the development of a computer program that is used to present an item pair of behavioral statements based upon the previous response of the person who is doing the evaluation, one that also calculates the performance rating given by that person for that performance dimension. This program is based upon Item Response Theory and is very complex to write.

The Problem of Bias. Skepticism of judgmental measures centers on the problem of intentional and inadvertent bias by the supervisor making the judgment. Intentional bias is very difficult, if not impossible, to detect. The general thinking among selection specialists, however, is that it is not a widespread problem. As we explain later in the chapter, when criteria data are collected specifically for validation, these data are not used for any other purpose. This creates circumstances in which there is little to be gained if a rater were to intentionally distort his ratings. It is thought that this minimizes the problem.

Inadvertent bias in responses is a more frequently found problem. Commonly called *rater error,* this bias most frequently is described in one of the following four ways: halo, leniency, severity, and central tendency. *Halo* is rating the subordinate equally on different performance scales because of a rater's general impression of the worker. Specific attention is not paid to each individual scale used. *Leniency* or *severity* occurs when a disproportionate number of workers receive either high or low ratings respectively. This bias is commonly attributed to distortion in the supervisor's viewpoint of what constitutes acceptable behavior. For example, leniency has been found to be a consistent bias of some managers.[17] *Central tendency* occurs when a large number of subordinates receive ratings in the middle of the scale. Neither very good nor very poor performance is rated as often as it actually occurs. The effect of all these forms of bias on validation work is usually to lower the calculated correlation. Generally, bias lowers the range of scores on the criteria measures, which mathematically lowers the magnitude of the validity coefficient.

Training Supervisors. The major tactic in overcoming rater bias is to train supervisors to avoid these errors. Gary Latham, Kenneth Wexley, and Elliott Pursell described one such program that is representative of a type of training called rater-error training.[18] This program consisted of five videotaped interactions in which a manager was to rate another person. At the end of each interaction, each person in the training program was asked to give ratings for the following two questions: (a) How would you rate the person? and (b) How do you think the manager rated this person? Each of the five interactions demonstrated a different form of rating error. Each interaction was followed by a discussion in which the particular rating error was pointed out and various solutions were developed to minimize this error.

Another form of training uses another tactic by stressing rater accuracy rather than avoidance of errors.[19] In this training, supervisors are first taught about the multidimensionality of jobs and the need to pay close attention to employee performance in relation to these dimensions. Supervisors are then given rating scales, and the trainer reads the general definition of each dimension as well as the scale anchors associated with varying levels of performance. The group then specifically discusses the types of behavior that are indicative of various levels within each dimension, and the performance associated with each scale point. Videos and role-playing examples can be used as illustrations.

Several studies have demonstrated positive effects from training programs. For example, one study examined these two types of training programs and found benefits from each.[20] Rater-error training was associated with a reduced halo effect, and rater accuracy with reduced leniency. The use of both types of training was recommended. Another study examined the use of rater-error training in conjunction with each of three types of judgmental scales: trait, BES, and BOS.[21] Training resulted in a reduction of errors regardless of the type of scale used. In addition, the two types of behavioral scales resulted in fewer rating errors than did trait scales, even without training. Perhaps the most dramatic finding was from a criterion-related validity study for journeyman electricians.[22] The authors correlated scores from five predictors with supervisors' ratings using a 9-point scale with three behavioral anchors. The anchors were taken from job analysis information. Nonsignificant correlations were found for all of the predictors, indicating no validity for the test battery. The authors decided that this failure was due to rating errors of the supervisors rather than deficiencies in the predictors. It was decided to give these supervisors an eight-hour, rater-error training program. New performance ratings were obtained on the same sample of journeyman electricians one month after the supervisors completed the training. A second set of analyses indicated significant validity coefficients for four of the five predictors.

Systematic Data Collection.   Incomplete data about the job performance of subordinates is an additional source of bias. Such incompleteness forces the manager to base judgments on partially formed impressions. One example, known as the *primacy effect,* describes situations in which judgments are based on events that occurred during the first part of the evaluation period. The term *recency effect* is used when the judgments are based on events that occurred in the latter part of the period. To avoid this source of bias, managers have been taught to record behavior systematically during the complete period of evaluation. Usually this entails making written notes at fixed intervals describing the actual work behavior of each subordinate. These notes are not summary evaluations of the goodness or badness of the behavior; rather, they are nonevaluative descriptions. Often these notes are also shared with the subordinate. At the time of the appraisal, the manager reviews the file and bases his or her judgment on all of the notes gathered over the complete time period of evaluation.

Psychometric Characteristics of Judgmental Data.   You may be asking yourself at this point, "How good are these judgmental methods?" Several recent studies have come up with answers to this question.

Relationship of Judgment and Production Measures.   One study examined the relationship between judgmental measures and production measures of job performance through meta-analysis and found a significant, but small, correlation of 0.39 between the two.[23] This means that judgmental and production measures are not interchangeable—they probably measure different aspects of job performance. Our idea is that production measures are usually very narrow. They focus on end products, not on the behaviors that are necessary to get to end products. Judgments, especially of overall job performance ratings, logically take into account a variety of actions that are part of job performance. These may include helping behaviors with other employees, communication with the supervisor, interaction with customers, and punctuality at meetings. Neither measure is right or wrong. Both measure job performance, but they measure different characteristics of it.

A related topic is the similarity of ratings and objective production measures as criteria for validation. Calvin Hoffman, Barry Nathan, and Lisa Holden compared four criteria for their predictability by a composite measure of several cognitive ability tests—two objective (production quantity and production quality) and two subjective (supervisor and self-ratings). Although both supervisory ratings and production quantity resulted in validity coefficients of about 0.25, production quality and self-appraisal ratings resulted in validities of 0.00.[24] Another study found that the overlap in the distributions of validity coefficients between production quantities and supervisor ratings ranged from 80 to 98 percent.[25] We can conclude that judgmental ratings do correlate with objective measures.

Reliability and Validity of Performance Ratings. Other research has examined the reliability of judgments of job performance. One study determined that the test-retest reliability of supervisors' ratings of overall job performance was 0.79 and that the test-retest reliability estimates for specific job performance dimensions averaged 0.57.[26] The specific dimensions of knowledge, problem solving, aspirations (goal orientation), and initiative had the highest reliability estimates. One problem with interpreting reliability estimates is the question of whether an individual's work performance changes over time or whether differences between ratings at two different times are error. Some research has developed the concept of dynamic job performance. This concept means that an individual's work performance does change over time due to experience, learning, and motivation.[27] Such causes of differences in performance over time would mean that the individual's true work performance has changed during the time period. However, the change in ratings over time could also be due to situational variables such as equipment conditions, performance demands, amount of supervisory guidance, and availability of input materials. Differences in ratings due to these factors could be considered as sources of error leading to unreliability in job performance measurement. The problem is determining which of these two options to take into account when interpreting a test-retest reliability estimate of .79 or .57. Did the true performance change and the estimate is an underestimate? Or did situational factors affect performance, creating error and lowering the estimate? In one study about this issue of sources of changes in performance, it was found that the effect of situational factors on performance varied according to how "strong" or "weak" the situation was for performance.[28] The strength of a situation depends upon the extent to which characteristics of the situation promote consistency of individuals' perceptions of expected behavior. Strong situations lead to uniform perceptions among workers as to appropriate work behavior. Therefore, there is less variance either among individual workers at any one time or even for the same individual worker at two different times. Weak situations are not characterized as having common perceptions of appropriate work behavior and work performance can vary between people at any one time or for the same individual at two different times. A related study found that reliability estimates are affected by the type of measurement instrument used and the length of the interval in between test-retest administrations. Stability of measurement is higher for shorter time intervals and when judgmental measures of job performance are used. It was also found that objective performance measures are very unstable for highly complex jobs and therefore not very useful.[29]

Another study looked at raters and what effects they could have on reliability estimates of performance.[30] The researchers found five factors that they thought influenced performance ratings: the ratee's general level of performance, the ratee's performance on a specific performance dimension, the rater's idiosyncratic rating tendencies (rater error of halo and leniency), the rater's organizational perspective (position relative to ratee), and random measurement error. Quite clearly, we (and the person being rated) would hope that the two dimensions of ratee performance (ratee's general level of performance and ratee's performance on a specific performance dimension) would account for most of the performance rating being given by the raters. Do you think that's what was found? You're right ... nope!! Rater idiosyncratic effects accounted for over 50 percent of the differences among ratings of individuals' performance. The *combined effects* of the two ratee performance dimensions accounted for only about half as much as did the rater idiosyncratic effects.

The somewhat low reliability estimates found in several studies as well as the identification of factors that influence performance ratings have lead to the development and successful use of the training programs for supervisors that we described previously. As a result of such programs, the reliability of judgment data can be improved. As you should remember from Chapter 3, reliability is good. High reliability can lead to high validity. Rater bias that we have described is an error component of the performance ratings; error lowers the reliability and validity of the selection program. That is, unreliability of the performance measure lowers the correlation coefficient between the predictor and the criterion. Such lowering would make it more difficult to establish a statistically significant validity coefficient. However despite the estimated unreliability of many performance measures, they have been used often over the years as criteria measures, and validity coefficients have reached statistically significant levels. In the case of meta-analytic studies, these coefficients have often been corrected statistically for unreliability with the resulting validity coefficients being in the 0.30–0.50+ range. Said another way, any calculated validity coefficient may be an underestimate of the true validity. That is, scores on the selection instruments should not correlate with the error component of performance ratings but only with the true score components of these ratings. Obviously, if the performance ratings used in validation are unreliable ratings with large error components, the correlation of those performance ratings with scores on a selection instrument could be expected to be quite low. The selection instruments could be much more valid that the magnitude of the validity correlation indicates. This lack of reliability in judgments may partially explain why validity coefficients that have been calculated using training proficiency as the criterion measure are higher estimates of the validity of selection instruments than are validity coefficients that have been calculated using job performance as the criterion measure.

360-Degree Feedback.   As we mentioned previously, judgment data are used when 360-degree performance reviews are conducted. In this technique, superiors, peers, and subordinates of the individual being reviewed are each given a performance evaluation form that requests ratings on a number of work behaviors and work results. These ratings are averaged, and the results are given to the individual being assessed. Because all raters are guaranteed anonymity, the ratings are usually summarized according to the relationship with the individual being reviewed (superiors, peers, and subordinates are averaged separately, which provides three scores on each scale). In some cases, the ratings of all respondents are averaged and reported as one score.

Given what we have already said about the bias of raters in making performance ratings, it is logical that the ratings made by the various rating groups in 360-degree performance reviews would be the subject of research. One main question this research has addressed is whether the three groups of raters are similar in their ratings. If they are, ratings can be combined across the three groups. If they are not, then the ratings should only be averaged within each of the three groups. The results of such research are mixed. Some studies have found that there is marginally acceptable equivalence among rater groups in 360 assessments that would allow for combining ratings across groups.[31] However, other research has repeatedly found that the three groups, (manager, peer, and subordinates) do not agree with one another in ratings of the same person.[32] These differences among groups may be caused by several things:

- Individuals from the various groups (manager, peers, subordinates) conceptualize the rating instrument differently (the items do not mean the same thing to raters at different levels)

- The raters have different perspectives of the performance of the person being rated because they interact in different ways with the individual being rated

- Raters have individual biases

The first explanation has been ruled out by a study that found that the rating instrument and its items are conceptualized similarly by raters with different working relationships with the ratee.[33] The second explanation that rating differences are a function of different working perspectives is questionable because another study found differences even among individuals who are at the same job level (differences even among peers and subordinates).[34] One would expect that subordinates would all have approximately the same perspective about the work performance of a superior and would substantially agree in the ratings of the performance behavior of the superior. It seems that the explanation of individual rater bias is appearing more feasible than the other explanations. In support of the third explanation, another research study found that a group of raters (subordinates) differed in ratings of the same individual when the purpose of the evaluation differed.[35] That is, ratings by subordinates of their superiors changed as the result of two different explanations given to the raters about how the ratings would be used: (a) the ratings would be used for development purposes (training) and (b) the ratings would be used for administrative purposes (compensation and promotion). This is evidence that the perspective of the rater can influence the ratings.

The real issue is how to use the results of these research studies. One recommendation is to present each rater's ratings to the ratee individually (without names or positions). For example, if six raters participated, the ratee would receive six ratings of each of the performance dimensions being judged.[36] To interpret the ratings, the person being reviewed could then examine both the patterns across individual raters and the relative order of the scores of the dimensions. We have referred to other methods: one is to average all ratings and the other is to average ratings within each of the three groups. There is support for each method and evidence against it. Our thought is to compare the average ratings of the three groups. If average scores clearly and consistently vary among groups then it seems logical to report the average scores of each of the three groups rather than combine them into one group score. If average scores of the three groups are similar, then they can be reported as one combined group or three separate groups. If there seems to be as much variance within each group as between the three groups, then it may be the most informative to the person who was rated to report the individual anonymous scores of all who completed the 360 questionnaire.

Concluding Comments on Judgmental Scales.   To maximize the effectiveness of judgmental scales, it's important to keep in mind the principles that were presented in this section. First, the use of job-behavior scales rather than trait scales is recommended. The role of selection is to identify individuals who will perform well on the job, not to identify those with desirable personality characteristics. Therefore, job-behavior dimensions are the only acceptable kind.

Second, the history of selection argues that the dimensions used be fairly broad statements of performance or job behaviors.[37] We hope the following example will clarify what we mean by this statement. Directors of management information systems have multiple, diverse activities. If we were validating a set of selection instruments for this job, we would probably use some form of judgmental data as part of the criterion measures. Suppose that one performance dimension is the design and implementation of information systems for various groups within the company. This behavior is actually made up of several more specific job behaviors—for example, the discussion of user information needs, the development of a report describing the nature of the recommended system, the design of a detailed hardware plan, the development of software packages, and the training of users in software packages. It is better to determine one rating that is a measure of the general performance dimension than it is to treat each of these separate behavioral dimensions as a criterion measure. Generally, selection measures correlate less well with specific, narrow job dimensions than with broad dimensions. For this reason, criterion data should be collected by asking the supervisor to make one judgment of the overall job dimension; if he or she is asked to rate the more specific dimensions, the dimensions should be combined into a single score.

Third, it is obvious that extensive training must be done with the supervisors who will use the instrument. The studies we have summarized demonstrate that sometimes the training of supervisors has a dramatic effect in reducing the rater error that artificially lowers a validity correlation. This training should address how to record and evaluate job behaviors accurately and how to avoid the judgmental errors of halo and leniency.

APPROPRIATE CHARACTERISTICS OF SELECTION CRITERIA MEASURES

As we have mentioned, it is possible to use in validity studies each of the performance measurement devices we have presented. It is the role of the selection specialist to choose those measures that are the most appropriate for the selection program under consideration. This choice depends in part on how the strengths and limitations of each device match the work situation under which the validation must be carried out. In addition, this choice is dependent on the extent to which the criterion measure possesses the characteristics that we will discuss in this section. Possession of these characteristics helps ensure that the criterion has the information that is necessary for conducting validation. We briefly mentioned a few of these characteristics in Chapter 3. In the following section, we discuss them more completely.

Individualization

Selection programs are designed to furnish data used in employment decisions. As we have described these programs, the applicant completes various selection instruments, each of which is designed to measure specific KSAs. In validation, these measures of KSAs are gathered for each member of a group and correlated with corresponding measures of job performance. The logic of this is that the job performance measure must also be a measure of the individual. If we are attempting to determine whether high scores on the selection instruments are indicative of high scores on job performance, it would be dysfunctional to have the job performance be representative of anyone except the individual. This may seem obvious, but many work situations create job performance outputs that violate this principle. For example, team or group tasks are becoming increasingly popular. Even traditional manufacturing operations have formed groups of 10 to 12 workers who are assigned all operations necessary for completion of the product. Workers are interchangeable and move unsystematically from work station to work station. It would not be appropriate to use the number of items produced as a criterion measure for selection. Such a number would not measure the distinct performance of an individual and therefore is not appropriate for correlation with individual selection instrument scores.

Controllability

The logic of selection also indicates that measuring the KSAs of applicants is important because these KSAs affect job performance. Those workers who possess more of the desirable KSAs should perform better. This can be tested only if the work performance measure is one that the employee can affect or control. That is, the employee can change her score on the performance measure.

Again, many frequently used measures of job performance do not have this characteristic. For example, it has been common to evaluate branch managers' performance for financial service institutions partially on the basis of profits generated by the branch. Offhand this seems accurate, because profits are of central importance to financial institutions and branch managers are commonly assumed to be the chief executive of the unit and in charge of operations. But this assumption often does not hold. Interest rates for deposits are set by the highest level of management. Loans are often controlled by standard policy. Loans over a certain amount must be approved by others, and guidelines concerning loan evaluation are used for smaller loans. Other items, such as size and salary of staff are dictated by company headquarters. Many factors that greatly affect the profits of the branch are not influenced by the branch manager. To use profits as a criterion measure in selection may be an error in such a situation. Logically, differences in the KSAs of various branch managers may be reflected in other performance aspects such as completeness and timeliness of reports. The branch manager can make a difference in the reports; therefore, reports are controllable by the branch manager. He or she does not make a difference in profits—profits are not controllable by the manager.

Other examples exist. Job scheduling and quality of materials frequently affect production output of workers, even though neither may be controlled by the worker. Repair records of maintenance workers in plants are often evaluated based on time spent on service visits and frequency of return calls. In many instances, these factors are more attributable to the performance of the operators of the machinery than they are to the maintenance worker who repairs the machine.

Relevance

Selection is designed to contribute to the productivity of the organization. Individuals are employed primarily to perform well on the critical or important parts of a job. It is these parts, therefore, that should be included in job performance measures. Sometimes this principle is overlooked because other job performance measures are easy to obtain. For example, promptness and attendance usually are easily obtainable records. However, as we have mentioned, in many jobs such attendance is not a critical dimension of performance. This is commonly the case for managers and professionals in an organization in which little attention is paid to coming and going, or to the use of company time for doctor visits. Such events are irrelevant as long as "the work gets done." Our point is that this may also be true of other jobs for which attendance records are carefully kept. Therefore, these records are not appropriate criteria measures. The primary method of judging the relevance of a criterion measure is job analysis. Job analysis should identify the important, critical, or frequently performed job activities. The question of relevance relates to whether the job performance measure corresponds to this information.

Measurability

Given the nature of validation, this is one of the more obvious characteristics. It is not possible to perform an empirical validation study unless behavior on both the selection and the job performance instruments is quantified. This quantification is how we have defined measurement (see Chapter 3). As we discussed in the previous section, the source of this measurement can be production output units, an individual's judgment, training examinations, work sample tests, attendance records, and so on. The most frequently experienced difficulty in meeting this measurement characteristic is determining how to quantify a job behavior dimension. For example, a regional sales manager may be in charge of advertising for the region. Ultimately, the purpose of advertising is to increase sales.

However, this end may not be achieved for a long period of time. This creates a problem. What should be measured in place of sales that will measure the effectiveness of the advertising? In many cases, some associated measure is obtained. For example, a judgment is made about the quality of the advertising campaign based on its correspondence to accepted standards of advertising. This judgment becomes the job performance measure.

Reliability

Chapter 4 discussed in detail the importance of reliability in measurement. Frequently, HR specialists are greatly concerned with the reliability of selection instruments but pay less attention to the reliability of job performance measures. This is unfortunate, because unreliability in these measures can also negatively affect validation coefficients. As we have noted, the unreliability of supervisors' "judgments" of subordinates has been of great concern to selection specialists.

Unreliability in other criteria measures is not often thought about, but it does exist and it must be corrected. Monthly sales volume for many jobs, such as a furniture or clothing representative, fluctuates with seasonal buying patterns. In these cases, it is necessary to accumulate sales data for a period of time longer than a month to compensate for these seasonal fluctuations. As we mentioned, a major difficulty in using absenteeism as a criterion variable has been unreliability in some cases. This is especially true if total days absent is used as a measure. One severe illness could distort the data.

Variance

It is conceptually useless and statistically difficult to validate a selection program in cases in which there is little, if any, variance in worker performance levels. If every worker performs at the same level, the amount of workers' KSAs is apparently irrelevant—the difference in KSAs makes no difference in performance levels. This lack of variance can be caused by two factors: (a) standardization in output due to work process, or (b) inappropriate use of the measurement device. Output for machine-paced manufacturing is an example of the former. If an assembly line is set to move continuously at a certain speed, all workers should produce the same output. The latter case is often demonstrated in supervisors' judgments of subordinates. At one time, the military experienced severe problems with its appraisal forms. Theoretically, 100 scale points were to be used for rating, with a score of 70 being designated as average performance. In practice, however, the great majority of personnel were rated between 90 and 100 to ensure their chances for promotion. The same problem has been repeated in other situations in which a supervisor thinks that all the subordinates are exceptionally good workers.

A problem for selection specialists is determining whether such supervisory judgments reflect actual similarity in performance, or misuse of the rating instrument. After all, it is possible that members of a work group, especially one that is experienced and well trained, could all perform at the same general level. In most cases, this possibility is ignored; the decision is made that the appraisal form is being used incorrectly, and a training program is implemented. (Selection specialists are suspicious people, sometimes inappropriately.)

Practicality

Practicality refers to the cost and logistics of gathering data. In those rare circumstances in which these factors are not constraints, this can be ignored. In most cases, however, time and money become major issues. For example, most companies that have direct sales operations think that both sales volume and customer service are important performance dimensions. The problem is that to collect customer service data accurately, many time-consuming and costly steps must be carried out. A representative sample of customers for each salesperson must be compiled. Then, each must be contacted and questioned, using a standardized interview, about the behaviors of the salesperson and the customer's reaction to the services rendered. Obviously, this is not a practical operation in most cases. Instead, less time-consuming and less costly measures are used. For example, often the number of complaints made by customers is used. To do this, however, the logical assumptions must be made that (1) the opportunity for customers to file complaints is the same for all sales personnel, and (2) that complaints are caused by the salesperson rather than any other store factors—lateness of delivery, difficult order process, or incorrect record keeping. If such assumptions cannot be made, then this measure is not useful as a job performance measure.

Lack of Contamination

Criterion contamination occurs when the applicants' scores on the selection instruments are used to make employment decisions about these individuals; these employment decisions, in turn, have a bearing on criterion scores. One of the best examples has occurred in the use of assessment centers (ACs). Most often, ACs are used for internal selection for higher-level management jobs. For this example, let us assume that an AC for lower-level managers has been designed to determine their suitability for higher management positions. The lower-level managers complete the AC and receive formal feedback from the assessors. In many cases, the assessment ratings and descriptions are given to the supervisors of those who have completed the AC and are also placed in central HR files. Contamination occurs when these assessment center data are used to make decisions about whom among the group should be promoted, and then promotion is used as the criterion variable. Obviously such an action would increase the magnitude of the validity coefficient artificially. These events would constitute a self-fulfilling prophecy: Individuals would be promoted because they scored well at the AC, and the AC scores would be validated against promotion records of individuals. Similar contamination could occur when scores on selection devices are used for placement of employees into desirable sales territories or fast-track positions.

Specificity for Selection

Selection specialists generally prefer to use job performance data in validation that are specifically collected for selection program development rather than primarily for one of the other human resource management purposes. This is the difference between the administrative and research use of performance data within organizations.[38] For our purposes, the major difference is that validation is impersonal. The emphasis is on using quantitative performance and predictor scores of individuals who are virtually unknown by the selection specialist. The administrative uses of performance data, in contrast, focus on the individual on whom the measurement is taken. Especially when judgmental methods are used, this sometimes means that other factors affect the measured. For example, when performance measures are used for salary increases, supervisors may consider such factors as the worker's experience, market demand, the worker's potential career, and personal relationships when making the evaluation.

What If Some of the Characteristics Aren't There?

After this discussion of characteristics, the question that undoubtedly arises in your mind is, "What happens if these characteristics are not present?" Without going into a long explanation, the general conclusion is that *major violations of these characteristics can lower the correlation coefficient artificially and reduce the probability of demonstrating empirical validity.* This is because such violations would introduce unsystematic errors into the measures. We said previously that the effect of unsystematic error is usually to lower both reliability and validity. We use the word *artificially* because the lowering is due to extraneous factors that could be controlled. In other words, the validity coefficient provides an indication of the relationship between predictor and criterion. It should be low if no relationship exists and high if such a relationship is present. Under the circumstances we have mentioned, however, the relationship could still be high in reality, but the magnitude of the validity coefficient would be low because of the presence of unsystematic error. The low correlation would not be representative of the actual relationship between predictor and criterion.

ISSUES IN CRITERION USE

Single versus Multiple Criteria

One of the most perplexing issues for selection specialists involved in validation is how to decide on the number of measures of job performance to use. This issue is commonly referred to as the choice between single or multiple criteria. In validation, the use of a single measure of job performance translates into viewing it as overall or global performance. This single measure could exist in either of two forms. One form consists of a single aspect of performance. For example, for sales personnel a measure of dollar sales volume has frequently been used. For social service workers, the measure has been the number of clients interviewed. The second form consists of two or more measures that are combined algebraically to yield one overall measure. For example, a district sales manager's rating of quality of customer service may be combined in some manner with the sales volume figures to arrive at one total composite of job performance for sales personnel.

The argument for using a single performance measure in validation is partially based on the fact that validation procedures become more straightforward with one criterion. The predictors are correlated with this one measure in the manner we described in Chapter 5. In most instances, only one correlation coefficient would be tested to determine significance. This makes both the interpretation of the findings and the judgment about the adequacy of the selection program relatively simple.

The argument for the use of multiple criteria measures is made on the basis of research findings and logic. Essentially, this argument starts with the fact that job analysis studies identify multiple tasks within jobs. Multiple tasks are indicative of the multiple aspects of job performance. Also, studies of job performance have concluded that a global measure of performance may not reflect all of the job activities even for simple entry-level jobs.[39]

One example of this diversity of performance within jobs can be found in Project A, which we described in Chapter 11. This project identified multiple components of performance for 19 entry-level army jobs. John Campbell, Jeffrey McHenry, and Lauress Wise utilized multiple job analysis methods and criterion measurement to yield more than 200 performance indicators, which were further reduced to 32 criterion scores for each job.[40] The same argument can be made for other types of jobs, such as manufacturing operations, in which days present and lack of defective assembly items are, at the minimum, thought to be important. Even in typing and stenography jobs, the importance of both speed and accuracy serving as performance measures is obvious.

When to Use Each. Wayne Cascio has presented the a straightforward solution to the dilemma, and the following discussion reflects his writings.[41] Cascio has made the distinction between using job performance measures to assist in managerial decision making and using them to serve research purposes. In most cases, a validity study is done to identify a set of selection devices that assist in managerial decision making. That is, the applicants' scores on the selection devices are used in making decisions about to whom to extend job offers. In these cases a composite criterion would generally be used. Managers are essentially interested in selecting individuals who, all things considered, perform well in an overall manner. The use of the composite criterion reflects this thinking.

In a few cases, a validity study is done for research purposes. For example, we may wish to study the relationship between specific mental abilities (mathematical reasoning, spatial visualization, and so on) and different parts of a research engineering job (development of research plans, preparation of technical reports, and so on). In such a case, the major emphasis is on linking a specific mental ability to each subpart of the job. Such information could later be used in selection, training, and career development work. It would therefore be appropriate to use multiple criteria and to validate the mental ability tests against each separate measure of job performance.

Forming the Single Measure. If a composite measure is desired, the immediate problem is how to combine the different measures into one. Essentially, three methods are used for doing this: dollar criterion, factor analysis, or expert judgment.

Dollar Criterion. The first method, which Cascio points out is the logical basis of combination, is to develop a composite that represents economic worth to the organization. This entails expressing the various job performance measures that we have discussed as a monetary amount that represents the value of worker performance to the organization. Put simply, the main purpose of selection is to improve the economic position of the firm through better workers, who are identified through a valid selection program. Expressing job performance in dollars would be a direct reflection of this thinking.

This line of reasoning was first expressed many years ago by Hubert Brogden and Erwin Taylor, who developed the dollar criterion.[42] In the years after this first work, refinements have been made in how to practically estimate the monetary worth of job performance. These refinements are part of the general topic of utility analysis (yes, Chapter 5). Without going through a detailed description of this topic, at least three major methods are used to determine this dollar value of job performance. One method requires that job experts estimate the monetary value of various levels of job performance.[43] A second method assumes that the dollar value of job performance is a direct function of yearly salary.[44] The third method also uses employee salary but partitions this among a job's activities, so that each activity is assigned a proportion of that salary in accord with the job analysis results.[45]

Factor Analysis. The second method of combining separate criteria measures into one composite relies on statistical correlational analysis. In this approach, all individual criteria measures are correlated with one another. The intercorrelation matrix is factor analyzed; this, statistically, combines these separate measures into clusters or factors. Ideally, a majority of the separate measures would be combined into one factor that would then serve as the composite performance measure. The factor analysis procedure also provides weights that could be applied to each specific measure in forming the composite.

Expert Judgment.   A third method uses judgments of job experts to form the composite. Essentially, the problem for these judges is to identify the relative weights of the specific performance aspects. For example, let us assume that the job of laboratory technician has five components we wish to combine. The role of the job experts is to specify the numerical value that each component should be multiplied by to derive the overall performance score. This weighting should reflect the importance of each of the five components with regard to overall performance. If all five components are regarded as equally important, then all five parts carry a weight of "1" and are directly added. If the five components are thought to be unequal in importance, there are, at that point, two different procedures that are often used to determine the appropriate weights. Under the first procedure, each judge is given 100 points and asked to divide them among the five parts. The weight for each part is the average number of points assigned to it by the judges. The second procedure asks each judge to assign a value of 1.0 to the most unimportant part. The number assigned to each of the other four is to represent how many times more important each part is to this least important one. The weight is again the average of these values. Both procedures assume reliability among the judges—in deciding the order of the five parts as well as in determining the relative importance among them. This means that if the judges do not closely agree on which components are unimportant and which are very important, the computed averages are conceptually meaningless and ought not to be used.

Another judgment method describes how a single score can be compiled by using preferences obtained from individuals, such as customers, who derive value from the organizations' outputs.[46] These preference values on such variables as product or service performance can be ordered and weighted to identify the critical performance criteria to be used for evaluating individual and organizational effectiveness.

JOB PEFORMANCE MEASUREMENT AND EEO ISSUES

The effect of EEO principles on job performance measurement is not as clear as it is for other areas of selection. Partially, this is because only a small part of *The Uniform Guidelines on Employee Selection Procedures,* published by the EEOC, explicitly treats job performance measurement; it does not fully discuss the necessary features of such systems. Similarly, although a number of court cases have addressed job performance measurement, on only a few occasions has it been the major issue in the case. Moreover, the major proportion of even this sketchy treatment has focused on judgmental data, not the complete topic of job performance measurement. For these reasons, it is difficult to state specifically what actions HR specialists should take to minimize the chances of having a court disagree with a performance evaluation system.

To provide an understanding of what is known about this topic, in this section we indicate those parts of the *Uniform Guidelines* that pertain to job performance measurement, summarize the results of relevant court decisions, and present some recommendations regarding necessary features of job performance measurement systems. As other authors have put it, these recommendations ought to be treated as "a set of hypotheses regarding the legal ramifications" rather than a strict set of guidelines.[47]

The Uniform Guidelines

Three sections of the *Uniform Guidelines* contain the most direct statements about work measurement. Of these, section 2.B is the most often cited. Its purpose is to make clear that any procedure that contributes to any employment decision is covered by the *Uniform Guidelines*. This is addressed by this statement: "These guidelines apply to tests and other selection procedures which are used as a basis for any employment decision."[48] Some experts interpret this section of the *Uniform Guidelines* to mean that all data collection instruments used in employment decisions are to be labeled as "tests" and subject to all the statements of the *Uniform Guidelines* directed at tests.

The second statement, section 14.B (3) (see Table 15.2), serves several purposes. For one, it makes explicit that three of the four types of data we have discussed are permissible: production data, HR data, and training proficiency. More detail is provided about training proficiency than about the others. It is pointed out that the relevance of the training to actual important dimensions of job performance must be demonstrated, and that various measures of training proficiency may be used, including instructor evaluations, performance samples, and paper-and-pencil tests. The statement is also made that these three types of criteria measures may be used without a previous job analysis "if the user can show the importance of the criteria to the particular employment context." Presumably, this is done by pointing out the direct relationship of these criteria measures to the purpose of the job. Other issues in section 14 refer to some of the points we made in "Appropriate Characteristics of Selection Criteria Measures," an earlier section of this chapter. These points include preventing contamination and ensuring relevance. A statement is also made in section 14 to the effect that it is permissible to develop one overall measure for job performance. Earlier in the chapter, we discussed appropriate methods for doing this.

A third section, 15.B (5), makes clear that the data that are used to identify and develop the validation criterion measures must be made explicit: "The bases for the selection of the criterion measures should be provided." This includes the description of the criterion and how the measure was developed and collected. Explicit statements are also made recognizing the fourth type of work measurement data (which we previously discussed)—judgmental data. When judgmental data are used, both the forms used to collect the judgments and the explicit instructions given to the judges must be provided.

Court Decisions

Several reviews of court decisions have been completed regarding discrimination in performance measurement. These reviews examine whether the decision was in favor of the plaintiff or the defendant and which, if any, characteristics of the performance measurement system seem to be related to the decisions.[49] One of these reviews was done by

---

TABLE 15.2   Statements from the Uniform Guidelines Pertaining to Work Measurement

Section 14.B.(3).

(3) Criterion measures. Proper safeguards should be taken to insure that scores on selection procedures do not enter into any judgments of employee adequacy that are to be used as criterion measures. Whatever criteria are used should represent important or critical work behavior(s) or work outcomes. Certain criteria may be used without a full job analysis if the user can show the importance of the criteria to the particular employment context. These criteria include but are not limited to production rate, error rate, tardiness, absenteeism, and length of service. A standardized rating of overall work performance may be used where a study of the job shows that it is an appropriate criterion. Where performance in training is used as a criterion, success in training should be properly measured and the relevance of the training should be shown either through a comparison of the content of the training program with the critical or important work behavior(s) of the job(s), or through a demonstration of the relationship between measures of performance in training and measures of job performance. Measures of relative success in training include but are not limited to instructor evaluation, performance samples, or tests. Criterion measures consisting of paper and pencil tests will be closely reviewed for job relevance.

Source: *Adoption of Four Agencies of Uniform Guidelines on Employee Selection Procedures*, 43 Federal Register 38, 290–315 (Aug. 25, 1978).

Jon Werner and Mark Bolino, who summarized 295 U.S. circuit court decisions that were rendered from 1980 to 1995.[50] Their analysis first examined whether contextual variables influenced court decisions. That is, they wanted to determine how issues regarding disparate treatment versus disparate impact, individual versus class action, the year of decision (before or after the 1991 Civil Rights Act), the circuit court district, the type of organization, the purpose of the appraisal, and the race and gender of the evaluator affected the outcome of the decision. Their findings determined that none of these variables was significantly related to the decisions, indicating that rulings were apparently made on the basis of the features of the appraisal systems rather than on features that were not directly relevant.

The features that were strongly related were the use of job analysis, the development and use of written instructions by the evaluators, the employee's right to review the performance appraisal that the rater completed, and whether multiple raters were used in the performance appraisal. As you can probably guess, the court's decision usually was in favor of the organization if these characteristics were present. If they were not present, the plaintiff usually won. The authors also found that it did not make a difference if the appraisal system used traits or behaviors. Very few cases addressed the measurement properties of appraisal systems, such as reliability or validity. The effect of the raters' training on courts' rulings was unknown, because so few cases used this as an important factor in the decision. However, the authors noted that its absence was mentioned in several cases, and that these cases usually were decided in favor of the plaintiff.

Werner and Bolino concluded from their findings that courts are primarily concerned with the fairness of the process of the appraisal system—that is, whether the procedures of the appraisal system indicate that it is based on job information, is carried out in a systematic manner, and is open to the individual being reviewed. The unimportance of measurement features and behavioral measures similarly indicates that courts are more interested in the procedures of appraisal than the quality of the data that are collected and used. This is not unexpected. Issues of quality are very technical—often debated among practitioners—and are of less concern to many employees than the manner in which they are treated. The findings of this study provide excellent guidelines for the process of performance review in organizations.

There is research whose results complicate any issue of adverse impact or discrimination in selection. That is, meta-analysis has determined differences in the average job performance scores of black and white employees. One study explored differences across a large variety of performance measures: overall performance ratings, quality ratings, quantity ratings, objective measures of quantity, objective measures of quality, job knowledge scores, work samples, absenteeism, on-the-job training, and promotion.[51] Whites scored higher on all of these measures than did blacks. Specific findings were that:

- Whites and blacks differed by about one-third of a standard deviation unit ($d = 0.31$) across all measures of job performance.

- The average difference between the two groups was $d = 0.21$ for both quality and quantity performance ratings.

- The difference for all measures of job knowledge as performance criteria was $d = 0.48$.

- The difference for work sample tests as performance criteria was $d = 0.59$.

- The difference for absenteeism was $d = 0.19$.

- The differences for objective and subjective measures of quality were equal, $d = 0.27$ and 0.26, respectively.

- The differences for objective and subjective measures of quantity were 0.32 and 0.09, respectively. That is, the difference between the two groups was higher for objective measures of quantity than for subjective measures.

- The differences between objective and subjective measures of job knowledge were 0.55 and 0.15, respectively. Again, the difference between the groups was greater for objective measures of job knowledge than subjective measures.

- Differences occur at all levels of job complexity.

- Differences between white and Hispanic employees were smaller than those between white and black employees.

Some of the general conclusions were that (a) whites score higher on all measures of job performance, (b) the differences between blacks and whites are smaller for subjective measures than for objective measures, and (c) differences on work samples and job knowledge criteria are larger than for other types of criteria.

A second, larger meta-analysis had similar findings.[52] These findings were that:

- There were differences between the two groups across all types of performance measures ($d = 0.27$).

- Differences in training proficiency criteria were $d = 0.46$.

- Differences are largest for performance criteria that are highly dependent on cognitive ability (work samples and job knowledge tests).

- Differences on performance measures that stress personal interaction or personality are much smaller than on other measures.

- Differences in work performance have decreased over the years that studies have been done.

The importance of these meta-analyses is that they indicate that there are measured differences between blacks and whites on some predictors (an observation that we have made at various points in this book) and on performance measures. This is additional evidence that adverse impact on predictor scores is indicative (predictive) of differences in job performance. Therefore, adverse impact may occur but not be an indication of discrimination.

PERFORMANCE REVIEW FOR TEAMS

As we mentioned in Chapter 1 (see how tightly interwoven this book is!), organizations are moving toward the use of work teams, away from the traditional collection of individuals working in series. This movement from individual jobs to teams poses problems for selection specialists in terms of collecting data appropriate for validation work. The major issue is that validation must be done at the individual level of analysis and that team-based jobs hinder the development of such data. Some organizations that are strongly committed to work teams only collect performance data for each team as a whole, not the individuals who make up the teams. For example, indicators of quality or quantity of performance for a team are collected at the team level, (amount produced, amount of scrap, customers' comments, total sales). Such measures indicate the results of team performance. If no individual performance measures are usually gathered, then the selection specialist will have to develop and implement special individual measures in order to carry out a validation study. For example, the specialist could ask each member of a team to make judgments about the behaviors of others on the team. These judgments could be about how much each team member has contributed to either overall production of the team or to individual aspects of production. If the team behavior toward one another is a work performance criterion, then the team members could be asked to judge one another on specific behaviors that are essential for effective team functioning (for example, discussion of possible alternative ways of getting to the end result, instructing other team members in how to carry out specific tasks, resolving conflicts among teams members, taking initiative in group activities, and volunteering for additional work).[53] One difficulty in having team members evaluate each other is that such evaluation, because it focuses on individual performance rather than team performance, is somewhat contrary to the philosophy of teams. Some teams either refuse to carry out this request or rate each member equally and highly on each performance question. If it is not appropriate to collect data from individual team members, an alternative is to have a supervisor make such judgments. However, the supervisor can only make such ratings if he/she has many opportunities to observe the team at work. If the contact between the team and the supervisor is limited, then it is unlikely that the supervisor can make valid evaluations of team interaction or individual contribution to team output.

Performance Measurement in Small Business

Measuring performance in small businesses is easy, and we will be brief. Everything we said in this chapter should be directly applicable to businesses of all sizes. Production, personnel, training proficiency, and judgmental data are all applicable to small businesses. The only topic that we have mentioned in this chapter that could differ with regard to the size of the business is the conducting of criterion-related validity studies. Because of the large number of employees necessary for such studies, small businesses, as a general rule, would not be able to carry out these studies. Although this inability may be disappointing, it does not preclude the use of the information contained in this chapter about performance data for other parts of selection, such as the development of KSAs and content validation.

THAT'S ALL, FOLKS!

Well, that's it. We don't know much more about selection, and we are sure that you don't want to know any more right now. If you do, ask your professor. Like all faculty, he or she enjoys talking and will be flattered. Asking may even help your grade. We know you are now ready to be a selection specialist and earn at least $125,000 per year (plus a car, expense account, and stock options) for doing what you read in this book. We will even say nice things about you if you want us to serve as references when you apply for employment—provided that you show us your receipt from purchasing this text and promise us 10 percent of your first year's salary!

REFERENCES

1. Frank J. Landy and James L. Farr, *The Measurement of Work Performance Methods, Theory, and Applications* (New York: Academic Press, 1983); Kevin R. Murphy and Jeanette N. Cleveland, *Understanding Performance Appraisal: Social, Organizational, and Goal-Based Perspectives* (Sage Publications: Thousand Oaks, CA, 1995); and Robert L. Cardy, *Performance Management, Concepts, Skills, and Exercises* (Armonk, NY: M. E. Sharpe, 2004).

2. William W. Ronan and Erich P. Prien, *Perspectives on the Measurement of Human Performance* (New York: Appleton-Century-Crofts, 1971), 73.

3. Ibid., 94.

4. Landy and Farr, *The Measurement of Work Performance Methods, Theory, and Applications*, 30.

5. Ibid., 33.

6. David A. Harrison and Charles L. Hulin, "Investigations of Absenteeism: Using Event History Models to Study the Absence-Taking Process," *Journal of Applied Psychology* 74 (1989): 300–316.

7. J. B. Carroll, "The Nature of the Data, or How to Choose a Correlation Coefficient," *Psychometrika* 26 (1961): 347–372.

8. David A. Harrison and Charles L. Hulin, "Investigations of Absenteeism: Using Event History Models to Study the Absence-Taking Process," *Journal of Applied Psychology* 74 (1989): 300–316.

9. Charles Williams, "Deciding When, How, and If to Correct Turnover Correlations," *Journal of Applied Psychology* 75 (1990): 732–737.

10. Dan R. Dalton and William D. Todor, "Manifest Needs of Stewards: Propensity to File a Grievance," *Journal of Applied Psychology* 64 (1979): 654–659.

11. Hannah Rothstein Hirsh, Lois Northrup, and Frank Schmidt, "Validity Generalization Results for Law Enforcement Occupations," *Personnel Psychology* 39 (1986): 399–429.

12. Sidney Gael, Donald L. Grant, and Richard J. Ritchie, "Employment Test Validation for Minority and Nonminority Telephone Operators," *Journal of Applied Psychology* 60 (1975): 411–419; and Sidney Gael, Donald L. Grant, and Richard J. Ritchie, "Employment Test Validation for Minority and Nonminority Clerks with Work Sample Criteria," *Journal of Applied Psychology* 60 (1975): 420–426.

13. H. John Bernardin and Richard W. Beatty, *Performance Appraisal: Assessing Human Behavior at Work*, (Boston: West Publishing Co., 1984).

14. Gary P. Latham and Kenneth N. Wexley, *Increasing Productivity through Performance Appraisal*, (Reading, MA: Addison-Wesley Publishing Co., 1982), 51–55.

15. Kevin Murphy and Joseph Constans, "Behavioral Anchors as a Source of Bias in Ratings," *Journal of Applied Psychology* 72 (1987): 573–577.

16. Walter C. Borman, Daren E. Buck, Mary A. Hanson, Stephan J. Motowidlo, Stephen Stark, and Fritz Drasgow, "An Examination of the Comparative Reliability, Validity, and Accuracy of Performance Ratings Made Using Computerized Adaptive Rating Scales," *Journal of Applied Psychology* 86 (2001): 965–973.

17. Jeffrey S. Kane, H. John Bernardin, Peter Villanova, and Joseph Peyretitle, "Stability of Rater Leniency: Three Studies," *Academy of Management Journal* 38 (1995): 1036–1051.

18. Gary P. Latham, Kenneth N. Wexley, and Elliott Pursell, "Training Managers to Minimize Rating Errors in the Observation of Behavior," *Journal of Applied Psychology* 60 (1975): 550–555.

19. Elaine Pulakos, "A Comparison of Rater Training Programs: Error Training and Accuracy Training," *Journal of Applied Psychology* 69 (1984): 581–588.

20. Ibid.

21. Charles H. Fay and Gary P. Latham, "The Effects of Training and Rating Scales on Rating Errors," *Personnel Psychology* 35 (1982): 105–116.

22. Elliott D. Pursell, Dennis L. Dossett, and Gary P. Latham, "Observing Valid Predictors by Minimizing Rating Errors in the Criterion," *Personnel Psychology* 33 (1980): 91–96.

23. William H. Bommer, Jonathan L. Johnson, Gregory A. Rich, Philip M. Posdsakoff, and Scott B. Mackenzie, "On the Interchangeability of Objective and Subjective Measures of Employee Performance: A Meta-Analysis," *Personnel Psychology* 48 (1995): 587–605.

24. Calvin C. Hoffman, Barry R. Nathan, and Lisa M. Holden, "A Comparison of Validation Criteria: Objective versus Subjective Performance Measures and Self versus Supervisor Ratings," *Personnel Psychology* (1991): 601–619.

25. Barry Nathan and Ralph Alexander, "A Comparison of Criteria for Test Validation: A Meta-Analytic Investigation," *Personnel Psychology* 41 (1988): 517–535.

26. Jesus F. Salgado, Silvia Moscoso, and Mario Lado, "Test-Retest Reliability of Ratings of Job Performance Dimensions in Managers," *International Journal of Selection and Assessment* 11 (2003): 98–101.

27. Diana L. Deadrick and Robert M. Madigan, "Dynamic Criteria Revisited: A Longitudinal Study of Performance Stability and Predictive Validity," *Personnel Psychology* 43 (1990): 717–744. See also Edwin E. Ghiselli, "Dimensional Problems of Criteria," *Journal of Applied Psychology* 40 (1956): 1–4.

28. Erich C. Dierdorff and Eric A. Surface, "Placing Peer Ratings in Context: Systematic Influences beyond Ratee Performance," *Personnel Psychology* 60 (2007): 93–126.

29. Michael C. Sturman, Robin A. Cheramie, and Luke H. Cashen, "The Impact of Job Complexity and Performance Measurement on the Temporal Consistency, Stability, and Test-Retest Reliability of Employee Job Performance Ratings," *Journal of Applied Psychology* 90 (2005): 269–283.

30. Steven E. Scullen, Michael K. Mount, and Maynard Goff III, "Understanding the Latent Structure of Job Performance Ratings," *Journal of Applied Psychology* 85 (2000): 956–970.

31. Kelly M. Hannum, "Measurement Equivalence of 360° Assessment Data: Are Different Raters Rating the Same Constructs?" *International Journal of Selection and Assessment* 15 (2007): 293–301.

32. Dennis P. Bozeman, "Interrater Agreement in Multi-Source Performance Appraisal: A Commentary," *Journal of Organizational Behavior* 18 (1997): 313–316. See also Leanna E. Atwater, Cheri Ostroff, Francis J. Yammarino, and John W. Fleenor, "Self-Other Agreement: Does It Really Matter?" *Personnel Psychology* 51 (1998): 577–598.

33. Jeffrey D. Facteau and S. Bartholomew Craig, "Are Performance Appraisal Ratings from Different Rating Sources Comparable?" *Journal of Applied Psychology* 86 (2001): 215–227.

34. Michael K. Mount, Timothy A. Judge, Steven E. Scullen, Marcia R. Systsma, and Sarah A. Hezlett, "Trait, Rater, and Level Effects in 360-Degree Performance Ratings," *Personal Psychology* 51 (1998): 557–576.

35. Gary J. Greguras, Chet Robie, Deidra J. Schleicher, and Maynard Goff III, "A Field Study of the Effects of Rating Purpose on the Quality of Multisource Ratings," *Personnel Psychology* 56 (2003): 1–21.

36. Mount, Judge, Scullen, Systsma, and Hezlett, "Trait, Rater, and Level Effects in 360-Degree Performance Ratings."

37. Neal Schmitt and Benjamin Schneider, "Current Issues in Personnel Selection," *Research in Personnel and Human Resources Management*, vol. 1 (Greenwich, CT: JAI Press, 1983), 93.

38. Landy and Farr, *The Measurement of Work Performance Methods, Theory, and Applications*, 191–207.

39. Wayne F.Cascio, *Applied Psychology in Personnel Management*, 3rd ed. (Reston, VA: 1987), 116–118.

40. John P. Campbell, Jeffrey J. McHenry, and Lauress L. Wise, "Modeling Job Performance in a Population of Jobs," *Personnel Psychology* 43 (1990): 313–333.

41. Cascio, *Applied Psychology in Personnel Management*, 109.

42. Hubert E. Brogden and Erwin K. Taylor, "The Dollar Criterion—Applying the Cost Accounting Concept to Criterion Construction," *Personnel Psychology* 3 (1950): 133–154.

43. Frank L. Schmidt, John E. Hunter, Robert C. Mckenzie, and Tressie W. Muldrow, "Impact of Valid Selection Procedures on Workforce Productivity," *Journal of Applied Psychology* 64 (1979): 609–626.

44. Frank L. Schmidt, John E. Hunter, and Kenneth Pearlman, "Assessing the Economic Impact of Personnel Programs on Workforce Productivity," *Personnel Psychology* 35 (1982): 333–348.

45. Wayne F. Cascio, *Costing Human Resources: The Financial Impact of Behavior in Organizations* (Boston: Kent, 1982), 163.

46. Peter Villanova, "A Customer-Based Model for Developing Job Performance Criteria," *Human Resource Management Review* 2 (1992): 103–114. See also James T. Austin and Peter Villanova, "The Criterion Problem: 1917–1992," *Journal of Applied Psychology* 77 (1992): 836–874.

47. Bernardin and Beatty, *Performance Appraisal: Assessing Human Behavior at Work*, 43.

48. *Adoption of Four Agencies of Uniform Guidelines on Employee Selection Procedures*, 43 Federal Register 38, 290–38, 315 (Aug. 25, 1978).

49. Hubert S. Feild and William H. Holley, "The Relationship of Performance Appraisal System Characteristics to Verdicts in Selected Employment Discrimination Cases," *Academy of Management Journal* 25 (1982): 392–406. See also Hubert S. Feild and Diane Thompson, "A Study of Court Decisions in Cases Involving Performance Appraisal Systems," *The Daily Labor Report*, 26 December 1992, p. E1–E5; and Glenn M. McEvoy and Caryn L. Beck-Dudley, "Legally Defensible Performance Appraisals: A Review of Federal Appeals Court Cases," paper presented at the Sixth Annual Conference of the Society for Industrial and Organizational Psychology, April 1991, St. Louis, Missouri.

50. Jon M. Werner and Mark C. Bolino, "Explaining U.S. Courts of Appeals Decisions Involving Performance Appraisal: Accuracy, Fairness, and Validation," *Personnel Psychology* 50 (1997): 1–25.

51. Philip L. Roth, Allen I. Huffcutt, and Philip Bobko, "Ethnic Group Differences in Measures of Job Performance: A New Meta-Analysis," *Journal of Applied Psychology* 88 (2003): 694–706.

52. Patrick F. McKay and Michael A. McDaniel, "A Reexamination of Black-White Mean Differences in Work Performance: More Data, More Moderators," *Journal of Applied Psychology* 91 (2006): 538–554.

53. Jon M. Werner, "Dimensions That Make a Difference: Examining the Impact of In-Role and Extrarole Behaviors on Supervisory Ratings," *Journal of Applied Psychology* 79 (1994): 98–107. See also Stephan J. Motowidlo and James R. Van Scotter, "Evidence That Task Performance Should Be Distinguished from Contextual Performance," *Journal of Applied Psychology* 79 (1994): 475–480.

AUTHOR INDEX

SUBJECT INDEX